XIX CENTURY FICTION

A BIBLIOGRAPHICAL RECORD

BASED ON HIS OWN COLLECTION
BY

MICHAEL SADLEIR

IN TWO VOLUMES

VOLUME I

Martino Publishing
Mansfield Centre, CT
2004

Martino Publishing
P.O. Box 373,
Mansfield Centre, CT 06250 USA

web-site: www.martinopublishing.com

ISBN 1-57898-032-1

Library of Congress Cataloging-in-Publication Data

Sadleir, Michael, 1888-1957.
XIX century fiction: a bibliographical record based on his own collection / by Michael Sadleir.
p. cm.
Originally published: London: Constable, 1951, in 2 v.
Includes indexes.
ISBN 1-57898-032-1
1. English fiction--19th century--Bibliography. 2. Fiction--19th century--Bibliography. I. Title: 19th century fiction. II. Title: Nineteenth century fiction. III. Title.

Z2014.F4S16 2004
[PR861]
016.823'8--dc22 2003064873

Printed in the United States of America On 100% Acid-Free Paper

XIX CENTURY FICTION

A BIBLIOGRAPHICAL RECORD

BASED ON HIS OWN COLLECTION
BY

MICHAEL SADLEIR

IN TWO VOLUMES

VOLUME I

PRINTED AT THE UNIVERSITY PRESS, CAMBRIDGE
AND PUBLISHED

in Great Britain by
CONSTABLE & CO LTD
10–12 ORANGE STREET
LONDON W.C. 2

in the U.S.A. by the
UNIVERSITY OF CALIFORNIA
PRESS
BERKELEY AND LOS ANGELES

First published 1951

TO

RICHARD JENNINGS ESQUIRE

My dear Richard,

The pleasure which I have had from your friendship over a number of years, and the cheerful intimacy into which that friendship has developed, would be justification enough for my dedicating to you this product of a hobby we have for so long shared and enjoyed.

But I have another reason for wishing your name to appear on this page—a reason more closely interwoven than that of personal affection with the inception and compilation of my Catalogue. Although your bibliomania embraced other and older periods than mine, I had the sense, when I looked at your books (little though I understood their minutiae and complexity), to realise that *condition* is three-quarters of the battle for any fine collection of any epoch. This—you having set the English-speaking world a standard of 'condition', to which many pay parrot-lip-service, of which a few have the honesty to recognise the rare achievability—may read as a polite platitude. But it is nothing of the kind. Your seventeenth- and eighteenth-century books taught me to apply the requirements of 'Jennings Condition' to the collecting of the boards and cloth of the nineteenth century, and I was fortunate enough to begin collecting while really fine copies could—with assiduity and intelligence—still be found. Now that specimens in Jennings condition of scarce books of my period, no less than of yours, have become virtually undiscoverable, we—you and I—risk relegation to the horrid category of Old Caspar, whose tedious tales of valour in years gone by bored the incredulous young.

Never mind. In your library can be seen the tangible results of your prevision and of your sense of biblio-perfection. In this Catalogue are recorded the results of whatsoever sense of perfection I may have learnt from your example.

Yours ever,

M. S.

CONTENTS

ILLUSTRATIONS

AT END

PASSAGES FROM THE AUTOBIOGRAPHY OF A BIBLIOMANIAC

To write any sort of an account of the formation of my collection of Nineteenth Century Fiction would be impossible without a continual use of the first person singular, and without reference to phases of my individual bibliolatry which, though intense and absorbing in their day, are now things of the past and are not reflected in this catalogue. I will not, therefore, apologise either for egotism or apparent irrelevance, seeing that both are implicit in the job which, to please myself, I have undertaken.

I began collecting books at the age of eighteen. As an undergraduate my favourites were contemporary 'firsts'—poets, prose writers and novelists; but I soon extended operations into French literature of the schools which styled themselves *Symboliste* and *Décadent.* I think I must from the very beginning have had a penchant for group-collecting, that is to say, for seeking out the first editions of authors who belong to one movement, and adding to them the manifestoes, pamphlets and ephemeral periodicals which, in larger or smaller numbers, are produced by every movement. In any event, I now recognise in this *Symboliste* phase of my collecting the same impulse which later turned me to the pursuit, in non-fiction, of nineteenth-century Londoniana, of books on coloured paper, of certain obscure nineteenth-century private press issues (Lee Priory, Great Totham), of the literature of publishing; in fiction, of Gothic Romance, of Silver Fork novels, of yellow-backs and, of course, first and other editions of the cloth period in one to four volumes.

I no longer possess my main collection of Gothic Romances (and of such as I still have, only very few—e.g. by Porter and Maturin—qualify for inclusion in this Catalogue); but the gathering of that collection had its impulse so far back in my book-hunting career that I must advance-mention it at this early stage and return to it later and at greater length.

My youthful enthusiasm for the Symbolist movement in French literature inevitably included the great inspirers of that movement—Baudelaire and Mallarmé. Now both these poets—the latter under the influence of the former—were profound admirers of Edgar Allan Poe, and made translations of writings by Poe, which themselves have become classics. As a collector of *Symbolisme,* my ambition would naturally have urged me to collect the works of the American master; but he, in first edition, was far beyond my financial reach, and I had to content myself with reprints as respectable as possible. Nevertheless, through reading Poe, I found myself exploring into the past in search of the work of Charles Brockden Brown; and from Brown to the English, German and French romances of the 'Terror' school became (when the time was ripe) a step both easy and natural.

This, however, was not yet. I was ready for a new adventure; but among Victorian, not pre-Victorian, allurements.

I had been brought up in a household devoted to Jane Austen and Dickens, and with a limited but genuine fondness for Anthony Trollope. Largely, I daresay, in reaction from the fevers, furies and languors of the French aesthetes, and as my interest in moderns began to wane, I became possessed by childish memories of the Barsetshire novels, and half-frivolously began to experiment in collecting Trollope. In a very short time I was completely absorbed in this new and fascinating task. At that time—I suppose about 1918—Trollope presented an ideal problem to the book-collector who really loved the job of collecting. He had written a very large number of books; he was little sought after and therefore (with one or two exceptions) moderately priced; and he was desperately difficult to find in tolerable original condition. I spent four enchanted years making my first collection of Anthony Trollope, which (on orthodox group lines) was extended to include the numerous works of his mother Frances, with, in support, the solitary production of his sister Cecilia, and a selection of the novels of his brother Thomas Adolphus, and of his sister-in-law Frances Eleanor. These four years left a permanent mark on my bibliomania. They taught me to love the Victorian novel *as a material thing*, and therefore—for their very multiplicity of volumes if for no other reason—to be susceptible to old novels generally.

Collecting Trollope was combined with collecting various other novelists of his period. These had to be chosen from among the, at that time, un-sought-for and therefore cheaply priced. My own inclination (based on memories of books read, or read to me, in youth) turned toward Marryat, Disraeli, Mrs Gaskell and Wilkie Collins. To the intelligence and kindly enthusiasm of Everard Meynell at his Serendipity Shop in Shepherd's Market, I owed a realisation of Herman Melville and many of his 'firsts'. Charles Reade and Whyte-Melville just happened, the former becoming in time a respect-worthy bore, the latter being quickly recognised as an error of judgment.

But the hunt was a delight and the examination of my captures an education. In 1922 there appeared a volume of critical essays and first edition bibliographies entitled *Excursions in Victorian Bibliography*. The essays were very unequal and the bibliographies elementary; but the book had its interest as a piece of pioneer research. The authors dealt with were those just enumerated, plus of course Anthony Trollope.

After the publication of *Excursions*, I settled to the writing of a biography of Anthony Trollope and his mother. This was the first full-length application of a principle which had from the beginning influenced my book-collecting policy and was to become an integral part of it. I have never undertaken the intensive collection of any author or movement without the intention of ultimately writing the material collected into biography, bibliography or fiction. Admittedly in early days that intention produced only trifling results (for a portfolio of unprinted analyses of the Symbolist movement, an elaborate chart of the Rougon-Macquart novels and a decent essay on the poetry of Verhaeren are more or less their sum), but it existed; and with the ambition to follow up a volume of sketchy bibliographies of seven Victorian novelists with a solid critical biography of one of them, it definitely imposed itself. The book, *Trollope: a Commentary*, was published in 1927, and a year later appeared a full-length Bibliography of his works.

My Trollope material had now been transferred from the collecting department of my mind to that concerned with literary production. Naturally I remained on the look-out for additional or better-condition titles by him or by any of the chosen Victorian authors; but there was a vacancy for a new collecting interest and that vacancy was quickly filled.

One day in the autumn of 1922 I was in Bumpus' bookshop at 350 Oxford Street. There were at least two upstairs floors of second-hand books in that original shop (this was before the old Marylebone Court House was taken in, and of course long before the move to Messrs Bumpus' present premises), and poking about on the uppermost floor of all I came across a little run of books in three-quarter morocco with the book-plate of Samuel Whitbread, the wealthy brewer and enlightened Foxite politician, who quarrelled with Sheridan over the rebuilding of Drury Lane Theatre and died by his own hand in 1815. There were, I think, five titles—all novels—in about sixteen volumes; and I remember clearly that one was Regina Roche's *The Children of the Abbey*, another *Horrid Mysteries*, another *The Carpenter's Daughter of Dereham Down*, and another *Duncan and Peggy* by Mrs Helme. I carried them home. Though I hardly realised it, I was in the toils of a new entanglement. My Gothic collection had started.

It was not long before the lust for Gothic Romance took complete possession of me. Some instinct—for which I can only be thankful—told me not to stray into 'Sensibility', 'Pastoral' or 'Epistolary' novels of the period 1770–1820, but to stick to Gothic novels and Tales of Terror.

Of course in the case of several prolific authors (whom it was a natural ambition to complete) sensibility, pastoral and even improving fictions were intermingled with Gothics and had to be secured; but in the main I kept to my restricted field, and so obeyed with tolerable accuracy the influences which (from Baudelaire to Poe and Brockden Brown, through *Northanger Abbey* and the 'Terror' elements in Dickens to a generalised passion for old novels as things for their own sake desirable) had guided me to my new and absorbing interest.

I soon discovered that Gothic Romance as a collecting subject perfectly illustrated a truth about book-collecting which is not everywhere realised. In itself it was an untrodden and an uncharted field; but among Gothic Romancers were a few writers famous either as individuals or on other grounds. In consequence, among the Gothic titles which I ought logically to acquire were certain items already of great celebrity and therefore sought after by collectors. These titles were expensive; but paradoxically they were comparatively easy to find. The genuinely difficult ones were those no one had bothered to want. It is worth remarking that a collector will often have this same experience—that the high spots in his subject, though costly, do not test his assiduity or his skill as a collector; the real snags are hidden among the crowd of titles hitherto despised and rejected. Actually, as in time I came to understand, to have stumbled on 'firsts' of *The Children of the Abbey* and *Horrid Mysteries* at the very outset of my career as a collector of Gothics was as phenomenal a piece of beginner's luck as can be imagined. Never since have I set eyes on a 'first' of Mrs Roche's best-known novel, and on only two 'firsts' of *Horrid Mysteries*; and although it was regrettable that Samuel Whitbread's binders had destroyed half-titles, I soon knew enough of the difficulties of my subject to treasure with gratitude what they had left behind.

It follows from what has just been said that my next lot of acquisitions were mainly 'high spots'. I bought Mrs Radcliffe's *Mysteries of Udolpho* and *The Italian*; I bought Horace Walpole's *Castle of Otranto* and Lewis' *The Monk* (both the London and Waterford editions) and his *Tales of Wonder* and Sophia Lee's *Recess*. If I had had the money, I could without difficulty have bought Shelley's *Zastrozzi* and *St Irvyne*. But the supply of well-known (and therefore available) titles which were within my reach soon ran out, and I might have suffered a considerable check, but for my second piece of good luck within a few months.

In the spring of 1923 Sothebys held a sale of the final portion of the famous library from Syston Park. At the end of the sale—or of one session—were several bundles of old novels. There were forty or fifty volumes in each bundle, and the cataloguers had naturally wasted neither time nor space on detailed description. With some inward trepidation I went to Sothebys myself, and at about half-past four in the afternoon bought all but (I think) two of the bundles, at prices which reflected the fatigue, the satiation or the indifference of the trade. When I got the books home and sorted them up, I found that my Gothic collection had ceased to be an aspiration and had become a reality. No title of, at that date, current market importance was in the bundles; but there were a few which have since become bill-toppers (the first novels of Mrs Radcliffe and Jane Porter—*The Castles of Athlin and Dunbayne* and *Thaddeus of Warsaw*—were among them) as well as a large number of genuine minor Gothics of the kind most difficult to locate. Further, the majority showed an admirable taste on the part of Sir John Thorold or his binders, and virtually all had their half-titles and their incidental advertisements.

From the date of the Syston Park sale until approximately 1930 the pursuit of 'Gothics' was my main book-collecting preoccupation. But before anthologising the events of those few years, I would like to describe a friendship which contributed largely to the building-up of the collection, and pay a tribute to a man whose peculiar quality as a bibliomaniac and his abundant generosity alike to fellow-collectors and to aspiring authors have not been celebrated as they deserved.

It was, I suppose, some time in 1923 that at a dinner of the Omar Khayyam Club I made the acquaintance of Arthur Hutchinson. He was nearly twenty years my senior and had been editor of the popular and successful *Windsor Magazine* since before the turn of the century. He was a bald, large-faced, solid-built but terrifically energetic and always bustling man, with a more tireless capacity for talk than anyone I ever met. Nothing could stop Hutchinson talking; and the luncheons to which, in his hospitable way, he would continually invite both friends and strangers, would persist until late in the afternoon, unless the guests were adamant in returning to work or keeping another engagement. He was kindness personified, and only needed to know that in some way he could help a friend to set about doing so. But the process involved torrents of words, long telephone harangues, and pages covered with his fierce black handwriting, and often left the person helped—though duly grateful—more exhausted than his helper.

Hutchinson's hobby was the collecting of fiction from the mid-eighteenth century to the early nineteen-hundreds—not necessarily fiction in first edition or fiction in original state, but just *fiction*, with a very strange but quite definite predilection for fiction by women authors. It was a devouring hobby; and, as he spent a large part of his life striding about London, he practised it off and on every day. He was terrified of leaving a parcel in a taxi, so regularly strapped or tied his purchases to his wrist. He sometimes came to see me with a whole cluster of parcels dangling and bumping on his arm. It must have been a very uncomfortable system, but it fulfilled its purpose. He was the kind of collector conventionally called 'omnivorous', his lust for fiction being uncontrolled either by selective design or problems of space. There were also certain non-fiction lines which he worked no less energetically—notably the publications of the Daniel Press, the works of Oscar Wilde, and books dealing with various towns in which he had a special interest. That he was not hampered by the difficulty of housing his purchases was due to his curious way of living. He had a bedroom in a hotel off the Strand, and in that room were always two packing cases supplied by a big furniture repository. As each parcel of books was delivered, he packed it in a case, often not removing the outer wrapping. When the cases were full, he telephoned to the repository, who collected the full cases and left two empty ones in their place. He was always talking of taking a house in the country and spending a happy retirement sorting and arranging his books. But quite suddenly, on the evening of Friday, August 26, 1927, he died in his room. He had invited a number of people to a tea-party on the following afternoon at a large west-end hotel (these Saturday tea-parties were one of his regular pleasures) and not until they had waited an hour for their host and then telephoned to his address, did they learn what had happened.

During my four years' acquaintanceship with Hutchinson we had grown intimate as only persons can whose hobbies are identical. We exchanged lists of desiderata; we made up check-lists of works by specified authors from the advertisement leaves at the end of volumes; we had a common enthusiasm for Robert Bage, and planned to republish his cynical and strangely modern novels with a biographical introduction and critical comments. Hardly a day passed without our either meeting or telephoning or writing, and whenever I could play truant from my office, we would visit those booksellers who dealt in our particular quarry. I was, therefore, not altogether surprised—though highly complimented, for after all I was only a recent friend compared with many others—to find that in his will he had appointed me one of two 'library-executors' to dispose of his books to the best advantage of two nephews, who were his nearest relatives and of whom he was very fond. But I had no idea, until we came to tackle the job, what a tremendous (and in some ways a macabre) task had been laid upon me.

I say 'upon me' designedly, for my fellow-executor was compelled by ill-health to throw in his hand almost immediately, and shortly afterwards died. It was only in the very early stages that we worked together, and even then—owing to his other commitments—my colleague was unable to spare more than a very occasional hour. For the handling of Hutchinson's library 'very occasional hours' were to prove worse than useless.

I shall never forget the first sight of that astonishing collection. After sending our credentials to the repository and fixing a time for a preliminary view, we asked for certain sample cases to be unpacked in readiness for our visit. Having arrived at the huge building, we were conducted to a sort of mezzanine floor—low-ceilinged and in complete darkness. There were, we were told, one hundred and forty packing cases of books, of which a random dozen or fifteen had been unpacked. We were given torches and left to investigate.

The rays of light flickered across the vast floor on which—spines upward—were ranged row after row of books. It looked as though an over-floor of books had been laid down, with the narrowest passages here and there through which we crept, flashing the torches on to title after title, and feeling every moment more appalled at the prospect of having to sort these thousands of volumes and prepare them for sale. For they were completely unclassified and desperately miscellaneous; quite half were still parcelled and would have to be undone and distributed before even a start could be made. Out in the daylight my colleague and I stared at one another in despair. What in the world were we to do?

What indeed? The repository naturally charged storage on this bulk of books, as well as rent for the cases in which they were packed. To allow these expenses to run indefinitely would hardly fulfil an executor's duty toward the estate he was directed to benefit. On the other hand, to invite a bookseller to make an offer for the library would involve giving him a chance to examine it, and this he could only do *in situ* and after the entire collection had been spread out. Such an arrangement, even if the repository were able to spare the necessary space, would still further increase the cost to the estate, for examination would be an affair of weeks, for which—and properly—the bookseller would recoup himself by an adjustment of the price offered. Equally subject to preliminary inspection would be an offer of the library to a firm of auctioneers, and the result would at best be a choice of special items and the rest left behind. We knew enough of Hutchinson's tastes and methods to be sure that only a small minority of the books were up to the level of individual cataloguing; and no auctioneer could afford to take delivery of a vast mass of miscellaneous material and sort it through, without the certainty of finding more money-bringers than were here available.

Eventually, after consultation with the executor proper of Hutchinson's will, it was decided that I be allowed to make an offer for the whole collection and take responsibility for its disposal. This arrangement was highly speculative, because, although I had a general idea of the nature of the library, I had only *seen* a fraction of it and that under difficult conditions. Further, no one could estimate the length of time needed to go through and classify all the hundred and forty cases, and during the period of classification the books must be stored somewhere and at the buyer's expense. On the other hand, being nearly as great an old-novel maniac as Hutchinson (perhaps at that time the only other one in the country), I could reckon on finding more books in the collection which I wanted for myself than could any other single buyer, and must regard the acquisition of these as equivalent to monetary return. As matters turned out, the arrangement proved scrupulously fair to both parties. Leaving entirely out of account the time and labour spent in sorting, I got back by sale of unwanted or duplicate material almost exactly what I paid the estate for them. The incidental costs, when set against the books I kept, represented fairly enough the price I should have had to pay for those books, *had I been able to find them elsewhere.*

The work of sorting the Hutchinson library was at once infinitely laborious and continuously exciting. I was lent a small empty room in the London office of my firm's binders (there was no space available in my own office) and relays of packing cases—about ten at a time—were delivered there from the repository. With the valiant assistance of two or three friends (and often until late at night) these relays were opened up, classified and distributed in various directions. In one place was collected the material for sale at auction; in another junk, only fit for stall-holders in street-markets; in another the certain 'keeps'; in another the 'doubtfuls'; in another the 'imperfects'. These last were the most troublesome, for until the work was finished there was no knowing whether a missing volume or volumes would or would not turn up. Hutchinson's curious system of filling case after case and storing them away, actually bred imperfections. If he came back to his room with a four-volume novel and there only remained space in one case for two volumes, he would split the work so that two volumes were at the top of one case and the other two at the bottom of another. The cases were neither labelled nor numbered in sequence, and once back in the repository were stacked wherever convenience required. Consequently when they emerged again and were successively unpacked, the original order was hopelessly lost, and the number of titles awaiting completion became a real embarrassment.

Two other queer characteristics of this queer collector increased the labour of sorting, but in compensation added to its piquancy. Not only (as I have said) were hundreds of parcels still unopened, but their contents were bafflingly miscellaneous. Hutchinson made no attempt to separate his important 'finds' from the valueless stuff which he would also buy. If in one shop on one morning he bought six books, of which two were Gothic items and the others modern reprints, he had them all parcelled together and probably packed them as they were. As a result, one could never be sure that something of interest was not hidden in a package of junk, and every volume had to be carefully examined. For example, a beautiful little copy of Mrs Radcliffe's poems was sandwiched between two fiction-cheaps for bookstall sale, the three items wrapped in newspaper and tied with string. Similarly, many of the Gothic chap-books were discovered in bundles of paper-covered oddments—modern novels, local guides, time-tables and odd numbers of magazines. Every moment, therefore, had its potential thrill.

The second element of excitement related to *condition.* Hutchinson was indifferent to condition and bought his novels in any state available. Also he often bought more than one copy of the same title. Now and again fortune threw in his way a really beautiful copy; more often it did not. But all the time there was just a chance that a wanted novel in fine original state *might* turn up—and any collector will understand that in such circumstances those weeks of dust and toil and ceaseless carrying of books were weeks of delicious tension.

The contribution of the Hutchinson library to my collection of Gothic Romances was very extensive. From no other single source were so many new titles obtained. But the outstanding discovery was that which completed the series of 'Northanger Novels'—the seven novels recommended by Isabella Thorpe to her friend Catherine Morland in Jane Austen's Gothic pastiche.

I had, of course, determined in early days to find these novels if I possibly could, and have already told of the good fortune which brought me *Horrid Mysteries* at the very outset of my career. The next one to turn up was *Clermont*—a lovely copy in original wrappers bought in a South Coast town. Next came *The Mysterious Warning*, which for some reason is the one I have since seen most frequently. Then for long enough nothing happened, until one blessed morning, on my way to the office, I went on a sudden impulse into (of all places) the shop which has made Grafton Street famous. This monarch of the antiquarian trade was perhaps the least likely bookseller in London to have such obscure trifles as Gothic Romances; but my good angel guided me, and there—straight opposite the door in a shelf under the broad central table—was a copy of *The Midnight Bell.* It was a very nice copy in contemporary calf and had its half-titles.

It was, I think, the miracle of *The Midnight Bell* which stimulated me, when invited to read a paper before the English Association, to offer one on the Northanger Novels. This was in the autumn of 1926. I consulted Arthur Hutchinson as to where I could get access to the three missing titles: *The Castle of Wolfenbach, The Necromancer* and *The Orphan of the Rhine*, no one of which was to be found in the Statutory Libraries. He declared that he possessed the first two and, by some mysterious means, contrived to produce them. *The Orphan of the Rhine*, however, he definitely had not, nor had ever seen. Borrowing his two and working on my copies of four, I wrote my paper, read it in the Hall of Westminster School in February 1927, and in preparation for its ultimate printing, obtained photographs of the six title-pages for reproduction. The paper ended with a lament that no copy of *The Orphan of the Rhine* could be located.

In August 1927, Hutchinson died, and during September and October the frenzied struggle to classify and distribute his library was at its height. One evening in late October, stupefied with fatigue and dust and feeling I never wanted to see a book again, I was listlessly unpacking perhaps the hundredth packing case, when my jaded intelligence suddenly awoke to the fact that I was holding in my hand the four volumes of *The Orphan of the Rhine*. Hutchinson, though he did not know it, had had a copy after all. There was just time to add a postscript to my paper and photograph the title-page, with the result that English Association Pamphlet No. 68 is really complete, and that the seven Northanger Novels in first edition became—and will remain—a part of the Gothic collection, which has now found a worthy home elsewhere.

Collecting Gothics was the perfection of collecting. Like Trollope 'firsts' up to 1922, they were both rare and unwanted. And they had an extra quality which Trollope could not claim. Being the works of a generation of writers and not one writer only, they were potentially far more numerous and, representing a fashion in novel-writing and not a single characteristic authorship, they tended to turn up (when they *did* turn up) in groups. This meant that my collection increased in spasms, which were the more exciting for the blank periods in between. I have already mentioned some of the windfalls which good fortune brought me—the small starting windfall from Bumpus, the important windfall from Syston Park, the melancholy but tremendous windfall from Arthur Hutchinson. There were others, some of which dropped in my path as I toured the bookshops of the United Kingdom, while others came my way thanks to information from friendly booksellers, who tipped me off when they heard of small lots in the possession of any of their confrères. One of these was, in fact, the very last of my Gothic 'buys'—a dozen or more titles from the library of Harriet Mellon, the actress who had a fortune from Coutts the banker and became Duchess of St Albans. They were in unusually sumptuous bindings which, with their silk or coloured end-papers, agreeably suggested the pleasure the good lady always took in squandering her millions.

That, I suppose, was about 1937; and a twelve-month later, except for a few duplicates, I parted with the whole collection. I did this for more than one reason. From the first I had intended to use my Gothics as material for some kind of a book, and up to a point (though not very discernibly) I did so, for they were the basis of a considerable element in the opening volume of *Bulwer: a Panorama* (later entitled *Bulwer and his Wife*). Several of Bulwer Lytton's early novels are the direct projections of Gothic Romance (after it had undergone strengthening and improving treatment at the sometimes didactic hands of Scott, Maturin and the Porter sisters), and link the Gothic period proper with the debased horror-fiction of the mid-nineteenth century. But I never tackled outright the task of criticism or bibliography of Gothic Romance *per se* because, long before I got round to it, other people were on the job. More than one critical examination of the period of Gothic taste in fiction, poetry, architecture and decoration appeared during the late nineteen-twenties and early nineteen-thirties, and when—three or four years before it actually appeared in 1939—Miss Dorothy Blakey started on her great bibliography of the Minerva Press, it became obvious that not enough in either department remained undone to justify my keeping Gothic Romance as an item on a future writing programme, or as an exorbitant competitor for urgently needed shelf-room. For although I had continued throughout the early thirties to collect the now infrequent Gothics which came my way, I had as long ago as 1927 started another line, and by the middle thirties several more, and the pressure on space was becoming intolerable.

My second reason for disposing of the Gothic collection was partly that I was restless, partly that I felt as though a hitherto unspoilt holiday resort had been found out. A point had been reached when there was not enough doing to keep my mania busy, and further, the subject was becoming 'smart'. During the late nineteen-twenties it had become increasingly difficult to find fresh titles in Gothic Romance, and when they occurred they were much more highly priced than had been usual. Competition had unmistakably begun; and it was noticeable that the 'Old Novel' section in catalogues (previously more or less of a rag-bag and none too frequent at that) became not only fairly general, but also emphatic as to type and often important in content.

To put it frankly, my growing disinclination (except in outstanding cases) to buy on a rising and publicised market arose from a queer sense that obscure Gothic Romances should be hunted out and not bought from write-ups; also that they ought not to cost much above the average price which I had been accustomed to pay. Illogical, I admit; but there it was. I wonder whether other collectors are conscious of a similar feeling of frustration when, after some years of more or less solitary pursuit of a particular quarry, that quarry becomes suddenly more expensive and, instead of lurking in obscure shelves and basements, is thrust on their attention by ingenious cataloguing.

I hope this does not read like a complaint, or as implying that at their enhanced prices the books were over-charged. They were always genuinely scarce, and only absence of demand had kept them cheap. Now buyers (notably certain American libraries) were multiplying, and of course prices rose. No doubt I had myself done something to create a more general interest in this particular class of book, and so raised the market against myself. But that was not all of it. I am convinced that taste in book-collecting obeys some influences far bigger than a few individual collectors can exercise. The era of poetry and old plays (that during which the Ashley Library was formed) was giving place to an era of fiction. Novels from the early eighteenth century to the end of the Victorian period were due to become the prevailing taste, and I was lucky in being a little ahead of their coming, and so earning the early bird's reward. It is quite possible that the wastage of old novels which took place during the war of 1914–18 hastened the swing of the pendulum in favour of fiction. In 1917 and 1918 thousands of novels in two to five volumes were sold for pulp. Prices of paper and strawboard rose to famine height, and second-hand booksellers all over the country gladly turned into cash forgotten fictions which no one would buy. There used to be a bookshop in Barnsley (the West Riding town from which both my parents came) whose stock of three-deckers was regularly exposed outside and stretched a dozen feet across a wide pavement. In those days I passed them by, caring nothing for such things. The whole lot were sold for pulp between 1914 and 1918, and I sometimes wonder wistfully what may not have been among them. Is it not possible that this wholesale destruction threw a shadow of coming scarcity over collector-land and gave to some collectors a second sense of what was destined soon to disappear?

Once again, therefore, in default of all but very occasional Gothics, the way was open for me to engage in a new enterprise in novel-collecting, and once again chance put one in my way. In July 1927 was offered for sale at Hodgson's Rooms a quantity of board and label books from the Rhiwlas Library in North Wales. I wandered into Hodgson's one morning, and found the greater part of the large sale room walled on both sides with spines of brown or buff or blue or white, across which ran gleaming, undulating lines of paper-labels. It was a staggering sight; and the memory of Frances Price who began the collection, and of R. L. Ll. Price who (maybe) inherited and certainly carried it on, should ever be held in respect and gratitude, for though they read their books, they did not bind them, and they kept them for the most part scrupulously clean.

You will say it was no particular good luck of mine to see at Hodgson's a Welsh library offered for public sale. Nor was it; and lots of other people saw it too. But there was, I think, luck in these three facts: first, the Price fiction-purchases were nearly all made between (roughly) 1825 and 1840, when the prevalent fashion among regular novel-readers was for novels of what was derisively known as the 'Silver Fork School' and when writers destined to a great reputation a hundred years later were very few. Second, I was at this period more than normally short of money to spend on books and would, whatever the contents of the library, have had to be content with the cheaper because less wanted lots. It was impossible for me to compete for the Rhiwlas high spots—for example, *Mansfield Park*, or Leigh Hunt's *Sir Ralph Esher*. I went, therefore, for the novels offered in lots of twelve to twenty volumes. Third, whereas at this very time, I *needed* Silver Fork fiction as part of the documentation for the first section of *Bulwer: a Panorama*, nobody else cared very much about it. The position was curious. Mid-Victorian novels by authors of repute were now sought after by collectors and readers alike; Gothic and sensibility novels of the eighteenth and very early nineteenth centuries were also in demand. But between these two categories of desired fiction lay the output of upwards of fifteen still neglected years—and precisely of that output was the Rhiwlas Library principally composed.

From the Hutchinson library I had already acquired certain of the novels of Mrs Gore and was eager to find more of these witty, experienced and (as evidence of social background) unrivalled books. Through the garish and crudely cheerful spectacles of Frances Trollope and of Theodore Hook, I had studied the vulgarities and ostentations of those who aped the *ton*. But to understand the arrogance and money-pride and bland assumption of superiority of the self-appointed leaders of that society to which the young Bulwer and the young Disraeli aspired to belong, it was necessary to find Lord Normanby, and Lady Charlotte Bury, and Lady Stepney and T. H. Lister and L. E. L. and Mrs Maberly and such anonyma as *Almacks* and *Herbert Milton* and *English Fashionables Abroad* (and *At Home*) and, of course, all (if possible) of Mrs Gore. Anyone who has the patience to study the provenance of the novels catalogued in this volume will see how considerable was the Rhiwlas contribution to the achievement of these and similar ambitions.

It is not feasible beyond this point to continue my book-collecting story as a single, coherent narrative. Several distinct interests were now running concurrently and have continued to do so to this day. Three-decker firsts—in boards or in cloth—were always welcome, and increased attention was paid to changing styles of binding material and ornament. In 1930 these physical characteristics were discussed in a monograph on the history of Publishers' Binding Styles between 1770 and 1900—a subject later developed with much skill and constructive argument by John Carter. The social background of the thirties having been worked into *Bulwer*, investigation was prolonged into the forties (which meant an extension of search for novels of manners in various grades of society, in order to cover that critical and revolutionary decade). It had been my intention to follow *Bulwer* with a second, and maybe a third, book on the later phases of his pathetic, preposterous yet impressive career; but that plan was abandoned when it became clear that the reading public had no interest whatsoever either in Bulwer Lytton himself or his miserable marriage, or the papier-maché splendours of the high society of his day. The extent to which *Bulwer* flopped still astonishes me. Now and again I dip into it; and find all manner of ironies, absurdities and pathos, as well as glimpses of the life and shams of the period displayed or betrayed in contemporary periodicals and literature, which offer uneasy parallels to those of a few years ago. These elements of the book at least should, in my judgment as a publisher, have found their mark. But my judgment as a publisher was at fault. No one wanted *Bulwer* nor ever pretended that he did.

So I revised my scheme of work; and, instead of centring a second volume on the luckless Bulwer Lytton, took as main theme the bizarre story of the lovely Lady Blessington, bringing in Bulwer by a side-door. The writing of *Blessington-d'Orsay* (which appeared in 1933) was at once reflected in my book-collecting. Apart from Lady Blessington's own works (and in particular the association set *par excellence* bound to d'Orsay's taste and left for decades after his death to be forgotten in the remote desolation of Chambourcy), I gradually acquired a series as complete as possible of d'Orsay's lithographed portraits, as well as the Part- and Volume-issues of John Mills' *d'Horsay or the Follies of the Day*; and works by Lord Blessington, Harriet Gardiner and Lady Blessington's nieces.

Blessington-d'Orsay was as widely read as *Bulwer* was ignored. Whether I felt vaguely that I had avenged a failure and could now relax, or whether—having once let them go—I could not pick up the threads of social and literary history which I had once intended to follow out to the end of Bulwer Lytton's strenuous but throttled life, I hardly know. But I do know that the zest for biography and literary history was temporarily lost, and that for a while book-collecting and book-writing ceased to be connected.

As I have said, I can no longer observe a strict chronology; but three events of major importance in the story of my bibliomania occurred between 1928 and the middle thirties. The first in enduring influence if not in date was the beginning of my friendship with Richard Jennings, to whom this catalogue is dedicated. Jennings is not a book-collector on a lavish scale, because his standard of 'condition' is so high that acceptable copies of all the books he wishes to possess simply do not exist. He is inexorable in maintaining this standard; and, in consequence, although his collection shows many gaps which on titles alone he would wish to fill, there is hardly a book in his possession—whether of the seventeenth, eighteenth or nineteenth centuries—which is not in a state of preservation as nearly faultless as one could hope to see.

Now I had from the earliest days been a stickler for *original* condition—that is to say, I had never deliberately bought a re-bound nineteenth-century book save for purposes of mere utility, and did not regard such reading copies as part of my collection. A number of re-bound novels were in the Hutchinson library and a few (they are recorded in this catalogue) I retained, because I wanted the texts. Also, as will be seen, there is an occasional bound run of a collected author (e.g. the d'Orsay set of Blessington and the Gaisford set of Peacock) which, in my opinion, carry their own justification. But insistence on 'original condition' had often, until I became familiar with Jennings' books, been too tolerantly maintained. Where, in the attempt to complete some author's first editions, I had been able to find no copy of one or more titles without library labels or marks of library labels on the covers, I had (though reluctantly) incorporated such discreditable specimens in my collection. Henceforward I rejected many books which, in pre-Jennings days (though certainly without enthusiasm), I should have taken.

The second major event of this period (actually the latest in date) was the discovery in the West of Ireland of the fabulous board-and-label library at Mount Bellew. My friend M. J. MacManus of Dublin, whose adventure the discovery was, will some day tell the whole amazing story. My record shall therefore begin when in May 1933 the first MacManus catalogue of Bellew books reached this country. In the course of the present volume will be found descriptions of a *Scottish Chiefs*, by Jane Porter, two or three Maturins and a few other novels from Mount Bellew. All are in a pristine condition which has to be seen to be believed. I had many other books from the Bellew Library which, because they are of too early date or because they are non-fiction, have no place in this catalogue; they too were in the same miraculous condition. The library, formed between 1800 and 1830, was a very large one and with certain exceptions of earlier date, consisted mainly of books published between 1770 and 1830. There was a sensational sale at Sothebys of certain high-spot titles which every collector and dealer will recall, including two Jane Austens, Mary Shelley's *Frankenstein*, *Essays of Elia*, several plate-books in parts and other notabilia. Then came three or four more MacManus catalogues, while parcels of minor books made their appearance in quite a succession of Hodgson sales. Practically without exception the books were not only in wrappers or boards as issued (occasionally in full morocco of publishers' origin, cf. *Harrison's Novelists Magazine*, Section III below) but as clean and new as the day they had first appeared.

I shall never forget the arrival by post of the first slim Bellew catalogue. After tearing through the catalogue's eight pages, I felt so breathless that I had to sit a few moments before I was capable of going through the whole thing item by item. I made pencil-crosses; I drafted a long telegram. Then I commended my cause to Providence and went through the catalogue all over again.

Here are some sentences from a preface which MacManus included in his third or fourth Bellew selection:

BOOKS IN BOARDS

At the beginning of the Nineteenth Century there lived in an old mansion in a remote part of the western Irish seaboard a man whose hobby was book-collecting. Disdaining the fox-hunting tradition of his family and class he devoted his days to literary pursuits and the acquisition of a library. He stored his books in specially-constructed cupboards, dust-proof and damp-proof. Many of them he did not live to read, but even those which he read suffered nothing in the process. When he died, the fox-hunting tradition prevailed once more, and the books, safe behind locked doors, were forgotten for a century.

Here is a wide range of uncommon and attractive volumes, offered in a condition so dazzlingly fine that by their very appearance they will lend distinction to the bookshelves of the most fastidious collector.

Not one word of over-statement do these paragraphs contain. Indeed it would hardly be possible to over-state the perfection of Bellew condition or the excitement of those Bellew days, with parcels from Dublin trickling in and immaculate treasures slowly encumbering my table. Long before the residue of the huge library had been liquidated I went to Dublin at MacManus' invitation and spent happy hours in a warehouse above a furniture shop, where faultless Bellew volumes of every size and kind lay in piles, overflowed from bureau drawers, stood close-ranked in shelves. Some were books of extreme dullness; some were books about which nothing was known; some were precisely the sort of scarce but unreputed trifles which I delight to find. But *all*—literally *all*—were crisp and radiant, with labels dead white and perfect, with spines sound and round and flawless at the hinge, with strawboards clear-cut and fore-edges sinuous and sharp. The opening up of the Bellew Library was surely one of the peak moments in the history of modern book-collecting. It is one privilege to have been alive when it happened, and another to have enjoyed the friendship of the man most concerned and therefore to have been among the earliest to hear the news. In Mount Bellew MacManus found a few copies of a private folio catalogue of which fifteen copies were printed for Christopher Bellew in 1813 (that is to say, about half-way through his collecting life). One of those he gave me, and an occasional reference to it will be found in the pages which follow.

The third incident which during these years affected my bibliomania will seem (and admittedly is) of much smaller stature than the tremendous exhumation of the Bellew Library. But it was very important to me, in that it launched me on my (to the time of writing) latest new large-scale operation in nineteenth-century fiction. For that reason—namely that its influence on my collecting activity became effective later than that of the Bellew Library—I have given the latter priority, although chronologically it does not merit it.

One day in the autumn of 1928 a bookseller, who then occupied a charming shop in St Martin's Lane (now, alas, abandoned), told me he had a queer lot of miscellaneous stuff in the basement which I might like to look over. I was conducted to two small and poorly lighted rooms (not the usual basement, which was one of my regular haunts) the floors of which were piled and littered with wrappered magazines, with small books of all kinds and with hundreds of yellow-backs. It was the collection of an old gentleman named Molineux, an insatiable collector recently dead, who had bought books for decades and always wrapped his purchases carefully and put them away. A lovelier lot of obscure fictional oddments I never hope to see again. There were pictorial board issues, *Parlour* and *Railway Library* books, the Annuals of Routledge and Tinsley, the Christmas Numbers of *Belgravia* and *London Society*, and all manner of other ephemera.

I was, of course, conscious of the yellow-back as a feature of Victorian publishing; but the word suggested a rather dispiriting and almost illegible crown 8vo reprint of Ouida or James Payn or Walter Besant, with a spine (where present) of conventional design and tail-ends of cheap canvas fluffing through worn patches in the glazed paper boards. The Molineux yellow-backs, on the other hand, were mainly of small format, with admirably designed front covers and spines, and in new condition. Similarly, the Parlour Library volumes and those belonging to other Series, as well as the wrappered Annuals from about 1860 onwards, were unsoiled and untorn. It seemed a case for buying in bulk, and instituting a small-scale Hutchinson sort-out. The bookseller was quite agreeable (with the market as it then was, the labour of arranging and cataloguing would have been quite uneconomic, for the material—apart from its condition—was mostly of the kind at that time suited to outside shelves or boxes where, if it sold at all, it would sell at from threepence to two-shillings a go). He quoted me a flat price per volume, and in a few days' time I had entered into the Molineux inheritance.

Since then my yellow-back and board-series collections were considerably enlarged. During the nineteen-thirties I received welcome reinforcements from the collection of the late John Browne of Croydon (who bought his books from Mann Nephews, Cornhill, as loyally as Frances Price bought hers from Seacome or from Harding of Chester and took as good care of them) and a few from that of the excellent Mary Rumfitt, who went in for 'Series' and (most admirable habit) always dated her signature. Latest accretion of all (it could not for obvious reasons find a place in this catalogue) was the extensive file of yellow-back covers *in proof*—many in several states—which belonged to the famous firm of Edmund Evans. Evans printed by far the largest proportion of pictorial board covers produced between the early fifties to the mid-nineties, and their file is very comprehensive.

Nevertheless the original Molineux contribution to my Yellow-back collection (see Section II) remained the foundation of the whole. Nearly all the Detection yellow-backs were part of it, as also the elegant little Marryats and other naval novels, the *pictorial* examples of the Railway Library, and the bulk of the small format reprints of the fifties and early sixties, copies of which nowadays are hardly ever seen.

To one small group of yellow-backs nothing (so far as I recall) accrued from any one of the three respected book-buyers above mentioned. Mary Rumfitt would certainly have disapproved; John Browne might well have hesitated before the raised eyebrows of Mann Nephews; but that J. R. Molineux (to whom they would strongly have appealed) passed them by implies that their extreme scarcity goes farther back than the last twenty years. Because this group (though very incomplete in first issue and unequal as to condition in any shape) acts as a link between my fiction library and a non-fiction collection to which I have already referred and to which I am especially attached, I would take leave to mention it.

In Section II will be found a heading: *Anonyma Series*, and beneath that heading a list of ostensibly raffish fictions dealing with the fast life of Victorian London. A few pages back, I mentioned as an example of the group-collecting to which I have always been prone, Londoniana of the nineteenth century. I started on this subject early in the nineteen-twenties, with a number of folio periodicals (Renton Nicholson's *The Town* was the most respectable) which had been the property of the late W. Robertson Nicoll. Continuously (though very slowly, because reliable evidence of what went on behind the façade of early and mid-Victorian propriety is extremely scarce) I extended this collection, and to it the *Anonyma* novels may fairly claim to belong.

In two respects the formation and possession of this assemblage of London periodicals, chapbooks, night-life guides, crime-sheets, street-maps and what not, has a flavour no other one of my collections possesses. In the first place, when on the prowl, one has no idea, not merely where to look for new material, but even what new material to look for. A Gothic Romance, a three-decker, a yellow-back, however bad as to condition and however unwanted, are manifestly a Gothic Romance, a three-decker and a yellow-back. But data on Under-London may turn up anywhere, may be of any format or pushed into any corner. So the search for them tests the patience and intelligence of the collector to the utmost—confronts him, in other words, with a job of collecting in its noblest form. In the second place, while I have collected fiction with the idea of transmuting some of its contents into décor for historical biography, I have from the first looked forward to using predominantly non-fictional Londoniana as décor for fiction. That process began with the writing of *Fanny by Gaslight* and *Forlorn Sunset*, and may, I daresay, be further pursued. I find a peculiar relish in thus turning the tables on my own previous practice.

To conclude this record of what has been the most exciting continuous experience of my life, there remains to be told the story of the Bentley Fiction File.

In a large brick house in Slough, surrounded by a large garden and looking across the water-meadows to Eton, lived Richard Bentley the Second, the last of the family which in direct succession had for over sixty years conducted the famous publishing firm of Bentley. In 1898 Macmillan purchased the business of Bentley and Son, taking over the firm's publishing copyrights and stocks, and Richard Bentley retired to the imposing residence which his father, George Bentley, had built a few years before his death in 1895. In his retirement Richard the Second became a meteorologist and antiquarian of repute, as well as a prominent figure in various spheres of scholarship and administration. He was President of the Royal Meteorological Society in 1905; Master of the Stationer's Company in 1924–25; for many years Vice-Chairman of the King Edward VII Hospital at Windsor, and an influential member of the Committee of the Royal Literary Fund. Continuously for sixty-three years (the longest period on record in the history of British railways) he held a season ticket between Slough and Paddington.

Mr Bentley was a remarkable man, both in appearance and character. Short, very stout, bald-headed and with pure white whiskers of the Emperor-Francis-Joseph type, he might have stepped straight from an illustration to a mid-Victorian novel. Right up to the end of a long life (he was eighty-one when he died in February 1936) he retained his sight, hearing, physical activity and magnificent appetite. In no single respect was Mr Bentley's life a niggardly one. His house was very large and very red and white, the lawns were very extensive and very smooth, the shrubs luxuriant and of many kinds. Inside, the paint-work shone with cleanliness and good quality, the furnishings were lavish, various and ornate; there were books and pictures everywhere. Gadgets abounded—service lifts; ingenious cupboards; even electric fixtures to throw beams of light across the garden, should he feel suddenly in gala-mood, or suspect that burglars were lurking in the bushes. In his hall stood a full-size scarlet pillar-box of regulation design, in which letters were placed for posting. In the hall also, an impressive clock, largely labelled: REAL TIME, expressed his disapproval of daylight-saving nonsense. His hospitality was almost overwhelming. Never, between 11 a.m. and 5 p.m., have I been pressed to eat so many and such excellent meals as on day-visits to this cordial home.

When he wrote letters (which in reply to my queries he would do most punctually and generously), he not only covered sheets of notepaper of the very finest quality with large and beautiful handwriting, but used red as well as black ink and even other devices to emphasise his points. Here, after a paragraph or two of regulation black, would come three lines in scarlet; here a hand pointing in the margin, or a rigid railway-signal with the word STOP! would jerk the reader sharply to attention.

In short, he was a memorable and highly individual figure—a very embodiment of full-blooded mid-Victorian security, and the perfect culmination of a publishing dynasty whose productions were more lavish in design and of choicer material than any of their period.

I first made Mr Bentley's acquaintance when I was working on *Excursions in Victorian Bibliography*, and from the beginning found him ready with information and accessible to requests for help. But it was not until I had known him for some years that he really accepted me as a serious student of Victorian publishing. Once that stage was reached, no trouble was too great for him. I do not think I misrepresent him if I say that he actually welcomed enquiries; and I have no doubt whatever that the too-few visits which I was able to pay to Slough were a real pleasure to him. He loved to conduct a genuinely interested visitor from one book-room to another—unlocking cases, pulling out volumes, expatiating on this old memory or that.

The house was crowded with books. But the portion of it most attractive to me was the attic; for there was the file of Bentley fiction from (roughly) 1860 onwards, which had been removed to Slough from the offices in New Burlington Street when the firm of Bentley and Son was finally merged in Macmillan. It was not a complete file. It contained only scattered examples from the thirties and forties; a fair representation from the fifties; the vast majority of novels published by the firm from the early sixties to the early nineties; and then again a mere selection from the four or five final years. At each end, in short, it was very imperfect, but the middle period was terrific. I judge that the last years of all had been transferred to Macmillan, for I found several Bentley titles among the Macmillan File Copies from the eighties and nineties, when these were put at my disposal through the kindness of the publishers.

'Proved later to be terrific' I should rather say; for it must be confessed that, owing to the structure of the attic and under the ever-vigilant eye of Mr Bentley, no very clear idea of what was actually there could be obtained. Access to the attic was up a steep ladder and through a trap-door. You (or rather Mr Bentley, with you in his wake) mounted the ladder, pushed back the trap, grasped a convenient rope (of superlative marine quality) and pulled yourself into a prolonged triangular tunnel, criss-crossed with beams and floored with duck boards laid over joists, between which ran water-pipes. For light you (and Mr Bentley) held an electric bulb on a handle, and crept forward as nearly upright as the available clearance allowed. The Bentley Fiction File was kept in long low book cases right under the slope of the roof. These cases were set so far into the angle that there were, I think, only three shelves to each; and while the hand-lamp shone uncertainly on those immediately to right and left, they stretched away into what seemed an infinity of shadowy distance. When the *visite* was over (I can only think of those expeditions in terms of an official sightseeing tour of a French chateau), one extinguished the lamp, grasped the rope and clambered carefully downward to a man-height corridor once more. The whole performance was a miracle of agility on the part of Mr Bentley and an uncompleted thrill to the favoured visitor.

In February 1936, as I have said, Mr Bentley died and was buried in the churchyard of St Laurence, Upton, alongside his father and near to the old church for whose antiquarian repute he had worked so hard. Fourteen months later (in April 1937) the Bentley Fiction File came up for sale at Hodgson's Rooms in Chancery Lane. Once again was seen the fabulous sight of the large room lined with novels of the nineteenth century in virtually new condition. This time, however, instead of the muted allurements of pale paper spines and snowy labels, brilliant gold patterning and cloths of every colour dazzled the beholder. No novel publishers of the second half of the century went in so thoroughly and persistently as Bentley and Son for golden ornament, for brilliant cloths, for bevelled boards, for all the panoply of glitter and colour which (perhaps for the last time in the whole history of publishing) signalised a period of prosperity, confidence and peace.

The Bentley novels were catalogued in 145 lots, of which the first 140 (comprising over 1700 volumes) were put up for sale *en bloc*. If as a single lot they failed to reach the reserve, they would be offered separately. The remainder of the lots consisted of sets of *Temple Bar*, *Bentley's Favourite Novels*, the works of Mrs Henry Wood and some oddments.

The first composite lot represented the Fiction File from the great attic at Slough, plus a number of other novels scattered about the house and now added to the attic-series. A few titles were damp-stained or mildewed, but the vast majority were new. Possibly dust and years had slightly dulled their pristine brilliance, but not sufficiently to disqualify them from being described as in 'mint state'. Thanks to the darkness in which the attic-books had been kept, no one was faded; such fading as had occurred affected an occasional book from other parts of the house. It is not too much to say that nowhere else in the world could such a collection of two- and three-deckers of the cloth period, and in such superb condition, conceivably exist.

The opening lot reached the reserve, and all the titles of any intrinsic interest appear in this catalogue. Those whose authors or contents seemed to me irrevocably (or better) forgotten—and they were fairly numerous—I arranged in exact chronological order in glass cases in my office, where they presented an impressive and glowing picture of the changes in binding taste, decade by decade, from about 1860 to 1895. Then, in two successive night raids, bombs fell on Garlands Hotel which backed on to our office building. Our top three floors were condemned and had to be cleared of their contents—among which were the binding specimens so laboriously dated and set in order. No visual chart survived of mid-Victorian binding enthusiasms—from the comparative simplicity of grained cloths, blind-blocked and plainly lettered; through an intensifying orgy of heavily gilt spines with ever more fanciful lettering; through a brief and modish period of floral- or filigree-blocking in gold, silver and pale colours on dark smooth cloths, with patterned edges and a general air of tricksy elegance, to a new severity of unglazed, unblocked linens with straightforward titling on the spines. For a while I planned to reconstitute it, but lacked the patience and leisure to do so. Then more space was urgently needed, and the books were sold.

In conclusion, a few words in explanation of certain peculiarities of the collection catalogued in this volume. It presents certain obvious gaps, and also certain unexpected amplitudes. Some comment is due on both these phenomena.

Like Archdeacon Wrangham I have always been more interested in hunting 'difficult' and unusual books than in the acquisition of famous and therefore expensive ones. Wrangham quotes with approval these sentences from the library catalogue of a fellow bibliophile, and applies them to his own collection:

> This collection is by no means to be considered as an Essay towards a perfect Library. Here are few publications of great price; but it is believed that not many private collections contain a greater number of really curious and scarce books.

I would venture to make the same claim on behalf of the books here described, naturally using the final words in a modern sense and as is compatible with a Library of Fiction. A preference for the rare but unsought was, of course, virtually forced on me (as on the Archdeacon) by limitations of finance; indeed only in very recent years have I been justified in paying other than really modest prices, even for books I badly wanted. But I must insist that it was from the first—and has remained—an ingrained characteristic of my collecting mania. When I started in earnest on nineteenth-century fiction in first edition, there were a few novelists already keenly sought for by important collectors of the day (e.g. Scott, Dickens, Thackeray, Borrow, the Brontës, George Eliot, Meredith, Gissing, Stevenson and Hardy) and therefore at the same time charted. The first editions of these writers, if available, were easily located. Booksellers knew they had them, and kept them on a first-edition shelf, often behind glass. Even in cases when I could have afforded to pay the prices, I should have had little satisfaction in acquiring such easy game. In consequence, these authors (and two or three others of their class) were regarded as outside my territory. Admittedly, during more recent years, I was lucky enough to obtain satisfactory specimens of several of these once-avoided novelists; but not of all of them. I never attempted to collect Scott, Borrow or Stevenson. Of Thackeray (modestly enough) I desired nothing except a really fine *Vanity Fair* and a really fine *Esmond*—both in cloth, for the bound *Esmond* in the collection is there for the sake of its charming appearance and connection with Delane. I freely recognise that the absence (or virtual absence) of certain giants in nineteenth-century fiction destroys any pretension to completeness which this book might be so rash as to make. Fortunately, however, their failure to appear does not seriously affect my catalogue's reference value, for all have been bibliographised already, so that other books exist to which, for better or for worse, the curious may turn.

At the other end of the scale from the missing great are a few ostensibly over-distended small. Why, it may be asked, such lavish provision of Lady Georgiana Chatterton, B. L. Farjeon, Charles Gibbon, Katherine S. Macquoid, Hawley Smart? I can only reply that I am weakly susceptible to runs of 'family' copies or to longish presentation series of novels once belonging to some friend of the author. Such runs, when they turn up, are usually in fine condition and those with presentation inscriptions sometimes throw an amusing light on the character of the writer. On behalf of three of the novelists above-mentioned I would further plead a definite intrinsic interest. Lady Georgiana Chatterton ranks with the so-similarly-named Lady Georgiana Fullerton as a Catholic authoress with a devoted and well-merited following of her own; Farjeon, Australian by origin, was one of the most popular writers of sensation fiction of his day, whatever degree of oblivion may now have overtaken him; while Hawley Smart can surely claim his share of whatsoever respect be considered due, on the one hand to dashing writers of the G. A. Lawrence and Whyte-Melville order, on the other to the spirited and inexhaustible turf-lore of Nat Gould. Had I been lucky enough to strike Lawrence or Whyte-Melville in presentation-series, they would appear in this catalogue. Nat Gould (who *did* to some extent come my way in a highly desirable form) is debarred from inclusion, because he published no story in two or three volumes.

In conclusion a paragraph is due in explanation of the virtual absence of Part-Issues, which will strike every knowledgeable student of this catalogue. Except in a few very special cases, I have not collected Parts. They are a nuisance to preserve and impossible to read without damage, while few things are more dismal to look at than a shelf of cloth or morocco boxes. Consequently only my brightest of star-authors—Le Fanu, Marryat, Frances Trollope (and one or two more whose Part-issues are publishing curiosities)—offer their Part- as well as their Volume-issues; the rest are in boards or cloth, and not necessarily the more easily obtained for being so.

Further inconsistencies will doubtless strike the reader and user of these pages. Some must be charged to the luck or ill-luck of the chase; others to a personal preference for one author over another.

MICHAEL SADLEIR

EXPLANATORY GUIDE

Something must be said about the arrangement, mechanics, scope and limitations of this Catalogue. It is in three Sections:

I. An Alphabet of Authors, describing their first (and certain subsequent) editions, with a subsection 'Comparative Scarcities'.

II. The Yellow-back Collection, arranged in a mixed alphabet of Authors' Names, Series-titles and a few group-headings.

III. 'Novelists Libraries', 'Standard Novel' Series and Collections of Tales, alphabetically listed under the key-word in the title of each such Library or Series.

All three Sections are primarily concerned with books actually in the Collection, but in each one some titles not present have been added. In Section I this has been done where the run of first editions of any one hitherto unbibliographised author (whether of his complete works or of his fiction*) is very nearly complete. In order to compile a complete bibliography of such an author, I have obtained from some outside source (usually a Statutory Library) a description as nearly accurate as possible of the missing titles. In Sections II and III titles not in the Collection are added to the lists of several important Series, the record of which must, if it is to be of reference-value, be made as complete as possible. In every case, and in each Section, items recorded but never in my possession are distinguished by asterisks.

As regards scope and limitations, those must first be clearly understood which govern the Catalogue as a whole, and then those relevant to the three Sections. The choice of Authors for inclusion has been governed by three quite simple rules. Any novelist whose writing-life was comprised within the limits of the nineteenth century is entitled to a place, assuming of course that he was represented in the Collection. No novelist who published fiction prior to the year 1800 has been admitted.† Any writer who began publishing late in the century and issued a fiction in two or three volumes (provided a novel by him or her in this form was in the Collection) has been regarded as eligible for inclusion.

My interpretation of 'eligibility' has, admittedly, been arbitrary and personal. In some cases fiction by authors who really belong to the later one-volume period, but chance to have one or two early titles issued in two- or three-decker form, is given full treatment (e.g. Harland, Hudson, Pryce, Mark Rutherford, Somerville and Ross) or treatment as full as the Collection allows (e.g. Bret Harte). In others, authors of the kind are only recorded up to, and including, the year 1900 (e.g. Doyle, Haggard, Flora Annie Steel). Authors fully established during the three-decker period, whose writing-lives nevertheless stretched well into the twentieth century, received extended treatment if I consider they merit it (e.g. Braddon, Broughton, Henry James, Ouida); but some are stopped at 1900, even though I had titles of later date, because their work does not in my view merit further pursuit (e.g. Hall Caine and Marie Corelli). An exception is made of Mrs Humphry Ward (who would normally have been closured in 1900) because the series of presentation copies to Bishop and Mrs Creighton are of sufficient interest to justify prolonging her catalogue to the year 1911. Finally, in several cases (e.g. Barclay, Everett Green, Fletcher, Marriott Watson, Moore, Philpotts) the author's single three-decker has been considered sufficient representation.

* Although the work is overridingly a catalogue of fiction, a certain number of non-fiction titles find a place in it. Where I can offer a complete record of the first editions of some significant author who is mainly known as a novelist, it seemed pedantic to omit his few non-fiction books and to that extent damage the utility of the list of his works.

† To this rule one near-exception has been made in Section I. Maria Edgeworth's first *novel* appeared in 1800, but she published during the eighteenth century two or three books which were in the Collection and are here recorded.

Naturally I have not felt bound, in order to honour the second of my rules, to include every in-itself-admissible novel which may have been in my possession. To an enthusiast for novels published in Victorian shape a really fine copy of a work, though itself wholly negligible, can give pleasure; but to occupy space in a printed catalogue with particulars of books no one is ever likely to wish to remember would be wasteful of effort. On the other hand, many titles do appear, of which nothing is known or recollected. Each of these has in my view something of interest—whether textual or as a specimen of book-making or as evidence of publishing method—and seems in consequence worthy of record.

At the end of Section I is a subsection presenting lists of Comparative Scarcities of the first editions of the fictions (or the principal fictions) of the more important authors whose works are adequately represented in the preceding pages.

With a single exception, the condition that eighteenth-century publications shall be excluded is imposed on Sections II and III, as well as on Section I. That exception is HARRISON'S NOVELISTS MAGAZINE (1780–1788) in Section III. It would have been wilful, in a work purporting to record the Contents and bibliographical features of the principal 'Novelists' Libraries' of the nineteenth century, to ignore their grandiose prototype.

The caption 'Yellow-back Collection' given to Section II must not be understood too literally. It comprises books issued in all colours, styles and forms of non-cloth binding employed by publishers during the cloth-period. Thus, Section II includes pictorial boards on bases of yellow, white, pink and blue; decorated and lettered boards; stiffened and unstiffened wrappers. Each variety is recorded, as and when it occurs. Further, the Section contains nearly as many titles *first published in one of these forms* as it does straight reprints. It is not generally realised how many fictions (some by well-known authors) first made their appearance in boards or wrappers and, since throughout the Section first editions are typographically differentiated from reprints,* there will be no difficulty in distinguishing them.

Section III seeks to provide what I have often wished were available, i.e. descriptions and schedules of the contents of the principal Libraries of Fiction and Novel Series of the nineteenth century. Inevitably these are somewhat miscellaneous, and contain work both original and reprinted; but they are of much interest, alike as evidence of the continued vitality of certain authors or titles, and as stages in the development of cheap-edition publishing.

Naturally no complete list of nineteenth-century fiction Series has been attempted. Such a list would be enormously long and the greater part of it useless. I have, therefore, sought to select only those Series which have a bearing on publishing history; and though my selection may well be incomplete, it can, I think, claim to contain nothing that has not some justification.

But justifications vary, and therefore the fullness with which the Series are recorded varies also. For example, it would have been sheer waste of labour and space to provide a complete list of ROUTLEDGE'S RAILWAY LIBRARY, which only very rarely has textual importance, and as a piece of progressive publishing was a direct imitation of the PARLOUR LIBRARY. The latter, on the other hand, deserves and has received extended treatment. Similarly, BENTLEY'S STANDARD NOVEL SERIES, as a collection of titles and as a publishing venture, so far outweighs in importance COLBURN'S MODERN NOVELISTS or ROUTLEDGE'S STANDARD NOVELS that I have devoted several times as much space to it as to both the others put together.

One other point. At several places reference is made to the BENTLEY PRIVATE CATALOGUE. This remarkable compilation was the work of Mr Richard Bentley, ably assisted by Mr F. E. Williams who for many years worked in New Burlington Street. These two, between 1893 and 1923, working on the ledgers and records of the firm, drew up a descriptive, partially annotated and in the main accurate catalogue of its publications from 1829 to 1898. A very small edition of this

* First editions are in caps., reprints in caps. and l.c.

catalogue was privately printed by the late Mr Bentley and labelled 'For Official Use Only'. I have to thank Mrs Bentley for kindly giving me access to a record which has proved very valuable in establishing dates, authorship, Series-details, etc. in connection with a number of Bentley books.

* * * * *

In the descriptive entries I have tried to observe the following rules:

(*a*) Title and subtitle are given verbatim (though with standardised punctuation), but no further title-page wording.

(*b*) Where no size is given, the volumes are either (in the parlance of the period) 'Post 8vo' or what we now call 'Crown 8vo.' Larger and smaller formats are designated as '8vo' or 'small' or 'fcap' 8vo, and where a book is quarto it is so described. I have purposely not gone into closer detail in this matter of sizes nor tackled the vexed question of whether a book, just because it is printed in twelves, should be described as 12mo, for such problems do not affect the identification of any particular issue of the books in this Catalogue.

(*c*) Where a book was published anonymously, or as 'by the author of', etc., or under a pseudonym, or in collaboration, or as 'Edited by' someone, the fact is stated. Where nothing is said, the author's name appears quite simply on the title-page.

(*d*) Publishers' imprints are abbreviated in all well-known cases. Certain obscure imprints are given in full. Where place of publication was elsewhere than London, the fact is stated and the place given before the publisher's name.

(*e*) Colour of cloth used on 'half-cloth-board' books is not given because the material employed, whether by the original publishers or by the novel distributors who bought sheets in bulk, had no overriding sanction. The same book may exist with spines of several different textures and colours, no one of which can claim priority or official prescription.

(*f*) Details of blocking on covers are given only for important authors not elsewhere described or where significant variants or issue-points exist.

(*g*) Where no colour of end-papers is given, these are yellow or pale yellow or buff or white. Other colours are recorded throughout. Only in the case of a few important authors have I subdivided these shades.

(*h*) Books with title-pages undated are described as 'n.d.' If a date appears elsewhere (for example in a dedication or preface or—as sometimes—among advertisements), this date is added in *round* brackets. A date in *square* brackets has been established on external evidence.

(*i*) I have tried to be severe on blemishes in the copies described, and correspondingly restrained in words of praise. With very occasional exceptions, I have used only the terms 'very fine' and 'fine'. Both should be taken literally—the former as meaning virtually above criticism, the latter as something highly exceptional, but not peerless.* Where no description is given, the book lacks specific faults and would normally be described as very good indeed, or even fine, but it does not in my opinion really qualify for the latter epithet. Every book with Bentley provenance is labelled (B), and must be understood to be in pristine condition unless some flaw is recorded. Similarly, all yellow-backs catalogued are really fine unless otherwise stated, with a few exceptions among Series such as the PARLOUR LIBRARY, HODGSON'S NOVELS, etc., where titles in imperfect state are listed *as titles* in order more clearly to achieve a complete record.

(*j*) Where a half-title or other leaf or leaves should precede title-page I have said so. No comment means that no half-title (or preceding leaf or leaves) is called for.

*** It must be borne in mind that a cloth book can be 'very fine' and still have some trifling external defect such as a rust-spot or small scratch. The description applies to the over-all brilliance of gold and glaze and the sharpness of edges and blocking.**

I am afraid that absolute uniformity in the formulas used, and in the wording and arrangement of entries, has not been achieved. The annotations have been done over a long period, and it was impossible to prevent slight variations of phrasing and arrangement. I hope, however, that the same amount of information has been given throughout.

(*k*) The Index at the end of this volume is an index of titles in the Collection and of significant titles mentioned in *Notes* throughout the Author-Alphabet.

Throughout Section I, where indicated by book-plate or signature, I have noted the provenance of books described. Apart from the obvious interest (sometimes the evidential value as to priority of issue) of inscriptions or signatures dated contemporaneously with a book's publication, it seemed to me that users of the Catalogue might be glad to recognise a copy earlier noted by themselves, or perhaps to find the name of some connection or forbear of their own recorded as a previous owner. Then, as the entries accumulated, I found that this evidence of provenance connected up in a queer way and quite independently of the individual significance of the original owners. There emerged the names or initials of half a dozen persons—persons previously quite unknown to me—who at some time during the nineteenth century had been in the habit of *buying* three-volume, two-volume, or single-volume novels, and treating them with varying degrees of respect.

I do not, of course, include in this group of former proprietors such large-scale book-owners as Christopher Bellew, or the Prices of Rhiwlas, or George or Richard Bentley, or Coningsby Disraeli. Their books, and those from one or two other prolific or family sources, came to me in bulk and at specified times. They lack, therefore, the unexpected (indeed, until I began to relate them to one another, the unsuspected) interest of books bought up and down the country at any time during the last twenty-five years, and now—quite fortuitously—reünited.

To the inspired purchasers and scrupulous custodians of certain yellow-backs, volumes of boarded series and the like, reference has been made in the autobiographical essay which precedes this Preface. John Browne, J. R. Molineux and Mary Rumfitt are the triumvirate who rule this kingdom. But there are also a few cloth-bound-fiction addicts, and to them also I would like to pay the tribute they deserve. The care they lavished on their books was not wasted, and they will be no less scrupulously treated in future.

First come 'Moretino' (who was he?); then the enthusiast for Henry James, of whom I know nothing but the initials 'L. M. V. de W.' and from whose collection I have never seen a book by another author; then Radclyffe Walters. All these three kept their books superbly. The last-named (who, like Mary Rumfitt, dated his signature in every book) would appear to have been the most recent of the trio to become a victim of posthumous dispersal. The great majority of the 'Walters books' were acquired during 1944 and 1945. And yet *Under the Greenwood Tree*, which belonged to Walters' collection, was bought ten years earlier!

Lady Georgiana Codrington's only failing was a habit—shared with (perhaps, in social aspiration, borrowed from) the Duke of Leeds—of writing her name in ink on the outside of cloth covers.* Lady Emily Fitzroy was kind to her books—kinder than 'Ingram' or 'Mary C. Ingram', who bought with discrimination but read a little roughly. The book-plates of Geo. Evelyn Cower and A. H. Christie nowadays survive, I am glad to say, less frequently than was at one time the case. When I began on nineteenth-century fiction, books from the Cower and Christie collections appeared oftener than specimens from other recognisable sources (I presume their libraries had been recently dispersed), and my zeal for titles outran my sense of condition. Neither gentleman was a stickler

* It is interesting to find her mentioned in the first volume of Osbert Sitwell's autobiography, *Left Hand, Right Hand*, as the half-sister of the Sitwells' grandmother Lady Londesborough. She lived at Doddington Park, near Bath, and her books—so far as I had the luck to come across them—were scattered among the Bath bookshops.

for cleanliness or even for original state, and much replacement was necessary to bring what were once Cower or Christie items up to a satisfactory standard of unimproved normality.

* * * * *

A second non-bibliographical interest emerges from an examination of this considerable assembly of nineteenth-century fiction.

There take shape several subject-groups which cut across authorships and have a chronology of their own. These groups are of different kinds. Some formed themselves without conscious effort on my part; others resulted from a deliberate collecting pursuit. One or two have no cohesion save the theme common to all their members; the majority can be related to some historical happening, some new exploring enterprise, some specific outburst of social protest, even to some sudden popularity of a particular sport.

To the first category belongs the group of novels of School and University life—a group which is a respectable example of spontaneous accumulation. From Arnold's *Christ Church Days* to Mrs Henry Wood's *Orville College* it persists throughout the alphabet; and unusual specimens appear under Annie Edwards, Hewlett, Lister, Melly and Winwood Reade, as well as the more widely known books of Cuthbert Bede, Dean Farrar, Thomas Hughes and Henry Kingsley.

Roughly analogous is the spasmodic sequence of novels reflecting the perpetual conflict between Protestant and Catholic. This series of fictions merges on the one side into those concerned with Ireland and the Irish question (of which more below), on the other into stories of clerical life and vaguely religious colouring. But it retains a core of mutual disputatiousness and eager self-justification to which both sides contribute. In addition to the well-known books by Mark Rutherford, Shorthouse and Mrs Humphry Ward, works belonging to this central core will be found under Archdeacon, Beste, Reynolds, Sinclair, and the section headed 'Authorship Unknown'.

Of the second and more numerous category of subject groups—representing the *Schwärmereien* which, at different epochs and at the prompting of various events at home and abroad, possessed our novel-reading forbears—it suffices to mention, and briefly, a few only. There are the stories of Persia and the near Orient (Morier, Baillie Fraser); the stories, spaced over a longer period, whose theme is India (Hockley, Meadows-Taylor, Flora Annie Steel); tales of the Sea and of life in the Navy; tales of the Wars and of life in the Army; propaganda novels written in defence of the down-trodden; novels of the Race Course and the Hunting Field.

There is, however, one specimen of period-fashion in fiction-making which merits a few paragraphs of comment—the craze during the twenty years preceding 1848 for what are familiarly known as 'Silver Fork' novels.

I have already recounted the opportune disposal of the Rhiwlas library, which made it possible for me to acquire a representative selection of these highly ephemeral fictions. I would now venture a brief comment on their intrinsic quality and interest.

In my opinion, these books, though frequently absurd, deserve more attention than they have yet received. An American student has published a monograph on the subject which gives evidence of much careful research and has value as a work of reference.* But its reading quality is flat, because it lacks the understanding of the English social background from 1825 to 1840 essential to an appreciation of a class of novel whose significance is more social than literary. The Silver Fork School (if a jostle of writers so predominantly amateur can be termed a 'school') produced a higher proportion of downright bad novels than any similar group, with the possible exception of the Gothic Romancers; but the flimsiest and gaudiest specimen bears inevitably the marks of the hectic period which produced it. Snobbery, title-hunting, parvenu-arrogance, the worship of fashion, the

* *The Silver Fork School*, by Matthew Whiting Rosa. Columbia Univ. Press, 1936.

aping by mushroom-aristocrats of the manners of aristocracy at the expense of its spirit, all the shrill ferment of a post-war and pre-revolutionary carnival pervade these otherwise worthless books and give them documentary value.

Only one individual Silver-Fork novelist (and to her also reference has already been made) deserves survival in her own right. She is Catherine Frances Gore—Disraeli's 'full-blown rose of a woman'—who gave Sunday parties at her flat in the Place Vendôme; whose piquante saucy daughter, Cecilia, played the flapper-coquette with young Coventry Patmore to such cruel effect that the shy tormented youth was driven almost to suicide. It may be that Hook must be regarded as the founder of the School; it is certain that Disraeli and Bulwer and Frances Trollope wrote novels which rank as School-products; but no one of these claims survival as a Silver Forkist. Mrs Gore, on the other hand—apart from some early 'costume' work and a few tales of foreign lands—devoted her considerable talents during a long and active life to the delineation of precisely the gilded absurdity which during the thirties and forties was known as the *ton*. Further, being herself a woman of fashion who was also a gentlewoman, she knew what she was writing about and that all was not gold which glittered. Her novels are usually too long for their content (she was no rebel and, if publishers and libraries asked for three volumes, three volumes they should have), are often written in careless haste, and pretend to be only what they are—the caustic comments of a witty and observant woman on the vagaries of feminine character and on the follies of a society and an epoch of which she was well qualified to write. But, as such, they have humour, epigram, and a perceptive malice which is almost frightening.

It is unlikely that Mrs Gore will ever be reprinted. She is too loose in texture, too topical in reference, too dated in implication to be a 'revival' proposition. But no student of social history during the two garish decades when the jumble of ennobled profiteers, lickspittles and impoverished gentry staged a pseudo-eighteenth century jamboree can afford to neglect her books. The difficulty will be to find them.

In conclusion, I wish to draw attention to one particular section of this Novel-Collection, partly because I regard its successful assembling with unashamed complacency, mainly because it has an importance far transcending that of any of the subject-groups above mentioned. Here is a representative collection, in original (and for the most part in fine) condition, of the works of the novelists of Ireland. These Irish novels do not represent a response to some sudden new awareness, whose very novelty spells transience, but constitute a national literature in terms of fiction and, as such, have permanent significance. Their authors, from Maria Edgeworth to Somerville and Ross, include writers of every shade from the now despised Anglo-Irish to the now venerated nationalists.

Ideological labels to literature are distasteful to me. The quality of such novelists as Miss Edgeworth, Lady Morgan, Miss Somerville, Le Fanu, Lever, Maxwell, is something as independent of their attitude (or indifference) to Irish political and religious disputatiousness as is the quality of Carleton, Lover, or other contributors to Duffy's 'Library of Ireland'. Similarly the half-way-houseness of Griffin and the Banim Brothers is as irrelevant to their writing achievements as it would be if they had been Highlanders or Bashi-basouks. Irish fiction comprises much fiction of genius; but it is a *literary* genius, with superb local material superbly used. Its attitude to Pope or Protestantism or England or Orangism or Ribbon-Men or Absentee Landlords or any one of the bones of contention of that bony and contentious race, is in my opinion altogether beside the point.

ACKNOWLEDGEMENTS

Dozens of people, in greater or less degree, have contributed of their knowledge or experience to the compilation of this catalogue. To acknowledge them all by name would be frankly impossible, as notes derived from sources no longer remembered have been incorporated, and numerous members of the trade, both in England and America, have over a period of years confirmed or disputed some of my tentative conclusions.

To certain helpers, however, I must give individual thanks for protracted and often laborious assistance. Messrs F. C. Francis of the British Museum, Strickland Gibson, R. H. Hill, C. J. Hindle of the Bodleian, and Alwyn Scholfield of the University Library, Cambridge, have with unfailing patience answered queries or had books looked out and set aside for me to examine at my convenience. Messrs Richard Jennings, John Carter, Percy Muir, Simon Nowell-Smith, with all of whom I am fortunate enough to be in fairly constant touch, grew accustomed to being asked for opinions on points or policy or terminology and were always ready with considered replies. They also read the proofs to disruptive but admirable effect.

For specialised assistance I have to thank Mr Douglas Munro, who put at my disposal his great knowledge of English editions of Dumas; Mr M. J. MacManus and Mr P. S. O. O'Hegarty, both of whom answered questions about Irish issues in the nineteenth century, many of which are puzzling indeed; and Professor Harold Butler who helped with Maria Edgeworth.

To those members of the Cambridge University Press, who, during the years this Catalogue has been in progress, have helped it forward with care and skill, I must say a generalised 'Thank you'. The Printer and his immediate staff; the keyboard operators; the readers—indeed everyone concerned—have done all that was possible, in the teeth of delays and frustrations for which no one of us was to blame, to maintain standards of elegance, clarity and accuracy.

There remain two persons without whose devoted collaboration the Catalogue could never have come into being. The transcription of a mass of often almost undecipherable manuscript, the checking-over of the hundreds of figure-entries and the compilation of the index to this volume were all undertaken by Miss Martha Smith. To Mr Dudley Massey I owe skilful and continuous help—day after day, even week after week—not only with proof-reading but also with the actual handling and collation of the books. His experience, his retentive memory and his swift competence in examining and analysing a volume were indispensable.

SECTION ONE

AN AUTHOR-ALPHABET OF FIRST (AND CERTAIN SUBSEQUENT) EDITIONS: ALSO A SUB-SECTION 'COMPARATIVE SCARCITIES'

GENERAL NOTES

(i) When a book is described as 'n.d.' followed by a date in *square* brackets, it means that no date appears anywhere in the book itself, but that one has been established from an outside source. Where the date is in *round* brackets, it means that, although the title-page is undated on recto or verso, a date appears somewhere in the volume, usually at the end of a preface or dedication, sometimes as part of the printer's imprint at the end.

(ii) At certain points in this section an 8vo novel is described as 'bound from the parts'. This means that the stab-holes caused by sewing the parts are visible throughout the text and in the margin of the plates. A novel which first appeared in parts and is not so described shows no trace of having been sewed for serial issue, with the implication that sheets and plates were cloth-bound from the first.

It is very difficult to estimate the issue significance (if any) of these differences of state. In some cases (e.g. *Pickwick, Orley Farm, The Last Chronicle of Barset*) we know that the novel was reprinted after part-issue, because of textual changes in later issues. Such reprinting probably took place on most occasions when a story proved very popular, and the demand continued after part-issue was finished. But there were other circumstances which had other results. For example, the advance-subscription to a part-issue sometimes fell short of the publisher's anticipation, so that he had on hand copies already stabbed for part-issue but not required. Such copies, though we would have to describe them as 'bound from the parts', would in fact be book-issues consisting of unwanted parts. On the other hand, a publisher sometimes underestimated part-demand, having judged from the reception of the early numbers of a story which gained unexpected popularity as it proceeded. He would, therefore, have prepared what proved to be an inadequate supply of parts, keeping a large portion of his original printing unstabbed, ready for cloth-issue. This issue he would now hurry out, and the books would belong to the original printing, but show no stab-holes. Finally, a considerable proportion of part-subscribers would send in their parts to be cased at the end of serial-issue, and such copies, when returned to their owners in cloth, would genuinely be 'bound from the parts'. This phrase, then, is used in the pages which follow merely as giving an additional descriptive detail, and without any attempt at historical reconstruction.

(iii) Reference to existing bibliographies is made, where such exist and are, in my experience, reliable. Advanced students of Bulwer Lytton, Dickens, Hardy, Meredith, Trollope and several other writers should note that the Morris L. Parrish Library of Nineteenth-Century Literature (mainly fiction) bequeathed to Princeton University—and I believe already (1949) available to researchers—contains numerous variants of first editions of Victorian novels not recorded in any published bibliography. The special number of *The Princeton Library Chronicle* (vol. VIII, No. 1, November 1946), dedicated to Morris L. Parrish, gives sufficient particulars of this marvellous collection to enable a reader to judge what, in his particular line, may there (and frequently nowhere else) be examined.

AINSWORTH, W. HARRISON (1805–1882)

A Bibliographical Catalogue of the Published Novels and Ballads of William Harrison Ainsworth by Harold Locke (London 1925) gives title readings, brief binding descriptions, etc., but no collations. *William Harrison Ainsworth and his Friends* by S. M. Ellis (2 vols. 1911) contains much useful information.

[1] AURIOL (originally entitled 'Revelations of London')

For the hitherto unrecorded first book-edition of this unfinished romance, see 3396 in Section II: AINSWORTH, FIRST UNIFORM COLLECTED EDITION. Chapman & Hall 1850, Vol. XII.

[2] BEATRICE TYLDESLEY

3 vols. Tinsley 1878. Bright brown diagonal-fine-ribbed cloth.

Half-title in each vol.

Vol. I x+(288) T_8 blank.
II viii+(274) Final leaf, T_1, a single inset.
III (viii)+(268)

Fine.

[3] BEAU NASH, or Bath in the Eighteenth Century

3 vols. Routledge, n.d. [1879]. Dark olive diagonal-fine-ribbed cloth.

Half-title in Vol. I

Vol. I viii+288
II iv+288
III iv+(304)

Very fine.

[4] CARDINAL POLE, or The Days of Philip and Mary

3 vols. Chapman & Hall 1863. Bright brown dot-and-line-grain cloth.

Half-title in each vol.

Vol. I x+(302) Last leaf of prelims. and final leaf of text, Y_1, are inset leaves.
II viii+(306) Final leaf, X_1, a single inset.
III viii+302 Final leaf, Y_1, a single inset.

Dedicatee's copy (Edward Watkin Edwards) with his book-plate in each vol. Very fine.

[5] CHETWYND CALVERLEY

3 vols. Tinsley 1876. Lilac-grey diagonal-fine-ribbed cloth.

Vol. I viii+(278) Final leaf [T_1, mis-signed U_1] a single inset.
II vi+294 Final leaf, X_1, a single inset.
III vi+290 Final leaf, U_1, a single inset.

Presentation Copy: 'Mrs E. W. Edwards, with the Author's Kind Regards' in ink on verso of fly-leaf in Vol. I. Fine.

COMBAT OF THE THIRTY (The). From a Breton Lay of the Fourteenth Century [6]

Chapman & Hall 1859. Green glazed stiff printed wrappers.

pp. 32

Presentation Copy: 'The Rev^{d}. T. Corser. With W. Harrison Ainsworth's kind regards' in ink on fly-leaf.

CONSTABLE DE BOURBON (The) [7]

3 vols. Chapman & Hall 1866. Maroon sand-grain cloth.

Vol. I (viii)+(288) T_8 blank.
II vi+(288)
III vi+(292)

E. W. Edwards' copy with his book-plate in each vol. Fine.

CONSTABLE OF THE TOWER (The) [8]

3 vols. Chapman & Hall 1861. Red bead-grain cloth. Wood-engraved front. in each vol., and in I two, in II one illust. after John Gilbert.

Vol. I (viii)+(308)
II (viii)+(316)
III (viii)+332

Anthony Trollope's copy with his book-plate and shelf-label in each vol.

CRICHTON [9]

***First Edition.** 3 vols. Bentley 1837. Boards, labels.

Half-title in each vol.

Vol. I (xlviii) [paged (i) to (iv)+(i) to xliv]+(336)
II vi+410 Final leaf, T_1, a single inset.
III vi+340+(i)–(xx) Appendix

First Illustrated Edition: Royal 8vo. Chapman & Hall 1849. 'Third revised edition.' Olive-green morocco cloth. Etched front., pictorial title and 16 plates by Hablot K. Browne. [9*a*]

pp. vi+(354)

Fine.

DECEMBER TALES [anon] [10]

G. & W. B. Whittaker 1823. Boards (re-covered and spine renewed. No label).

Half-title. pp. (xii)+(232)

Printed label 'RUDING. Shelf 1' pasted on title.

FALL OF SOMERSET (The) [11]

3 vols. Tinsley 1877. Chocolate-brown diagonal-fine-ribbed cloth.

Vol. I viii+290
II vi+(288) T_8 imprint leaf.
III (viii)+(280)

From E. W. Edwards' Library but with no book-plate or inscription. Very fine.

[12] GOLDSMITH'S WIFE (The)
3 vols. Tinsley 1875. Bright blue sand-grain cloth.
Vol. I (viii)+(278) Final signatures, T, 2 leaves, U, a single inset.
II vi+296
III (viii)+300
From E. W. Edwards' Library, but with no book-plate or inscription. Very fine.

[13] GUY FAWKES; or the Gunpowder Treason. An historical romance
3 vols. Bentley 1841. Claret fine-diaper cloth, blocked in blind on front and back, gold-lettered and blind-banded on spine. Pale yellow end-papers. Etched front. to each vol., and in Vols. I and II six, in Vol. III seven etched plates, all by George Cruikshank.
Half-title in Vol. I
Vol. I xvi+(304)
II iv+(308)
III iv+(360) Q_{12} adverts.
The illustrations for all three volumes are listed on pp. (xv) xvi of Vol. I.
Book-plate of Lord Esher. An extremely good—almost a fine—copy of one of the most difficult Ainsworths in any sort of original condition.

[14] JACK SHEPPARD
3 vols. Bentley 1839. Dark grey-green ribbed cloth. Front. portrait of the author in Vol. I and 8 etchings by George Cruikshank; 9 etchings in Vol. II; 10 etchings in Vol. III.
Half-title in Vol. III
Vol. I (xii)+352
II iv+292
III (viii)+312
Book-plate of T. Fardinando in each vol. Binder's ticket: 'Bunting' inside front cover of Vol. 1.
Fine. One corner of back cover of Vol. II damp-stained.

[15] JAMES THE SECOND; or the Revolution of 1688. An Historical Romance. (Edited by W. Harrison Ainsworth, Esq.)
3 vols. Colburn 1848. Half-cloth boards, labels. Etched front. in each vol. by R. W. Buss.
Half-title in Vols. I and II; advert. leaf and half-title precede title in Vol. III
Vol. I (xxviii) [paged (i)–(iv)+(i)–(xxiv)]+278. Final leaf, N_7, a single inset.
II (iv)+(298) Final leaf, O_5, a single inset.
III (vi)+308 pp. (vii) (viii) are cut away and probably constituted label-leaf.
Fine.

JOHN LAW: THE PROJECTOR [16]
3 vols. Chapman & Hall 1864. Dark purple-brown diagonal-wide-bead-grain cloth.
Vol. I vi+300
II vi+(304)
III vi+314 Final leaf, Y_1, a single inset.
Presentation Copy: 'Mrs E. W. Edwards with the Author's Best Regards 1st August 1864' in ink on title of Vol. I. Book-plate of Edward Watkin Edwards, and 'Mrs Edwards. Blackhurst' in pencil on fly-leaf of each vol. Very fine.

LANCASHIRE WITCHES (The) [17]
3 vols. Colburn 1849. Half-cloth boards, labels.
Vol. I (vi)+320 The fourth leaf of prelims. is neatly cut away and was probably the label-leaf.
II iv+(320) X_8 adverts.
III iv+(360)
Very fine.

LEAGUER OF LATHOM (The): a Tale of the Civil War in Lancashire [18]
3 vols. Tinsley 1876. Bright blue diagonal-fine-ribbed cloth.
Vol. I viii+(294) Final signatures, U, 2 leaves, X, a single inset.
II vi+(288)
III vi+326 Final signatures, Y, 2 leaves, Z, a single inset.
Fine.

LORD MAYOR OF LONDON (The), or City Life in the Last Century [19]
3 vols. Chapman & Hall 1862. Magenta wavy-grain cloth.
Vol. I (x)+304 pp. ix (x), signed *b*, a single inset.
II vi+302
III vi+316
Fine. Spines a little faded.

MANCHESTER REBELS (The), or The Fatal '45 [20]
Tinsley 1874. Blue sand-grain cloth, blocked on front in gold and black with standardised design of Tinsley's Popular Half-Crown Series.
Half-title. pp. xvi+356
'With the Author's compliments' (not in Ainsworth's hand) in ink on fly-leaf, and ink signature: 'J. G. Boiney. Tunbridge Wells', inside front cover.
Note. This is a New Edition of *The Good Old Times*, (3 vols, 1873) with a new preface.

MERVYN CLITHEROE [21]
Copy I: Part Issue (entitled on wrappers: 'The Life and Adventures of Mervyn Clitheroe') *Pl. 1*
Twelve-in-eleven monthly 8vo parts, priced at one shilling (except final double part, which is two

shillings). Nos. I–IV were published by Chapman & Hall from December 1851 to March 1852; Nos. V–XI / XII by Routledge from December 1857 to June 1858. The Chapman & Hall Nos. are wrappered in cream, the Routledge Nos. in blue, all printed in black—on front as described below, on inside covers and outside back covers with adverts.

Front covers carry an all-over design by Phiz, incorporating incidents from the story and fancy lettering, also wording in type which shows changes as the publication proceeds. Thus: No. I [II, III etc.] DECEMBER [*JANUARY, FEBRUARY* etc.] *Price* 1s. [final part 2s.] / (*top of design*—unframed on Nos. I–IV, enclosed in single line frame on V–XI/XII) / THE / LIFE AND ADVENTURES / OF / MERVYN CLITHEROE / BY / W. HARRISON AINSWORTH / ILLUSTRATED BY PHIZ. / *bottom of design* / Then, on Nos. I–IV, LONDON: CHAPMAN AND HALL, 193, PICCADILLY. / J. MENZIES, EDINBURGH: T. MURRAY, GLASGOW: J. M'GLASHAN, DUBLIN. / WHITING,] (on No. I: C. WHITING) 1851 [1852]. / [BEAUFORT HOUSE.

On No. V the wording below the design but enclosed in the frame reads: LONDON: GEORGE ROUTLEDGE AND CO., FARRINGDON STREET./ NEW YORK: 18, BEEKMAN STREET. / WHITING,] 1857 [1858]. [BEAUFORT HOUSE.

On Nos. VI–XI/XII, below the frame, appears the legend: (*hand pointing*) NOTICE.—The Author of this work reserves the Right of Translation.

No. I. Inside front cover: (i) Robert Cocks, Music Publishers; (ii) Heal & Sons; (iii) small Chapman & Hall advert.
Two plates by Phiz, imprinted and dated 1851. pp. (1)–32 of text.
Inside back cover: Pulvermacher's Hydro-Electric Voltaic Chain.
Outside back cover: Price list of E. Moses & Son, tailors, preceded by a long and punning paragraph headed: THE MOST IMPORTANT MONTH FOR THE GARDEN.

Note. Locke calls for an inset slip advertising *Mr Sponge's Sporting Tour.* No trace of such a slip appears in this copy.

No. II. Inside front cover: (i) Chapman & Hall composite advert.; (ii) *Punch* Office advert. of *Mr Sponge's Sporting Tour*; (iii) Bradbury & Evans' advert. of Dickens' *Child's History of England.*
Two plates by Phiz, imprinted and dated 1852. pp. 33–64 of text.
Inside and outside back covers as No. I.

No. III. Inside front cover: (i) Chapman & Hall advert. of Macgregor's *History of the British Empire*; (ii) Coles's Truss; (iii) Pulvermacher's Hydro-Electric Chain.
Two plates by Phiz, imprinted and dated as in No. II. pp. 65–96 of text.
Inside back cover: Chapman & Hall composite advert. including *Alton Locke*, Second Edition.
Outside back cover: Moses' Price List, preceded by a facetious par. headed: NOTICE OF MERVYN CLITHEROE.

No. IV. Inside front cover: (i) Chapman & Hall advert. as in No. III, plus Penny's *Letter to the Lords Commissioners of the Admiralty*; (ii) Pulvermacher slightly re-worded from No. III.
Two plates by Phiz, imprinted and dated as in No. III. pp. 97–126 of text (ending with the words: END OF THE FIRST PART / OF / MERVYN CLITHEROE, the two final words being a line block from fancy Phiz lettering), followed by I_8, printed on recto with a 'Notice' from the author, dated February 1852, apologising for an inevitable delay in the continuation of the story, on verso with the words: 'Due Notice will be given of the appearance of No. V'.
Inside back cover: Chapman & Hall composite advert., substituting *Reade's Poetical Works* for *Alton Locke*, otherwise as in No. III.
Outside back cover: Moses' Price List, preceded by a poem headed: POSSIBLE VERY! JUST SO! INDEED!

No. V. Inside front cover: Routledge composite advert. Slip of blue paper tipped on to verso of first plate reading: NOTICE:—*Four Numbers of this Work* / (*containing the First Book*) *are already* / *published*, with illustrations by HABLOT / K. BROWNE. *Price One Shilling each* / *Number.* / 2, Farringdon Street, December 1.
Two plates by Phiz, neither imprinted nor dated. pp. (129)–160 of text.
Inside back cover: Routledge advert. of Ainsworth's Works.
Outside back cover: Moses' Price List, re-designed and headed: OLD FRIENDS.

Note. At the front of this copy is a trace of adverts. on white paper, presumably the 8 pp. to which Locke refers.

No. VI. Inside front cover: Press Opinion on *five* Numbers of *Mervyn Clitheroe.*
Two plates by Phiz. pp. 161–92 of text.
Leaf of yellow paper, printed on recto with Routledge list of Children's Books, verso blank.
Two leaves of white paper headed 'British Expedition Advertiser' and printed with various adverts. Two leaves of thinner white paper printed with Routledge adverts.
Inside back cover: continuation of inside front cover.
Outside back cover: Moses, with no Price List, but a long Address headed: THE NEW YEAR'S WELCOME.

No. VII. Inside front cover: Press Opinion on *six* Numbers of M. C. Slip of yellow paper

tipped to following sheet, advertising *The Royal Princesses of England* published by Routledge.
Two leaves of white paper advertising *The National Cyclopaedia* published by Routledge.
Two plates by Phiz. pp. 193–224 of text.
Inside back cover: continuation of inside front cover.
Outside back cover: Moses' Price List, headed: ARTICLES OF ATTIRE.

No. VIII. Inside front cover: Press Opinion on *seven* numbers of M. C.
Two plates by Phiz. pp. 225–56 of text.
Inside back cover: continuation of inside front cover.
Outside back cover: Moses' Price List, headed: SPRING NOVELTIES.

No. IX. Inside front cover: Routledge composite advert.
Two leaves of white paper advertising Routledge publications and dated 'April 1858'.
Two plates by Phiz. pp. 257–88 of text.
Inside back cover: Routledge composite advert.
Outside back cover: Moses' Price List, headed: SPRING AND SUMMER ATTIRE.

No. X. Inside front cover: Announcement regarding Completion of M. C. and Press Opinions on No. IX.
Two leaves of white paper, advertising Routledge publications and dated 'May 1858'.
Two plates by Phiz. pp. 289–320 of text.
Inside back cover: Routledge advert. of Ainsworth and G. P. R. James.
Outside back cover: Moses' Price List, headed: ANGOLA SUITS.

Nos. XI/XII. Inside front cover: Press Opinion on M. C. Front. and pictorial title (the latter imprinted and dated 1858) by Phiz. Two plates by Phiz. (*a*) 4 leaves paged (i)–viii + *b*, 2 leaves unpaged, forming a 12-page prelim. incorporating a fly-title to Book I (in the actual Number the sequence of these leaves is ignored for reasons of folding). pp. 321–72 of text.
Inside back cover: Routledge advert. as in No. X.
Outside back cover: Moses' Price List, headed: MIDSUMMER VACATIONS, EXCURSIONS etc.

Nos. I–IV carry bookseller's ticket: 'Meehan, Bath' inside front cover. The parts are uniformly fine, except that the spine of the final part has been pasted down.

Note. I have described this issue rather fully, because in complete and original form (the four first parts were re-wrappered by Routledge in blue and re-issued to form sets with the seven later parts as these were periodically published) it is one of the rarest part-issues of the period, and for obvious reasons. The change of publishers suggests a parallel with Mayne Reid's *Headless Horseman* (q.v.), but whereas there was no interruption in the appearance of that work and the history of its adventures remains a mystery, a break of five and a half years occurred in the publication of *Mervyn Clitheroe* and was publicly foretold. S. M. Ellis tells the story in his biography of Ainsworth, stating that the part-issue fell so flat that, after four numbers had appeared, the author deliberately broke off his narrative, as he was publishing at a loss. He only resumed composition in 1857 in response to the urgent requests of a few friends. Surprisingly enough, when the tale began to re-appear, it proved as popular from No. V onward as it had previously been neglected.

Copy II: First Book Edition. [21*a*]

8vo. Routledge 1858. Dark blue bead-grain cloth. Etched front., pictorial title and 22 plates by Hablot K. Browne.

pp. (xii) + 372

'Carrie Faber from her loving mother' in ink on fly-leaf. Very fine.

Notes. (i) The irregularity of paging between Nos. IV and V of the part-issue, where the text, having ended on p. 126, continues on p. (129) is remedied in the book-issue by the insertion of a fly-title to Book II in place of the leaf carrying the Author's Notice. Unfortunately this fly-title was misprinted: 'Book the First.' The line block rendering of *Mervyn Clitheroe* on p. 126 of the parts is omitted from the book-issue.

(ii) In the book-issue, the Chapman & Hall imprint and date at the foot of the plates survive on the plates facing pp. 17 and 27, are partially erased from that facing p. 47, and wholly erased in the remaining five cases.

MYDDLETON POMFRET: a Novel [22]

3 vols. Chapman & Hall 1868. Plum patterned-sand-grain cloth, blocked in blind on front and back, blocked and lettered in gold on spine. Cream end-papers.

Half-title in Vol. I

Vol. I (viii) + (288)
II (vi) [paged (viii)] + (288) T_8 blank. The title a single inset, and p. (iii) signed *b*.
III vi + (316) Title a single inset, p. (iii) signed *b*, and p. iv mispaged v.

Book-plate of Lord Esher.

OLD COURT: a Novel [23]

3 vols. Chapman & Hall 1867. Light brown sand-grain cloth.

Half-title in each vol.

Vol. I (viii) + 288
II viii + (292)
III viii + (292)

Binders' ticket: 'W. Bone & Son' at end of Vol. I.

Presentation Copy: 'Mrs E. W. Edwards from W. Harrison Ainsworth, June 19, 1867' in ink on fly-leaf of Vol. I. Fine.

[24] **OLD ST PAUL'S**: a Tale of the Plague and the Fire
3 vols. Cunningham 1841. Dark brown fine-diaper-grain cloth. 10 engraved plates by John Franklin in Vol. I, 5 each in Vols. II and III.

Vol. I (viii) + 352
II (iv) + (336) P_{12} adverts.
III (iv) + (328) Single advert. leaf, paged (1) 2, inset at end.

Very fine.

[25] **OVINGDEAN GRANGE**
8vo. Routledge 1860. Blue bead-grain cloth. Wood-engraved front. and 7 illustrations after Hablot K. Browne.

pp. (x) [(*a*) 4 leaves, *b* 1 leaf] + (358) Final signatures, 2A, 2 leaves, 2B, a single inset.

Fine. Also issued in red cloth, uniformly blocked.

[26] **ROOKWOOD**: a Romance [anon]
3 vols. Bentley 1834. Boards, labels.

Blank leaf and half-title in Vol. I, half-title only in II and III

Vol. I (x) + 324 [B unsigned].
II (vi) + 364 [B unsigned].
III (iv) + 464 [B signed].

Very fine.

[27] **SIR JOHN CHIVERTON**: a Romance [anon]
John Ebers 1826.

Copy I: First Edition. Boards, label. Half-title. pp. (viii) + (320) X_8 adverts. Longman cat., 4 pp. dated May 1826, inset between front end-papers. Doubtless Longman acted as distributors.

Ink signature: 'F. Price. Rhiwlas. 1826' inside front cover. Top of spine neatly repaired. Boards and label fine.

[27*a*] **Copy II: Second Edition,** W. Harrison Ainsworth, 1827. Contemporary half-calf, marbled edges. Collation as I, but lacking X_8.

Presentation Copy: 'Mrs Gore Langton with the Author's respects. May, 1827' in ink on half-title (probably in the hand of John Aston).

Note. Sir John Chiverton was written in collaboration with a school friend J. P. Aston (cf. Ellis, Vol. I, pp. 134 seq.). The 'Second Edition' consists of first edition sheets with a cancel title, carrying Ainsworth's name as publisher.

[28] **SPANISH MATCH** (The), or Charles Stuart in Madrid
3 vols. Chapman & Hall 1865.

Copy I. Olive-green pebble-grain cloth.

Vol. I viii + (294) Final signatures, U, 2 leaves, X, a single inset.
II vi + (294) Final signatures, U, 2 leaves, X a single inset.
III vi + 324

Binders' ticket: 'Bone & Son' at end of Vol. I.

Presentation Copy: 'E. W. Edwards Esq. from his friend W. Harrison Ainsworth' in ink on title of Vol. I. 'Mrs Edwards, Blackhurst' in pencil on fly-leaves of II and III.

Copy II. Violet-blue pebble-grain cloth. Collation as I, but without binders' ticket. [28*a*]

Presentation Copy: 'E. W. Edwards Esq. with the author's comp[ts]' (not in Ainsworth's hand) on title of Vol. I.

Both copies very fine. Copy II is the regulation colour. I have never seen another as Copy I.

SPENDTHRIFT (The): a Tale [29]
8vo. Routledge 1857. Yellow boards, pictorially printed and lettered in dark blue. Wood-engraved front. and 7 plates after Phiz, of which that facing p. 290 is reproduced on front cover.

Half-title. pp. (viii) [paged (vi)] + 332

Blind stamp: 'W. H. Smith & Son' on fly-leaf. Fine.

This volume was also issued in blue, red and green cloth, gilt.

TALBOT HARLAND: a Tale of the Days of Charles II [30]
8vo. John Dicks, n.d. [1870]. Buff paper wrappers pictorially printed in red, green and black. Inside covers and outside back cover printed with adverts. Wood-engraved front. and 9 illustrations after F. Gilbert.

Half-title. pp. (128) [paged (iv) + (110). D_{16} adverts]. The 9 internal plates, though on text paper with blank versos, are not reckoned in the pagination.

'John S. Hayden. London. Jan. 25th, 1883' in ink on half-title.

A volume in Dicks' Sixpenny English Novels. Copies in pale green wrappers, printed in black and carrying a portrait of Ainsworth, are re-issues.

TOWER OF LONDON (The): a Historical Romance [31]
8vo. Bentley 1840. Publisher's dark green morocco, pictorially blocked and lettered in gold, uniform with cloth issue. All edges gilt. Etched front., 39 plates and numerous wood-engravings in the text by George Cruikshank.

pp. xvi + (440) Fine.

Note. This is the first issue, the plates facing pp. 16, 28 and 45 showing the earliest features as set out by Cohn (*George Cruikshank*, London, 1924. Page 7, No. 14).

[32] WINDSOR CASTLE: an Historical Romance
3 vols. Colburn 1843. Half-cloth boards, labels. Etched front. in each vol. by George Cruikshank.
Half-title in Vol. III
Vol. I (vi) [paged (iv)] + 296 Slip 'DIRECTIONS TO THE BINDER' tipped in between pp. (vi) and (1).
II (vi) [paged (iv)] + 300
III (viii) + (326) First leaf of final sig., Y_1, a single inset.
Boards a little frayed and labels discoloured, but an honest, untouched copy.

ALEXANDER, MRS (ANNIE HECTOR) (1825–1902)

[33] ADMIRAL'S WARD (The)
3 vols. Bentley 1883. Pale olive diagonal-fine-ribbed cloth; mauve decorated end-papers.
Vol. I (ii) + 322 Final leaf, 21_1, a single inset.
II (ii) + 324
III (ii) + (316) B

[34] EXECUTOR (The): a Novel
3 vols. Bentley 1883. Navy-blue diagonal-fine-ribbed cloth, lettered in silver; grey floral end-papers.
Half-title in each vol.
Vol. I (iv) + (324)
II (iv) + 320
III (iv) + (324) 62_2 blank. B
This novel is printed throughout in dark blue ink.

[35] FRERES (The): a Novel
3 vols. Bentley 1882. Greenish grey diagonal-fine-ribbed cloth; black end-papers.
Vol. I (ii) + 324
II (ii) + (310) First leaf of final sig., 41_1, a single inset.
III (ii) + (368) 64_8 adverts. B

[36] HER DEAREST FOE: a Novel
3 vols. Bentley 1876. Slate diagonal-fine-ribbed cloth.
Vol I (ii) + 350 First leaf of final sig., 22_1, a single inset.
II (ii) + 306 Final leaf, 20_1, a single inset.
III (ii) + 298 Final leaf, 19_5 [signed 19_3] a single inset. B

[37] HERITAGE OF LANGDALE (The): a Novel
3 vols. Bentley 1877. Plum diagonal-fine-ribbed cloth, bevelled boards.
Half-title in Vol. I
Vol. I (iv) + 300
II (ii) + (280)
III (ii) + 272 Publisher's cat., 4 pp. undated, at end. B
Back cover of Vol. I slightly marked.

LIFE INTEREST (A) [38]
3 vols. Bentley 1888. Dark red cloth spines and corners, glazed paper sides with floral design in dark red and white; pale olive-brown floral end-papers.
Half-title in Vol. I: blank leaf and half-title precede title in II and III
Vol. I viii + (300)
II (viii) [paged vi] + (288) 37_8 adverts.
III (viii) [paged vi] + (268) $54A_2$ adverts. B

RALPH WILTON'S WEIRD (by the author of 'The Wooing O't') [39]
Copy I: First Edition. 2 vols. Bentley 1875. Red diagonal-fine-ribbed cloth; grey-chocolate end-papers, bevelled boards.
Vol. I (ii) + (272)
II (ii) + 268 B
Copy II: First one-volume Edition. Bentley 1878. Scarlet fine-ribbed cloth. No. 3 of Bentley's Half-Crown Empire Library (Section III, 3733). [39*a*]

SECOND LIFE (A): a Novel [40]
3 vols. Bentley 1885. Burnt-umber diagonal-fine-ribbed cloth; grey floral end-papers.
Half-title in Vol. I
Vol. I (vi) + 318 First leaf of final sig., 20_1, a single inset.
II (ii) + 348
III (ii) + (368) B

WOOING O'T (The): a Novel [41]
3 vols. Bentley 1873. Smooth red cloth.
Half-title in Vol. I
Vol. I (iv) + (330) Third leaf of final sig., Y_3, a single inset.
II (ii) + (326) First leaf of final sig., Y_1, a single inset.
III (ii) + (328) Y_4 blank. B
Binders' ticket: 'Leighton, Son & Hodge' at end of Vol. I.
Cloth rather damp-stained.

ALEXIS, W.

BURGOMASTER OF BERLIN (The). Translated from the German of W. Alexis by W.A.G. [42]
3 vols. Saunders & Otley 1843. Scarlet fine-morocco cloth, blocked in blind and lettered in gold.

Half-title in Vol. I
Vol. I (xx) [paged (xviii)] + (316) P_2 adverts.
II (ii) + 332
III (ii) + 336

This copy belonged to Richard Monckton Milnes. 'Fryston' is written in ink, and in his hand, on inside cover of each vol.

Note. Entitled in the original *Der Roland von Berlin*, this story of the fifteenth century describes the conquest of the Mark of Brandenburg by the Hohenzollern, the second of which line embodies the principle of absolute monarchy in its most favourable light. Alexis supplies an 'Author's Preface', specially written for this English edition.

ANSTEY, F. (1856–1934)

This entry is a compromise. Predominantly it consists of orthodox prose-fiction (including a three-decker of which I am not conscious of having seen another copy outside a Library); but, on account of their established reputation and frequent new editions, I have admitted four 4to volumes of the humorous dialogues in dramatic form for which Anstey had both talent and liking. It seemed stupid to omit *Voces Populi* and *The Man from Blankley's*, seeing that to many people they, with *Vice Versâ*, constitute this author's work.

[43] BABOO JABBERJEE, B.A.
J. M. Dent & Co. 1897. Smooth blue cloth, pictorially blocked in gold on front, gold-lettered on spine, back plain. Half-tone front. and 28 illustrations in half-tone and line after Bernard Partridge, all on plate paper. Title printed in red and black.

Half-title (reading: BABOO / HURRY BUNGSHO JABBERJEE, B.A.) Pp. xvi + 272.

Booksellers' stamp: 'Hodges Figgis & Co. Ltd. Dublin' on fly-leaf.

[44] BRASS BOTTLE (The)
Smith, Elder 1900. Light olive-green linen, lettered on front and spine in red-brown. Back plain. Line-engraved front. after H. R. Millar on plate paper. Blank leaf and half-title precede front. Pp. (viii) + (320). Final sigs. X and Y each four leaves. Y_1–Y_4 adverts.

Fine. A correspondence card in Anstey's hand to a Miss Bowker, dated 27 June 1900 and referring to *The Brass Bottle*, is inserted in the book.

[45] FALLEN IDOL (A)
Smith, Elder 1886. Orange diagonal-fine-ribbed cloth, blocked in black on front, in blind on back; blocked in black and lettered in gold on spine. Glazed pale-yellow end-papers.

Half-title. Pp. (viii) + (336) Y_8 adverts.

Pencil signature: 'Radclyffe Walters. 1887' facing half-title. Library label removed from front cover. Cloth fresh.

GIANT'S ROBE (The) [46]
Smith, Elder 1884. Dark blue-green diagonal-fine-ribbed cloth, blocked in black on front, in blind on back; blocked in black and lettered in gold on spine. Glazed pale-yellow end-papers.

Half-title. Pp. viii + 440

Pencil signature: 'Radclyffe Walters 1884' facing half-title. Very fine.

LOVE AMONG THE LIONS: a Matrimonial Experience [47]
J. M. Dent & Co. [1898]. Dark red diagonal-fine-ribbed cloth, blocked and lettered in gold on front and spine; back plain. Line-engraved illustrations, full-page and in the text, all on text-paper, after 'Forrest'. Title-page printed in red and black.

Blank leaf and half-title precede title. Pp. (viii) [paged vi] + (120). Fine.

LYRE AND LANCET: a Story in Scenes [48]
Small sq. 8vo. Smith, Elder 1895. Blue-grey ribbed cloth, blocked and lettered in black and gold on front and spine, back plain. Line illustrations on text paper after Bernard Partridge.

Half-title. Pp. viii + (258) Final leaf (S_1) adverts and a single inset. Very fine.

Note. This was Vol. II in The Novel Series (3753 in Section III).

MAN FROM BLANKLEY'S (The) and Other Sketches [49]
Fcap 4to. Longmans, Green & Co. 1893. White parchment spine blocked and lettered in gold, uniform with the Second Series of *Voces Populi*; patterned paper-board sides (in dark blue, light blue and gold). Fawn-on-white Swan-and-Ship end-papers. 25 line engraved illustrations after Bernard Partridge, all on text paper and that appearing on p. 6 repeated as front. and printed on verso of half-title.

Half-title. pp. (viii) + (152)

Pencil signature: 'Radclyffe Walters 1893' facing half-title. Fine.

PARIAH (The) [50]
3 vols. Smith, Elder 1889. Smooth grey-blue cloth, blocked and lettered in red on front and spine; back plain. Pale-green-on-white patterned end-papers. Blank leaf and half-title precede title in each vol.

Vol. I (viii) + (296)
II (viii) + (296)
III (viii) + (312) X_3 X_4 adverts.

Pencil signature: 'Radclyffe Walters 1889' in each vol. Very fine.

Note. Although Anstey's name appears on title, the front and spine of each vol. read 'By the Author of Vice Versa'.

[51] PUPPETS AT LARGE. Scenes and Subjects from Mr Punch's Show

Bradbury, Agnew 1897. Green ribbed cloth, pictorially blocked and lettered on front in black and brown, gold-lettered on spine, back plain. Black end-papers. 16 illustrations in line on text paper after Bernard Partridge. Title-page printed in red and black.

Half-title. pp. (viii) + (280) R_3 R_4 adverts.

Pencil signature: 'Radclyffe Walters 1897' facing half-title. Very fine, in salmon dust-jacket printed in brown.

[52] TALKING HORSE (The) and Other Tales

Smith, Elder 1892. Blue fine-diaper cloth spine, lettered in gold; smooth fawn cloth front and back, the former lettered in blue. Glazed yellow end-papers.

Half-title. pp. (viii) + (328) Y_1–Y_4 adverts.

Pencil signature facing title: 'Radclyffe Walters 1892'. Very fine.

[53] TINTED VENUS (The): a Farcical Romance

Copy I: First Edition. Fcap 8vo. Bristol, Arrowsmith 1885. Scarlet diagonal-fine-ribbed cloth, blocked and lettered in black. Pale yellow end-papers.

pp. (iv) + 192. 4 pp. of adverts (publishers' and commercial) at end. Fine. Vol. VI of Arrowsmith's Bristol Library. Also issued in wrappers.

[53*a*] **Copy II: First Illustrated Edition.** Extra cr. 8vo. Harper & Brothers 1898. Dark red unglazed linen, pictorially blocked and lettered in gold on front and spine; back plain. Half-tone front. and 14 illustrations after Bernard Partridge, all on plate paper.

Half-title. pp. (viii) + (280) [mispaged 3–(282)]

Ink signature: 'Nellie (?) Dasent' on title.

[54] TOURMALIN'S TIME CHEQUES

Bristol, Arrowsmith [1891]. Smooth apple-green cloth, lettered on front and spine in dark green. White end-papers.

pp. (iv) [paged ii] + 172. Publisher's cat., 16 pp. on text paper undated, at end.

Pencil signature: 'Radclyffe Walters 1891' on flyleaf. Very fine.

TRAVELLING COMPANIONS (The): a Story in Scenes. (Reprinted from *Punch*) [55]

Fcap 4to. Longmans, Green & Co. 1892. Smooth rose-red cloth spine lettered in gold; smooth salmon-cloth front and back, the former pictorially blocked and lettered in rose-red. Red chocolate end-papers. 26 line-engraved illustrations after Bernard Partridge, all on text paper, and that appearing on p. 127 repeated as front.

Half-title. pp. (viii) + (152)

Pencil signature: 'Radclyffe Walters 1892' facing half-title. Fine.

UNDER THE ROSE: a Story in Scenes [56]

Bradbury, Agnew [1894]. Green ribbed cloth, gold-lettered on front and spine. Olive-green end-papers. Fifteen line-engraved illustrations on text paper after Bernard Partridge.

Half-title. pp. (viii) + (218) Final leaf, Q_1, a single inset.

Pencil signature: 'Radclyffe Walters 1894' on half-title. Very fine.

VICE VERSÂ: or A Lesson to Fathers [57]

Smith, Elder 1882. Brownish-slate diagonal-fine-ribbed cloth, blocked in black on front and spine, gold-lettered on spine, blind blocked on back. Primrose end-papers.

Half-title. pp. (viii) + 364

Bookplate removed from inside front cover. Cloth fine, apart from small soiled patch on spine.

VOCES POPULI. (Reprinted from *Punch*) [58]

Fcap 4to. Longmans, Green & Co. 1890. Smooth apple-green cloth spine lettered in gold, marbled paper-board sides. Chocolate end-papers. Line-engraved front. and 19 illustrations after Bernard Partridge, all on text paper.

Blank leaf and half-title precede front. pp. (xii) + 136

Pencil signature: 'Radclyffe Walters 1891' on recto of first blank leaf.

VOCES POPULI. (Reprinted from *Punch.*) Second Series [59]

Fcap 4to. Longmans, Green & Co. 1892. White parchment spine blocked and lettered in gold, patterned paper-board sides (in dark green, light green and gold). Fawn-on-white Swan-and-Ship end-papers. 25 line-engraved illustrations after Bernard Partridge, all on text paper, and that appearing on p. 86 repeated as front.

Half-title precedes front. pp. (viii) + 156

Pencil signature: 'Radclyffe Walters 1892' facing half-title. Fine.

ARCHDEACON, M.

[60] PRIEST-HUNTER (The): an Irish Tale of the Penal Times
Dublin: James Duffy 1844. Red fine-ribbed cloth, blocked in blind on front and back, all-over blocked and lettered in gold on spine.
pp. (viii) + 416
Note. The title also appears in Irish on title and first page of text: 'Shawn na Soggarth'. The author is described as 'author of *Connaught in 1798*, *Legends of Connaught*, *Everard*, etc.'

ARNOLD, REV. FREDERICK (1832–1891)

[61] CHRIST CHURCH DAYS: an Oxford Story
2 vols. Bentley 1867. Red moiré fine-ribbed cloth, bevelled boards.
Vol. I (iv) + (316)
II (ii) + (332) Y_6 blank. B
Front cover of Vol. I ink-smeared on fore-edge.

AUSTEN, JANE (1775–1817)

For full bibliographical detail see Keynes, *Jane Austen: a Bibliography*, London 1929, to which work references are made below.

[62] SET OF FIRST EDITIONS
16 vols. 1811–1818. Full dark green polished morocco; marbled end-papers; all edges gilt. Lord Rosebery's set, with his book-plate in each vol.

[62*a*] **Sense and Sensibility** [*Keynes p.* 3
3 vols. Egerton 1811.
Half-title (correct by Keynes' facsimiles) in Vols. II and III; lacking from Vol. I.

[62*b*] **Pride and Prejudice** [*Keynes p.* 8
3 vols. Egerton 1813.
No half-titles.

[62*c*] **Mansfield Park** [*Keynes p.* 11
3 vols. Egerton 1814.
Half-title (correct by Keynes' facsimiles) in each vol. Vol. II, O_4 (blank) and Vol. III, R_4 (advert. and blank) lacking.

[62*d*] **Emma** [*Keynes p.* 14
3 vols. Murray 1816.
Half-title in each vol.

[62*e*] **Northanger Abbey** and **Persuasion** [*Keynes p.* 16
4 vols. Murray 1818.
Half-title in Vol. I; lacking in II, III, IV. Vol. IV, P_7 P_8 (blanks) lacking.
See also: *Bentley's Standard Novels* etc. in Section III.

'BENTLEY'S FAVOURITE NOVELS' EDITION [63]

These are first issues of this frequently reprinted edition, and the title in caps is a first edition of the Jane Austen material.
Green cloth, gilt, in standard Favourite Novel style.

Sense and Sensibility [63*a*]
Pride and Prejudice [63*b*]
Mansfield Park [63*c*]
Emma [63*d*]
Northanger Abbey and **Persuasion** [63*e*]
(each 1 vol. Bentley 1870.)

MEMOIR OF JANE AUSTEN (A) by her nephew, J. E. Austen Leigh. Second Edition. To which is added LADY SUSAN AND FRAGMENTS OF TWO OTHER UNFINISHED TALES BY MISS AUSTEN. [63*f*]
Bentley 1871.
Blank leaf and half-title precede title.
pp. (xii) [paged (x)] + 364
Contains a new preface by J. Austen Leigh dated November 1, 1870, considerable additions to the Memoir, the cancelled chapter of *Persuasion*, *Lady Susan* and *The Watsons*.

AUSTIN, ALFRED (1835–1913)

Some time in the early 1930's I bought a small collection of the works of Alfred Austin which had belonged to him and been sold from his home. Most of the books here described constituted that collection, and it is a fair presumption that he was the author of certain anonymous and pseudonymous items.

ARTIST'S PROOF (An) [64]
3 vols. Tinsley 1864. Green sand-grain cloth.
Half-title in each vol.
Vol. I vi + (320)
II (iv) + 316
III (iv) + (314) Final leaf, X_5, a single inset.
Back cover of Vol. III dented by a nail.

FIVE YEARS OF IT [65]
2 vols. J. F. Hope 1858. Grey-blue morocco cloth.
Vol. I (iv) + (320) Publisher's cat., 12 pp. undated, at end.
II (ii) + 324 Final leaf Y_3; Y_4 probably title. Publisher's cat., 12 pp. undated, at end.
Stain on front cover of Vol. II.

GOLDEN AGE (The): a Satire [66]
Chapman & Hall 1871. Smooth brown cloth, greenish-black end-papers.
Half-title. pp. (xii) + (128) I_8 blank. Erratum slip between pp. (iv) and (v).

Ink-inscription: 'Katharine C. Blake, with much love and best wishes from [initials illegible] 18 Jan. 1896', on half-title in handwriting undoubtedly Austin's (cf. that in *The Season*, Copy II).

From the Austin collection.

[67] HUMAN TRAGEDY (The): a Poem

8vo. Robt Hardwicke 1862. Smooth glazed brown cloth, bevelled boards, chocolate end-papers.

Half-title. pp. (iv) + (220) Errata slip between pp. (iv) and (1). Binder's ticket: 'Burn' at end.

From the Austin collection. Very fine.

[68] JESSIE'S EXPIATION (by Oswald Boyle)

3 vols. Tinsley 1867. Purplish-maroon sand-grain cloth.

Vol. I (iv) + (316)
II (iv) + (312)
III (iv) + (304) 19_8 imprint leaf.

From the Austin collection of his own works. It is difficult to account for its presence there unless it were a pseudonymous work.

[69] LORD OF ALL (The): a Novel [anon]

2 vols. Chapman & Hall 1867. Brown fancy-diaper cloth.

Half-title in each vol.

Vol. I viii + (360)
II viii + (360) AA_4 blank.

From the Austin collection of his own works, with pencil corrections in his manner and apparently in his handwriting.

Back cover of Vol. I damp-stained.

[70] MY SATIRE AND ITS CENSORS

8vo. George Manwaring 1861. Purple wavy-grain cloth; dark terra-cotta end-papers.

Half-title. pp. (iv) + (60) E_3–E_6 adverts.

From the Austin collection. Fine.

[71] RANDOLPH: a Poem in two cantos [anon]

Saunders & Otley 1855. Blue morocco cloth.

Half-title. pp. viii + (112) F_6, F_7 Notes. F_8 adverts.

From the Austin collection. Fine.

[72] SEASON (The): a Satire

Copy I: First Edition. 8vo. Hardwicke 1861. Magenta bead-grain cloth; dark green end-papers. Lithographed front. after T. G. Cooper.

Half-title. pp. (76) (E_6) blank.

[72*a*] **Copy II: Second Edition revised.** 8vo. George Manwaring 1861. Blue bead-grain cloth; dark brown end-papers. Front. as first edition.

pp. (88) F_4 adverts.

Copy III: Third Edition revised. Small 8vo. Hotten 1869. Smooth brown cloth; grey-chocolate end-papers, all edges gilt. Bevelled boards. [72*b*]

Half-title. pp. (xxviii) + 80. Publisher's cat., 4 pp. undated, at end.

Binders' ticket: 'W. Bone & Son', at end.

Inserted in Copy II are 20 pp. corrected by A. for the third edition, and inscribed in ink on half-title 'To my Mother. April 1, 1861' in his hand.

All three copies from the Austin collection.

SHOTS AT SHADOWS: a Satire; but —— a poem (by 'Proteus') [73]

Robt Hardwicke 1859. Blue bead-grain cloth; chocolate end-papers.

pp. (42)

From the Austin collection. Pencil corrections in his hand suggest that he was the author.

WON BY A HEAD: a Novel [74]

3 vols. Chapman & Hall 1866. Scarlet sand-grain cloth.

Half-title in Vol. I

Vol. I viii + 292
II iv + 296
III iv + (308)

From the Austin collection, with a few corrections in ink and pencil.

AUTHORSHIP UNKNOWN

AUTOBIOGRAPHY OF AN IRISH TRAVELLER [75]

3 vols. Longman etc. 1835. Boards, labels.

Half-title in each vol.

Vol. I (viii) + (300)
II (iv) + 312
III (iv) + 296

Book-label of the Imperial Library, St Petersburg, inside front cover of each vol. Fine.

Note. The book is dedicated to the Tsar Nicholas I, and this is therefore the copy presented to the dedicatee.

BIBLICALS (The): or Glenmoyle Castle. A Tale of Modern Times [76]

Keating & Brown, 38 Duke Street, Grosvenor Square 1831. Half-cloth boards, label.

pp. (294) (2 A_1) Errata leaf and a single inset, preceded by traces of a cancel. Except for sig. (A), 8 leaves, the book collates in sixes. Sigs. R and W are each 7 leaves on account of cancellations. In R, R_4–R_6 have been cancelled and replaced by 4 leaves (pp. 203, 204, 204*, 205, 205*, 206, 207, 208). In W, W_5 has been cancelled and replaced by 2 leaves (pp. 253, 253*, 254, 254*).

Dedication leaf torn and text slightly affected.

Note. A Catholic novel, attacking Biblicism and rather defiantly dedicated to the Protestant Archbishop of Tuam.

[77] BOB NORBERRY: or Sketches from the Note Book of an Irish Reporter (edited by Captain [T] Prout)

8vo. Dublin: James Duffy 1844. Plum ribbed cloth, pictorially blocked in gold. Etched front. and pictorial title by W. H. Holbrooke, and 7 full-page etched plates by Henry MacManus.

pp. viii + 360

Armorial book-plate 'si dieu veult'.

[78] CASTLE MARTYR: or a Tale of Old Ireland

2 vols. Hugh Cunningham 1839. Dark green fine-diaper cloth.

Vol. I (l) + (352)

II (ii) + (368) R_4 advert., announcing two three-volume novels by the same author: *The Ormonde Annals* and *Reginald the Bachelor*.

Note. In October 1837 Lady Blessington called Bentley's attention to the MS. of this novel and hoped he would publish it.

[79] CHARLEY CHALK: or the Career of an Artist

8vo. G. Berger, Holywell Street, n.d. Yellow pictorial boards, printed in red and black. Engraved front., pictorial title and 18 full-page plates by 'Jacob Parallel'. (The front. is reproduced on front cover, and title vignette and List of Plates on back.)

pp. (viii) + (312) [paged 310] Pagination of pp. 191, 192, is duplicated. Fine.

Notes. (i) Also issued in maroon diaper cloth, blind-blocked front and back, gold blocked on spine with title, figure of Chalk from frontispiece and all-over design.

(ii) It would seem certain that this book was first published about 1840. It is included in Vol. VI of *The Romancist and Novelist's Library* (3757 *a* in Section III) with another tale dated 1839, and the book-issue here described undoubtedly appeared in 1842 or 1843. In these circumstances I imagine the cloth binding to be the original one. Pictorial yellow boards, even in this unusual style and format, are hardly conceivable at so early a date.

[80] CONVERTS (The): a Tale of the Nineteenth Century, or Romanism and Protestantism brought to bear in their true Light against one another

Keating & Brown, 38 Duke Street, Grosvenor Square, 1837. Navy-blue fine-pebble-grain cloth, paper label.

pp. 388 Text ends 353, (354) blank, (355)–359 Preface to the Appendix, (360) blank, (361) to 388 Appendix.

Ink signature: 'Miss Fairfax' inside front cover. Very fine.

Notes. (i) The title-page is a cancel. As the printer's imprint on verso is that of a Guernsey printer, I suspect the book appeared locally in the Channel Islands, and that a consignment of sheets with reprint title was sent to Keating & Brown for the mainland market.

(ii) This 'Tale' is a fighting defence of Catholicism on a frail foundation of narrative. Footnotes and a long Appendix, quoting authorities, support an unobtrusive story, whose characters discuss faiths and creeds, the Confessional, whether or not to go into convents and so forth, while leading a life of elegant anguish. The author deals heatedly with the 'Revelations' of the notorious Maria Monk, who is declared 'a most profligate character' as well as a liar and a calumniator.

COUNTRY HOUSES [81]

3 vols. Saunders & Otley 1832. Boards, labels.

Vol. I (ii) + 312 4 page leaflet announcing the first number of *Tait's Edinburgh Magazine* on March 31, 1832, inserted between front end-papers.

II (ii) + (354) First leaf of final signature, R_1, a single inset.

III (ii) + (372)

Book-label of R. J. Ll. Price, Rhiwlas Library (stuck over the signature of Frances Price, 1832) and bookseller's ticket: 'Seacome, Chester', inside front cover of each vol. Very fine.

Note. A 'silver fork' novel, which remains obstinately anonymous.

'Silver fork' fiction is commented on in the Introduction to this Catalogue. It is treated more fully in my book *Bulwer and his Wife*.

DOMESTIC MANNERS OF THE PARISIANS [82]

3 vols. Whitaker, Treacher, Arnot & Co. 1834. Half-cloth boards, labels.

Vol. I (ii) + (312) O_{12} blank.

II (ii) + (316)

III (ii) + (312) O_{11} adverts., O_{12} blank.

Book-plate of Richard Brinsley Sheridan in each vol.

Note. In all probability this book was inspired by the success of Mrs Trollope's *Domestic Manners of the Americans*. Perhaps it was commissioned by the publishers, who had themselves published Mrs Trollope's book in 1832.

DOZEN PAIR OF WEDDING GLOVES (A) [83]

[anon]

James Blackwood 1855.

Copy I. Red morocco cloth, pictorially blocked and fancy lettered on front in gold with blind decoration, gold lettered on spine WEDDING GLOVES. All edges gilt. Wood-engraved front., designed title and 2 illustrations after Phiz: also 4 illustrations after other artists.

Half-title. pp. xvi + (208) O_6–O_8 adverts.

[83*a*] **Copy II.** White ornamental boards, printed in red and green, up-lettered on spine, advert. on back-cover. Plain edges. Illustrations, collation, etc. as I.

Notes. (i) On the front cover of this issue is printed: ILLUSTRATED BY 'PHIZ' and the price: one shilling.

(ii) Dedicated to 'My Friend Albert Smith'.

[84] ENGLISH LIFE: or Manners at Home. In Four Pictures

Copy I: First Edition. 2 vols. G. Wightman, Fleet Street. 1825. Boards, labels.

Half-title in each vol.

Vol. I (iv) + (280)
II (iv) + (288) T_8 adverts.

Ink signature: 'Miss Susannah Coke', on title of each vol. Fine.

[84*a*] **Copy II: New (unavowed) Edition,** sub-titled: 'or Characters and Manners at Home'. 2 vols. Wightman 1829. Boards, labels.

No half-titles: otherwise as I.

Spines a little worn.

Note. Four unconnected long-short stories of aristocratic and upper-class life. They have none of the brittle dandyism of 'silver fork' fiction, nor of its occasional wit; but are sententious, exclamatory, moralising, and considerably concerned with broken engagements. The title, in so far as it suggests a book offering interesting period-background, is misleading.

[85] FAMILY SECRETS AND FAMILY INTERESTS: a Story Taken from Life

Hope & Co., n.d. [circ. 1855]. Magenta wavy-grain cloth. Steel-engraved front. after Smirke.

pp. (ii) + (268) S_5 S_6 adverts.

Note. The suggested dating of this book is based on an advert. at end of *Willy Reilley* by Carleton, in which it is described as 'Now Ready'.

[86] GRIMMS' [sic] GOBLINS: Part-Issue

4to. George Vickers, Angel Court, n.d. [? 1860].

42 penny parts (the last 'double' part, 2*d.*) each 8 pp. (the last 12 pp.), preceded by a 4 pp. prelim. (pictorial title, verso blank: Preface, 2 pp.).

In original state, unstitched, each part numbered at foot and up-printed along spine: FAIRY BOOKS FOR BOYS AND GIRLS.—'Grimm's Goblins'. No. 1 [2, 3, 4, etc.]. Price One Penny. London: GEORGE VICKERS. Angel Court, Strand.

Coloured wood-engraved title (p. i of prelims.) and 42 illustrations (on first page of each part) after Phiz. Also uncoloured text illustrations after other artists. The final part opens with Contents and List of 'Coloured Illustrations Designed by Phiz' (2 pp.) and then continues with pp. 329 to (338) of text, with coloured illustration on p. 329.

pp. (iv) + 1–(338) + (ii)

No printer's imprint appears anywhere. Very fine.

Notes. (i) This (in the words of the Preface) is a 'Collection of Fairy Tales and Goblin Lore combining the best legends of all nations and languages...and illustrated by a new process of Chromoxylography.' The Editor's name is not given. He discourses briefly on the history of Goblin and Fairy lore and states that 'collections of stories from such various sources as *Grimm's Goblins* are rare in the English language, most of them hitherto having been compiled from French originals only, too many of them being, if not entirely frivolous, often vulgar in language and gross in details, thus rendering them unfit for home purposes'.

Having thus reassured the guardians of the British hearth, the Editor pays a more interesting tribute to illustrator and producer. He 'trusts the public will join him in appreciating the talent of the artists, especially Mr Hablot K. Browne, some of whose designs in this work will be acknowledged in after years as his masterpieces: and the especial skill of Mr Edmund Evans, in engraving these designs and printing them in colours—a singular and successful novelty'.

(ii) This is undoubtedly the earliest issue of a compilation whose bibliography is in itself perplexing and is further complicated by the appropriation of its title, nearly twenty years later, for the benefit of a totally different book.

Of the work now under discussion the only copies in two of the principal National Libraries show important differences between one another, as well as between themselves and the Part Issue above described.

The B.M. has a run of 6 sixpenny parts, each containing 6 of the penny parts (i.e. 48 pp.), in yellow pictorial wrappers carrying the coloured illustration which forms the title of the Penny Part Issue. These wrappers carry titling: FAIRY BOOKS FOR BOYS AND GIRLS / PART I[–VI] / GRIMMS' GOBLINS / PRICE SIXPENCE / LONDON: GEORGE VICKERS, ANGEL COURT, STRAND. No date appears on the wrappers or anywhere else. There is no Preface in any of the six parts. The back wrappers (that of Part VI is missing) are printed with adverts. of Vickers' publications. That on Part V carries, not only Vickers' imprint, but also that of Edmund Evans as printer. This B.M. set is incomplete, as it contains only 288 of the 340 pages which compose the complete work. It is unfortunately not possible to say whether an overall printed title and/or an Editor's Preface was issued with the missing Part VII. The reception dates were:

Parts I–III: April 1861.
Part IV: May 1861.
Part V: July 1861.
Part VI: August 1861.

The Bodleian copy is a book-edition in yellow pictorial boards with the coloured title of the Part Issue appearing on the front cover. The prelims. (4 pp.) are on whiter paper than the text and typographically later in appearance. They consist of (i) (ii) title: GRIMM'S GOBLINS / A Collection / of / FAIRY TALES FOR BOYS AND GIRLS / / *rule* / ILLUSTRATED BY PHIZ. / *rule* / LONDON: / GEORGE VICKERS, ANGEL COURT, STRAND / 1861.; verso: London / Printed by Edmund Evans / etc.; (iii) Contents; (iv) ILLUSTRATIONS, / DESIGNED BY PHIZ. There is no Editor's Preface. The outside back cover carries publisher's advert., including a Gulliver and a collection of tales: *The Battle and the Breeze*, both illustrated by Phiz.

I have, therefore, guessed at 1860 as the date of publication of the Penny Part Issue, a period which suits with the heyday of Vickers' activities, and was indeed early in the history of chromoxylography.

It is very curious that the Bodleian copy should be manifestly of later issue than the parts and that the Preface should have been suppressed. One wonders whether the Part Issue as originally published ever actually came out in volume form.

Finally, as said above, the title 'Grimms' Goblins' made a later and unrelated reappearance on the covers of a different work. In 1876, over the imprint R. Meek & Co., Wine Office Court, a small 4to was published in pictorial boards entitled GRIMM'S GOBLINS, with illustrations by Cruikshank. This collection of stories, translated from the German of the Brothers Grimm and all from their pen, is merely a new edition under a new title of *Grimm's Household Stories* originally published in fcap 8vo in 1823. The illustrations are from the original plates and much too small for the new format. This is the only work under this title listed by the *C.B.E.L.*, and is a different book altogether from the one here described.

(iii) *Grimms' Goblins* is one of the books I remember most vividly as a beloved friend in childhood. To possess it in original parts gives me a pleasure no one can be expected to share: but it is due to the memory of the Editor and of Phiz to record that the stories and the illustrations can still, nearly fifty years later, bring back in meticulous detail my grandfather's house in Barnsley, where, together with *Aunt Judy*, this book (in deplorable half-calf) transformed a hundred dark West Riding afternoons into one child's particular version of fairyland.

HAROLD THE EXILE [87]

3 vols. * * * * [Colburn] 1819. Boards, new labels on Vols. I and III.

Half-title in each vol.

Vol. I (iv) + 284
II (iv) + 312
III (iv) + (324) F_6 adverts. (no imprint, but the books listed were published by Henry Colburn).

Ink signature: 'Walcot', on inside front cover of each vol.

Note. This curious novel is a satire on Byron, Caroline Lamb and other contemporaries. The asterisked imprint is unique in my experience of nineteenth-century publishing.

HIGH LIFE [88]

3 vols. Saunders & Otley 1827. Boards, labels.

Half-title in each vol.

Vol. I (iv) + (304)
II (iv) + 372
III (iv) + (384) R_9–R_{11} adverts., R_{12} blank.

Fine.

Note. Another unattributable 'silver fork' novel.

MAGIC AND MESMERISM: an Episode of the Eighteenth Century, and Other Tales [89]

3 vols. Saunders & Otley 1843. Black ribbed cloth.

Half-title in Vols. II and III

Vol. I viii + (300) O_6 adverts.
II (iv) + (296) O_4 adverts.
III (iv) + 288

Fine.

Note. At first sight merely a minor member of the large family of 'Canterbury Tales', this work has in fact a definite and curious interest. A stormbound party of English tourists in Germany escape boredom by telling stories. Three tales fill the three volumes, of which the title story occupies the first and two-thirds of the second.

This story is nothing less than a flamboyant narration in fictional form of the notorious Jesuitical scandal involving Mademoiselle Cadière and Father Girard. It is told in the first person by the youngest son and fifteenth child of Chaudon, who appeared for Catherine Cadière as prosecuting counsel. A postscript to the tale says: 'This singular trial is recorded in Pittaval's *Causes célèbres*.' No other indication is given of the historical basis of the narrative.

AUTHORSHIP UNKNOWN

The trial of Father Girard for mesmeric domination, seduction and abandonment of the young girl Catherine Cadière took place in Toulon in 1731. It provoked a swarm of pamphlets, and the contemporary sensation infected most European countries. Michelet treats of it at length in his *Histoire de France* (*Louis XV*, pp. 102 seq.). Lowndes (Vol. II, p. 896) records four contemporary English versions of the actual trial. Ashbee, in *Absconditorum* (pp. 225 seq.), lists numerous continental and English versions of the trial, but these are all either contemporary or near-contemporary polemics, or frankly erotica-after-the-event (e.g. *La Religieuse en Chemise*).

The only serious nineteenth-century English reference to the case which I can trace is in Cooper's *History of the Rod* (1869) which post-dates *Magic and Mesmerism* by over twenty-five years. One is tempted to wonder whether the latter is not in fact the first appearance in England of the story, presented as a chapter from the lives of the various human beings who, though not necessarily taking part or even attending the trial, formed the social background of the whole strange episode.

[90] MAURICE ELVINGTON: or One out of Suits with Fortune. An Autobiography (edited by Wilfrid East)

3 vols. Smith, Elder 1856. Claret diagonal-wavy-grain cloth.

Half-title in each vol.

Vol. I vi+272 Publishers' cat., 16 pp. dated Dec. 1858 at end.
II (iv)+290 Final leaf, N_1, a single inset.
III (iv)+(288) M_{12} adverts.

Binders' ticket: 'Westleys & Co.' at end of Vol. I.

Note. This was the publishers' file copy and only came to light in 1942. Evidently it did not belong to the first binding. It is in new condition.

[91] NAVY 'AT HOME' (The)

3 vols. small 8vo. William Marsh 1831. Boards, labels.

Vol. I (xx) [paged (xiv)]+(278) Final leaf, N_7, a single inset.
II (ii)+320
III (ii)+364

Fine.

[92] POOR PADDY'S CABIN: or Slavery in Ireland. A True Representation of Facts and Characters ('by an Irishman')

Wertheim and Macintosh, Paternoster Row; Dublin: M'Glashan 1853. Bright green glazed-ornamental-boards, printed in gold. Decoration and titling on front repeated on back cover. Uplettered and patterned on spine. Engraved front. and 1 plate.

pp. (vi)+(260) Text ends p. 248, followed by folding sheet of three versions of the Ten Commandments; (249) (250) 'Irish Keens' in the vernacular, verso blank; (251)–255 Appendix; (256) blank; (257)–(260) Supplement to the Appendix.

The stitching has given way in the middle, but the boards and text are in very fine state. The binding is signed: 'W. Scraggs. Lith. Cork', by whom also the book was printed.

Note. An anti-Romanist tale, avowedly modelled on *Uncle Tom's Cabin.*

ROWLAND BRADSHAW: his Struggles and Adventures on the Way to Fame (by the author of 'Raby Rattler') [93]

8vo. Sherwood, Gilbert and Piper 1847 (on engraved title); Sherwood and Co. 1848 (on printed title). Dark gun-metal-grey fine-ribbed cloth, blocked in gold and blind and lettered in gold. Steel-engraved front., decorative title and 26 plates by S. P. Fletcher.

pp. vi+(434)

Book-plate, crest over 'CRESCIT SUBPONDERE VIRTUS'. Fine.

SCHOOL OF FASHION (The): a Novel [94]

3 vols. Colburn 1829. Boards, labels.

Half-title in Vol. I

Vol. I viii+288
II (ii)+300
III (ii)+312

Very fine.

SOCIETY: or the Spring in Town [95]

3 vols. Saunders & Otley 1831. Boards, labels.

Half-title in each vol.

Vol. I (iv)+(324) P_6 blank.
II (iv)+(312) O_{12} adverts.
III (iv)+(300) O_4–O_6 adverts.

Ink signature: 'Frances Price, 1832 Rhiwaedog', inside front cover of each vol. Very fine.

Note. Both this and its predecessor are 'silver fork' novels.

SWEENEY TODD, THE DEMON BARBER OF FLEET STREET [96]

4 vols. royal 8vo. C. Fox, 4 Shoe Lane, n.d. Yellow wrappers cut flush, printed on front with all-over pictorial design in full colour, incorporating titling. Above design 'Volume I [*II etc.*]....Price 1s.'; below, imprint.

Unlettered spines. Back covers printed with publisher's advert.

Each vol. contains twelve 12-page parts, printed in double column, each with large wood-engraved illustration on first page with title of book above, underline, and No. 1 [2, 3, etc.] below. The second page (verso of illustration) is blank. Both are reckoned in the pagination.

Vol. I (1)–144 [Parts 1–12]
II (145)–288 [Parts 13–24]
III (289)–432 [Parts 25–36]
IV (433)–576 [Parts 37–48]

No preliminary matter for single-volume issue is provided, and as the advert. on back covers includes Sweeney Todd 'complete in Four Vols. Price 1*s.* each' it may be presumed that no such issue was made.

Note. Montague Summers (*A Gothic Bibliography*, 1941) and E. C. Turner (*Boys will be Boys*, 1948) attribute to the late 'seventies this refurbishment of a story called *A String of Pearls*, published by Edward Lloyd in 1846.

[97] WOMAN WITH THE YELLOW HAIR (The) and other Modern Mysteries. Chiefly from 'Household Words' [anon]

Saunders, Otley & Co. 1862. Magenta coarse-morocco cloth, blocked and lettered in gold and blocked in blind. Chocolate end-papers.

Blank leaf and half-title (reading 'MODERN MYSTERIES') precede title. pp. (xii) [paged x] +(384) R_{12} blank. Cloth faded.

AYTOUN, W. E. (1813–1865)

[98] NORMAN SINCLAIR

3 vols. Blackwood 1861. Violet wavy-grain cloth. Half-title in each vol.

Vol. I (vi)+344
II (vi)+326
III (vi)+308

Binders' ticket: 'Edmonds & Remnants', at end of Vol. I. Front fly-leaf of Vol. I torn.

BALLANTYNE, ROBERT MICHAEL (1825–1894)

Ballantyne, whose popularity with young people still persists, published his first 'story for boys' over ninety years ago. Seeing that his hold on youthful affection has proved so durable, he deserves more adequate bibliographical charting than he has yet received. Allibone (*Supp.* Vol. I, p. 84) gives a comprehensive check list of his works, but is not always accurate over first edition dates. *C.B.E.L.* (Vol. III, p. 568) limits him to a selective entry in one of its less satisfactory sections—that of 'Children's Books'—repeats certain of Allibone's errors and adds one or two of its own.

That the dates of first publication be definitely established is important in the case of a number of Ballantyne's books. Unlike many 'juveniles' they were *dated*: but as new printings were called for, the dates were altered and no sign given that editions with earlier dates had previously appeared.

What follows is by no means a complete list of his works, but it includes the best-known and most sought-after titles and the only reasonably exhaustive analysis in existence of *Ballantyne's Miscellany.* Two important tales, not being in the Collection, are described from a Statutory source and asterisked.

The bindings in which the boys' stories were first issued fall into a chronological series of groups. His first publishers, Nelson, devised the squat crown 8vo. format which persisted for several years. They also decorated the spines with pictorial blocking and lettering in gold. Their front covers, however, were various, sometimes conventionally blind-blocked, sometimes lettered, sometimes embellished with a vignette in gold. With *Gascoyne the Sandalwood Trader* (1864) Ballantyne became a Nisbet author. For their first few titles Nisbet more or less maintained the Nelson style; but with, I think, *The Iron Horse* (1871) they adopted a uniform front cover blocking in black, with scroll decoration and title and author's name boldly lettered in reverse. Their earlier titles were systematically re-issued in this uniform style and do not always give any indication of previous publication. The spine designs of this Nisbet period are vigorous and unconventional. Each one is special to the volume it adorns, and the bold use of black and gold on bright coloured cloths is highly effective. The format remains squat crown 8vo. This style of binding, described below under *The Iron Horse*, is elsewhere referred to as 'Nisbet 1'.

In or about 1880 (I think with *Post Haste*, published in that year) was introduced 'Nisbet 2'. This is a grievous change for the worse, as the description given below under *Post Haste* will, I hope, make manifest. Henceforward the books are full crown 8vo. in size.

Finally in 1886 came 'Nisbet 3', a modification (and slight gaudification) of Nisbet 2. This style is described under *Red Rooney*.

Nisbet 3 was not obligatory during its active years. For example *The Prairie Chief* (1886), though it has elements in common with Nisbet 3, differs in lay-out from its predecessor *Red Rooney*, while *The Big Otter* (1887) is entirely different. In 1893 the style was replaced by a rather timid exercise in Hentyism.

It should be noted that the earlier titles (pre-Nisbet 1) were published simultaneously in cloths of different colours. The colour given below is that of the specimen described, and should not be regarded as compulsory.

BATTERY AND THE BOILER (The): or Adventures in the Laying of Submarine Electric Cables [99]

Nisbet 1883. Dark green cloth (Nisbet 2). Dark grey end-papers. Wood-engraved front., pictorial title (undated) and 4 illustrations after drawings by the author.

pp. (viii)+(424) $2D_3$ $2D_4$ adverts.

Note. The sub-title on cover reads: AN ELECTRICAL STORY.

[100] BLOWN TO BITS: or the Lonely Man of Rakata. A Tale of the Malay Archipelago

Nisbet 1886. Blue-grey cloth (Nisbet 3). Very dark grey end-papers. Front. and 2 illustrations in half-tone, pictorial title (undated) and 2 illustrations in line, all after drawings by the author.

pp. (viii) + (440) $2E_4$ adverts. Fine.

[101] BLUE LIGHTS: or Hot Work in the Soudan. A Tale of Soldier Life in several of its Phases

Nisbet 1888. Scarlet cloth (Nisbet 3). Very dark grey end-papers. Wood-engraved front., pictorial title (undated) and 4 illustrations after E. Giberne.

pp. (viii) + (428) $2D_6$ adverts. Publishers' cat., 8 pp. undated, at end. A poor copy.

[102] CHARLIE TO THE RESCUE: a Tale of the Sea and the Rockies

Nisbet 1890. Smooth scarlet cloth (Nisbet 3). Very dark brown end-papers. Half-tone front., vignette title (preceding printed title) and 4 illustrations after drawings by the author.

pp. (viii) + (424) Fine.

[103] CORAL ISLAND (The): a Tale of the Pacific Ocean

Pl. 3 Nelson 1858. Rose-pink diagonal-wavy-grain cloth, blocked on front and back in blind, on spine pictorially in gold. Front., pictorial title and six plates, all in full colour, after drawings by the author.

pp. (440) [paged (i)–viii + (9)–438 + (2)] $2E_4$ blank.

Note. Another (and presumably a simultaneous) issue had the illustrations reproduced in two colours only. The book is misdated in Allibone.

[104] DEEP DOWN: a Tale of the Cornish Mines

Pl. 3 Nisbet 1868. Violet sand-grain cloth, blocked in blind on front and back, pictorially blocked and lettered in gold on spine. Grey end-papers. Wood-engraved front., pictorial title (undated) and 4 illustrations.

pp. (viii) + (424) $2D_3$ $2D_4$ adverts.

Cloth faded. Front internal hinge broken.

[105] DOG CRUSOE (The): a Tale of the Western Prairies

Nelson 1861. Violet bead-grain cloth, pictorially blocked in gold on front and spine; also blind-blocked on front and back and gold-lettered on spine. Front. and 3 plates in full colour.

pp. 356 [paged (i)–viii + (9)–356]

Inscription dated 31 May 1861 inside front cover. Cloth rubbed.

Note. This copy has no half-title or blank leaf preceding title nor is there a sign of either; but the pagination from (iii) (title-page) to viii is as given above, which implies that an additional prelim. leaf should be present.

The book is misdated in Allibone and *C.B.E.L.*

DUSTY DIAMONDS Cut and Polished: a Tale of City-Arab Life and Adventure [106]

Nisbet 1884. Reddish brown cloth (Nisbet 2). Chocolate end-papers. Wood-engraved front., pictorial title (undated) and 4 illustrations.

pp. (viii) + (432) $2D_8$ adverts.

ERLING THE BOLD: a Tale of the Norse Sea-Kings [107]

Nisbet 1869. Grass-green sand-grain cloth, blocked in blind on front and back, pictorially blocked and lettered in gold on spine. Grey end-papers. Wood-engraved front., pictorial title (undated) and 4 illustrations after drawings by the author.

pp. (viii) + (440) $2E_4$ adverts. Publishers' cat., 16 pp. undated, at end.

Ink inscription dated 'Christmas. 1869' on verso of fly-leaf.

FIGHTING THE FLAMES: a Tale of the London Fire Brigade [108]

Nisbet 1867. Maroon sand-grain cloth, blocked in blind on front and back, pictorially blocked and lettered in gold on spine. Grey end-papers. Wood-engraved front., pictorial title (undated) and 4 illustrations.

pp. (viii) + (424), $2D_3$ $2D_4$ adverts. Publishers' cat., 16 pp. undated, at end.

Cloth slightly split at head.

FLOATING LIGHT OF THE GOODWIN SANDS (The): a Tale [109]

Nisbet 1870. Royal-blue sand-grain cloth, blocked in blind on front and back, pictorially blocked and lettered in gold on spine. Grey end-papers. Wood-engraved front., pictorial title and 4 illustrations after drawings by the author.

pp. (viii) + (408) $2C_3$ $2C_4$ adverts. of works by the same author. Publishers' cat., 16 pp. undated, at end. Fine.

Note. When this title was re-issued in the style 'Nisbet 1', with title and author in black on front, a black printing was incorporated in the spine-blocking, with the result that the later issue of the spine-design looks more elaborate than the original one.

*GORILLA HUNTERS (The): a Tale of the Wilds of Africa [110]

Nelson 1861. Purple bead-grain cloth, pictorially blocked and lettered in gold and blind-blocked on front; blind-blocked on back; on spine pictorially blocked and lettered in gold. Wood-engraved front., pictorial title and 5 illustrations.

pp. (424) $2D_4$ blank.

Note. The front. and pictorial title are reckoned in pagination as pp. (1)–(4) although they are on plate paper. The other illustrations, also on plate paper, are not so reckoned. Text begins p. (9) and the first foliation is p. 10.

[111] HOT SWAMP (The): a Romance of Old Albion

Nisbet 1892. Scarlet cloth (Nisbet 3). Black end-papers. Half-tone front., pictorial title (undated) and 4 illustrations after S. W. Burton.

pp. (viii) + 408 8 pp. of adverts. of Ballantyne's works on text paper at end.

[112] HUDSON'S BAY: or Every Day Life in the Wilds of North America, during six years' residence in the Territories of the Honourable Hudson's Bay Company (Non-fiction)

'Edinburgh: for Private Circulation, and copies to be had of William Blackwood & Sons, 45 George Street.' 1848. Dark gun-metal grey perpendicular-ribbed cloth, blind-blocked with plain quadruple frame on front and back, gold-blocked and lettered (title only) on spine. White end-papers. Wood-engraved front. and 3 full-page illustrations on plate paper and 15 cuts in the text, all after drawings by the author.

Half-title. pp. (xii) + 328

Ink signature: 'Margaret Clay, Newwaterhaugh. 1848' on fly-leaf. Fine.

Note. The Second Edition (first published edition) of this work appeared in the same year as the original private edition. It was bound in almost, but not quite, uniform style; and as the private edition is a rare book and rising in value, it is desirable to note the differences, in case a copy be met with of first edition sheets 'improved' by a second edition binding.

(i) The first edition has no imprint on spine but a double gold rule at foot; the second has imprint: BLACKWOODS / EDINBURGH / AND / LONDON. and no rules (this because Blackwood assumed the responsibility for putting the book on the ordinary market). (ii) The first edition has plain quadruple blind framing on front and back, but no other ornament; the second has identical framing, but with corner ornaments sloping inward toward the centre.

Internally, the Second Edition collates (xvi) [paged (xiv)] + 328. The prelims. carry an advert. leaf before the half-title, and the Contents are spread to occupy two instead of one leaf. The entire text is re-set or re-arranged, though uniform in appearance.

[113] IN THE TRACK OF THE TROOPS: a Tale of Modern War

Pl. 3 Nisbet 1878. Brown sand-grain cloth (Nisbet 1). Dark grey end-papers. Wood-engraved front., pictorial title (undated) and 4 illustrations.

pp. viii + 400. 8 pp. of adverts. of Ballantyne's works on text paper at end.

IRON HORSE (The): or Life on the Line. A Tale of the Grand National Trunk Railway [114]

Nisbet 1871. Orange-scarlet sand-grain cloth, blocked and lettered in black on front, with conventional scroll work, title and author in reverse in oblong panels, and sub-title in black between the panels; blind-blocked on back; pictorially blocked and lettered in gold and black on spine (Nisbet 2). Dove-grey end-papers. Wood-engraved front., pictorial title (undated) and 4 illustrations. *Pl. 3*

pp. (viii) + (408) Publishers' cat., 16 pp. dated October 1871, at end.

LAKES OF KILLARNEY (The) (Non-fiction) [115]

Fcap 8vo. Nelson 1859. Violet wavy-grain cloth, blocked and lettered in gold and blind on front, pictorially and ornamentally blocked and lettered in gold on spine. Front. and 11 plates, all in colour-lithography and probably after drawings by the author; also a folding-map.

Half-title. pp. (112) [paged (i)–viii + (9)–(112)]

A volume in the Series: Nelsons' Hand-books for Tourists.

LONELY ISLAND (The): or the Refuge of the Mutineers [116]

Nisbet 1880. Green cloth (Nisbet 2). Chocolate end-papers. Wood-engraved front., pictorial title (undated) and 4 illustrations.

pp. (viii) + (416) $2C_8$ adverts. Publishers' cat., 16 pp. undated, at end. Fine.

MAN ON THE OCEAN: a Book for Boys [117]

Copy I: First Edition. Nelson 1863. Magenta bead-grain cloth, pictorially blocked on front in gold and blind, and gold-lettered; blocked and lettered in gold on spine; blind-blocked on back. The front and spine design are signed 'J. L.' (John Leighton). Pale yellow end-papers. Front. and 7 plates in colour, and numerous wood-engraved text illustrations by unavowed artists. *Pl. 3*

Blank leaf precedes front. pp. 408 [paged (i)–viii + (9)–408].

Ink signature: 'W. H. Lindley, Christmas, 1862' on title. Booksellers' ticket 'S. & T. Gilbert, Copthall Buildings' inside front cover. Cloth fine. Early signatures slightly loose.

Notes. (i) This is not a work of fiction, as it narrates several true stories of sea-adventure.

(ii) Allibone dates this book 1862, but, although the book was published for the Christmas market of 1862, it was dated forward. B.M. copy, dated 1863, was received on 11 December 1862.

[117a] **Copy II: New Edition (unavowed) in collaboration.** MAN ON THE OCEAN. A Book about Boats and Ships. Pictorial and Descriptive (by R. M. Ballantyne and Robert Richardson). Nelson 1883. Bright blue diagonal-fine-ribbed cloth, pictorially blocked in gold and black and lettered in black on front and spine; blind-blocked on back. Sand-brown-on-white floral end-papers. 68 wood-engraved illustrations, some full page, some in text, all on text paper.

pp. (288) 18_4–18_5 publishers' adverts.

Book-label of H. G. and G. M. Spicer.

Note. There is no indication that this book had an earlier incarnation. Large sections are repeated verbatim from the edition of 1863, but the chaptering is virtually transformed, much new material links up the extracts from the original, and nearly all Ballantyne's Part II (narratives of adventure) is omitted in favour of factual descriptions of ship-construction and seamanship. In short the new edition is less romantic and, in a technical sense, more instructive. The illustrations differ throughout.

[118] MARTIN RATTLER: or a Boy's Adventures in the Forests of Brazil

Nelson 1859. Sage-green bead-grain cloth pictorially blocked in gold on front and spine, also blind-blocked front and back and gold-lettered on spine. Wood-engraved front. and 3 illustrations.

Leaf bearing advert. on recto precedes title.

pp. (336) [paged (i)–viii + (9)–330 + (6)] X_6–X_8 blank.

A used copy, lacking front.

Note. The book is misdated in Allibone, and in *C.B.E.L.*

[119] NORSEMEN IN THE WEST (The): or America Before Columbus. A Tale

Pl. 3 Nisbet 1872. Orange-scarlet sand-grain cloth, blocked in black and gold; grey end-papers. Wood-engraved front., pictorial title (undated) and 4 illustrations after Pearson.

pp. (viii) + (408) $2C_4$ adverts. Publishers' cat., 16 pp. dated July 1872, at end.

Ink inscription dated Christmas 1872, on fly-leaf.

[120] PIRATE CITY (The): an Algerine Tale

Nisbet 1874. Green sand-grain cloth (Nisbet 1). Grey end-papers. Wood-engraved front., pictorial title (undated) and 4 illustrations.

pp. (viii) + 400 Publishers' cat., 16 pp. undated, at end.

Notes. (i) The book is mis-dated in *C.B.E.L.* It was reissued the following year in brown cloth uniformly blocked. No indication was given of an earlier appearance.

(ii) Collation of Second Edition identical with First, but cat. at end quite different. That in First Edition begins with 8 pp. of 'Works by the same author,' numbered i–xiv + Ballantyne's Miscellany and leading off with *Black Ivory*, *Tales of Adventure on the Sea*, *The Norsemen in the West*, etc. There follow 8 pp. of general adverts. dated January 1874. That in Second Edition opens in the same way, but the numbered titles begin *Pirate City*, *Black Ivory*, *The Norsemen in the West* and continue in a different order. The final 8 pp. are undated and different.

POST HASTE: a Tale of Her Majesty's Mails [121]

Nisbet 1880. Brown diagonal-fine-ribbed cloth, blocked in black and gold—on front, with title in reverse on oblong gold panel, sub-title in black beneath, conventional ornamentation in black behind and below the lettering, below this ornament a vignette with arched top in black and gold and, below that, author's name in black and more ornament; on spine, with title and author in reverse on gold panels at head and tail, between them sub-title in black in oval frame, and black ornament; on back, with central ornament (later replaced by publishers' monogram) in blind. Bevelled boards (Nisbet 2). Plum end-papers. Wood-engraved front., pictorial title (undated) and 4 illustrations.

pp. (viii) + 424 Publishers' cat., 16 pp. undated, at end.

Note. Subsequent examples of Nisbet 2 omit author's name from front, carrying title on curved panel, and substitute design of fern leaves for the conventional ornament.

RED ERIC (The): or the Whaler's Last Cruise. A Tale [122]

Routledge 1861. Magenta morocco cloth, pictorially blocked in gold on front with blind ornamental framing, in blind on back, pictorially gold blocked and lettered on spine. Wood-engraved front. and 7 illustrations after Coleman.

Half-title. pp. viii + 400 Publishers' cat., 64 pp. undated, at end.

RED ROONEY: or The Last of the Crew [123]

Nisbet 1886. Smooth scarlet cloth, blocked in gold, black and a third colour (in this case green) —on front, with a scattered design of palm and other leaves on which is imposed an oblong panel carrying title, a vignette blocked in gold, black and red, and author's name in gold; on spine, with title at head on gold panel, author below in gold, vignette and leaf ornament in three colours, and imprint in gold at tail; on back with publishers' monogram in black. Bevelled boards (Nisbet 3). Very dark grey end-papers. Wood-engraved front., pictorial title (undated) and 4 illustrations signed A. P.

pp. (vi) + (442) Final leaf $2F_1$ a single inset. Publishers' cat., 24 pp. undated, at end.

[124] RIVERS OF ICE: a Tale illustrative of Alpine Adventure and Glacier Action
Nisbet 1875. Dark red sand-grain cloth (Nisbet 1). Grey end-papers. Wood-engraved front., pictorial title (undated) and 4 illustrations.
pp. (viii) + (432) $2D_8$ adverts. Publishers' cat., 16 pp. undated, at end.
Fine.

[125] ROVER OF THE ANDES (The): a Tale of Adventure in South America
Nisbet 1885. Brown cloth (Nisbet 2). Dark grey end-papers. Wood-engraved front., pictorial title (undated) and 4 illustrations after drawings by the author.
pp. (viii) + (432) 8 pp. of adverts. of Ballantyne's works on text paper at end.
Very fine.

[126] SETTLER AND THE SAVAGE (The): a Tale of Peace and War in South Africa
Nisbet 1877. Bright blue sand-grain cloth (Nisbet 1). Grey end-papers. Wood-engraved front., pictorial title (undated) and 4 illustrations.
pp. (viii) + (424) $2D_4$ adverts. Publishers' cat., 16 pp. undated, at end.
Ink signature: 'W. Russell Thompson. 25th Decr 1879' on fly-leaf.

[127] SHIFTING WINDS: a Tough Yarn
Nisbet 1866. Maroon sand-grain cloth, blocked in
Pl. 3 blind on front and back, pictorially blocked and lettered in gold on spine. Grey end-papers. Wood-engraved front. and 5 illustrations.
Half-title. pp. viii + (408) $2C_4$ adverts. Publishers' cat., 16 pp. undated, at end.

[128] SNOW FLAKES AND SUN BEAMS: or the Young Fur Traders
Nelson 1856. Blue diagonal-ripple-grain cloth, blocked on front and back in blind, on spine pictorially in gold. The title on the spine reads THE / YOUNG FUR TRADERS / a Tale of / THE FAR NORTH. Wood-engraved front. and pictorial title (undated) and 6 full-page illustrations after drawings by the author.
pp. (viii) [paged vi] + (432) $2E_4$ blank.
Note. Re-issued the following year, bound in red morocco cloth with different blind blocking on front and back, but uniform spine. No indication was given of an earlier appearance. The book is misdated in *C.B.E.L.*.

[129] UNDER THE WAVES: or Diving in Deep Waters. A Tale
Nisbet 1876. Royal-blue sand-grain cloth (Nisbet 1). Grey end-papers. Wood-engraved front., pictorial title (undated) and 4 illustrations.
pp. (viii) + (416) $2C_8$ adverts. Publishers' cat., 16 pp. undated, at end.
Very fine. Also in the Collection in brown cloth.

UNGAVA: a Tale of Esquimaux-Land [130]
Nelson 1858. Puce wavy-grain cloth, blocked on
front and back in blind, on spine pictorially in *Pl. 3*
gold. Wood-engraved front., pictorial title (undated) and 6 full-page illustrations after drawings by the author.
pp. viii + (512) $2I_8$ blank.
Ink inscription dated 'Christmas 1859,' on recto of frontispiece. Fine.
Note. The book is misdated in Allibone.

WILD MAN OF THE WEST (The): a Tale of [131]
the Rocky Mountains
Small 8vo. Routledge 1863. Red wide-bead-grain cloth, pictorially blocked and lettered in gold on front and spine, blind ornamental blocking on front and back. Wood-engraved front. and 7 illustrations after Zwecker.
pp. viii + 408
Book-plate of Cooke, Detlong, and ink signature: 'R. Cooke. Aug. 21st, 1864', on fly-leaf.
Note. Also issued in grass-green wavy-grain cloth, uniformly blocked and lettered.

*WORLD OF ICE (The): or Adventures in the [132]
Polar Regions
Nelson 1860. Violet ripple-grain cloth, blocked on front with two lozenge-shaped vignettes in gold and all-over blind decoration, on back in blind, on spine gold-blocked and lettered. Wood-engraved vignette title and 3 illustrations.
pp. (iv) + (316) Sig. A, 6 leaves, comprises pp. (i)–(iv) + (1)–8, sig. B beginning p. 9. Final sig. X, 2 leaves. It is possible that pp. (1)–4 of text were printed with X_1 X_2.
Note. By 1863 this book was redressed with an elaborate design on front signed 'J.L.' (John Leighton) and incorporating title, a Polar Bear, a compass, etc. All edges were gilt and the vignette title had been replaced by a front.

Although not one of them is a first edition, the following additional Ballantyne titles in the Collection are appended, on account of their external attraction. They are all admirable specimens of Nisbet 1. First edition dates are given in brackets.

Black Ivory: a Tale of Adventure among the Slaves of East Africa. 1875 (1873). Red cloth. No indication is given of previous issue.

Golden Dream, The: a Tale of the Diggings. 'New Edition' 1876 (1860). Green cloth.

Lifeboat, The: a Tale of Our Coast Heroes. 'Thirteenth Edition' 1876 (1864). Green cloth.

Lighthouse, The: being the Story of a Great Fight between Man and the Sea. 'Eleventh Edition' 1875 (1865). Royal-blue cloth.

[133] BALLANTYNE'S MISCELLANY 1863–1886

The bibliography and publishing history of this series is obscure. What follows is as complete a reconstruction of the truth as I can contrive, on the basis of such volumes as are in the Collection and with the help of notes kindly contributed by P. H. Muir.

List of titles 1863–1869

Vol. 1. **Fighting the Whales**
2. **Away in the Wilderness**
3. **Fast in the Ice**
4. **Chasing the Sun**
5. **Sunk at Sea**
6. **Lost in the Forest**
7. **Over the Rocky Mountains**
8. **Saved by the Life Boat**
9. **The Cannibal Islands**
10. **Hunting the Lions**
11. **Digging for Gold**
12. **Up in the Clouds**
13. **The Battle and the Breeze**
14. **The Pioneers**
15. **The Story of the Rock**
16. **Wrecked but not Ruined**

In 1883 and 1886 (with V below) two further volumes were published.

[133] I. *First Edition.* $3\frac{7}{8} \times 5\frac{1}{2}$. With 4 coloured lithographed illustrations after drawings by the author. Bubble-grain cloth, with series and story title blocked in gold on front, spine unlettered; red-chocolate end-papers.

Vol. 1. *Not in the Collection.*
2. Violet cloth. Nisbet 1863.
Vol. 3. Dark brown cloth. Nisbet 1863.
4. Red cloth. Nisbet 1864.

How far the series went in this format I do not know. An advert. leaf at the end of Vols. 2–4 gives a list 'In course of publication' of 15 titles; but beyond Vol. 4 the order given in the list differs from that actually adopted, and contains titles not included in the series at all.

[133*a*] II. *New Edition* (*at any rate of earlier vols.*). 13 vols. Nisbet 1869. $3\frac{7}{8} \times 5\frac{3}{4}$. Uniform green sand-grain cloth, blocked on front in gold with same decorative treatment of series and story title as on first edition, but also blocked and lettered in gold on spine; red-chocolate end-papers.

Each vol. contains wood-engraved front., pictorial title and 2 full-page illustrations. In the earlier vols. (where comparison is possible) these illustrations are re-drawn from the author's original coloured versions.

The set in the Collection of these thirteen vols. is, as issued, in a red cloth box, blocked in black and gold with a list of titles on the lid.

It seems likely that this issue is the first of some of the later vols.

[133*b*] III. *Collected Edition* (*Rearranged*). TALES OF ADVENTURE. 4 vols. Nisbet 1873–1875.

Although this series is only a re-issue, it is sufficiently uncommon and curious in construction to merit description. In the Collection vols. 1–3 are not first editions. Vol. 1 appeared in 1873, vols. 2 and 3 in 1874.

(1) **Tales of Adventure on the Sea**

1875 (1873). Purple sand-grain cloth, blocked in black and gold; grey end-papers. Wood-engraved front. and 11 illustrations on plate paper after drawings by the author.

pp. viii + (5)–124 + (5)–124 + (5)–124 + (5)–126 + 6–2$H_{6,7,8}$–adverts. Publishers' cat., 16 pp. undated, at end.

The book is paginated in four sections, each section beginning with an engraved title, verso blank, on text paper (by implication paged (5)), followed by first page of text, which starts on page (7).

(2) **By Flood, Field and Mountain**

1875 (1874). Red sand-grain cloth, blocked in black and gold; grey end-papers. Wood-engraved front. and 11 illustrations on plate paper after drawings by the author.

pp. viii + (5)–126 + (5)–126 + (5)–126 + (5)–126. Publishers' cat., 16 pp. undated, at end.

Pagination arrived at as in Vol. I.

(3) **Wild Work in Strange Places**

1875 (1874). Blue sand-grain cloth, blocked in black and gold; grey end-papers. Wood-engraved front. and 11 illustrations on plate paper after drawings by the author.

pp. (viii) + (5)–126 + (iv) [paged vi] + (9)–128 + (5)–124 + (5)–126. Publishers' cat., 16 pp. undated, at end.

Pagination arrived at as in Vol. I except that the second section begins with page (iii) engraved title, p. (iv) blank, Preface (v)–vi, text beginning on p. (9).

(4) **On the Coast**

1875. Red sand-grain cloth, blocked in black and gold, grey end-papers. Wood-engraved front. and 11 illustrations on plate paper after drawings by the author.

pp. (viii) + (5)–(128) + (5)–128 + (5)–124 + (5)–(126). $2I_2$ blank. Between $2I_1$ and $2I_2$ is a 16 pp. publishers' cat. undated.

Pagination arrived at as in Vol. I.

Vols. 1, 2 and 3 are marked with asterisks on titles. Vol. 4 is marked Vol. IV. No numbering on spines. The distribution of tales from Ballantyne's Miscellany over these four volumes is as follows:

Vol. I. 'On the Sea' contains 1, 3, 9, 13.
II. 'By Flood, Field and Mountain' contains 5, 6, 7, 11.
III. 'Wild Work in Strange Places' contains 2, 14, 10, 12.
IV. 'On the Coast' contains 15, 16, 8, 4.

'Ballantyne's Miscellany' in 16 vols. 16mo, 1*s.* each, is advertised in a publishers' cat. at the end of each vol.

[133*c*] IV. *Third Separate-volume Edition.* 16 vols. 1874–1875.

In format and illustration similar to No. II. The set in the Collection is in royal-blue cloth and mint condition.

[133*d*] V. *Fourth Separate-volume Edition.* 18 vols. 1883–1886.

Not in the Collection. Larger format. Illustration as II. Various coloured cloths, but new blocking. With this Edition two new stories were published for the first time.

The Thorogood Family (1883) was issued in bright brown diagonal-fine-ribbed cloth, elaborately blocked in black and gold. No series-indication appeared on the case, but among adverts. at the end the story was listed as 'No. 17 (new volume)'. The standard vignette title of the series preceded the printed title. *The Lively Poll* (1886) was published uniform with *The Thorogood Family*, but in grass-green cloth, and with similar vignette and printed titles. No adverts. were included at the end, nor did the number in the series (18) appear anywhere.

BALZAC, HONORÉ DE (1799–1850)

[134] CAT AND BATTLEDORE (The) and Other Tales

Translated into English by Philip Kent, B.A. 3 vols. Sampson Low, etc., 1879. Blue diagonal-fine-ribbed cloth blocked in blind on front and back with publisher's monogram and triple frame, gold-lettered on spine.

Half-title in each vol.

Vol. I [The Cat and Battledore. The Vendetta] (iv) + (300) X_2 blank.
II [The Purse. The Ball at Sceaux] (iv) + (252)
III [Madame Firmiani. A Double Family] (iv) + (252) R_6 imprint leaf.

Publishers' cat., 32 pp. dated April 1878, at end.

BANIM, JOHN (1798–1842) AND MICHAEL (1796–1874)

This is a complete collection of the works of the Banim brothers except *The Anglo-Irish*, 3 vols. 1828, *The Bit o' Writin'*, 3 vols. 1838 (of both of which a description is given from the most complete copies discoverable) and a pamphlet about George IV's visit to Ireland, 1822.

*ANGLO-IRISH OF THE NINETEENTH CENTURY (The): a Novel [anon] [135]

3 vols. Colburn 1828. Boards, labels.

Half-title in each vol.

Vol. I (iv) + 308
II (iv) + ? (308) P_4 blank or adverts. (lacking from copy examined, which ends with P_3, p. 306).
III (iv) + (304)

(*From Bodleian copy, bound* 3 *vols. in one.*)

*BIT O' WRITIN' (The) and other Tales (by the O'Hara Family) [136]

3 vols. Saunders & Otley 1838. Half-cloth boards, labels.

? Half-title in each vol. (certainly in II and III).

Vol. I (vi) + 304
II (vi) + (308) O_{10} adverts. pp. (v) (vi), Contents, a single inset.

III (vi) + 296 pp. (v)(vi), Contents, a single inset.

(*Vol. I from Bodleian copy, bound 3 vols. in one. Vols. II and III from copies in original state in my possession.*)

[137] BOYNE WATER (The): a Tale (by the O'Hara Family)

3 vols. W. Simpkin & R. Marshall 1826. Boards, labels.

Half-title in each vol.

Vol. I (xxxiv) [(*a*) (i)–(iv); *b* (v)–(xxviii), paged (i)–xxiv; *c* (xxix)–(xxxiv), paged xxv–(xxx), c_4 cancelled] + (376)

II (iv) + (424) U_2 blank.

III (iv) + 436

Spines rather worn.

[138] CELT'S PARADISE (The): in four Duans. By John Banim

Fcap 8vo. John Warren 1821.

Copy I. Boards, label.

pp. (iv) + 96 (text) + xxvi (notes; final leaf C_1 a single inset)

'Robt G. Mooney T.C.D.' (in ink) and 'John F. Haydon. 1879' (in pencil) on title. Soiled. Spine repaired. Label defective.

[138*a*] **Copy II.** Full polished olive-green calf.

Presentation Copy to dedicatee: 'To Lord Cloncurry with the author's respects', in ink facing title.

Collation as Copy I.

[139] CHAUNT OF THE CHOLERA (The): Songs for Ireland (by the author of 'The O'Hara Tales', 'The Smuggler', etc. etc.)

Tall 12mo. James Cochrane 1831. Green paper boards, printed in black. Back cover announces a novel in 3 vols.: *The Dwarf Bride*, by the O'Hara Family, of which I can find no trace.

pp. iv + 92

Book-plate of Seumas O'Sullivan: 'R. Keating', in ink on title.

[140] CROPPY (The): a Tale of 1798 (by the authors of 'The O'Hara Tales', 'The Nowlans' and 'The Boyne Water')

3 vols. Colburn 1828. Boards, labels.

Half-titles in vols. II and III

Vol. I (iv) + (316) P_2 adverts.

II (iv) + (300)

III (iv) + (320) P_4 adverts.

[141] DAMON AND PYTHIAS: a Tragedy in 5 acts [anon]

8vo. John Warren 1821. New boards, cut.

pp. (viii) + 70 [i.e. to F_3] ? F_4 blank [lacking in this copy].

Between (viii) and B_1 is inserted a Playbill of the play, starring Macready, C. Kemble and Abbott, dated May 28, 1821, but headed: 'Never Acted'.

Note. This play was No. 363 of *Cumberland's British Theatre* and No. 19 of *Dick's English Plays.*

DENOUNCED (The) (by the authors of 'Tales of the O'Hara Family') [142]

Copy I: First Edition. 3 vols. Colburn & Bentley 1830. Half-cloth boards, labels.

Half-titles in Vols. II and III

Vol. I viii + (312) O_{12} adverts.

II (iv) + (316)

III (iv) + 292

'Mr Murray of Simpson' in ink on front covers. Spines split at hinges.

Note. THE DENOUNCED ends on p. 187 of Vol. II. The running headlines throughout read THE LAST BARON OF CRANA. Vol. II, p. (188) is blank, pp. (189), (190) fly-title to THE CONFORMISTS, verso blank.

Copy II: 'New Edition, with Introduction and Notes by Michael Banim, Esq. (survivor of the "O'Hara Family").' Dublin: James Duffy 1866. Dark green dotted-line-ribbed cloth, blocked in gold and blind. Lettered on spine (and title) THE DENOUNCED; OR THE LAST BARON OF CRANA. All edges gilt. [142*a*]

Half-title. pp. viii + 444. P. (v) is occupied by Michael Banim's Introduction, dated November 16, 1865, stating that neither of the tales in the volume (both written by his brother) was seen by him until after publication. THE DENOUNCED (headlines throughout THE LAST BARON OF CRANA occupies pp. (1)–235; THE CONFORMISTS occupies pp. 236–430; NOTES (not previously published) to both stories occupy pp. (431)–444.

Note. See also *Mayor of Wind-Gap*, Copy II. I presume the green cloth and decorated board issues were simultaneous. Similar 'New Editions', with Introductions and Notes, were published of *Bit o' Writin'*, *Boyne Water, Croppy, Peep o' Day* (these in 1865) and *Peter of the Castle and Fetches*, 1866.

FATHER CONNELL (by the O'Hara Family) [143]

3 vols. T. C. Newby & T. & W. Boone 1842. Half-cloth boards, labels.

Half-title in each vol.

Vol. I (iv) + 306 3rd leaf of final sig., O_3, a single inset.

II (iv) + (274) 1st leaf of final sig., N_1, a single inset.

III (iv) + (336) P_{12} adverts.

Book-plate: 'Castle Freke Library'. Fine.

[144] GHOST HUNTER AND HIS FAMILY (The) (by the O'Hara Family)

Smith, Elder 1833. Dark green morocco cloth; watered end-papers.

pp. (xvi) + (332) Z_2 advert. of No. II in the Library. Fine.

Note. This is No. I of Smith, Elder's Library of Romance (3760*a* in Section III). The Series title precedes the individual title.

[145] LETTER TO THE COMMITTEE (A)...NATIONAL TESTIMONIAL etc. By John Banim, Esq.

8vo. Dublin: Millikin 1822. Brown unlettered wrappers.

pp. (32)

'Peter La Touche jun. Esqr' in ink on title.

[146] LONDON AND ITS ECCENTRICITIES IN THE YEAR 2023: or Revelations of the Dead Alive (by the author of 'Boyne Water', 'Anglo-Irish', etc.)

Newman 1845. Half-cloth boards, label.

pp. (ii) + 376

'5/6/20 Ex Libris P. S. O'Hegarty' in ink on fly-leaf. Bookseller's ticket: 'J. Darcy. Dublin', inside front cover.

Note. This is a re-issue, under another title, of the sheets of *Revelations of the Dead-Alive* (see below) with half-title and adverts. dropped. The Errata are still uncorrected.

[147] MAYOR OF WIND-GAP (The) and CANVASSING (by the O'Hara Family)

Copy I: First Edition. 3 vols. Saunders & Otley 1835. Boards, spines and labels renewed.

Half-title in each vol.

Vol. I (iv) + 336
II (iv) + (402)
III (iv) + 316

Haywards Library, Bath, labels pasted on front covers.

[147*a*] **Copy II: 'New Edition,** with Introduction and Notes by Michael Banim (the survivor of the O'Hara Family).' Dublin: James Duffy 1865. Decorated boards; white end-papers printed with adverts.

pp. iv + (396)

Note. This, like the 'New Edition' of *The Denounced* described above, is an edition of considerable interest. Michael Banim's Introduction to the *Mayor of Wind-Gap* [pp. (iii), iv] states that he wrote the story years before his brother John, paralysed by spinal disease, retired to a cottage on Wind-Gap-Hill and became locally known as 'the Mayor of Wind-Gap'. Pp. (191)–196 are occupied by 'Notes on the *Mayor of Wind-gap*', here first printed. An introductory Note to *Canvassing* on p. (199) confirms that the author was Miss Martin of Ballynahinch Castle and states that Michael Banim cannot explain why the tale was originally included with the *Mayor of Wind-Gap* as 'by the O'Hara Family'.

REVELATIONS OF THE DEAD-ALIVE [anon] [148]

W. Simpkin & R. Marshall 1824. Probably original boards, re-covered. Cloth spine and MS. label.

Half-title. pp. (iv) + 376 Errata slip after p. 376 followed by 2 leaves of publishers' adverts. on text paper. P. S. O'Hegarty reports his copy as in original all-over boards, label. It contains neither Errata slip nor publishers' adverts., but is tight in cover. See *London* etc. above.

Note. The narrator, by a process vaguely indicated, contrives to 'die' for 198 days, each day representing a year of ordinary life, and at the end of them become alive again and report his adventures in London. His experiences are not progressive, but all relate to the year 2023 which is the last year of his 'living death'.

The result is not prophetic but satirical. A few scientific ingenuities are devised (there are, for example, mechanical knives and forks which feed you on their own); but mainly the London of 1825 is turned topsy-turvy. Bond Street has become a Jews' market; Regent Street, derided as 'theatrical lath and plaster', has fallen to ruin and been rebuilt; the Achilles Statue has been destroyed on grounds of decency; Primrose Hill is now the smart West-end. The latter half of the book deals with art and letters, the prominent practitioners of 1825 being criticised or declared forgotten, or (occasionally) praised by learned critics of 2023. In short, the work is a semi-humorous outburst against current fashions and reputations, in the form of retrospective comment at a far distant date. As an indication of the taste and preoccupations of the intelligentsia of the early 1820's, it has a certain value.

SMUGGLER (The): a Tale (by the author of 'Tales by the O'Hara Family', 'The Denounced', etc.) [149]

3 vols. Henry Colburn & Richard Bentley 1831. Boards, labels.

Vol. I iv + 302 Final leaf, P_1, a single inset.
II (ii) + (300)
III (ii) + 326 Final leaf, Q_1, a single inset.

This copy is misbound, pp. 301–302 [P_1] from Vol. I appearing at the end of Vol. III, and pp. 325–326 [Q_1] from Vol. III at end of Vol. I.

Fine.

[150] TALES BY THE O'HARA FAMILY [anon]
3 vols. W. Simpkin & R. Marshall 1825. Boards, labels.

Half-title in each vol.

Vol. I (iv) + (368)
II (iv) + 392
III (iv) + 404

Contents: Crohoore of the Bill-Hook—The Fetches—John Doe.

Labels a little chafed, but a remarkable copy of a book very rare in boards.

[151] TALES BY THE O'HARA FAMILY: Second Series [anon]
3 vols. Colburn 1826. Boards, labels.

Vol. I (iv) + (324) P_4–P_6 adverts.
II (iv) + 360
III (iv) + (384) R_{12} adverts.

Contents: The Nowlans—Peter of the Castle.

Armorial book-plate: 'Virtute non Vi' surmounted by coronet, in each vol. Labels darkened. The vols. have been covered with paper at some time, and the paste has left discoloration.

[152] TOWN OF THE CASCADES (The) (by Michael Banim)
2 vols. Chapman & Hall 1864. Green diagonal-wide-bead-grain cloth.

Half-title in each vol.

Vol. I xvi + 284
II viii + 284

Fine.

Note. This work was re-issued in 1866, two vols. in one, under the title *Irish Tales.* The re-issue was in green cloth, duller than on first edition, with less blind blocking but spines elaborately gilt.

Banimiana

[153] CROHOORE OF THE BILL HOOK: a Dramatisation by W. A. Mitchell from *The O'Hara Tales*
Mitchell, Newcastle-on-Tyne 1828. New boards.

Half-title. pp. (56), paged (iv) + 52

Presentation Copy: 'To Mr Robert Storey from his friend the author W. A. Mitchell' in ink on half-title.

BANKS, MRS LINNAEUS (1821–1897)

[154] THE MANCHESTER MAN
3 vols. Hurst & Blackett 1876. Grass-green sand-grain cloth; old rose end-papers.

Half-title in each vol.

Vol. I (iv) + 308
II (iv) + (292) (U_2) adverts.
III (iv) + (308) (X_2) [wrongly signed U] fly-title to publishers' cat. which follows, 16 pp. undated. Text of novel ends 299; 300 blank; (301)–306 Appendix.

Fine.

Note. A factual story of old Manchester during the first 30 years of the nineteenth century. The author claims that her descriptions of the town, her account of the 'Peterloo Massacre', the bulk of the incidents and most of the actual characters in the book are true to life, being based on her own research or on personal reminiscences of people and events communicated to her by survivors from the period of the tale.

A handsome new edition was published in 1896, in quarto, with illustrations by Charles Green and Hedley Fitton.

BARCLAY, FLORENCE S. (1862–1920)

GUY MERVYN: a Novel ('by Brandon Roy') [155]
3 vols. Spencer Blackett (on titles), Griffith Farran & Co. (on spines) 1891. Smooth claret cloth, blocked and lettered on front in bronze and yellow, gold-lettered and colour blocked on spine, backs plain; deep plum end-papers.

Half-title in each vol.

Vol. I (iv) + 238 First leaf of final signature, 15_1, a single inset.
II (iv) + 242 Final leaf, 31_1, a single inset.
III (iv) + (272) Publishers' (Spencer Blackett) cat., 32 pp. dated October 1890, at end.

Presentation Copy: 'To my friend G. H. Grubb from the writer Florence S. Barclay. Early work of long ago!' in ink on verso of fly-leaf of Vol. I.

Fine.

Notes. (i) The half-title has been torn from Vol. I. I suspect it had an earlier inscription to some vanished recipient: and that when Mrs Barclay wanted a copy to give to Grubb (he was manager of Putnam's London office, which published *The Rosary* and her other hugely successful novels) she only had this one, which for some reason or other had returned to her.

(ii) The differing imprints on title and spine have an exact parallel in the second edition of Conan Doyle's *Sign of Four* (1890). The first *edition* of the *Sign of Four* and the first *issue* of *Guy Mervyn* have 'Spencer Blackett' both on title and spine. The second *edition* of the Conan Doyle story, like this second *issue* of Mrs Barclay's novel, retains its Blackett title but has spine imprint of Griffith, Farran. The latter firm took over Blackett's business in 1891.

BARHAM, R. HARRIS (1788–1845)

[156] INGOLDSBY LEGENDS (The): or Mirth and Marvels (by Thomas Ingoldsby Esquire)
First Series. Bentley 1840.

[156*a*] **Copy I: Private Edition limited to 12 copies.**

Pl. 4 Full brown russia, tooled and lettered in gold. The title appears on front; title and imprint *and the date* 1840 on spine. All edges gilt. Yellow end-papers. Etched pseudo-armorial title-page on plate paper, with fancy lettering in dark purple and black, signed 'J. S. Gwilt invt' and based on plates in the book. Also 6 etchings, one by Buss after Dalton Barham, three by Leech and two by Cruikshank (all imprinted and dated: 'London, Richard Bentley 1840') and two wood-engravings in the text. There is no printed title-page.

pp. (viii) [paged (x)] + 340

Notes. (i) The make-up of the prelims. is eccentric because adapted from that of the Public Edition (see below). pp. (i) (ii) are represented by the etched title; (iii)–v Author's letter to Richard Bentley Esq.; (vi) blank; (vii) Contents; (viii) Illustrations; (ix) (x) inset sheet printed on recto: 'This Edition consists of Twelve Copies only. / No....'

(ii) The book is printed on thick cream-toned paper.

(iii) This copy is No. 8, was the property of the publisher, and carries the names of Samuel Bentley and Richard Bentley (in the hand of the latter) on p. (ix).

[156*b*] **Copy II: Public Edition** (1000 copies issued simultaneously with Copy I).

Pl. 4 Very dark brown perpendicular-ribbed cloth, blocked in blind on front, back and spine and gold-lettered on front and spine. The lettering on front is identical with that on Copy I, but the spine-lettering is different and the imprint is undated.

Etched title and plates as in Copy I, except that the first is printed in orange-red and black.

Collation as Copy I, but the make-up of the prelims. is different. The etched title is (rightly) omitted from collation, and is followed by a half-title, which represents pp. (i) (ii). The leaf stating limitation of edition is not present, so that the prelims. are a regulation 4-leaf gathering.

The book is printed on white paper, considerably thinner than that used for Copy I.

This copy carries bookseller's ticket: 'Bain, Haymarket' inside front cover, and is in flawless condition. Except that the pages have been carefully opened, the book is new.

[156 *c* & *d*] **Copies III and IV: Public Edition**

As Copy II, except that III has p. 236 blank with slip inserted (see below, *General Note*) and IV carries the complete Ballad of 'The Franklyn's Dogge' and is in (*c*) style binding (again see below). III is good unsophisticated copy; IV also is untouched.

General Note on the First Series (for the reprinting of part of which I am indebted to the courtesy of *The Times Literary Supplement*).

The bibliography of this famous work becomes the more obscure the more closely it is examined. Although I can demonstrate that certain statements hitherto accepted are incorrect, the solution of the main problem—i.e. the true sequence of issues—defeats me.

A. TEXT. What are our principal authorities?

The Statutory Copies; the Bentley Private Catalogue; Douglas, and Cohn.

All agree that a blank page 236 (preceding 'Gengulphus') is a feature of the first published issue. But this engaging unanimity is made meaningless by the categorical statement in B.P.C. that a *Private Edition* of twelve copies printed on thick paper and bound in full leather was issued gratis to the author and his friends on the same day (30 January 1840) as the first *Published Edition* appeared, and enjoyed priority of manufacture.

The B.P.C. goes on to say that in these Private copies p. 236 carried the incomplete version (first and last couplets only) of the Ballad of 'The Franklyn's Dogge', quoting as its authority the Annotated Edition of the Legends, published in 1894 by Barham's daughter, Mrs E. A. Bond. In this work (Vol. I, p. 247) Mrs Bond writes:

"Of the first edition of the Collected Legends (first series) twelve presentation copies were printed in which these verses were omitted, the notice of Gengulphus stating in respect of the primitive ballad: 'I regret that I am compelled to confine my present account of it to the first and last couplets.' In some of the copies, however, even these lines are wanting and the space for them is left blank, the following lines being inserted in MS.:

By a blunder for which I have no one to thank
But myself, here's a page has been somehow left blank,
Ah! Ah! Master Critic, I have you! You'll look
In vain for a fault in *one* page of my book.
Thos. Ingoldsby.

"In some instances the author substituted for the words 'Master Critic' the name of the person to whom the volume was presented."

The only specimens of the Private Edition of which I have knowledge are

(i) the one in my possession in its original brown leather;

(ii) the Owen D. Young copy in the New York Public Library which was Barham's own copy and is also in the original brown leather;

(iii) a copy—from catalogue description only—(rebound, with plates on India paper inserted) sold in New York in February 1836, from the

Library of D. Phoenix Ingraham. *All these copies have p. 236 printed with the incomplete version of 'The Franklyn's Dogge'.*

But there is in the Widener Collection in Harvard College Library a copy of the *Public* Edition, presented by Barham to E. R. Moran, which has p. 236 blank; and on it, in Barham's hand, couplets which differ in one word only from that quoted by Mrs Bond. Worse still, there are three other copies of the Public Edition in the Harvard Library *all with p. 236 blank*! The only conclusion to which we can tentatively come is that the Private Edition carried the incomplete 'Franklyn's Dogge', that the blank 236 only occurs in *some* copies of the Public Edition, while other (presumably later) copies of the Public Edition contained the Ballad complete, and still other copies (my own, for example, described above) were uniform with the Private Edition and showed only the first and last couplets.

In what order should these be ranged? From the point of view of publishing procedure (though without any authority) I suggest the most likely sequence to have been as follows: (*a*) Private, with incomplete Ballad; (*b*) Public, *ditto*; (*c*) Public, with 236 blank, Barham having decided to complete the Ballad and, while he was doing so, some copies having got out with the page already cleared ready for the new version; (*d*) Public, with Ballad complete.

The next problem is the printed slip, found inserted in some published copies which have p. 236 blank (as in Copy III above). As regards this slip, B.P.C. quotes Mr Edwin Truman (the well-known Cruikshank collector) as saying "that in other copies [issued later] the couplets [i.e. the four line verse] were printed on a separate slip and merely 'thrown into' the volume, and that owing to its rarity fabrications of this slip are not unknown".

But the text of the printed slip is not identical with that of the verse said to have been written into a few of the private copies by Barham himself. The printed version reads:

TO THE CRITICAL READER

By a blunder—for which too myself I may thank—
Page Two thirty-six has been somehow left blank.
Aha!—*pour le coup je te tiens*—you'll look
In vain for a fault in *one* page of the book.

T.I.

At this point our authorities begin to differ seriously. The opinion of B.P.C. has above been reported. Statutory Copies available have the blank but no slip; Douglas says 'some' copies have the slip; Cohn, that the blank page and a printed slip facing it constitute 'the chief point of a 1st issue'. Of copies examined by me in the possession of the trade six were sufficiently untampered with to be used as a basis for argument, and of them three had a slip and three had not—which leaves us very much where we were. In my own copy (III above) the slip is tipped in on title-page—an easy process at any time, even in a copy otherwise in good untouched condition.

In this matter of the slip, therefore, we are left with two (by me unanswerable) questions.

(1) Why is the text of the printed slip different from that of the verse said to have been written in a few copies by Barham? It is possible that Dr Bond mistranscribed the manuscript text; but the differences between the two versions are so great as to make this almost inconceivable. Alternatively Barham may have revised the verse, when a printed slip was decided upon.

(2) If it were considered desirable to print this slip at all, there must have been a considerable number of copies with the page blank. The Statutory Copies (blank page but no slip) must have been part of a genuine edition, and as only 1000 copies of the First Edition were printed (this on the authority of B.P.C.) how were these sub-divided into partial-ballad, blank without slip, blank with slip, and whole-ballad?

Let us finally, so far as the *text* of the First Series is concerned, simplify the position by clearing away so-called 'points' which are definitely invalid. Mr Cohn, in his great Cruikshank Bibliography, gives three further points of a first issue.

(*a*) 'Ralph de Shurland' in error for 'Robert de Shurland' throughout 'Grey Dolphin'. In fact this error persists in all issues of the First Edition seen by me and is not corrected until the second edition of 1843.

(*b*) Motto on p. 260 set in Gothic type. It is so set in all issues of the first seen by me *and* in the second edition.

(*c*) Presence of final leaf Q_2 Appendix. This leaf appears in all issues of the first seen by me *and* in the second edition. In the last-named, however, the misprint 'Paisley' is corrected to 'Pasley'.

B. BINDING.

There are three styles of binding on copies of the first edition. (*a*) Copies with partial-ballad (e.g. Copy II above) have an elaborate ornamental design, oval in shape, blind-blocked in centre of front and back covers and blind quadruple framing (thick, thin, *gap*, thin, thick). (*b*) Copies with p. 236 blank (including two Statutory Copies and Copy III above) have *corner ornaments* in addition to the central ornament which is identical with (*a*). The framing on these copies is uniform with (*a*). (*c*) Copies with the whole-ballad (e.g. Copy IV above) have a simpler central ornament, rectangular in shape, no corner ornaments and a double frame only (medium thick, very thick). The imprint on (*a*) and (*b*) is tall and rather condensed and has no period after BENTLEY; that on (*c*) is small and uncondensed and *has* a period after BENTLEY. It should be noticed that (c) is the style subsequently used on the Second and Third Series.

[156e] **Second Series.** Bentley 1842. Binding Style (c) as described above. Etched pseudo-armorial title-page on plate paper (similar in style to that in First Series but quite different in detail) with fancy lettering in burnt-umber and black, signed 'C. Cook Sculpt.' and based on plates in the book. Also seven etchings, four by Cruikshank and three by Leech of which (in this copy) only the last ('St Medard') shows an imprint and that is dated '1843'. Also three text-cuts and decorative initials, wood-engraved. There is no printed title or list of illustrations.

Half-title. pp. (viii) [paged (x), the etched title being reckoned in collation] + 288

Notes. (i) A private edition of 12 copies on thick paper was issued simultaneously with the public edition of 1500 copies on 30 December 1842.

(ii) The imprint dated 1843 is explained by the fact that 'St Medard' appeared in Bentley's Miscellany for January 1843 and the plate was engraved for magazine issue.

[156f] **Third Series.** Bentley 1847. Binding as Second Series. Etched pseudo-armorial title-page on plate paper re-designed to introduce features of the other plates, with fancy lettering in burnt-umber and black, and signed 'Cook sc.'. Also two engraved portraits of the author (one after Lane A.R.A., the other after 'Dalton', i.e. Rev. Dalton Barham), two etchings by Leech and two by Cruikshank, of which (in this copy) three show imprints, dated 1846 (one) and 1847 (two). There is no printed title.

Half-title. pp. (viii) + 364 Pp. (1)–183 are occupied by a Memoir of Barham, pp. (185)–364 by the further series of Legends.

Notes. (i) No private edition was issued. The public edition numbered 1500 copies and was published on 26 December 1846. It is curious that whereas the Second Series, despite publication late in December, was dated with the actual year of issue, the Third Series was dated forward.

(ii) The first Cruikshank plate is unsigned and the second was 'scamped' by the artist who, ever since the end of 1843, had sabotaged most of his work for Bentley in order to force the publisher to release him from a contract to supply one plate a month to the *Miscellany*.

[157] SOME ACCOUNT OF MY COUSIN NICHOLAS (by Thomas Ingoldsby, Esq.... To which is added: 'The Rubber of Life')

3 vols. Bentley 1841.

Copy I: Half-cloth boards, labels.

Half-title in Vols. II and III

Vol. I (viii) + 304
II (iv) + 300
III (iv) + (288) N_{12} blank.

Ink signature: 'James Royds, Woodlands' on fly-leaf of each vol. Re-cased; boards and labels in fine state.

The Rubber of Life by Dalton Ingoldsby begins on p. 261 of Vol. II and occupies the whole of Vol. III.

Copy II, Another: Three-quarter roan, cloth sides [latter original, spines exact replica of decayed originals]. [157a]

Half-title in Vols. II and III are lacking in this copy.

Presentation Copy to Dedicatee (Thomas Hughes)—with inscription to Hughes in the author's hand: 'To / Thomas Hughes Esq. / with the best regards / of his sincere Friend / Thomas Ingoldsby / (for the nonce) / or / R. H. Barham. / "Jack Falstaff with my familiars / John with my relations and Sir John with all the world."'

Also A.L.S. from Barham to Mrs Hughes and one from her to her son.

BARING-GOULD, SABINE (1834–1924)

ARMINELL: a Social Romance (by the author of 'Mehalah', 'John Herring', etc.) [158]

3 vols. Methuen 1890. Smooth scarlet cloth; black end-papers.

Half-title in each vol.

Vol. I (iv) + 306 Final leaf, U_1, a single inset.
II (iv) + (304) Final leaf, X_1, a single inset.
III (iv) + (298)

'With the publisher's compliments' in ink on fly-leaf of Vol. I.

BOOK OF WERE WOLVES (The): being an Account of a Terrible Superstition [159]

Smith, Elder 1865. Red sand-grain cloth; grey chocolate end-papers. Wood-engraved front.

Half-title. pp. xii + (268) 17_6 adverts.

Book-label of John H. Rossall and bookseller's ticket: 'T. Edmondson Lancaster', inside front cover.

CHEAP JACK ZITA

3 vols. Methuen 1893. Blue ribbed cloth. [160]

Half-title in each vol.

Vol. I (208)
II 200
III (200) Publisher's cat., 20 pp. dated May 1893, at end.

JOHN HERRING: a West of England Romance (by the author of 'Mehalah') [161]

3 vols. Smith, Elder 1883. Smooth light-apple-green cloth; floral end-papers.

Half-title in Vol. I

Vol. I (viii) + (292) U_2 adverts.
II (iv) + (320) X_8 adverts.
III (iv) + 308

Book-plate: coronet over 'C.B' in each vol. Fine.

[162] MEHALAH: a Story of the Salt Marshes [anon]
2 vols. Smith, Elder 1880. Grey diagonal-fine-ribbed cloth; floral end-papers.

Blank leaf and half-title precede title in each vol.

Vol. I (viii) + (304) U_8 adverts.
II (viii) + (280) T_4 adverts.

Spines slightly browned.

[163] THROUGH FLOOD AND FLAME: a Novel [anon]
3 vols. Bentley 1868. Apple-green morocco cloth, blocked in blind on front and back, blocked and lettered in gold on spine.

Half-title in each vol.

Vol. I (iv) + (306) Final leaf, X_1, a single inset.
II (iv) + 308
III (iv) + (302) Final leaf, X_1, a single inset. In this vol. penultimate sig., U, is only six leaves, whereas in Vol. I it is eight.

Covers of Vol. I damp-stained. B

Note. Baring-Gould's first novel.

BARKER, M. H.

[164] LAND AND SEA TALES (by The Old Sailor, author of 'Tough Yarns', etc.)
2 vols. Fcap 8vo. Effingham Wilson 1836. Dark grey-blue morocco cloth, pictorially blocked and lettered on spine in gold, front and back plain. Etched front. and vignette title in each vol. by George Cruikshank.

Half-title, printed on verso with adverts., precedes front. and vignette title in each vol.

Vol. I (x) + 408 Half-title, (A_1), a single inset.
II (vi) + 390 pp. (v), (vi), (A_3), and first leaf of final signature, $2C_1$, are single insets.

Ink inscription: 'Editor of the Naval & Military Gazette', on half-title of Vol. I. Very fine.

BARRIE, JAMES MATTHEW (1860–1937)

There may exist a more intimate series than this of association copies of Barrie's earliest and most important books. But there can hardly be one more relevant to the vital phase of his literary career. Frederick Greenwood, successively editor of *The Queen*, *The Cornhill*, *The Pall Mall* and *The St James's Gazette*, was the man who gave Barrie his chance in London; who by his encouragement and gusty kindness launched him on his triumphant career; who, suitably enough, was dedicatee of his first truly 'published' book. These copies remained in the possession of Greenwood's daughter until, thanks to a friendly bookseller, they passed to me.

AULD LICHT IDYLLS [165]
Hodder & Stoughton 1888. Navy blue buckram, bevelled boards, dark grey end-papers.

Half-title. pp. (viii) + (252) 18_2 adverts. (17 four leaves, 18 two leaves).

Presentation and Dedicatee's Copy: 'To Frederick Greenwood from J. M. Barrie' in ink on half-title. Fine, though buckram very slightly rubbed in places.

Note. A variant in pale buff cloth is recorded in Carter's *Binding Variants*, p. 92.

EDINBURGH ELEVEN (An): Pencil Portraits from College Life [166]
Sm. 8vo. British Weekly Office 1889. Cream paper wrappers, cut flush, printed in red and black. Inside front- and back- and outside back-covers printed with adverts.

Half-title. pp. (120) 8_3 8_4 adverts.

Presentation Copy: 'F. Greenwood from J. M. Barrie' in ink on half-title.

Note. No. 3 of The 'British Weekly' Extras, as stated on front cover and title. On the former the author's name appears as 'Gavin Ogilvy', on the latter as J. M. Barrie. Fine.

LITTLE MINISTER (The) [167]
3 vols. Cassell 1891. Pinkish ochre diagonal-fine-ribbed cloth. Pale-fawn-on-white foliage end-papers.

Blank leaf and half-title precede title in each vol.

Vol. I viii + 232 Publishers' cat., (16) pp. dated '9.91', at end.
II viii + (240)
III viii + 232

Presentation Copy: 'F. Greenwood from J. M. Barrie Oct. 91' in ink on first blank leaf of Vol. I. Fine. The only flaw is a small stain on front cover of Vol. I.

Note. One curious feature of make-up is unique in my experience. In Vol. I the signature lettering is in roman caps., in Vol. II in ital. l.c., in Vol. III in ital. caps.

MARGARET OGILVIE (by her son J. M. Barrie) [168]
Hodder & Stoughton 1896. Navy blue buckram, bevelled boards. Etched portrait front. Title printed in red and black.

Half-title. pp. viii + (208) N_7 N_8 adverts.

Presentation Copy: 'To F. Greenwood from J. M. Barrie. Dec. 1896' in ink on fly-leaf. Fine.

[169] MY LADY NICOTINE

Hodder & Stoughton 1890. Navy blue buckram, bevelled boards. Dark green end-papers.

Blank leaf and half-title precede title. Pp. (276) [paged (272)] 17_6–17_8 adverts.

Presentation Copy: 'F. Greenwood from J. M. Barrie' in ink on first blank leaf. Fore-edges of covers damp-stained.

[170] WHEN A MAN'S SINGLE: a Tale of Literary Life

Hodder & Stoughton 1888. Navy blue buckram, bevelled boards. Dark green end-papers.

Half-title. pp. (292) 19_2 adverts.

Presentation Copy: 'F. Greenwood from J. M. Barrie' in ink on half-title. Apart from faint spotting of back cover, a fine copy.

[171] WINDOW IN THRUMS (A)

Hodder & Stoughton 1889. Navy blue buckram, bevelled boards. Green end-papers.

Half-title. pp. (8) [paged in arabic]+(224) 15_6–15_8 adverts.

Presentation Copy: 'F. Greenwood from J. M. Barrie' in ink on half-title. Fore-edges of covers very slightly damp-stained.

BARROWCLIFFE, A. J. (ALBERT MOTT)

[172] AMBERHILL

2 vols. Smith, Elder & Co. 1856. Very dark green morocco cloth, blocked in blind on front and back, gold-lettered and blind-banded on spine.

Half-title in each vol.

Vol. I (iv)+328
II (iv)+(280) T_4 advert.

Publishers' cat. 16 pp. dated December 1855, at end.

Cloth used and spine of Vol. I frayed.

Note. It is a curious fact that this novel is printed (in London) partly on white, partly on dusky cream paper, the latter of poor quality. Precisely the same phenomenon occurs in Wilkie Collins' *After Dark*, published almost simultaneously (it is advertised on Vol. II T_4 as 'now ready') but printed in Edinburgh. In the copy of *After Dark* now in the Collection only prelims are on white paper, but in my earlier (discarded) copy several text signatures also were so printed.

[173] NORMANTON

Smith, Elder 1862. Magenta honeycomb-grain cloth.

pp. iv+340 Publishers' cat., 16 pp. dated November 1862, at end.

Very fine.

Note. This remarkable novel was acclaimed, sometime in the early nineteen-thirties, by Siegfried Sassoon, who later presented me with the copy of *Amberhill* above described. The *Normanton* here recorded is the only copy which I have ever seen outside a Library.

The story is a fine period specimen, with a stern father who drives two erring daughters out of his house and so to suicide by drowning, with a sensational case of eavesdropping followed by a tremendous confession and, as a climax, the killing of the wicked seducer. But this somewhat traditional tale is told with a delicacy, with a sense of landscape and seasonal characteristics, with a tenderness for animals and weak things generally, and with a mastery of prose-rhythm, which raise it to a high level of achievement. Henry Kingsley at his best never wrote anything more thrilling and tuneful than Barrowcliffe's long description of a moonlit orchard, than his account of Lilla's early rising on a spring morning, than his faultless rendering of a dozen fleeting moods of nature and of weather.

I bought the book, of which I knew nothing, in 1930 in a second-hand furniture shop for 1*s.* 6*d.*, merely because its magenta cloth was brilliant and unfaded. Never before or since have I, so cheaply and so unawares, secured a masterpiece.

BATEMAN, MRS J. C.

NETHERWOODS OF OTTERPOOL (The): a Novel [anon] [174]

3 vols. Bentley 1858. Dark green bead-grain cloth, paper labels.

Vol I (iv)+(314) Final leaf, P_1, a single inset.
II (ii)+(338) Final leaf, Q_1, a single inset.
III (ii)+(314) Final leaf, P_1, a single inset. B

Note. This novel is stated in the Bentley Private Catalogue to have been published in violet cloth, and certainly the binding on the present copy looks unconvincing for 1858. As it was in the publisher's personal file, it is hardly likely to have been a 'secondary' in the ordinary sense, and I suspect it was an early, unofficial copy, supplied by the binders (perhaps to show bulk) or sent in with a few earlies from the printer for office use.

WHO IS TO HAVE IT? a Novel (by the author of 'The Netherwoods of Otterpool') [175]

Routledge 1859. Red bead-grain cloth. Author's name on spine. Wood-engraved front.

pp. (iv)+(444) $(2F_2)$–$(2F_6)$ adverts., signed 'B' on $(2F_2)$.

Binder's ticket: 'Burn', at end. Booksellers' ticket: 'Mann Nephews', inside front cover.

Note. This story was announced as an intended volume in Routledge's New Library of Fiction, a series of original works to be published at five shillings or less, with specially drawn frontispieces. Other titles announced were *Hollywood Hall* by James Grant, *The Wife and the Ward* by Lt.-Col. Money, *The Man of Fortune* by Albany Fonblanque and one or two more. I have never seen a specimen of this Series, and Mrs Bateman's *Who is to Have it?* bears no trace of belonging to it or to any other Series.

BEAZLEY, SAMUEL (1786–1851)

[176] ROUÉ (The) [anon]

3 vols. Colburn 1828. Boards, labels.

Vol. I (iv) + 350 Final sigs., P, six leaves, Q, one leaf.
II (ii) + 362 Final sigs., P, twelve leaves, Q, one leaf.
III (ii) + 408

Very fine.

Note. This novel and its sequel *The Oxonians* were reprinted in Philadelphia about 1850 'attributed to Sir E. L. Bulwer'. The attribution persisted until, at any rate, about 1870. (See Trollope, Anthony, *Macdermots of Ballycloran.*)

BESANT, WALTER (1836–1901) [and BESANT & JAMES RICE (1843–1882)]

Books written in collaboration by Besant and Rice are lettered: B. & R. Description is provided of one important item not in the Collection.

[177] ALL IN A GARDEN FAIR: a Simple Story of Three Boys and a Girl

3 vols. Chatto & Windus 1883. Smooth blue cloth; pale green floral end-papers.

Blank leaf and half-title precede title in Vol. I

Vol. I (viii) + 312
II (iv) + (320)
III (iv) + 264 Publishers' cat., 32 pp. dated December 1883, at end.

Book-plate of Nicholas West.

[178] *ALL SORTS AND CONDITIONS OF MEN: an Impossible Story

3 vols. Chatto & Windus 1882. Smooth light grey cloth, blocked and lettered on front and back in brown and black, blocked in brown and black and gold-lettered on spine. Grey on white flowered end-papers. Wood-engraved front. and 3 plates in each volume after Fred Barnard, all on plate paper.

Blank leaf and half-title precede title in Vol. I, half-title only in II and III

Vol. I (xvi) [paged (xiv)] + (316) X_6 publishers' device.
II (viii) + (308)
III (viii) + 284 Publishers' cat., 32 pp. dated July 1882, at end.

Note. This novel is dedicated to the memory of James Rice who died on 25 April 1882. The Besant and Rice collaboration had lasted ten years, and the preface to the present work pays an affectionate tribute to the dead man and states that the publishing arrangements for *All Sorts and Conditions of Men* were made by the two in partnership, although the task of writing had from the first been allotted to Besant.

AS WE ARE AND AS WE MAY BE [179]

Chatto & Windus 1903. Red buckram. Title printed in red and black.

Half-title. pp. (viii) + (316) 20_6 imprint leaf. Publishers' cat., 32 pp. dated September 1902, at end.

BELL OF ST PAULS (The) [180]

3 vols. Chatto & Windus 1889. Dark red sand-grain cloth, blocked on front and spine in bronze green and spine lettered in gold. Grey-on-white floral end-papers.

Blank leaf and half-title precede title in each vol.

Vol. I (viii) + (312) X_4 publishers' device.
II (viii) + (316) X_6 publishers' device.
III (viii) + 304 Publishers' cat., 32 pp. dated September 1889, at end.

Presentation Copy: 'A. P. Watt from Walter Besant' in ink on title of Vol. I. Fine.

BEYOND THE DREAMS OF AVARICE [181]

Chatto & Windus 1895. Ochre linen cloth; light brown floral ends.

Blank leaf and half-title precede title. pp. (viii) [paged vi] + (332) Publishers' cat., 32 pp. dated December 1894, at end.

Presentation Copy: 'To A. P. Watt, with the author's kindest regards. Jan. 28, 1895' in ink on first blank.

CHANGELING (The) [182]

Chapman & Hall 1898. Red buckram.

Blank leaf and half-title precede title. pp. (viii) + 344

CHAPLAIN OF THE FLEET (The): a Novel [B. & R.] [183]

3 vols. Chatto & Windus 1881. Blue diagonal-fine-ribbed cloth, blocked and lettered in black and gold.

Half-title in Vol. I

Vol. I vi + 330 Final leaf, 21_5, a single inset.
II (iv) + 276
III (iv) + 260 Publishers' cat., 32 pp. dated March 1881, at end.

Bookplates of Walter Radcliffe and Roy Truscott inside front covers in each vol. W. H. Smith Library label inside back cover of Vols. I and III. Some sections of Vol. III loose.

[184] CITY OF REFUGE (The)

3 vols. Chatto & Windus 1896. Dark red ribbed cloth; ochre-brown flowered end-papers.

Half-title in each vol.

Vol. I (viii) + 218 Final leaf, 14_5, a single inset.
II (vi) + 248
III (vi) + (212) Publishers' cat., 32 pp. dated July 1896, at end.

Pencil signature: 'Radclyffe Walters 1896' facing title of Vol. I. Fine.

Note. A second copy of the same edition, with cat. dated *September* 1896, is bound in dark *blue* cloth in uniform style. Presumably the colour was changed for the second 'binding-up'.

[185] DEMONIAC (The)

Small 8vo. Bristol, Arrowsmith 1890. White paper wrappers, printed in dark blue and yellow—with title, author, etc. on front and spine, with adverts. on inside front and both back covers.

Two leaves of adverts. precede title.

pp. (232) [paged (4) + 212 + (16)] 15_1–15_8 adverts.

Note. This story was Arrowsmith's Christmas Annual for 1890.

[186] FOUNTAIN SEALED (A)

Chatto & Windus 1897. Red ribbed cloth; olive-green floral end-papers. Half-tone front. after H. G. Burgess.

Half-title. pp. viii + (312) 19_8 publishers' device. (20_1)–(20_4) adverts., unsigned and paged (1)–8. Publishers' cat., 32 pp. dated May 1897, at end.

[187] GLORIOUS FORTUNE (A)

Large 8vo. Extra Christmas No. of *All the Year Round* 1883. Blue wrappers printed in red and black. Back and inside covers printed with adverts.

pp. 72 [Besant's story ends p. 55] Five leaves of adverts. of differing size and colour inset at end.

[188] GOLDEN BUTTERFLY (The): a Novel (by the authors of 'Ready Money Mortiboy' etc.) [B. & R.]

3 vols. Tinsley 1876. Bright brown diagonal-fine-ribbed cloth, blocked in black on front with triple frame and with butterfly in blind; on back with triple frame in black; on spine with butterfly in gold, and black and gold lettering and bands.

Half-title in each vol.

Vol. I (iv) + (280)
II (iv) + (288) T_8 blank.
III (iv) + (292)

Book-label of A. J. Payne. Covers rather worn.

HERR PAULUS: His Rise, His Greatness, His Fall [189]

3 vols. Chatto & Windus 1888. Brown sand-grain cloth, blocked in shaded blue; grey floral end-papers.

Vol. I (iv) + (308) X_2 publishers' device.
II (iv) + 284 Publishers' cat., 32 pp. dated December 1887, at end.
III (iv) + 300

Pencil signature: 'Radclyffe Walters 1889' facing title of Vol. I. Very fine.

HOLY ROSE (The), etc. [190]

Chatto & Windus 1890. Dark blue diagonal-fine-ribbed cloth, florally blocked; grey floral end-papers. Wood-engraved front. after Fred Barnard.

pp. (iv) + 316 Publishers' cat., 32 pp. dated October 1889, at end.

IN LUCK AT LAST [191]

Large 8vo. Extra Christmas No. of *All the Year Round* 1884. Blue wrappers printed in red and black. Back and inside covers printed with adverts.

pp. 72 Three leaves of adverts., of two colours, inset at end.

INNER HOUSE (The) [192]

Bristol: Arrowsmith 1888. White paper wrappers printed in black, blue and yellow.

2 leaves of adverts. precede title.

pp. (viii) + (208) 14_4–14_8 adverts.

Note. This story was Arrowsmith's Christmas Annual for 1888.

IVORY GATE (The) [193]

3 vols. Chatto & Windus 1892. Smooth light brown cloth.

Half-title in Vol. I: blank leaf and half-title precede title in Vols. II and III

Vol. I (viii) + (288) T_8 publishers' device. Publishers' cat., 32 pp. dated May 1892, at end.
II (viii) + (304) U_8 publishers' device.
III (viii) + (296) U_4 publishers' device.

Fine.

[194] JACK O'LANTERN. The Christmas Annual of *Once a Week* (by the authors of 'Ready Money Mortiboy') [B. & R.]

4to. Office, 19 Tavistock Street 1872. Lilac wrappers, cut flush, pictorially printed and fancy-lettered in black: spine unlettered: back and inside covers printed with adverts. Wood-engraved front. on plate paper and numerous text illustrations after Frederick Waddy.

pp. 96 4 page leaflet advert. inserted before front.; slip between pp. 12, 13, announcing serialisation of *My Little Girl* (by B. & R.), and 5 leaves of adverts. (of different sizes) at end.

Fine.

[195] KATHARINE REGINA

Bristol: Arrowsmith 1888. Scarlet fine-ribbed cloth.

pp. (iv)+(240) 14_8 and 15_1–15_{10} adverts.

Note. This story was No. XXVI of Arrowsmith's Bristol Library.

[196] LADY OF LYNN (The)

Chatto & Windus 1901. Apple-green cloth, pictorially blocked. Half-tone front. and 11 illustrations after Demain Hammond.

Half-title. pp. (viii)+(456) 29_4 blank. Publishers' cat., 32 pp. dated May 1901, at end.

[197] NO OTHER WAY

Chatto & Windus 1902. Smooth red cloth, decoratively blocked. Half-tone front. and 11 illustrations after Charles D. Ward.

Half-title. pp. (viii)+(392) 25_4 publishers' device. Publishers' cat., 32 pp. dated March 1902, at end.

[198] 'OVER THE SEA WITH THE SAILOR' [B. & R.]

Large 8vo. Extra Christmas No. of *All the Year Round* 1880. **Presentation Edition** in white linen, lettered on front in gold with title, authors, date, etc. and 'With the Authors' Compliments'.

pp. 72

[199] READY-MONEY MORTIBOY: a Matter of Fact Story [B. & R.]

3 vols. Tinsley 1872. Dark maroon sand-grain cloth. Initial designs by F. W. Waddy.

Half-title in Vol. I

Vol. I (iv)+300
II (ii)+312
III (ii)+(300)

Presentation Copy: 'W. R. Spicer Esq[re] from J. S. Rice with comp[ts] and regards June 1872' in ink on half-title of Vol. I. The first novel of the collaboration.

REBEL QUEEN (The) [200]

3 vols. Chatto & Windus 1893. Bright blue morocco cloth; pale grey flowered end-papers.

Half-title in Vol. I: blank leaf and half-title precede title in Vols. II and III

Vol. I (viii)+(296)
II (viii)+(300) U_6 publishers' device.
III (viii)+(292) U_2 publishers' device. Publishers' cat., 32 pp. dated April 1893, at end.

Fine.

REVOLT OF MAN (The) [201]

Copy I: First Edition [anon]. Blackwood 1882. Orange-scarlet sand-grain cloth, blocked and lettered in black on front, in gold on spine. Edges uncut.

Half-title. pp. (vi)+(362) Z_4 Z_5 adverts. 1st leaf of final signature, Z_1, a single inset.

Spine darkened. Besant's first independent novel.

Copy II: 'New Edition' (by Walter Besant). [201*a*]
Blackwood 1882. Smooth scarlet cloth, pictorially blocked in black on front and back, gold lettered on spines; dark chocolate end-papers. Edges uncut.

Collation as Vol. I, but adverts. on Z_4, Z_5 different. Publisher's cat., 24 pp. undated, at end.

Book-plate of John Browne. Very fine.

SWEET NELLY MY HEART'S DELIGHT [202]
[B. & R.]

Large 8vo. Extra Christmas No. of *All The Year Round* 1879.

Copy I: Presentation Edition. White linen, lettered on front in gold with title, authors, date, etc. and 'With the Authors' Compliments'.

pp. 48

Copy II: Ordinary Edition. Blue wrappers printed [202*a*]
in red and black. Back and inside covers printed with adverts. Three leaves of adverts. (of different sizes) inset at end.

TEN YEARS' TENANT (The), and Other Stories [203]
[B. & R.]

3 vols. Chatto & Windus 1881. Smooth grey blue cloth; grey floral end-papers.

Blank leaf and half-title precede title in each vol.

Vol. I (viii)+272 Publishers' cat., 32 pp. dated January 1881, at end.
II (viii)+276 Publishers' cat., 32 pp. dated October 1880, at end.
III (viii)+280 Publishers' cat., 32 pp. dated January 1881, at end.

Ink signature: 'Lillie C. Rice, April, 1882', on fly-leaf of Vol. I.

[204] TO CALL HER MINE, etc.
Chatto & Windus 1889. Maroon sand-grain cloth, florally blocked, grey floral end-papers. Wood-engraved front. and 8 illustrations after A. Forestier.

pp. (iv) + 432 Publishers' cat., 32 pp. dated October 1889, at end.

[205] 'TWAS IN TRAFALGAR BAY, and Other Stories [B. & R.]
Chatto & Windus 1879. Grey diagonal-fine-ribbed cloth, blocked in black and lettered in gold in the series style of the publishers' Piccadilly Novels.

Advert. leaf and half-title precede title.

pp. (viii) [paged vi] + (344) Publishers' cat., 40 pp. dated February 1879, at end.

Book-plates of Walter Radcliffe and Roy Truscott. Spine a little faded.

[206] UNCLE JACK, etc.
Chatto & Windus 1885. Grey cloth, pictorially blocked in black and red; pale green floral end-papers.

Leaf of adverts. and half-title precede title.

pp. (viii) + (340) Publishers' cat., 32 pp. dated October 1884, at end.

[207] VERBENA, CAMELLIA, STEPHANOTIS etc.
Chatto & Windus 1892. Blue-grey diagonal-fine-ribbed cloth, blocked and lettered in black and gold in the style of the publishers 'Piccadilly Novels'. Fawn-on-white flowered end-papers. Wood-engraved front. after Gordon Browne.

Two leaves of adverts. precede title. pp. (xii) [paged viii] + (340). 22_2 publishers' device. Publishers' cat., 32 pp. dated January 1892, at end.

Very fine.

[208] WITH HARP AND CROWN: a Novel [B. & R.]
3 vols. Tinsley 1875. Green diagonal-fine-ribbed cloth.

Half-title in each vol.

Vol. I (iv) + 268
II (iv) + (268)
III (iv) + (348) 22_6 blank.

[209] WORLD WENT VERY WELL THEN (The)
3 vols. Chatto & Windus 1887. Dark green sand-grain cloth, blocked on front in brick-red, darker green and dark brown with title on tasselled stole, on spine gold-lettered and blocked in brick red with similar stole, on spine blocked in dark green with publishers' monogram. Grey-on-white floral end-papers. Etched portrait front. in Vol. I after John Pettie, R.A., also wood-engraved illustrations after A. Forestier—of which 4 full-page on plate paper and several in text; in Vol. II, front. and 1 full-page and 1 text illustration; in Vol. III, front. and 2 full-page illustrations—all after Forestier.

Blank leaf and half-title precede title in Vol. I; half-title only in II and III

Vol. I (xvi) [paged xiv)] + (320)
II (viii) + (320)
III (viii) + (288) Publishers' cat., 32 pp. dated September 1886, at end.

Fine.

BESTE, HENRY DIGBY (1768–1836) [210]

POVERTY AND THE BARONET'S FAMILY: a Catholic Novel
T. Jones, 63 Paternoster Row 1845. Grey-green morocco cloth, blocked in blind and gold-lettered on spine: POVERTY / A / CATHOLIC NOVEL.

pp. xxxii + (420) T_5, T_6 adverts.

Note. Pp. (iii)–xxxii are occupied by a 'Biographical Memoir of the Author', unsigned but dated 'Botleigh Grange, August 1845'. On the title the author is described as 'the late Henry Digby Beste Esq. M.A. Fellow of St Mary Magdalen College, Oxford; originator of the Religious Opinions of Modern Oxford'.

Ink signature: 'Pattison Ellames', on fly-leaf.

BLACK, WILLIAM (1841–1898)

BEAUTIFUL WRETCH (The), THE FOUR MACNICOLS, THE PUPIL OF AURELIUS [211]
3 vols. Macmillan 1881. Dark blue diagonal-fine-ribbed cloth, dark chocolate end-papers.

Half-title in each vol., that in I and II reading THE BEAUTIFUL WRETCH only, that in III bearing titles of all three stories.

Vol. I (iv) + 224 Publishers' cat., 24 pp. dated April 1881, at end.
II (iv) + (252) R_6 blank.
III (iv) + (230) Q_3 adverts., and a single inset.

BRISEIS [212]
Sampson Low 1896. Blue fancy-grain cloth; decorated end-papers.

Blank leaf and half-title precede title.

pp. (viii) + (320) X_8 adverts.

Ex libris R. D. Blackmore and sold from his house in Teddington. Very fine.

DAUGHTER OF HETH (A) [anon] [213]
3 vols. Sampson Low 1871. Maroon morocco cloth, blocked in black and gold.

Half-title in Vols. I and III

Vol. I vi + 298 Final leaf, X_1, a single inset.
II iv + 268
III vi + 282 Final leaf, U_1, a single inset. Publishers' cat., 16 pp. dated September 1870, at end.

A Library label has been removed from front cover of Vol. III.

[214] IN SILK ATTIRE: a Novel
3 vols. Tinsley 1869. Plum fine-ribbed moiré cloth, blocked in blind on front and back, blocked and lettered in gold on spine.

Half-title in each vol.

Vol. I (viii) + (264)
II (vi) + 292
III (vi) + (312) 20_3 20_4 adverts.

Pencil signature: 'Radclyffe Walters 1889' facing half-title of Vol. I.

Note. Black's third novel, preceded by *James Merle* (Glasgow, Murray, 1863) and *Love or Marriage* (1868) and followed by *Kilmeny*.

[215] KILMENY
3 vols. Sampson Low 1870. Bright green diagonal-fine-ribbed cloth.

Blank leaf and half-title precede title in Vol. III

Vol. I iv + (300) U_6 adverts.
II iv + (308)
III (viii) [paged vi] + (304) U_8 adverts.

Very fine.

[216] MONARCH OF MINCING LANE (The): a Novel
3 vols. Tinsley 1871. Royal-blue patterned-sand-grain cloth, blocked in blind on front and back, blocked and lettered in gold on spine. Bright primrose end-papers.

Half-title in Vol. III

Vol. I (iv) + 292
II (iv) + 300
III (vi) + 282 Pp. (v) (vi) and final leaf, U_1, single insets.

Fine.

[217] STRANGE ADVENTURES OF A HOUSE-BOAT (The)
3 vols. Sampson Low 1888. Fourth Edition. Smooth apple-green cloth, pictorially blocked and lettered on front in ochre, blue and black, gold-lettered on spine, back plain. Olive-brown-on-white floral end-papers.

Half-title in each vol.

Vol. I (iv) + (268) S_6 blank.
II (iv) + (272) S_8 blank.
III (iv) + 256 Publishers' cat., 32 pp. dated April 1888, at end.

Presentation Copy: 'To Mrs Roller. With William Black's very kind regards. Brighton March 1890' in ink on half-title of Vol. I.

Note. There is also in the Collection a first edition, identical in style and collation but in cloth of a less yellow green. Copies of the first edition also occur in light blue cloth, similarly blocked.

WHITE HEATHER: a Novel [218]
3 vols. Macmillan 1885. Blue sand-grain cloth, blocked in black and blind and lettered in gold. Very dark grey-brown end-papers.

Half-title in each vol.

Vol. I (viii) + 216
II (viii) + 208
III (viii) + 208

Pencil signature: 'Radclyffe Walters 1888. 3 vols' facing half-title of Vol. I. Very fine.

BLACKMORE, R. D. (1825–1900)

This is a complete collection (and in superlative condition) of Blackmore's prose-fiction.

ALICE LORAINE: a Tale of the South Downs [219]
3 vols. Sampson Low 1875. Royal blue morocco cloth. Cream end-papers.

Half-title in Vol. I

Vol. I viii + 298 First leaf of final sig., U_1, a single inset. Publishers' cat., 40 pp. dated February 1875, at end.
II iv + (328) Y_4 blank
III iv + 356

Presentation Copy: 'To My dear niece "The Maid of Sker" Eva Pinto Leite. April 1875. R. D. Blackmore' in ink on half-title of Vol. I. Very fine.

CHRISTOWELL: a Dartmoor Tale [220]
3 vols. Sampson Low 1882. Maroon diagonal-fine-ribbed cloth. Cream end-papers.

Vol. I (iv) + (304) U_8 blank.
II (iv) + 300
III (iv) + (320) X_8 blank.

CLARA VAUGHAN: a Novel [anon] [221] *Pl. 4*

Copy I: First Edition. 3 vols. Macmillan 1864. Dark blue morocco cloth ('Kingsley style'); chocolate end-papers.

Half-title in each vol.

Vol. I (iv) + (308)
II (iv) + (340)
III (iv) + (340) Z_2 adverts.

Presentation Copy to Author's wife: 'Lucy Blackmore. Feb. 25 1864' in ink on half-title of Vol. I, and numerous ink corrections, all in the author's hand. Fine.

[221*a*] **Copy II: Second Edition.** 3 vols. 1864. Cloth and end-papers uniform with Copy I. Collation as Copy I.

Book-plate of Alexander Macmillan in each vol. and blind stamp 'FILE' on front cover. Binder's ticket: 'Burn', at end of Vol. I.

[222] *Pl. 4* CRADOCK NOWELL: a Tale of the New Forest
3 vols. Chapman & Hall 1866. Apple-green morocco cloth. Cream end-papers.

Vol. I (iv) + 324
II (ii) + (320) X_8 blank.
III (ii) + 320

Presentation Copy to the Author's wife: 'Lucy Blackmore, Sept. 11, 1866' in ink on fly-leaf of Vol. I in the author's hand. Very fine.

Note. There is a secondary binding of beach-leaf brown wavy-grain cloth, with no spine imprint.

[223] CRIPPS THE CARRIER: a Woodland Tale
3 vols. Sampson Low 1876. Olive-green sand-grain cloth. Cream end-papers.

Vol. I iv + (282) First leaf of final sig., T_1, a single inset.
II (iv) + 280
III (iv) + (296) U_4 blank.

Presentation Copy to the Author's wife: 'Lucy Blackmore, May 17, 1876' in ink facing title of Vol. I in the author's hand.

Very fine.

[224] DARIEL: a Romance of Surrey
Blackwood 1897. Dark blue morocco cloth, blocked in blind and lettered in gold. White end-papers. Line front. and 13 illusts. after Chris Hammond.

Half-title. pp. (viii) + (532) [paged (506)]

Presentation Copy: 'Dolly Pinto Leite from her affectionate uncle, R. D. Blackmore. Dec[r] 10th, 1897' in ink on fly-title. Very fine.

Note. The structure of this book is curious. With the exception of the front. which is inset and on plate-paper, each illust. is on text paper with blank verso and part of the sheet. But they are not reckoned in collation. Consequently every signature in which an illust. occurs, although actually of 16 pp. only, paginates as 14. In addition, the first leaf of sig. 3 (pp. 33–4) was cancelled, but the pagination altered so as to run on. This results in sig. 3 being unsigned, containing 7 leaves only and being paged 33–46. Sig. 4 begins p. 47. My total pagination, given in brackets above, includes therefore the leaves carrying an illust. on recto which are integral parts of the sheets, but omits the missing leaf of sig. 3.

EREMA: or My Father's Sin [225]
3 vols. Smith, Elder 1877. Slate diagonal-fine-ribbed cloth, blocked in black on front; black blocked and gold lettered on spine; blind blocked with double frame on back. Primrose end-papers.

Blank leaf and half-title precede title in each vol.

Vol. I (viii) [paged vi] + (284) T_6 adverts.
II (viii) [paged vi] + (296) U_4 adverts.
III (viii) [paged vi] + 308

Presentation Copy to the Author's Wife: 'Lucy Blackmore from her affectionate husband. Septr. 29th 1877. Bridlington Quay, Yorkshire' on first blank of Vol. I; 'Lucy Blackmore' in Vols. II and III—in ink and in the author's hand. Also pencil corrections throughout the text. Very fine.

KIT AND KITTY: a Story of West Middlesex [226]
3 vols. Sampson Low 1890. Smooth grey-blue cloth, decoratively blocked on front in black and red, gold-lettered on spine; pale-green-on-white floral end-papers.

Vol. I iv + (304) U_8 blank.
II iv + (316)
III iv + 308

Presentation Copy: 'Eva Pinto Leite, with best love from her affectionate uncle, R.D.B. Dec. 5th 1889' in ink facing title of Vol. I; 'Eva Pinto Leite Dec. 5th, 1889', also in ink in Blackmore's hand, facing title of Vols. II and III. Fine.

LORNA DOONE: a Romance of Exmoor [227] *Pl. 4*
3 vols. Sampson Low 1869. Blue moiré fine-ribbed cloth, blocked in blind on front and back with plain triple frame, blocked and lettered in gold on spine (no author's name). Cream end-papers.

Blank leaf precedes title in Vol. I

Vol. I (viii) [paged vi] + 332
II iv + 340
III iv + (344) Z_4 blank. Publishers' cat., 16 pp. dated March 1869, at end.

Presentation Copy to the Author's Wife: 'Lucy Blackmore, March 20 1869' in ink in his hand on fly-leaf of Vol. I. Throughout text 84 pencil corrections have been made by Blackmore. Fine.

Note. The binding is Carter A (*More Binding Variants* 1938, p. 1).

MAID OF SKER (The) [228] *Pl. 4*
3 vols. Blackwood 1872. Bright blue morocco cloth; dark chocolate end-papers.

Half-title in I and II; leaf of adverts. and half-title precede title in III

Vol. I vi + (320)
II vi + 324
III (viii) [paged vi] + 304

Presentation Copy to the Author's wife: 'Lucy Blackmore. Withypool. August 2, 1872' on half-title of Vol. I and ink-corrections throughout, all in Blackmore's hand. Very fine.

[229] MARY ANERLEY: a Yorkshire Tale
3 vols. Sampson Low 1880. Blue diagonal-fine-ribbed cloth, blocked in blind on front and back with publishers' monogram and triple frame; blocked and lettered in gold on spine. Cream end-papers.

Half-title in Vol. I

Vol. I viii + (324)
II iv + (324) Y_2 imprint leaf.
III iv + (308) Publishers' cat., 32 pp. dated April 1880, at end.

As new. From the author's home in Teddington.

[230] PERLYCROSS: a Tale of the Western Hills
3 vols. Sampson Low 1894.

Copy I. Dark blue diaper cloth (normal binding); decorated monogram end-papers. Spine imprint: SAMPSON LOW & CO.

Vol. I (iv) + (300) U_6 blank.
II (iv) + 280
III (iv) + (292) U_2 blank.

[230*a*] **Copy II.** Dark red diaper cloth; same end-papers. Spine imprint: LONDON / SAMPSON LOW & CO. Collation as I.

[230*b*] **Copy III.** Smooth olive-green cloth; same end-papers. Spine imprint as II. Collation as I.

All very fine. The three copies came from the author's home at Teddington and had been in the possession of his niece E. Pinto Leite.

[231] REMARKABLE HISTORY OF SIR THOMAS UPMORE, BART. M.P. (The), formerly known as 'Tommy Upmore'
2 vols. Sampson Low 1884. Bright blue diagonal-fine-ribbed cloth, blocked in blind on front and back, gold-lettered on spine. Primrose end-papers.

Vol. I viii + (324) Y_2 blank.
II iv + (340) Z_2 blank.

Presentation Copy to the Author's Wife: 'Lucy Blackmore, with best love. May 9, 1884' on fly-leaf of Vol. I; 'Lucy Blackmore, May 9, 1884' in Vol. II—in ink and in the author's hand. Also notes regarding the 1 vol. edition facing title of Vol. I and occasional corrections in the text. Very fine.

[232] SPRINGHAVEN: a Tale of the Great War
Copy I: First Edition. 3 vols. Sampson Low 1887. Smooth grey-green cloth, pictorially blocked in colours. Pale yellow end-papers.

In Vol. I leaf precedes title, printed on verso with adverts; blank leaf and half-title precede title in II and III

Vol. I viii + (300)
II (viii) [paged vi] + 296
III (viii) [paged vi] + (300) U_6 blank.

Presentation Copy to Eva Pinto Leite inscribed by Blackmore in ink in each vol. with her name and date: March 3, 1887, and in Vol. I, 'with best love'. Very fine.

Copy II: First Illustrated Edition. Square demy 8vo. Sampson Low 1888. Smooth pale green cloth, pictorially blocked in black and blocked and lettered in gold on front and spine. Publishers' monogram in black on back. Dark-green-on-white foliage end-papers. All edges gilt. Wood-engraved front. and 63 illustrations (some full page, others in the text), all on text paper and reckoned in collation, after Alfred Parsons and F. Barnard. [232*a*]

pp. viii + 512

Presentation Copy to the Author's wife: ink inscription 'Lucy Blackmore. With kind love. Nov. 25th, 1887. R.D.B.' on verso of front fly-leaf. Very fine.

Note. It may be noted that the girl's figure on the spine of this edition is a re-drawing of the vignette printed in colour on the front covers of the first edition, which vignette was doubtless drawn by Fred Barnard.

TALES FROM THE TELLING HOUSE. [233]
1. Slain by the Doones. 2. Frida; or the Lover's Leap. 3. George Bowring. 4. Crocker's Hole.

Sampson Low 1896. Sand-brown canvas cloth, lightly glazed, and blocked and lettered in dark green and gold. White end-papers. Pictorial title, printed in red and black, and tissued.

Blank leaf and half-title precede title. pp. (xvi) [paged (xiv)] + (252) [paged (246)] R_6 imprint leaf.

Presentation Copy: 'Eva Pinto Leite. With best love. March 16th 1896' in ink in Blackmore's hand on fly-leaf. Very fine.

Notes. (i) The irregularity in paging is due to the non-inclusion in pagination of the three fly-titles to stories 2–4, although they are part of the sheet and reckoned in the signature lettering.

(ii) The book was issued in a light grey paper dust jacket printed in red.

(iii) The Collection also includes a curiosity—a dummy copy, formerly the property of the author, consisting of the first 126 pp. of text and the rest blank—bound in dark olive-green cloth blocked and lettered in light green and gold. The design in centre of front cover is the one finally adopted, but the titling and author's name are quite different in style. Presumably this was a specimen binding submitted to Blackmore and rejected.

BLESSINGTON-D'ORSAY

BLESSINGTON, CHARLES GARDINER, EARL OF (1782–1829)

[234] OBSERVATIONS ON THE STATE OF IRELAND...etc.

8vo. Longman etc. 1822. Boards, label.

Half-title. pp. (xii) + 88

Presentation Copy: originally to the Duke of Gloucester (inscription erased), secondly to 'The Earl of Gosford, from his friend the author' in ink on half-title.

BLESSINGTON, MARGUERITE, COUNTESS OF (1789–1849)

This is a complete collection of the authentic works of Lady Blessington, but three of the novels are not in their original covers. Catalogued as by her (because described as 'by the author of *The Magic Lantern*') are two little books: *Sketches and Fragments* and *Journal of a Tour through the Netherlands to Paris in 1821*, both published by Longman in 1822. I can find no evidence that the Blessingtons made a continental tour in 1821; but the colourless triviality of the style of both booklets might be blamed on anyone. In case, therefore, they were from her pen, I put on record that each has a half-title, and that *Sketches and Fragments* collates (xii) + (140) and *Journal of a Tour* viii + (172).

Comment on a number of the titles under this heading will be found in my book *Blessington-d'Orsay*, of which a revised edition was published in 1947.

[235] BELLE OF A SEASON (The): a Poem

4to. Longman etc. 1840. Crimson watered silk. Pictorial title and nine full-page engravings after A. E. Chalon, R.A.

Blank leaf (not text paper) and engraved title precede printed title. pp. (ii) + (94). First leaf of final sig., N_1, a single inset.

Ink signature: 'Margaret Kay, 1st January 1840', on fly-leaf. Rebacked.

[236] CONFESSIONS OF AN ELDERLY GENTLEMAN (The)

Longman etc. 1836.

Copy I. Light olive-green ribbon-embossed cloth. Steel-engraved front. and 5 portraits after E. T. Parris.

Half-title. pp. (iv) + (288)

Presentation Copy: 'To the Duchesse de Gramont from her affectionate friend the author' in ink on half-title. Fine.

[236*a*] **Copy II.** Light maroon ribbed cloth. Collation etc. as I.

Book-plate of William F. Ross. Binder's ticket: Remnant & Edmonds, inside front cover.

Apart from its association, the style of Copy I is more elegant and less machine-made than that of Copy II, and certainly represents the primary binding.

CONFESSIONS OF AN ELDERLY LADY (The) [237]

Longman etc. 1838. Dark blue fine-diaper cloth. Steel-engraved front. and 7 portraits after E. T. Parris.

Half-title. pp. (iv) + 342

CONVERSATIONS OF LORD BYRON with the COUNTESS OF BLESSINGTON [238]

8vo. Colburn 1834. Maroon diaper cloth; black paper label lettered in gold. Lithographed portrait front. after d'Orsay.

pp. iv + 412 $2D_2$ adverts. foliated as part of text and followed by inset publisher's cat. which has been removed from this copy.

COUNTRY QUARTERS: a Novel. With a memoir of Lady Blessington by her niece, Miss Power [239]

3 vols. Shoberl 1850. Boards, labels. Tinted lithographic portrait-front. in Vol. I, after d'Orsay.

Advert. leaf, dated January 1850, and half-title (forming sig. (*a*)) precede front. Title begins *b*.

Vol. I (xxviii) [paged xxiv] + 312
II (ii) + 304
III (ii) + (376)

Spine of Vol. I defective.

Note. The advert.-leaf in vol. I sometimes occurs at the end of Vol. III.

DESULTORY THOUGHTS AND REFLECTIONS [240]

Fcap 8vo. Longman etc. 1839.

Copy I: First Edition. Half-calf.

pp. (iv) + (124) I_6 blank. Lacking half-title and I_6.

Copy II: Second Edition. Pale blue diaper limp cloth. Collation as I. With half-title and I_6. [240*a*]

GOVERNESS (The) [241]

2 vols. Longman etc. 1839. Dark green fine-diaper cloth. Steel-engraved front. in Vol. I after E. T. Parris.

Half-title in each vol.

Vol. I (iv) + 308 Publishers' cat., 16 pp. dated October 1840, at end.
II (iv) + (332)

Ink signature: 'Margaret New Locke, January 1842', on fly-leaf of each vol.

GRACE CASSIDY. See *Repealers, The*

[242] HONEYMOON (The), and Other Tales

2 vols. Philadelphia: Carey & Hart 1837. Half-cloth boards, labels.

2 leaves of adverts. inserted before title in each vol.

Vol. I (iv)+(13)–(204) 17_6 blank.
II (iv)+(13)–216

'W. R. London, Feb. 25, 1837' in pencil on p. (13) in each vol.

Selected contents: The Honeymoon (Blessington); *Grace Falkiner* (author of *Cecil Hyde*); *Mimia Mordaunt* (Mrs Hall); *Nourmahal* (L. E. L.); *Juliet's Tomb in Verona* (Bulwer); *Félicité* (Blessington); *The Parvenus* (Mary Shelley); *To a Maiden Sleeping* (Disraeli); *Walstein* (Disraeli); *A Sentimental Adventure* (Miss Mitford); *Rigour of the Law* (Mrs Gore) and tales by G. P. R. James, Crofton Croker, Louisa Sheridan and others.

[243] IDLER IN FRANCE (The)

2 vols. 8vo. Colburn 1841. Grey-purple ribbed cloth.

Half-title in Vol. I

Vol. I (iv)+356
II (ii)+270 First leaf of final sig., S_1, a single inset.

Two publisher's catalogues: (*a*) 8 pp. dated May 1841, (*b*) 16 pp. dated January 1841, at end.

[243*a*] **Copy I.** *Presentation Copy:* 'To Sir E. L. Bulwer with the kindest regards of his sincere friend the author' in ink on half-title of Vol. I. Fine.

[243*b*] **Copy II.** *Presentation Copy:* 'To my dear Louisa Fairlie from her fond aunt M. Blessington' in ink on half-title of Vol. I, and on fly-leaf of Vol. II in ink 'Mrs Fairlie'. Also in ink on each fly-leaf: 'Mrs King. Tunbridge Hall.'

Copy III. *Presentation Copy:* 'To the Duchesse de Gramont from her affectionate friend M. Blessington' in ink on half-title. On the title of each vol. is violet ink stamp: 'Le Manoir, Chambourcy.'

See also 251: SET OF WORKS.

[244] IDLER IN ITALY (The)

2 vols. 8vo. Colburn 1839. Grey-purple ribbed cloth. Engraved portrait front. in Vol. I after Landseer.

Vol. I viii+400 Publisher's cat., 16 pp. dated March 1839, precedes front.
II x+(566) First leaf of final sig., OO_1, a single inset.

Blind monogram in circular wreath on titles. Small stain on front cover of Vol. I.

Note. For 'Second Edition', incorporating an entirely new Vol. III, see 251: SET OF WORKS.

LOTTERY OF LIFE (The) See 251: SET OF WORKS

MAGIC LANTERN (The), or Sketches of Scenes in the Metropolis [anon] [245]

8vo. Longman etc. 1822. Boards, label.

pp. (ii)+72 Errata slip follows p. 72.

Presentation Copy: 'To the Lord Erskine with the best wishes of the author' in ink on title. Fine.

MARMADUKE HERBERT. See 251: SET OF WORKS

MEMOIRS OF A FEMME DE CHAMBRE: a novel [246]

3 vols. Bentley 1846. Boards, labels.

Half-title in Vol. I

Vol. I (iv)+(316)
II (ii)+(316)
III (ii)+318 First leaf of final sig., P_1, a single inset.

The labels give title as 'The Femme de Chambre'.

'Moretino' in ink on title of each vol.

MEREDITH. See 251: SET OF WORKS

REPEALERS (The): a Novel [247]

Copy I: First Edition. 3 vols. Bentley 1833. Boards, labels.

Half-title in each vol.

Vol. I (iv)+316
II (iv)+348
III (iv)+320

In each vol. book-plate of Baron Dickinson Webster and in ink on fly-leaf 'Baron D. Webster, Penns'. Also in Vol. I on inside cover: 'Elizabeth Strutt.

Copy II: Second Edition. GRACE CASSIDY, or THE REPEALERS: a Novel [247*a*]

3 vols. Bentley 1834. Boards, labels.

In ink on inside cover of each vol. 'Frances Price, Rhiwlas 1834'. Very fine.

This issue consists of sheets of the first edition with new prelims., and in Vol. I a Preface (2 pp.) dated January 1834.

In the possession of the late Richard Bentley was a 'Key' to the characters in *The Repealers*, in Lady Blessington's hand. It read as follows:

Duchess of Heaviland . . .	Duchess of Northumberland
Marchioness of Bowood . .	Marchioness of Lansdowne
Countess of Grandison . . .	Countess of Grantham
Lord Albany	Lord Alvanley
Lady Elsinore	Lady Tullamore
Lady Kidney	Lady Sidney
Duke of Lismore	Duke of Devonshire
Mrs Grantly	Mrs Norton
Countess of Guernsey . . .	Countess of Jersey
Lord Key	Earl Grey
Marchioness of Stuartville . .	Marchioness of Londonderry
Lord Montagu	Lord Rokeby
Duchess of Lenox	Duchess of Richmond
Marchioness of Burton . . .	Marchioness of Conyngham
Marquis of Mona	Marquis of Anglesey
Marchioness of Mona . . .	Marchioness of Anglesey

Lady Augusta Garing . . .	Lady Augusta Baring
Marchioness of Glanricarde .	Marchioness of Clanricarde
Lady Emmeline Hart-Burtley .	Lady E. Stuart Wortley
Lady Yesterfield	Lady Chesterfield
Mrs Branson	The Hon. Mrs Anson
Lady Lacre	Lady Dacre
Lady Norely	Lady Morley
Mr Manley	Mr Stanley
Sir Robert Neil	Sir Robert Peel
Mrs Butler Ferguson . . .	Mrs Cutler Ferguson
Mr Errice	Mr Edward Ellice
Mr Thiel	Mr Shiel
Lord Rafton	Lord Sefton
Lady Castlemount	Lady Charlemont
Lord Leath	Lord Meath
Duke of Cartoun	Duke of Leinster
Duchess of Cartoun	Duchess of Leinster

[248] STRATHERN; or Life at Home and Abroad: a Story of the Present Day

4 vols. Colburn 1845. Half-cloth boards, labels. Lithographed portrait front. in Vol. I after Landseer (same portrait as in *Idler in Italy*).

Vol. I (ii)+(316)
II (ii)+(306)
III (ii)+(316) P_2 adverts.
IV (ii)+(300) O_5 O_6 adverts.

Fine.

[249] VICTIMS OF SOCIETY (The)

Copy I: First Edition. 3 vols. Saunders & Otley 1837. Boards, labels.
Half-title in each vol.

Vol. I (viii)+288
II (iv)+288
III (iv)+(296) O_2–O_4 adverts.

Fine.

[249*a*] **Copy II: Paris Edition.** 8vo. Paris: Baudry 1837.

Paper wrappers printed in black with Series design for 'Baudry's Collection of...British Authors', of which this is Vol. CXC.

[250] WORKS OF LADY BLESSINGTON (The)

2 vols. Large 8vo. Philadelphia: Carey & Hart 1838. Full contemporary (? publishers') calf. Steel-engraved portrait front. in Vol. I after Chalon.

Vol. I (388)
II (356)

Ink signature: 'Mamie Thomson', on recto of front.
Contents: The Two Friends—The Repealers—Confessions of an Elderly Gentleman—Confessions of an Elderly Lady—Victims of Society—Conversations with Lord Byron—The Honeymoon... Galeria—Flowers of Loveliness—Gems of Beauty.

[251] *SET OF LADY BLESSINGTON'S WORKS FORMERLY BELONGING TO COUNT D'ORSAY*

Three-quarter vellum (in one case full vellum), dark green morocco cloth (occasionally glazed green paper) sides, spines gold-tooled and inlaid with red and green. Pink iridescent satin-paper end-papers (in one or two cases plain pinkish brown).

In certain cases Count d'Orsay's book-plate is inserted and Zaehnsdorf's label as binder (31 Hyde Street, Bloomsbury) is also in many cases present. Somewhere in every volume appears the violet ink stamp: 'Le Manoir, Chambourcy'—the home of d'Orsay's sister, the Duchesse de Gramont.

In the schedule following collations are only given of the titles not otherwise represented in the Collection. These titles are in caps.

Confessions of an Elderly Gentleman [251*a*]
Book-plate. Collation as given above.

Confessions of an Elderly Lady [251*b*]
Book-plate. Collation as given above.

Conversations of Lord Byron [251*c*]
Full vellum. Book-plate. Collation as above, no cat. *Pl. 6*

Country Quarters [251*d*]
No book-plates. Collation as given above, but Vol. III S_5 lacking.

IDLER IN ITALY. Second Edition [251*e*]
3 vols. post 8vo. Colburn 1839. Portrait in Vol. I as in first edition. Half-title in Vols. I and II

Vol. I (xii)+(364)
II (xii) [paged x]+358
III iv+324

Vol. III contains entirely new matter not included in the earlier edition. Probably issued in full cloth.

Idler in France [251*f*]
Book-plates. Collation as given above, but publisher's cat. lacking.

LOTTERY OF LIFE (THE) [251*g*]
3 vols. Colburn 1842.
Half-title in each vol.

Vol. I (vi)+312
II (vi)+308
III (vi)+(338) Final leaf (Q_1) [? Q_2 blank].

Presentation Copy: 'To Henry F. Chorley Esq. from his sincere friend the Author', in ink on half-title of Vol. I.
Book-plate in each vol. Issued in half-cloth boards, labels.

MARMADUKE HERBERT, or the Fatal Error: a Novel founded on Fact. [251*h*]
3 vols. Bentley 1847.

Vol. I (ii)+304
II (ii)+(298) Final leaf O_5.
III (ii)+304

No book-plates.

Memoirs of a Femme de Chambre [251*i*]
No book-plates. Lacks half-title in Vol. I.

[251*l*] MEREDITH
3 vols. Longman etc. 1843.
Half-title in each vol.
Vol. I (iv)+(312)
II (iv)+306 Final leaf P_1 [? P_2 blank].
III (iv)+(326) Final leaf P_7 [? P_8 blank].
Book-plate in each vol.

[251*m*] **Repealers, The**
Book-plate in each vol. Lacks half-titles.

[251*n*] **Strathern**
No book-plates. Lacks Vol. III P_2 and Vol. IV $O_5 O_6$.

Blessingtoniana

[252] SHILLING BOOK OF BEAUTY (The). See 3440 in Section II: Yellow-Back Collection; BEDE, CUTHBERT

[253] CATALOGUE OF THE GORE HOUSE SALE: May 7, 1849
Binder's cloth lettered 'Catalogue of Lady Blessington's Effects'. Issued in blue paper wrappers.

D'ORSAY, ALFRED, COUNT (1800–1852), and d'Orsayana

[254] MARIE. From the French. Edited by Count d'Orsay
Fcap 8vo. Chapman & Hall 1847. [Probably issued in cloth; this copy in plain wrappers.] Four wood-engravings.
Half-title. pp. (iv)+152
A translation of *La Mare au Diable.*

[255] PORTRAITS BY COUNT D'ORSAY
This assemblage of 117 portraits and a caricature represents a fusion of the collections formed by the late Lord Rosebery and the late Miss J. M. Seymour, with a few added by myself. According to Madden a further nineteen portraits were produced. In untrimmed state (as are the Seymour plates) the majority have the imprint of John Mitchell, Royal Library, Old Bond St., and were presumably offered for sale by him. Practically all are dated by d'Orsay and the dates demonstrate that his years of especial activity were 1845–47, at which time he was virtually a prisoner in the grounds of Gore House.

[256] L'OMBRE DU BONHEUR (par la Comtesse d'Orsay [Harriet d'Orsay])
3 vols. in one. Paris: Comon 1851. Three-quarter morocco, marbled sides.
Half-title to each vol.
Presentation Copy: 'Anne Denys, from her affec. friend the author. Lausanne. September 6th 1851.'
See also: MILLS, JOHN; POWER, MARGUERITE A.

BOLDREWOOD, ROLF [T. A. Browne] (1826–1915)

BABES IN THE BUSH [257]
Macmillan 1900. Dark blue ribbed cloth.
Half-title. pp. viii+(424) $2E_3$–$2E_4$ adverts., followed by publishers' cat., 16 pp. dated '15.9. 1899.'
Very fine.

CROOKED STICK (The), or Pollie's Probation [258]
Macmillan 1895. Dark blue diaper cloth.
Half-title. pp. (iv)+(344) Z_3 Z_4 adverts. Publishers' cat., 56 pp. dated September 1895, at end.
Very fine.

GHOST CAMP (The), or the Avengers [259]
Macmillan 1902. Dark blue ribbed cloth.
Blank leaf and half-title precede title. pp. (viii)+(400) CC_8 blank. Publishers' cat., 16 pp. dated 20.9.02, at end.
Pencil signature: 'J. Browne. 1902. 4/6', on inside front cover. Very fine.

OLD MELBOURNE MEMORIES [260]
Melbourne: George Robertson 1884. Glazed yellow boards, printed pictorially in red and black on front, in black on spine and back.
Pp. (184) [paged viii+(9)–182] 12_8 blank. Text of 'Memories' ends p. (164); pp. (165)–182 Poems.
Presentation Copy: 'Lady Jersey. With the Author's Compliments and best wishes. Albury, March 25, 1891' in ink on fly-leaf, and annotations in the author's hand on pp. 171, 176 and 180.
Bookseller's stamp: 'T. F. Hughes, Albury', on fly-leaf.

ROBBERY UNDER ARMS: a Story of Life and Adventure in the Bush and in the Goldfields of Australia ('by Rolf Bolderwood' [sic]) [261]
3 vols. Remington 1888. Smooth grass-green cloth, blocked in black on front, gold-lettered on spine; pale grey floral end-papers.
Half-title in each vol.
Vol. I (iv)+300
II (iv)+300
III (iv)+(292)
Presentation Copy: on the half-title of Vol. I is the following inscription in ink: '*With the Author's compliments*' (in the hand of a publisher's clerk), continued in Boldrewood's hand: 'not exactly, but his love and tender memories for his dear old Mother who was so proud of her boy's learning to read and has now lived to hear of people liking to read *his* books. Casabella, 20th Jan[y]. 1888'. On the half-title of Vols. II and III, in ink in Boldrewood's hand: 'With the Author's love to his dearest Mother. Casabella. 20th Jan[y]. 1888.'

[262] SEALSKIN CLOAK (The)
Macmillan 1896. Dark blue diaper cloth.

Half-title. pp. (iv)+(508) KK_6 adverts. Publishers' cat., 56 pp. dated July 1896, at end.

Very fine.

[263] SYDNEY-SIDE SAXON (A)
Macmillan 1891. Scarlet diaper cloth.

Blank leaf and half-title precede title. pp. (viii)+(240) Q_8 adverts. Publishers' cat., 56 pp. dated May 1891, at end.

Book-plate of John Browne. Very fine.

BOYD, ARCHIBALD (d. 1854)

A historical novelist of potential importance, who unfortunately published only three books. The titles which follow deal—*The Cardinal* with Alberoni, *The Crown Ward* with the Scottish Court under James VI, and *The Duchess* with Louise of Savoy, Duchess of Angoulême.

[264] CARDINAL (The) (by the author of 'The Duchess')
3 vols. Bentley 1854. Half-cloth boards, labels.

Half-title in Vols. II and III

Vol. I xii+292
II (iv)+316
III (iv)+(318) 1st leaf of final sig., P_1, a single inset.

Ink signature: 'Paulina Curteis, Windmill Hill, 1855' and booksellers' ticket: 'King & Co. Brighton' inside front cover of each vol. Titles foxed; one label defective.

[265] CROWN WARD (The)
3 vols. Bentley 1856.

Copy I: First Edition. Rose-pink diagonal-ripple-grain cloth.

Vol. I (vi) [paged (iv)]+(310) First leaf of final sig., O_1, a single inset.
II (vi) [paged (iv)]+314 Final leaf, P_1, a single inset.
III (vi) [paged (iv)]+(318) Text ends O_4; O_5–O_{12}, P_1–P_3 Appendix. First leaf of final sig., P_1, a single inset.

[265*a*] **Copy II: Another.** Publisher's half leather, marbled sides, spines decoratively blocked in blind.

Book-plate of J. Leveson Douglas Stewart, Glenogil.

[266] DUCHESS (The): or Woman's Love and Woman's Hate: a Romance [anon]
3 vols. Bentley 1850.

Copy I: Olive-green fine-wavy-grain cloth. Half-title in each vol.

Vol. I (viii)+(316)
II (viii)+(328)
III (viii)+300

Copy II: Another. Dark green ripple-grain cloth. [266*a*]
Bound without half-title in Vol. I, otherwise as Copy I.

Author's Copy extensively corrected in his hand for a new edition to appear over his name. Cloth very fine.

BRADDON, MARY ELIZABETH (1837–1915)

The most adequate check lists of Miss Braddon's voluminous bibliography are those in the C.B.E.L. (Vol. III) and in *A Gothic Bibliography* by Montague Summers. While this Catalogue was going through the press, I was given the chance to acquire the Braddon collection of the late Mrs P. S. Bysshe (a close connection of the Maxwell family). Previously I was many titles short of completeness; now, although many of the Bysshe copies are in poor condition, I seem to lack only one three-decker and three volumes of novelettes or short stories. Novels 'edited by Miss Braddon' are excluded from this calculation, as also are disputable attributions and American issues.

One or two observations will increase the utility of the section, imperfect though it be.

(i) Rather than use space by continual repetition of the words 'by the author of Lady Audley's Secret' I have condensed them to 'by the a.o.L.A.S.'

(ii) The phrase 'Standard Style' denotes what became from 1872 a more or less regulation binding style for Braddon three-deckers, viz. dark green cloth with plain front and back, and on spine gold lettering of peculiar elongated caps. with drop tails. See ROBERT AINSLEIGH (*Note*), which was the earliest novel to be issued in this style.

(iii) Several titles are presentation copies to Mr and Mrs Henry Whiting (or belonged to them), and more than one shows a curious double end-paper at front or back or both. These double end-papers were certainly inserted at the moment of original binding, but are in my experience special to the Whiting copies. I conclude, therefore, that Mr Whiting was connected, either with the publishing department of Simpkins, or with Leighton Son & Hodge the binders. If he were thus concerned with the actual production of Miss Braddon's books, he could easily have caused the set of sheets she intended to inscribe for him to be bound with an extra fly-leaf (cf. especially, *Ishmael*).

It is a pity, having gone to this special trouble, that he did not keep the books in a dry place.

ALL ALONG THE RIVER: a Novel (by the author of 'Ishmael') [267]
3 vols. Simpkin 1893. Dark green cloth, standard style.

Vol. I (iv)+316
II iv+296
III (iv)+(312) X_4 blank.

Very fine.

[268] ASPHODEL: a Novel (by the a.o.L.A.S.)
3 vols. Maxwell 1881. Dark green cloth, standard style.

Vol I (vi)+312
II (iv)+(340) Z_2 blank.
III (iv)+344

Ink-stamped in each vol. 'Rehearsal Club'.

[269] AURORA FLOYD
3 vols. Tinsley 1863.

Pl. 5 **Copy I.** Dark blue dot-and-line-grain cloth, blocked in blind on front and back, blocked and lettered in gold on spine.

Half-title in each vol.

Vol. I viii+(306) Final leaf, X_1, a single inset.
II vi+(328)
III (viii)+(320) [paged vi+(1)–(322)] Y_8 adverts.

Presentation Copy: 'Mrs Wolfenden, with the author's affectionate regards. Feb. 21, 1863' in ink on fly-leaf of Vol. I. 'John Baldwin Buckstone Esq.' [dedicatee of *Henry Dunbar*] 'With the Author's most sincere regards' on fly-leaf of Vol. III. Fine.

[269*a*] **Copy II: Another.** Violet-blue ripple-grain cloth, similarly blocked. Collation as I.

Book-plate of John P. Ellames.

ana AURORA FLOYD OF THE DARK DEED IN THE
[269*b*] WOOD. A Drama in Three Acts. By C. H. Hazlewood

French's Acting Edition (late Lacy's) No. 856 n.d. Pink paper wrappers, printed in black. pp. 36.

Note. Mr Montague Summers (*T.L.S.* 24 April 1943) stated that this was the third unauthorised stage version of Miss Braddon's novel to be produced in London between 11 March and 21 April 1863. Whether the other versions were printed he did not know. It will be observed that Hazlewood makes no acknowledgment to the author on the title-page of this play, whereas he does so on *Lady Audley's Secret* (q.v. below).

This copy is probably not of the first wrappering-up, for the back wrapper lists Nos. 1441–1610 of French's Acting Edition. The front cover states that the 'Country Right of this Piece belongs to Samuel French.'

[270] BEYOND THESE VOICES
Hutchinson 1910. Scarlet linen-grain cloth.

Half-title. pp. (iv)+(374) First leaf of final sig., $2B_1$, a single inset.

Cloth faded. Library label inside front cover.

BIRDS OF PREY: a Novel (by the a.o.L.A.S.) [271]

Copy I: First Edition. 3 vols. Ward, Lock & Tyler 1867. Bright green moiré fine-ribbed cloth (uniform with *Charlotte's Inheritance*).

Vol. I (viii)+(332) Y_6 blank.
II (iv)+(292) U_2 imprint leaf.
III (iv)+(320) X_8 blank.

Copy II: First One-volume Edition. Ward, Lock & Tyler 1868. Blue dot-and-line-grain cloth. Tinted front. and pictorial title. [271*a*]

Blind stamp 'W. H. Smith & Son' on fly-leaf.

CAPTAIN OF THE VULTURE (The) [272]

Copy I: First Edition. Ward & Lock 1863. Cont. half-calf, cut edges.

pp. (iv)+252

A volume in Ward & Lock's Shilling Volume Library. See 3711 (14) in Section II. A trace of the original wrapper can be seen on title.

Copy II: 'Revised Edition.' Ward, Lock & Tyler 1867. Blue dot-and-line-grain cloth. Tinted front. and pictorial title on plate paper. pp. iv+364. Publishers' adverts., 4 pp. undated at end. [272*a*]

Ink signature 'F. D. Finlay' (and two addresses) on front fly-leaf. Short A.L.S. from Mary Maxwell, undated, pasted inside front cover. Not a nice copy, soiled and shaken.

Note. On a rough reckoning the story is about 20,000 words longer in this version than when it was first published in 1863 in the Shilling Volume Library. The number of chapters, however, remains the same.

CHARLOTTE'S INHERITANCE: a Novel (by the a.o.L.A.S.) [273]

Copy I: First Edition. 3 vols. Ward, Lock & Tyler 1868. Bright green moiré fine-ribbed cloth.

Vol. I (viii)+(320) X_8 blank.
II iv+(296) U_4 blank.
III iv+(288) T_8 blank.

Very fine.

Presentation Copy: 'Mrs Basden, with the Author's affectionate regards. February 1868' in ink on fly-leaf of Vol. I.

Copy II: First One-volume Edition. Ward, Lock & Tyler 1868. Blue dot-and-line-grain cloth. Tinted front. and pictorial title. [273*a*]

Pencil signature: 'G. H. Strutt', on fly-leaf. Fine.

CHRISTMAS HIRELINGS (The) [274]

Square 8vo. Simpkin 1894. Buff linen sides, blue morocco spine; patterned end-papers. Half-tone front. and numerous illustrations after F. H. Townsend all on text paper and reckoned in collation.

Half-title. pp. (272) R_3 adverts., R_4–R_8 Publishers' cat. undated and paged (1)–8.
Ink signature: 'M. J. Braddon', on half-title.

[275] CLOVEN FOOT (The): a Novel (by the a.o.L.A.S.)
3 vols. J. & R. Maxwell n.d. [1879]. Dark green cloth, standard style. Maxwell imprint on titles but Simpkin Marshall on spines. First issue was Maxwell throughout.

Vol. I (iv) + (308)
II (iv) + (304) U_8 blank.
III (iv) + (288)

'J. Whiting' in ink on 2nd fly-leaf of Vol. I (this is the only vol. with double fly-leaf). Cloth damp-stained at edges.

[276] CONFLICT (The): a Novel
Simpkin 1903. Smooth blue linen-grain cloth, blocked and lettered in scarlet and black on front, blocked and lettered in gold on spine.

Blank leaf and half-title precede title. pp. (viii) + (400)

[277] DAY WILL COME (The): a Novel (by the a.o. L.A.S.)
3 vols. Simpkin n.d. [1892]. Dark green cloth, standard style.

Half-title in each vol.

Vol. I (iv) + 316
II (iv) + 308
III (iv) + (324) Y_2 blank.

Presentation Copy: 'To dear Juliette from her attached friend the author, May 1892' in ink on title of Vol. I.

[278] DEAD LOVE HAS CHAINS
Hurst and Blackett 1907. Grey diagonal-fine-ribbed cloth, lettered in white on front and spine.

Half-title. pp. (iv) + (272) 17_8 adverts.

[279] *DEAD MEN'S SHOES: a Novel (by the a.o.L.A.S.)
3 vols. Maxwell 1876. Green cloth, standard style.

Half-title in Vol. I

Vol. I viii + (304)
II iv + 324
III iv + (344)

[280] DEAD SEA FRUIT: a Novel (by the a.o.L.A.S.)
3 vols. Ward, Lock & Tyler 1868. Dark blue moiré fine-ribbed cloth.

Half-title in Vol. I.

Vol. I (vi) + 316
II (iv) + (324) Y_2 blank.
III (iv) + 336

'Mary Basden' in violet ink in the author's hand on each title. Inserted in Vol. I is the original drawing for the spine-design by 'Luke Limner' (J. Leighton).

DOCTOR'S WIFE (The) (by the a.o.L.A.S.) [281]
3 vols. Maxwell 1864. Second Edition. Green diagonal-dot-and-line-grain cloth.

Vol. I (iv) + (320)
II (iv) + (328)
III (iv) + 304

Presentation Copy: 'Mrs Basden with the Author's affectionate regards, October 1864' in ink on fly-leaf of Vol. I. Very fine.

The collation of the First Edition is identical. A copy is in the Collection, handsomely bound in full crimson morocco, all edges gilt.

DURING HER MAJESTY'S PLEASURE [282]
Hurst & Blackett 1908. Smooth dark grey cloth, lettered in white.

Half-title. pp. (iv) + (276) 18_2 adverts.

This copy was mis-bound, signature 7 being duplicated and signature 16 omitted.

ELEANOR'S VICTORY [283]
3 vols. Tinsley 1863. Green dot-and-line-grain cloth, blocked and lettered in black *both on front and back*, blocked in black and lettered in gold on spine.

Half-title in each vol.

Vol. I viii + (320) X_8 adverts. (commercial).
II vi + (320) X_8 adverts. (commercial).
III vi + (316) X_5 X_6 adverts. (publishers').

Presentation Copy: 'Mrs Basden with the Author's love, November 1863' in ink on fly-leaf of Vol. I; and 'Braddon, 38 Park Street' written in pencil on half-title of Vols. I and II and fly-leaf of Vol. III.

Note. Also issued in cloth of same colour, but with a diagonal grain of which I have seen two variants.

FATAL THREE (The): a Novel (by the a.o.L.A.S.) [284]
3 vols. Simpkin n.d. [1888]. Dark green cloth, standard style.

Vol. I (iv) + 308
II (iv) + (276)
III (iv) + (256) R_6–R_8 adverts.

Presentation Copy: 'To dear Mrs Dobson with the Author's affectionate regards. July 1888' in ink facing title of Vol. I.

FENTON'S QUEST: a Novel (by the a.o.L.A.S.) [285]
3 vols. Ward, Lock & Tyler 1871. Green morocco cloth.

Half-title in each vol.

Vol. I (vi) + (290) Final leaf, (U_1), a single inset.
II (vi) + (298) Final leaf, U_5, a single inset.
III (vi) + 306 Final leaf, X_1, a single inset.

Presentation Copy: 'Jno Willis' [dedicatee of *Robert Ainsleigh*] 'from John Maxwell Esq. Feb[y] 1871' in ink on title of each vol. Cloth a little worn.

[286] *FLOWER AND WEED: a Novel
Tauchnitz Edition, Vol. 2163. Leipzig 1883. Half red roan (binding of Milan Lending Library).

Half-title. pp. 256

Note. Opinions conflict as to the first English edition of the short novel. The *C.B.E.L.* gives the title at the end of Miss Braddon's fiction as 'n.d.'; Mr Summers records it as a Maxwell three-decker dated 1884; the English Catalogue gives it as published by Maxwell in 1884 at 2/6 and 2/-, and it does not appear at all in the catalogues or shelves of B.M. or Bodley.

I include it here, although no copy is in the Collection, because I have reason to disagree with all these presumptions. *Flower and Weed* constituted the entire *Mistletoe Bough Annual* for, I think, 1877 (cf. *Under the Red Flag* below, which formed the Annual for 1883). I cannot be certain of the date, for the run of *Mistletoe Bough* in the Collection begins with 1878 and is continuous until 1885; but I have *seen* a copy of *Flower and Weed* in Mistletoe Bough shape, bound without wrappers (where alone the date appears) in one vol. with Mrs Riddell's *The Haunted River* (q.v.) which was the *Routledge Annual* for 1877. Further, I believe that 1877 was the first year of *The Mistletoe Bough,* which Miss Braddon substituted for *The Belgravia Annual,* and might well have launched with a complete novelette from her own pen.

Similar obscurity hangs over the first edition of her novelette, *Cut by the County,* which may well prove also to have made its appearance as an Annual. But with regard to this I have no evidence.

[287] GARIBALDI AND OTHER POEMS
Small square 8vo. Bosworth & Harrison 1861. Olive green-ribbed cloth.

Half-title. pp. viii+(320) X_8 adverts. Publishers' cat., 12 pp. undated, at end.

Binders' ticket: 'Westleys & Co.', at end.

[288] GERARD: or the World, the Flesh and the Devil (by the a.o.L.A.S.)
3 vols. Simpkin 1891. Dark green cloth, standard style.

Vol. I (iv)+(300) U_6 blank.
II (iv)+(284) T_6 blank.
III (iv)+(240) Q_8 blank.

Presentation Copy: To dear Madame Trübner with the Author's love' in ink on title of Vol. I. Pencil signature: 'Trübner' on fly-leaf of II and III.

Very fine.

[289] GOLDEN CALF (The): a Novel (by the a.o.L.A.S.)
3 vols. J. and R. Maxwell 1883. Dark green cloth, standard style.

Vol. I (iv)+(324)
II (iv)+296
III (iv)+(284) T_6 blank.

GREEN CURTAIN (The) [290]
Hutchinson 1911. Dark green diagonal-fine-ribbed cloth, blocked in white and gold-lettered on front, blocked and lettered in gold on spine. Title printed in green and black.

Half-title. pp. (iv)+(468). Publishers' cat., 32 pp. dated August 1911, at end.

Ink signature: 'Maggie Matheson, 50 Prince's Gate' on fly-leaf. Fine.

HENRY DUNBAR: the Story of an Outcast (by the a.o.L.A.S.) [291]
3 vols. Maxwell 1864. *Pl. 5*

Copy I: First Edition. Brown diagonal-dot-and-line-grain cloth.

Vol. I viii+(308) X_4 blank.
II iv+324
III (iv)+276

Book-plate: Coronet over L.R. in monogram. Binders' ticket: 'Leighton, Son & Hodge', at end of Vol. I.

Copy II: Third Edition. 3 vols. 1864. Binding and collation as Copy I. [291*a*]

Presentation Copy: 'Mrs Basden with the author's love. May 1864' in ink on fly-leaf of Vol. I.

Both very fine.

HER CONVICT [292]
Hurst & Blackett 1907. Smooth red cloth.

Half-title. pp. (iv)+(368) One leaf of publishers' adverts. inset at end.

HIS DARLING SIN [293]
Simpkin n.d. [1899]. Powder-blue cloth. Title printed in blue and black.

Half-title. pp. (iv)+(348)

Violet stamp on title: 'With the publisher's compliments.'

HOSTAGES TO FORTUNE: a Novel (by the a.o.L.A.S.) [294]
3 vols. Maxwell 1875. Dark green cloth, standard style.

Half-title in Vols. II and III

Vol. I (iv)+280
II (iv)+284
III (iv)+(296)

Fine.

INFIDEL, (The): a Story of the Great Revival [295]
Simpkin n.d. [1900]. Black ribbed cloth.

Half-title. pp. viii+(344) Z_4 adverts.

IN HIGH PLACES [296]
Copy I: First Issue. Extra cr. 8vo. Hutchinson 1898. Scarlet ribbed cloth, blocked and lettered in gold and black. Edges uncut.

Blank leaf and half-title precede title. pp. (viii) [paged vi] + (376) 24_3 24_4 adverts.

[296a] **Copy II: Cheaper Re-issue.** Cut to cr. 8vo. Undated. Dark green ribbed cloth, gold blocked on spine uniform with *The Mighty Atom* by Marie Corelli. Edges cut. Collation as Copy I.

[297] ISHMAEL: a Novel (by the a.o.L.A.S.)

3 vols. John & Robert Maxwell n.d. [1884]. Dark green cloth, standard style. Maxwell imprint on titles; Simpkin on spines. First issue was Maxwell throughout.

Vol. I (328) Y_4 blank.
II (336)
III 304

'J. Whiting' in ink on 2nd fly-leaf of Vol. I; 'Henry Whiting' on 2nd fly-leaf of Vol. III. Vol. II has single fly-leaf.

Note. There should be a half-title in each vol., but none are present in this well-preserved copy. I feel sure that Whiting was connected with the binders or with Simpkin (probably the latter), and fancy that, at his instructions, second fly-leaves were deliberately substituted for the half-titles when the books were bound, and one was omitted in error from Vol. II. It will be noticed that the Braddon-Whiting friendship was in force at the time (approximately 1891) when the Braddon copyrights were formed into a company and, with the retirement from publishing of J. & R. Maxwell, were entrusted to Simpkin for exploitation. In consequence Maxwell sheets, transferred to Simpkin, would have been bound to Simpkin order with their imprint on spines, and Mr Whiting could easily have arranged for the insertion of fly-leaves in his own copies.

[298] JOHN MARCHMONT'S LEGACY (by the a.o.L.A.S.)

3 vols. Tinsley 1863.

Copy I: First Edition. Violet-blue pebble-grain cloth.

Half-title in each vol.

Vol. I viii + (348) Z_6 adverts. (publishers'), followed by a single inset leaf of adverts. (partly commercial).
II vi + (332) Y_6 adverts. (publishers').
III vi + (328) Single inset leaf of adverts. (partly commercial) at end.

'Shaw, Westwood House' roughly inked on end-papers. Cloth shabby.

[298a] **Copy II: Second Edition.** 3 vols. 1863. Binding as Copy I.

Vol. I As Copy I, but no inset leaf at end.
II As Copy I, plus inset leaf of adverts. (partly commercial) between pp. (330), (331).
III As Copy I.

Presentation Copy: 'Mrs Basden with the Author's love, December 1863', in ink on fly-leaf of Vol. I. Very fine.

Note. I have seen a Third Edition (3 vols. 1863) in claret morocco cloth, plainly lettered on spine in gold and without spine-imprint. Presumably a secondary.

JOSHUA HAGGARD'S DAUGHTER: a Novel (by the a.o.L.A.S.) [299]

3 vols. Maxwell 1876. Dark green cloth, standard style.

Half-title in each vol.

Vol. I (viii) + 312
II (vi) + (312)
III (vi) + (300) U_6 blank.

Presentation Copy: 'William Tinsley Esqre with the author's kind regards October 16th 1876' in ink on fly-leaf of Vol. I.

Binders' ticket: 'Leighton Son & Hodge', at end of Vol. I.

JUST AS I AM: a Novel (by the a.o.L.A.S.) [300]

3 vols. J. & R. Maxwell n.d. [1880]. Dark green cloth, standard style.

Vol. I iv + (306) Final leaf, X_1, a single inset.
II iv + (296)
III iv [p. iv is mispaged v] + (316)

A soiled copy, with labels inside covers.

LADY AUDLEY'S SECRET [301]

Serial Issues

I. ROBIN GOODFELLOW (edited by Charles Mackay)

8vo. 'Published at the Office: 122 Fleet Street.' No. 1, July 6, 1861—No. 13, Sept. 28, 1861, containing Chaps. I–XVIII. In original unstitched numbers, as issued.

II. THE SIXPENNY MAGAZINE [301a]

8vo. Ward & Lock. Vol. I, 1861—Vol. V, 1863, containing the whole novel. Publishers' maroon morocco cloth.

LADY AUDLEY'S SECRET

Book Issues

3 vols. Tinsley 1862.

Copy I: Vols. I and II, Second Edition; Vol. III, First Edition. Royal blue dot-and-line-grain cloth, blocked in blind on front and back, blocked and lettered in gold on spine. [302]

Half-title in each vol.

Vol. I viii + 306 Final leaf, X_1, a single inset.
II vi + 308
III vi + (284) T_4–T_6 adverts., paged (1)–6.

'Alfred Stourton' in ink on fly-leaf of each vol.

Notes. (i) One copy in U.S.A. was reported with Vol. I, X_2 adverts. This leaf is not in this copy (see Schedule below).

(ii) The novel was first published on October 1. It may be observed that this copy carries an identical owner's signature on each fly-leaf, the original pencilled pricing '3 vols. 1/11/6' in Vol. I, and shows every sign of having been bought new in this mixed condition.

[302*a*] **Copy II: Second Edition.** 3 vols. 1862. Grass-green cloth, same grain and blocking as Copy I.

Pl. 5 Half-title in each vol. Collation as Copy I.

Presentation Copy: 'Mrs Basden, with the affectionate regards of her niece, the author October, 1862' in ink on fly-leaf of Vol. I. In pencil, on inside front cover of Vol. I and fly-leaf of Vols. II and III: 'Braddon 38 Park Street.' Very fine.

[302*b*] **Copy III: Third Edition, Revised.** 3 vols. 1862. Royal blue cloth as Copy I.

Half-title in each vol.

Vol. I viii+(308) X_2 adverts. paged (1) 2.
II vi+(312) X_3 X_4 adverts. paged (1)–4.
III vi+(284) T_5 T_6 adverts. paged (1)–4.

Very fine.

Schedule of Editions. I append to this description of the copies of *Lady Audley's Secret* in the Collection a more complete bibliographical record compiled from copies in other ownerships than my own, so that an adequate survey of this famous and rare novel shall be available to students.

First Edition. 3 vols. 1862.

Title-page: LADY AUDLEY'S SECRET / BY / M. E. BRADDON, / AUTHOR OF 'AURORA FLOYD'. / IN THREE VOLUMES. / VOL. I. [II. III.] / LONDON: TINSLEY BROTHERS, / 8, [*sic* in Vol. I; 18, in Vols. II and III] CATHERINE STREET, STRAND. / 1862. / [*The right of Translation is reserved.*]

Collation: Half-title in each vol.

Vol. I viii+306 [*a* (4 leaves)+B–X_1 text+X_2 adverts.].
II vi+308 [*a* (3 leaves)+B–X_2].
III vi+278+6 [*a* (3 leaves)+B–T_3 text+T_4–T_6 adverts., paged (1)–6].

Binding: Royal blue dot-and-line-grain cloth (*Carter: Binding Variants.* Plate II l.), blocked on front and back with elaborate conventional design in blind; in gold on spine: *decorative band* / LADY / AUDLEY'S / SECRET / *rule* / Vol. I. [II. III.] / *ornament* / M. E. BRADDON / *triple rule* / LONDON. / TINSLEY BRO[S]. Very pale yellow end-papers. Tops and fore edges uncut, tails trimmed.

Notes. (i) In Vol. I the '*i*' of '*is reserved*' (last line of title-page) is undotted. In Vols. II and III it is dotted.

(ii) In the Contents List to Vol. III, Chapter V is misprinted 'DR MGSGRAVE'S ADVICE', and Chapter VI 'BUOIED ALIVE'.

Second Edition. 3 vols. 1862.

Title-page: As first edition, with same misprinted street number and missing dot in Vol. I (both correct in Vols. II and III) but with the words SECOND EDITION. in small sans-serif caps between vol. no. and imprint. This addition necessitated pushing up IN THREE VOLUMES etc. about one-eighth of an inch nearer to the author's name.

Collation: As first edition throughout. Half-title in each volume.

Binding: Two variants have been noted: (*a*) As first edition, both cloth and end-papers. (*b*) Grass-green instead of blue cloth, of similar grain, similarly blocked. End-papers a deeper yellow. (See Copy II above.)

Note. Title-page misprints are exactly as in first edition, but the mistakes in the Contents List of Vol. III have been rectified to read DR MOSGRAVE'S ADVICE and BURIED ALIVE respectively.

Third Edition Revised. 3 vols. 1862.

Title-page: As second edition, except that under vol. no. appear the words in sans-serif caps: THIRD EDITION, REVISED. and the imprint is altered to read: LONDON: / TINSLEY BRO[S]., 18, CATHERINE STREET, STRAND. / 1862. / [*The right of Translation is reserved.*] Once again the '*i*' of '*is reserved*' is undotted in Vol. I, but dotted in Vols. II and III.

Collation: Half-title in each vol.

Vol. I viii+306+2 [*a* (4 leaves)+B–X_1+X_2 adverts., paged (1) 2].
II vi+308+4 [*a* (3 leaves)+B–X_2+X_3 X_4 adverts., paged (1)–4].
III vi+280+4 [*a* (3 leaves)+B–T_4+T_5 T_6 adverts., paged (1)–4].

Binding: As first edition. End-papers very pale yellow.

Notes. (i) The difference in collation between Vol. III, first and third editions, is due to the re-writing of the last two paragraphs of Chapter IX, which are extended by several hundred words. The chapter now runs over pp. 274 and 275, instead of, as originally, ending on p. 273. Presumably this is the 'revision' recorded on the title-page. It may be observed that Tinsley did not think to alter the Contents List, which still records Chapter X as beginning on p. 274, although actually it now begins on p. 276.

(ii) The advertisements at the end of Vol. III are textually the same as those in the first edition, but re-set to occupy four pages instead of six.

(iii) The copy of the third edition examined is a presentation copy from the author with an inscription dated 'December 24. 1862'.

Fourth Edition. Not located.

Fifth Edition. Not located.

Sixth Edition Revised. 3 vols. 1862.

Title-page: As third edition, except for the word SIXTH instead of THIRD. The '*i*' of '*is reserved*' is dotted in each volume.

Collation: As third edition throughout. The mis-paging of Chapter x in the Contents List of Vol. III persists.

Binding: As first edition. End-papers a deeper yellow.

Note. A curious feature of the sixth edition examined is that the prelims. of Vol. I are printed on a *white* paper as used for all earlier editions seen, but that the text and adverts. of Vol. I and the whole of Vols. II and III (prelims. text and adverts.) are printed on a dingy cream paper of slightly bulkier quality.

Seventh Edition Revised. 3 vols. 1862. Uniform with the sixth edition as to title-page (apart from reading 'SEVENTH' instead of 'SIXTH'), collation, binding and end-papers. Printed throughout on white paper.

Notes. (i) A new feature is a panel advertisement printed on the verso of the title-page of each volume. Vol. I advertises *Guy Livingstone* and *The Public Life of Lord Macaulay*; Vol. II *A Tangled Skein* and *The Literature of Society*; Vol. III *My Private Note Books* (Watts), *The House by the Churchyard* and *Aurora Floyd*.

(ii) The advertisement in Vol. III is of interest. Both Lefanu's *House by the Churchyard* and Miss Braddon's *Aurora Floyd* are scheduled for 'January next'. In addition to evidence of publishing dates of two important novels, the promise of *Aurora Floyd* for January, 1863, proves that date on the title-pages of the novel to be genuine. It has been suggested, from the fact that 'author of *Aurora Floyd*' is printed on the title-pages of *Lady Audley's Secret*, that the former novel was really published earlier than the latter. Actually this reference is to the serial, which was running in *Temple Bar* during 1862. Book-issue did not take place until early in 1863—I imagine in February, as a fine presentation copy is recorded above dated 'February 21st, 1863'.

Eighth Edition Revised. 3 vols. 1862. Unseen, but listed in a catalogue of about 1937.

Ninth (first illustrated) Edition. 1 vol. 1863. Blue dot-and-line-grain cloth. Curious photographic front.

From these necessarily incomplete descriptions one consoling fact emerges—that owing to tiny differences between the various 'Editions' of this popular work (and even between the individual volumes of each edition) it would be virtually impossible to create a first—or indeed a second or third—edition by skilful manipulation of miscellaneous material.

ana [302*c*]

LADY AUDLEY'S SECRET. An Original Version of Miss Braddon's popular Novel, in Two Acts. By C. H. Hazlewood. Lacy's Acting Edition, No. 849 n.d. Pale pink paper wrappers, printed in black. pp. (30). Final leaf, C_3, a single inset. Advert. leaf on thin paper at end.

Note. According to Mr Montague Summers (*T.L.S.* 24 April 1943) this was the fourth unauthorised stage version of Miss Braddon's novel to be produced in London between 2 February and 25 May 1863. Mr Summers informed me that one at least of the earlier dramatisations (by George Roberts) was privately printed (but not published) on 28 February 1863. He was doubtful whether the other versions were printed.

The copy in the Collection is not of the first wrappering-up, for the back wrapper lists up to No. 986 of Lacy's Acting Edition.

LADY LISLE (The) [303]

Ward & Lock 1862. Magenta morocco cloth.

pp. iv+(268)

Presentation Copy: 'Mrs Cowland with the affectionate regards of her niece the author. October 1862' in ink on fly-leaf. Cloth faded.

A volume in Ward & Lock's Shilling Volume Library. See 3711 (4) in Section II.

LADY'S MILE (The) (by the a.o.L.A.S.) [304]

3 vols. Ward, Lock & Tyler 1866.

Copy I: Dark green sand-grain cloth. *Pl. 5*

Half-title in Vol. I

Vol. I (viii)+(308) X_2 blank (cut away from this copy).
II (iv)+(284)
III (iv)+(336)

Book-plate: Coronet over L.R. in monogram, and 'E. W. Cowderry' pencilled facing half-title or title in each vol. Fine.

Copy II: Presentation Binding. Full dark green morocco, fully gilt, all edges gilt. Dedicatee's copy (Sir Edwin Landseer) with his signature at the end of Vols. I and II, and on front fly-leaf of Vol. III. Book-label of Sir Hugh Walpole. [304*a*]

LIKE AND UNLIKE: a Novel (by the a.o.L.A.S. etc.) [305]

3 vols. Spencer Blackett (successor to J. & R. Maxwell) n.d. [1887]. Dark green cloth, standard style.

Vol. I (iv)+320
II (iv)+(316) X_8 blank.
III (iv)+(322) Y_2 blank.

Cloth worn. Library labels inside covers.

[306] LONDON PRIDE: or When the World was Younger
Simpkin 1896. Dark green ribbed cloth.
Half-title. pp. (viii) + (512)
Book-plate of Henry Kent; ink signature: 'Kent. 1896' and blind stamp 'W. H. Smith & Son' on fly-leaf. Fine.

[307] LOST EDEN (A)
Hutchinson 1904. Crimson diaper-grain cloth.
Half-title. pp. (iv) + (476) $2H_{4-6}$ adverts. Publisher's cat., 16 pp. dated February 1904, at end.

[308] LOST FOR LOVE: a Novel (by the a.o.L.A.S.)
3 vols. Chatto & Windus 1874. Dark green cloth, standard style: but spine-lettering more conventional and Chatto's imprint in the form of a device.
Blank leaf and half-title precede title in Vol. I, half-title only in Vols. II and III.
Vol. I (viii) + (288) Publishers' cat., 40 pp. dated September 1874, at end.
II (iv) + (288)
III (iv) + 296
Blind stamp 'W. H. Smith & Son' on fly-leaf of Vol. I. Fine.

[309] LOVELS OF ARDEN (The): a Novel (by the a.o.L.A.S.)
3 vols. Maxwell 1871. Grass-green horizontal-fine-ribbed cloth, diagonally blocked and lettered in black on front and back (generally in the style of *Fenton's Quest*), lettered in gold and in reverse and elaborately blocked in gold and black on spine, uniform with *Run to Earth*.
Vol. I (iv) + 312
II (iv) + 300
III (iv) + (300) U_6 blank.
Pencil signature: 'Trübner' on fly-leaf of each vol.
Binders' ticket: 'Leighton, Son & Hodge' at end of Vol. I. Very fine.
Note. A panel advert. of Ward, Lock & Tyler editions of Miss Braddon's works appears on p. (iv) of Vol. I. This Maxwell would hardly have included voluntarily, and one must conclude that its insertion was part of the agreement for his release from obligations incurred to Ward, Lock. *Lovels of Arden* was the first Maxwell 'Braddon', after the seven Ward, Lock novels which Miss Braddon wrote in order to secure freedom to publish with whom she chose.

[310] LUCIUS DAVOREN: or Publicans and Sinners: a Novel (by the a.o.L.A.S.)
3 vols. Maxwell 1873. Royal blue cloth, standard style.
Half-title in Vol. I
Vol. I viii + (320)
II iv + 314 Final leaf, Z_1, a single inset.
III (ii) + 336 [paged iv + 334]
Binders' ticket: 'Leighton Son & Hodge', at end of Vol. I.

MARY [311]
Hutchinson 1916. Crimson linen-grain cloth.
Half-title. pp. (iv) + 336 Publisher's cat., 32 pp. dated Autumn 1916, at end.
Ink signature: 'Rita Teare (?)' on front cover.

MILLY DARRELL and other Tales (by the a.o.L.A.S.) [312]
3 vols. Maxwell 1873. Dark green cloth, standard style.
Half-title in Vol. I
Vol. I (viii) + 292
II (iv) + (288) T_8 blank.
III (iv) + (292)
Contents: (*Vol. 1*) Milly Darrell—Old Rudderford Hall—The Splendid Stranger—Hugh Damer's Lost Leger. (*Vol. 2*) The Sins of the Fathers—Mr and Mrs de Fontenoy—A Good Hater—The Dreaded Guest—Colonel Benyon's Entanglement. (*Vol. 3*) The Zoophyte's Revenge—At Chrighton Abbey—Three Times—On the Brink.

MIRANDA [313]
Hutchinson 1913. Crimson fine-ribbed cloth. Title printed in red and black.
Half-title. pp. (iv) + 416 Publisher's cat., 36 pp. dated Autumn 1913, at end.

MOHAWKS: a Novel (by the a.o.L.A.S.) [314]
3 vols. J. & R. Maxwell n.d. [1886]. Dark green cloth, standard style.
Vol. I (iv) + (338) Final leaf, (Z_1), a single inset.
II (iv) + (318) First leaf of final sig., X_1, a single inset of thicker paper.
III (iv) + 308
Date inserted in ink under imprint on title of Vol. I. Binders' ticket: 'Leighton Son & Hodge', at end of Vol. I.

MOUNT ROYAL: a Novel (by the a.o.L.A.S.) [315]
3 vols. J. & R. Maxwell 1882. Dark green cloth, standard style.
Vol. I (iv) + 300 U_6 blank.
II (iv) + (288)
III (iv) + (320) X_8 blank.
Pencil signature: 'Trübner' on fly-leaf of each vol. Very fine.

ONE LIFE, ONE LOVE: a Novel (by the a.o.L.A.S. etc.) [316]
3 vols. Simpkin 1890. Dark green cloth, standard style.

Vol. I (iv) + 300
II (iv) + (276)
III (iv) + 260

A poor copy. Labels removed from covers.

[317] ONE THING NEEDFUL, etc. (by the a.o.L.A.S.)
3 vols. J. & R. Maxwell 1886. Dark green cloth, standard style.

Vol. I (iv) + (304) U_8 blank.
II (iv) + 356
III (iv) + (312) X_4 blank.

'Mrs Henry Whiting, from the author Aug. 1886' in ink on fly-leaves—not in Miss Braddon's hand. Cloth damp-stained.

Contents: (*Vols. 1 and 2*) One Thing Needful—Cut by the County (*to end of Vol. 3*).

[318] ONLY A CLOD (by the a.o.L.A.S.)
3 vols. Maxwell 1865.

Copy I: First Edition. Bright blue pebble-grain cloth.

Half-title in Vol. I.

Vol. I (viii) + (316) X_6 blank.
II (iv) + (288) T_8 blank.
III (iv) + (308)

Book-plate: Coronet over L.R. in monogram and 'E. W. Cowderry' pencilled, facing half-title or title in each vol. Fine.

[318*a*] **Copy II: Second Edition.** 3 vols. 1865. Binding and collation as Copy I.

Presentation Copy: 'Mrs Basden with the author's affectionate regards. May 1865' in ink on fly-leaf of Vol. I. Fine.

[319] OPEN VERDICT (An) (by the a.o.L.A.S.)
3 vols. Maxwell 1878. Dark green cloth, standard style.

Vol. I (iv) + (332) Y_6 blank.
II (iv) + (328) Y_4 blank.
III (iv) + 348

Binders' ticket: 'Leighton, Son & Hodge' at end of Vol. I.

[320] OUR ADVERSARY
Hutchinson 1909. Smooth maroon cloth. Title printed in red and black.

Half-title. pp. (iv) + (428) Publisher's cat., 32 pp. dated February 1909, at end.

Presentation Copy to Lady Dorothy Nevill, with A.L.S., signed 'Mary Maxwell', dated 30 March, pasted to front fly-leaf.

[321] PHANTOM FORTUNE: a Novel (by the a.o.L.A.S.)
3 vols. Maxwell 1883. Dark green cloth, standard style.

Vol. I (iv) + (356) $2A_2$ blank.
II (iv) + 336
III (iv) + 336

Book-plate of T. C. Venables in each vol. Letter from Maxwell to Venables presenting the copy, pasted to fly-leaf of Vol. I. Fine.

RALPH THE BAILIFF and other Tales (by the a.o.L.A.S.) [322]
Ward, Lock & Tyler n.d. [1867]. Blue wide-dot-and-line-grain cloth in the standard style of the Library Edition (cf. *Birds of Prey*, *Captain of the Vulture*, etc.). Wood-engraved front. and pictorial title, with tint background and printed on plate paper, precede printed title.

pp. iv + (428) EE_5 EE_6 adverts.

A tired copy, loose in covers.

Note. This is partially a first edition. There was published in 1862, under the same title, a volume in Ward & Lock's Shilling Volume Series, which contained the first eight of the twelve stories in the present work, viz.: *Ralph the Bailiff—Captain Thomas—The Cold Embrace—My Daughters—The Mystery at Fernwood—Samuel Lowgood's Revenge—The Lawyer's Secret—My First Happy Christmas.* The four stories now first issued in book form are: *Lost and Found* (a novelette of 23 chapters consisting of episodes printed in the *London Journal* as part of *The Outcasts*, but cut out when that story was published in 3 vols. as *Henry Dunbar*)—*Eveline's Visitant—Found in the Muniment Chest* and *How I heard my Own Will Read.*

The date 1867 is suggested, despite the fact that on p. (425) *The Ladies Mile* (3 vols. 1866) is advertised as 'Just Published', because *Eveline's Visitant* and *How I heard my Own Will Read* both appeared in Vol. I of *Belgravia* which was published in February 1867. (For these details I was indebted to Mr Montague Summers.)

ROBERT AINSLEIGH (by the a.o.L.A.S.) [323]
3 vols. Maxwell 1872. Dark green moiré fine-ribbed cloth, with plain sides and gold lettering on spine (see *Note*).

Half-title in Vol. I

Vol. I (viii) + (316)
II (iv) + (316) X_6 blank.
III (iv) + (352) Z_8 blank.

'Jno F. Monsey [?]' in ink on each fly-leaf. Cloth tired.

Notes. (i) This was the earliest novel to be issued in Braddon 'Standard Style'. It and its successor *Lucius Davoren* were the only 'Standard Style' Braddons issued in moiré or in blue cloth. Thereafter the cloth used was dark green, with a fine-dotted-line-rib-grain.

(ii) *Robert Ainsleigh* was serialised in *Belgravia* as *Bound to John Company*, and an American edition was published under that title.

[324] ROSE OF LIFE (The)
Hutchinson 1905. Rose-pink fabric-grain cloth.
Blank leaf and half-title precede title. pp. (viii) [paged vi] + 352 Publisher's cat., 16 pp. dated January 1905, at end.

[325] ROUGH JUSTICE
Simpkin 1898. Red linen-grain cloth. Title printed in red and black.
Half-title. pp. viii + 392 Publisher's cat., 16 pp. undated, at end.

[326] RUN TO EARTH: a Novel (by the a.o.L.A.S.)
3 vols. Ward, Lock & Tyler 1868. Dark green horizontal-fine-ribbed moiré cloth, blocked in blind on front and back, lettered in gold and in reverse and ornately blocked in gold on spine.
Half-title in Vol. I
Vol. I (xii) [paged (x)] + 306 Final leaf, 20_1, a single inset.
II (iv) + 306 Final leaf, 20_1, a single inset.
III (iv) + 304
Fine.

[327] RUPERT GODWIN (by the a.o.L.A.S.)
3 vols. Ward, Lock & Tyler 1867. Magenta fine-ribbed cloth, blind-blocked on front and back, blocked and lettered in gold on spine.
Half-title in Vol. I
Vol. I (viii) + 340
II (iv) + 316
III (iv) + 312
Book-plate of Isaac Latimer. Cloth water-stained.

[328] SIR JASPER'S TENANT (by the a.o.L.A.S.)
3 vols. Maxwell 1865.
Copy I: First Edition. Grass-green morocco cloth.
Half-title in Vol. I
Vol. I (viii) + (316) 20_6 blank.
II (iv) + (288)
III (iv) + (324) (21_2) blank.

[328*a*] **Copy II: Fourth Edition.** 3 vols. 1865. Darker green sand grain cloth. Collation as Copy I.
Presentation Copy: 'Mrs Basden with the author's affectionate regards, October 1865' in ink on fly-leaf of Vol. I; in pencil on fly-leaf of Vol. III 'Miss Braddon, 38 Park Street'.
Both very fine.

[329] SONS OF FIRE: a Novel (by the a.o.L.A.S.)
3 vols. Simpkin n.d. [1895]. Smooth dark green glazed cloth.
Vol. I (iv) + (288) T_8 blank.
II (iv) + (280)
III (iv) + (276) T_2 blank.
Presentation Copy: 'Madame Whiting, with affectionate greetings from M. E. Braddon. September 1895' in ink facing title of Vol. I. Fine.

STORY OF BARBARA (The): her Splendid Misery, and her Gilded Cage [330]
3 vols. J. & R. Maxwell n.d. [1880]. Dark green cloth, standard style.
Half-title, reading 'BARBARA', (?) in each vol.
Vol. I (x) + (286)
II (? vi) + 268
III (vi) + 254
Note. This is such an abominable copy that I cannot be certain of its structure. Actually no half-title appears in Vol. II, but I suspect there should be one, leaving a single leaf in each prelim. which was originally printed as T_8 in Vol. I, as S_8 in II, and as R_8 in III.

STRANGERS AND PILGRIMS: a Novel (by the a.o.L.A.S.) [331]
3 vols. Maxwell 1873. Dark green cloth, standard style.
Half-title in each vol.
Vol. I (iv) + (284)
II (iv) + 298 1st leaf of final sig., U_1, a single inset.
III (iv) + (286) 1st leaf of final sig., T_1, a single inset.
A very bad copy.

STRANGE WORLD (A): a Novel [332]
3 vols. Maxwell 1875. Dark green cloth, standard style.
Vol. I (iv) + (296) U_4 blank.
II (iv) + (296) U_4 blank.
III (iv) + 312
Cloth good. Library labels inside covers.

TAKEN AT THE FLOOD: a Novel (by the a.o.L.A.S.) [333]
3 vols. Maxwell 1874. Dark green cloth, standard style.
Half-title in Vol. I
Vol. I (viii) + 312
II (iv) + 312
III iv + (304) U_8 blank.
'From the publishers' in pencil on fly-leaf of Vol. I. Book-plate of Thomas Charles Venables in each vol., and 'Thos C. Venables' in pencil on each title. An invitation, in Miss Braddon's hand, to Mr and Mrs Venables, pasted on to fly-leaf of Vol. I. Fine.

THOU ART THE MAN: a Novel (by the a.o.L.A.S.) [334]
3 vols. Simpkin n.d. [1894]. Dark green cloth, standard style.
Vol. I (iv) + (288) T_8 blank.
II (iv) + 272
III (iv) + (256) R_8 blank.

Presentation Copy: 'M. J. Braddon from M. E. Braddon' in ink facing title in each vol. (not in author's hand). Fine.

[335] THREE TIMES DEAD: or the Secret of the Heath

8vo. W. M. Clark, Warwick Lane and C. R. Empson, Beverley n.d. [1854]. Old three-quarter morocco. Wood engravings in text.

pp. (ii) + 218

Inserted are various cuttings; an A.L.S. from Maxwell to Empson; one from Empson to James Mills of Beverley; and one from Mary Maxwell to the same, all concerning this story and *The Trail of the Serpent* (q.v. below).

James Mills, who read the proof for Empson originally, annotates this copy and certifies it as a set of revised proofs.

Some torn pages roughly mended.

[336] TO THE BITTER END: a Novel (by the a.o.L.A.S.)

3 vols. Maxwell 1872. Dark green cloth, standard style.

Half-title in Vols. I and III

Vol. I (viii) + (300)
II (iv) + (284)
III (viii) [(vii) (viii), first leaf of text, paged 1 (2)] + 290 Owing to irregular pagination at the beginning, each sig. apparently ends on an odd leaf. But as p. 3 is B_1 and p. 18 B_8, so is p. 290 T_8.

[337] TRAIL OF THE SERPENT (The) (by the a.o.L.A.S.)

Ward, Lock & Tyler 1866. Dark blue dot-and-line-grain cloth. Tinted front. and pictorial title precede printed title.

Half-title. pp. viii + 456 Publishers' cat., 4 pp. undated, at end.

Ex-Basden collection but not inscribed. Fine.

Note. Until the late summer of 1942 this volume had been accepted (certainly by me) as the first re-issue of Miss Braddon's first story *Three Times Dead: or the Secret of the Heath* (q.v. above). But on 29 August 1942, Mr Montague Summers (in a contribution to the *Times Literary Supplement*) reported the existence in the Bodleian of an edition dated 1861. This is a yellow-back, published by Ward & Lock, entitled *The Trail of the Serpent: or Three Times Dead*, and contains various revisions of the original Beverley text, of which revisions Mr Summers gave details (briefly some chapter-titles and a number of names were altered, and about 10,000 words cut out). The cover-drawing is quite different from that on the yellow-back of 1867 recorded in Section II.

The survival of this 1861 edition is of importance to anyone interested in the bibliography of Miss Braddon, and raises a curious problem as to the policy of Ward, Lock & Tyler in their handling of the cloth edition of 1866 above described.

It is not surprising that the 1866 volume has been regarded as the first re-issue of *Three Times Dead*, for it contains a Publishers' Announcement dated July 1866 which, although it does not mention the story's original title, to all intents and purposes says as much:

'*The Trail of the Serpent* was written originally for serial publication....In its serial form it was subjected to all the vicissitudes which can afflict a literary undertaking; but although always hastily and sometimes recklessly produced, the Novel was written *con amore*, with very little hope of fee or reward except the thrilling pleasure which the literary aspirant feels on seeing a first work in print....

'The work now reprinted has been carefully revised and in part re-written....For what it is, the Publishers submit *The Trail of the Serpent* to the generous appreciation of both critical and non-critical readers.'

It would be difficult, without saying so outright, to imply more definitely that the volume thus introduced was the first, and revised, re-appearance of a story issued some years ago in serial numbers. Nevertheless, there exists in the Bodleian an edition dated 1861, also published by Ward & Lock (as they then were), and containing the same differences from the original Beverley text as appear in the edition of 1866.

Why should Ward, Lock & Tyler in their cloth issue of 1866, not merely make no mention of the board issue of 1861, but go out of their way to imply that no intermediate edition had appeared since the original publication in Beverley? A possible explanation is suggested by a document in my possession which had not hitherto had much meaning for me. This is a letter from John Maxwell to Empson of Beverley, written on the paper of the *St James's Magazine* and dated 19 April 1861. It says:

'I bought and paid for the copyright of *The Trail of the Serpent*, taking at the time of my purchase a receipt and assignment from the Author, Miss M. E. Braddon, of No. 20, High Street, Camden Town. I am wholly taken by surprise, therefore, at your claim, and will feel obliged if you will forward to a friend of your own in London any documents sustaining your position, etc., etc....'

Now suppose that Miss Braddon, not fully understanding her position *vis-à-vis* Empson or considering that he had defaulted from the contract which was therefore void (Mr Summers informed me that Empson not only asked her to cut her story by half and accept £5 instead of £10, but in fact never paid a penny beyond the 50*s*. given in advance), sold her copyright twice over. Suppose that Maxwell (on the staff of Ward & Lock and ignorant of the earlier basis of contract) arranged for the story to appear in 1861 under a new title but rashly retained the old one as a sub-title. Suppose that Empson saw this book, or an announcement of it, and challenged the new publishers' rights, provoking in reply this letter from Maxwell. Is it not possible that when the two parties got down to brass tacks Empson was able to prove his case? The immediate result would be the withdrawal of the Ward & Lock edition of 1861 and, in 1866 (the difficulty with Empson may or may not have been resolved in the interval), the issue of a cloth-bound edition, published without the original title and prefaced by a publishers' note suggesting that this was the first revival of a forgotten and anonymous story.

[338] UNDER LOVE'S RULE (by the a.o.L.A.S.)
Simpkin 1897. Lime-green linen-grain cloth.
pp. (iv) + (308) U_7 U_8 and X_1 X_2 adverts.
Front cover water-stained.

[339] UNDER THE RED FLAG
8vo. J. & R. Maxwell 1883. White wrappers, cut flush, pictorially printed and lettered in blue, green and yellow: up-lettered on spine MISS BRADDON'S NEW CHRISTMAS ANNUAL. 1/-. Back and inside covers printed with adverts. Wood-engraved front. and 3 full-page illustrations after Henry French. 24 pp. of adverts. on text paper dated Nov. 1883 precede front.
pp. 104 Very fine.
Note. This—the 1883 issue of the Annual called *The Mistletoe Bough*—has no other contents than *Under the Red Flag* and is, therefore, the first edition of the novel published in regulation cloth-bound form in 1884.

[340] VENETIANS (The): a Novel (by the a.o.L.A.S.)
3 vols. Simpkin 1892. Dark green cloth, standard style.
Vol. I (iv) + (292) U_2 blank.
II (iv) + (284) T_6 blank.
III (iv) + 304
Presentation Copy: 'To Mrs Henry Whiting with the author's affectionate regards, June 1892' in ink on title of Vol. I. 'Mrs Henry Whiting' in recipient's hand on fly-leaf of Vols. II and III.

[341] WEAVERS AND WEFT, and other Tales (by the a.o.L.A.S.)
3 vols. John Maxwell 1877. Dark green cloth, standard style.
Vol. I (iv) + (316)
II (iv) + (318) Final leaf, X_7, a single inset.
III (iv) + (320)
Presentation Copy: 'Henry Whiting Esq with the author's kind regards, March 2nd, 1877.' 'Henry Whiting' in ink on 2nd fly-leaf of Vols. II and III. 'Juliette E. M. Turner, 16 Chelsea Embankment' on 1st fly-leaf of Vols. I and II. Inside edges of Vol. I badly affected by damp.
Contents: (*Vols. 1 and 2*) Weavers & Weft—In Great Waters—Sebastian Levison's Victim—Christmas in Possession—John Granger. (*Vol. 3*) Prince Ramji Rowdedow—Too Bright to Last—The Scene-Painter's Wife—Sir Luke's Return—Her Last Appearance—Sir Hanbury's Bequest—A Very Narrow Escape—My Unlucky Friend.
Note. This copy has Maxwell imprint on titles but Simpkin, Marshall & Co. on spines. 1st issue was Maxwell throughout.

WHITE HOUSE (The) [342]
Hurst & Blackett 1906. Smooth grey-blue linen-grain cloth, blocked and lettered in dark blue on front, in gold on spine; pale grey monogram end-papers.
Half-title. pp. (iv) + 444

WYLLARD'S WEIRD: a Novel (by the a.o.L.A.S.) [343]
3 vols. J. & R. Maxwell n.d. [1885]. Dark green cloth, standard style.
Vol. I (iv) + (316)
II (iv) + 296
III (iv) + (304)
Book-plate of T. C. Venables in Vol. I and rhyme on pink paper pasted on fly-leaf. Fine.

American Editions and Attributions [344]
The following fictions published in U.S.A. carry Miss Braddon's name on wrapper and title. Those asterisked were certainly her work:

(*a*) Published by Robert M. de Witt, New York, in 8vo. Pale brown wrappers printed in black.

***Oscar Bertrand,** n.d. ('De Witt's Choice Novels', No. 9.) [344*a*]

***The Octoroon or The Lily of Louisiana,** n.d. ('De Witt's Choice Novels, No. 17.) [344*b*]

The Blue Band or A Story of a Woman's Vengeance, n.d. ('Miss Braddon Series', No. 6.) [344*c*]

Leighton Grange or Who killed Edith Woodville? n.d. ('Miss Braddon Series', No. 7.) [344*d*]

Note. The other titles in the 'Miss Braddon Series' are: No. 1, **The White Phantom or the Nameless Child.* No. 2, **The Factory Girl or All is not Gold that Glitters.* No. 3, **The Black Band or the Mysteries of Midnight.* No. 4, **Oscar Bertrand or the Black Band Unmasked.* No. 5, **The Octoroon or the Lily of Louisiana.* Probably all the titles originally appeared in 'De Witt's Choice Novels'.
No. 3 is the only title of which Mr Summers could trace a separate English edition.

(*b*) Published by T. B. Peterson & Brothers, Philadelphia. Red-brown wrapper printed in black.

[344e] *The Lawyer's Secret, n.d. (1863).

(c) Published in the 'Leisure Hour Library', 4to, no wrappers, decorative series heading and titling at head of p. 1.

[344f] *Dudley Carleon (*Ralph the Bailiff*) L.H.L. No. 25, New Series. April 26, 1884.

[344g] Jasper Dane's Secret. L.H.L. No. 67, New Series. Feb. 1885.

[344h] The Fatal Marriage. L.H.L. No. 90, New Series. June 30, 1886.

[344i] His Second Wife. L.H.L. No. 109, New Series. Sept. 4, 1886.

[344j] *The Lawyer's Secret (a story in *Ralph the Bailiff*). L.H.L. No. 140, New Series. May 28, 1887.

[344k] *George Caulfield's Journey. L.H.L. No. 200, New Series. July 21, 1888.

[See also HAMILTON, WALTER.]

BRONTË, REV. PATRICK (1777–1861)

[345] MAID OF KILLARNEY (The); or, Albion and Flora: A Modern Tale; in which are interwoven some Cursory Remarks on Religion and Politics [anon]

Slim Cr. 8vo. Baldwin, Cradock & Joy 1818. Boards, label.

pp. (168) [paged (i)–vi+(7)–(168)] O_6 Errata, with Printer's imprint on verso.

Very fine. From the Bellew Library.

BRONTË SISTERS, THE

CHARLOTTE (1816–1855); EMILY (1818–1848); ANNE (1820–1849)

For further bibliographical detail see Parrish, *Victorian Lady Novelists*, London, 1933, to which work references are made below.

[346] JANE EYRE: an Autobiography (Edited by Currer Bell)

Copy I: First Edition. 3 vols. Smith, Elder 1847. Grey-purple fine-ribbed cloth. Dark cream end-papers. [*Parrish*, p. 87

Half-title in each vol.

Vol. I (iv)+304 Publishers' cat., 32 pp. dated October 1847, at end, preceded by inset fly-title dated June 1847 and followed by inset leaf of thicker paper advertising the *Calcutta Review*.
II (iv)+304
III (iv)+(312)

Binders' ticket: 'Westleys & Clark', at end of Vol. I. The cloth sides of each volume are a little rubbed, and there is a water-stain (though not a disfiguring one) on the front cover of Vol. III. The spines, uniformly faded, are sharp and clean. The copy is absolutely untouched and, although frail at the joints, is, for this book, an excellent one.

Copy II: Second Edition. 3 vols. Smith, Elder 1848. Plum fine-ribbed cloth, blocked in blind and lettered in gold. [*Parrish*, p. 89 [346a]

Half-title in each vol., that in Vol. I preceded by a 12 pp. signature of text paper, giving extracts from reviews of *Jane Eyre*. This signature is signed 'VOL. III X' and paged (1)–9. Pp. (10) (11) (12) are blank.

Vol. I (xii)+(xii) [prelims., paged (i)–xi, p. (xii) blank]+304 Publishers' cat., 32 pp. dated October 1847, preceded by a single inset leaf serving as fly-title to cat. and dated April 1847. Back fly-leaf of this vol. missing.
II (iv)+304
III (iv)+304

Vol. I. pp. (v) (vi) carry Dedication to Thackeray and (vii)–xi carry Author's Preface, dated 21 Dec. 1847. Book-label of Hugh Walpole.

PROFESSOR (The): a Tale (by Currer Bell) [347]
[*Parrish*, p. 96

2 vols. Smith, Elder 1857. Grey-purple morocco cloth.

Half-title in each vol.

Vol. I viii+(296) U_4 adverts.
II (iv)+(268) S_2 imprint leaf, S_3–S_6 adverts. Publishers' cat., 16 pp. dated June 1857, at end.

Binders' ticket: 'Westleys', at end of Vol. I. Cloth fine. A grease spot affects pages (1)–10 of Vol. II.

SHIRLEY: a Tale (by Currer Bell) [348]

Copy I: First Edition. 3 vols. Smith, Elder 1849. Claret horizontal-fine ribbed cloth. [*Parrish*, p. 93

Vol. I iv+(304) Publishers' cat., 16 pp. dated November 1849, at end.
II iv+308
III iv+(320) X_8 adverts.

Ink signature: 'Moretino', on title of each vol. Binders' ticket: 'Westleys', at end of Vol. I. A brilliant copy.

Copy II: First one-volume Edition. Smith, Elder 1853. 'New Edition.' Grey-purple morocco cloth. [348a]

Ink signature: 'Jane Carrington 1853', on fly-title.

VILLETTE (by Currer Bell) [349]

3 vols. Smith, Elder 1853. Olive-brown morocco cloth. [*Parrish*, p. 95

Vol. I (iv) + 324 Publishers' cat., 12 pp. dated January 1853, at end.
II (iv) + (320)
III (iv) + (352) Z_8 imprint leaf.

Ink signature: 'J. Julia L. Gordon', on title of Vol. I. Binders' ticket: 'Westleys', at end of Vol. I. Fine.

[350] WUTHERING HEIGHTS: a Novel (by Ellis Bell) and AGNES GREY: a Novel (by Acton Bell)

Pl. 5 **Copy I: First Edition.** 3 vols. Newby 1847. Half-cloth boards, labels. [*Parrish*, p. 85

Vol. I (ii) + 348
II (ii) + 416
III (ii) + (364)

Each title is a single leaf, and the fourth leaf required to complete the preliminary folding was almost certainly a label-leaf. The stub, conjugate with title of Vol. III, is clearly seen in this copy.

A magnificent copy. The only blemishes are a few tiny holes in the label of Vol. II and that the front fly-leaf of Vol. I is missing. I believe I am right in saying that more copies of this very rare book survive in full cloth than in half-cloth boards.

[350*a*] **Copy II: 'A New Edition Revised',** with a Biographical Notice of the Authors, a Selection from their Literary Remains and a Preface by Currer Bell. Smith, Elder 1850. Grey-purple morocco cloth. [*Parrish*, p. 94

Advert. leaf and half-title precede title. pp. xxiv [of which (i)–(xviii) are paged (i)–xvi and (xix)–xxiv correctly paged] + 504.

Ink signature: 'Mary Anne Humble, March 14th 1851', on fly-leaf, and in same hand on inside front cover 'Mrs Richard Roberts'. Binders' ticket: 'Westleys', at end. Very fine.

Note. This highly important edition contains Biographical Notice (10 pp.) and Editor's Preface (6 pp.) by Charlotte Brontë and Selections from the Literary Remains of Emily and Anne Brontë, edited by Charlotte Brontë, occupying pp. (470)–505 and never before printed.

This copy lacks Publishers' cat. called for by Parrish, which cat., being dated 1855, presumably belonged to a subsequent binding.

Brontëana

[351] TRANSACTIONS AND OTHER PUBLICATIONS OF THE BRONTË SOCIETY

9 vols. 1898–1939.

Vol. I Parts I–VIII. Also Catalogue of Brontë Museum, 1895–1898. Three-quarter blue calf. Original wrappers retained.
II Parts IX–XV, 1899–1906. Three-quarter red morocco. Original wrappers of Part X only.
III (Supplementary) 'Persons and Places in the Brontë Novels', 1906. Three-quarter red morocco.
IV Parts XVI–XXII, 1907–1912. Three-quarter red morocco.
V Parts XXIII–XXIX, 1913–1919. Three-quarter red morocco. Original wrappers retained.
VI Parts XXX–XXXV, 1920–1925. Three-quarter red morocco. Original wrappers retained.
VII Parts XXXVI–XLI, 1926–1931. Three-quarter red morocco. Original wrappers retained.
VIII Parts XLII–XLV. Also 'Sources of Charlotte Brontë's Novels' (Supplementary) 1932–1935. Three-quarter red morocco. Original wrappers retained (except for Part XLV.
IX Parts XLVI–XLIX, 1936–1939. Original wrappers.

BROOKS, SHIRLEY (1816–1874)

ASPEN COURT: a Story of Our Own Time [352]

3 vols. Bentley 1855. Dark brown morocco cloth.

Vol. I (vi) + (340)
II (iv) + (320)
III (iv) + 322 First leaf of final signature, P_1, a single inset.

Booksellers' ticket: 'G. & J. Robinson, Liverpool', on inside front cover of Vol. I. Cloth very fine. Lacks final end-paper in Vol. III. The story is dedicated to Charles Dickens.

BROUGHAM, HENRY, LORD (1778–1868)

ALBERT LUNEL: or the Château of Languedoc [353]
[anon]

3 vols. Charles Knight & Co. 1844. Boards, labels.

Half-title in Vols. I and II

Vol. I viii + (256) M_8 adverts.
II vi + (242) Final leaf, M_1, a single inset.
III iv + 284

Very fine.

Notes. (i) A secondary issue was made, many years later, of first edition sheets in cherry bubble-grain cloth, with no spine imprint and end-papers printed with Chapman & Hall adverts.

(ii) A tertiary issue of original sheets, with half-titles cancelled and reprint-titles, was published by C. H. Clarke in 1872. A Note facing the title in each vol., dated March 1872, says that the novel had been written in 1844 'but for private reasons of his Lordship's was not published'. This edition was issued in maroon sand-grain cloth with spine-lettering from type. The title-pages are undated.

(iii) This novel in first edition form is one of the false rarities, whose legend haunts the book-trade. The legend originates, I believe, in the 1865 edition of Lowndes' *Bibliographers' Manual*, where we read: 'it is said not above five copies are extant.'

Brougham told Forsyth that the bulk of the original edition was sealed in a cellar and, later on, 'I dare say many years hence someone will dig this up and publish it'. Did he mean the balance of edition would be re-issued or that the story would be reprinted? Further, on whose authority did Henry G. Bohn, when preparing the 1865 edition of Lowndes (Brougham was still alive) report that 'not above five copies are extant'?

Lowndes' assertion continues to appear in booksellers' and auctioneers' catalogues, despite the fact that the new edition of Halkett & Laing says in so many words that the stock of the sheets were sold off after Brougham's death.

Certainly the novel, even today, is not of great rarity, and of the twenty odd copies I have seen the majority were in boards and in fine condition. There are two board copies in the Collection, one immaculate, the other less so—and the latter, I think, offers a solution of what happened.

This copy, with the bookplate of Frederick Locker in Vols. I and III, can only have belonged to Brougham himself. It carries a pencil-note in his hand on p. 1 of the dedication to Samuel Rogers: 'The only persons who ever saw this book were Rogers, Lyndhurst, Croker, Lady C. Lindsay & Mrs Dawson Damer.' Elsewhere, also in Brougham's hand, are identifications of certain characters. Thus Vol. II p. 110 identifies 'M. la Croasse' with Croker, Vol. III pp. 32 and 156 identify 'M. de Chapeley' with Copley Lyndhurst, p. 104 'Earl of Mornton' with Lord Wellesley, p. 155 'M. Velour' with Sir John Leach, and p. 172 'Chevalier André Agneau' with Sir Andrew Agnew. On p. 156 'M. Balaye' (with bi-lingual humour which does not quite come off) is endorsed 'Myself'. Further the passages in Vol. III describing the heroine (Brougham's daughter who died in 1839) are heavily scored in the margin. There is also a note in Locker's hand on fly-leaf of Vol. I verifying Brougham's hand and remarking on the copy's intrinsic interest.

It would appear obvious that Brougham genuinely believed the authorship of this novel—a *roman à clé* about an intimate circle, actually staged in the Château at Cannes built in his daughter's memory in 1840 but ostensibly a tale of pre-revolutionary France—to be known only to the five friends named; also that he thought to have secured its complete suppression. It seems equally clear that, by chance or by design, his orders were not properly carried out, and that, as Halkett & Laing state, *a* (rather than '*the*') stock of sheets came to light after Brougham's death and were sold off, boarded and with original labels.

There exist, therefore, four states of *Albert Lunel*: (i) first edition, first boarding, of which it is very likely only five copies survived; (ii) first edition, second and posthumous boarding, of which an unknown number of copies came into existence, probably immediately after Brougham's death; (iii) first edition, cloth bound; and (iv) the C. H. Clarke re-issue, both of which are really scarce.

BROUGHTON, RHODA (1840–1920)

Though this is not a complete collection of Broughton first editions—it lacks four one-volume novels and a one-volume collaboration—it is a noteworthy one, and well illustrates the debt owed by the Collection to the Bentley Fiction File. Broughton 'firsts' are not common in any state, and some seem virtually undiscoverable. Descriptions of those not in the collection are provided from copies in the Statutory Libraries, and asterisked.

It is permissible to refer to my essay on Rhoda Broughton, included in a volume called *Things Past* (1944), which provides much information about the publishing history of her books.

ALAS! a Novel [354]

3 vols. Bentley 1890.

Copy I. Light mottled blue fabric-grain cloth, blocked in bronze and lettered in gold. Titles printed in red and black; grey monogram end-papers.

Half-title in each vol.

Vol. I (iv)+(300)
II (iv)+(304)
III (iv)+(320) 58_6-58_8 adverts. **B**

Small ink sketch on p. 299, Vol. I.

Copy II. A paler smoother cloth, otherwise identical. Lettering and collation as Copy I. **B.** [354*a*]

BEGINNER (A) [355]

Bentley 1894. Standard style binding for the Favourite Novel Series, but in smooth white cloth. Sides blocked in blind; grey monogram end-papers.

Half-title. pp. (iv)+(396) 25_6 blank. Publisher's cat., 32 pp. dated Spring 1894, at end. **B**

With two corrections in George Bentley's hand. Cloth slightly soiled.

No. 149 of the Favourite Novels.

Note. Occasionally Bentley prepared a few copies of novels originally published in Favourite Novel style in white cloth for presentation to the authors and others (*cf.* Maarten Maartens, below).

[356] BELINDA: a Novel
3 vols. Bentley 1883.

Copy I. Unglazed chintz-cloth with black and white acorn design; pale grey floral end-papers.

Half-title to Vol. I Leaf of adverts. precedes title in Vols. II and III

Vol. I (iv) + 300
II (iv) + (300)
III (iv) + (292) (57_2) adverts. B

[356*a*] **Copy II.** Smooth glazed black cloth; pale grey leafy end-papers. Spine-lettering and collation as Copy I. Very fine.

Note. Of these two copies that in chintz cloth came from the Bentley file, and I have no doubt that it represents the original binding-style. Its predecessor (*Second Thoughts*) was chintz-bound; its successor (*Doctor Cupid*) was in smooth black cloth. I think it may be taken for certain that the Circulating Libraries objected to the *clinging* quality of chintz bindings, and that these were abandoned under pressure from important customers.

[357] BETTY'S VISIONS and MRS SMITH OF LONGMAINS
Routledge, n.d. [1886]. Buff paper wrappers, printed in red, green and black. Spine up-lettered.

pp. (180). Single leaf of adverts. inset at end.

Fine. This is a volume in Tillotson's Shilling Fiction.

[358] *BETWEEN TWO STOOLS
Stanley Paul & Co., n.d. [1912]. Olive-green linen-grain cloth, blocked and lettered on front in dark green, gold-lettered on spine.

Half-title. pp. (368) Publishers' cat., 48 pp. dated January 1912, at end.

[359] COMETH UP AS A FLOWER: an Autobiography [anon]

Pl. 5 2 vols. Bentley 1867. Grass-green sand-grain cloth.

Half-title in Vol. II

Vol. I (iv) + (328)
II (iv) + (296) U_4 blank. B

[360] *CONCERNING A VOW
Stanley Paul & Co. 1914. Smooth dark blue linen-grain cloth, blocked and lettered on front in black, on spine in gold.

Half-title. pp. (352) Publishers' cat., 48 pp. dated November 1913, at end.

Issued in an orange jacket, printed in black.

[361] DEAR FAUSTINA
Bentley 1897.

Copy I. Standard style binding for the Favourite Novel Series, but in white dot-and-line-grain cloth, blocked in gold on front, spine and back; grey monogram end-papers.

Half-title. pp. (iv) + 400 Publisher's cat., 32 pp. dated Autumn 1896, at end. B

Copy II. Regulation dark green Favourite Novel style. Collation as Copy I. B [361*a*]

No. 158 of the Favourite Novels.

DEVIL AND THE DEEP SEA (The) [362]
Macmillan 1910. Smooth red cloth.

Half-title. pp. (iv) + 288 Publisher's cat., 8 pp. undated, at end.

Fine.

Note. There is also in the Collection a *Presentation Copy*, inscribed in ink on title: 'To Beloved C.M.S. from R.B. Oct. 3rd 1910.'

DOCTOR CUPID: a Novel [363]
3 vols. Bentley 1886. Smooth glazed black cloth. Titles printed in red and black.

Vol. I (ii) + 298 Final leaf, 19_5, a single inset.
II (ii) + (286) Final leaf, 37_7, a single inset.
III (ii) + 270 Final leaf, 54_7, a single inset. B

FOES IN LAW [364]
Macmillan 1900. Blue linen-grain cloth.

Half-title. pp. (vi) + (364) $2A_4$–$2A_6$ adverts., paged 1–6. Publisher's cat., 16 pp. dated August 5, 1900, at end. pp. (v), (vi) of prelims. form inset Dedication Leaf.

Ink signature: 'A. L. Ripley', on fly-leaf. Covers slightly stained.

FOOL IN HER FOLLY (A) Foreword by Mrs Belloc Lowndes [365]
Odhams, n.d. [1920]. Scarlet linen-grain cloth.

Half-title. pp. 352

Very fine, with picture jacket.

GAME AND THE CANDLE (The) [366]
Macmillan 1899. Regulation dark green Favourite Novel Series style; grey monogram end-papers.

Half-title. pp. (iv) + 396

Presentation Copy, inscribed in ink on title: 'Priscilla Brackenbury. With Rhoda's fondest love. May 17th 99.'

GOOD-BYE SWEETHEART: a Tale [367]
3 vols. Bentley 1872. Red sand-grain cloth. Titles printed in red and black.

Vol. I iv + 312
II iv + 300
III iv + (312) 20_4 adverts. B

Covers of Vol. I stained and wormed.

JOAN: a Tale [368]
3 vols. Bentley 1876. Blue-grey diagonal-fine-ribbed cloth, bevelled boards.

Leaf of adverts. precedes title in Vol. III

Vol. I (ii) + (310) First leaf of final sig., 20_1, a single inset.

II (ii) + 278 First leaf of final sig., 38_1, a single inset.

III (iv) + (316) **B**

[369] *LAVINIA

Macmillan 1902. Smooth blue linen-grain cloth, blocked and lettered on front in white and gold, gold-lettered on spine.

Half-title. pp. (iv) + 320 Publishers' cat., 16 pp. dated Autumn 1902, at end.

Issued in a very pale green jacket lettered in black.

[370] MAMMA

Macmillan 1908. Powder-blue sand-grain cloth.

Half-title. pp. (iv) + (300) Publisher's cat., 8 pp. dated August 30, 1908, at end.

Very fine, with dust jacket.

[371] MRS BLIGH: a Novel

Bentley 1892. Standard style binding for the Favourite Novel Series, but in smooth white cloth blocked in gold on front, spine and back; grey monogram end-papers.

Half-title. pp. (vi) + (362) 23_4 23_5 adverts. 23_5 a single inset. Publisher's cat., 32 pp. dated Autumn 1892, at end. **B**

No. 140 of the Favourite Novels.

[372] NANCY: a Novel

3 vols. Bentley 1873. Ochre sand-grain cloth. Titles printed in red and black.

Vol. I (iv) + (316)

II (ii) + (284)

III (ii) + 280 **B**

[373] NOT WISELY BUT TOO WELL: a Novel (by the author of 'Cometh Up as a Flower')

Pl. 5 3 vols. Tinsley 1867. Dark blue wavy-grain cloth.

Half-title in each vol.

Vol. I (iv) + (288)

II (iv) + 288

III (iv) + 292 **B**

Presentation Copy: 'Mr Bentley, with the author's comp[ts] October 17, 1867' in ink on fly-leaf of Vol. I.

[374] RED AS A ROSE IS SHE: a Novel (by the author of 'Cometh up as a Flower')

Pl. 5 3 vols. Bentley 1870. Bright blue sand-grain cloth.

Vol. I (ii) + (304)

II (ii) + 300

III (ii) + (300) **B**

SCYLLA OR CHARYBDIS? [375]

Bentley 1895.

Copy I. Standard style binding for the Favourite *Pl. 5* Novel Series, but in white dot-and-line-grain cloth, blocked in gold on front, spine and back; grey monogram end-papers.

Half-title. pp. (iv) + (380) 24_{4-6} adverts. Publisher's cat., 32 pp. dated Autumn 1895, at end.

Copy II. Regulation dark green Favourite Novel [375*a*] Series style. Collation as Copy I. Both copies **B**

Note. There is also in the Collection a *Presentation Copy*, inscribed in ink on title: 'With the author's best love. Oct. 28. 95.'

SECOND THOUGHTS [376]

2 vols. Bentley 1880. Unglazed multicoloured floral chintz cloth; black end-papers.

Half-title in each vol.

Vol. I (vi) + (308)

II (iv) + (296) Text ends 38_3; 38_4 fly-title to Publisher's cat., 16 pp. on text paper, dated May 1880 and occupying 38_5–38_8, (39_1)–(39_4).

Binder's ticket: 'Burn' at end. **B**

TALES FOR CHRISTMAS EVE [377]

Copy I: First Edition. Bentley 1873. Plum fine-pebble-grain cloth, bevelled boards; grey *Pl. 5* end-papers.

Half-title. pp. (vi) + (218) Final leaf, 14_5, a single inset. **B**

Publisher's 'Copyright Copy', with his File Label pasted inside front cover.

Copy II: New Edition, under a new title: TWILIGHT STORIES. Bentley 1879. Scarlet [377*a*] diagonal-fine-ribbed cloth.

No. XII in Bentley's Half-Crown Empire Library.

*THORN IN THE FLESH (A) [378]

Stanley Paul & Co. 1917, 'Third Edition'. Medium blue linen-grain cloth, blocked and lettered in bluish white on front and spine.

Leaf of adverts. and half-title precede title. pp. (320) U_8 blank. Publishers' cat., 48 pp. dated 1916, at end.

TWILIGHT STORIES

See TALES FOR CHRISTMAS EVE.

WAIF'S PROGRESS (A) [379]

Macmillan 1905. Blue linen-grain cloth.

Half-title. pp. (iv) + (404) $2D_2$ blank. Publisher's cat., 8 pp. dated August 16, 1905, inserted between pp. 402 (403).

*WIDOWER INDEED (A) (by Rhoda Broughton [380] and Elizabeth Bisland)

Osgood, McIlvaine 1892. 'Second Edition.' Pale glazed Nattier-blue cloth spine, lettered in gold; flecked blue and white diagonal-fine-ribbed cloth sides with decorative panel and lettering on front, blocked in darkish grey-blue and gold; pale grey floral end-papers.

Blank leaf (single inset) and half-title precede title. pp. (vi)+(290) Final leaf, (U_1), blank and a single inset, presumably originally conjugate with leaf preceding half-title.

Note. Described from the Bodleian copy. I have been unable to trace a first edition.

Broughtoniana

[381] BAZALGETTES (The): a Tale [anon]

Hamish Hamilton 1935. Black wide-dot-and-line grain cloth, blocked and lettered in the Series style of Bentley's Favourite Novels.

Half-title. pp. (384)

Note. A 'Publisher's Note' says: 'This anonymous novel of the years 1870–1876 is something of a literary conundrum.... When it came to us the style seemed faintly familiar and we suspected who might have written it.' Not long before she died, I was given permission by E. M. DELAFIELD to disclose that she was the author.

The book is a brilliant pastiche of the bouncing Broughton of the early three-deckers, which does not guy its victim (as does Burnand's slapstick parody: *Gone Wrong*, by Rhody Dendron†) but gently heightens her absurdities while re-creating her high spirits. The earliest parody of Rhoda Broughton with which I am familiar is *Groweth Down like a Toadstool*, by Lucius Broughton which began in *The St James's Magazine*, October 1876.

BUCHANAN, ROBERT (1841–1901)

[382] GOD AND THE MAN

3 vols. Chatto & Windus 1881. Blue sand-grain cloth. Wood-engraved front. and 4 plates in Vol. I, 2 each in Vols. II and III.

Half-title in each vol.

Vol. I (viii)+(284)

II (viii)+(286) First leaf of final sig., T_1, a single inset.

III (viii)+244 Publishers' cat., 32 pp. dated October 1881, at end.

Very fine. Front. to Vol. I detached.

Dedication: 'To an old enemy' etc., is addressed to D. G. Rossetti, and is an offer of peace after the controversy over Buchanan's *Fleshly School of Poetry*.

Notes. (i) Also issued in smooth sand-brown cloth, similarly blocked in black and lettered in gold. I cannot determine priority, but the general effect of the blue cloth style is richer.

(ii) The first one-volume edition, published in the style of the Piccadilly Series in 1883 and retaining the illustrations, contained two stanzas by the author addressed by name to the now dead Rossetti, dated August 1882 and celebrating a lily laid on the corpse by Buchanan. There is also a 2 pp. 'Preface to the New Edition', signed and dated August 18, 1882, the second paragraph of which freely acknowledges that *The Fleshly School of Poetry* was a lapse into Philistinism which 'must remain to me a matter of permanent regret'.

† See 3648 (5) in Section II.

ana FLESHLY SCHOOL OF POETRY (The), and Other Phenomena of the Day [382*a*]

Strahan & Co. 1872. Pale lilac wrappers, cut flush, pictorially printed and lettered in black on front; inside covers and outside back cover blank.

pp. (x)+(98) Final leaf, H_1, a single inset.

Note. This copy, bound in white buckram lettered in gold, retains original wrappers, and has pencil signature: 'Countess of Lovelace', on verso of title.

MASTER OF THE MINE (The) [383]

2 vols. Bentley 1885. Blue-grey diagonal-fine-ribbed cloth; floral end-papers, bevelled boards.

Blank and half-title precede title in each vol.

Vol. I (viii) [paged vi]+(292)

II (viii) [paged vi]+(272) S_8 adverts. **B**

Small ink stain on back cover of Vol. II.

SHADOW OF THE SWORD (The) [384]

3 vols. Bentley 1876. Bright blue diagonal-fine-ribbed cloth, bevelled boards.

Vol. I (iv)+(292) T_8 and U_1 adverts. U_2 blank.

II (iv)+(276)

III (iv)+(312) **B**

THAT WINTER NIGHT: or Love's Victory [385]

Bristol, Arrowsmith 1885. White wrappers, cut flush, front printed in black; inside and back wrappers plain.

pp. (iv)+(176)

Vol. XVIII of Arrowsmith's Bristol Library.

BULWER, EDWARD LYTTON (Sir Edward Bulwer Lytton—Lord Lytton) (1803–1873)

This is virtually a complete collection of the first editions of Bulwer Lytton, with, in support, a considerable number of his many 'revised' or re-prefaced editions.† The condition is not, in a few cases, as good as I could wish; but Bulwer Lytton (certain titles apart) is an extremely difficult author to get in fine state.

My schedule of Comparative Scarcities at the end of this Section applies only to the fiction. But Bulwer's non-fiction includes two groups of books which present equally interesting contrasts in their degree of survival in original state, and may be here summarised.

First the plays. The two most frequently met with are *Not So Bad as We seem* and *Walpole.* Clearly the effort to launch 'The Guild of Literature and Art' involved printing a large edition of the inaugural play, while *Walpole*, published during the years when Messrs Blackwood were treating Bulwer Lytton as a 'star-author', was over-priced for a single play and probably over-produced. Next (for some reason I cannot guess) ranks *The Sea Captain*, with the *Duchesse de la Vallière* not far behind. *Richelieu* presents, in my experience, considerable difficulty; *Money* is really rare; while *The Rightful Heir* (in any state) and *The Lady of Lyons* (in wrappers) have never come my way at all.

Secondly the various books of poems, poetical plays, translations and so forth. Here we run into complications. Among the earliest books of verse are four (*Ismael*: *Delmour*: *Sculpture* and *Weeds and Wildflowers*) which, for a period in recent years, became comparatively common in new condition. This is because a 'balance of copies' (not a 'remainder', for they were Author's Books and in consequence the undistributed stock properly remained in his hands) was discovered at Knebworth and put on the market.

But beyond this explicable group of frequencies, we become involved in the queerest jumble of findables and unfindables. One would expect that poetry published late in a long life by a prolific and quickly out-moded writer would have found its way into the remainder market. Yet on the contrary the latest of Bulwer Lytton's minor works are scarce in any degree of original state and in fine condition practically undiscoverable.

The best I can produce as a schedule of comparative scarcities (beginning with the scarcest) is as follows:

1. *Lost Tales of Miletus* (private edition; this is really *hors-concours*).
2. *O'Neill*: *The Boatman*: *Odes and Epodes of Horace* (fine).
3. *The New Timon* (parts or boards): *King Arthur* (parts).
4. *Eva*: *St Stephens.*
5. *Siamese Twins*: *Odes and Epodes of Horace* (any state).
6. *Poems of Schiller*: *King Arthur* (cloth): *Lost Tales of Miletus* (public edition).

† The fiction and poetry are complete. Two plays are lacking: *The Lady of Lyons* and *The Rightful Heir*, the latter represented by the first American edition. Several of his speeches and certain books edited or prefaced by him are not in the Collection, nor is the 2 vol. *Athens: Its Rise and Fall.*

ADDRESS OF SIR EDWARD BULWER LYTTON, BART., M.P., D.C.L. to the... University of Edinburgh...delivered Jan. 18, 1854 and his Speech on Jan. 20, 1854 [386]

8vo. Blackwood 1854. Stitched in green paper wrappers.

pp. 28.

ALICE OR THE MYSTERIES: a Sequel to 'Ernest Maltravers' (by the author of 'Pelham', etc.) [387]

3 vols. Saunders & Otley 1838. Half-cloth boards, labels.

Leaf of adverts. precedes title in Vol. I: half-title in Vols. II and III.

Vol. I (viii) + 368
II (iv) + (356)
III (iv) + 324

Bookseller's ticket: 'Martin Keene, Dublin', inside front cover of Vol. I. The binding of this copy is rather worn.

ASMODEUS AT LARGE (by the author of 'Pelham', etc.) [388]

Philadelphia: Carey, Lea & Blanchard 1833. Half-cloth boards, label.

pp. iv + (216) [paged iv + (13)–(228)] Text starts p. (13).

Publishers' adverts., 4 pp. undated, precede title and there is a Publishers' cat., 24 pp. undated, at end.

Note. This is the first book-edition of a work originally printed in the *New Monthly Magazine.*

BOATMAN (The) (by Pisistratus Caxton) [389]

8vo. Blackwood 1864. Cream paper wrappers printed in black, all edges gilt.

pp. 16

Ink signature: 'H. T. Taverner Nov. 10 '69', on front wrapper.

CALDERON THE COURTIER: a Tale (by the author of 'Leila', etc.) [390]

Philadelphia: Carey, Lea & Blanchard 1838. Half-cloth boards, label.

pp. 144

Ink signature: 'Miss M. Patterson', on title.

Note. First separate edition of a Tale published with *Leila* in the same year in England.

CAXTONIANA: a Series of Essays on Life, Literature and Manners (by Sir E. Bulwer Lytton, Bart.) [391]

2 vols. Blackwood 1863. Chocolate pebble-grain cloth, blocked in blind and gold, bevelled boards; green end-papers.

Half-title in Vol. I. Blank leaf and half-title precede title in Vol. II

Vol. I viii + (368)
II (viii) + (352) Y_8 L'Envoi. Publishers' cat., 20 pp. undated, at end.

Very fine.

[392] CAXTONS (The): a Family Picture (by Sir E. Bulwer Lytton, Bart.)

3 vols. Blackwood 1849. Dark brown ribbed cloth, blocked in blind and lettered in gold.

Half-title in each vol.

Vol. I (viii) [paged (iv)] + (328)
II (iv) + 346 Final leaf, Z_1, a single inset.
III (iv) + 308 Publishers' cat., 32 pp. dated 1849, at end.

Bookseller's ticket 'Cawthorn, Cockspur St' inside front cover of Vol. I. Binders' ticket: 'Remnant and Edmonds', at end of Vol. I. Very fine.

[393] COMING RACE (The) [anon]

8vo. Blackwood 1871. Orange-scarlet sand-grain cloth, blocked in black and gold; red chocolate end-papers.

Half-title. pp. (vi) + 292 [pp. (v) (vi) Dedication, single inset leaf.]

Book-plate of Frank C. Hills. Fine. Slight paste-mottling on spine.

[394] CONFESSIONS OF A WATER-PATIENT in a Letter to W. Harrison Ainsworth, Esq. (by Sir E. Bulwer Lytton, Bart.)

Colburn 1846. Bright green moiré paper wrappers, printed in black. All edges gilt.

Half-title. pp. (iv) + (100) H_2 imprint leaf.

Signature partially erased from title. Spine defective.

[395] CRISIS (The): a Satire of the Day [anon]

John Ollivier, December 1845. Unbound.

pp. (16)

[396] CRITICAL AND MISCELLANEOUS WRITINGS (The) of Sir Edward Lytton Bulwer

2 vols. Philadelphia: Lea & Blanchard 1841. Grey-purple morocco cloth, lettered in gold; white end-papers.

Vol. I (viii) + 356 First page of text misfoliated (13), so actually text-pages number 344.
II (iv) + (304) 26_2 blank. As in Vol. I, first page of text misfoliated (13), so actually text-pages number 292.

Ink signature: 'W. H. Sparshott 1894', on fly-leaf of each vol. Fine. Spines a little faded.

Note. A reprint of contributions to the *New Monthly* (15), the *Monthly Chronicle* (9, including the unfinished tale *Zicci*) and the *Edinburgh Review* (2), of which all but three, printed in 1832 in *The Student*, had not previously been issued in book-form, and the great majority were never so issued in Great Britain.

DELMOUR, or a Tale of a Sylphid: and other Poems [anon] [397]

8vo. Carpenter & Son 1823. Original blue-grey wrappers, unlettered. Half-title. pp. (viii) + 64

Very fine.

DEVEREUX: a Tale (by the author of 'Pelham') [398]

3 vols. Colburn 1829. Boards, labels.

Vol. I (viii) + (300)
II (ii) + (312) O_{12} adverts.
III (ii) + 344

Errata slip precedes first page of text in each vol.

Book-plate of Robert William Duff, Fetteresso, in each vol. Fine.

DISOWNED (The) (by the author of 'Pelham') [399]

4 vols. Colburn 1829. Boards, labels.

Vol. I (lii) [paged (ii) + (l)] + 384
II (ii) + (342) Final leaf, Q_3, a single inset.
III (ii) + (274) First leaf of final sig., N_1, a single inset.
IV (ii) + 352 [pp. 353–354 (R_3) adverts. are not present in this copy]

Book-plate of Coningsby Disraeli, Hughenden, in each vol. Fine.

DRAMATIC WORKS OF SIR EDWARD LYTTON BULWER, BART. (The). Now first Collected. To which are added Three Odes on the Death of Elizabeth, Cromwell and The Death of Nelson [400]

8vo. Saunders & Otley 1841. Brown ribbed cloth, blocked in blind and lettered in gold.

Half-title. pp. (xx) + 8 (a prefatory inset to the 3rd edition of *The Duchesse*, etc.) + (528) $2O_4$ imprint leaf.

Book-plate of Sliochd Ian Dubh. Fine.

Note. This volume contains: The Duchesse de la Vallière—The Lady of Lyons—Richelieu—Odes—Money. Its style is identical (though in larger format) with the First Uniform Edition of Bulwer Lytton's works. See 'Bentley's Standard Novels and their Bye-products' (3735*b* in Section III.)

DUCHESSE DE LA VALLIÈRE (The): a Play in Five Acts (by the author of 'Eugene Aram', etc.) [401]

8vo. Saunders & Otley 1836. Brown paper wrappers, white label on front printed in black.

Half-title. pp. (xx) + (184) N_2 Epilogue, N_3 N_4 adverts.

Spine renewed.

ENGLAND AND THE ENGLISH (by Edward Lytton Bulwer, Esq., M.P.) [402]

Copy I: First Edition. 2 vols. Bentley 1833. Boards, labels.

Half-title in Vol. II

Vol. I xii + (400) Text ends p. (380), (381)–(400) Appendix.
II (xii) + (356) Text ends p. 318, (319)–(356) Appendix.

Book-label of 'R. J. Ll. Price, Rhiwlas Library' in each vol. Bookseller's ticket: 'Seacome, Chester', inside front cover of each vol. Fine.

[402a] **Copy II: Third Edition.** 2 vols. Bentley 1834. Half-cloth boards, labels.

Half-title in Vol. II

Vol. I (xxxvi) + (340)
II (xii) + (332) P_4 blank.

This edition contains a new Preface of 23 pp. The words 'Third Edition' appear on labels as well as on titles.

[402b] **ana:** A LETTER FROM C. M. WESTMACOTT TO E. L. BULWER

8vo. James Ridgeway 1833. Stitched as issued.

pp. 16

Note. This is the reply to the attack on Westmacott in *England and the English*, Vol. II, pp. 234–236.

[403] ERNEST MALTRAVERS (by the author of 'Pelham', etc.)

3 vols. Saunders & Otley 1837. Half-cloth boards, labels.

Half-title (in this copy) in Vols. I and II

Vol. I x + (312) O_{11} O_{12} adverts.
II (iv) + 306
III (ii) + 312 (half-title probably lacking)

Ink signature: 'Thomas Mackenzie Esq., Applecross', on title of each vol. Binding worn and loose.

[404] EUGENE ARAM: a Tale (by the author of 'Pelham', 'Devereux', etc.)

3 vols. Colburn & Bentley 1832. Half-cloth boards, labels.

Half-title in each vol.

Vol. I (xii) + (300)
II (iv) + 308
III (iv) + (308) O_{10} adverts.

Book-plate of Coningsby Disraeli, Hughenden, in each vol.

[405] EVA: A TRUE STORY OF LIGHT AND DARKNESS: The Ill-Omened Marriage, and Other Tales and Poems (by Sir Edward Lytton Bulwer, Bart.)

Saunders & Otley 1842. Dark grey-green diaper cloth, blocked in blind and lettered in gold.

pp. xii + (224) P_5–P_8 adverts. paged 1–8.

[406] FALKLAND [anon]

Colburn 1827. Boards, label.

pp. (xii) + 264

Book-plate of 'J. R. P. Forrest, Edinburgh'.

Note. Another edition was published in 1834 by Colburn and Bentley (copy noted in grey-brown cloth) as 'by the author of *Pelham*, *Devereux*, *The Disowned*, etc.', with a cancel title and no indication of the book having appeared previously.

GODOLPHIN: a Novel [anon] [407]

3 vols. Bentley 1833. Boards, labels.

Half-title in Vols. II and III.

Vol. I iv + (308)
II (iv) + (282) First leaf of final sig., N_1, a single inset, conjugate with N_{10} label leaf; offset clearly visible on verso of N_9.
III (iv) + (308)

Ink signature: 'Edw[d] Sidebottom, Pledwick, 1835', inside front cover of each vol. Spine of Vol. I defective and labels rubbed.

HAROLD, the Last of the Saxon Kings (by the author of 'Rienzi', etc.) [408]

3 vols. Bentley 1848. Half-cloth boards, labels.

Half-title in each vol.

Vol. I xx + (330) Text ends p. 314, pp. (315)–329 Notes. Final leaf P_9; P_{10} probably label-leaf, of which stub remains.
II (iv) + (348) Text ends p. 336: pp. (337)–347 Notes.
III (iv) + (404) Text ends p. (382): pp. (383)–396 Notes: pp. (397)–(404), S_7–S_{10}, adverts.

HAUNTED AND THE HAUNTERS (The) [409]

The first book edition of this famous story of the supernatural is Vol. X of the First Series of TALES FROM BLACKWOOD, 1858–1861 (3739a(ii) in Section III).

ISMAEL: an Oriental Tale, with other Poems (by Edward George Lytton Bulwer) [410]

J. Hatchard & Son 1820. Boards, label.

Half-title. pp. (xvi) + (200) K_4 adverts.

Book-plate of Lord W. Kerr, G.C.B.

Note. The presence of the book-plate shows that this copy did not belong to the recently dispersed 'balance of stock'. In fact it was bought long before that balance was discovered. It is a fine copy, but not in new state.

KENELM CHILLINGLY: his Adventures and Opinions (by the author of 'The Caxtons') [411]

3 vols. Blackwood 1873. Violet sand-grain cloth, lettered in gold; dark green end-papers.

Half-title in each vol.

Vol. I (vi) + 358 First leaf of final signature, Z_1, a single inset. Publishers' cat., 64 pp. undated, at end.
II (vi) + 394 Final leaf, $2C_1$, a single inset.
III (iv) + (456) $2G_4$ blank.

Errata slip between pp. (iv) and (v) in Vols. I and II. Binder's ticket: 'Burn', at end of Vol. I.

Book-plate (monogram under coronet) in each vol. Ink inscription in title of Vol. I: 'From Robert L. March 27, 1873' (i.e. from the author's son). Fine.

Note. Copies of this book bound by Edmonds & Remnants show a less condensed fount for titling and a slightly larger fount for imprint. I have no evidence as to priority, and the variations are very trifling. A secondary binding is described by Carter in *More Binding Variants*, p. 5.

[412] KING ARTHUR

Copy I: Part Issue: [by the author of the New Timon' (*Part I*); by Sir E. Bulwer Lytton—Author of the New Timon (*Parts II and III*).] 3 Parts. Colburn 1848, 1849, 1849. Buff paper wrappers printed in black.

Part I. (ii)+(200). Publisher's cat., 24 pp. undated, at end. Slip worded *To be Continued* follows p. (200).

II. xvi (half-title, title and Preface to Vol. I of Book Issue)+(201)–296+(ii) (title to Vol. II of Book Issue)+(1)–(78)+single inset leaf of Errata.

III. (79)–(306)+single inset leaf of Errata.

Signature erased from front covers.

[412*a*] **Copy II: First Book Edition.** 2 vols. Colburn 1849. Powder-blue horizontal-ribbed cloth, blocked in blind and gold.

Half-title in Vol. I

Vol. I xvi+296 Publisher's cat., 24 pp. undated, at end.

II (ii)+(308) O_9 Notes to Book XII, O_{10} Erratum.

Book-plate monogram 'J.H.P.' in each vol. Fine.

[412*b*] **Copy III: Second Edition.** Chapman & Hall 1851. Olive-green morocco cloth. pp. xiv+(454). U_{11} Note to Book XII. First leaf of final sig., U_1, a single inset.

Ink inscription: 'Eva Mackintosh from H.E.B. 2nd May 1859', on title. Fine.

This Edition contains a revised Preface and comments on the Notes.

[412*c*] **Copy IV: Revised Edition:** 'A Poem by Edward Bulwer, Lord Lytton'. Charlton Tucker 1870. Carmine sand-grain cloth, blocked in blind and gold. Bevelled boards, all edges gilt. Wood-engraved front., designed title and illustrations (full page and vignettes) throughout the text after Edward Hughes.

Half-title. pp. (xvi) [paged xiv]+(444)

Ink inscription inside front cover dated Christmas 1871.

Note. This edition contains a New Preface dated October 1870. It was also published in green cloth.

LADY OF LYONS (The), or Love and Pride: a Play (by the author of 'Eugene Aram', etc.) [413]

8vo. Saunders & Otley 1846 (not 1st edition). Stitched as issued, half-title serving as front cover. Edges uncut.

Half-title. pp. 72 [paged (i)–(xii)+(13)–72] Text begins p. (13). Final signature, E, 4 leaves; Advert. leaf inset at end.

Note. This reprint is not recorded in *C.B.E.L.* It bears no indication of previous issue. The play was first published in 1838.

LAST DAYS OF POMPEII (The) (by the author of 'Pelham', etc.) [414]

3 vols. Bentley 1834. Half-cloth boards, labels.

Half-title in Vols. II and III.

Vol. I xvi+(316) Text ends p. 312: pp. 313–315 Notes.

II (iv)+296

III (iv)+(316) Text ends p. 312: pp. 313–315 Notes.

Errata slip precedes fly-title in each vol.

Book-plate of Lord James Butler in each vol., and ink signature: 'Wm Humphrys, Ballyhaise House', on fly-leaf of each vol.

Note. For several variants see Carter, *Binding Variants*, p. 99, and *More Binding Variants*, p. 4.

LAST OF THE BARONS (The) (by the author of 'Rienzi') [415]

3 vols. Saunders & Otley 1843.

Copy I. Boards, labels.

Half-title in each vol.

Vol. I (xxx)+(318) Text ends p. 312: pp. 313–314 'Note to Vol. I': p. (315) Errata, pp. (317) (318), P_3, adverts. Second leaf of final sig., P_2, a single inset.

A blank leaf precedes half-title in some copies. It is not reckoned in the pagination of the prelims. nor, if one reckons (a_1)–(a_3)+P_1–P_3, essential to collation: but probably P_4 was label-leaf. The blank leaf is not present in this copy (cf. Copy II).

Vol. II (iv)+(372) Text ends p. 368: pp. 369–370 'Note to Vol. II': pp. (371) (372), S_2, adverts.

III (iv)+(488)

Fine.

Copy II. Half-cloth boards, labels. As Copy I except [415*a*]

(i) Blank leaf precedes half-title in Vol. I.

(ii) Errata leaf (P_2 in Copy I) here precedes B_1 in Vol. I.

Bookseller's ticket: 'R. Spencer, High Holborn', inside front cover of Vol. I.

LEILA or The Siege of Granada, and CALDERON THE COURTIER (by the author of 'Eugene Aram', 'Rienzi', etc.) [416]

Copy I: First Edition. 8vo. Longman etc. 1838. Grey-blue fine-diaper cloth, blocked in blind on front and back, gold-lettered on spine and lettered BULWER'S / SIEGE OF / GRANADA. Steel-engraved portrait front., vignette title and 14 plates after various artists.

pp. (xii) + 400 Advert. leaf inset at end.

Binders' ticket: 'Remnant & Edmonds', inside front cover.

[416*a*] **Copy II: Another.** Full publishers' morocco, gilt. All edges gilt. As Copy I, but without advert. leaf at end.

Note. I am not aware that this book was issued in glazed boards with a label in the style of *The Pilgrims of the Rhine*, but quite possibly it was. If so, the cloth binding above described is of a date subsequent to first publication.

[416*b*] **Copy III: Re-issue in Parts** (by Sir Edward Lytton Bulwer). Nine 8vo parts. J. & D. A. Darling 1850, 'New Edition'. Glazed green paper wrappers, printed in black.

This re-issue contains the engravings of the original edition, but the text is re-set.

[417] LETTERS TO JOHN BULL ESQUIRE, etc. (by Sir Edward Bulwer Lytton, Bart.)

8vo. Chapman & Hall 1851. New boards.

Half-title. pp. (iv) + 104.

[417*a*] **ana:** LETTER TO SIR E. BULWER LYTTON BART., COMMENTING UPON THE POLICY ADVOCATED IN HIS LETTERS TO JOHN BULL, ESQ. (by W. Bull, one of John's sons)

8vo. Pelham Richardson, 23 Cornhill, 1851. Stitched as issued.

Half-title. pp. 24

Presentation Copy: 'From the Author' in ink on half-title, which serves as front cover.

[418] LOST TALES OF MILETUS (The)

Copy I: First (private) Edition [anon]. 8vo. 'Strictly Private. Only 12 copies printed', n.d.

Pl. 6 [Autumn 1865] Full dark green morocco, t.e.g.

pp. 84

Note by Richard Garnett on fly-leaf, dated July 24 1883; also A.L.S. from Robert Lytton to Garnett, dated June 2 1883, in which he says: 'The Tales were privately printed by my father for the perusal only of a few friends, whose opinions and wishes about them afterwards induced him to publish them with considerable alterations and, I think, improvements.' A blank corner of the title and last leaf have been mended.

Note. The suggested date of this private issue seems at once inevitable and unconvincing. Writing to Robert Lytton on September 21 1865 from Mont Dore, Bulwer said: 'I have been scribbling and may send you some proofs for your criticism.' On October 17, the proofs were sent, together with a letter discussing certain of the 'Lost Tales'. On December 26, Bulwer wrote: 'I am glad you prefer *Sisyphus*—so do I. But I do not think it is the favourite with the few who have seen the poems.'

Yet on February 13 1866 he writes commenting on an 'unfair and carping article in *The Saturday Review*', adding 'I think they [the "Tales"] are making their way and are generally favoured by the critics'.

Manifestly by this final date the *published* edition was out and being reviewed. It is, however, not easy to see how poems, still being written on September 21, 1865, could have been privately printed, sent to friends, commented on, re-cast in the light of these comments, prepared for *public* issue, despatched to Murray, printed and bound and sent for review and published by early February 1866—especially as the author was in Auvergne, and speed in manufacture must have been offset by slowness of communication.

Copy II: First (published) Edition ('By the Rt. Hon. Sir Edward Bulwer Lytton, Bart., M.P.) [418*a*]

John Murray 1866. Smooth bright-brown cloth, blocked in gold, bevelled boards; sea-green end-papers.

Blank leaf and half-title precede title. pp. (xvi) [paged (xiv)] + 168.

Ink inscription to John Eliot Hodgkin from his sister, dated June 1866, on first blank leaf.

LUCRETIA or The Children of Night (by the author of 'Rienzi', etc.) [419]

3 vols. Saunders & Otley 1846.

Copy I: First Edition. Half-cloth boards, labels.

Blank leaf and half-title precede title in Vol. I, half-title only in Vols. II and III.

Vol. I (xiv) [paged as (xii)] + (294) [paged as 296] The irregularity of collation is due to the first leaf of text (B_1) being paged as part of the prelims.

II (iv) + 306 First leaf of final sig., O_1, a single inset.

III (iv) + (312) O_{10}–O_{12} adverts.

Leaflet advertising Whittaker's Popular Library pasted on fly-leaf of Vol. I. Very fine.

Copy II: 'Second Edition, to which is Prefixed A Word to the Public'. 3 vols. Saunders & Otley 1847. Boards, labels. [419*a*]

Half-title in each vol. Collation as Copy I except that 'A Word to the Public', printed from the type of the original pamphlet issue (see below), is inserted between pp. (iv) (v) of Vol. I and is separately paged (1)-60.

[420] MISCELLANEOUS PROSE WORKS (by Edward Bulwer, Lord Lytton)

Copy I: English Edition. 3 vols. 8vo. Bentley 1868. Maroon sand-grain cloth; dark green end-papers.

Vol. I (vi)+494 First leaf of final sig., $2I_1$, a single inset.

II (iv)+(418) First leaf of final sig., $2E_1$, a single inset.

III (iv)+498 Final leaf, $2K_1$, a single inset.

Damp-stained.

Note. This is the first book-edition of all the Essays in Vol. I except the *Life of Schiller* and *Sir Thomas Browne*; also of the Section in Vol. II: 'Influence of Love upon Literature'. (Bentley Private Cat. Feb. 14, 1868.)

[420*a*] **Copy II: American Edition.** 2 vols. New York: Harper 1868. Brown coarse morocco cloth; brown end-papers.

Note. This contains the material in Vols. I and II of the English edition.

[421] MONEY: a Comedy in Five Acts (by the author of 'The Lady of Lyons', etc.)

8vo. Saunders & Otley 1840. Pinkish buff paper wrappers, white label on front printed in black.

Half-title. pp. (vi)+(160) L_8 imprint leaf. Publishers' cat., 4 pp. undated, at end.

Spine defective.

[422] "MY NOVEL" (by Pisistratus Caxton) or Varieties in English Life

4 vols. Blackwood 1853. Dark brown ribbed cloth, blocked in blind and lettered in gold.

Half-title ("MY NOVEL") in each vol.

Vol. I (viii)+374 First leaf of final sig., $2A_1$, a single inset.

II (vi)+(380)

III (iv)+(370) Final leaf, ($2A_1$), a single inset.

IV (vi)+(300) Publishers' cat., 8 pp. undated, at end.

In Vols. I, II and IV appears a leaf, recto reading MY NOVEL (unquoted), verso Printers' imprint. This follows dedication in Vol. I and titles in Vols. II and IV. These leaves appear to be part of a half-gathering of four leaves, carrying Dedication *plus* these leaves.

In some copies of the book pp. (vii) and (viii) of Vol. I may appear as pp. (v) and (vi) of Vol. III.

Book-label of J. R. P. Forrest in each vol. Portrait cut from a newspaper, mounted and inserted before half-title of Vol. I, and binders' ticket: 'Remnant and Edmonds', at end. Fine.

[423] NEW TIMON (The): a Romance of London [anon] 8vo. Colburn 1846.

Copy I: Part Issue. Four one-and-sixpenny 8vo parts, published between late December 1845 and January 31 1846. Cream paper wrappers printed in black—on front: *plain multiple frame* / THE / NEW TIMON. / A ROMANCE OF LONDON. / IN FOUR PARTS. / PART I. / LONDON: / HENRY COLBURN, PUBLISHER, / GREAT MARLBOROUGH STREET. / *short rule* / 1846. / *Price One Shilling and Sixpence* / *bottom of frame.* Spine unlettered; other wrappers unprinted or printed as stated.

Part I: Other wrappers plain.

Inset title-page. pp. (1)–(46) of text. 1st leaf of final sig., D_1, a single inset. Two publisher's cats., 8 pp. dated May 1845 and 6 pp. undated, at end.

Part II: Outside back wrapper announces Part Three for January 15 and Part Four for January 31; inside wrappers plain. Fly-title to Part II [actually E_1 but omitted from pagination, E_2 being signed 'E'], pp. (47)–108 of text [E, 4 leaves, F.G.H. 8 leaves each, I 4 leaves].

Part III: 'Opinions of the Press' and announcement of a reprint of Parts I and II pasted to outside back wrapper; inside wrapper plain.

Inset advert. leaf of Press Opinions as on back wrapper; inset fly-title to Part III; pp. (109)–(150) of text. [K.L.M. 8 leaves each.]

Part IV: Other wrappers as in Part III.

Inset fly-title to Part IV; pp. (151)–200 [N.O.P. 8 leaves each] Text ends Q_1; Q_2 adverts.

Book-plate of Lord Esher. Part III at one time stabbed by a nail and subsequently repaired.

Copy II: First Book Edition. Publisher's morocco, all edges gilt. [423*a*]

pp. (ii)+200. Final leaf, Q_1, a single inset. In the book-edition the fly-titles are suppressed, reducing E to 3 leaves. Morocco worn at hinge. Normal binding—half cloth, label.

NIGHT AND MORNING (by the author of 'Rienzi', etc.) [424]

3 vols. Saunders & Otley 1841. Half-cloth boards, labels.

Vol. I (ii)+336

II (ii)+(356)

III (ii)+(344) Publishers' cat., 4 pp. undated, at end.

Errata slip precedes B_1 in each vol. In one copy examined the errata slips, undivided, appeared at the end of Vol. III.

Very fine.

NOT SO BAD AS WE SEEM: or Many Sides to a Character. A Comedy in Five Acts (by Sir Edward Bulwer Lytton, Bart.) [425]

8vo. 'Published for the Guild of Literature and Art by Chapman & Hall' 1851. Drab paper wrappers, printed in black.

pp. iv+(140)

Single leaf of instructions (sm. cr. 8vo) for performance of the Play tipped in between p. iv and p. (1). This was probably written by Charles Dickens who acted as producer. Prospectus of the Guild of Literature and Art, 16 pp. at end.

[426] ODES AND EPODES OF HORACE (The): a Metrical Translation into English. With Introduction and Commentaries (by Lord Lytton)

Blackwood 1869. Smooth plum cloth, blocked in black and gold, bevelled boards; greenish-black end-papers.

Half-title. pp. (xliv) + (486) Final leaf, $2H_3$, a single inset.

Binder's ticket: 'Burn', at end. Fine.

[427] O'NEILL, or The Rebel [anon]

Colburn 1827. Boards, label.

Half-title. pp. (viii) [p. viii misfoliated v] + 140

Ink signature: 'John Gibbons 1777–1851', on fly-leaf. In ink on title 'E. L. Bulwer'. Fine.

[428] PARISIANS (The) (by Edward Bulwer, Lord Lytton)

Copy I: Wrappered Edition. 4 vols. Blackwood, n.d. [1873]. Yellow paper wrappers printed in black, with 'Price Six Shillings' on front wrapper of each vol. Back-wrappers printed with adverts. Four full-page wood-engravings after Sydney Hall in each vol.

Half-title in Vols. I, III and IV: leaf of adverts. and half-title in Vol. II

Vol. I (x) + (300) Publishers' cat., 8 pp. undated, at end.

II (viii) + (312) Publishers' cat., 8 pp. undated, at end.

III (vi) + (294) First leaf of final sig., T_1, a single inset.

IV (x) + (326) (Y_2) (Y_3) adverts. pp. (v)–viii 'Prefatory Note by the Author's Son' signed 'L'; pp. (ix) (x)—List of Illustrations—an odd leaf, probably printed as (Y_4).

In Vol. I a slip worded: 'Reprinted from Blackwood's Magazine', is inserted between half-title and title. In other vols. these words are printed on verso of half-title.

Blind stamp: 'With the Publishers' Compliments', at various points in each vol.

Note. The purpose of this wrappered edition is obscure. According to Carter (*Binding Variants*, p. 100) the publishers stated that it pre-dated the cloth edition, as one would presume from internal evidence. According to an advert. on the back wrapper of Vol. II, the volumes were published monthly at 6*s*., whereas the cloth-edition was issued at 26*s*. (i.e. 6*s*. 6*d*. per vol., which suggests a binding charge of 6*d*.); and an advert. of the book appearing in Vol. I of the cloth edition makes no mention of monthly issue. Yet the wrappered edition was in no sense a Part Issue, for its four volumes are identical in content with those of the cloth edition. Was it possibly an advance-edition for export, wrappered in the French manner, and designed mainly for the obviously promising French market?

Copy II: Cloth Edition. 4 vols. Blackwood, n.d. [428*a*]
[1873]. Bright blue pebble-grain cloth, on front pictorially blocked in gold (Vendôme column) and black, on spine in black and gold, on back in blind; dark brown end-papers.

Collation as I, but no slip in Vol. I, the reference to Blackwood's Magazine being printed on verso of half-title in all four vols.

Ink signature: 'F. H. Armitage. Oulton House Sept. 28, 1873', on fly-leaf of each vol.

Notes. (i) A curious variant-issue (not in the Collection) merits record. Printed on much thinner paper the vols. are bound in blue sand-grain cloth, of same colour as first edition but differently blocked and with different spine-lettering. Prelims. are reprinted, and on verso of half-title of Vol. I is an acknowledgement to Blackwood, as owners of the copyright, of their consent to the publication of this edition. There is no mention anywhere of *Blackwood's Magazine*, nor are there any illustrations or advert. leaves. Following the title of Vol. I is the PREFATORY NOTE BY THE AUTHOR'S SON, signed 'L' and paged (i)–iv, followed by the 'Introductory Chapter' [(v)–viii], as in first edition. This Prefatory Note appears in Vol. IV of preceding editions.

(ii) I have noted a secondary binding in dark green cloth, blocked in gold and black, and with dark green end-papers. No imprint appears on spine and the sheets are cut to a smaller size. No catalogue at end of Vol. I or II; no advert. leaf preceding half-title in Vol II; no adverts. at end of Vol. IV.

PAUL CLIFFORD (by the author of 'Pelham', [429]
'Devereux', etc.)

3 vols. Colburn & Bentley 1830. Boards, labels.

Half-title in Vol. I

Vol. I (xxiv) + 288

II (ii) + 324

III (ii) + (332) Q_4 adverts.

PAUSANIAS THE SPARTAN: an Unfinished [430]
Historical Romance (by the late Lord Lytton. Edited by his Son)

Routledge 1876. Purple-brown diagonal-fine-ribbed cloth, blocked in black and gold, bevelled boards.

Half-title. pp. (384) [paged (i)–(xxviii) + (29)–376 + BB_{5-8} adverts.]

Fine.

[431] **PELHAM**, or the Adventures of a Gentleman [anon]
3 vols. Colburn 1828. Boards, labels.

Half-title in each vol.

Vol. I (iv) + (330)
II (iv) + 316
III (iv) + (368) R_4 adverts.

Ink signature: 'P. Davies Cooke', on fly-leaf of each vol. Bookseller's ticket: 'Lloyd, Mold', inside front cover of each vol. Fine.

Note. In Vol. I the following pages are cancels: 165–168 (H_{11} H_{12}); 193–204 (K_1–K_6); 255–258 (M_6 M_7); and possibly 337–339 (Q_1 Q_2—re-signed *q*, uniform with earlier re-signings and therefore presumably cancels).

In this copy pp. 205–216 are misbound after 192.

[432] **PILGRIMS OF THE RHINE** (The) (by the author of 'Pelham')
8vo. Saunders & Otley 1834.

Copy I. Greenish-buff glazed boards, label. Engraved front., vignette title, portrait bust of author and 24 plates after various artists.

Half-title. pp. xxxvi + (344) X_8 advert. Final leaf of text, with vignette, is on plate paper, but is foliated 341 (342) Inset leaf advertising proof issues of the illustrations follows front fly-leaf. Fine.

[432*a*] **Copy II.** Full publishers' morocco gilt: all edges gilt. As Copy I, but without half-title and inset leaves.

[432*b*] **Copy III: Large Paper.** Full publishers' morocco, gilt: all edges gilt; cherry-red end-papers. Plates on India Paper. Collation as Copy I.

[432b_2] **Copy IIIa: Engravings.** The 27 plates in the first edition on India Paper, with letters, $10\frac{1}{2} \times 14\frac{1}{4}$ ins., contained in original half-morocco portfolio, leather title-label on spine.

[433] **POEMS** (by the Rt Hon. Sir Edward Bulwer Lytton, Bart., M.P.).
John Murray 1865. 'A New Edition Revised.' Grass-green fine-morocco cloth, blocked in gold, bevelled boards; rose-pink end-papers.

Two blank leaves and half-title precede title. pp. (xvi) [paged as xii] + (384) BB_8 adverts.

Ink note on last fly-leaf dated Nov. 15, 1866. Binders' ticket: 'Edmonds & Remnants', at end. Cloth fine. The front fly-leaf has been torn out.

[434] **POEMS AND BALLADS OF SCHILLER** (The) (Translated by Sir Edward Bulwer Lytton, Bart.). With a Brief Sketch of Schiller's Life
2 vols. Blackwood 1844. Orange-brown ribbed cloth, blocked in blind and lettered in gold.

Half-title in each vol.

Vol. I (x) + (clvi) + (140)
II viii + (238) R_3 (a single inset) adverts.

Monogram book-plate 'A.W.S.' in each vol.

POETICAL AND DRAMATIC WORKS of Sir Edward Bulwer Lytton, Bart. [435]
5 vols. Chapman & Hall 1852–54. Vols. I–III bright blue, wavy-grain cloth, Vols. IV–V royal blue, bead-grain cloth (all vols. blocked in blind and lettered in gold). Engraved portrait front. after Maclise in Vol. I: engraved vignette title in each vol. preceding printed title.

Half-title in Vols. II–V

Vol. I (viii) + 344
II (iv) + (340)
III (viii) + (328) Y_4 blank.
IV (iv) + 392
V (iv) + (300) U_6 adverts.

Book-label of 'James D. Gaff' in each vol. Vol. II has printed ends, and bookseller's label 'Arthy, Chelmsford' inside front cover. Fine.

Notes. (i) A Prefatory Note, dated December 1851, states that this edition contains some material 'not before printed and some entirely rewritten from the more imperfect productions of earlier years. Few, if any, of the poems that have previously appeared have escaped revision and alteration'.

(ii) The contents of Vols. I–III were reprinted by Routledge in 1860 as a 'New Edition', and issued in a single small cr. 8vo volume bound in green cloth.

POETICAL WORKS OF E. L. BULWER (The) [436]
8vo. Paris: Baudry 1836. Buff wrappers, printed in blue and black with standard design for Baudry's Collection of Ancient and Modern British Authors, of which this is No. cxxxi. The wrapper is dated 1835. Engraved portrait front. after Blanchard.

Series half-title. pp. viii + 392

Note. This volume (published also by Galignani in 1836) contains, in addition to *O'Neill* and *The Siamese Twins*, an enlarged and revised version of *Milton*, first printed in *Weeds and Wildflowers*: a fragment of *Eugene Aram: a Tragedy* which appeared in the *New Monthly Magazine*, and '*Elegy to the Memory of H*(*arriet*) *W*(*heeler*), *buried by Père Lachaise*'.

RICHELIEU; or the Conspiracy. A Play in Five Acts. To which are added Historical Odes on The Last Days of Elizabeth; Cromwell's Dream and the Death of Nelson (by the author of the 'Lady of Lyons', 'Eugene Aram', etc.) [437]

Copy I: First Edition. 8vo. Saunders & Otley 1839. Buff wrappers, white side-label printed in black, giving author's name as 'Sir E. Lytton Bulwer, Bart.'

Half-title. pp. (xii) + 144

Spine renewed.

[437*a*] **Copy II: First American Edition.** New York: Harper 1839. Half-cloth boards, label.

Blank leaf precedes title. pp. (160) N_6–N_8 adverts., paged 1–6.

[438] RIENZI, the Last of the Tribunes (by the author of 'Eugene Aram', 'Last Days of Pompeii', etc. etc.)

3 vols. Saunders & Otley 1835. Half-cloth boards, labels.

Half-title in each vol.

Vol. I (xiv)+302 pp. xiii (xiv) signed *b* and a single inset. Final leaf, P_1, a single inset.

II (iv)+364 Errata slip, six lines, tipped on to p. (1).

III (iv)+(360) Errata slip, five lines, tipped on to p. (1). Text of novel ends p. 343; (344) blank; (345)–356 Notes; (357)–(360), Q_{11} Q_{12}, adverts.

Cloth spines perished at hinges, so that vols. are frail and loosened in covers, but a wholly unsophisticated copy. The book was also issued in grey moiré cloth with paper labels, but copies so bound almost certainly belong to a later binding-up.

[439] *RIGHTFUL HEIR (The): a Drama in Five Acts (by the author of 'Richelieu', 'The Lady of Lyons', etc.)

First Edition. 8vo. John Murray 1868. [? Wrappers.]

pp. (iv)+(64). E_8 blank

Note. I cannot locate a copy in original wrappers. The Preface explains that the play is a re-writing of *The Sea Captain*, which itself had been suggested by a situation in Dumas' *Le Capitaine Paul*

[439*a*] **First American Edition.** New York: Harper & Brothers 1868. Buff paper wrappers, printed in black.

Leaf precedes title, printed on recto with the authorisation to Messrs Harper to publish the play in America, dated October 8, 1868.

pp. (64) pp. (63) (64) adverts.

[440] ST STEPHENS: a Poem [anon]

Blackwood 1860. Royal-blue morocco cloth, blocked in blind and gold.

Half-title. pp. (viii)+136

Binders' ticket: 'Edmonds and Remnants', at end.

[441] SCULPTURE: a Poem (by E. G. Lytton Bulwer)

8vo. Cambridge, July 1825. No imprint. Original blue wrappers, unlettered.

pp. 16 Erratum slip follows p. 16.

Fine.

[442] SEA CAPTAIN (The), or the Birthright. A Drama in Five Acts (by the author of 'The Lady of Lyons', etc.)

8vo. Saunders & Otley 1839. Pinkish-buff paper wrappers, white paper label on front printed in black.

Blank leaf and half-title precede title. pp. (xii) [paged (x)]+112 Two leaves of adverts. at end, on text paper, probably originally (A_7) (A_8).

Book-plate of Holland House, and ink inscription: 'Holland House', on front cover. Spine renewed.

SIAMESE TWINS (The): a Satirical Tale of the Times. With other Poems (by the author of 'Pelham', etc.) [443]

8vo. Colburn & Bentley 1831. Boards, label. Etched front. and 5 plates by W. H. Brooke on tinted paper.

pp. xvi+(392). CC_4 adverts., dated Jan. 1, 1831. Errata slip precedes B_1.

Catalogue of Whittaker Treacher, 12 pp. undated, inserted between front end-papers.

STRANGE STORY (A) (by the author of 'Rienzi', 'My Novel', etc.) [444]

2 vols. Sampson Low, Son & Co. 1862. Red-brown coarse-morocco cloth, blocked in blind and gold.

Half-title in Vol. I

Vol. I (xii) [paged x]+(354) Final leaf, $2A_1$, a single inset.

II (ii)+384 Publishers' cat., 16 pp. dated January 1862, at end.

Pencil signature: 'Eliz[th] Frances Bulwer', on title of Vol. I. Binders' ticket: 'Leighton, Son & Hodge', at end of Vol. I. Fine.

Note. I cannot identify the original owner of this copy.

STUDENT (The): a Series of Papers (by the author of 'Eugene Aram', 'England and the English', etc.) [445]

2 vols. Saunders & Otley 1835.

Copy I. Boards, labels.

Half-title in each vol.

Vol. I (xiv)+(336)

II (viii)+(364) (R_2) adverts.

Book-plate of Hansard Watt (irregularly placed) in each vol. Ink signature: 'Wm. Watson', inside front cover of Vol. I. Spines a little worn.

Copy II. Dark green ribbon-embossed fine-morocco cloth, labels. [445*a*]

12 pp. Catalogue of Longman, etc. dated April 1835 inset between front end-papers of Vol. I. Collation as Copy I. Fine.

TAXES ON KNOWLEDGE. Debate in the House of Commons on the 15th June, 1832, on Mr Edward Lytton Bulwer's Motion 'For a select committee to consider the propriety of [446] establishing a cheap postage on Newspapers and other Publications', etc. etc.

8vo. Printed by W. Barnes, Newington Causeway, Southwark. 1832.

pp. 48: unbound.

No. 13 of the pamphlets issued by the National Political Union. Bulwer's speech occupies pp. (3)–16; Notes on the Speech (by an anonymous editor) pp. 30–36; and an article reprinted from the *Examiner* in support of the Motion, pp. 43–48.

[447] WALPOLE, or Every Man has his Price: a Comedy in Rhyme (by Lord Lytton)

Blackwood 1869. Smooth blue cloth blocked in gold; bevelled boards, all edges gilt; pale chocolate end-papers.

Half-title. pp. (vi) + (124)

Binder's ticket: 'Burn', at end.

[448] WEEDS AND WILDFLOWERS (by E.G.L.B.)

Large 8vo. Paris 'Not Published' 1826. Green paper wrappers printed in black.

Half-title. pp. (xii) + (106) pp. 97, 98 single leaf: 99–102 (wrongly paged 103) conjugate; (103), 104 Errata, conjugate with (105) (106), which leaf is pasted down to inside back cover and serves as final end-paper.

Note. This copy does not belong to the 'balance of stock' recently discovered. It was bought a long while ago and, while in good condition, is not 'as new'.

[449] WHAT WILL HE DO WITH IT? (by Pisistratus Caxton)

4 vols. Blackwood 1859. Scarlet morocco cloth, blocked in blind and lettered in gold.

Half-title in each vol.

Vol I (vi) + 404
II (iv) + 360 Publishers' cat., 16 pp. undated, at end.
III (iv) + 334 First leaf of final sig., X_1, a single inset.
IV (iv) + (316)

Ink signature: 'Mrs Baker Cresswell, Cresswell 1859', on fly-leaf of each vol. Binders' ticket: 'Edmonds & Remnants', at end of Vol. I.

Note. Copies of this book were also issued in sand-grain cloth of rather darker red, with thinner straw-boards and spine lettering of vaguely meaner proportions. I suspect these to be of later date. Carter describes two certain secondaries in *Binding Variants*, p. 100.

[450] WORD TO THE PUBLIC (A) (by the author of 'Lucretia', etc.)

Saunders & Otley 1847. Uncut and stitched, as issued.

pp. 60

ZANONI (by the author of 'Night and Morning', etc.) [451]

3 vols. Saunders & Otley 1842.

Copy I: Half-cloth boards, labels.

Half-title in Vols. II and III

Vol. I (xxiv) + (308)
II (iv) + (308) O_8–O_{10} adverts., paged 1–6.
III (iv) + (324) P_6 adverts.

Errata slip precedes B_1 in each vol.

Copy II. Grey-brown ribbed cloth, lettered on spine. ZANONI / *short rule* / BULWER / VOL. I etc. As Copy I, except that Errata, undivided, form a single inset leaf following last page of text in Vol. III. [451*a*]

Book-plate of Frederick Lovell Keays in each vol. Fine.

Partially written by Bulwer Lytton

SKETCHES FROM LIFE: by the late Laman Blanchard. With a Memoir by Sir Edward Bulwer Lytton, Bart. [452]

3 vols. Colburn 1846. Dark brown ribbed cloth. Steel-engraved portrait front. after Maclise and wood-engravings in the text by Cruikshank and others.

Vol. I xliv + 296 Publisher's cat., 24 pp. dated 1845, at end.
II iv + 396
III iv + 416

For Bulwer Lytton see also HAMILTON, WALTER, below, and 'Bentley's Standard Novels and Bye-Products' (3735*b* in Section III).

BULWER, ROSINA (LADY LYTTON BULWER—LADY BULWER LYTTON—THE LADY LYTTON) (1804–1882)

This is a complete collection of the writings of Lady Bulwer Lytton, except *Cheveley*, 3 vols. 1839 (no first edition of which is in the B.M. or Bodley, nor has any copy of the second or third editions in three volumes and in original state ever been seen by me), and a pamphlet of 1857 about her wrongs.

Most of Lady Bulwer Lytton's books are very uncommon and, when they turn up, are usually in poor state. She is an excellent illustration of the argument put forward in my *Trollope Bibliography* (p. 252) that an obscure imprint always has an unfavourable effect on the survival-power of a nineteenth-century novel. Her publishers were all second-grade firms (or worse), with inferior distributive organisation, little publicity-pull, and in some cases a habitual tendency to shoddy manufacture.

[453] BEHIND THE SCENES: a Novel (by Lady Bulwer Lytton)

3 vols. C. J. Skeet 1854. Bright blue fine-diagonal-wavy-grain cloth.

Vol. I (xxii) [paged xvi] + (326) Final leaf, Y_3, a single inset.
II (ii) + (328)
III (ii) + 332

Pencil signature: 'C. Tyler', on title of each vol. The cloth of this copy is somewhat chafed in places.

[454] BIANCA CAPELLO: an Historical Romance (by Lady Lytton Bulwer)

3 vols. Edward Bull 1843. Half-cloth boards, labels.

Half-title in each vol.

Vol. I (iv) + (284) O_2 adverts.
II (iv) + 276
III (iv) + 264 M_9–M_{12} adverts., but paged as part of the text.

Ink signature: 'W. Greenwood', on each half-title.

[455] BUDGET OF THE BUBBLE FAMILY (The) (by Lady Lytton Bulwer)

3 vols. Edward Bull 1840. Dark blue ribbed cloth. Etched front. and 1 plate in each vol. by Hervieu.

Half-title in each vol.

Vol. I (xii) + (356) Q_{10} blank.
II (iv) + (376) R_8 blank.
III (iv) + (376) R_7 R_8 adverts.

Copy I. Copy belonging to the author's mother, Mrs Wheeler, with her signature in ink on half-title of Vol. I and recto of front. in Vol. II: also numerous scorings and violent notes in her hand throughout (particularly in the Dedication to Frances Trollope) directed against Bulwer-Lytton. Later ink signature: 'Edward Cutler, K. C., Edgeware' inside front cover and on title of each vol. This copy is loose in covers and dog's-eared.

[455*a*] **Copy II: Another.** No association, but sound and clean.

[456] *CHEVELEY, or the Man of Honour (by Lady Lytton Bulwer)

3 vols. Edward Bull 1839. 'Third Edition.' Boards (and/or half-cloth boards), labels.

Half-title in each vol.

Vol. I viii + 308
II (iv) + (372)
III (iv) + (336)

Note. Description taken from B.M. copy bound three-vols.-in-one.

HOUSEHOLD FAIRY (The) (by the Lady Lytton) [457]

Hall & Co. 1870. Red fine-morocco cloth; red chocolate end-papers. Head and tail pieces and initial letters throughout printed in red.

Half-title. pp. (vi) + (258) (Z_1)–(Z_4) publishers' cat. dated 1870. Y a five-leaf signature, Y_5 a single inset.

A poor copy, cloth soiled and back hinge split.

MIRIAM SEDLEY, or the Tares and the Wheat: a Tale of Real Life (by Lady Bulwer Lytton) [458]

3 vols. Shoberl 1851. Half-cloth boards, labels.

Two leaves of adverts., dated April 1851, precede title in Vol. I

Vol. I (xii) [paged (viii)] + (312) O_{11} O_{12} adverts.
II (ii) + (316)
III (ii) + (362) Final leaf, (R_1), a single inset.

Fine.

Note. Also issued in full pink cloth, blocked in blind and gold-lettered.

PEER'S DAUGHTERS (The): a Novel (by Lady Bulwer Lytton) [459]

3 vols. Newby 1849. Half-morocco, cloth sides.

Vol I (viii) + 340 p. vii misfoliated v. Text ends p. 333, pp. 334–340 Notes.
II (ii) + 358 First leaf of final sig., Q_1, a single inset.
III (ii) + 372

Dates erased from titles. Labels of Lovejoy's Library, Reading, on and inside front covers.

Note. The original binding was of claret fine-diaper cloth, blocked in blind on front and back, gold-lettered on spine with title, vol. no. and imprint (no author's name).

SCHOOL FOR HUSBANDS (The): or Molière's Life and Times (by Lady Bulwer Lytton) [460]

3 vols. Chas. J. Skeet 1852.

Copy I: Ochre morocco cloth.

Vol. I (xxxiv) [paged (xxviii)] + (280) Leaf 3 of prelims., carrying epigraphs, is a single inset.
II (ii) + (270) First leaf of final sig., N_1, a single inset.
III (ii) + 256

Copy II: Half-cloth boards, labels. Collation as Copy I. Very fine. [460*a*]

(Above entries are transposed to save correction.)

The running headlines throughout read 'Molière's Tragedy: his Life and Times' which (as the long polemical preface states) was the title the author wished to use but was dissuaded.

SHELLS FROM THE SANDS OF TIME (by the Dowager Lady Lytton) [461]

Square 8vo. Bickers & Son 1876. Grey diagonal-fine-ribbed cloth, bevelled boards; dark brown end-papers. Title printed in red and black.

Half-title. pp. vi + (244)

Inside front hinge broken, but cloth in good order.

[462] VERY SUCCESSFUL (by Lady Bulwer Lytton)
3 vols. Whittaker & Co., London; Frederick R. Clarke, Taunton 1856. Half-cloth boards, labels. Titles and chapter-heads and decorative initial letters printed throughout in red. Vol. I contains 2 satirical portraits and 2 views, all lithographed. Of the former, one is of Bulwer, and the views are of Knebworth House and Knebworth School House. Bulwer becomes 'Sir Gregory Kempenfelt' and Knebworth 'Barons Court'.

Vol. I (xii)+(348)
II (ii)+(280) S_4 imprint leaf.
III (ii)+(328) W_4 blank.

Note. A bye-product of this novel was a pamphlet: LADY BULWER LYTTON'S APPEAL TO THE JUSTICE AND CHARITY OF THE ENGLISH PUBLIC; SHEFFIELD; PUBLISHED BY ISAAC IRONSIDE AT THE 'FREE PRESS' OFFICE, 1857. I have only seen a third edition of this pamphlet; but as the authoress states in a Dedicatory Letter to Ironside dated May 1857 that this third edition has been called for within six weeks of the first, we may presume that in format and contents (Dedicatory Letter apart) the two were identical. The pamphlet is an 8vo of 36 pp., p. (1) and verso serving as front cover and title. A 'Preliminary Announcement' occupies pp. (4)–16; 'Preface' to the Second Edition of *Very Successful* occupies pp. (17)–34 and is dated March 1857. Pp. (35) (36)—the latter mis-paged 33—carry Press Opinions of *Very Successful.* An errata slip is tipped on to the verso of title and I cannot say whether this appeared in the first edition. The preliminary Announcement explains that, a Second Edition of *Very Successful* having been prevented by threat of legal action, the projected Preface was not able to appear and is therefore now offered to the public in pamphlet form.

[463] WORLD AND HIS WIFE (The): or a Person of Consequence. A Photographic Novel (by Lady Bulwer Lytton)
3 vols. Charles J. Skeet 1858. Rose-madder wavy-grain cloth.

Half-title in each vol.

Vol. I (iv)+292 Errata slip faces p. 292.
II (iv)+(336)
III (iv)+(336) Y_6 Y_7 adverts., Y_8 blank.

Edited by Lady Bulwer Lytton

[464] MEMOIRS OF A MUSCOVITE
3 vols. Newby 1844. Half-cloth boards, labels.

Vol. I (vi) [paged iv]+292
II (ii)+324
III (ii)+(298) Final leaf, O_5, a single inset.

PRINCE-DUKE AND THE PAGE (The): a Historical Novel [465]
3 vols. T. & W. Boone 1841. Half-cloth boards, labels.

Vol. I (ii)+360 [paged (i)–vi+(7)–360] Title a single inset; B_1–B_3 paged (i) vi.
II (ii)+364
III (ii)+340

Book-plates removed and ink signature: 'S. Hall', in each vol. Labels rubbed.

ana

BLIGHTED LIFE (A) (by the Rt. Hon. Lady Lytton) [466]
London Publishing Office 1880. Red sand-grain cloth, blocked in black and gold (measure of front cover $4\frac{7}{8} \times 7\frac{5}{8}$); black end-papers. 3 wood-engraved illustrations.

Half-title. pp. (viii) [paged (iv)]+(112) [mis-paged (3)–111 because (*a*) text begins p. (3) [there is no p. 1 or 2], (*b*) 3 engravings, in fact occupying pp. (9), (39) and (69), are not foliated, but the text on verso of each engraving carries on the foliation in direct sequence].

Note. This copy is in the first binding, seldom seen, with gold blocking and price (2/6) on front, and gold decoration as well as up-lettering on spine. Most copies have no gold blocking and are cut to smaller size.

REFUTATION OF AN AUDACIOUS FORGERY OF THE DOWAGER LADY LYTTON'S NAME TO A BOOK [A BLIGHTED LIFE] [467]
(No publisher or imprint) 1880. Stitched as issued.

pp. 16 Pp. [i–ii] blank+pp. 1–14 text.

BURDETT, MRS C. D.

AT HOME: a Novel (by the author of 'English Fashionables Abroad') [468]
3 vols. Colburn 1828. Boards, labels.

Half-title in each vol.

Vol. I (iv)+300
II (iv)+300
III (iv)+(360)

Ink signature: 'Frances Price, 1832. Rhiwaedog', inside front cover of each vol. Fine.

Note. The headlines throughout read: ENGLISH FASHIONABLES AT HOME, clearly the title originally intended.

ENGLISH FASHIONABLES ABROAD: a Novel [anon] [469]
3 vols. Colburn 1827. Boards, labels.

Half-title in each vol.

Vol. I (iv)+(324) O_6 adverts. Text ends p. 310: pp. (311)–322 Notes.
II (iv)+348 Text ends p. 345: pp. (346)–348 Notes.
III (iv)+(348) P_6 adverts. Text ends p. 340: pp. (341)–346 Notes.

Ink inscription: 'F. Price from her much obliged and affte friend S. Iles. Nov. 24, 1828', on title of each vol. Book-label of R. J. Ll. Price, Rhiwlas Library, inside front cover of each vol. Back cover of Vol. II damaged.

BURY, LADY CHARLOTTE (NÉE CAMPBELL) (1775–1861)

A daughter of the Duke of Argyll, of great personal beauty and everywhere acclaimed for her charm and intelligence, Lady Charlotte Bury was prominent in Society from early girlhood. She was not a good novelist; but she contrived to introduce a vein of thoughtfulness into even the most conventional of her many Silver Fork fictions. Her name will survive as the now accepted author (or foundation-author at any rate) of *Diary Illustrative of the times of George IV*, which first appeared with Colburn in two octavo volumes in 1838, and of which a Second Edition in post 8vo, offering two additional volumes of new matter, followed in 1838/39.

[470] ALLA GIORNATA, or To the Day [anon]
3 vols. Saunders & Otley 1826. Boards, labels.
Half-title in each vol.
Vol. I (iv)+348 B_1 (pp. (1) (2)) carries a Note explaining the title.
II (iv)+300
III (iv)+(312) O_{12} adverts.
Bookseller's ticket: 'D. Lawrence, Dublin', on front cover of Vol. I.

[471] CONDUCT IS FATE [anon]
3 vols. sm. 8vo. Blackwood 1822. Boards, labels.
Half-title in each vol.
Vol. I (iv)+312
II (iv)+(304) N_8 blank.
III (iv)+352 Publishers' cat., 12 pp. on text paper undated, at end.
Bookseller's ticket: 'Bowdery & Kirby Junr, Oxford Street', inside front cover. Small piece torn from spine of Vol. II.

[472] DEVOTED (The) (by the authoress of 'The Disinherited', 'Flirtation', etc.)
3 vols. Bentley 1836. Boards, labels.
Half-title in each vol.
Vol. I (iv)+(296) O_4 adverts. Errata slip tipped in preceding p. (1).
II (iv)+(328)
III (iv)+330 First leaf of final sig., P_1, a single inset.
Spines of Vols. I and II chipped.

DISINHERITED (The), and The ENSNARED (by the authoress of 'Flirtation') [473]
3 vols. Bentley 1834. Boards, labels.
Half-title in Vols. II and III
Vol. I (iv)+316 Longman etc. cat., 12 pp. dated May 1834, inserted between front end-papers. Pp. 313–316 wrongly bound at the end of Vol. II.
II (iv)+312 (followed by pp. 313–316 of Vol. I)
III (iv)+296
Ink signature: 'Frances Price, Rhiwlas, 1834', inside front cover of each vol. Spines cracked.

DIVORCED (The) (by Lady Charlotte Bury, authoress of 'Flirtation', etc. etc.) [474]
2 vols. Colburn 1837. Boards, labels.
Half-title in each vol.
Vol. I (iv)+(270) B_1 (pp. (1) (2)) carries fictitious Press-extract. Final leaf of text, N_1, a single inset. N_2 N_3 adverts., paged (1)–4.
II (iv)+(248) M_4 adverts.
Ink signature: 'Glencairn Caster, Edgeworth, 1837', on fly-leaf of each vol. Re-cased. Spine of Vol. I laid down on new back. End-papers not original.

EXCLUSIVES (The) [anon] [475]
3 vols. Colburn & Bentley 1830. Boards, labels.
Half-title in each vol.
Vol. I (iv)+312
II (iv)+(286) N_{11} advert. First leaf of final sig., N_1, a single inset. N_{12} (cut away) probably label-leaf.
III (iv)+(336) P_{12} adverts.
Book-label of R. J. Ll. Price, Rhiwlas Library, inside front cover of each vol., pasted above ink-inscription: 'Frances Price. Given by her kind friend Miss Iles.'
Fine.

Note. The attribution of this novel to Lady Charlotte Bury, for which Halkett and Laing quote the authority of the University Library, Cambridge, is quite definite in the Bentley Private Catalogue, and must therefore be accepted—with or without reservations. There was published by Marsh & Miller, shortly after the novel appeared, a pamphlet 'Key to the Royal Novel *The Exclusives*'. In this pamphlet the chief characters are thus identified:

Lady Tilney	Lady Jersey
Duchess of Hermanton .	Princess Esterhazy
Princess Leinsengen . .	Princess Lieven
Lady Ellersby . . .	Lady Cawdor
Lord Tonnerre . . .	Lord Trelawne
Mr Leslie Winyard . .	Hon. H. de Ros
Frank Ormbre . . .	Frank Russell
Spencer Newcombe . .	Hon. Spencer Perceval
Lord & Lady Glenmore .	Lord & Lady Ellenborough

Lord Albert d'Esterre .	Lord G. L. Gower
Lady Dunmelraise . .	Dowager Duchess of Leeds
Lady Tenderden . . .	Lady Tankerville
Lady Marchmont . .	Lady Hopetoun
Lord Arlingford . . .	Lord Sefton
Duke of Mercington . .	Duke of Wellington
Lord Gascoigne . . .	Lord Alvanley
Sir William Temple . .	Sir G. Warrender
George Foley	George Anson

[476] FAMILY RECORDS, or the Two Sisters
3 vols. Saunders & Otley 1841. Half-cloth boards, labels.

Vol. I (ii) + 304
II (ii) + (320) P_4 adverts.
III (ii) + (288)

Ink signature: 'Jane Royds 1842', inside front cover of each vol. A sound but dingy copy, with faded spines and discoloured labels.

[477] FLIRTATION: a Novel [anon]
3 vols. Colburn 1827. Boards, labels.

Half-title in each vol.

Vol. I (iv) + 304
II (iv) + 316
III (iv) + (384) R_{11} R_{12} adverts.

Ink signature: 'Frances Price, Rhiwlas, 1828', inside front cover of each vol. Fine.

[478] MANŒUVRING MOTHER (The) (by the author of 'The History of a Flirt')
3 vols. Colburn 1842. Half-cloth boards, labels.

Vol. I (ii) + 332 Longman etc. two-part cat., 16 + 16 pp. dated April 1842, at end.
II (ii) + (320) P_2–P_4 adverts.
III (ii) + (336)

Vols. I and II have been re-cased and the titles are slightly soiled.

[479] SEPARATION (The): a Novel (by the authoress of 'Flirtation')
3 vols. Colburn & Bentley 1830. Boards, labels.

Half-title in each vol.

Vol. I (vi) + (268) Pp. (v) (vi) inset leaf of Errata. N_2 adverts.
II (iv) + (256) M_8 adverts.
III (iv) + 268

Ink signature: 'Frances Price, Rhiwlas, 1830', and bookseller's ticket: 'Seacome, Chester', inside front cover of each vol. Fine.

[480] THREE GREAT SANCTUARIES OF TUSCANY (The), VALOMBROSA, CAMALDOLI, LAVERNA: a Poem, with Historical and Legendary Notices
Oblong folio. John Murray 1833. Brown diagonal-fine-ribbed watered cloth; dark brown leather side-label lettered in gold: THE / THREE GREAT SANCTUARIES / OF TUSCANY / BY / THE LADY CHARLOTTE BURY. Lettering enclosed in ornamental frame. No spine lettering. Red chocolate end-papers.

Etched ornamental title-page by Thos. Landseer precedes printed title, with the names of the three Sanctuaries in gothic script emblazoned on a baroque shield. Engraved portrait of Lady Charlotte Bury after G. Hayter, printed on India paper, mounted on plate paper, and with facsimile of her signature at foot, follows title.

6 full-page engravings in warm sepia after drawings by the late Rev. Edward Bury, husband of the author, each with a stout tissue.

pp. (xiv) [pp. (xiii) (xiv) 'List of Royal Subscribers', a single inset] + (140). pp. (1) (2) fly-title, verso blank; (3)–9 Notices of Valombrosa; 10–37 Poem: 'Valle Ombrosa'; 38–64 Notices of Camaldoli; 65–87 Poem: 'Camaldoli'; 88–113 Notices of Laverna; 114–39 Poem: 'Laverna'.

Note. This pious memorial to her late husband (he died in 1832) was surely erected at Lady Charlotte's expense. The drawings are of considerable merit and beautifully reproduced. I include the book, despite its poetical character, for the sake of these drawings and in order that its existence may be known.

At the foot of the 'List of Royal Subscribers' it is stated that 'the remaining Portion of the List of Subscribers' Names will be published when the Subscription is closed'. There may, therefore, be copies containing this full and longer list.

See also GORE, MRS and SCOTT, LADY LYDIA.

CAINE, HALL (1853–1931)

As in a few other cases (e.g. Corelli, Doyle, Haggard), I have excluded such Caine novels as I possess which post-date 1900.

BONDMAN (The): a New Saga [481]
3 vols. Heinemann 1890. Scarlet diagonal-fine-ribbed cloth.

Half-title in Vol. I. Blank leaf and half-title precede title in Vols. II and III

Vol. I (xii) + (256) Q_8 blank. Publishers' cat. 4 pp. dated January 1890, at end.
II (viii) + (320) U_8 blank. Publishers' cat., as in Vol. I, at end.
III (viii) + (276) Publishers' cat., as in Vol. I, at end.

Presentation Copy: 'To my dear friend J. S. Cotton. Hall Caine. 3/Feb./90' in ink on fly-leaf of Vol. I.

[482] CAPT'N DAVY'S HONEYMOON: THE LAST CONFESSION: THE BLIND MOTHER

Heinemann 1893. Scarlet bubble-grain cloth.

Half-title. pp. (viii) + (280) S_2–S_4 adverts.

Presentation Copy: 'Js. S. Cotton Esqr with affectionate greetings. Hall Caine' in ink on fly-leaf.

[483] CHRISTIAN (The): a Story

Heinemann 1897. Dark cherry-red fine-ribbed cloth.

Leaf carrying list of author's works on verso and half-title precede title. pp. (viii) + (472). $2F_{4-8}$ and $2G_{1-4}$ adverts.

Book-plate of Coningsby Disraeli, Hughenden. Blind stamp: 'W. H. Smith & Son', on fly-leaf. Fine.

Note. On verso of title appear these words: 'First Edition in One Volume, Six Shillings, consisting of 50,000 copies.'

[484] DEEMSTER (The): a Romance

3 vols. Chatto & Windus 1887. Bright blue sand-grain cloth, blocked in colours; grey floral end-papers.

Leaf of adverts. precedes title in Vols. I and III. Leaf of adverts. and half-title in Vol. II

Vol. I (viii) + 304 Publishers' cat., 32 pp. dated July 1887, at end.
II (viii) + (336) Y_8 adverts.
III (vi) + 346†

Ink inscription: 'H. T. Mackenzie Bell, from the publishers, Nov. 1887', on verso of fly-leaf, and pencilled MS. insertion by him on Vol. III, p. 344. Fine.

[485] MANXMAN (The)

Heinemann 1894. Dark cherry-red diagonal-fine-ribbed cloth, lettered in gold and blocked in dark green and blind.

Advert. leaf and half-title precede title. pp. (viii) + (440). Publisher's cat., 20 pp. dated June 1894, at end.

Blind stamp 'Presentation Copy' on title. Very fine.

[486] SCAPEGOAT (The): a Romance

2 vols. Heinemann 1891. Scarlet diagonal-fine-ribbed cloth.

Half-title in Vol. I. Blank leaf and half-title precede title in Vol. II

Vol. I (viii) + (260) R_2 blank. Publisher's cat., 16 pp. dated June 1891, at end.
II (viii) + (316) X_2 adverts.

This copy was ex libris J. S. Cotton but not inscribed.

† The make-up, and consequently the pagination of this vol. are irregular. It opens with (A), a 6 leaf sig., the fourth leaf of which is paged (1) 2 and begins the text. B_1 is p. 7 and the book runs on to Y_8 in eights + Z, 2 leaves. My description, therefore:— (vi) + 346, follows the pagination but misrepresents the structure.

SHADOW OF A CRIME (The) [487]

3 vols. Chatto & Windus 1885. Smooth light brown cloth, floral blocking; pale green floral end-papers.

Blank leaf and half-title precede title in each vol.

Vol. I (xii) [paged (x)] + (340) Z_2 publishers' device.
II (viii) + 296
III (viii) + (260) S_2 publishers' device. Publishers' cat., 32 pp. dated October 1884, at end.

Book-plate of Johannis Lovett in each vol.

SON OF HAGAR (A): a Romance of our Time [488]

3 vols. Chatto & Windus 1887. Grey-green sand-grain cloth, blocked in dark blue; yellow floral end-papers.

Leaf of adverts. precedes title in Vol. I

Vol. I (xvi) + 318 First leaf of final sig., 20_1, a single inset.
II (iv) + (320) Publishers' cat., 32 pp. dated November 1886, at end.
III (iv) + 324 Cat. as in Vol. II at end.

Ink inscription: 'H. T. Mackenzie Bell from Alex. H. Japp, Feb. 10, 1887', on verso of fly-leaf in Vol. I.

CALABRELLA, BARONESS DE

DOUBLE OATH (The), or the Rendezvous [489]

3 vols. Bentley 1850. Gun-metal-grey morocco cloth; yellow end-papers printed with adverts.

Half-title in each vol.

Vol. I (290) Final leaf, N_1, a single inset.
II 268
III (284) L_{10} imprint leaf; (M_1)–(M_{12}) [mis-signed N] adverts., dated September 1850 and paged (1)–24. **B**

EVENINGS AT HADDON HALL ('Edited by the Baroness de Calabrella') [490]

Royal 8vo ($6\frac{1}{4} \times 9\frac{5}{8}$). Colburn 1846. Cream morocco cloth elaborately blocked with gold ornamentation on front, back and spine and gold-lettered on spine. All edges gilt. Steel-engraved front. and 23 plates after Cattermole.

Half-title. pp. (viii) + (456). GG_8 adverts. Two Publisher's cats., each 8 pp. undated, at end.

Binders' ticket: 'Westleys & Clark', at end. Fine.

CARLETON, WILLIAM (1794–1860)

'Carleton was a great Irish historian. He is also the great novelist of Ireland by right of the most Celtic eyes that ever gazed from under the brows of story-teller. His equals in gloomy and tragic power, Michael and John Banim, had nothing of his Celtic humour....

'There is no wistfulness in the works of Carleton. I find there a kind of clay-cold melancholy. When I read any portion of the *Black Prophet* or the scenes with Raymond the Madman in *Valentine M'Clutchy*, I seem to be looking out at the wild, torn storm-clouds that lie in heaps at sundown along the western seas of Ireland; all nature, and not merely man's nature, seems to pour out for me its inbred fatalism.'

This extract from W. B. Yeats' Preface to a selection of Carleton's stories, published in Walter Scott's Camelot Series in 1889, justifies the emphasis laid in the present catalogue on his first and early editions.

Although incomplete and containing a few unsatisfactory copies, the following is a really remarkable collection of Carleton's works. His bibliography is complex in the extreme, but nowhere hitherto has the degree of scope and accuracy here reached been achieved. Even the *C.B.E.L.* (whose Carleton section I myself revised) lacks one or two titles and gives a few incorrect dates which, since that revision, I have been fortunate enough to establish.

Mainly of Irish origin, Carleton's books were frequently of shoddy manufacture, and more or less disintegrated under rough usage. Also their supply to the Statutory Libraries was apt to be irregular. Finally his (or his publishers') habit of re-issuing stories in different order under new titles and, conversely, giving almost identical titles to quite different collections, has made the identification of genuine first editions baffling and hazardous.

So far as possible I have supplied descriptions of titles not in the Collection from copies in the Statutory Libraries. These titles are asterisked.

[491] ALLEY SHERIDAN and Other Stories
Dublin: P. Dixon Hardy & Sons, n.d. (1857).

Copy I. Red bead-grain cloth, pictorially blocked in gold on front and spine, all edges gilt. Wood-engraved front. and vignette title preceding printed title on plate paper, and cuts in text.

pp. (iv)+(260) [paged (i), ii, iii, (iv), (5), (6), (7), 8–259, (260)]. First 4 unnumbered pp. are title, verso blank; contents, verso blank. Pp. (i)–iii, Publishers' Preface, dated December 1857, stating that these early tales appeared in the *National Magazine*; (iv) blank; (5) (6) fly-title to *Alley Sheridan*, verso blank; text begins (7).

[491*a*] **Copy II.** Yellow pictorial boards; yellow end-papers printed with adverts. Outside back cover advertises: 'HARDY'S GENUINE EDITION OF TALES AND STORIES OF THE IRISH PEASANTRY: The Present volume ALLEY SHERIDAN contains etc. etc.'

Collation as Copy I.

Contents: Alley Sheridan*—Laying a Ghost*—Owen M'Carthy or The Landlord and Tenant†—Condy Cullen and the Gauger‡—The Donagh or the Horse-Stealers§—Sir Turlough or the Churchyard Bride.†

* In *Popular Tales and Legends of the Irish Peasantry*, 1834.

† In *Characteristic Sketches of Ireland*, 1845.

‡ An extended version of the tale which appears as 'Condy Cullen or the Gauger Outwitted' in *Tales and Sketches*, 1845, and as 'The Gauger Captured' in *The Irishman at Home*, 1849.

§ In *Traits and Stories: Second Series*, 1833. The present volume, therefore, can only claim to offer one amended text.

ART MAGUIRE, or the Broken Pledge: a Narrative [482] *Pl. 7*

Dublin: James Duffy 1845. Olive-green ribbed cloth (with binder's imprint—O. BELLEW, DUBLIN—in blind at foot of front cover) and lettered on spine 'The Broken Pledge'.

Half-title: 'Tales for the Irish People.' pp. (xii)+252.

In ink on title: 'Annie Prendergast, Sept. 15, 1845. J.E.P.', and facing title: 'Rev. J. H. O'Donnell, from Ellen Phelan. May 1903.'

Notes. (i) I think this is certainly the first edition, despite the fact that Lib. of Congress gives date of first as 1841, but no detail. The Preface is dated July 4, 1845, and gives no suggestion that the story had previously appeared. This is the only edition in B.M. O'Donoghue (see 523 below: *Life of Carleton*) states that the story was written in 1845 and was originally published at three shillings as the first of a series of 'Tales for the People'. Clearly he could not locate a copy and therefore does not record the book in his bibliography until 1847, in which year it appeared in Duffy's 'National Library'.

(ii) Also issued in red. There is a 'secondary' in red cloth with spine heavily gilt and a coloured front.

BATTLE OF THE FACTIONS (The) and Other Tales of Ireland [493]

8vo. Philadelphia: Carey and Hart. 1845. Buff wrappers cut flush, printed in black, up-lettered on spine, inside and back covers printed with adverts. Etched front. and pictorial title, spirited in drawing and finely engraved, on plate paper, and one cut in the text.

pp. (iv) [plate paper]+(96) [paged (9)–(104)]

Contents: The Battle of the Factions—The Geography of an Irish Oath—Neal Malone—The Donagh or the Horse Stealers—The Station.

Notes. (i) On front wrapper the publishers' imprint has been cancelled, and a slip over-pasted imprinted 'New York: Burgess, Stringer & Co.'

(ii) This volume contains five stories originally published in *Traits and Stories*, First Series (2), Second Series (2) and *Tales of Ireland* (1).

[494] **BLACK BARONET** (The), or the Chronicles of Ballytrain

Dublin: James Duffy 1858. Yellow-back pictorial boards. Wood-engraved front. and vignette title on plate paper after Geo. Measom. Printed end-papers.

pp. viii + 476. Fine.

Note. This novel was first published as *Red Hall or the Baronet's Daughter* in 3 vols. 1852 (q.v.). The present edition contains a Preface (pp. iv–viii) dated October 26, 1857.

[495] *Pl. 8* **BLACK PROPHET** (The): a Tale of the Irish Famine

Copy I: First Edition: first issue. Belfast: Simms & M'Intyre 1847. [Parlour Library, No. 1.] Pale green glazed boards, printed in brown on front and back with standard Series design of Parlour Library. No decoration on spine (only lettering). White (or pale green) unprinted end-papers. Back cover announces Parlour Library, No. 2.

Series half-title (no frame or imprint) precedes title imprinted as above. pp. (324) [paged (1)–(4) + (i)–iv + (5)–320]. Two leaves (Dedication and Preface) paged (i)–iv are inset between pp. (4) and (5). A pink slip (4 pp.) announcing the Parlour Library is inset between front end-papers. Very fine.

[495*a*] *Pl. 8* **Copy II: First Edition: second issue.** Differs from Copy I as follows:

(*a*) Spine patterned in Series style to range with front and back cover decoration.

(*b*) Back cover announces Parlour Library, No. 8. (This is the case to the best of my knowledge. The two copies in boards which I have seen both carried such an announcement. It is, however, possible that copies were issued advertising earlier volumes in the Series.)

(*c*) Series half-title has become a Series title in decorative frame and imprinted.

(*d*) Imprint on Series title (with slight variations): Simms & M'Intyre, 13 Paternoster Row; and 26 Donegall Street, Belfast. P. S. O'Hegarty reports that in his copy the individual title has Belfast imprint only, as in first issue. This is probably the earlier state.

(*e*) End-papers green and printed with adverts.

Very fine.

[495*b*] *Pl. 8* **Copy III: Illustrated Edition.** 8vo. Simms & M'Intyre, London and Belfast 1847. Pale yellow glazed boards, printed in gold and red with elaborate all-over arabesque design. Pictorial half-title (not reckoned in collation) and 5 wood-engravings by Dickes after W. Harvey.

pp. (xii) + (456)

Ink signature: 'Rebecca Pleyer, 1848', on fly-leaf. Fine.

This edition is advertised as 'Illustrated Edition' in the pink-inset to Copy I, and as a 'Christmas Gift Book' on the end-papers of Copy II.

CHARACTERISTIC SKETCHES OF IRELAND AND THE IRISH [by Carleton, Lover and Mrs Hall] [496]

Copy I: First Edition. Fcap 8vo. Dublin: P. D. Hardy 1845. Maroon diaper cloth, gold-lettered on spine SKETCHES OF IRISH CHARACTER. Etched front. and 5 illustrations by Kirkwood. *Pl. 7*

pp. (iv) + 288

Copy II: Re-issue (unavowed). Halifax: William Milner 1849. Red ribbed cloth, gold blocked and lettered on spine: IRELAND AND THE IRISH: GOOD ENTERTAINMENT WITHIN. Illustrations and collation as Copy I. Doubtless original sheets with new prelims. [496*a*] *Pl. 7*

Note. This is not the first Milner issue, which appeared in 1846 in maroon cloth.

Copy III: Second Re-issue (still unavowed) under the title TALES AND STORIES OF IRELAND. Halifax: Milner & Sowerby 1852. Bright green boards, printed in black. Illustrations and collation as Copy I. [496*b*] *Pl. 7*

Contents: Carleton: The Horse-Stealers—Owen M'Carthy—Squire Warnock—The Abduction—Sir Turlough.

Lover: Paddy Mullowney—Legend of Clanmacnoise—Ballads and Ballad Singers.

Hall: The Irish Agent—Philip Garraty.

DENIS O'SHAUGHNESSY GOING TO MAYNOOTH [497]

Routledge 1845. Dark green ribbed cloth. Two etchings by W. H. B[rooke].

pp. (ii) + 200

Re-issue of a story from *Traits and Stories, Second Series*, 1833. Either composed of Irish sheets, or from the type of the fourth (5 vol.) edition of 1836. Spine-lettering: 'Going to Maynooth'.

***DOUBLE PROPHECY** (The), or Trials of the Heart [498]

2 vols. Dublin: James Duffy 1862. Magenta wavy-grain cloth, conventionally blocked in blind on front and back, gold-lettered on spine.

Two blank leaves and half-title precede title in Vol. I. Half-title only in Vol. II

Vol. I (xvi) [paged viii] + (232)
II (vi) [paged viii] + (226) P_8 blank. Final leaf, (Q_1), a single inset, carries Errata for both vols. Text ends p. 220; (221) 222, 'Postliminous Preface'.

[499] EMIGRANTS OF AHADARRA (The): a Tale of Irish Life
Pl. 7
Simms & M'Intyre 1848. [Parlour Library, No. 11.] Pale green glazed boards, printed in brown (possibly also in green cloth gilt—but this later). Pale green Parlour Library end-papers, printed with adverts. Back cover announces Parlour Library, No. 12.

Series title precedes title. pp. viii + (312) U_4 blank. Publisher's (McGlashan) cat., 16 pp. dated December 1847, at end.

'Emily Mary Purnell' in ink on Series title. Very fine.

[500] EVIL EYE (The), or the Black Spectre: a Romance
Pl. 7
Dublin: James Duffy 1860. Violet morocco cloth (also red, and maybe other colours). All edges gilt. Wood-engraved portrait front., vignette title and 11 plates after Edmund Fitzpatrick.

Half-title. pp. viii + (520) $2L_4$ adverts. Fine.

Note. Also issued in bead-grain cloth, similar blocking.

[501] *FAIR OF EMYVALE (The)

I am unable to describe the first edition of this story, which was, presumably, No. 10 of The Parlour Library: Sixpenny Series, published by Ward, Lock & Tyler in 1869–70 (3755*b* (ii) in Section III). O'Donoghue dates the First Edition 1870. No copy is available either in B.M., Bodley or the U.L.C.

The Fair of Emyvale was serialised in *The Illustrated London Magazine* from July to September 1853 with illustrations by Phiz.

[502] FARDOROUGHA THE MISER, or the Convicts of Lisnamona

Pl. 7 **Copy I: First Edition.** Dublin: William Curry Jun. & Co. 1839. Boards, label.

Leaf of adverts. and half-title precede title. pp. (xii) [paged x] + 468 Leaf of adverts. defective.

Note. Also issued in very dark green cloth with label.

[502*a*] **Copy II: New Edition: 'With an Introduction written for the Present Edition'.** Sm. 8vo. Simms & McIntyre 1848. (Parlour Library, No. 21.) Green glazed boards printed in brown in standard Parlour Library style. Green end-papers printed with adverts.

Series title precedes title. pp. xvi + 296 Pp. (v)–xvi carry an Introduction dated September 16, 1848. Fine.

[503] *FATHER BUTLER: THE LOUGH DEARG PILGRIM: being Sketches of Irish Manners [anon]

12mo. Dublin: William Curry Jun. & Co. 1829. Smooth sage-green cloth, label. Wood-engraved front. after George Petrie, not on text paper.

pp. iv + 302 Final leaf, S_1, a single inset.

Note. Preface states that the sketches originally appeared in the *Christian Examiner* and *The Church of Ireland Magazine.*

*FAWN OF SPRING-VALE (The), The Clarionet and Other Tales [504]

3 vols. Dublin: William Curry Jun. & Co. 1841. ? Half-cloth boards, labels (copies in B.M. and Bodley rebound).

Vol. I (xii) + (368) (i) (ii) title, verso printers' imprint; (iii) (iv) Dedication to Wordsworth, verso blank; (v) [signed *a*]–viii Preface; (ix) (x) Contents of the 3 vols., verso blank; (xi) (xii) fly-title to *Jane Sinclair*, verso blank.

II (iv) + (352) (iii) (iv) fly-title to *The Clarionet*, verso blank.

III (iv) + 328 (iii) (iv) fly-title to *Barney Branagan*, verso blank.

Contents: Vol. I: Jane Sinclair or the Fawn of Spring-Vale—Lha Dhu or The Dark Day. Vol. II: The Clarionet—The Dead Boxer. Vol. III: The Misfortunes of Barney Branagan—The Resurrections of Barney Bradley.

Note. JANE SINCLAIR OR THE FAWN OF SPRING VALE, etc., 3 vols., Dublin: William Curry, London: George Routledge, 1843, is a re-issue of the sheets of the above book, with reprinted inset title in Vol. I, reprinted title and new leaf of Errata inserted between fly-title and B_1 in II, reprinted title inset between fly-title and B_1 in III. This re-issue is bound in dark green diaper cloth (also boards, labels).

IRISHMAN AT HOME (The): Characters and Sketches of the Irish Peasantry [anon] [505]

Dublin: McGlashan 1849. Dark green fine-ribbed cloth. Wood engravings.

pp. (304) [paged 302]

Contents: The Whiteboys—The Rockite—The Wrestlers—The Mowin' Match—The False Step—The Fatal Meeting—The Gauger captured and the Gauger Outwitted.†

PARRA SASTHA, or the History of Paddy-go-Easy [506]

12mo. Dublin: James Duffy 1845. (Duffy's Library of Ireland, No. 5.) Glazed white paper wrappers printed in green and red. Pl. 6

pp. xvi + (212) M_4–M_{10} Publishers' cat., 14 pp. dated November 1, 1845.

This little book, and others in the series, was also issued in green cloth, and (later) in full morocco with gold harp on front and back and gilt edges.

Note. An advertisement in No. 11 (May 1846) of Duffy's Library of Ireland (*Poems of Thomas Davis*) states that a second edition of *Parra Sastha* is ready, 'of which the greater portion is

† Previously published in *Tales and Sketches etc.* 1845.

re-written'. P. S. O'Hegarty kindly provides details of this re-writing. The last par. of the Preface is omitted, also the end of Chap. VI and the 'Observations on Farming'. Four new chapters are added, occupying pp. 175–228.

Duffy re-issued the Library of Ireland in dumpy red cloth volumes, each containing two of the original numbers. By that time *Parra* was still in a Second, and *Rody* (q.v. below) in a Sixth edition.

[507] POOR SCHOLAR (The), Frank Martin and the Fairies, The Country Dancing Master and Other Irish Tales

Dublin: James Duffy 1869. Green sand-grain cloth.

pp. (iv) + 252

Ink signature: 'J. McGarry', on fly-leaf.

Contents: The Poor Scholar—Mickey M'Rorey, The Irish Fiddler—Buckram Back (*sic*), The Country Dancing Master—Mary Murray, the Irish Match Maker—Bob Pentland or The Gauger Outwitted—The Fate of Frank M'Kenna—The Rival Kempers—Frank Martin and the Fairies—A Legend of Knockmany.

Note. Not a first edition. All the stories except *The Poor Scholar* appeared in *Tales and Sketches*, etc. 8vo. 1845 (q.v.) and *The Poor Scholar* in *Traits and Stories*.

[508] POPULAR TALES AND LEGENDS OF THE IRISH PEASANTRY [by Carleton, 'Denis O'Donoho', Mrs S. C. Hall, etc.]

Dublin: Wakeman 1834. Glazed dark green (or plum) linen, paper label. Etched front. and 4 plates by Samuel Lover.

pp. (vi) + (406) Y_6 advert. Z_1–Z_5 renewal of text, Z_6 blank. Pp. (ii) (iii), 'To the Reader', a single inset.

Contains *Alley Sheridan* and *Laying a Ghost* by Carleton.

Note. Lover, in the Preface to his *Legends and Stories of Ireland* (2nd Series), makes a strong protest against the implication that he had anything to do with the work here described, save as illustrator. Certainly the title is so designed as to fit his name to the text as well as the illustrations.

[509] RED HAIRED MAN'S WIFE (The)

8vo. Dublin: Sealy, Bryers & Walker; London: Simpkin, Marshall 1889. Scarlet diagonal-fine-ribbed cloth, gold-lettered on front and spine.

Half-title. pp. viii + (276) (S_2) blank.

Note. A Publishers' Note states that this last work of William Carleton was put in their hands many years ago but that its publication had been delayed 'owing to a serious mishap', now remedied. O'Donoghue states (Vol. II, p. 321) that the original MS., completed in 1867, was partially burnt and that the missing portions were supplied after Carleton's death by one MacDermott, who then serialised the tale in 1870 in the *Carlow College Magazine.*

*RED HALL or The Baronet's Daughter [510]

3 vols. Saunders & Otley 1852. Boards, labels. (? also issued in cloth. Copy in U.L.C. as above, those in B.M. and Bodley rebound).

Half-title in each vol.

Vol. I (iv) + 308
II (iv) + 316
III. (iv) + (320) Publishers' cat., 4 pp., at end.

*REDMOND COUNT O'HANLON, the Irish Rapparee: an Historical Tale [511]

Fcap 8vo. Dublin: James Duffy 1862. Blue-grey (or dark green) morocco cloth, conventionally blocked in blind on front and back, gold-lettered on spine.

pp. 174

RODY THE ROVER, or The Ribbonman [512]

12mo. Dublin: James Duffy 1845. (Duffy's Library of Ireland, No. 3.) Glazed white paper wrappers, printed in green and gold. *Pl. 6*

pp. iv + 260 Two leaves of adverts. inset before title.

This copy lacks back wrapper.

*SILVER ACRE (The) and Other Tales [513]

Ward & Lock 1862. Pale blue wrappers printed in black.

pp. (ii) + 238 Final leaf, Q_7, a single inset.

No. 15 of Ward & Lock's Shilling Volume Library. First printed serially in *The Illustrated London Magazine* from November 1853 to (?) February 1854 with illustrations by Phiz.

SQUANDERS OF CASTLE SQUANDER (The) [514]

2 vols. Illustrated London Library, 1852. Scarlet ribbed or blue morocco cloth, blocked on front and spine in silver. Design initialled J. L[eighton]. In each vol. wood-engraved front., 4 plates after Topham, and printed title—all on plate paper. *Pl. 7*

Vol. I (iv) [paged vi, because the title, although on plate paper, is reckoned in the pagination] + (328) Y_4 adverts.
II. (ii) + (312)

Copy I: (Red). Book-plate of John Browne. Binders' ticket, 'Leighton, Son & Hodge', at end of each vol. Fine.

Copy II: (Blue). Booksellers' ticket: 'Greene & Co. Dublin.' [514*a*]

Copy III: Green morocco cloth, blocked in blind on front and back, on spine lettered (title and vol. number only) and blocked in gold, with a design incorporating a palette and brushes. [514*b*]

This issue is slightly taller ($7\frac{11}{16}$ as against $7\frac{1}{2}$) than I and II.

Notes. (i) Front. and title are conjugate in each vol.

(ii) Two further variants are reported by P. S. O'Hegarty: (*a*) grey-green cloth, lettered in gold on front and spine: ILLUSTRATED FAMILY NOVELIST and also on spine with title vol. number and imprint (Nathaniel Cooke), the whole interspersed with gold scroll work. Front and back are also blind-blocked. (*b*) Very dark (or medium) green cloth, blind-blocked on front and back, gold-lettered on spine: THE / SQUANDERS / BY / CARLETON / VOL. I. ILLUSTRATED. This issue is of the tallness of Copy III above, and is, I fancy, the variant described by Carter, *Binding Variants*, p. 102.

How are we to order these variants?

I am satisfied that the first issue is represented by Copies I and II above and for this reason—the elaborate front- and back-blocking and lettering are exactly uniform with those on *Ivar the Skjüts-Boy* and *Lady Felicia* by Cockton, both published from the 'Office of the Illustrated London Library' in 1852. In no one of the three books is there any mention of the Illustrated Family Novelist (3747 in Section III), which was a later creation of Nathaniel Cooke, whose imprint did not exist before 1853, and in which *Squanders*, *Ivar* and *Felicia* were subsequently incorporated. An advert. leaf at the end of *Ivar* describes *Squanders* as 'recently published, uniform with "Ivar"', and announces *Felicia*. Further, the Bodleian Statutory copy is in Style I.

Probably O'Hegarty (*a*) is the next issue, but I see no way of deciding whether the third is copy III above or O'Hegarty (*b*). The tallness of these two last is not in my view an argument for priority. The *Squanders-Ivar-Felicia* non-series issue, as well as the volumes of the Illustrated Family Novelist, are all cut close; and it is quite likely that, when a balance of sheets were bound up in style III or in O'Hegarty (*b*), the sheets by chance were only trimmed.

The final incarnation was 2 vols. in one, in bright blue morocco cloth, gold-blocked on spine.

[515] TALES AND SKETCHES, illustrating the Character, Usages, Traditions, Sports and Pastimes of the Irish Peasantry

Copy I: First Edition. 8vo. Dublin: James Duffy 1845. Green horizontal-fine-ribbed cloth, blocked in blind on front, spine and back, and gold-lettered on spine: CARLETON'S / TALES &C / OF / THE IRISH / PEASANTRY / DUFFY. DUBLIN. The binding is 'signed' in blind: G. BELLEW BINDER DUBLIN, twice on front and back and once on spine.

Half-title (reading: TALES AND SKETCHES).

pp. (xii) + (396) 2C_6 advert. of Duffy's Library of Ireland.

Copy II: Illustrated Re-issue. Scarlet moiré cloth; spine pictorially blocked in gold and lettered: CARLETON'S / TALES AND STORIES (*sic*) / OF / THE IRISH PEASANTRY / ILLUSTRATED / BY PHIZ. Etched front. and pictorial title (dated 1846), preceding printed title (dated 1845), and 6 plates by Phiz. No list of plates. [515*a*] *Pl. 8*

Collation as Copy I. Sheets of First Edition with plates inserted.

Ink signature: 'Edmund Lowe, Kingston-on Thames', on fly-leaf. Also heavy pencil scribble by unknown young.

Contents: Mickey M'Rorey, the Irish Fiddler*—Buckramback, the Country Dancing-master*—Mary Murray, the Irish Matchmaker*—Bob Pentland or the Gauger Outwitted*—The Fate of Frank M'Kenna*—The Rival Kempers*—Frank Martin and the Fairies*—A Legend of Knockmany—Rose Moan, the Irish Midwife*—Talbot and Gayna, Irish Pipers—Frank Finnigan, the Foster Brother*—Tom Gressiey, the Irish Senachie*—The Castle of Aughentain or A Legend of the Brown Goat*—Barney M'Haigney, the Irish Prophecy Man*—Moll Roe's Marriage or the Pudding Bewitched—Barney Brady's Goose or Dark Doings at Slath Beg—Condy Cullen or the Exciseman Defeated—A Record of the Heart or the Parents' Trial—The Three Wishes, an Irish Legend—The Irish Rake—Stories of Second Sight and Apparition.

Notes. (i) The 12 stories asterisked were first printed in the *Irish Penny Journal* (Dublin: Gunn & Cameron) and under slightly different titles. Thus: The Irish Fiddler (Aug. 15, 1840)—The Country Dancing Master (Aug. 29, 1840)—The Irish Matchmaker (Oct. 10, 1840)—Bob Pentland or the Gauger Outwitted (Oct. 17, 1840)—Irish Superstitions: I, Ghosts and Fairies; II, The Rival Kempers; III, untitled (Nov. 21 and Dec. 12, 1840: Feb. 20, 1841). [These three are The Fate of Frank M'Kenna, The Rival Kempers, Frank Martin and The Fairies]—The Irish Midwife (in three parts, Dec. 26, 1840, Jan. 2 and April 3, 1841)—The Foster Brother (April 24, 1841)—The Irish Shanahus (May 29, 1841). [This is Tom Gressiey, the Irish Senachie]—The Castle of Aughentain (June 5, 1841)—The Irish Prophecy Man (June 12, 1841).

(ii) The book was re-issued in 1849 and 1851 without Dedication, Preface, or indication of previous issue.

TALES OF IRELAND (by the author of 'Traits and Stories', etc.) [516] *Pl. 7*

Copy I. Fcap 8vo. Dublin: Curry 1834. Grey-purple morocco cloth. Etched front. and 5 plates by W. H. Brooke.

Leaf of adverts. precedes half-title. pp. (xvi) [paged (xiv)] + (368) $2A_8$ adverts.

Book-plate of Andrew Ferguson. Bookseller's ticket: 'Wm. Campbell, Londonderry', inside front cover.

Contents. The Death of a Devotee—The Priest's Funeral—Neal Malone—The Brothers—The Illicit Distiller—The Dream of a Broken Heart—Lachlin Murray and the Blessed Candle.

[516a] **Copy II.** Dark green embossed morocco cloth, uniform design with *Traits and Stories*, 5 vols. 1836. Collation as Copy I.

Bookseller's ticket: 'Coupland's Library, Southampton', inside front cover.

Note. The copy in the Nat. Lib. Dublin is in glossy brown cloth, and M. J. MacManus' copy in dull brown ribbed cloth, differently lettered on spine

[517] TITHE PROCTOR (The): a Novel. Being a Tale
Pl. 7 of the Tithe Rebellion in Ireland

Simms & M'Intyre, 1849. (Parlour Library, No. 24.) Pale green glazed boards, printed in brown. Pale green Parlour Library end-papers, printed with adverts. Back cover announces Parlour Library, No. 25.

Series title precedes individual title. pp. xvi + 288 Single advert. leaf of white paper pasted between front end-papers.

[518] TRAITS AND STORIES OF THE IRISH PEASANTRY: **First Series.**

Pl. 7 **Copy I: First Edition.** 2 vols. Dublin: W. Curry Jun. & Co. 1830. Glazed green (or blue) linen, paper labels. Etched front. and 2 plates in each vol. by W. H. Brooke.

Half-title in each vol.

Vol. I xii + (276)
II (iv) + 304 Publishers' cat., 4 pp. undated on text paper, at end.

Book-label of Henry McCall and his ink-signature, inside front cover and on title of each vol.

Also issued in boards with labels. Copy reported in this style had the 4 pp. adverts. at end of Vol. II.

Contents: Ned M'Keown—The Three Tasks—Shane Fadh's Wedding—Larry M'Farland's Wake—The Battle of the Factions—The Funeral and Party Fight—The Hedge School and the Abduction of Mat Kavanagh—The Station.

[518a] **Copy II: 'Second Edition, Corrected'.** Dublin: W. Curry Jr. 1832. Dark green moiré cloth, green paper label lettered in white. Front. and 5 etchings by W. H. Brooke.

pp. viii + (568) Publishers' cat., 12 pp. undated, inserted between front end-papers.

The cloth of this copy is rather worn and the label defective.

Contents: as first edition.

Copy III: 'Third Edition Corrected'. 2 vols. fcap 8vo. Dublin: William Frederick Wakeman 1834. Dark green (or plum) morocco cloth, labels. 6 etchings (and wood engravings in the text) by W. H. Brooke. [518b]

Vol. I (xii) + (342) $2A_4$ blank. Pp. (xi) (xii) are fly-title to the first story—*Ned M'Keown*, verso blank.
II (iv) + (372)

Vol. II loose in cover. There is also in the Collection another example of this edition in plum cloth (lacking labels) and, uniform with it, a set of the three volumes of the Second Series (Copy II, 1834), q.v. below.

Contents: as first edition.

Copy IV: 'Fourth Edition Corrected'. 2 vols. fcap 8vo. Dublin: Wakeman 1835. Binding and illustrations as in Copy II. [518c]

Half-title in each vol.

Vol. I (xii) + (342) $2A_4$ blank (the overall half-title takes the place of the fly-title to *Ned M'Keown*, which drops out).
II (iv) + (372) pp. (1) (2) Contents leaf, text begins p. (3).

Contents: as first edition.

Book-plate of J. H. Shorthouse (author of *John Inglesant*). Fine.

TRAITS AND STORIES OF THE IRISH PEASANTRY: **Second Series** [519]

Copy I: First Edition. 3 vols. Dublin: William Frederick Wakeman 1833. Boards, labels. *Pl. 7*

Vol. I viii + (472) Publishers' cat. (Whittaker, Treacher), 12 pp. undated, inserted between front end-papers.
II (iv) + (476)
III (iv) + 448

Contents: The Midnight Mass—The Donagh or the Horse-Stealers—Phil Purcell, the Pig Driver—An Essay on Irish Swearing—The Geography of an Irish Oath—The Lianhan Shee—The Poor Scholar—Wildgoose Lodge—Tubber Derg, or the Red Well—Denis O'Shaughnessy going to Maynooth—Phelim O'Toole's Courtship.

Copy II: Second and First Illustrated Edition. 3 vols. Dublin: Wakeman 1834. Dark green (or plum) morocco cloth, labels; pale brown watered end-papers. Etched front. and 3 plates (and wood-engravings in the text) in each vol. by W. H. Brooke. [519a]

Vol. I vi + 364
II (iv) + (376)
III (iv) + (344) Z_4 imprint leaf.

Vol. II loose in cover. (See First Series Copy III).

This edition contains a 'Preface to the Second Edition' (Vol. I pp. (v) vi) and is wholly re-set. Two stories in Vol. I are in different order, but

Contents the same as Copy I. In the plum cloth set the prelims. of Vol. I show a variant. They consist of *twelve* pages, there being inserted between pp. (v) vi three leaves, of which the first blank and a single inset, and the other two carrying 'Preface to the First Edition' paged (vii)–x. The Preface to the First Edition is not included in the green-cloth volume.

Note. It may be noted that the first five stories of this Second Series were issued in 1854 as a volume in Routledge's New Series, bound in blue morocco cloth and with two illustrations by Phiz, reproduced from the two-vol. 8vo edition of *Traits and Stories* (see below) originally published by Curry in 1843 and taken over and re-issued by Routledge about 1850.

[520] TRAITS AND STORIES OF THE IRISH PEASANTRY: **Both Series**

Pl. 7 **Copy I: First Collected Edition.** 5 vols. Baldwin & Cradock (Dublin: Wakeman) 1836. Olive-brown embossed morocco cloth. Portrait front. in Vol. I after Roe. Etchings (and wood engravings in the text) by W. H. Brooke.

Vol. I (x) + (340)
II (iv) + (372)
III x + 364
IV (iv) + (376)
V (iv) + (344) Z_4 blank.

Book-label of J. P. Brown-Westhead, Lee Castle in each vol. Very fine.

Contents: as previously, but the sixth story is now called *The Party Fight and Funeral.*

[520*a*]
Pl. 8 **Copy II: 'A New Edition, with an Autobiographical Introduction, Explanatory Notes and Numerous Illustrations in Wood and Steel'.** 2 vols. 8vo. Dublin: Curry 1843. Red morocco cloth, spines pictorially blocked (figures and wreathed shamrocks) and lettered in gold. Tinted portrait front. and designed title in Vol. I: tinted landscape front. and designed title in Vol. II, preceding printed title. 22 full-page etchings in Vol. I and 14 in Vol. II by Phiz, Sibson, Wrightson, Franklin, MacManus, Lee and Gilbert, and occasional wood-engravings.

Half-title in each vol.

Vol. I (xxxii) [paged xxiv] + (432) EE_7 EE_8 adverts.
II (viii) + (432) EE_8 adverts.

Ink signature: 'Hunter', on fly-leaf of Vol. I and half-title of Vol. II. Fine.

Notes: (i) This edition includes two additional stories: *The Lough Derg Pilgrim* † and *Neal Malone* ‡; and omits *The Geography of an Irish Oath* and *Phelim O'Toole's Courtship*. The 'General Introduction' occupies pp. (ix)–(xxxii), is paged (i)–xxiv and dated: Dublin, August, 1842.

(ii) This handsome binding, undoubtedly the earliest, was also issued in green and blue cloth. Black cloth, with no pictorial blocking, is, I suspect, of later date.

(iii) This two-vol. 8vo edition was taken over by Routledge and re-issued about 1850, and again re-issued by Tegg in 1864 as 'Fifth Edition'. In 1854, as above stated, the first five stories in the Second Series were issued as a volume in Routledge's New Series.

† See *Father Butler* (1829). ‡ See *Tales of Ireland* (1834).

Copy III: Another edition 'With the Author's Latest Corrections'. J. & R. Maxwell, 4 Shoe Lane and George Vickers, Angel Court, n.d. [1880/1]. Glazed green boards, pictorially printed and lettered in black. Etched front. and 3 plates by Daniel Maclise, and a wood-engraved vignette title after a drawing by Maclise. [520*b*]

pp. (iv) + 780 Published at half a crown.

Notes: (i) The dating above is suggested by an advert., on back cover, of the cheap edition of Miss Braddon's novels which ends with No. 36, *The Story of Barbara*, and states that 'Miss Braddon's other Novels will follow in due succession'. Clearly *The Story of Barbara* was her latest, and it was first published in 1880.

(ii) This edition was issued in 26 penny parts of which 1–23 were of 32 pp., 24–25 of 16 pp. and 26 of 12 pp.

(iii) I am puzzled to account for two features of this edition:

(*a*) *the Contents.* These consist of the Introduction to the 2 vol. 8vo edition of 1843, all the stories in that edition, and in addition *The Silver Acre, The Fair of Emyvale* and *Master and Scholar. The Silver Acre* was published in 1862 in Ward & Lock's Shilling Volume Series; *The Fair of Emyvale* and *Master and Scholar* formed No. 10 of the Parlour Library: Sixpenny Series (1869–70). Is this Maxwell-Vickers edition the first in which they are joined to the bulk of *Traits and Stories*? It looks uncommonly like it, because a Vickers edition of 1875 with Maclise etchings (see (*b*) below) does *not* include them, but stops with *Neal Malone*—the story which immediately precedes *The Silver Acre* in this Maxwell-Vickers edition.

(*b*) *the Illustrations.* Where did these originally appear? I have seen an edition dated 1875, *with Vickers imprint only*, in which the etchings are included; but seeing that Maclise died in 1870 (the year after Carleton) they must in all likelihood have been used earlier than 1875.

As a postscript to this entry, I would quote from *A Diary* by William Allingham (1917). The diarist gives an account of an evening with Tennyson, in the course of which occurs the following:

'Carleton's *Traits and Stories*—with which he

(Tennyson) is delighted. I said I knew Carleton a little. "Then you knew a man of genius" said Tennyson. He thinks Carleton is not appreciated. I told him that in Ireland he is, highly. Also that Carleton, Catholic born, turned Protestant in youth, wrote the *Traits*, then returned to his old Church and wrote many stories, in which priests and other matters were handled in a different way. "Those are not so good, I should think" Tennyson said.'

[521] VALENTINE McCLUTCHY, THE IRISH AGENT: or Chronicles of the Castle Cumber Property

Copy I: First Edition. 3 vols. Dublin: James Duffy 1845. Scarlet morocco cloth.

Half-title in each vol.

Vol. I xii + 300
II (iv) + (320) X_8 blank.
III (iv) + 336

[521*a*] **Copy II: Illustrated Edition.** 8vo. Dublin: James Duffy 1847. Light claret horizontal-fine-ribbed cloth, spine pictorially blocked in gold, and lettered with title, sub-title and 20 / ILLUSTRATIONS / BY / PHIZ. Etched front. and 19 plates by Phiz.

Half-title. pp. xii + 468 Cloth rather worn.

Note. This edition is sub-titled on title 'The Chronicles of Castle Cumber'. pp. (ix)–xii are occupied by a Preface dated Nov. 1846. The work was re-issued, undated, by Henry Lea in blue morocco cloth, text and illustrations poorly printed from the original plates.

[521*b*] **Copy III: another.** Red morocco cloth, blocked in blind and gold-lettered on spine *with title only.* Collation, etc., as II. Very fine.

I give II priority on account of the more elaborate and informative spine-blocking.

[522] WILLY REILLY AND HIS DEAR COLLEEN BAWN: a Tale, Founded upon Fact

Copy I: First Edition. 3 vols. Hope & Co. 1855. Dark blue ribbed cloth, blocked in blind on front and back, blind-banded and gold-lettered on spine. Primrose end-papers.

Half-title in each vol.

Vol. I xvi + 300
II (iv) + 296
III (iv) + 284

Ink signature: 'A. G. Smith' on fly-leaf of Vol. I. A sound non-library copy which, although slightly darkened, is sharp and firm. For this book (of which in my whole experience I have only seen one other cloth specimen, and that ex-library, stained, loose in covers and imperfect) I venture to claim that the copy described is 'fine'.

[522*a*] **Copy II: Second Edition.** Dublin: Duffy 1857. Yellow pictorial boards. Wood-engraved front. and vignette title after Geo. Measom, on plate paper but reckoned in collation.

pp. 454. Contains a new Preface (pp. (9)–12) dated December 1856.

partly by Carleton

LIFE OF WILLIAM CARLETON (The): being his Autobiography and Letters; and an Account of his Life and Writings, from the point at which the Autobiography breaks off, by David J. O'Donoghue. With an Introduction by Mrs Cashel Hoey [523]

2 vols. Downey & Co., 12 York Street, Covent Garden, 1896. Olive-green buckram, bevelled boards, black end-papers. Half-tone portrait front. in each vol.

Half-title in each vol.

Vol. I lxiv + (292) U_2 adverts. pp. (ix)–xvi Preface; (xvii)–lv Introduction by Mrs Cashel Hoey; (lvi) blank; (lvii)–lxiv Bibliography of Carleton's Writings.
II viii + (364) Bb_2 imprint leaf.

Note. Inasmuch as the whole of Vol. I (prelims. apart) consists of Carleton's hitherto unprinted Autobiography, this book merits record as an item in his bibliography.

For its own sake, also, it cannot be neglected by students of his work. Not only is it based on first-class unpublished material, which makes it the only informative record in existence of the self-tormented life of an unreasonable, feckless, vain, contentious, yet very great writer, but it also provokes an inevitable comparison with *The Life of Holcroft*, which also begins with an unfinished autobiography, followed by its completion by another hand. Hazlitt did his work with an ostentatious dullness in almost tragic contrast to the vigorous simplicity of Holcroft's fragment. The fact that he was a writer of genius rendered his disservice to Holcroft's memory the more lamentable. Mr O'Donoghue, who does not pretend to be a man of letters, who is pedestrian, in a polite way prejudiced, at times repetitive and bibliographically unreliable, is nevertheless carefully self-effacing. Carleton remains as much the central figure of the continuation of the narrative as he is of its opening portion. His vivid and moving account of his childhood and adolescence merges, therefore, agreeably enough into a painstaking and well-documented biography, its individual quality not only unobscured but actually enhanced by the pious self-subordination of its sequel.

The faults in the bibliography in the first volume are clearly due in most cases to failure to locate (or even to realise the existence of) certain issues. O'Donoghue was born in London, and lived there until about 1900 when he went to Ireland. His researches into Carleton were carried out in the B.M. He died in 1917 at the age of fifty-one.

CHAMEROVZOW, LOUIS ALEXIS

[524] YULE LOG (The) for Everybody's Christmas Hearth etc. (by the author of 'The Chronicles of the Bastile')

Fcap 8vo. Newby 1847. Dark blue horizontal-fine-ribbed cloth, pictorially blocked and lettered on front and spine, blind-blocked on front and back. Etched front. and three illustrations by George Cruikshank on plate paper; also wood-engraved pictorial title (preceding printed title) and vignette in the text, both after Cruikshank and on text paper.

Advert. leaf and half-title precede front. and pictorial title. pp. (viii) + (192) N_8 imprint leaf.

Very fine. Pencil signature: 'Radclyffe Walters 1885' facing advert. leaf.

Note. The author's name is incorporated in the design of the pictorial title. The printed title reads as above.

CHAMIER, CAPT. FREDERICK, R.N. (1796–1870)

[525] ARETHUSA (The): a Naval Story

3 vols. Bentley 1837. Boards, labels.

Half-title in each vol.

Vol. I (iv) + (308)
II (iv) + (312) O_{12} blank.
III (iv) + 356

Fine.

[526] BEN BRACE: the Last of Nelson's Agamemnons

3 vols. Bentley 1836. Half-cloth boards, labels.

Half-title in Vols. II and III

Vol. I (ii) + (304) O_8 adverts.
II (iv) + (320)
III (iv) + (336) P_{12} blank.

[527] LIFE OF A SAILOR (The) ('by a Captain in the Navy')

3 vols. Bentley 1832. Boards, labels.

Half-title in Vol. I: advert. leaf precedes title in Vol. II and follows title in III

Vol. I (xvi) [paged (xii)] + (284) Publishers' cat. (Whittaker), 12 pp. undated, at end.
II (iv) + (324)
III (iv) + (316)

[528] MY TRAVELS: or an Unsentimental Journey through France, Switzerland and Italy

3 vols. Hurst and Blackett 1855. Olive-brown morocco cloth; royal-blue end-papers.

Vol. I (ii) + 324 Publishers' cat., 16 pp. undated, at end.
II (ii) + 324 Publishers' cat., 24 pp. dated March 1855, at end.
III (ii) + (342)

Binders' ticket: 'Leighton, Son & Hodge', at end of Vol. I.

SPITFIRE (The): a Tale of the Sea [529]

3 vols. Colburn 1840. Boards, labels. Steel-engraved portrait front. after L. Schmitz and etching by Phiz headed 'Frontispiece Vol. I' (but following title) in Vol. I: etched front. by Phiz in Vols. II and III similarly headed. All three fronts. imprinted and dated 1840.

Vol. I (ii) + (312)
II (ii) + (324)
III (ii) + 328

Title of Vol. III tipped in. Spines of Vols. I and II renewed.

TOM BOWLING: a Tale of the Sea [530]

3 vols. Colburn 1841. Boards, labels.

Half-title in Vols. I and II

Vol. I (iv) + 312 Publisher's cat., 4 pp. undated, precedes half-title.
II (iv) + 332
III (ii) + (312)

Book-plate: Coronet and mitre over 'Virtute non Vi'. Spines and labels renewed.

Edited by Capt. Frederick Chamier

PASSION AND PRINCIPLE: a Novel [531]

3 vols. Colburn 1842. Half-cloth boards, labels.

Vol. I (ii) + 342
II (ii) + (346) First leaf of final sig., Q_1, a single inset.
III (ii) + 324

A poor copy.

CHATTERTON, GEORGIANA, LADY (1806–1876)

Lady Chatterton (*née* Lascelles) was married at seventeen and, until Sir William Chatterton's death in 1855, lived a life of cultivated fashion. She travelled, wrote novels and diaries, painted in oils and water-colours, was a friend of the majority of what nowadays we would call the aristocratic intelligentsia. She was always a religious woman, but did not join the Catholic Church until the year before her death.

Four years after her husband died, she married E. Heneage Dering, and, with him, paid a visit to her niece Rebecca Ferrers, who had married Marmion Ferrers of Baddesley Clinton. The visit developed into permanent residence, and the two couples—Dering and Ferrers—lived a peaceful life, cultivating the arts and gradually withdrawing into a communal mystical retirement. Marmion Ferrers and E. H. Dering wore costumes of the seventeenth century, and Mrs Ferrers painted large portraits and conversation-pieces of her husband and relatives. Lady Chatterton (Mrs Dering) died in 1876 and Marmion Ferrers in 1884. Rebecca Ferrers, his widow, thereupon married E. H. Dering, so that 'Mrs Ferrers' and 'R. Dering' were the same person.

Dering went over to Rome in 1865, and questions of faith and creed preoccupied the household increasingly.

When at last Georgiana Chatterton (as she continued to sign herself) sought admission to the Church, she declared in a letter to Newman, printed by Dering in his *Memoirs of Georgiana, Lady Chatterton* (1878), that her husband's novel *Sherborne* really decided her to take the final step. For this reason I include that story in the entry which follows, under the heading *ana*.

All the titles which follow, with the exception of those marked †, came from Baddesley Clinton Hall, Warwickshire, the home of the families of Dering and Ferrers. Lady Chatterton, after her marriage to E. H. Dering, lived at Baddesley Clinton and died there. The books, therefore, were either her own copies or belonged to her husband.

[532] ALLANSTON, or the Infidel: a Novel ('Edited by Lady Chatterton')

Copy I: First (? private) Edition. 3 vols. Newby 1843. Full vellum, leather lettering piece and gold tooling on spine. Marbled end-papers, sprinkled edges.

Vol. I vi+(360) A_2 a single inset. Q_{11} Q_{12} advert.
II (ii)+(342) Final leaf, Q_3, a single inset.
III (ii)+(364)

[532*a*] **Copy II: Second (? first public) Edition.** 3 vols. Newby 1844. Grey-purple fine-diaper cloth, blocked in blind and lettered in gold. Primrose end-papers, edges uncut.

Collation as Copy I, except that in the prelims. of Vol. I, A_1 is the inset.

Very fine. Unopened.

Note. The portions of Lady Chatterton's diary printed in her husband's memoir state categorically that she was the author of this novel, despite the pretence of 'editorship'. It is only a guess that Copy I was a private edition, predating a public one by one year. But the binding is clearly a presentation one; both I and II came from Baddesley Clinton; and it seems possible that the author hesitated to make formal publication until, at her own expense, she had approved the story in printed form. The sheets of both editions are identical; but the titles differ as to publisher's imprint—those in Copy I reading: LONDON / T. C. NEWBY, 65, MORTIMER STREET. / *rule* / 1843, those in Copy II: LONDON: / T. C. NEWBY, PUBLISHER, / 65, Mortimer Street, Cavendish Square. / *rule* / 1844. It will be noted that in Copy II the title of Vol. I, and not A_2, is the single inset.

[533] AUNT DOROTHY'S TALE or Geraldine Moreton: a Novel [anon]

2 vols. Bentley 1837. Half-cloth boards, labels.

Half-title in each vol.

Vol. I (iv)+(348)
II (iv)+(304)

Inset slip after title in Vol. I apologises, on author's behalf, for bad proof-correcting. Vol. II roughly opened.

CATHEDRAL CLOISTER (The). 'Edited by E. H. Dering') [534]

Art & Book Co. Leamington, n.d. Brown paper boards, printed in green and red. With illustrations in half-tone.

pp. (ii)+136 Very fine.

COMPENSATION: a Story of Real Life Thirty Years Ago [anon] [535]

2 vols. Fcap 8vo. John W. Parker & Son 1856. Claret fine-ripple-grain cloth, blocked in blind on front and back, gold-lettered on spine. Red chocolate end-papers.

Vol. I iv+(316) Publishers' cat., 4 pp. on text paper and undated, at end.
II iv+(312) X_3 X_4 adverts.

Note. I have another copy in which the authorship is authenticated on title by Mrs Ferrers.

COUNTRY COTERIES [536]

3 vols. Hurst & Blackett 1868. Dark blue dot-and-line-grain cloth; chocolate end-papers.

Half-title in each vol.

Vol. I (iv)+(316)
II (iv)+(304)
III (iv)+296 Publishers' cat., 16 pp. undated, at end.

Fine.

EXTRACTS FROM ARISTOTLE'S WORKS ('Selected and translated by Georgiana, Lady Chatterton') [537]

Printed for Private Circulation by J. Masters & Co. New Bond Street 1875. White sand-grain cloth; black end-papers. All edges gilt.

pp. iv+(68) (F_2) blank. Fine.

†GREY'S COURT. ('Edited by Georgiana, Lady Chatterton') [538]

2 vols. Smith, Elder 1865. Grass-green diagonal-fancy-wide-bead-grain cloth.

Half-title in Vol. II

Vol. I (iv)+(324) 21_2 adverts.
II (iv)+(344) 43_4 adverts.

Note. This was the publishers' file copy and only came to light in 1942. Apart from a water-stain on the back of Vol. I, it is in fine condition.

Dering's memoir states that this novel was a collaboration between his wife and himself. Lady Georgiana wrote 'Lora Grey's Diarys' (virtually all of Vol. I) and he wrote the rest.

†HEIRESS AND HER LOVERS (The) [539]

3 vols. Bentley 1863. Maroon dot-and-line grain cloth.

Vol. I (ii)+316
II (ii)+320
III (ii)+302 Final leaf, Y_1, a single inset. B

CHATTERTON

[540] HOME SKETCHES AND FOREIGN RECOLLECTIONS (by Lady Chatterton)
3 vols. Saunders & Otley 1841. Maroon morocco cloth. Tinted lithographic front. and 3 plates in each vol. after (admirable) drawings by the author; also a few cuts in text.

Vol. I vi+300
II iv+(300) O_6 blank.
III iv+(336) P_{10}–P_{12} adverts.

[541] LADY MAY: a Pastoral
Thomas Richardson & Son 1869. Original vellum gilt, bevelled boards, all edges gilt; rose-pink patterned end-papers.

Half-title. pp. (iv)+(112) 7_8 blank. Very fine.

[542] LOST BRIDE (The)
3 vols. Hurst & Blackett 1872. Green fine-ribbed cloth; dark rose-pink end-papers.

Half-title in each vol.

Vol. I (iv)+308
II (iv)+(312)
III (iv)+320 Publishers' cat., 16 pp. undated, at end.

Cloth fine. Some pages in Vol. I roughly opened.

[543] PYRENEES (The) with Excursions into Spain (by Lady Chatterton)
2 vols. 8vo. Saunders & Otley 1843. Plum fine-diaper cloth, blocked in blind on front and back, blind-banded on spine and gold-lettered: THE / PYRENEES / AND / SPAIN etc. Coloured lithographic front. and 7 plates in each vol. after drawings by the author.

Half-title in each vol.

Vol. I (x) [paged (viii)]+(384) Half-title a single inset.
II (viii) [paged vi]+(404) [paged (406)] (D_1) (D_2) [pp. (401)–(404)] adverts. Sig. A, one leaf, is, although paged (1) 2, in fact the final leaf [pp. (vii) (viii)] of the prelims. Sig. B is paged 3–18.

Faded strip along top of covers; otherwise very fine.

Note. Lady Chatterton's quality as a landscape artist is well shown by the excellent lithographs in these volumes.

[544] RAMBLES IN THE SOUTH OF IRELAND DURING THE YEAR 1838 (by Lady Chatterton)
2 vols. Saunders & Otley 1839. Grass-green ribbed cloth. Tinted lithographic front. and 3 plates in each vol. after drawings by the author; also cuts in text. The plates are imprinted and dated 1839.

Half-title in each vol.

Vol. I (xii)+(336) P_{11} P_{12} adverts.
II (viii)+328

Extensively corrected for second edition by one 'S.A.MB.' whose initials are on outside covers.

WON AT LAST [545]
3 vols. Hurst & Blackett 1874. Chocolate diagonal-fine-ribbed cloth; greenish-black end-papers.

Half-title in each vol.

Vol. I (iv)+300
II (iv)+(304)
III (iv)+304 Publishers' cat., 16 pp. dated January 1873, at end.

Ink signature: 'R. Dering, Baddesley Clinton', on half-title of Vol. I. Fine.

ana

SHERBORNE; OR, THE HOUSE AT THE FOUR WAYS. By EDWARD HENEAGE DERING. [546]
3 vols. Smith, Elder 1875. Cherry-red diagonal-fine-ribbed cloth blocked and lettered in black on front, in gold on spine, blind-blocked on back.

Half-title in each vol.

Vol. I (iv)+(296) U_4 blank.
II (iv)+296 Slip of 'Errata to Vol. II' precedes p. (1).
III (iv)+(332) Y_6 blank.

Fine.

Notes. (i) On the title-page Dering claims the authorship of *Grey's Court* (q.v. above).
(ii) The story is a protracted argument between suavely ingenious Catholics, and Protestants who are at best dialectically incompetent, at worst merely comic. All belong to the landed gentry, and there is sufficient pother over a disputed inheritance to carry the controversy through three stout volumes. Finally: 'There are four of us here' says Mrs Atherstone, 'whose life has been in different ways influenced by the ownership of a property—The House at the Four Ways. Now all four of us have had to do with another sort of meeting of the ways. We have all come by different roads into the unity of the Church.'

CHESNEY, GENERAL SIR GEORGE (1830–1895)

LESTERS (The), or a Capitalist's Labour [547]
3 vols. Smith, Elder 1893. Smooth brown cloth, blocked and lettered in dark blue on front, gold-lettered on spine.

Half-title in each vol.

Vol. I (iv)+(300)
II (iv)+(308) X_2 adverts.
III (iv)+(292) U_2 adverts.

Note. General Chesney became well known as the author of *The Battle of Dorking* (1871), an account of an imaginary invasion of England, designed to urge the cause of National Defence through the Volunteer movement. *The Lesters* is also a propaganda work—this time on behalf of the control of speculative building, especially in the suburbs. Wimbledon is quoted as a typical case of tasteless crowded development. Improvement is to be carried out by an enlightened millionaire, who will unite business sense with public spirit; and the novel leaves him prepared to tackle rural housing on the same lines.

CHOLMONDELEY, MARY (1859–1925)

This is a complete collection of the first editions (one rebound) of Mary Cholmondeley. She is an excellent example of the not-so-long-ago front-rank novelist, whose books in good condition are extraordinarily difficult to find. Thanks to the Bentley file, and to the presence in a bookshop of a number of novels from the library of Mr Edward Dent (among them several of the later Cholmondeleys), I have been able to reach a high level. Specimens seen elsewhere could be numbered on one hand, and were far from attractive.

With Rhoda Broughton, an analogous case, I have also been fortunate; but to what shifts one is driven without the help of windfalls, when collecting the books of the 1890's and early 1900's by established and popular novelists, is demonstrated by the imperfect showing achieved on behalf of Mrs Oliphant and Mrs Riddell.

[548] DANVERS JEWELS (The) [anon]

Copy I: First Edition. n.d. [1887]. Blue-grey wrappers (indescribable because never seen).

pp. (128)

The copy in the Collection is in binder's cloth. Book-plate of Laurence Hardy; ink-signature 'Evelyn Hardy 1891' on fly-leaf.

[548*a*] **Copy II: 'New Edition'.** Bentley 1898. Ochre diagonal-fine-ribbed cloth.

Blank leaf and half-title precede title. pp. (viii) + (224). B

The authorship is avowed in this edition.

[549] DEVOTEE (A): an Episode in the Life of a Butterfly

Arnold 1897. Greenish-grey ribbed cloth, blocked in dark grey and lettered in gold.

Half-title. pp. (224) 14_3–14_8 adverts.

[550] DIANA TEMPEST

3 vols. Bentley 1893.

Pl. 12 **Copy I: First Edition.** Half grey-blue cloth, flowered board sides—blue flowers on an ochre ground; monogram end-papers. Titles printed in red and black.

Half-title in each vol.

Vol. I (viii) + 296
II (iv) + (272) 36_8 blank.
III (iv) + (268) B

Copy II: Second Edition. Three-quarter smooth apple-green cloth, dark olive-green cloth sides; monogram end-papers. Titles in black only.

Half-title in each vol. Collation as Copy I. B

LOWEST RUNG (The). Together with THE HAND ON THE LATCH, ST LUKE'S SUMMER and THE UNDERSTUDY [551]

John Murray 1908. Smooth greenish-buff linen-grain cloth, blocked and lettered in dark green and white.

Half-title. pp. (184) 23_4 adverts. Fine.

MOTH AND RUST. Together with GEOFFREY'S WIFE and THE PITFALL [552]

John Murray 1902. Light grey-green linen-grain cloth, blocked in white and gold and lettered in gold. Title printed in red and black.

Blank leaf and half-title precede title. pp. (xii) + (320) U_5 U_6 adverts., U_7 imprint leaf, U_8 blank.

Blind stamp: 'W. H. Smith & Son', on fly-leaf.

NOTWITHSTANDING

John Murray 1913. Smooth powder-blue linen-grain cloth, lettered in gold. [553]

Half-title. pp. (vi) + (386) 25_2–25_4 adverts.

Spine faded.

PRISONERS (fast bound in Misery and Iron) [554]

Hutchinson 1906. Smooth claret cloth, lettered in gold.

Blank leaf and half-title precede title. pp. (viii) + (344) 22_4 adverts.

Publishers' cat., 24 pp. on text paper dated August 1906, at end.

Note. E. F. Benson in *Final Edition* (1940) records that the publication of PRISONERS got the author into bad trouble with a large number of her middle-aged bachelor friends.

'About a hundred claimed or complained that they were her models for one of the gentry whom with manifest glee she exhibited in this book as a selfish and complacent prig. She protested that she had none of them in mind when she invented the peculiarly odious character Wentworth, who was the making of her book. She ought to have left it at that. Instead, stimulated perhaps by the resentment of her victims, she retorted that now her attention had been called to this undesigned resemblance she saw it herself. Now they had put on the cap, she admitted that it fitted them admirably.

'My brother Arthur became the test case among the injured. He had been great friends with her and they had had many sibylline talks together and now she had put verbatim into the mouth of Wentworth many of his contributions to these conversations.... My mother thought that Arthur had been grossly caricatured, but she remained on perfectly friendly terms with Mary, slightly amused at the hullaballoo. Arthur, however, was not at all amused. He was hurt and angry and never visited her again.'

[555] RED POTTAGE
Edward Arnold 1899. Dark red ribbed cloth.

Pl. 12 Blank leaf and half-title precede title. pp. (viii) + (376) Text ends $2A_3$, $2A_4$ Postscript.

Publisher's cat., 32 pp. dated October 1899, at end. 'M.S.S. 1899' in ink on fly-leaf.

[556] ROMANCE OF HIS LIFE (The) and other Romances
John Murray 1921. Smooth grey-green linen-grain cloth, blocked and lettered in black.

Half-title. pp. (256) A_1 A_2 form front end-papers, Q_7 Q_8 back end-papers.

As new, with picture jacket.

[557] SIR CHARLES DANVERS (by the author of 'The Danvers Jewels')
2 vols. Bentley 1889. Greenish-blue diagonal-fine-ribbed cloth.

Half-title in Vol. II

Vol. I (iv) + (284)
II (iv) + (304) B

The titles are cancels. Possibly they originally bore the rejected title: *Deceivers Ever*, or alternatively the author's name. B.P.C. does not explain.

[558] UNDER ONE ROOF: a Family Record
Small square 8vo. John Murray 1918. Smooth mauve linen-grain cloth, blocked and lettered in dark blue. Line-block front. on text paper of Hodnet Rectory, after a sketch by Hester Cholmondeley.

Half-title. pp. (xviii) + (192) [paged (xviii) + 1–166] This pagination ignores blanks. In fact, the book collates in eights from 1–12. 1_1 1_2 form *front* end-papers, 12_7 12_8 *back* end-papers.

As new, with picture jacket.

CHORLEY, HENRY F. (1808–1872) [559]

LION (The): a Tale of the Coteries
3 vols. Colburn 1839. Half-cloth boards, labels.

Vol. I (xii) + 296
II (iv) + (318) Final leaf, P_1, a single inset.
III (iv) + 302 First leaf of final sig., O_1, a single inset.

This novel is dedicated to Lady Blessington.

CLARKE, MARCUS (1846–1881)

HIS NATURAL LIFE [560]

Copy I: First Edition. Melbourne: George Robertson 1874. Grass-green diagonal-fine-ribbed cloth, blocked in black and gold; grey-chocolate end-papers. Pl. 9

pp. viii + 480 (pp. (477)–480 Appendix). Publisher's cat., 12 pp. dated January 1874, at end.

Booksellers' ticket: 'F. W. Arthur. Carlisle', inside front cover. Fine.

Copy II: First English Edition. 3 vols. Bentley 1875. Dark red diagonal-fine-ribbed cloth, blocked in black and gold. No author on spines. [560*a*]

Vol. I viii + (320) 20_8 adverts. Pl. 9
II iv + 326 First leaf of final sig., 21_1, a single inset.
III iv + 322 Text ends p. 317; (318)–322 Appendix. Final leaf, 21_1, a single inset. B

Notes. (i) A secondary binding of green cloth lacks ornate blocking and carries name: 'M. CLARKE' on spines. With the first one-vol. edition (Bentley's Favourite Novels, 1878) the title was elaborated to *For the Term of his Natural Life*.

(ii) Two letters from Marcus Clarke to Messrs Bentley & Son throw an interesting light on the history of this famous novel.

The Public Library
Melbourne
Victoria.

30th Dec. 1874

Dear Sirs,

I have received through Messrs Baillière of this city, London and Paris, an intimation from Mr Sterry (of Messrs Kelly & Co. Lincolns Inn) that your firm would publish my novel 'His Natural Life' and secure me the copyright, provided that certain alteration was made in the end of the story.

Mr Sterry informs me that it is your wish that the book ends happily, and suggests to me to correct the sheets accordingly. I have by this mail forwarded to Mr Sterry the last pages of the novel altered as he desires, and concluding with an additional chapter putting that pleasant construction upon events which I believe you think to be best suited to your purchasers.

The story—if you will recall it—originally ended in the death of the hero and the death of the woman whom he loves. Mr Sterry informs me that you object to that end. It would be monstrous to make the hero—a convict—*marry* his love, so I have given the woman a daughter and contrived that the hero shall rescue that daughter from death and see in her the mother whom he once loved.

As I have informed Mr Sterry by this mail, I desire *that the correction which I send him be the only correction in the novel.* Unless you can see your way to publish 'His Natural Life' as I have written it (replacing the original end by the MS sent to Mr Sterry) and retaining the Appendices etc. I would rather not have it re-published at all. I hope however that the MS and this letter may arrive in time to prevent any correction by a strange hand.

Mr Sterry gives me—through Mr Baillière—to understand, that you give no price for the book, but publish an edition at your own cost, securing to *me* the copyright of future editions. I shall be glad to have a reply from you to this note.

I am, dear sirs, Yours faithfully,
Marcus Clarke.

21st April 1875

Dear Sirs,

This letter will be enclosed to you by Mr George Robertson the Melbourne publisher of my novel 'His Natural Life'.

Mr Sterry writes to say that you expressed yourself willing to print the work for library circulation in England in the customary 3 vols. on the following terms:

£50 on publication
£50 on sale of 750 copies
£50 for every other 250 copies sold

but that this offer being contingent upon the fact that Mr Robertson send *no* copies for sale in England.

I was ignorant of the condition and asked Mr Robertson to send home some copies for review. He sent home 250 which did not sell (one vol. 8vo. 488 pages 7/6*d.*) nor did any English journal review the work. Mr Robertson will, however, withdraw the copies from the market if you will publish the book.

Will you oblige me by making terms with his London agent and bring out the book? I have authorised Mr Robertson to do the best he can with the book, and to receive any money paid for its republication.

Sir Charles Gavan Duffy, writes me by the mail to say that he had—through Mrs Cashel Hoey—communicated with you. I have written to him to tell him the arrangement I have made with Mr Robertson, and to ask him to see you himself.

I am, my dear sirs, faithfully yours
Marcus Clarke.

After all this, Bentley published the Australian text with no alteration whatsoever—a fact of which the compilers of the Private Catalogue were clearly unaware, for they say that the original Melbourne edition (which they ascribe to the wrong publisher) was 'very different' from the Bentley three-decker. Clearly they never saw a copy of the Australian edition, guessed at the publisher and took the above two letters at face-value.

LONG ODDS: a Novel [561]

8vo. Melbourne: Clarson, Massina & Co. 1869. Dark green diagonal-fine-ribbed cloth, blocked in black and gold. Wood-engraved front. and 7 illustrations after Thomas Carrington.

Half-title. pp. xii + 344

'A. Robson' in pencil on fly-leaf. Fine.

CLIFFORD, LUCY (MRS W. K. CLIFFORD) (*circ.* 1860–1929) [562]

AUNT ANNE

2 vols. Bentley 1892. Smooth dark blue cloth; monogram end-papers. Edges salmon-yellow, printed with dark blue filigree design.

Half-title in each vol.

Vol. I (iv) + (308)
II (iv) + (312) **B**

LAST TOUCHES (The) and Other Stories [563]

Adam & Charles Black 1892. Royal blue morocco cloth, blocked in black and lettered in gold.

Half-title. pp. (viii) + (244) 16_2 advert. Publishers' cat., 56 pp. undated, at end.

MRS KEITH'S CRIME: a Record [anon] [564]

2 vols. Bentley 1885. Dark blue diaper cloth, bevelled boards; floral end-papers.

Blank leaf precedes title in Vol. II

Vol. I (iv) + (276)
II (iv) + (292) **B**

CLIVE, CAROLINE (MRS ARCHER CLIVE) (1801–1873) [565]

PAUL FERROLL: a Tale (by the author of 'IX Poems by V')

Saunders & Otley 1855. Blue ribbed cloth.

Half-title. pp. (iv) + 336 Publishers' cat., 4 pp. undated, at end.

Loose in cover.

[566] POEMS (by the author of 'Paul Ferroll'). Including a new edition of 'IX Poems by V' with former and recent additions

Fcap 8vo. Saunders & Otley 1856. Blue ribbed cloth.

Half-title. pp. (vi) [paged iv]+(236) Q_4–Q_6 adverts.

Note. In 1928 a new edition of *IX Poems by V* was published by the Scholartis Press, with an interesting and valuable essay on Mrs Archer Clive by Eric Partridge.

[567] WHY PAUL FERROLL KILLED HIS WIFE (by the author of 'Paul Ferroll')

Saunders & Otley 1860. Blue morocco cloth.

pp. (ii)+(342) First leaf of final sig., P_1, a single inset. Publishers' cat., 4 pp. on text paper undated, at end.

Book-plate of Augustine Birrell. Binder's ticket: 'Burn', at end. Part of front end-paper cut away.

COBBOLD, REV. RICHARD (1797–1877)

This is a complete collection of the *fiction* by Richard Cobbold in first edition. Of his non-fiction titles, poetry and prose, four are lacking.

For convenience sake, and to demonstrate the popularity of this strange author-illustrator, I have included in this entry boarded and wrappered re-issues which belong properly to Section II. Cobbold was a member of a prominent and wealthy Suffolk family, the son of a poetess well-known in her day, and his legend was still alive in East Anglia when war broke out in 1939.

[568] CHARACTER OF WOMAN (The). A Lecture delivered April 13, 1848

8vo. Diss: Printed for the author, n.d. [presumably 1848]. Sky-blue ribbed cloth, gilt.

pp. 64 [paged (i)–(viii)+(9)–64]

Binders' ticket: 'Remnant and Edmonds', at end. Fine.

[569] FRESTON TOWER, or the Early Days of Cardinal Wolsey

Copy I: First Edition. 3 vols. Colburn 1850. Grass-green ribbed cloth. Etched front. in each vol., two other plates in Vol. I and one other in Vol. III by Alfred Ashley.

Half-title in Vol. II

Vol. I (viii)+320
II (iv)+(288)
III (ii)+288 Publisher's cat., 16 pp. undated, at end.

Pencil-signature: 'Reed' (on recto of front or half-title) in each vol. Fine.

Copy II: 'Run and Read Library' Edition. [569*a*]
Simpkin, Marshall & Co., n.d. (1856). Light blue glazed boards, printed in dark blue. Wood-engraved front. and pictorial title precede printed title.

Preface, although dated January 15, 1856, is identical with that in first edition, except that three lines are added at the end referring to the gift by the author of any profits of this edition to the East Suffolk Hospital.

A volume in the 'Run and Read Library' (3673 (18) in Section II), whose series title appears on front cover and spine. Published at 1*s*. 6*d*.

GEOFFERY GAMBADO, or a Simple Remedy [570]
for Hypochondriacism and Melancholy Splenetic Humours ('by a Humourist Physician')

Small 4to. Printed for the author by Dean & Son, n.d. Green sand-grain cloth, all edges gilt. 18 lithographic plates, tinted in pink, 16 of which are apparently after re-drawings by Cobbold of original sketches by Henry Bunbury, for each is signed 'Henry Bunbury inv^{t}' and initialled 'R.C.'

pp. 116

HISTORY OF MARGARET CATCHPOLE [571]
(The): a Suffolk Girl [anon]

Copy I: First Edition. 3 vols. Colburn 1845. Plum weave-grain cloth. Engraved front. in each vol., 2 other plates in Vols. I and III and 1 other in Vol. II after drawings by the author.

Vol. I xii+316
II (iv)+(292)
III iv+284 Publisher's cat., 24 pp. dated 1845, at end.

Ink signature: 'Agnes Moore, 19th April 1845', inside front cover or on verso of front. in each vol. Fine.

Copy II: 'Twentieth Thousand'. Small 8vo. [571*a*]
Ward Lock & Tyler, n.d. [? circ. 1870]. Bright blue sand-grain cloth, bevelled boards; all edges gilt. Tinted lithographic front.

Ink signature: 'M. H. Shaw. Dec. 15, 1870', on fly-leaf. Fine.

JACK RATTLER, or the Horrors of Transporta- [572]
tion. A Memoir of his Life, written in the year 1852 by John Rattler Esq. a Pauper in the Scorpion Union House

A 4to MS. of 233 pages (29 chapters), all in Cobbold's hand, bound in royal blue morocco cloth, blocked and lettered in gold on front and spine. All edges gilt.

Note. This is a complete unpublished novel based on the real life-story of an ex-convict and dedicated to 'The Judges of Old England'. Cobbold's name appears nowhere on the MS., but the pedigree (it came from the family) and the handwriting make the authorship certain.

It may be noted that Cobbold originally called his hero 'Bragg', but when he had reached Chapter 18 altered the name (probably to avoid confusion with Hook's novel). Throughout the first part of the MS. 'Rattler' is substituted for 'Bragg'.

[573] MARY ANNE WELLINGTON: the Soldier's Daughter, Wife and Widow

Copy I: First Edition. 3 vols. Colburn 1846. Claret weave-grain cloth. Engraved front. in each vol., 1 other plate in Vols. I and III and 3 others in Vol. II after drawings by the author.

Half-title in Vol. I

Vol. I (xii) + 300
II (ii) + (300)
III (ii) + 236 Publisher's cat., 24 pp. undated, at end.

Fine.

[573*a*] **Copy II: 'New and Improved Edition.'** Clarke, Beeton & Co. 1853. Royal-blue glazed boards, printed in black. Wood-engraved front. and pictorial title precede printed title. Published at 1*s*. 6*d*. See 3673 (6) in Section II.

[573*b*] **Copy III: 'Rose Library' Edition.** Small 8vo. Ward Lock & Tyler, n.d. Series style paper wrappers, florally printed in colours, cut flush. A volume in the Rose Library, published at 1*s*.

[574] ORIGINAL, SERIOUS AND RELIGIOUS POETRY

Ipswich: R. Deck 1827. Half-cloth boards, label. Half-title. pp. viii + 224.

[575] VALENTINE VERSES: or Lines of Truth, Love and Virtue

8vo. Ipswich: E. Shalders 1827. Half-linen boards, label. 2 engraved portraits and numerous lithographed plates by the author.

Half-title. pp. (xviii) [paged (xvi)] + 262 Errata slip inset between back end-papers.

[576] ZENON THE MARTYR: a Record of the Piety, Patience and Persecution of the Early Christian Nobles

Copy I: First Edition. 3 vols. Colburn 1847. Half-cloth boards, labels.

Half-titles in Vols. I and II

Vol. I xii + (244)
II (iv) + (236)
III (ii) + (304)

The second leaf of prelims. in Vol. III was almost certainly label-leaf. The stub remains in this copy.

[576*a*] **Copy II: 'Run and Read' Library: New Edition.** Clarke and Beeton 1855. Pale green glazed boards, printed in black. Wood-engraved front. and pictorial title precede printed title.

Booksellers' ticket: 'Mann Nephews', inside front cover. A volume in the 'Run and Read Library', whose series title appears on front cover and spine. Published at 1*s*. 6*d*.

Edited by Richard Cobbold

COURTLAND: a Novel ('By the daughter of Mary Anne Wellington. Edited by the Rev. Richard Cobbold') [576 *bis*]

3 vols. Newby 1852. Light ochre morocco cloth.

Leaf of adverts. (dated Feb. 28, 1852, in Vols. I and II) precedes title in each vol.

Vol. I (iv) + (300)
II (iv) + (288)
III (iv) + (372) R_6 adverts.

Oval book-plate, crest over 'C', in Vol. I.

Note. According to *C.B.E.L.* this novel was 'largely written by Cobbold'.

JOHN H. STEGGALL: a Real History of a Suffolk Man (edited by the author of 'Margaret Catchpole') [577]

Copy I: First Edition. Simpkin Marshall 1857. Brown morocco cloth, gold-lettered on front: 'THE HISTORY OF A SUFFOLK MAN'; on spine: 'LIFE OF J. H. STEGGALL'. Wood-engraved front. and vignette title on plate paper.

pp. 312 [paged (i)–(viii) + 9–312]

Ink signature: 'J. Shaw', on fly-leaf.

Copy II: 'Enlarged Edition', under new title: THE SUFFOLK GIPSY. Ward & Lock, n.d. Yellow pictorial boards. (Library of Popular Authors.) [577*a*]

COLLINS, MORTIMER (1827–1876)

IVORY GATE (The) [578]

2 vols. Hurst & Blackett 1869. Smooth orange-scarlet cloth; greenish-black end-papers.

Half-title in each vol.

Vol. I (vi) + 328
II (iv) + 310 First leaf of final signature, X_1, a single inset. Text ends p. 308. Pp. 309, 310 'Epilogue' (in verse). Publishers' cat., 16 pp. undated, at end.

Cloth a little dust-soiled.

MARQUIS AND MERCHANT [579]

3 vols. Hurst & Blackett 1871. Plum sand-grain cloth; greenish-black end-papers.

Half-title in each vol.

Vol. I (vi) + (322) Final leaf, (Y_1), a single inset.
II (iv) + 312
III (iv) + (320) Publishers' cat., 16 pp. dated January 1871, at end.

Presentation Copy: 'George and Josephine Stevens from Mortimer and Frances Collins' in ink on half-title of Vol. I.

[580] SQUIRE SILCHESTER'S WHIM

3 vols. H. S. King 1873. Red fine-morocco cloth; greenish-black end-papers.

Half-title in Vols. I and III

Vol. I (viii) + (260) Publishers' cat., 32 pp. dated November 1872, at end.
II (iv) + (248)
III vi + (250) pp. (249) (250) carry a poem (misprinted: THE IDYL OF THE BBIDGE) with printers' imprint on verso.

Note. My former copy of this novel (in poor condition) showed a fly-leaf variant in each vol. The end-papers were dead-black and blank on verso. In the present copy, each verso of the greenish-black fly-leaf carries a panel-advert.—in Vol. I, of Collins' *Inn of Strange Meetings*; in Vol. II, of his *Princess Clarice*; in Vol. III, of *The Secret of Long Life* [anon]. As the cat. in Vol. I of the former copy was dated February 1873 and the volumes carried an inscription from Frances Collins to Percy Cotton dated 1877, it may, I think, be presumed that the greenish-black end-papers printed on verso are signs of a first issue.

[581] SWEET AND TWENTY

3 vols. Hurst & Blackett 1875. Green sand-grain cloth; rose-pink end-papers.

Half-title in each vol.

Vol. I (vi) + (288)
II (iv) + (272)
III (iv) + (262) Final sig., S, 2 leaves + single inset leaf, serving as fly-title to publishers' cat., 16 pp. undated, at end of vol.

Binders' ticket: 'Leighton, Son & Hodge', at the end of Vol. I. 'Dodgson' in ink on half-title of Vol. I.

[582] SWEET ANNE PAGE

3 vols. Hurst & Blackett 1868. Magenta moiré fine-ribbed cloth.

Half-title in each vol.

Vol. I (iv) + 308
II (iv) + (304) U_8 blank.
III (iv) + (280) T_4 serves as fly-title to publishers' cat., 16 pp. on text paper undated, at end.

Book-plate, 'Malo Mori Quam Fœdari' (V. de Payen Payne), in Vol. I. Two A.L.s in Collins' hand signed 'Anak' and addressed to 'My dear Chang' (i.e. J. Bertrand Payne) inserted in Vol. I. Covers dull and a little darkened and some signatures loose, but an honest, untouched copy of a very rare novel, which was undoubtedly 'Chang's' own copy inherited by his son V. de Payen Payne.

Note. See S. M. Ellis, *Wilkie Collins, Le Fanu and Others*, London, 1931, pp. 83 seq. for facts regarding the suppression of *Sweet Anne Page*, and the friendship between 'Chang' and 'Anak'.

TWO PLUNGES FOR A PEARL [583]

3 vols. Tinsley 1872.

Half-title in each vol.

Vol. I (viii) + (226) Final leaf, (Q_1), a single inset.
II (vi) + 216
III (vi) + (218) First leaf of final three-leaf sig., P_1, a single inset. pp. (215)–(218) 2 leaves of adverts. paged 1–4.

Copy I: Presentation binding. Bright green morocco cloth, blocked in gold on front and spine; grey-chocolate end-papers, all edges gilt.

Presentation Copy: 'George and Josephine Stevens from Mortimer and Frances Collins' in ink on half-title of Vol. I and 8 lines of verse on Dedication page. Very fine.

Copy II: Regular binding. Red fine-morocco cloth, blind-blocked on front in Tinsley's advertisement style, publicising *Tinsley's Magazine.* Pale yellow end-papers. [583*a*]

Book-plate of A. H. Christie in each vol. Covers worn. This novel has a Swinburne interest.

VILLAGE COMEDY (The) ('by Mortimer and Frances† Collins') [584]

3 vols. Hurst & Blackett 1878. Green diagonal-fine-ribbed cloth; plum end-papers.

Half-title in each vol.

Vol. I (vi) + (312)
II (iv) + (300)
III (iv) + (306) Final leaf, X_1 a single inset. Publishers' cat., 16 pp. undated, at end.

Book-plate of Charles J. Billson in each vol.

VIVIAN ROMANCE (The) [585]

3 vols. Hurst & Blackett 1870. Plum bubble-grain cloth, bevelled boards. 'R.D.B. / FROM / M.C.' in gold on front covers. All edges gilt; black end-papers.

Half-title in each vol.

Vol. I (vi) + (320)
II (iv) + (320)
III (iv) + (304)

Binders' ticket: 'Leighton, Son & Hodge', at end of Vols. II and III. This is a specially bound copy, prepared for presentation to the dedicatee R. D. Blackmore.

YOU PLAY ME FALSE ('by Mortimer and Frances† Collins') [586]

3 vols. Bentley 1878. Grey diagonal-fine-ribbed cloth.

Vol. I (vi) + 268
II (iv) + (268)
III (iv) + 282 Final leaf, 52_5, a single inset. B

† Frances Collins, née Cotton, lived till 1886.

COLLINS, W. WILKIE (1824–1889)

For further bibliographical detail, see *Wilkie Collins and Charles Reade* by M. L. Parrish, London, 1940. The references which follow are to this work.

[587] AFTER DARK [*Parrish* p. 26
2 vols. Smith, Elder 1856. Dark green wavy-grain cloth.

Half-title in each vol.

Vol. I viii + (316) Publishers' cat., 16 pp. dated April 1856, at end.
II (iv) + (324) X_2 advert. Prelims. of this vol. are on a whiter paper than the rest of the work.

Binders' ticket: 'Westleys', at end of Vol. I. Facing half-title of Vol. II in ink: 'Adelaide Dorothea Forbes. Dec. 1857', 'Lady Selina Henry', 'Eva G. Henry' (the first two names scored through). Fine.

[588] ARMADALE
Demy 8vo. 2 vols. Smith, Elder 1866. Bright brown fine-morocco cloth, pictorially blocked and lettered in gold on front with triple framing in blind, decoratively blocked and lettered in gold on spine, blind blocked with triple framing on back. Pale yellow end-papers. Wood-engraved front. in each vol., and in Vol. I, 8, in Vol. II, 10 illustrations, all after George H. Thomas and all on plate paper.

Vol. I (viii) + 304
II (iv) + (372)

Bookplate of Agnes E. Barker; ink signature 'Mrs T. R. Barker, The Edge', and book-label of Hugh Walpole, in each vol.

Very fine. This is the only fine copy of this book I have ever seen. A comment on its rarity will be found below, under 'Collins', in the sub-section 'Comparative Scarcities'.

[589] BASIL: a Story of Modern Life (by W. Wilkie Collins) [*Parrish* p. 18
3 vols. Bentley 1852.

Copy I: Half-cloth boards, labels.

Half-title in Vol. I

Vol. I 300 [paged (i)–(xxiv) + (25)–300]
II (ii) + (304)
III (ii) + (302) First leaf of final signature, P_1, a single inset.

Ink signature: 'Edward T. W. Wood. Nov. 1854', on fly-leaf of each vol. Inner front hinge and final page of Vol. II repaired.

[589*a*] **Copy II:** Bright blue ripple-grain cloth; terra-cotta end-papers. Collation as Copy I.

Oval blind stamp, coronet over S.C.S. in monogram, on fly-leaf of each vol.

DEAD SECRET (The) [*Parrish* p. 30 [590]
2 vols. Bradbury & Evans 1857. Grey-purple morocco cloth.

Half-title in Vol. I

Vol. I viii + (304)
II (iv) + (332)

Ink signature: 'Emily Louisa Fitzroy', on title-page of each vol. Fine. Spines a little faded.

FROZEN DEEP (The), and other Stories [591]
[*Parrish* p. 61

Copy I: First Edition. 2 vols. Bentley 1874. Bright blue sand-grain cloth, bevelled boards.

Half-title in each vol., that in Vol. II preceded by leaf printed with advert. on verso.

Vol. I viii + 248
II (viii) [paged vi] + (284) U_2 adverts.

Binders' ticket: 'Leighton, Son & Hodge', at end of Vol. I. **B**

MS. comment in George Bentley's hand on p. 5 of Vol. I directing a re-arrangement of type and spacing. In no first edition seen by me was this re-arrangement carried out.

Copy II: First American and First Illustrated Edition. Boston: William F. Gill & Co. 1875. Grass-green dotted-line-ribbed cloth, pictorially blocked and fancy-lettered in gold and black on front and spine. Wood-engraved front. and 3 illustrations after Alfred Fredericks, all on plate paper. [591*a*]

pp. (240) 20_6 blank.

Ink signature: 'F. W. Cram' on fly-leaf.

Pages 185–237 are occupied by *A Terribly Strange Bed*, first published in 1856 in *After Dark*. A Publisher's Note states that this story has not previously been printed in any authorised American edition of Collins' work.

GUILTY RIVER (The) [*Parrish* p. 120 [592]
Bristol: Arrowsmith 1886. Cream paper wrappers printed on front in black, blue and yellow, elsewhere in black only. Spine, outside back and both inside covers printed with adverts (commercial).

pp. (viii) [(i)–(vi) adverts., (vii) title, (viii) advert.] + (200) [13_7 13_8 and 14_1–14_8 adverts., mostly commercial].

Arrowsmith's Christmas Annual for 1886. Re-issued 1887 as No. 19 in Arrowsmith's Bristol Library.

HIDE AND SEEK (by W. Wilkie Collins) [593]
3 vols. Bentley 1854. [*Parrish* p. 22

Copy I: Half-cloth boards, labels.

Half-title in each vol.

Vol. I viii + (300) Text ends 295, 296–297 Note to Chapter VIII, (298) blank, (299) (300), O_6, adverts. dated June 1854.

Vol. II (iv)+(324) P_6 adverts, dated June 1854.
III (iv)+332

Copy II: Light pinkish-brown wavy-grain cloth.

Both copies fine.

[594] LAW AND THE LADY (The): a Novel [*Parrish* p. 94

3 vols. Chatto & Windus 1875. Grass-green diagonal-fine-ribbed cloth, blocked in blind on front and back, gold-lettered on spine.

Vol. I (viii)+(248) R_4 advert. Publishers' cat., 40 pp. dated December 1874, at end.
II iv+(272) S_8 advert.
III iv+(344) Z_4 advert.

Binders' ticket: 'Leighton, Son & Hodge' at end of Vol. I. Book-plates of Pickford Waller and Oliver Brett (Lord Esher). Fine. Slight denting at one or two places by auctioneer's string.

[595] LEGACY OF CAIN (The) [*Parrish* p. 126

3 vols. Chatto & Windus 1889. Ultramarine fine-morocco cloth; pale grey floral end-papers.

Half-title in each vol.

Vol. I viii+(290) Final leaf, unsigned, a single inset.
II vi+(264)
III vi+(282) Final leaf, 53_5, a single inset. Publishers' cat., 32 pp. dated October 1888, at end.

Presentation Copy: 'To A. P. Watt from Wilkie Collins, 11th Decr 1888' in ink on p. (v). Fine. Presented to me by W. P. Watt, son of the recipient.

[596] LITTLE NOVELS [*Parrish* p. 123

3 vols. Chatto & Windus 1887. Bright blue smooth fine-morocco cloth; grey floral end-papers.

Half-title in each vol., that in Vol. III preceded by a blank leaf.

Vol. I (vi)+(320)
II (vi)+(332)
III (viii)+(304) Publishers' cat., 32 pp. dated April 1887, at end.

Fine.

[597] MISS OR MRS? and other Stories in Outline [*Parrish* p. 86

Bentley 1873. Brown sand-grain cloth.

pp. viii+(328) Y_4 advert.

Presentation Copy: 'To F. Carr Beard from Wilkie Collins January 18th 1873' in ink on title.

Spine darkened and covers a bit dulled.

[598] MOONSTONE (The): a Romance

3 vols. Tinsley 1868.

Copy I: First Edition. Purple sand-grain cloth. [*Parrish* p. 72

Half-title in each vol., that in Vol. II preceded by leaf of adverts.

Vol. I viii+(316)
II (vi)+(298) First leaf of final sig., U_1, a single inset, originally conjugate with (i), (ii) (i.e. advert. leaf) which is also a single inset.
III (iv)+(312) X_4 adverts.

'J. K. July', on inside cover of Vol. I, which was not originally part of the same set as Vols. II and III, nor as fine as they.

Copy II: Second Edition. [*Not in Parrish* [598*a*]

Binding as Copy I, except for SECOND EDITION on spines. Collation as Copy I, except that the prelims. of Vol. II are only pp. (iv) and the advert. leaf appears as U_6 at the end, conjugate with U_1. 'Library B' in pencil on each fly-leaf.

MY MISCELLANIES [*Parrish* p. 51 [599]

2 vols. Sampson Low 1863. Grass-green diagonal-wide-bead-grain cloth, greenish buff end-papers.

Vol. I (viii)+(292) Publishers' cat., 16 pp. dated Nov. 1863, at end.
II (iv)+(300) Publishers' cat., 16 pp. dated Nov. 1863, at end.

Blind stamp: 'W. H. Smith & Son' on fly-leaf of Vol. I. Very fine.

NEW MAGDALEN (The): a Novel [*Parrish* p. 89 [600]

2 vols. Bentley 1873. Bright brown diagonal-fine-ribbed cloth, blocked and lettered in black on front, in gold on spine, blocked in black on back.

Vol. I vi+(298) pp. (v) vi, Contents, and final leaf, 19_5, single insets.
II iv+(300) 19_6 adverts.

Presentation Copy: 'To Caroline Graves from Wilkie Collins June 10th 1873' in ink on title of Vol. I. Ink signature: 'Lady Georgiana Codrington' on title of Vol. II. Cloth bruised and a little tired, but an honest untouched copy and, I think, an unmixed set. Lady Georgiana Codrington liked to write her name on the title-pages of her books, but she could not have done this on Vol. I of this book without over-writing the presentation inscription.

NO NAME [601]

Copy I: First Edition. 3 vols. Sampson Low 1862. Orange-scarlet morocco cloth. [*Parrish* p. 45

Half-title in Vols. I and II

Vol. I (x)+(340)
II (iv)+(364)
III (ii)+408

Copy II: First One-volume Edition. Sampson Low 1864. Dark green bead-grain cloth. Steel engraved front. after J. E. Millais. [*Parrish* p. 48 [601*a*]

[602] POOR MISS FINCH [*Parrish* p. 83
3 vols. Bentley 1872. Smooth chocolate cloth.

Vol. I (xii) + (316) Pp. (xi) (xii) fly-title to Part I; 20_6 adverts.
II iv + 316
III iv + 320

Very fine. '1st Edition' in pencil in George Bentley's hand on title of Vol. I. B

[603] QUEEN OF HEARTS (The)

Copy I: First Edition. 3 vols. Hurst & Blackett 1859. Sage-green wavy-grain cloth. [*Parrish* p. 33

Vol. I (vi) [paged (iv)] + 314 First leaf of final sig., X_1, a single inset, probably originally conjugate with title, which is also single. Publishers' cat., 16 pp. undated, at end.
II (ii) + (360)
III (ii) + (308)

Presentation Copy to Dedicatee: 'To Emile Forgues from Wilkie Collins. October 1859' in ink on title of Vol. I. Booksellers' ticket: 'Veuve Boyveau, Paris' in each vol. Binders' ticket: 'Leighton, Son & Hodge', at end of Vol. I. Covers sharp and bright; a few spots here and there the only blemish.

[603*a*] **Copy II: First One-volume Edition.** Sampson Low 1862. Magenta bead-grain cloth. Steel-engraved front. after John Gilbert. Very fine. [*Parrish* p. 36

[604] ROGUE'S LIFE (A): from his Birth to his Marriage
Bentley 1879. Scarlet diagonal-fine-ribbed cloth; black end-papers.

pp. iv + 188

No. VII in Bentley's Half Crown Empire Library. Very fine.

[605] WOMAN IN WHITE (The)

Copy I: First Edition. 8vo. Harper, N.Y. 1860. Dark brown morocco cloth; brown end-papers. Numerous wood-engraved text-illustrations after John McLenan. [*Parrish* p. 40

Advert. leaf precedes title. pp. (264) R_3, R_4 adverts.

Inserted is pictorial handbill on proof paper of the play produced at the Olympic. Front cover and spine in brilliant state: back cover badly creased by damp. Preceded English edition by one month.

[605*a*] **Copy II: First English Edition.** 3 vols. Sampson, Low 1860. Violet bead-grain cloth. [*Parrish* p. 39

Vol. I viii + 316
II (ii) + 360
III (ii) + 368 Publishers' cat., 16 pp. dated August 1, 1860, at end.

'Winthrop, U.S.A.' in pencil on fly-leaf of each vol. Very fine.

Copy III: First One-volume English Edition. [605*b*]
Sampson Low 1861. Magenta bead-grain cloth. [*Parrish* p. 42

[*See also* HAMILTON, WALTER, *below*]

CONWAY, HUGH (1847–1885)

AT WHAT COST, and other Stories ('by the late Hugh Conway') [606]
J. & R. Maxwell, n.d. [1885]. White paper wrappers printed in black. Inside front and both sides back cover printed with adverts.

pp. (176) M_6 adverts.

BOUND TOGETHER: Tales [607]
2 vols. Remington 1884. Third Edition. Sage-green diagonal-fine-ribbed cloth; black end-papers.

Vol. I (iv) + 268
II (iv) + (272)

Fine.

CALLED BACK [608]
Small 8vo. Bristol: Arrowsmith 1884 (83rd thousand). Dark green diagonal-fine-ribbed cloth, blocked and lettered in gold. Dark grey end-papers.

pp. (iv) + (196) O_2 blank. Inset between O_1 and O_2 is 32 pp. cat. of Griffith and Farran, dated '2 84.'

No. 1 of Arrowsmith's Bristol Library.

Note. I am unable to trace a first edition. The Bodleian Copy, '10th–14th thousand', has O_2 printed with adverts., lacks Griffith and Farran cat., and is in white wrappers printed in black.

CARDINAL SIN (A) [609]
3 vols. Remington 1886. Dark red fine-diaper cloth; green end-papers patterned in dark red.

Half-title in each vol.

Vol. I (iv) + (272) S_8 blank.
II (iv) + (256) R_8 blank.
III (iv) + 264

Ink signature: 'Ingram', on half-title of each vol.

CARRISTON'S GIFT: A FRESH START, JULIAN VANNECK and A DEAD MAN'S FACE [610]
Small 8vo. Bristol: Arrowsmith, n.d. [1886]. White paper wrappers printed in black, with title, etc. on front and spine: with adverts. on inside front and both back wrappers. Front. monument to Conway erected in Bristol Cathedral, March 5, 1886.

pp. (iv) + (192) 13_3–13_8 Publisher's cat., undated and paged (1)–12.

No. 12 of Arrowsmith's Bristol Library.

[611] DARK DAYS
Small 8vo. Bristol: Arrowsmith 1884.

Copy I. Greenish-buff paper wrappers, printed in red and black—with title, etc. on front: with adverts. on spine, inside front and both back covers.

Leaf of adverts. and dedication leaf precede title. pp. (viii) + 192 13_2–13_8 adverts.

Yellow slip advertising publications of Griffith, Farran, Okeden and Welsh tipped in between pp. (182) and 183.

[611*a*] **Copy II.** Dark green diagonal-fine-ribbed cloth. Collation as Copy I. Book-plate of Geo. Evelyn Cower.

Note. This story was Arrowsmith's Christmas Annual for 1884. It was re-issued in 1885, without indication of any earlier appearance, as No. 3 of Arrowsmith's Bristol Library, presumably both in wrappers and in dark brown cloth.

[612] FAMILY AFFAIR (A): a Novel

Copy I: First Edition. 3 vols. Macmillan 1885. Smooth salmon-pink cloth; black end-papers.

Half-title in each vol.

Vol. I (viii) + 260
II (viii) + (252) R_6 blank.
III (viii) + 236 Publishers' cat., 32 pp. dated May 1885, at end.

Pencil signature: 'Clay, West House', facing half-title in Vol. II. Fine.

[612*a*] **Copy II: First One-volume Edition.** Macmillan 1885. Scarlet diaper cloth; black end-papers. Fine.

[613] LIVING OR DEAD: a Novel
3 vols. Macmillan 1886. Smooth salmon-pink cloth; black end-papers.

Half-title in each vol.

Vol. I (viii) + 250 Final leaf, S_1, a single inset.
II (viii) + 248
III (viii) + (208) Publishers' cat., 32 pp. dated March 1886, at end.

Stain on front cover of Vol. II.

[614] SLINGS AND ARROWS
Small 8vo. Bristol: Arrowsmith 1885. Pale grey paper wrappers, printed in red and black—with title, etc. on front: with adverts. on spine, inside front and both back covers.

Three leaves of adverts. precede title. pp. (viii) + 200. 16 pp. adverts. on text-paper at end.

Arrowsmith's Christmas Annual for 1885. Re-issued 1886 as No. 8 of the Bristol Library.

Conwayana

MUCH DARKER DAYS (by A. Huge Longway, author of 'Scrawled Black', 'The Mystery of Paul Targus', 'Unbound', etc.) [615]

Longman etc. 1884. Pale blue paper wrappers, printed in red and black—with title, etc. on front and spine: with adverts. on outside back cover.

Half-title. pp. (viii) + (112) I_1–I_4 adverts.

COOPER, THOMAS, THE CHARTIST (1805–late '80s.) [616]

WISE SAWS AND MODERN INSTANCES
2 vols. Jeremiah How, 209 Piccadilly 1845. Very dark grey morocco cloth.

Advert. leaf and half-title precede title in Vol. I, half-title only in Vol. II

Vol. I (xii) [paged x] + (264) M_{10}–M_{12} adverts.
II (240) K_{10}–K_{12} adverts.

Dedicated to Douglas Jerrold. Author's 'Advertisement' states the sketches were mostly written in Stafford Gaol.

CORELLI, MARIE (1864–1924)

Of Marie Corelli's works published to the year 1900 (beyond which date this entry does not go) two are not in the Collection: *My Wonderful Life* (1889) and *The Silver Domino* (1892), neither of which I have been able to find in fine enough condition.

ARDATH: the Story of a Dead Self [617]
3 vols. Bentley 1889. Smooth slate-grey cloth, with harp and wreath and title in black on front; gold lettered on spine. Blue grey end-papers in Vol. I, patterned dark grey on grey in Vols. II and III

Blank leaf and half-title precede title in each vol.

Vol. I (viii) + (332)
II (viii) + (364)
III (viii) + 362 B

BARABBAS: a Dream of the World's Tragedy [618]
3 vols. Methuen 1893. Olive-brown ribbed cloth, lettered in gold on front and spine; white end-papers.

Half-title in each vol.

Vol. I 248
II (240) 15_8 blank.
III 240 Publishers' cat., 24 pp. dated October 1893, at end. B

Presentation Copy: 'To George Bentley Esq. my first pilot through the doubtful sea of literature, this work is offered as a testimony of lasting regard and friendship from the author Marie Corelli. Oct. 23/1893' in ink, facing half-title of Vol. I.

[619] BOY: a Sketch
Hutchinson 1900. Crimson diagonal-fine-ribbed cloth, blocked in gold. Title printed in red and black.
Half-title. pp. 352
Slip, printed in red, dated May 31, 1900 and tipped in facing title, emphasises the importance of this new work.

[620] CAMEOS: Short Stories
Hutchinson, n.d. (1896). Dark green ribbed cloth, blocked in brown, white and gold, on front with oval cameos, title and author, on spine with title and author; dark green end-papers. Half-tone front. and decorated title inset on art paper.
Half-title. pp. (viii) [paged (xii), reckoning 2 leaves of art paper] + (360) Very fine.

[621] JANE: a Social Incident
Small narrow 8vo. Hutchinson 1897. Pale yellow buckram, blocked and lettered in dark blue. Half-tone front. and 7 illustrations after G. H. Edwards. Title (a cancel) printed in red and black.
Half-title. pp. (152) K_3 K_4 adverts.

[622] MASTER CHRISTIAN (The)
Methuen 1900. Scarlet diagonal-fine-ribbed cloth, blocked in white and gold. On front Papal insignia.
Half-title. pp. (iv) + (636) 40_5 Appendix, 40_6 blank. Publishers' cat., 48 pp. dated August 1900, at end.

[623] MIGHTY ATOM (The)
Hutchinson 1896. Dark green ribbed cloth, blocked and lettered in gold; black end-papers.
Half-title. pp. (352) 22_{3-8} adverts.
Uniform with the re-issue of *In High Places* by Miss Braddon.

[624] MURDER OF DELICIA (The)
Skeffington 1896. Dark red straight-grain morocco cloth, lettered in gold; floral end-papers.
Half-title. pp. (xx) + 292 T_1 T_2 adverts.
Ink signature: 'S. R. Strickland, 68 Canfield Gardens', on fly-leaf.

[625] ROMANCE OF TWO WORLDS (A): a Novel
2 vols. Bentley 1886. Indigo diagonal-fine-ribbed cloth; white end-papers patterned in pale lilac.
Half-title in Vol. I
Vol. I (viii) + 316
II (iv) + 304 **B**

SORROWS OF SATAN (The), or the Strange Experience of one Geoffrey Tempest, Millionaire [626]
Methuen 1895. Dark green morocco cloth, blocked in silver and gold—on front the fallen star, the wings of Lucifer, title and quotation; on spine title, author and single star.
Half-title. pp. (iv) + (488) Publishers' cat., 32 pp. dated September 1895, at end.

SOUL OF LILITH (The) [627]
3 vols. Bentley 1892. Blue morocco cloth, title and facsimile of author's signature in gold on front. Publisher's monogram end-papers.
Half-title in each vol.
Vol. I (vi) + 288
II (iv) + (278)
III (iv) + (244) Publisher's cat., 32 pp. on text paper dated Summer 1892, at end. **B**

THELMA: a Society Novel [628]
3 vols. Bentley 1887. Smooth olive-yellow cloth, with creeper on a wall in violet and black on front; gold-lettered on spine. White end-papers patterned in pale grey.
Half-title in Vols. II and III
Vol. I (iv) + (324) 21_2 blank.
II (iv) + (288)
III (iv) + (308) 59_2 blank. **B**

VENDETTA! or the Story of One Forgotten: a Novel [629]
3 vols. Bentley 1886. Dark red diagonal-fine-ribbed cloth, hand clasping dagger and title in gold on front; gold-lettered on spine. Black end-papers.
Half-title in each vol.
Vol. I viii + (268)
II (iv) + 284
III (iv) + 288
'Copyright Copy', with Bentley's slip pasted in each vol. **B**

WORMWOOD: a Drama of Paris [630]
3 vols. Bentley 1890. Smooth dark green cloth, crossed scarlet satin ribbons on spine, gold serpent on front, gold lettered on spine. Publisher's monogram end-papers.
Half-title in Vol. I; blank leaf and half-title in Vols. II and III
Vol. I (xvi) + (268) Page (xiii) is printed in red and black. 17_6 blank.
II (viii) + (256) Page (vii) is printed in red and black.
III (viii) + 252 Page (vii) is printed in red and black. **B**

Note. Copies were issued to the Circulating Libraries *without* the crossed ribbons on spine.

[631] ZISKA: the Problem of a Wicked Soul
Bristol: Arrowsmith 1897. Cambridge-blue ribbed cloth, blocked and lettered in gold—on front with view of the Pyramids, title and author; on spine with title and author.
Half-title. pp. (368) 23_8 adverts.
Ink signature: 'J. S. Percival, Bramerton', on half-title. Fine.

CRAVEN, MRS AUGUSTUS (PAULINE DE LA FERRONAYS) (1808–1891)

[632] ANNE SEVERIN (by the author of 'Le Récit d'une Sœur')
3 vols. Bentley 1869. Grass-green fine-bead-grain cloth.
Half-title in Vol. I
Vol. I vi+250 First leaf of final sig., 16_1, a single inset.
II iv+(260)
III iv+244 B

[633] ELIANE: a Novel. Translated by Lady Georgiana Fullerton
2 vols. Bentley 1882. Dark grey diagonal-fine-ribbed cloth, blocked in silver; patterned end-papers.
Half-title in each vol.
Vol. I (iv)+(304) 19_8 blank.
II (iv)+(284) B

[634] NATALIE NARISCHKIN: Sister of Charity of St Vincent of Paul. Translated by Lady Georgiana Fullerton
2 vols. Bentley 1877. Pinkish-grey diagonal-fine-ribbed cloth, gold-lettered on front and spine SISTER NATALIE
Vol. I xii+312
II vi+292, followed by a single advert. leaf, presenting a facsimile of the title of the 'Popular Edition' of *A Sister's Story.* B

[635] SISTER'S STORY (A). Translated from the French by Emily Bowles
3 vols. Bentley 1868. Maroon sand-grain cloth.
Leaf of adverts. precedes title in Vol. I
Vol. I (viii)+316
II (ii)+324
III (ii)+(292) 19_2 adverts.
The word 'query' in George Bentley's hand is written in pencil alongside the emotional dedication 'to the Almighty'. B

CRAWFORD, F. MARION (1854–1909)

My ambition in respect of Marion Crawford has been limited to his two- and three-deckers, and even within these limits has not been fully achieved. The only one-volume book here recorded (*The Upper Berth*) appears by virtue of its membership of a fiction-series referred to elsewhere. It seems desirable to explain the absence of such important early works as *Mr Isaacs* and *Dr Claudius*, as well as of the numerous one-volume novels of his period of maturity and greatest popularity.

Two of the titles which follow (*Casa Braccio* and *The Ralstons*) are American-printed and possibly appeared in the U.S. earlier than in England.

Finally a note on the cloth-bindings.

For all their 2- and 3-vol. Crawfords Macmillans used a style of binding which is generally standardized but which exhibits three variations. The variations, while they do not correspond absolutely with dates, were introduced in the following order:

Standard binding (1). Smooth Cambridge-blue cloth, blocked in white with five continuous rules along top and bottom of front and spine, and with Publishers' monogram on back; plain gilt lettering on spine, with vol. no. near foot.

Standard binding (2). Smooth Cambridge-blue cloth (except *Katharine Lauderdale*, in dark blue diaper cloth), gilt-lettered on front and spine. Vol. no. under title on spine, Publishers' circular monogram near foot. Lettering is in peculiar square-seriffed caps, with the elongated tails of the A, G, K or R serving to underline the word. (The same lettering was used on many of Mrs Oliphant's novels published by Macmillan at this period.)

Standard binding (3). Generally similar in design and lettering to (1), but in smooth Oxford- (instead of Cambridge-) blue cloth with greenish-yellow (instead of white) blocking.

These bindings are noted as S.B. 1, 2 and 3. Certain titles are recorded as 'M.F.'. This indicates that they came from the Macmillan File, have 'File Copy', stamped in blind on front cover, and sometimes also the book-plate of Macmillan & Co.

AMERICAN POLITICIAN (An): a Novel [636]
2 vols. Chapman & Hall 1884. Olive-brown diagonal fine-ribbed cloth (uniform with Meredith's *Tragic Comedians*).
Half-title in each vol.
Vol. I (vi)+240
II (iv)+(220)
Fine.

CASA BRACCIO [637]
2 vols. Macmillan 1895. S.B. 3.
Half-title in each vol.
Vol. I (viii)+(336) Z_2 blank.
II (vi)+332
Fine.

[638] CHILDREN OF THE KING (The): a Tale of Southern Italy
2 vols. Macmillan 1893. S.B. 1.
Blank and half-title in Vol. I. Half-title only in Vol. II
Vol. I (viii)+(236) Q_3 Q_4 adverts.
II (iv)+(232) Q_6 adverts.
Fine.

[639] CIGARETTE MAKER'S ROMANCE (A)
2 vols. Macmillan 1890. S.B. 1.
Half-title in each vol.
Vol. I (iv)+(236)
II (iv)+(240)
Fine.

[640] DON ORSINO
3 vols. Macmillan 1892. S.B. 2.
Half-title in each vol.
Vol. I (iv)+(292)
II (iv)+(308)
III (iv)+(300) U_5 U_6 adverts.
Fine.

[641] GREIFENSTEIN
3 vols. Macmillan 1889. S.B. 2; black end-papers.
Blank leaf and half-title precede title in Vol. I. Half-title only in Vols. II and III
Vol. I (viii)+(304) U_8 adverts.
II (iv)+(296) U_4 adverts.
III (iv)+284
Very fine.

[642] KATHARINE LAUDERDALE
3 vols. Macmillan 1894. S.B. 2, but dark blue diaper cloth. Lettering in gold on front and spine uniform with Henry James' *The Tragic Muse.*
Half-title in each vol.
Vol. I (iv)+280
II (iv)+280
III (iv)+(280) T_4 adverts.
Very fine.

[643] KHALED: a Tale of Arabia
2 vols. Macmillan 1891. S.B. 1.
Half-title in each vol.
Vol. I (iv)+(236) Q_{4-6} adverts.
II (iv)+(236)
Fine.

[644] MARION DARCHE: a Story without Comment
2 vols. Macmillan 1893. S.B. 1.
Half-title in each vol.
Vol. I (iv)+184 Publishers' cat., 48 pp. on thin paper and dated August 1893, at end.
II (iv)+(248)
Very fine.

MARZIO'S CRUCIFIX [645]
2 vols. Macmillan 1887. S.B. 1. M.F.
Half-title in each vol.
Vol. I (iv)+220
II (iv)+(220)
Covers soiled.

PAUL PATOFF [646]
3 vols. Macmillan 1887. S.B. 2: dark chocolate end-papers. M.F.
Half-title in each vol.
Vol. I (iv)+308
II (iv)+(284) T_6 adverts.
III (iv)+(284) T_6 adverts., followed by Publishers' cat., 32 pp. dated September 1887.
Covers soiled.

PIETRO GHISLERI [647]
3 vols. Macmillan 1893. S.B. 2.
Half-title in each vol.
Vol. I (iv)+280
II (iv)+(268)
III (iv)+(264) S_4 adverts.
Fine.
Note. This, the Publishers' file copy, has Vol. II in Second Edition, while the vol. no. on spine is corrected from III to II.

RALSTONS (The) [648]
2 vols. Macmillan 1895. S.B. 3.
Half-title in each vol.
Vol. I (iv)+340
II (iv)+336
Blind stamp: 'Presentation Copy', on title of Vol. I. Fine.

ROMAN SINGER (A) [649]
2 vols. Macmillan 1884. S.B. 1. M.F.
Half-title in Vol. I. Blank leaf and half-title in Vol. II
Vol. I (iv)+(260) S_2 adverts.
II (iv)+(252) Title-page, verso, form pp. (1) (2).
Covers soiled.

SANT' ILARIO [650]
3 vols. Macmillan 1889. S.B. 2; black end-papers.
Half-title in each vol.
Vol. I (iv)+(300) U_4–U_6 adverts.
II (iv)+(304)
III (iv)+296
Very fine.
Note. Mr Nowell Smith's copy has an inset dedication-leaf in Vol. I. No such leaf is present in this copy, although in new condition.

[651] SARACINESCA

3 vols. Blackwood 1887. Smooth salmon-brown cloth, blocked in dark brown and gold; dark green end-papers.

Half-title in each vol.

Vol. I (vi)+290 pp. (v) (vi) 'Note' and final leaf, T_1, single insets.
II (iv)+(280) S_4 blank.
III (iv)+306 Final leaf, U_1, a single inset.

'With the publishers compliments' blind-stamped on title of each vol. Fine.

Note. This novel was also issued in pale olive-green cloth with similar blocking.

[652] TALE OF A LONELY PARISH (A)

2 vols. Macmillan 1886. S.B. 1.

Blank leaf and half-title in Vol. I. Half-title only in Vol. II

Vol. I (viii)+(300)
II (iv)+(284)

'Presentation Copy' in violet ink on title of each vol. Covers soiled and nail hole in spine of Vol. II.

Note. Mr Nowell Smith's copy has half-title and title only in Vol. I, neither blank (i) (ii) nor dedication-leaf (vii) (viii) being present.

[653] THREE FATES (The)

3 vols. Macmillan 1892. B.S. 2.

Half-title in each vol. 2 leaves of Publishers' adverts. on thin paper inset, dated '20. 2. 92', at end of each vol.

Vol. I (viii)+300
II (iv)+(260)
III (iv)+(276) T_2 blank.

Fine.

[654] UPPER BERTH (The)

Narrow 8vo. Fisher Unwin 1894. Brick-red paper wrappers printed in black.

Series half-title precedes individual title. pp. (192) M_8 imprint and advert. leaf.

No. I of Unwin's Autonym Library.

[655] WITCH OF PRAGUE (The)

3 vols. Macmillan 1891. S.B. 2.

Half-title in each vol.

Vol. I (iv)+(260)
II (iv)+(268) S_6 imprint leaf.
III (iv)+(268)

Fine.

[656] ZOROASTER

2 vols. Macmillan 1885. S.B. 1.

Blank leaf and half-title precede title in Vol. I. Half-title only in Vol. II

Vol. I (viii)+(232) Q_3 Q_4 adverts.
II (iv)+(220) P_6 adverts.

Very fine.

CREASY, EDWARD (1812–1878)

FIFTEEN DECISIVE BATTLES OF THE WORLD (The): from Marathon to Waterloo (by E. S. Creasy, M.A.) [657]

2 vols. Bentley 1851. Scarlet ribbed cloth; pale yellow end-papers.

Vol. I xii+308
II iv+(336) P_{12} blank.

Ink signature: 'Emily Leach', on fly-leaf of each vol. Very fine.

Notes. (i) Creasy appears in this fiction catalogue by virtue of his 3-vol. novel, described below. The *Fifteen Decisive Battles* is recorded, not as fiction, but because, besides being the book on which his fame rests, it is one of the most difficult cloth books of the period to find in undamaged condition. The cloth must be of brittle quality, for almost invariably it has split at the hinges. A parallel case is Mayne Reid's *Rifle Rangers*, published the previous year and bound in similar cloth. Creasy is known to *C.B.E.L.* only as an historian of Eton.

(ii) The chapter on Waterloo was published separately, with additions in 1852, as No. 13 of Bentley's Railroad Library (3444 in Section II).

OLD LOVE AND THE NEW (The): a Tale of Athens (by Sir Edward Creasy, M.A.) [658]

3 vols. Bentley 1870. Grass-green bubble-grain cloth.

Half-title in each vol.

Vol. I viii+314 Final leaf, Y_1, a single inset.
II (iv)+(326) Final leaf, $2A_1$, a single inset.
III (iv)+304 **B**

CROKER, T. CROFTON (1798–1854)

ADVENTURES OF BARNEY MAHONY (The) [659]

Fisher, Son & Jackson 1832. Half-cloth boards, label.

pp. (iv)+(300)

Ink signature: 'Waldegrave', on title. Fine.

FAIRY LEGENDS AND TRADITIONS OF THE SOUTH OF IRELAND [anon] [660]

3 vols. Murray 1825, 1828, 1828. Vol. I boards, label. Vols. II and III glazed plum cloth, labels. Vol. I illustrated with wood-engraved vignettes after W. H. Brooke. Vols. II and III have each 6 full-page etchings by him, as well as vignettes. Of the etchings, 1 serves as front. to each vol. and all the other 5 follow immediately after Contents List. No indication in Vol. I of further vols. to come. Vols. II and III described as Part II and Part III.

Vol. I (viii) + (364)

Green booksellers' ticket: 'Hodges and McArthur Dublin', on front cover. From the Bellew Library. Very fine.

Vol. II xii + (328)
III xxxii + 300

Fine.

Note. Four of the tales in Vol. I are by William Maginn.

CROLY, REV. GEORGE (1780–1860)

[661] SALATHIEL: a Story of the Past, the Present and the Future [anon]

3 vols. Colburn 1828. Boards, labels.

Vol. I viii + 338 Final leaf, P_1, a single inset.
II (ii) + 324
III (ii) + (418) First leaf of final sig., S_1, a single inset.

Very fine.

[662] TALES OF THE GREAT ST BERNARD [anon]

3 vols. Colburn 1828. Boards, labels.

Half-title in Vols. II and III

Vol. I (iv) + 336
II (iv) + 336
III (iv) + (324) O_6 adverts.

Book-label: 'R. J. Ll. Price, Rhiwlas Library, Bala, Merionethshire', inside front cover of each vol. Very fine.

CROWE, CATHERINE (1800–1876)

[663] ADVENTURES OF SUSAN HOPLEY, or Circumstantial Evidence [anon]

Copy I: First Edition. 3 vols. Saunders & Otley 1841. Purple-brown ribbed cloth.

Half-title in each vol.

Vol. I (iv) + (336) Q_3–Q_6 adverts.
II (iv) + 348
III (iv) + (348) Q_6 blank.

A rather dull copy, with edges of front covers weakened by too emphatic blocking.

[663*a*] **Copy II: New Edition.** SUSAN HOPLEY, or the Adventures of a Maid Servant.

8vo. Edinburgh: William Tait 1842. Grey-blue ribbed cloth. Wood-engraved front. on text paper. Leaf printed with reviews of first two monthly parts and half-title precede front. and title.

pp. (viii) + 280. Fine.

This edition was first issued in Weekly numbers, and Monthly parts. Nos. 1–6 are of 8 pp. each and the numbering then changes to Nos. IV–XVII, each of 16 pp., and ends with No. XVIII, 8 pp. It is curious to find a cheap re-issue (the cloth volume sold for 3*s*. and is priced on the spine) so soon after the first edition and over another imprint. Presumably Saunders & Otley owned the copyright and sold or leased it to Tait.

Note. In 1842 T. P. Prest wrote, and E. Lloyd published in 56 8vo. numbers at one penny, SUSAN HOPLY, OR THE TRIALS AND VICISSITUDES OF A SERVANT GIRL (by the author of 'Kathleen', 'Hebrew Maiden', etc.). This violent romance, illustrated with fierce woodcuts, has no connection with Mrs Crowe's story beyond the purposely adapted title. It became the basis of a melodrama, which played for many years in theatres addicted to such productions.

GHOSTS AND FAMILY LEGENDS: a Volume for Christmas [664]

T. C. Newby 1859.

pp. (viii) + (340)

Copy I. Sage-green ripple-grain cloth. Spine-titling ¾ high and imprint at extreme base, with four blind-blocked panels as decoration. Presumably a 'family copy'. Book-plate of I. W. Crowe, Folkestone, and ink signature: 'E. Crowe', on fly-leaf.

Copy II. Aloe-green bead-grain cloth. Spine-titling ⅞ high and imprint ⅞ low. Elongated blind-ornament between the two, incorporating publisher's monogram. U.L.C. copy similar. [664*a*]

LIGHT AND DARKNESS, or Mysteries of Life [665]

3 vols. Colburn 1850. Half-cloth boards, labels.

Half-title in each vol.

Vol. I (viii) [paged (vi)] + 314 First leaf of final sig., X_1, a single inset.
II (vi) + 320
III (vi) + 312

Monckton Milnes' (Lord Houghton's) copy, with his autograph 'R. M. Milnes, Fryston' in ink on inside cover of each vol.

NIGHT SIDE OF NATURE (The): Ghosts and Ghost Seers [666]

2 vols. Newby 1848. Dark brown fine-ribbed cloth.

Vol. I viii + 422 Final sig., $2O_1$, Appendix to Chapter VI, and a single inset.
II (iv) + 384

Back end-paper of Vol. I torn out. Cloth very fine.

This book collates throughout in sixes.

[667] STORY OF LILLY DAWSON (The)
3 vols. Colburn 1847. Boards, labels.
Vol. I (ii)+324
II (ii)+(292)
III (ii)+312 Publisher's cat., 24 pp. undated, at end.
Ink signature: 'W. Selby Lowndes, Whaddon Hall' on title of each vol. Very fine.
Note. The labels read 'BY THE AUTHOR OF "SUSAN HOPLEY"'.

CUNNINGHAM, ALLAN (1784–1842)

[668] PAUL JONES: a Romance
3 vols. Edinburgh: Oliver & Boyd 1826. Boards, labels.
Half-title in each vol.
Vol. I (vi)+380
II (iv)+372
III (iv)+(372)

CUNNINGHAM, SIR HENRY STEWART (1832–1920)

[669] COERULEANS (The): a Vacation Idyll
2 vols. Macmillan 1887. Cambridge-blue sand-grain cloth, blocked in dark blue and lettered in gold (uniform with *Portrait of a Lady* and other Henry James three-deckers). Dark chocolate end-papers.
Half-title in each vol.
Vol. I viii+(232) Q_4 adverts.
II (viii)+(228) Q_2 adverts.
Presentation Copy: 'Mrs Goschen with the author's compliments. April 28. 1887' in ink on half-title of Vol. I. Very fine.

[670] HERIOTS (The)
3 vols. Macmillan 1890. Cambridge-blue sand-grain cloth, gold-lettered uniform with *Katharine Lauderdale* and other Marion Crawfords. Black end-papers.
Half-title in Vol. I, blank leaf and half-title preceding title in II and III
Vol. I (viii)+(220)
II (viii)+228
III (viii)+212. Inset advert. leaf on thinner paper at end.
Very fine.

CURLING, CAPTAIN HENRY (1803–1864)

[671] FRANK BERESFORD, or Life in the Army
Charles J. Skeet 1858. Orange-scarlet bead-grain cloth, blocked in blind and lettered in gold.
Half title. pp. (viii)+(412)
Ink signature: 'W. S. Lowndes J[nr]' on fly-leaf. Fine.
The *D.N.B.* mis-dates the first appearance of this book as 1847.

RECOLLECTIONS OF THE MESS-TABLE AND THE STAGE [672]
T. Bosworth 1855. Orange-brown perpendicular-fine-ribbed cloth, blocked in gold on front, back and spine, but gold-lettered on front only.
Half-title. pp. viii+248
Ink signature: 'Selby Lowndes' on title. Cloth rather stained.
Note. Only partially fictional, this book is here included for the sake of its unusual binding design. The spine is gold-blocked into panels of an antique pattern and is unlettered; the front and back have an elaborate design of trellis-work and leaves which, on the front, encloses the book's title.

DACRE, CHARLOTTE ('ROSA MATILDA': MRS BYRNE) (1782–*circ.* 1841)

ZOFLOYA, or the Moor. A Romance of the Fifteenth Century [673]
3 vols. sm. 8vo. Longman etc. 1806. Cont. half-green leather; marbled sides and end-papers; sprinkled edges.
Vol. I (ii)+(284)
II (ii)+(288) N_{11} N_{12} adverts.
III (ii)+236
Book-plate of R. H. A. Bennet.
Notes. (i) Each vol. was printed by a different firm: I by Woodfall; II by Mercier; III by Brooke.
(ii) This novel was the model for Shelley's ZASTROZZI. T. J. Wise (*Ashley Catalogue*, Vol. x, p. 184) believed that only four copies were known. I suspect this to be rather below the mark, but the book is undoubtedly of great rarity. In Vol. V of the *Ashley Catalogue* (p. 131) is reproduced a letter from Swinburne to H. Buxton Forman describing at length the effect on Shelley of the reading of *Zofloya*.

DALRYMPLE, MRS HUGH ELPHINSTONE

LIVINGSTONES (The): a Story of Real Life [anon] [674]
3 vols. Colburn & Co. 1851. Olive-brown ripple-grain cloth.

Vol. I (ii) + 324 Publishers' cat., 8 pp. undated, plus a single inset advert. leaf, at end.
II (ii) + 314 3rd leaf of final sig., X_3, a single inset.
III (ii) + (282) Publishers' cat., 24 pp. undated, at end. 3rd leaf of final sig., T_3, a single inset.

Ink signature: 'J. R. McQueen', inside front cover of each vol. Fine.

Note. Inserted, in the handwriting of McQueen, is a 'Key' to the characters in the novel. The 'Livingstones' are the Elphinstone-Dalrymples and 'Magdalen Livingstone' is the author of the book.

DANIEL, GEORGE (1789–1864)

[675] MERRIE ENGLAND IN THE OLDEN TIME

2 vols. Bentley 1842.

Copy I: Dark brown ribbed cloth. In Vol. I etched front. and 3 plates by Leech and 7 illustrations in the text by Robert Cruikshank and others; in Vol. II etched front. by Leech and 16 illustrations in the text by Cruikshank and others.

Half-title in each vol.

Vol. I (viii) + 292
II (iv) + 296

Presentation Copy: 'To Edward Walker Esqr from his attached friend George Daniel' in ink on half-title of Vol. I. Fine.

[675*a*] **Copy II:** Scarlet morocco cloth, blocked in blind on front and back, ornate pictorial gold-blocking and lettering on spine. Collation and illustration as Copy I.

Presentation Copy to Henry (afterwards Lord) Cunliffe, with A.L.S. from Daniel inserted and the Cunliffe book-plate. Very fine.

Note. I will not venture to allot priority between these bindings. I is a good quality dignified style, II is suggestive of a gift-book market. The Bentley Catalogue merely says 'cloth'.

DAVIDSON, JOHN (1857–1909) and C. J. WILLS

[676] LAURA RUTHVEN'S WIDOWHOOD

3 vols. Lawrence & Bullen 1892. Olive-green morocco cloth, blocked in blind with plain double frame on front and back, gold-lettered on spine. Dark yellow-on-greenish-drab floral end-papers.

Blank leaf and half-title precede title in each vol.

Vol. I (viii) + (244) Publishers' cat., 16 pp. dated Autumn 1892, at end.
II (viii) + 236 Cat. as in I at end.
III (viii) + 224 O_7 O_8 adverts. Cat. as in I and II at end.

Book-plate of Oliver Brett (Lord Esher). Very fine.

DAVIES, REV. CHARLES MAURICE [677]

PHILIP PATERNOSTER: a Tractarian Love-Story ('by an Ex-Puseyite')

2 vols. Fcap 8vo. Bentley 1858. Dark green bead-grain cloth, blocked in blind on front and back, blocked and lettered in gold on spine.

Vol. I (iv) + 246 Final sigs. R, 2 leaves, S, one leaf and a single inset.
II (iv) + (250) Final leaf, S_1, a single inset. **B.**

Note. A bitter attack on Anglo-Catholicism by a man who in youth had belonged to the sect, but later (as he explains at length) saw the error of his ways. The book is a strange mixture of doctrinal rhetoric and melodrama, denunciations of Tractarianism alternating with two seductions, a suicide, glimpses of social gaiety and earnest protracted conversations. It culminates in marriage and parenthood. Davies wrote several more novels of a disputatious kind which are recorded by Alibone. The Bentley Catalogue states that the hero of this first book was named after a member of an Anglo-Catholic Secret Society, who was later charged with embezzlement.

DAVIS, JOHN (1775–1854)

POST CAPTAIN (The), or the Wooden Walls Well Manned; comprehending a view of Naval Society and Manners [anon] [678]

8vo. Thomas Tegg 1806. Boards, (?) label.

pp. (xii) + 300

Ink signature (partially erased): 'W. Waddell', on title. Spine renewed.

Note. This book was reprinted (from the Third Edition of 1808) in 1928 by the Scholartis Press, with valuable Introduction and Notes by R. H. Case. He establishes the authorship beyond doubt; but, not having seen a First Edition, concludes from remarks by contemporary reviewers that this edition carried on the title an ascription of the work to the author of *Zeluco.* Such an attribution *does* appear on the Third Edition (and perhaps also on the Second), but it is now made certain by the discovery of the present copy that the book originally appeared anonymously. So far as I know, no other copy of the First Edition has been reported since Dr Case declared himself unable to locate one.

[DIBDIN, THOMAS FROGNALL] (1776–1847)

[679] CRANMER ('by a Member of the Roxburghe Club')
3 vols. Colburn 1839. Dark blue morocco cloth, labels.

Vol. I (vi)+(324)
II iv+322 Final leaf, P_3, a single inset.
III iv+(286) O_1, leaf of corrigenda, a single inset.

A leaf following title in Vol. I (probably label-leaf) is cut away.

Dedication Copy: 'Hudson Gurney Esq. With the Author's grateful "Reminiscences" May 31, 1839' in ink facing title of Vol. I. Printed dedication to Gurney appears on p. (iii).

DICKENS, CHARLES (1812–1870)

As Dickens collections go, this one is, of course, insignificant. But it has one claim to distinction which, because the basis of that claim is insufficiently appreciated, merits emphasis. It offers a complete series of Dickens' 8vo fictions (except *Master Humphrey's Clock*) *in cloth* and mostly in fine condition.

Although their part issues are valued far more highly than the 8vo first editions in cloth, these are (with the exception of a *Pickwick* with all the minutiae of points) considerably easier to find and in fine state. And even *Pickwick* (ignoring points) is rarer 'fine in original cloth' than fine in parts. It would I think surprise many experienced collectors to discover how extremely difficult it is to get these 8vo first editions in original cloth and really clean. The great majority of copies which survive are re-bound, and those which have retained their original clothing (most of the volumes being too heavy for their cases) are usually in poor condition.

The bibliographical and semi-bibliographical literature dealing with Dickens is very extensive, yet includes no single comprehensive and satisfactory work. The most ambitious general book is *The First Editions of Charles Dickens* by J. C. Eckel (revised edition 1932) which gives much detailed information, but is unhelpful as to original bindings and frequently so clumsy in style as to be meaningless. The Part-Issues are dealt with very fully in *A Bibliography of the Periodical Works of Charles Dickens* by T. Hatton and A. H. Cleaver, but no discussion of Book-Issues is included. Incidental, but scattered information may be found in three works by F. G. Kitton: *Dickensiana* (1886), *The Novels of Charles Dickens* (1897), *The Minor Writings of Charles Dickens* (1900); in the file of *The Dickensian* and in certain other books listed in the *C.B.E.L.*

[680] BARNABY RUDGE
Royal 8vo. Chapman & Hall 1841. Maroon fine-diaper cloth; marbled end-papers and edges.

pp. vi+(229)–420, with irregularities.

This separate edition of *B.R.* is made up of sections from the 3 vols. of *Master Humphrey's Clock.*

BATTLE OF LIFE (The): a Love Story [681]
Fcap 8vo. Bradbury & Evans 1846. Red horizontal-fine-ribbed cloth, blocked in blind and gold on front; in gold on spine; in blind on back. Pale yellow end-papers. All edges gilt. Engraved front. and title by Maclise; also wood-engravings in text after Maclise, Leech, Stanfield and Doyle.

Half-title. pp. (viii)+(178) (N_1) adverts., a single inset. Fine.

Note. Described by Eckel as the Second Issue, with the scroll: 'A Love Story' part of the engraved title, but without cherub; also with imprint: LONDON: / PUBLISHED BY BRADBURY & EVANS, WHITEFRIARS. / 1846.

BLEAK HOUSE [682]
8vo. Bradbury & Evans 1853. Green fine-diaper cloth. Etched front. and 38 plates by Phiz. Also engraved title dated 1853 preceding printed title.

Half-title. pp. xvi+624. Fine.

CHIMES (The): a Goblin Story of some Bells that rang an Old Year out and New Year in [683]
Fcap 8vo. Chapman & Hall 1845. Red fine-ribbed cloth, blocking, etc., similar to *The Battle of Life.* Engraved front. and title by Maclise; also wood-engravings in text after Leech, Stanfield and Doyle.

Advert. leaf and half-title precede title. pp. (viii)+(176) Slight flaw on front cover. Fine.

Note. First issue, with publishers' imprint a part of the engraved title-page, and not type-set under the engraving.

CHRISTMAS CAROL (A). In Prose, being a Ghost Story of Christmas [684]
Fcap 8vo. Chapman & Hall 1843. Brown-salmon fine-ribbed cloth, blocked in blind and gold on front; in gold on spine; in blind on back. Yellow end-papers. All edges gilt. Coloured etched front., 3 plates and cuts in text—all by Leech. Title printed in red and blue.

Half-title (printed in blue). pp. (viii)+(168) M_4 adverts. Ink signature: 'Thomas Lister Marsden, London' on fly-leaf.

Note. This issue, with yellow end-papers and 'Stave I', is now accepted as the first. All known presentation copies are of this variant.

CRICKET ON THE HEARTH (The): a Fairy Tale of Home [685]
Fcap 8vo. 'Printed and published for the Author by Bradbury and Evans' 1846. Red fine-ribbed cloth, blocking, etc., similar to *The Battle of Life.* Engraved front. and title by Maclise; also wood-engravings in text after Leech, Stanfield, Doyle and Landseer.

Half-title. pp. (viii)+(176) M_8 adverts. Fine.

[686] DAVID COPPERFIELD

8vo. Bradbury & Evans 1850. Green fine-diaper cloth. Etched front. and 38 plates by Phiz. Also engraved title dated 1850 preceding printed title.

Half-title. pp. (xvi) + 624

Blind stamp of Stephen Moore, Bookseller, Cork, on fly-leaf. Fine. Spine a little faded.

[687] DOMBEY AND SON

8vo. Bradbury & Evans 1848. Green fine-diaper cloth. Etched front. and 38 plates by Phiz. Also engraved title dated 1848 preceding printed title.

Half-title. pp. xvi + 624 Leaf printed with Errata precedes half-title in this copy.

Binder's label: 'Burn', at end. Label of John Duffus, bookseller of Aberdeen, inside front cover. Fine. Small tear in front hinge.

[*See also* NICHOLSON, RENTON, *below*.]

[688] GREAT EXPECTATIONS

3 vols. Chapman & Hall 1861. Violet wavy-grain cloth.

Vol. I (iv) + 344
II (ii) + 352
III (ii) + 344 Publishers' cat., 32 pp. dated May 1861, at end.

In this copy title and dedication leaf in Vol. I are not conjugate: but the copy (which came from a country Reading Institute and Library, where it had been ever since publication) is absolutely untouched, and the leaves must have been divided by the original binder.

Blind stamp: 'W. H. Smith & Son, Strand', on fly-leaf of Vol. I. Fine.

[689] HARD TIMES: for these Times

Bradbury & Evans 1854. Olive-green moiré horizontally-ribbed cloth, blocked in blind and lettered in gold. Price at foot of spine.

Half-title. pp. viii + 352

Bookseller's blind stamp: 'H. J. Wallis, Exeter', on fly-leaf. Fine. Spine slightly faded.

Note. This is Carter A in *More Binding Variants*, p. 7.

[690] HAUNTED MAN (The) and the Ghost's Bargain. A Fancy for Christmas Time

Fcap 8vo. Bradbury & Evans 1848. Red fine-ribbed cloth, blocking, etc., similar to *The Battle of Life*. Engraved front. and title after Tenniel, printed in black and white with a deep ivory surround, on plate paper; also wood-engravings in text after Tenniel, Leech, Stanfield and F. Stone.

Advert. leaf precedes title. pp. (viii) + 188

[691] LITTLE DORRIT

8vo. Bradbury & Evans 1857. Green fine-diaper cloth. Etched front. and 38 plates by Phiz. Also engraved title dated 1857 preceding printed title.

pp. (xiv) + (626) (A_7) and SS_1 are single insets.

This copy was bound from the Parts. Ink signature: 'William Hanson Box', inside front cover. Small ink stain on front cover.

MARTIN CHUZZLEWIT [692]

8vo. Chapman & Hall 1844. Blue diagonal-ribbed cloth. Etched front. and 38 plates by Phiz. Also engraved title dated 1844 preceding printed title.

Half-title. pp. (xvi) + 624

Book-label of William Hardcastle. Engraved title reads '£100 REWARD'. Bound from the Parts.

MUDFOG PAPERS ETC. (The). Now First Collected [693]

Bentley 1880. Scarlet diagonal-fine-ribbed cloth; black end-papers.

pp. iv + (204) 13_6–13_8 adverts.

No. XIII of Bentley's Half-Crown Empire Library. Very fine.

MYSTERY OF EDWIN DROOD (The) [694]

8vo. Chapman & Hall 1870. Green fine-bead-grain cloth. Portrait front. Engraved title (undated), and 12 wood-engraved illustrations, all after Fildes.

pp. (viii) + (192) N_8 adverts.

Book-label of Henry T. Wood. This copy was bound from the Parts and contains at end W. H. Smith's Secondhand Catalogue, 32 pp. dated May 1872, and four leaves of miscellaneous adverts.

NICHOLAS NICKLEBY [695]

8vo. Chapman & Hall 1839. Green fine-diaper cloth. Engraved portrait front. and 39 etched plates by Phiz.

Half-title. pp. xvi + 624

Booksellers' ticket: 'Boult and Catherall, Chester' inside front cover. Ink signature: 'Mr C. Potts, Chester' on fly-leaf.

Bound from the Parts. Fine.

OLIVER TWIST [696]

Copy I: First Edition. 3 vols. Bentley 1838. 'Boz' on all titles and spines. Publisher's imprint on spines. Maroon fine-diaper cloth. Etched front. in each vol. and 8 plates in I, 6 plates in II and 7 plates in III, all by Geo. Cruikshank. No List of Plates, and the 'Fireside Plate' in Vol. III.

Half-title in Vols. I and II. Leaf of adverts. precedes title in Vol. III

Vol. I (iv) + (336) P_{11} P_{12} adverts.
II (iv) + (308)
III (iv) + (316)

Fine. Book-label of G. W. M. Henderson in each vol.

[696a] **Copy II: Another (partially Second Issue)** 'Boz' and publisher's imprint on all spines, but 'By Charles Dickens' on title of Vol. I. Illustration and Collation as I. No List of Plates.

Note. There can be no question of this being a made-up set. It is absolutely homogeneous, crisp and clean, and must have been sent out by the publisher with titles non-uniform. For an interesting discussion of Issues see Carter, *Binding Variants*, p. 107, and *More Binding Variants*, p. 7.

[696b] **Copy III: Third Edition** 'with an Introduction by the author'. 3 vols. Chapman & Hall 1841. Plates as First Edition except that 'Tomb Plate' replaces 'Fireside Plate' in Vol. III.

Vol. I (xiv) [paged xii] + (332) Title a single inset leaf.
II (ii) + (308)
III (ii) + (316)

Pp. (iii)–(xiv) [paged (i)–xii] of Vol. I are occupied by 'Author's Introduction to the Third Edition', dated April 1841.

Notes. (i) I can record three bindings of this edition, of which A and B are in the Collection. In what I take to be their correct chronology they are: A. Grey-purple fine-diaper cloth, in general appearance similar to the First Edition but without fancy lettering for author's pseudonym and vol. numbers, no publishers' imprint, and different blind-blocking on front and back. Spine lettering reads: OLIVER / TWIST / *rule* / BOZ. / VOL. I [II III]. Blind bands across spine as on First Edition. B. Sage-green fine-diaper cloth, blocked in blind and spine lettered from type (though elegantly) OLIVER / TWIST / BY / CHARLES DICKENS / I [II III]. The publisher's own copy was in this binding, but the signature on fly-leaf of Vol. I 'Henry Garnett, Wynside, 1858' shows that Bentley purchased it some while after the event. C. Grass-green fine-diaper cloth of an altogether later appearance, lettered from type on spine.

(ii) The Introduction is of considerable importance. The Author replies to critical strictures on his action in staging a story in the London underworld. 'It is, it seems, a very coarse and shocking circumstance that some of the characters in these pages are chosen from the most criminal and degraded of London's population; that Sikes is a thief, and Fagin a receiver of stolen goods; that the boys are pickpockets and the girl is a prostitute.' He goes on: 'I confess I have yet to learn that a lesson of the purest good may not be drawn from the vilest evil....I saw no reason, when I wrote this book, why the very dregs of life should not serve the purpose of a moral, at least as well as its froth and cream. Nor did I doubt that there lay festering in St Giles's as good materials towards Truth as any flaunting in Saint James's.'

Copy IV: First 8vo Edition. Bradbury & Evans 1846. 'A New Edition, Revised and Corrected.' [696c]

Slate-grey fine-diaper cloth, blocked on front in gold and blind, on spine pictorially blocked and lettered in gold, on back blind-blocked uniform with front. Cream endpapers. Etched front. and 23 plates by Cruikshank—the same as in III but with imprint and date erased. The plate listed as facing p. 82 appears as front.

Half-title. pp. xii + (312) p. (viii) 'List of Illustrations', pp. (xi)–xii 'Author's Preface to the Third Edition'.

Ink signature: 'Jane F. Luttrell' inside front cover. Fine.

Note. Sigs. B–I and L–N are bound from the Parts, Prelims. and sigs. K and O–X are not.

OUR MUTUAL FRIEND [697]

2 vols. 8vo. Chapman & Hall 1865. Maroon sand-grain cloth. Wood-engraved front. and 19 illustrations in each vol. after Marcus Stone.

Half-title in each vol.

Vol. I (xii) + 320 Slip explaining title tipped on to p. (1). Publishers' cat., 36 pp. dated January 1865, at end.
II (viii) + (312) $X_2 X_3$ Postscript. X_4 adverts. Publishers' cat., 4 pp. dated November 1865, at end.

Very fine.

POSTHUMOUS PAPERS OF THE PICKWICK CLUB (The) [698]

8vo. Chapman & Hall 1837. Slate-black fine-diaper cloth; pale yellow end-papers. Etched front., vignette title and 41 illustrations by Seymour and Phiz. Engraved title (second state) dated 1837 precedes printed title.

Half-title. pp. (xvi) + (610)

Ink signature: 'Jemima Williams', on fly-leaf. Very fine.

Note. The book collates as follows: (A) 8 leaves; B–D in fours; E five leaves; F–G in fours; H–TT in eights. E_1 (pp. 25/26), a single inset, was originally the final leaf of Part I in the Part Issue; it is followed by a normal four-leaf gathering, also (on p. 27) signed E, which began the original Part II. In this copy, belonging to the second issue, both pp. 25 and 27 are signed E.

SKETCHES BY 'BOZ', Illustrative of Every-Day Life and Every-Day People [699]

2 vols. John Macrone 1836. Dark green regular-patterned straight-grain morocco cloth, gold blocked and lettered on spine; yellow end-papers. Etched front. and 7 plates by George Cruikshank in each vol.

Vol. I viii + 348
II (iv) + 342 Last two sigs., Q two leaves, R a single inset.

Ink signature: 'Lady Burdett' and book-plate of Kenneth H. M. Connal in each vol. Very fine.

[700] SKETCHES BY BOZ. Illustrative of Every-Day Life and Every-Day People. The Second Series. Complete in one volume.

John Macrone 1837 [on printed title, engraved title dated 1836]. Rose-pink morocco cloth, blind-blocked in relief on front, back and spine. At head of spine is overlaid a panel of black cloth decoratively framed in gold, which carries title in gold lettering; at base of spine is a narrow oblong panel of similar cloth also framed in gold, and gold-lettered: SECOND SERIES. / *rule* / MACRONE 1837. Dark-blue-on-white filigree-patterned end-papers. Etched front, pictorial title incorporating fancy titling, and eight plates by George Cruikshank.

Half-title precedes front. and engraved title.

pp. (x) + (378) [pp. (ix) (x), c_1, and first leaf of final sig., R_1, single insets.] Publisher's cat., 20 pp. on text paper, dated December 1836, at end.

Book-plate of Kenneth H. M. Connal. Very fine.

Notes. (i) The prelims. are eccentrically paged. pp. (v)–(viii) are paged (i)–(iv) and signed *b*; pp. (ix) (x) are paged (vii)–viii and signed *c*.

(ii) In view of the extreme elegance of binding and the stylish typography, the carelessness with which the book was prepared for press is curious. The List of Illustrations gives the frontispiece-plate twice, once 'To face title', again 'To face 216', and omits altogether 'Mr Minns and his Cousin' which faces 263. Three pages are mis-numbered: p. 25 is numbered '52', 32 '23' and 62 '46'. Each story has a fly-title, verso blank, except 'The Hospital Patient' and 'Mr Minns and his Cousin', which have their titles printed on the verso of the last leaf of text of the preceding story, so that on pp. 131 and 255 a story-title appears on the page *facing* the opening of the story to which it applies.

(iii) Uniformly with those in the two vols. of the First Series, the plates are all imprinted: 'London: John Macrone 1836' and carry face-page numbers. In front of these numbers 'Vol. III' has been erased.

(iv) Eckel implies that the presence of a List of Illustrations on p. (x) [following Contents] is a sign of a second issue; but he does not make clear why this should be so, nor does he make any reference to the erasure of 'Vol. III' from the plates. Nevertheless, a few copies are known with no List of Illustrations and with 'Vol. III' *un*erased and these would certainly seem to represent an earlier (and perhaps suppressed) issue of the book, which was evidently unknown to J. F. Dexter who in 1900 stated to F. G. Kitton that the errors in typography and make-up detailed in (ii) above were distinguishing marks of 'the absolutely *first* issue'.

Of the erasure (taken in conjunction with the imprint dated 1836) the only possible explanation seems to be that Macrone and Dickens planned *Sketches by Boz* as a three-volume work, and that the plates were prepared for the third volume in uniform style with those for Vols. I and II. Possibly Dickens then insisted on adding more material than a normal third volume could accommodate, and a Second Series in one bulky vol. was forced on the publisher. There is no evidence of this in Forster's *Life* nor, to my knowledge, anywhere else; but the irregular spacing of the plates certainly implies that they had been engraved ahead, as embellishments for a portion only of the Sketches.

TALE OF TWO CITIES (A) [701]

8vo. Chapman & Hall 1859. Red morocco cloth. Etched front. and 14 plates by Phiz. Also engraved title, undated, preceding printed title.

pp. (x) + 254 [pp. (ix) (x), signed *b* [List of Plates], and final leaf, T_1, single insets.]

Booksellers' ticket: 'Gilbert Brothers, Gracechurch Street' inside front cover. Bound from the Parts. Page 213 misprinted 113. Very fine.

Partly by Dickens

'ALL THE YEAR ROUND', EXTRA CHRISTMAS NUMBERS [702]

The series of 5 numbers, complete and in exceptionally fine condition. These issues are common, because very large editions were printed, but they rarely survive in such admirable state.

Large 8vo. Blue paper wrappers printed in black. Back and inside covers printed with adverts. pp. (in each case) 48.

1863 MRS LIRRIPER'S LODGINGS. [702*a*]

1864 MRS LIRRIPER'S LEGACY. This issue has an additional leaf of blue wrapper-paper in front, printed with adverts., and a slip announcing Vol. I of *Our Mutual Friend*, tipped in before p. (1) of text. [702*b*]

1865 DR MARIGOLD'S PRESCRIPTIONS. [702*c*]

1866 MUGBY JUNCTION (in collaboration with Andrew Halliday, Charles Collins, Hesba Stretton and Amelia B. Edwards). [702*d*]

1867 NO THOROUGHFARE (in collaboration with Wilkie Collins). [702*e*]

PIC NIC PAPERS (The). By Various Hands. Edited by Charles Dickens Esq. etc. [703]

3 vols. Colburn 1841. Grass-green fine-ribbed cloth, blocked in blind and lettered in gold. The spine-lettering gives title etc. and EDITED BY BOZ. In Vol. I etched front. and one plate by Cruikshank, also 2 plates by Phiz; in Vol. II front. and 3 plates by Phiz; in Vol. III lithographed front. and 4 plates after R. J. Hamerton.

Vol. I (viii) + (324) p. (vii) carries List of Illustrations to all three vols.

II (iv) + 298 First leaf of final sig., O_1, a single inset. Publisher's cat., 8 pp. dated May 1841, at end.

III (ii) + (382) S_2 S_3 adverts. S_3 a single inset.

Booksellers' ticket: 'Philip and Evans, Bristol' inside front cover of Vols. II and III.

Despite a small stain on front cover of Vol. II, very fine.

Note. In addition to Dickens, the authors contributing to this work included Agnes Strickland, Leitch Ritchie, Allan Cunningham, W. H. Maxwell, Thomas Moore, W. Harrison Ainsworth and Horace Smith. Vol. III which (according to Eckel) Shelton Mackenzie in his *Life of Dickens* (Philadelphia, 1870) accuses Dickens of lifting without acknowledgement from *Charcoal Sketches* by J. C. Neal, actually contains only two long stories, one of which is by Horace Smith and the other manifestly of English and not American origin. One might assume that Eckel had written Vol. III in mistake for Vol. II, which consists of a number of brief sketches, all anonymous and all conceivably written by an American. But in this case the quotation from Dickens' letter of 1859 to Edmund Yates in which he disclaims any connection with 'the third volume', made up of 'American reprint' for trade purposes by Colburn personally, needs explanation. And explanation is not easy. Vol. II is illustrated by Phiz, who was intimate with Dickens and would not have been likely to work for Colburn against his friend's wishes. Vol. III is illustrated by a comparative outsider, who might well have been brought in by the publisher after a breach with Dickens. Also Vol. III is fifty per cent by Horace Smith, who was on good terms with Colburn and is known to have helped the publisher with other ventures. Smith is just the man Colburn would have employed to edit (and contribute to) a third volume; but in this case Vol. II *must* have been edited by Dickens, and its miscellaneous anonymous contents chosen by him.

[*See also* HAMILTON, WALTER, *below*.]

Postscript to Dickens. Specimens of "Droodiana"

The Collection makes no claim to be able to offer even a reasonable selection from the immense bibliography of Droodiana. It does, however, contain four items, which are not only among the earliest of the Drood interpretations, but merit record on account of their rarity in original state and their interest as specimens of book-production. They are listed chronologically.

[704] PICCADILLY ANNUAL (The)

Square royal 8vo. John Camden Hotten n.d. [1870].

Cream paper wrappers (stiffened with cream end-papers) pictorially printed and lettered on front. by coloured lithograph, with circular Alpine view and lettering in gold, red and black; up-lettered on spine; printed with advert. of Asser and Sherwin's Games on back. End-papers unprinted. Wood-engraved front., vignette title and numerous illustrations, all on text-paper.

pp. 96

Fine.

Note. pp. (5)–13 occupied by 'Hunted Down' by Charles Dickens; pp. 25–29 by 'Memoranda' by Mark Twain; pp. 59–62 by 'The Mystery of Mr. E. Drood. Specimen of an Adaptation' by Orpheus C. Kerr, the earliest of all Droodiana; pp. 66–72 by 'Some Memories of Charles Dickens' by J. Field, his American publisher; pp. 73–81 by reproductions of sketches from Thackeray's Note Books. There are also contributions by Blanchard Jerrold, Albert Smith, Robert Brough, Bret Harte, H. W. Longfellow and James Russell Lowell.

The greater part of this Annual, being of American origin, was probably appropriated by Hotten for publication in England.

JOHN JASPER'S SECRET: being a Narrative of Certain Events following and explaining 'The Mystery of Edwin Drood' [anon, attributed to Henry Morford] [705]

Copy I: Part Issue. Eight 8vo Shilling Parts, published monthly from 'Publishing Offices, No. 342 Strand' from October 1871 to May 1872. Month and year of issue appear on front cover of each part. Blue paper wrappers printed in black—on front with rope-like frame knotted and twisted to enclose twelve vignette-scenes (unsigned) from the story, with JOHN JASPER'S SECRET / A SEQUEL TO EDWIN DROOD in fancy caps on two strip-panels set cross-wise in the centre of the composite design. Above the frame are the words: Part 1.] (etc.) October, 1871. (etc.) [Price 1*s*.; below the frame: LONDON: PUBLISHING OFFICES, NO. 342, STRAND, / Where Advertisements are received. / [*The Right of Translation is reserved.*] Inside front- and back-, and outside back-covers printed with adverts.

Part I. Inside front cover: Great Bazaar of Oriental Curiosities, (Farmer & Rogers).

Leaf of adverts., headed 'John Jasper Advertiser' on text paper.

Two wood-engraved illustrations on plate paper, the second signed 'R.H.'.

'PROSPECTUS' (single leaf of text paper), explaining the work and stating that 'the authors' have worked on hints left by Dickens as to his intentions, together with 'many more particulars, laboriously but lovingly procured'. This Prospectus does *not* appear in the book-edition.

pp. 1–32 of text.

Two leaves of adverts. on text paper.
Inside back cover: J. Lobb, Bootmaker.
Outside back cover: Harman & Co. Tailors.
Inset between pp. 16 and 17 of text are two leaves of cheaper paper advertising the Willcox and Gibbs Sewing Machine.

Part II. Inside front cover: 'Virgin Cork' and Notices of *John Jasper's Secret.*
Two leaves of adverts. on text-paper enclosing two illustrations, the second signed 'R.H.'.
pp. 33–64 of text.
Two leaves of cheaper paper advertising the Willcox and Gibbs Sewing Machine. Copy differs from that in Part I.
Ward Lock & Tyler's catalogue of S. O. Beeton's Books and Serials, 8 pp. of good quality paper in post 8vo and undated.
Inside back cover: Rowlands Preparations; Lobb, Bootmaker.
Outside back cover: Harman, Tailors. Copy differs from Part I.

Part III. Inside front cover: Notices of *John Jasper's Secret.* Copy identical with Part II, but set to full page.
Two leaves of adverts. on text paper, enclosing two illustrations unsigned.
pp. 65–96 of text.
Two leaves of cheaper paper advertising (again with fresh copy) the Willcox and Gibbs Sewing Machine.
Inside back cover: Rowlands Preparations (copy differs from II); Lobb, Bootmaker (as in II).
Outside back cover: as II.

Part IV. Inside front cover: Holloway's Pills; Almond's Crochet Cotton; Bass' Claret Cup; The American Sewing Machine; a Ballad 'Ever the Same'.
Two illustrations, unsigned.
pp. 97–128 of text.
Inside back cover: Whelpton's Pills; Lobb, Bootmaker (new copy); Atkinson's Plate Polish.
Outside back cover: as II.
Inset between pp. 112 and 113 are two leaves of decent paper advertising (with new and humorous copy) the W. and G. Sewing Machine.

Part V. Inside front cover: Morris and Yeoman's Penny Needles; Almond's Cotton; Claret Cup; American Sewing Machine and 'Ever the Same'—the last four as in IV.
Two illustrations, unsigned.
pp. 129–160 of text.
Inside back cover: Notices of *John Jasper's Secret* (copy as in II and III); Holloway's Pills.
Outside back cover: as inside-back of Part IV.
Inset between pp. 144–145 are two leaves of cheaper paper, advertising (again new copy) the W. and G. Sewing Machine.

Part VI. Inside front cover: Morris & Yeoman; Almond's Cotton; Claret Cup; American Sewing Machine (these four as in V); Mole's Boots.
Two illustrations, unsigned.
pp. 161–192 of text.
Inside back cover: as V.
Outside back cover: as V.

Part VII. Inside front cover: as VI, except that a new Song 'Gone' takes the place of the American Sewing Machine.
Two illustrations, unsigned. Two more, also unsigned, are inset between pp. 208 and 209 of text.
pp. 193–224 of text.
Inside back cover: as V.
Outside back cover: as V.

Part VIII. Inside front cover: as VII.
Two illustrations, unsigned. Two more, also unsigned, are inset between pp. 240 and 241 of text.
pp. 225–252 of text, which ends on R_6.
R_7 R_8: title, verso printer's imprint; List of Illustrations, verso blank.
Inside back cover: as V.
Outside back cover: as V.
The condition of this set is uniformly very fine.

Copy II: Volume Issue. 'Publishing Offices. No. 342 Strand' 1872. Dark green sand-grain cloth, blocked in blind on front and back, blocked in blind and lettered in gold on spine. Primrose end-papers. Wood-engraved front. and 18 illustrations. pp. (iv)+252 [705*a*]

Ink signature: 'John Holgate' on fly-leaf and title. Booksellers' ticket: 'Mann Nephews' inside front cover. A sound but rather dingy copy. One plate loose.

GREAT MYSTERY SOLVED (A); being a Sequel to 'The Mystery of Edwin Drood'. By Gillan Vase (Mrs Richard Newton). [706]

3 vols. Remington 1878. Grey sand-grain cloth, blocked in black on front, spine and back, and lettered on spine in gold and black. Dark chocolate end-papers.
Leaf bearing panel-advert. on verso precedes title in each vol.

Vol. I (vi)+(320) X_8 blank.
II (iv)+(320)
III (iv)+336

Book-plate of Charles Augustus Oliver. Very fine.

WATCHED BY THE DEAD by Richard A. Proctor [707]
W. H. Allen & Co. 1887.

Copy I. Cream paper boards, pictorially printed in black. Pictorial title (as front cover) inset before printed title.
pp. viii+(168) 11_4 imprint leaf. Publishers' cat., 48 pp. dated December 1887, at end.

Copy II. Slate-grey diaper cloth. Title and author fancy-lettered in gold on front. Chocolate end-papers. [707*a*]
Collation as Copy I. Publishers' cat., 48 pp. dated November 1887, at end.

Both copies fine.

DILLON (HENRY AUGUSTUS DILLON-LEE, VISCOUNT) (1777–1832)

[708] LIFE AND OPINIONS OF SIR RICHARD MALTRAVERS, an English Gentleman of the Seventeenth Century [anon]

2 vols. G. & W. B. Whittaker 1822. Boards, labels.

Half-title in each vol.

Vol. I (iv)+(278) T_2 T_3 adverts. T_1 a single inset.
II (iv)+(288)

First five leaves of Vol. II wormed in margin. Boards (pink) and labels fine. Ink signature: 'Tho[s]. Strickland' inside front cover of each vol.

This curious and discursive novel contrasts the manners of the seventeenth century with those of the author's own day. The latter make a poor showing. The book's original owner was the father of Agnes Strickland.

DISRAELI, BENJAMIN (1804–1881)

This is a complete collection of the fiction, poetry and political writings of Disraeli as set out in *C.B.E.L.*† with certain additions. His speeches, volumes of letters, etc. (though some are in my possession) have not been regarded as within the scope of the Collection.

[709] CONINGSBY, or the New Generation (by B. D'Israeli, Esq., M.P.)

Copy I: First Edition. 3 vols. Colburn 1844. Half-cloth boards, labels.

Vol. I iv+(320)
II (ii)+314 Final leaf, P_1, a single inset.
III (ii)+354 R_2 R_3 adverts. Final sigs., Q (6 leaves) R (3 leaves), in fact constituting one 9-leaf sig., of which Q_1 a single inset.

Ink signature: 'Vyall Vyvyan, Trelowanen', on fly-leaf of Vol. I. Label of Vol. I slightly defective.

[709*a*] **Copy II: Fifth Edition.** Fcap 8vo. Colburn 1849. Dark green fine-ribbed cloth. Engraved portrait front. after A. E. Chalon.

Half-title reading: WORKS/OF/B. DISRAELI, M.P. pp. viii+(472) HH_4 adverts.

Binders' ticket: 'Westleys & Co.', at end. This edition contains a new Preface on pp. (v)–viii, dated May 1849. Very fine.

ana

[709*b*] ANTI-CONINGSBY, or the New Generation Grown Old (by an Embryo M.P. [William North q.v. below])

2 vols. Newby 1844. Half-cloth boards, labels.

Vol. I (xii) [paged (x)]+(312) O_{12} adverts.
II (ii)+(262) M_8–M_{11} adverts. First leaf of final sig., M_1, a single inset.

Boards worn, labels discoloured.

KEY TO THE CHARACTERS IN CONINGSBY: comprising about Sixty of the Principal Personages of the Story [anon]

Sherwood, Gilbert & Piper 1844. Stitched as issued. pp. (8)

CONSUL'S DAUGHTER (The) (by the author of 'Vivian Grey') [710]

Publishing Office, 44 Essex Street, n.d. [? 1881/2].

pp. (32)

Page (1) serves as front cover, pictorially printed in black and worded: EARL BEACONSFIELD'S / FIRST NOVEL / THE CONSUL'S DAUGHTER / HITHERTO UNPUBLISHED /1d. / PUBLISHING OFFICE, 44, ESSEX STREET, STRAND. Pages (2) (31) (32) printed with adverts.

Note. The Consul's Daughter was first printed in 'The Book of Beauty' for 1836 and it may be hazarded that this catch-penny reprint was made just after Disraeli's death in 1881. Although it is a false statement that the tale is 'hitherto unpublished', the pamphlet is in fact the first 'book' (i.e. separate) edition. The story was again reprinted in *Tales and Sketches*, 1891 (q.v.).

CONTARINI FLEMING: a Psychological Autobiography [711]

Copy I: First Edition. [Anon.] 4 vols. Murray 1832. Boards, labels. *Pl. 9*

Half-title in each vol.

Vol. I (iv)+288
II (iv)+(248)
III (iv)+(196) O_2 adverts.
IV (iv)+(232) Q_4 imprint leaf.

Ink signature of M. A. Disraeli (the author's wife) on fly-leaf of Vols. I, II and III and on half-title of Vol. IV. Fine.

Copy II: Second Edition (by Disraeli the Younger, author of 'Vivian Grey', etc.) 4 vols. Moxon 1834. Glazed pink linen, paper labels. [711*a*]

Half-title in each vol.

Vol. I viii+288; other vols. as Copy I.

Book-plate of Sylvain van de Weyer in each vol.

Note. Vol. I contains a new preliminary signature, containing a Preface explaining the author's action in putting his name to the book. [711*b*]

Copy III: 'Second Edition', with *Alroy* (actually the third of *Contarini*, second of *Alroy*). CONTARINI FLEMING. ALROY. (Romances by B. D'Israeli, M.P.). 3 vols. Colburn 1846. Boards and labels. Steel-engraved portrait front. after A. E. Chalon in Vol. I.

† The listing by *C.B.E.L.* as a separate item of *The Spirit of Whiggism*, 1836, is a mistake. It was published as a pendant to *The Letters of Runnymede* (q.v. below).

Vol. I vi + (288)
II (ii) + (372) $2B_2$ adverts.
III (ii) + 360 Publisher's cat., 24 pp. undated, at end.

Fine. Bought at the Coningsby Disraeli sale at Sothebys, March 1937. The copy, therefore, came from Hughenden.

Note. A New Preface to *Contarini* (Vol. I, pp. (iii)–vi) and one to *Alroy* (Vol. II, pp. (287)–290) are both dated July 1845. *The Rise of Iskander*, which originally appeared with Alroy, is not included in this edition.

[712] ENDYMION (by the author of 'Lothair')

Copy I: First Edition. 3 vols. Longman etc. 1880. Scarlet diagonal-fine-ribbed cloth, lettered in silver; pale grey floral end-papers.

Half-title in each vol.

Vol. I (iv) + (332)
II (iv) + (340) Z_2 blank.
III (iv) + (348) Z_6 adverts.

Fine. Book-plate of Coningsby Disraeli, Hughenden in each vol.

[712*a*] **Copy II: Another.** Identical with Copy I, except that Vol. II, Z_2 carries an Erratum.

Ink signature: 'Guy Lloyd, Cwyhan 1880', on half-title of each vol. Fine.

The error corrected by the Erratum in Copy II is *un*corrected in the text of all copies examined.

[713] ENGLAND AND FRANCE, or a Cure for the Ministerial Gallomania

Murray 1832. Boards, label.

pp. (x) + 268 Contents leaf (pp. (ix) (x)) a single inset.

[714] HENRIETTA TEMPLE: a Love Story (by the author of 'Vivian Grey')

Pl. 9 3 vols. Colburn 1837. Boards, labels.

Half-title in each vol.

Vol. I (vi) + (300)
II (iv) + (312) O_{12} adverts.
III (iv) + (332)

Ink signature: 'H. C. Beaujolois Charleville Feb[y] 1837', on title and front cover of each vol. Bookseller's ticket: 'Milliken, Dublin', on front cover of Vol. I. Fine.

[715] INQUIRY INTO THE PLANS, PROGRESS AND POLICY (An) of the American Mining Companies [anon]

8vo. Murray 1825. Three-quarter red morocco.

pp. 88

Presentation Copy: 'William Geo Meredith Esq. Ex auctoris et amici donis' in ink on title. Inscription very slightly shaved.

IXION IN HEAVEN and THE INFERNAL MARRIAGE. See below: [721*g*]

LAWYERS AND LEGISLATORS, or Notes on the American Mining Companies [anon] [716]

8vo. John Murray 1825. Three-quarter red morocco.

pp. (viii) + (100)

LETTERS OF RUNNYMEDE (The) [717]

Copy I: Private, incomplete and probably unauthorised Edition: LETTERS ADDRESSED TO LORD VISCOUNT MELBOURNE and Others etc. Copied from the Times Newspaper, commencing January 19, 1836 [anon]

8vo. 'Printed by Cullum, Exeter.' No publisher. Issued stitched. This copy bound in three-quarter red morocco.

pp. 40 Slip of errata follows p. 40.

This pamphlet contains the first nine 'Letters of Runnymede', the latest being dated February 11, 1836. It is hitherto unrecorded.

Copy II: First Complete Edition: THE LETTERS OF RUNNYMEDE [anon] [717*a*]

8vo. John Macrone 1836. Dark green diagonal-fine-ribbed and embossed cloth, blocked in gold.

Leaf of adverts. paged (i) (ii), and half-title precede title. pp. (xxiv) [paged (xxii)] + (240) K_{10}–K_{12} adverts. *The Spirit of Whiggism* occupies pp. (175)–234.

Book-plate of Frederick William Irby. Fine.

LIFE OF PAUL JONES (The): from Original Documents in the Possession of John Henry Sherburne, Esq. etc. [anon] [718] Pl. 9

Murray 1825. Dark green morocco cloth, paper label.

Half-title. pp. xii + 320 Publisher's cat., 16 pp. dated August 1835, at end. Very fine.

Note. The earliest issue of this book was in boards, with paper label. This copy was probably bound in the early thirties.

LORD GEORGE BENTINCK: a Political Biography (by B. Disraeli) [719]

8vo. Colburn 1852. Dark brown ribbed cloth.

pp. (iv) + 588 Publisher's cats. at end: (i) 8 pp. cr. 8vo undated; (ii) 24 pp. 8vo undated; (iii) 2 pp. cr. 8vo undated.

Binders' ticket: 'Westleys & Co.', at end. Book-plate of Charles George Milnes-Gaskell. Two autograph letters of Bentinck's pasted on front fly-leaf. Very fine.

LOTHAIR (by the Right Honourable B. Disraeli) [720]

3 vols. Longman etc. 1870. Green dot-and-line-grain cloth; chocolate end-papers.

Blank leaf and half-title precede title in Vol. I. Half-title only in Vols. II and III

Vol. I (viii) + 328 Publishers' cat., 32 pp. dated January 1870, at end.
II (iv) + (324) Y_2 adverts.
III (iv) + (336) Y_8 adverts.

Ink signature: 'Lady Georgiana Codrington', on title of each vol. Very fine.

Note. The following variants in copies of this work have been noted:

(*a*) In Vol. II: Y_2 blank (not adverts.) and printers' imprint missing from p. (322).

(*b*) In Vol. III: Y_8 blank (not adverts.) and sometimes followed by Y_9 Y_{10} adverts.

There are also variant blind panels and corner ornaments on covers.

[721] 'POPULAR EDITION' (the title in caps is a First Edition)

9 vols. (out of 10) fcap 8vo. David Bryce 1853. Pink paper boards, printed in black. The volumes appeared in the order here given but are not numbered in Series.

[721*a*] **Venetia**

[721*b*] **Henrietta Temple**

[721*c*] **Sybil**

[721*d*] **Contarini Fleming**

[721*e*] **Alroy and The Rise of Iskander** (this volume reproduces the Preface to the three-vol. issue of *Contarini* and *Alroy* which, omitting *Iskander*, appeared in 1845)

[721*f*] **Coningsby**

[721g] IXION IN HEAVEN. THE INFERNAL MARRIAGE. Popanilla. Count Alarcos

Pl. 10

pp. (304). This is the first book edition of *Ixion* and *The Infernal Marriage* which were originally printed in the *New Monthly Magazine*.

[721*h*] **The Young Duke** (this volume contains a short new 'Advertisement' dated October 1853).

[721*i*] **Tancred**

[Vol. (10), not in the Collection, was *Vivian Grey* with a short new 'Advertisement' dated 1853.]

[722] PRESENT STATE OF MEXICO etc. (The): with Notes and a Memoir of Don Lucas Aleman [anon]

8vo. Murray 1825. Three-quarter red morocco.

Half-title (lacking in this copy). pp. 152

[723] REVOLUTIONARY EPICK (The): the Work of Disraeli the Younger

Copy I: First Edition. 2 vols. 4to. Moxon 1834. Boards, white side labels printed in black, spines unlettered.

Half-title in each vol.

Vol. I (xii) [paged viii] + (92) N_2 announcement: 'The Plea of Lyridon forms The Second Book.'
II (xii) + (93)–(208) [paged (91)–206]

Presentation Copy: 'To J. G. Lockhart Esq. From the Author' in ink on half-title of Vol. I. This copy has been re-backed.

Copy II: New Edition (by the Rt. Honourable Benjamin Disraeli). Longman etc. 1864. Smooth brown cloth; chocolate end-papers. [723*a*]

Blank leaf and half-title precede title. pp. (xiv) [paged (xii)] + (178) M_6 blank.

Binders' ticket: 'Edmonds and Remnants', at end. A Dedication to Lord Stanley, dated Easter 1864 (pp. (v), vi) first appears in this edition.

RUMPEL STILTSKIN: a Dramatic Spectacle (by B.D. and W.G.M.) [724]
Pl. 10

4to. 'Oxoniae 1823.' Cherry-red boards, green leather spine label, up-lettered 'RUMPEL STILTSKIN. 1823'.

A MS. of 36 pages, handwritten, illustrated and illuminated on one side of the page only.

Note. This is Disraeli's earliest completed work of imagination. Inserted in the copy is an article signed 'W. Hutcheon' from the *Morning Post* of January 13, 1914, telling the whole story of the playlet—a collaboration between Disraeli and William George Meredith. Only two copies exist—one was in 1914 in the possession of the Meredith family and is now in America: the other (now in the Collection and here described) had remained with Disraeli's sister Sarah and passed to the late Coningsby Disraeli. The Meredith MS. lacks the inserted Preface and the illuminated dated colophon present in this copy. The handwriting and ornamentation were the work of Meredith. Of the actual text of the extravaganza, Coningsby Disraeli told Hutcheon that Disraeli wrote the Arias and Songs and Meredith the remainder.

STAR CHAMBER (The). Nos. 1–9 (all published) April 19–June 7, 1826 [725]

8vo. William Marsh. Boards, label. Pl. 9

pp. iv + 154

No. 5, pp. (75)–84, and No. 6, pp. (91)–100, contain *The Dunciad of Today* by Disraeli (cf. the final essay in my book *Things Past*, London, 1944).

Bookseller's ticket: 'William Hutt', inside front cover. Fine.

SYBIL, or the Two Nations (by B. Disraeli, M.P.) [726]

Copy I: First Edition. 3 vols. Colburn 1845. Half-cloth boards, labels.

Half-title in Vols. I and II

Vol. I viii + (316) Longman cat., 32 pp. undated, at end.
II (iv) + 324
III (ii) + (328) Y_4 adverts.

The advert. on recto of Y_4 includes 'The Collected Works of B. Disraeli, M.P. in Three Vols. In the Press.'

[726*a*] **Copy II: First Edition in unbound sheets.** This set shows the label leaf intact, conjugate with title of Vol. III. The advert. on recto of Y_4 does *not* include the announcement of Disraeli's Collected Works in three vols.

[726*b*] **Copy III: Third Edition.** 3 vols. Colburn 1845. Boards, labels. Collation as Copy I, only prelims. reprinted. A word is corrected in second line of p. viii in Vol. I. The advert. on recto of Y_4 is uniform with Copy II.

Ink signature: 'Dis', on half-title of Vol. I. Fine. The copy was bought at the Coningsby Disraeli sale at Sothebys, March 1937, and presumably belonged to the author.

[727] TALES AND SKETCHES, by the Right Hon. Benjamin Disraeli, Earl of Beaconsfield, K.G. With a Prefatory Memoir by J. Logie Robertson. William Paterson 1891. Three-quarter cream buckram, blue cloth sides, leather label, top edges gilt. Etched portrait front.

Half-title. pp. (xxiv) + (392) $2B_4$ adverts.

No. 19 of 55 copies on hand-made paper.

Note. Of this collection of stories and sketches a number are here first printed in book-form.

[728] TANCRED: or the New Crusade (by B. Disraeli, M.P.)

Copy I: First Edition. 3 vols. Colburn 1847. Half-cloth boards, labels.

Vol. I (ii) + 338 Final leaf, Q_1, a single inset.
II (ii) + 340 Title probably conjugate with label-leaf.
III (ii) + (310) O_6–O_{11} adverts. First leaf of final sig., O_1, a single inset.

Ink signature: 'Spottiswoode', on title of Vols. II and III and on front cover of each vol. Very fine.

[728*a*] **Copy II: Second Edition.** 3 vols. Colburn 1847. Boards, labels. Collation as Copy I. Very fine.

Bought at the Coningsby Disraeli sale at Sothebys, March 1937.

[729] TRAGEDY OF COUNT ALARCOS (The) (by the author of 'Vivian Grey')

8vo. Colburn 1839. Buff paper wrappers printed in black.

pp. (viii) + (112) H_7 H_8 adverts. Erratum slip precedes B_1.

Book-label: 'S.A.C.', inside front cover. Fine.

[730] UNFINISHED NOVEL (without a title) by the late Benjamin Disraeli, Earl of Beaconsfield

Originally and only printed in *The Times* for January 20, 21 and 23, 1905. The three numbers as issued.

VELVET LAWN: a Sketch written for the Benefit of the Buckinghamshire Infirmary (by the author of 'Vivian Grey') [731] *Pl. 10*

Wycombe: E. King 1833. Glazed yellow wrappers lettered in black, 'VELVET LAWN' on front cover.

pp. (14). Final leaf a single inset. Fine.

Enclosed in an envelope, inscribed by Coningsby Disraeli, with a signed statement that the copy belonged to William Meredith, and was bought by him (C. Disraeli) at Sothebys in July 1911.

VENETIA (by the author of 'Vivian Grey', etc.) [732]
3 vols. Colburn 1837. Boards, labels.

Leaf of adverts. precedes title in Vol. III.

Vol. I (iv) + 346 Final leaf Q_5. Q_1 a single inset, probably conjugate with (A_1) (A_2) and label-leaf.
II (ii) + (378) Final leaf S_3. S_1 a single inset, probably conjugate with (A_1).
III (iv) + 324

Book-plates of Lords Birkenhead and Esher. Very fine.

VINDICATION OF THE ENGLISH CONSTITUTION in a Letter to a Noble and Learned Lord (by Disraeli the Younger) [733]

8vo. Saunders & Otley 1835. Boards, label.

Half-title. pp. viii + 210 [B_1, though reckoned as p. (1) is paged ix]. Final leaf, P_1, a single inset. Errata slip follows title.

Presentation Copy: 'The Countess of Jersey from the Author' in ink on half-title.

Note. A second (very fine) copy in the Collection contains P_2, an advert. leaf, at end and the book-label of W. Berryman, Jun. The Presentation Copy above described is in untouched original state and has certainly never included P_2. Possibly the advert. leaf was purposely omitted from copies intended for presentation.

VIVIAN GREY [anon] [734]
5 vols. Colburn: Vols. I, II 1826; III–V 1827. Boards, labels. *Pl. 9*

Half-titles in Vols. II and V

Vol. I (iv) + (268) N_2 adverts.
II (iv) + (240) L_{11} L_{12} adverts.
III (ii) + (336) P_{12} adverts. Publishers' cat. (Saunders & Otley), 4 pp. undated, inserted between front end-papers.
IV (ii) + (364) R_2 adverts.
V (iv) + 324 Verso of half-title carries one line Erratum for Vol. III.

Book-plate of Robert William Duff, Fetteresso. Very fine.

ana

[734*a*] KEY TO VIVIAN GREY [anon]

William Marsh 1827: re-sewn in grey wrappers.

Half-title. pp. (iv)+(28) (E_2) adverts.

This first appeared in the *Star Chamber*, No. 7.

[735] VOYAGE OF CAPTAIN POPANILLA (The) (by the author of 'Vivian Grey')

Pl. 9 **Copy I: First Edition.** Colburn 1828. Boards, label.

Half-title. pp. viii+(244)

[735*a*] **Copy II: 'New Edition, with Illustrations.** Colburn 1829. Boards, label. 8 full-page engraved plates after Maclise.

pp. viii+(244) Two leaves, paged (1)–4, advertising the third edition of *Vivian Grey*, are inserted after p. (vi).

Book-label of H. I. McClary.

[735*b*] **Copy III: Another of the same.** Old half-calf.

Presentation Copy: 'Edward Lytton Bulwer Esq. from his obliged friend and servant the author' in ink on the title. The inscription is shaved. This copy lacks pp. (vii), viii. Otherwise identical with Copy II.

[736] WHAT IS HE? (by the author of 'Vivian Grey')

8vo. Ridgeway 1833. Unbound.

Half-title (lacking in this copy). pp. 16

[737] WONDROUS TALE OF ALROY (The). THE RISE OF ISKANDER (by the author of 'Vivian Grey', etc.)

3 vols. Saunders & Otley 1833. Boards, labels.

Half-title in each vol.

Vol. I (xxviii)+(304) Text ends p. (270): pp. (271)–(303) Notes. 12 page undated cat. of William Curry, Jun. & Co. at end.
II (iv)+(308) O_4 adverts. Text ends p. (292): pp. (293)–(305) Notes.
III (iv)+(328) P_7 adverts., P_8 blank.

Ink signature: 'Thomas Mornington Esq[re]. Somesfield Court' on half-title of each vol. Book-plate of Oliver Brett (Lord Esher).

[See also CONTARINI FLEMING, Copy III]

[738] YOUNG DUKE (The) (by the author of 'Vivian Grey')

3 vols. Colburn & Bentley 1831. Half-cloth boards, labels.

Half-titles in Vols. II and III

Vol. I iv+300 O_5 fly-title to Notes. O_6 Notes.
II (iv)+(272) N_4 Notes.
III (iv)+(268) (N_2) adverts.

Fine.

[*See also* HAMILTON, WALTER, *below*.]

D'ORSAY, ALFRED. See BLESSINGTON

DOYLE, SIR ARTHUR CONAN (1859–1930)

This collection of Doyle first editions is capricious, even to the year 1900. An adequate Doyle Bibliography by Harold Locke was published in 1928 by D. Webster, Tunbridge Wells.

ADVENTURES OF SHERLOCK HOLMES (The) [739]

Royal 8vo. Newnes 1892. Smooth Cambridge-blue cloth, pictorially blocked in black with vignette of 'The Strand Library' and lettered in black and gold on front, blocked and lettered in black and gold on spine. Bevelled boards, fawn-on-white floral end-papers. Numerous half-tone illustrations in the text after Sidney Paget. The series-title 'The Strand Library' is repeated on spine.

Half-title. pp. (iv)+(320) 21_8 blank.

Very fine.

DOINGS OF RAFFLES HAW (The) [740]

Slim cr. 8vo. Cassell 1892. Smooth navy-blue cloth, gold-lettered on spine.

Half-title. pp. 256 [paged (i)–viii+(9)–256] Publishers' cat., 8 pp. foliated, on text paper, at end.

DREAMLAND AND GHOSTLAND: an Original Collection of Tales and Warnings from the Borderland of Substance and Shadow etc. [741]

3 vols. George Redway n.d. [1887]. Scarlet sand-grain cloth, blocked in black on front, gold-lettered on spine, backs plain.

Half-title and leaf bearing quotations on recto and verso precede title in Vols. II and III

Vol. I pp. (320) [paged (i)–viii+(9)–318] U_8 blank.
II pp. 320 [paged (i)–(viii)+(9)–320]
III pp. (320) [paged (i)–(viii)+(9)–308] U_3–U_8 Publishers' cat., paged (1)–12 and undated.

Ink inscription 'From the Publisher' on title of Vol. I. Front cover of Vol. I slightly scuffed; otherwise fine.

Notes. (i) This collection includes the following contributions by Conan Doyle (signed Δ): 'J. Habakuk Jephson's Statement' (in Vol. II) 'The Great Keinplatz Experiment', 'The Mystery of Sasassa Valley', 'The Captain of the Pole-Star' and 'John Barrington Cowles' (in Vol. III).

(ii) For an illustration of the three issues of the work, see P. H. Muir's *Points: Second Series*, London 1934.

(iii) If a statement in a bookseller's catalogue (June 1945), that only six copies of the first issue are said to exist, is correct, I have seen them all, and one or two of them twice over.

[742] EXPLOITS OF BRIGADIER GERARD (The)
Newnes 1896. Scarlet ribbed cloth, pictorially blocked in black and lettered in gold on front, gold-lettered on spine, publisher's device in black on back. Wood-engraved front. and 23 illustrations after W. B. Woollen, all on plate paper.

Half-title. pp. (viii) + (336) 21_8 blank. Publishers' cat. 8 pp., with incidental date 'March 2, 1896', at end.

Very fine.

Note. This book was later re-issued in small cr. 8vo with cut edges, bound in smooth red cloth less ambitiously blocked, and with no indication of having previously appeared.

[743] FIRM OF GIRDLESTONE (The): a Romance of the Unromantic
Chatto & Windus 1890. Claret patterned-sand-grain cloth, blocked and lettered in black on front, blocked in black and gold-lettered on spine, publishers' monogram in blind on back. Light-green-on-white floral end-papers.

pp. viii + (400). Publishers' cat., 32 pp. dated January 1890, at end.

Fine. Single spot on front cover.

[744] GREAT SHADOW (The)
Fcap 8vo. Arrowsmith n.d. [1892]. Brown diagonal-fine-ribbed cloth in series-style of the publisher's Bristol Library.

Advert. leaf and half-title precede title. pp. (216) [paged (212)]. 12_7 12_8, 13_1–13_8, (14_1)–(14_4), adverts., publisher's and commercial.

Book-plate of W. U. L. Unwin. Fine.

[745] GREEN FLAG (The) and other Stories of War and Sport
Smith, Elder 1900. Smooth scarlet cloth, pictorially blocked in black and lettered in gold on front and spine. Very dark grey end-papers. Half-tone front. unsigned.

Half-title. (pp. viii) + (352) Z_7 Z_8 adverts.

Fine.

[746] MEMOIRS OF SHERLOCK HOLMES (The)
Royal 8vo. Newnes 1894. Smooth Oxford-blue cloth, uniformly blocked with the ADVENTURES and with uniform end-papers. Bevelled boards. Half-tone front. (preceding half-title and on text paper) and numerous illustrations in the text after Sidney Paget.

Front. and half-title precede title.

pp. (viii) + 280 Very fine.

[747] MICAH CLARKE: his Statement as made to his three grandchildren etc. etc.
Longman etc. 1889. Smooth navy-blue cloth, lettered in gold on front and spine. Ochre-on-white Swan and Ship end-papers, bevelled boards.

Half-title. pp. (viii) [paged vi] + (424) Text ends 412, (413)–(421) Appendix, (422) blank, (423) (424)—EE_4—adverts. Publishers' cat., 16 pp. dated June 1888, at end.

PARASITE (The) [748]
Narrow fcap 8vo. Constable 1894. Issued simultaneously in grey-green paper wrappers lettered in dark blue and in dark blue ribbed cloth, blocked and lettered in gold. Blank leaf (cut away before publication) and half-title precede title. pp. (viii) + (128) Final leaf, H_8, blank and cut away before publication.

Fine (both wrappered and cloth issues). Bookseller's ticket: 'Thornton Oxford' on front cover of former; book-plate of W. U. L. Unwin in latter.

Notes. (i) This was Vol. I of the ACME LIBRARY (3393 in Section II).

(ii) The Series was not a success. A big price was paid for the copyright of this story and a correspondingly large edition printed, with the result that a considerable balance of sheets was left on the publishers' hands. In 1897 they re-issued *The Parasite* in smooth canary-yellow cloth, blocked and lettered in black. New prelims. were printed and all mention of the Acme Library was eradicated.

RODNEY STONE [749]
Smith, Elder 1896. Navy-blue fine-diaper cloth, pictorially blocked and lettered in gold on front and spine. Very dark mushroom-brown end-papers. Half-tone front. and 7 illustrations after Sidney Paget, all on plate paper.

Half-title. pp. (viii) + (376) Text ends 366 ($2A_7$ verso), $2A_8$ and $2B_{1-4}$ adverts.

Fine. Spine very slightly faded.

TRAGEDY OF THE KOROSKO (The) [750]
Smith, Elder 1898. Smooth scarlet cloth, pictorially blocked and lettered in gold on front and spine. Black end-papers. Half-tone front. and 39 illustrations after Sidney Paget, all on text paper with blank versos, and reckoned in collation.

Half-title. pp. xii + (340) Text ends 333, (334) blank (335) (336)—X_8—and (337)–(340)—Y_1 Y_2—adverts.

Pencil signature: 'Radclyffe Walters 1898' on verso of front fly-leaf. Very fine.

UNCLE BERNAC: a Memory of the Empire [751]
Smith, Elder 1897. Smooth scarlet cloth, pictorially blocked and lettered in gold on front, gold-lettered on spine. Black end-papers. Half-tone front. and 11 illustrations after Sauber, all on plate paper. Also headpiece to Chapter 1.

Blank leaf and half-title precede title. pp. (xii) [paged x] + (308) Text ends 300 (U_6). X_1–X_4 adverts.

Fine. Spine very slightly faded.

[752] WHITE COMPANY (The)
3 vols. Smith, Elder 1891. Red-brown diagonal-fine-ribbed cloth, blocked and lettered in black on front, blocked in black and lettered in gold on spine. Pale-grey-on-white foliage end-papers.

Half-title in Vol. I; blank leaf and half-title precede title in Vols. II and III

Vol. I viii + (312)
II (viii) [paged vi] + (304) U_8 adverts.
III (viii) [paged vi] + (280) T_4 adverts.

Slight marks on back covers. Fine.

DRURY, ANNA H.

[753] BROTHERS (The): a Novel
2 vols. Chapman & Hall 1865. Chocolate sand-grain cloth.

Vol. I vi + (310)
II iv + (292)

Very fine.

This was a review copy, the publishers' blind stamp (R in a circle) appearing on title of Vol. I. But it is over-stamped by blind stamp of W. H. Smith's Library, which suggests that even in those days Circulating Libraries economised at the expense of authors and publishers by buying review copies at a cheap rate for issue to their subscribers. Nevertheless this copy, being in mint state and unlabelled, never went into circulation and was perhaps not such an economy for W.H.S. after all.

[754] CALLED TO THE RESCUE
3 vols. Bentley 1879. Yellow-brown diagonal-fine-ribbed cloth.

Vol. I (iv) + (356) 23_2 blank.
II (iv) + (352) 45_8 blank.
III (iv) + 344 B

[755] DEEP WATERS: a Novel
3 vols. Chapman & Hall 1863. Dark green morocco cloth.

Half-title in each vol.

Vol. I viii + 334 Final leaf, $2A_1$, a single inset.
II vi + 294 Final leaf, X_1, a single inset.
III (vi) + 248 Publishers' cat., 32 pp. dated Nov. 1862, at end.

Booksellers' ticket: 'H. & C. Treacher, Brighton' inside front cover of each vol.

Fine.

[756] FURNISHED APARTMENTS
3 vols. Bentley 1875. Red diagonal-fine-ribbed cloth, blocked in black on front with conventionalised representation of a lodging-house window, with hanging card, looped curtains and plant in a pot. A very unusual case of a three-decker so blocked as pictorially to express, not an incident or character in the novel, but its actual title.

Half-titles in Vols. II and III

Vol. I (iv) + (292)
II (iv) + (248)
III (iv) + (308) X_2 blank. B

GABRIEL'S APPOINTMENT: a Novel [757]
3 vols. Bentley 1877. Brown diagonal-fine-ribbed cloth.

Vol. I iv + (324)
II iv + (320) X_8 blank.
III iv + (340) B

Outside cover of Vol. III damp-stained.

STORY OF A SHOWER (The): a Novel [758]
2 vols. Bentley 1872. Smooth orange cloth.

Vol. I (ii) + (288)
II (ii) + 288 B

The cloth is badly discoloured, probably by paste-action.

EDEN, HON. ELEANOR

DUMBLETON COMMON [759]
2 vols. Bentley 1867. Reddish-brown sand-grain cloth.

Advert. leaf precedes title in Vol. I

Vol. I (viii) [paged vi] + (296) 19_4 adverts.
II iv + (300) B

This copy, which came from the Bentley collection at Slough, has the title of Vol. II misprinted 'Vol. I' and altered in ink to the correct number. Eleanor Eden was the niece of Emily Eden (see below).

EDEN, HON. EMILY (1797–1869)

SEMI-ATTACHED COUPLE (The) (by the author of 'The Semi-Detached House') [760]
2 vols. Bentley 1860. Olive-green morocco cloth.

Half-title in each vol.

Vol. I (vi) [paged iv] + 266 First leaf of final sig., S_1, a single inset.
II (iv) + (260)

SEMI-DETACHED HOUSE (The) [anon. 'Edited by Lady Theresa Lewis'] [761]
Bentley 1859. Dark green bead-grain cloth, striped horizontally with light green.

Half-title. pp. (iv) + (328)

Binders' ticket: 'Westleys & Co.', inside back cover. This copy lacks final end-paper.

EDGEWORTH, MARIA (1767–1849) and RICHARD LOVELL (1744–1817)

It should be sufficient testimonial to the worthiness of this Edgeworth collection to say that, so far as the books written by Maria are concerned—alone or in collaboration with her father—it was one of the main bases of Bertha Coolidge Slade's *Maria Edgeworth: a Bibliographical Tribute* (London, 1937). In that work will be found full bibliographical details (from some of which I dissent) and much important information about the writing and publication of the books. Of the titles dealt with by Mrs Slade, the only ones lacking from the Collection in first edition are *The Parent's Assistant* (? 1796: no set has been anywhere located), one of the ten small volumes of *Early Lessons* (1801), and *Essays on Professional Education* (1809).

Books written by R. L. Edgeworth alone were not treated by Mrs Slade.

A. Maria

[762] BELINDA [*Slade* 8A

Copy I: First Edition. 3 vols. Johnson 1801. Cont. half-calf (issued in boards, labels).

Half-title in each vol.

Vol. I 8+372 R_6 blank.
II (iv)+(388)
III (iv)+(360)

Ink signature: 'Mary Pine. Maidstone', on fly-leaf of each vol.

[762*a*] **Copy II: First French Edition.** (Bélinde, Conte Moral. Traduit de l'anglais par le Traducteur d'Ethelwina [Octave Ségur].)

4 vols. 12mo. Paris: Maradan, 1802. [*Slade* p. 97

4 vols. in 2. Full contemporary calf. Book-plate of Richard Lovell Edgeworth.

Presentation Copy: 'To my dear kind aunt Mary Sneyd with thanks for correcting and loving Belinda so well' in ink in Maria Edgeworth's hand on title of Vol. I. Ink signature: 'M. Sneyd' on title of Vol. II.

[763] CASTLE RACKRENT: an Hibernian Tale etc. [anon]

Pl. 13 **Copy I: First Edition.** Johnson 1800. Boards, label. [*Slade* 5A

Half-title. pp. (xlviii) [paged xliv]+182 First leaf of final sig., N_1, a single inset.

Signature 'R S' on inside front cover and title, both crossed through in ink.

Fine. When purchased, the spine and label were covered with brown paper, the removal of which has given a pale, washed look to the original cream spine.

[763*a*] **Copy II: Dublin Edition.** Dublin: P. Wogan etc. 1800. Boards (re-backed and label renewed). [*Slade* 5D

pp. (xlvi) [paged xliv]+182

Signatures: 'Richard Lovell Edgeworth' and 'Harriet Edgeworth June 1817' on title.

COMIC DRAMAS in Three Acts [*Slade* 19A [764]

R. Hunter 1817. Boards, label.

Half-title. pp. (viii)+(384) R_{12} adverts.

Very fine. From the Bellew Library.

CONTINUATION OF EARLY LESSONS: Frank, Rosamund and Harry and Lucy [765] [*Slade* 15A

2 vols. Sm. 12mo. Johnson 1814. Publisher's half-roan, marbled sides, labels.

Vol. I xxxvi+(288)
II (ii)+324

Label (defective) on Vol. II only.

EARLY LESSONS [*Slade* 6A(i)–6A(iv) [766]

10 vols. Sm. 16mo, approx. $4\frac{1}{4} \times 3$ in. Johnson 1801.

Set I: First Editions.

Vol. I. HARRY AND LUCY, Part I. **1st Issue** (printed by Woodfall) bound with Part II in cont. sheep. Half-titles. pp. (iv)+112. *Presentation Copy:* 'To Honora Edgeworth from the Author' in ink on title. **2nd Issue** (printed by Bryer) bound in publisher's marbled boards, roan spine, vellum corners, numbered '1' on spine. Collation as 1st Issue.

Vol. II. HARRY AND LUCY, Part II. **1st Issue** (printed by Woodfall) bound with Part I as stated above. Half-title. pp. (iv)+(120). **2nd Issue** (printed by Bryer) bound as 2nd Issue of Part I and numbered '2' on spine. Collation as 1st Issue.

Vol. III. ROSAMUND, Part I. Not in the Collection.

Vol. IV. ROSAMUND, Part II. Marbled wrappers, cut flush, white side label printed in black. Half-title. pp. (iv)+(68) *Pl. 13*

Vol. V. ROSAMUND, Part III. Wrappered as Vol. IV. Half-title. pp. (iv)+(96)

Vol. VI. FRANK, Part I. Wrappered as Vol. IV. Half-title or blank leaf precedes title (pasted down to inside front wrapper). pp. (112)

Vol. VII. FRANK, Part II. Wrappered as Vol. IV. Half-title or blank leaf precedes title (pasted down to inside front wrapper). pp. (112) G_8 blank.

Vol. VIII. FRANK, Part III. Bound as Vol. I, 2nd Issue, and numbered '8' on spine. Half-title. pp. (92)

Vol. IX. FRANK, Part IV. Wrappered as Vol. IV. Half-title (pasted down to inside front wrapper). pp. (iv)+(96)

Vol. X. LITTLE DOG TRUSTY, THE ORANGE MAN, THE CHERRY ORCHARD. Bound as Vol. I, 2nd Issue, and numbered '10' on spine.

Half-title. pp. (iv) + (108) H_6 ? blank or adverts. (lacking from this copy). [*Slade* 6 C

Note. Throughout this series the name 'Maria Edgeworth' appears on front-cover label, but title-page reads: 'by the author of The Parents Assistant, Six Volumes.'

[766*a*] **Set II: Edition of 1809.** 10 vols.

This edition is in the main a reprint of that of 1801, but with revised pagination in certain of the volumes owing to the prelims. being reckoned as part of the text and not paged separately [thus *Rosamund, Part II* now collates (72); *Rosamund, Part III* (100); *Frank, Part III* 96; *Little Dog Trusty* (110)] and in a single case, *Frank, Part IV*, completely re-set. *Frank, Part IV* now collates (iv) + 96, and the page-content varies from p. 3 onward.

Maria Edgeworth's name appears on all title-pages of the 1809 edition except on *Harry and Lucy, Parts I* and *II* which are anonymous.

A complete set is in the Collection, bound in four volumes in contemporary sheep, lacking half-titles and the occasional blank (or advert.) leaf. There are also copies of *Rosamund, Part II* and *Little Dog Trusty* in original marbled wrappers with side-labels. These contain half-titles.

[767] FRANK: A SEQUEL TO 'FRANK', IN EARLY LESSONS [*Slade* 22 A

3 vols. Sm. 12mo. R. Hunter 1822. Orig. half-roan, marbled boards, gold-lettered on spine.

Blank leaf precedes title in each vol.

Vol. I (xxviii) [paged xxvi] + 324
II (iv) + 346 First leaf of final sig., $2G_1$, a single inset.
III (iv) + (300)

[768] GARRY OWEN, or THE SNOW WOMAN

Copy I: First Printing. THE CHRISTMAS BOX: an Annual Present for Young Persons (Edited by T. Crofton Croker). John Ebers 1829. Pink glazed boards, unlettered and unlabelled.

Blank leaf, half-title and presentation leaf precede title. pp. (xii) [paged viii] + (244) (R_1) adverts., (R_2) blank.

On special presentation leaf preceding title, in ink: 'From the author of Garry Owen to C. Sneyd Edgeworth.' Pasted above, fragment of a letter from C. Sneyd Edgeworth. On inside cover later inscription dated 1915.

Binder's ticket: 'F. Westley', at end. GARRY OWEN occupies pp. 33–88.

[768*a*] **Copy II: First separate Edition.** John Murray 1832. Orig. half-roan, marbled boards, lettered on spine (also issued in *drab* boards, spine as above). Cuts in text. [*Slade* 25 A

pp. 116

Ink signature: 'V. M. Baxter', on title.

HARRINGTON: a Tale, and ORMOND: a Tale [*Slade* 18 A

3 vols. R. Hunter 1817. Boards, labels.

Blank leaf precedes title in each vol.

Vol. I (viii) [paged (iv) + iv] + (524) $2A_2$ blank.
II (iv) + (424) T_8 imprint leaf.
III (iv) + (354) (R_1) adverts.

Labels discoloured.

HARRY AND LUCY CONCLUDED, being the last part of 'Early Lessons' [*Slade* 23 A [769]

Copy I: First Edition. 4 vols. R. Hunter 1825. Boards, labels.

Half-title in each vol.

Vol. I xviii + (288)
II (iv) + 340
III (iv) + (320)
IV (iv) + 336 Publisher's cat., 4 pp. on text paper paged (1)–4 and undated, at end.

Labels rather worn.

Copy II: 'Second Edition, Corrected'. 4 vols. Baldwin, Cradock & Joy 1827. [*Slade* 23 B [769*a*]

Full contemporary rose-pink straight-grain morocco.

Presentation and Association Copy: 'Mrs Beaufort either for herself or for any of her children to whom she chooses to give it from Maria Edgeworth, Jany. 1st, 1829, a day which adds another strong link to family connexion & friendship' in ink on half-title of Vol. I; 'Mrs Beaufort from Maria Edgeworth, Jany. 1st, 1829' in ink on title of Vol. I; and, facing title, ink inscription, signed 'D.A.B.': 'The whole of this work was revised in MS. by Capt. Beaufort & many passages were re-written by him.' The work is dedicated to Captain Beaufort's children.

Copy III: Third Edition 'Revised and corrected'. [770]

HARRY AND LUCY: Complete in 3 vols. Baldwin & Cradock and George Routledge 1840. Dark brown fine-diaper cloth. [*Slade* 23 C

Book-plate and two book-labels of the Llanover Library in each vol. Fine.

HELEN: a Tale [*Slade* 26 A [771]

Copy I: First Edition. 3 vols. Bentley 1834. Boards, labels. *Pl. 13*

Half-title in each vol.

Vol. I (iv) + 336
II (iv) + 336
III (iv) + 322 First leaf of final sig., P_1, a single inset. P_6, probably label-leaf, has been cut away.

Very fine.

Copy II: First French Edition. (Hélène. Traduit de l'Anglais par Louise Sw.-Belloc.) [*Slade* 26 C [771*a*]

3 vols. Demy 8vo. Paris: Adolphe Guyot 1834. Sand-brown wrappers lettered in black, white spine labels.

Presentation Copy: Ink inscription: 'à Miss Edge worth, hommage du plus tendre respect, et de la plus sincère admiration de sa toute devouée Louise Sw.-Belloc. 29 mars 1834' on half-title of Vol. I.

[771*b*] **Copy III: First American Edition.** 2 vols. Carey, Lea & Blanchard, Philadelphia 1834. Blue diced cloth, paper labels. [*Slade* 26 C

Author's own copy with 'Maria Edgeworth' on title of Vol. II. Labels defective.

[772] I FANCIULLI O I LORO CARATTERI ('di Miss Edgeworth. Prima Traduzione Italiana')

Fcap 8vo. Firenze: Pietro Bigazzi 1828. Publisher's full red morocco, fully gilt. Spine lettered: CARATTERI / DEI / FANCIULLI. All edges gilt. Engraved front. by Zignani after Sabatelli.

pp. (vi) + (248)

Presentation Copy, with two ink inscriptions on recto of fly-leaf: [i] (slightly cut into): 'A Miss Edgeworth in segno di grato animo ital[ia]no per le sue belle opere [ ] educazione offre l' Editore Pietro Big[azzi]. Firenze.' [ii] (in Maria's hand): 'To my very dear niece Mary Anne Fox, April 21st, 1849, from her old aunt & friend Maria Edgeworth.'

Note. This is not a regular translation of any single work of Maria Edgeworth's. Almost certainly it is translated from a French publication of 1822 entitled *Les Enfans ou Les Caractères Par Miss Edgewoets* (see Slade, p. 73) which contained a few of the stories in *Early Lessons* considerably adapted, as well as stories for children by other (unnamed) authors.

[773] LEONORA [*Slade* 12 A

2 vols. J. Johnson 1806.

Copy I. Boards, labels.

Vol. I (ii) + (292)
II (ii) + (292)

Spines and labels worn.

Copy II. Contemporary tree calf. Collation as Copy I.

[773*a*] *Presentation Copy:* 'Richard Lovell Edgeworth from his partner the author' and underneath 'Harriet Edgeworth June 1817' in ink on each title.

Book-plate of Richard Lovell Edgeworth in each vol. Pencil annotations in Maria's hand in text of both vols.

[774] LETTERS FOR LITERARY LADIES

Copy I: First Edition. [anon] Johnson 1795. Orig. boards (re-backed, label renewed). [*Slade* 1 A

pp. (iv) + (204) [paged (1)–(76) [G_2 advert.] + (1)–(80) + (1)–(48)].

Signature: 'Miss Hookham's', on front cover.

Pp. 33–34 misbound between 46–47.

Copy II: Second Edition: Corrected and Much Enlarged. [Second Issue, with author's name] Johnson 1799. New half-calf, marbled boards. [*Slade* 1 B (b) [774*a*]

pp. (viii) + 240

Ink signature: 'Francis Wrangham 1804', on title.

Copy III: Third Edition. Johnson 1805. Cont. tree calf. [Not in *Slade* [774*b*]

Assuming a half-title (not present in this copy). pp. (viii) + 232

Ink signatures: 'S. Ferris, M.D.' and 'Ethelberta Lucy Emily Ferris', on fly-leaf.

LITTLE PLAYS FOR CHILDREN [775]
[*Slade* 24 A

Sm. 12mo. R. Hunter 1827. Orig. half-roan, marbled boards, lettered on spine.

pp. viii + (256)

Presentation Copy: 'Mrs Mary Sneyd from the author' in ink on fly-leaf.

Note. This book is described on title as 'VOL. VII OF THE PARENT'S ASSISTANT'.

MODERN GRISELDA (The): a Tale ('by Miss Edgeworth, author of' etc.) [776]

Copy I: First Edition. Johnson 1805. Cont. half-calf (issued in boards, label). [*Slade* 11 A

pp. (iv) + 170

Book-plate of John Hughes, and signature M. A. Hughes on fly-leaf.

Copy II: Second Edition. Johnson 1805. Cont. half-calf (issued in boards, label). [*Slade* 11 B

pp. (ii) + (204)

MORAL TALES FOR YOUNG PEOPLE [777]
[*Slade* 7 A

5 vols. Johnson 1801. Boards, glazed dark blue paper spines, paper labels. Engraved front. in each vol., 2 after C. Edgeworth, 1 after F. Edgeworth, 2 unsigned. *Pl. 13*

Half-title in Vols. I, II and V (? lacking from III and IV)

Vol. I (xii) + (240) L_{12} blank.
II (iv) + (198) Second leaf of final sig., K_2, a single inset.
III (ii) + 192
IV (ii) + (192) I_{12} blank, pasted to back cover.
V (iv) + 190 6th leaf of final sig., I_6, a single inset.

Spines of Vols. I, II and V defective. Title of Vol. V repaired.

[778] ORLANDINO [*Slade* 27A
Sm. sq. 16mo. Edinburgh: W. & R. Chambers 1848.

Copy I. Illuminated boards (Slade, First Binding Variant). Engraved front. on plate paper and 1 illustration on text paper.

Half-title. pp. (vi)+(178) (M_1), a single inset, carries advert. of Chambers' Series, dated Oct. 15, 1847.

[778*a*] **Copy II.** Ditto re-backed.

Presentation Copy: 'Honora Beaufort from the Author' in ink on title (only last three words in M.E.'s hand).

[779] PARENT'S ASSISTANT (The)

Copy I: Illustrated Edition. 6 vols. sm. 8vo. Johnson 1800. Cont. tree calf. [*Slade* 2C(i)

Ink signature: 'Emily Addison', on inside cover of each vol.

[779*a*] **Copy II: Sixth Edition.** 6 vols. sm. 12mo. Johnson 1813. Orig. half-roan, marbled boards, labels. [Not in Slade
Fine.

[779*b*] **Copy III: French Edition.** (L'Ami des Parens.) 2 vols. Geneva, n.d. Original boards (re-covered).

Association Copy: Ink signatures: 'Rich[d] Lovell Edgeworth, 1817' on half-title, and 'Harriet Edgeworth June 1817' on title of Vol. I; both signatures on title of Vol. II.

Notes. (i) Slade (p. 33) provisionally dates this work [1826?]. The signatures in this copy may be taken to demonstrate the actual date of issue.
(ii) The author's name first appeared on the third (unillustrated) edition of 1800 (*Slade* 2C).

[780] PATRONAGE [*Slade* 16A
Pl. 13 4 vols. J. Johnson 1814. Boards, labels.

Half-title in Vols. II, III, IV

Vol. I (iv)+418 First leaf of final sig., T_1, a single inset.
II (iv)+(432)
III (iv)+402 Final sigs., S (6 leaves) T (3 leaves). T_1 a single inset.
IV (iv)+(390) Final leaf, S_3, a single inset carrying Errata for all 4 vols.

Book-label of Rhiwlas Library, and signature: 'F. Price 1814', in each vol. Fine.

[781] POPULAR TALES [*Slade* 10A
3 vols. J. Johnson 1804. Cont. half-calf, marbled boards (issued in boards, labels).

Vol. I (viii) [paged (vi)]+(386) Final leaf, (S_1), a single inset carrying Errata.
II (iv)+(370) Sig. R, 4 leaves; final leaf, (S_1), a single inset carrying Errata.
III (iv)+(396) S_6 Errata (pasted on a stub).

RATIONAL PRIMER (A) (by the Authors of Practical Education) [*Slade* 4, pp. 47–51 [782]
Small 8vo. 'Printed for J. Johnson, St. Paul's Church-Yard, London, by Messrs Biggs and Cottle, St. Augustine's-Back, Bristol. 1799.'

Bound with a copy of *Poetry Explained for the Use of Young People* (1802) in full cont. calf, spine-lettered POETRY EXPLAINED / EDGEWORTH. (Probably originally issued in wrappers, plain or lettered. An advert. on p. (116) of *Poetry Explained* (q.v. below) lists it as '2s. 6d. sewed').

pp. (vi) [unpaginated; p. (iii) signed *a*]+(1)–40 'Preface' [signed A, 4 leaves, B, C, each 8 leaves] +1–(70) 'Text' [unsigned, and paged 1–69 because p. (4), blank, is unpaginated and what is really p. 5 is paged '4'].

Analysis of Text: pp. 1, 2 'Alphabet'; 3 'Vowels'; (4) blank and unpaginated; (5) [paged 4]–(37) [paged 36] 'Dipthongs, Consonants'; (38) [paged 37]–(61) [paged 60] 'Words'; (62) blank; (63) [paged (64)]–(70) [paged 69] a story: 'The Way to my Grandmother's', printed from engraved plates, showing accenting and underlining according to the principle adopted by R.L.E. in *Practical Education* (Lichfield, 1780) q.v. below.

Note. This is the rarest Edgeworth item after *The Parent's Assistant.* In addition to my own I am aware of two copies, one in the possession of the Butler family, the other formerly in the possession of Archdeacon Wrangham, now in the Library of Trinity College, Cambridge. The Wrangham copy is identical with mine, and as described above. The Butler copy (kindly analysed for me by Professor Harold Butler) is highly eccentric as to make-up and pagination. It seems to me probable that this Butler copy, a 'family' copy with a 'family' inscription, was an early or trial copy, and that all the blanks but two (pp. (4) and (62)) were removed and all the irregularities of pagination save one (p. (4)) corrected before formal publication.

ROSAMUND: a Sequel to Early Lessons [783]
[*Slade* 21A
2 vols. Sm. 12mo. R. Hunter (succ. to Johnson) 1821. Orig. half-roan, marbled boards, labels. *Pl. 13*
Blank leaf precedes title in Vol. II

Vol. I (viii)+252
II (iv)+(274) First leaf of final sig., $2A_1$, a single inset, $2A_6$ probably label-leaf.

Book-label of E. M. Philipps in each vol. In Vol. I, ink signature on fly-leaf: 'Arthur Hughes from E. M. Herbert. July 1864'; in Vol. II 'Arthur Hughes' only.

TALES AND MISCELLANEOUS PIECES: First Collected Edition [*Slade* 29A [784]
14 vols. Fcap 8vo. Printed for R. Hunter; Baldwin, Cradock & Joy, etc. etc. 1825. Very dark purple straight-grain morocco, fully gilt. A.e.g. Grey-

green end-papers. Certainly a publishers' binding.

This edition is of extreme scarcity. It was for years, and in vain, on the Bodleian list of desiderata.

[785] TALES AND NOVELS: Second Collected Edition [*Slade* 29B

18 vols. Baldwin & Cradock etc. 1832–33. Maroon moiré cloth. Fine.

Note. In this set the engraved front. and title to each vol. (after Harvey) are in three states: the first before letters on India paper; the second on India lettered in all margins; the third, as usual, on plate paper.

As Mrs Slade states (p. 222), the set is in the regulation style of binding and externally shows no sign of the extra-embellishments within; nor is there any indication of previous ownership to account for them.

[786] *Pl. 13* TALES OF FASHIONABLE LIFE

6 vols. J. Johnson 1809–1812. Boards, labels.

Vols. I–III Second Edition 1809. [*Slade* 14B

Vols. IV–VI First Edition 1812. [*Slade* 14A

Half-title in each vol.

Vol. I viii + (420) T_6 blank.
II (iv) + (392) S_4 blank.
III (iv) + 388
IV (xii) [paged (viii)] + 460
V (iv) + 392
VI (iv) + (468) X_6 blank.

Very fine. From the Bellew Library.

Partially by Maria Edgeworth

[787] COTTAGE DIALOGUES AMONG THE IRISH PEASANTRY (by Mary Leadbeater). With Notes and a Preface by Maria Edgeworth, author of 'Castle Rackrent' [*Slade* 28(i)*a*

London: J. Johnson, 1811. Boards, label.

Half-title. pp. (xii) [paged (x)] + (344) Longmans' cat., 36 pp. dated Feb. 1812, at end.

Very fine. From the Bellew Library.

Note. pp. (v)–(vii) are occupied by M.E.'s Preface, and her 'Glossary and Notes' occupy pp. 269–343.

B. Maria and Richard Lovell

[788] *Pl. 13* ESSAY ON IRISH BULLS [*Slade* 9A

J. Johnson 1802. Boards, label.

pp. (iv) [paged ii] + 316

Engraved vignettes on pp. (1) and 316. These pages are of thicker paper, and although paginated do not form part of the ordinary signatures. pp. (1) 2 are signed *b*.

Very fine. From the Bellew Library.

MEMOIRS OF RICHARD LOVELL EDGEWORTH, ESQ. ('begun by himself and concluded by his daughter, Maria Edgeworth') [789]

Copy I: First Edition. 2 vols. 8vo. R. Hunter 1820. Boards, labels. Engraved portrait front. in each vol. (in I of R.L.E., in II of Edward, Lord Longford); also in I engraved portrait of Thomas Day, and in II engraved portrait of Erasmus Darwin and 5 facsimiles (2 of them folding) of drawings by Charlotte Edgeworth. [*Slade* 20A

Half-title in each vol.

Vol. I (iv) + 392
II (xii) [paged (viii)] + (500) Text ends 448; 449–450 Directions for Burial; (451)–493 Appendix; 494–498 Notes on the Plates; (499)–(500) adverts. and Directions to Binder.

Very fine. From the Bellew Library.

Copy II: Third Edition. 8vo. Bentley 1844. Maroon fine-diaper cloth. Engraved portrait front. of R.L.E., also the 3 other portraits as in Copy I, but imprint on plates altered to Richard Bentley, 1844. [*Slade* 20C [789*a*]

pp. (iv) + (488) Text ends 486; 487 Directions for Burial; 488 List of Periodical contributions by R.L.E.

Signature: 'R. J. Gomperts', on inside front cover and extract from Maxwell's *Noontide Essays* written on fly-leaf. Fine.

Note. Maria's part in this work was 'nearly rewritten' for this edition.

PRACTICAL EDUCATION [790]

Copy I: First Edition. 2 vols. 4to. J. Johnson 1798. Boards, labels. Engraved plate constitutes pp. 45–46 in Vol. I; 2 folding engraved plates at end of Vol. II are not reckoned in collation. [*Slade* 3A

Half-title in each vol.

Vol. I (xii) + (386) Final leaf, ($3D_1$), a single inset.
II (iv) + 387–(794) Text ends 730; (731)–775 Appendix; (776) blank; (777)–(792) Index; (793) (794), $5I_1$, Corrections, and a single inset leaf. pp. 387–388 are $3D_2$.

Very fine.

Copy II: Another. With original blank leaf (pp. 45–6 Vol. I) uncancelled by binder. Plate intended for this page at end of Vol. II. Boards, backs defective. [790*a*]

Copy III: Another. Cont. tree calf, mottled edges. [790*b*]

Copy IV: Second Edition (Revised). 3 vols. 8vo. J. Johnson 1801. Cont. mottled calf, mottled edges. Engraved plates as in Copy I, but re-engraved to new scale. [*Slade* 3B [790*c*]

Half-title in each vol. (not present in this copy).

Vol. I (xvi) + 412
II (iv) + 386 Final leaf, Cc_1, a single inset.
III (iv) + (388) Text ends 319; (320) blank; (321)–357 Appendix; (358) blank; (359)–387 Index.

Book-plate of George Pemberton in each vol., and notes by him in Vol. III.

[790*d*] **Copy V: French Edition.** 2 vols. Paris and Geneva 1801. Cont. tree calf, gilt, marbled edges. 'Nouvelle Edition, revue, corrigée et augmentée.' [*Slade* 3D

Presentation Copy: 'Madame Edgeworth de la part de Maria E'; lower down: 'de l'Anglais de R. L. Edgeworth'—all in Maria's hand on each title.

Note. The first edition of this translation was published in 1800. The second contains an exchange of letters between the translator, Charles Pictet, and R. L. Edgeworth, not in the first edition.

C. Richard Lovell

[791] ESSAY ON THE CONSTRUCTION OF ROADS AND CARRIAGES (An)
8vo. J. Johnson 1813. Orig. boards (re-backed, label renewed).

Half-title. pp. (xii) [paged (x)] + (196) [paged (i)–iii + (4)–(196)] n_2 adverts.

Book-label of E. & F. N. Spon at end.

[792] LETTER TO THE EARL OF CHARLEMONT ON THE TELLOGRAPH (A) etc.
8vo. Dublin printed, London reprinted, Johnson 1797. New boards, but uncut and front wrapper preserved.

Half-title. pp. iv + 54

Signature of Maria Edgeworth on title.

[793] POETRY EXPLAINED FOR THE USE OF YOUNG PEOPLE
J. Johnson 1802. Orig. grey paper wrappers, unlettered.

pp. (xvi) + (116) Tear in p. 13.

[794] PRACTICAL EDUCATION, or The History of Harry and Lucy, Vol. II [*Slade* pp. 3–7
16mo. Lichfield, Jackson 1780. Orig. half sheep, marbled boards, unlettered. Copper-plate engraving faces p. 101.

Blank leaf precedes title. pp. (xxii) [paged (iv) + (ii) + (xvi)] + (128) (A_3) a single inset. Text ends 104; 105–127 Glossary.

Maria Edgeworth's copy, with her signature on inside cover, and on Dedication leaf in the author's hand 'from the author to his partner June '97'. Spine defective.

Note. See Slade, pp. 3–6, for a history of this book and reasons for doubting the existence of Vol. I. In my opinion the most likely explanation is that Vol. I existed *in manuscript only*, and that R.L.E., finding its utility as a text-book for his children greater than expected, caused the second vol. to be printed.

READINGS ON POETRY [795]
Copy I: First Edition. 12mo. Hunter 1816. Orig. half-roan, marbled boards, paper label. [*Slade* 17A

pp. xxviii + (216) T_6 adverts. Publishers' cat., 8 pp. undated, at end.

Copy II: Second Edition, Corrected. 12mo. Hunter 1816. Binding as Copy I. [*Slade* 17B [795*a*]

pp. xxviii + (216) Text ends 212; (213)–(216), T_5 T_6, 'Advertisement' and adverts. Publisher's cat., 8 pp. undated, at end. Fine.

SCHOOL LESSONS [796]
Sm. sq. 8vo. Dublin: Printed for the Author by John Jones 1817. Full cont. calf, marbled edges.

pp. viii + 92

In ink facing title: 'H. Beaufort. The gift of L.E. October 3, 1817.' [Honora Beaufort was R.L.E.'s daughter by his 3rd wife; L.E. was Lovell Edgeworth, son of R.L.E. to whom this book is dedicated.]

SUBSTANCE OF THREE SPEECHES (The) on the subject of Union with Great Britain [797]
8vo. J. Johnson 1800. Bound in cloth with four other tracts relating to the Edgeworth family.

Half-title. pp. (iv) + 48

From the library of C. Sneyd Edgeworth, with his book-plate and various inscriptions.

Edgeworthiana

MEMOIR OF THE ABBE EDGEWORTH, by C. Sneyd Edgeworth. [798]
Hunter (succ. to Johnson) 1815. Boards, label. Engraved portrait front.

pp. iv + (224)

Very fine. From the Bellew Library.

A MEMOIR OF MARIA EDGEWORTH: With a Selection of Her Letters. By the late Mrs Edgeworth. Edited by her Children. Not published. [799]
3 vols. Printed by Joseph Masters & Son, London 1867. Calf extra by Riviere & Son. Top edges gilt.

Half-title in Vols. I and III

Vol. I (iv) + (326)
II (ii) + 300
III (iv) + 290

From the Rosebery Library, with Durdan's Library book-plate in each vol. and blind stamp on title and p. 99 in each volume.

EDWARDES, MRS ANNIE (*circ.* 1830–1896)

[800] BALLROOM REPENTANCE (A) (by Annie Edwardes)
2 vols. Bentley 1882. Oxford-blue diagonal-fine-ribbed cloth; dark chocolate end-papers. Printed throughout in dark blue ink.
Half-title in each vol.
Vol. I (viii) + 344
II (viii) + (344) B

[801] GIRTON GIRL (A) (by Mrs Annie Edwardes).
3 vols. Bentley 1885. Blue-grey diagonal-fine-ribbed cloth, with oval wood-engraved medallion of a Girton Girl pasted on front in a gold surround; dark grey-chocolate end-papers.
Blank leaf and half-title precede title in each vol.
Vol. I (viii) [paged vi] + (304) U_8 blank.
II (viii) [paged vi] + (292) U_2 blank.
III (viii) [paged vi] + (300) U_6 adverts. B

[802] LEAH: A WOMAN OF FASHION (by Mrs Edwardes).
3 vols. Bentley 1875. Royal-blue diagonal-fine-ribbed cloth, blocked and lettered in black and gold.
Vol. I (iv) + 296
II (iv) + (290) Final leaf, (U_1), a single inset.
III (iv) + (300) B

[803] OUGHT WE TO VISIT HER? (by Mrs Edwardes).
3 vols. Bentley 1871. Grass-green sand-grain cloth; café-au-lait end-papers.
Vol. I (ii) + 290 Final leaf, U_2, a single inset.
II (ii) + (302) First leaf of final sig., U_1, a single inset.
III (ii) + (298) Final leaf, U_5, a single inset. B

[804] PEARL POWDER: a Novel (by Mrs Annie Edwardes).
2 vols. Bentley 1890. Indigo diagonal-fine-dot-and-line-grain cloth; monogram end-papers.
Vol. I (iv) + 300
II (iv) + (288) B
Hinge of Vol. I mouse-eaten.

[805] PLASTER SAINT (A) (by Annie Edwardes).
Chatto & Windus 1899. Red linen-grain cloth; flowered end-papers.
Half-title. pp. (iv) + (260) (17_2) publishers' device. Publishers' cat., 32 pp. dated September 1899, at end.

[806] STEVEN LAWRENCE, YEOMAN (by Mrs Edwards (sic), author of 'Archie Lovell', 'The Morals of Mayfair', etc.)
3 vols. Bentley 1868. Earth-brown sand-grain cloth.
Vol. I (ii) + (330) Final leaf, Y_5, a single inset.
II (ii) + (330) Y, 2 leaves; Z, 3 leaves. Z_1 a single inset.
III (ii) + 344 B
Back cover of Vol. I damp-stained.

SUSAN FIELDING (by the author of 'Archie Lovell' and 'Steven Lawrence, Yeoman') [807]
3 vols. Bentley 1869. Maroon diagonal-fine-dot-and-line-grain cloth.
Vol. I iv + (296)
II iv + 320
III iv + (324) B

EDWARDS, AMELIA B. (1831–1892)

HALF A MILLION OF MONEY
3 vols. Tinsley 1866. Green sand-grain cloth. [808]
Advert. leaf and half-title precede title in Vol. I. Half-title only in Vols. II and III.
Vol. I (viii) [paged vi] + (324)
II vi + 332
III vi + (400) CC_8 blank.
Presentation Copy: 'To my dear old friend and cousin, M. Betham Edwards, A.B.E. 1865' on fly-leaf of Vol. I. Label of Tunbridge Wells Library and Reading Room in each vol.

EDWARDS, M. BETHAM (1836–1919)

WHITE HOUSE BY THE SEA (The): a Love Story [809]
2 vols. Smith, Elder 1857. Cambridge-blue ribbed cloth.
Half-title in each vol.
Vol. I (iv) + 280
II (iv) + (224) P_8 adverts. Publishers' cat., 16 pp. dated November 1857, at end.
Presentation Copy: 'Amelia B. Edwards from her loving friend and cousin M. Betham Edwards 1857' on title of Vol. I. Book-plate of Amelia B. Edwards in each vol. Also book-plates of the 'Edwards Library' at Somerville College.
Note. It is a curious coincidence (of the kind which gives peculiar savour to the hobby of collecting) that there should have come my way from totally different sources mutual presentation copies of Amelia Edwards' best-known and most popular story and the first novel of her prolific cousin M. Betham Edwards.

EGAN, PIERCE (1772–1849)

[810] **PILGRIMS OF THE THAMES** (The), in Search of the National!

8vo. Thomas Tegg 1839. Plum ribbed cloth. Etched front. and 23 plates, also wood-engravings in the text, by Pierce Egan the Younger.

pp. (viii) [paged iv] + (376)

EGAN, PIERCE, the Younger (1814–1880)

[811] **FLOWER OF THE FLOCK** (The)

3 vols. W. S. Johnson & Co. n.d. [1858]. Magenta morocco cloth.

Vol. I iv + 328
II iv + 304
III iv + 320

Blind stamp of W. H. Smith's Library on fly-leaf of Vol. I. Fine.

Note. There is a secondary binding of orange-scarlet sand-grain cloth, with type-set spine and no imprint.

ELIOT, GEORGE (MARION EVANS) (1819–1880)

For further bibliographical detail see *Victorian Lady Novelists* by M. L. Parrish (London, 1933). Reference is also made to Carter, *Binding Variants* (London, 1932).

[812] **ADAM BEDE** [*Parrish* p. 12

3 vols. Blackwood 1859. Bright brown ripple-grain cloth.

Half-title in each vol.

Vol. I (viii) + (326) Final leaf, X_3, a single inset.
II (viii) + 374 Final leaf, $2B_1$, a single inset. (2A two leaves.)
III (vi) + (334). 1st leaf of final sig., X_1, a single inset. Text ends 324; (325)–334 Epilogue. Publishers' cat., 16 pp. undated, at end.

Ink signature: 'Cath[e] Greaves, 1859', on fly-leaf of Vol. I; Booksellers' stamp: 'Cooke & Son, Warwick', on fly-leaf of each vol. Binders' label: 'Edmonds & Remnants', at end of Vol. I.

[813] **DANIEL DERONDA** [*Parrish* p. 39

4 vols. Blackwood 1876. Dark maroon diagonal-fine-ribbed cloth; dark chocolate end-papers.

Half-title in each vol.

Copy I: 1st Issue.

Vol. I (iv) + (368) [Final leaf is Z_8.]
II (iv) + 364
III (iv) + (394) Final leaf, $2C_3$, a single inset. Erratum slip tipped on to p. (394).
IV (iv) + (370) Final leaf, $2A_8$, adverts.

Very fine.

The discrepancy between the signature-numbering of Vols. I and IV is due to the fact that sig. L in Vol. IV is a one-leaf signature. L_1 (pp. 161, 162) is a single inset leaf and is followed by the fly-title to Book VIII. This fly-title is in fact M_1 but is not signed. Consequently Vol. IV is seven leaves ahead of Vol. I, and what was Z_8 in I becomes $2A_7$ in IV.

Copy II, 2nd Issue. As Copy I, but the prelims. in each vol. are (vi), on account of the addition of a single inset Contents leaf. In my experience the part issue contained no Contents leaves, nor do they appear either in the Bodleian copy of the book issue (fine in original cloth) or in the one described by Parrish. I think the first book issue was without them, and that they were later inserted for readers' convenience. Their appearance is somewhat fortuitous, for in a previous copy of my own such a leaf was only present in Vol. I, and I have seen other copies incompletely furnished. [813*a*]

The Parts also contain an Erratum slip (in Part III) referring to Book II, p. 336. I have not located a book issue with this slip (in Vol. I), and the quotation is printed with the correction duly made.

FELIX HOLT: the Radical [*Parrish* p. 20 [814]

3 vols. Blackwood 1866.

Copy I: Bright brown sand-grain cloth. Spine: 'Carter B.'

Half-title in each vol.

Vol. I (iv) + (304)
II (iv) + 290 Final leaf, T_1, a single inset.
III (iv) + (288) S_7 S_8 adverts.

'Carlingford 1885' in ink on half-title of Vol. I. Very fine.

Copy II: Bright blue sand-grain cloth, blocked in black on front, in blind on back, blocked and lettered in gold on spine. 'Carter E.' [814*a*]

Collation as Copy I. Blind stamp of W. H. Smith 'Library' on fly-leaf of Vol. I.

Fine.

MIDDLEMARCH: a Study of Provincial Life [815]
[*Parrish* p. 32

4 vols. Blackwood 1871. Bright blue sand-grain cloth; chocolate end-papers.

Half-title in each vol.

Vol. I (xii) + 410 First leaf of final sig., $2D_1$, a single inset.
II (vi) + (378) Pp. (v) (vi), Contents, and final leaf, $2A_5$, single inset leaves.
III (vi) + 384 Pp. (v) (vi), Contents, form a single inset leaf.
IV (vi) + (372) Pp. (v) (vi), Contents, form a single inset leaf.

Fine.

[816] MILL ON THE FLOSS (The) [*Parrish* p. 14
3 vols. Blackwood 1860. Bright brown ripple-grain cloth.

Half-title in each vol.

Vol. I (viii)+(364) Z_6 blank.
II (viii)+(320)
III (viii)+(314) Final leaf, U_5, a single inset. Publishers' cat., 16 pp. undated, at end.

Copy I. Spine 'Carter A'. Binder's ticket: 'Burn', at end of Vol. I.

[816*a*] **Copy II.** Spine 'Carter B'. Binders' ticket: 'Edmonds and Remnants', at end of Vol. I.

Both copies very fine. Neither copy contains the advert. leaf [Vol. I (ix) and (x)], advertising *Clerical Life* and *Adam Bede*, recorded by Parrish and demonstrated by Carter to be a later insertion.

[817] ROMOLA [*Parrish* p. 17

Copy I: First Edition. 3 vols. Smith, Elder 1863. Green dot-and-line-grain cloth.

Vol. I iv+336
II iv+(336) 42_8 adverts.
III iv+292

Fine.

Presentation Copy from the publisher: 'The Rev. F.D. Maurice with Henry King's very kind regards July 30th, 1863' in ink facing title of Vol. I. Cross, in his *Life of George Eliot*, records from the diary of Henry King (a member of the firm of Smith, Elder) a meeting with Maurice and a conversation about George Eliot's new novel, *Romola*, just published. Clearly the publisher sent Maurice this copy the next day.

[817*a*] **Copy II: First one-volume and first illustrated Edition.** Smith, Elder 1865: 'Illustrated Edition.' Red morocco cloth, blocked in blind and gold, uniform with Gaskell's *Cousin Phillis*, Copy I. Inset wood-engraved front. and engraved title dated 1865 precede printed title similarly dated. Three other plates in text.

Book-plate of John Browne. Fine.

[818] SCENES OF CLERICAL LIFE [*Parrish* p. 7
2 vols. Blackwood 1858. Dark maroon morocco cloth; chocolate end-papers.

Half-title in each vol.

Vol. I (vi)+366 Pp. (v) (vi), Contents, and 1st leaf of final sig., Z_1, are single insets.
II (vi)+(382) Pp. (v) (vi), fly-title, and 1st leaf of final sig., $2A_1$, are single insets.

Binders' ticket: 'Edmonds & Remnants', at end of Vol. I. Very fine.

[819] SILAS MARNER: the Weaver of Waveloe [*Parrish* p. 15
Blackwood 1861. Bright brown ripple-grain cloth. Spine: 'Carter B.'

Half-title. pp. (vi)+364. Pp. (v) (vi), fly-title to Part I, form a single inset leaf. 2 leaves on thinner paper advertising *Autobiography of Alexander Carlyle* at end, followed by Publishers' cat., 16 pp. undated.

Very fine.

ELLIS, MRS SARAH STICKNEY (*circ.* 1810–1872)

DAUGHTERS OF ENGLAND (The): their Position in Society, Character and Responsibilities [820]
Fisher, Son & Co. n.d. (1842). Dark olive-green fine-diaper cloth. Steel-engraved front. after Allom.

pp. (iv)+396 Preface dated January 20, 1842. Publishers' cat., 16 pp. also dated January 20, 1842, at end.

Signature: 'Katherine Bowman, Loughborough Rd. Brixton, S.', on fly-leaf.

ENGLISHWOMAN'S FAMILY LIBRARY (The) [821]
4 vols. Fisher, Son & Co. 1843. Uniform rose-madder fine-diaper cloth, blocked in blind on front and back with floral decoration and royal crown over V.R. in monogram, gold-lettered on spine.

The four books are contained in a dark red leather box, with hinged glass front, tooled in gold and surmounted by a pediment gold-lettered: THE ENGLISHWOMAN'S FAMILY LIBRARY. The vols. are not numbered, so I have given them chronological sequence.

Vols. I and II had been published before their inclusion in this Library, in 1838 and 1842 respectively. Vols. III and IV are first editions.

(Vol. I) **The Women of England**, their Social Duties and Domestic Habits. n.d. Twentieth Edition. Preface dated 1839. [821*a*]

Half-title. pp. (360) [paged 356]

Binders' ticket: 'Westleys and Clark', at end.

(Vol. II) **The Daughters of England**, their Position in Society, Character and Responsibilities. n.d. Preface dated as in First Edition, but re-set. Steel-engraved front. [821*b*]

pp. (viii)+400. Publishers' cat., 12 pp. undated, at end.

Binders' ticket as in Vol. I.

(Vol. III) THE WIVES OF ENGLAND, their Relative Duties, Domestic Influence and Social Obligations (by the author of 'The Women of England') [821*c*]

Dedicated, by permission, to the Queen. n.d. Preface dated 1843.

pp. (xii)+(372) R_6 adverts.

Binders' ticket as in Vol. I.

[821*d*] (Vol. IV) THE MOTHERS OF ENGLAND, their Influence and Responsibility (by the author of the 'Women of England'), 1843

pp. (viii) + (400) S_4–S_8 adverts., which include an illustration of this boxed 'Library' which was sold at 39*s.* in cloth; 47*s.* in cloth elegant, gilt edges; 63*s.* in morocco elegant, while for 10*s.* extra the box could be had in morocco.

Except for a very slight fading of the spines, these volumes are in fine condition.

[822] FAMILY SECRETS: or Hints to those who would make Home happy

3 vols. 8vo. Fisher, Son & Co. [1843]. Publishers' full calf gilt; gilt edges. Steel-engraved front. and vignette title after E. Corbould in Vol. I, after T. Allom in II and III; also, in I, 9 steel-engraved plates after Corbould and Allom, in II 9 plates after Allom, in III 7 plates, all after Allom save one unsigned.

Vol. I (iv) + 328
II (iv) + 312
III (iv) + 308

Bookseller's label: 'Price Booklander, Bilston.'

Originally published in monthly parts.

[823] LOOK TO THE END, or the Bennets Abroad

2 vols. Fisher, Son & Co. n.d. [1845]. Claret fine-diaper cloth. Copies in dark green bead-grain are later.

Vol. I viii + (360)
II (ii) + (348)

[824] MOTHER'S MISTAKE (The)

Houlston & Stoneman n.d. Red morocco cloth, blocked and lettered in gold and blind. Steel-engraved front. and text illustrations after Anelay.

pp. viii + (208)

Ink inscription: 'H. Davies from his Mother. July 21st/57' on fly-leaf. This date is probably approximately that of publication, as the work was re-issued by Ward and Lock in 1860.

Note. This story is printed in double columns on cheap paper, and has the appearance of work first published in penny parts. Its most interesting feature is a 'Sketch of the Literary Career of Mrs Ellis' which is not only informative, but curiously outspoken in occasional criticism of her style and matter. At the time the 'Sketch' was written she was conducting a school, for young ladies, and applying to its conduct 'her ideas of the qualifications necessary for an honourable, useful and happy female character'.

[825] PICTURES OF PRIVATE LIFE: Second Series (by Sarah Stickney)

Fcap 8vo. Smith, Elder 1834. Purple-brown morocco cloth, blocked and lettered in gold on spine. Steel-engraved front., 'The Misanthrope', after Howard, R.A.

pp. (xii) + (412) DD_6 advert. Publishers' cat., 24 pp. undated, at end.

Note. The Second of three Series of *Pictures of Private Life,* which constituted the future Mrs Ellis' earliest work. Each series was issued in morocco as well as in cloth. This Second Series contains two tales: *The Misanthrope* and *The Pains of Pleasing.*

SOCIAL DISTINCTION, or Hearts and Homes [826]

3 vols. 8vo. J. & F. Tallis, n.d. [1848–49]. Pale apple-green cloth, gilt; gilt edges. Steel-engraved front. and vignette title in each vol. after H. Warren; also in Vol. I 9, in II and III 8 plates each, all after Warren.

Vol. I pp. 480
II pp. 480
III Inset leaf 'Directions to Binder' follows engraved title. Text pp. 478. 1st leaf of final sig., $3P_1$, a single inset.

Booksellers' ticket: 'Hunt & Son, Ipswich', at end of Vols. I and II. Pencil signature: 'M. A. Cole', on fly-leaf of each vol.

Note. This book is sumptuously produced. Each plate has an elaborate frame specially designed, and all are tissued. The work was originally published in monthly parts.

TEMPER AND TEMPERAMENT: or Varieties of Character [827]

2 vols. 8vo. Fisher, Son & Co. n.d. [1846]. Dark blue morocco cloth. Steel-engraved plates and engraved titles after various artists.

Vol. I (iv) + (268)
II (iv) + 272

ELTON, SIR ARTHUR HALLAM, BART., M.P. (1818–1883) [828]

BELOW THE SURFACE: a Story of English Country Life [anon]

3 vols. Smith, Elder 1857. Grey-purple morocco cloth.

Half-title in Vol. I

Vol. I (viii) + 272 Publishers' cat., 16 pp. dated August 1857, at end.
II (iv) + (296) U_4 blank.
III (iv) + (336)

Binders' ticket: 'Westleys & Co.', at end of Vol. I.

Note. This was the publishers' file copy and only came to light in 1942. It is in new condition. The story is an exposure of abuses prevalent in Lunatic Asylums and Workhouses.

EVERETT-GREEN, EVELYN (1856–1932)

[829] TORWOOD'S TRUST: a Novel
3 vols. Bentley 1884. Pale sage-green cloth; flowered end-papers.
Vol. I vi [paged iv] + 306 Final leaf, 20_1, a single inset.
II iv + 298 Final leaf, 39_5, a single inset.
III iv + (314) 59_5 'Note', and a single inset.
The only three-decker of this well-known writer of historical fiction for young people. B

FAITHFULL, EMILY (1835–?)

[830] CHANGE UPON CHANGE: a Love Story
Emily Faithfull, Victoria Press, Princes Street, 1868. Dark brown sand-grain cloth, bevelled boards.
pp. (iv) + (412)
Ink signature: 'Octavia A. Duse' on p. (iii).
See also TROLLOPE (ANTHONY), *A Welcome.*

FARJEON, B. L. (1838–1903)

This extensive collection is mainly of family origin. The great majority of the books came from the novelist's North London home and were the residue of his 'author's' copies. The set is, however, far from complete, at least six three-deckers and as many one-volume titles recorded in the *C.B.E.L.* being absent. The run of Annuals and Christmas Numbers is more nearly comprehensive; and these are interesting as showing the great popularity won by Farjeon as a purveyor of such characteristic mid-Victorian fare.

[831] AARON THE JEW
3 vols. Hutchinson 1894. Smooth dark red cloth, blocked and lettered in gold; patterned end-papers.
Half-title in each vol.
Vol. I (viii) + (208) 13_8 adverts.
II (viii) + 204
III vi + (198) Final leaf, 13_3, a single inset.
'S. S. RALLI' stamped on half-title in each vol.

[832] BASIL AND ANNETTE: a Novel
3 vols. F. V. White & Co. 1890. Plum morocco cloth, blocked and lettered in black on front, gold-lettered on spine; pale grey floral end-papers.
Half-title in each vol.
Vol. I (viii) + (156)
II (viii) + (252)
III (viii) + (248) 49_4 imprint leaf. Publishers' cat., 16 pp. undated and on text paper, at end.
Very fine.

BELLS OF PENRAVEN (The) [833]
Xmas No. of *Tinsley's Magazine*, 1879. White pictorial wrappers, printed in red, blue and black. Text illustrations.
pp. 96. Fine.

BETRAYAL OF JOHN FORDHAM (The) [834]
Hutchinson 1896. Red ribbed cloth, blocked and lettered in gold.
Blank leaf and half-title precede title. pp. (viii) + 358 First leaf of final sig., (Z_1), a single inset. Publishers' cat., 16 pp. on text paper dated August 1896, at end.

BLADE O' GRASS [835]
Xmas No. of *Tinsley's Magazine*, 1871. White pictorial wrappers, printed in red, blue and black. Front. and text illustrations.
pp. 96. Very fine.

BREAD AND CHEESE AND KISSES [836]
Xmas No. of *Tinsley's Magazine*, 1872. White pictorial wrappers, printed in red, blue and black. Front. and text illustrations.
pp. 104. Very fine.

CHRISTMAS ANGEL [837]
Ward & Downey n.d. [1885]. Glazed coloured pictorial boards, yellow edges. Illustrations in the text by Gordon Browne.
Half-title. pp. 152 Publishers' cat., 8 pp. on text paper dated October, 1885, at end. Very fine.

CLAIRVOYANTE (The) [838]
Hutchinson 1905. Grey-blue linen-grain cloth, with title and author in white on smooth dark blue panel on front, gold-lettered on spine.
Leaf of adverts. precedes half-title. pp. (viii) + (280) 18_4 adverts., followed by Publishers' cat., 16 pp. dated January 1905. Fine.

DEATH TRANCE (The) [839]
'The Penny Library of Fiction.' S.P.C.K. n.d. Coloured pictorial wrappers.
pp. (32). Final leaf adverts. Fine.

DEVLIN THE BARBER [840]
8vo. Ward & Downey 1888. Pictorial boards, red cloth spine.
Half-title. pp. (viii) + (192). Fine.

DUCHESS OF ROSEMARY LANE (The): a Novel [841]
3 vols. Tinsley 1876. Grass-green diagonal-fine-ribbed cloth; blocked in black on front and back, gold-lettered and blocked in gold and black on spine.

Blank leaf and half-title precede title in Vol. I. Half-title only in Vols. II and III.

Vol. I (viii) [paged vi] + 272
II (viii) + (304) U_8 blank.
III (viii) + 268

Ink-signature 'Collins' on fly-leaf of each vol. Half-title and title in Vol. III torn.

[842] FOR THE DEFENCE: a realistic and sensational story of human nature

Trischler & Co. 1891. 'Fifteenth thousand.'

Advert. leaf precedes half-title. pp. 216

Copy I: Pictorial wrappers. Fine.

[842*a*] **Copy II:** Black sand-grain cloth, blocked and lettered in pink. Very fine.

Note. Both these were author's copies; and I imagine an entire first edition of fifteen thousand was thus described. Almost certainly the same procedure was followed with the English edition of Fergus Hume's *Mystery of a Hansom Cab* (3597 in Section II).

[843] GOLDEN GRAIN

Xmas No. of *Tinsley's Magazine,* 1873. White pictorial wrappers, printed in red, grey-blue and black. Front. and text illustrations.

pp. 96. Very fine.

[844] GOLDEN LAND (The), or Links from Shore to Shore

Ward, Lock 1886. Smooth olive-green cloth, pictorially blocked in red, black and gold; chocolate end-papers. Wood-engraved front. and 27 illustrations after Gordon Browne, of which 24 in the text.

Half-title. pp. 344 [paged (i)–viii + (9)–344] Fine.

[845] GREAT PORTER SQUARE: a Mystery

3 vols. Ward & Downey 1885. Grey diagonal-fine-ribbed cloth, blocked and lettered in black and gold; silver-grey floral end-papers.

Vol. I iv + 272
II iv + (256) 33_8 imprint leaf.
III iv + (240)

Fine.

[846] GRIF

Copy I: First Edition. 'A Story of Colonial Life.' Dunedin: William Hay 1866. Stiff glazed salmon paper wrappers, pictorially printed in brown on front cover. Spine and back cover plain. Wood-engraved version of front cover picture as front.

pp. (viii) + (254) Very fine.

[846*a*] **Copy II: First English Edition.** 'A Story of Australian Life.' 2 vols. Tinsley 1870. Bright blue fine-dot-and-line cloth, bevelled boards.

Half-title in each vol.

Vol. I vi + 286. First leaf of final sig., T_1, a single inset.
II vi + (278) Final leaf, T_3, a single inset.

Very fine.

Copy III: Dramatic Version: 'Grif: A Drama in Four Acts.' Imprint '12 Buckingham St., Strand.' n.d. [1891]. Unwrappered. Page (1) lettered 'Grif'. [846*b*]

pp. (1)–(80), interleaved with blanks

IN A SILVER SEA [847]

3 vols. Ward & Downey 1886. Smooth very-pale-blue cloth, blocked in brown and lettered in silver; olive-grey end-papers.

Vol. I iv + 272
II iv + (272) S_8 imprint leaf.
III iv + (264) S_4 blank.

ISLAND PEARL (An) [848]

Xmas No. of *Tinsley's Magazine,* 1875. White pictorial wrappers, printed in red, grey-blue and black. Front. after R. Knight and text illustrations.

pp. 96 Very fine.

Note. This story was re-issued about 1902 by Hutchinson, as a sixpenny 8vo in pictorial boards, undated and without evidence of previous publication. At least two others of the Tinsley-Farjeon Christmas stories were similarly re-issued (*Blade o' Grass* and *Bread, Cheese and Kisses*), but only *An Island Pearl* is in the collection.

JOSHUA MARVEL [849]

3 vols. Tinsley 1871. Dark green bubble-grain cloth, with Tinsley's standard blocking, advertising *Tinsley's Magazine,* in blind on front and back, blocked and lettered in gold on spine.

Half-title in each vol.

Vol. I (vi) + 326 First leaf of final sig., Y_1, a single inset.
II (vi) + 328
III (vi) + (296) U_4 blank.

Fine.

KING OF NO-LAND (The) [850]

Xmas No. of *Tinsley's Magazine,* 1874. White pictorial wrappers, printed in red, greenish-grey and black. Front. after R. Knight and text illustrations.

pp. 96 Very fine.

LIFE'S BRIGHTEST STAR. The Sunday Magazine Christmas Story [851]

4to. Isbister & Co. 1886. Pale yellow wrappers, pictorially printed and fancy lettered in red and black: spine unlettered; back and inside covers printed with adverts. Wood-engraved front. on plate paper and numerous text illustrations after R. Barnes.

pp. 64 Fine.

[852] **LITTLE MAKE-BELIEVE**
Xmas No. of *Tinsley's Magazine*, 1883. White pictorial wrappers, printed in red, blue and black. Text illustrations.

pp. 96 Fine.

[853] **LONDON'S HEART**
3 vols. Tinsley 1873. Ultramarine patterned-sand-grain cloth, blocked in black on front and back, blocked and lettered in gold on spine.

Half-titles in Vols. I and II

Vol. I (vi) [paged iv]+(302) First leaf of final sig., U_1, a single inset.
II (vi)+308
III (iv)+294 First leaf of final sig., U_1, a single inset.

[854] **LOVE'S VICTORY**: a Novel
2 vols. Tinsley 1875. Brown diagonal-fine-ribbed cloth, blocked in black on front and back, blocked in black and lettered in gold on spine.

Blank leaf and half-title precede title in each vol.

Vol. I viii+(284) T_3–T_6 adverts., followed by publishers' cat., 16 pp. dated March 1874.
II viii+288

[855] **MARCH OF FATE** (The): a Novel
3 vols. F. V. White & Co. 1893. Olive diagonal-fine-ribbed cloth, blocked and lettered in black on front., publishers' monogram in black on back, blocked in black and gold-lettered on spine. Very dark brown end-papers.

Half-title in each vol.

Vol. I (viii)+(240) 15_8 blank.
II (viii)+(240) 30_8 imprint leaf.
III (viii)+(240) 45_8 blank, followed by publishers' cat., 16 pp. on text paper, undated.

Very fine.

[856] **MESMERISTS** (The): a Novel
Copy I: First Edition. Hutchinson 1900. Smooth bright red cloth, lettered in white.

Half-title. pp. 400

The Mesmerists ends p. 262; pp. (263)–400 are occupied with *The Mesmerist, an Original Play in four Acts.*

[856*a*] **Copy II: Dramatic Version.** 'The Mesmerist: an original play in four Acts.' No imprint or date. Grey printed wrappers.

pp. (144) i_7 i_8 blank.

Two copies, of which one corrected in pencil. Both came from the family source. Unpaginated, but printed from the type set up for book issue (Copy I).

MYSTERY OF ROARING MEG (The) [857]
Xmas No. of *Tinsley's Magazine*, 1878. White pictorial wrappers, printed in red, blue and black. Text illustrations.

pp. 96 Very fine.

MYSTERY OF THE ROYAL MAIL (The) [858]
Hutchinson 1902. Dark green diagonal-fine-ribbed cloth, with title in gold on red panel on front, gold-lettered on spine.

Half-title. pp. (viii)+376 Publishers' cat., 8 pp. on text paper dated Sept. 1902, at end. Fine.

PERIL OF RICHARD PARDON (The): a Novel [859]
F. V. White & Co. 1890.

Advert. leaf precedes title. pp. (viii)+(120) 8_4 adverts.

Copy I: Pictorial wrappers. Fine.

Copy II: Smooth cherry red cloth, patterned ends. Cloth a little faded.

SECRET INHERITANCE (A) [860]
3 vols. Ward & Downey 1887. Smooth scarlet cloth, blocked and lettered in black on front, publishers' monogram in blind on back, gold-lettered on spine. Grey-on-white flowered end-papers.

Half-title in each vol.

Vol. I (iv)+292
II (iv)+284
III (iv)+(284) T_6 imprint leaf.

Spines darkened.

SELF-DOOMED [861]
Griffith, Farran, Okeden & Welsh, n.d. [1885]. Stiff pictorial wrappers.

Half-title. pp. (124) Fine.

SHADOWS ON THE SNOW: a Christmas Story [862]

Copy I: First Edition. Dunedin: William Hay [1865]. Cream pictorial wrappers, printed in black on front. Spine and back cover plain. Illustrations by N. Chevalier.

pp. viii [p. (vi) is foliated ii]+(128) H_8 blank.

Dedicated to Charles Dickens. Fine.

Copy II: First English Edition. With a New Preface. Xmas No. of *Tinsley's Magazine*, 1876. White pictorial wrappers, printed in red, blue and black. Front. and text illustrations after Harry Furniss. [862*a*]

pp. 96 Fine.

SHIELD OF LOVE (The) [863]
Sm. 8vo. Bristol: Arrowsmith 1891. White paper wrappers printed in dark blue and yellow—with title, author, etc. on front and spine, with adverts. on inside front and both back covers.

Two leaves of adverts., forming part of first sheet but not reckoned in collation, precede title. pp. (212) [paged 194+(14)] 13_2–13_8 advert. Spine worn.

Note. This story, Arrowsmith's Christmas Annual for 1891, reappeared as No. 48 of the Bristol Series in 1892.

[864] SNOWED UP: a New Year's Story
William Macintosh, 24 Paternoster Row, January 1869. White pictorial wrappers, printed in greenish-drab and black.

3 leaves of adverts. precede title. pp. (viii)+64

No. 1 of *The Sixpenny Magazine*, New Series. p. (vi) announces the serialisation of *Grif*, beginning in the February no.

[865] SOLOMON ISAACS
Xmas No. of *Tinsley's Magazine*, 1877 [Second Edition]. White pictorial wrappers, printed in red, grey-blue and black. Front. and text illustrations.

pp. 96 Fine.

[866] SOMETHING OCCURRED
Routledge 1893. Smooth buff linen-grain cloth, blocked and lettered in gold, blue and dark red. Bevelled boards; monogram end-papers.

Half-title. pp. (viii)+328 Fine.

[867] THREE TIMES TRIED
'The Penny Library of Fiction.' S.P.C.K. n.d. Coloured pictorial wrappers.

Pp. 32 Fine.

[868] TOILERS OF BABYLON
3 vols. Ward & Downey 1888. Royal-blue diagonal-fine-ribbed cloth, blocked and lettered in black and silver on front and spine, publishers' monogram in blind on back. Pale grey-on-white floral end-papers.

Half-title in each vol.

Vol. I (iv)+268
II (iv)+(264)
III (iv)+264

[869] TRAGEDY OF FEATHERSTONE (The): a Novel
3 vols. Ward & Downey 1887. Smooth grey cloth, blocked and lettered in black on front, publishers' monogram in blind on back, gold-lettered on spine. Grey-on-white flowered end-papers.

Half-title in each vol.

Vol. I vi+(274) Final leaf, (18_1), a single inset.
II vi+274 Final leaf, (35_1), a single inset.
III vi+266 Final leaf, 51_5, a single inset.

VERY YOUNG COUPLE (A): a Novel [870]
F. V. White & Co. 1890.

Advert. leaf precedes title. pp. (viii)+(120) 8_4 adverts.

Copy I: Pictorial wrappers. Very fine.

Copy II: Brown bubble-grain cloth; floral end-papers. Very fine. [870*a*]

WHILE GOLDEN SLEEP DOTH REIGN: [871]
Good Words Christmas Story (*Good Cheer*, 1887)
4to. Isbister & Co. 1887. Pale salmon-pink wrappers, decoratively printed and lettered in black: spine unlettered, back and inside covers printed with adverts. Wood-engraved front. on plate paper and text illustrations after Gordon Browne.

pp. 64 Pp. 27, 28 torn.

YOUNG GIRL'S LIFE (A): a Novel [872]
3 vols. Ward & Downey 1889. Bright blue diagonal-fine-ribbed cloth, blocked in blind and lettered in silver; green-on-white patterned end-papers.

Blank leaf and half-title precede title in each vol.

Vol. I (viii) [paged vi]+(260)
II (viii) [paged vi]+(256)
III (viii)+(240) Publishers' cat., 16 pp. dated Midsummer 1889, at end.

Very fine.

FARRAR, FREDERIC W. (1831–1903)

ERIC: or Little by Little [873]
Edinburgh: Adam & Charles Black 1858.

Copy I: First Edition. Dark brownish-purple bead-grain cloth; cream end-papers. *Pl. 12*

Half-title. pp. x+(398) S_6 S_7 adverts. Half-title and final leaf, S_7, single insets. Publishers' cat., 48 pp. undated, at end.

Presentation Copy: 'R. C. Cann Lippincott. With thanks for help in correcting proof sheets etc. From the author. Harrow, Nov. 8' in ink on inside cover.

Fine.

Copy II: Another (binding variant). Grey-purple bead-grain cloth (no brownish tinge) with publishers' monogram in circular frame blocked in the centre panel of front and back. This monogram is absent from Copy I. Brick red end-papers. Collation as Copy I. [873*a*]

Ink inscription: 'Headworth Williamson. Praemium Diligentiae from his affectionate friend E. R. Hastings. Harrow. Decr. 8. 1858' on fly-leaf.

Fine. Spine a little faded.

[874] JULIAN HOME: a Tale of College Life
Edinburgh: Adam & Charles Black 1859.

Copy I. Maroon morocco cloth; café-au-lait end-papers.

Blank leaf and half-title precede title. pp. xii+(448) Publishers' adverts., 8 pp. on text paper undated, at end. Publishers' advert. slip tipped in between front end-papers.

Ink inscription: 'Julia Cann Lippincott from R.C.C.L.', on title.

Fine. Cloth a little bubbled.

[874*a*] **Copy II: Another** (with variants). Maroon bead-grain cloth; café-au-lait end-papers. Collation as Copy I.

Binding stained and a little torn.

The Prefaces in these two copies are different. That in Copy I makes reference to *Eric*; that in Copy II half apologises lest this 'Tale of College Life' give offence to readers. The mental processes behind the two Prefaces are in arguable sequence. Neither Preface is a cancel: the leaves were reprinted.

Note. Copy I is presented to his wife, by the recipient of *Eric* described above. The binding of Copy II is more nearly uniform with *Eric*.

[875] ST WINIFRED'S, or the World of School [anon]
Edinburgh: Adam & Charles Black 1862. Green honeycomb-grain cloth; chocolate end-papers.
Pl. 12

Half-title. pp. (xii)+(540) $2M_5$ $2M_6$ adverts.

Ink signature: 'Charles Pelham Lane, July 1863 from Papa', on fly-leaf. Bookseller's ticket: 'Henry Wright, Birmingham', on inside front cover. Binder's ticket: 'Burn', at end.

This is the first issue, with title in black and no author's name. In 1863 a cancel title was issued, printed in red and black and carrying Farrar's name. In this copy, as in all others seen of first and second issues, pp. 241–244 are cancels.

FARRIE, HUGH. See WESTBURY, HUGH

FITZGERALD, PERCY (1834–1925)

Several of the copies described below (inscribed and otherwise) originally belonged to John Forster. How they became separated from the bulk of the Forster Library now in South Kensington, I do not know. They were sold on October 24, 1934, at the Thomas Hughes Keely sale in New York.

[876] BEAUTY TALBOT
3 vols. Bentley 1870. Orange-vermilion sand-grain cloth.

Half-title in Vol. II.

Vol. I (ii)+(302) First leaf of final sig., U_1, a single inset.
II (iv)+(288)
III (ii)+318 First leaf of final sig., X_1, a single inset.

Binders' ticket: 'Bone & Son', at end of Vol. I. **B**

BELLA DONNA, or the Cross before the Name (by Gilbert Dyce) [877]
2 vols. Bentley 1864. Second Edition. Bright blue pebble-grain cloth; chocolate end-papers.

Vol. I iv+(332) Y_6 blank.
II iv+(332) **B**

Note. The first of three novels, dealing with the life and provocations of 'Jenny Bell', a sort of Becky Sharp with a twist. The second of the trilogy is entitled *Jenny Bell* and the third *Seventy Five Brook Street.*

DEAR GIRL (The) [878]
3 vols. Tinsley 1868. Bright blue sand-grain cloth.

Half-title in each vol.

Vol. I (iv)+(276) [paged (i)–(x)+(11)–(276)] T_2 adverts.
II (280) [paged (i)–(viii)+(9)–(280)] T_3 T_4 adverts.
III 300 [paged (i)–(viii)+(9)–300]

From the John Forster collection, but uninscribed. Very fine.

FAIRY ALICE [879]
2 vols. Bentley 1865. Green sand-grain cloth.

Vol. I iv+312
II iv+344 **B**

JENNY BELL: a Story [880]
3 vols. Bentley 1866. Violet-blue sand-grain cloth.

Vol. I vi+314 pp. (v) (vi), signed *a*, (Contents) and final leaf, Y_1, single insets.
II iv+324
III iv+(324)

The binding of this copy, which was in the Bentley collection, looks like a secondary, having plain lettering from type on spines. But the Bentley catalogue gives 'Violet Cloth' as colour of binding, so the style may be a primary one, as the provenance would lead one to expect. **B**

MIDDLE-AGED LOVER (The): a Story [881]
2 vols. Bentley 1873. Pale chocolate-brown diagonal-fine-ribbed cloth; earth-brown end-papers.

Vol. I iv+(312)
II iv+(344) 22_4 adverts.

Presentation Copy: 'John Forster Esq. with the affect. regards of the author' in ink on title of Vol. I.

Very fine.

[882] MILDRINGTON THE BARRISTER: a Romance [anon]

2 vols. Bentley 1864. Second Edition. Dark green morocco cloth, chocolate end-papers.

Vol. I (iv)+292
II (ii)+312 **B**

Note. The story was anonymously serialised in the *Dublin University Magazine* and the book-edition is dedicated to J. S. Le Fanu. It was first published by Saunders & Otley in 1863 and the present 'edition' is a re-issue of S. & O. sheets with cancel Bentley titles. In the running headlines the sub-title reads: 'A Romance of Two Syrens'. Presumably Bentley preferred to omit the last three words from his title-pages.

[883] NEVER FORGOTTEN

3 vols. Chapman & Hall 1865. Green sand-grain cloth.

Vol. I (viii)+(326) Y, 2 leaves; Z, 1 leaf and a single inset.
II (vi)+328 pp. v (vi), signed *b*, a single inset.
III vi+(346) Z, 4 leaves; 2A, 1 leaf. pp. v vi, signed *b*, and 2A, single insets.

Presentation Copy: 'John Forster Esq., from his friend the author, Easter 1865' in ink on title of Vol. I; and in pencil on fly-leaf opposite 'One of two copies only printed on toned paper, No. 1' (same legend in Vol. III).

Dedicated to Charles Dickens. Very fine.

[884] PARVENU FAMILY (The), or Phoebe, Girl and Wife

3 vols. Bentley 1876. Bright green diagonal-fine-ribbed cloth.

Vol. I (iv)+278 Final leaf, 18_3, a single inset.
II iv+(282) Final leaf, 18_5, a single inset.
III iv+316

Presentation Copy: 'Mr Forster, with the affect. regards of the author, December 1876' on title of Vol. I.

Very fine.

[885] SECOND MRS TILLOTSON (The): a Story

3 vols. Tinsley 1866. Ultramarine dot-and-line-grain cloth.

Half-title in Vol. I

Vol. I viii+320
II iv+(324)
III iv+(378) First leaf of final sig., BB_1, a single inset.

From the Forster collection, but uninscribed. Very fine.

[886] SEVENTY-FIVE BROOK STREET: a Story

3 vols. Tinsley 1867. Blue dot-and-line-grain cloth.

Half-title in each vol., preceded in Vol. I by inset leaf of adverts.

Vol. I (xiv)+(292)
II (viii)+284
III (viii)+282 Final leaf, U_1, a single inset.

From the Forster collection, but uninscribed. Very fine.

TWO FAIR DAUGHTERS [887]

3 vols. Hurst & Blackett 1871. Orange-vermilion sand-grain cloth; greenish-black end-papers.

Half-title in each vol.

Vol. I (iv)+320
II (iv)+322 Final leaf, Y_1, a single inset.
III (iv)+(360) Publishers' cat., 16 pp. undated, at end.

Presentation Copy: 'John Forster Esq. with the author's kindest regards, 1870' in ink on title of Vol. I. A similar inscription has been erased from title of Vol. III, tearing the paper and defacing the title.

Cloth very fine.

FLETCHER, J. S. (1863–1935)

WHEN CHARLES THE FIRST WAS KING [888]

3 vols. Bentley 1892. Smooth sand-brown cloth spines and corners, dark red marbled paper sides. Crimson and dark blue marbled edges.

Vol. I iv+(296) 19_4 blank.
II iv+(272)
III iv+(280) **B**

Note. I include this single item from the immense production of J. S. Fletcher because it had, perhaps, a longer life than any other of his books. It was not his first work (three novels are mentioned on the title-page); but as late as 1905, by which time Boots Library Catalogue credited him with 27 novels, advertisements of new stories by him put out by Digby, Long & Co. were headed: 'By the author of *When Charles the First Was King*.' The novel is listed both in Baker's *Guide to the Best Fiction* (1903) and Nield's *Guide to the Best Historical Novels and Tales* (1904).

FOOT, ROSE

BLIGHT, or the Novel Hater: a Tale of Our Own Times (by the author of 'Good in Everything') [889]

3 vols. J. F. Hope 1859. Pale pink wavy-grain cloth, blocked in blind on front and back, gold lettered and decorated on spine. Tinted lithographic front. to each vol.

Half-title in each vol.

Vol. I (viii) + (304) Publishers' cat., 16 pp. headed 'January Catalogue', at end.
II (iv) + (312)
III (iv) + 328

Very fine. The volumes have double end-papers at front and back.

Note. This absurd work is produced with extreme elegance and (one presumes) at the author's expense. A Preface signed 'Rose Foot' (Vol. I, pp. (v)–vii) implies that the novelist's genius was unrecognised in youth and severely blighted. It also apologises for the many misprints in the author's preceding novel, *Good in Everything*.

FOTHERGILL, JESSIE (1851–1891)

[890] BORDERLAND: a Country Town Chronicle
3 vols. Bentley 1886. Olive-green fancy-ribbed cloth; floral end-papers. Title in red and black.

Vol. I (iv) + (300) 19_6 imprint leaf.
II (iv) + (300)
III (296) [paged (vi) + (290)] 39_1, blank, precedes title; 39_8 is pp. 9, 10 of text; pp. 11, 12 constitute 40_1. 57_4 blank. B

[891] FIRST VIOLIN (The): a Novel.

Copy I: First (unpublished) Edition. By JESSIE FOTHERGILL, / AUTHOR OF 'HEALEY', 'ALDYTH' etc./*German Quotation in small rom. caps and l.c.*/IN THREE VOLUMES / VOL. I/ *publishers' device*/LONDON:/RICHARD BENTLEY AND SON./1877./(*All Rights Reserved.*)

3 vols. Violet diagonal-fine-ribbed cloth, blocked in black on front with title and decorative frame, with lettering and decoration in gold and black on spine, with blind frame on back. Yellow end-papers.

Binders ticket: 'Leighton, Son and Hodge', at end of Vol. I.

Vol. I vi [title, verso blank; dedication, verso blank; Contents (2 pp.)] + 288. Text $1–18_8$ in eights.
II iv [title, verso blank; Contents (2 pp.)] + 258. Text 19–35, in eights. Final leaf a single inset.
III iv [title, verso blank; Contents (2 pp.)] + (272). The title in this vol. is a cancel. Text $36–52_8$ in eights. B

[891*a*] **Copy II: Second (published) Edition** [anon]. *German Quotation in Gothic type* / IN THREE VOLUMES./VOL. I/*publishers' device*/LONDON:/ RICHARD BENTLEY AND SON, / Publishers in Ordinary to Her Majesty the Queen. (*in Gothic caps and l.c.*) / 1878. / [*All Rights Reserved.*]

3 vols. Binding and collation as Copy I.

Notes. (i) According to the Bentley Private Catalogue five Statutory copies of the first edition were sent out, and only four others bound. None was sold. It seems that no publishing purpose (e.g. the securing of copyright) was served by the first edition. The late Mr Bentley (speaking presumably from memory) told me that the author's father intervened at the last moment and insisted that the book be anonymous.

(ii) In addition to the removal of the author's name and certain other variants between the title of the two editions, the following differences may be noted:

(*a*) First Edition has no chapter titles in Contents List or at head of chapters. Second Edition has chapter titles in both places.

(*b*) First Edition has *large* signature number on first leaf of each gathering. Second Edition has *small* number.

(*c*) First Edition is set throughout in slightly larger stronger type than second, most noticeable in comparing running heads (ital. caps) and 'Chapter I' etc. (rom. caps). Differences of arrangement, alinement etc. also show that the book was re-set.

(*d*) In Copy I title, in Copy II Dedication, is a single inset, because Title and Contents were reprinted for Second Edition but not the Dedication.

(iii) The cancel title to Vol. III of the above copy of the First Edition has the wording and arrangement of the Second Edition, of which it is a 'proof title only before printing' (stated in a pencil note by the publisher). The date is erased. The copy, therefore, is a 'trial copy' in intermediate state. The Statutory copies have all three titles uniform and dated 1877.

FROM MOOR ISLES: a Love Story [892]
3 vols. Bentley 1888. Dark blue cloth spines, embossed wall-paper sides with all-over design in blue and white; green end-papers.

Vol. I (iv) + (308)
II (iv) + 296
III iv + 340

The spine of Vol. II shows 'Vol. III' over-stamped 'Vol. II'. B

KITH AND KIN: a Novel [893]
3 vols. Bentley 1881. Flowered chintz, cream paper title-panels on spines.

Vol. I (vi) + (304) 19_8 adverts.
II (iv) + 304
III (iv) + 306 Final leaf 20_1. B

MADE OR MARRED [894]
Bentley 1881. Scarlet diagonal-fine-ribbed cloth; black end-papers.

pp. (iv) + 188

No. XV of Bentley's Half-Crown Empire Library. B

[895] MARCH IN THE RANKS (A)
3 vols. Hurst & Blackett 1890. Brown diagonal-fine-ribbed cloth, blocked in black and lettered in gold. Grey end-papers. Blank leaf and half-title precede title in each vol.

Vol. I (viii)+(320) X_8 blank.
II (viii)+316
III (viii)+300

An unopened copy, wholly unused but slightly dust-darkened. Two leaves in the final sig. of Vol. III are torn.

[896] 'ONE OF THREE': a Fragment
Bentley 1881. Scarlet diagonal-fine-ribbed cloth; black end-papers.

Half-title. pp. viii+(216) 14_1–14_4 adverts.

No. XVI (and last) of Bentley's Half-Crown Empire Library. B

[897] PERIL: a Novel
3 vols. Bentley 1884. Smooth navy-blue cloth; floral end-papers.

Vol. I (iv)+308
II iv+312
III iv+(332)

Cloth of Vols. I and III damp-stained. B

[898] PROBATION: a Novel (by the author of 'The First Violin')
3 vols. Bentley 1879. Brown diagonal-fine-ribbed cloth.

Vol. I (iv)+(284) 18_6 blank.
II (ii)+308
III (ii)+(336)

Vol. I Second Edition. Vols. II and III First Edition. B

[899] WELLFIELDS (The): a Novel
3 vols. Bentley 1880. Flowered chintz; black end-papers.

Half-title in Vol. I.

Vol. I (viii)+300
II (iv)+(272)
III (iv)+(268)

Binder's ticket: 'Burn', at end of Vols. II and III. B

FRANCIS, FRANCIS (1822–1886)

[900] NEWTON DOGVANE: a Story of English Country Life
3 vols. Hurst & Blackett 1859. Light-claret ribbed cloth. Etched front. by Leech in each vol.

Vol. I (ii)+(330) Y_5 (a single inset) adverts.
II (ii)+(340)
III (ii)+(318) First leaf of final sig., X_1, a single inset.

Binders' ticket: 'Leighton, Son & Hodge', at end of each vol. Covers of Vol. I spotted.

Note. This copy came from the Morden Hall sale in September 1941.

FRASER, JAMES BAILLIE (1783–1856)

This is a complete collection of the fiction of J. B. Fraser with the exception of *The Dark Falcon*, a description of which is provided from another source.

ALLEE NEEMROO: the Buchtiaree Adventurer: a Tale of Louristan [901]
3 vols. Bentley 1842. Half-cloth boards, labels.

Half-title in each vol.

Vol. I (iv)+344
II (iv)+328
III (iv)+(306) Final leaf (P_1) a single inset.

Book-plate of Charles Brownell in each vol. In pencil on each half-title, signature and address of Wm. Nicholson, 1864.

*DARK FALCON (The): a Tale of Attruck [902]
4 vols. Bentley 1844. Boards (or half-cloth boards), labels.

Vol. I vi+306
II (ii)+312
III (ii)+320
IV (ii)+308

HIGHLAND SMUGGLERS (The) (by the author of 'Adventures of a Kuzzilbash' etc.) [903]
3 vols. Colburn & Bentley 1832. Boards (re-backed and labels renewed).

Vol. I (viii)+358
II (ii)+(348)
III (ii)+(420)

'Bretley Park' in ink on front covers.

KUZZILBASH (The): a Tale of Khorasan [anon] [904]
3 vols. Colburn 1828. Boards, labels.

Half-title in each vol.

Vol. I (iv)+348
II (iv)+(360)
III (iv)+(336) P_{11} P_{12} adverts.

Spines worn.

The running headlines read: ADVENTURES OF A KUZZILBASH.

PERSIAN ADVENTURER (The), being the Sequel of 'The Kuzzilbash' [905]
3 vols. Colburn & Bentley 1830. Half-cloth boards, labels.

Half-title in Vol. I

Vol. I xii+(366) Final leaf, R_1 a single inset.
II (ii)+(366) Final leaf, R_1 a single inset.
III (ii)+392

[906] TALES OF THE CARAVANSERAI: the Khan's Tale

Smith, Elder 1833. Dark green morocco cloth, standard Series style.

pp. iv+(372)

Vol. VII in Smith, Elder's Library of Romance (3760*a* in Section III).

FRASER, JULIA AGNES

[907] SHILRICK THE DRUMMER, or Loyal and True: a Romance of the Irish Rebellion of 1798

3 vols. Remington 1894. Dark grass-green diagonal-fine-ribbed cloth, pictorially blocked in gold and black; yellow and brown patterned end-papers. Photographic front. to each vol.—in I a portrait of the author in fancy dress: in II a reproduction of a drummer boy in period uniform (this figure appears on front cover): in III a portrait of a pet dog.

Half-title, with verses on verso, in each vol.

Vol. I viii+336
II (iv)+(344) Z_4 recto carries 2 verses by Moore.
III (iv)+(368) AA_7 AA_8 'List of Patrons and Subscribers prior to publication'.

Book-plate of the Mount Edgcumbe Library. An eccentric publication, presumably issued at the author's expense. Very fine.

FRISWELL, HAIN (1825–1878)

[908] DAUGHTER OF EVE (A)

2 vols. Bentley 1863. Green wavy-grain cloth.

Half-title in each vol.

Vol. I viii+(296)
II (vi) [paged iv]+270 Half-title and first leaf of final sig., S_1, single insets. B

[909] GHOST STORIES AND PHANTOM FANCIES

Bentley 1858. Pictorial boards (broken).

pp. viii+222 First leaf of final sig., P_1, a single inset.

[910] OTHER PEOPLE'S WINDOWS

2 vols. Sampson, Low 1868. Smooth grass-green cloth; grey-chocolate end-papers.

Vol. I viii+(304)
II iv+(308) Publishers' cat., 24 pp. dated May 1868, at end.

Presentation Copy: 'William Stephens Esq. from his Attached Friend the Author...June 17, 1868' in ink facing title of Vol. I.

Book-label of A. B. Stevens in each vol. Binders' ticket: 'Bone & Son', at end of Vol. I.

OUT AND ABOUT: a Boy's Adventures written for Adventurous Boys [911]

Fcap 8vo. Groombridge & Sons 1860. Blue straight-grain-morocco cloth. Blocked and lettered in gold on front, in blind on back; spine pictorially blocked in gold and fancy-lettered. Wood-engraved pictorial title (serving as front., and facing printed title) and five illustrations, all after George Cruikshank and on plate paper.

Half-title. pp. xvi+(328) 21_4 adverts.

Ink inscription on fly-leaf: 'George D. Murray from his "Auntie". Christmas 1867.'

Fine.

FULLERTON, LADY GEORGIANA (1812–1885)

Née Leveson-Gower, Lady Georgiana Fullerton was a daughter of Earl Granville and a granddaughter of the Marquis of Stafford and the Duke of Devonshire. Brought up in simplicity and retirement, she took little part in fashionable life, but by training and preference spent her time on charitable work and gave much thought to religious questions. Her father's diplomatic appointments kept the family in Paris and in Rome, with only brief intervals of English residence, and it was in Paris that in 1833 she married Mr Fullerton, an attaché to the Embassy. He was converted to Catholicism in 1843 and Lady Georgiana, after an interval of devout Puseyism, also joined the Roman church in 1846. Her first novel *Ellen Middleton* was a product of her Anglo-Catholic period and provoked considerable criticism by representing the heroine confessing to, and being absolved by, an Anglican clergyman. Her second novel *Grantley Manor* was frankly Roman Catholic in inspiration and in the message it sought to convey. The rest of her life was spent in the practice and propagation of the Catholic faith. She was intimately concerned in the founding of *The Month.*

Perhaps her most intimate friend was Mrs Augustus Craven (q.v. above), several of whose works she translated into English, and Mrs Craven wrote a memoir in French of Lady Georgiana which was translated and published in London in 1888.

CONSTANCE SHERWOOD: an Autobiography of the Sixteenth Century [912]

3 vols. Bentley 1865. Royal-blue fine-morocco cloth.

Half-title in each vol.

Vol. I (iv)+(308) X_2 adverts.
II (iv)+(312)
III (iv)+(280) T_3 T_4 adverts.

[913] ELLEN MIDDLETON: a Tale

3 vols. Moxon 1844. Grey-purple perpendicular fine-ribbed cloth.

Half-title in each vol.

Vol. I (iv)+280 Publishers' cat., 8 pp. dated March 1, 1844, inserted between front end-papers.

II (iv)+(288)

III (iv)+(260), (N_1) (N_2) adverts. Publisher's cat., 14 pp.+blank leaf dated May 1844, at end.

'Guy's Cliffe' in ink in each vol. Cloth bright; a little foxed internally.

[914] GRANTLEY MANOR: a Tale

3 vols. Moxon 1847. Dark maroon fine-diaper cloth.

Half-title in each vol.

Vol. I (iv)+288 Publishers' cat., 8 pp. dated April 1, 1847, inserted between front end-papers.

II (iv)+(288) N_{11} adverts., N_{12} blank.

III (iv)+(264) M_{10-12}, publisher's cat., paged (1)–6 and dated June 1847.

[915] LADY-BIRD: a Tale

3 vols. Moxon 1852. Dark maroon fine-diaper cloth.

Half-title in each vol.

Vol. I (iv)+(292) O_2 adverts. Publisher's cat., 8 pp. dated January 1852, inserted between front end-papers.

II (iv)+272

III (iv)+(272)

Ink-signature: 'Lady Elizabeth Stucley', on title of each vol. Fine.

[916] LAURENTIA: a Tale of Japan

'Printed in aid of the Fund for Orphan and Destitute Catholic Children', 1861. Violet bead-grain cloth; glazed white end-papers starred in gold.

pp. viii+(264)

Ink-signature of authoress, dated May 16, 1861, on title. Very fine.

[917] MRS GERALD'S NIECE

3 vols. Bentley 1869. Grass-green dot-and-line-grain cloth.

Vol. I (vi)+(346) pp. (v) (vi) fly-title to Part I and a single inset. First leaf of final sig., 22_1, a single inset.

II (iv)+340

III (iv)+376 B

[918] NOTARY'S DAUGHTER (The): a Tale (from the French of Mme Léonie d'Aulney) and THE HOUSE OF PENARVAN· a Tale (from the French of M. Jules Sandeau).

2 vols. Bentley 1878. Plum diagonal-fine-ribbed cloth. Bevelled boards.

Half-title in each vol.

Vol. I viii+324

II vi+(310) Final leaf, 41_3, a single inset. B

The Notary's Daughter occupies all of Vol. I and pp. 1–45 of Vol. II. *The House of Penarvan* is not mentioned on the title-pages, but appears at foot of front covers.

STORMY LIFE (A): a Novel [919]

3 vols. Bentley 1867. Carmine sand-grain cloth.

Vol. I (iv)+(288)

II (iv)+(304) U_8 blank.

III (iv)+(260)

Back cover of Vol. II stained. B

TOO STRANGE NOT TO BE TRUE: a Tale [920]

3 vols. Bentley 1864. Green bead-grain cloth.

Half-title in each vol.

Vol. I vi+306 Half-title and final leaf, X_1, single insets.

II (iv)+266 First leaf of final sig., S_1, a single inset.

III (iv)+296 B

WILL AND A WAY (A) [921]

3 vols. Bentley 1881. Greenish-grey diagonal-fine-ribbed cloth; floral end-papers.

Vol. I (vi)+(316) 20_6 adverts.

II (iv)+(266) 37_5 adverts. (a single inset leaf).

III (iv)+(268) 54_6 adverts. B

A Will and a Way occupies Vols. I and II and pp. 1–126 of Vol. III. It is followed by two short tales: *The Handkerchief at the Window* and *The Lilies of the Valley.*

GARIBALDI, GENERAL GIUSEPPE (1807–1882) [922]

RULE OF THE MONK (The): or Rome in the Nineteenth Century

2 vols. Cassell, Petter & Galpin, n.d. [1870]. Orange-scarlet patterned-sand-grain cloth, blocked in blind on front and back, blocked and lettered in gold on spine.

Half-title in each vol.

Vol. I xvi+252

II vi+(270) First leaf of final sig., R_1, a single inset. Text of novel ends p. 238; pp. (239)–254 Appendix, 'The Campaign of Mentana' by Ricciotti Garibaldi; pp. (255)–269 Notes.

Note. This novel was written during the late sixties, while the author was under detention at Varignano. It appeared in Italian in the same year as this English edition, under the title: *Clelia, ovvero il Governo del Monaco.* The anonymous translator's preface to the Cassell edition describes the English version as having been prepared from 'the Italian MS. itself, written throughout in the autograph of the General', but whether the work appeared in book-form first in Milan or in London I cannot say.

The story is a fragile cloak for an attack on the corruption and hypocrisies of Papal rule in Rome. The Appendix (by the General's son) attributes the defeat of the Garibaldians by the French at Mentana in November 1867 to treachery by the Italian Government.

GARTSHORE, MRS MURRAY

[923] CLEVELAND: a Tale of the Catholic Church [anon] Bentley 1847. Brown fine-diaper cloth, blocked in blind and lettered in gold.

pp. (ii)+(394) 1st leaf of final sig., S_1, a single inset.

'Guys Cliffe' in ink on fly title.

Note. A well-written uncompromising story of the struggle between a forceful and fanatical Catholic priest and an Anglican clergyman for the soul of the latter's wife.

GASKELL, ELIZABETH CLEGHORN (1810–1865)

For further bibliographical detail, see *Victorian Lady Novelists* by M. L. Parrish, London, 1933.

[924] COUSIN PHILLIS and Other Tales

Copy I: First Edition. Smith, Elder 1865: 'Illustrated Edition.' Red morocco cloth blocked in blind on front and back with ornamental frame and publishers' imprint and device; on spine blocked and lettered in gold. (The binding style is the first of the two adopted for the firm's one-volume illustrated editions.) Wood-engraved front., pictorial title dated 1865 and 2 plates after du Maurier. [*Parrish* p. 71

pp. (288) 18_8 adverts.

Ink signature: 'John A. Dorsett, Sept. 1866', inside front cover. Dorsett was an intimate friend of Mrs Henry Wood (q.v.). Fine.

[924*a*] **Copy II: Re-issue.** Smith, Elder 1866 (1867). Smooth brown cloth, ornamentally blocked in black on front and back; in gold with publishers' monogram on front; blocked and lettered in black and gold on spine. (The binding style is the second of the two adopted for the firm's one-volume illustrated editions.) Illustrations and collation as Copy I. Date on pictorial title 1867; date on printed title 1866.

CRANFORD (by the author of 'Mary Barton', 'Ruth', etc.) [*Parrish* p. 60 [925]

Copy I: First Edition. Fcap. 8vo. Chapman & Hall 1853. Green diagonal-fine-ripple-grain cloth, blocked in blind on front and back, gold-lettered and blocked in gold and blind on spine.

pp. iv+324

Booksellers' ticket: 'Kerby & Son, 190 Oxford Street' inside front cover. Spine a little spotted, but a sharp, firm copy in a fine state.

Note. This book originally lacked the front fly-leaf. In a mistaken desire to improve matters, a former owner removed the back fly-leaf, inserted it before the title page, and provided a new back fly-leaf. This sort of tinkering-about is just silly.

Copy II: Illustrated Edition. Smith, Elder 1867. Binding as *Cousin Phillis*, Copy II. Wood-engraved front., pictorial title dated 1867 and 2 plates after du Maurier. [925*a*]

pp. (248) $8a_3$ $8a_4$ adverts.

This edition was first published in 1864 with that date on both titles.

DARK NIGHT'S WORK (A) [926]

Copy I: First Edition. Smith, Elder 1863. Chocolate dot-and-line-grain cloth. [*Parrish*, p. 71

Half-title. pp. iv+(304) 19_7 19_8 adverts. Publishers' cat., 16 pp. dated April 1863, at end.

Book-plate of Alan F. Maclure, and ink signature on fly-leaf: 'V. T. Thompson'. Fine.

Copy II: Illustrated Edition. Smith, Elder 1864. Binding as *Cousin Phillis*, Copy I. Wood-engraved front., pictorial title dated 1864 and 2 plates after du Maurier. Inside front and back covers printed with adverts. [926*a*]

Half-title. pp. (252) Publishers' cat., 24 pp. dated March 1864, at end.

Book-plate of John Browne. Very fine.

LIBBIE MARSH'S THREE ERAS (by the author of 'Mary Barton', 'Ruth' etc.) [*Parrish* p. 62 [927]

Fcap. 8vo. Chapman & Hall 1855. Half-calf by Zaehnsdorf, original yellow wrappers preserved.

pp. 24

Book-plate of Clement K. Shorter.

LIFE OF CHARLOTTE BRONTË (The) [*Parrish* p. 64 [928]

Copy I: First Edition. 2 vols. Smith, Elder 1857. Dark brown wavy-grain cloth. Engraved portrait front. after G. Richmond in Vol. I and a facsimile page of MS.; view of Haworth after a drawing by Mrs Gaskell as front. in Vol. II.

Half-title in each vol.

Vol. I viii + 352
II viii + (328) Publishers' cat., 16 pp. dated March 1857, at end.

Booksellers' stamp: 'Cooke & Son, Warwick', on fly-leaf and at foot of title in each vol. Cloth fine. Vol. I loose in covers.

[928a] **Copy II: 'New Edition.'** Smith, Elder 1860. Glazed orange linen, printed in black, uniform with the cheap edition of the Brontë novels published 1857–1858.

[929] LIZZIE LEIGH: a Domestic Tale (From 'Household Words', by Charles Dickens) [*Parrish* p. 58

New York: Dewitt & Davenport 1850. Buff paper wrappers printed in black. Spine unlettered; inside front and inside and outside back wrappers printed with adverts. Front wrapper serves as title.

pp. 36

Book-plate of Lord Esher. Fine.

[930] MOORLAND COTTAGE (The) (by the author of 'Mary Barton' etc.) [*Parrish* p. 60

Fcap. 8vo. Chapman & Hall 1850. Maroon fine-diaper cloth, elaborately blocked, first in blind and then in gold; gilt edges. Wood-engraved front., vignette title (both on text paper) and illustrations in the text after Birket Foster.

Half-title. pp. (viii) + (184) N_4 advert.

Fine.

[931] NORTH AND SOUTH (by the author of 'Mary Barton', 'Ruth', 'Cranford', etc.)

2 vols. Chapman & Hall 1855. Dark brown fine-ripple-grain cloth, blocked in blind on front, spine and back, gold-lettered on spine.

Advert. leaf and half-title precede title in Vol. I; half-title only in Vol. II

Vol. I (viii) + 320 Publishers' adverts, 4 pp. on text paper at end.
II (iv) + (364) AA_6 blank.

Ink signature: 'F. W. Balfour' on fly-leaf and booksellers' ticket 'W. Whyte & Co. Edinburgh' inside front cover of Vol. I.

Fine. Small circular stain on back cover of Vol. II.

[932] ROUND THE SOFA (by the author of 'Mary Barton' etc.) [*Parrish* p. 66

Copy I: First Edition. 2 vols. Sampson, Low 1859. Orange-red bead-grain cloth.

Vol. I (iv) + 340
II (iv) + (298) Publishers' cat., 12 pp. dated March 1859, at end.

Book-plate of Charles Walter Lyon in each vol. and his signature in ink, dated 1859, on fly-leaf of each vol. Binders' ticket: 'Bone & Son', at end of each vol. Very fine.

Copy II: First one-volume Edition, entitled: MY LADY LUDLOW and Other Tales included in 'Round the Sofa'. Sampson, Low 1861. Green bead-grain cloth. Steel-engraved front. after J. Gilbert. [932a]

pp. (iv) + (320) X_8 adverts.

Book-plate of Alan F. Maclure. Very fine.

RUTH: a Novel (by the author of 'Mary Barton') [*Parrish* p. 61 [933]

3 vols. Chapman & Hall 1853. Purple-maroon fine-net-grain† cloth; yellow end-papers, printed with advertisements in Vols. I and II, plain in Vol. III

Vol. I (ii) + 298 U, 4 leaves; X, 1 leaf.
II (ii) + 328
III (ii) + (312)

Fine. Spines a little faded.

SEXTON'S HERO (The) and CHRISTMAS STORMS AND SUNSHINE (contributed by the authoress of 'Mary Barton' for the Benefit of the Macclesfield Public Baths and Wash-houses) [*Parrish* p. 58 [934]

Slim cr. 8vo. Manchester: Johnson, Rawson & Co. 1850. Pale pink paper wrappers printed in black on front, spine unlettered, elsewhere blank.

pp. 28

Book-plate of Lord Esher.

SYLVIA'S LOVERS [*Parrish* p. 70 [935]

3 vols. Smith, Elder 1863. Plum pebble-grain cloth; greenish-drab end-papers.

Half-title in Vol. I

Vol. I (viii) + (312) 20_4 imprint leaf.
II (iv) + 294
III (iv) + (288) 57_7 57_8 adverts.

Presentation Copy: 'To my dear Mary, who helped me by her sympathy and counsel during the composition of "Sylvia"—from her ever affectionate friend—E. C. Gaskell. February 1863' in ink on fly-leaf of Vol. I.

Fine.

WIVES AND DAUGHTERS: an Every-Day Story [*Parrish* p. 74 [936]

2 vols. 8vo. Smith, Elder 1866. Plum fine-morocco cloth. Wood-engraved front. and in Vol. I 9, in Vol. II 7 illustrations after du Maurier.

Vol. I (iv) + 336
II (iv) + 332

Book-plate of Alan F. Maclure. Very fine.

† I do not know how else to describe this grain which I have not met with on any other book.

GIBBON, CHARLES (1843–1890)

This, with two or three contributions from the Bentley file, is as intimate a family series of 'firsts' as one could wish to see. Gibbon was the sentimental counterpart of the sensational Farjeon, and in his way as popular: nor does he disguise his talent for wholesome romance in the inscriptions written in these novels. They provide a condensed version of his own love-story, beginning with a restrained message to Miss Robertson, passing to a respectful one to her mother, then to the fond playfulness of early married life, and finally to affectionate exhortations (one so prolix that I had not the patience to transcribe it) to his sons, who at the dates in question were very small boys indeed.

Gibbon was of working-class origin, and by dogged self-education raised himself first to clerkship, then to journalism and finally to the writing of successful fiction.

[937] AMORET: a Romance

Sm. 8vo. J. & R. Maxwell, n.d. White paper wrappers printed in dark blue with title, author, etc. on front and spine, with adverts. inside front and on both back covers.

pp. (ii) + 206

Yellow slip inset after p. (ii) announcing publication on February 20, 1886 of *A Maiden Fair* by the same author (at 1*s*. in wrappers, 1*s*. 6*d*. in cloth). Fine.

[938] BEYOND COMPARE: a Story

3 vols. Sampson Low 1888. Grey-green morocco cloth.

Half-title in Vol. I

Vol. I (viii) + 268
II (iv) + 268
III (iv) + (248) Publishers' cat., 32 pp. dated April 1888, at end.

Presentation Copy: 'To R. M. M. Robertson from Margaret J. M. R. Gibbon and Charles Gibbon, 22nd June 1888.' Very fine.

[939] BLOOD MONEY and other Stories

2 vols. Chatto & Windus 1889. Dark royal-blue diaper cloth, blocked in scarlet; floral end-papers.

Half-title in each vol.

Vol. I viii + 232 Publishers' cat., 32 pp. dated February 1889, at end.
II vi + (322) Final leaf (36_1) a single inset.

Fine.

[940] BRAES OF YARROW (The): a Romance

3 vols. Sampson Low 1881. Dark purple-brown diagonal-fine-ribbed cloth.

Blank leaf precedes title in Vol. I

Vol. I (viii) + (312) X_4 blank.
II (iv) + 324
III (iv) + 304 Publishers' cat., 32 pp. dated January 1881, at end.

Binders' ticket: 'Bone & Son', at end of each vol. Fine.

BY MEAD AND STREAM: a Novel [941]

3 vols. Chatto & Windus 1884. Smooth brown cloth, florally blocked in green and yellow, and gold-lettered. Light-green-on-white foliage end-papers.

Half-title in each vol.

Vol. I (viii) + (264)
II (vi) + (288)
III (vi) + (260) S_2 publishers' device. Publishers' cat., 32 pp. dated Sept. 1884, at end.

Fine.

CLARE OF CLARESMEDE: a Romance [942]

3 vols. Sampson Low 1886. Smooth grey-green cloth, blocked in dark green.

Blank leaf precedes title in Vol. I

Vol. I (viii) [paged vi] + (276)
II (iv) + 280
III iv + (262) First leaf of final sig., S_1, a single inset. Publishers' cat., 32 pp. dated October 1885, at end.

Presentation Copy: 'To our son "Bertie", born 1st October 1882, from his father Charles Gibbon, and his mother Margaret J. M. R. Gibbon. 1st Oct. 1886' in ink on first blank leaf of Vol. I.

The novel is dedicated to his two sons. Very fine.

DANGEROUS CONNEXIONS: a Novel [943]

3 vols. John Maxwell & Co. 1864. Blue fine-morocco cloth.

Vol. I (iv) + (306) Final leaf, 20_1, a single inset.
II (302) [p. (4) mispaged ii] Sig. 19, 4 leaves. Final leaf, 20_1, a single inset.
III 300

Spines slightly worn at tail.

FOR THE KING [944]

2 vols. Henry Edward Knox, 29 Paternoster Row, 1872. Blue dotted-line-ribbed cloth; chocolate end-papers.

Half-title in each vol.

Vol. I (viii) + (272) R_7 R_8 adverts.
II (viii) + 244

Fine.

GARVOCK: a Romance [945]

3 vols. J. & R. Maxwell n.d. [1885]. Smooth olive-green cloth, blocked in brown.

Half-title in Vols. I and II. Blank leaf and half-title precede title in Vol. III

Vol. I vi + 316
II vi + 312
III (viii) [paged vi] + 316

This copy contains two copies of a prospectus of *Garvock*, slipped into Vol. III. Very fine.

[946] GOLDEN SHAFT (The)

3 vols. Chatto & Windus 1882. Smooth dark blue cloth, blocked with arrow and ribbon in yellow; floral end-papers.

Blank leaf and half-title precede title in each vol.

Vol. I (xii) [paged x] + 320
II (viii) [paged vi] + (308)
III (viii) [paged vi] + (276) T_2 publishers' device. Publishers' cat., 32 pp. dated October 1882, at end.

Binder's ticket: 'Burn', at end of Vol. I.

Presentation Copy: 'To Charles Robertson Gibbon. My dear Son...' etc., signed and dated 'Edinburgh 10 Dec. 1882' in ink on first blank leaf of Vol. I. (This inscription takes the form of a letter of about 100 words, describing the novel as the boy's 'twin brother' and as 'my best work, the beginning of what I call my New Life'. The letter is sincere and moving, but a little shame-making.) Fine.

[947] HEART'S DELIGHT: a Novel

3 vols. Chatto & Windus 1885. Smooth powder-blue cloth, blocked in black, silver and gold; pale green-on-white floral end-papers.

Half-title in each vol.

Vol. I vi + (288) 18_8 publishers' device.
II (viii) + (296)
III vi + (272) Publishers' cat., 32 pp. dated April 1885, at end.

Presentation Copy: 'To Mama, with very much love from M.G. and C.G.' in ink on half-title of Vol. I. Very fine.

This novel seems to have been a collaboration, for certain chapters in Vol. III are initialled by Mrs Gibbon 'M.G.'

[948] HEART'S PROBLEM (A)

2 vols. Chatto & Windus 1881. Smooth powder-blue cloth, blocked in black; chocolate-on-white floral end-papers.

Half-title in Vol. I; blank leaf and half-title precede title in Vol. II

Vol. I (viii) + (232) Q_4 publishers' device. Publishers' cat., 32 pp. dated November 1881, at end.
II (viii) + (280)

Presentation Copy: 'To Mrs Robertson, with sincere regards Charles Gibbon. 25 Dec. 1881' in ink on half-title of Vol. I. Very fine.

[949] IN CUPID'S WARS: a Novel

3 vols. F. V. White 1884. Jade-green moiré fine-ribbed cloth; decorated end-papers.

Blank leaf and half-title precede title in each vol.

Vol. I (viii) + (256) R_8 blank.
II (viii) + (272) S_8 blank.
III (viii) + (328)

Covers discoloured, probably through paste-action.

IN HONOUR BOUND [950]

3 vols. Bentley 1874. Olive-green sand-grain cloth; chocolate end-papers.

Half-title in Vol. I

Vol. I viii + (296) 19_3 19_4 adverts.
II iv + 308
III iv + (260) B

IN LOVE AND WAR: a Romance [951]

3 vols. Bentley 1877. Grey diagonal-fine-ribbed cloth.

Blank signature-leaf and half-title precede title in each vol.

Vol. I (viii) + 300
II (viii) + 312
III (viii) + 320 B

Also issued in red cloth, similarly blocked. The Bentley Catalogue records the colour as 'grey'. A secondary binding has been noted, in scarlet cloth with plainly lettered spine and no imprint, and with sheets cut down.

IN PASTURES GREEN and Other Stories [952]

Chatto & Windus 1880. Smooth olive-brown cloth, blocked in light green and yellow; blue-on-white floral end-papers.

Blank leaf and half-title precede title.

pp. (viii) + (276) T_2 blank. Publishers' cat., 32 pp. dated April 1880, at end. Fine.

OF HIGH DEGREE: a Story [953]

3 vols. Chatto & Windus 1883. Smooth greenish-blue cloth, blocked in red and gold; green-on-white floral end-papers.

Half-title in Vol. I; blank leaf and half-title precede title in Vols. II and III

Vol. I viii + (336) Y_8 publishers' device.
II (viii) [paged vi] + (280) T_4 publishers' device.
III (viii) [paged vi] + 248 Publishers' cat., 32 pp. dated December 1882, at end.

Presentation Copy: 'To my dear Collaborator and Best Self from Her "Frankenstein" C.G. 24 Feby. 1883 (see CHAPTER XXXI)' in ink on half-title of Vol. I. Very fine.

Note. In chapter XXXI Stephen Meredith, laughingly commanded by pretty Dahlia to find the Queen of the Fairies in the Green Lane, finds Ruth instead.

QUEEN OF THE MEADOW: a Novel [954]

3 vols. Chatto & Windus 1880. Smooth dark green cloth, blocked in light green; blue-on-white floral end-papers. Front. and 3 wood-engraved illustrations after A.H. in each vol.

Half-title in each vol. Blank leaf precedes that in Vol. I

Vol. I (xii) + (268) S_6 publishers' device.
II (viii) + (264) S_4 publishers' device.
III (viii) + (248) R_4 publishers' device. Publishers' cat., 32 pp. dated December 1879, at end.

Presentation Copy: 'To Miss M. J. M. Robertson from her friend Charles Gibbon, 19 Jan. 1880' in ink on first blank leaf of Vol. I. Binder's ticket: 'Burn' at end of vol. I. Fine.

[955] ROBIN GRAY: a Novel
3 vols. Blackie & Son 1869. Green morocco cloth.

Half-title in each vol.

Vol. I viii + (334)
II vi + 306 Final leaf 41_1 a single inset.
III vi + 288

Very fine. A few very small ink-spots on spines.

[956] WHAT WILL THE WORLD SAY? a Novel
3 vols. Bentley 1875. Red diagonal-fine-ribbed cloth.

Vol. I (vi) + (284) (v) (vi), Contents, a single inset.
II (iv) + 296
III (iv) + 282 Final leaf, T_5, a single inset. B

GIFT, THEO [DOROTHY HENRIETTA HAVERS, afterwards MRS BOULGER]

[957] PRETTY MISS BELLEW
3 vols. Bentley 1875. Royal-blue diagonal-fine-ribbed cloth.

Vol. I (iv) + (308)
II (iv) + (368)
III (iv) + 304 B

Note. To *Harper's New Monthly Magazine* for May 1888 R. R. Bowker (the founder of the famous firm who publish the New York *Publishers' Weekly*) contributed a long illustrated article entitled 'London as a Literary Centre'. Dealing with contemporary women novelists, he singled out as of sufficient importance to merit mention Miss Braddon, Ouida, Rhoda Broughton, Helen Mathers, Charlotte Yonge, Mrs Cashel Hoey, Mrs Alexander and 'Theo Gift', making particular mention of *Pretty Miss Bellew*. An earlier novel by 'Theo Gift' was *True to Her Trust*.

GILBERT, WILLIAM (1804–1890)

[958] DR AUSTIN'S GUESTS
2 vols. Strahan 1866. [Copy in the Collection two-vols-in-one in blue morocco cloth, and lacking pp. 313–314.]

Half-title in each vol. Blank leaf precedes half-title in Vol. I

Vol. I (viii) + 310 1st leaf of final sig., X_1, a single inset.
II (vi) + (320) X_7 X_8 adverts.

Note. A case-book describing the various inmates of a private asylum. Recorded, despite its imperfections, as a companion piece to *Shirley Hall Asylum*.

KING GEORGE'S MIDDY [959]
Sq. 8vo. Bell & Daldy 1869. Green sand-grain cloth, blocked in black and gold; bevelled boards; red chocolate end-papers. All edges gilt. 150 illustrations by W. S. Gilbert.

Half-title. pp. viii + (504) KK_4 blank.

Ink signature (of a child): 'C. J. Norman, 56 Crystal Palace Park Road, Sydenham', on fly-leaf.

LANDLORD OF 'THE SUN' (The): a Novel [960]
3 vols. Bentley 1871. Smooth pinkish-ochre cloth, blocked in black and lettered in gold; café-au-lait end-papers.

Vol. I (ii) + (328)
II (ii) + 314 Final leaf, X_5, a single inset.
III (ii) + 304 B

Back cover of Vol. I damp-stained.

Note. There is a secondary binding of ochre diagonal-fine-ribbed cloth, blocked in black and lettered in gold. No spine-imprint.

LEGION: or the Modern Demoniac [961]
Tinsley 1882. Smooth navy-blue cloth, blocked on front in lime-green, gold-lettered on spine.

Half-title. pp. (iv) + (272) S_8 adverts.

Note. This book is the result of the author's many years' study of insanity and its causes, and deals particularly with alcoholism. It is only 'fictional' by courtesy, in that it introduces anecdotes of real life in disguised form; but as a direct pendant to *Shirley Hall Asylum* it deserves inclusion in this catalogue.

SHIRLEY HALL ASYLUM: or the Memoirs of a Monomaniac (Edited by the author of 'Dives and Lazarus', 'The Weaver's Family', 'Margaret Meadows', etc.) [962]
William Freeman, 102 Fleet Street 1863. Dark green morocco cloth.

pp. (vi) + (394) First leaf of final sig., $2B_1$, a single inset. Fine.

Partly by Gilbert

BUNCH OF KEYS (A). Where they were found and what they might have unlocked. A Christmas Book. Edited by T. Hood [963]

Groombridge & Sons 1865. Claret morocco cloth, blocked on front in gold with a bunch of keys labelled with contributors' names and in blind with ornamentation, blocked and lettered in gold on spine. Bevelled boards, red chocolate end-papers. Gilt edges. Wood-engraved front., and vignette title (bunch of keys as on binding) after Paul Gray, on plate paper but reckoned in collation.

Half-title. pp. (xiv) + (294) Half-title and 19_1 single insets. Publishers' cat., 16 pp. undated, at end.

Ink inscription to Charles Bolton, signed 'T. F. Dillon Croker' and dated 'Christmas/64' on half-title. Very fine.

pp. (89)–144 are occupied by THE KEY OF THE STRONG ROOM by W. S. Gilbert. Other contributors: Thomas W. Robertson, Thomas Archer, Thomas Hood, William J. Prowse and Clement W. Scott.

[964] RATES AND TAXES and how they were collected. Edited by T. Hood

Groombridge & Sons 1866. Bright-blue morocco cloth, uniformly blocked with *A Bunch of Keys*, except that the gold vignette on front represents a spike-file for bills. Bevelled boards, plum end-papers. Gilt edges. Wood-engraved front. and vignette title (spike-file as on binding) after Paul Gray, on plate paper. Title only is reckoned in collation.

Half-title. pp. (xii) + 274 Final leaf, 18_1, a single inset. Publishers' cat., 12 pp. undated, at end. Binders' ticket 'Westleys' at end.

Ink inscription to Charles Bolton, signed 'T. F. Dillon Croker' and dated '2nd December 1865' on half-title. Very fine.

pp. (185)–230 are occupied by THE INCOME TAX READS A STORY, FOUND IN A DRAWER, AND CALLED 'MAXWELL AND I' by W. S. Gilbert. Other contributors as in *A Bunch of Keys*.

GISSING, GEORGE (1857–1903)

[965] DENZIL QUARRIER: a Novel

Lawrence & Bullen 1892. Olive-green morocco cloth, blocked in blind on front with publishers' device, gold-lettered on spine, back plain. Dark blue-green end-papers.

Half-title. pp. (iv) + (342) Final leaf, Z_3, a single inset. Fine.

[966] EMANCIPATED (The): a Novel

3 vols. Bentley 1890. Smooth olive-brown cloth spine, patterned paper sides in grey and olive-brown. Gold-lettered on spine. Grey monogram end-papers.

Vol. I (iv) + 308
II (iv) + (306) 40_1 a single inset.
III (iv) + 308

Fine.

IN THE YEAR OF JUBILEE [967]

3 vols. Lawrence & Bullen 1894. Milky-blue morocco cloth, blocked and lettered uniformly with *The Odd Women* (q.v.). Plain white end-papers.

Half-title in each vol.

Vol. I (iv) + 236
II (iv) + (268) R_6 blank.
III (iv) + 268

ISABEL CLARENDON [968]

2 vols. Chapman & Hall 1886. Dark sage-green straight-grain-morocco cloth, blocked in black on front and spine with band of decoration and rules at head and tail, on back with publishers' monogram: gold-lettered on spine.

Half-title in each vol.

Vol. I (iv) + (294) 1st leaf of final sig., U_1, a single inset.
II (iv) + 328

Very fine.

LIFE'S MORNING (A) [969]

3 vols. Smith, Elder 1888. Smooth red-brown cloth spine and corners, sides of morocco cloth of uniform colour. Black double-rules on front, spine and back; gold lettering on spine.

Blank leaf and half-title precede title in each vol.

Vol. I (viii) + (316)
II (viii) + (304)
III (viii) + (336) Y_8 adverts.

Fine.

Note. The B.M. copy is in grey-blue cloth, uniformly designed. The copy here described belonged to the author, and is uniform with the copy in Bodley.

NETHER WORLD (The): a Novel [970]

3 vols. Smith, Elder 1889. Smooth grey-blue cloth, blocked and lettered on front in red and apple-green, blocked in same colours on spine and gold-lettered, back plain.

Blank leaf and half-title precede title in Vol. I; half-title only in II and III

Vol. I (viii) + (292)
II (312) [paged (i)–(vi) + (1)–306]. Sig. (A) consists of prelims + (1)–10 of text.
III (316) [paged (i)–(vi) + (1)–310]. Sig. (A) as in Vol. II.

Cloth rather tired and spines darkened.

Note. The copy here described belonged to the author. That in Bodley is uniform in design but the basic cloth is reddish-brown, while that in B.M. (also uniform in design) has cloth of a light green.

[971] NEW GRUB STREET: a Novel

3 vols. Smith, Elder 1891. Dark blue-green morocco cloth, blocked and lettered in black on front, blocked in black and gold-lettered on spine, back plain.

Blank leaf and half-title precede title in each vol.

Vol. I (viii) + (308) X_2 adverts.
II (viii) + 316
III (viii) + (336)

Fine.

[972] ODD WOMEN (The)

3 vols. Lawrence & Bullen 1893. Dark red morocco cloth, blocked with blind rules on front, spine and back, gold-lettered and blocked with single rule on spine. Fawn-on-white foliage end-papers.

Blank leaf and half-title precede title in each vol.

Vol. I (viii) + (298) Final leaf, U_5, blank and a single inset.
II (viii) + (332) Final leaf, (Z_2), blank. Penultimate sig., Y, 4 leaves.
III (viii) + (328) Final leaf, Y_4, blank.

Note. The copy here described belonged to the author, and is uniform with the copy in Bodley. That in B.M. is in cloth of a royal blue.

[973] OUR FRIEND THE CHARLATAN

Chapman & Hall 1901. Dark grey-blue glazed linen, blocked and lettered in gold on front and spine; back plain. Front. and 4 half-tone illustrations after Launcelot Speed.

Half title. pp. (viii) + (428) EE_6 blank.

Fine.

[974] PAYING GUEST (The)

Narrow fcap. 8vo. Cassell 1895. Dark yellow unglazed buckram, blocked and lettered in red.

Series half-title, with list of volumes in the series on verso. pp. (160) Publishers' cat., 4 pp. on text paper dated '9. 95', at end.

Note. This was the sixth volume to appear of Cassell's Pocket Library (3741 in Section III).

[975] PRIVATE PAPERS OF HENRY RYECROFT (The)

Archibald Constable & Co. 1903. Dark green ribbed cloth, blocked and lettered in gold on front and spine, back plain.

Blank leaf and half-title precede title. pp. (xvi) [paged xiv] + (304). Text ends U_3 recto, verso blank, U_4 U_5 Index, U_6–U_8 adverts., paged 1–6.

Monogram bookplate of Dryburgh House, St Boswells. Very fine.

[976] SLEEPING FIRES

Slim 8vo. Fisher Unwin 1895. Terra cotta paper wrappers, printed in black.

Advert. leaf and half-title precede title. pp. (240) P_4–P_8 publishers' cat. undated.

Book-plate of W. U. L. Unwin. Fine.

No. 13 in Unwin's Autonym Library. Simultaneously issued in buff linen, blocked and lettered in dark blue.

TOWN TRAVELLER (The) [977]

Methuen 1898. Scarlet ribbed cloth, blocked and lettered in gold on front and spine; back plain.

Half-title. pp. (320) [paged vi + (314)] Sig. (A) of eight leaves is paginated (i)–vi + 1–10. Publishers' cat., 40 pp. dated September 1898, at end.

Fine.

UNCLASSED (The): a Novel [978]

3 vols. Chapman & Hall 1884. Greenish-blue fine-diaper cloth, blocked in black on front and spine, also gold-lettered on spine. Publisher's monogram in blind on back. Pinkish-cream endpapers.

Half-title in each vol.

Vol. I viii + 300
II vi + (316) Half-title a single inset.
III vi + 304 Half-title a single inset.

Presentation Copy: 'Thomas Hardy (from George Gissing)' in ink and in Hardy's hand on verso of fly-leaf in Vol. I. Also inserted two ALS from Gissing to Hardy, dated June 30, 1886 and July 25, 1887. The former apologises for sending an other than new copy of *The Unclassed* but it is the only one in the writer's possession. The letter goes on to comment on the novel ('I myself should not dare to read it now; it is too saturated with by-gone miseries of every kind'), and then to express his deep pleasure at having met and talked with Hardy. The second letter sends thanks for a copy of *The Mayor of Casterbridge*, discusses the book and speaks of his own writing plans.

Labels removed from front covers, but cloth otherwise bright. Two pages roughly opened and one or two sections loose.

VERANILDA: a Romance [979]

Archibald Constable & Co. Ltd. 1904. Crimson glazed linen, blocked in blind and lettered in gold on front and spine; back plain.

Blank leaf and half-title precede title. pp. (xii) [paged x] + 348. Publishers' cat., 16 pp. undated, at end. pp. v–vii are occupied by a preface by Frederic Harrison.

VICTIM OF CIRCUMSTANCES (A) and Other Stories [980]

Constable 1927. Blue unglazed linen, blocked and lettered in navy blue.

Half-title. pp. (xii) + 308

Issued in a white dust jacket, printed in ochre and dark blue. As new.

GLASCOCK, CAPT. W. N., R.N. (? 1787–1847)

[981] NAVAL SERVICE (The), or Officers' Manual for Every Grade in His Majesty's Ships

2 vols. Saunders & Otley 1836. Dark green fine-diaper cloth, blocked in blind on front and back, blocked with naval emblems and lettered in gold (NAVAL / OFFICERS / MANUAL) on spine.

Half-title in each vol.

Vol. I viii + 336
II (iv) + (344) Q_3 Q_4 adverts.

Presentation Copy: 'To Sir E. L. Bulwer, Bart. with the author's kind regards' in ink on title of Vol. I. Fine.

[982] NAVAL SKETCH-BOOK (The), or the Service Afloat and Ashore etc. (by an Officer of Rank)

2 vols. 'Printed for the Author and sold by H. Colburn, Geo. B. Whittaker' etc. 1826. Boards, labels.

Half-title in each vol.

Vol. I xxiv + (252)
II vi + 286 Text ends 244; 245–286 Appendix. First leaf of final sig., T_1, a single inset.

Spines discoloured.

[983] SAILORS AND SAINTS, or Matrimonial Manœuvres (by the authors of 'The Naval Sketch Book')

3 vols. Colburn 1829. Boards, labels.

Half-title in Vol. I

Vol. I (viii) + (316) Errata slip tipped in preceding p. (1) of text.
II (ii) + (328)
III (ii) + 316

Two labels slightly defective.

[984] TALES OF A TAR: Characteristic Anecdotes (by one of the authors of 'The Naval Sketch Book')

Colburn & Bentley 1830. Boards, labels.

Leaf of adverts. and half-title precede title. pp. (xii) [paged (x)] + (334) First leaf of final sig., P_1, a single inset.

Note. The authorship of this, and the previous, work is curious, as no indication of more than one author appears on *The Naval Sketch-Book.*

GOGOL, NICOLAI VASELIVICH (1810–1852)

[985] HOME LIFE IN RUSSIA (by a Russian Noble. Revised by the Editor of 'Revelations of Siberia')

2 vols. Hurst & Blackett 1854. Green morocco cloth, blocked in blind on front and back, blind-blocked and gold-lettered on spine.

Vol. I (vi) [paged iv] + 308
II (ii) + (316) P_2 adverts.

Note. This is the first English translation of *Dead Souls.*

GORE, MRS CATHERINE GRACE FRANCES (née MOODY) (1799–1861)

This, I think, is a complete record of Mrs Gore's fiction. Titles asterisked are not in the Collection; and as neither B.M. nor Bodley possess such titles in boards and I have been unable to locate board copies elsewhere, the descriptions provided are necessarily a little conjectural. Such non-fiction titles as are in the Collection are also included.

In the Preface to this Catalogue the importance of Mrs Gore's novels as source-books for the student of manners has been briefly indicated. No one, seeking to recreate the affectations, arrogance and pasteboard splendours of smart Society during the eighteen-thirties and forties, can afford to ignore them. Nor would one wish to do so; for her tongue is as witty as it is cruel, and oblivion can never be the fate of a woman who coined epigrams of such permanent significance as 'the sort of society in which a Lord is always a Lord, even if the Lord knows whom'.

AGATHONIA: a Romance [anon] [986]

Fcap 8vo. Edward Moxon 1844.

Copy I: Regulation binding. Dark green fine-diaper cloth, blocked in blind on front and back, in gold on spine with scroll-work and titling and blind decoration.

Half-title. pp. (iv) + (176) M_8 adverts. Text ends 153: (155)–173 Notes.

Bookseller's ticket: 'Sharland, Southampton', inside front cover.

Copy II: Presentation binding. Ivory fine-diaper cloth, spine unlettered, title in gold and blind frame on front, blind frame on back. Collation as Copy I. Sheets ¼ in. taller. [986*a*]

Presentation Copy: 'From the Author' in ink on half-title. Ink inscription: 'Queen Anne's Mead', on fly-leaf.

Note. A letter from Mrs Gore to Ollier was catalogued by Colbeck Radford in June 1939, in which, sending a copy of *Agathonia,* she said: 'to which I own only among my friends'.

According to a rumour of long-standing William Beckford helped Mrs Gore with this story. The rumour is supported by a letter from John Forster to Bulwer Lytton of May 1844 (cf. Chapman and Hodgkin, *Bibliography of Beckford,* p. 89).

AMBASSADOR'S WIFE (The) [987]

3 vols. Bentley 1842. Half-cloth boards, labels.

Half-title in each vol.

Vol. I (iv) + (312)
II (iv) + (312)
III (iv) + (322) First leaf of final sig., P_1, a single inset.

Labels slightly rubbed.

[988] BANKER'S WIFE (The), or Court and City: a Novel
3 vols. Colburn 1843. Half-cloth boards, labels.
Vol. I (iv)+296 Longman etc. cat., 32 pp. dated July 1843, at end.
II (ii)+324
III (ii)+346 First leaf of final sig., Q_1, a single inset.
Fine.

[989] BIRTHRIGHT (The) and Other Tales
3 vols. Colburn 1844. Half-cloth boards, labels.
Vol. I (iv)+(324) P_6 adverts.
II (ii)+(312)
III (ii)+314 Final leaf, P_1, a single inset.
Ink signature: 'J. V. Gaskell', inside front cover of each vol.
Contents: (*Vol. I*) The Birthright. (*Vol. II*) The Smuggler's Dog—The Man of the Day—Autobiography of Squire Ganderfield. (*Vol. III*) Old Families and New—The Childless Mother—Family Secrets—St Cecilia.

[990] CABINET MINISTER (The) (by the authoress of 'Mothers and Daughters', 'Mrs Armytage', 'The Heir of Selwood', etc.)
3 vols. Bentley 1839. Boards, labels.
Half-title in each vol.
Vol. I (iv)+300
II (iv)+296
III (iv)+288
Fine.
Note. This was William Beckford's copy. The front fly-leaf in each vol. (in Vols. II and III on verso as well as recto) carries notes in his hand.

[991] CASTLES IN THE AIR: a Novel
3 vols. Bentley 1847. Marbled boards, labels.
Half-title in Vols. I and II
Vol. I (iv)+302 First leaf of final sig., O_1, a single inset.
II (iv)+(308)
III (ii)+(338) Errata slip tipped in preceding p.(1) of text. Final leaf, Q_1, a single inset.
Note. A late boarding-up of sheets, with original labels. Although the top edges are uncut, the fore edges and tails are trimmed. The labels are set *high* on the spines (as on *Esmond* and certain books by Borrow) which suggests that this rather fanciful boarding was done in the early fifties. Labels slightly rubbed.

[992] CECIL: or the Adventures of a Coxcomb: a Novel [anon]
3 vols. Bentley 1841. Cont. half-calf (originally issued in boards with labels).
Half-title in each vol. (lacking in this copy).
Vol. I xii+312
II (iv)+324
III (iv)+300 Tear in title of Vol. III.
Note. Many years ago I had a fine board copy of *Cecil.* I threw it out as junk, and have never seen another.

CECIL: A PEER: 'A Sequel to "Cecil: or the Adventures of a Coxcomb" by the same author' [993] *Pl. 11*
3 vols. T. & W. Boone 1841. Boards, labels.
Half-title in each vol.
Vol. I (viii) [paged vi]+(314) Final leaf, P_1, a single inset.
II (iv)+298 Second leaf of final sig., O_2, a single inset.
III (iv)+308 Cat. of John Cumming, Dublin, 8 pp. dated 1841, at end.
Ink signature: 'Charleville', on title of each vol. Bookseller's label: 'Milliken, Dublin', on front cover of Vol. I. Very fine. At the end of Vol. I, pp. 301–(310) of vol. I of a novel called *The Expectant* are bound in by mistake.
Note. Re-issued in 1842 under the title *Ormington*, with a brief preface by the author.

COURTIER OF THE DAYS OF CHARLES II [994]
(The) with Other Tales
I cannot establish the true first edition of this collection of stories. *C.B.E.L.* says 'Paris 1839' and a volume in Baudry's European Library is the only specimen of 1839 publication in B.M. There is in the Collection an American edition of 1839 which, in default of an alternative, is here described.
2 vols. New York: Harper 1839. Dark brown morocco cloth, labels.
Vol. I pp. (228)
II pp. 208
Contents: The Courtier, etc.—The Leper-House of Janval—The Household Hospital—Dives and Lazarus; or Ireland!—Rigour of the Law in 1657—The Patriot Martyr of Old England—Married and Single—The Sisters; or Nature and Art—Ursel—Les Enfans Trouvés—The Royalists of Peru—The Red Man—The Christening Cloth.
Note. A 'Notice' at the beginning of Vol. I, signed 'C. F. Gore', states that, contrary to assertions made in more than one quarter, all the tales in this collection and in *Mary Raymond* (q.v.) are original and not translations from the French.

DACRE OF THE SOUTH, or the Olden Time: [995]
a Drama
8vo. Bentley 1840. Stiffened brown paper wrappers, white side-label printed in black.
pp. (iv)+(96)
Dedicated to 'The Author of Vathek...as a slight token of sincere admiration'. Very fine.

[996] *Pl. 11* DEAN'S DAUGHTER (The), or the Days We Live In

3 vols. Hurst & Blackett (successors to Colburn & Co.) 1853. Cream morocco cloth, blocked in blind on front and back, on spine blocked and lettered in gold.

Vol. I (vi) + 312 Publishers' cat., 8 pp. dated January 1853, at end.
II (ii) + 304 Publishers' cat., 16 pp. undated, at end.
III (ii) + (318) First leaf of final sig., X_1, a single inset. Publishers' cat., 8 pp. undated, at end.

Book-plate of Sir William Molesworth. Fine.

Notes. (i) The catalogues at the end of Vols. II and III are imprinted Colburn & Co., that in Vol. I Hurst & Blackett. (ii) I have also seen this book in half-cloth boards, labels.

[997] DEBUTANTE (The), or the London Season

3 vols. Bentley 1846. Half-cloth boards, labels.

Vol. I (ii) + (308) O_{10} imprint leaf.
II (ii) + 302 First leaf of final sig., O_1, a single inset
III (ii) + (320)

Spines dull: those of Vols. I and III nibbled by mice.

[998] DIAMOND AND THE PEARL (The): a Novel

3 vols. Colburn 1849. Boards, labels.

Vol. I (ii) + (320) X_8 adverts. Two undated Publishers' cats. at end: (*a*) 8 pp., (*b*) 24 pp.
II (ii) + (312) X_4 adverts.
III (ii) + (336)

Book-label of Alexander Durn on front cover of Vol. I.

[999] DIARY OF A DÉSENNUYÉE (The) [anon]

2 vols. Colburn 1836. Half-cloth boards, labels.

Advert. leaf precedes title in Vol. I

Vol. I (iv) + (300)
II (ii) + (296)

A leaf advertising four publications of John Cumming, Dublin, is pasted inside front cover of Vol. I. The advert. leaf preceding title in Vol. I announces, under date July 1, 1836, that Colburn has restarted his London publishing business, and lists ten new works (of which *The Diary of a Désennuyée* is No. VIII) as forming his first list from Great Marlborough Street.

Note. This is not a parody of Mrs Jameson's *Diary of an Ennuyée* (1826), but was almost certainly suggested by that work.

[1000] DOWAGER (The), or the New School for Scandal

3 vols. Bentley 1840. Half-cloth boards, labels.

Vol. I (ii) + (324) P_6 advert.
II (ii) + (320) P_4 advert.
III (ii) + 320

Book-plate of A. H. Royds. Not a very fresh copy. Vol. I loose in covers and label defective.

FAIR OF MAY FAIR (The) [anon] [1001]

3 vols. Colburn and Bentley 1832. Boards, labels.

Vol. I (viii) + 348
II (ii) + (332) Q_4 adverts.
III (ii) + (376)

Ink signature: 'Frances Price, Rhiwlas. 1832' and bookseller's ticket: 'J. Seacome, Chester', inside front cover of each vol. Very fine.

Contents: (*Vols. I, II*) The Flirt of Ten Seasons—The Separate Maintenance. (*Balance of Vol. II and into Vol. III*) Hearts and Diamonds. (*Balance of Vol. III*) A Divorce—My Granddaughter—The Special License.

GREVILLE, or a Season in Paris [1002]

3 vols. Colburn 1841. Half-cloth boards, labels.

Vol. I (ii) + 306 First leaf of final sig., O_1, a single inset.
II (ii) + 300
III (ii) + 332

Ink signature: 'E. Evans, Highmead', on verso of fly-leaf in each vol. Subscribers' list of the Carmarthen Reading Society pasted inside front cover of Vol. I. Loose in covers. Oil-stain at beginning of Vol. III.

HAMILTONS (The), or the New Æra (by the author of 'Mothers and Daughters') [1003] *Pl. 11*

3 vols. Saunders & Otley 1834. Boards, labels.

Half-title in Vol. I

Vol. I (iv) + 308
II (iv) + 308 Page (iii) carries a quotation from *Gulliver.*
III (ii) + (324) P_6 adverts.

Book-label: 'R. J. Ll. Price. Rhiwlas Library', and bookseller's ticket: 'Seacome, Chester', inside front cover of each vol. Very fine.

Note. One title has been cut from the list of novels on p. (323) of Vol. III.

See also 3735c *in Section III.*

HECKINGTON: a Novel [1004] *Pl. 11*

3 vols. Hurst & Blackett 1858. Dark green bead-grain cloth, double blind frame on front and back, gold lettered on spine.

Vol. I (ii) + 304 Publishers' cat., 24 pp. undated, at end.
II (ii) + 316
III (ii) + (318) X_6 X_7 adverts. X_7 a single inset.

Ink signature: 'Lady Molesworth of Pencanon 1859', on fly-leaf of Vols. I and III. Binders' ticket: 'Leighton, Son & Hodge', at end of Vol. I. Very fine.

[1005] HEIR OF SELWOOD (The), or Three Epochs of a Life (by the authoress of 'Mothers and Daughters', 'Mrs Armytage' and 'Stokeshill Place')

3 vols. Colburn 1838. Boards, labels.

Half-title in each vol.

Vol. I (iv)+300
II (iv)+314 Final leaf, P_1, a single inset.
III (iv)+(320) P_3 P_4 adverts.

Very fine.

Note. This was William Beckford's copy. The front fly-leaf of each vol. carries pencil notes by him. On the verso of that of Vol. III he makes a shrewd general comment: 'The clever authoress, a little tired—or so I suspect—of *all* her characters, tumbles events over events in a strangely confused, incoherent manner, and drives on to the end of the required third volume as fast as she is able. W.B. 12 Nov. 1838.'

[1006] HISTORICAL TRAVELLER (The): Comprising Narratives connected with the Most Curious Epochs of European History, and with the Phenomena of European Countries ('by Mrs Charles Gore')

2 vols. Sm. 8vo. Colburn & Bentley 1831. Maroon watered cloth, paper labels.

Half-title in each vol.

Vol. I viii+(320) X_8 adverts.
II (viii)+(312)

Note. Also issued in green watered cloth with black and gold label.

[1007] HUNGARIAN TALES (by the author of 'The Lettre de Cachet')

3 vols. Saunders & Otley 1829. Boards, labels.

Half-title in each vol.

Vol. I (xii)+328 pp. (xi) (xii) are fly-title to *Cassian.*
II (vi)+(350) [paged (329)–(428)+(1)–250] Half-title and 1st leaf of final sig., single insets.
III (viii)+(340) pp. (vii) (viii) adverts. Spines worn and labels defective.

Contents: (*Vol. I*) Cassian. (*Vol. II*) Cassian (*concluded*). The Tzigany, or Hungarian gipsy—The Tavernicus—The Elizabethines—The Ferry on the Danube. (*Vol. III*) The Balsam-seller of Thurotzer—The Festival of the Three Kings—The Infanta at Presburg.

[1008] *Pl. 11* INUNDATION (The), or Pardon and Peace: a Christmas Story

Fcap 8vo. Fisher, Son & Co. n.d. [1847]. Red morocco cloth, pictorially blocked in gold and blind uniform with *The Snow Storm.* All edges gilt. Etched front. and 3 plates by George Cruikshank.

pp. (iv)+222 Final leaf, P_7, a single inset. Publishers' cat., 16 pp. undated, at end.

Ink inscription dated December 1847 on title. Loose in covers. On front cover the sub-title reads: PEACE & PARDON.

Note. Sheets of this story, and of *The Snow Storm* and *New Year's Day,* were re-issued, undated, in eleven parts by Peter Jackson (late Fisher, Son & Co.) in buff paper wrappers printed in black entitled: CHRISTMAS STORIES by MRS GORE. Parts 1, 4, 6 and 9 are in the Collection.

Still later, Willoughby made a re-issue of unsold sheets under the original title, in red wavy-grain cloth, blocked in blind and lettered (from type) in gold.

*LETTRE DE CACHET (The): a Tale. THE REIGN OF TERROR: a Tale [anon] [1009]

J. Andrews, 167 New Bond Street 1827. Boards, label.

pp. (viii)+(408) $2D_4$ Imprint leaf. Pp. (vii) (viii) are fly-title to *Lettre de Cachet,* verso blank.

Note. I assume the book was issued in boards with a label. The B.M. copy has an Errata slip pasted on a blank end-paper. I cannot say where this slip was originally tipped in.

LIFE'S LESSONS (A) [1010]

3 vols. Hurst & Blackett 1856. Dull-salmon (or green) morocco cloth: double blind frame on front and back: spine lettered and blocked in gold; bright yellow end-papers.

Vol. I (iv)+(316) X_6 adverts.
II (ii)+(318) X_7 adverts. and a single inset.
III (ii)+(318) X_7 adverts. and a single inset.

Binders' ticket: 'Leighton, Son & Hodge', at end of Vols. I and III.

Note. I have also seen this book in green cloth of similar grain and similarly blocked.

MAMMON, or the Hardships of an Heiress [1011]

3 vols. Hurst & Blackett 1855. Dark green ripple-grain cloth, blocked in blind on front and back: blocked and lettered in gold and blocked in blind on spine; thick sand-coloured end-papers.

Vol. I (ii)+(304) Publishers' cat., 24 pp. dated January 1855, at end.
II (ii)+(320)
III (ii)+(336) Y_8 adverts.

Ink signature: 'H. B. Westerman, 1856' inside front cover of Vol. I and bookseller's stamp: 'Byrne, Leeds' at end. Vol. I loose in covers.

*MAN OF FORTUNE (The) and Other Tales [1012]

3 vols. Colburn, n.d. [1842]. Boards (and/or half-cloth boards), labels.

Vol. I (ii)+(318)
II (iv)+(320) P_4 blank.
III (iv)+(360) Q_{11} Q_{12} adverts.

Contents: (*Vol. I*) The Man of Fortune. (*Vol. II*) Ango, or the Merchant Prince—The Queen's Comfit Maker, a Legend of Tottenham Cross—The Young Soldier, or Military Discipline—A Lucky Dog—The Fatal Window—The Railroad—The Mariners of the Pollet. (*Vol. III*) The Wife of an Aristocrat—Neighbour Gray and her Daughter—The Jewess—The Cost of a Reputation—Mr Prattles, the Dining-out-man—A House of Five Stories.

[1013] MARY RAYMOND and Other Tales (by the authoress of 'Mothers and Daughters')

3 vols. Colburn 1838. Boards (and/or half-cloth boards), labels. This copy in cont. half calf.

Half-title in Vol. I

Vol. I (viii) + (338) (Q_1) a single inset.
II (iv) + (332) P_{10} adverts.
III (iv) + (368)

Contents: (*Vol. I*) Mary Raymond—The Abbey—Xaviera. (*Vol. II*) Pierre L'Ecrevissier—Burgher of St Gall—The Scrap-Stall—The Soldier's Return—The Lit de Veille—The Miller of Corbeil—The Champion—Sir Roger de Coverley's Picture Gallery. (*Vol. III*) St John of the Island—Dorathea—Verrex—Wine—Napoleon at Fontainebleau—Lady Evelyn's Three Trials—La Tarantata—Now or Never—Victoria—The Hair-Market of Evreux.

Note. I do not know whether Vol. I should end with (Q_2), blank or adverts.

[1014] MEMOIRS OF A PEERESS, or the Days of Fox ('edited by Lady Charlotte Bury')

Copy I: First Edition. 3 vols. Colburn 1837. Boards, labels.

Half-title in each vol.

Vol. I (vi) [paged iv] + 282 First leaf of final sig., N_1, a single inset.
II (iv) + 308
III (iv) + (296) O_4 adverts.

Book-plate of James Francis Anderton. Spines of Vols. I and II shaken and label of Vol. II slightly imperfect.

Note. The running headline throughout is 'Posthumous Memoirs'.

[1014*a*] **Copy II: 'A New Edition Revised by the Author.'** Knight & Son 1859. Grass-green bead-grain cloth, blocked and lettered in gold: blind-blocked on front and back.

pp. iv + (312)

Presentation Copy: 'With Mrs Gore's Comps' in ink and in her hand inside front cover.

Binders' ticket: 'Lewis & Sons', at end. Fine.

Note. Pp. (iii) iv are occupied by a Preface, dated 1858 and signed C.F.G., stating that Colburn put Lady Charlotte Bury's name as 'Editor' on the first edition against Mrs Gore's wishes and when she was living abroad.

MEN OF CAPITAL [1015]

3 vols. Colburn 1846. Boards, labels. *Pl. 11*

Half-title in Vols. II and III

Vol. I (x) + 328
II (iv) + (322) Final leaf, (P_1), a single inset.
III (iv) + (360) Q_{12} adverts.

Ink signature: 'Moretino', on title of each vol. Very fine.

*MODERN CHIVALRY, or a New Orlando Furioso [anon] [1016]

2 vols. John Mortimer 1843. Boards (or half-cloth boards), labels. Etched front. in each vol., and in Vol. I one, in Vol. II two plates by George Cruikshank. Also vignettes on titles.

Half-title in each vol.

Vol. I viii + (294)
II (290)

Note. Robson had several copies of this book in Hanover Street at the period when I discarded *Cecil.* I did not buy one.

*MONEY-LENDER (The) [1017]

3 vols. Colburn 1843. Boards (and/or half-cloth boards), labels.

Vol. I iv + ? (296) U_4 ? blank or adverts.
II (ii) + 294
III (ii) + 284

Note. I assume that Vol. II originally ended with U_3, U_4 being title, and that Vol. III ended with T_6, T_7 and T_8 being title and label leaf. This description is taken from B.M. copy bound three-vols.-in-one.

MOTHERS AND DAUGHTERS: a Tale of the Year 1830 [anon] [1018] *Pl. 11*

3 vols. Colburn & Bentley 1831. Boards, labels.

Vol. I (ii) + 318 First leaf of final sig., P_1, a single inset.
II (ii) + (332)
III (ii) + (360) Q_{11} Q_{12} adverts.

Ink signature: 'Frances Price, Rhiwlas, 1831' and bookseller's ticket: 'Seacome, Chester' inside front cover of each vol. Fine.

MRS ARMYTAGE, or Female Domination (by the authoress of 'Mothers and Daughters') [1019]

Copy I: First Edition. 3 vols. Colburn 1836. Half-cloth boards, labels.

Vol. I (ii) + (306) Final leaf, P_1, a single inset.
II (ii) + (292) O_2 adverts.
III (ii) + (356)

Copy II: New Edition. FEMALE DOMINATION. Bryce, n.d. [circ. 1854]. Bright green [1019*a*] glazed boards printed in black; printed end-papers.

pp. (viii) [paged (x)] + 364 Very fine.

Note. Pp. (v)–(vii) of prelims. are occupied by a Preface, written for this edition and signed 'C.F.G.', in which the author states that the murdered Duchesse de Praslin was reading *Mrs Armytage* on the night of her assassination.

[1020] *Pl. 11* NEW YEAR'S DAY: a Winter's Tale

Copy I: First Edition. Fcap 8vo. Fisher, Son & Co. n.d. (Dedication dated Nov. 1846.) Pale apple-green morocco cloth, pictorially blocked in gold and blind on front and spine, in blind on back. All edges gilt. Etched front. and 3 plates by George Cruikshank.

Half-title. pp. (vi) + (204) Publishers' cat., 8 pp. undated, at end.

[1020*a*] *Pl. 11* **Copy II:** THE LOST SON. Dean & Son, n.d. [1854]. White paper boards, printed with decoration and fancy titling in blue, red and brown. Up-lettered on spine. Printed end-papers.

Note. An exact reprint of Copy I on cheaper paper, with 3 plates omitted, a new title, and the front. printed on text paper and conjugate with title.

[1021] OPERA (The): a Novel (by the author of 'Mothers and Daughters')

3 vols. Colburn & Bentley 1832. Boards, labels.

Half-title in each vol.

Vol. I (iv) + (320) Cat. of Simpkin & Marshall, 4 pp. undated, inset at end.
II (iv) + 304
III (iv) + (320) P_4 adverts.

Ink signature: 'Frances Price, Rhiwlas, 1832' and bookseller's ticket: 'J. Seacome, Chester' inside front cover of each vol. One title has been carefully cut from the list of books advertised on Vol. III, P_4.

[1022] PARIS IN 1841

Large 8vo. Longman etc. 1842. Light apple-green fine-morocco cloth, blocked on front in blind and gold, on back in blind; spine gold-lettered: THE / PICTURESQUE / ANNUAL. / *rule* / 1842. All edges gilt. Steel-engraved vignette title [HEATH'S / PICTURESQUE ANNUAL, / FOR 1842. / PARIS / *By Mrs Gore*] preceding printed title, and 20 illustrations after Thomas Allom, some full page, others on the same page as text, and all on plate paper. Each engraving is tissued.

pp. (viii) + (270) Final leaf, Q_8, blank.

Rather dingy, and spine darkened.

Note. That the final leaf should be Q_8, yet be paged (270), is due to an eccentricity in the construction of this volume. 15 of the engraved illustrations are treated as vignettes in the text, with letter-press above or below them and on verso. They are on plate-paper, but are paginated as part of the text. The full-page plates, on identical paper, are not paginated. But although the pagination is thus extended to include 30 pages of plate-paper, the signature lettering takes account only of the text-paper. Consequently Q_8 is really p. (240), but is numbered (270).

PEERS AND PARVENUS: a Novel [1023]

3 vols. Colburn 1846. Half-cloth boards, labels.

Vol. I (ii) + 304
II (ii) + (300) O_6 adverts.
III (ii) + 336

Ink signature: 'Lady Carew, Marley', on title of each vol. Bookseller's ticket: 'Sam[l] Hannaford, Totnes', inside front cover of each vol. A few small scribbles by some youthful Carew on fly-leaf and inside cover of Vols. II and III. Fine.

PIN MONEY: a Novel (by the authoress of 'The Manners of the Day') [1024]

3 vols. Colburn & Bentley 1831. Boards, labels.

Vol. I (iv) + (336) P_{11} P_{12} adverts., dated 1st June, 1831.
II (ii) + 312
III (ii) + (328)

Book-plate of R. J. Ll. Price, Rhiwlas Library, in each vol. Fine.

Note. Vol. I, P_{11} recto carries the interesting advert. of the Standard Novel Series to which reference is made in Section III [Vol. 2, p. 94].

POLISH TALES (by the authoress of 'Hungarian Tales') [1025]

3 vols. Saunders & Otley 1833. Boards, labels.

Half-title in each vol.

Vol. I (viii) + 330 Final leaf, R_1, a single inset. Text ends p. 325; (327)–330 Notes.
II (iv) + 332
III (iv) + 326 Final leaf, Q_1, a single inset. Publishers' cat., 4 pp. on text paper dated March 1833, at end. Text ends p. 314; (315)–326 'Notes to Vols. II and III'.

Ink inscription: 'Hamsterley' in R. S. Surtees' hand, on title of each vol. Joints cracked and covers of Vol. I almost detached.

Contents: (*Vols. I and II*) The Confederates of Lubionki. (*Balance of Vol. II and into Vol. III*) The Mill of Mariemont or the Fortunes of Stanislas. (*Balance of Vol. III*) The Pasieka or the Bee Farm.

POPULAR MEMBER (The): THE WHEEL OF FORTUNE, etc. [1026]

3 vols. Bentley 1844. Cont. half-calf (probably originally issued in half-cloth boards).

Vol. I (ii) + 304
II (ii) + 320
III (ii) + 306 Final leaf, P_2 (instead of P_3 as it would normally be) because sig. O is of seven leaves.

Contents: (*Vol. I*) The Popular Member. (*Vol. II*) The Popular Member (*concluded*)—True Love—The Last of the Knights. (*Vol. III*) Blanks and Prizes, or The Wheel of Fortune.

[1027] PREFERMENT, or My Uncle the Earl
Pl. 11 3 vols. Colburn 1840. Boards, labels.

Half-title in each vol.

Vol. I (iv) + (302) First leaf of final sig., O_1, a single inset.
II (iv) + 292
III (iv) + 340

Fine.

Note. This was William Beckford's copy. Inside front and back covers and fly-leaf of Vols. I and II, fly-leaf and inside back cover of Vol. II carry notes in his hand. Two architectural sketches in pencil are inside front cover of Vol. III, and are dated March 30, 1840. The notes inside front cover of Vol. I were originally written in March 1840, and gone over in ink in May. Other notes elsewhere are dated 'March'.

[1028] PROGRESS AND PREJUDICE
3 vols. Hurst & Blackett 1854. Smooth cloth, glazed and marbled in blue, ochre, crimson and black, blocked in blind with neat key-pattern frame on front and back, and lettered in gold on spine.

Vol. I (ii) + 296 4 pp. of publishers' adverts. and publishers' cat., 24 pp. undated, at end.
II (ii) + 324
III (ii) + (308) O_9 O_{10} adverts.

Presentation Copy: 'Charles Prideaux Bruac (?) from the Author 1854' in ink inside front cover of Vol. I. Fine.

Note. This is undoubtedly a special presentation binding, and was reproduced (not very satisfactorily) facing p. 54 of my *Evolution of Publishers' Binding Styles.* The normal publishers' binding of *Progress and Prejudice* is of light grey-blue ripple-grain cloth, blocked ornamentally in blind on front, back and spine and gold-lettered on spine.

[1029] ROMANCES OF REAL LIFE (by the author of 'Hungarian Tales')

Copy I: First Edition. 3 vols. Colburn 1829. Boards, labels.

Half-title in Vols. I and II

Vol. I (viii) + (330) Final leaf, Q_3, a single inset.
II (vi) + (324) pp. (v) (vi), Contents, form a single inset.
III (iv) + (360) Q_{10}–Q_{12} adverts.

Book-label of R. J. Ll. Price, Rhiwlas Library, and bookseller's ticket: 'J. Seacome, Chester' in each vol. Fine.

Copy II: Cheap Edition. Knight & Son 1859. [1029*a*]
Blue bead-grain cloth, blocked in gold on spine, and in blind on front and back. Wood-engraved front. on text paper included in the collation.

pp. (iv) + (328) Y_3 Y_4 adverts.

Presentation Copy: 'From C. F. Gore' in ink inside front cover, and ink signature: 'Lady Molesworth of Pencanon /59', on fly-leaf.

Note. The spine imprint is: STANDARD NOVELS, but Knight used this term only for his editions of Mrs Gore.

Contents: (*Vols. I and II*) The Maid of Honour—The Soldier Priest—The Bride of Zante—The Court at Tunbridge in 1664—The Lettre de Cachet. (*Continuing Vol. II and into Vol. III*) The Princess's Birthday—The Hindoo Mother—The Reign of Terror. (*Balance of Vol. III*) The Queen of May—Ehrenbreitstein—The Abbey of Laach—Subordination—The Deserted House—The Last Day of the Year in Vienna.

ROSE FANCIER'S MANUAL (The) [1030]
Colburn 1838. Plum ribbed cloth, blocked in blind on front and back, gold blocked and lettered on spine. Engraved title, with rose-wreath hand-coloured and fancy lettering, precedes printed title.

Half-title. pp. xx + (436) U_2 adverts.

SELF (by the author of 'Cecil') [1031]
3 vols. Colburn 1845. Boards, labels.

Half-title in Vol. II

Vol. I viii + 324
II (iv) + 372
III 380 Publisher's cat., 24 pp. on text paper dated 1845, at end.

Very fine.

SKETCH BOOK OF FASHION (The) (by the author of 'Mothers and Daughters') [1032]
3 vols. Bentley 1833. Boards, labels.

Half-title in Vol. II

Vol. I iv + (308) Cat. of Simpkin & Marshall, 4 pp. undated, inset at end.
II (iv) + 312
III (ii) + 330 First leaf of final sig., P_1, a single inset.

Ink signature: 'Frances Price. Rhiwlas 1833' and bookseller's ticket: 'J. Seacome, Chester' inside front cover of each vol. Fine.

Contents: (*Vols. I and II*) The Pavilion—My Place in the Country—The Second Marriage. (*Balance of Vol. II and into Vol. III*) The Old and the Young Bachelor. (*Balance of Vol. III*) The Manœuvrer outwitted or Relations from India—The Intriguante.

[1033] SKETCHES OF ENGLISH CHARACTER
2 vols. Bentley 1846. Dark brown ribbed cloth, blocked in blind and lettered in gold.

Half-title in each vol.

Vol. I (vi)+348
II (vi)+324

[1034] SNOW STORM (The): a Christmas Story
Pl. 11 Fcap 8vo. Fisher, Son & Co. n.d. [1845]. Red morocco cloth, pictorially blocked in gold on front and spine, in blind on back. All edges gilt. Etched front. and 3 plates by George Cruikshank.

pp. (iv)+(256) R_8 adverts.

Two illustrations coloured by hand. Loose in covers.

Note. I have seen a re-issue, imprint Darton & Co. n.d., in magenta wavy-grain cloth, pictorially blocked in gold on spine. Plates as in first edition.

[1035] STOKESHILL PLACE, or the Man of Business (by the authoress of 'Mrs Armytage', 'Mothers and Daughters', etc.)
3 vols. Colburn 1837. Boards, labels.

Half-title in each vol.

Vol. I (iv)+(330) First leaf of final sig., P_1, a single inset.
II (iv)+320
III (iv)+320 P_3 P_4 adverts., paged (317)–320.

Labels slightly rubbed.

[1036] STORY OF A ROYAL FAVOURITE (The)
3 vols. Colburn 1845. Half-cloth boards, leather labels pasted over original paper ones.

Vol. I (ii)+288
II (ii)+(308)
III (ii)+(296) O_3 O_4 adverts.

Book-label: Coronet over 'S.E.H.B. & C.'

[1037] TEMPTATION AND ATONEMENT, and Other Tales

Copy I: First Edition. 3 vols. Colburn 1847. Half-cloth boards, labels.

Half-title in Vol. I

Vol. I (iv)+312
II (iv)+332
III (iv)+(328)

Book-plate of John Henry Smith in each vol.

Contents: (*Vol. I*) Temptation and Atonement. (*Vol. II*) Judge Not, that ye be not Judged—A Passage in the Civil Wars—A Vision of a Royal Ball—An Account of a Creditor—The Hot Water Cure—May Fair at Bruges—Hush! (*Vol. III*) The Next of Kin—Second Thoughts are best—Uncle Moseley and the Railroad—The Spinster's Home—A Chapter on Grandmothers—The Fatal Window.

Copy II: Revised Edition of title-story only, i.e. Vol. I of Copy I. Knight & Son, n.d. Red fine-morocco cloth, pictorially blocked in gold and blind. All edges gilt. Wood-engraved front. on text paper. pp. (iv)+(188) N_3–N_6 adverts. [1037*a*]

Presentation Copy: 'From C. F. Gore' in ink inside front cover.

THERESA MARCHMONT, or the Maid of Honour: a Tale ('by Mrs Charles Gore') [1038]
Sm. 8vo. Printed for J. Andrews 1824. Boards.

pp. (ii)+120

Ink inscription: 'For Maria from William E.', on title. Back-strip missing. I cannot say whether the book was issued with or without a label.

TRANSMUTATION, or The Lord and the Lout ('by N or M') [1039]

***First Edition.** Chapman & Hall 1854. Claret fine-ribbed cloth in the style of Chapman & Hall's Monthly Series.

Half-title. pp. (iv)+288

Binders' ticket: 'Bone & Son', at end (of Bodleian copy).

Note. This volume contains no mention of the Monthly Series (q.v. in Section III). The author has not previously been identified as Mrs Gore.

New Edition. THE LORD AND THE LOUT (by Mrs Gore). Knight & Son, n.d. Blue bead-grain cloth, uniform in colour and blocking with *Romances of Real Life*, Copy II. [1039*a*]

Half-title. pp. (288) T_2–T_8 adverts.

Presentation Copy: 'A reprint, from C. F. Gore' in ink inside front cover.

TUILERIES (The): a Tale (by the author of 'Hungarian Tales', 'Romances of Real Life', etc.) [1040]
3 vols. Colburn & Bentley 1831. Boards, labels.

Half-title in Vol. I

Vol. I (iv)+(316) P_2 adverts.
II (ii)+(344) Q_4 adverts.
III (ii)+352

Spine of Vol. I a little chipped and label defective.

TWO ARISTOCRACIES (The): a Novel [1041]
3 vols. Hurst & Blackett 1857. Dark green morocco cloth, double blind frame on front and back, spine blocked in blind and lettered in gold.

Vol. I (ii)+308 Publishers' cat., 24 pp. undated, at end.
II (ii)+316
III (ii)+330 Final leaf, Z_1, a single inset.

Ink signature: 'Elisabeth Fortescue', on title of each vol. A dull copy, and covers of Vol. II stained.

[1042] TWO BROKEN HEARTS (The): a Tale [anon]
8vo. J. Andrews, 167 New Bond St. 1823. Full polished calf (originally issued in boards with or without spine label). Probably half-title (lacking from this copy); in which case, pp. (viii) + 100. Text ends p. 94; (95) (96) fly title to Notes: (97)–100 Notes.

Ink signature on title: 'Katherine Annabella Bisshopp' and 'J.D.P. July 1823'. Lower down, in the hand of 'J.D.P.' 'By Mrs Gore. 1823'. Book label 'Castle Goring'.

[1043] WOMAN OF THE WORLD (The): a Novel (by the authoress of 'The Diary of a Désennuyée')
3 vols. Colburn 1838. Boards, labels.

Half-title in Vols. I and III

Vol. I viii + 300
II (ii) + 320
III (iv) + (324)

Fine.

Note. This was William Beckford's copy. The front fly-leaf of each vol., and in Vol. III the verso of half-title also, are covered with notes in his hand. On back inside cover of Vol. III are two pencil sketches of a large house and the date (in his hand) '28 Sept. 1838'. Inserted in Vol. I is a draft letter from Beckford to Mrs Gore praising this book in enthusiastic terms. This letter, written in ink by Beckford, is dated September 5, 1838, but is neither finished off nor signed.

[1044] WOMEN AS THEY ARE, or Manners of the Day [anon]
3 vols. Colburn & Bentley 1830. Second Edition. Boards, labels.

Half-titles in Vols. I and II

Vol. I (iv) + 332
II (iv) + 326 Final leaf, P_7, a single inset.
III (ii) + (316)

Book-label of R. J. Ll. Price, Rhiwlas Library, and bookseller's ticket: 'Seacome, Chester', in each vol. Spines worn. The first edition appeared in the same year.

Edited by Mrs Gore

[1045] FASCINATION and Other Tales ('Edited by Mrs Gore')
3 vols. Colburn 1842. Half-cloth boards, labels.

Vol. I (iv) + 320
II (ii) + 320
III (ii) + (298) Final leaf, P_1, a single inset, probably conjugate with label-leaf.

Booksellers' ticket: 'Meyler & Son, Bath', inside front cover of Vol. I. Pencil initials 'T.C.' on fly-leaf of Vol. II. I bought this copy in Bath with some other novels from Doddington Park, recently occupied by the family of Codrington.

Contents: (*Vol. I*) Fascination—First Love. (*Vol. II*) The Modern Scipio—The Silver Ring—Retribution—Lex Talionis. (*Vol. III*) The Cossack's Grave—Theresa.

Note. An Editor's 'Advertisement' in Vol. I explains that the stories now offered were translated from the French by a man who, though an excellent linguist, lacked literary experience and invited Mrs Gore to revise his manuscript.

LOVER AND THE HUSBAND (The): THE WOMAN OF A CERTAIN AGE ('Edited by Mrs Gore') [1046]
3 vols. Bentley 1841. Half-cloth boards, labels.

Half-title in each vol.

Vol. I (viii) [mispaged vii] + (320)
II iv + (314) Final leaf, (P_1), a single inset.
III iv + (324)

Labels rubbed and that of Vol. I defective. Title of Vol. III stained.

Contents: (*Vols. I and II*) The Lover and The Husband. (*Balance of Vol. II and into Vol. III*) The Woman of a Certain Age. (*Balance of Vol. III*) Persecution—The Goldsmith's Wife.

Note. Title-story translated from the French of GERFAUT by Charles de Bernard.

QUEEN OF DENMARK (The): an Historical Novel ('Edited by Mrs Gore') [1047]
3 vols. Colburn 1846. Half-cloth boards, labels.

Vol. I vi + (288) 4 pp. leaflet, advertising publications of Gilbert, inserted at end.
II (ii) + 302 First leaf of final sig., O_1, a single inset. Leaflet as in I at end.
III (ii) + 308 Leaflet as in I at end.

Spines stained and labels discoloured.

Note. From the Danish of T. C. HEIBERG.

GRAND, SARAH [MRS FRANCES ELIZABETH MCFALL] (1862–1943)

HEAVENLY TWINS (The) [1048]
3 vols. Heinemann 1893.

Copy I: Trial Issue. Smooth scarlet cloth, unblocked on front and back, gold-lettered on spine.

Half-title in each vol.

Vol. I (xviii) [paged (xvi)] + (300) Half-title a single inset.
II (iv) + (284)
III (iv) + 274 Final leaf, T_1, a single inset. Publishers' cat., 16 pp. dated Nov. 1892, at end.

Association Copy (*from the author's collection*): Ink inscription inside front cover of Vol. I:

'This copy of *The Heavenly Twins* is one of the three copies of *advanced sheets* made up by the

Guardian Office for Heinemann; and contains the matter cut by Sarah Grand before the final publication of the book. There is one copy in my possession, of the book, between the galley proofs and this issue. [signed] C. Haldane McFall.'

On fly-leaf of Vol. I, ink signature, 'C. Haldane McFall' and note: 'presented by W. Heinemann, July 13, 1893'. Similar ink signature on fly-leaves of Vols. II and III.

Note. I fear that Haldane McFall (Sarah Grand's son) has confused matters. This copy appears to be identical as to text with the regular first edition (so far at any rate as can be gathered from a systematic checking of page-endings throughout the three volumes) and the similar red-cloth copy which belonged to Sir Edmund Gosse also showed no textual variation from the green-cloth published edition. No doubt McFall is correct in stating that only three trial copies in this style were submitted to Heinemann; but I think the still earlier copy to which he refers must be the one containing the cancelled matter.

[1048*a*] **Copy II: First Published Edition.** Smooth dark green cloth, blocked and lettered in black on front, publishers' monogram in blind on back, gold-lettered on spine. Collation as Copy I.

Spine of Vol. II a little bruised, but generally very fine.

Presentation and Association Copy: Ink inscription on the fly-leaf of Vol. I, unsigned but in Sarah Grand's handwriting:

'To dear old Chambers. In grateful and affectionate acknowledgment of all I owe to his help and patience, and in memory of the long, long weary hours he devoted to reducing the amorphous mass of manuscript, and carving the story out of the redundant rubbish in which it was encrusted. 7th February 1893.'

Ink inscription on recto and verso of back fly-leaf and inside back cover of Vol. I in Sarah Grand's handwriting and signed S.G.:

'*George Meredith, his life and friends in relation to his work*, by S. M. Ellis (1919) page 247.

'And concerning *The Heavenly Twins* by Sarah Grand, he wrote: "The author is a clever woman and has ideas; for which reason she is hampered at present in the effort to be a novelist. Her characters have ideas, but they are not made to express them, and are incapable of helping the story to move. Such story as there is pertains to their individual fortunes. There is no main current: Evadne would kill a better work with her heaviness. It matters little what she does—she has her ideas; the objection is the tedium in the presentation of her. The writer should be advised to put this manuscript aside until she has got the art of driving a story. She has ability enough, and a glimpse of humour here and there promises well for the future—if only she would practise, without thought of publishing, until she can narrate and sketch credible human creatures without harping on such trash as she gives them."

'Meredith, as a reader for Chapman & Hall, rejected *The Heavenly Twins* for the above reason. He probably saw the book before it was revised, and it may have been revised on his advice, transmitted to me when the manuscript was returned, but I cannot remember. When I was staying at the Burford Bridge Hotel, Sept. 1896, writing the Beth book, I asked him one day, as we walked together on Box Hill, why he rejected *The Twins.* He sighed deeply, at the same time drawling: "It was such a very long book, Sarah."

'Mrs Meynell's children were staying with him at Flint Cottage. She slept at the Hotel. I had refused an introduction to Meredith from Mrs Gordon (afterwards Mrs Butcher) because I thought if he cared to know me he would call, and if he did not I should save him trouble by not forcing my acquaintance on him. He heard of my arrival from Mrs Meynell and immediately sent her to ask me to tea, and to excuse his not calling on account of his lameness. We immediately became fast friends. I dined, or walked, or had tea with him every day. Nothing could exceed his kindness. He took great interest in my work and helped me much both with advice and encouragement. His conversation was a feast of ideas, witticisms, anecdotes, and verses improvised at a moment's notice on any theme that occurred to him. I never saw him serious; his great mind was always at play with me. He was like a grown-up person who himself enjoys the game as much as the child he is trying to amuse.

S.G. 27th March, 1919.
T. Wells.'

IDEALA: a Study from Life [anon] [1049]

Bentley 1889. (Fourth [Bentley] Edition.) Smooth dark blue cloth, banded in blind and lettered in gold. Green end-papers.

Half-title. pp. (x) [paged viii] + (306) pp. vii viii and (X_1) single insets.

Presentation Copy: 'C. Haldane McFall from the Author' in ink on half-title.

Notes. (i) The first [Bentley] edition, also dated 1889, was identical with this, apart from the words 'Fourth Edition' on title.

(ii) There was, however, an earlier edition still, published in July 1888 by E. W. Allen of Ave Maria Lane. This edition collated as above, consisting as it did of the sheets printed from the same setting at the Guardian Office, Warrington.

I cannot describe the binding, as I have never seen a copy as issued.

GRANT, JAMES (1822–1887)

[1050] ADVENTURES OF AN AIDE-DE-CAMP, or a Campaign in Calabria

3 vols. Smith, Elder 1848. Scarlet ribbed cloth.

Vol. I (xii)+(332) Y_6 blank, followed by single leaf of adverts. on text paper.
II iv+(316) X_6 blank.
III iv+324

Signature 'E. J. Shirley' on fly-leaf of each vol. Binders' ticket: 'Westleys and Clark', at the end of Vol. I. Fine.

[1051] CAMERONIANS (The): a Novel

3 vols. Bentley 1881.

Copy I. Maroon paper boards in imitation of morocco cloth; floral end-papers (pearl grey).

Vol. I viii+316
II iv+(312)
III iv+(316) 60_5 60_6 adverts. B

[1051*a*] **Copy II.** Smooth red cloth; green-on-white floral end-papers. Collation as Copy I except that 60_5 60_6 have been cut away from Vol. III.

The Bentley Catalogue describes the binding as 'claret cloth'. Fine.

[1052] DEAD TRYST (The): a Christmas Story

Routledge's Christmas Annual 1874. White pictorial wrappers printed in red, blue and yellow. Illustrations by A. C. Corbould.

pp. 96 Very fine.

[1053] HAUNTED LIFE (A): a Ghost Story

Routledge's Christmas Annual 1876. White pictorial wrappers printed in red, yellow and black. Illustrations.

pp. 96

[1054] MISS CHEYNE OF ESSILMONT

3 vols. Hurst & Blackett 1883. Olive-brown fine-diaper cloth, blocked and lettered in black on front, gold-lettered and black-blocked on spine. Dark grey end-papers.

Half-title in each vol.

Vol. I (iv)+324
II (iv)+324
III (iv)+332 Publishers' cat., 16 pp. undated, preceded by inset fly-title, at end.

Presentation Copy: Ink inscription: 'To Mrs Alforth with best love of the Author 28 Feb. 1883' on half-title of Vol. I.

[1055] PHANTOM REGIMENT (The), or Stories of 'Ours'

Thomas Hodgson, n.d. [1856].

Copy I. Pale green glazed boards printed in brown; white printed end-papers.

Half-title. pp. 352

Bookseller's ticket: 'Andrews, Guildford', inside front cover.

Copy II. Dark green fine-ribbed cloth, with Parlour Library Medallion in blind on front and back, spine gilt; yellow end-papers. Collation as Copy I. 4 pp. of adverts. (end-papers of board edition) precede half-title. [1055*a*]

Book-plate of George Wackerbath. Parlour Library, No. 142.

PHILLIP ROLLO, or the Scottish Musketeers [1056]

2 vols. Routledge 1854. Grey-purple morocco cloth; yellow printed end-papers.

Vol. I viii+308
II iv+(340)

Ink signature: 'M. J. Lobeden. Goguddan', on p. 1 of text in each vol. Cloth a little bubbled at hinges.

ROMANCE OF WAR (The), or The Highlanders in Spain [1057]

4 vols. Colburn, Vols. I–III, 1846; Vol. IV, 1847. Half-cloth boards, labels.

Half-title in Vol. IV only.

Vol. I (vi)+322 Title and first leaf of final sig., P_1, single insets.
II (ii)+(362) Final leaf, (R_1), carries Erratum and is a single inset.
III (ii)+(336)
IV vi+(352) Q_8 adverts. Half-title a single inset.

In this copy, preceding half-title of Vol. IV, is a Whittaker & Co. Catalogue, 24 pp. dated October 1846. Very fine.

SECOND TO NONE: a Military Romance [1058]

3 vols. Routledge, Warne & Routledge 1864. Grey-purple coarse-morocco cloth.

Vol. I vi+(316) pp. (v) vi, Contents, form a single inset.
II iv+316
III iv+332

Binders' ticket: 'Bone & Son', at end of Vol. I. This copy lacks front fly-leaf of Vol. II. Cloth very fine.

See also 3560–3567, 3672 (5) (8) and (10) in Section II.

GRATTAN, T. C. (1792–1864)

CAGOT'S HUT (The) and THE CONSCRIPT'S BRIDE Simms & M'Intyre 1852. Pale green glazed boards printed in brown. [1059]

Half-title. pp. 384

Parlour Library No. 82. Very fine.

[1060] CURSE OF THE BLACK LADY (The) and Other Tales. Legends of the Rhine
Thomas Hodgson n.d. [1857]. Pale green glazed boards printed in brown.
Half-title. pp. 224
Parlour Library No. 165. Fine.

[1061] FORFEIT HAND (The) and Other Tales. Legends of the Rhine
Thomas Hodgson n.d. [1857]. Fancy boards printed in colours.
Half-title. pp. 216
Parlour Library No. 163.
Note. There are two copies in the Collection, with boards similarly designed, but one on a yellow, the other on a cream base and with title in different lettering.

[1062] HEIRESS OF BRUGES (The): a Tale of the Year 1600
4 vols. Colburn & Bentley 1830. Boards, labels.
Vol. I (iv) + 302 Final leaf, P_1, a single inset.
II (ii) + (334) First leaf of final sig., P_1, a single inset.
III (ii) + (316) P_2 adverts.
IV (ii) + (320) P_4 adverts.
Bookseller's ticket: 'Robert Robinson, Manchester', inside front cover of each vol. Very fine.

GRAY, MAXWELL [MISS M. G. TUTTIETT] (?1850's–1923)

[1063] SILENCE OF DEAN MAITLAND (The): a Novel
3 vols. Kegan Paul, Trench & Co. 1886. Scarlet diagonal-fine-ribbed cloth, blocked on front with double frame in black, gold-lettered on spine and blocked on back in black with double frame and publishers' monogram; black end-papers.
Half-title in each vol.
Vol. I (iv) + 324
II (iv) + (304) U_8 imprint leaf.
III (iv) + (292) U_2 blank. Publishers' cat., 44 pp. dated '3.86', at end.
Fine.

GREENWOOD, FREDERICK (1830–1909)

[1064] MARGARET DENZIL'S HISTORY: annotated by her husband [anon]
2 vols. Smith, Elder 1864. Green sand-grain cloth.
Vol. I iv + (316) 20_6 adverts.
II iv + (316) 40_6 adverts.
Fine.
Note. Greenwood completed Mrs Gaskell's *Wives and Daughters*. He was successively editor of the *Cornhill*, and of the *Pall Mall* and *St James's* Gazettes. See also BARRIE, J. M.

GRIFFIN, GERALD (1803–1840)

This (with a single 'fractional' exception) is a complete collection of the works of Gerald Griffin. Most of the books are of the utmost rarity; and it is evidence of the difficulty of establishing a correct bibliography that the entry in the *C.B.E.L.* omits one three-decker altogether, mis-dates another, and prints as first editions five stories which had previously appeared in collections of tales already recorded. The Collected Edition (of which one volume is missing from the set here described) is also of extreme scarcity in its original form. The Duffy re-issues are fairly common, but usually as odd volumes.

CHRISTIAN PHYSIOLOGIST (The): Tales Illustrative of the Five Senses. (Edited by the author of 'The Collegians') [1065]
Bull 1830. Cont. half-calf, marbled edges (originally issued in boards,? with label).
Half-title. pp. xxvi + 376 [(xxv) xxvi, signed *b*, a single inset.]
Ink inscription: 'James Armstronge to Anna E. Boyce', on fly-leaf.
From this copy, half-title [pp. (i) (ii)] is missing, and, judging from P. S. O'Hegarty's report of his copy, also 6 pp. of publisher's adverts. at end, forming part of final gathering. Collation of text should therefore presumably read: (380) Final leaf blank.'
Contents: The Kelp-Gatherer—The Day of Trial—The Voluptuary Cured—The Self-Consumed—The Selfish Crotarie—A Story of Psyche.

COLLEGIANS (The) [anon] [1066]
3 vols. Saunders & Otley 1829. Half-cloth boards, labels.
Half-title in each vol. reading: A SECOND SERIES/OF/TALES OF THE MUNSTER FESTIVALS.
Vol. I (iv) + 330
II (iv) + (350) Final leaf, Q_7, a single inset.
III (iv) + 322 First leaf of final sig., P_1, a single inset.
Bookseller's ticket: 'Milliken, Dublin' on front cover of Vol. I, and ink signature: 'Clive' on inside cover of Vol. I. Fine.

DUKE OF MONMOUTH (The) (by the author of 'The Munster Festivals') [1067]
3 vols. Bentley 1836. Boards, labels.
Half-title in each vol.
Vol. I (iv) + (304)
II (iv) + (312)
III (iv) + 284
Fine.

[1068] GISIPPUS, or the Forgotten Friend: a Play in Five Acts

8vo. Maxwell & Co. Southampton Street, Strand 1842. Buff wrappers, yellow side-label printed in black. Spine unlettered.

Half-title. pp. [viii] + (iv) + (78) First leaf of final sig., L_1, a single inset. Single advert. leaf inset at end.

[1069] HOLLAND TIDE, or Munster Popular Tales [anon]

Simpkin & Marshall 1827. Boards, label.

pp. (iv) + 378

Book-plate of R. J. Ll. Price, Rhiwlas Library. Fine. Spine jarred at head.

Contents: The Aylmers of Bally-Aylmer—The Hand and Word—St Martin's Day—The Brown Man—The Persecutions of Jack Edy—The Unburied Legs—Owney and Owney-na-Peak.

[1070] INVASION (The) (by the author of 'The Collegians')

4 vols. Saunders & Otley 1832. Cont. half-leather, original board sides, original labels laid down.

Half-title in each vol.

Vol. I (xvi) + 300
II (iv) + (312) O_{12} blank.
III (iv) + 312
IV (iv) + (348)

Ink inscription: 'H. Mocketts Public Library, 8 Broadway, Westm[r]', on inside front cover of each vol. Labels worn.

[1071] RIVALS (The): TRACY'S AMBITION (by the author of 'The Collegians')

3 vols. Saunders & Otley 1829. Boards, labels.

Half-title in each vol. reading: THIRD SERIES / OF / TALES OF THE MUNSTER FESTIVALS

Vol. I (iv) + (xxxii) [(i) signed *a*, xxv signed *b*] + 306 First leaf of final sig., P_1, a single inset. Preceding sig., O, 6 leaves.
II (iv) + (322) First leaf of final 5-leaf sig., P_1, a single inset. Sig. O, 12 leaves.
III (iv) + (304) P_4 adverts.

Spines chipped at head and tail.

Note. An unavowed Second Edition of this book was published in 1830, bearing no indication at all of previous publication. Internally, the only difference between the two editions is the date on the titles; externally, the labels of the Second Edition have been reset. TRACY'S AMBITION / THE COLLEGIANS and IN THREE VOLS. / VOL. I [II, III] are all smaller on the Second Edition (on the First THE COLLEGIANS almost fills the entire width of the label) while the thick rule to head and tail is little more than half as thick as on the First. The copy of the 1830 edition in the Collection is in boards, half-cloth.

TALES OF THE MUNSTER FESTIVALS (by the author of 'Holland Tide or Irish (*sic*) Popular Tales') [1072]

3 vols. Saunders & Otley 1827. Boards, labels.

Half-title in each vol.

Vol. I (iv) + (xxiv) [(i) signed *b*, (iv) mispaged vi] + (356)
II (iv) + (328) Q_6 advert.
III (iv) + (324) P_9–P_{12} adverts.

Book-label of Samuel Rigby, Liverpool, in each vol.

Contents: Card-Drawing—The Half-Sir—Suil Dhuv, the Coiner.

TALES OF MY NEIGHBOURHOOD (by the author of 'The Collegians') [1073]

3 vols. Saunders & Otley 1835. Boards (re-backed), labels renewed. New end-papers.

Half-title in each vol. Advert. leaf precedes half-title in Vol. I

Vol. I (viii) + (292) [pp. 289–(292) mispaged 291–(294)]
II (viii) + 304
III (viii) + (336) P_{12} adverts. Text ends p. 328, (329)–334 Notes.

Haywards (of Bath) Library labels on front and back covers.

Contents: The Barber of Bantry—The Great House—A Night at Sea—Touch my Honour, Touch my Life—Sir Dowling O'Hartigan—The Nightwalker—The Village Ruin—Shanid Castle—The Cavern—The Force of Conscience—The Sun-Stroke—Send the Fool Farther—Mount Orient—Orange and Green—The Philanthropist—The Blackbirds and Yellow Hammers—Notes to Shanid Castle.

TALIS QUALIS, or Tales of the Jury Room [1074]

3 vols. Maxwell & Co. 1842. Olive-green fine-diaper cloth.

Half-title in each vol. Preceding half-title in Vol. I is inset an 8 pp. prospectus of 'The Life and Works' (q.v. and also *Note* below).

Vol. I (x) [(viii) paged ii] + 314 Half-title and final leaf, (P_1), single insets.
II (viii) + (302) Final leaf, O_7, a single inset.
III (viii) + (300) O_6 blank.

Signature of 'W. M. Praed' on verso of half-title of Vol. I, on verso of fly-leaf in Vols. II, III.

Contents: The Jury Room—Sigismund—The Story-Teller at Fault—The Knight without Reproach—The Mistake—Drink, my Brother—The Swans of Lir—McEneiry, the Covetous—Mr Tibbot O'Leary, the Curious—The Lame Tailor of Macel—Antrim Jack—The Prophecy—Sir Dowling O'Hartigan*—The Raven's Nest.

* This story first appeared in *Tales of My Neighbourhood*, 1835.

Notes. (i) The prospectus of the 'Works' here inset forecasts a more extensive series of volumes than actually appeared. It announces twelve volumes, of which the first six are as ultimately published. Vol. VII is *Here and There or Tales of the Day*, Vol. VIII is *Tales of the Jury Room*, Vol. IX is *The Invasion*, Vol. X is *The Christian Physiologist and other Tales*, Vol. XI is *Miscellaneous Tales and Fragments*, Vol. XII is *Poetical Works*. It may be noted that the Series is advance-described as 'Uniform with the Standard Novels'.

(ii) This work was re-issued by Duffy in 1846, three vols. in one, bound in green cloth. Overall Duffy title in front, Maxwell titles preserved for Vols. II and III. Engraved portrait front. No prospectus included.

[1075] LIFE AND WORKS OF GERALD GRIFFIN (The)

8 vols. Fcap 8vo. 1842–43.

This series is so rarely seen, that it is difficult definitely to establish its complex publishing history and what material constitutes a perfect set. But I think the collations, binding descriptions and statements as to re-issues which follow are correct, and the analysis of the set in the First Binding has been confirmed in detail by comparison with the set in original condition in Bodley (8d 320–7 BS.). Vol. I: LIFE and Vol. VIII: POETICAL WORKS are first editions. Vol. V: HOLLAND-TIDE contains a story transferred from *Tales of My Neighbourhood* and one story at least not previously published.

Collations:

Vol. I. LIFE OF GERALD GRIFFIN, ESQ. by his Brother (Daniel Griffin, M.D.).

Simpkin & Marshall 1843. [Although numbered Vol. I, this was the last of the series to appear.]

Engraved portrait front. and title-page (the latter dated 1843) precede printed title. Series half-title *and* individual half-title precede engraved front.

pp. [viii] + (viii) [paged (v)–xii] + [ii], inset leaf of Errata, + 484 + inset leaf of adverts.

Vol. II. THE COLLEGIANS, A Tale of Garryowen [thus on engraved title; printed title reads: TALES OF THE MUNSTER FESTIVALS. FIRST SERIES, THE COLLEGIANS.]

Maxwell & Co. 30 Southampton St. 1842. Engraved front. and title (the latter dated 1842) precede printed title. Series half-title *only* precedes engraved front.

pp. (viii) + (468) 2G 4 leaves. (2H) 6 leaves. pp. (459)–(466), paged (1)–8, prospectus of the work, as recorded above in Vol. I of *Talis Qualis*. ($2H_6$) blank.

Vol. III. CARD DRAWING, THE HALF-SIR AND SUIL DHUV [thus on printed title, preceded by TALES OF THE MUNSTER FESTIVALS. SECOND SERIES; on engraved title THE HALF-SIR only. Front. headed THE COINER subtitle to 'Suil Dhuv'.]

Maxwell 1842. Engraved front. and title (the latter dated 1842) precede printed title. Series half-title *only* precedes engraved front.

pp. (xiv) + (480) $2H_8$ blank. pp. xiii (xiv) form a single inset leaf.

Vol. IV. THE RIVALS AND TRACY'S AMBITION [thus on printed title, preceded by: TALES OF THE MUNSTER FESTIVALS. THIRD SERIES; on engraved title: THE RIVALS only. Front. headed: TRACY'S AMBITION].

Maxwell 1842. Engraved front. and title (the latter dated 1842) precede printed title. Series half-title *only* precedes engraved front.

pp. (x) [paged vi] + (384). pp. (v) (vi), Introduction, not present in this copy, but present in a copy seen in the Second Binding (see below). $2B_8$, blank or adverts., has been cut away from this copy (and also from that in Bodley).

Vol. V. HOLLAND-TIDE [thus on printed title; engraved title reads: THE AYLMERS OF BALLY-AYLMER, and the front. is headed THE HAND AND WORD, both stories in the volume, the latter of which is omitted from the Contents List.]

Maxwell 1842. Engraved front. and title (the latter dated 1842) precede printed title. No half-title preceding front.

pp. (iv) [(iii) (iv) Advertisement and Contents, not present in copy seen in Second Binding] + 432.

Vol. VI. THE DUKE OF MONMOUTH

Maxwell 1842. Engraved front. and title (the latter dated 1842) precede printed title. All are worded as above. Series half-title precedes front.

pp. (424)

Note. This vol. is lacking from the set in the collection. Description compiled in Bodley.

Vol. VII. TALIS QUALIS or TALES OF THE JURY ROOM [thus on printed title; engraved title reads: SIGISMUND (a story in the book) and front. is headed: THE JURY ROOM].

Maxwell 1842. Engraved front. and title (the latter dated 1842) precede printed title. Blank leaf and Series half-title precede front.

pp. (viii) + (504)

Vol. VIII. THE POETICAL WORKS [thus on printed and engraved titles; front. is headed: THE FATE OF CATHLEEN, the first poem in the book.] Spine-titling: POETRY.

Simpkin & Marshall 1843. Engraved front. and title (the latter dated 1842) precede printed title. Advert. leaf precedes front.

pp. (x) [paged vi] + 384 pp. (v) (vi), Advertisement, verso blank, form a single inset leaf.

Note on Material in the Collection: The Collection includes a First Issue set, lacking Vol. VI, fine throughout, and with binders' ticket: 'Westleys & Clark', at end of each vol. It has one sample vol. (VIII) of the Second Issue.

Bindings:

Pl. 13 **First Binding:** Very dark blue-green (in the case of Vols. III and IV sage-green)† fine-diaper cloth, blind-blocked on front and back with conventional framing of flowers and foliage; on spine blocked with three blind panels and gold-lettered. On Vols. II–VIII the lay-out is: blind panel; WORKS / OF / G. GRIFFIN. ESQ[R] / *rule* / VOL. II [III, IV, etc.]; blind panel; title of vol.; blind panel. On Vol. I: blind panel; LIFE / OF / G. GRIFFIN ESQ. / *rule* / VOL. I; blind panel; BY HIS / BROTHER.; blind panel.

End-papers: Vols. I, IV, VIII: pale yellow; Vols. II, III, V, VI, VII: bright yellow.

Pl. 13 **Second Binding:** Dark grass-green fine-ribbed cloth, blind-blocked on front and back with conventional and more or less geometrical framing; on spine blocked with cross-bars and three blind panels (more elaborately traceried than those on first binding) and gold-lettered. The lay-out, uniform for all vols., is: cross-bar; blind panel; GERALD / GRIFFIN'S / WORKS.; two cross-bars; I [II, III, etc.] / *rule* / title of vol.; two blind panels; two cross-bars.

The spine wording differs considerably from that on first binding. Not only is the series-title differently expressed, but the vol. titles also vary.

Vol. I reads: LIFE / AND / LETTERS

Vols. II–V read: TALES OF THE / MUNSTER / FESTIVALS., instead of giving the individual story titles.

Vol. VI was lacking from the set examined so I cannot say how TALIS QUALIS was handled (see Note below).

Vol. VII reads: DUKE / OF / MONMOUTH., as does first binding.

Vol. VIII reads: POEMS / AND SONNETS., as opposed to POETRY on first binding.

Note. A curious feature of this Second Issue is the rearrangement of some of the vols. Vols. I, II, III are as in First Issue. Vol. IV is *Holland-Tide*, which in First Issue is V. Vol. V is *The Rivals*, etc. which in First Issue is IV. Vol. VI is (presumably) *Talis Qualis*, which in First Issue is VII. Vol. VII is *Duke of Monmouth*, which in First Issue is VI.

All Series half-titles are omitted from Second Issue, except from Vol. III. I imagine this was done purposely to facilitate the re-numbering of the volumes.

In Vol. V *The Rivals*, etc. (Vol. IV in First Issue), a blank leaf at end of prelims. [pp. (xi) (xii)], completes the sheet in place of the suppressed half-title.

One or two other imperfections—a missing front., a missing printed title, etc.—were probably not intentional, but caused by imperfect sheet and engraving stock (e.g. *The Life of Griffin* in the Second Issue has neither engraved front. nor title), or careless binding, or rough usage.

A faulty imprint:

In the collection, in addition to the vols. of the First Issue above described, is (as stated) Vol. VIII (*Poetical Works*) in the *Second* Binding, of which the imprint on printed title is flagrantly misprinted. It reads: SIMPKIN AMD MARCHALL. / JOHN CUMMING, DUBLIN; AND BELL AND BFADFUTE, / EDINBUFGH. / 1843. This imprint, however, in Vol. VIII of a complete Second Issue set which I was permitted to examine, is correct. But, strangely enough, Vol. I of this borrowed set (the only other vol. with a Simpkin & Marshall imprint) shows exactly the same misprints as set out above.

In explanation I suggest that the misprinted titles were discovered before the original issue of these vols. and discarded in favour of corrected ones. Then, when the balance of sheets was being prepared for re-issue in rearranged sequence, the discarded titles were used in Vols. I and VIII to save the expense of reprinting. This theory is borne out by the facts that the imprints on the sets in B.M. and Bodley are throughout correct, and that, in the possession of P. S. O'Hegarty, is a copy in an obviously 'gift' binding of later date (scarlet ribbed cloth, lavishly gilt on spine and all edges gilt) showing the faulty imprint.

Priority of Bindings:

That the very dark green style preceded the grass-green is, I think, certain. In the first place the full complement of half-titles, engravings and advert. material; the informative spine-titling; the binders' tickets; and the volume sequence which conforms exactly to that announced on the advert. leaf in Vol. III and, within its limits, to the Prospectus at the end of Vol. II—all imply an original and more or less carefully planned venture.

In the second place, Vol. II (*Collegians*) of the borrowed set of Second Issues has a printed title with the imprint of James Duffy of Dublin and dated 1847. The date 1842 has been removed from the engraved title. Duffy, as is recorded below, took over the whole series in due course and re-issued it; and it can be safely argued that, if one of his re-issues is in grass-green cloth, that style is later than the one with which he had no concern.

Duffy re-issues:

The plates and type of this edition were acquired by Duffy of Dublin in the middle forties. We know that one vol. at least was re-issued in 1847,

† Variations probably fortuitous. Of the Bodleian set Vols. II, III, V, VI, VII are in dark blue-green, Vols. I, IV and VIII in sage-green.

and a complete re-issue was made in 1857, with no indication of any previous publication. In most cases the dates were erased from the engraved titles, but occasionally the date 1857 was substituted. The Duffy editions are in dark green (or sometimes scarlet) cloth, ornately blocked in black and gold. I have seen variants of cloth grain and blocking. In 1857 Duffy also issued a 'Second, Revised and Enlarged Edition' of the *Life of Griffin*. This book was bound in bright green cloth.

GRUNDY, SIDNEY (1848–1914)

[1076] DAYS OF HIS VANITY (The): a Passage in the Life of a Young Man

3 vols. Samuel Tinsley 1876. Red-brown diagonal-fine-ribbed cloth, blocked in blind and lettered in gold.

Vol. I (iv) + (248)
II (iv) + 272
III (iv) + 296

Note. The first (clearly autobiographical) work and only novel of a subsequently well-known and popular dramatist.

GWYNNE, TALBOT (JOSEPHA GULSTON)

[1077] LIFE AND DEATH OF SILAS BARNSTARKE (The): a Story of the Seventeenth Century

Smith, Elder 1853. Olive-brown fine-ribbed cloth, label.

pp. (iv) + (344) Z_4 adverts. Publishers' cat., 16 pp. dated June 1853, at end. Binders' ticket 'Westleys' at end.

Note. This book is produced exactly uniform with Thackeray's *Esmond*, the Second Edition of which is featured in the publishers' cat. 'Talbot Gwynne' published two other single-volume stories, one of which forms the next entry.

[1078] SCHOOL FOR FATHERS (The): an Old English Story

Smith, Elder 1852. Glazed marbled cloth in black and shades of red, paper label. Terracotta end-papers.

pp. iv + (336) Y_8 blank. Publishers' cat., 16 pp. dated June 1853, at end.

Binders' ticket: 'Westleys' at end. Book-plate of Shirley, Eatington Park.

Note. Produced in the antique manner favoured by the publishers of the works of Ann Manning (q.v.), this story of *Tatler* and *Spectator* days was, at the time of its appearance, widely praised. Clearly this copy does not belong to the first binding-up, for the catalogue advertises Gwynne's second novel *The School for Dreams* and is identical with that bound at the end of her third novel, *Life and Death of Silas Barnstarke*, described above.

HAGGARD, SIR HENRY RIDER (1856–1925)

Rider Haggard is treated in the same way as Marie Corelli and Conan Doyle—that is to say, none of his works published after 1900 is here included. Several books of fiction issued prior to 1900 do not appear because they are not in the Collection; and as a good bibliography is in existence, I have not used space in describing these from other sources. It may be remarked that Haggard is a good example of the long-lived and prolific author, whose *late* books—published at a time when his vogue had largely passed—are among his most difficult to find in fine state, although of comparatively recent date.

References are made to *A Bibliography of Sir Henry Rider Haggard* by J. E. Scott. Mathews 1947.

ALLAN QUATERMAIN, being an Account of his further Adventures and Discoveries, etc. [1079]

[*Scott* p. 43

Longmans 1887. Smooth navy-blue cloth, blocked and lettered in gold. Bevelled boards, brown-on-blue-grey Swan-and-Ship end-papers. Front. and 19 wood-engraved illustrations after C. H. M. Kerr on plate paper, and numerous cuts in the text.

Half-title. pp. (viii) + (280) T_4 'Authorities', with panel advert. on verso.

A sound copy, but lacking 'bloom'.

ALLAN'S WIFE and other Tales [1080]

[*Scott* pp. 57–59

Spencer Blackett 1889.

Copy I: Ordinary Edition. Brown cloth, smooth for spine and corners; coarse morocco grain on front and back; smooth panel lettered in gold on front. Smooth areas ruled off in black. Plum end-papers. Half-tone front. and 7 illustrations after Maurice Greiffenhagen (5) and Charles Kerr (3), on text paper, reckoned in collation and foliation but with blank versos. Also 26 illustrations in the text after the same artists.

Half-title. pp. (336) 21_7 advert., 21_8 imprint leaf. Publisher's cat., 32 pp. dated Sept. 1889, at end. Fine.

Copy II: Large Paper Edition. Cr. 4to. Smooth claret cloth sides, brown calf spine lettered in gold. Gold-on-crimson patterned end-papers. Title-page printed in red and black. [1080*a*]

Half-title. pp. (336) 41_3 adverts., 41_4 imprint leaf.

The book collates in fours; hence difference in signature-numbering from ordinary edition in eights.

Pencil signature: 'Radclyffe Walters 1895' on a thin paper blank preceding half-title. No. 15 of 100 copies. Fine.

Note. Spencer Blackett's imprint on spine indicates an original issue (as in this case). The later Griffith, Farran imprint is a 'take-over' imprint, which occurs on other Spencer Blackett books (*cf.* Barclay, Florence, above).

[1081] BLACK HEART AND WHITE HEART and other Stories [*Scott* p. 88

Longmans 1900. Smooth navy-blue cloth, lettered in gold. Bevelled boards, black end-papers. Half-tone front. and 5 illustrations in the first story after Charles Kerr (the front. is repeated facing p. 34 but not listed in the List of Illustrations); 8 line-illustrations in the second story after F. H. Townsend; 19 half-tone illustrations in the third story after Charles Kerr. All the illustrations are on text paper and reckoned in collation, but with the exception of the front. *not* included in pagination.

Half-title. pp. xii + 414 Publishers' cat., 4 pp. undated, at end.

Fine.

[1082] CETAWAYO AND HIS WHITE NEIGHBOURS etc. [*Scott* p. 27

Demy 8vo. Trübner & Co. 1882. Olive green, diagonal-fine-ribbed cloth, blocked on front in gold and black, lettered in gold and blocked in black on spine, blind-blocked on back. Dark chocolate end-papers.

Blank leaf, half-title and leaf carrying quotations on verso precede title. pp. (xxiv) [paged (xxii)] + (296) T_4 blank. Text ends 236, (237)–294 Appendix.

Pencil signature: 'Radclyffe Walters 1896' on verso of fly-leaf. Very fine.

Note. This is not fiction, but is included because it was the author's first book and is rare in this remarkable condition.

[1083] CLEOPATRA etc. [*Scott* p. 55

Longmans 1889. Smooth navy-blue cloth, blocked and lettered in gold. Bevelled boards, yellow-ochre-on-white Swan-and-Ship end-papers. Half-tone front. and 28 illustrations in half-tone and line, after Maurice Greiffenhagen (18) and R. Caton Woodville (11), all on plate paper. A slip acknowledging the Caton Woodville illustrations to the *Illustrated London News* is tipped to p. (xv).

Half-title. pp. xvi + 336 Publishers' cat., 16 pp. dated January 1889, at end.

Pencil signature: 'Radclyffe Walters 1889' on verso of fly-leaf. Very fine.

COLONEL QUARITCH, V. C. A Tale of Country Life [*Scott* p. 53 [1084]

3 vols. Longmans 1888. Scarlet diagonal-fine-ribbed cloth, lettered in black.

Half-title in each vol.

Vol. I (viii) + (248)
II (viii) + (264)
III (viii) + (264) 50_4 blank.

Pencil signature: 'Radclyffe Walters 1889' on fly-leaf of Vol. I. Very fine.

Note. The Dedication to Charles J. Longman is repeated in each vol.

DAWN [*Scott* p. 30 [1085]

3 vols. Hurst & Blackett 1884. Smooth pale-apple-green cloth, blocked and lettered on front in red and a darker green, gold-lettered and blocked in red and green on spine. Grey end-papers.

Half-title in each vol.

Vol. I (iv) + (326) Final leaf, Y_3, a single inset.
II (iv) + 334 1st leaf of final sig., Y_1, a single inset.
III (iv) + (336) Y_7 fly title to adverts., Y_8 adverts. Publishers' cat., 16 pp. undated on text paper, at end.

Not an ex-library copy, and clean as to sides and text. But the spines have been washed and the volumes tightened in covers, though this last not unduly.

DOCTOR THERNE [*Scott* p. 81 [1086]

Longmans 1898. Light tan linen-grain cloth, lettered in brown on front, gold-lettered and brown-blocked on spine. Brown-on-white Swan-and-Ship end-papers.

Blank leaf and half-title precede title. pp. (xii) [paged (x)] + (256) 17_2 imprint leaf. Penultimate sig., 17, four leaves.

Fine.

ERIC BRIGHTEYES [*Scott* p. 63 [1087]

Longmans 1891. Smooth navy-blue cloth, lettered in gold on front and spine. Black end-papers, bevelled boards. 17 full-page wood-engraved illustrations, of which 16 on plate paper but one on text paper with blank verso and reckoned in collation [pp. (107) (108)]; also numerous cuts in the text. All the illustrations are after Lancelot Speed. There is no front.

Blank leaf and half-title precede title. pp. (xvi) [paged xiv] + (320) Publishers' cat., 16 pp. dated '12/90', at end.

Pencil signature: 'Radclyffe Walters 1891' on first blank leaf.

Fine.

[1088] HEART OF THE WORLD [*Scott*, p. 76

New York: Longmans 1895. Greenish-blue linen-grain cloth, blocked and lettered on front in red and gold, gold-lettered on spine. Half-tone front. and 12 illustrations, probably all after Amy Sawyer though mostly unsigned, and all on plate paper.

Blank leaf and half-title precede title. pp. (xii) + (348). Publishers' cat., 16 pp. undated at end.

Rider Haggard's copy, with his signature on fly-leaf. Fine.

Note. Pre-dated London edition by nearly a year.

[1089] KING SOLOMON'S MINES [*Scott* p. 34

Cassell 1885. Smooth scarlet cloth, pictorially blocked in black on front and back, black-lettered on front, on spine lettered in gold (title) and black (author) and pictorially blocked in black. Coloured lithographic folding-map serves as front.

Half-title. pp. (iv) + 320 [paged (i)–vi + (7)–320] Publishers' cat., 16 pp. dated '10. 85', at end.

Ink signature: 'J. Vyre' on fly-leaf. Spine slightly dulled but an unusually good copy of this particular book. The catalogue indicates that it belonged to the second 'binding-up' of 500 copies.

[1090] MR MEESON'S WILL [*Scott* p. 48

Demy 8vo. Spencer Blackett ('Successor to J. & R. Maxwell') 1888. Smooth scarlet cloth, pictorially blocked in black and lettered in black and gold on front; lettered in black and gold on spine. Black end-papers. Wood-engraved front. and 15 illustrations on text paper, with blank versos but reckoned in collation, after A. Forestier and A. Montbard.

Half-title. pp. (288) [paged (xviii) + (19)–(288)] S_8 blank. Publisher's cat., 32 pp. dated October 1888, at end.

Pencil signature: 'Radclyffe Walters 1888' facing half-title. Very fine.

[1091] PEOPLE OF THE MIST (The) [*Scott* p. 70

Longmans 1894. Smooth navy-blue cloth, lettered in gold on front and spine. Black end-papers, bevelled boards. Line-engraved front. and 15 illustrations after Arthur Layard, all on plate paper.

Half-title. pp. (x) [paged viii, and real p. (viii) mispaged ii] + (344) Publishers' cat., 24 pp. dated '9/94', at end. pp. (ix) (x) of prelims. [Contents and Illustrations] form a single inset leaf.

Very fine.

[1092] SHE: a History of Adventure [*Scott* p. 36

Longmans 1887. Smooth navy-blue cloth, blocked and lettered in gold on front and spine. Brown-on-blue-grey Swan-and-Ship end-papers, bevelled boards. Two plates in coloured litho, facing one another on a single folding of heavy plate paper, precede title.

Half-title. pp. (viii) + (320) X_8 adverts.

SWALLOW: a Tale of the Great Trek [1093]
[*Scott* p. 83

Longmans 1899. Smooth navy-blue cloth, lettered in gold on front and spine. Black end-papers, bevelled boards. Half-tone front. and 7 illustrations after Maurice Greiffenhagen, all on plate paper.

Half-title. pp. (x) + 348 pp. v (vi) [Dedicatory letter] form a single inset leaf.

Front. detached; otherwise very fine.

WIZARD (The) [*Scott* p. 79 [1094]

Fcap. 8vo. Bristol: Arrowsmith (1896). Dark brown diagonal-fine-ribbed cloth, blocked and lettered in black on front, in gold on spine; blind blocked on back. Very dark brown end-papers.

Half-title. pp. (240) [paged (i)–(iv) + (1)–208 + (209)–(240)] Text ends 208. (209)–(240) constitute two final sigs., 14–15, signed but irregularly paginated, which carry adverts., publisher's and commercial.

Vol. LXXII of Arrowsmith's Bristol Library. Previously issued as Arrowsmith's Christmas Annual for 1896.

WORLD'S DESIRE (The) (In collaboration with [1095]
Andrew Lang) [*Scott* p. 62

Longmans 1890. Smooth navy-blue cloth, lettered in gold on front and spine. Black end-papers, bevelled boards.

Half-title. pp. viii + (320) X_7 'Palinode', verso blank; X_8 imprint leaf. Publishers' cat., 16 pp. dated '10/90', at end.

Fine. Spine very slightly faded.

Note. Scott calls for *green* cloth.

HALL, MRS S. C. (1800–1881)

BUCCANEER (The): a Tale [1096]

3 vols. Bentley 1832. Half-cloth boards, labels.

Half-title in each vol.

Vol. I (iv) + (344)
II (iv) + (308) P_4 adverts.
III (iv) + (320) P_3 P_4 adverts.

Signature 'Eliza Jane Alcock April 1833' in ink on p. 1 of the text in Vols. I and II and on title of Vol. III. Fine.

STORIES OF THE IRISH PEASANTRY [1097]

Edinburgh: W. & R. Chambers 1850. Red perpendicular-fine-ribbed cloth, blocked in gold and blind on front, in blind on back, blind-blocked and gold-lettered on spine.

Half-title. pp. (304) [mispaged 302, p. (9) being wrongly reckoned as p. (7)]

Presentation Copy: 'Enock Gibbon Salisbury Esq. With the best regards of Mr and Mrs S. C. Hall. May 30th, 1850' in ink, in the hand of S. C. Hall, on fly-leaf.

Note. The Dedication to the Landlords and Tenants of Ireland, which appears on p. (5) is wrongly dated 'May 20, 1840'. The stories appeared in *Chambers' Journal* during 1849 and the book was published in 1850. The title-page is correctly dated.

[1098] WOMAN'S STORY (A)

3 vols. Hurst & Blackett 1857. Olive-brown wavy-grain cloth.

Vol. I (ii) + 320
II (ii) + 304
III (ii) + 318 First leaf of final sig., X_1, a single inset.

Book-plate and labels (2) of the Llanover Library in each vol. Very fine.

See also below 3398*c*, 3572–3, 3742 (1, 2), 3755*a*.

HAMEL, FELIX JOHN

[1099] HARRY ROUGHTON, or Reminiscences of a Revenue Officer ('by Lionel J. F. Hexham')

Simpkin, Marshall 1859. Royal-blue morocco cloth. Engraved front. and 11 plates by the author.

pp. viii + (336) X_8 adverts.

Note. I include this obscure work because it adds a fragment to our knowledge of pseudonymous authorship. A letter from Hamel to Sir Thomas Fremantle, Bart., dated February 3, 1859, is pasted to inside front cover. This letter, presenting the copy of the book, points out that the nom-de-plume is an anagram of the writer's real name. The engravings are amateurish and crude, and somewhat reminiscent of the drawings with which the Rev. Richard Cobbold illustrated several of his own works.

HAMILTON, CAPTAIN THOMAS (1789–1842)

[1100] MEN AND MANNERS IN AMERICA (by the author of 'Cyril Thornton', etc.)

2 vols. Blackwood 1833. Boards, labels.

Half-title in each vol.

Vol. I (xvi) [paged (xii)] + (396) $2K_6$ adverts.
II (vi) + 402 Final leaf, $2L_1$, a single inset.

Book-label of R. J. Ll. Price, Rhiwlas Library, and bookseller's ticket: 'Seacome, Chester', inside front cover of each vol. Very fine.

Note. These vols. collate alternately in eights and fours.

YOUTH AND MANHOOD OF CYRIL THORNTON [anon] [1101]

3 vols. Blackwood 1827. Boards, labels.

Half-title in each vol.

Vol. I (vi) + (366) pp. (v) (vi), Dedication, and first leaf of final sig., Z_1, single insets.
II (iv) + 384
III (iv) + (384) $2A_7$ $2A_8$ adverts.

Book-label of R. J. Ll. Price, Rhiwlas Library, in each vol. Fine.

HAMILTON, WALTER (EDITOR) (1844–1899)

PARODIES [1102]

6 vols. 4to. Reeves & Turner 1884–9. Dark green bubble-grain cloth, blocked and lettered in gold and black.

The Editor's own copy with his marginal notes, book-plate and signature in each vol. Vol. I is endorsed 'my proof copy', Vols. II–VI 'Working copy'. Numerous cuttings and autograph letters are inserted. Fine.

Notes. (i) This remarkable compilation was published in 73 sixpenny parts, published monthly from December 1883 to December 1889. The parts were wrappered in pink paper printed in black on all covers. The earlier parts, having been printed in editions of a tentative size, were soon exhausted, but were reprinted to keep complete sets available.

The set in the collection consists of first issues throughout, as the Editor clearly had each series of Parts bound up in publishers' cloth as it was completed. He retained all the original wrappers except those of Parts 25–48, forming Vols. III and IV.

(ii) Hamilton's collection of Parodies consists predominantly of Parodies in Verse. In Vol. VI, however, he ventures into prose, and provides specimens (many of them gathered from magazines and not previously published in book form) of the following novelists represented in this Catalogue: Braddon, Bulwer Lytton, Collins, Dickens, Disraeli, Harte, Hugo, Marryat, Morgan (Lady), Ouida, Reid (Mayne) and Sketchley.

Under 'Dickens' he provides a bibliography of Parodies, imitations and dramatisations, including a list of 'Droodiana'. Under 'Disraeli', he reprints a conjectural 'key' to *Endymion* published in *Notes and Queries*.

Finally, at the end of the volume, he gives a check list of other parodies of English novelists 'which are either of less merit in themselves or mimic authors of less importance than those already dealt with'. This list includes the following additional relevant names: Ainsworth, Black, Blessington, Brontë, Broughton, Conway, Gore, Hume, James (G. P. R.), Lever, Reade, Smart, Smith (Horace), Thackeray and Trollope.

Naturally, among the Parodies quoted are a few from books already listed in this Catalogue, viz. *Mr Punch's Prize Novelists* (Thackeray) in Section I, and in Section II *Shilling Book of Beauty* (Bede), *Our Novel Shilling Series* (Burnand), *Our Miscellany* (Yates and Brough).

HAMLEY, EDWARD BRUCE [GENERAL SIR E. HAMLEY] (1824–1893)

[1103] LADY LEE'S WIDOWHOOD

2 vols. Blackwood 1854. Royal-blue moiré cloth. Engraved front. and vignette title in each vol., and in Vol. I, 5, in Vol. III, 3 plates after drawings by the author.

Half-title in each vol.

Vol. I (iv) + 344
II (iv) + (368) Z_7 Z_8 adverts.

Hinges slightly rubbed.

See also 3739*a* and *b* in Section III.

HARDY, THOMAS (1840–1928)

Two bibliographies of Hardy, by Henry Danielson and A. P. Webb, were published in London in 1916; but more satisfactory than either is the late Carroll A. Wilson's Catalogue of the Grolier Club Centenary Exhibition of Hardy's works, issued by Colby College, Waterville, Maine, in 1940. A full-scale bibliography has recently (1948) been completed by Professor R. L. Purdy of Yale. From the list which follows non-fiction is excluded.

[1104] CHANGED MAN (A), THE WAITING SUPPER AND OTHER TALES, concluding with the Romantic Adventures of a Milkmaid

Macmillan 1913. Dark green ribbed cloth, blocked in gold. Photogravure front. Also at end a map of Wessex on plate paper.

Half-title ('The Wessex Novels, Volume XVIII'). pp. (viii) + (416) $2D_8$ adverts.

Book-plate of J. A. Fuller Maitland. Faded strip at top of front cover, otherwise fine. With dust-jacket.

[1105] FAR FROM THE MADDING CROWD

Copy I: First Edition. 2 vols. 8vo. Smith, Elder 1874. Bright green diagonal-fine-ribbed cloth, blocked in black, gold and blind—on front with two vignettes in black and fancy-titling in gold (latter signed G.S.L. in monogram), on spine with lettering and decoration in black and gold, on back with blind framing; coffee-coloured end-papers. Wood-engraved front. and 5 illustrations in each vol. after H. Paterson.

Vol. I iv + (336) Y_8 blank.
II iv + 344 Z_4 blank.

Book-plate of S. Mercer. Fine.

Copy II: Second Edition. 2 vols. 8vo. Smith, Elder 1874. In general appearance identical with Copy I, but the following two small differences should be noted: [1105*a*]

(i) On back covers of the First Edition the triple blind framing consists of an outside and inside frame of uniform thinness and between them one very slightly broader ($\frac{1}{16}$ in.). On the Second Edition the centre frame is nearly twice as broad (practically $\frac{1}{8}$ in.).

(ii) The end-papers of the Second Edition are dark chocolate.

Collation as Copy I.

The words 'Second Edition' are inserted on title below volume number, which has been pushed up to make more room.

Blind stamp: 'W. H. Smith Library', on front end-paper of Vol. I. Very fine.

Copy III: First one-volume edition: 'New Edition.' Smith, Elder 1877. Bright green diagonal-fine-ribbed cloth, blocked in black and gold; grey-chocolate end-papers. The upper vignette on front of First Edition reappears centred on this edition. Front. and 5 illustrations after H. Paterson, selected from those in the First Edition. [1105*b*]

Half-title. pp. (viii) + (408)

Binders' ticket: 'Simpson & Renshaw', at end. From the Library of Thomas Hardy. Very fine.

GROUP OF NOBLE DAMES (A) [1106]

Osgood, McIlvaine 1891. Smooth pale straw (sometimes drab) linen-grain cloth, blocked on front in gold, on spine blocked in gold and lettered in brown.

Blank leaf and half-title precede title. pp. (viii) + (272). A single blank leaf follows final leaf of text, S_8.

HAND OF ETHELBERTA (The): a Comedy in Chapters [1107]

Copy I: First Edition. 2 vols. 8vo. Smith, Elder 1876. Bright brown diagonal-fine-ribbed cloth, blocked in black and gold; café-au-lait end-papers. Wood-engraved front. in each vol. and, in Vol. I, 5, in Vol. II, 4 full-page illustrations after du Maurier.

Half-title in each vol.

Vol. I (viii) + (324) Y_2 adverts.
II (viii) + (320) X_8 adverts.

Presentation Copy: 'E. L. Hardy from the author' in recipient's hand in ink on title of Vol. I. From the Library of Thomas Hardy. Very fine.

Copy II: First one-volume edition: 'New Edition.' Smith, Elder 1877. Bright green diagonal-fine-ribbed cloth, blocked in black and gold; grey-chocolate end-papers. Front. and 5 illustrations after du Maurier selected from those in the First Edition. [1107*a*]

Half-title. pp. (viii) + (416) D_7 D_8 adverts.

Binders' ticket: 'Simpson & Renshaw', at end. From the Library of Thomas Hardy. Very fine.

[1108] JUDE THE OBSCURE
Osgood, McIlvaine & Co. 1896. Dark green ribbed cloth, blocked in gold. Etched front. with underline on separate inset leaf preceding title. Also, at end, map of Wessex on text paper.

Half-title ('The Wessex Novels, Volume VIII'). pp. (x) [paged (viii)] + (518) $2K_3$ map, and a single inset. Very fine. With dust-jacket.

Note. A copy in the possession of a friend collates to (520), $2K_3$ map, $2K_4$ blank, making 2K a normal 4 leaf gathering. The copy above described has no such blank and is in new condition.

[1109] LAODICEAN (A), or the Castle of the de Stancys. A Story of To-Day
3 vols. Sampson, Low 1881. Grey sand-grain cloth, blocked in blind and gold.

Half-title in each vol.

Vol. I (iv) + 312
II (iv) + (276)
III (iv) + (272) S_8 blank.

Fine. Rust spot on spine of Vol. II.

Note. Regulation issue, with 'OR' on half-title of Vol. I. Harper's Franklin Square Library edition preceded this by one week.

[1110] LIFE'S LITTLE IRONIES: a Set of Tales with some Colloquial Sketches entitled 'A Few Crusted Characters'
Osgood, McIlvaine 1894. Sage-green sand-grain cloth, blocked in brown and lettered in gold.

Blank leaf and half-title precede title. pp. (viii) + (304) U_8 blank.

Book-plate of Walter C. Parker. Very fine.

[1111] MAYOR OF CASTERBRIDGE (The): the Life and Death of a Man of Character
2 vols. Smith, Elder 1886. Smooth dark blue cloth: blocked in black and lettered in gold; pale grey-on-white floral end-papers.

Half-title in each vol.

Vol. I (iv) + (316) X_6 adverts.
II (iv) + (316) X_5 X_6 adverts.

Very fine.

Note. There is a secondary binding of lightish sage-green cloth, blocked and lettered in black on front, gold-lettered from type on spine.

[1112] PAIR OF BLUE EYES (A): a Novel
3 vols. Tinsley 1873. Bright blue pebble-grain cloth, blocked in black and blind on front and back, blocked and lettered in gold on spine. Pale yellow end-papers printed with Chapman & Hall adverts.

Half-title (a single inset) in each vol.

Vol. I (vi) + (304)
II (vi) + (312)
III (vi) + 262 First leaf of final sig., S_1, a single inset.

Fine.

Note. This is the secondary issue, 'Carter C' (cf. *More Binding Variants*, p. 9).

RETURN OF THE NATIVE (The) [1113]
3 vols. Smith, Elder 1878. Brown diagonal-fine-ribbed cloth, blocked in black and gold. Sketch-map on plate paper as front. in Vol. I.

Blank leaf and half-title precede title in each vol.

Vol. I (viii) [paged vi] + (304)
II (viii) [paged vi] + (300) X_2 adverts. Sig. U 4 leaves.
III (viii) [paged vi] + 320

Copy I: Binding '*A*'. Fine. Book-label of Hugh Walpole.

Copy II: Binding '*B*'. Also fine. [1113*a*]

Note. As with *The Trumpet Major* (q.v. below) there are two bindings of this novel which show slight differences. '*A*' has spine imprint in small caps about $\frac{3}{32}''$ in height, and a *triple* blind frame on back; '*B*' has a larger spine imprint (about $\frac{5}{32}''$) and a *double* blind frame on back. The cloth of '*A*' is of a slightly warmer brown.

The only evidence of priority at present available is that a copy of '*A*' sold at Sotheby's in March 1941 had a pencil date on the fly-leaf of Vol. III: '6/10/78', whereas the B.M. copy, received December 1878, is '*B*'. As serialisation was not complete until December 1878, the book edition would hardly have been published earlier than November (Carroll Wilson, p. 19, says 'the English first was not printed until November') and the dating of these two copies may possibly indicate that '*A*' copies were review copies sent out before publication, and that the B.M. copy was delivered (as usual with Statutory Copies) on publication or shortly afterward. The question must, however, be regarded as a matter for surmise only.

TESS OF THE D'URBERVILLES. A Pure Woman. Faithfully presented by Thomas Hardy [1114]
3 vols. Osgood, McIlvaine 1891. Smooth sand-brown cloth, blocked and lettered in gold.

Half-title in Vols. I and II: blank leaf and half-title precede title in Vol. III

Vol. I (viii) + (264) Final page [(264), S_4 verso] unpaginated, though carrying text.
II (viii) + (280) T_4 blank. Chap. XXXV (p. 199) misnumbered XXV.
III (viii) + (280) T_4 blank.

Fine.

[1115] TRUMPET-MAJOR (The): a Tale

Copy I: First Edition. 3 vols. Smith, Elder 1880. Scarlet diagonal-fine-ribbed cloth, blocked in black and gold.

Blank leaf and half-title precede title in each vol.

Vol. I (viii) [paged vi] + (296)
II (viii) [paged vi] + 276
III (viii) [paged vi] + (260)

Fine.

Note. There are two variants in the blocking of this novel, which seem to have definite issue-significance.

Variant A: B.M. copy (12640. bb5 recd Dec. 17 1880), Bodleian copy (recd. February 1881), and a soiled copy sold at Sothebys, March 17, 1941 (Lot 156) showed (i) Vol. I (*II, III*) in caps slightly swelling at top and bottom but not definitely seriffed; (ii) the period between SMITH and ELDER in spine-imprint *centred*, and not on base line; (iii) two well-separated blind frames on back.

Variant B: The Faux copy (Lot 356 at Sothebys, March 17, 1941) and other very fine copies seen showed: (i) Vol. I (*II, III*) in markedly seriffed caps; (ii) period between SMITH and ELDER on *base* line; (iii) *triple* blind frame on back.

This copy is Variant A. It seems likely that there was a small remainder of the first edition of *The Trumpet Major*, for the copies surviving in mint condition are to the best of my knowledge predominantly Variant B, which almost certainly represents a second binding-up.

[1115*a*] **Copy II. First one-volume edition: 'Cheap Edition.'** Sampson Low 1881. Scarlet diagonal-fine-ribbed cloth, blocked in black and gold; dark grey end-papers.

pp. iv + 428 Publishers' cat., 32 pp. dated January 1881, at end.

Book-plate of John Browne. Very fine.

[1116] TWO ON A TOWER: a Romance

3 vols. Sampson Low 1882. Dark green diagonal-fine-ribbed cloth, blocked in blind on front and back with publishers' monogram and triple plain frame, gold-lettered on spine. Pale yellow end-papers.

Half-title in each vol.

Vol. I (iv) + (248) R_4 imprint leaf.
II (iv) + 240
III (iv) + (224)

A mixed set. All three vols. are very good; but I and II have book-plate crest: over 'Broadbent', while III has ink-signature 'Ino Jones' dated '24. 9. 83', also book-label and ink-signature of Hugh Walpole.

UNDER THE GREENWOOD TREE: a Rural Painting of the Dutch School (by the author of 'Desperate Remedies') [1117]

Copy I: First Edition. 2 vols. Tinsley 1872. Green patterned-sand-grain cloth, blocked in black and gold, bevelled boards.

Half-title in each vol.

Vol. I (vi) + (216)
II (vi) + 216

Pencil signature: 'Radclyffe Walters 1889', on front fly-leaf of Vol. I. Very fine.

Copy II: 'A New Edition. With a Portrait of the Author and Fifteen Illustrations' (by Thomas Hardy). Chatto & Windus 1891. Olive-green morocco cloth blocked and lettered in black and gold in the style of the publishers' 'Piccadilly Novels'; floral end-papers. Wood-engraved portrait front., vignette title and 15 illustrations. [1117*a*]

Leaf of adverts. and half-title precede front. pp. (x) [paged (viii)] + (344) Z_4 publishers' device. Publishers' cat., 32 pp. dated September 1891, at end.

Book-plate of John Browne. Very fine.

WELL-BELOVED (The): a Sketch of a Temperament [1118]

Osgood, McIlvaine & Co. 1897. Dark green ribbed cloth, blocked in gold. Etched front., with underline on separate inset leaf preceding title. Also, at end, a map of Wessex on text paper.

Blank leaf and half-title ('The Wessex Novels, Volume XVII') precede front. pp. (xiv) [paged (x)] + (340) Y_2 carries the map.

Book-plate of J. A. Fuller Maitland. Fine.

WESSEX TALES: Strange, Lively and Commonplace [1119]

2 vols. Macmillan 1888. Smooth dark green cloth, blocked in light green and lettered in gold.

Blank leaf and half-title precede title in each vol.

Vol. I (viii) + (248)
II (viii) + (216) P_3 P_4 adverts.

Book-plate of Albert Laker in each vol. and 'With the Publishers Compliments' stamped in violet ink on the title of Vol. I. Very fine.

WOODLANDERS (The) [1120]

Copy I: First Edition. 3 vols. Macmillan 1887. Dark green very-fine-bead-grain cloth, blocked in black and lettered in gold; dark chocolate end-papers.

Half-title in each vol.

Vol. I (iv) + (304) U_8 adverts.
II (iv) + 328
III (iv) + 316

Fine. This is first issue cloth. Later issue is coarse bubble grain.

[1120*a*] **Copy II: First one-volume Edition.** Macmillan 1887. Scarlet fine-diaper cloth.

Half-title. pp. (iv) + 352

Book-plate of John Browne. Very fine. This edition bears no evidence of the book having been published before.

Partly by Hardy

[1121] IN SCARLET AND GREY (with Florence Henniker). Stories of Soldiers and Others by Florence Henniker and The Spectre of the Real by Thomas Hardy and Florence Henniker

John Lane 1896. Smooth scarlet cloth, pictorially blocked in black, and gold-lettered on spine in standard Keynotes Series style, of which this is No. XXVI. Pictorial title (as front cover) after P.W.; key design on p. (viii) after Beardsley.

Half-title. pp. (viii) + (224) Sig. (O) (8 leaves unsigned) carries adverts. of the Keynotes Series. Publisher's cat., 16 pp. on text paper dated 1896, at end. Very fine, with dust-jacket.

Note. pp. 164–208 are occupied by the story *The Spectre of the Real.*

HARLAND, HENRY (1861–1905)

This is a complete schedule of Harland's fiction published over that name. Two or three 'Luska' titles are lacking.

[1122] AS IT WAS WRITTEN: a Jewish Musician's Story (by Sidney Luska)

Square cr. 8vo. Cassell (1885). Stiff orange and yellow wrappers, cut flush and printed in black. Spine up-lettered. Back outside wrapper printed with adverts.

A volume in Cassell's 'Rainbow Series of Original Novels' and outset 'Cassell' (for collation, see 3657 in Section II).

Cassell also published this book in New York in cloth at $1, and I presume the American edition pre-dated the English one. *As It Was Written* was Harland's first book.

[1123] CARDINAL'S SNUFF-BOX (The)

John Lane 1900. Smooth crimson linen-grain cloth, lettered in gold on front and spine.

Half-title. pp. (322) (21_1) a single inset leaf of adverts. Publisher's cat., 16 pp. dated 1900, at end.

Ink signature: 'Frederic Chapman', inside front cover. (Frederic Chapman was reader for John Lane.)

[1124] COMEDIES AND ERRORS

John Lane 1898. Rough olive-green canvas-cloth, blocked in dark green with conventional design on front and spine, lettered in dark green on front and in gold on spine, blocked on back with centre decoration in dark green.

Advert. leaf, printed on verso only, and half-title precede title. pp. (viii) + 344 Publisher's cat., 12 pp. dated 1898, at end.

Fine.

Note. The cover-design was by Mrs (Mabel) Dearmer, as is established by a presentation copy from the author to her reported to me by a bookseller.

GRANDISON MATHER, or an Account of the Fortunes of Mr and Mrs Thomas Gardiner ('by Sidney Luska (Henry Harland)') [1125]

New York: Cassell (1889). Smooth light-apple-green cloth, lettered in gold. Pale-green-on-white floral end-papers.

Half-title. pp. (396) [paged (vi) + (390)] (395) (396) adverts.

The book is unsigned.

A.L.S. from Harland inserted, dated April 26, 1887. Book-plate of Lord Esher. Cloth soiled.

Note. An English edition, consisting of American sheets, was published in smooth red cloth, blocked and lettered in black on front and gold-lettered on spine. It was undated, but contained a publisher's cat. dated '6. 90'.

GREY ROSES [1126]

John Lane 1895. Smooth slate cloth, blocked in pinkish cream, and gold-lettered on spine in standard Keynotes Series style, of which this volume is No. X. Decorated title (as on front cover) and key-design on p. (vi) after Beardsley.

Half-title. pp. (vi) + (264) Text ends on Q_7. There follow 5 leaves of text paper advertising the Keynotes Series, and paged (1)–10, of which pp. 9, 10 form a single inset leaf (? printed as Q_8). Publisher's cat., 16 pp. on text paper dated 1895, at end.

Very fine.

LADY PARAMOUNT (The) [1127]

John Lane 1902. Smooth blue linen-grain cloth, lettered in gold on front and spine.

Half-title. pp. (336) X_5–X_8 adverts.

Front cover damp-spotted.

LATIN-QUARTER COURTSHIP (A), and other Stories ('by Sidney Luska (Henry Harland)') [1128]

Cassell (1889). Smooth red cloth, blocked and lettered in black on front, gold-lettered on spine.

pp. (iv) + (270) Final sig. 2 leaves. Publishers' cat., 16 pp. dated '11. 89', at end. The book is unsigned.

This is the English edition, consisting of American sheets, of a work previously published in New York. Bookplate of Lord Esher.

[1129] MADEMOISELLE MISS, and other Stories
Heinemann 1893. Smooth brown-salmon cloth, blocked in dark brown on front and spine with design of peacock's feathers, lettered in brown on front and in gold on spine. Publisher's monogram in brown on back cover.

Half-title. pp. (iv) + 192 [half-title, verso; title, verso, are not reckoned in the pagination, which begins with the first leaf of the first signature, i.e. Contents, verso]. Publisher's cat., 16 pp. dated October 1892, at end.

Very fine.

[1130] MEA CULPA: a Woman's Last Word
3 vols. Heinemann 1891. Greenish-blue diagonal-fine-ribbed cloth spines, smooth olive-brown cloth sides, blocked and lettered in gold.

Half-title in each vol.

Vol. I (vi) + 214 Final leaf, 14_3, a single inset. Publisher's cat., 16 pp. dated April 1891, at end.
II (iv) + 216
III (iv) + 266 Final leaf, 45_5, a single inset.

Very fine.

[1131] MRS PEIXADA (by Sidney Luska)
New York: Cassell (1886). Smooth pinkish-ochre cloth, blocked in black and lettered in gold.

Half-title. pp. (320) (319) (320) adverts.

The book is unsigned. Double end-papers at front and back. Book-plate of Lord Esher. Cloth rather used. Harland's second book.

[1132] MY FRIEND PROSPERO
John Lane 1904. Olive-green ribbed cloth, lettered in gold on front and spine.

Blank leaf and half-title precede title. pp. (viii) + (320) X_3 X_4 adverts.

[1133] MY UNCLE FLORIMOND ('by Sidney Luska (Henry Harland)')
Boston: D. Lothrop Company (1888). Light apple-green diagonal-fine-ribbed cloth, pictorially blocked and lettered on front and spine in chocolate, dark green and gold. Half-tone front. and six illustrations, both line and half-tone, after various artists. All are on plate paper, but are reckoned in collation.

pp. (192) [paged (206) on account of 14 pages of plate paper being included] (185) (186) blank (187)–(192) adverts. The book is unsigned.

Book-plate of Lord Esher. Fine.

[1134] ROYAL END (The): a Romance.
Hutchinson 1909. Royal-blue diagonal-fine-ribbed cloth, blocked in white and lettered in gold. Title printed in old-rose and black.

Blank leaf and half-title precede title. pp. (viii) + (320). Publishers' cat., 32 pp. on text paper dated February 1909, at end.

Booksellers' ticket: 'Whiteleys', at end.

TWO WOMEN OR ONE? From the manuscripts of Doctor Leonard Benary [1135]
Cassell 1890. Light blue paper wrappers, cut flush, printed on front in dark blue. Spine up-lettered. Publisher's device on back.

Half-title. pp. (viii) + 152. Publishers' cat., 16 pp. dated '11. 89', at end.

Book-plate of Oliver Brett (Lord Esher).

YOKE OF THE THORAH (The) (by Sidney Luska) [1136]
New York: Cassell (1887). Blue diagonal-fine-ribbed cloth, blocked in dark red and lettered in gold. Olive-green-on-white floral end-papers.

Half-title. pp. (332) [paged (vi) + (326)] (321)–(324) adverts. (325) (326) blank. The book is unsigned.

Book-plate of Lord Esher.

HART, ELIZABETH

WILFRED'S WIDOW: a Novel (by the author of 'Mrs Jerningham's Journal', etc.) [1137]
2 vols. Bentley 1883. Smooth pinkish-brown cloth spines; board sides veneered with real wood, cut very thin and blocked in black with a sprig of holly. Spine lettered in gold.

Vol. I (ii) + 304
II (ii) + 336 B

Note. My only reason for including this forgotten novel is that it is probably one of the very few copies of the actual first edition to survive. Here are two extracts from the Bentley catalogue:

(*a*) 'Excepting some early copies sent to the country and some review copies to the press, the whole of the first issue of this novel was consumed in a fire on the premises of Mr Matthew Bell, bookbinder, in Cursitor St.' [Feb. 10, 1883].

(*b*) 'With great promptitude a second issue was put into circulation on this day, made up from reserve copies lying at the printers in the country and bound by Messrs Simpson. There is a slight variation in the covers of the two editions' [Feb. 13, 1883].

The Catalogue then proceeds to describe both bindings as 'plain dark blue cloth, cut edges'—manifestly a jump to a conclusion on the strength of some note made at the time and in the absence of any specimen of the real first issue. The rather elaborate binding of this copy could not possibly have been duplicated so quickly; and it is therefore a fair assumption that the destroyed first issue was as here described, and the second issue was hastily clothed in plain dark blue which was conveniently to hand.

This copy, coming from the Bentley file, was in all likelihood one of the very few of the original issue delivered in advance of publication to the publisher's office.

HARTE, BRET (1836–1902)

Reference should be made to *Anglo-American First Editions: West to East*, by I. R. Brussel, London, 1936, pp. 22–45.

T. Edgar Pemberton, to whom belonged several of the books here catalogued, was Bret Harte's biographer. His *Life of Bret Harte* appeared in 1903.

[1138] ARGONAUTS OF NORTH LIBERTY (The)

Small square 8vo. Boston and New York: Houghton Mifflin & Co. 1888. Smooth blue cloth, blocked and lettered in black on front, blind-blocked on back, blocked in black and lettered in gold on spine. Orange edges. Inset blank leaf and leaf carrying panel of adverts. on verso precede title. pp. (vi) + (208) Final leaf blank. The book is unsigned throughout.

Presentation Copy: 'Lady Shrewsbury from Bret Harte. London, July 1888' in ink on fly-leaf. Fine.

[1139] BARKER'S LUCK, and other Stories

Boston: Houghton, Mifflin & Co. 1896. Smooth dark-salmon cloth; grey-green end-papers.

Two leaves precede title, of which the second is printed on verso with panel-advert. pp. (viii) + (274) Pp. (267)–(272) adverts.; (273) (274) blank. No signature lettering.

Presentation Copy: 'T. Edgar Pemberton Esq. from Bret Harte. Xmas-'96' in ink on title.

Book-plate of T. Edgar Pemberton. Fine.

Note. This edition preceded the English by a week or two.

[1140] BELL-RINGER OF ANGELS (The), etc. (First English Edition)

Chatto & Windus 1894. Scarlet morocco cloth, pictorially blocked in black, pink and gold. Front. and illustrations by various artists, all on text paper.

pp. viii + (280) + 4 T_2 publishers' device, T_3 T_4 adverts. Publishers' cat., 32 pp. undated, at end. Fine.

Note. This edition followed the American by a week or two.

[1141] CLARENCE

Chatto & Windus 1895. Bright blue morocco cloth, blocked in peacock-blue, black, bronze and gold; patterned end-papers. Front. and 7 half-tone plates after A. Jule Goodman.

Leaf of adverts. precedes half-title. Title printed in red and black. pp. (viii) + (256) R_8 publishers' device. Publishers' cat., 32 pp. dated July 1895, at end.

Presentation Copy: 'To A.T. (sic) Watt Esq., with kind regards of Bret Harte. November '95.' in ink on recto of front. Fine. Presented to me by W. P. Watt, son of the recipient.

Note. This edition preceded the American by over three weeks.

COLONEL STARBOTTLE'S CLIENT, and Some Other People (First English Edition) [1142]

Chatto & Windus 1892. Blue morocco cloth, pictorially blocked in black and ochre; lettered in black on front and in gold on spine; publishers' monogram in black on back. Pale grey floral end-papers. Wood-engraved front. after Fred Barnard.

Advert. leaf and half-title precede title. pp. (viii) + (312) X_3 X_4 adverts. Publishers' cat., 32 pp. dated October 1891, at end.

Note. This edition followed the American, which was dated 1891.

CONDENSED NOVELS. New Burlesques [1143]

Chatto & Windus 1902. Smooth red linen-grain cloth, blocked in black and white and lettered—on front, in white: NEW / BUR- / LESQUES / Bret Harte; on spine, in gold: CONDENSED / NOVELS / Bret / Harte and imprint. Photogravure portrait front. after John Pettie, R.A.

Advert. leaf and half-title precede title. pp. (viii) + (224) P_7 P_8 adverts. Publishers' cat., 32 pp. dated March 1902, at end.

Ink signature: 'T. E. Pemberton', on fly-leaf. Fine.

Note. This edition preceded the American by a few days.

CRESSY [1144]

2 vols. Macmillan 1889. Smooth blue cloth banded with yellow on front, publisher's monogram in yellow on back, gold-lettered and yellow banded on spine (a blend of Marion Crawford S.B. 1 and 3).

Half-title in each vol.

Vol. I (iv) + 204
II (iv) + (236) Q_4–Q_6 adverts.

Presentation Copy: 'A. P. Watt, with regards of Bret Harte, January 1889' in ink on fly-leaf of Vol. I. Given to me by W. P. Watt, son of the recipient.

Note. Brussel (p. 45) records date of American issue as January 9, but cannot fix English date more precisely than 'in January'. It is unfortunate that Harte, who usually dated his inscriptions in detail, failed to do so in this case.

[1145] CRUSADE OF THE 'EXCELSIOR' (The): a Novel

2 vols. F. V. White 1887. Smooth blue-green cloth, blocked and lettered in black on front, in black and gold on spine, in black on back with publishers' monogram. Magenta-on-pale-blue floral end-papers.

Half-title in each vol.

Vol. I (viii) + (244) (Q_2) blank.
II (viii) + (248) Q_4 blank.

Pencil signature: 'Radclyffe Walters 1888 2 vols' facing half-title in Vol. I. Fine, despite ink spot on back cover of Vol. II.

First English edition, later than the American by six weeks.

[1146] DEVIL'S FORD, etc. (First English Edition)

Chatto & Windus 1896. Dark crimson morocco cloth, blocked in light blue and bronze and lettered in black and gold; blue-on-white foliage end-papers. Half-tone front. after W. H. Overend.

Half-title. pp. (vi) + 332 Publishers' cat., 32 pp. dated July 1895, at end.

[1147] FIRST FAMILY OF TASAJARA (A)

2 vols. Macmillan 1891. Smooth blue cloth banded with yellow on front, publishers' monogram in yellow on back, gold-lettered and banded on spine (a blend of Marion Crawford S.B. 1 and 3).

Half-title in each vol.

Vol. I (iv) + (228) Q_2 blank.
II (iv) + (208)

Ink signature: 'Bayliss' on title of each vol. Fine.

[1148] FROM SAND-HILL TO PINE

Copy I: First Edition.

C. Arthur Pearson 1900. Smooth dark-claret cloth, pictorially blocked in red, blue and cream, and lettered in cream.

Leaf, printed on verso with panel advert., and half-title precede title. pp. (376)

Book-plate of T. Edgar Pemberton. Fine.

Note. This edition was published a day or two before the American.

[1148*a*] **Copy II: First American Edition.** Boston and New York: Houghton Mifflin & Co. 1900. Smooth claret cloth, blocked and lettered in black on front, gold-lettered on spine.

Blank leaf and leaf carrying panel advert. on verso precede title.

pp. (viii) + (332) Final leaf but one adverts., final leaf blank. The two final sigs. are each seven leaves. I think the first leaf of one (pp. 305/306) and certainly the penultimate (advert. leaf) of the other are single insets. The book is unsigned throughout.

Presentation Copy: 'Theresa, Countess of Shrewsbury, from Bret Harte. 1900' in ink on fly-leaf. Covers rubbed.

GABRIEL CONROY: a Novel [1149]

3 vols. Frederick Warne (1876). Brown diagonal-fine-ribbed cloth, blocked in black on front with title of book and decoration, blocked and lettered in gold on spine.

Half-title in each vol.

Vol. I viii + (300) 19_6 adverts.
II vi + (316)
III vi + (292)

Signature 'J. W. M. Smith, 17/9/94' in ink on fly-leaf of each vol. Spine of Vol. I slightly darkened and cloth of Vol. III a little bubbled; but a sharp bright copy.

Note. Brussel (p. 26) describes Parts I and II of an 8vo Part-Issue started in November, 1875. As he could not trace any further Part, it seems likely that the publication was abandoned—very likely for lack of support.

HERITAGE OF DEDLOW MARSH (The), and Other Tales [1150]

2 vols. Macmillan 1889. Smooth blue cloth, blocked in light green and gold-lettered on spine (uniform with *The First Family of Tasajara*).

Half-title in Vol. I, blank leaf and half-title in II

Vol. I (viii) + 208
II (viii) + (200) O_3 O_4 adverts.

Pencil signature: 'Radclyffe Walters 1890' facing half-title of Vol. I. Fine.

First English edition, later than the American by about a month.

IN A HOLLOW OF THE HILLS [1151]

Slim cr. 8vo. Chapman & Hall 1895. Glazed dark blue fold-over wrappers decoratively printed and lettered in terra-cotta and white—on front with Series-title: CHAPMAN'S STORY SERIES and publishers' monogram; on spine (almost illegibly) with Series-title, author's name and imprint; on back with Series-title in white. Line engraved front. on text paper after St M. Fitzgerald.

Blank leaf over which front wrapper is folded, inset leaf carrying Series-advert. on verso, half-title and leaf carrying front. precede title.

pp. (x) + (224) Back wrapper is folded over final leaf, P_8, blank.

Presentation Copy: 'Lady Shrewsbury from Bret Harte Nov[r] 1895' in ink on inset leaf.

LUCK OF ROARING CAMP (The), and other Sketches (by Francis Bret Harte) [1152]

Copy I: First Edition. Boston: Fields, Osgood & Co. Plum sand-grain cloth blocked in blind on front and back, gold-blocked and lettered on spine. Chocolate end-papers.

pp. (viii) + (240)

This volume has double end-papers at front and back.

[1152*a*] **Copy II: First English Edition.**

John Camden Hotten n.d. Green sand-grain cloth, blocked in blind on front and back, blocked and lettered in gold on spine. Bevelled boards, café-au-lait end-papers.

Half-title. pp. (viii) + 216 Publisher's cat., 24 pp. headed 'Special List of 1870', at end.

Note. Presumably the first English edition, dated 1871 by Brussel. There seems reason to suspect that it was actually published in 1870. Not only the date on the catalogue implies this possibility. A stronger argument is the absence of the episode 'Brown of Calaveras'. This episode was not included in the first issue of the first American edition (see above), but appeared in the second issue which followed rapidly on the first.

[1153] MR JACK HAMLIN'S MEDIATION and other Stories

Copy I: First Edition. C. Arthur Pearson 1899. Red-brown very fine bead-grain cloth, blocked in dark brown and lettered in gold.

Blank leaf and half-title precede title. pp. (viii) + (332) X_6 blank.

Book-plate of T. Edgar Pemberton. Fine.

[1153*a*] **Copy II: First American Edition.** Boston: Houghton, Mifflin & Co. 1899. Olive-brown fine-diagonal-ribbed cloth.

Blank leaf precedes title-page. pp. (vi) + (294) Pp. (291) (292) adverts.; (293) (294) blank. No signature lettering.

Presentation Copy: 'To T. Edgar Pemberton Esq. from Bret Harte 1900' in ink on fly-leaf.

Book-plate of T. Edgar Pemberton. Fine.

Note. The English edition preceded the American by a day or two.

[1154] ON THE OLD TRAIL (First English Edition)

C. Arthur Pearson 1902. Smooth brownish-red linen-grain cloth, pictorially blocked and lettered on front in pale blue, stone colour and black; gold-lettered on spine.

Half-title. pp. (320) U_8 adverts.

Book-plate of T. Edgar Pemberton. Fine.

Note. Brussel records that the American edition of this book appeared on April 26 under the title *Openings in the Old Trail*, and that, though he cannot establish the actual date of issue of the English edition, it was not recorded in the *Publisher's Circular* until May 10.

PROTÉGÉE OF JACK HAMLIN'S (A), etc. (First English Edition) [1155]

Chatto & Windus 1894. Blue morocco cloth, pictorially blocked in black and ochre; lettered in black on front and in gold on spine; pale grey floral end-papers. Half-tone front. and 25 illustrations, all on text paper and reckoned in collation, after Stanley L. Wood, William Small, A. S. Boyd and others.

Half-title. pp. (viii) + 320 Publishers' cat., 32 pp. dated February 1894, at end.

Presentation Copy: 'A. P. Watt from Bret Harte. London, March 1894' in ink on fly-leaf.

Note. This edition followed the American by two months.

QUEEN OF THE PIRATE ISLE (The) [1156]

Square demy 8vo. Chatto & Windus, n.d. [1886]. Pale silver-green linen, pictorially blocked in colours and lettered in black and gold. Ivory end-papers. Red edges. Coloured front., title vignette, and illustrations in text after Kate Greenaway, all reckoned in collation.

Half-title. pp. 58. pp. (1) (2), half-title, a single inset.

Very fine.

Note. This is the first edition of the story. The American edition consisted of English sheets and appeared later (Brussel, p. 34).

SALLY DOWS, etc. [1157]

Chatto & Windus 1893. Scarlet morocco cloth pictorially blocked in black and light brown, lettered in black on front, in gold on spine; greenish-yellow floral end-papers. Line front. and 46 line and half-tone illustrations after Almond, Hutchinson, Jacomb Hood and Morrow, all on text paper.

Blank leaf and half-title precede front. pp. (xii) [paged x] + (296) Publishers' cat., 32 pp. dated November 1896, at end.

Note. This edition pre-dated the American by two weeks.

SAPPHO OF GREEN SPRINGS (A), and other Tales [1158]

Chatto & Windus 1891. Myrtle-green sand-grain cloth, blocked in bronze and gold; greenish-yellow floral end-papers. Half-tone front. and pictorial title after Hume Nisbet on plate paper.

Half-title. pp. (iv) + (316) X_4 publishers' device, X_5 X_6 adverts. Publishers' cat., 32 pp. dated January 1891, at end.

Note. This edition preceded the American by two weeks.

[1159] SNOWBOUND AT EAGLES: a Novel
Ward & Downey 1886. Smooth brown cloth, blocked and lettered on front in black and white, gold-lettered and white-blocked on spine, blocked in black with publisher's monogram on back. Grey-on-white flowered end-papers.

Half-title. pp. (iv)+(256) R_2 imprint leaf. Publishers' cat., 16 pp. dated February 1886, at end.

Fine.

Note. This edition followed the American by a few days.

[1160] STORIES IN LIGHT AND SHADOW
Boston and New York: Houghton Mifflin & Co. 1898. Smooth brownish-red cloth, blocked and lettered in black on front, gold-lettered on spine.

Blank leaf and leaf carrying panel advert. on verso precede title. pp. (viii)+(310) Final leaf but two, Imprint leaf; but one, advert.; final leaf blank. The book is unsigned throughout. The final sig. has 6 leaves.

Presentation Copy: 'Lady Shrewsbury from Bret Harte 1898' in ink on fly-leaf.

[1161] TALES OF TRAIL AND TOWN (First American Edition)
Boston: Houghton, Mifflin & Co. 1898. Smooth brick-red cloth; grey-green end-papers.

Two leaves precede title, of which the second printed on verso with panel advert. pp. (viii)+(352) Pp. (349) (350) Imprint leaf; (351) (352) blank. No signature lettering.

Presentation Copy: 'To T. Edgar Pemberton from Bret Harte 1898' in ink on recto of second blank leaf.

Book-plate of T. Edgar Pemberton. Fine.

Note. This edition was later than the English by two days.

[1162] THREE PARTNERS: or the Big Strike on Heavy Tree Hill
Chatto & Windus 1897. Dark blue ribbed cloth, sand-brown-on-white foliage end-papers. Half-tone front. and 7 plates after H. Gülich.

Half-title. pp. (vi)+(298) Publishers' cat., 32 pp. dated February 1897, at end.

Book-plate of Walter Wren, and on List of Illustrations his signature dated 17/9/97.

Note. This edition preceded the American by two weeks.

[1163] TRENT'S TRUST and other Stories
Eveleigh Nash 1903. Black buckram, blocked and lettered in gold, bevelled boards.

Blank leaf and half-title precede title. pp. (viii)+(324) X_2 blank.

Book-plate of T. Edgar Pemberton.

Note. This edition preceded the American by ten days.

UNDER THE REDWOODS (First English Edition) [1164]
C. Arthur Pearson 1901. Smooth claret cloth, pictorially blocked in flame, cream and black, black-lettered on front, gold-lettered on spine.

Blank leaf and half-title precede title. pp. (352) $Y_7 Y_8$ adverts. Two publisher's cats. at end, each 8 pp. on text paper, the first dated 'Spring 1901', the second undated. Fine.

Note. This edition was later than the American by a week.

WAIF OF THE PLAINS (A) [1165]
Chatto & Windus 1890. Smooth scarlet cloth, pictorially blocked on front in orange, green, blue and black, uniform pictorial blocking and gold lettering on spine. Pale grey-on-white floral end-papers. Line engraved front., vignette on title and 59 text illustrations and decorative initial letters after Stanley L. Wood, all on text paper.

Half-title. pp. viii+(240) Q_8 publishers' device. Publishers' cat., 32 pp. dated October 1889, at end.

Pencil signature: 'Radclyffe Walters 1890' facing half-title. Very fine.

WARD OF THE GOLDEN GATE (A) [1166]
Boston and New York: Houghton Mifflin & Co. 1890. Smooth dark green cloth, blocked and lettered in black on front, gold-lettered on spine.

Blank leaf precedes title. pp. (iv)+(252) Final leaf blank. The book is unsigned throughout.

Presentation Copy: 'Lady Shrewsbury from Bret Harte. London. Novem. '90.' in ink on fly-leaf.

See also HAMILTON, WALTER, *above and* 3578–84 *in Section II*

HARWOOD, JOHN BERWICK (1828–? late '80s)

This novelist is, to me, one of the minor mysteries of mid-nineteenth century authorship. According to the Bentley catalogue he was born in 1828, published a volume of poems with Pickering in 1849, married in 1850 and celebrated his honeymoon abroad in a book (regrettably) entitled *The Bridal and the Bridle.* His first novel appeared in 1854 and his last in 1885. He wrote at least nineteen.

The novels published by Bentley (the list which follows lacks two or three titles) are, in so far as I have seen them, produced with the ostentatious solidity these publishers gave to the works of authors they respected (the outstanding example is Mrs Henry Wood)—that is to say, they have a look of importance. Yet, until finding him in the Bentley collection, I had never heard his name nor, until after this catalogue was in proof, had seen a book of his in a second-hand shop. At first I assumed he was a rich man, who published at his own expense. But this assumption (in itself improbable with a publisher of Bentley's standing) collapsed, when he was discovered writing wild-west serials for Cassell's *Saturday Magazine* in the early eighties.

Harwood is not in the *D.N.B.*; Allibone lists his works, but without personal comment; and no one of his books, except *Lord Lynn's Wife* and *Lady Flavia*, seems to have reached a second edition.

[1167] HELENA LADY HARROGATE: a Tale
3 vols. Bentley 1878. Dark green diagonal-fine-ribbed cloth, blocked in black and gold.
Half-title in each vol.
Vol. I (vi) + 320
II (vi) + 320
III (vi) + 288
In each case (v) (vi), Contents, form a single inset. B

[1168] *LADY FLAVIA (by the author of 'Lord Lynn's Wife')
3 vols. Bentley 1865. Crimson sand-grain cloth, blocked in blind and blocked and lettered in gold.
Half-title in Vols. I and III
Vol. I vi + 300
II iv + 300
III vi + (302) Final sigs. U (1 leaf), X (6 leaves).

[1169] LADY LIVINGSTON'S LEGACY: a Novel (by the author of 'Lady Flavia', 'Lord Lynn's Wife', etc.)
3 vols. Bentley 1874. Dark green close-bead-patterned cloth blocked in black and gold; grey-chocolate end-papers.
Vol. I (iv) + 308
II (iv) + (296)
III (iv) + (284) 18_6 adverts. B

[1170] LORD LYNN'S WIFE [anon]
2 vols. Bentley 1864. Red fine-morocco cloth, blocked in blind and lettered in gold.
Vol. I (ii) + 280
II (ii) + (266) Final leaf, T_1, a single inset. B

[1171] LORD ULSWATER: a Novel (by the author of 'Lord Lynn's Wife', 'Lady Flavia', etc.)
3 vols. Bentley 1867. Bright blue sand-grain cloth, blocked in blind and lettered in gold.
Blank leaf and half-title precede title in Vol. I; half-title only (a single inset) in Vols. II and III
Vol. I viii + (320)
II (vi) [paged viii] + 310 Final sigs. X (1 leaf), Y (2 leaves).
III vi [paged viii] + 310 Final sigs. X (1 leaf), Y (2 leaves). B

MAJOR PETER (by the author of 'Lord Lynn's Wife', 'Lady Flavia' and 'Odd Neighbours') [1172]
3 vols. Bentley 1866. Grass-green fine-morocco cloth, blocked in blind and lettered in gold.
Vol. I (x) + (298) (ix) (x), Contents, and final leaf, U_5, single insets.
II (iv) + (290) Final leaf, (U_1), a single inset.
III (iv) + (298) Final leaf, U_5, a single inset. B

MISS JANE, THE BISHOP'S DAUGHTER (by John Harwood) [1173]
3 vols. Bentley 1867. Claret fine-morocco cloth, blocked in blind and lettered in gold; pale terra-cotta end-papers.
Vol. I (iv) + (304)
II (iv) + (308)
III (iv) + (296) 19_4 adverts. B

ODD NEIGHBOURS (by the author of 'Lord Lynn's Wife') [1174]
3 vols. Bentley 1865. Plum fine-morocco cloth, blocked in blind and lettered in gold.
Vol. I (vi) + 316 Title-page a single inset.
II (ii) + (304)
III (ii) + (316) B
Vol. II discoloured by damp, Vol. III damp-spotted on lower covers.

PAUL KNOX, PITMAN [1175]
3 vols. Bentley 1878. Bright blue fine-ribbed cloth, grained herring-bone fashion in broad stripes, blocked in black and gold.
Vol. I (iv) + (272)
II (iv) + (288) 35_8 blank.
III (iv) + (272) 52_8 blank. B

PLAIN JOHN ORPINGTON (by the author of 'Lord Lynn's Wife', 'Lady Flavia', etc.) [1176]
3 vols. Bentley 1866. Royal-blue fine-morocco cloth, blocked in blind and lettered in gold.
Vol. I (iv) + 292
II (iv) + (304)
III (iv) + 320 B

SIR PEREGRINE'S HEIR [1177]
3 vols. Bentley 1875. Maroon fine-dot-and-line-grain cloth, heavily blocked with horizontal bars in blind and gold-lettered.
Vol. I (iv) + (316)
II (iv) + 324
III (iv) + 292 B

TENTH EARL (The) [1178]
3 vols. Hurst & Blackett 1880. Smooth blue-grey cloth, blocked and lettered in black on front and in gold on spine. Puce-on-white floral end-papers.
Half-title in each vol. (v) (vi), Contents, form a single inset in each vol.

Vol. I (vi)+298 First leaf of final sig., U_1, a single inset.
II (vi)+(284)
III (vi)+280 Publishers' cat., 16 pp. undated, at end.

Rather soiled; front cover of Vol. II damp-stained.

Note. *Lady Flavia* is still Harwood's oriflamme. It is displayed in large letters on front cover and spine of this fifteen-year-later novel.

HAWTHORNE, JULIAN (1846–1934)

[1179] ARCHIBALD MALMAISON
Bentley 1879. Scarlet diagonal-fine-ribbed cloth; black end-papers.

Half-title. pp. (iv)+(188) (12_1)–(12_6) adverts. dated May 1879. B

No. XI of Bentley's Half Crown Empire Library.

[1180] BRESSANT: a Romance
2 vols. Henry S. King & Co. 1873. Violet fine-bead-grain cloth, blocked in black and lettered in gold. Dark green end-papers. A panel advert. is printed on the white verso of the fly-leaf in each vol.

Vol. I iv+(276) T_2 (missing from this copy) blank or adverts.
II iv+248 Publishers' cat., (ii)+32 pp. dated March 1873, plus a single inset leaf of additional adverts., at end.

Spines faded.

[1181] GARTH: a Novel
3 vols. Bentley 1877. Crimson moiré diagonal-fine-ribbed cloth, blocked and lettered in black and gold.

Vol. I vi+(320) 20_8 adverts. (iii) (iv) Dedication, form a single inset.
II iv+(346) Final leaf, 42_5, a single inset.
III iv+(280) 60_4 adverts. B

[1182] SEBASTIAN STROME: a Novel
3 vols. Bentley 1879. Black fancy-diaper cloth, blocked in blind and gold and lettered in gold.

Half-title in Vol. I

Vol. I viii+(298) Final leaf, 19_5, a single inset.
II iv+284
III iv+258 Final leaf, 54_1, a single inset. B

HAWTHORNE, NATHANIEL (1804–1864)

[1183] OUR OLD HOME
2 vols. Smith, Elder 1863. Dark moss-green wavy-grain cloth, blocked front and back in blind and on spine blocked and lettered in blind and gold.

Half-title in each vol.

Vol. I xii+272
II (iv)+(304) U_7 U_8 adverts.

Note. This edition preceded the American issue by two months.

Very fine. This superb copy was bought at the Yates Thompson sale in Portman Square (summer of 1941).

PANSIE: a Fragment. 'The Last Literary Effort of Nathaniel Hawthorne' [1184]
Hotten [1864]. Yellow printed wrappers.

pp. 48 Publisher's cat., 16 pp. undated, at end. Spine repaired.

Note. This edition preceded the American issue by over eighteen months (Brussel, p. 49).

TRANSFORMATION, or the Romance of Monte Beni [1185]
3 vols. Smith, Elder 1860. Claret fine-ripple-grain cloth, blocked in blind and spine-lettered in gold.

Half-title in Vol. I

Vol. I (xvi)+(276) 18_2 imprint leaf.
II (iv)+(296) 37_4 imprint leaf.
III (iv)+(288) 55_8 adverts. paged (1) 2. Publishers' cat., 32 pp. dated February 1860, at end.

Fine, despite slight spine-bubbling of Vol. I.

Note. Brussel (p. 48) demonstrates that in fact the American edition of this novel, under the title *The Marble Faun*, appeared a day or two before the English one; but I record the Smith, Elder edition on account of its different title and rumoured priority.

HELPS, SIR ARTHUR (1813–1875)

CASIMIR MAREMMA (by the author of 'Friends in Council', 'Realmah', etc.) [1186]
2 vols. Bell & Daldy 1870. Red-brown sand-grain cloth; greenish-black end-papers.

Half-title in Vol. I, blank leaf and half-title in Vol. II

Vol. I (l)+238 Pp. xlix and (l) are a single leaf signed *d.* First leaf of final sig., Q_1, a single inset.
II (viii) [paged vi]+276

Dedication Copy to Lord Northbrook, a note to whom in the author's hand, dated 'Jan. 31/70' and stating this to be the first copy in existence, is inserted in Vol. I.

Book-plate of Lord Northbrook and his ink signature on the title of Vol. I.

IVAN DE BIRON, or the Russian Court in the Middle of Last Century (by the author of 'Friends in Council', etc.) [1187]
3 vols. Isbister & Co. 1874. Magenta diagonal-fine-ribbed cloth; very dark green end-papers.

Half-title (a single inset) in each vol.

Vol. I vi+256
II vi+252
III vi+220 Final sigs. P, 4 leaves, Q, 2 leaves. Publishers' cat., 6 pp. on text paper, undated, at end.

Book-plate of Michael Tompkins in each vol. has been over-pasted with another book-plate, and then both have been badly defaced.

HENTY, G. A. (1832–1902)

[1188] **MARCH TO MAGDALA (The)**

8vo. Tinsley 1868. Bright blue fine-morocco cloth, blocked in blind and lettered in gold in the style adopted by the publishers for several non-fiction 8vos at this period; café-au-lait end-papers.

Half-title. pp. (viii)+(432). Fine.

Notes. (i) This straightforward account of the Magdala campaign was Henty's second published book. Although not fiction, it is recorded as a specimen of a characteristic Tinsley style.

(ii) Other Tinsley titles generally uniform with this work are *English Photographs by An American*, 1869: *The Battle Fields of Paraguay* by Richard Burton, 1870: and *Wonderful London*, 1878.

[1189] **RUJUB, THE JUGGLER**

3 vols. Chatto & Windus 1893. Blue morocco cloth, blocked in bronze on front and back and gold-lettered on spine; buff-on-white flowered end-papers.

Half-title in each vol.

Vol. I (iv)+(296) T_4 blank.
II (iv)+(280) S_4 blank.
III (iv)+(268) R_6 blank. Publishers' cat., 32 pp. dated October 1892, at end.

Very fine.

[1190] **SEARCH FOR A SECRET (A): a Novel**

3 vols. Tinsley 1867. Royal-blue moiré fine-ribbed cloth.

Vol. I iv+(300) U_6 imprint leaf.
II iv+(372) S_8 blank.
III iv+(264)

Fine.

Note. This was the author's first published book.

[1191] **SEASIDE MAIDENS**

8vo. Tinsley 1880. White wrappers, cut flush, pictorially printed in blue and black with a drawing after Harry Furniss. Ten full-page illustrations after Harry Furniss.

Pp. (14) [paged 16]+98 Pp. (1)–(12) adverts. (pp. 11, 12 a single inset leaf), (13) (14) [mispaged 16] title-leaf. Final leaf, h_1, a single inset.

Summer Number of *Tinsley's Magazine.* Spine defective.

Also issued in brown cloth blocked and lettered (with title only) in black and gold.

Note. Edmund Downey, in *Twenty Years After* (1905), states that William Tinsley forced the title of this collection of straightforward and rather charming love-stories on the unwilling author. Presumably he also chose the wrapper-drawing, which is of the C. H. Ross-Stage-Whispers school and unsuited both to Henty and his work.

YOUNG FRANC-TIREURS (The), and Their Adventures in the Franco-Prussian War [1192

Griffith & Farran 1872. Vermilion pebble-grain cloth, pictorially blocked in black and gold; gilt edges; pinkish buff end-papers. Wood-engraved front. and 7 full-page illustrations after R. T. Landells, all on plate paper.

pp. (viii)+376 Publishers' cat., 32 pp. undated, at end.

Binders' ticket: 'Burn', at end.

Note. The second of Henty's long series of Books for Boys. The first was *Out on the Pampas*, 1868.

HEWLETT, JOSEPH THOMAS JAMES (1800–1847)

Hewlett took Orders in 1826 and was shortly afterwards appointed headmaster of Abingdon Grammar School. His career there was brief and unfortunate, and he retired to Dorset where he struggled to support himself by writing. He was an intimate friend of Theodore Hook, who lent his name to two of Hewlett's works in order to help their sale.

GREAT TOM OF OXFORD (by the author of 'Peter Priggins') [1193

3 vols. Colburn 1846. Boards, labels.

Half-titles in Vols. I and II

Vol. I (iv)+(320)
II (iv)+(324)
III (ii)+(292) Publishers' cat., 24 pp. undated, at end.

Pencil (and incorrect) statement on inside cover of Vol. I: 'Author—Theodore Hook.' Fine.

PARISH CLERK (The) (by the author of 'Peter Priggins'). 'Edited by Theodore Hook, Esq.' [1194

3 vols. Colburn 1841. Plum fine-diaper cloth.

Vol. I (ii)+312
II (ii)+330
III (ii)+(322)

Cloth stained and worn.

[1195] PETER PRIGGINS: the College Scout [anon]. 'Edited by Theodore Hook, Esq.'
3 vols. Colburn 1841. Dark-ivory ribbed cloth. Etched front. and 3 plates by Phiz in each vol.
Vol. I (iv)+336 Publishers' cat., 8 pp. undated, at end.
II (ii)+326 1st leaf of final sig., P_1, a single inset.
III (ii)+338 Final leaf, Q_1, a single inset.
Fine.

HOCKLEY, W. B. (1792–1860)

[1196] PANDURANG HARI, or Memoirs of a Hindoo [anon]
3 vols. Whittaker 1826. Boards, labels.
Half-title in each vol.
Vol. I (xvi)+346 Second leaf of final sig., Q_2, a single inset.
II (iv)+(360) Q_{10}–Q_{12} adverts.
III (iv)+398 Final leaf, T_1, a single inset.
From this copy Q_{12} in Vol. II has been cut away. Fine.

Note. This novel was actually written by Cyrus Redding, from rough notes sent from India by Hockley. A new edition was published in 1872 with a Preface by Sir Bartle Frere, from which the following interesting extract is taken: 'When PANDURANG HARI was first published the book was received as an authentic picture of Native Indian society. I well remember my gratitude to a friend who recommended it to me, with HAJJI BABA and THE KUZZILBASH, as the only books he could find which gave any idea of what would now be called the inner life of the Oriental. The works of Morier and Fraser have long since secured a permanent place in Anglo-oriental literature; but PANDURANG HARI has been so completely forgotten, that when Dr George Birdwood recommended its republication, the publishers were indebted to the liberality of Lord Talbot de Malahide for one of the few copies of the book which could be traced by Captain Meadows Taylor in any library in the United Kingdom....'

[1197] ZENANA (The), or a Nuwab's Leisure Hours (by the author of 'Pandurang Hari')
3 vols. Saunders & Otley 1827. Boards, labels.
Vol. I viii+(424)
II (ii)+(440) U_4 adverts.
III (ii)+(436)
There is a fly-title in each vol., so placed as to be B_1, i.e. to follow the last page of the Introduction in Vol. I and the title in Vols. II and III. Fine.

HOGG, JAMES (1770–1835)

PRIVATE MEMOIRS AND CONFESSIONS OF A JUSTIFIED SINNER (The), written by himself [anon] [1198]
Longman, etc. 1824. Half-cloth boards, label. Engraved front.
pp. iv+(392) $2C_4$ blank.

THREE PERILS OF MAN (The), or War, Women and Witchcraft. A Border Romance [1199]
3 vols. Longman etc. 1822. Boards, labels.
Half-title in each vol.
Vol. I (vi)+(344) P_4 blank. (v) (vi), Dedication, form a single inset. Publishers' cat., 4 pp. dated June 1822, inset between front end-papers.
II (iv)+(356) Q_4 blank.
III (iv)+(450) First leaf of final sig., U_1, a single inset.
Ink signature: 'G. O. Callaghan', on front cover of each vol. Very fine.

HOOK, THEODORE (1788–1841)

This is a complete collection of Hook's fiction in first edition. I have excluded such non-fiction as I possess, making an exception of *The Ramsbottom Letters* (which may reasonably claim to be semi-fiction, at least) because this little volume contains some of Hook's most characteristic and vigorous absurdities. These 'Letters' appeared serially in *John Bull* from 1822–1831, but were not issued in volume form until 1872.

BIRTHS, DEATHS AND MARRIAGES (by the author of 'Sayings and Doings', 'Maxwell', 'Jack Brag', etc.) [1200]
3 vols. Bentley 1839. Half-cloth boards, labels.
Half-title in each vol.
Vol. I (viii)+(308)
II (iv)+(320)
III (iv)+306 First leaf of final sig., O_2, a single inset.
Presentation Copy: 'To Mrs Lyon with the author's best compliments and regards. Theodore E. Hook' in ink on title of Vol. I.

FATHERS AND SONS: a Novel [1201]
3 vols. Colburn 1842. Boards, labels. Steel-engraved portrait front. in Vol. I.
Half-title in each vol., printed with adverts.
Vol. I (xxii)+304 Final leaf of prelims., a_9, a single inset.
II (iv)+336
III (iv)+312 8 pp. cat. dated 1841, of John Cumming, Dublin, at end.
Spines repaired.

Note. Cumming was a publisher, who, in addition to issuing his own books, imported titles in sheets from England and boarded them in Dublin. He usually inserted a catalogue of his publications.

[1202] GILBERT GURNEY (by the author of 'Sayings and Doings', 'Love and Pride', etc.)
3 vols. Whittaker & Co. 1836. Boards, labels.

Blank leaf precedes title in Vol. III

Vol. I (iv)+(340) Q_2 adverts.
II (ii)+(332) P_{10} adverts.
III (iv)+(368)

Book-plate of Sir Moses Montefiore. Very fine.

[1203] GURNEY MARRIED: a Sequel to Gilbert Gurney (by the author of 'Sayings and Doings')
3 vols. Colburn 1838. Boards, labels.

Half-title in each vol.

Vol. I (iv)+(324)
II (iv)+312
III (iv)+(334) First leaf of final sig., P_1, a single inset.

[1204] JACK BRAG (by the author of 'Sayings and Doings', 'Maxwell', etc.)
3 vols. Bentley 1837. Half-cloth boards, labels.

Half-title in each vol.

Vol. I (iv)+(312)
II (iv)+324 Errata slip tipped on to p. (1) of text.
III (iv)+336

Book-plate of the Earl of Charlemont in Vols. I and II. Booksellers' ticket: 'Kerr and Richardson, Glasgow', inside back cover of each vol. Fine.

[1205] LOVE AND PRIDE (by the author of 'Sayings and Doings', etc.)
3 vols. Whittaker & Co. 1833. Boards, labels.

Half-title in each vol.

Vol. I (viii) [paged vi]+(308) O_{10} adverts.
II (iv)+(304)
III (iv)+(340) Q_2 adverts.

Book-label of R. J. Ll. Price, Rhiwlas Library, in Vols. I and II. Signature of Frances Price, Rhiwlas, 1833 in Vol. III. Spine of Vol. I defective.

[1206] MAN OF SORROW (The): a Novel. ('By Alfred Allendale, Esq.')
3 vols. Sm. 8vo. Samuel Tipper 1808. Cont. half-calf.

Vol. I (vi) [paged (iv)]+(264)
II (ii)+274
III (ii)+236

Signature of Caroline Page on title of Vols. I and III. Vol. II lacks title. (See 3590 in Section II.)

Note. (i) (ii) of Vol. II represent the missing title. It is possible there should be a half-title in each vol.

MAXWELL (by the author of 'Sayings and Doings') [1207]
3 vols. Colburn & Bentley 1830. Grey-purple glazed figured linen, labels. Edges trimmed.

Half-titles in Vols. I and II

Vol. I (iv)+(348)
II (iv)+336
III (ii)+(360) Q_{11} Q_{12} adverts.

A leaf of Errata (verso blank) is inset after p. 356. It lists 7 Errata in Vol. I, 6 in Vol. II and 1 in Vol. III, i.e. fourteen lines. See *Note.*

This looks like a late binding-up of first-edition sheets. The labels are original and complete.

Note. Three issues of this Errata leaf have been noted. The earliest carried only *five* lines and followed the title of Vol. III; the next was as described above; the third carried *fifteen* lines and was inset at the end of Vol. I.

PARSON'S DAUGHTER (The) (by the author of 'Sayings and Doings', etc.) [1208]
3 vols. Bentley 1833. Boards, labels.

Vol. I (ii)+300 4 pp. cat. of Simpkin Marshall inserted at end.
II (ii)+(332)
III (ii)+(322) Final leaf, Q_1, a single inset.

Fine.

PEREGRINE BUNCE, or Settled at Last. A Novel [1209]
3 vols. Bentley 1842. Half-cloth boards, labels.

Half-title in each vol.

Vol. I (iv)+312
II (iv)+(312)
III (iv)+312

Book-plate of Horatio Austen Smith and ink signature: 'P. K. Smith', in each vol.

PRECEPTS AND PRACTICE [1210
3 vols. Colburn 1840. Earth-brown ribbed cloth. Steel-engraved portrait front. and 4 etchings by Phiz in Vol. I, 4 etchings by Phiz in Vol. II, and 2 in Vol. III.

Vol. I (vi)+316 Pp. (v) (vi), 'Illustrations', a single inset leaf. 8 pp. leaflet, fcap 8vo, advertising Colburn's Standard Novelists, at end.
II (iv)+312
III (iv)+(332) P_{10} advert.

Presentation copy: 'Mrs Lyon, with the author's best compliments and regards. Theodore E. Hook' in ink on title of Vol. I.

[1211] RAMSBOTTOM LETTERS (The)
Fcap 8vo. Bentley 1872. Buff paper wrappers, cut flush, printed in black on front, unprinted on spine and back; white end-papers.
pp. 96 [paged (i)–iv + (5)–96]
Blind stamp: 'W. H. Smith & Son', on fly-leaf. Spine chipped.

[1212] SAYINGS AND DOINGS: a Series of Sketches from Life [anon]
3 vols. Colburn 1824. Boards, labels.
Vol. I (viii) + 336
II (ii) + 350 Final leaf, R_1, a single inset.
III (ii) + 358 [mispaged 258] First leaf of final sig., Q_1, a single inset.
From the Clumber Library, October 1937. Very fine. A small piece is missing from foot of spine of Vol. II.

[1213] SAYINGS AND DOINGS: or Sketches from Life. Second Series [anon]
3 vols. Colburn 1825. Boards, labels.
Half-titles in Vols. II and III.
Vol. I viii + 326 Final leaf, Q_1, a single inset.
II (iv) + 344
III (iv) + (416) T_3 T_4 adverts.
Ink signature: 'Joseph Walters Daubeny, 1826', inside front cover of each vol. Fine.

[1214] SAYINGS AND DOINGS: or Sketches from Life. Third Series [anon]
3 vols. Colburn 1828. Boards, labels.
Half-title in each vol.
Vol. I (vi) + 378 Pp. (v) (vi), 'Advertisement', a single inset leaf. Final leaf, S_3, a single inset.
II (iv) + 326 Final leaf, Q_1, a single inset.
III (iv) + (336) P_{12} adverts.

Edited by Hook

[1215] PASCAL BRUNO: a Sicilian Story. 'Edited by Theodore Hook'
Colburn 1837. Boards, label. Steel-engraved portrait front. by G. Murray.
pp. viii + (288) Publishers' cat., 6 pp. on text paper dated 1837, at end.
Spine defective.
Note. This story is translated from Alexandre Dumas.

[*See also* HEWLETT, J. T. J., *above*.]

HOOTON, CHARLES

ADVENTURES OF BILBERRY THURLAND [anon] [1216]
3 vols. Bentley 1836. Boards, labels. Etched front. and 2 plates in each vol., all by Hervieu.
Half-title in Vols. II and III
Vol. I (vi) + 344 pp. (v) (vi) form a single inset leaf.
II (iv) + 300
III (iv) + (280)
Fine.

HOPE, THOMAS (1770–1831)

ANASTASIUS, or Memoirs of a Greek written at the close of the Eighteenth Century [anon] [1217]
Copy I: First Edition. 3 vols. Murray 1819. Boards, labels.
Half-title in each vol.
Vol. I (viii) [paged (iv)] + 376 Aa_3–Bb_4 Notes.
II (iv) + (432) Ee_2–Ee_7 Notes. EE_8 blank, serving as inside back end-paper.
III (iv) + (460) Gg_3–Gg_5 Notes, Gg_6 adverts.
Very fine. From the Bellew Library.
Copy II: Another. Squarer format, width of open page $5\frac{1}{8}$ ins. against usual $4\frac{7}{8}$ ins. Deliberately uneven folding as in a French large-paper copy. Also boards, labels. [1217*a*]
Collation as (i) save that in Vol. II the blank leaf, Ee_8, is followed by a regulation inside back end-paper. Fine.

HOPPUS, MARY A. M. (MRS ALFRED MARKS)

MASTERS OF THE WORLD [1218]
3 vols. Bentley 1888. Smooth navy-blue cloth; black end-papers.
Vol. I iv + 332
II iv + (336) 42_8 imprint leaf.
III iv + (328) 63_4 blank. B
Note. The Bentley Private Catalogue rates this novel of Rome under Domitian, which culminates in the murder of the Emperor, as one of the 'four classical stories of pre-eminent merit issued from New Burlington Street'. The other three were *The Last Days of Pompeii* (414), *Dion and the Sybils* (1335), and *Acte* (3306). It also quotes high praise from John Ruskin. Although dated 1888 the novel was not actually published until February 5, 1889.

HORT, LT.-COL.

I can find no mention of this man in any work of reference, nor trace of initials or Christian name. He appears here rather as a vehicle for bringing forward his admirable illustrator, Alfred Ashley, than for his own sake as an author.

Nor can I find much more information about Ashley, who published a handbook on the technique of engraving in 1849. W. Shaw Sparrow dismisses him as 'poor in figures, only moderately good in landscape'. Other Ashley illustrations are recorded below under SWEPSTONE.

[1219] EMBROIDERED BANNER and Other Marvels (The)

8vo. J. & D. A. Darling 1850. Red morocco cloth. Eight coloured etchings on steel by Alfred Ashley, of which two are front. and engraved title, inset between half- and printed title.

Half-title pp. (viii) + 288 Publishers' cat., fcap 8vo, 8 pp. undated, followed by 2 leaves of cheap paper advertising the works of Lieut.-Colonel Hort, at end.

Book-plate of Astley Terry. Fine.

[1220] GUARDS AND THE LINE (The)

Oblong folio. J. & D. A. Darling 1851. Quarter crimson cloth, drab boards, printed by lithography in black with a design by Alfred Crowquill. The imprint on the cover is dated 1850. Twelve full-page lithographed and hand-coloured illustrations after Crowquill, each consisting of two scenes depicting (with considerable bitterness) the luxury life of an officer of the Guards and the hardships and neglect experienced by an officer of a Line Regiment. Each plate has a satirical text, set in two columns and elaborating the contrast between the Guards and the Line.

pp. (viii) + 78 Collates in fours, but C only 3 leaves of which C_1 a single inset, signed C_2 on verso.

[1221] *Pl. 21* HORSE GUARDS (The) (by the author of 'Two Mounted Sentries')

8vo. J. & D. A. Darling 1850. Buff paper boards, with coloured lithographic illustration on front and back covers. Thirteen coloured lithographs, of which two on covers and one a frontispiece. The title and List of Illustrations announce only 12 illustrations, omitting that on back cover, although the one on front cover is reckoned and listed.

pp. viii + 104

Book-plate 'Malacrida'.

Note. The title of the book is stated pictorially on the front cover, and not set out in words, so that in more than one respect it is a curious piece of book-making.

A second edition was published in the same year, bound in claret morocco cloth, pictorially blocked and spine-lettered in gold. The plates were printed in stronger, coarser colours. No indication anywhere of authorship.

MAN WHO ELOPED WITH HIS OWN WIFE (The) [1222]

8vo. J. & D. A. Darling 1850. Stiff wrappers engraved in colours by Alfred Ashley. Spine unlettered; back printed with advert. Yellow end-papers. Three coloured etchings by Ashley, of which one on front cover, one a frontispiece, and the third at the end, advertising Hort's books.

Half-title. pp. (iv) + 68, followed by the Ashley advertising plate and 2 leaves of yellow paper carrying publishers' adverts. Outside back wrapper printed with list of Hort's works.

Book-plate of Astley Terry. Front cover of this copy has been repaired.

PENELOPE WEDGEBONE: The Supposed Heiress [1223]

8vo. J. & D. A. Darling. (Preface dated June 1st, 1850). Deep sea-blue morocco cloth. Eight coloured etchings on steel by Alfred Ashley, of which two are front. and engraved title, preceding printed title.

pp. (vi) + 196. Publishers' cat., fcap 8vo, 8 pp. undated, followed by 2 leaves of salmon-pink paper advertising the works of Col. Hort.

Book-plate of the Duke of Leeds and his ink signature on outside and inside front cover. Very fine.

Note. Also issued in red and in green morocco cloth, uniformly blocked and probably of simultaneous issue.

HOWARD, HON. EDWARD GRANVILLE (?–1841)

This is a complete schedule of Howard's fiction, and rounds off in a satisfactory manner the equally complete collection of Captain Marryat.

JACK ASHORE (by the author of 'Rattlin the Reefer', 'Outward Bound', etc. etc.) [1224] *Pl. 18*

Copy I: First Edition. 3 vols. Colburn 1840. Boards, labels. Engraved portrait front. to Vol. I, dated December 1838.

Half-title in Vols. II and III

Vol. I xvi + 310 First leaf of final sig., O_1, a single inset.

II viii + 300

III (viii) + (328) P_7 P_8 adverts.

Presentation Copy: 'To Mrs Howard, his best friend, from the author Ed. Howard' in ink on title of Vol. I.

Very fine.

[1224a] **Copy II: First American Edition.** 2 vols. Philadelphia: Carey & Hart 1840. Half-cloth boards, labels.

Advert. leaf precedes title in Vol. I; two such leaves in Vol. II

Vol. I pp. 196 [paged (i)–xii + (13)–196]
II pp. (198) [paged (i)–viii (in mistake for x) + (13)–(200) (in mistake for (11)–(198)] 17_4 blank.

Ink signature: 'G. H. Kissel', on fly-leaves.

[1224b] **Copy III: First French Edition.** LE MARIN À TERRE (par l'auteur de 'Rattlin le Marin', 'Du Vieux Commodore', et 'd'Ardent Troughton'). Traduit par A. J. B. Defauconpret.

2 vols. 8vo. Paris: Charles Gosselin 1841. Half red roan gilt, red morocco paper sides. Edges uncut.

Half-title in each vol.

Vol. I (iv) + 328
II (iv) + 312

From the Library of the Empress Marie Louise, with her monogram on front and back covers.

Note. 'Avertissement de l'Editeur' explains that hitherto he had included Howard's novels under a series half-title: 'Œuvres Complètes du Capitaine Marryat', but has just learnt that they are not in fact from his pen. *Le Marin à Terre* in consequence makes no reference to Marryat on the half-titles.

[1225] OLD COMMODORE (The) (by the author of 'Rattlin the Reefer')

3 vols. Bentley 1837. Issued in boards, labels; this copy in three-quarter brown morocco by Riviere, t.e.g., others uncut.

Half-title in each vol.

Vol. I (iv) + 306
II (iv) + 304
III (iv) + (312) O_{11} O_{12} adverts.

Book-plate of John Croft Deverell.

Note. I have been unable to locate another copy of this novel, even in decently bound state, let alone in original condition. Vol. I ends with O_9 and the final leaf is, in the copy described, a single inset. I wondered whether, when Deverell bought the book and had it bound, this vol. already lacked one or more advert. leaves. But at the eleventh hour P. S. O'Hegarty found a board copy, which confirms as correct the collation given above. This bears out my impression that Deverell (from whose library I have seen numerous books) was very scrupulous over half-titles, blanks and advert. leaves.

OUTWARD BOUND, or a Merchant's Adventures (by the author of 'Rattlin the Reefer', 'The Old Commodore', etc.) [1226]

Copy I: First Edition. 3 vols. Colburn 1838. Boards, labels.

Half-title in Vols. II and III

Vol. I (iv) + (300) Publishers' cat. (Longman etc.), 16 pp. dated March 1838, inserted between front end-papers.
II (iv) + (310) O_{11} adverts., O_{12} probably label-leaf. First leaf of final sig., O_1, a single inset.
III (iv) + (328) P_8 [pp. (327) (328)] cut away from this copy: either blank or adverts.

Spine of Vol. I repaired at tail.

Copy II: First French Edition. ARDENT TROUGHTON OU LE COMMERÇANT NAUFRAGÉ (publié par le Capitaine Marryat). Traduit par A. J. B. Defauconpret, etc. [1226a]

2 vols. 8vo. Paris: Charles Gosselin, etc. 1838. Half red roan gilt, red morocco paper sides. Edges uncut.

Half-title in each vol.

Vol. I (iv) + (344)
II (iv) + 392

From the Library of the Empress Marie Louise, with her monogram on front and back covers.

RATTLIN THE REEFER. Edited by the author of 'Peter Simple' [1227] *Pl. 18*

3 vols. Bentley ('Successor to Henry Colburn') 1836. Boards, labels. Etched front. and 2 plates in each vol. by Hervieu.

Half-title in Vol. I

Vol. I xii + ii [inset List of Illustrations, found preceding or following Contents] + (304) O_8 advert.
II viii + 300
III viii + 344

Book-label of Thos. Shepheard. Fine.

Note. The Second Edition, 1836, has no half-title in Vol. I and the List of Illustrations is printed on verso of 'Advertisement'. The words 'Successor to Henry Colburn' are dropped from the publisher's imprint on titles.

SIR HENRY MORGAN THE BUCCANEER [1228]
(by the author of 'Rattlin the Reefer', etc.)

3 vols. Colburn 1842. Half-cloth boards, labels. Lithographed portrait front. to Vol. I.

Half-title in Vol. I

Vol. I (viii) + (300) O_5 O_6 adverts.
II vi + (308)
III (viii) + (316)

Fine. Label of Vol. II slightly defective.

HUBBACK, MRS

[1229] WIFE'S SISTER (The), or the Forbidden Marriage (by 'Mrs Hubback, Niece of Miss Austen')

3 vols. Shoberl 1851. Half-cloth boards, label.

Vol. I (iv)+(298) Third leaf of final sig., O_3, a single inset.

II (ii)+294 First leaf of final sig., O_1, a single inset.

III (ii)+298 Third leaf of final sig., O_3, a single inset.

HUDSON, W. H. (1841–1922)

[1230] CRYSTAL AGE (A) [anon]

T. Fisher Unwin 1887. Smooth black cloth, blocked and lettered on front in scarlet, gold-lettered and scarlet-blocked on spine, scarlet-blocked on back. Olive-on-cream floral end-papers.

Half-title. pp. (iv)+(288) Publisher's cat., 32 pp. dated Autumn–Christmas 1886, at end.

Presentation Copy: 'Dr P. L. Sclater with the Author's compliments' in ink in Hudson's hand on title. Dr Sclater collaborated with Hudson in *Argentine Ornithology*, 2 vols., 1888–9.

[1231] EL OMBU

Duckworth 1902. Grass-green linen-grain cloth, blocked and lettered in black. Publishers' device in black on back cover.

Half-title. pp. (viii)+(184) N_4 blank.

Book-label of Charles Whibley. Fine.

No. II in Duckworth's 'Greenback Library': published at 1*s.* 6*d.* in wrappers, 2*s.* in cloth.

[1232] FAN: the Story of a Young Girl's Life (by Henry Harford)

3 vols. Chapman & Hall 1892. Olive-green diagonal-fine-ribbed cloth, blocked in black and gold.

Half-title in each vol.

Vol. I (iv)+(312) X_4 imprint leaf.

II (iv)+292

III (iv)+(300) U_6 imprint leaf.

Ink signature: 'E. M. Nichols', on half-title of each vol. A brilliant copy.

[1233] GREEN MANSIONS: a Romance of the Tropical Forest

Duckworth 1904. Grey-green buckram, bevelled boards.

Half-title. pp. (iv)+(316)

Ink signature: 'W. F. Clare. 5 March 1904', on fly-leaf. Very fine.

Note. This copy has no publishers' device in blind on back cover.

HUGHES, THOMAS (1822–1896)

TOM BROWN AT OXFORD (by the author of 'Tom Brown's Schooldays') [1234] *Pl. 5*

[*Parrish: Kingsley/Hughes* p. 120

3 vols. Cambridge: Macmillan 1861. Royal-blue morocco cloth (Kingsley style). Deep cream end-papers.

Half-title in each vol.

Vol. I xii+(320) Publishers' cat., 24 pp. dated '15.10.61', at end.

II (viii)+(340) Z_2 adverts.

III (viii)+(312) X_4 blank.

Binder's ticket: 'Burn', at end of Vol. I. Very fine.

Note. For convenience and ease of identification the style of blue cloth binding used on *Westward Ho* and many other Macmillan books of the period is described as 'Kingsley style'.

TOM BROWN'S SCHOOL DAYS ('by an Old Boy') [1235]

[*Parrish* p. 106

Macmillan 1857. Blue straight-grain morocco cloth, Kingsley style. Primrose end-papers.

Half-title. pp. viii+420 Inset advert. leaf and 24-page publishers' cat., dated February 1857, signed A and paged (1)–24, at end.

Ink signature: 'Edward F. Randolph' on fly-leaf. Letter inserted from Augustus Orlebar, dated March 11, 1911 and endorsed 'the original of "Tom Brown"'.

Hinges worn in places and frail internally, but a remarkable copy of a book, which I have never seen or heard of in really fine condition. It belonged to Frank Hogan.

A copy with publishers' cat. dated *January* 1857 was in the possession of Mr Gilbert Fabes in 1944.

HUGO, VICTOR (1802–1885)

BY ORDER OF THE KING. The Authorised English Translation of Victor Hugo's 'L'Homme qui Rit' [1236]

Copy I: First Edition. 3 vols. Bradbury, Evans & Co. 1870. Smooth apple-green cloth, pictorially blocked in black and blocked and lettered in gold; slate end-papers. Wood-engraved front. and vignette title (on plate paper) in each vol.; also, in Vol. I, 6, in Vol. II, 3, in Vol. III, 3 illustrations after S. Luke Fildes. Titles printed in red and black.

Half-title (reading: BY ORDER OF THE KING. / A Romance of English History) in each vol.

Vol. I (xii) [4 pp. of plate paper and 8 pp. of text paper, paged (x)]+(300) U_6 adverts.

II (xii) [as in I]+(290) Final leaf, (U_1), a single inset.

III (xii) [as in I]+(310) Final leaf, X_3, a single inset.

Binders' ticket: 'Leighton. Son & Hodge', at end of Vols. I and II.

[1236*a*] **Copy II: First one-vol. Edition.** Bradbury & Evans 1871. Smooth bright blue cloth blocked in black and lettered in gold; café-au-lait end-papers. Wood-engraved front., vignette title and 10 illustrations after Fildes, all on plate paper.

Half-title. pp. (xii) [vignette title but *not* front. is reckoned in collation] + (522) Final leaf, MM_1, a single inset.

Book-plate of John Browne, and ink signature: 'J. Browne, Southend, July 1871', on title. Fine.

[1237] HISTORY OF A CRIME (The): the Testimony of an Eye-Witness. Translated by T. H. Joyce and Arthur Locker

4 vols. Sampson Low, etc. 1877 (Vols. I & II), 1878 (Vols. III & IV). Very dark brown sand-grain cloth, blind-blocked front and back with framing and publishers' monogram, gold-lettered on spine.

Half-title in Vol. I

Vol. I xii + (256)
II 244 [paged (i)–iv + (5)–244]
III (viii) + (248) R_4 imprint leaf.
IV (248) Q_4 blank. In this vol. sig. B begins p. 17, as against p. 1 in Vol. III.

Binders' ticket 'Bone & Son' at end of Vol. I.

Note. Vols. I and II are spine-lettered with title, author's name and imprint; Vols. III and IV with title and imprint only.

[1238] LAST DAYS OF A CONDEMNED (The). With Observations on Capital Punishment by Sir P. Hesketh Fleetwood, Bart., M.P.

Smith, Elder 1840. Grass-green ribbed cloth, pictorially blind-blocked in relief on front and back with view of a cathedral in decorative frame; gold-lettered (title only) on spine.

Half-title. pp. (xliv) + 192 Text of story ends p. 154; (155)–192 'Preface of M. Victor Hugo'.

Ink signature: 'Jennett Chambers, 88 Union Road, Rotherhithe' on fly-leaf. Fine.

[1239] NINETY THREE

Translated by Frank Lee Benedict and J. Hain Friswell. 3 vols. Sampson Low. 1874. Scarlet diagonal-fine-ribbed cloth, blocked in blind on front and back with publishers' monogram and triple frame, gold-lettered on spine.

Vol. I iv + 336
II iv + (298) First leaf of final sig., U_1, a single inset. Publishers' cat., 48 pp. dated October 1873, at end.
III iv + 324

'E. R.' 74' in ink inside front cover. Fine.

NOTRE-DAME: a Tale of the 'Ancien Regime'. With a Prefatory Notice, Literary and Political, of his Romances, etc. [1240]

3 vols. Effingham Wilson 1833. Half-cloth boards, labels. Lithographed portrait front. in Vol. I

Vol. I xxviii + (332)
II iv + (356) Q_{10} blank.
III iv + (376) S_2 blank.

Ink signature: 'Hugh de Selincourt, July 1896' inside front covers of Vols. I and II, erased from Vol. III.

TOILERS OF THE SEA. Authorised English Translation by W. Moy Thomas [1241]

3 vols. Sampson Low 1866. Grass-green morocco cloth; grey chocolate end-papers.

Vol. I (x) [ix (x) signed *b*, a single inset] + (332)
II (vi) [v (vi) signed *b*, a single inset] + (328)
III (iv) + (288) T_8 adverts. dated March 30, 1866. Publishers' cat., 16 pp. on text paper dated February 1, 1866, at end.

Blind stamp: 'Doidge, Booksellers, Redruth', on fly-leaf of each vol.

[*See also* HAMILTON, WALTER, *above*.]

HUMPHREYS, MRS DESMOND. See 'RITA'

HUNT, MRS ALFRED (mother of VIOLET HUNT) (1831–1912)

GOVERNESS (The) (finished by Violet Hunt). With a Preface by Ford Madox Hueffer [1242]

Chatto & Windus 1912. Grey-green cloth. Title printed in red and black.

Blank leaf and half-title precede title. pp. (xx) [paged xviii] + (316) Publishers' cat., 32 pp. dated '9.11', at end.

Fine. Ford Madox Hueffer's copy with his violet ink book-stamp.

Note. Hueffer's Preface is interesting. It begins with a lament for the three-decker and an attack on the mania for cheapness which foisted the six-shilling novel on authors and public. After a character-sketch of Mrs Hunt with comments on her earlier novels, he praises *The Governess* as a valuable social document. He concludes by comparing the proceeds of one of Mrs Hunt's best-known 3 vol. fictions with that of the last book published in her lifetime, which was in 1 vol. at 6*s*. *Thornicroft's Model* (3 vols.) and *Mrs Juliet* (1 vol.) each sold 2000 copies: on the former the author received 10*s*. per copy, i.e. £1000: on the latter 1*s*. per copy, i.e. £100.

[1243] MAGDALEN WYNYARD, or the Provocations of a Pre-Raphaelite ('by Averil Beaumont')
2 vols. Chapman & Hall 1872. Full royal-blue polished calf gilt, marbled edges (issued in plum sand-grain cloth, gold-lettered on spine).
Vol. I (ii) + 284
II (ii) + 264
Note. I imagine this book in its original state either has a half-title in Vol. II or, if the titles were printed together, a blank or advert. leaf at the end of Vol. I.

[1244] THORNICROFT'S MODEL. A New Edition with a Preface by Violet Hunt
Chatto & Windus 1912. Scarlet linen-grain cloth, blocked in blind and lettered in gold.
Advert. leaf and half-title precede title.
pp. (xvi) + (388) Very fine.
Note. This was Violet Hunt's own copy. Her mother was to this extent fortunate in her daughter and son-in-law, in that the books published (or re-published) under their auspices had introductions which added considerably to the interest of the original stories (cf. *The Governess* above). In the Preface to this edition of *Thornicroft's Model*, first published by Chapman & Hall in 1873 under the pseudonym 'Averil Beaumont', Violet Hunt gives a delightful account of her mother's meeting with and adoration of Rossetti; of the dominance of the Royal Academy at the time the book was written; of the harm this indiscreet championship of an anti-Academician (Rossetti: for Rossetti, likeness apart, is 'Thornicroft') did to her poor husband's career. At the same time she truly says that *Thornicroft's Model* is a 'rattling good story'; and, although I would welcome a first edition if I could find a clean one, it is certain that the book reads better after Violet Hunt's preliminary gloss, than in its original pseudonymous and unannotated form.

HUNT, LEIGH (1784–1859)

[1245] SIR RALPH ESHER, or Adventures of a Gentleman of the Court of Charles II [anon]
3 vols. Colburn & Bentley 1832. Boards, labels.
Vol. I (ii) + (300)
II (ii) + (356) R_4 adverts. (of books published in 1830).
III (ii) + (344)
Fine.
Note. In the *Bookman's Journal*, Vol. XVII, No. 12, 1930, Mr Luther A. Brewer published an article about this novel, in which he demonstrated (I think conclusively) that the work was prepared for issue in 1830 but not actually published till 1832. The reasons for the postponement (still obscure) are bibliographically irrelevant; what matters is that one or two copies undoubtedly exist (e.g. that in B.M. which belonged to Reynell, the printer of the book) with an 1830 title in each vol. and that mixed sets have appeared at auction from time to time (e.g. Lot 988 in the Esher Sale, Sotheby, May 21, 1946). It should be noted that the 1830 titles read: MEMOIRS OF A GENTLEMAN, and the 1832 titles: ADVENTURES OF A GENTLEMAN. Running heads read: MEMOIRS throughout.
One point which implies that the sheets were completed and ready for issue in 1830 and seems to dispose of the theory that Hunt was dilatory and had not finished his book in time, has not, to my knowledge, been noted. R_4 in Vol. II advertises as 'Just published' seven novels (among them works by Mrs Gore, G. P. R. James, Godwin, Galt and Gleig), all of which were actually published in the first six months of 1830; and as 'preparing for publication' a further seven novels, all of which appeared during the second half of the same year. It is highly improbable that so slick a publisher as Colburn would have compiled up-to-date copy for an advert. leaf to be included in a novel not yet fully delivered.

HURTON, WILLIAM

HEARTS OF OAK, or Naval Yarns (by the author of 'Vonved the Dane'). [1246]
Bentley 1862. Royal-blue coarse-morocco cloth, blocked in blind on front and back, pictorially blocked and fancy-lettered in gold on spine. Blank leaf and half-title precede title.
Pp. (viii) + 296 B
Note. This volume contains what must be the earliest English tribute to the novels of Herman Melville who, with Cooper and Dana, is studied in an essay called 'A Trio of American Sailor Authors'. Also included are a lengthy discussion of Marryat's novels, and three original stories. The material appeared originally in the *Dublin University Magazine*.

JAMES, G. P. R. (1799–1860)

Except in yellow-back form, the Collection makes no pretence of offering anything comprehensive in the way of James; but, by way of comment on the ephemeral fame of best-sellers, students may be asked to note the evidence of his astonishing contemporary popularity provided by the yellow-backs listed in Section II and the various novel series in Section III. Even Harpers in America were on him like a flash for their Select Novels, while Bentley's Standard Novels and, later, the Parlour Library, made tremendous play of the titles they offered. Routledge hastily swept up the unsecured crumbs and served them, slightly stale, as Railway fare.

James was not a good writer: but he was conscientious, suitable for home consumption and superbly prolific. He had his reward. May his kind (of whom there are one or two or three in every generation) profit by his example and make money while the uncritical sun of library subscribers' favour still shines.

S. M. Ellis' *The Solitary Horseman* (London, 1927) may be recommended to anyone curious about James. Ellis also did not write very well: but he was no less conscientious as a researcher, and had a sympathetic interest in vanished splendours. He makes of James a pathetic yet noteworthy figure—as indeed he was.

This much, however, can be said on behalf of the titles here described—that they include fine association copies of several of James' late novels which, because he lost ground toward the end of his life and was reduced to publishing with Newby, are much scarcer (and in any condition) than his earlier ones.

[1247] AGNES SOREL, an Historical Romance

3 vols. Newby 1853. Grass-green horizontal-fine-ribbed cloth, blocked in blind and spine-lettered (title and imprint only, no author) in gold.

Vol. I (iv) + (344) [paged (i)–iv + (5)–(344)]
II (ii) + 352
III (ii) + (344) Q_4 adverts.

Ink signature: 'Wellington 1853' on fly-leaf of each vol. Very fine.

This and the other presentation copies came from Strathfield Saye House, and belonged to the Second Duke, who succeeded to the main title in September 1852.

[1248] ARRAH NEIL, or Times of Old

3 vols. Smith, Elder 1845. Half-cloth boards, labels. Advert. leaf and half-title precede title in Vols. I and II, half-title only in III

Vol. I (vi) + 320
II (vi) + 332
III (iv) + (308)

Presentation Copy: 'Jan. 1846/Douro/the gift of the author' in ink, inside front cover of Vols. I and II.

[1249] BEAUCHAMP, or the Error

3 vols. Smith, Elder 1848. Half-cloth boards, labels.

Vol. I (ii) + (302) 1st leaf of final sig., U_1, a single inset. Publishers' cat., 16 pp. dated May 1848, at end.
II (ii) + (312)
III (ii) + 322 Final leaf, Y_1, a single inset.

Presentation Copy: "Douro/from the author/1851" in ink, inside front cover of each vol.

[1250] BERNARD MARSH: a Novel (by the late G. P. R. James)

2 vols. Bentley 1864. Smooth dark-chocolate cloth.

Vol. I (ii) + (302) First leaf of final sig., U_1, a single inset.
II (ii) + (286) First leaf of final sig., T_1, a single inset. **B**

CASTLE OF EHRENSTEIN (The); its Lords Spiritual and Temporal, its Inhabitants Earthly and Unearthly [1251]

3 vols. Smith, Elder 1847. Half-cloth boards, labels. Titles printed in red and black.

Half-title in each vol.

Vol. I (iv) + (304) Publishers' cat., 36 pp. dated January 1847, + single advert. leaf, at end.
II (iv) + (304) U_8 blank.
III (iv) + (308) X_2 adverts.

Note. The principal interest of this book is that, like *Russell* below, it lay in the publishers' warehouse for over ninety years from publication. The novels were transferred with the rest of the stock to John Murray when he bought Smith, Elder's business, and came to light by degrees between 1937 and 1942. They are in virtually new condition.

COMMISSIONER (The), or De Lunatico Inquirendo [anon] [1252]

8vo. Dublin: Wm. Curry Jun. & Co. 1843. Dark green fine-ribbed cloth, blocked in blind front and back, pictorially and decoratively blocked and lettered in gold on spine. Etched front. and 27 plates by Phiz.

8 pp. of Curry adverts. on cheap paper precede front. pp. (xvi) + 440

Ink inscription: 'With the Publishers' Compliments', on title. Slight fading on front cover, but a fine, sharp copy.

Notes. (i) The binding is signed at the base of front cover: 'J. MOWAT BINDER.'

(ii) There is in the collection a second copy of this book bound in scarlet diagonal-ribbed cloth, differently blind-blocked on front and back, but on spine uniformly gold-lettered and blocked with all-over scroll design and vignette. This binding is unsigned.

CONVICT (The): a Tale [1253]

3 vols. Smith, Elder 1847. Half-cloth boards, labels.

Half-title in Vols. II and III

Vol. I iv + 326. 1st leaf of final sig., Y_1, a single inset. Publishers' cat., 36 pp. dated—on fly-title June 1847, on first page October 1847—at end.
II (iv) + (304) U_8 blank.
III (iv) + (292)

Presentation Copy: 'Douro/from the author/1851' in ink, inside front cover of each vol.

[1254] FATE (The): a Tale of Stirring Times
3 vols. Newby 1851. Ink-blue perpendicular-fine-ribbed cloth, blocked in blind and spine-lettered (title and imprint only, no author) in gold.

Advert. leaf precedes title in Vol. I and two advert. leaves in Vol. III

Vol. I (iv)+(300)
II (ii)+(304)
III (vi)+(326) Title and final leaf, Q_1, single insets.

Presentation Copy: 'Douro/from the author 1852' in ink, inside front cover of each vol.

[1255] LEONORA D'ORCO: a Historical Romance
3 vols. Newby 1857. Rose-pink horizontal-fine-ribbed cloth, elaborately blocked in blind on front and back, all-over gold-blocked and lettered (title and imprint only, no author) on spine.

Advert. leaf precedes title in each vol.

Vol. I 276
II 284
III 312

From the Library at Strathfield Saye, but unsigned. Very fine.

Note. The binding of this novel is exceptionally elegant and, for Newby, barely credible. Was it a special style devised by James, for both *Ticonderoga* and *Vicissitudes of a Life* (see below) are uniform in design?

[1256] RUSSELL: a Tale of the Reign of Charles II
3 vols. Smith, Elder 1847. Half-cloth boards, labels.

Half-title in each vol.

Vol. I (iv)+(312) X_4 blank.
II (iv)+(308)
III (iv)+316

See Note to *The Castle of Ehrenstein.*

[1257] TICONDEROGA, or the Black Eagle. A Tale of Times Not Long Past
3 vols. Newby 1854. Claret morocco cloth, blocked and lettered uniform with *Leonora d'Orco*, but only spine-lettering in gold.

Advert. leaf precedes title in Vols. II and III

Vol. I (iv)+(312)
II (iv)+(300) O_6 adverts.
III (iv)+(324)

Ink signature: 'June 1854/The Duke of Wellington' on fly-leaf of each vol. Very fine.

[1258] VICISSITUDES OF A LIFE (The): a Novel
3 vols. Newby 1853. Dark-blue diagonal-wavy-grain cloth, blocked and lettered uniform with *Ticonderoga.*

Half-title in each vol.

Vol. I (iv)+(274) N_4 N_5 adverts; N_1, a single inset. Publisher's cat., 16 pp. undated, at end.
II (iv)+(288) N_{11} N_{12} adverts.
III (iv)+(288)

Ink signature: 'Wellington/July 17, 1853' on title of Vol. I and half-title of II and III. Very fine.

WOODMAN (The): a Romance of the Times of Richard III [1259]
3 vols. Newby 1849. Dark grey-purple fine-ripple-grain cloth, blocked in blind and spine-lettered (title and imprint only, no author) in gold.

Vol. I (ii)+(356)
II (ii)+(342) 1st leaf of final sig., Q_1, a single inset.
III (ii)+(358) 1st leaf of final sig., Q_1, a single inset. Q_{11} adverts.

Presentation Copy: 'Douro/from the author/1851' in ink, inside front cover of each vol.

JAMES, HENRY (1843–1916)

This (*The Ivory Tower* apart) is a complete collection of the fiction of Henry James published earlier in England than in America, together with such American first editions as I have been able to obtain in fine state, and a few 'first English editions'. Facts as to priorities I owe to I. R. Brussel's *Anglo-American First Editions, West to East* (London, 1936).

AMBASSADORS (The) [1260]
Methuen 1903. Scarlet ribbed cloth.

Half-title. pp. (iv)+(460) $2G_6$ imprint leaf. Publishers' cat., 40 pp. dated July 1903, at end. Last leaf of cat. blank. Fine.

AMERICAN (The) (first Macmillan edition) [1261]
Macmillan 1879. Dark blue fine-bead-grain cloth, ornamentally banded across front and spine in black and gold; gold-lettered on spine; blind-banded on back. Chocolate end-papers. (This binding style is hereafter referred to as '*American* Style'. It was used by Macmillan with slight variations for a few other authors—e.g. Shorthouse—as well as for James' one-vol. editions.)

Half-title. pp. (352) Y_8 adverts.

Book-plate: 'L. M. V. de W.' Fine.

ASPERN PAPERS (The) · LOUISA PALLANT · THE MODERN WARNING [1262]
2 vols. Macmillan 1888. Smooth steel-blue cloth, banded in gold; black end-papers.

Half-title in each vol., that in Vol. I preceded by a blank leaf

Vol. I (viii)+(240)
II (viii)+(264) S_{2-4} adverts.

'With the Publishers' Compliments' stamped in blue on title of Vol. I. Very fine.

[1263] AWKWARD AGE (The)
Heinemann 1899. Cambridge-blue diagonal-fine-ribbed cloth, blocked in blind on front with design of four conventional pansies. Title-page printed in red and black.

Blank leaf and half-title precede title. pp. (viii) [paged vi] + (416) $2C_8$ adverts. Publisher's cat., 32 pp. undated, on thin paper, at end.

Spine somewhat darkened.

Notes. (i) I have seen two variants of the catalogue at the end of this vol. The earlier in date is certainly that of which the last page is occupied with a list, without 'quotes', of 'The Latest Fiction'. In the other catalogue seven of the novels given in this list are included with quotations from reviews, which demonstrates that between the issue of the first and second catalogues these books had been published and criticised.

(ii) Secondary issues of this book, and also of *Embarrassments*, *The Spoils of Poynton*, *The Two Magics* and *What Maisie Knew*, have a design of *tulips* blind-blocked on front cover and gilt lettering of somewhat cheaper-looking appearance. Tertiary issues of these books, and of *Terminations*, also with the tulip blocking, consist of colonial sheets, on thin smooth paper: title is printed in black only and half-title cancelled.

[1264] BETTER SORT (The)
Methuen 1903. Red ribbed cloth.

Blank leaf and half-title precede title. pp. (viii) + 312 Publishers' cat., 40 pp. dated February 1903, at end.

[1265] BOSTONIANS (The): a Novel
Copy I: First Edition. 3 vols. Macmillan 1886. Dark blue-green fine-bead-grain cloth; chocolate end-papers.

Half-title in each vol.

Vol. I (iv) + 244
II (iv) + (228) Q_2 adverts.
III (iv) + (236) Q_5 Q_6 adverts.

Very fine.

[1265*a*] **Copy II: First one-vol. Edition.** Macmillan 1886. Dark blue fine-bead-grain cloth, *American* style.

[1266] CONFIDENCE
2 vols. Chatto & Windus 1880. Smooth olive-brown cloth, blocked in black and lettered in gold. Blue-on-white floral end-papers.

Half-title in each vol.

Vol. I (iv) + (312) X_4 publishers' device.
II (iv) + (256) R_8 publishers' device. Publishers' cat., 32 pp. dated December 1879, at end.

Book-plate: 'L. M. V. de W.', in each vol. Fine.

DAISY MILLER: a Study [1267]
32mo. New York: Harper & Brothers 1878. Dark olive-green diagonal-fine-ribbed cloth, blocked and lettered in red and black in the Series Style of Harper's Half-Hour Series, of which this is No. 82. Drab end-papers.

Four pp., advertising the Series to No. 120 precede title. pp. (128) 8_3–8_8 adverts.

Note. Series-advert. shows this is not a first issue.

DAISY MILLER: a Study · AN INTERNATIONAL EPISODE · FOUR MEETINGS [1268]
2 vols. Macmillan 1879. Bright blue sand-grain cloth; chocolate end-papers.

Half-title in each vol.

Vol. I (viii) + (272)
II (viii) + (264) Publishers' cat., 40 pp. dated November 1878, at end.

Book-plate: 'L. M. V. de W.', in each vol. Fine.

EMBARRASSMENTS · THE FIGURE IN THE CARPET · GLASSES · THE NEXT TIME · THE WAY IT CAME (first English edition) [1269]
Heinemann 1896. Cambridge-blue diagonal-fine-ribbed cloth. Title printed in red and black.

Half-title. pp. (viii) + (264) Publisher's cat., 32 pp. undated, at end.

Notes. (i) This edition post-dated the American by two days.
(ii) The title (black only) of the secondary issue does not carry the names of the four stories.

ESSAYS IN LONDON and Elsewhere [1270]
Osgood, McIlvaine 1893. Pale salmon ribbed cloth.

Half-title. pp. (viii) + 320

Book-plate of Sir Julius Wernher, Bart. Very fine.

Note. Included for the sake of *An Animated Conversation* which may fairly claim to rank as fiction.

EUROPEANS (The): a Sketch [1271]
Copy I: First Edition. 2 vols. Macmillan 1878. Bright blue sand-grain cloth; chocolate end-papers.

Half-title in each vol.

Vol. I (iv) + (256) Publishers' cat., 40 pp. dated June 1878, at end.
II (iv) + 272

Spines slightly darkened and that of Vol. I a little worn.

Copy II: First one-vol. Edition. Macmillan 1879. [1271*a*]
Dark blue fine-bead-grain cloth, *American* style.
Book-plate: 'L. M. V. de W.' Fine.

[1272] FINER GRAIN (The)
Methuen 1910. Smooth pinkish-brown linen-grain cloth, gold decorative blocking on spine.
Blank leaf signed 'a' precedes half-title. pp. (viii) + (308) Publishers' cat., 32 pp. dated September 1910, at end.
Very fine.

[1273] GOLDEN BOWL (The)
2 vols. New York: Scribner 1904. Smooth silky pinkish-biscuit cloth.
Half-title in each vol.
Vol. I (iv) + 412
II (iv) + (380) 24_6 blank.
Fine.

[1274] INTERNATIONAL EPISODE (An)
32mo. New York: Harper 1879. Buff paper wrappers, cut flush, printed in red and black in the Standard style of Harper's Half Hour Series, of which this is No. 91.
pp. (144) A_1 A_2 adverts. preceding title; I_5–I_8 adverts. at end. Fine.

[1275] IN THE CAGE
Duckworth 1898. Buff canvas, blocked and lettered in black.
Half-title. pp. (iv) + (204) M_7 M_8 and N_1–N_6 adverts. Fine.

[1276] LESSON OF THE MASTER (The) · THE MARRIAGES · THE PUPIL BROOKSMITH · THE SOLUTION · SIR EDMUND ORME (first English edition)
Macmillan 1892. Blue diaper cloth, blocked in gold; green end-papers.
Blank leaf precedes half-title. pp. (viii) + (304) T_8 blank. Publishers' cat., 44 pp. dated December 1891, at end. Fine.
Note. This edition, consisting of American sheets, post-dated the American by two months.

[1277] LONDON LIFE (A) · THE PATAGONIA · THE LIAR · MRS TEMPERLY
2 vols. Macmillan 1889. Smooth steel-blue cloth, banded in gold; black end-papers.
Half-title in each vol., that in Vol. II preceded by a blank leaf
Vol. I (viii) + (284) T_6 adverts.
II (viii) + (364) $2A_6$ adverts.

[1278] MADONNA OF THE FUTURE (The) and Other Tales
2 vols. Macmillan 1879. Steel-blue fine-bead-grain cloth; chocolate end-papers.
Half-title in each vol.
Vol. I (viii) + 288
II (viii) + (248) R_4 adverts.
Book-plate: 'L. M. V. de W.', in each vol. Fine.
Contents. The Madonna of the Future—Longstaff's Marriage—Madame de Mauves—Eugene Pickering—The Diary of a Man of Fifty—Benvolio.

OUTCRY (The) [1279]
Methuen 1911. Green linen-grain cloth, gold decorative blocking on spine.
Half-title. pp. (iv) + (312) Publishers' cat., 32 pp. dated August 1911, at end.
'(Name erased). October 1911, Caversfield' in ink on inside cover. Fine.

PASSIONATE PILGRIM (A), and other Tales (by Henry James, Jr.) [1280]
Boston: James R. Osgood & Company 1875. Grass-green sand-grain cloth, blocked with double blind frame on front and back, blocked and lettered in gold on spine. Bevelled boards. Red-chocolate end-papers.
Inset blank leaf of slightly thinner paper precedes title and follows final page of text. pp. 496
Contents: A Passionate Pilgrim—The Last of the Valerii—Eugene Pickering—The Madonna of the Future—The Romance of Certain Old Clothes—Madame de Mauves.

PORTRAIT OF A LADY [1281]
3 vols. Macmillan 1881. Dark blue-green fine-bead-grain cloth; dark chocolate end-papers.
Half-title in each vol.
Vol. I (iv) + (268) S_6 blank.
II (iv) + (256) R_8 blank.
III (iv) + 248 Publishers' cat., 24 pp. dated April 1881, at end.
Book-plate: 'L. M. V. de W.', in each vol. Very fine.

PRINCESS CASAMASSIMA (The): a Novel [1282]
Copy I: First Edition. 3 vols. Macmillan 1886. Dark blue-green fine-bead-grain cloth; chocolate end-papers.
Half-title in each vol.
Vol. I (iv) + 252
II (iv) + (260) S_2 adverts.
III (iv) + (244) R_2 adverts.
Very fine.
Copy II: First one-vol. Edition. Macmillan 1887. Dark blue fine-bead-grain cloth, *American* style. [1282*a*]
Ink-signature: 'L. M. Aug. 1887', on fly-leaf.

PRIVATE LIFE (The) · THE WHEEL OF TIME · LORD BEAUPRE · THE VISITS · COLLABORATION · OWEN WINGRAVE [1283]
Osgood McIlvaine 1893. Grey-blue ribbed cloth, blocked and lettered in gold.
Blank leaf and half-title precede title. pp. (viii) + (332)
Note. These stories were issued some months later in America in two volumes.

[1284] **REAL THING** (The) and Other Tales (first English edition)

Macmillan 1893. Blue diaper cloth, blocked in gold; dark green end-papers.

Half-title. pp. (x)+(278) Last leaf blank. The signatures are not registered. Publishers' cat., 48 pp. dated January 1893, at end.

Signature 'L. M. V. de W.' in pencil on half-title. Fine.

Contents. The Real Thing—Sir Dominick Ferrand—Nona Vincent—The Chaperon—Greville Fane.

Note. This edition, consisting of American sheets, post-dated the American by three months.

[1285] **REVERBERATOR** (The)

2 vols. Macmillan 1888. Smooth steel-blue cloth, banded in gold; black end-papers.

Half-title in each vol.

Vol. I (iv)+(192) N_8 advert.
II (iv)+(208)

Very fine.

[1286] **RODERICK HUDSON**

Copy I: First Edition. Boston: James R. Osgood & Co. 1876. Green patterned-sand-grain cloth, bevelled boards; chocolate end-papers.

Blank leaf precedes title. pp. (vi)+(486) 31_2 31_3 blank. Prelims. and final sig., 31, probably printed together. pp. (i) (ii) and (485) (486) form single insets.

Book-label of Hugh Walpole. Very fine.

Note. Also issued in bright brown fine-bead-grain cloth, and possibly other colours also.

Copy II: Second English and First one-vol. Edition. Macmillan 1880. Dark blue fine-bead-grain cloth, *American* style.

Book-plate: 'L. M. V. de W.' Fine.

[1287] **SACRED FOUNT** (The)

New York: Scribner 1901. Smooth silky biscuit cloth, blocked and lettered in gold.

Half-title. pp. (vi)+(320) pp. (v) (vi) form fly-title and a single inset. Fine.

Note. A signed presentation inscription dated March 4 1901 appears in a copy reported, which lacks pp. (v) (vi). Possibly the earliest copies did not contain the fly-title.

[1288] **SENSE OF THE PAST** (The)

Collins 1917. Smooth dark blue cloth. Photogravure portrait front.

Half-title. pp. (viii)+(352) As new, with dust jacket.

SPOILS OF POYNTON (The) [1289]

Heinemann 1897. Cambridge-blue diagonal-fine-ribbed cloth, blocked in blind on front uniform with *Awkward Age*, etc. Title printed in red and black.

Half-title. pp. (iv)+(288) T_8 adverts. Publisher's cat., 32 pp. undated, at end.

Presentation Copy: 'Edmund Gosse from Henry James' in ink on half-title. Book-plate of Edmund Gosse. Letter from James inserted.

STORIES REVIVED [1290]

Copy I: First Edition. 3 vols. Macmillan 1885.

Vol. I THE AUTHOR OF 'BELTRAFFIO' · PANDORA · THE PATH OF DUTY · A DAY OF DAYS · A LIGHT MAN

II GEORGINA'S REASONS · A PASSIONATE PILGRIM · A LANDSCAPE PAINTER · ROSE-AGATHE

III POOR RICHARD · THE LAST OF THE VALERII · MASTER EUSTACE · THE ROMANCE OF CERTAIN OLD CLOTHES · A MOST EXTRAORDINARY CASE

Dark blue-green fine-bead-grain cloth; chocolate end-papers.

Half-title in each vol., that in Vol. II and in Vol. III preceded by a blank leaf

Vol. I (viii)+280
II (viii)+280
III (viii)+(272) S_8 adverts.

Very fine.

Copy II: 'First Series.' First one-vol. Edition. [1290*a*]
Macmillan 1885. Dark blue fine-bead-grain cloth, *American* style. Containing the 5 stories in Vol. I and from Vol. II the 1st story and the 3rd.

Ink signature: 'L. M. Bombay. Feb. 1887', on fly-leaf.

TALES OF THREE CITIES (first English edition) [1291]

Macmillan 1884. Smooth dark green cloth.

Blank leaf precedes half-title. pp. (viii)+(312) X_4 adverts.

Book-plate: 'L. M. V. de W.'

Contents. Lady Barberina—A New England Winter—The Impressions of a Cousin.

Note. This edition was later than the American by two or three weeks.

A secondary binding was carried out to the order of Messrs Bickers many years later, in similar cloth and colour, but of cheaper quality. Spine lettering squatter and more heavily seriffed. Initial of 'James' a drop-cap. Cf. P. H. Muir, *Points* 1874–1930 (London 1931). Similar variations between the original and later 'bindings-up' exist also on *French Poets and Novelists* and *Partial Portraits.*

[1292] TERMINATIONS · THE DEATH OF THE LION · THE COXON FUND · THE MIDDLE YEARS · THE ALTAR OF THE DEAD

Heinemann 1895. Cambridge-blue diagonal-fine-ribbed cloth.

pp. (x) + 260 [Pp. (i) (ii) pasted to inside front cover, (iii) (iv) blank.]

Note. This is the tertiary issue (see Note (ii) to *Awkward Age*). The title (black only) does *not* carry the names of the four stories.

[1293] TRAGIC MUSE (The)

Copy I: First Edition. 3 vols. Macmillan 1890. Blue diaper cloth; black end-papers.

Half-title in each vol.

Vol. I (iv) + 248
II (iv) + 252
III (iv) + (260) S_2 blank.

Fine.

The lettering on covers is of the angular long-tailed kind, used on several of Marion Crawford's novels.

[1293*a*] **Copy II: First one-vol. Edition.** Macmillan 1891. Scarlet diaper-cloth.

[1294] TWO MAGICS (The) · THE TURN OF THE SCREW · COVERING END

New York: Macmillan 1898. Smooth crimson linen-grain cloth.

Half-title. pp. (iv) + (396) $2C_6$ adverts. Fine.

[1295] WASHINGTON SQUARE

Copy I: First Edition. New York: Harper 1881. Dull olive-green diagonal-fine-ribbed cloth, pictorially and decoratively blocked in brown and gold; liver-brown end-papers. Wood-engraved front. and 5 full-page illustrations on text paper (tissued and reckoned in collation), also vignettes in the text, all after du Maurier.

pp. (272) 17_6–17_8 adverts., paged (1)–6. Extra end-papers (blank) inset at front and back.

[1295*a*] **Copy II: English Edition and First Edition of** THE PENSION BEAUREPAS **and** A BUNDLE OF LETTERS. 2 vols. Macmillan 1881. Dark blue-green fine-bead-grain cloth; chocolate end-papers.

Half-title in each vol.

Vol. I (viii) + (268) Final sigs., S four leaves, T two leaves, T_2 blank.
II (iv) + (272) [mispaged (372)] Publishers' cat., 40 pp. dated December 1879, at end.

Book-plate of 'L. M. V. de W.' in each vol. Very fine.

This copy is of the First Issue, i.e. in Vol. II, pp. 268–271 are misfoliated 368–371.

Note. There is a second copy in the Collection, identical as to text and catalogue but showing slight external differences from that above described. The binding is not quite $7\frac{3}{4}''$ tall, as opposed to $7\frac{13}{16}$, although sheet measurements are identical. On spine, the imprint is only $\frac{1}{8}''$ above the black band at foot, as opposed to $\frac{3}{16}''$, and MACMILLAN is in caps. slightly less condensed. Seeing that the taller copy has the book-plate of L.M.V. de W. (whose James' titles seem to have been bought on publication and are of uniform size), I incline to regard the shorter copy as belonging to a later binding-up. It is in new condition.

WATCH AND WARD [1296]

Square 12mo. Boston: Houghton, Osgood 1878. Bright green diagonal-fine-ribbed cloth, blocked in blind and gold, red edges; liver-brown end-papers.

pp. (224) [paged (222)] First and last leaves blank.

Very fine. The signatures of this book are not registered. Copies frequently occur in brown cloth.

WHAT MAISIE KNEW [1297]

Heinemann 1898. Cambridge-blue diagonal-fine-ribbed cloth, blocked in front in blind uniform with *Awkward Age.* Title printed in red and black.

Half-title. pp. (iv) + 304 Publisher's cat., 32 pp. undated, at end.

Presentation Copy: 'Edmund Gosse from Henry James. Sept. 24 1897' in ink on fly-leaf: book-plate of Edmund Gosse. Letter from James inserted. Fine.

WINGS OF A DOVE (The) [1298]

Copy I: First Edition. 2 vols. New York: Scribner 1902. Smooth silky biscuit cloth.

Blank leaf precedes half-title in each vol.

Vol. I (vi) + (332) 21_6 blank.
II (vi) + (444) 28_5 28_6 blank.

Fine.

Copy II: First English Edition. Constable 1902. Blue ribbed cloth. [1298*a*]

Half-title. pp. (iv) + 576

Presentation Copy: 'To Violet Hunt, her faithful old friend Henry James. April 3d 1903' in ink on fly-leaf. Fine.

JARNAC, COMTE DE

DARK AND FAIR ('by Sir Charles Rockingham, author of 'Rockingham', 'Electra', etc.') [1299]

3 vols. Hurst & Blackett 1857. Dark green morocco cloth.

Vol. I (ii) + 328
II (ii) + 320
III (ii) + 302 First leaf of final sig., U_1, a single inset.

Book-plate and labels of the Llanover Library in each vol.

[1300] ELECTRA: a Story of Modern Times (by the author of 'Rockingham')
3 vols. Hurst & Blackett 1853. Light blue wavy-grain cloth. Engraved front. and one plate in each vol. after drawings by Lord Edward Fitzgerald.
Vol. I (iv) + 320 Publishers' cat., 16 pp. undated, at end.
II (ii) + 348
III (ii) + 356
Ink signature: 'John Fairbairn 1855', on title in each vol. Some signatures loose in Vol. III.

[1301] ROCKINGHAM, or the Younger Brother [anon]
3 vols. Colburn 1849. Half-cloth boards, labels.
Half-title in Vol. I
Vol. I (xii) + (296) O_3 O_4 adverts.
II (ii) + (312)
III (ii) + (310) First leaf of final sig., O_1, a single inset.
Ink signature: 'Lady Georgiana Codrington' and (in her writing) 'by Le Comte de Jarnac' in violet ink on each title. Bookseller's blind stamp: 'John Ollivier, Pall Mall' on fly-leaf of each vol. Boards damp-stained at foot.

JEFFERIES, RICHARD (1848–1887)

To divide the works of Jefferies into fiction and non-fiction is not easy. For example, there are several books which are certainly not novels or stories yet can be, *pace C.B.E.L.*, justifiably classified as semi-fiction. I have, therefore, included in the list which follows all the titles in the Collection except those which are Nature Essays pure and simple, and two specialist pamphlets.

[1302] AFTER LONDON, or Wild England
Cassell 1885. Ochre diagonal-fine-ribbed cloth; pinkish-brown-on-white floral end-papers; bevelled boards.
Half-title. pp. (viii) + (444) CC_6 adverts. Publishers' cat., 8 pp. dated '4. 85', at end.
Ink signature: 'J. S. Chapman. August 1885', on reverse of fly-leaf. Fine.

[1303] AMARYLLIS AT THE FAIR: a Novel
Sampson Low, Marston, Searle & Rivington 1887. Smooth dark green cloth, blocked in black, yellow and gold; bevelled boards.
Blank leaf signed 'A' precedes half-title. pp. (viii) + 260
'Reine, August 1899' in ink on fly-leaf. Very fine.

[1304] AMATEUR POACHER (The) (by the author of 'The Gamekeeper at Home' and 'Wild Life in a Southern County')
Smith, Elder 1879. Dark brown fine-pebble-grain cloth, blocked in black and gold. Black end-papers.
Half-title. pp. (viii) + 240
The Preface is signed 'R.J.'

BEVIS: the Story of a Boy [1305]
3 vols. Sampson Low, Marston, Searle & Rivington 1882.
Copy I. Brown diagonal-fine-ribbed cloth, blocked in black and gold; pale yellow end-papers.
Half-title in Vol. I only
Vol. I viii + (288)
II iv + (296) U_4 imprint leaf.
III iv + (296) U_4 imprint leaf.
Publishers' cat., 32 pp. dated December 1881, at end.
Presentation Copy: 'Ellen Harrild from the author. July 1882' in ink facing title of Vol. I and 'E. H. from R. J. Jefferies' in pencil on title of Vol. III. Very fine.
Imprint on spine: LONDON/SAMPSON LOW & CO. Publishers' name in tall condensed caps.

Copy II. Cloth, blocking, end-papers and collation as Copy I, except that there is no cat. at end of Vol. III. [1305*a*]
'To J. A. Jingo from H. C. F. Christmas 1887' etc. in ink on fly-leaf of Vol. I. Fine.
Imprint on spines worded as I, but publishers' name in squat caps.

Copy III. Green diagonal-fine-ribbed cloth, blocked in black and gold; blue-grey patterned end-papers. Collation as Copy II. [1305*b*]
Book-plate of Waldo Leon Rich in each vol. Blind stamp of W. H. Smith Library on fly-leaf of Vol. I. Fine.
Imprint on spines: S. LOW, MARSTON & CO./ LONDON.
In *Binding Variants* (p. 122) Carter gives priority to the brown cloth of Copies I and II.

DEWY MORN (The): a Novel [1306]
2 vols. Bentley 1884. Green pebble-grain cloth, silver-grey-on-white patterned end-papers.
Vol. I (ii) + 296
II (ii) + (328) B

GAMEKEEPER AT HOME (The): Sketches of Natural History and Rural Life [anon] [1307]
Copy I: First Edition. Smith, Elder 1878. Dark green diagonal-fine-ribbed cloth, blocked in black and gold. Chocolate end-papers.
Half-title. pp. (viii) + 216
Front cover slightly marked, but a sharp, bright copy.
The Preface is signed 'R.J.'

[1307a] **Copy II: First Illustrated Edition** [also anon]. Sq. extra cr. 8vo. Smith, Elder 1880. Smooth dark olive-green cloth, pictorially and decoratively blocked in black and gold on front and spine, blocked in black on back. Bevelled boards. Green-on-white patterned end-papers. Wood-engraved front. and 41 illustrations in text after Charles Whymper, all on text paper.

Half-title. pp. xii + (220)

Book-plate: William Crampton. Booksellers' ticket: 'Matthews & Brooke, Bradford & Leeds' inside front cover. Fine.

[1308] GREEN FERNE FARM
Smith, Elder 1880. Olive-green linen-grain cloth, blocked and lettered in black and gold.

Half-title. pp. viii + (296) U_2–U_4 adverts.

Ink signature: 'E. (?) Rogers' inside front cover. Fine.

[1309] HODGE AND HIS MASTERS
2 vols. Smith, Elder 1880. Dark brown fine-pebble-grain cloth, blocked in black and gold; black end-papers.

Blank leaf precedes half-title in each vol.

Vol. I (xii) + (360)
II (viii) + (316) Y_1 Y_2 adverts.

Very fine.

Note. This is one of the few two-or-three volume books, of which the front cover blocking is not uniform. The vignette, blocked in gold, shows quite a different scene on each of the two volumes. Another example is Nansen's *Farthest North.*

[1310] JACK BRASS: Emperor of England
8vo. T. Pettitt & Co. 23 Frith Street, Soho 1873. Drab paper wrappers, printed in black on front, spine unlettered, elsewhere blank.

pp. 12

Book-plate of Oliver Brett (Lord Esher).

Note. This letter to an imaginary multi-millionaire is included by *C.B.E.L.* among Jefferies' fiction.

[1311] RED DEER
Longmans 1884. Smooth grey-green cloth, blocked in red-brown. Grey-chocolate end-papers.

pp. (iv) + (208)

Book-plate: Randolph Behrens. Binders' ticket: 'Simpson and Renshaw', at end. Fine.

[1312] RESTLESS HUMAN HEARTS: a Novel
3 vols. Tinsley 1875. Scarlet diagonal-fine-ribbed cloth, blocked in black and gold.

Half-title in each vol.

Vol. I (iv) + (314) Final leaf, X_5, a single inset.
II (iv) + (300)
III (iv) + 296

Ink inscription: 'Jefferies. Coate', on fly-leaf of each vol. (the copy came from a family source). Very fine.

Note. There is a secondary binding of green sand-grain cloth, blind-blocked on front and gold-lettered from type (without imprint) on spine.

ROUND ABOUT A GREAT ESTATE [1313]
Smith, Elder 1880. Royal-blue diagonal-fine-ribbed cloth, blocked on front in gold with drawing of leaf signed 'RJ' (drawing repeated on title-page) and in black with decorative bands; spine lettered in gold and blocked in black. Dark green end-papers.

Blank leaf and half-title precede title. pp. (xii) [paged (x)] + (208) O_7 O_8 adverts.

Book-plate of Herbert Massey. Very fine.

Note. I have seen an identical copy with dark *brown* end-papers.

SCARLET SHAWL (The): a Novel [1314]
Tinsley 1874. Red sand-grain cloth.

Advert. leaf precedes half-title. pp. (viii) + (312) 20_4 adverts.

Ink-signature: 'N. Dickinson, 1877' on half-title; blind stamp 'W. H. Smith & Son' on fly-leaf. Fine.

This copy has First Issue binding and error in Dedication to Ellen Harrild. (For my notes on the three bindings cf. Carter, *More Binding Variants*, p. 12.)

STORY OF MY HEART (The): my Autobiography [1315]
Longman, etc. 1883. Smooth sage-green cloth, blocked in black and gold; grey end-papers.

Half-title. pp. (iv) + 188 Publishers' cat., 12 pp. dated April 1883, at end. Very fine.

Note. The Second Edition of this book appeared in 1891 with an etched portrait-frontispiece by William Strang and a preface by C. J. Longman, who tells the publishing history of *The Story of My Heart* and quotes, not only Jefferies' letters to his publisher, but also the 'blurb' which, at Longman's request, he wrote for publicity use. This blurb, being about a thousand words long, was possibly an embarrassment to the advertising manager, but to posterity it is a document of considerable interest. The Second Edition was issued in smooth dark-red cloth, lettered in silver.

[1316] SUEZ-CIDE!! or How Miss Britannia bought a dirty Puddle and lost her Sugar-Plums

John Snow & Co. 2 Ivy Lane, Paternoster Row 1876. Magenta paper wrappers, printed in black on front, spine unlettered, elsewhere blank.

pp. 20

Book-plate of Lord Esher. Fine.

Note. This political squib has at least as good a claim as *Jack Brass* to rank as fiction, for it is cast in ordinary conversational form, and Miss Britannia, Cousin Ben, Fritz and the Bull family are presented as characters in a tale.

[1317] WOOD MAGIC: a Fable

Extra cr. 8vo. 2 vols. Cassell, Petter & Galpin 1881. Dark green diagonal-fine-ribbed cloth, blocked in black and lettered in gold. Dark grey end-papers.

Half-title in each vol.

Vol. I (viii)+(236) Publishers' cat., 8 pp. on text paper dated '5. 81' and paged 1–8, at end.

II (vi)+(264) Publishers' cat., as in Vol. I, at end.

[1318] WORLD'S END: a Story in Three Books

3 vols. Tinsley 1877. Dove-grey diagonal-fine-ribbed cloth, blocked in black and gold.

Half-title in each vol.

Vol. I (iv)+(252) 16_6 adverts.

II (iv)+278 First leaf of final sig., 18_1, a single inset.

III (iv)+(290) Final leaf, 19_1, a single inset.

Presentation Copy: 'E. Jefferies. With the Author's love. July 5. 1877' in ink on half-title. Very fine.

Partly by Jefferies

[1319] SOCIETY NOVELETTES

2 vols. 8vo. Vizetelly 1883. Smooth violet cloth; dark green end-papers. Wood-engraved front. and numerous illustrations.

Half-title in each vol.

Vol. I (vi)+(336) Containing 'Kiss and Try' by R. J.

II (vi)+(340) Z_2 advert. Containing 'Out of the Season' by R. J.

Note. In 1886 Vol. I of this work was re-issued with a cancel title as NO ROSE WITHOUT A THORN AND OTHER TALES, in royal-blue cloth, patterned end-papers.

JENKINS, JOHN EDWARD (1838–1910)

DEVIL'S CHAIN (The) [1320]

Strahan 1876. Red-brown diagonal-fine-ribbed cloth, elaborately blocked and lettered in black and gold on front and spine, triple blind-framing on back. Cafe-au-lait end-papers.

Half-title. pp. (xii)+276

Very fine.

Note. This lurid story of the evils of alcoholism is dedicated to Sir Wilfred Lawson. In his Dedicatory Letter the author says: 'I do not attempt to describe the purge. My aim is here—as it was in "Ginx's Baby"—rather to exhibit in rude, stern, truthful outlines the full features and proportions of the abuses I would humbly help to remove.'

GINX'S BABY: His Birth and other Misfortunes [1321]
[anon]

Strahan & Co. 1870. Bright blue sand-grain cloth, blocked in black and lettered in gold on front and spine, with single blind frame on back. Red-chocolate end-papers.

Half-title. pp. (viii)+224 Publishers' cat., 8 pp. on text paper undated, at end. Binder's ticket: 'Burn', at end.

Fine.

Note. This rare book is a social document of great importance. It is an unshrinking exposure of life in the slums of Westminster, the miseries of the slum child, and the hypocrisy and heartlessness of so-called 'charitable' folk, of clergy, of parish authorities and Boards of Guardians, of politicians and comfortable reformers. It provoked great excitement and violent controversy, and was reprinted again and again. The author's name was avowed on the 6th edition (1871) and in 1876 appeared the 36th Edition with illustrations by Fred Barnard.

Jenkins followed *Ginx's Baby* with other outspoken novels on contentious social themes (alcoholism, the plight of the agricultural labourer, the sins of Society) but so far I have only succeeded in finding two of them in suitable condition.

LORD BANTAM (by the author of 'Ginx's Baby') [1322]

2 vols. Strahan 1872. Brown morocco cloth, diagonally ruled in black and gold-lettered on front and spine; greenish-black end-papers.

Blank leaf and half-title in Vol. I, half-title only in Vol. II

Vol. I (viii) [p. (viii) mispaged iii]+(ii)+(204) The leaf following prelims. is a List of Errata, tipped in and on different paper.

II vi+230 Final leaf, R_1, a single inset.

Ink signature: 'J. Harry Pakington, Kings End Worcester. Jan. '72', on half-title of Vol. I. Fine.

JENNINGS, HARGRAVE (*circ.* 1817–1890)

[1323] MY MARINE MEMORANDUM BOOK
3 vols. Newby 1845. Deep-sea-blue fine-diaper cloth.

Vol. I (viii) [paged (vi)] + (320)
II (iv) + 304 pp. (iii) (iv) 'Dedication' of the whole work.
III (iv) + 300 (iii) (iv) fly-title '*Felicia Wayland*'.

Binder's stamp: 'Marrow, Cecil St. Strand', on inside front cover of each vol. Fine.

Note. A hotch-potch of a book. Vol. I consists of nineteen chapters of a single narrative—in fact, the story *Felicia Wayland or the Cuba Merchantman,* whose fly-title is conjugate with the title-page of Vol. III. Vols. II and III contain a series of stories and sketches about sailormen and life at sea. There is no Contents List, and the running headlines throughout repeat the book's overall title.

[1324] SHIP OF GLASS (The), or the Mysterious Island. A Romance
3 vols. Newby 1846. Grey-blue diagonal-fine-ribbed cloth.

Half-title in Vol. III

Vol. I (iv) [paged ii] + 306 First leaf of final sig., P_1, a single inset.
II (iv) + 296
III (iv) + (296) O_4 blank.

Author's signature: 'Hargrave Jennings. 1st November 1846', in ink on fly-leaf of Vol. II. Ink signature: 'Eliza Anne Boyle. Sept^{ber} 3rd. 1846', on fly-leaf of Vol. I. Binder's stamp: 'Marrow 3 Cecil Street, Strand', inside front cover of each vol.

Note. Another example (reminiscent of *Wuthering Heights*) of Newby's queer methods of book-making. These three vols. contain two wholly separate stories, both by Jennings. *The Ship of Glass* ends on p. 65 of Vol. II; p. (67) is fly-title for *Atcherley,* which runs to the end of Vol. III. The half-title in Vol. III reads: ATCHERLEY / *rule* / VOL. III.

JENNINGS, LOUIS J. (1836–1893)

[1325] MILLIONAIRE (The) [anon]
3 vols. Blackwood 1883. Yellow-ochre diagonal-fine-ribbed cloth, blocked and lettered in black on front, black-blocked and gold-lettered on spine, blind-blocked on back. Dark chocolate end-papers.

Blank leaf and half-title precede title in Vols. I and III, half-title only in Vol. II

Vol. I (viii) + (288) S_8 blank.
II (vi) + 278 Half-title and S_1 single insets.
III (viii) + (276)

Note. A novel based on the life of Jay Gould, by the father of this catalogue's dedicatee.

PHILADELPHIAN (The) [1326]
3 vols. Hurst & Blackett 1891. Three-quarter smooth brown cloth, marbled paper sides, bevelled boards. Marbled end-papers, uniform with binding. Blank leaf and half-title precede title in each vol.

Vol. I (viii) + 300 U, 4 leaves; X, 2 leaves.
II (viii) + (284)
III (viii) + (272) Publishers' cat., 16 pp. dated 1891, at end.

JEWSBURY, GERALDINE E. (1812–1880)

ANGELO, or The Pine Forest in the Alps [1327]
Small square 8vo. Grant & Griffith 1856. Red morocco cloth, pictorially blocked and lettered in gold after a design (signed) by J. L[eighton]. All edges gilt. Wood-engraved front. and 3 illustrations, all coloured, after John Absolon.

pp. (iv) + 96 Publishers' cat., 16 pp. undated, at end.

Binder's ticket: 'Burn', at end.

CONSTANCE HERBERT [1328]
3 vols. Hurst & Blackett 1855. Dark green diagonal-ripple-grain cloth, blocked in blind on front and back, gold and blind-blocked and gold-lettered on spine. Dark green end-papers.

Vol. I (iv) + 304
II (ii) + 298 1st leaf of final sig., U_1, a single inset.
III (ii) + (304) Text ends 302, 303 'L'Envoy', (304) advert. Publishers' cat. 24 pp., dated January 1855 at end.

MARIAN WITHERS [1329]
3 vols. Colburn & Co. 1851. Half-cloth boards, labels.

Vol. I (iv) + 298 Final leaf, X_1, a single inset.
II (ii) + (292)
III (ii) + (304)

RIGHT OR WRONG [1330]
2 vols. Hurst & Blackett 1859. Violet bead-grain cloth.

Vol. I (iv) + 320 followed by inset leaf of adverts.
II (ii) + 312 followed by inset leaf of adverts. Publishers' cat., 16 pp. undated, at end.

Ink signature: 'Henry Elwell, Wandsworth 1859', in fly-leaf of Vol. I and title of Vol. II. Booksellers' ticket: 'Napper & Wright, Birmingham', inside front covers. Fly-leaf missing from Vol. II. Cloth faded.

[1331] SORROWS OF GENTILITY (The)
2 vols. Hurst & Blackett 1856. Orange wavy-grain cloth; bright blue end-papers.

Vol. I (iv)+(304) U_8 adverts. Publishers' cat., 24 pp. undated, at end.
II (ii)+(322) Final leaf, (Y_1), a single inset.

Bookseller's blind stamp: 'Hicks, Wakefield', on fly-leaf of each vol.

[1332] ZOE: the History of Two Lives
3 vols. Chapman & Hall 1845. Maroon morocco cloth.

Vol. I (ii)+(320) X_8 blank.
II (ii)+316
III (ii)+310 First leaf of final sig., X_1, a single inset.

Note. This was one of the few contemporary novels by (at the time) unknown writers which provoked Bulwer Lytton to favourable comment in private letters (cf. 1524 below). On 12 June 1847 he wrote to Forster:

'I have just read Miss Jewsbury's book. The first volume and much of the second made me exclaim: "At last an honest woman speaks out, right or wrong, to the world." There are in this volume a strength and independence of thought which are sufficient to [? predict] a great and startling writer—one who may pursue society, though I do not agree with her in much, and though if her friend and relation I would rather for her sake she let society alone. The third volume falls off and Mirabeau devastates you. But there—he represents animal passion and that but coarsely.'

Three days later, in reply to a letter from Lady Lovelace to whom he seems to have sent a copy of *Zoe* with a recommendation, he writes:

'I cannot recover my amazement at one or two passages being written by a young lady of three or four and twenty. They would be striking in a woman ten years older and married, but what may be the simple result of experience after a certain age is in a younger person extremely distasteful to one's feelings as implying a monstrosity of development.'

Unless (and there seems to be no evidence that this was the case) *Zoe* was written more than ten years before it was published, Bulwer was mistaken about the lady's age. Miss Jewsbury was born in 1812.

In May 1880 Miss Jewsbury wrote to George Bentley (she acted as reader and editor for the firm): 'After being put into a *dark cupboard* in the Manchester Library of that day—because *Zoe* was calculated to injure the morals of the *young men*—I was, a long time afterwards, promoted to write a book for *Young Girls* of fourteen to sixteen! Wh. I did.'

KEMBLE, ADELAIDE (Mrs Sartoris) (1814–1879)

MEDUSA and Other Tales (by the author of 'A Week in a French Country-House') [1333]
Large square 8vo. Smith, Elder 1868. Plum moiré ribbed cloth; grey end-papers; bevelled boards. Wood-engraved front. after Millais.

Half-title. pp. (viii)+228

Dedicated 'To Henry Greville. For Auld Lang Syne, my dear.' Fine.

WEEK IN A FRENCH COUNTRY-HOUSE [1334]
(A) (by Adelaide Sartoris)
Large square 8vo. Smith, Elder 1867. Violet morocco cloth; grey end-papers; bevelled boards. Wood-engraved front. and 1 illustration, printed on tinted background.

pp. (iv)+(204) O_5 O_6 adverts. Fine.

KEON, MILES GERALD (1821–1875)

DION AND THE SYBILS: a Romance of the First Century [1335]
2 vols. Bentley 1866. Dark green fine-morocco cloth.

Half-title in Vol. I

Vol. I (iv)+308
II (ii)+346 Final leaf, $2A_1$, a single inset. B

See Note to 1218 above.

HARDING THE MONEY-SPINNER [1336]
3 vols. Bentley 1879. Carmine diagonal-fine-ribbed-cloth.

Half-title in each vol.

Vol. I (xii)+300
II (iv)+(272)
III (iv)+(276) B

Vol. I contains as Preface a brief memoir of the author, who died comparatively young and had been intimate with Bulwer Lytton.

KINGSLEY, CHARLES (1819–1875)

For further bibliographical detail, see Parrish, *Charles Kingsley and Thomas Hughes* (London, 1936).

ALTON LOCKE: Tailor and Poet [*Parrish* p. 11 [1337]
Copy I: First Edition. 2 vols. Chapman & Hall 1850. Rose-madder fine-ribbed cloth.

Vol. I iv+(308) X_2 adverts.
II iv+300

Binders' ticket: 'Bone & Son', at end of Vol. I. Very fine.

Copy II: First one-vol. Edition. 'New Edition with a New Preface.' Cambridge: Macmillan [1337*a*]

1862. Royal-blue sand-grain cloth; red-chocolate end-papers.

Half-title. pp. (xxxii) + (312) X_4 adverts. Publishers' cat., 56 pp. dated November 1869, at end. Pp. (v)–xxiv are occupied by a 'Preface to the Undergraduates of Cambridge', undated; and pp. (xxv)–xxx by a 'Preface Written in 1854 etc.'

Blind stamp: 'W. H. Smith & Son, Strand.' Fine

[1338] HEREWARD THE WAKE: 'Last of the English' [*Parrish* p. 59

2 vols. Macmillan 1866. Crimson-lake fine-morocco cloth, blocked and lettered in gold; greenish-black end-papers.

Half-title in each vol.

Vol. I viii + (368) AA_8 adverts.
II viii + (404) DD_2 adverts.

Blind stamp: 'W. H. Smith & Son', on half-title of Vol. I.

[1339] HYPATIA, or New Foes with an Old Face. [*Parrish* p. 17

2 vols. John W. Parker 1853. Dark olive-brown morocco cloth.

Half-title in Vol. I

Vol. I xxiv + (324)
II iv + (384) BB_6–BB_8 adverts., paged (1)–6.

Fine.

[1340] WESTWARD HO! or the Voyages and Adventures of Sir Amyas Leigh, Knight, etc. [*Parrish* p. 26

3 vols. Cambridge: Macmillan 1855. Blue morocco cloth (Kingsley style†).

Inset advert. leaf and half-title precede title in Vol. I; half-title only in Vols. II and III

Vol. I (x) [paged viii] + (304) Publishers' cat., 16 pp. dated February 1855, at end.
II vi + 356
III vi + (374) Final leaf, BB_3, a single inset.

Bookseller's ticket: 'William Hutt', inside front cover of Vol. I. The Yates-Thompson copy (Sotheby, August 1941). Covers of Vol. I slightly spotted, back hinge of Vol. III a little blurred by damp, but, for this book, a fine copy.

Note. On p. 7 of the cat. at end of Vol. I the home of Sir Amyas Leigh is spelt 'Burrow' and not 'Burrough' as on title. This error was corrected in later catalogues.

YEAST: a Problem [anon] [*Parrish* p. 8

[1341] John W. Parker 1851. Rose-madder wavy-grain cloth.

pp. (viii) + (388) R_{11} R_{12} S_1 S_2 adverts. paged (1)–8.

Ink signature: 'John Rutson. Trin. Coll.', on fly-leaf. Fine.

† See note to 1234, above.

KINGSLEY, GEORGE H.

FOUR PHASES OF LOVE, by Paul Heyse. Translated by G. H. Kingsley [1342]

Sm. 8vo. Routledge 1857. Smooth brown-orange cloth printed in black.

pp. (ii) + (190) Title and N_1 single insets. Back outside cover printed with adverts.

SOUTH SEA BUBBLES (by 'The Earl and the Doctor'—i.e. Lord Pembroke and G. H. K.) [1343]

8vo. Bentley 1872. Vermilion diagonal-fine-dot-and-line-grain cloth blocked in gold and blind; chocolate end-papers; bevelled boards.

Half-title. pp. (viii) + 312 Publishers' cat., 12 pp. dated 1872, at end.

KINGSLEY, HENRY (1830–1876)

This is a complete collection of the works of Henry Kingsley. Titles issued in the blue morocco cloth style used by Macmillan for *Westward Ho!* and other novels are again described as in 'Kingsley style'.

AUSTIN ELLIOT [1344]

2 vols. Macmillan 1863. Binding: Kingsley style; deep cream end-papers. *Pl. 14*

Half-title in each vol., that in Vol. I preceded by a leaf of adverts.

Vol. I (viii) + (292) T_{10} adverts.
II (iv) + (272) Publishers' cat., 16 pp. undated, at end.

Very fine.

BOY IN GREY (The) [1345]

Strahan 1871. Maroon pebble-grain cloth, blocked in black and gold; red-chocolate end-papers. Wood-engraved front. and 13 illustrations after Arthur Hughes, all on plate paper.

Half-title. pp. (iv) + (204) 13_2–13_6 Publishers' cat. paged (1)–10.

Blind stamp: 'Palmer & How, Manchester', on fly-leaf. Binder's ticket: 'Burn', at end.

Note. This is the first issue binding. A secondary binding was issued, similarly blocked but in grey-blue smooth cloth, thinner boards and with cut edges.

FIRESIDE STUDIES [1346]

2 vols. Chatto & Windus 1876. Maroon diagonal-fine-ribbed cloth, blocked in black and gold; dark green end-papers.

Half-title in each vol.

Vol. I (x) + 322 Final leaf, 21_1, a single inset.
II (vi) + 254

Book-plate of W. K. D'Arcy in each vol. Binders' ticket: 'W. Bone & Son', at end of each vol. Fine. Spines a little faded.

[1347] GRANGE GARDEN (The): a Romance
3 vols. Chatto & Windus 1876. Green diagonal-fine-ribbed cloth, blocked in black and gold; cream end-papers.
Blank leaf and half-title precede title in each vol.
Vol. I (viii) [paged vi] + (268) S_6 publishers' device.
II (viii) [paged vi] + (252)
III (viii) [paged vi] + 240
Publishers' cat., 32 pp. dated March 1876, at end.
Binders' ticket: 'W. Bone & Son', at end of each vol. Very fine.

[1348] HARVEYS (The)
2 vols. Tinsley 1872. Brown sand-grain cloth, blocked with Tinsley's standard blocking, advertising *Tinsley's Magazine*; cream end-papers.
Half-title in each vol., that in II a single inset.
Vol. I viii + 250
II vi + 204 Publishers' cat., 16 pp. dated December 1871, at end.
Fine.

[1349] HETTY
Copy I: First Edition. Royal 8vo. New York: Harper & Brothers 1869. Pinkish-buff wrappers, printed in black.
Advert. leaf precedes title. pp. (80) E_4–E_8 adverts.
No. 325 of Harpers Library of Select Novels. Book-plate of Lord Esher.

[1349*a*] **Copy II: First English Edition.** 'HETTY' (alone). Bradbury & Evans 1871. Smooth dark blue cloth; dark grey end-papers. Wood-engraved front. and vignette title on plate paper, but reckoned in collation.
Half-title. pp. (viii) [paged (xii)] + (384) BB_8 advert.
Ink inscription: 'Minnie Lawson from Edmund 1872', on fly-leaf. Binders' ticket: 'Leighton, Son & Hodge', at end. Cloth rather soiled and stain on front cover.

[1349*b*] *Pl. 14* **Copy III: Enlarged Edition.** 'HETTY AND OTHER STORIES.' Text re-set throughout and every page in a frame. Binding, end-papers, front. and vignette on title as Copy II, but in this edition the 2 leaves of plate paper are *not* reckoned in collation.
Blank leaf precedes half-title. pp. viii + 344
Book-label of General Wynne.

[1350] *Pl. 14* HILLYARS AND THE BURTONS (The): a Story of Two Families
3 vols. Macmillan 1865. Binding: Kingsley style; chocolate end-papers.
Half-title in each vol.
Vol. I xii + 288
II viii + (284) T_6 adverts.
III viii + (320) X_8 adverts.
Fine. Spine of Vol. III slightly bubbled.

HORNBY MILLS, and Other Stories [1351]
2 vols. Tinsley 1872. Blue sand-grain cloth, blocked in blind with Tinsley's standard blocking, advertising *Tinsley's Magazine*; cream end-papers.
Half-title in each vol., that in II a single inset.
Vol. I (viii) + (250) Final sig., R, is unsigned and final leaf, (R_5), a single inset.
II (vi) + 234 Final leaf, Q_5, a single inset.
Book-label: Coronet over 'L. R.' in monogram. Blind stamp: 'H. S. Eland, Exeter', on fly-leaf. Fine.

LEIGHTON COURT: a Country House Story [1352]
2 vols. Macmillan 1866. Brown sand-grain cloth; dark green end-papers.
Half-title in each vol., that in Vol. I preceded by a blank leaf.
Vol. I (viii) + (264) Publishers' cat., 32 pp. undated, at end, of which last leaf blank.
II (iv) + (268) S_6 adverts.
Presentation Copy: 'The Revd A. J. W. Blunt with the Author's kindest regards and remembrances' in ink on first blank leaf of Vol. I.

LOST CHILD (The) [1353]
4to. Macmillan 1871. Green morocco cloth, blocked in black and gold; red-chocolate end-papers. Wood-engraved front., vignette title and 6 illustrations after Frölich.
Half-title. pp. (44) C_2 adverts.
The vignette-title and seven plates are on plate paper and do not form part of the text signatures. They are, however, reckoned in the pagination, so that what are in fact 28 pp. of text are paginated as 44.
Blind stamp: 'W. H. Smith & Son', on fly-leaf. Binder's ticket: 'Burn', at end. Fine.
Note. This is a reprint of Chapter XIII of Vol. II of *Reflections of Geoffry Hamlyn*, with a Preface by the author, (pp. (7) 8) two paragraphs added at the beginning of the text, and one at the end.

MADEMOISELLE MATHILDE: a Novel [1354]
3 vols. Bradbury & Evans 1868. Dark green sand-grain cloth; cream end-papers.
Half-title in each vol.
Vol. I xii + 282 Final leaf, U_1, a single inset.
II vi + (274) Half-title and final leaf, (T_1), single insets.
III vi + 284 Half-title a single inset.
Spines slightly darkened.

MYSTERY OF THE ISLAND (The) [1355]
William Mullan & Son 1877. Olive-green diagonal-fine-ribbed cloth, pictorially blocked in black and gold; bevelled boards; black end-papers.

Half-title. pp. (vi) + 266 pp. (v) (vi), Contents, and final leaf, S_5, single insets.

Signature: 'W. Webb', on title. Cloth fine, end-papers damaged. Also issued in red cloth.

[1356] NUMBER SEVENTEEN: a Novel

2 vols. Chatto & Windus 1875. Dark green diagonal-fine-ribbed cloth; pale yellow end-papers.

Advert. leaf and half-title precede title in each vol.

Vol. I (viii) [paged vi] + 236 Publishers' cat., 32 pp. undated, at end.
II (viii) [paged vi] + 244 Publishers' cat., 32 pp. undated, at end.

Very fine.

[1357] OAKSHOTT CASTLE: being the Memoir of an Eccentric Nobleman, written by Mr Granby Dixon and edited by Henry Kingsley

3 vols. Macmillan 1873. Red fine-pebble-grain cloth, blocked in black and gold; green end-papers.

Half-title in each vol.

Vol. I (viii) + (276)
II (viii) + 260
III (viii) + (256) R_8 adverts.

Blind stamp: 'With the Publishers' compliments', on title of Vol. I.

[1358] OLD MARGARET: a Novel

2 vols. Tinsley 1871. Blue sand-grain cloth, blocked in blind with Tinsley's standard blocking, advertising *Tinsley's Magazine*; cream end-papers.

Half-title in each vol.

Vol. I (iv) + (236) Publishers' cat., 16 pp. on text paper dated May 1871, at end.
II (iv) + (268)

Spines darkened.

[1359] RAVENSHOE

3 vols. Cambridge: Macmillan 1862.

Copy I: First Edition. Binding: Kingsley style; deep cream end-papers.

Half-title in each vol.

Vol. I (xii) [paged viii] + (300) U_6 adverts.
II viii + (276) Publishers' cat., 16 pp. undated, at end.
III (viii) + (268) S_2 adverts.

Book-label: 'Percy Scawen Wyndham', in each vol. Fine.

[1359*a*] **Copy II: Second Edition**, re-set. 3 vols. 1862. Binding and collation show the following differences from the first edition:

(*a*) On spines, Vol. I [II, III] is smaller and more closely set. Imprints are in *serif* caps, whereas in first edition they are block caps.

(*b*) End-papers chocolate.

(*c*) Collation:

Vol. I xii + 312
II viii + (312) U_4 adverts.
III (viii) + (304) Publishers' cat., 24 pp. dated '11. 7. 63', at end.

Pencil signature: 'Augustine Birrell, Sheringham', on half-title of Vol. II and fly-leaf of Vol. III. The half-title of Vol. III has been torn out.

Notes. (i) The reason for the rapid re-setting is obscure. No textual changes seem to have been made; the chapters tally as to numbers and titles in both editions. The Second Edition is more leaded than the first and with more 'whites'. The words 'Second Edition' appear on titles.

(ii) The first one-vol. edition appeared in 1864.

RECOLLECTIONS OF GEOFFRY HAMLYN (The) [1360]

3 vols. Cambridge: Macmillan 1859. Binding: Kingsley style; pale yellow end-papers.

Half-title in each vol.

Vol. I (viii) [paged vi] + (276) Publishers' cat., 24 pp. on text paper dated April 15, 1859, at end.
II (viii) + 324
III (viii) + (276) Publishers' cat., as in Vol. I, at end.

Ink signature: 'John Gordon E. Sibbald, September 1867' on half-title of each vol. Very fine.

Note. The second edition was in one volume, 1860.

REGINALD HETHEREGE [1361]

3 vols. Bentley 1874. Smooth ivory linen-grain cloth, blocked in black and gold; cream end-papers.

Vol. I (iv) + 284
II (iv) + (284) T_6 blank.
III (iv) + 292 B

Note. This copy is in first issue binding. For secondary variants see Carter, *Binding Variants*, pp. 41–42. To the two secondaries there described I can add a third: pinkish sand-grain cloth, blocked on front with triple-frame in black, ditto on back in blind; on spine with black-rules and gold-lettering from type. Buff end-papers, all edges cut.

SILCOTE OF SILCOTES [1362]

3 vols. Macmillan 1867. Brown sand-grain cloth; greenish-black end-papers. *Pl. 14*

Half-title in each vol.

Vol. I (viii) + (272) Publishers' cat., 48 pp. dated September 1867, at end.
II (viii) + (280) T_4 adverts.
III (viii) + 304

'C. Downshire' in ink on title of each vol.

[1363] STRETTON: a Novel

Pl. 14 3 vols. Tinsley 1869. Royal-blue sand-grain cloth; pale yellow end-papers.

Half-title in each vol.

Vol. I (iv) + 296
II (iv) + (284)
III (iv) + (288) T_8 adverts.

Cloth very fine. Half of back end-paper of Vol. I torn away.

Note. Also issued in apple-green very-fine-bead-grain cloth, similarly lettered.

[1364] TALES OF OLD TRAVEL

Macmillan 1869. Bright green sand-grain cloth, pictorially blocked in gold and blind; pinkish-chocolate end-papers. Wood-engraved front., vignette title and 7 plates. Front. and plates on plate-paper, vignette title on text paper and reckoned in collation.

Half-title. pp. (viii) + 368 Publishers' cat., 56 pp. dated August 1869, at end. Fine.

[1365] VALENTIN: a French Boy's Story of Sedan

Copy I: (presumably) First Edition. 2 vols. Tinsley 1872. Royal-blue dot-and-line-grain cloth, blocked in black and gold; cream end-papers.

Half-title in each vol.

Vol. I (iv) + 254
II (iv) + 244 Publishers' cat., 16 pp. dated February 1872, at end.

Monogram 'L. H.' stamped in violet ink on fly-leaf of each vol. Back hinge of Vol. I torn at head.

Note. Valentin, in serial form, was included in *Routledge's Every Boy's Annual for 1873* (published in the autumn of 1872). Presumably it had run during the year through the numbers of *Every Boy's Magazine.* The respective publication dates of the *Annual* and of Tinsley's edition cannot be established, so just in case the former predated the latter and could claim priority as a quasi-book-edition, I record the presence in the Collection of this *Annual for 1873,* in mint condition with dust-jacket of dark yellow paper, printed in black.

[1365*a*] **Copy II: First Illustrated Edition.** 'Revised and Corrected'

Routledge n.d. [1874]. Brown bubble-grain cloth, pictorially blocked and lettered in gold and black on front and spine. Wood-engraved front. and 5 illustrations, all on plate paper.

pp. (ii) + 310 1st leaf of final sig., X_1, a single inset. Publishers' cat., 32 pp. undated at end.

This dumpy volume is a typical 'juvenile' of the period.

LANDON, LAETITIA E. (1802–1838)

FRANCESCO CARRARA (by the author of 'Romance and Reality', 'The Venetian Bracelet', etc. etc.) [1366]

3 vols. Bentley 1834. Boards, labels.

Half-title in Vols. II and III

Vol. I (iv) + (324)
II (iv) + 328
III (iv) + 368

Bookseller's ticket: 'Seacome, Chester', inside front cover of each vol. Very fine.

Dedicated to Mrs Wyndham Lewis (afterwards Mrs Disraeli).

LADY ANNE GRANARD: or Keeping Up Appearances ('by L. E. L. (the late Mrs Maclean), authoress of' etc.) [1367]

3 vols. Colburn 1842. Half-cloth boards, labels. Steel-engraved portrait front. in Vol. I after D. McClise (*sic*).

Vol. I iv + (312) O_{10}–O_{12} adverts.
II (ii) + (320)
III (ii) + 318 First leaf of final sig., P_1, a single inset.

Book-label of Edward Ellice, Invergary inside front cover of each vol. Labels rubbed.

ROMANCE AND REALITY (by L. E. L., author of etc.) [1368]

3 vols. Colburn & Bentley 1831. Boards, labels.

Advert. leaf precedes title in Vols. I and III, half-title in Vol. II

Vol. I (viii) + 328
II (iv) + (344)
III (iv) + 332

Book-label of R. J. Ll. Price, Rhiwlas Library, and bookseller's ticket: 'Seacome, Chester', inside front cover of each vol.

According to his occasional practice, Price has cut two titles from the advert. leaf preceding title in Vol. III (presumably as a preliminary to ordering them). Otherwise the copy is very fine.

See also STEPNEY, LADY (3146 below).

LE FANU, JOSEPH SHERIDAN (1814–1873)

Except for one pamphlet (THE PRELUDE: being a contribution toward a History of the Election for the University, by John Figwood. Dublin [1865]), this is a complete collection of the first editions of Joseph Sheridan Le Fanu. As Messrs Pickering & Chatto said, in the preface to their remarkable catalogue 'The Victorian Novel, 1837–1901' (issued in the spring of 1939), Le Fanu is an author 'now widely but vainly sought'; and I do not pretend to regard this series of his books otherwise than with pride. The copies which came from the Bentley File are in absolutely new condition, and several of the others carry presentation inscriptions in the author's hand.

A full-dress bibliography of Le Fanu by Dudley Massey and M. J. MacManus is in preparation and will, in due course be published by the Bibliographical Society. For this reason I have not described the material features of the books much more elaborately than those of less distinguished authors. I have, however, felt it essential to discuss at some length the various issues and editions of *The House by the Church-Yard*, as without explanation they would be unintelligible.

[1369] ALL IN THE DARK

2 vols. Bentley 1866.

Copy I: First Edition: Regulation Binding. Claret pebble-grain cloth; cream end-papers.

Vol. I vi+(300) Contents leaf, (A_3), a single inset.

II iv+290 Final leaf, 19_1, a single inset. B

[1369*a*] **Copy II: Another: Presentation Binding.** White pebble-grain cloth; cream end-papers. Collation as Copy I.

Book-label of T. Mackenzie Fowler, and booksellers' ticket: 'Gawthorn and Hutt' inside front cover of each vol. Fine.

[1370] BEAUTIFUL POEM OF SHAMUS O'BRIEN

Pl. 17 (The): a Story of Ninety-Eight [anon]

Manchester: John Heywood 1867. Orange wrappers, cut flush, printed in black on front. Inside front, and inside and outside back wrappers blank.

pp. 16

[1371] CHECKMATE

3 vols. Hurst & Blackett 1871. Apple-green sand-grain cloth, blocked in black and lettered in gold; old rose end-papers.

Half-title in each vol.

Vol. I (vi)+310 Dedication, (A_3), and final leaf, Y_1, single insets.

II (iv)+320

III (iv)+(336) Publishers' cat., 16 pp. dated January 1871, at end.

[1372] CHRONICLES OF GOLDEN FRIARS

Copy I: First Edition. 3 vols. Bentley 1871. Violet dotted-line-ribbed cloth; cream end-papers. Line-engraved decorative titles with fancy titling.

Vol. I viii+(304)

II (ii)+328

III (ii)+298 Final leaf, U_5, a single inset. B

Contents. A Strange Adventure in the Life of Miss Laura Mildmay—The Haunted Baronet—The Bird of Passage.

Copy II: First Illustrated Edition, entitled: A CHRONICLE OF GOLDEN FRIARS, and other Stories. Downey & Co. 1896. Blue ribbed cloth, blocked in blind and gold; white end-papers. Half-tone front. and illustrations in the text, both half-tone and line, after Brinsley Le Fanu (the author's younger son) and John F. O'Hea. [1372*a*]

pp. viii+(332) Z_2 advert. and imprint leaf.

Note. This volume contains the story which occupies Vol. III of the first edition of *Chronicles of Golden Friars* (and is there entitled *A Bird of Passage*) and five stories from *The Purcell Papers.*

COCK AND THE ANCHOR (The): being a Chronicle of Old Dublin City [anon] [1373]

Copy I: First Edition. 3 vols. Dublin: William Curry Jun. & Co. 1845. Dark green binders' linen, original labels laid down, edges trimmed (the only specimens yet discovered in more nearly original state were a set roughly rebacked and without labels in Lord Esher's library, and an odd volume in all-over boards).

Half-title in each vol.

Vol. I (iv)+(348)

II (iv)+(328)

III (iv)+(348) Q_6 adverts.

Label of Churton's Subscription Library on front cover of each vol. and the novel's Library Number stamped in gold on spine.

Note. P. S. O'Hegarty reports a curious re-incarnation of this edition. It consists of first edition sheets (i.e. Irish-printed by Folds of Dublin) with new and typographically different titles (probably London-printed), dated 1847 and imprinted: LONDON: LONGMAN & CO. / PARRY & CO., 32 & 33 LEADENHALL STREET.

Copy II: New Edition in Small Format. [anon] 3 vols. Fcap 8vo. Dublin: Curry 1845. Library half-morocco, top edges uncut. Pagination as Copy I, but as this edition collates in eights instead of in twelves, Q_6 at end of Vol. III becomes (Z_6) [mis-signed Q]. [1373*a*]

Note. Small differences in setting (full details of which will be given in the forthcoming Massey-MacManus bibliography) establish that this small-format edition post-dated that represented by Copy I, though no indication is given that the novel had previously appeared.

Copy III: Third Edition, entitled: SIR HENRY ASHWOODE: THE FORGER. A Chronicle of Old Dublin City [anon]. 3 vols. Fcap 8vo. Parry & Co. 1851. Library half-morocco, uniform with Copy II. No half-titles, otherwise as Copy II. [1373*b*]

Note. This edition consists of the sheets of Copy II, with new titles. Ink signature: 'Ira W. Carter', on title of Vol. I.

[1373c] **Copy IV: First Illustrated Edition.** Downey & Co. (1895). Smooth brown cloth, blocked in black and gold; black end-papers. Half-tone front. and pictorial title and 8 full-page plates (all on plate-paper and not reckoned in collation), as well as numerous illustrations in the text, after Brinsley Le Fanu. Authorship avowed.

Half-title. pp. (viii) + (360) AA_4 adverts. Fine.

[1373d] **Copy V: Yellow-back Edition** ('by the author of "Uncle Silas"' entitled: MORLEY COURT: 'NEW EDITION'. Chapman & Hall 1873. Cover by Phiz. *Select Library of Fiction.*

S. M. Ellis (*Wilkie Collins, Le Fanu and Others*) says that the text was corrected for this edition.

[1374] EVIL GUEST (The)

Downey & Co. (1895). Smooth dark green cloth, blocked in black and gold; very dark grey end-papers. Half-tone front. and pictorial title printed in sanguine, and illustrations in the text, both half-tone and line, after Brinsley Le Fanu.

pp. (iv) + (240) Q_8 adverts. Publishers' cat., 8 pp. on text paper dated March 1895, at end, of which pp. (7) (8) are blank.

Very fine.

Note. This text of a story first published in *Ghost Stories* is re-written more or less throughout, though mostly in matters of detail.

[1375] FORTUNES OF COLONEL TORLOGH O'BRIEN (The): a Tale of the Wars of King James [anon]

Pl. 1 **Copy I: Part Issue.** Eleven (as ten) monthly shilling 8vo parts, published by McGlashan from April 1846 to January 1847. Pink paper wrappers printed in black—on front: No. 1 (etc.) APRIL (etc.) PRICE 1*s*. / all-over pictorial design by Phiz incorporating fancy-titling as follows: THE FORTUNES / OF / TURLOGH (sic) O'BRIEN / A TALE OF / THE WARS OF KING / JAMES; imprint at foot: 'James McGlashan' etc.; on back with adverts. Inside front and back wrappers printed with adverts.

Part I: Inside front wrapper: *Cock and Anchor.*
Two etchings by Phiz. pp. (1)–32 of text.
Inside back wrapper: *Dublin Literary Observer.*
Outside back wrapper: *Dublin University Magazine:* April, March, February, January.

Part II: Inside front wrapper: as Part I.
Two etchings by Phiz. pp. 33–64 of text.
Inside back wrapper: as Part I.
Outside back wrapper: *D.U.M.* May, April, March, February, January.

Part III: Inside front wrapper: as Part I.
Two etchings by Phiz. pp. 65–96 of text.
Inside back wrapper: Works published by McGlashan.
Outside back wrapper: *D.U.M.* June, May, April, March.

Part IV: Inside front wrapper: *Douglas Jerrold's Weekly Newspaper* and *Cock and Anchor.*
Two etchings by Phiz. pp. 97–128 of text.
Inside back wrapper: as Part III.
Outside back wrapper: *D.U.M.* July, June, May, April.

Part V: Inside front wrapper: New Works sold by McGlashan.
Two etchings by Phiz. pp. 129–160 of text.
Inside back wrapper: as Part III.
Outside back wrapper: *D.U.M.* August, July, June.

Part VI: Inside front wrapper: *Dublin and its Environs.*
Two etchings by Phiz. pp. 161–192 of text. Single leaf advertising *Dombey & Son* and Dickens' Works.
Inside back wrapper: Works published by McGlashan.
Outside back wrapper: *D.U.M.* September, August, July, June.

Part VII: Inside front wrapper: Works published by McGlashan.
Two etchings by Phiz. pp. 193–224 of text.
Inside back wrapper: Works for Farmers.
Outside back wrapper: *D.U.M.* October, September, August.

Part VIII: Inside front wrapper: *D.U.M.* November, October, September.
Two etchings by Phiz. pp. 225–256 of text.
Inside back wrapper: Works recently published (McGlashan).
Outside back wrapper: *Dublin Evening Herald.*

Part IX: Inside front wrapper: Works recently published (McGlashan).
Two etchings by Phiz. pp. 257–288 of text.
Inside back wrapper: Works for Farmers.
Outside back wrapper: *D.U.M.* December, November.

Parts X and XI (wrapper very pale pink): Price Two Shillings.
Inside front wrapper: Works preparing for publication (McGlashan).
Four etchings by Phiz. pp. 289–342 of text. Text ends $2A_1$ (preceding sig., Z, 2 leaves). $2A_2$–$2A_6$ prelims., paged (i)–(x). Final leaf of prelims. pp. (ix) (x), carrying List of Illustrations, is signed *b*.
Inside back wrapper: Works recently published (McGlashan).
Outside back wrapper: *D.U.M.* January, December.

Copies II and III: First Book Edition. 8vo. [1375 *a,b*]
Dublin: James McGlashan 1847. Dark grass-green morocco cloth, and scarlet fine-ribbed cloth, blocked on front and back in blind, on spine pictorially blocked and lettered in gold;

yellow end-papers. Etched front. and 21 plates by Phiz.

pp. (x)+342

Green copy fine; red copy very fine.

Note. These copies are in the first binding. The same style also exists in dark blue. The second binding (which I have seen in red and black) is much plainer and lacks pictorial blocking on spine.

[1376] GHOST STORIES and Tales of Mystery [anon] Sm. 8vo. Dublin: James McGlashan 1851.

Copy I: First Binding: red fine-ribbed cloth, pictorially blocked in gold on front. and spine (see Carter, *Binding Variants*, p. 127: Style A). Pale yellow end-papers. Etched front. and 3 plates by Phiz.

Half-title and title printed in red and blue. pp. 304

Contents. The Watcher—The Murdered Cousin—Schalken the Painter—The Evil Guest.

[1376*a*] **Copy II: Second (Gift) Binding:** violet cloth, elaborately blocked in gold on front and spine, all edges gilt (see Carter, p. 165, but for 'bead grain' read 'coarse morocco' cloth). Pale yellow end-papers. Illustrations and Collation as Copy I.

[1376*b*] **Copy III: Secondary Binding:** red morocco cloth, meanly blocked in gold on spine only (see Carter, p. 127: Style C). Illustrations and Collation as Copy I. This copy re-sewn and with new end-papers (see also *The Watcher* and *The Evil Guest*).

[1377] GUY DEVERELL
3 vols. Bentley 1865. Carmine sand-grain cloth; cream end-papers.

Vol. I vi+(298) pp. (v) vi, Contents, signed 'a', and first leaf of final sig., U_1, single insets.
II iv+(304) U_6–U_8 adverts.
III iv+280 B

[1378] HAUNTED LIVES: a Novel
3 vols. Tinsley 1868. Dark green sand-grain cloth; cream end-papers.

Half-title in each vol.

Vol. I viii+(292) 19_2 adverts.
II vi+(284) 18_6 adverts. pp. (v) vi, Contents, a single inset.
III vi+(276) 18_2 adverts. pp. (v) vi, Contents, a single inset.

Very fine.

Notes. (i) This novel is dedicated to the 'Mrs Fitzgerald of Fane Valley' to whom some of the copies in the Collection are inscribed.

(ii) I have noted a variant binding on this book. The copy described above is in a sand-grain cloth, flecked or spangled with spots of a larger grain; also on spine between AUTHOR OF / "A LOST NAME" and Vol. I [*II, III*] is a short fancy rule with a central ornament. Another copy is in ordinary sand-grain cloth and the short rule on spine is quite plain. This latter copy has a pencil inscription dated 'Xmas 1871', i.e. three years after the book had been published.

HOUSE BY THE CHURCH-YARD (The) [the last word is printed thus throughout the *text* of every 3 vol. issue; on the *spines* it is in two words *un*hyphened] [1379] *Pl. 14*

Copy I: First Issue (All Irish). 3 vols. Tinsley 1863. Royal-blue bead-grain cloth; yellow end-papers.

Half-title in Vol. III

Vol. I (ii)+310 Title and O_1 single insets; final leaf O_{11}.
II (ii)+318 Title and X_1 single insets; final leaf X_7.
III (iv)+312

Copy II: First Issue with English Prelims. 3 vols. Tinsley 1863. Grass-green coarse-morocco cloth; cream end-papers. [1379*a*] *Pl. 14*

Half-title in each vol.

Vol. I (iv)+310 O_1 single inset as in Copy I.
II (iv)+318 X_1 single inset as in Copy I.
III (iv)+312

Ink signature: 'Hugh R. (?) Wolfe 18 April '94', on half-title of each vol. (date in Vol. I only). Photograph (presumably of the House by the Church-Yard) pasted on verso of half-title in Vol. I and annotated 'In 1894'. Newspaper cutting about Chapelizod pasted to fly-leaf of Vol. I. Fine.

Copy III: 'Second Edition'.† 3 vols. Tinsley 1863. Royal-blue morocco cloth; chocolate end-papers. [1379*b*] *Pl. 14*

Collation as Copy I, except that half-title in Vol. III has been suppressed. The words: 'Second Edition', appear on titles.

Ink signature: 'F. E. Abbott', on title and inside front cover of each vol. Book-plate of Paul S. Seybolt.

Copy IV: 'Third Edition'.† 3 vols. Bentley 1865. Binding exactly uniform with Copy II (imprint apart), but the cloth a slightly darker green; pale cream end-papers. [1379*c*]

Collation as Copy III, i.e. no half-titles, reprinted titles and original sheets. B

Copy V: Remainder Issue. 3 vols. Tinsley 1863. Bright blue morocco cloth; chocolate end-papers printed with Chapman & Hall adverts. [1379*d*] *Pl. 14*

Collation as Copy I, but while Vols. II and III have first ('all Irish') issue titles, Vol. I has a 'Second Edition' title.

† These are, of course, not 'editions' at all but 'issues'. I quote the phrase because it appears on titles.

Ink initial: 'E. R. 1871', inside front cover of each vol. Blind stamp: 'W. H. Smith & Son', on fly-leaf of Vol. I.

Note. The dated initials probably give the year when this remainder issue was put on sale.

[1379*e*] **Copy VI: First one-vol. and first Illustrated Edition, Revised and Enlarged.** Bentley 1866: 'A New Edition.' Standard green cloth style of Bentley's Favourite Novels. Wood-engraved front. and vignette title on plate paper after H. E. Doyle. 'Church-Yard' thus in text and on spine.

pp. (iv) + 476

Binders' ticket: 'Edmonds and Remnants', at end.

Note. No. 14 of 'Bentley's Favourite Novels'. This edition is dedicated to Percy Fitzgerald, and was considerably re-written and enlarged. It contains 99 chapters as against 88 in the three-vol. editions.

Note to 'The House by the Church-Yard'

The only first-hand account of the publishing history of *The House by the Church-Yard* is the following paragraph from William Tinsley's *Random Recollections of an Old Publisher* (1900, vol. II, pp. 222–3):

'Mr Le Fanu was, at the time we purchased *The House by the Church-Yard* from him, the proprietor and editor of the *Dublin University Magazine.* He had had the book printed and part of the edition bound in Dublin before we saw or agreed to publish it; but when he sent us a specimen copy, we found it was very badly produced indeed. Paper, printing, and binding were all of an inferior quality. We did not alter the printing and paper, but we got our binders to re-bind those sent us in the binding done in Dublin, in fact, we made the volumes look as well as we could, and the book sold very well indeed.

'In after years I published several novels for Le Fanu, etc.... '

This paragraph is, and must remain, the starting-point of any investigation into the history of a very puzzling book.

Puzzling it certainly is, because the problem is not merely one of variant bindings. The make-up of the printed sheets also varies oddly, and not always in tune with changing binding-styles. Nevertheless, the recent discovery of copies in good original state of the SECOND and THIRD three-vol. 'editions', and some letters from Le Fanu to Bentley the publisher, help us as nearly to a final solution as can be expected.

It must be clearly understood at the outset that there was never more than one printing (carried out in Ireland) of the *text* of the novel in 3 volumes. The *prelims.* were set (or re-aligned) three times, but the *sheets* of Copies I to V described above all belonged to an original, far-too-extensive printing.

With this all-important fact in mind, let us examine Copies I to V, first as regards prelims. and text, then as regards binding, aware that, despite the appearance of 'Second (or Third) Edition' on three of their title-pages, they are in fact variants of one edition. We can then conclude with a general comment on the publishing-history of this interesting work.

A. Sheets

Copy I [First Issue, all-Irish]. Text and prelims. poorly printed on toned paper of commonish quality in a fount with markedly narrow caps. At foot of title under imprint appears a Note reserving Translation Rights, printed in italics and *un*bracketed. Occasional half-titles are found, but not according to any recognisable plan. These half-titles bear no vol. number—merely the title of the novel. No printer's imprint appears anywhere on these sheets.

Copy II [First Issue with English prelims.]. Text as I, but prelims. on a smoother, whiter paper and set in a different more rounded and more cleanly seriffed fount. The Note reserving Translation Rights is in italics but *bracketed.* Sometimes half-titles occur in all three vols. of this state, sometimes in two, sometimes, I believe, only in one.

This is the normal type of first edition (for binding see below), but various specimens examined show sheet-variations. For example the Bodleian copy and that in U.L.C. have Vols. I and II as in Copy I, though without half-titles, and Vol. III as Copy II—with half-title. I have seen this same mixture in a copy in a bookshop.

As Copy I is the only specimen so far known of a completely furnished production with sheets as described, there can be little doubt that it is Irish throughout and represents the novel as actually received by Tinsley from Dublin, and by him furbished up in order to 'look as well' as possible. (Again see below for binding.)

Copy III [so-called **'Second Edition'** (Tinsley)]. Sheets as Copy I but without half-titles and title-page adapted.

The titles of this 'Second Edition' show the type re-aligned, i.e. the vol. number and author's name have been pushed up to leave a larger space between the vol. number and publishers' imprint, into which have been dropped the words SECOND EDITION, in a peculiar elongated Gothic type, familiar to readers of the *Dublin University Magazine* and other Irish periodicals. That it is a case of re-alignment and not of re-setting is suggested by the fact that the imprint in Vol. III shows traces of exactly the same faulty letters as appeared in the imprint to Vol. III of Copy I, and in each case the Note reserving Translation Rights under the imprint is *un*bracketed as in Copy I.

It may safely be assumed (especially in the light of Le Fanu's letters to Bentley quoted below) that this 'Second Edition' was prepared in Ireland and despatched by the author to Tinsley for binding.

Copy IV [so-called **'Third Edition'** (Bentley)]. The *text* throughout as Copy I; *prelims.* consist of a single inset title in each vol. on whiter paper and clearly of English origin. These titles, which carry Bentley's imprint and device and the words 'Third Edition', were of course specially set. This is the only copy known to me of this issue.

Copy V [Remainder Issue]. Sheets all-Irish, but title of Vol. I is 'Second Edition' as Copy III and of Vols. II and III as Copy I. There is a half-title in Vol. III. The imprints, of course, are Tinsley throughout. This is the only copy known to me of the remainder issue.

B. Bindings

Copy I. Blue bead-grain cloth. There is no decorative blocking on spine, but only title and imprint in gold, in caps. and l.c. differing from those on Copy II. Vol. numbers (also different) are from a brass. Publishers' imprint, on *one* line, in caps. Front and back are blocked with a blind frame.

Copy II. Usually green, sometimes blue, morocco cloth (an occasional copy has also been noted in blue dot-and-line pattern cloth), with considerable gilt decoration on the spine and elaborate blind blocking on front and back. Title and author are blocked on the spine in gold from a brass cut in caps. and l.c. Vol. numbers are in fancy caps., i.e. blocked from a brass. Publishers' imprint on two lines, in caps.

Copy III. Royal-blue morocco cloth (graining different from that on Copy II) with conventional blind-blocking on front and back (design quite different from that on Copy II); but on the spine are title and author (no imprint) *blocked in gold from the same brass as that used on* Copy II. A little gold ornament is added and the vol. numbers are blocked from type. Fairly obviously this binding was produced in England and by Tinsley's binders, who used the title and author-brass previously employed.

Copy IV. Green morocco cloth, identical in colour, grain and blocking with that on Copy II. Evidently the brasses were bought or borrowed by Bentley and cut at the foot of the spine to substitute BENTLEY / LONDON for Tinsley's imprint.

Copy V. Bright blue morocco cloth, blind-blocked on front and back, gold-lettered on spine from *type* in sans serif italic caps., with title, author and vol. number (no imprint). Also on spine are meagre decoration and rules. Each vol. has brown end-papers printed with *Chapman & Hall advertisements*, dated by implication by a quotation in praise of Jane Austen from the *Quarterly Review* of Jan. 1870.

C. A Comment on Publishing History

Copies I to III speak for themselves to this extent—that they are clearly—I, the novel as printed and bound in Ireland; II, the novel as tidied-up by Tinsley for the English market; III, a fake 'Second Edition', produced in the hope of working-off the balance (or a portion of the balance) of still unsold sheets.

Copies IV and V, however, call for examination in the light of letters, recently discovered, from Le Fanu to Bentley. Here are the relevant extracts:

March 23. 1865. 'Very many thanks for your trouble about *The House by the Church-Yard.* The stock remaining is mine and shall be packed and despatched forthwith.'

April 3. 1865 (to Bentley junior). 'Mr Bentley about a week since wrote to me to say that he could sell the remaining copies of *The H. by the C.* The return of the stock states 450 copies. They were packed and sent by the Dublin publisher of the *Dublin University Magazine.* This explains the 4 mysterious bales. Would you be so good as to ask Mr B. to retain 6 copies for me, and to have them bound in the ordinary cloth, and to accept one from me, as I do not think he has got one?'

April 16. 1865. 'If the one vol. edition of the *H. by the C.* would interfere with the sale of the remainder in sheets, I would rather defer it.... I wrote to Tinsley to ask him about bound copies of the *H. by the C.* but he has not yet written to say whether he has any. I believe all his were exhausted at the regular price.'

April 29. 1865. 'With regard to the remainder of *The H. by the C.* I would rather sell the lot at 2/- a set than have them travelled on the chance of selling them at 5/- or 6/-.'

May 3. 1865. 'I should be very glad to sell the sheets of *H. by the C.* at 2/-... I would be glad that it were quite out of the way of a cheap edition.'

May 11. 1865. 'Accept any bidding pretty near 2/- a set for *The H. by the C.*'

May 14. 1865. 'I am sorry that nothing worth while can be had for the remainder of *The H. by the C.* Tinsley said sometime ago that the regular thing for remainders was 1/- per set, but whatever price fortune assigns I must be content with. So, as I am quite tired of possessing them, perhaps you will kindly dispose of the remainder sheets for whatever they will bring—by auction or otherwise—unless you think that disposing of them at such a price would injure you.'

These letters encourage more than one assumption:

(i) Obviously Le Fanu greatly over-produced his novel when—at his own expense—he had it printed in Dublin.

(ii) He either leased 3 vol. book rights to Tinsley or, maybe, got him to publish on commission. He did not part with copyright or ownership of sheets.

(iii) The 'Second Edition' was prepared by him in Dublin, possibly on his own initiative.

(iv) He never intended Bentley to publish a full-price new edition in England. From the first the balance of 450 sets of sheets was destined to be sold off *in sheets* and at a reduced price.

(v) Therefore his request that six copies be bound in regulation style was a private whim, for which he was prepared to pay. I suspect he meant Bentley just to borrow (or hire) Tinsley's brasses, to produce the six copies with their existing title pages and imprints, and not connect his own firm with them in any way. Bentley, however, perhaps from self-respect, perhaps also from gratification at the offer of a copy, preferred to bear the cost of a new title page and a new spine-imprint brass, even though they were only to occur six times. A gesture of the kind would have appealed to George Bentley. As a final touch, he called this amusing little venture a 'Third Edition'. The copy he kept for himself is the copy now in the Collection, which came from the Bentley file. Presumably the other five were sent to the author.

Admittedly the Bentley Private Catalogue confuses matters and, if taken at face value, challenges assumptions (iv) and (v). It says: 'Published July 3. 1865. 31*s.* 6*d.* SECOND EDITION OF REISSUE OF THE FIRST EDITION with a new Title-page. The First Edition was published by Tinsley Brothers, 1863, from whom the work was taken over.' There follows a collation—*not* of the Bentley 'third edition', but of the first Tinsley issue.

Now the B.P.C. was compiled long after the event (the section for 1864 in 1909), and the compilers were evidently unaware there had been a Tinsley 'Second', failed to locate (or forgot the existence of) the gift-copy of the Bentley 'Third', did not look up the letters and assumed that the title had been formally taken over from Tinsley for issue at 31*s.* 6*d.* I am of opinion, therefore, that their entry may be ignored; that the 'Third Edition' in fact consisted of *six copies only* and that the remainder of 444 sets of sheets was sold off at 1*s.* or less each, and ended up in the jobbing department of Chapman & Hall. These remainder sheets would naturally be a mixture of first and second editions, if, as would seem almost certain, Le Fanu only 'treated' a portion of the balance lying in Dublin when Tinsley's 'Second' was prepared for the market. Remainder-publishers cared nothing for 'editions', being merely concerned to sell such three-vol. sets as came most easily to a packer's hand. Why only one copy of the remainder issue has so far been discovered I cannot explain.

[1380] IN A GLASS DARKLY

Copy I: First Edition. 3 vols. Bentley 1872. Claret sand-grain cloth; pale cream end-papers.

Vol. I (iv)+(300)
II (iv) [*see Note below*]+(286) First leaf of final sig., T_1, a single inset.
III (ii)+270 Final leaf, S_7, a single inset. B

Note. The prelims. of Vol. II are thus constructed: single inset title-leaf; fly-title signed B and first leaf of first text-signature; a further single inset leaf, carrying 'Prologue', signed *a* and paged (i) ii. B_2 [first page of text and paged (3)] follows.

Contents: Green Tea—Mr Justice Harbottle—The Dragon Volant—Carmilla.

[1380*a*] **Copy II: First one-vol. Edition.** Bentley 1884: 'A New Edition.' Standard dark green cloth style of Bentley's Favourite Novels.

Half-title. pp. (viii)+(472)

No. 99 of Bentley's Favourite Novels.

[1381] LOST NAME (A)

3 vols. Bentley 1868. Scarlet sand-grain cloth; cream end-papers.

Vol. I iv+314 Final leaf, 20_5, a single inset.
II iv+(310) Final leaf, 20_3, a single inset.
III iv+(300) Publishers' cat., 32 pp. dated March 1868, at end. B

Note. This novel was issued in a secondary binding of red-brown sand-grain cloth, spine lettered from type and without imprint. A curious feature (common to the three copies I have seen) is a line-engraved front. in Vol. I, set sideways and printed on different paper. It looks like a cut extracted from a magazine, where there would have been space for it to be set across-page in a normal way.

POEMS OF JOSEPH SHERIDAN LE FANU (The). Edited by Alfred Perceval Graves [1382]

Downey & Co. 1896. Olive-green diagonal-fine-ribbed cloth, blocked and lettered in gold on front and spine, publishers' monogram in blind on back. Half-tone portrait front.

Half-title. pp. xxviii+(168) M_4 imprint leaf.

Ink signature: 'Mary Bennett 1896', on title and 'J. M. Bennett, Eastholme', on fly-leaf. Bookseller's ticket: 'Westley, Cheltenham', inside front cover.

Note. There was a remainder issue of this book in a plainer binding of cheaper quality, which I have never seen.

PURCELL PAPERS (The) (by the late Joseph Sheridan Le Fanu). With a Memoir by Alfred Perceval Graves [1383]

3 vols. Bentley 1880. Navy-blue diagonal-fine-ribbed cloth, gold-lettered on front and spine, back plain. Bevelled boards; pale yellow end-papers.

Vol. I (xxxii)+236
II (iv)+(274) Final leaf, 17_9, a single inset.
III (iv)+(290) Final leaf, 18_9, a single inset. B

Note. This is the first of the four styles of binding in which copies of *The Purcell Papers* are known (cf. Carter, *Binding Variants*, p. 130). I have ventured to differ from Carter in my description of the cloth.

Contents. The Ghost and the Bone-Setter—The Fortunes of Sir Robert Ardagh—The Last Heir of Castle Connor—The Drunkard's Dream—Passage in the Secret History of an Irish Countess—The Bridal of Carrigvarah—Strange Event in the Life of Schalken the Painter—Scraps of Hibernian Ballads—Jim Sullivan's Adventures in the Great Snow—A Chapter in the History of a Tyrone Family—An Adventure of Hardress Fitzgerald, a Royalist Captain—'The Quare Gander'—Bill Malowney's Taste of Love and Glory.

See also *The Watcher* and *Chronicles of Golden Friars*, Copy II.

ROSE AND THE KEY (The) [1384]

3 vols. Chapman & Hall 1871. Brown dotted-line-ribbed cloth, blocked in black and gold and lettered in gold; pale cream end-papers.

Half-title in Vol. I

Vol. I (viii) [paged iv] + 290 Final leaf, U_1, a single inset.
II iv + (310) Final leaf, Y_1, a single inset.
III iv + (312)

Ink signature, virtually erased, on half-title of Vol. I and title of Vols. II and III. Fine.

[1385] TENANTS OF MALORY (The): a Novel
3 vols. Tinsley 1867. Scarlet sand-grain cloth; cream end-papers.

Half-title in each vol.

Vol. I viii + 280
II vi + 280 Half-title a single inset.
III vi + 272 Half-title a single inset.

Presentation Copy: 'Mrs Fitzgerald. With the Author's kindest regards' in ink on fly-leaf of Vols. I and III. Fore-edge of Vol. I slightly affected by damp.

[1386] UNCLE SILAS: a Tale of Bartram-Haugh
Copy I: First Edition. 3 vols. Bentley 1864. Claret pebble-grain cloth; cream end-papers.

Half-title in each vol.

Vol. I (xiv) [paged (xii)] + (326) Half-title, (A_1), and final leaf, Z_1, single insets.
II (vi) [paged iv] + (316) Half-title, (A_1), a single inset.
III (vi) [paged iv] + 324 Half-title, (A_1), a single inset. B

[1386*a*] **Copy II: Another.** Three-quarter contemporary vellum, spine tooled in gold with inlaid red and green calf ornamental letter-pieces; marbled end-papers; red edges.

Half-titles missing: otherwise collation as Copy I.

Presentation Copy: 'To J. T. Delane Esqre in gratitude for generous and powerful encouragement. From the Author. May 1865' in ink on first blank leaf of Vol. I.

Note. The following extract from a letter written by Le Fanu to George Bentley serves as pedigree for this copy:

'May 3, 1865

'I am going to send a copy of UNCLE SILAS handsomely bound in half vellum inlaid, a presentation copy to Mr Delane, which his generous encouragement calls for—with an inscription from "the author". I am sure you will permit me to forward it through the post, under cover, to you—to send on to his *private* address—as I should be glad to be assured it had reached its destination.'

[1386*b*] **Copy III: First one-vol. and first Illustrated Edition.** Bentley 1865: 'A New Edition.' Standard green cloth style for Bentley's Favourite Novels. Wood-engraved front. and vignette title on plate paper after H. E. Doyle.

Half-title. pp. viii + (464) GG_8 blank.

No. 11 of Bentley's Favourite Novels. New Preface (2 pp.) dated December, 1864.

WATCHER (The), and other Weird Stories [1387]
Downey & Co. n.d. (1894). Grey linen flecked with white, blocked in black and silver; pale green leafy end-papers. Half-tone front., pictorial title printed in red and black, and illustrations in the text, both half-tone and line, after Brinsley Le Fanu.

pp. (viii) + (272) Publishers' adverts., 8 pp. on text paper undated, at end. Fine.

Note. Of the six stories in this volume, two first appeared in *Ghost Stories* and four in *The Purcell Papers*. *The Watcher* was re-published in 1942 by Mr Alan Downey at 'The Carthage Press, Waterford and Dublin' under the title 'No Escape'.

WILLING TO DIE [1388]
3 vols. Hurst & Blackett 1873. Brown diagonal-fine-ribbed cloth; greenish-black end-papers.

Half-title in each vol.

Vol. I (iv) + (312)
II (iv) + 320
III (iv) + (284) T_6 serves as fly-title to publishers' cat., 16 pp. undated, at end of volume.

Presentation Copy: 'To Mrs Lynch. With kind regards from Philip S. Lefanu', in ink on half-title of Vol. I. (Philip Lefanu was the author's elder son. He died in 1878.)

Binders' ticket: 'Leighton, Son & Hodge', at end of Vol. I. Covers slightly rubbed.

WYLDER'S HAND: a Novel [1389]
3 vols. Bentley 1864. Grey-purple coarse morocco cloth; cream end-papers.

Blank leaf precedes title in Vols. II and III

Vol. I (iv) + (314) Final leaf, Y_1, a single inset, preceded by sig. X, 4 leaves.
II (iv) + (324) Y_2 blank.
III (iv) + 310 Final leaf, Y_1, a single inset, preceded by sig. X, 2 leaves. B

WYVERN MYSTERY (The): a Novel [1390]
3 vols. Tinsley 1869. Smooth dark maroon cloth; cream end-papers.

Half-title in each vol.

Vol. I viii + (276)
II vi + (280) T_4 adverts. Half-title a single inset.
III vi + 264 Half-title a single inset.

Presentation Copy: 'Mrs Fitzgerald. With the Author's kindest regards' in ink on fly-leaf of Vol. I. Front cover of Vol. II badly stained: back cover of Vol. III spotted.

LENNOX, LORD WILLIAM

[1391] PHILIP COURTENAY, or Scenes at Home and Abroad

3 vols. Hurst & Blackett 1855. Claret ripple-grain cloth; royal-blue end-papers.

Vol. I (ii) + 324
II (ii) + 296
III (ii) + (290) U_1 adverts. and a single inset leaf. Publishers' cat., 24 pp. dated March 1855, at end.

Binders' ticket: 'Leighton, Son & Hodge', at end of Vol. I. Front cover of each vol. dulled by damp: rest of binding and interior of vols. unaffected.

[1392] TUFT HUNTER (The)

3 vols. Colburn 1843. Boards, labels.

Vol. I (ii) + 250 First leaf of final sig., M_1, a single inset.
II (ii) + (258) Final leaf, M_9, a single inset.
III (ii) + 240 Publishers' cat., 8 pp. undated, at end.

Book-plate: Coronet and Mitre, over 'Virtute non Vi'. Spine of Vol. III split at hinge, but a fine copy.

LEVER, CHARLES (1806–1872)

It has proved impossible to locate a copy of *A Rent in a Cloud* [1865]. This entry is otherwise a complete record of Lever's fiction in British volume-form.

[1393] ARTHUR O'LEARY: His Wanderings and Ponderings in Many Lands. Edited by his friend Harry Lorrequer and Illustrated by George Cruikshank

3 vols. Colburn 1844. Green fine-ribbed cloth, blocked in blind on front and back, gold-lettered and blocked with blind bands on spine; primrose yellow end-papers. Etched front. in each vol. and, in Vol. I, 3, in Vols. II and III, 2 plates each, by George Cruikshank.

Half-titles in Vols. II and III

Vol. I (iv) + 290 Final leaf, U_1, a single inset.
II (iv) + 320
III (iv) + (330) Final leaf, Y_5, Errata and a single inset.

At end of Vol. II bookseller's ticket: 'Sold by Lovejoy, Reading etc.', and of Vol. III binder's ticket: 'Bound by Lovejoy. Reading.' Very fine.

[1394] BARRINGTON

8vo. Chapman & Hall 1863.

Copy I: Brown trefoil-grain cloth (i.e. rows of tiny trefoils, giving the regular effect of 'bead-grain' but shamrock leaves instead of beads) blocked in blind and gold; cream end-papers. Etched front., vignette title and 24 plates by Phiz.

pp. (viii) + (412) Very fine.

Copy II. Another. Maroon coarse-morocco cloth. Blocking and collation as Copy I. [1394*a*]

Note. This copy is bound from the parts, so that possibly the binding-style (though less handsome than I) should have priority.

BRAMLEIGHS OF BISHOP'S FOLLY (The) [1395]

3 vols. Smith, Elder 1868. Dark plum sand-grain cloth, blind-blocked on front and back, gold-blocked and lettered (title and author in *itals*, former in caps and l.c., latter in caps). Cream end-papers. *Pl. 15*

Blank leaf precedes title in Vol. I

Vol. I viii + (340)
II iv + 356
III iv + (352) 67_8 blank.

Blind stamp: 'W. H. Smith', on fly-leaf of Vol. I.

Very fine.

Note. The Statutory copies examined are in dark *green* cloth, otherwise uniform, and were possibly 'earlies'. The very few copies of the book I have seen in the market were all plum-colour. There was a secondary binding of light crimson fine-pebble-grain cloth, blocked in black and lettered in gold, title and author in rom. caps and l.c.

CHARLES O'MALLEY: the Irish Dragoon (Edited by Harry Lorrequer) [1396]

2 vols. 8vo. Dublin: William Curry Jr. 1841. Dark green ribbed cloth, blocked in blind and gold; pale yellow end-papers. Etched front., vignette title, and 20 plates by Phiz in each vol.

Vol. I (xii) + 348 Publishers' cat., 8 pp. undated, inserted before front.
II (x) [paged (viii); pp. (iii) (iv) inset Dedication to the Marquis of Douro] + 336

Cloth of Vol. II rather bubbled.

Book-label of Stratford Public Library at beginning of Vol. I; and of T. Sowler, Manchester in Vol. II.

Notes. (i) This copy contains 'L'Envoy'—a Poem to G. P. R. James and a letter from him to Lever, forming signature Y_8–Z_6 in Vol. I. In later editions text ends on Y_7; Y_8 is blank.

(ii) The inset Dedication leaf appears variously in the prelims. to Vol. I.

(iii) P. S. O'Hegarty reports a later issue in rose-madder cloth, side-blocked uniform with *Our Mess* but with quite individual spine. In this issue prelims. to I are only x (and so paged), the List of Plates being printed on verso of last page of Contents.

[1397] CONFESSIONS OF CON CREGAN: the Irish Gil Blas [anon]

2 vols. Wm. S. Orr & Co., Amen Corner, n.d. [1849]. Scarlet morocco cloth, blocked with blind framing on front and back, pictorially blocked and lettered in gold on spine (title and vol. no. only, no imprint). Yellow end-papers. Etched front., vignette title and in Vol. I 12, in Vol. II 13 plates by Phiz; also wood-engraved drawings in the text after Phiz.

Half-title in Vol. II

Vol. I viii + 336
II viii + (308), X_4 adverts.

Booksellers' blind stamp: 'Burge and Perrin, Manchester' on front fly-leaf of Vol. I. Fine.

[1398] CONFESSIONS OF HARRY LORREQUER (The) [anon]

8vo. Dublin. William Curry Jun. 1839. Rose-madder fine-ribbed cloth, blocked in blind on front and back with martial emblems and decoration (cloth and blocking uniform with the bindings of *Our Mess*), on spine gold-blocked with all-over scroll decoration and gold-lettered: HARRY / LORREQUER / DUBLIN / CURRY & CO. Primrose end-papers. Etched front. and undated pictorial title (preceding printed title) and 20 plates by Phiz.

pp. (xviii) [(i) (ii), printed title and verso, a single inset; (iii) signed *a*] + (342) [paged 344, pp. (1) 2 being wrongly paged (3) 4].

Owing to this mis-paging (the final leaf of *a* being mistakenly reckoned as the first leaf of A), sig. A has 7 leaves, of which A_7 is a single inset.

Binder's ticket: 'Pilkington, Dublin', at end. Very fine.

Note. Carter (*Binding Variants*, p. 131) records three bindings for this novel. P. S. O'Hegarty reports a fourth, and the copy above described supplies a fifth. O'Hegarty supports Carter's chronology, dating A as 1839; Carter B and his own C (a different shade of green cloth and different side blocking; spine and advert. of *O'Malley* No. I as in Carter) as early 1841; Carter C (now D) as late 1841, and my E as 1842 or 1843.

[1399] CORNELIUS O'DOWD UPON MEN AND WOMEN AND OTHER THINGS IN GENERAL [anon]

3 vols. (1st, 2nd and 3rd Series). Blackwood 1864 (1st Series), 1865 (2nd and 3rd Series). Dark grass-green sand-grain cloth, with facsimile signature in gold on front, and elaborate scroll lettering in gold on spines; bevelled boards; dark chocolate end-papers.

Half-title in each vol.

First Series xii + (300)
Second Series (viii) [paged xii] + 322 Final leaf, X_1, a single inset.
Third Series viii + (288)

Book-plate of James du Pre in each vol. Fine. Small mark on front cover of 1st and back cover of 3rd Series.

Note. The first issue of the First Series has no Series indication on spine. The second issue (to which my copy belongs) carries the words *First Series.*

DALTONS (The), or Three Roads in Life [1400]

2 vols. 8vo. Chapman & Hall 1852. Dark brown ripple-grain cloth, blocked in blind, lettered in gold; yellow end-papers. Etched front., vignette title and 24 plates by Phiz in Vol. I; front. only and 22 plates in Vol. II.

Half-title in each vol.

Vol. I (viii) + 384
II (viii) + 360

Book-plate: 'J. C. Frampton', in each vol. Spines slightly dulled.

Note. Bound from the Parts. This is first issue binding. For later variants see Carter, *Binding Variants*, p. 132.

*DAVENPORT DUNN, or the Man of the Day [1401]

8vo. Chapman & Hall 1859. Plum ripple-grain cloth, blocked in blind on front and back, blocked and lettered in gold on spine. Etched front., vignette title and 42 plates by Phiz.

pp. (viii) + 696

Note. This is one of the titles later issued in the uniform Lever style (see below, under *One of Them*) and it may be noted that what I presume to be the first issue binding was of colour and grain as above, with title and author in an ornamental and roughly hexagonal medallion on spine, the word DAVENPORT curving over the top of DUNN.

DAY'S RIDE (A): a Life's Romance [1402]

2 vols. Chapman & Hall 1863. Bright green (occasionally dark blue) dot-and-line-grain cloth, with blind frames and gold lettering; pale cream end-papers.

Vol. I (ii) + (320) X_8 adverts. (on verso).
II (ii) + (328)

Blind stamp: 'W. H. Smith & Son', on fly-leaf of Vol. I. Very fine.

Although described on titles as Second Edition, this is the first book issue, the implied 'first edition' being the serial appearance in 'All the Year Round'.

DIARY AND NOTES OF HORACE TEMPLETON ESQUIRE, late Secretary of Legation at —— [anon] [1403]

2 vols. Chapman & Hall 1848. Dark grass-green fine-diaper cloth, blocked in blind and lettered in gold; cream end-papers.

Half-title in each vol.
Vol. I (iv) + 308
II (iv) + 280

Signature: 'R. M. Milnes' [Richard Monckton Milnes, Lord Houghton], on half-title of Vol. I and a few annotations by him identifying the originals of certain characters. Cloth very fine, but vols. recased.

[1404] DODD FAMILY ABROAD (The)
8vo. Chapman & Hall 1854. Olive-brown ripple-grain cloth, blocked in blind on front and back, blocked and lettered in gold on spine. Pale yellow end-papers. Etched front., vignette title (preceding half-title) and 38 plates by Phiz.
Half-title. pp. (xvi) + 624
Bound from the parts.

[1405] FORTUNES OF GLENCORE (The)
3 vols. Chapman & Hall 1857. Myrtle-green morocco cloth, blocked in blind and lettered in gold; yellow end-papers.
Vol. I x + (304) Title-page a single inset, p. (iii) signed *b*.
II (ii) + 296
III (ii) + (312)
Book-plate of George Hamilton Seymour on inside front cover, and of Henry Hampden Dutton on fly-leaf of each vol. Fine.

[1406] GERALD FITZGERALD: The Chevalier. A Novel
Ward & Downey 1899 (First English Edition). Green canvas, blocked and lettered in gold; white end-papers. Etched front. by A. D. M'Cormick.
Half-title. pp. viii + 408 Publishers' cat., 16 pp. dated May 1899, at end.
Note. The first book edition of this story was published in New York by Harper in 1859.

[1407] KNIGHT OF GWYNNE (The): a Tale of the Time of the Union
8vo. Chapman & Hall 1847. Rose-madder fine-ribbed cloth, spine-blocked in gold (title and author in fancy frame, no imprint); yellow end-papers. Etched front., title and 38 plates by Phiz.
Half-title. pp. (xii) + 628
Covers slightly worn at base.
Note. I am not sure whether this is a first issue binding. I have only seen the book, either in this style or in the standardised rose-madder binding adopted for several Lever titles and known to be of later date.

[1408] *Pl. 15* LORD KILGOBBIN: a Tale of Ireland in our Own Time
Copy I: First Edition. 3 vols. Smith, Elder 1872. Dark green dotted-line-ribbed cloth, blocked in black on front and back, black-blocked and gold-lettered on spine. Pinkish cream end-papers.
Half-title in Vol. I
Vol. I viii + (296) 19_4 blank.
II iv + 288
III iv + (260) 54_2 imprint leaf.
Fine.

Copy II: First one-vol. and first Illustrated Edition. Smith, Elder 1872: 'New edition.' Dark green sand-grain cloth; chocolate end-papers. Wood-engraved front. and 4 illustrations signed S. L. F. (S. Luke Fildes). [1408*a*]
pp. (viii) + (472) 30_4 adverts.
Book-plate of John Browne. Very fine.

LUTTRELL OF ARRAN [1409]
8vo. Chapman & Hall 1865. Plum sand-grain cloth, blocked in blind and gold; light-chocolate end-papers. Etched front., pictorial title and 30 plates by Phiz.
pp. (viii) + (504)
Book-plate of James Stewart. Very fine.
Note. The binding of this copy has every appearance of being a primary. Title and author in an elaborate ornamental frame, not unlike that used on *Barrington*, are gold-blocked from a specially cut brass, and the whole effect is considered and important. Copies in dark green wide dot-and-line grain cloth with a blind panel-design on spine and, gold-lettered from type, not only with title and author, but also with 'ILLUSTRATIONS BY H. K. BROWNE', are certainly secondaries.

MARTINS OF CRO MARTIN (The) [1410]
8vo. Chapman & Hall 1856. Grass-green morocco cloth, blocked in blind and gold; yellow end-papers. Etched front., vignette title and 38 plates by Phiz.
Half-title. pp. (xiv) + (626) pp. xiii (xiv) and final leaf, $2S_1$, single insets.
Fine. Bound from the parts.

MAURICE TIERNAY, or The Soldier of Fortune (by the author of 'Sir Jasper Carew') [1411]
Thomas Hodgson, n.d. [1855]. Green glazed printed boards in standard Parlour Library style; printed end-papers.
Half-title. pp. (496)
Book-plate of Stephen George Holland on verso of half-title.
No. 119 in the Parlour Library.

NUTS AND NUTCRACKERS [anon] [1412]
Copy I: First Edition. Fcap 8vo. Wm. S. Orr & Co. 1845. Scarlet smooth-morocco cloth, pictorially blocked in gold on front and spine;

decoratively blocked in blind on front and back. All edges gilt. Etched front. and 5 plates by Phiz and numerous wood-engravings in the text after Phiz.

Half-title. pp. viii + 232

The second edition collates identically, and is uniformly bound.

[1412*a*] **Copy II: Third Edition.** Small 8vo. Chapman & Hall 1857. Yellow paper boards, pictorially printed and lettered in black. Spine down-lettered; back cover printed with adverts. Illustrations and collation as Copy I.

This edition was printed from Orr's type or plates, but the frame enclosing each page of text was omitted and the type imposed on taller paper.

[1413] O'DONOGHUE (The): a Tale of Ireland Fifty Years Ago

8vo. Dublin: W. Curry Jr. 1845. Scarlet (later issue in rose-madder) fine-morocco cloth, blocked on front and back in blind and on spine elaborately blocked and lettered in gold; yellow end-papers. Etched front. and 25 plates by Phiz.

Half-title. pp. (xii) + 410 First leaf of final sig., $2D_1$, a single inset.

Bookseller's ticket: 'G. Mann, Bookseller, Cornhill', inside front cover. Very fine. Bound from the parts.

[1414] ONE OF THEM

8vo. Chapman & Hall 1861. Rose-madder ribbed cloth, spine-blocked in gold; pale cream end-papers. Etched front., vignette title and 28 plates by Phiz.

pp. (viii) + (472)

Ink signature: 'W. Gardner Bird', on fly-leaf.

Note. This is almost certainly a late style of binding, which occurs on several other 8vo Levers and was carried forward to later editions also. Title and author form part of a medallion design with a pipe-smoking Irishman at the top of it. There is no spine-imprint. I have seen the book catalogued as in blue cloth but never handled such a copy.

[1415] OUR MESS (edited by Charles Lever)

3 vols. 8vo. Dublin: William Curry Jr. 1843–1844.

Vol. I: JACK HINTON, THE GUARDSMAN.

Vols. II, III: TOM BURKE OF OURS.

Rose-madder fine-ribbed cloth, blocked in blind and gold with martial emblems; pale yellow end-papers. Steel-engraved portrait front. after S. Lover, 26 etched plates and 9 wood engravings in Vol. I; etched front. and 23 plates in Vol. II; etched front. and 19 plates in Vol. III—all by Phiz.

Half-titles in Vols. I and II

Vol. I (xx) [paged (xii)] + 396 First 4 leaves consist of 6 pp. of adverts. and half-title.

II (xii) + 372 The half-title serves for the 2 vols. of *Tom Burke*, as does also B_1, fly-title.

III (viii) + (304) U_4 adverts., U_5 leaf of directions for separate binding of *Jack Hinton* and *Tom Burke*. U_{6-7} titles for *Tom Burke*, Vols. I and II; U_8 title for *Jack Hinton* (all dated 1844).

Bookseller's ticket: 'Deighton, Worcester', inside front cover of Vol. II. Spines faded. Back cover of Vol. I slightly damp-stained. Covers of Vols. II and III fine.

PAUL GOSSLETT'S CONFESSIONS IN LOVE, LAW AND THE CIVIL SERVICE [1416]
[anon]

Virtue & Co., 26 Ivy Lane 1868. Royal-blue sand grain cloth, pictorially blocked and lettered in gold on front, up-lettered in gold on spine. Pale yellow end-papers. Wood-engraved front. after Marcus Stone.

pp. (iv) + (156) L_5 L_6 adverts.

Book-plate of F. J. Meijer. Fine.

*ROLAND CASHEL [1417]

8vo. Chapman & Hall 1850. Dark plum ripple-grain cloth, blocked in blind on front and back, blocked and lettered in gold on spine. Etched front., vignette title and 38 plates by Phiz.

Half-title. pp. viii + 628

Note. Another of the titles later issued in uniform Lever style as described under *One of Them.* The binding above indicated is, I think, the primary one. Title and author (the former in fancy lettering on a curve) are enclosed in a decorative oval frame, and at the base of the spine, also in gold, appears the standing figure of a girl—a reproduction of the girl shown in the frontispiece.

SIR BROOK FOSSBROOKE [1418]

3 vols. Blackwood 1866. Bright blue sand-grain cloth, blocked in blind front and back, blocked and lettered in gold on spine (title in rom. caps, author in ital. caps). Plum end-papers. *Pl. 15*

Blank leaf and half-title precede title in Vol. I; half-title only in Vols. II and III

Vol. I (viii) + 324

II (iv) + 328

III (iv) + 324 Publishers' cat., 20 pp. undated, at end.

Fine. Ink-spot on front cover of Vol. III.

Note. A secondary binding in similar cloth was issued later, but without publisher's imprint on spine and lettered from type (I think in ital. caps).

[1419] *Pl. 15* SIR JASPER CAREW: His Life and Experiences (by the author of 'Maurice Tiernay')
Thomas Hodgson, n.d. [1855].

Copy I. Green glazed printed boards in standard Parlour Library style; printed end-papers.

Half-title. pp. 480 [paged (1)–viii + (9)–480]

Book-plate of Stephen George Holland on verso of half-title.

No. 123 of the Parlour Library.

[1419*a*] *Pl. 15* **Copy II.** Specially designed boards in sapphire-blue, ruby and black, on white, symbolising jewellery (probably one of the 'brilliant fancy covers by Alfred Crowquill' advertised at end).

Bookseller's yellow label: 'Thomas W. Arthur Carlisle', tipped in between front end-papers.

The half-title, with name of series and number of vol., has been cancelled. Otherwise collation as Copy I.

Both vols. fine. The bindings were reproduced as frontispiece to Carter's *Binding Variants.*

[1420] ST PATRICK'S EVE
Small sq. cr. 8vo. Chapman & Hall 1845. Green fine-ribbed cloth, pictorially blocked and lettered in gold on centre of front and all down spine, blind-blocked on front and back. All edges gilt. Etched front. and 3 plates by Phiz and numerous wood-engraved text illustrations after Phiz.

pp. (iv) + (204)

Ink-inscription: 'Henry Thomas Mousley with the sincere regards of Prince L. Crawford, April 3rd 1845.' on fly-leaf. Very fine.

Note. This issue measures (sheet size) $6\frac{5}{8} \times 4\frac{7}{8}$. I am indebted to P. S. O'Hegarty for a note of two further (and undoubtedly later) issues in cloth of a lighter green. The first of these lacks gilt edges, lower half of spine blocking and gold design on front cover. It measures $6\frac{13}{16} \times 4\frac{1}{2}$. The second is uniform, but in addition lacks the four harps blocked in blind in the corners of front and back covers.

[1421] TALES OF THE TRAINS: being some Chapters of Railroad Romance (by Tilbury Tramp, Queen's Messenger)
Sq. fcap 8vo. William S. Orr 1845. Red morocco cloth, blocked in on front with title and railway-engine in gold surrounded by blind ornament, on spine in gold with title and scroll-work, on back in blind. Gilt edges; pale yellow end-papers. Wood-engravings in the text.

Pp. 160 [paged (i)–viii + (5)–156]

Bookseller's ticket: 'S. W. Theakston, Scarboro', inside front cover. Fine.

Notes. (i) This work was first issued in five (? monthly) parts, wrappered in buff. I have only seen a specimen of Part I, lacking front wrapper, and leading off with a title-page dated 1845 and carrying the name of the first story. No preface or overall title (as in book issue) is included in this part.

(ii) P. S. O'Hegarty reports a variant, in very dark brown diagonal-ribbed cloth vertically striped in red (same style used on *Bon Gaultier Ballads*) with an oval in gold on front.

THAT BOY OF NORCOTT'S [1422]
8vo. Smith, Elder 1869. Smooth apple-green cloth, blocked in blind front and back, on spine pictorially blocked and lettered in gold; bevelled boards; slate end-papers. Wood-engraved front. and 4 plates after Mary Ellen Edwards.

Half-title. pp. viii + (276) 18_2 adverts.

Book-plate of Frederick William Brown. Fine. Small scrape on front cover.

TONY BUTLER [anon] [1423]
3 vols. Blackwood 1865. Green sand-grain cloth, blocked in blind and gold; chocolate end-papers. *Pl. 15*

Half-title in each vol.

Vol. I (iv) + 322 Final leaf, X_1, a single inset.
II (iv) + 324
III (iv) + 322 Final leaf, X_1, a single inset.

Very fine.

Note. A 'New Edition' of *Tony Butler* was published in 3 vols. by Chapman & Hall in 1872. It consisted of Blackwood's sheets with new prelims., and was bound in bright apple-green diagonal-dotted-line-grain cloth, blocked in black and lettered in gold. The end-papers were plain chocolate, and a panel advert. of Chapman & Hall's 'Library Edition' of Lever faced the title in each vol.

It is curious that Blackwood should have sold three-decker sheets for a Chapman & Hall 'secondary', and that the latter should have bound the book with considerable pretension. This edition has no appearance of being a remainder, for the binding is handsome, the spines imprinted, and the whole effect important. The only copy I have seen had W. H. Smith blind stamps on fly-leaves, and possibly the edition was a Smith venture on the lines of the blue-cloth issue of *Felix Holt.*

LEWES, G. H. (1817–1878)

RANTHORPE [anon] [1424]
Chapman & Hall 1847. Rose-madder fine-ribbed cloth.

pp. viii + (352) Publishers' cat., 32 pp. dated June 1847, at end.

A volume in Chapman & Hall's Monthly Series (3742 (13) in Section III), but with regulation imprint on spine. Two spots on covers.

[1425] ROSE, BLANCHE AND VIOLET

3 vols. Smith, Elder 1848. Dark green wavy-grain cloth.

Vol. I xii + 304
II iv + (316) X_6 adverts.
III iv + 320

Booksellers' ticket: 'Simms & Dinham, Manchester', inside front cover of Vols. I and II. Book-plate: stag over monogram, in each vol. Small tear at head of spine of Vols. II and III.

LEWIS, LADY THERESA. See Eden, Hon. Emily

LINTON, MRS E. LYNN (1822–1898)

[1426] AMYMONE: a Romance of the Days of Pericles (by the author of 'Azeth the Egyptian')

3 vols. Bentley 1848. Half-cloth boards, labels.

Vol. I (viii) + 336
II (ii) + 328
III (ii) + 348

Bookseller's ticket: 'Bentham, Southsea', on inside front cover of each vol.

Note. Although no author's name appears on titles, the Dedication is signed 'E. Lynn' and the Preface 'Eliza Lynn'.

[1427] ATONEMENT OF LEAM DUNDAS (The): a Novel

3 vols. Chatto & Windus 1876. Slate-grey diagonal-fine-ribbed cloth, blocked and lettered in black on front, blocked with blind framing on back, blocked in black and lettered in gold on spine.

Half-title in each vol.

Vol. I (x) + (316) Pp. (ix) (x), fly-title to Book I, form a single inset leaf.
II (viii) + (292)
III (viii) + (272) S_8 publishers' device. Publishers' cat., 32 pp. dated April 1876, at end.

Pencil signature: 'W. D. Gainsford' on fly-leaf of each vol. Fine.

Note. An unusual specimen of Chatto binding, belonging to the very brief period when the firm used the same designers (or designers with similar ambitions) as worked for Bentley and, in a lesser degree, for Smith, Elder, Tinsley, and Chapman & Hall. This period only lasted during 1876 and 1877, and other examples of the style then adopted are the definitive edition of the *Reliques of Father Prout* 1876 (see Mahony) and Mallock's *New Republic* 1877. Chatto soon evolved their characteristic tricksy but elegant binding style, using smooth cloths, often of pale colouring, with floral blocking in colours.

AUTOBIOGRAPHY OF CHRISTOPHER KIRKLAND (The) [1428]

3 vols. Bentley 1885. Dark blue fancy-grain (intersecting circles) cloth; pale green flowered end-papers.

Vol. I (viii) + (298) Final leaf, 19_5, a single inset.
II (ii) + 302 First leaf of final sig., 38_1, a single inset.
III (ii) + 320 B

AZETH: THE EGYPTIAN. A Novel [anon] [1429]

3 vols. Newby 1847. Half black morocco, cloth sides, with Crewe crest in gold on front and Egyptian emblems on spine.

Vol. I (viii) [paged iv] + (340)
II (ii) + (436) U_2 blank (lacking in this copy).
III (ii) + (384) R_{12} blank (lacking in this copy).

Crewe book-plate in Vol. II. R. Monckton Milnes' (Lord Houghton's) copy, with a letter to him from E. Lynn dated 21 May 1847 pasted to end-paper of Vol. I.

Originally issued in puce diagonal-fine-ribbed cloth, blocked in blind and spine-lettered in gold.

GIRL OF THE PERIOD (The) and other Social Essays [1430]

2 vols. 8vo. Bentley 1883. Brown diaper cloth; black end-papers.

Blank leaf and half-title precede title in each vol.

Vol. I (xii) [paged x] + (344)
II (viii) + (336) Y_8 adverts.

Book-plate of A. M. Broadley in each vol., and note by him on blank leaf of Vol. I stating this was Mrs Lynn Linton's own copy, given by her to him. Inserted (by A. M. B.) are a caricature, letters *from* Mrs L. L. on various themes, letters *to* Mrs L. L. from Lady Dilke about the Dilke scandal, etc.

Note. This work is not, of course, fiction. But the title-essay, when it appeared in the *Saturday Review* on 14 March 1868, caused such a furore that its heading became a catch-phrase for nearly two years, and provoked several and various by-products, some of which are represented in the Collection and are at least partly fictional.

The immediate reactions to the original *Saturday* article (of which an unauthorised reprint in two-penny pamphlet form was produced in Bristol) were bitterly hostile. The authorship was, of course, unknown; but cartoons depicted an ugly and jealous harridan deliberately blackening the reputations of the young and pretty women of the time.

The first comparatively serious counterstroke was the publication by Robert Hardwicke, 192 Piccadilly, of a small square 8vo pamphlet (16 pp. stitched, pp. (1) (2) serving as front cover, pp. (15) (16) adverts.) entitled: THE MAN OF THE PERIOD. A Companion to 'The Girl of the

Period'. Unsigned and dated 3 September 1868, this pamphlet matches against feminine vanity and extravagance the parallel masculine failings, leaving the final advantage with the ladies.

As the months passed, however, journalistic enterprise saw a chance of profit in farcical exaggeration of the *Saturday's* charges. A magazine called *Echoes from the Clubs* published, late in 1868, THE GIRL OF THE PERIOD ALMANACK FOR 1869. This publication—a large 4to of 8 pages, issued at 3*d.* as 'Echoes No. 82' from 'Echoes' Office, 19 Catherine Street—consisted of letters to 'Miss Echo' from a number of young women, describing (with illustrations) various 'all-girl' clubs, formed in imitation of men's clubs, for rowing, betting, swimming, shooting, etc. The emancipation was genteel and undress was carefully avoided. But monocles, cigarettes and an occasional d—— showed that the young persons were definitely out and about.

In March 1869 (owing, according to the leading article, to the immense success of the Almanack) appeared No. 1 of THE GIRL OF THE PERIOD MISCELLANY, a sixpenny monthly magazine of 32 pages with an attractive coloured cover, containing prose, verse and pictures and a serial story: 'The Wooing and the Winning' by 'an ex-girl of the Period.' This Miscellany ran for 9 numbers (March to November), was issued as to Nos. 1–7 from 342 Strand, as to Nos. 8 and 9 from 183 Strand, and appeared each month with its pictorial cover printed in different and very dashing colours. Towards the end of the year an ALMANACK FOR 1870 appeared from the latter address, more or less uniform with the previous Almanack for 1869.

Meantime, on 30 October 1869, had appeared, also from 183 Strand, No. 1 of a twopenny weekly paper: THE PERIOD. This paper, in folio, with a front page in colours, ran until 26 February 1870 (No. 18). It then changed hands; and, after a short interval, began a New Series in smaller format from Wyman's offices at 75 Great Queen Street, of which No. 1 appeared on 14 May. Whether this New Series ran beyond 15 October (No. 23) I do not know, for it is not recorded at all in *The Times* Handlist.

The last item of 'Girl of the Periodiana' in the Collection is a story by Bracebridge Hemyng, as always tireless in pursuit of topicality, entitled *The Man of the Period.* This is recorded under his name (3587 in Section II below).

The Girl of the Period captured the stage as well as journalism. During 1869 a play called 'The Girl of the Period' was acted at Drury Lane, and another at the Lyceum: 'Hypermnestra, the Girl of her Period'.

IONE [1431]

3 vols. Chatto & Windus 1883. Smooth grey-green cloth; pale-green-on-white flowered end-papers.

Half-title in Vol. I

Vol. I (viii) + 296
II (iv) + (296)
III (iv) + (292) Publishers' cat., 32 pp. dated October 1883, at end.

Very fine.

LIZZIE NORTON OF GREYRIGG: a Novel [1432]

3 vols. Tinsley 1866. Green fine-morocco cloth.

Half-title in Vol. I

Vol. I (viii) + 320
II (iv) + (312) X_4 adverts.
III (iv) + 308 Text ends on 306; 307/308 'Explanation'.

Very fine.

"MY LOVE!" [1433]

3 vols. Chatto & Windus 1881. Smooth olive-brown cloth; dark-brown-on-white flowered end-papers.

Half-title in Vol. I; leaf carrying advert. on verso and half-title precede title in Vols. II and III

Vol. I (viii) + (304)
II (viii) + (324)
III (viii) + (300) Publishers' cat., 32 pp. dated March 1881, at end.

Very fine.

REALITIES: a Tale (by E. Lynn) [1434]

3 vols. Saunders & Otley 1851. Half-cloth boards, labels.

Half-title in Vols. II and III

Vol. I (viii) + (304) O_8 imprint leaf.
II (iv) + 304
III (iv) + 264

R. Monckton Milnes' (Lord Houghton's) copy with 'Mr Milnes' in his hand in ink on front cover of Vol. I. Bookseller's ticket: 'Folthorp, Brighton', on inside front cover of each vol.

REBEL OF THE FAMILY (The) [1435]

3 vols. Chatto & Windus 1880. Smooth grey-blue cloth; pale-grey-on-white flowered end-papers.

Half-title in Vol. I; leaf carrying advert. on verso and half-title precede title in Vols. II and III

Vol. I (viii) + 304
II (viii) + (284) T_6 publishers' device.
III (viii) + 288 Publishers' cat., 32 pp. dated October 1880, at end.

Very fine.

[1436] TRUE HISTORY OF JOSHUA DAVIDSON (The) [anon]
Strahan 1872. Brown sand-grain cloth; very dark green end-papers.
Blank leaf and half-title precede title. pp. viii + (280)
Book-label of Rev. Wm. Major Scott, M.A.
Note. In the guise of a biography of a fictitious Cornish carpenter during the mid-nineteenth century, this is a novelised version of the Life of Christ.

[1437] UNDER WHICH LORD?
3 vols. Chatto & Windus 1879. Smooth brown cloth; blue-on-white flowered end-papers. Wood engraved front. and 3 plates in each vol. after Arthur Hopkins.
Blank leaf and half-title precede title in Vol. I; half-titles in Vols. II and III
Vol. I (xii) + (332) Y_6 publishers' device.
II (viii) + 292 Publishers' cat., 40 pp. dated August 1879, at end.
III (viii) + 308
Binder's ticket: 'Burn', at end of Vol. I. Very fine.

[1438] WITCH STORIES (Collected by E. Lynn Linton)
Chapman & Hall 1861. Light-claret bead-grain cloth, blocked in blind and lettered in gold.
pp. iv + 428
Ink signature: 'T. H. Kersley L.L.D.' inside front cover. Fine.

[1439] WITH A SILKEN THREAD and other Stories
3 vols. Chatto & Windus 1880. Smooth dark blue cloth; blue-on-white flowered end-papers.
Leaf carrying advert. on verso and half-title precede title in each vol.
Vol. I (xii) + (292)
II (viii) + (288) T_8 blank.
III (viii) + (332) Y_6 blank.
Very fine.

LISTER, CHARLES

[1440] COLLEGE CHUMS (The): a Novel
2 vols. Newby 1845. Dark grey-blue ribbed cloth.
Vol. I (ii) + 290 Final leaf, O_1, a single inset.
II (ii) + (282) Final leaf, N_9, a single inset.

LISTER, MRS MARIA THERESA (later Lady G. Cornwall Lewis)

[1441] DACRE: a Novel [anon]. Edited by the Countess of Morley
3 vols. Longman etc. 1834. Boards, labels.
Half-title in each vol.
Vol. I (iv) + 298 First leaf of final sig., O_1, a single inset.
II (iv) + 348
III (iv) + (348)
Book-label of R. J. Ll. Price, Rhiwlas Library, and bookseller's ticket: 'Seacome, Chester', inside front cover of each vol. Very fine.

LISTER, T. H. (1800–1842)

This is a complete schedule of the fiction, original and 'edited', by T. H. Lister. *C.B.E.L.* credits him with three further novels, which were in fact written by Lady Charlotte Bury, Mrs Gore and Lord Normanby. He is in the front rank of silver-fork novelists, and *Granby* is an essential document to the student of Lady Caroline Lamb (*cf.* my *Bulwer and his Wife*, pp. 53 *note* and elsewhere) and of personalities and manners of her time.

ARLINGTON: a Novel (by the author of 'Granby') [1442]
3 vols. Colburn & Bentley 1832. Boards, labels.
Vol. I (ii) + 326 Final leaf, P_7, a single inset.
II (ii) + (350) Final leaf, Q_7, a single inset.
III (ii) + (324) Errata slip tipped in after p. (324).
Book-label of R. J. Ll. Price, Rhiwlas Library, in each vol. Very fine.

GRANBY: a Novel [anon] [1443]
3 vols. Colburn 1826. Boards, labels.
Half-title in Vols. I and III
Vol. I (iv) + 324
II (ii) + 342 Final leaf, Q_3 [mis-signed Q_2] a single inset.
III (iv) + (332) Q_4 adverts.
Fine, though a little frail. This important book is extremely rare in original state.

HERBERT LACY (by the author of 'Granby') [1444]
3 vols. Colburn 1828. Boards, labels.
Half-title in each vol.
Vol. I vi + (306) pp. (v) vi, Dedication, and final leaf, O_9, single insets. 4 pp. cat. of John Taylor and James Duncan inserted between back end-papers.
II (iv) + (292) (O_2) adverts.
III (iv) + (288) N_{12} adverts.
Fine.

Edited by T. H. Lister

ANNE GREY: a Novel [anon] Edited by the author of 'Granby' [1445]
3 vols. Saunders & Otley 1834. Boards, labels.
Vol. I (vi) + (308) P_4 blank. Title-page a single inset.
II (ii) + 320
III (ii) + (324) P_6 adverts.

Bookseller's ticket: 'Seacome, Chester', inside front cover of each vol. Very fine.

Notes. (i) This novel was written by Lister's sister, Lady Harriet Cradock.

(ii) 'Editor's Advertisement' occupies pp. (iii)–(vi) of Vol. I. The size of gatherings varies between different vols., e.g. in vol. I O is 6 leaves, in Vol. III, 12 leaves.

LOCKHART, JOHN GIBSON (1794–1854)

[1446] REGINALD DALTON (by the author of 'Valerius' and 'Adam Blair')

3 vols. Edinburgh: Blackwood 1823. Pink boards, labels.

Half-title in each vol.

Vol. I (vi) + 346 pp. (v) (vi), Dedication, and final leaf, Y_5, single insets.
II (iv) + (344)
III (iv) + (352) (Y_2)–(Y_8) adverts.

Dedicated to Henry Mackenzie (author of *The Man of Feeling*), this is the dedicatee's copy, with his ink signature on title of each vol. The volumes were covered with plain paper when I bought them, and in the course of it being removed, the spine of Vol. I became detached and that of Vol. II weakened. The former has been repaired. Otherwise the novel's condition is nearly as fresh as new.

[1447] SOME PASSAGES IN THE LIFE OF MR ADAM BLAIR, Minister of the Gospel at Cross-Meikle [anon]

Edinburgh: Blackwood 1822. Boards, label.

Half-title. pp. (iv) + (350) Y_3–Y_8 adverts. Longman etc. cat., 12 pp. dated August 1822, inserted between front end-papers. Very fine.

[1448] VALERIUS: a Roman Story [anon]

3 vols. Edinburgh: Blackwood 1821. Mottled pink and white boards, labels.

Half-title in each vol.

Vol. I (iv) + (312)
II (iv) + (348)
III (iv) + 312

Very fine.

See also WILSON, JOHN, *Noctes Ambrosianae*, 5 vols., 1863.

Edited by J. G. Lockhart

[1449] JANUS, or the Edinburgh Literary Almanack

Edinburgh: Oliver & Boyd 1826. Brown paper boards printed in black.

Half-title. pp. viii + (544)

Bookseller's ticket: 'D. Lawrence, Dublin', on front cover. Spine a little stained, but a fine sound copy.

Note. Edited by Lockhart, this Miscellany contains hitherto unpublished contributions by 'Christopher North' (John Wilson), Maria Edgeworth, D. M. Moir and Lockhart himself.

LONG, LADY CATHARINE (? –1867) [1450]

SIR ROLAND ASHTON: a Tale of the Times

2 vols. Nisbet 1844. Bright blue morocco cloth, gold-lettered on spine (title and author only).

Half-title and Errata-slip in each vol.

Vol. I (viii) + 380
II (iv) + 420

Book-label: 'Sandrock Hill' in each vol. Binders' ticket: 'Westleys' at end of Vol. I. Fine.

Note. An anti-tractarian story, and the first work of a well-known writer on religious themes and composer of sacred music. Lady Catharine was the daughter of the third Earl of Orford.

LOVER, SAMUEL (1797–1868) [1451]

HANDY ANDY: a Tale of Irish Life *Pl. 22*

8vo. Frederick Lover and Richard Groombridge 1842. Dark green fine-diaper cloth, blocked in gold and blind; yellow end-papers. Front. and 23 illustrations on steel by the author, each imprinted 'F. Lover....1842'.

pp. iv + 380

Bookseller's stamp: 'Williams Library, Cheltenham', on inside front cover. Very fine.

RORY O'MORE: a National Romance [1452]

3 vols. Bentley 1837. Boards, labels. Steel-etched front. and 4 plates by the author in each vol.

Half-title in Vols. II and III

Vol. I (iv) + 300 Catalogue of James Duncan, 8 pp. dated March 1837, at end.
II (iv) + 300
III (iv) + (316)

Labels discoloured, but a fine sharp copy.

TREASURE TROVE: the First of a Series of Accounts of Irish Heirs: being a Romantic Irish Tale of the Last Century [1453]

8vo. Frederick Lover, Aldine Chambers, Paternoster Row 1844. Light-claret fine-ribbed cloth, blocked in blind on front and back, gold-lettered on spine. Pale yellow end-papers. Etched front. and 25 plates by the author.

pp. iv + (412) [curiously paged, i.e.: B_1, 'A Few Words about £. S. D.', is paged (i) ii; B_2 is paged (3) 4, and so on, correctly. The List of Illustrations is printed on verso of final page of text, i.e. on p. (412).

Ink signature: 'Sir G. Napier', on verso of flyleaf. Spine repaired at head, binding a little shaken; but a good unsophisticated copy bound from the Parts, which bore the title., £. S. D.: TREASURE TROVE. The sheets of the book-issue are thus head-lined.

LYALL, EDNA (1857–1903)

[1454] AUTOBIOGRAPHY OF A SLANDER (The)

Copy I: First Edition. Longman etc. 1887. Pale grey-blue wrappers, printed in red and black.

Half-title. pp. (viii) + (120)

Spine defective at tail.

[1454*a*] **Copy II: Illustrated Edition.** Sq. 8vo. Longman etc. 1892. Smooth navy-blue cloth, elaborately blocked in light blue, white and gold; black end-papers; all edges gilt. Wood-engraved front. and 19 illustrations after L. Speed, all on text paper. Title printed in red and black.

Half-title. pp. (xii) [including front.] + (148) K_2 blank.

Ink signature: 'H. E. Talbot fr. D. T. Sept. 12/1892' on half-title. Fine.

[1455] AUTOBIOGRAPHY OF A TRUTH (The)
Longman etc. 1896.

Copy I. Pale grey wrappers, printed in red and black.

Half-title. pp. (viii) + (116) Text ends p. 112 (H_8). I_1 Author's Note, I_2 adverts. Very fine. Ink-signature: 'Priscilla E. Weight. February 1903' on half-title.

[1455*a*] **Copy II.** Smooth apple-green cloth lettered in chocolate; black end-papers. Collation as Copy I. Very fine.

[1456] DONOVAN: a Novel
Pl. 12 3 vols. Hurst & Blackett 1882. Smooth blue-grey cloth, blocked in black and lettered in gold; grey-chocolate end-papers.

Half-title in each vol.

Vol. I (vi) + 322 pp. (v) (vi), Dedication, and final leaf, Y_1, single insets.

II (iv) + 326 First leaf of final sig., Y_1, a single inset.

III (iv) + 338 Final leaf, Z_1, a single inset. Publishers' cat., 16 pp. undated, at end.

Binders' ticket: 'Leighton, Son & Hodge', at end of Vol. I. Very fine.

[1457] DOREEN: the Story of a Singer
Longman etc. 1894. Sage-green linen-grain cloth; black end-papers.

Blank leaf and half-title precede title. pp. (viii) + 496

Presentation Copy: 'Hypatia Bradlaugh Bonner. With the Author's Love' in ink on title. (The recipient was Bradlaugh's daughter.)

Note. This book was printed from American plates.

HARDY NORSEMAN (A) [1458]
3 vols. Hurst & Blackett 1890. Three-quarter smooth blue cloth, blue-green marbled sides, gold-lettered on spine; grey end-papers.

Half-title in each vol., those in II and III single insets.

Vol. I (viii) + 302 First leaf of final sig., U_1, a single inset.

II (vi) + 302 First leaf of final sig., U_1, a single inset.

III (vi) + (304) Publishers' cat., 8 pp. undated, at end.

Presentation Copy: 'To dear Cousin Martha with the author's love. 1 Oct. 89' in ink on title of Vol. I.

HINDERERS (The): a Story of the Present Time [1459]
Longman etc. 1902. Green linen, mottled in white; black end-papers.

Blank leaf and half-title precede title. pp. (viii) + (184) N_3 N_4 adverts. Very fine.

IN SPITE OF ALL: a Novel [1460]
Hurst & Blackett 1901. Bright brown sand-grain cloth; very dark chocolate end-papers.

Leaf carrying list of works by same Author on verso, and half-title precede title. pp. (viii) + (392) 25_3 25_4 adverts.

Rubber stamp: 'Major P. G. Shewell, Cotswold, Cheltenham', on verso of fly-leaf and Bookseller's ticket: 'John J. Banks, Cheltenham', inside front cover. Fine.

KNIGHT ERRANT [1461]
3 vols. Hurst & Blackett 1887. Scarlet sand-grain cloth; black end-papers.

Half-title in each vol.

Vol. I (viii) + 300

II (vi) + 300 pp. (v) (vi), Contents, form a single inset.

III (vi) + (300) pp. (v) vi, Contents, form a single inset. Publishers' cat., 8 pp. [paged 6] undated, at end.

Ink signature: 'F. Cashel Hoey, March 1887', on half-title of Vol. I. (This is the novelist Mrs Cashel Hoey.) Covers rather soiled.

WE TWO: a Novel [1462]
3 vols. Hurst & Blackett 1884. Smooth chocolate-brown cloth, blocked in black and lettered in gold; darkish brick-red end-papers.

Half-title in each vol.

Vol. I (vi) + (314) pp. (v) (vi), Dedication, and final leaf, X_5, single insets.

II (iv) + 332

III (iv) + (300) U_6 serves as fly-title to Publishers' cat. and carries adverts. on verso. Publishers' cat., 16 pp. undated, at end.

Very fine.

LYSTER, ANNETTE

[1463] RIDING OUT THE GALE: a Novel
3 vols. Samuel Tinsley 1877. Royal blue diagonal-fine-ribbed cloth, with bold nautical design and titling gold-blocked on spine.
Vol. I (ii)+288
II (ii)+320
III (ii)+254 First leaf of final sig., 16_1, a single inset.
Very fine. Recorded as an unusual binding specimen.

LYTTON, THE EARL OF ('Owen Meredith') (1831–1891)

[1464] BALDINE and other Tales (from the German of K. E. Edler)
2 vols. Bentley 1886. Light blue diagonal-fine-ribbed cloth; dark brown end-papers. Titles printed in red and black.
Half-title in each vol.
Vol. I xliv+(292) 19_2 blank.
II (iv)+(292) B

[1465] RING OF AMASIS (The): a Romance [anon]
No date or imprint (1888). Cream parchment fold-over wrappers, printed in brown.
2 leaves, the first blank, the second printed on recto MOST PRIVATE & CONFIDENTIAL, precede title. pp. (158) First leaf of final sig., L_1, a single inset.
Presentation Copy: 'Austin Lee. With affectionate wishes for the year that is coming and grateful recollections of the year that is gone—from his already old friend Lytton. Paris 30 Dec[r]. 1888' in ink on first blank.
MOST PRIVATE AND CONFIDENTIAL appears also on front cover. Spine defective.
Note. The first public edition of this work appeared in 1890.

MAARTENS, MAARTEN (J. VAN DER POORTEN SCHWARTZ) (1858–1915)

[1466] GOD'S FOOL: a Koopstad Story
3 vols. Bentley 1892.
Copy I. Smooth olive-green cloth; monogram end-papers. All edges printed with filigree design in black on pale green. Titles printed in red and black.
Half-title in each vol.
Vol. I (viii) [paged vi]+(280)
II vi+290 pp. (v) vi, Contents, and final leaf, (37_1), single insets.
III vi+(296) (55_2) (55_3) adverts., (55_4) blank. pp. (v) vi, Contents, form a single inset. B

[1466*a*] **Copy II.** Smooth dark blue cloth, otherwise as Copy I. B

GREATER GLORY (The): a Story of High Life [1467]
3 vols. Bentley 1894. Smooth black cloth, blocked in bronze with all-over design of butterflies and foliage; monogram end-papers. All edges black, over-printed in bronze with same design. Titles printed in red and black.
Half-title in each vol.
Vol. I (xvi) [paged (x)]+(288)
II vi+(270) pp. (v) vi, Contents, and first leaf of final sig., 35_1, single insets.
III vi+(306) 54_8 (55_1) adverts., the latter a single inset. pp. (v) vi, Contents, also form a single inset. B
Binder's ticket: 'Burn', at end of Vol. I.

MY LADY NOBODY: a Novel [1468]
Bentley 1895. Standard binding style for the Favourite Novel Series, but in white dot-and-line-grain cloth, blocked with all-over design in gold; monogram end-papers.
Half-title. pp. viii+(536) B
This copy is in the special presentation binding issued in certain cases by Bentley for authors' copies (cf. Broughton). The ordinary binding is the dark green cloth used for Bentley's Favourite Novels (of which this is No. 153).

OLD MAID'S LOVE (An): a Dutch Tale told in English [1469]
3 vols. Bentley 1891. Smooth dark blue cloth, three-quarter-blocked front and back with all-over floral design in yellow, and gold-lettered.
Vol. I viii+(272)
II (iv)+(264) 34_4 blank.
III (iv)+(280) 52_3 adverts., 52_4 blank. B

SIN OF JOOST AVELINGH (The): a Dutch Story [1470]
2 vols. Remington & Co. 1889. Smooth brownish-salmon cloth, diagonally blocked on front in red, white and blue and gold-lettered; pale grey-on-white foliage end-papers.
Blank leaf and half-title precede title in each vol.
Vol. I (viii)+(256) Q_8 blank.
II (viii)+248 B

MABERLY, HON. MRS

EMILY, or the Countess of Rosedale. A Novel [1471]
3 vols. Colburn 1840. Half-cloth boards, labels. Mezzotint front. in Vol. I after J. Wood.
Half-title in each vol.
Vol. I (iv)+(312)
II (iv)+310 First leaf of final sig., O_1, a single inset.
III (iv)+(348) Q_6 adverts.
Very fine.

MABERLY

[1472] LADY AND THE PRIEST (The)

3 vols. Colburn & Co. 1851. Half-cloth boards, labels.

Half-title in Vols. I and II

Vol. I viii + (330) Final leaf, Q_3, a single inset.
II (iv) + 304
III (ii) + (310) First leaf of final sig., O_1, a single inset. The single leaf prelim. was almost certainly conjugate with label leaf.

[1473] LEONTINE, or the Court of Louis the Fifteenth

3 vols. Colburn 1846. Boards, labels.

Half-title in Vols. I and III

Vol. I (iv) + 312
II (ii) + (386) Final leaf, S_1, a single inset.
III (iv) + 294 First leaf of final sig., O_1, a single inset.

Ink signature: 'Cloncurry', on title of each vol. Spines of Vols. II and III chipped at tail: otherwise fine.

MACDONALD, GEORGE (1824–1905)

[1474] AT THE BACK OF THE NORTH WIND

Strahan & Co. 1871.

Copy I: First Edition, first binding. Bright blue fine-morocco cloth, elaborately blocked: *On front:* in gold with picture of Nanny looking out of the round window in the moon, scroll bearing title in reverse, three-sided rustic frame; and in black with a second similar frame, author's name and minor scroll-work. *On back:* in blind with framing and publishers' device (anchor and ANCHORA SPEI in circle). *On spine:* in gold with title, author's name, large anchor, scroll-work and rustic bands at head and tail; in black with panel under title, scroll-work, the initials A. S. on either side of the anchor, and two more rustic bands. Red chocolate end-papers. All edges gilt. 76 wood-engraved illustrations in the text after Arthur Hughes.

Half-title. pp. viii + (392) 24_{6-8} 25_{1-4} Publishers' cat., undated and paged 1–13, (14) blank.

Presentation Copy: 'Mary Rachel Lucas / with love from / George MacDonald— / —the old man that wrote the book' in ink on half-title.

Binder's ticket: 'Burn', at end.

[1474*a*] **Copy II: First Edition, second binding.** Cloth as I, but gold rustic framing omitted from front and publishers' device from back. Simpler framing in blind on back. On spine similar blocking to I, but imprint (in gold) STRAHAN / & CO. Pinkish-buff end-papers. Illustrations and collation as I.

Ink signature: 'L. Paget June 1874', on fly-leaf.

Copy III: First Edition, third binding. Magenta bubble-grain cloth, blocked on front as II; on back with framing as I but no publishers' device; on spine as I, but imprint (in gold) DALDY / ISBISTER / & CO. Pinkish-buff end-papers. Illustrations and collation as I. [1474*b*]

Blind stamp: 'W. H. Smith & Son, Strand', on fly-leaf.

Copy IV: First American Edition. New York: George Routledge, n.d. Dark green dotted-ribbed cloth, blocked on front as I, except that the double frame round the gold picture is in black and gold and not in gold alone, and the author's name is drawn larger; on back with plain frame and central ornament in blind; on spine as I, except that there is only an anchor (re-designed) in gold at tail and no initials or name. Pale yellow end-papers. Illustrations as I. [1474*c*]

Blank leaf and half-title precede title, which is differently worded, mentioning other works by G. M. and the existence and number of illustrations. pp. (x) [paged viii] + 378 Penultimate sig., 24, 4 leaves; final leaf, 25, a single inset.

Presentation Copy: 'Jessie M. McMickan / with love from her father's friend / George Macdonald. / S.S. Calabria, May 30, 1873' in ink on half-title.

This edition was almost certainly printed from English plates, with prelims. re-set.

Note. I have seen another copy of I (in magenta cloth) with a contemporary inscription dated 'Xmas '71'. Also a copy of III in green cloth. The imprint 'Daldy, Isbister' came into existence during 1874.

DEALINGS WITH THE FAIRIES [1475

Sm. sq. 8vo. Alexander Strahan 1867. Smooth blue cloth, blocked with all-over decoration in black and gold; pale chocolate end-papers; all edges gilt. Wood-engraved front. and 11 illustrations after Arthur Hughes.

Half-title. pp. (viii) + (312) X_3 X_4 adverts. dated December 1866.

Book-plate of Constance Flower. Fine.

DONAL GRANT [1476

3 vols. Kegan Paul 1883. Scarlet diagonal-fine-ribbed cloth; black end-papers.

Blank leaf and half-title precede title in each vol.

Vol. I (viii) [paged vi] + (292) U_2 blank. Publishers' cat., 40 pp. dated '10. 83', at end.
II (viii) [paged vi] + (292) U_2 blank.
III (viii) [paged vi] + (316) X_6 blank.

Very fine.

ELECT LADY (The) [1477

Kegan Paul 1888. Scarlet diagonal-fine-ribbed cloth; black end-papers; bevelled boards. Wood-engraved front. signed L. H.

Half-title. pp. vi + (346) Final leaf, Y_5, a single inset. Publishers' cat., 48 pp. dated '11. 87', at end.

Presentation Copy: 'A. P. Watt from his friend George Macdonald' in ink on title. Book-plate of A. P. Watt.

[1478] LILITH: a Romance

Chatto & Windus 1895. Black ribbed cloth, lettered in gold; blue-on-white patterned end-papers. Title printed in red and black.

Half-title. pp. viii + (352) Very fine.

[1479] PHANTASTES: a Faerie Romance

Pl. 16 **Copy I: First Edition.** Smith, Elder 1858. Olive-green morocco cloth, blocked in blind, front and back, and blocked and lettered in gold on spine; cream end-papers.

Half-title. pp. (iv) + (324) Publishers' cat., 24 pp. dated July 1859, at end.

Bookseller's blind stamp: 'Ledger, Limerick', on front fly-leaf. Binders' ticket; 'Westleys', at end.

Note. This is an exceptionally fine copy of a book very uncommon in good state. Two spots on front cover are the only blemishes.

[1479*a*] *Pl. 16* **Copy II: First Illustrated Edition.** Chatto & Windus 1894. Smooth sky-blue cloth, pictorially blocked on front and spine in black and white, gold-lettered on spine; blue-on-white patterned end-papers. Sky-blue edges. Half-tone front. and 24 illustrations after John Bell, on text paper and reckoned in collation.

Half-title. pp. viii + 280 Publishers' cat., 32 pp. dated September 1894, at end. Very fine.

[1480] RINCESS AND CURDIE (The)

Chatto & Windus 1883. Smooth pale green cloth, blocked in red, brown and gold; pale grey flowered end-papers. Front. and 10 lithographed illustrations by James Allen.

Blank leaf and half-title precede title. pp. (viii) [paged vi] + (256) Publishers' cat., 32 pp. dated July 1882, at end.

Ink inscription: 'Ina K. Sandeman from her affec^ate^ Sister Ella V. G. Sandeman Xmas 1882.' This is a poor copy, soiled and worn at hinges.

[1481] PRINCESS AND THE GOBLIN (The)

Strahan & Co. 1872. Chocolate-brown pebble-grain cloth, blocked in gold and black—on front with title and circular vignette showing the Princess surrounded by Goblins: on spine with title, author and publishers' imprint (STRAHAN & CO.) and picture of the Princess at foot of lighted stairway: on back in blind with plain double frame. Cream end-papers, with slip advertising Mrs George Macdonald's *Chamber Dramas*, tipped in at front. All edges gilt. Numerous wood-engraved illustrations in text after Arthur Hughes.

Half-title. pp. vi + (314) pp. (v) vi, Contents, and final leaf, X_5, single insets. Fine.

RANALD BANNERMAN'S BOYHOOD [1482]

Strahan & Co. 1871. Orange-red fine-pebble-grain cloth, blocked in black and gold; pinkish buff end-papers. Wood-engraved front. and 23 illustrations on plate paper, also cuts in text, all after Arthur Hughes.

Half-title (a single inset). pp. (vi) [paged iv] + (300)

Binder's ticket: 'Burn', at end.

WITHIN AND WITHOUT: a Dramatic Poem 'by George Mac Donald' [1483]

Longman 1855. Olive-brown morocco cloth, blind framing on front and back, blocked in blind and lettered in gold on spine. Terra-cotta end papers.

pp. (iv) + (188) N_5 N_6 adverts. Publishers' cat., 24 pp. dated March 1856, and binders' ticket: 'Edmonds and Remnants', at end. Frederick Locker's copy, with his book-plate. Fine.

Note. Macdonald's first book. The catalogue includes Trollope's *Warden*, which was also published in 1855 and in very similar style.

MACKAY, CHARLES (1814–1889)

LUCK, and what came of it. A Tale of our Times [1484]

3 vols. W. H. Allen & Co. 1881. Scarlet diagonal-fine-ribbed cloth, blocked in black on front, in blind on back, gold-blocked and lettered on spine.

Vol. I iv + (266) Final leaf, 18_1, a single inset. Publishers' cat., 40 pp. dated August 1880, at end.

II (ii) + (388)

III (ii) + 326 1st leaf of final sig., 21_1, a single inset.

Presentation copy (*to Marie Corelli*), inscribed in ink on fly-leaf of Vol. I: 'To my dear, very dear and most beloved Minnie, my daughter and my friend, these volumes are presented by the author, who is proud to be her father. April 5th, 1881.' Book-plate of Charles Mackay in Vols. II and III. Fine.

I suspect this copy came from the sale at Mason Croft after Miss Bertha Vyver's death. Why, in conjunction with the lavish inscription in Vol. I, Dr Mackay put his own plate in II and III, I cannot explain. Possibly Marie Corelli inserted the plates after his death, to identify the books more closely with him. The inscription has interest and importance in view of stories current at one time regarding Marie Corelli's parentage.

[1485] TWIN SOUL (The), or The Strange Experiences of Mr Rameses. A Psychological and Realistic Romance [anon]

2 vols. Ward & Downey 1887. Smooth crimson cloth, blocked and lettered in black on front, gold-lettered and black-blocked on spine. Grey-on-white floral end-papers.

Half-title in each vol.

Vol. I (viii)+(260) 17_2 imprint leaf.
II (viii)+264

MACQUOID, KATHERINE S. (1824–1917)

Katherine S. Macquoid (née Gadsden) married a Yorkshire artist (she collaborated with him in two travel books and he illustrated many works of hers). C. Clough Robinson, to whom the great majority of the novels in the Collection were presented, was a dialectologist who published a Glossary and Grammar of mid-Yorkshire dialect.

[1486] APPLEDORE FARM

3 vols. Ward & Downey 1894. Olive-green diagonal-fine-ribbed cloth; flowered end-papers (those in Vol. II differ from Vols. I and III).

Half-title in each vol.

Vol. I (viii)+(216) P_4 adverts.
II (iv)+196 [mispaged 199]
III (iv)+(196) O_2 blank.

Very fine. This copy belonged to the Clough Robinson collection, but is not inscribed.

[1487] AT AN OLD CHÂTEAU: a Novel

Ward & Downey 1891. Smooth dark green cloth, pictorially blocked in black and lettered in gold; pale green flowered end-papers.

Half-title. pp. (viii)+(224)

Presentation Copy: 'To my friend C. Clough Robinson. With much regard. Whitsuntide 1891 K. S. M.' in ink facing half-title. Fine.

[1488] AT THE RED GLOVE: a Novel

3 vols. Ward & Downey 1885. Smooth blue-grey cloth, blocked in red and black, a picture of a hanging glove (preceded by the word AT) on front cover doing duty as the book's title; pale green flowered end-papers.

Half-title in each vol.

Vol. I (xii)+264
II (viii)+264
III (viii)+(260)

Presentation Copy: 'To my kind friend C. Clough Robinson Nov. 25, 1885. K. S. M.' in ink on half-title of Vol. I.

Covers rather stained.

BERKSHIRE LADY (The): a Romance [1489]

Macmillan 1879. Orange-scarlet pebble-grain cloth; black end-papers.

Half-title. pp. xii+300

Presentation Copy: 'To C. Clough Robinson Esq. With much regard K. S. M. October 3rd' in ink facing title.

BERRIS [1490]

2 vols. Ward & Downey 1893. Dark blue pebble-grain cloth.

Half-title in Vol. I; blank leaf and half-title precede title in Vol. II

Vol. I viii+(240) Q_8 adverts.
II (viii) [paged vi]+(216)

Fine. This copy belonged to the Clough Robinson collection, but is not inscribed.

BESIDE THE RIVER: a Tale [1491]

3 vols. Hurst & Blackett 1881. Dark olive-green diagonal-fine-ribbed cloth; olive-green flowered end-papers.

Half-title in each vol.

Vol. I (viii)+(340)
II (vi)+304 pp. (v) (vi), Contents, form a single inset.
III (vi)+(312) pp. (v) (vi), Contents, form a single inset. Publishers' cat., 16 pp. undated, at end.

Presentation Copy: 'To C. Clough Robinson. With much regard K. S. M. March 12, 1881' in ink on half-title to Vol. I. Fine.

DRIFTING APART: a Story [1492]

Percival & Co. 1891. Dark blue morocco cloth; dark green end-papers.

Two blank leaves and half-title precede title. pp. (xiv) [paged (x)]+(320) X_8 blank. pp. (xiii) (xiv) form a single inset.

Presentation Copy: 'C. Clough Robinson. With much regard and all good wishes for a Happy Easter. 1891' in ink on first blank leaf. Fine.

ELINOR DRYDEN'S PROBATION [1493]

3 vols. Charles J. Skeet 1867. Violet-blue sand-grain cloth.

Vol. I iv+(320)
II iv+(298) Final leaf, 19_5, a single inset.
III iv+314 Final leaf, 21_1, a single inset.

ELIZABETH MORLEY [1494]

Bristol: Arrowsmith 1889. Greenish-buff boards, printed in brown, in standard style of Arrowsmith's 2*s*. Series.

pp. (iv)+(256)

Presentation Copy: 'To my dear friend C. Clough Robinson. With best wishes for a Happy Easter. 1889. K. S. M.' in ink on fly-leaf.

Vol. IV in Arrowsmith's 2*s*. Series.

[1495] FAITHFUL LOVER (A)
3 vols. Hurst & Blackett 1882. Smooth pale grey cloth; very dark brown end-papers.
Half-title in each vol.
Vol. I (viii)+(318) First leaf of final sig., X_1, a single inset.
II vi+308 pp. (v) vi, Contents, form a single inset.
III (vi)+(288) Publishers' cat., 16 pp. undated, at end. pp. (v) (vi), Contents, form a single inset.
Presentation Copy: 'To my kind friend and critic C. Clough Robinson. With much regard. K. S. M. May 26, 1882' in ink on half-title of Vol. I.

[1496] HAUNTED FOUNTAIN (The)
Spencer Blackett 1890. Glazed buff wrappers printed in black; end-papers printed with adverts.
pp. 192
Presentation Copy: 'To C. Clough Robinson Esq. with much regard. Easter 1890. K. S. M.' in ink on title.
Spine defective. A volume in Blackett's Select Shilling Novel Series.

[1497] HIS LAST CARD
Ward & Downey 1895. Olive-green ribbed cloth.
Half-title. pp. viii+(376)
Presentation Copy: 'To my dear friend C. Clough Robinson. With much regard Nov. 7th 1895. K. S. M.' in ink on fly-leaf.
Covers spotted.

[1498] IN AN ORCHARD
2 vols. Bliss, Sands & Foster 1894. Smooth pale green linen, threaded with white.
Half-title in each vol.
Vol. I pp. (192) Publishers' cat., 8 pp. on text paper dated 1894, at end.
II pp. (176) L_7 L_8 blank. Publishers' cat., as in Vol. I, at end.
Very fine. This copy belonged to the Clough Robinson collection, but is not inscribed.

[1499] IN THE SWEET SPRING TIME: a Love Story
3 vols. Hurst & Blackett 1880. Apple-green diagonal-fine-ribbed cloth; dark chocolate end-papers.
Half-title in each vol.
Vol. I (viii)+(298) Final leaf, U_5, a single inset.
II vi+298 pp. (v) vi, Contents, and final leaf, U_5, single insets.
III vi+262 pp. (v) vi, Contents, and first leaf of final sig., S_1, single insets. Publishers' cat., 16 pp. undated, at end.
Publishers' compliment slip, endorsed 'By desire of the author', inserted in Vol. I. Spines rather discoloured.

LITTLE FIFINE and other Tales [1500]
3 vols. Hurst & Blackett 1881. Chocolate diagonal-fine-ribbed cloth; chocolate flowered end-papers.
Half-title in each vol.
Vol. I (iv)+(310) Final leaf, X_3, a single inset.
II (iv)+304
III (iv)+(294) First leaf of final sig., U_1, a single inset. Publishers' cat., 16 pp. undated, at end.
Presentation Copy: 'To my kind friend C. Clough Robinson September 20th 1881. K. S. M.' in ink on half-title of Vol. I. Fine.

LOUISA: a Novel [1501]
3 vols. Bentley 1885. Smooth olive-green cloth.
Half-title in Vols. I and II (the latter a single inset). Blank leaf and half-title precede title in Vol. III
Vol. I (viii)+(312)
II (vi)+(290) Final leaf, (39_1) [signed 38*], a single inset.
III (viii)+(304)
Presentation Copy: 'To my kind friend C. Clough Robinson. With best wishes. Katharine S. Macquoid. April 11th, 1885' in ink on half-title of Vol. I. Fine.

MAISIE DERRICK: a Story [1502]
2 vols. A. D. Innes 1892. Pearl-grey patterned-sand-grain cloth; light olive-green flowered end-papers.
Half-title in each vol.
Vol. I (xii)+248
II (xii)+(228)
'With the Publishers' Compliments' stamped in red ink on title of Vol. I. Fine.
Note. Dedication and poem by dedicatee (Margaret Veley) appear in both volumes.

MISS EYON OF EYON COURT [1503]
Ward & Downey 1892. Smooth grey cloth; very dark brown end-papers.
Blank leaf and half-title precede title. pp. (viii) [paged vi]+300 X_2 adverts.
Slightly soiled. Auctioneer's ticket on front cover. This copy belonged to the Clough Robinson collection but is not inscribed.

MY STORY [1504]
3 vols. Hurst & Blackett 1875. Sage-green patterned-sand-grain cloth; chocolate end-papers.
Half-title in each vol.

Vol. I (vi)+(320) pp. (v) (vi), Dedication, form a single inset.
II (iv)+324
III (iv)+(350) First leaf of final sig., Z_1, a single inset. Publishers' cat., 16 pp. undated, at end.

Binders' ticket: 'Leighton, Son & Hodge', at end of Vol. I.

Presentation Copy: 'To C. Clough Robinson. With best Christmas wishes. K. S. M. 1877' in ink on p. (iv) of Vol. I.

[1505] PATTY
2 vols. Macmillan 1871. Orange-scarlet pebble-grain cloth; greenish-black end-papers.

Half-title in each vol.

Vol. I viii+360
II viii+(336) Y_8 adverts. Publishers' cat., 28 pp. dated October 1871, at end. B

Presentation Copy: 'To George Bentley Esq. with very kind regards November 1871 K. S. M.' in ink facing half-title in Vol. II.

[1506] PICTURES ACROSS THE CHANNEL (by the author of 'Patty', etc.)
2 vols. Bentley 1873. Green small-patterned cloth.

Half-title in each vol. (that in I a single inset).

Vol. I (x)+316
II (vi)+274 pp. (v) (vi), Contents, and final leaf, T_1, single insets. B

This work is dedicated to G. H. Lewes.

[1507] PRINCE'S WHIM (The) and other Stories
A. D. Innes (late Walter Smith & Innes) 1891. Smooth dark red cloth; yellow-green flowered end-papers.

Leaf of adverts. and half-title precede title. pp. (viii)+(320) X_{5-8} adverts.

'With the Publishers' Compliments' stamped in violet ink on title. Fine.

[1508] ROGER FERRON and other stories
2 vols. Ward & Downey 1889. Smooth greenish-blue cloth; pale grey flowered end-papers.

Half-title in each vol.

Vol. I (viii)+212
II (viii)+196

Presentation Copy: 'To C. Clough Robinson Esq. with much regard K. S. M. August 1889', in ink on half-title of Vol. I.

Very fine. Auctioneer's ticket on front cover of Vol. II.

[1509] ROOKSTONE: a Novel (by the author of 'Wild as a Hawk', 'Hester Kirton', etc.)
3 vols. Bentley 1871. Grass-green pebble-grain cloth.

Half-title in Vol. I

Vol. I (vi) [paged iv]+278 pp. (v) (vi), Contents, and final leaf, 18_3, single insets.
II iv+296
III iv+(292) B

SIR JAMES APPLEBY, BART.: a Novel [1510]
3 vols. Ward & Downey 1886. Smooth pale blue cloth; pale grey flowered end-papers.

Half-title in Vol. III

Vol. I iv+(268) S_6 imprint leaf
II iv+(268)
III (viii)+(240) Publishers' cat., 32 pp. dated October 1886, at end.

Presentation Copy: 'To C. Clough Robinson. With much regard from Katharine S. Macquoid Nov. 1886' in ink on verso of title of Vol. I.

Covers a little soiled.

TOO SOON: a Study of a Girl's Heart (by the author of 'Patty', etc.) [1511]
3 vols. Bentley 1873. Dark green dotted-ribbed cloth.

Vol. I (iv)+284
II (iv)+(284) T_6 imprint leaf.
III (iv)+(260) S_2 imprint leaf. B

Front cover of Vol. III damp-stained.

MAGINN, WILLIAM (1793–1842)

This is a complete collection of the first editions in book-form of the works of Maginn, with the exception of Parts IX and X of *Magazine Miscellanies* and Vol. III of the Shelton Mackenzie edition of the Miscellaneous Writings.

'FRASER GALLERY, THE' [1512]
EDITION I: LITERARY PORTRAITS FROM FRASER'S MAGAZINE (A Collection of)
4to. James Fraser, 215 Regent Street 1833. Brown paper wrappers, printed in black; dark green leather spine unlettered. Inside covers and back cover blank. All edges gilt.

pp. (iv)+(68), i.e. title, verso blank; Contents, verso blank; and 34 portrait drawings after Maclise, versos blank, printed on single unfoliated sheets of variously tinted paper, interleaved with tissues.

Note. The following words appear on the title: 'A very small number of this Edition is printed; with only Twenty Four Copies on India Paper. The drawings were destroyed immediately after their first appearance in the above work [i.e. *Fraser's Magazine*]—and not one has been suffered to get abroad detached from the Magazine.'

I include this rare item under Maginn despite the fact that the text he supplied for the portraits is not included, because it was the direct precursor of *A Gallery of Illustrious Literary Characters. Edited by William Bates* (see below)—a precursor of whose existence Bates was apparently unaware.

[1513] EDITION II: ILLUSTRIOUS LITERARY CHARACTERS (1830–1838) (A Gallery of). Drawn by the late Daniel Maclise, R.A. and accompanied by Notices chiefly by the late William Maginn, LL.D. (Edited by William Bates, B.A. with a Preface and Copious Notes etc.)

4to. Chatto & Windus, n.d. (1873).

[1513*a*] **Copy I.** Bright blue diagonal-fine-ribbed cloth, blocked on front, in black with facsimile signatures of the persons portrayed, in gold with double frame and title: The / MACLISE / PORTRAIT / GALLERY /; on spine in gold: MACLISE / PORTRAIT / GALLERY / *rule* / DR MAGINN / CHATTO & WINDUS; on back with double blind frame. Café-au-lait end-papers; bevelled boards. All edges gilt. Front. and 83 full-page facsimiles of portrait-drawings by Maclise on plate paper.

Half-title. Pp. (244) [paged (xii) + (9)–(240)]

Ink signature: 'Mary G. Salisbury, 17th January 1874', on half-title. Binders' ticket: 'Leighton, Son & Hodge', at end. Very fine.

Note. The error in pagination occurs with p. (9). The prelims. consist of (*a*) 4 leaves, *b* 2 leaves.

[1513*b*] **Copy II.** Original red morocco, gilt, lettered on spine: ILLUSTRIOUS / LITERARY / CHARACTERS / 1830–1838 / MACLISE. Marbled end-papers; bevelled boards. All edges gilt. Illustrations and collation as Copy I. A white end-paper follows and precedes the marbled one at front and back.

Inside joints repaired.

Notes. (i) It is not surprising that the publishers issued copies of this book solidly bound in leather. Copies in cloth are virtually always in ruins, because the book was cased with rubber solution and, being heavy and full of plates, came to pieces as soon as the adhesive mixture lost its resilience. The cloth copy in the collection is in superb condition, but I hardly dare to open it.

(ii) The work contains three portraits (Hallam, Thackeray and Maclise himself) not published in *Fraser's Magazine*. To these, naturally, no 'Notice' by Maginn or any other contemporary is appended. Of the 'Notices' collected from *Fraser's*, all were written by Maginn except: Maginn himself (by Lockhart); Goethe (by Carlyle); Miss Landon (L. E. L.), Béranger and O'Brien (by Mahony).

(iii) Bates published a new edition of his version in 8vo, Chatto & Windus 1898. To this he added a photograph of Father Prout, and used extracts only from Maginn's original notices which extracts he incorporated with his own (rewritten) 'memoirs'. This edition is entitled THE MACLISE GALLERY.

HOMERIC BALLADS: with Translations and Notes (by the late William Maginn, LL.D.) [1514]

Parker 1850. Smooth dark brown cloth; chocolate end-papers; bevelled boards, red edges.

Half-title. pp. xii + (308) 19_7 19_8, (20_1) (20_2) adverts.

Ink signature: 'E. A. Whittuck', on title.

Note. Also issued in black cloth, differently blocked and lettered, and with no spine imprint.

JOHN MANESTY, the Liverpool Merchant (by the late William Maginn, LL.D.) [1515]

2 vols. John Mortimer 1844.

Copy I. Half-cloth boards, labels. Two etchings by George Cruikshank in each vol., one a front., the other immediately following Contents.

Vol. I (viii) + (292)
II iv + (296)

Ink signature: 'Lord Cloncurry', on each title. Fine.

Copy II. Maroon ribbed cloth. Three etchings in Vol. I and one in Vol. II. No front. in either vol. Collation as Copy I. Fine. [1515*a*]

Note. According to Cohn, some copies contain six plates, of which he gives the titles. The two absent from these copies are: 'The Robbery of Lord Silverstick' and 'The Fatal Duel'.

MAGAZINE MISCELLANIES [1516]

4to. No imprint or date [1840]. No wrappers. New boards, edges uncut.

pp. 128

This curious publication was brought out by Maginn at his own expense (or rather on his own credit, for he went to gaol in 1842 for not having paid the bills) in weekly numbers of 16 pp. each. Ten numbers in all were issued, and the only copy recorded comprising them all was in the possession of Maginn's friend Edward Kenealy, defender of the Tichborne claimant (cf. *Miscellaneous Writings*, edited by R. Shelton Mackenzie, vol. v, p. xcii). This set lacks Parts IX and X. There is no indication or numbering where a fresh part begins and no signature-lettering after B on p. (1).

MAXIMS OF SIR MORGAN O'DOHERTY BART. [anon] [1517]

Sm. sq. 8vo. Blackwood 1849. Limp red-brown (or green) wavy-grain cloth, cut flush; all edges gilt.

Half-title. pp. (iv) + 138 First leaf of final sig., I_1, a single inset. Fine.

[1518] MISCELLANEOUS WRITINGS (Edited by R. Shelton Mackenzie)

5 vols. New York: J. S. Redfield 1855–1857. Brown cloth.

Vols. I, II	**The O'Doherty Papers**	1855
Vol. III	**Homeric Ballads**	Not in the Collection
IV	**The Shakespeare Papers**	1856
V	**The Fraserian Papers**	1857

Note. This series (particularly Vols. I, II and V) contains a mass of Maginn material not previously published in book-form.

Miscellanies, Prose and Verse, ed. R. W. Montague, 2 vols. Sampson Low 1885 consists of reprinted material.

[1519] SHAKESPEARE PAPERS: Pictures Grave and Gay

Bentley 1859. Red bead-grain cloth.

pp. (iv)+368

Ink signature: 'Fanny Romans (?)', on fly-leaf. Binders' ticket: 'Westleys', at end.

[1520] WHITEHALL, or The Days of George IV [anon]

William Marsh, n.d. [1827]. Three-quarter polished calf, t.e.g., others trimmed. (Issued in boards, with label reading: WHITEHALL, / OR, GEORGE IV / *rule* / 10*s*. 6*d*.)

pp. vi+330 pp. (v) vi, Preface, and final leaf, Z_1, single insets.

See also CROKER, T. C., *Fairy Legends and Traditions of the South of Ireland* 1825 and WILSON, JOHN, *Noctes Ambrosianae*, 5 vols. 1863.

Attributed to Maginn

[1521] RED BARN (The): a Tale, Founded on Fact [anon]

8vo. Knight & Lacey, 55 Paternoster Row, 1828. Publishers' full mottled calf, fully gilt, red leather spine-lettering-piece lettered in gold: RED / BARN. Marbled edges and end-papers. Aquatint front. and 7 plates, of which one signed R. Seymour, another probably by him, and the rest by an unidentifiable artist. All plates imprinted and dated 1, 7 or 14 June 1828 (as to 5 of them), 1 August 1828 (as to 2 of them), 1 October 1828 (as to the remaining plate). Also folding facsimile of letter from Corder to his mother, written on his way to Bury Gaol.

pp. (viii) [pp. (vii) (viii) fly-title to text of novel]+716 Text of THE RED BARN ends p. 615; (616) blank; (617)–680 TRIAL OF WILLIAM CORDER; (681)–690 Appendix; (691)–716 LETTERS SENT BY VARIOUS LADIES IN ANSWER TO CORDER'S MATRIMONIAL ADVERTISEMENT.

Note. Halkett & Laing attribute this work to William Maginn on the strength of a paragraph by Charles Welch, printed in *The Library Journal*, Vol. v, p. 88, March 1880. This paragraph reads:

'The Red Barn, a tale of truth [*sic*] (8vo. London, 1828, Knight and Lacy). This story was written by Dr William Maginn, and is founded upon the murder of Maria Marten by William Corder. It was published in parts and had a great success. I cannot find it in any book-list, nor does it appear in the Catalogue of the British Museum. The wrapper of part I is lettered "Subscription Copy". See Hindley's *Life of Catnach* 1878, pp. 189–90.'

The statement of Hindley's to which Welch refers is as follows:

'It is not generally known that Dr Maginn wrote for Knight and Lacey, the publishers in Paternoster Row, a novel embodying the strange story of the Polstead Murder, in 1828, under the title of the "Red Barn". The work was published anonymously, in numbers, and by its sale the publishers cleared many hundreds of pounds.'

Charles Welch was Guildhall Librarian and one of the founders of the Bibliographical Society. His positive acceptance of Hindley's attribution of THE RED BARN to Maginn cannot be disregarded, even though *D.N.B.*, *C.B.E.L.*, Shelton Mackenzie, Bates and other biographers and bibliographers make no mention of it.

Offsetting in this copy shows that in the part-issue the prelims. were sent out sandwiched between the final blank page of the actual story, p. (616), and the first page of the account of the Trial, p. (617). The book was re-issued in 1831 without indication of an earlier edition.

MAHONY, REV. FRANCIS ('Father Prout') (1804–1866)

FACTS AND FIGURES FROM ITALY (by Don Jeremy Savonarola, Benedictine Monk). Addressed during the last two winters to Charles Dickens, Esq., being an appendix to his 'Pictures' [1522]

Bentley 1847

Copy I: First Edition, probably first or trial binding. Cream-coloured ribbed cloth, blocked in gold on front with the Papal Arms, and in blind with decoration and the words: 'COLOUR SEE PAGE 157'. Spine of standard Bentley style of the period, blind-banded and gold-lettered with title, author and imprint. Edges uncut.

pp. (iv)+(316) P_4 P_5 adverts., P_6 blank.

Note. The blind wording on the front cover is very curious. Page 157, describing the Papal Arms, states that the hereditary colours of the Feretti family are white and yellow. Is it a binder's query and therefore the case a trial one?

Possibly: for P. S. O'Hegarty reports a copy in canary yellow with Papal Arms in gold on front, in blind on back, and no ref. to 'colour', etc. This is a presentation copy, and may represent the style finally adopted.

[1522*a*] **Copy II: First Edition, probably later binding.** Canary yellow ribbed cloth, blind blocked on front, back and spine; title and imprint only (no author) on spine. Edges trimmed. Collation as Copy I.

Stamped crest of Charles Bosworth Thurston on title and his signature on fly-leaf dated January 1857.

[1523] *Pl. 16* RELIQUES OF FATHER PROUT (The) (collected and arranged by Oliver Yorke, Esq. Illustrated by Alfred Croquis, Esq.)
2 vols. Sm. cr. 8vo. James Fraser 1836.

Copy I: First Edition, first binding. Dark green morocco cloth, blocked in blind with all-over embossed decoration and lettered in gold. Etched front. and vignette title (printed in brown and black) in each vol., and one plate in Vol. I, all by Daniel Maclise and on plate paper; also, in Vol. I 6, in Vol. II 7 etchings by Maclise, ingeniously printed on text paper.

Half-title in each vol. (that in II a single inset)
Vol. I (xvi) + 324
II (vi) + (324)
Very fine.

[1523*a*] *Pl. 16* **Copy II: First Edition, later binding.** Grey-purple fine-diaper cloth, conventionally blocked in blind and lettered in gold (the price: £1 : 1 : -, gold-blocked on spine). Illustrations and collation as Copy I. Fine.

Note. I have seen another variant binding which, because the sheets are slightly cut down, I should suspect of being a tertiary. It is of pale pink silky watered cloth, blocked in gold on front and back with a wreath, and gold-lettered (from type) on spine with meagre ornamentation. The general appearance is that of an inferior Annual.

[1523*b*] **Copy III: 'New Edition, Revised and Largely Augmented.'** Bohn 1860. Grass-green ribbed cloth, blind blocked in series style of Bohn's Illustrated Library, of which this is No. 63. Triple end-papers, front and back, printed in blue with adverts. Folding engraved front. ('The Fraserians'); engraved vignette title as in Copy I and 19 plates by D. Maclise.

pp. (xiv) + 578 Pp. (xiii) (xiv), List of Engravings, and final leaf, PP_1, single insets.

A 'Preface to the Present Edition', dated Nov. 20, 1859, occupies pp. (iii)–vii.

[1523*c*] **Copy IV.** FINAL RELIQUES OF FATHER PROUT (the Rev. Francis Mahony). Collected and Edited by Blanchard Jerrold. Chatto & Windus 1876. Slate diagonal-fine-ribbed cloth, blocked in black and lettered in gold. Steel-engraved portrait front. and facsimile of Prout's writing.

Half-title. pp. (xvi) + 532 Publishers' cat., 36 pp. dated October 1877, at end. Very fine. Copies exist with publishers' cat. dated November 1875.

Note. Much material not previously issued in book-form is contained in this vol., woven together with a biographical account of the author.

ana. THE ILLUSTRATIONS TO THE RELIQUES OF FATHER PROUT...BEING A SERIES OF VIGNETTES, DRAWN AND ETCHED BY DANIEL MACLISE ESQ. A.R.A. Proofs before Letters [1523*d*]
8vo. James Fraser 1836. Dark green morocco-cloth sides, very dark green morocco-leather spine up-lettered in gold. (*a*) 2 leaves + B–F in fours (unfoliated).

Note. This volume contains the 18 etchings included in the first book-edition, all on plate paper and proofed before letters. The relevant portion of the text follows each etching, usually occupying one leaf, occasionally two leaves. These extracts from the text are specially set to 8vo format, and headed with an exact reference to their whereabouts in the book-edition.

It may be noted that the etchings are openly credited to Maclise, whereas in the first book-edition he appears as 'Alfred Croquis'.

MALET, LADY

VIOLET, OR THE DANSEUSE: a Portraiture of Human Passions and Character [anon] [1524] *Pl. 22*
2 vols. Colburn 1836. Boards, labels.

Half-title in each vol.
Vol. I (iv) + (288)
II (iv) + (290) Final leaf, O_1, a single inset leaf.
Very fine.

Note. It is strange how completely forgotten is this in many ways remarkable book. It moved Bulwer Lytton (who, for all his grandiloquence, did not easily praise his contemporaries' work) to three separate panegyrics over a period of twenty-five years, and is warmly praised in a sympathetic article on L. E. L. by 'A Middle-Aged Man', printed in *Bentley's Miscellany* for 1845.

Here are Bulwer Lytton's tributes:

(*a*) In a letter to Lady Blessington, Oct. 20, 1836: 'I have read *Violet*. It has great truth of painting and knowledge of a certain kind of life.'

(*b*) In a letter to Mrs Cunningham, April 16, 1837: 'Have you read *Violet*? Is it not pretty? That and the *Pickwick Papers* are the best things I have seen for years.'

(*c*) In an interview, given on June 21, 1861: 'Lady Malet has written *Violet or The Danseuse*, the best novel of the sort I know. It came out twenty years ago. When I saw it, I said I must look out for a rival. The circle of interest is limited—it is descriptive of the back scenes of theatrical life—but it beats *Adam Bede* and everything which has since appeared.'

I believe that this last comment provides the only certain statement extant as to the novel's authorship. Halkett & Laing, on the strength of a correspondence in *Notes & Queries*, attribute the story to '—— Beasley'. Perhaps this was the maiden name of the lady who later became Lady Malet. I can find nothing to show which Lady Malet she was.

MALLOCK, W. H. (1849–1923)

[1525] HEART OF LIFE (The)

3 vols. Chapman & Hall 1895. Green unglazed buckram, blocked and lettered in black on front, gold-lettered on spine, back plain.

Half-title in each vol.

Vol. I (iv)+(280) T_4 blank.
II (iv)+(280)
III (iv)+(268) S_6 blank.

Fine.

[1526] NEW PAUL AND VIRGINIA (The), or Positivism on an Island

Chatto & Windus 1878. Pinkish-slate diagonal-fine-ribbed cloth, blocked in black and blind and lettered in gold uniform with *The New Republic* (see below). Grey-on-grey-blue floral end-papers.

Advert. leaf and half-title precede title. pp. (viii) [paged vi]+144. Text ends 134. (135)–144 Notes. Publishers' cat., 36 pp. dated March 1878, at end.

Book-plate of E. A. Abbey. Binders' ticket: 'Bone & Son' at end.

Fine.

[1527] NEW REPUBLIC (The), or Culture, Faith and Philosophy in an English Country House [anon]

2 vols. Chatto & Windus 1877. Slate diagonal-fine-ribbed cloth blocked in black on front, in blind on back, on spine blocked and lettered in gold and black. Titles printed in red and black.

Blank leaf and half-title precede title in Vol. I, half-title only in Vol. II

Vol. I (viii)+(244) R_2 publishers' device. Publishers' cat., 36 pp. dated October 1876, at end.
II (iv)+(260)

Presentation Copy: 'Wentworth. From W. H. Mallock. March 5, 1877' in ink on slip of paper tipped on to first blank of Vol. I. Book-plate of the 2nd Earl of Lovelace and 13th Baron Wentworth. Fine.

Note. Dedicated to 'Violet Fane', this Peacockian symposium in novel-form introduces her as Mrs Sinclair. Other characters admittedly drawn from life are 'Dr Jenkinson' (Jowett), 'Mr Herbert' (Ruskin), 'Mr Storks' and 'Mr Stockton' (Huxley and Tyndal), 'Mr Luke' (Matthew Arnold), 'Mr Rose' (Walter Pater). One could hardly wish for a more intimate copy of the book than the one presented to Lord Wentworth (afterward Earl of Lovelace), who was for many years Mallock's hero and close friend.

OLD ORDER CHANGES (The): a Novel [1528

3 vols. Bentley 1886. Smooth grey-blue cloth, pictorially blocked in dark blue, and gold-lettered on spine; black end-papers. Titles printed in red and black.

Half-title in each vol.

Vol. I (iv)+(312)
II (iv)+(340) Z_2 adverts.
III (iv)+(352) B

Note. A 'New Edition' in one vol. was published in 1887, bound in dark green cloth, with same pictorial blocking in light green, chocolate end-papers, and a wood-engraved front. after a drawing by the Earl of Mount Edgcumbe.

ROMANCE OF THE NINETEENTH CENTURY (A) [1529

2 vols. Chatto & Windus 1881. Smooth greenish-grey cloth, blocked on front and back with stars and crescent-moon in dark blue, gold-lettered on spine. Blue-on-white foliage end-papers.

Half-title in each vol.

Vol. I (iv)+(256) Publishers' cat., 32 pp. dated April 1881, at end.
II (iv)+308

Note. This copy belonged to Frances (Mrs Mortimer) Collins, whose maiden name was Cotton. Her ink signature and that of Percy Cotton appear on the half-title of Vol. I, her signature and the initials FPC on that of Vol. II, both inscriptions being dated 1881. Four documents are inserted at the beginning or end of the volumes. There are three letters from Mallock to Mrs Collins dated Jan. and Feb. 1882, concerning a critical explanation of his aims in writing this novel, which he begs her to prepare for publication in a periodical. There is also a copy of the printed prelims. of Vol. I of the *Second Edition*, containing a Preface of eleven pages, in which Mallock defends himself against the charge of having written a licentious book. This Preface is in places mutilated, Mrs Collins having evidently cut passages away, possibly for quotation in her article.

MANNING (ANN) (1807–1879)

This selection from her works (it is by no means a complete collection) serves to illustrate what are, perhaps, the two most interesting characteristics of Miss Manning as a published writer. The earlier and considerably larger portion of her output was of a historical kind, and written with great 'period' solemnity. It was not on that account by any means a phenomenon, though it soon lost favour with conservative publishers of severe taste. In June 1854 Daniel Macmillan wrote to Kingsley in the course of a preliminary discussion of *Westward Ho!*: 'Of course you will not adopt that pseudo-antique manner in which *Esmond* and *Mary Powell* are written. That style is now getting a bore.' What *was* remarkable was the degree to which her archaistic manner (which undoubtedly became something of an affectation) was reflected in the design of her printed books. Her publishers cultivated an 'antique style' as carefully as their author; and this style (at its date highly unusual) had a definite though transient influence on other authors and publishers. The design (maybe to some extent the archaism) of Thackeray's *Esmond* can be directly attributed to the example of Hall, Virtue's experiments with Miss Manning, while the publications of the resuscitated firm of Saunders & Otley in the late fifties and early sixties were equally their debtors.

The second striking characteristic of this popular writer was that through a bibliography predominantly historical ran a vein of quiet comedy of village and small-town contemporary life. Her second book *Village Belles* (1838) was of this class, but not until twenty years later did she repeat the experiment with *The Ladies of Bever Hollow*. This novel had a success as striking as her 'period' stories, and was followed by several others of the same kind. That a retiring spinster should have excelled in two so different categories of fiction is sufficiently unusual to merit remark.

[1530] BELFOREST: a Tale of English Country Life (by the author of 'Mary Powell' and 'The Ladies of Bever Hollow')

2 vols. Bentley 1865. Dark green morocco cloth, blocked in blind on front and back, blocked and lettered in gold on spine.

Half-title in each vol.

Vol. I (viii)+(312) X_4 adverts.
II (viii)+(336) Y_8 blank. B

[1531] CALIPH HAROUN ALRASCHID

Arthur Hall, Virtue & Co. 1855. Dark brown ribbed cloth, elaborately blocked in blind on front and back, ditto and gold-lettered on spine. Bevelled boards, orange-brick edges. Terra-cotta end-papers.

Half-title. pp. (viii)+(296) U_3 U_4 adverts.

Title printed in red and black. Pages framed. Binders' ticket: 'Westleys', at end.

[1532] CHERRY AND VIOLET: a Tale of the Great Plague (by the Author of 'Mary Powell')

Virtue Bros. & Co. 1863. Fourth Edition. Plum honey-comb-grain cloth, blocked in blind and lettered in gold. Bevelled boards, red-chocolate ends. All edges scarlet. Wood-engraved front. on plate paper. Title printed in red and black.

pp. iv+234 Final leaf, Q, a single inset. Publishers' cat., 16 pp. dated November 1863, at end.

Fine. First published 1853.

CHRONICLE OF ETHELFLED (The) (set forth by the author of 'Mary Powell') [1533]

Arthur Hall, Virtue & Co. 1861. Violet wavy-grain cloth, all-over blind blocked on front and back, blocked and lettered in gold on spine (title and author only). Bevelled boards, terra-cotta end-papers, brick-red edges.

pp. iv+(212) P_2 adverts. Publishers' cat., 24 pp. dated June 1861, at end. Binders' ticket: 'Westleys', at end.

CHRONICLES OF MERRY ENGLAND (The), rehearsed unto her People. Books I–VI [all published] (by the author of 'Mary Powell') [1534]

Arthur Hall, Virtue & Co. 1854. Brown diagonal-ripple-grain cloth, blocked in blind on front and back, blind-blocked and gold-lettered on spine (title only, no imprint).

Advert. leaf (inset) precedes title. pp. (viii) [paged vi]+252. Publishers' cat., 24 pp. dated December 1853, at end. Booksellers' blind stamp: 'Kruuy and Slater, Manchester' on fly-leaf.

CLAUDE THE COLPORTEUR (by the author of 'Mary Powell') [1535]

Arthur Hall, Virtue & Co. 1854. Black, flecked with red, fine-ribbed moiré cloth, blocked in blind on front and back, blocked and lettered in gold and blind-blocked on spine. Light pink end-papers. Coloured front. by W. Dickes after Henry Warren on plate paper.

pp. iv+(300) U_3–U_6 adverts. Publishers' cat., 24 pp. dated May 1854, at end. Binders' ticket: 'Westleys', at end.

COLLOQUIES OF EDWARD OSBORNE (The), Citizen and Clothworker of London. (As reported by ye Authour of 'Mary Powell') [1536]

Arthur Hall, Virtue & Co., n.d. [1852]. Brown morocco cloth, blocked in blind on front and back, gold-lettered (title and imprint) on spine. Bevelled boards. Brick-red end-papers and edges. Engraved view of Old London Bridge as front., and engraved decorative title printed in red and black, both on plate paper, precede printed title, also in red and black.

Half-title. pp. (viii) [of which (iii)–(vi) on plate paper]+(300) U_4–U_6 adverts. This book collates in eights. Each page of text is framed, with marginal dates, etc.

Ink signature: 'James Kershaw' on recto of front fly-leaf; booksellers' blind stamp: 'Simms and Dinham, Manchester' on verso. Binders' ticket: 'Remnant & Edmonds', at end.

[1537] **DAY OF SMALL THINGS** (The) (by the author of 'Mary Powell')

Arthur Hall, Virtue & Co. 1860. Full maroon embossed morocco (presentation binding), lettered in gold. Bevelled boards, all edges gilt and patterned. Title printed in red and black.

Blank leaf precedes half-title. pp. (viii) + 236

Presentation Copy: 'To dear Florence from her affectionate aunt Anne, 1864' in ink on leaf preceding half-title; also 'Florence Powell 1864' on fly-leaf.

Fine.

[1538] **DEBORAH'S DIARY:** a Sequel to 'Mary Powell' [anon]

Copy I: First Edition. Arthur Hall, Virtue & Co., n.d. [1859]. Black (or dark violet) morocco cloth, blind-blocked on front and back, blocked and lettered in gold on spine. Bevelled boards, brick-red end-papers and edges. Title printed in red and black.

Half-title. pp. (iv) + 192 Publishers' cat., 24 pp. dated October 1858, at end. 4-page leaflet, advertising books by the same author, inset between front end-papers. Binders' ticket: 'Westleys', at end.

[1538*a*] **Copy II: New (and first illustrated) Edition.** 'Deborah's Diary: a Fragment'. Sm. 8vo. 1860. Wood-engraved front and vignette title on plate paper. Title printed in red and black. Claret bead-grain cloth, blocked and lettered in blind, also gold-lettered on front and gold up-lettered on spine. Terra-cotta end-papers, brick-red edges.

pp. (iv) [plate paper] + 140 Publishers' cat., 24 pp. dated January 1860, at end. 4-page leaflet of publishers' adverts. inset after front fly-leaf. Binders' ticket: 'Westleys', at end.

Note. A secondary binding was of claret sand-grain cloth with simpler lettering and no cat. at end. There is no indication in this New Edition that the book had previously appeared.

[1539] **DIANA'S CRESCENT** (by the author of 'Mary Powell')

2 vols. Fcap 8vo. Bentley 1868. Grass-green sand-grain cloth, blocked on front in gold and blind, on back in blind, on spine blocked and lettered in gold. Dark green end-papers. Titles printed in red and black.

Vol. I iv + (200)
II iv + 192 B

[1540] **DUCHESS OF TRAJETTO** (The) (by the author of 'Mary Powell')

Arthur Hall & Co., 26 Paternoster Row, 1863. Mauve (or green) ripple-grain cloth, all-over blocked in blind and gold on front, in blind only on back, blocked and lettered in gold on spine. Plum end-papers. Title printed in red and black.

pp. iv + (302) Final leaf, U_7, adverts. and a single inset.

Binders' ticket: 'Westleys', at end.

GOOD OLD TIMES (The): a Tale of Auvergne (by the author of 'Mary Powell') [1541]

Arthur Hall, Virtue & Co. 1857. Orange morocco cloth, all-over blind-blocked front and back, blind-blocked and gold-lettered on spine. Wood-engraved front. on plate paper. Title, a single inset, printed in red and black.

pp. (vi) + (282) T_3–T_5 adverts. Third leaf of final sig., T_3, a single inset. Publishers' cat., 24 pp. dated August 1856, at end. Binders' ticket: 'Westleys', at end.

Note. There is also in the Collection a Second Edition (1857) as follows:

Presentation Copy: 'To dear Florence, from her affectionate aunt Anne. 1864' in ink on leaf preceding front; also in ink: 'Florence Powell 1864' on fly-leaf. Full dark green embossed Morocco (publishers'), all edges gilt and patterned.

***HELEN AND OLGA:** a Russian Tale (by the author of 'Mary Powell') [1542]

Arthur Hall, Virtue & Co. 1857. Dark grey-green morocco cloth, blocked in blind and spine-lettered in gold. Wood-engraved front. on plate paper. Title printed in red and black.

pp. iv + (308) (V_1) (V_2) adverts. Publishers' cat., 24 pp. dated January 1857, at end.

HILL SIDE (The) (by the author of 'Mary Powell') [1543]

Sm. 8vo. Arthur Hall, Virtue & Co., n.d. (1854). Maroon morocco cloth, blocked in blind and spine-lettered in gold. Title printed in red and black.

pp. iv + (92) G_6 adverts. Publishers' cat., 24 pp. dated August 1854, at end.

Presentation Copy: 'Frances & Lydia Manning from their affectionate sister A.M. Sept. 15, 54' in ink on title. Binders' ticket 'Westleys' at end.

HOUSEHOLD OF SIR THOS. MORE (The) [anon] [1544]

Arthur Hall, Virtue & Co., n.d. [1851]. Brownish-red marbled fine-ripple-grain cloth, blocked in blind on front and back, gold-lettered on spine (title only, no imprint). Bevelled boards. Brick-red end-papers and edges. Engraved portrait front. and decorative title, printed in red and black, precede printed title (also in red and black). These three leaves are on plate paper.

pp. (vi) [on plate paper] + (272) Publishers' cat., 4 pp. on text paper, at end. The book collates in fours throughout. Each page of text is framed, with marginal dates.

Ink signature: 'Edward Owen M.A.' on fly-leaf. Bookseller's ticket: 'W. Graham, Oxford' inside front cover. Binders' ticket: 'Westleys', at end.

Note. A New Edition of this book, with a valuable introduction by the Rev. W. H. Hutton and illustrations by John Jellicoe and Herbert Railton, was published by Nimmo in 1899. The book was issued in green ribbed cloth, pictorially blocked and lettered in gold. Uniform with it were published new editions of three other works by the same author. A complete series was promised, but the promise was not fulfilled.

[1545] IDYLL OF THE ALPS (An) (by the author of 'Mary Powell')

Hall & Co., 1876. Grass-green diagonal-fine-ribbed cloth, blocked and lettered in black, gold and blind. Bevelled boards.

Half-title. pp. (viii) [vii, mispaged vi] + 312 Publishers' cat., 8 pp. undated on text paper, at end.

Presentation Copy: 'Frances and Lydia Manning with their sister Anne's true love. Nov. 1, 1876' in ink on half-title.

[1546] LADIES OF BEVER HOLLOW (The): a Tale of English Country Life (by the author of 'Mary Powell')

2 vols. Fcap 8vo. Bentley 1858. Red-brown ribbed cloth, blocked in blind on front and back, blocked and lettered in gold on spine. Pinkish-brown powdered edges. Title printed in red and black.

Vol. I (vi) [pp. (v) (vi) 'To the Reader', signed *b* and a single inset] + (292)
II iv + 250 First leaf of final sig., R_1, a single inset. B

[1547] LADY OF LIMITED INCOME (The): a Tale of English Country Life (by the author of 'Mary Powell')

2 vols. Bentley 1872. Bright blue sand-grain cloth, blocked in black on front and back, gold-lettered and black-blocked on spine. Titles printed in red and black.

Vol. I (iv) + 298 Final leaf, 20_1, a single inset.
II (iv) + (334) First leaf of final sig., 21_1, a single inset. B

[1548] LORD HARRY BELLAIR: a Tale of the Last Century (by the author of 'Mary Powell')

2 vols. Bentley 1874 Blue diagonal-fine-ribbed cloth, blocked and lettered in black, gold and blind. Titles printed in red and black.

Half-title in each vol.

Vol. I vi + 244
II vi + (228) Final leaf, 15_2, blank. B

MAIDEN AND MARRIED LIFE OF MARY POWELL (The), afterwards Mistress Milton [anon] [1549]

Arthur Hall, Virtue & Co. at 25 Paternoster Row, n.d. [1849]. Light claret morocco cloth blocked in blind on front and back, gold-lettered on spine (title only, no imprint), bevelled boards. Brick-red end-papers and edges. Line engraving of Milton's Arms, printed in red and black, serves as front. on text paper. Title-page also printed in red and black.

pp. (iv) + (272) Publishers' cat., 4 pp. on text paper, at end. The book collates in fours throughout. Each page of text is framed, with marginal dates, etc.

Bookseller's ticket: 'H. Scott, Carlisle' inside front cover. Binders' ticket: 'Westleys', at end.

Note. There is also in the Collection a Third Edition (1864) as follows:

Presentation Copy: 'To dear Florence: from her affectionate Aunt Anne. 1864' in ink on leaf preceding front; also 'Florence Powell. 1864' on verso of fly-leaf. Full claret morocco, embossed in black. Marbled end-papers, all edges gilt. This edition has front. portrait of Cromwell, and eagle-coat on p. (272).

MEADOWLEIGH: a Tale of English Country Life (by the author of 'The Ladies of Bever Hollow') [1550]

2 vols. Bentley 1863. Very dark brown fine-ribbed cloth, all-over blocked in blind on front and back, gold-lettered on spine. Titles printed in red and black.

Half-title in Vol. II

Vol. I (iv) + (308)
II (iv) + (316) B

MISS BIDDY FROBISHER: a Salt-Water-Story (by the author of 'Mary Powell') [1551]

Sampson Low, etc. 1866. Grass-green sand-grain cloth, blocked in blind and lettered in gold. Bevelled boards, chocolate end-papers.

Half-title. pp. (iv) + [300] T_6 blank.

Presentation Copy: 'Florence Powell from her affectionate aunt Anne. New Year's Day. 1865' in ink on half-title.

Fine.

MONKS NORTON: a Tale of English Country Life (by the author of 'Mary Powell' etc.) [1552]

2 vols. Bentley 1874. Violet diagonal-fine-ribbed cloth, blocked and lettered in blind and gold. Bevelled boards; café-au-lait end-papers. Titles printed in red and black.

Vol. I (ii) + (288) T_8 blank.
II (ii) + (272) B

[1553] NOBLE PURPOSE NOBLY WON (A): an Old Old Story (by the author of 'Mary Powell')

Arthur Hall, Virtue & Co. Second Edition 1862 (same year as First). Full very dark green morocco, bevelled boards. All edges gilt and patterned. Title printed in red and black.

pp. (iv)+420

Presentation Copy: 'To dear Florence from her affectionate aunt Anne. 1864' in ink on leaf preceding title; also 'Florence Powell 1864' on fly-leaf. Corners a little worn.

[1554] ONE TRIP MORE, and other Stories (by the author of 'Mary Powell')

Cassell, Petter and Galpin n.d. [1870]. Violet sand-grain cloth, blocked and lettered in gold, black and green. All edges gilt. Wood-engraved front. on plate paper (but reckoned in pagination) and one other plate, also on plate paper but *not* reckoned in pagination.

pp. (1)–(160) Publishers' cat., 16 pp. undated, at end.

Binders' ticket: 'Straker & Son' at end.

[1555] PASSAGES IN THE LIFE OF THE FAIRE GOSPELLER, MISTRESS ANNE ASKEW (by the author of 'Mary Powell')

Bentley 1866. Smooth chocolate cloth, blocked in gold and blind and lettered in gold on front, blocked and lettered in gold on spine, blind blocked on back. Very dark blue-green end-papers. Bevelled boards. Title-page printed in red and black.

Half-title. pp. (viii)+296

Ink inscription: 'S. C. B[entley] from dear George [Bentley] Aug[st] 1866' facing half-title. **B**

[1556] SPANISH BARBER (The): a Tale (by the author of 'Mary Powell')

Nisbet 1869. Smooth red-brown cloth, blocked and lettered in gold, black and blind. Dark green end-papers. Wood-engraved front. on plate paper.

Half-title. pp. (viii)+232

Presentation Copy: 'Florence Powell, with her aunt Anne's sincere affection, Oct. 22, 1869' in ink on half-title. Binder's ticket: 'Burn', at end.

[1557] TASSO AND LEONORA: the Commentaries of Ser Pantaleone degli Gambacati, Gentleman Usher to the august Madama (*sic*) Leonora d'Este (by the author of 'Mary Powell')

Arthur Hall, Virtue & Co. 1856. Drab (or crimson) ribbed cloth, blocked in black on front and back, blocked in black and gold-lettered on spine. Wood-engraved front., signed C. P. Nicholls, on plate paper but reckoned in pagination. Title-page printed in red and black.

pp. (vi) [paged viii]+(298) U_3–U_5 adverts. Title and first leaf of final sig., U_1, single insets. Publishers' cat., 24 pp. dated April 1856, at end. Binders' ticket: 'Westleys', at end.

TOWN AND FOREST (by the author of 'Mary Powell') [1558]

Bentley 1860. Grass-green morocco cloth, blocked in blind on front and back, blocked and lettered in gold on spine. Brown-on-white patterned end-papers. Wood-engraved front. Title printed in red and black.

pp. iv+(288) N_{12} adverts. Single advert. leaf of thinner paper, fcap 8vo in size, inset at end.

Binders' ticket: 'Westleys' at end. **B**

YEAR NINE (The): a Tale of the Tyrol (by the author of 'Mary Powell') [1559]

Arthur Hall, Virtue & Co. 1858. Dark green bead-grain (or morocco) cloth, blocked in blind on front and back, blocked and lettered in gold on spine. Wood-engraved front. on plate paper. Title printed in red and black.

pp. iv+(284) T_6 adverts. Publishers' cat., 24 pp. dated January 1857, at end. Also 4-page leaflet, advertising works by the same author, inset between front end-papers. Binders' ticket: 'Westleys', at end.

MARIOTTI, L.

BLACK GOWN PAPERS (The) [1560]

2 vols. Wiley & Putnam 1846. Black fine-ribbed cloth. Tinted lithographic front. in each vol. by John Leslie.

Half-title in Vol. I, blank leaf and half-title in II

Vol. I (viii)+256
II (viii)+276

Binders' ticket: 'Remnant & Edmonds' at end of Vol. I.

Note. This apparently desultory work contains matter of interest. Writing of America, the author develops the theme of Martin Chuzzlewit's 'Eden' in a strong and detailed account of the haphazard raising of a mushroom-city by speculators, sharpers and thugs of all kinds. Writing of London, he describes the sufferings of the Italian boy-organ-grinders, hounded daily from the slums of Clerkenwell to earn a few pence in distant quarters of the city.

MARRYAT, FLORENCE (daughter of Captain Marryat, became (i) MRS ROSS CHURCH, (ii) MRS LEAN) (1838–1899)

During the first part of her writing life Florence Marryat was bracketed with Annie Thomas as a purveyor of dangerously inflammatory fiction, unsuitable for reading by young ladies, yet highly to their taste. (Note the dedication to *The Girls of Feversham*, below.) Subsequently she took much interest in spiritualism and, like Frances Eleanor Trollope, introduced the subject into certain of her novels.

[1561] CONFESSIONS OF GERALD ESTCOURT (The)
3 vols. Bentley 1867. Claret fine-morocco cloth.

Half-title in each vol.

Vol. I (iv)+(320)
II (iv)+(312)
III (iv)+(292) U_2 imprint leaf. B

[1562] FOR EVER AND EVER: a Drama of Life
3 vols. Bentley 1866. Claret fancy-diaper cloth.

Half-title in Vol. I

Vol. I (viii)+(320) X_8 adverts.
II (iv)+(316) X_6 adverts.
III (iv)+(308) B

[1563] GIRLS OF FEVERSHAM (The)
2 vols. Bentley 1869. Chocolate fine-morocco cloth.

Vol. I (iv)+314 First leaf of final sig., X_1, a single inset.
II (ii)+312 B

Binder's ticket: 'W. Bone', at end of Vol. I.

Note. The novel is dedicated to the author's mother, with a plea that it is the first of her books to have nothing 'sensational' about it. The plea is a little pathetic and wholly justified.

[1564] LOVE'S CONFLICT
3 vols. Bentley 1865. Green fine-morocco cloth.

Vol. I (vi) [paged iv]+338 pp. (v) (vi), Contents, signed *b*, and final leaf, Z_1, single insets.
II iv+(320) X_8 blank.
III iv+320 B

Badly stained by damp.

Note. The novel is dedicated to the memory of Captain Marryat, the author's father. Her surname, spelt correctly on titles, is spelt Marrya*tt* on spines.

[1565] MAD DUMARESQ: a Novel
3 vols. Bentley 1873. Orange-scarlet diagonal-fine-ribbed cloth, blocked in black with all-over design from a 'period' binding.

Vol. I (iv)+(292) U_2 blank.
II (iv)+(284)
III (iv)+304 B

The back cover and spine of Vol. III are damp stained.

"MY OWN CHILD": a Novel [1566]
3 vols. Tinsley 1876. Royal-blue sand-grain cloth, blocked in black and gold.

Half-title in each vol.

Vol. I (viii)+(300) U_6 blank.
II (viii)+(288)
III (viii)+(272) S_8 blank.

Presentation Copy: 'To Arthur Cöhnan (?) With the author's very kind regards. August 1876' in ink on fly-leaf of Vol. I. Fine.

Note. The dedication to the author's daughter and son-in-law appears in all three volumes.

NELLY BROOKE: a Homely Story [1567]
3 vols. Bentley 1868. Bright blue fine-morocco cloth.

Half-title in Vol. I

Vol. I viii+(334) First leaf of final sig., 21_1, a single inset.
II iv+(320)
III iv+(306) Final leaf, 20_1, a single inset. B

NO INTENTIONS: a Novel [1568]
3 vols. Bentley 1874. Red-brown diagonal-fine-ribbed cloth; chocolate end-papers.

Blank leaf precedes title in Vol. II

Vol. I (iv)+(312)
II (iv)+(288)
III (ii)+310 First leaf of final sig., X_1, a single inset. B

PETRONEL: a Novel [1569]
3 vols. Bentley 1870. Apple-green fine-pebble-grain cloth.

Vol. I (iv)+(332)
II (iv)+320
III (iv)+296 B

Note. For all its luxuriance and enterprise, mid-Victorian binding-design was rigidly subject to certain conventions, of which one governed the placing of the spine lettering. As the period when novels were paper-labelled gradually receded, the titling was pushed up from three-quarter high to nearly the head of the spine, while either the author's name or the volume number or both were placed low-central (until Chatto & Windus dominated the novel market in the 'eighties and kept all lettering, except their imprint, high up on the spine). Florence Marryat's *Petronel*, therefore, instantly draws the modern eye, because title, author and vol. number are all central and closely grouped. I do not think I know of another novel of the period 1860–1890 designed in this way.

[1570] PREY OF THE GODS (The): a Novel

3 vols. Bentley 1871. Grass-green fine-morocco cloth.

Vol. I (iv) + 308

II (iv) + 294 Penultimate sig., 19, 2 leaves; final leaf, 20_1, a single inset.

III (iv) + (316) **B**

[1571] VÉRONIQUE: a Romance

3 vols. Bentley 1869. Apple-green fine-diaper cloth.

Vol. I (xii) + 322 Final leaf, 21_1, a single inset.

II (iv) + 306 Final leaf, 20_1, a single inset.

III (iv) + 340 **B**

Note. The novel is dedicated, by permission, to Charles Dickens.

[1572] WRITTEN IN FIRE: a Novel

3 vols. Tinsley 1878. Grass-green diagonal-fine-ribbed cloth.

Half-title in each vol.

Vol. I viii + (260)

II (viii) + (260) (S_2) adverts.

III (viii) + 248

Fine.

MARRYAT, CAPTAIN FREDERICK, R.N. (1792–1848)

This is a complete collection of the first editions of Captain Marryat, both fiction and non-fiction (supported by variant copies, significant American issues and numerous subsequent editions), with the single exception of his *Code of Signals*, which is represented by a Second, a Seventh and a Tenth edition. It would be false modesty to hesitate to describe it as a very fine collection indeed—perhaps the finest in existence. Nowadays several of Marryat's 'firsts' are almost undiscoverable in any state, and here the whole series appears, for the most part in excellent original condition and in numerous cases in really brilliant shape.

In addition to the non-first editions here recorded, those should be noted which formed part of BENTLEY'S, COLBURN'S and MACMILLAN'S STANDARD NOVELS, as well as one or two other series (see Section III of this catalogue). All are in the Collection, together with numerous 'yellow-back' issues.

[1573] CHILDREN OF THE NEW FOREST (The)

Pl. 17 **Copy I: Part Issue.** Part I (? all published, see below), published by H. Hurst, 27 King William Street, Strand, n.d. [April 1847].

Buff paper wrapper, printed on front in navy-blue with ornamental frame and wording as follows: THE / JUVENILE / LIBRARY / BY / CAPTAIN MARRYAT, R.N. / NO. I. / THE CHILDREN OF THE NEW FOREST. / LONDON; / H. HURST, 27 KING WILLIAM STREET, / STRAND. / Price One Shilling. / *bottom of frame* / HATTON AND CO., KING STREET, COVENT GARDEN. Back wrapper printed with advert. of Rowland's Preparations. Inside front and back wrappers blank.

The Contents of the Part are as follow: Publisher's cat., 8 pp. undated, headed 'The Juvenile Library Advertiser'. Two steel-engraved plates by Frank Marryat. pp. (1)–72 of text.

Note. The catalogue at the front of this Part schedules four Parts for publication, to make up Vol. I of the story. It is certain that Parts III and IV never appeared and practically certain that not even Part II was issued. No copy of a second Part is recorded as having been seen, and I have never heard of another copy of Part I (see 'General Note on *The Children of the New Forest*' below).

Copy II: First Book Edition. 2 vols. Small 8vo. H. Hurst, n.d. [1847]. [1573a]

The volumes of this set show binding differences. The fact is curious, as both bear the same contemporary inscription (that in Vol. I dated 1847) showing that they were presented to a youthful member of the Belcher family by her 'Aunt Kate'. The copy came from the same source as that of *Midshipman Easy* (Second Edition) described below and presented by Marryat himself to Frederick Belcher. 'Aunt Kate' was the sister of Captain (later Admiral) Sir Edward Belcher, with whom Marryat's son Frank sailed in the *Samarang*, 1846–1849. She became the second wife of Marryat's brother Charles. Pl. 17

With this provenance, the binding differences have sufficient significance to merit separate treatment, and consequently the two volumes are described separately.

Volume I. Dark green *morocco* cloth, blocked and lettered on front in gold and blind, on back in blind, and spine lettered in gold; pale yellow end-papers. Steel-engraved front. and *seven* plates by Frank Marryat. Title printed in red and green—an inset leaf not on text paper nor reckoned in the collation.

Half-title. pp. (iv) + 288

Ink inscription: 'Henrietta Belcher from her Aunt Kate 1847', on fly-leaf. Very fine.

Note. Of this volume pp. (1)–72 and 145–216, as well as the engravings included in these pages, show stab-holes (see 'General Note' below).

Volume II. Dark green *pebble-grain* cloth, similarly blocked to Vol. I, but showing the following differences: (i) lettering on front is larger and less condensed, (ii) lettering on spine less condensed but smaller (particularly the author's name), (iii) blind blocking slightly different in design. End-papers a darker yellow than in Vol. I. Steel-engraved front. and *three* plates by Frank Marryat. Title as in Vol. I.

Half-title. pp. (iv) + (302) CC_6 CC_7 adverts., paged (1)–4. CC_7 is a single inset. The adverts. recommend 'The Juvenile Library'.

Ink inscription: 'Henrietta Belcher from her Aunt Kate', on fly-leaf. Very fine.

Notes. (i) Obviously there are no stab-holes in this or any other copy of Vol. II, as the latter half of the work was never prepared for part issue.

(ii) Of the two bindings on this copy, that on Vol. II is the style regularly met with, alike on *The Children of the New Forest* and *The Little Savage*. As the two volumes did not appear simultaneously, and as the provenance implies a connection with the author's family, it seems possible that this specimen of Vol. I was peculiarly early—perhaps one of the copies sent to Marryat on or before publication.

[1573*b*] **Copy III: Another.** Binding and end-papers uniform with Vol. II of Copy II. Plates identical with Copy II. Collation as Copy II, with the addition at the end of Vol. I of Publisher's adverts., 4 pp. not on text paper, undated. Neither text nor plates in Vol. I show stab-holes.

A somewhat worn copy. Plate facing p. 266, Vol. I, inserted from another copy.

[1573*c*] **Copy IV: Another.** Binding and end-papers uniform with Vol. II of Copies II and III. Collation as Copy I except that there is a front. and *three* plates in *each* vol.

Half-title in Vol. II only.

Ink signature: 'Anne H. Weston', and bookseller's ticket: 'King, Brighton', inside front cover of each vol. Fine.

Notes. (i) Of Vol. I of this copy pp. (1)–144, as well as two of the four engravings included in these pages, show stab-holes.

(ii) The half-title to Vol. I was suppressed, when the plates were reduced from 8 to 4 and the List of Plates reprinted.

(iii) A Second Edition, bound uniform with the First, was undated. A Third Edition in the same binding was dated 1849. The first volume of both these editions contained 4 plates only and showed no stab-holes.

General Note on 'The Children of the New Forest'

Any attempt to reconstruct in detail the publishing history of this little work would occupy more space than is here available. But a few words must be said about the non-completion of the Part Issue and a justification of Copy IV (above) being catalogued as subsequent to Copies II and III.

We know that Part I actually appeared during April, 1847.† We know also that the sheets at any rate were prepared for Parts II–IV, though probably in diminishing quantity. This is proved by the presence, in the fourteen tolerably perfect copies which I have been able to examine, of stabbed signatures of all the four quarters of Vol. I of the novel. Stabbed signatures of the first quarter are the most frequent, of the second a little less so, of the third much less so, while of the fourth I have only seen one example. Whether any wrappers beyond those for Part I were printed, I do not know.

Why was the Part Issue interrupted, and why was the number of plates in Vol. I reduced at some stage from 8 to 4? I think the main reason was in all probability Marryat's health, which caused irregularity—perhaps in the arrival of instalments of the story itself, certainly in the supply of illustrations from Frank Marryat. Captain Marryat began to fail early in 1847, and during the last six months of the year was seriously ill. Frank, like all at Langham, was very anxious for his father's health and much occupied in caring for the sick man. It is more than likely that he fell behind on his schedule, and that Hurst, the publisher, found himself pledged to give the public Vol. II of *The Children of the New Forest* but unable to obtain more than 4 engravings from the distracted illustrator. He could not continue Part Issue without a full quota of plates, but he *could* publish Vol. II with fewer illustrations than Vol. I. I suggest, therefore, that he decided, very early in the course of its appearance, to abandon Part Issue altogether and publish the story in book form with the volumes unequally illustrated. Then, when his original bound stock of Vol. I was exhausted, he deliberately reduced the amount of its plates to the equivalent of that in Vol. II.‡

CODE OF SIGNALS (A) for the Use of Vessels employed in the Merchant Service [1574]

Copy I: 'Second Edition, to which is added a List of the Agents to Lloyds.' 8vo. Sold by J. M. Richardson etc. 1818. Boards, side-label. Three plates of coloured flags on one folding sheet of vellum precede title.

Half-title. For collation see *Note* below.

Note. This book is unfoliated. It opens with a 4-leaf sig. unsigned; followed by another 4-leaf sig. also unsigned and carrying the List of Agents to Lloyds, first appearing in this edition and dated at end Feb. 25 1818; followed by 5 leaves, unsigned, carrying 'Introduction'. Thereafter it collates B–G in eights.

Copy II: 'Seventh Edition', Corrected and Enlarged etc. 8vo. J. M. Richardson 1840. [1574*a*]

† The *Dublin University Magazine* for April 1847 carries a display advertisement of this 'New Periodical Work'. It says: 'Each number will consist of seventy-two pages of letterpress and two illustrations engraved on steel.' Part I is reviewed and advertised in *The Examiner* for May 1.

‡ The publisher naturally announced the change of plan without reference to Marryat's disability, In *The Examiner* for July 10, 1847 is a Hurst advert. stating: 'In consequence of the difficulty of having the steel-engravings properly executed in so short a space of time, the Juvenile Library will in future be published in Volumes, instead of Monthly Parts. Vol. I...is now ready', etc. Vol. II is advertised as ready on October 16. No statement is made as to the number of engravings.

Boards (re-backed in cloth), side label; new end-papers. Coloured front. and 2 coloured plates (one folding) all of flags.

For collation see *Note* below.

Note. Also unfoliated. It opens with a 4-leaf sig. unsigned, and thereafter collates B–T in fours (omitting I and K) plus a single inset leaf unsigned.

[1574*b*] **Copy III: 'Tenth Edition', Entirely Revised and Corrected.** 8vo. J. M. Richardson 1847. Boards (re-backed in cloth), side label. Coloured folding plate of flags precedes title.

For collation see *Note* below.

Note. Also unfoliated. It opens with a 4-leaf sig. unsigned, and thereafter collates B (4 leaves), C (2 leaves), D–L in fours (omitting J), M (8 leaves), N–2I in fours.

Preface, signed F. M. but undated, occupies pp. (5)–(8) and presumably first appeared in the edition of 1841 (? the eighth), which edition, according to a note in the twelfth edition of 1854, was the last personally revised by Marryat.

[1575] DIARY IN AMERICA (A): with Remarks on its Institutions

Copy I: First Edition. 3 vols. Longman etc. 1839. Boards, labels.

Half-title in each vol.

Vol. I (iv)+(324) P_6 blank. Publishers' cat., 16 pp. dated July 1839, at end.
II (iv)+(320)
III (iv)+(312)

Binders' blind stamp: 'Westley & Co.', at end of Vol. III.

[1575*a*] **Copy II: Another.** Pink ribbed cloth, blocked in blind and lettered in gold; yellow end-papers. Collation as Copy I, but no cat. at end of Vol. I. Very fine.

Note. Copy I is an earlier issue than Copy II. Its labels make no mention of the work being a 'First Part' or 'First Series', whereas Copy II is described on the spines as 'First Series' and was manifestly bound up simultaneously with sheets of the Second Series.

[1575*b*] **Copy III: First American Edition.** 2 vols. Philadelphia; Carey & Hart 1839 (late July). Half-cloth boards, labels.

Vol. I pp. 242
II pp. 228

Labels defective.

Note. This edition preceded the English edition by three months. A Copyright Notice appears on verso of title in each volume recording the book as 'entered for (*c*)' on November 1838. The English edition was published during October 1839. Capt. Marryat copyrighted this work, while in America, to test the law. Shortly after it appeared, it was pirated in New York and issued in one volume. Upon losing the case, the Philadelphia publishers issued the work in one volume, omitting the (*c*) notice.

DIARY IN AMERICA (A), PART SECOND [1576]

Copy I: First Edition. 3 vols. Longman etc. 1839. Boards, labels. Two folding maps follow title of Vol. II.

Half-title in each vol.

Vol. I (iv)+304
II (iv)+(294) First leaf of final sig., O_1, a single inset. Slip of 'Directions to Binder' tipped on to guard of the first map.
III (iv)+362

The labels of this edition say 'Part Second'.

Copy II: Another. Pink ribbed cloth, blocked in blind and lettered in gold; yellow end-papers. Uniform with First Series, Copy II. Collation as Copy I, but without slip 'Directions to Binder'. Spine lettering reads 'SECOND SERIES'. Very fine. [1576*a*]

Copy III: American (? unauthorised) Edition, entitled 'Second Series of a Diary in America.... Complete in One Volume'. Philadelphia: T. K. & P. G. Collins 1840. Half-cloth boards, label. [1576*b*]

pp. (ii) [inset title-page]+300

The words 'Cheap Edition' appear on the label.

DIARY OF A BLASÉ (by the author of 'Jacob Faithful', 'Peter Simple', etc.) [1577

Philadelphia: Carey & Hart 1836. Half embossed-cloth boards, label.

Half-title. pp. (196) [paged (1)–(4)+(7)–(198)]

Pencil signature: 'Helen Frederica King', on first page of text. Label defective.

Notes. (i) This is the first appearance in book form of material published in the *Metropolitan Magazine* to July 1836. It was not so issued in England until *Olla Podrida* (1840). The label carries the name 'Maryatt' (*sic*) and spells the title 'Blazé'.

(ii) In a number of American editions of English novels at this period there is a discrepancy of pagination between prelims. and text. I suspect the reason for this to have been that composition of text was started immediately serial issue began to reach the United States, and continued in instalments. Until the text was complete, the American publisher could not know for certain how extensive his prelims. would have to be. He therefore set aside what seemed to him an adequate allowance of prelim. pages, and started his text-paging with the number following his estimated prelim. length. If, as frequently happened, the prelims. fell short of this estimate, his book went forth with a numerical gap between the final page of prelims. and the first page of text. Cf. below *Japhet, Privateersman, Snarleyyow.*

[1578] JACOB FAITHFUL (by the author of 'Peter Simple', 'The King's Own', etc.)

Copy I: First Edition. 3 vols. Philadelphia and Baltimore: Carey & Hart 1834.

Leaf carrying adverts. on verso inset before title in Vols. II and III

Vol. I pp. 204
II pp. (164) Two publishers' cats., each of 12 pp., the first dated March 1834, the second October 1833, at end.
III pp. (160) Cats. as in Vol. II.

Very fine.

Notes. (i) This American edition preceded the first English.

(ii) Vols. I and III have side-boards of buff, Vol. II of pale green.

(iii) This edition (and the corresponding one of *Peter Simple* [Copy II] are not abbreviations but full texts. The type used is small, and the great majority of chapter-divisions are suppressed, several English chapters being run into one American one. Hence the small number of pages per vol.

[1578*a*] *Pl. 18* **Copy II: First English Edition.** 3 vols. Saunders & Otley 1834. Boards, labels.

Vol. I viii + 304
II (viii) + (304) O_8 adverts.
III (viii) + (308)

Ink signature: 'J. Osborne, Nov. 11, 1834', inside front covers of Vol. I: name only in Vols. II and III. Very fine.

[1578*b*] **Copy III: Third Edition in 'Ship Binding'.** 3 vols. Saunders & Otley 1835. Dark blue diagonal-fine-ribbed cloth, uniform with that used on *Peter Simple* Copy III. Blocked pictorially in blind as *Jacob Faithful* Copy IV, but with different gold spine-titling. On this edition the wording is CAPT. MARRYAT'S / NOVELS / *rule* / JACOB FAITHFUL / VOL. I [*II. III*] enclosed in a decorative frame, shortened from that used on Copy IV by breaking the sides and closing up. Pale yellow end-papers.

Half-title in each vol.

Vol. I (x) + (312) O_{12} adverts.
II (x) + (304) O_8 adverts.
III (x) + (308)

Bookseller's ticket: 'Yates, Goswell St', inside front cover of Vol. I.

Notes. (i) The appearance on this Third Edition of 1835 of the elaborate ship binding invented in 1837 for the Illustrated Edition is very curious. Beyond those here listed (cf. *Japhet in Search of a Father*, *King's Own* and *Pacha of Many Tales*) I have only seen one other example of its use on an ordinary unillustrated Marryat. The normal binding for the book is, of course, boards and labels. The collation is identical with the Illustrated Edition, and either the type of this Third Edition or surplus sheets were used when the Illustrated Edition was manufactured. Then, when the Illustrated Edition was abandoned, the publishers seem to have used their balance of blue cloth and their binding-brasses on a few ordinary Marryat editions.

A slight rearrangement was carried out in this 'Third Edition', doubtless in order to equalize the bulk of the volumes. Vol. I contains 16 instead of 17 chapters, and Vol. II 13 instead of 12.

(ii) For the Illustrated Edition, only the half-titles and titles were re-set and printed on rather different paper.

Copy IV: 'Illustrated Edition.' 3 vols. Saunders & Otley 1837. Claret diagonal-fine-ribbed cloth, blocked in blind on front and back uniform with *Peter Simple* Copy III. Spine blocked in blind with capstan, trident, pike, etc. and in gold with title, etc. in ornamental frame. The wording is: CAPT^{N} MARRYAT'S / NOVELS / *rule* / Illustrated / Edition. / *rule* / JACOB FAITHFUL / VOL. I [*II. III*] enclosed in an elongated decorative frame. Yellow end-papers. Hand-coloured etched front. and 3 plates by R. W. Buss in each vol. [1578*c*] *Pl. 19*

Leaf of adverts., verso blank, precedes title in Vol. I. Half-titles in Vols. II and III. Collation as Copy III. Very fine.

Note. There was published in London in 1928 an edition of *Jacob Faithful* in two volumes, with binding design and illustrations (in colour) facsimiled from this Illustrated Edition of 1837. The work also contained an Introduction by George Saintsbury.

JAPHET IN SEARCH OF A FATHER (by the author of 'Peter Simple', 'Jacob Faithful', etc.) [1579] *Pl. 18*

Copy I: First English Edition. 3 vols. Saunders & Otley 1836. Boards, labels.

Half-title in Vol. I

Vol. I viii + 304
II viii + (300)
III viii + (324) P_5 P_6 adverts.

Bookseller's stamp: 'Williams, Cheltenham', inside front cover of Vol. I. Very fine.

Copy II: First American Edition. Part Issue. Four post 8vo Parts. New York: Wallis & Newell, 9 John Street, 1835 [Parts 1 and 2], 1836 [Parts 3 and 4]. Light blue wrappers printed in black—on front: double (thick-thin) frame; PART 1 (2 etc.) PRICE 12½ CTS [Part 1], 6¼ CTS [Parts 2–4], / JAPHET / IN SEARCH OF A FATHER. / BY THE AUTHOR OF / 'Peter Simple', 'Jacob Faithful', 'Naval Officer', &c. / *rule* / (FRANKLIN LIBRARY EDITION.) / NEW-YORK. / WALLIS & NEWELL, PUBLISHERS, / etc. etc. The sub-imprint alters with Part 3, [1579*a*] on which is printed a long list of booksellers in various cities who sell the work instead of merely: 'Sold by the Principal Booksellers etc.'. Spine unlettered. Back printed with advert. of the Franklin Library which offers useful information (see below). Inside wrappers plain.

Part 1 pp. (92) [paged (5)–96]
2 pp. 97–144
3 pp. 145–192
4 pp. 193–(224)

The first leaf of Part 1 is title, verso blank; the first page of text is paged (7).

[1579*b*] **Copy III: Second American Edition. Vol. I only.** Philadelphia and Baltimore: Carey & Hart 1835. Half-cloth boards, label.

Blank leaf precedes title and is conjugate with it. pp. (188) [paged (1)–(4)+13–196] Publishers' cat., 24 pp. dated January 1835, at end.

Pencil inscription: 'Anna L. Whites. Presented by George Clark', on fly-leaf.

Note. This portion of the American edition preceded English book issue (but see 'General Note' below). Neither title nor label suggest a further volume to come, but on last page of text is stated 'End of Volume One'.

General Note on American Editions of 'Japhet'

I have no authority for this sequence of American editions but it can be defended on grounds of internal evidence. Of the Wallis & Newell Part Issue (recently discovered by Mr I. R. Brussel and hitherto quite unknown) Parts 1 and 2, both dated 1835, contain up to p. 282 of Vol. II of the English edition (the second page of Chap. XXIX), whereas Vol. I of the Carey & Hart edition (the second vol. is dated 1836) only goes to p. 166 of the English Vol. II—i.e. to the middle of Chap. XVII. Therefore under date 1835 a considerably longer section of the novel appeared in U.S.A. (and preceded English issue) in the Wallis & Newell, than in the Carey & Hart edition.

There is further evidence in favour of Wallis & Newell in their 'Advertisement' on the back wrappers of their Part Issue. This Advertisement is unusually careful and specific for American pirated editions at this period. On the back of Part 1, over date April 22, 1835, we read:

'This day is published Part 1 of JAPHET IN SEARCH OF A FATHER, [etc. etc.]. In consequence of the numerous applications for the above Work, the Publishers of the FRANKLIN LIBRARY have been induced to issue Part 1, which contains all that has yet been received of this interesting tale. They also beg leave to inform the numerous Patrons of the Franklin Library that they receive the very earliest copy that can be procured, and will issue it complete immediately upon the receipt of the remainder from England.'

This announcement is repeated verbatim on the back cover of Part II.

Japhet appeared serially in the *Metropolitan Magazine* from November 1834 to January 1836. The material contained in Part I was that printed in the *Metropolitan* up to March 1835, so it took about seven weeks for Wallis & Newell to receive a text and publish it in America. The material contained in Part II appeared in the *Metropolitan* for April, May and June, so we may conclude that Part II appeared toward the end of July.

On the back of Part III the Advertisement is dated January 29, 1836, and on Part IV February 1836. Part III covers *Metropolitan* publication up to October 1835 and one would have expected this to be issued in America by the end of November; but the front wrapper and Advertisement are specifically dated 1836, and this date must be accepted at face value. A possible reason for delay is that, whereas Parts I and II were Nos. 21 and (probably) 22 of the Franklin Library, Parts III and IV were Nos. 47 and 49, twenty-eight additional titles having appeared in the interval. The wish to issue these may have caused the publishers deliberately to hold up a continuation of *Japhet*.

The Franklin Library was published weekly, either in full Parts at 12½ cents or half Parts at 6¼ cents. The list of works issued up to Part IV of *Japhet* comprises such important English novels as *The Last Days of Pompeii* (Bulwer); *Tylney Hall* (Hood); *Brambletye House* (Horace Smith); *Lodore* (Mary Shelley); *The Cruise of the Midge* and *Tom Cringle's Log* (Scott); and the following Marryat novels in addition to *Japhet*: *Jacob Faithful, Peter Simple, Naval Officer* and *Pacha of Many Tales*. There seems reason to suppose that the Part Issues of some of these at any rate will, if sets can be located, prove to be hitherto undetected priorities over the English issue and therefore of bibliographical importance.

Copy IV: Second Edition in 'Ship Binding'. [1579*c*]
3 vols. Saunders & Otley 1836. Dark blue diagonal-fine-ribbed cloth, blocked in blind and gold as *Jacob Faithful* Copy III (q.v.). Collation as Copy I. First Edition sheets with title overprinted.

JOSEPH RUSHBROOK, or the Poacher (by the author of 'Peter Simple') [1580]

3 vols. Longman etc. 1841. Half-ribbed cloth boards, labels.

Half-title in each vol.

Vol. I viii+(276) Publishers' cat., 16 pp. dated July 1841, inserted between front endpapers.
II viii+(296) O_4 imprint leaf.
III viii+(276) N_4 N_6 adverts.

Fine.

Note. I have seen a copy with the cat. in Vol. I dated February, 1841.

KING'S OWN (The) (by the author of 'The Naval Officer') [1581]

Copy I: First Edition. 3 vols. Colburn & Bentley 1830. Boards, labels.

Half-title in each vol.

Vol. I (iv) + 324
II (iv) + (326) Final leaf, P_7, a single inset, probably conjugate with label-leaf.
III (iv) + (332) Q_3 Q_4 adverts. Final sigs. P, six leaves; Q, four leaves.

Ink signature: 'Wollaton, 1830', on front cover of each vol., and name only inside front cover of each vol. Bookseller's ticket: 'C. Price', inside front cover of Vol. I. Fine.

[1581*a*] **Copy II: Second Edition in 'Ship Binding'** (by the author of 'Peter Simple', etc.). 3 vols. Saunders & Otley 1836. Dark blue diagonal-fine-ribbed cloth, blocked in blind and gold as *Jacob Faithful* Copy III (q.v.).

Half-title in each vol.

Vol. I (iv) + (308)
II (iv) + (308)
III (iv) + (308)

Ink signature: 'Scarnett. May 1876', on fly-leaf of Vol. II. Bookseller's ticket: 'Yates, Goswell Street', inside front cover of Vol. I.

[1582] LITTLE SAVAGE (The)

Copy I: First Edition. 2 vols. Small 8vo. 'Part I', H. Hurst 1848; 'Part II', H. Hurst and Co. 1849. Dark green morocco cloth, blocked on front in gold and blind and gold-lettered with the words 'THE JUVENILE LIBRARY'; on back in blind; and gold-lettered on spine with title, author and 'PART I [*II*]'. Wood-engraved front. and 3 plates in each vol. Titles printed in red and green—inset leaves not on text paper nor reckoned in the collation—and printed with the words 'First Edition'.

Half-title in each vol.

'Part' I (iv) + (302) CC_6 CC_7 adverts., paged (1)–4. CC_7 is a single inset. The adverts. recommend 'The Juvenile Library'.
II (iv) + (284) BB_3 BB_4 adverts., paged (1)–4.

Binders' ticket: 'Weemys & Co.', at end of Vol. II. Ink signature: 'Anne H. Weston. 1848 (1849)', inside front cover of each vol. Bookseller's ticket: 'King, Brighton', inside front cover of Vol. I. Very fine.

Note. The cloth on these volumes is not quite uniform. That on Vol. I is pebbly morocco, that on Vol. II coarse morocco. The end-papers also differ—Vol. I, yellow; Vol. II, cream. There can be no question of this being a mixed set. It is in perfect condition, with identical provenance, and was plainly sold on publication in its present form.

[1582*a*] **Copy II: Another.** 'Part I', First Edition; 'Part II', Second Edition. 2 vols. 1848/1849. Part I (H. Hurst) identical with Copy I, Part I. Part II: straight-grain coarse morocco cloth, blocked and lettered uniform with Copy I, Part II. Uniform end-papers. Plates as in Copy I. Title of Part II bears the words 'Second Edition, and imprint 'H. Hurst and Co.'

Half-title in each vol.

'Part' I Identical with Copy I.
II Leaf of adverts. precedes half-title. pp. (viii) + 280 Page (v) carries a short new preface dated February 1849, signed by Frank Marryat and referring to his father's death and to the consequent delay in publication.

Binders' ticket: 'Westleys & Co.', at end of Vol. II. Ink signature: 'Philip Williams', inside front cover of each vol. Bookseller's stamp: '? Library, Cheltenham', in Vol. I and Bookseller's ticket: 'R. Davies, Birmingham', in Vol. II.

Copy III: Another. 'Part I, Third Edition' (Hurst & Co. 1849); 'Part II, Fourth Edition' (Hurst & Co. 1850). Dark green fine-diaper cloth, blocked and lettered uniform with foregoing; yellow end-papers. Plates as in Copy I. Titles in red and green. [1582*b*]

Half-title in each vol.

'Part' I Identical with Copy I.
II Identical with Copy I.

Binders' ticket: 'Westleys and Co.', at end of Vol. I. Ink signature: 'Cecile Holford', on title of each vol.

MASTERMAN READY, or the Wreck of the Pacific. Written for Young People [1583]

3 vols. Small 8vo. Longman etc. Vol. I, 1841; Vols. II and III, 1842.

Vol. I. Navy-blue fine-diaper cloth, pictorially blocked in blind on front and back, and gold-lettered on spine: MASTERMAN / READY / BY / CAPTAIN / MARRYAT. / Yellow end-papers. Wood-engraved front. on text paper (reckoned in the collation as (A_1)) and vignettes in the text.

pp. viii + (288) Publishers' cat., 12 pp. dated February 1, 1841, at end.

Vols. II and III. Dark slate fine-diaper cloth, blocked on front and back uniform with Vol. I, gold-lettered on spine: MASTERMAN / READY / BY / CAPTAIN MARRYAT. / *rule* / VOL. II [*III*]. Cream end-papers. Wood-engraved front. on text paper, reckoned in collation as (A_1), and vignettes in text in each vol.

Vol. II (iv) + (272) S_8 imprint leaf.
III (iv) + (228) Q_2 carries 'Note' on recto and printers' imprint on verso.

Ink signature: 'John A. F. Luttrell etc. 1844 (1845)', on fly-leaf of each vol. Very fine.

Notes. (i) Later issues of Vol. I, bound at the time of publication of Vol. II or thereafter, have VOL. I on spine.

(ii) Some copies of this book contain no advertisement material, which may be regarded as optional.

(iii) To the courtesy of 'Taffrail', the well-known writer of sea stories, I owe the information that Marryat himself drew the illustrations, or at least supplied the sketches from which drawings were finally prepared for engraving. On February 13, 1841, he wrote to a friend: 'I am positively forbidden to write a line...and have been amusing myself with drawing all the illustrations myself.'

(iv) The following later editions of this story have been noted:

(*a*) Of Vol. III only: 1845, with printers' imprint on verso of title and of Q_2 reading 'J. & H. Cox Brothers, 74 and 75 Great Queen Street etc.' instead of 'J. L. Cox and Sons, 75 Great Queen Street etc.' as in edition of 1842.

(*b*) Of Vols. I and II: 1850, with printers' imprint as in 1845 edition of Vol. III, except that 'Brothers' is bracketed.

[1584] MISSION (The), or Scenes in Africa. Written for young People

Copy I: First Edition. 2 vols. Small 8vo. Longman etc. 1845. Dark brown horizontal-ribbed cloth, blocked in blind on front, back and spine, and gold-lettered on spine; cream end-papers. Wood-engraved front. on text paper in each vol., reckoned in the collation as (A_1); and a map in Vol. I, also on text paper and forming p. (vi) of prelims.

Vol. I (vi)+328 Publishers' cat., 32 pp. undated, at end.
II (iv)+(376) $2B_4$ imprint leaf.

Fine. Two small stains on back cover of Vol. I.

[1584*a*] **Copy II: 'New Edition', with illustrations by John Gilbert.** Bohn 1860. Grass-green ribbed cloth, blind-blocked in series style of 'Bohn's Illustrated Library', of which this is No. 64. Triple end-papers front and back, printed in blue with adverts. Wood-engraved front. and 6 plates after John Gilbert and a map.

Half-title. pp. (x) [paged viii]+446 Publisher's cat., 32 pp. undated, at end.

Fine. From the Library, Windsor Castle. Book-plate: 'Library' and Royal Arms.

Note. Bohn's Illustrated Library also included newly illustrated editions of *Masterman Ready* (engravings unsigned), *The Privateersman* (engravings after Stothard) and *The Settlers in Canada* (engravings after Gilbert).

[1585] MR MIDSHIPMAN EASY (by the author of 'Japhet in Search of a Father', 'Peter Simple', 'Jacob Faithful', etc.)

Copy I: First Edition. 3 vols. Saunders & Otley 1836. Half-cloth boards, labels.

Half-title in each vol.

Vol. I (viii)+(292)
II (viii)+(308) O_{10} adverts.
III viii+(316) P_2 adverts.

Ink signature: '(one name illegible) Coote', on title of each vol. Publisher's advert. (John Cumming, Dublin) dated 1836 pasted inside front cover of Vol. I. Labels slightly rubbed and volumes loose in covers.

Copy II: 'Second Edition.' 3 vols. Saunders [1585*b*]
& Otley 1836. Boards, labels. The words 'Second Edition' appear on the labels. Collation as Copy I. First Edition sheets, with titles over-printed (not re-set).

Presentation Copy: 'Fredk Belcher from Capt Marryat' in pencil on fly-leaf of Vol. I and on half-title of Vol. II. On fly-leaf of Vol. III Marryat had begun a similar inscription, but left it unfinished so that only 'Fredk' survives.

Note. For further presentation copies to the Belcher family, cf. *The Children of the New Forest.*

NARRATIVE OF THE TRAVELS AND ADVENTURES OF MONSIEUR VIOLET IN CALIFORNIA, SONORA, AND WESTERN TEXAS [1586]

3 vols. Longman etc. 1843.

Copy I: First Edition, in boards. Half-cloth boards, labels. Labels worded: MONSIEUR / VIOLET. / BY / CAPT. MARRYAT / *rule* / VOL. I [*II. III*]. Folding map precedes title of Vol. I.

Half-title in each vol.

Vol. I viii+312
II (iv)+(320) P_4 imprint leaf.
III (iv)+(300)

Book-plate of Sir Benjamin Morris, Waterford, in each vol. Spines faded and labels discoloured.

Copy II: First Edition in pictorial cloth. Scarlet [1586*a*]
fine-morocco cloth, pictorially and decoratively blocked in blind on front and back, pictorially blocked and lettered in gold on spine: ADVENTURES / OF / MONS*R* VIOLET / AMONG THE / SNAKE IND*NS* / *rule* / MARRYAT / *rule*/ VOL. I. [*II. III*]. Cream end-papers.

Folding map, half-titles and collation as in Copy I. Spine of Vol. I repaired and P_4 torn away from Vol. II. Cloth fine. Bookseller's ticket: 'Sharland, Southampton' inside front cover of each vol.

Note. Although I say below that this binding and that on the re-issue are uniform, there is one minute difference which should be recorded. On Copy II, the caps and numerals used for VOL. I, etc. are a shade taller, sharper and more condensed than those used on Copy III. The production of the re-issue, therefore, involved the making of new cases.

[1586b] **Copy III: Re-issue (under different title):** THE TRAVELS AND ROMANTIC ADVENTURES OF MONSIEUR VIOLET, AMONG THE SNAKE INDIANS AND WILD TRIBES OF THE GREAT WESTERN PRAIRIES. 3 vols. Longmans, etc. 1843. Binding as Copy II. Folding map in Vol. I as in Copies I and II.

Half-title in Vol. III only (reading, as in Copy I: NARRATIVE / OF / TRAVELS AND ADVENTURES, / &c / *rule* / VOL. III).

Vol. I (vi) [paged viii] + 312
II (ii) + (320) P_4 imprint leaf.
III (iv) + (300)

Note. Whether the original half-title which appears in this copy survives by exception I do not know. In Vols. I and II the original halves have been eliminated and the new titles are single insets; in Vol. III the new title is pasted to the stub of the old one. The sheets throughout are those of the first edition.

I have little doubt that this issue, with its more exciting title, was designed for the gift-book market, and presented as a book for boys.

[1587] *Pl. 18* NAVAL OFFICER (The), or Scenes and Adventures in the Life of Frank Mildmay [anon] 3 vols. Colburn 1829. Boards, labels.

Half-title in each vol.

Vol. I (iv) + (300) O_6 adverts.
II (iv) + (312) O_{12} adverts.
III (iv) + (276) N_4–N_6 adverts., paged (1)–6.

Ink signature: 'W. Bayfield (?)', on title of each vol., and printed book-label: 'Walters', on title of Vol. I. Booksellers' ticket: 'Owen, Homers Head, Little Bell Alley', tipped in on fly-leaf of Vol. III.

Note. This, Marryat's first novel, is one of the rarest three-deckers in original shape.

[1588] *Pl. 18* NEWTON FORSTER, or THE MERCHANT SERVICE (by the author of 'The King's Own') 3 vols. James Cochrane, 11 Waterloo Place 1832. Half-cloth boards, labels.

Half-title in each vol.

Vol. I (iv) + (272) M_4 adverts.
II (iv) + (296)
III (iv) + 260 L_7–L_{10} adverts. paged as continuation of text (253)–260.

Book-plate of Joseph Shrimpton in Vol. I. Fine. Pp. 165, 166 of Vol. II torn at corner.

[1589] OLLA PODRIDA (by the author of 'Peter Simple', etc.)

Copy I: First Edition. 3 vols. Longman etc. 1840. Pink ribbed cloth, blocked in blind and lettered in gold, uniform with *A Diary in America* Copy II; yellow end-papers.

Vol. I (viii) + 310 First leaf of final sig., O_1, a single inset.
II (iv) + (364) R_2 blank.
III (iv) + 332

Spines faded and chipped at head.

Copy II: Re-issue, under title 'OLLA PODRIDA: or a Medley of Adventures on the Continent, Tales, etc. By Capt. Marryatt (*sic*) C. B. Author of, etc.' 3 vols. Longman etc. 1842. Half ribbed-cloth boards, labels. [1589a]

Half-title in each vol.

Vol. I (viii) [paged vi] + 310 First leaf of final sig., O_1, a single inset.
II (vi) + (364) R_2 blank
III (vi) + 332

Ink signature: 'J. M. Jerningham', and Bookseller's ticket: 'Bolster, Cork', inside front cover of each vol. Fine.

Note. First Edition sheets of text with new half-titles and titles. Vol. I, pp. (vii) (viii)—fly-title 'Diary on the Continent'—are not present in this re-issue.

PACHA OF MANY TALES (The) (by the author of 'Peter Simple', 'Jacob Faithful', etc.) [1590] *Pl. 18*

Copy I: First Edition. 3 vols. Saunders & Otley 1835. Boards, labels.

Half-title in each vol.

Vol. I (iv) + (312) O_{11} O_{12} adverts.
II (iv) + 300
III (iv) + 312

This copy was bought at the sale of the Clumber Library (Duke of Newcastle) October 1937. Very fine.

Copy II: Another. Olive-brown glazed linen, paper labels. Collation as Copy I. [1590a]

Note. A secondary issue, undated, was made subsequently, of the 3 vols. in one, red cloth, with cancel title carrying the author's name (misspelt) and a steel engraved front. after W. Daniell, R.A.

Copy III: Second Edition in 'Ship Binding'. 3 vols. Saunders & Otley 1835. Dark blue diagonal-fine-ribbed cloth, blocked in blind and gold as *Jacob Faithful* Copy III (q.v.). Collation as Copy I. First Edition sheets with reprinted prelims. [1590b]

Ink signature: 'M. E. Scarnett, May 1876', on fly-leaf of Vol. I. Bookseller's ticket: 'Yates, Goswell Street', inside front cover of Vol. I. I have seen one other copy of this issue of *The Pacha.*

PERCIVAL KEENE

Copy I: First Edition. 3 vols. Colburn 1842. Half diaper-cloth boards, labels. [1591]

Half-title in each vol.

Vol. I (iv) + (296) O_4 imprint leaf.
II (iv) + (280)
III (iv) + (316)

Very fine.

[1591*a*] **Copy II: Another.** Brown fine-diaper cloth, blocked in blind on front and back and gold-lettered on spine; yellow end-papers. Collation as Copy I. Very fine.

[1592] PETER SIMPLE (by the author of 'Newton Forster', 'The King's Own', etc.)

Copy I: First Edition. 3 vols. Philadelphia and Baltimore: Carey & Hart. Vols. I and II, 1833; Vol. III, 1834. Half-cloth boards, labels.

Leaf bearing 'Publishers Advertisement' on verso precedes title in Vol. I; blank leaf precedes title in Vol. III

Vol. I pp. 216 Publishers' cat., 18 pp. dated September 1833, at end.
II pp. (156) 11_2 blank. Publishers' cat., as in Vol. I, at end.
III pp. (186) [paged (184)] 16_2 blank. Publishers' cat., as in Vol. I, at end.

Ink signature: 'R. H. Ludlow', on title of Vols. I and III, and 'V. H. Ludlow', inside front cover of Vol. II. Signature 'H. Le R. Cox' in ink inside front cover of each vol. and in pencil on each fly-leaf.

Notes. (i) This American edition preceded the first English, so far as Vol. I, and possibly also Vol. II, are concerned.

(ii) The titles vary. Vol. I says: PETER SIMPLE: or Adventures of a Midshipman (by the author of 'The King's Own', 'The Naval Officer', etc.); Vols. II and III say: PETER SIMPLE (by the author of 'Newton Forster', etc.).

(iii) Vol. I has no vol. number either on title or label. Vols. II and III are numbered in both places.

(iv) The 'Publishers Advertisement' in Vol. I explains that, owing to there seeming 'no probability of the story's early completion', the first volume is published alone, after having been delayed 'for some time'. It seems evident that the story was pirated from the *Metropolitan Magazine*, in which it ran intermittently from June 1832 to December 1833. The English edition was published in December 1833.

(v) Vols. I and II have side boards of pale green, Vol. III of buff.

[1592*a*] **Copy II: First English Edition.** 3 vols. Saunders & Otley 1834. Boards, labels.

Half-title in Vol. II

Vol. I (viii) + 328 Errata slip (14 lines) to Vol. III inserted between p. (viii) and p. (1).
II viii + (344)
III viii + (384) R_{11} R_{12} adverts.

Ink signature: 'Ellen Anne Weir', on title of each vol. Re-backed, original labels (defective) laid down.

Copy III: 'Second Edition' (re-set). 3 vols. Saunders & Otley 1834. Half (pink and white glazed) cloth boards, labels. [1592*b*]

Vol. I (viii) + (310) First leaf of final sig., O_1, a single inset.
II (viii) + (324) P_6 adverts.
III viii + 316

The purpose of re-setting seems to have been to equalise more nearly the length of the volumes. The Second Edition contains one chapter more than the First in Vols. I and II and consequently two chapters less in Vol. III.

Copy IV: 'Illustrated Edition.' Title and authorship as in Copy I. 3 vols. Saunders & Otley 1837. Dark blue diagonal-fine-ribbed cloth, blocked in blind on front and back with elaborate design of full-rigged ship etc., in gold on spine with lion's head above framed title etc. No publishers' imprint. Yellow end-papers. Etched front. and 3 plates by R. W. Buss in each vol. [1592*c*]

Leaf, with an Advertisement of an Illustrated Edition of Marryat's Works (seven titles are promised) on recto, precedes front. in Vol. I

Vol. I (x) [paged (viii)] + (312) O_{12} adverts.
II (viii) + (324) P_6 adverts.
III viii + 316 Slip tipped on to title forecasts a 'striking improvement' in the next title of the Illustrated Edition (*Jacob Faithful*).

Very fine.

Notes. (i) An occasional copy of this edition has the etchings coloured. Such copies post-date original issue. When it was decided to publish future volumes in the series with coloured plates (only *Jacob Faithful* appeared), Saunders & Otley put out an advertisement that any owner of the uncoloured *Peter Simple* who so desired would in due course receive a set of coloured plates in exchange for his plain ones, and that notice would be given when such an exchange could be made. As Buss's etchings for *Peter Simple* were designed for uncoloured issue, the result of subsequently overlaying hand-colouring was somewhat unsatisfactory. There is a coloured copy in the Collection.

(ii) There was published in London in 1929 an edition of *Peter Simple* in two volumes with binding design and illustrations facsimiled from this edition of 1837. The work also contained 9 hitherto unpublished drawings by Buss, a gravure Portrait of Marryat and an Introduction by myself.

PHANTOM SHIP (The) [1593]

3 vols. Colburn 1839. Half watered-cloth boards, labels.

Half-title in Vol. I

Vol. I (iv) + 300
II (ii) + (290)
III (ii) + (276) N_2–N_6 adverts.

Note. In the same year as Marryat's novel there was published by W. Emans, Cloth Fair, in 15 parts, a work entitled *The Black Pirate or the Phantom Ship*. The story was 'dedicated to Captain Marryat' and this statement on the front wrapper of each part has misled cataloguers into attributing the work to him. It may be taken for certain that he had nothing to do with it. In all probability it was an attempt to profit by his popularity and, by using the title of his latest work as a sub-title, to achieve a few sales of a totally different story under false pretences.

[1594] PIRATE AND THE THREE CUTTERS (The)

Copy I: First Edition 8vo (6″ × 9¼″ sheet measure). Longman etc. 1836. Cream glazed paper boards, spine blocked in gold; yellow end-papers. Steel-engraved portrait front. after W. Behnes: steel-engraved title (preceding printed title) and 18 plates after Clarkson Stanfield, all dated December 1835.

Half-title. pp. (viii) + (316)

Binders' ticket: 'Westley', at end. Spine laid down.

[1594*a*] **Copy II: Another.** Dull plum fine-diaper cloth, blocked in blind and gold; yellow end-papers. Illustrations and collation as Copy I.

Book-plate of Spencer Eddy. Fine.

Note. I have seen another cloth style—pink ribbed cloth, gold blocked on front with a ship in full sail surrounded by blind decoration. Both cloth-styles are later than that in boards.

[1594*b*] **Copy III: Another. Large Paper.** (7¼″ × 10⅝″ sheet measure). Half dark-green ribbon-embossed cloth, green board sides, buff leather label blocked and lettered in gold; white end-papers. Plates (as in Copy I) on India Paper. Collation as Copy I.

Spine worn, label defective.

[1594*c*] **Copy IIIA. Proof Engravings, A Series of.** Folio. Full dark blue straight-grain morocco (by Zaehnsdorf, 1903); silk end-papers, gilt doublures.

Contains the full Series of Twenty Engravings to *The Pirate*, each in two states—Proof before Letters on India Paper and Lettered Proofs pulled on folio plate paper. Specially printed title and List of Plates, dating probably from 1903.

[1594*d*] **Copy IV: First American Edition.** 2 vols. Philadelphia: Carey & Hart 1836. Half-cloth boards, labels.

Vol. I pp. (192)
II (iv) + 188

Pencil signature: 'J. Williams Jr. 1836', on title of Vol. I and Contents Leaf of Vol. II.

This work contains not only *The Pirate and The Three Cutters*, but also a story *Moonshine*, hitherto only published in *The Keepsake* for 1836, and not issued in book-form in England until *Olla Podrida*, 1840.

See also *Stories of the Sea*

Copy V: Re-issue in Parts. Fifteen 8vo parts. [1594*e*]
A. Fullerton & Co., London, Dublin, Edinburgh 1845. Cream paper wrappers printed in brown.

This re-issue contains the engravings of the original edition, with Fullerton's imprint and no date. The text is re-set. The parts were later issued in one vol., bound in dark olive green cloth, with gold decoration on spine but no imprint.

This set lacks Part I. Ink signature: 'John Robins', on front wrapper of Parts II–XII.

POOR JACK [1595]

Copy I: Part Issue. (Two sets: A and B.) Twelve *Pl. 2*
8vo shilling parts, published monthly by Longman from January to December 1840. No monthly date of issue appears on Parts I to III; Parts IV to XII are dated April 1 to December 1.

Cream paper wrappers, printed in black with double frame and wording as follows: *on front*, No. 1. PRICE 1*s*. / *top of frame* / POOR JACK. / BY CAPTAIN MARRYAT, C.B. / WITH / ILLUSTRATIONS / BY CLARKSON STANFIELD, R.A. / LONDON: / LONGMAN, ORME, BROWN, GREEN, AND LONGMANS, / PATERNOSTER ROW. / 1840. / *bottom of frame*; *on back*, either blank (Parts I–III) or printed with publishers' adverts. (Parts IV–XII). *Inside* front and back wrappers of Parts I–V blank, of Parts VI–XII printed with publishers' adverts.

For small points of difference between A and B see *Note on the Parts* below.

Part I. Three wood-engraved plates after Clarkson Stanfield, pp. (1)–32 of text (B_1 fly-title, verso blank). Publishers' cat., 8 pp. dated January 1, 1840. Inset leaf advertising *Paul Periwinkle.*

Part II. Publishers' cat., 4 pp. dated February 1840. Prospectus of McCulloch's Dictionary, 8 pp. in buff wrappers dated February 1st, 1840. Three plates. pp. 33–64 of text.

Part III. Three plates. pp. 65–96

Part IV. Three plates. pp. 97–128

Part V. Slip, tipped on to first page of text, apologises for absence of plates and promises six for next number. pp. 129–160

Part VI. Six plates. pp. 161–192 Bohn's cat. of Valuable Books, 16 pp. dated March 1840.

Part VII. Slip, tipped on to first page of text, apologises for absence of plates on account of Stanfield's illness, and promises six for next number. pp. 193–224

Part VIII. Six plates. pp. 225–256

Part IX. Slip, tipped on to first page of text, states that plates are unavoidably postponed and promises six for next number. pp. 257–288

Part X. 4 pp. prospectus of Moore's Poetical Works. Six plates. pp. 289–320

Part XI. Three plates. pp. 321–352

Part XII. Three plates. pp. 353–384

There follow (i) Prelims. for volume issue paged (i)–x. Final leaf, *a*, a single inset, carries List of Plates. (ii) Two leaves of adverts. on wrapper paper, which, together with inside and outside back cover, are printed with adverts. and paged 3–8, reckoning front cover (unpaged) as 1–2. Both sets very fine.

Note on the Parts

The two sets above described are identical as regards wrappers, advertisement material and text. They show, however, two variants in the underlines to the plates.

		Set A	*Set B*
Part VIII.	The Arrival of the Privateer at Lanion	No engraver's name under block	'Vizetelly' under block
Part XI.	The Euphrosyne in the Downs	Underline in NARROW type (see below: 'Notes on Volume Issue')	No underline

[1595 *a,b,c*] **Copies II, IIa and III: First Book Editions.** 8vo. Longman etc. 1840. Dark navy-blue fine-diaper cloth, blocked on front in blind and pictorially in gold; on back in blind; on spine pictorially and with titling in gold. Pale yellow end-papers. Wood-engraved front., 35 full-page plates and 11 vignettes in the text after Clarkson Stanfield.

pp. x + 384

Copy III has binders' ticket: 'Remnant & Edmonds', inside front cover. Copies II and III very fine; Copy IIa bruised and cover a little spotted.

Note on the Book Editions

It is evident that the majority of the plates for *Poor Jack* were either at some stage re-engraved—probably transformed from wood-blocks into metal plates to meet the strain of what early promised to be a long run—or put simultaneously in the hands of different engravers. In either event two kinds of lettering were used for the underlines. One was designed with squarer letters, more emphatically seriffed, yet in result more condensed than the other. The difference is clearly seen in magnified facsimile, and here are the alternative underlines to the plate 'Fisher's Alley' included in Part I and facing p. 16 of book.

Style 'N' (narrow) **FISHER'S ALLEY.** Style 'S' (square) FISHER'S ALLEY.

Owing to the fact that the printing of the plates was a separate process from the printing of the text, it is impossible to establish a coherent chronology of 'states' of issue, particularly as even in the Parts a number of re-engraved plates occur, underlined in Style 'S'. Here, however, is a schedule of the underline differences (typographical and one textual) between the Parts and the three copies of the book-issue in the collection, which are numbered II, IIa and III according to their approximation to the Parts.

[1595*a*]	**Copy II:**	*face p.* 338	The Euphrosyne in the Downs	Style 'S' and high under block
		face p. 370	The Prize at Sheerness	Style 'S', more condensed and high under block

[1595*b*] **Copy IIa.** No underline differences from II, but the last page reference in the List of Plates: '248', is set in a different and larger fount from that used in all other copies, whether of Part or Volume issue.

[1595*c*]	**Copy III:**	*face p.* 110	Jack in Nanny's Room	More condensed
		face p. 153	Jack and Bramble *aboard* the Indiaman	Instead of, as in II and IIa: '*on board* the Indiaman'
		face p. 171	How's her Head, Jack?	More condensed
		face p. 253	The Arrival of the Privateer at Lanion	As Part-Set B, i.e. with engraver's name, but more spaced and lower under block
		face p. 304	The Wreck of the Galley	As Parts, but more spaced and lower under block than II and IIa
		face p. 305	The Rescue	As Parts, but more spaced and lower under block than II and IIa
		face p. 306	Bessy in Bed	As Parts, but lower under block than II and IIa
		face p. 374	Deal Beach	As Parts, but Style 'N' and lower under block in contrast to II and IIa

It will be seen from these notes how confused and contradictory is the incidence of the two styles of lettering. It would be foolish to attempt to define a first issue in detail, nor am I able to explain either the missing underline in Part XI of Set B or the different fount used for '248' in Copy IIa.

[1596] PRIVATEERSMAN (The), One Hundred Years Ago

2 vols. Small 8vo. Longman etc. 1846. Dark purple-grey horizontal-ribbed cloth, blocked in blind on front, back and spine, and spine-lettered in gold; cream end-papers.

Half-title in each vol.

Vol. I (iv)+(380) Publishers' cat., 32 pp. dated May 1846, at end.

II (iv)+(364) $2A_6$ imprint leaf.

Binders' ticket: 'Westleys & Clark', at end of Vol. I. Fine. Label partially removed from inside cover of Vol. II.

Notes. (i) Some copies have end-papers printed with advert. of *Lardner's Cabinet Cyclopaedia*. Copies in red morocco cloth, with gold ship on front, gold decoration on spine and no imprint, are secondaries.

(ii) The sheets of the first edition were re-issued (? in the early fifties) in blue cloth, blocked in gold on front and spine and with all edges gilt. This issue had 8 steel engravings by J. Stephenson.

(iii) A sectional issue of this story, under the title: LOG OF A PRIVATEERSMAN A HUNDRED YEARS AGO, was made (or at any rate begun) by Carey & Hart of Philadelphia. I possess only the first section—an octavo of 48 pages, paged (9)–48+4 leaves of adverts. (3_5–3_8), paged 1–8. The booklet is wrappered in brownish salmon paper, lettered in black.

The date on the front wrapper is 1846 and on p. 48 appear the words: END OF THE FIRST BOOK. An advert. of 'Library for the People' on back cover is dated April 1, 1846. Whether the story was completed in this form, and if so in how many sections, I do not know. The section examined contained about 300 of the 750 fcap. 8vo pages which constitute the text as published in London. Presumably the prelims. were destined to appear with the completing section, and pp. (1)–(8) were reserved for their accommodation.

It is very possible that this Philadelphia edition began publishing before Longman's edition was published. But the fact cannot be proved, as the April date on the back cover is not necessarily the date of the pamphlet's issue. Serialization in the *New Monthly Magazine* was completed in June, 1846, and the English book-edition was announced for early June but not actually published until early July. It should also be noted (in favour of the priority of at least the first Philadelphia instalment) that when the story started serial in the *New Monthly* in August, 1845, the title was LOG OF A PRIVATEERSMAN A HUNDRED YEARS AGO, but this was changed with the second serial section to THE PRIVATEERSMAN. That Carey & Hart should have used the original title suggests that they started printing their edition immediately on receipt of the August *New Monthly* in the autumn of 1845 and retained the title for convenience sake. But none of this is conclusive, and I prefer to record this American issue, without definitely deciding whether it has priority or not.

SETTLERS IN CANADA (The). Written for Young People [1597]

2 vols. Small 8vo. Longman etc. 1844. Dark brown fine-diaper cloth, blocked in blind on front, back and spine, and gold-lettered on spine; cream end-papers. Wood-engraved front. on text paper in each vol., conjugate with title and representing (A_1).

Vol. I (iv)+356 Publishers' cat., 32 pp. dated September 1844, at end.

II (iv)+(376) $2B_4$ imprint leaf.

Binders' ticket: 'Westleys & Clark', at end of Vol. I. Ink signature: 'Philip Williams', inside front cover of each volume. Very fine.

SNARLEYYOW, or THE DOG FIEND (by the author of 'Peter Simple', 'Frank Mildmay', etc.) [1598] *Pl. 18*

Copy I: First Edition. 3 vols. Colburn 1837. Boards, labels.

Half-title in each vol.

Vol. I viii+(312) O_{11} O_{12} adverts.

II (viii)+(300)

III viii+(308)

Very fine.

Note. The Second Edition (3 vols. 1840) was entitled: *The Dog Fiend: or Snarleyyow, and the King's Cutter.*

Copy II: First American Edition. Philadelphia: Carey & Hart 1837. Half-cloth boards, label. [1598*a*]

pp. (200) [paged (1)–4+13–(204) 17_6 blank.

Ink signature (illegible) dated April 1837 on title.

Note. This portion of the American edition preceded the English book issue (serialisation did not finish until August 1837). Neither title nor label suggest a further volume to come, but on last page of text is stated: 'End of Volume One.'

STORIES OF THE SEA [1599]

New York: Harper 1836. Dark green embossed cloth, paper label.

pp. 232

Spine a little worn at head and tail.

Note. This book, like the two-volume edition of *The Pirate and the Three Cutters* (q.v.), contains *The Pirate and the Three Cutters* (admittedly in competition with the expensive English edition) and *Moonshine*, a story published in *The Keepsake* for 1836, and not issued in book-form in England until *Olla Podrida*, 1840. Whether this volume or the Carey & Hart two-volume edition was the first to appear cannot be established.

[1600] SUGGESTIONS FOR THE ABOLITION OF THE PRESENT SYSTEM OF IMPRESSMENT, IN THE NAVAL SERVICE

8vo. J. M. Richardson 1822. Unbound.

Half-title. pp. (iv) + 64

Presentation Copy: 'His Excellency Sir Charles Stuart, G.B.C. etc. etc. etc. With Captn. Marryat's res[pects].' in ink on half-title. Inscription cut into.

The price, printed on half-title, has been erased from this copy.

[1601] VALERIE: an Autobiography

2 vols. Colburn 1849.

Copy I: First Edition. Half-cloth boards, labels.

Half-title in each vol.

Vol. I (iv) + 312
II (iv) + (288)

Book-plate of Thomas Best.

[1601*a*] **Copy II: Another.** Dark grass-green fine-ribbed cloth, blocked in blind and spine-lettered in gold; pale yellow end-papers. Collation as Copy I.

Book-plate of Octavius E. Coope.

French Editions

[1602] CAÏN LE PIRATE [*The Pirate and the Three Cutters*] (par le Capitaine Marryat)

2 vols. 8vo. Paris: Ollivier 1837. Half-red roan gilt, red morocco paper sides; edges uncut.

Half-title precedes, and two fly-titles follow, title in each vol. Half-title reads: ŒUVRES COMPLÈTES / DU CAPITAINE MARRYAT. / etc.

Vol. I (iv) + (302) 20_6–20_7 adverts. First leaf of final sig., 20_1, a single inset.
II (iv) + (328) 21_4 adverts.

From the Library of the Empress Marie Louise, with her monogram on front and back cover.

[1603] KING'S OWN, ou IL EST AU ROI (par le Capitaine Marryat)

2 vols. 8vo. Paris: Charles Gosselin 1837.

Half-title (as above) in each vol.

Vol. I (iv) + 394 First leaf of final sig., 25_1, a single inset.
II (iv) + (360)

Binding and provenance as *Caïn le Pirate.*

[1604] PACHA A MILLE ET UNE QUEUES (Le). Traduit par A. J. B. Defauconpret

2 vols. 8vo. Paris: Gosselin 1837.

Half-title in each vol.

Vol. I (iv) + 380
II (iv) + 356

Binding and provenance as *Caïn le Pirate.*

Note. M. Defauconpret's translation of Marryat's title is, I am afraid, a blunder, and one which does not argue well for his knowledge of English. One would like to regard it as a suitably Gallic joke: for a Pacha, more thoroughly than most men, would have been able to profit from such lavish furnishings.

PERCIVAL KEENE (par le Capitaine Marryat). Traduit...par A. J. B. Defauconpret [1605]

2 vols. 8vo. Paris: Charles Gosselin 1843.

Half-title in each vol.

Vol. I (iv) + (304) 19_8 blank.
II (iv) + (332) 21_6 blank.

Binding and provenance as *Caïn Le Pirate.*

PIERRE SIMPLE, ou Aventures d'un Officier de Marine (par le Capitaine Marryat). Traduit de l'anglais sur la deuxième édition par J. A. B. (*sic*) Defauconpret [1606]

2 vols. 8vo. Paris: Gosselin 1834.

Half-title in each vol.

Vol. I (iv) + (352)
II (iv) + 362 First leaf of final sig., 23_1, a single inset.

Binding and provenance as *Caïn le Pirate.*

PAUVRE JACK (Le) (par le Capitaine Marryat). Traduit...par A. J. B. Defauconpret [1607]

2 vols. 8vo. Paris: Charles Gosselin 1841.

Half-title in each vol.

Vol. I (iv) + (312)
II (iv) + (332) 21_6 blank.

Binding and provenance as *Caïn le Pirate.*

Continental Edition in English

Published in 8vo in Paris in Baudry's *Collection of British Authors.* Plain wrappers (drab or grey), paper spine labels printed in black. [1608]

Joseph Rushbrook	1841	**Percival Keene**	1842
King's Own, The	1840	**Phantom Ship, The**	1839
Naval Officer, The	1840	**Poor Jack**	1841
Newton Forster	1840	**Snarleyyow**	1837

[*See also* HAMILTON, WALTER, *above*]

Attributed to Marryat

FLORAL TELEGRAPH (The): a New Mode of Communication by Floral Signals (anon) [1609]

Copy I: First Edition. 12mo. Saunders & Otley 1836. Olive-green silk cloth, pictorially embossed in blind and gold-lettered on front and spine; all edges gilt. Hand-coloured engraved front. and 5 plates.

pp. (xvi) + (318) DD_5–DD_9 adverts. [? DD_{10} (lacking) blank or adverts.].

Re-jointed, new end-papers. Name cut from title. pp. xi, xii missing.

[1609a] **Copy II: New Edition,** entitled: 'THE FLORAL TELEGRAPH OF AFFECTION'S SIGNALS. BY THE LATE CAPTAIN MARRYAT, R.N.'

12mo. Saunders & Otley, n.d. [? circ. 1850]. Dark grass-green ripple-grain cloth, blocked in gold and blind on front and spine with designs signed J. L. [John Leighton], and gold-lettered on spine; yellow end-papers. Hand-coloured *lithographed* front. and 5 plates, as in Copy I, but more coarsely rendered.

pp. (xvi) + 324

This edition seems to consist of first edition sheets to p. 292 with new inserted title. pp. 293–324 show differences of text. Binder's ticket: 'J. Westley', at end.

Note. It has always seemed to me difficult to believe that Marryat had any share in this finical little work. The most masculine of authors, he cannot be imagined spending time and thought on a pretty-pretty boudoir trifle of the kind. It has been suggested to me by Dudley Massey (and I think the suggestion well worth recording) that the attribution to Marryat, which only appears on the later edition published after his death, was due to a confusion between *The Floral Telegraph* and *The Floral Calendar*, a small 8vo with coloured plates, compiled by a Commander James Mangles, R.N., privately printed and issued in 1839 over the imprint of F. W. Calder, Printer, 199 Oxford Street.

Between 1836 and 1850 the firm of Saunders & Otley ceased to exist, and was then revived under entirely new management. Supposing that, during the early forties, the two books had become confounded, is it not conceivable that a resurgent Saunders & Otley, without the records of its predecessor and aware that a Naval officer with a name not unlike Marryat's had once compiled a book very like one of which it had inherited unsold sheets and engraved plates, jumped to the conclusion that here was an opportunity to profit by the publicity attendant on Marryat's death?

Engravings after Original Drawings by Marryat

[1610] I. BIRMAN EMPIRE: Views taken at and near Rangoon.

Inevitably a few of the details regarding the early issues of this work have to be conjectured; for the publication, complete and in original state, is very scarce, and I have been unable to check my conclusions at one or two points. To the best of my belief, however, the following descriptions are correct.

Copy I: First Edition, First Issue

Three wrappered parts, loose in portfolio, *plus* two wrappered booklets of 'Notes'. The Portfolio is of marbled paper boards with red leather spine, and leather side-label lettered in gold RANGOON/VIEWS, the words enclosed in fancy frame. Spine unlettered.

The parts are in folio [sheet-measure $14\frac{1}{2}'' \times 21''$]; the booklets in 4to [sheet-measure: (i) $8\frac{3}{8}'' \times 10\frac{3}{8}''$, (ii) $8\frac{5}{8}'' \times 10\frac{3}{4}''$].

Published by Kingsbury & Co. Leadenhall Street and Thos. Clay, Ludgate Hill 1825, 1826. Each part is in a grey-brown paper wrapper, pictorially printed in black, folded round the sheets and carrying wording or engravings (as below). The sheets are merely inserted in the wrappers, not stitched. Marryat's contributions form part of the Second Series. Of the two booklets, the first is wrappered in greenish-brown, the second in a slightly lighter colour. Both are stitched and lettered in black on front, other wrappers plain.

[First Series]

Part I. Front wrapper carries a Burmese-style design, lithographed in black, incorporating the following wording in fancy caps. and caps. and l.c., as indicated: BIRMAN / PART I. / CONTAINING / *Six Views taken at and near* / RANGOON. / EMPIRE. Inside and back wrappers blank.

Contents. Pictorial dedication to the Court of Directors of the East India Company, signed by Joseph Moore, Lieut. of H.M. 89th Regt., engraved by R. W. Smart after a design by Thos. Stothard, R.A. Imprint: Published by Thos. Clay, 18 Ludgate Hill, London. The recto of this sheet is blank.

Pictorial List of Subscribers, headed by heraldic design engraved by J. Bromley after Stothard, below which appear eight names of eminent subscribers, also engraved. The verso of this sheet is blank.

Four leaves, printed by lithography on both sides with alphabetical lists in facsimiled handwriting of 'Subscriptions in India' (3 pp. + 1 page blank); 'Subscriptions in England' (half-page); 'Subscriptions in India, since received' (slightly over 3 pp.).

Six engravings in full colour after drawings by J. Moore. Each engraving is numbered in top right-hand corner.

1. 'The Harbour of Port Cornwallis, Island of Great Andaman, with the Fleet getting under weigh for Rangoon.' Engraved by G. Hunt. Imprint: Published Oct. 1, 1825 by Kingsbury & Co., 6 Leadenhall Str[t] & T. Clay, 18 Ludgate Hill, London. Area of engraving $10\frac{3}{16}'' \times 14\frac{5}{8}''$.
2. 'View of the Landing at Rangoon' etc. Engraved by H. Pyall. Imprint: Published October 1, 1825 by Kingsbury, Parbury & Allen, 6 Leadenhall Str[t] & T. Clay, 18 Ludgate Hill, London. Area of engraving $10'' \times 14\frac{1}{2}''$.
3. 'The Principal Approach to the Great Dagon Pagoda at Rangoon.' Engraved by T. Fielding.

Imprint: Published November 9, 1825 by Kingsbury & Co., Leadenhall Str[t] & T. Clay, 18 Ludgate Hill, London. Area of engraving 10″ × 14 5/16″.

4. 'View of the Great Dagon Pagoda' etc. Engraved by H. Pyall. Imprint as 3. Area of engraving 10″ × 14 9/16″.

5. 'Scene upon the Terrace of the Great Dagon Pagoda' etc. Engraved by G. Hunt. Imprint as 1. Area of engraving 10 3/16″ × 14 5/8″.

6. 'The Attack upon the Stockades near Rangoon' etc. Engraved by G. Hunt. Imprint (virtually) as 3 and 4. Area of engraving 10 1/4″ × 14 1/2″.

Parts II and III. Now we come to a query. The set of this first issue in the Collection has these two Parts enclosed in a single wrapper, which is identical with that enclosing Part I. The legend on the front has been altered by hand, very carefully in ink, to read: Part. (*sic*) II & III. / *each* CONTAINING / etc. as before. Whether correct wrappers for these two Parts were ever issued I do not know, but I doubt it. I have never seen another copy in loose portfolio form.

Contents. Twelve engravings in full-colour after drawings by J. Moore, numbered 7–18 in top right-hand corner. All engraved by Hunt unless otherwise stated.

7. 'The Gold Temple of the principal Idol Guadma' etc. Imprint as 1. Area of engraving 10 3/16″ × 14 5/8″.

8. 'Inside View of the Gold Temple' etc. Imprint as 6. Area of engraving 10 1/4″ × 14 9/16″.

9. 'Scene from the Upper Terrace of the Great Pagoda' etc. Engraved by Pyall. Imprint: Published Jan. 2, 1826 by Tho[s]. Clay, 18 Ludgate Hill & Kingsbury & Co., Leadenhall Str[t], London. Area of engraving 10 1/4″ × 14 11/16″.

10. 'The Storming of the Lesser Stockade at Kemmendine' etc. Imprint as 9. Area of engraving 10 5/16″ × 14 9/16″.

11. 'View of the Lake and part of the Eastern Road' etc. Engraved by Pyall. Imprint as 6. Area of engraving 10 1/16″ × 14 9/16″.

12. 'Rangoon. The Position of part of the Army' etc. Imprint as 2. Area of engraving 10 1/8″ × 14 1/2″.

13. 'Scene upon the Eastern Road from Rangoon' etc. Imprint as 3. Area of engraving 10 3/8″ × 14 9/16″.

14. 'Scene upon the Terrace of the Great Dagon Pagoda' etc. Imprint as 9. Area of engraving 10 1/4″ × 14 1/2″. This plate is lettered 'Proof' in bottom right-hand corner.

15. 'Rangoon. The Storming of one of the principal Stockades' etc. Imprint as 1. Area of engraving 10 1/8″ × 14 5/16″.

16. 'View of the Great Dagon Pagoda and ajacent (*sic*) Scenery' etc. Engraved by Fielding. Imprint as 6. Area of engraving 10 3/16″ × 14 1/2″.

17. 'The Conflagration of Dalla' etc. Imprint as 9. Area of engraving 10 3/8″ × 14 1/4″.

18. 'The Attack of the Stockades at Pagoda Point' etc. Engraved by Reeve Junr. Imprint as 9. Area of engraving 10 1/16″ × 14 9/16″.

[Second Series] Once again a query. The set under description shows the plates of this Series inserted in a wrapper identical with that used for Part I and with no ink-correction. I do not know whether, at the time of first issue, a special wrapper was prepared for the Second Series.

Contents. Six engravings in full colour, of which three painted by Stothard from original sketches by Marryat, one painted by D. Cox and one by G. Webster from sketches by Marryat, and one painted by Stothard from a sketch by Capt. Thornton, R.N. The engravings are numbered 1–6 in top right-hand corner. All engraved by Pyall.

1. 'The Storming of the Fort of Syriam' etc. (Stothard-Marryat). Imprint: Published Sep[r] 12, 1826, by Tho[s]. Clay, 18 Ludgate Hill, London. Area of engraving 9 3/4″ × 14 1/2″. This plate is lettered '*Proof*' in bottom right-hand corner.

2. 'The Attack of the Dalla Stockade' etc. (Stothard-Marryat). Imprint as above. Area of engraving 9 15/16″ × 14 1/2″. This plate is lettered '*Proof*' in bottom right-hand corner.

3. 'The Attempt of the Burmans to retake the Stockades of Dalla' etc. (Cox-Marryat). Imprint as above. Area of engraving 10 1/8″ × 14 9/16″. This plate is lettered '*Proof*' in bottom right-hand corner.

4. 'One of the Birman Gilt War Boats' etc. (Stothard-Marryat). Imprint as above. Area of engraving 9 15/16″ × 14 5/16″. This plate is lettered '*Proof*' in bottom right-hand corner.

5. 'H.M.S. Larne, H.C. Cruizer,...attacking the Stockades at the entrance of Bassein River' etc. (Webster-Marryat). Imprint as above. Area of engraving 10 1/16″ × 14 11/16″.

6. 'The Combined Forces...passing the Fortress of Donabue' etc. (Stothard-Thornton). Imprint as above. Area of engraving 10″ × 14 1/2″.

Booklet No. I. NOTES / TO ACCOMPANY / THE RANGOON VIEWS.

Engraved folding map as front. Slip: 'To Subscribers', tipped on to first page of text, explains that the Plates in the main work are not given in numerical order as planned, on account of the illness of one of the artists concerned. It also announces that Vignette, with Dedication and Names of Subscribers, will be given with the last Part. Text: 40 pp., unfoliated but signed B–F in fours, gives commentary on the series of Views and details of the war-incidents portrayed in them. *Pl. 20*

Pl. 20 **Booklet No. II.** NOTES / TO ACCOMPANY THE SECOND SERIES / OF / SIX COLOURED PRINTS, / ILLUSTRATIVE OF / THE COMBINED OPERATIONS OF THE BRITISH FORCES / IN THE BIRMAN EMPIRE, 1824 & 1825. / *rule* / PUBLISHED BY THOMAS CLAY, LUDGATE HILL, LONDON.

Text: 8 pp. unfoliated but signed B. Each leaf printed on recto only.

[1610*a*] **Copy II: First Edition, Second Issue**

2 vols., of which one in folio, the other in 4to.

(i) **Folio vol.** in three-quarter red leather, marbled board sides, leather side-label gold-lettered VIEWS / IN THE / BIRMAN EMPIRE, the words enclosed in fancy frames in blind and gold. Spine gold-blocked but unlettered. Drab end-papers. The sheet-measure of the contents of this volume $14\frac{1}{8}'' \times 20\frac{3}{8}''$.

Pl. 20 *Contents.* Grey brown wrapper, printed by lithography in black on front with same design as appears on the separate Parts of the First Issue, but re-worded: BIRMAN / EIGHTEEN / VIEWS, / *Taken at and near* / RANGOON. / EMPIRE. Verso blank.

Pictorial dedication and Pictorial List of Subscribers (2 leaves) as in First Issue. No lithographed sheets of subscribers in facsimile handwriting.

Eighteen engravings in full colour numbered 1–18, exactly as in First Issue, except where otherwise stated.

1. Engraving lettered 'Proof' in bottom right-hand corner.

8. Engraving lettered 'Proof' in bottom right-hand corner.

11. Word 'Proof' virtually erased in bottom right-hand corner.

16. The misprint 'ajacent' is corrected in the underline, which reads 'adjacent'.

Pl. 20 A second grey-brown wrapper, printed by lithography in black on front with a large drawing by Marryat of a group of natives with the Great Pagoda and a palm-tree in the background, and wording, in fancy caps. and italic caps. and l.c. SIX COLOURED PRINTS / *Illustrative of the Combined Operations* / OF THE BRITISH FORCES, / IN THE / BIRMAN EMPIRE. / *1824 and 1825.* / Second Series. Under the drawing is imprint: Pubd. by T. Clay, Ludgate Hill, 1826. Verso blank.

Six engravings in full colour numbered 1–6, exactly as in First Issue except where otherwise stated.

2. This plate is *not* lettered 'Proof'.

3. Word 'Proof' virtually erased.

4. This plate is *not* lettered 'Proof'.

(ii) **Quarto vol.**, bound uniform with (i). Side-label worded: NOTES / TO THE / BURMESE VIEWS. Sheet-measure $8'' \times 9\frac{15}{16}''$.

Contents. Folding map and 40+8 pp. of text exactly as in the separate booklets of the First Issue. The slip 'To Subscribers' is absent. Traces of the original booklet wrappers remain in the gully.

Copy III. Re-issue [1610*b*]

Oblong folio (sheet measure $13\frac{13}{16}'' \times 20\frac{1}{2}''$). Thomas Clay, n.d. Quarter blue cloth, greenish-drab paper sides, cut flush and printed in black on front: ILLUSTRATIONS OF / THE BURMESE WAR; / BOTH SERIES, WITH 24 PLATES, / AFTER DRAWINGS BY CAPTAIN MARRYAT, THORNTON, AND MOORE, / DISPLAYING THE OPERATIONS OF THE BRITISH FORCES. / (then follows abbreviated titles of the plates, set in three columns) / Price Six Pounds. / [*double rule*] / LONDON: PUBLISHED BY THOMAS CLAY. The wording is enclosed in a fancy frame. Back wrapper blank.

The volume contains no prelims. or text; merely the 24 plates uncoloured and printed in grey. Imprints as in original issues, but in several cases the dates have been erased.

The cloth spine is bead-grain, which suggests a post-1850 issue. Perhaps the venture was made in connection with Marryat's recent death.

II. PROGRESS OF A MIDSHIPMAN (The): exemplified in the Career of Master Blockhead. In Seven Plates and Frontispiece [1611]

Eight coloured engravings, signed with an Anchor (from left to right) and 'G. Cruikshank sculpt.' Pl. 21

Small oblong folio. G. Humphrey, St James's Street, May 15, 1820.

Albert Cohn (in *George Cruikshank: a Catalogue Raisonné*, 1924, No. 1874) gives the titles of the plates but does not record that the Frontispiece is numbered 8 and that consequently the other plates are all numbered one less than he states.

Notes. (i) This is the First State of these engravings, described by Cohn as 'of the greatest rarity'.

Also in the Collection are three sets of later States, published by McLean in 1835.

The first of these presents the eight plates in full colour, and exactly resembles the First State, save for the change of imprint and date. This copy is bound in dark grey boards, with a green leather lettering-piece up spine. The second variant consists of the eight plates in monochrome, printed on dark cream paper with very wide margins, and loose in series. The third variant is an *upright* small folio, stitched in amateur grey wrapper with MS. titling, with a new pictorial title, etched by Cruikshank and worded: THE / SAILORS / PROGRESS / Sic transit / gloria Mundi / LONDON / *Pub^{d} by Thos McLean*, 26 *Haymarket*, / *Augt. 1st*, 1835. The eight original plates follow in order of number (i.e. with original title-page at the end), printed in monochrome on white paper and set sideways on the page.

(ii) The survival of a letter from Marryat to Cruikshank (and my fortunate encounter with this letter while the present work was going through the press) enables me to put on record the hitherto unknown fact that a second series of Blockhead's adventures was contemplated by Marryat and the original drawings prepared. Why the scheme was abandoned we may never know; but it is possible that the sketches are in existence and, thanks to the letter printed below, may one day be discovered and recognized for what they are.

'My dear Cruikshank

I have often been requested to follow up the History of Master Blockhead and I have reason to suppose that Mr Humphries (*sic*) has found that it answered well as to the profits of the concern. I have arranged a new Series from Lieutenant to Commander. I am nearly finished and if you think it *worth your while* to publish them, they will all be very much at your service. Let me know your opinion and I will make an appointment with you. In the meantime

truly yours

F. Marryat.'

Sussex House
17 July 1827.

[1612] III. SINGLE ENGRAVINGS

(*a*) Funeral Procession of Bonaparte (The)

Coloured engraving, signed: 'Drawn on the spot by Capt. Marryat, R.N.... Engraved by Alken and Sutherland.'

Narrow oblong folio. S. and I. Fuller, July 25, 1821.

Ditto. Another copy, uncoloured. Stamp of Bibliotheca Lindesiana in corner.

(*b*) Interesting Scene on Board an East Indiaman (An). Showing the Effects of a Heavy Lurch—after Dinner. [*Cohn* 1238

Coloured engraving, signed with an Anchor (from right to left) and 'G. Cruikshank fec^t.'

Small oblong folio. G. Humphrey, November 9, 1818.

(*c*) Puzzled Which to Choose etc. [*Cohn* 1880

Coloured engraving, signed with an Anchor (from right to left) and 'G. Cruikshank sculp.'

Small oblong folio. G. Humphrey, October 10, 1818.

(*d*) Root of King's Evil (The) [*Cohn* 1913

Coloured engraving signed: 'Designed by an Amateur—G. Cruik^k fec^t' and imprinted: 'London Pub^d by G. Humphrey, July 8, 1819.' (Cohn gives the date as 1820.)

(*e*) Tomb of Bonaparte (The)

Sepia engraving, signed 'Capt. Marryat, R.N. del... T. Sutherland, sculp^t.'

Oblong folio. S. and I. Fuller, July 20, 1821.

MARSH, ANNE (MRS MARSH-CALDWELL (1791–1874)

ANGELA: a Novel (by the author of 'Emilia Wyndham', 'Two Old Men's Tales', etc.) [1613]

3 vols. Colburn 1848. Half-cloth boards, labels.

Half-title in Vol. II

Vol. I (iv)+312
II (iv)+(320) P_3 P_4 adverts.
III (ii)+(348) Q_6 adverts.

Ink signature: 'A. G. F. Griffin-Williams. Llwynhilig', inside front cover of Vol. I.

AUBREY (by the author of 'Emilia Wyndham') [1614]

3 vols. Hurst & Blackett 1854. Olive-green morocco cloth.

Vol. I (ii)+(308) Publishers' cat., 24 pp. undated, at end.
II (ii)+318 First leaf of final sig., X_1, a single inset. Publishers' cat., 16 pp. undated, at end.
III (ii)+344

Presentation Copy: 'Frances Mary Crofton, from her most affectionate mother, Anne Marsh. Oct. 28, 1854' in ink on fly-leaf of Vol. I, and the name only, in the author's hand, in Vols. II and III.

CASTLE AVON (by the author of 'Emilia Wyndham', 'Ravenscliffe', etc.) [1615]

3 vols. Colburn 1852.

Copy I: Half-cloth boards, labels.

Half-title in Vol. I

Vol. I (iv)+(298) Final leaf, U_5, a single inset.
II (ii)+294 First leaf of final sig., U_1, a single inset.
III (ii)+294 First leaf of final sig., U_1, a single inset. Publisher's cat., 16 pp. undated, at end.

Copy II: Olive-green diagonal-wavy-grain cloth. Collation as Copy I. Publisher's cat., 8 pp. undated, at end of Vol. I. A concurrent style. [1615*a*]

Cover of Vol. III stained and top hinge split.

CHRONICLES OF DARTMOOR (by Mrs Marsh) [1616]

3 vols. Hurst & Blackett 1866. Royal-blue fine-morocco cloth.

Half-title in Vol. I

Vol. I (vi) + (318) First leaf of final sig., X_1, a single inset.
II (ii) + (312)
III (ii) + (320) Publishers' cat., 16 pp. undated, at end.

Small crest book-plate (no name) in each vol. Fine.

[1617] *Pl. 22* EMILIA WYNDHAM (by the author of 'Two Old Men's Tales', 'Mount Sorel')
3 vols. Colburn 1846. Boards, labels.

Vol. I (iv) + 322 Final leaf, P_5, a single inset.
II (ii) + (328)
III (ii) + 360

Ink signature: 'Lady Georgiana Codrington, 3 Park Place, London Aug[st] 14. 1846', inside covers of Vols. II and III. Her pencil signature in Vol. I. Very fine.

Note. For a further reference to this, the author's best-known novel, see Chapman & Hall's Monthly Series, 3742 in Section III.

[1618] EVELYN MARSTON (by the author of 'Emilia Wyndham', 'Two Old Men's Tales', etc.)
3 vols. Hurst & Blackett 1856. Dark blue-green morocco cloth.

Vol. I (ii) + (308) Publishers' cat., 24 pp. undated, at end.
II (ii) + (314) Final leaf, X_5, a single inset.
III (ii) + (316) X_6 adverts.

[1619] FATHER DARCY (by the author of 'Mount Sorel' and 'Two Old Men's Tales')
2 vols. Chapman & Hall 1846. Rose-madder diagonal-ribbed cloth.

Half-title in Vol. I. Inset leaf of adverts. and half-title precede title in Vol. II

Vol. I pp. (318) First leaf of final sig., U_1, a single inset.
II (ii) + 368

Spines soiled, and inside hinges of Vol. II broken.

Note. This novel was a title in Chapman & Hall's Monthly Series (3742 (9) (10) in Section III) and carries the series imprint at base of spines. The advert. leaf in Vol. II concerns the series.

[1620] HEIRESS OF HAUGHTON (The), or The Mother's Secret (by the author of 'Emilia Wyndham', 'Two Old Men's Tales', etc.)
3 vols. Hurst & Blackett 1855. Dark blue-green morocco cloth; rose-pink end-papers.

Vol. I (ii) + (308) Publishers' cat., 24 pp. dated March 1855, at end.
II (ii) + (318) First leaf of final sig., X_1, a single inset.
III (ii) + (336) Y_8 adverts.

Binders' ticket: 'Leighton, Son & Hodge', at end of Vol. I. Fragments of auctioneer's ticket on cover of Vol. III.

MORDAUNT HALL, or a September Night (by the author of 'Two Old Men's Tales', 'Emilia Wyndham', 'Angela', etc.) [1621]
3 vols. Colburn 1849. Half-cloth boards, labels.

Half-title in Vol. I

Vol. I (iv) + (292)
II (ii) + 314 Final leaf, Y_1, a single inset.
III (ii) + (304)

Syston Park book-plate in Vol. III. A poor copy, loose, corners bruised and labels worn.

MOUNT SOREL, or the Heiress of the de Veres (by the author of 'Two Old Men's Tales') [1622]
2 vols. Chapman & Hall 1845. Rose-madder morocco cloth.

Half-title in each vol. 4 pp. prospectus of the Monthly Series, dated November 1844, precedes half-title in Vol. I

Vol. I (320)
II 330 This volume collates (B)–Z in eights, with the exception of N, a single-leaf signature.

Ink-signature: 'A. C. Bertie Percy' on fly-leaf of each vol. Very fine.

Note. This was the first novel to be published in Chapman & Hall's Monthly Series (3742 (3) (4) in Section III). The copy described is of the first issue, with series-imprint on spines. There is also in the Collection a copy (also very fine) of the second issue, in fine-ribbed cloth rather differently blocked, with publisher's imprint on spines, and a catalogue dated September 1846 at the end of Vol. II. In this second issue the prospectus is one leaf only, and announces the 'enlarged plan' by which the publishers hoped to save their series.

ROSE OF ASHHURST (The) (by the author of 'Emilia Wyndham', 'Two Old Men's Tales', 'Evelyn Marston', etc.) [1623]
3 vols. Hurst & Blackett 1857. Plum watered cloth.

Vol. I (ii) + 300 Publishers' cat., 24 pp. undated, at end.
II (ii) + 308
III (ii) + 306 Final leaf, X_1, a single inset.

TALES OF THE WOODS AND FIELDS: a Second Series of 'Two Old Men's Tales' [anon] [1624]
3 vols. Saunders & Otley 1836. Boards, labels.

Half-title in Vols. I and II

Vol. I viii + (300) Errata slip faces p. viii.
II (iv) + (276) N_5 N_6 adverts.
III (ii) + 288

Fine.

[1625] TIME, THE AVENGER (by the author of 'Emilia Wyndham', 'The Wilmingtons', etc.)

3 vols. Colburn 1851. Green morocco cloth.

Vol. I (ii)+300
II (ii)+292
III (ii)+(296) Publisher's cat., 24 pp. undated (though a work is announced on p. (3) for January 1 1851), at end.

Pencil signature: 'Crofton', in each vol. (Married name of the author's daughter, see *Aubrey.*)

Note. This novel has also been seen by me in half-cloth boards, labels—a concurrent style.

[1626 *Pl. 22* TWO OLD MEN'S TALES: the Deformed and the Admiral's Daughter [anon]

2 vols. Saunders & Otley 1834. Boards, labels.

Leaf of adverts. precedes title in Vol. II

Vol. I (iv)+(308)
II (iv)+308

Label of Rhiwlas Library on inside cover of each volume; also bookseller's ticket: 'Harding, Chester.' Inset between front end-papers of Vol. I is 8 pp. prospectus of Sacred Classics, published by Hatchard. Very fine.

Note. In her autobiography Harriet Martineau relates how, when she was spending two days with the Marshes in Kilburn, Mrs Marsh asked if she might read aloud 'one or two little stories' she had written. The first to be read was *The Admiral's Daughter*, which astounded Miss Martineau by its excellence. 'We cried so desperately', she says, 'that there was no concealing the marks of it.' She introduced the MS. to Saunders & Otley, who at once accepted it. The author's husband insisted on anonymity, lest his several daughters be embarrassed by an unsuccessful novelist-mother.

[1627] WILMINGTONS (The): a Novel (by the author of 'Two Old Men's Tales', 'Emilia Wyndham', 'Mordaunt Hall', etc.)

3 vols. Colburn 1850.

Copy I: Half-cloth boards, labels.

Vol. I (ii)+292
II (ii)+(302) First leaf of final sig., U_1, a single inset.
III (ii)+(278) First leaf of final sig., T_1, a single inset.

[1627*a*] **Copy II:** Dark green fine-ribbed cloth. Collation as Copy I. At end of Vol. III is publisher's cat., 16 pp. undated. Pencil signature: 'Crofton', in each volume. (Married name of the author's daughter, see *Aubrey.*)

Vol. I of this copy has a stain on back cover and fragment of auctioneer's ticket on front.

MARTINEAU, HARRIET (1802–1876)

This schedule includes all the principal fiction of Harriet Martineau (an unauthorized reprint of a short story, two insignificant items published later in her life and a posthumous fragment are missing), and I give descriptions of a number of her non-fiction books which are also in the Collection, because she is a writer of importance and provides some interesting specimens of publishing methods.

BRITISH FRIENDSHIP (A): and Memoir of the Earl of Elgin and Kincardine [1628]

Pamphlet. Windermere: Printed by J. Garnett for Private Circulation 1866. Grey wrappers, printed in black.

pp. (36)

Presentation Copy: 'Rosa E. Beaufort. With affectionate regards from Harriet Martineau. December 1866' in ink on front cover.

BRITISH RULE IN INDIA: a Historical Sketch [1629]

Smith, Elder 1857. Smooth light brown glazed linen, printed in black on front, spine and back; drab printed end-papers.

Half-title. pp. (viii)+(360) AA_3 AA_4 adverts.

Blind stamp: 'W. H. Smith Dublin', on fly-leaf. Fine.

COMPLETE GUIDE TO THE ENGLISH LAKES (A) [1630]

Copy I: First Edition. Small 8vo. Windermere: John Garnett (1855). Red morocco cloth, blocked in blind and lettered in gold on front; blocked, lettered and priced (5*s.*) on spine; blind blocked on back; cream end-papers. Front. and 15 steel engravings after Aspland and Banks; 6 outline panoramas, and a folding coloured map.

Half-title. pp. (xvi)+(252) The pagination is eccentric, thus: (iv) [half-title, verso; title, verso]+(iv) [Preface]+ii [Contents]+iv [Index] +(ii) [Illustrations, but reckoned as pp. (1) (2) of text]+(3)[signed A]–233, Text of Guide, + (234)–(250) [Adverts. of Hotels, paged (i)–(xix)] +(ii) [blank]. Sig. P runs from 223 to adverts. p. v; sig. Q from adverts. p. vi to final blank leaf, Q_8.

Binder's ticket: 'Banks Jr. Edinburgh', at end. Bookseller's ticket: 'King, Brighton', inside front covers.

Copy II: 4to Illustrated Edition. ('THE ENGLISH LAKES' on title-page). [1630*a*]

Cr. 4to. Windermere. John Garnett (1858). Orange-red morocco cloth, heavily blocked in gold on front, back and spine and gold-lettered 'THE ENGLISH LAKE DISTRICT' on spine. Bevelled boards. Steel-engraved front. and 5 plates after Aspland and Pettitt. Also numerous wood-cuts by W. J. Linton, printed on Chinese paper and mounted in text. Three double outline-panoramas (one folding) and a folding geological map in full colour.

Half-title. Pp. (viii) [paged ii] + (178) [paged (1)–(175) + (i)–iii]. Final sigs., OO, PP, QQ, RR, two leaves each.

Text ends 152; (153)–156 'Meteorology'; (157)–160 'List of Flowering Plants', etc.; (161)–166 'Botany of Cumberland'; (167)–173 'Geology and Mineralogy'; (174) (175) 'Tables'; (176) (178) Index, paged (i)–iii.

Note. The elaboration of this handsome edition is proof of the popularity won by Miss Martineau's Guide within three years of its first appearance. The steel engravings are all different from those in the original edition; the panoramas are re-engraved and the coloured map, although its centre-piece is that of the map of 1855, has sections of mountain-ranges in full colour in all four margins. The appendices dealing with Meteorology and Geology are new, as are also the Tables of heights, lake-areas and waterfalls.

But the most striking feature of the edition is the long series of Linton woodcuts, which are of a very high order, both artistically and technically.

[1630*b*] **Copy III: 'Third Edition,' Edited and Enlarged by Maria Martineau.** Windermere: John Garnett, n.d. [1862 or 1863]. Violet morocco cloth, blocked uniform with first edition. Steel engraved front., vignette title and 6 plates, some retained from first edition, others new. The vignette title shows the home of Harriet Martineau and a facsimile of her signature. The outline panoramas are retained from First Edition, and several folding ones added; 4 new finely engraved section-maps in colours are provided, while the large folding map published in colours in First Edition is now in black only and in a pocket inside back cover.

pp. (viii) [paged (ii) + ii + ii + (ii)] + (288) [(285)–(288), S_7 S_8, Index paged (i)–iv]. Hotel adverts., 16 pp. undated [signed A, and paged (i)–(xvi)], at end.

Pencil signature: 'S. H. (?) Harley 15 Sept. 1865', on fly-leaf. Very fine.

Note. The editor of this edition was the author's niece, whose death in 1864 gravely intensified her aunt's illness. A Fourth Edition, edited by the publisher Garnett, appeared in 1871.

[1631] DAWN ISLAND: a Tale. 'Written for the National Anti-Corn-Law Bazaar, May 1845'

Manchester: J. Gadsby. Deep-sea-blue fine-ribbed cloth, blocked in gold and blind. Etched front. and title by J. Stephenson precede printed title.

pp. (96) G_4 blank.

Ink signature: 'Wm. Day, Beverley, 1845', on fly-leaf. Also issued in red, green and possibly other colours.

DEERBROOK: a Novel [1632]

3 vols. Moxon 1839.

Copy I: Half-cloth boards; labels.

Vol. I (iv) + 336
II (iv) + (332)
III (iv) + 304

Book-plate of Castle Freke Library and booksellers' ticket: 'Caines & Co. Belgrave Square', on inside front cover of each vol. Very fine.

Copy II: Another. Olive-brown fine-diaper cloth, gold lettered on spine with title, author and vol. number (no imprint) in decorative frame. Collation as Copy I. [1632*a*]

Booksellers' ticket: 'Shield and Temple, North Shields', on inside front covers. Very fine.

EASTERN LIFE, PRESENT AND PAST [1633]

3 vols. Moxon 1848. Maroon fine-diaper cloth, blocked in blind and lettered in gold; pale yellow end-papers.

Half-title in each vol.

Vol. I x + 336
II (viii) + (324) P_6 adverts.
III (viii) + 344

Publisher's cat., 8 pp. dated July 1 1848, inset between front end-papers of Vol. I.

Ink signature: 'Mrs Beavan, Bryn y Hydd', on inside front covers of Vols. II and III. Fine.

FIVE YEARS OF YOUTH, or Sense and Sentiment [1634]

Small 8vo. Harvey & Darton 1831. Half-roan, marbled boards, as issued. Front. and 3 steel-engraved plates.

Half-title. pp. viii + 264

Binder's ticket: 'Russell, Guildford', on inside front cover.

FOREST AND GAME LAW TALES [1635]

3 vols. Moxon 1845.

Copy I: First Binding. Sage-green fine-diaper cloth, blocked in blind and lettered in gold; yellow end-papers.

Vol. I (xii) + 252
II (viii) + 304 U_8 adverts.
III iv + (260)

Publisher's cat., 8 pp. dated January 1 1846, inset between front end-papers of Vol. I.

Book-plate: 'Verum atque Decens', in Vols. I and II and ink signature: 'J. Lee, Hartwell, March 1846', on inside cover of Vol. I. Also, facing title of Vol. I, ink reference to favourable notices of the book in Oxfordshire papers. Fine.

Copy II: Secondary Binding. Grey-purple ribbed cloth, blocked in blind with gold decoration and lettering on spine. No inserted cat. Collation [1635*a*] as Copy I. I assume this style to be secondary because, although more showy than its predecessor, it is lettered from type, the decoration is from stock-brasses, and the strawboards are lighter. Style I is a typical Moxon primary—simple, dignified and of excellent quality.

A third binding is recorded in plain dark green cloth, with sheets slightly cut, and I have seen a copy in drab paper wrappers printed in black, which presumably represented a fourth style.

[1636] HAMPDENS (The): an Historiette

Small cr. 8vo. Routledge 1880. Slate-grey diagonal-fine-ribbed cloth, elaborately blocked and lettered in black and gold on front and spine, blind-blocked with ornament and publishers' initial on back. Bevelled boards. Wood-engraved front. and 9 illustrations after J. E. Millais, all on plate paper. The front. is listed in the List of Illustrations as facing p. 114.

Half-title. Pp. (viii) + (184). Text ends 177 (N_1 recto, verso blank), N_2–N_4 adverts.

Cloth worn at corners. Cover loose at one point.

[1637] HISTORY OF ENGLAND DURING THE THIRTY YEARS' PEACE: 1816–1846

2 vols. Sq. royal 8vo in format (covers measure $7\frac{1}{4} \times 10\frac{7}{8}$) but collating in fours. Charles Knight 1849 (Vol. I), 1850 (Vol. II). Dark brown fine-ribbed cloth, blocked in blind and lettered in gold; cream end-papers. Steel-engraved portrait front., 7 other engraved portraits and 7 folding coloured maps in Vol. I. Folding coloured map as front., 3 other maps and 8 engraved portraits in Vol. II.

Vol. I viii + (600)
II (xiv) + 722 Final leaf, ($4Z_1$), a single inset.

The irregularity of the prelims. of Vol. II is due to the insetting of a leaf—(xiii) (xiv)—'Directions for placing the portraits and maps'. No such Directions or any list of embellishments appears in Vol. I.

Presentation Copy: 'Mr Arthur Ryland. With kind regards from his friend Harriet Martineau. Birmingham Jan[y] 5th, 1850' in ink on title of Vol. I.

Very fine copies of books which, on account of their bulk and weight, are extremely rare in good state.

See also *Introduction to the History of the Peace*, 1643 below.

Note. This important and valuable work was begun by Charles Knight himself, who wrote the sections covering the years 1816–17. But business difficulties and want of assistance compelled him to suspend work. Harriet Martineau then took over the task and completed the three volumes. It was with reference to the *History of the Peace* and its supplementary 'Introduction' that she wrote to Lady Walshaw in 1850 or 1851:

'You will be glad to hear that poor Mr Knight sends me good news. The periodicals, most or all, will go on, and his host of poor authors be sustained. As for me, the chief creditors have decreed that I am not to lose, not even to be inconvenienced, and they have actually cashed K's first bill. Of course, I cannot drop the work immediately, on such a proof that it is valuable to the concern; so the 3d vol. is gone to press.'

HOUR AND THE MAN (The): a Historical Romance [1638]

3 vols. Moxon 1841. Maroon fine-diaper cloth, gold-lettered on spine with title and vol. number only, in decorative frame uniform with *Deerbrook.* Folding map in colours of 'Hayti, or St Domingo' as front. to Vol. I.

Vol. I (iv) + (316) P_2 imprint leaf.
II (iv) + (304) P_2 imprint leaf.
III (iv) + 304

Fine. Spines a little faded.

HOUSEHOLD EDUCATION [1639]

Moxon 1849. Sage-green ribbed cloth, blocked in blind and lettered in gold; yellow end-papers.

Half-title. pp. viii + (328) Y_4 adverts.

Ink inscription: 'Elma Howell Red Bank, N.J. 1904', on title. Fine.

HOW TO OBSERVE: Morals and Manners [1640]

Charles Knight 1838. Maroon morocco cloth.

pp. viii + (240) L_{12} adverts.

The prelims. are curious: (i) title, (ii) printers' imprint, (iii)–(v) [paged (v)–vii] Contents, (vi) blank, (vii) Advertisement, (viii) blank. Possibly in some copies the Advertisement precedes Contents.

[1641] ILLUSTRATIONS OF POLITICAL ECONOMY

25 numbers 12mo. Charles Fox 1832–1834. Drab wrappers, cut flush, printed in black on front and back. Spines unlettered. White end-papers. Except in No. I, a series title precedes individual title.

No. 1 LIFE IN THE WILDS 1832 pp. xx + 124
Ink inscription on fly-leaf: 'Rd Taylor Esq. with the Author's comps.', not in H. M.'s hand.

2 THE HILL AND THE VALLEY 1832 pp. (iv) + 140
Ink signature: 'Mr Sharpe', on front cover.

3 BROOKE OF BROOKE FARM 1832 pp. (8) + (148)

4 DEMERARA 1832 pp. (viii) [paged vi]+(144)

5 ELLA OF GARVELOCH 1832 pp. (viii)+144

6 WEAL AND WOE IN GARVELOCH 1832 pp. (vi)+140

7 A MANCHESTER STRIKE 1832 pp. (viii)+136

8 COUSIN MARSHALL 1832 pp. (iv)+132
Ink signature: 'P. D. Cooke. 8', on front cover.

9 IRELAND 1832 pp. (viii) [paged (iv)]+136

10 HOMES ABROAD 1832 pp. (iv)+128

11 FOR EACH AND FOR ALL 1832 pp. (iv)+132
Ink signature: 'P. D. Cooke. 11', on front cover.

12 FRENCH WINES AND POLITICS 1833 pp. (iv)+(148) O_2 imprint leaf.
'12' in ink on front cover.

13 THE CHARMED SEA 1833 pp. (iv)+136
Ink signature: 'P. D. Cooke. 13', on front cover.

14 BERKELEY THE BANKER. I 1833 pp. (viii)+172

15 BERKELEY THE BANKER. II 1833 pp. (iv)+(148) O_2 imprint leaf

16 MESSRS VANDERPUT AND SNOEK 1833 pp. (viii) [paged as vi]+140
'16' in ink on front cover.

17 THE LOOM AND THE LUGGER. I 1833 pp. (iv)+132
'17' in ink on front cover.

18 THE LOOM AND THE LUGGER. II 1833 pp. viii+144
Ink signature: 'P. Davies Cooke. 18', on front cover.

19 SOWERS NOT REAPERS 1833 pp. viii+148

20 CINNAMON AND PEARLS 1833 pp. (iv)+(126) First leaf of final sig., M_1, a single inset.
'20' in ink on front cover.

21 A TALE OF THE TYNE 1833 pp. (iv)+(136)

22 BRIERY CREEK 1833 pp. (iv)+(156)

23 THE THREE AGES 1833 pp. (iv)+(128) M_4 imprint leaf.

24 THE FARRERS OF BUDGE ROW 1834 pp. (viii)+136

25 MORAL OF MANY FABLES 1834 pp. (viii) [vii mis-paged vi]+144 At end are Titles, Contents Lists and labels for the 9 volumes of the book issue which appeared in cloth with labels. This material (20 leaves) is unsigned.

All fine; some very fine. This is an extremely difficult series to complete in first edition and in original state.

Notes. (i) The separate numbers were also issued in smooth unlettered olive-brown linen. Only one specimen (No. 2) in dilapidated state is in the Collection.

(ii) The outside back-wrapper of No. 1 merely announces the publication of No. 2 for March 1, 1832. That of No. 3 announces the publication of No. 4 on '1st of May' and gives Contents. The other numbers all combine an announcement of a forthcoming number with press-notices of the Series as a whole and of individual volumes.

[1642] ILLUSTRATIONS OF TAXATION

5 numbers 12mo. Charles Fox 1834. Drab wrappers, cut flush, printed in black on front and back. Spines unlettered. White end-papers. In each number a series title precedes individual title.

No. 1 THE PARK AND THE PADDOCK pp. (iv)+140

2 THE TENTH HAYCOCK pp. (iv)+144

3 THE JERSEYMEN MEETING pp. (iv)+(126) M_1 a single inset. M_2 M_3 serve as fly-leaf and backing to back wrapper. Printers' imprint on M_3 recto.

4 THE JERSEYMEN PARTING pp. (viii)+136

5 THE SCHOLARS OF ARNESIDE pp. (viii)+(138) N_1 a single inset. N_2 N_3 serve as fly-leaf and backing to back wrapper. Printers' imprint on N_3 recto.

Spines of Nos. 2 and 3 chipped.

MARTINEAU

[1643] INTRODUCTION TO THE HISTORY OF THE PEACE: from 1800–1815

Sq. royal 8vo, uniform with *History of the Thirty Years' Peace* but collating in eights. Charles Knight 1851. Dark brown fine-ribbed cloth, etc. uniform with *History of the Thirty Years' Peace.*

Paged throughout in roman numerals viii + (i)–(cccxii). $2D_6$ blank.

Ink signature: 'Arthur Ryland', and pencil-signature: 'Chavasse', on fly-leaf. The former was the recipient of the copy of the *Thirty Years' Peace* described above. Very fine.

LIFE IN THE SICK ROOM: Essays (by an 'Invalid') [1644]

Moxon 1849. Third Edition. [First Edition 1844.] Dark grey-purple ribbed cloth, blocked in blind and lettered in gold; cream end-papers.

Half-title. pp. (xvi) + 188 Publisher's cat., 8 pp. dated February 1 1849, inset between front end-papers.

Binder's ticket: 'Joseph Sanders, Ivy Lane', at end. Very fine.

[1645] PLAYFELLOW (The): a Series of Tales to be published Quarterly

4 vols. Sq. fcap 8vo. Charles Knight 1841. Dark brown fine-diaper cloth, blocked in blind and lettered in gold; yellow end-papers. In each vol. series title precedes individual title. Vols. I and III fine.

Vol. 1	THE SETTLERS AT HOME	pp. (vi) + (336) Y_7 Y_8 adverts. Fine.
2	THE PEASANT AND THE PRINCE	Advert. leaf precedes series title. pp. (viii) [paged vi] + (360) $2A_3$ $2A_4$ adverts.
3	FEATS ON THE FIORD	pp. vi + (378) $2C_1$ (foliated 377) adverts and a single inset. Ink signature: 'Letitia Philipps', on title.
4	THE CROFTON BOYS	pp. (viii) + 336

[1646] POOR LAWS AND PAUPERS ILLUSTRATED

4 numbers. 12mo. Charles Fox 1833–1834. Buff wrappers, cut flush, printed in black on front and back. Spines unlettered. White end-papers. Except in No. 1, series title precedes individual title. All fine.

No. 1	THE PARISH	1833	pp. (iv) + 216
2	THE HAMLETS	1833	pp. (iv) + 164
3	THE TOWN	1834	pp. (iv) + (172) Q_2, imprint leaf, serves as fly-leaf.
4	THE LAND'S END	1834	pp. (iv) + (180)

[1647] RETROSPECT OF WESTERN TRAVEL

3 vols. Saunders & Otley 1838. Boards, labels.

Half-title in each vol.

Vol. I (viii) + (320) P_4 imprint leaf.
II (vi) + 292
III (vi) + (296) O_4 adverts.

Fine. Labels dust-darkened.

[1648] SKETCHES FROM LIFE

Whittaker & Co. Windermere: J. Garnett (1856). Red-brown coarse-morocco cloth, blocked and lettered in gold and blind. Spine up-lettered. Bevelled boards. Engraved vignette title (no printed title) and 6 plates unsigned, all on plate paper. Also line-decoration on p. (1).

Blank leaf and half-title precede engraved title.

pp. (viii) [p. (vi) paged ii] + (168) L_4 blank.

Binders' ticket: 'Westleys' at end. Book-plate of David Martineau. Loose in covers.

[1649] SOCIETY IN AMERICA

3 vols. Saunders & Otley 1837. Half-cloth boards, labels.

Vol. I (xx) + 364
II (iv) + (372) R_6 adverts.
III (iv) [paged vi] + (368) R_4 adverts.

Book-plate: 'Eardiston', in each vol.

SUGGESTIONS TOWARDS THE FUTURE GOVERNMENT OF INDIA [1650]

8vo. Smith, Elder 1858. Grey-purple fine-diaper cloth, paper label up-lettered.

Half-title. Pp. viii + (156) M_2 adverts. Publishers' cat., 16 pp. dated January 1858, at end.

Author's own copy. 'H. Martineau. Feby. 6th/58.' in ink in her hand on half-title.

Partly by Harriet Martineau

SIMON DE MONTFORT, EARL OF LEICESTER. The Creator of the House of Commons. By Reinhold Pauli. Translated by Una M. Goodwin. With Introduction by HARRIET MARTINEAU [1651]

Trübner & Co. 1876. Olive-green sand-grain cloth; grey end-papers.

pp. xvi + (240) Miss Martineau's Introduction occupies pp. (iii)–viii and is dated May 1876.

Association Items

Although their Contents are only to a small degree fictional, her copies of two works by Charles Knight may suitably be included under Harriet Martineau, in view of the long-standing friendship between her and her publisher.

[1652] ONCE UPON A TIME, by CHARLES KNIGHT

2 vols. Fcap 8vo. John Murray 1854. Royal-blue wavy-grain cloth; brick end-papers.

Vol. I (viii)+(318) First leaf of final sig., X_1, a single inset.

II (iv)+(312) Publisher's cat., 32 pp. dated January 1853, at end.

Presentation Copy: 'Miss Martineau. With kind regards. Charles Knight' in ink on title of Vol. I.

Binders' ticket: 'Edmonds and Remnants', at end of each vol.

Note. In each volume a blank leaf of coarser quality paper than that used for text is inset between front fly-leaf and title.

[1653] PASSAGES OF A WORKING LIFE DURING HALF A CENTURY: with a Prelude of Early Reminiscences

3 vols. Bradbury & Evans 1864 (Vols. I and II), 1865 (Vol. III). Chestnut-brown (Vols. I and II) and tan (Vol. III) dot-and-line-grain cloth; chocolate (Vol. I), dark chocolate (Vol. II), café-au-lait (Vol. III) end-papers.

Vol. I (xvi)+346 Slip announcing that Vols. II and III 'will be published separately early next year' tipped in between front end-papers.

II (iv)+336 Text ends p. 330; (331)–336 Note to Chapter xv.

III (iv)+344 Text ends p. 328; (329) (330) farewell-quotation, verso blank; (331)–344 Index.

Presentation Copy: 'To Harriet Martineau. From Charles Knight. With affectionate regard. Dec. 8, 1863.' in ink on title of Vol. I.

Fine, despite stain on back cover of Vol. I.

MATHERS, HELEN (1853–1920)

[1654] AS HE COMES UP THE STAIR (by the author of 'Comin' Thro' The Rye', etc.)

Bentley 1878. Scarlet diagonal-fine-ribbed cloth; black end-papers.

pp. (iv)+(188) 12_4–12_6 adverts.

No. 5 of Bentley's Half-Crown Empire Library. Fine.

[1655] CHERRY RIPE: a Romance

3 vols. Bentley 1878. Cherry-red diagonal-fine-ribbed cloth, blocked in black and gold.

Vol. I (ii)+294 Final leaf, 19_3, a single inset.

II (ii)+330 Final leaf, 40_5, a single inset.

III (ii)+318 First leaf of final sig., 60_1, a single inset. **B**

Back cover of Vol. III discoloured, probably through paste action.

COMIN' THRO' THE RYE: a Novel [anon] [1656]

3 vols. Bentley 1875. Slate-grey diagonal-fine-ribbed cloth, blocked in black and gold. *Pl. 12*

Vol. I (iv)+324

II (iv)+(316) X_6 blank.

III (iv)+(292) U_2 blank. **B**

Publishers' slip: 'Copyright Copy', filled in by George Bentley with author's name and date of publication (June 12 1875), pasted into each vol.

EYRE'S ACQUITTAL [1657]

3 vols. Bentley 1884. Smooth powder-blue cloth, blocked in dark blue and green and lettered in gold; pale grey-on-white flowered end-papers.

Vol. I (ii)+(272)

II (ii)+262 Final leaf, 34_3, a single inset.

III (ii)+262 Final leaf, 51_3, a single inset. **B**

LAND O' THE LEAL (The) (by the author of 'Comin' Thro' The Rye', etc.) [1658]

Bentley 1878. Scarlet diagonal-fine-ribbed cloth; black end-papers.

pp. iv+(184) (12_2)–(12_4) adverts.

No. I of Bentley's Half-Crown Empire Library. Fine.

MAN OF TO-DAY (A): a Novel [1659]

3 vols. F. V. White 1894. Dark green diaper-cloth, bevelled boards; patterned end-papers.

Half-title in each vol.

Vol. I (viii)+(232)

II (viii)+(248)

III (viii)+(230) First leaf of final sig., 46_1, a single inset. Publishers' cat., 16 pp. undated, at end.

'With the Publishers' Compliments' stamped in violet ink on title of Vol. I. Very fine.

Note. The Dedication is repeated in each volume.

STUDY OF A WOMAN (A), or Venus Victrix: a Novel [1660]

F. V. White 1893. Cream paper wrappers, printed in blue. End-papers printed with adverts.

Leaf of adverts. precedes title. pp. (viii) [(vii) is fly-title]+(104) 7_4 adverts.

Publishers' cat., 16 pp. undated, at end. Spine torn and back wrapper detached.

[1661] WHAT THE GLASS TOLD: a Novel
F. V. White 1893. Cream paper wrappers, printed in red. End-papers printed with adverts.
Leaf of adverts. precedes title. pp. (viii) [(vii) is fly-title] + (120) 8_4 adverts.
pp. (viii) + (116) Play ends P_4; Q_1 Epilogue, Q_2 ? adverts. or blank.
This copy lacks Q_2.

MATURIN, REV. C. R. (1782–1824)

Apart from two volumes of Sermons and a Prize Poem, this is a complete collection of the works of Maturin.

[1662] ALBIGENSES (The): a Romance (by the author of 'Bertram, a Tragedy', 'Woman (sic), or Pour et Contre', etc.)
4 vols. Hurst, Robinson & Co. 1824. Cont. half-calf, sprinkled edges. Issued in boards, labels.
Half-title in each vol.
Vol. I viii + (440)
II (iv) + (366) R_4 adverts.
III (iv) + (336)
IV (iv) + (280) N_8 adverts.
Book-plate of John P. Ellames. This copy lacks all half-titles, and the advert. leaves in Vols. II and IV.

[1663] BERTRAM, or the Castle of St Aldobrand. A Tragedy in Five Acts (by the Rev. C. R. Maturin)
8vo. John Murray 1816. New wrappers, cut edges.
Half-title (almost certainly). pp. (viii) + (96) N_4 blank or adverts.
This copy lacks half-title and N_4.

[1664] FATAL REVENGE, or the Family of Montorio ('by Dennis Jasper Murphy')
3 vols. Longman etc. 1807. Cont. half-morocco, yellow edges. Issued in boards, labels.
Vol. I (xiv) + 400
II (ii) + (520) aa_2 blank.
III (ii) + (496) Y_8 adverts.
Ink signature: 'Harriet Townshend', and book-plate of 'Marmion Edwd Ferrers, Baddesley Clinton', inside front cover of each vol.
Note. Should this book have half-titles? I have examined more than half-a-dozen copies, and all were without them. Certainly seven leaves as prelims. to Vol. I suggest a half-title, yet the leaf following title is signed 'A_2'. In II and III the titles are single insets. The missing leaf from I may well have been label-leaf. Corners of one or two pages torn.

[1665] FREDOLFO: a Tragedy in Five Acts (by the Rev. C. R. Maturin)
8vo (but in fours). Edinburgh: Constable 1819. Boards (spine renewed).

MANUEL: a Tragedy in Five Acts (by the author of 'Bertram') [1666]
8vo (but in fours). John Murray 1817. New boards, cut edges.
pp. viii + (88) [paged (86)] Play ends M_3, M_4 Epilogue.
Dedicated to Sir Walter Scott. Ink signature: '(?) Graham', on title.

MELMOTH THE WANDERER: a Tale (by the author of 'Bertram') [1667] *Pl. 19*

Copy I. First Edition.

4 vols. Edinburgh: Constable 1820. Boards, labels.
Blank leaf (serving as fly-leaf) and half-title precede title in Vol. I. Half-title in Vols. II, III, IV
Vol. I xii + (342)
II (iv) + (324) O_6 blank and pasted down to inside back cover. A blank fly-leaf of text-paper is inset between O_5 and O_6.
III (iv) + (368)
IV (iv) + (456) T_{12} adverts.
Ink signature: 'Duchesse de Sagan', on title, and armorial book-label: 'P. H.' under royal crown, inside front cover of each vol. Very fine.
Note. An interesting reprint of *Melmoth* was published by Bentley in 1892. The work is in 3 vols., bound in smooth dark sage-green cloth with all-over blind embossing on front and back, and grey-on-white monogram end-papers. There is a portrait front. to Vol. I, and the title-page to each vol. is printed in claret ink.
Prefixed to the text of the novel are a Memoir of Maturin, a critical notice of his work and a bibliography, all anonymous. The first was the joint work of Robert Ross, More Adey and William Wilson; the second was by More Adey; the third by Ross and Adey. A Prefatory Note thanks Lady Wilde and Oscar Wilde for new details of Maturin's life, and George Saintsbury for help with the bibliography.
A secondary issue of this edition was bound in cloth of a lighter green without any decorative blocking on front or back.

Copy II. (?) First French Edition. [1667*a*]

L'HOMME DU MYSTÈRE, ou Histoire de Melmoth le Voyageur (par l'Auteur de 'Bertram', traduit de l'anglais par Madame E[ugénie] F[ournier-Pescay] B[égin])
3 vols. 12mo. Paris, à la Librairie Nationale et Étrangère 1821. Half-red russia, red glazed boards, stamped in gold front and back with Imperial Crown over Monogram. All edges uncut.

Half-title in each vol.

Vol. I (iv)+298 [paged (i)–iv+(5)–298] First leaf of final sig., 13_1, a single inset.
II (282)
III 228

Pencil inscription inside front cover of Vol. I giving full names of author and translator. From the Library of the Empress Marie Louise.

Note. The bibliography in the 1892 reprint noted above gives another French edition of 1821: *Melmoth ou L'Homme Errant.* Traduit par J. Cohen, 6 vols. 12mo. I do not know which of the two French editions first appeared.

[1668] MILESIAN CHIEF (The): a Romance (by the author of 'Montorio' and 'The Wild Irish Boy')
4 vols. Colburn 1812. Boards, labels.

Vol. I (viii) [paged vi]+228
II (ii)+218 Final leaf, L_1, a single inset.
III (ii)+(240)
IV (ii)+204

Very fine. From the Bellew Library and recorded in the private catalogue as 'Milisian'. Running headlines and labels read 'THE MILESIAN', so that possibly the addition of 'CHIEF' on the title-page was an afterthought.

[1669] WILD IRISH BOY (The) (by the author of 'Montorio')
3 vols. Longman etc. 1808. Boards, labels.

Half-title in each vol.

Vol. I (xii)+276
II (iv)+(344) Q_4 blank and pasted to inside back cover. A blank fly-leaf of text-paper is inset between Q_3 and Q_4.
III (iv)+(408) S_{12} adverts. Publishers' cat., 24 pp. dated August 1 1807, at end.

Very fine. From the Bellew Library and recorded in the private catalogue. '412' in ink on spine of Vol. II.

[1670] WOMEN, or Pour et Contre: a Tale (by the author of 'Bertram', etc.)
3 vols. Edinburgh: Constable 1818. Boards, labels.

Half-title in each vol.

Vol. I (viii) [paged (vi)]+(276)
II (iv)+276
III (iv)+408

Ink signature: 'Duchesse de Sagan', on title, and armorial book-label: 'P. H.' under royal crown, inside front cover of each vol. Fine.

ana

[1671] UNIVERSE (The): a Poem (by the Rev. C. R. Maturin)
8vo. Colburn 1821. Boards, label.

Half-title. pp. (viii)+(112) Poem ends H_1; H_2–H_6 Notes; H_7 H_8 adverts.

Ink signature: 'Matilda Page', on fly-leaf.

Note. This poem (dedicated to S. T. Coleridge) was actually written by the Rev. James Wills.

MAURICE, FREDERICK DENISON (1805–1872)

EUSTACE CONWAY, or the Brother and Sister [anon] [1672]

Copy I. 3 vols. Bentley 1834. Boards, labels.

Half-title in each vol.

Vol. I (iv)+300
II (iv)+(312)
III (iv)+288

In this copy a Longman etc. cat., 12 pp. dated February 1834, is stitched between front end-papers of Vol. I. The spine and label of Vols. I and II are rather chipped.

Copy II: Full cont. blue calf by Nutt of Cambridge. Collation as Copy I. [1672*a*]

Ink inscription on verso of fly-leaf in Vol. I: 'Georgiana F. Maurice from Freddy.' This was Maurice's second wife and the inscription, judging from the phrasing, is presumably in her hand. Also ink signature: 'J. M. Ludlow', in each vol.

Note. The running headlines throughout and the heading on p. (1) of each vol. read THE BROTHER & SISTER. The villain of the story is called 'Captain Marryatt', an error of judgement which brought Maurice a challenge to a duel.

MAURIER, GEORGE DU (1834–1896)

MARTIAN (The): a Novel [1673]

Ordinary Edition. Sq. crown 8vo. Harper 1898. Smooth navy-blue cloth, pictorially blocked and lettered in gold; very dark green end-papers. Wood-engraved portrait front.; also numerous illustrations, both full-page and in the text, after drawings by the author. All are on text paper and reckoned in collation.

Half title. pp. viii+(476) $2G_5$ $2G_6$ adverts., paged 1–4.

As new, with dust jacket.

Large Paper Edition. Cr. 4to. Apple-green buckram sides, vellum spine lettered in gold. The portrait-front. is reproduced on Jap vellum, and, in addition to the text illustrations in the ordinary edition, are included six facsimiles of pencil-studies for illustrations, finely lithographed on plate-paper. [1673*a*]

Leaf carrying notice of limitation to 250 numbered copies, and half-title, precede title; leaf carrying list of facsimiles follows List of Illustrations. As the portrait is not on text paper, prelims. now collate (x). Three fly-leaves (forming a 4-leaf signature, with inside front end-papers) precede limitation leaf. Text ends 471; (472) blank. $2G_5$ $2G_6$ are cut away and substituted by another 4-leaf signature of blanks, including inside back end-paper. Rather dust-soiled, but unopened.

[1674] PETER IBBETSON. With an Introduction by his cousin Lady * * * ('Madge Plunket'). Edited and illustrated by George du Maurier

Copy I: First Edition. 'New York and London. Harper Brothers.' 'Copyright 1891', etc., on verso of title. Smooth jade-green cloth, blocked and lettered in black and blocked in gold on front, blocked and lettered in gold on spine. Line-engraved front. and 83 illustrations (full-page and in the text), all on text paper and after drawings by the author.

pp. (432) [paged (viii) + (424)] 27_6–27_6 blank.

Note. This book was published on November 10 1891, the English edition not appearing till during December. Both English title-pages are dated 1892. The English edition contains no list of illustrations, but exactly the same number as in the Harper edition, and of the same size despite the larger English format. Presumably Osgood, McIlvaine obtained electros from Harper during or at the end of serialisation.

[1674*a*] **Copy II: First English Edition.** 2 vols. Sq. demy 8vo. Osgood, McIlvaine 1892. Pale buff linen flecked with white, pictorially blocked and fancy lettered in black; white end-papers. Vignette on title and numerous line-engraved illustrations, both full-page and in the text, after drawings by the author. All are on text paper and reckoned in collation.

Half-title in each vol.

Vol. I (iv) + (216) P_4 blank
II (iv) + (236)

Book-plate of Anna M. Thompson. Very fine.

Note. Carter (*Binding Variants*, p. 136) considers this all-black blocking and lettering to be subsequent to the black and brown.

[1675] TRILBY

3 vols. Osgood, McIlvaine 1894. Buff canvas, pictorially blocked and lettered in blue.

Half-title in each vol.

Vol. I (iv) + (248) R_4 blank.
II (iv) + (260)
III (iv) + (184) N_4 advert. on recto, verso blank. Publishers' cat., 44 pp. undated, at end.

Apart from a slight mark on the front cover of Vol. I, a very fine copy.

Notes. (i) I am inclined to regard this book as a parallel case to Trollope's *Rachel Ray*—that is to say, as a single edition which, in an attempt to whip up sales (or an illusion of sales) was subdivided by over-printing into seven 'Editions' so-called, all dated 1894.

It is almost inconceivable that at this late date seven editions of a three-decker, whose outsize popularity was in part made *after book-publication* by a play based on the story (and of which a one-volume illustrated edition was published in 1895) should have been required in the first year of its existence. The case is the more suspicious in that the schedule of pretended 'Editions' is not (in my experience at least) by any means complete. The Statutory copies in B.M., Bodley and U.L.C. are all of the *Seventh* Edition. I have had reported a set of which two volumes were *Second* Edition and the third undescribed, and another (imperfect) of which one volume at least was *Fifth* Edition, and have seen catalogued a *Sixth* Edition. But I have been unable to trace any record of a *Third* or *Fourth*. The statement of 'Edition' appears in every case on the verso of the titles and could easily have been over-printed on existing sheets; collation and quality of paper are constant in all complete sets seen by me, and the Publishers' Catalogue at the end of Vol. III shows no variation between the first and seventh editions.

(ii) There is also in the Collection the serial instalments of *Trilby* as they appeared in Harper's Magazine for 1894, extracted from the magazine, mounted, and bound in three-quarter morocco. This serial issue was not only lavishly illustrated by du Maurier with drawings not reproduced in the three-volume edition; it also contained a passage of nearly 1500 words, plus a drawing introducing, describing and depicting a character 'Joe Sibley'. This passage and drawing (of which the former would normally have appeared on pp. 216 seq. of Vol. I of the three-volume edition) were suppressed after serial issue, as, beyond a shadow of a doubt, they represented Whistler.

MAXWELL, WILLIAM HAMILTON (1792–1850)

BIVOUAC (The), or Stories of the Peninsular War [1676]

3 vols. Bentley 1837. Boards, labels.

Half-title in each vol.

Vol. I (viii) + 304
II (vi) + 292
III (vi) + 272

Ink signature: 'Samuel Horton, Rock House', on each title. Fine. Dedicated to Earl Mulgrave (afterwards Marquis of Normanby).

Note. Although Maxwell's name appears on titles the labels read: BY THE AUTHOR OF STORIES OF WATERLOO. Later entitled *Flood and Field.*

[1677] CAPTAIN O'SULLIVAN, or Adventures, Civil, Military and Matrimonial, of a Gentleman on Half Pay
3 vols. Colburn 1846. Half-cloth boards, labels.
Vol. I (ii)+(304)
II (ii)+298 First leaf of final sig., O_1, a single inset.
III (ii)+314 Final leaf, P_1, a single inset.
Fine.

[1678] ERIN-GO-BRAGH, or Irish Life Pictures
2 vols. Bentley 1859. Grass-green bead-grain cloth, blocked in gold with harp and blind decoration on front, blocked and lettered in gold on spine. Steel-engraved portrait front. after Samuel Lover.
Vol. I xii+358 First leaf of final sig., Q_1, a single inset.
II (iv)+368
Fine.
Note. Vol. I, pp. (vii)–xii are occupied by a Biographical Sketch of Maxwell by Dr Maginn, which originally appeared anonymously in *Bentley's Miscellany* (Vol. VII, 1840). There is no indication in *Erin-go-Bragh* of the Sketch's previous appearance.

[1679] *Pl. 22* HISTORY OF THE IRISH REBELLION IN 1798: with Memoirs of the Union, and Emmett's Insurrection in 1803
8vo. Baily Brothers, Cornhill 1845. Dark green ribbed cloth, pictorially blocked and fancy lettered on spine, blocked with ornament and decorative frame on front and back; pale yellow end-papers. Steel-engraved front. portrait of Lord Cornwallis after Lightfoot, 5 other engraved portraits, and 21 full-page etchings by George Cruikshank.
pp. (viii)+(480) $2H_8$ adverts. Publishers' cat., 16 pp. undated, at end (the last leaf, pp. 15, 16, has been torn out of this copy). Text ends p. 433; (435)–477 Appendix.
Bookseller's ticket: 'Charles Hutt, London', inside front cover. Cloth very fine.
The true first edition of this book (of which there were several unavowed re-issues) is now virtually undiscoverable in good shape.

[1680] *Pl. 22* MY LIFE (by the author of 'Stories of Waterloo', 'Wild Sports of the West', etc. etc.)
3 vols. Bentley 1835. Half-cloth boards, labels.
Half-title in each vol.
Vol. I xvi+288
II (iv)+300
III (iv)+340
Fine.

RAMBLING RECOLLECTIONS OF A SOLDIER OF FORTUNE [1681]
Dublin: William Curry, Jun. & Co. 1842. Dark brown horizontal-ribbed cloth, blocked with a harp in gold and blind decoration on front and back, gold-lettered on spine. Engraved portrait front. after C. Grey, R.H.A., imprinted and dated January 1 1842, and 4 wood-engraved plates after Phiz.
Half-title. pp. (xii)+(308) P_1–P_6 adverts., dated January 1842, and paged (1)–(12). Penultimate sig., O, 4 leaves. Fine.

STORIES OF WATERLOO and Other Tales [anon] [1682] *Pl. 22*
3 vols. Colburn & Bentley 1829. Boards, labels.
Vol. I (iv)+336
II (iv)+(280)
III (iv)+296
Spine of Vol. III split and chipped at base, but the copy is fresh and, in effect, fine.

WILD SPORTS OF THE WEST: with Legendary Tales and Local Sketches (by the author of 'Stories of Waterloo') [1683]
2 vols. 8vo. Bentley 1832. Boards, labels. Aquatint front. in each vol. unsigned but imprinted and dated 1832; also, in Vol. I two similar plates, in Vol. II one plate; also in each vol. 6 wood-engraved vignettes on text paper.
Half-title in Vol. I
Vol. I xvi+(328)
II (viii)+(344)
Book-plate of Thomas Clifton. Fine.

MELLY, GEORGE

SCHOOL EXPERIENCES OF A FAG at a Private and a Public School [1684]
Smith, Elder 1854. Mottled-red-and-black moiré fine-ribbed cloth, blocked in blind and lettered in gold.
pp. viii+(312) Publishers' cat., 16 pp. dated June 1854, at end.
Binders' ticket: 'Westleys', at end.

MELVILLE, HERMAN (1819–1891) [1685]

WHALE (The)
3 vols. Bentley 1851. Bright blue fine-ripple-grain cloth sides, cream morocco cloth spines, the former blocked in blind, the latter lettered in gold and gold-blocked with a rococo depiction of a whale plunging downwards. Deep cream end-papers.

Half-title in Vol. I, reading: THE WHALE; / or, / MOBY DICK. / *short rule* / Vol. I.

Vol. I viii + 312
II iv + (304)
III iv + 328 Text ends 312, (313) to 328 appendix.

Apart from slight damage through damp to the fore-edge of the back cover of Vol. III, a really fine copy of one of the rarest of three-deckers.

MEREDITH, GEORGE (1828–1909)

For further bibliographical detail see M. Buxton Forman, *Bibliography of George Meredith* (Bibliographical Society 1922), to which work (B. F.) the references which follow are made.

This is a complete collection of Meredith's fiction. Such non-fiction as I possess is not included.

[1686] ADVENTURES OF HARRY RICHMOND (The) [*B. F.* p. 45

3 vols. Smith, Elder 1871. Crimson fine-morocco cloth; cream end-papers.

Vol. I iv + (320) 20_8 imprint leaf.
II iv + (328) 41_4 blank.
III iv + (300) 60_6 imprint leaf.

Cloth tired, but an untouched copy.

[1687] AMAZING MARRIAGE (The) [*B. F.* p. 114

2 vols. Constable 1895. Sage-green ribbed cloth.

Half-title in Vol. I; blank leaf and half-title precede title in Vol. II

Vol. I viii + (272) R_8 blank.
II (viii) [paged vi] + (284) S_6 blank.

Fine.

[1688] BEAUCHAMP'S CAREER [*B. F.* p. 48

3 vols. Chapman & Hall 1876. Grass-green diagonal-fine-ribbed cloth.

Half-title in each vol.

Vol. I (viii) + 312
II (viii) + (320) X_8 blank.
III (viii) + (340)

Very fine.

[1689] CASE OF GENERAL OPLE AND LADY CAMPER (The) [*B. F.* p. 92

New York. John W. Lovell Company 1890. Dark salmon wrappers cut flush, printed in dark blue with standard cover lay-out of Lovell's Westminster Series, of which this is No. 3. Spine down-lettered. Front wrapper dated June 23, 1890.

Half-title. Pp. (128) 4_{16} blank (the book collates in sixteens).

Very fine. See also *The Tale of Chloe* below.

Note. The inside front wrapper of this book carries a list of the first 11 titles in the Westminster Series. That of *The Tale of Chloe* (No. 6 in the Series) carries a list of 12. I do not know whether earlier issues of the wrapper exist, carrying in the present case only 3 (or at any rate less than 11), in the case of *The Tale of Chloe* only 6 (or at any rate less than 12) titles. Buxton Forman gives no detail of these inside wrappers, and it would be interesting to know, either of earlier variants or details of the list given in Nos. 1 and 2 (*Her Last Throw* by the Duchess, and *The Moment After* by Robert Buchanan).

CELT AND SAXON [*B. F.* p. 156 [1690]

Constable 1910. Red ribbed cloth.

Blank leaf and half-title precede title. pp. (viii) [paged vi] + (300) T_6 blank. Fine, with grey dust-jacket printed in dark blue.

DIANA OF THE CROSSWAYS: a Novel [1691]

Copy I: First Complete Edition. 3 vols. Chapman & Hall 1885. Smooth red-brown cloth (see also Carter, *Binding Variants*, p. 140). [*B. F.* p. 73

Half-title in each vol.

Vol. I viii + 344
II vi + (336)
III vi + 330

Presentation Copy: 'To Mrs Alice Gordon from George M.' in ink on title of Vol. I (from Lady Butcher's collection). Fine.

Copy II: American Pirated and Incomplete pre-First Edition. New York: George Munro, Feb. 11 1885. White paper wrappers overprinted in light brown and black with standard Seaside Library design. [*B. F.* p. 77 [1691*a*]

Advert. leaf precedes title. pp. (128) Text ends p. 106 [4_5 verso]. 4_6–4_{16} adverts [4_6 4_7 commercial; 4_8–4_{16} Cat. of Seaside Library, undated and paged (1)–(18)].

Seaside Library, No. 350.

Note. It is difficult to state in a few words the relationship between the Munro text (which is that of the original serial issue in the *Fortnightly Review*) and the full text of the Chapman & Hall edition, because the re-writing and enlargement carried out by Meredith after serialisation affected the story at many points. Briefly C. & H. Vol. I (15 chapters) is contained in thirteen Munro chapters, of which the last three correspond to five of the extended text. Incidental passages are also introduced in earlier chapters which are absent from Munro. C. & H. Vol. II (13 chapters) is represented by only six chapters in Munro, the English chapters, I, III, IV, V, VI, VII, VIII, IX, XI, XII, XIII being extensive developments of Munro chapters XIV, XV, XVI, XVII and XIX, and English chapter II being absent altogether. Only English chapter X and Munro chapter XVIII are identical. In Vol. III the discrepancy is still greater. English chapters I–V correspond with Munro chapters XX–XXIV; Munro chapter XXV is a much shortened English chapter VI; Munro chapter XXVI combines (abbreviated) English chapters VII and VIII. The last seven chapters of C. & H. Vol. III do not appear at all in the Munro edition.

This copy can hardly be of the first issue, for the 'Patent Date' on front cover (part of the design) is 1887 and the Seaside cat. lists up to No. 1865. Nevertheless 'Feb. 11, 1885' is lightly printed at head of front cover. Another copy in the Collection carries the Seaside Library to 1813, and a date '1890' appears among the adverts.

[1692] EGOIST (The): a Comedy in Narrative [*B. F.* p. 57
3 vols. C. Kegan Paul & Co. 1879. Greenish-ochre small-patterned cloth; black end-papers.

Vol. I iv [p. (iv) mispaged v]+(340) Z_2 adverts.
II iv+320 Publishers' cat., 32 pp. dated '8. 79', at end.
III iv+(354) Final leaf, AA_1, a single inset.

Very fine.

[1693] EMILIA IN ENGLAND [*B. F.* p. 33
3 vols. Chapman & Hall 1864. Violet diagonal-wide-bead-grain cloth.

Vol. I iv+306 Final leaf, X_1, a single inset.
II iv+(288) T_8 blank.
III iv+338 Final leaf, Z_1, a single inset.

Book-label of Hugh Walpole. Fine.

[1694] EVAN HARRINGTON, or He Would be a Gentleman

Copy I: First Edition. New York: Harper 1860. Dark brown coarse-morocco cloth; red-chocolate end-papers. Pages measure $7\frac{5}{8}'' \times 4\frac{7}{8}''$. [*B. F.* p. 21

pp. iv+(504) X_7–X_{12} adverts. Three blank leaves at beginning and end (a half-gathering on text paper), one of which in each case is pasted on to reverse of chocolate end-paper.

Pencil signature: 'H. B. Hubbard', on first blank leaf. Fine.

Note. The coarse grain of the cloth and the page measurements suggest that this copy is of the original issue, and that the first edition was done in brown as well as in black and blue. Such colour variations were common form in American publishing at this period.

[1695] **Copy II: First English Edition.** 3 vols. Bradbury & Evans 1861. Pinkish-maroon bead-grain cloth. [*B. F.* p. 24

Blank leaf precedes title in Vol. III

Vol. I iv+(304) U_8 blank
II iv+(280)
III (viii)+(284) T_6 adverts. Publishers' cat., 12 pp. dated January 1861, at end.

Very fine.

FARINA: a Legend of Cologne [*B. F.* p. 17 [1696]
Smith, Elder 1857.

Copy I: Light jade-green straight-grain morocco cloth.

pp. (iv)+244 Publishers' cat., 16 pp. dated July 1857, at end.

Binders' ticket: 'Westleys', at end. Very fine.

Copy II: Binding variant. Dark olive-green pebble-grain cloth. Collation as Copy I but no cat. at end. [1696*a*]

Note. I agree with Carter (*Binding Variants*, p. 138) that this style is subsequent to the jade green above described, but suggest that it is less of a 'secondary' than of a 'substituted' binding. (Cf. Mayne Reid's *Wild Huntress* and Catherine Sinclair's *Beatrice.*) The jade cloth is both unusual and easily soiled. It is too experimental to have been chosen for anything but the original edition of a 'prestige' (as opposed to a popular) title such as *Farina*, and might well have been difficult to repeat. Complaints from the trade about its lack of durability and the difficulty of reading gold lettering on so vivid a ground, may have persuaded the publishers, when they ordered their second 'binding up', to use a cloth more usual and more practical.

The blind blocking on front and back is quite different on the two copies. That on Copy I has elaborate foliage corner decorations and a complicated central ornament; that on Copy II consists of a handsome but more or less rectangular frame with a plain centre. The spine lettering is identical on both copies, but the decorative bands top and bottom and the ornament under MEREDITH are more ambitious on Copy I than on Copy II.

This is the only specimen of Copy II I have ever seen.

GENTLEMAN OF FIFTY (The) AND THE DAMSEL OF NINETEEN. The Sentimentalists [1697]

No imprint or date [1920]. Olive-green limp linen wrappers, cream label on front printed in green, spine unlettered.

pp. (98) [paged (375)–(472)] (375) (376) fly-title, verso blank; (467)–(472) blank.

One of 12 copies. For the history of this curiosity see Buxton Forman, p. 303.

[1698] HOUSE ON THE BEACH (The): a Realistic Tale [*B. F.* p. 56

Pott 8vo. New York: Harper 1877. Grey paper wrappers.

pp. (144) 9_7 9_8 adverts. Two advert. leaves precede title and are included in collation. Fine.

No. 22 in Harper's Half-Hour Series.

See also *The Tale of Chloe* below.

[1699] LORD ORMONT AND HIS AMINTA: a Novel [*B. F.* p. 109

3 vols. Chapman & Hall 1894. Olive-green morocco cloth.

Half-title in Vol. I; blank leaf and half-title precede title in Vols. II and III

Vol. I (viii) + (236)
II (viii) + 240
III (viii) + (268) S_6 blank.

[1699*a*] **Copy I: Post 8vo, all edges uncut.** One of fifty copies thus issued (cf. *B. F.* p. 110).

[1699*b*] **Copy II: Cr 8vo, all edges cut.** Regulation first edition. The cloth is of a darker shade than that used on Copy I.

Both copies very fine.

See also Carter, *Binding Variants*, p. 140.

[1700] ONE OF OUR CONQUERORS [*B. F.* p. 97

3 vols. Chapman & Hall 1891.

Copy I. Royal-blue coarse-morocco cloth. Verso of front fly-leaves blank.

Vol. I (iv) + (304) U_8 blank.
II iv + 320
III iv + (308)

Very fine.

[1700*a*] **Copy II.** Powder-blue sand-grain cloth. Verso of front fly-leaves blank. Collation as Copy I.

Presentation Copy: 'To John of Verrell from his loving George Meredith' in ink on title of Vol. I. (John Deverell was Meredith's lawyer.) Very fine.

[1700*b*] **Copy III.** Smooth light-coffee-coloured cloth. Verso of front fly-leaves blank. Collation as Copy I.

Presentation Copy: 'To my dear Frederick Jameson & his wife. George Meredith' in ink on title of Vol. I. The sides of this copy are a little rubbed.

[1700*c*] **Copy IV.** Binding as Copy I, but panel of Meredith's works printed on verso of front fly-leaf in each vol. (this is the only style described by B. F.). Book-plate of J. M. Sagan-Musgrave in each vol. Very fine.

Note. As a pendant to this entry I reprint (by permission) an interesting statement contributed by John Carter to *The Times Literary Supplement* of July 27, 1940, regarding the variant bindings of *One of Our Conquerors* and of other nineteenth-century novels, in the course of which reference is made to several books described in this catalogue.

'The first edition of this novel (3 vols., Chapman & Hall, 1891) is familiar in royal-blue morocco cloth, with decoration in black on the front cover and spine lettering in gilt. Variant colours and fabrics, however, have been noted as follows, each in a single example:

(*a*) Biscuit-coloured smooth cloth.
(*b*) Cherry-red smooth cloth.
(*c*) Powder-blue very fine sand grain.
(*d*) Coffee-coloured smooth cloth.

'(In passing, it may be observed that all the freakish copies have the verso of the front free end-paper blank. This strongly suggests that, as between those copies of the first edition which have advertisements printed here and those which do not, the latter are the earlier, the advertisements in this unusual position being apparently an afterthought.)

'Variant (*a*) was described in my *Binding Variants* in 1932 (p. 141), variant (*b*) in *More Binding Variants* in 1938 (p. 27); and I then inclined to the view that these must be trial bindings, which (as sometimes happens) had got into circulation. The discovery by Mr Sadleir of (*c*) and (*d*), however, opens up a further possibility: for both these copies bear presentation inscriptions from the author (neither of them, unfortunately, dated). I do not think the suggestion can be entertained that these bindings were executed *for* the author. "Author's bindings" on novels were done for Mrs Henry Wood and Mortimer Collins, for Ouida (freely), for J. S. Le Fanu and Charles Reade (once each) and others; but in all cases known to me the special copies survive in more than one example and are uniform in colour. Again, straight variants of colour (and sometimes also of fabric) combined with standard blocking and lettering are found on novels from Mayne Reid's *The Scalp Hunters* (1851) to *Irene Iddesleigh* (1897), though infrequently among three-deckers.

'*One of Our Conquerors* must, I think, be differently classified. It is not without parallels. One of these is the same author's *Lord Ormont and his Aminta* (3 vols., Chapman & Hall, 1894), regularly bound in green, of which a solitary copy, identical except in colour, is known in maroon cloth. This came from the Meredith family. Thomas Hardy provides two examples (see *More Binding Variants*, p. 8), one of his own copies of *Desperate Remedies* being green instead of red, one of *Under the Greenwood Tree* terracotta instead of green. Again, a solitary bright blue copy of *Marion Fay* (3 vols., Chapman & Hall, 1882) belonged to Trollope himself, though normal copies are ochre. Finally Mr Sadleir possesses some pertinent variants of Blackmore's *Perlycross* (3 vols., Sampson, Low, 1894). Regularly found in dark blue diaper cloth, single examples of the first edition appear in (*a*) dark red cloth of the same fabric; (*b*) dark olive-green smooth cloth. These are blocked and lettered exactly as the normal copies, except for a different imprint brass. The first was given by the author to his nephew, the second retained by himself.

'We have, then, six novels between the years 1871 and 1894 which exhibit one or more variants (each at present unique) of the *type* of binder's trial copies—that is, samples in different colours and sometimes different fabrics, commonly made up after the general style (and decoration, if any) has been decided on and the lettering brasses cut. In five cases these copies are 100 per cent. author-derived; in the case of *One of Our Conquerors*, 50 per cent. demonstrably so. It looks in fact very much as if certain publishers used binder's trial copies—not for travelling, as often, nor for the copyright libraries, as occasionally, but sometimes also for their author's complimentary half-dozen. If this is so, it is likely that Tinsley, Chapman & Hall, and Sampson, Low were not the only ones to do so; and further examples would be welcome.

'One inscrutable case must be added, though its evidence has no more than an oblique bearing on our hypothesis. *The Spanish Match*, by W. Harrison Ainsworth (3 vols., Chapman & Hall, 1865)—earlier than any of the books cited above—is regularly found in green morocco cloth; but one copy is known in violet-blue morocco cloth. This freak has an inscription in the hand of the publishers' clerk to E. W. Edwards "with the author's compliments". But Mr Sadleir also possesses a normal copy, with a signed inscription in the author's hand—to the same recipient. This is obviously a case of what Lord Monomark used to call "bad tabulation": but does it also give us a glimpse of a publisher, not in this instance supplying his author with varicoloured trial copies, but using them up on the presentation list furnished by the unsuspecting Ainsworth?'

[1701] ORDEAL OF RICHARD FEVEREL (The): a History of Father and Son [*B. F.* p. 18

Copy I: First Edition. 3 vols. Chapman & Hall 1859. Dark sage-green ripple cloth.

Vol. I iv+(304)
II iv+348
III iv+(396) Publishers' cat., 16 pp. dated July 1, 1859, at end.

Fine. For this book 'very fine'.

See also Carter, *Binding Variants*, p. 138.

Note. The important textual changes made between the first and second English editions are recorded by *B. F.* p. 20.

[1701*a*] **Copy II: First Italian (and abridged) Edition.** ('RICCARDO FEVEREL')

2 vols. fcap 8vo. Milano: Emilio Croci 1873. Yellow paper wrappers pictorially printed and lettered in black. [*B. F.* p. 20

Half-title in each vol.

Vol. I pp. 128
II pp. 112

A curious feature is that the vignette on the wrapper of Vol. I reappears on the title of Vol. II and vice versa.

The story is divided into three parts and fifteen untitled sections, in all about 60,000 words. At the end of Vol. II (pp. 97–112) is a separate short story, authorship unstated, entitled *Uomo o Donna?*

RHODA FLEMING: a Story [*B. F.* p. 37 [1702]

3 vols. Tinsley 1865. Green fine-morocco cloth.

Half-title in each vol.

Vol. I vi+(332)
II vi+(292)
III vi+256

Binders' ticket: 'Bone & Son', at end of Vol. I. The finest copy (after the one in the Widener Library) I have ever seen. Buxton Forman's collation appears to be misprinted.

See also Carter, *More Binding Variants*, p. 26.

SHAVING OF SHAGPAT (The): an Arabian Entertainment [*B. F.* p. 11 [1703]

Chapman & Hall 1856. Scarlet horizontal-fine-ribbed cloth.

Half-title. pp. viii+384

In ink on inside front cover: 'A. E. Tress, 1857', and on fly-leaf: 'The Misses Tress, 1857' crossed through in ink. Fine.

For details of binding variants on this book see Carter, *Binding Variants* (p. 136) and *More Binding Variants* (p. 24).

Note. 'The variants of this book seem endless', says John Carter in *More Binding Variants* (1938), 'and nobody can be more weary of them than I.' The pursuit, however, must continue, though we faint by the way; for here is yet another, of which three examples certainly exist (one owned by me, the others reported) and in different colours:

Dark blue-green (also medium-light green, also dark purple-brown) coarse-morocco cloth, blocked in blind on front and back with (*a*) a $\frac{1}{4}$ in. frame, (*b*) a single line frame, (*c*) a five-framed panel, of which frames 1 and 4 are $\frac{1}{16}$ in. and the other three single-liners, (*d*) a central lozenge-shaped ornament; on spine, blind-blocked into four panels (each divided by a double decorated rule, and all, save the second from the top, subdivided by a double plain rule with ornamentation above and below) and gold-lettered in the second panel: THE SHAVING / OF / SHAGPAT / *short rule* / G. MEREDITH (no stop and no imprint at foot). Primrose end-papers; top edges uncut, fore-edges and tail trimmed.

The front covers measure $4\frac{15}{16} \times 7\frac{15}{16}$ in., i.e. they are as broad as the first binding (Carter A in *Binding Variants*, p. 136) and $\frac{1}{8}$ in. shorter. The sheets measure $4\frac{7}{8} \times 7\frac{5}{8}$ in., i.e. as broad as Carter A and $\frac{1}{16}$ in. shorter. The spine lettering of the title (except 'OF') is $\frac{3}{16}$ in. tall and, I think, blocked from type, although carefully and sharply done. The book, as seen by me, has all the appearance of an issue of the late fifties or very early sixties.

A curious feature of all three copies is an oval blind stamp on back cover of the two green, on front cover of the brown, not quite so deeply impressed as the blocking and just filling the space between the lower apex of the lozenge and the base of the quintuple frame. This stamp reads: C. MAURAIS (top curve of oval) BOOKSELLER (centre of oval) GOODGE ST. TOTTENHAM CT. RD. (bottom curve). It would be rash to assume that this blind stamp has any issue-significance—as, for example, that Maurais bought a quantity of sheets and bound them specially for his own shop; but it is strange that he should have stamped three copies, bound in identical style though in different colours, and others may, of course, exist. In any event, I do not recall another example of a retailer stamping his name on the outside cover of a mid-nineteenth century cloth book.

It remains to place this variant in Mr Carter's schedule; and I suggest it rank as B, inferior to A and to 'subsidiary-to-A', but taking precedence over the present B (see *Binding Variants* and *More Binding Variants*).

[1704] TALE OF CHLOE (The): an Episode in the History of Beau Beamish [*B. F.* p. 93

Copy I: First Edition. New York: John W. Lovell. 1890. Dark salmon paper wrappers, printed in black, uniform with *The Case of General Ople*, etc. (see above). Front wrapper dated July 7, 1890.

Half-title. pp. 144

No. 6 in Lovell's Westminster Series. Very fine.

[1704*a*] **Copy II: First English Edition** (with two other stories) THE TALE OF CHLOE—THE HOUSE ON THE BEACH—THE CASE OF GENERAL OPLE AND LADY CAMPER [*B. F.* p. 113

Ward, Lock & Bowden 1894. Smooth very dark olive-green cloth, gold-lettered on spine: THE TALE OF CHLOE / AND OTHER STORIES

Half-title. pp. (vi) [p. (v) mispaged vii] + (346) Final leaf, AA_1, a single inset. Very fine.

[1705] TRAGIC COMEDIANS (The): a Study in a Well Known Story [*B. F.* p. 61

2 vols. Chapman & Hall 1880. Dark sage-green diagonal-fine-ribbed cloth; black end-papers.

Half-title in each vol.

Vol. I (iv) + (200)
II (iv) + (184) N_4 adverts. Publishers' cat., 28 pp. dated November 1880, at end.

Presentation Copy: 'John of Verel from his friend George M.' in ink on the title of Vol. I. (Cf. above *One of Our Conquerors*, Copy II.) Very fine.

[1706] VITTORIA [*B. F.* p. 41

3 vols. Chapman & Hall 1867. Maroon fine-morocco cloth.

Half-title in Vol. I

Vol. I (vi) [paged iv] + (318) First leaf of final sig., X_1, a single inset.
II iv + (336). Y_8 blank (not recorded by Buxton Forman).
III iv + 288

Binders' ticket: 'Virtue & Co.', at end of Vol. I. A fine sharp copy. Spines flecked with tiny spots of white.

MERIVALE, HERMAN CHARLES (1839–1906)

FAUCIT OF BALLIOL: a Story in Two Parts [1707]

3 vols. Chapman & Hall 1882. Royal-blue diagonal-fine-ribbed cloth, blocked in black and lettered in gold. Very dark brown end-papers.

Half-title in each vol.

Vol. I viii + (272) S_8 blank.
II (viii) + (284)
III (viii) + (272) S_8 blank.

MERRICK, LEONARD (1864–1938)

CONRAD IN QUEST OF HIS YOUTH: an Extravagance of Temperament [1708]

Grant Richards 1903. Navy-blue ribbed cloth, blocked in bright blue and cream and lettered in gold.

Half-title. pp. (iv) + (304) T_3–T_8 adverts. paged 1–12. Very fine.

CYNTHIA: a Daughter of the Philistines [1709]

2 vols. Chatto & Windus 1896. Navy-blue ribbed cloth, florally blocked in blind on front and back, gold-lettered on spine. Blue-on-white foliage end-papers.

Half-title in each vol.

Vol. I (iv) + 200
II (iv) + (200) Publishers' cat., 32 pp. dated November 1896, at end.

Very fine.

MAN WHO WAS GOOD (The): a Novel [1710]

2 vols. Chatto & Windus 1892. Dark blue morocco cloth, blind-blocked with all-over impressed design; pale grey flowered end-papers.

Half-title in each vol.

Vol. I (iv) + (204) 13_6 adverts. Publishers' cat., 32 pp. dated October 1891, at end.
II (iv) + (212) Final signature, 27 (unsigned), has 2 leaves, of which the first, carrying adverts., follows p. (208) and the second, blank, follows Publishers' cat. (as in first vol.) which is bound in the middle of the two-leaf signature.

Fine.

[1711] QUAINT COMPANIONS (The)
Grant Richards 1903. Smooth green cloth flecked with white, blocked in violet and white and lettered in gold.
Half-title. pp. (iv)+(308) T_5–T_8 (U_1) (U_2) adverts. paged 1–12. Very fine.

[1712] VIOLET MOSES
3 vols. Bentley 1891. Light blue linen sides flecked with white, dark blue morocco cloth spines. All edges marbled in blue and white.
Half-title in each vol.
Vol. I (iv)+284
II (iv)+272
III (iv)+(240) 50_7 50_8 adverts. B

[1713] WORKS OF LEONARD MERRICK (The)
14 vols. Hodder & Stoughton [1918–19], of which the two last contain material now first published in book-form and are therefore set in caps. and bibliographically described. Uniform navy-blue ribbed cloth, blocked in gold with author's monogram on front, also with blind wreath and framing; blind-blocked and gold-lettered on spine, back plain. Title-pages in black and blue. Volumes unnumbered.
Conrad in Quest of his Youth. With an Introduction by Sir J. M. Barrie.
When Love Flies out of the Window. With an Introduction by Sir William Robertson Nicoll.
The Position of Peggy Harper. With an Introduction by Sir Arthur Pinero.
The Man Who Understood Women and other Stories. With an Introduction by W. J. Locke.
The Worldlings. With an Introduction by Neil Munro.
The Actor-Manager. With an Introduction by W. D. Howells.
Cynthia. With an Introduction by Maurice Hewlett.
The Quaint Companions. With an Introduction by H. G. Wells.
One Man's View. With an Introduction by Granville Barker.
The Man who was Good. With an Introduction by J. K. Prothero.
A Chair on the Boulevard. With an Introduction by A. Neil Lyons.
The House of Lynch. With an Introduction by G. K. Chesterton.

[1713*a*] WHILE PARIS LAUGHED: being Pranks and Passions of the Poet Tricotrin. (Fifth Edition)
Half-title. pp. (viii)+(280)

[1713*b*] TO TELL YOU THE TRUTH
Blank leaf and half-title precede title. pp. (viii) [paged vi]+(264)
The complete series very fine.
Note. This uniform edition of those works which Merrick wished to preserve represented an attempt by a group of fellow-writers to force on public notice and appreciation a delicate and conscientious artist in fiction, whose merits had never been recognised as they deserved. It is sad to have to record that the generous undertaking failed of its purpose. Merrick was, remained, and still is an "authors' author".

MERRIMAN, H. SETON [HUGH S. SCOTT] (1862–1903)

This is a complete collection of the fiction published over the pseudonym 'Merriman' except for *In Kedar's Tents*, 1897, details of which are supplied from a copy in a Statutory Library.

Norah Geraldine Hall, to whom some of these books were given and from whose family collection several of the others come, was sister to the lady who, as 'Stephen G. Tallentyre', collaborated with Merriman more than once. Norah was also sister to Ethel Frances Hall, whom Merriman married in 1889. He died at Melton near Woodbridge in November 1903.

The 'Standard blue cloth style', first used on *Roden's Corner*, is a royal-blue sand-grain cloth, blocked in black and gold, and with dark brown end-papers.

BARLASCH OF THE GUARD [1714]
Smith, Elder 1903. Standard blue cloth style; dark chocolate end-papers.
Blank leaf (signed *a*) and half-title precede title. pp. (viii) [paged vi]+(352) Z_7 Z_8 adverts.
Ink-inscription: 'A. Marjorie Allix from E. Barbara Allix, Nov[br] 1903' on first blank leaf. Very fine.

DROSS [1715]
Chicago and New York: Herbert S. Stone & Co. 1899. Dark red linen-grain cloth, blocked on front and back in white, and gold-lettered on spine. Front-cover lettering and design repeated on back cover. Half-tone front. and 27 full-page illustrations after Sauber.
Two blank leaves and half-title precede title. pp. (viii)+(336) Text ends p. 330; (331) (332) imprint leaf; (333)–(336) blank. No signature letters or numbers.
Ink signature: 'Evelyn Beatrice Hall', on fly-leaf. Fine.

FLOTSAM: The Study of a Life [1716]
Longman etc. 1896. Crimson linen-grain cloth, bevelled boards; black end-papers. Half-tone front. and vignette on title after H. G. Massey.
pp. (iv) [of plate paper]+(352) 22_8 blank. Publishers' cat., 24 pp. dated '4/96', at end.
Presentation Copy. 'Norah G. Hall from the author, 1902' in ink on verso of fly-leaf.

[1717] FROM ONE GENERATION TO ANOTHER
2 vols. Smith, Elder 1892. Pale sage-green diagonal-fine-ribbed cloth; pale grey flowered end-papers. [Carter A.]

Blank leaf and half-title precede title in each vol.

Vol. I (viii) + (264)
II (viii) + (244) R_2 adverts.

Damp has slightly affected the cloth at base of spines, but left little internal trace. Otherwise very fine. (See also Carter, *Binding Variants*, p. 141.)

[1718] FROM WISDOM COURT (with S. G. Tallentyre)
Heinemann 1893. Smooth scarlet cloth, pictorially blocked and lettered in black on front, gold-lettered on spine, publisher's monogram in black on back. Half-tone front. and illustrations in the text (all on text paper) after E. Courboin.

Half-title. pp. (xii) + (208) Publisher's cat., 16 pp. dated October 1892, at end.

Trace of rubber stamp on title (? review stamp). Blind stamp 'W. H. Smith & Son' on fly-leaf.

[1719] GREY LADY (The)
Copy I: First Edition. Sm. 8vo. Smith, Elder 1895. Slate-grey ribbed cloth.

Leaf of adverts and half-title precede title. pp. viii + (328)

A volume in 'The Novel Series' (q.v. in Section III), which series title is blocked on front cover. The spine of this copy is darkened.

[1719*a*] **Copy II: Illustrated Edition.** Full crown 8vo. Smith, Elder 1897. Pearl-grey fine-ribbed cloth; dark grey end-papers. Half-tone front. and 11 full-page illustrations after Arthur Rackham.

Half-title. pp. (viii) + (344) Z_4 adverts.

Presentation Copy: 'Norah G. Hall from the author, 1902' in ink facing half-title.

[1720] *IN KEDAR'S TENTS
Smith, Elder 1897. Standard blue cloth style; dark chocolate end-papers.

Blank leaf and half-title precede title. pp. (viii) [paged vi] + (344) Z_3 Z_4 adverts.

[1721] ISLE OF UNREST (The)
Smith, Elder 1900. Standard blue cloth style. Half-tone front. and 5 full-page illustrations after G. Wright.

Half-title. pp. viii + (352) Final sigs. Z (4 leaves), 2A (4 leaves), these last adverts.

Presentation Copy: 'Norah G. Hall from Henry Seton Merriman Sept. 1900' in ink on recto of front. Reviews of the novel from *The Times* and *The St James's Gazette* inserted.

LAST HOPE (The) [1722]
Smith, Elder 1904. Standard blue cloth style.

Blank leaf and half-title precede title. pp. (viii) [paged vi] + (352) Z_8 adverts.

Numerous cuttings (announcements and reviews) pasted in or inserted. Also holograph MS. of first portion of Chap. IV. From the Hall Collection. Very fine.

MONEY SPINNER (The): and other Character Notes (with S. G. Tallentyre) [1723]
Smith, Elder 1896. Scarlet diaper cloth; very dark brown end-papers. Half-tone front. and 11 full-page illustrations after Arthur Rackham.

Blank leaf and half-title precede title. pp. (xii) [paged x] + (244) R_2 adverts.

Book-plate of Sir Herbert Leon.

PHANTOM FUTURE (The) [1724]
2 vols. Bentley 1888. Smooth navy-blue cloth, blocked on front and spine with diagonal lines in silver, gold-lettered on spine; greenish-blue flowered end-papers.

Half-title in Vol. I; blank leaf and half-title precede title in Vol. II

Vol. I (viii) + (272) 17_8 blank
II (viii) + (256) **B**

PRISONERS AND CAPTIVES [1725]
3 vols. Bentley 1891. Pale greenish-blue diagonal-fine-ribbed cloth; pale grey end-papers with design of storks and palm leaves.

Half-title in Vol. I; blank leaf and half-title precede title in Vols. II and III

Vol. I (viii) + (276)
II (viii) + (264)
III (viii) + 248 **B**

Note. On front covers of Vols. I and II the author's first name 'Henry' (blocked in black) has been over-blocked on a previous faulty blocking in blind. It looks as though a capital J or Y in fancy italic had first been impressed by mistake. Vol. III is correct. Grease spot on back cover of Vol. I; otherwise brilliant.

RODEN'S CORNER [1726]
Smith, Elder 1898. Standard blue cloth style.

Blank leaf (signed *a*) and half-title precede title. pp. (viii) [paged vi] + (352) Z_5–Z_8 adverts.

Ink signature: 'Frances Hall, Eltham, 1898', on title, and review of the novel from *The Westminster Gazette* inserted. Fine. Ink spot on front cover.

[1727] SLAVE OF THE LAMP (The)
2 vols. Smith, Elder 1892. Smooth pale-greenish-blue cloth.

Blank leaf and half-title precede title in each vol.

Vol. I (viii) + 276
II (viii) + (292) U_2 adverts.

The tail of Vol. I has at some time been wetted. The damp has hardly affected the cloth, but has stained front and back end-papers. Otherwise very fine.

[1728] SOWERS (The)
Smith, Elder 1896. Blue patterned-sand-grain cloth; dark brown end-papers.

Half-title. pp. vi + (380) CC_2 adverts.

Presentation Copy: 'Norah Geraldine Hall from the author Jan. 1896' in ink facing half-title.

[1729] SUSPENSE
3 vols. Bentley 1890. Navy-blue diagonal-fine-ribbed cloth, blocked on front in silver with sword and scabbard, and gold-lettered; olive-brown end-papers with design of oak leaves and acorns.

Half-title in each vol.

Vol. I (viii) + (308)
II (vi) + (328)
III (vi) + 296 B

[1730] TOMASO'S FORTUNE and other Stories
Smith, Elder 1904. Standard blue cloth style.

Half-title. pp. (viii) + (312) U_6–U_8 and X_1–X_4 adverts.

Ink signature: 'E. B. Hall', on half-title. Very fine.

[1731] VELVET GLOVE (The)
Smith, Elder 1902: 'Third Impression.' Standard blue cloth style.

Blank leaf and half-title precede title. pp. (viii) [paged vi] + (348) Z_6 adverts.

Author's signature: 'Henry Seton Merriman' and 'Velvet Glove' written by him in ink facing half-title. Very fine.

[1732] VULTURES (The)
Smith, Elder 1902. Standard blue cloth style.

Blank leaf and half-title precede title. pp. (viii) [paged vi] + (344) Z_3 Z_4 adverts.

Bookseller's blind stamp: 'L. Bates, Buxton', on title. Review of the novel from *Punch* pasted on first blank leaf. Fine.

[1733] WITH EDGED TOOLS
3 vols. Smith, Elder 1894. Light olive-brown ribbed cloth. Primrose end-papers

Half-title in Vol. I; blank leaf and half-title precede title in Vols. II and III

Vol. I (viii) + (280) S_8 T_1–T_4 adverts.
II (viii) + (288) T_7 T_8 adverts.
III (viii) + (288) T_8 adverts.

Very fine. (See also Carter, *Binding Variants*, p. 142.)

YOUNG MISTLEY [anon] [1734]
2 vols. Bentley 1888. Royal-blue diagonal-fine-ribbed cloth; pale grey flowered end-papers.

Half-title in each vol.

Vol. I (iv) + 292
II (iv) + (292) (38_2) [unsigned] blank. B

MILLS, JOHN (1812–1873)

BELLE OF THE VILLAGE (The) [1735]
3 vols. Colburn & Co. 1852. Medium-green morocco cloth, blocked in blind and lettered in gold.

Vol. I (ii) + (298) Final leaf, U_5, a single inset. Publishers' cat., 16 pp., undated, at end, followed by inset advert. leaf on cheaper paper.
II (ii) + 296 Publishers' cat., 8 pp. undated, at end.
III (ii) + (272) T_3 T_4 adverts.

Pencil signature: 'Radclyffe Walters 1882' facing title of Vol. I. Very fine.

D'HORSAY, or the Follies of the Day (by a Man of Fashion) [1736]
Six Parts and 1 vol. W. Strange 1844.

Copy I: Part Issue. Six 8vo Parts—I–IV in yellow, V and VI in white wrappers, printed in black with an allegorical design incorporating a young Bacchus, a nymph, a Fool with cap and bladder and the sub-title of the book in fancy lettering. The number of the Part: the month of issue (January to June): 'Price 1*s*.'; the main title D'HORSAY; /OR, THE are printed above the design. Below it appear: WILLIAM STRANGE, 21 PATERNOSTER ROW; / AND TO BE HAD OF ALL BOOKSELLERS. / PRINTED BY C. REYNELL.] [LITTLE PULTENEY STREET. The whole is enclosed in a single frame.

Part I. Front. portrait (of Count d'Orsay): 'The Man of Fashion' and engraved plate: 'The Light of Other Days'.
B–C in eights (pp. (1)–32) Publisher's adverts. on thin paper, 8 pp. undated, at end.
Inside front, and inside and outside back wrappers blank.

Part II. Two engraved plates: 'Crockfords' and 'George Bobbins in his Glory'.
D–E in eights (pp. 33–64)
Inside front and inside back wrappers blank. Outside back wrapper printed with advert. of Rowlands' Preparations.

Part III. Two engraved plates: 'The Taglioni Drag / "Give 'em their Heads"' and 'Tattersall's / "As Precious a Screw as there is in London"'.
F–G in eights (pp. 65–96)
Inside front wrapper blank; inside back wrapper printed with synopsis of text and illustrations in Parts I–III; outside back wrapper printed with advert. of Panklibanon Iron Works.

Part IV. Two engraved plates: 'Mrs Theobald brushing a Cobweb. / "High Over!"' and 'The Queen's Bench as it was'.
H–I in eights (pp. 97–128)
Inside front and back wrappers as in Part III; outside back wrapper printed with advert. of Rowlands' Preparations.

Part V. Two engraved plates: 'Many steps but no rise' and 'Clara's charms divinely charming'.
K–L in eights + M (2 leaves) (pp. 129–156)
Inside front and inside and outside back wrappers blank.

Part VI. Engraved plate: 'The Finish' and engraved pictorial title: D'HORSAY / OR / FOLLIES OF THE DAY / *allegorical vignette* / Illustrated by George Standfast / London 1844 (in fancy lettering).
N (8 leaves) + O (4 leaves). Text ends on O_1 (pp. 157–174), O_2 Preface (verso blank), O_3 printed title (verso printer's imprint), O_4 blank.
Inside front, and inside and outside back wrappers blank.

[1736*a*] **Copy II: Volume Issue.** 8vo. William Strange 1844. Reddish-chestnut-brown ribbed cloth, unblocked but gold-lettered up-spine: D'HORSAY OR THE FOLLIES OF THE DAY. Engraved front., pictorial title and 10 plates by George Standfast. The plates are unsigned and there is no List of Illustrations, which appear facing pp. 34, 42, 48, 66, 73, 104, 112, 132, 140 and 172.

pp. (iv) + 174 The blank leaf, O_4, from the end of Part VI is omitted.

Ink inscription: 'Mr Cooper from N. Caister', on fly-leaf. Bookseller's ticket: 'J. G. Commin, Exeter', on inside front cover. Fine.

Note. For some comment on this book and the remarkable fact that it should have been published at all while many of the characters satirised (all easily recognisable) were still alive, see my *Blessington-D'Orsay*, pp. 283 seq.

[1737] FLYERS OF THE HUNT (The)
'The Field' Office, Strand, and Ward & Lock 1859. Scarlet bead-grain cloth, pictorially blocked and lettered in gold on front and spine. Coloured engraved front. and 5 coloured plates by John Leech.

Half-title. pp. (x) + (116) Pp. (ix) (x) form a single inset.

Binder's ticket: 'Burn', at end. Cloth very fine. Front fly-leaf torn out.

Note. Also issued with plates uncoloured.

OLD ENGLISH GENTLEMAN (The), or the Fields and the Woods [1738]
3 vols. Colburn 1841. Half-cloth boards, labels.

Vol. I viii + (294) First leaf of final sig., O_1, a single inset.
II (ii) + 280
III (ii) + (276) N_6 adverts.

Very fine.

Note. The really remarkable condition of this copy is due to its having been covered (probably at the time of purchase) with a paper wrapper, signs of the pasting down of which appear on inside front and back covers.

I remember an old bookseller in Edinburgh (who had been at one time employed by W. T. Spencer) telling me that Spencer regarded a board copy of *The Old English Gentleman* as one of the rarest three-volume items in his experience. It should be added that the bookseller was not trying to sell me this or any other copy. The statement was made in the course of a general conversation about nineteenth-century novels in original state.

STAGE COACH (The), or the Road of Life [1739]
3 vols. Colburn 1843. Dark brown ribbed cloth, blocked in blind and lettered in gold on spine with title and volume number only. Engraved front. in each vol. and in Vol. I two, in Vol. II three, in Vol. III one plate by Standfast.

Vol. I (viii) + (304) O_8 adverts.
II (ii) + (300)
III (ii) + (260)

Book-plate of Cecil George Assheton Drummond and bookseller's ticket: 'Wyllie, Aberdeen', in each vol. Trace of small label removed from spine of Vol. I and a few spots on the cloth, but a bright and sharp copy.

MITFORD, MARY RUSSELL (1787–1855)

There is only one significant gap in this collection of Miss Mitford's fiction: *Belford Regis*, 3 vols. 1835, a novel I have never been able to find in reliable (even though dingy) original condition. A tentative description from bound copies in Statutory Libraries is provided. Four volumes of verse or drama are also absent.

[1740] AMERICAN STORIES for Little Boys and Girls

First Series: 'Intended for Children under Ten Years of Age.' 3 vols. 12mo. Whittaker, Treacher 1831. Original glazed dark green embossed leather, sprinkled edges. Steel-engraved front. and title in each vol., preceding printed title. In Vol. I blank leaf precedes front.

Vol. I (viii) [paged iv] + (284)
II (iv) + (280) Bb_2 adverts.
III (iv) + 272

Ink signature: 'C. T. Calvert 1831', on fly-leaf of each vol. Booksellers' ticket: 'Bancks & Co. Manchester', on inside front covers of Vols. II and III. Vol. I of this set lacks back cover.

[1740*a*] **Second Series:** 'Intended for Children Above Ten Years of Age.' 3 vols. 12mo. Whittaker, Treacher 1832. Binding uniform with First Series. Steel-engraved front. and title in each vol., preceding printed title.

Vol. I (viii) + 284
II (iv) + (280) Bb_2 adverts.
III (iv) + (300) Cc_6 adverts.

Ink signature: 'C. T. Calvert, June 12, 1834', on engraved title in each vol. Vol. II of this set lacks printed title.

Note. The words 'Second Series' appear on spines only, not on titles.

Both Series were re-issued in 1835 with engraved titles omitted, and printed ones re-set so as to read 'Stories for Little Boys and Girls' (First Series) and 'Tales for Young People' (Second Series). Engraved front. as in first editions.

The First Series of this re-issue was bound in dark blue, the Second Series in plum-coloured fine diaper cloth, with gold decorations and lettering on spines.

[1741] ATHERTON and Other Tales

3 vols. Hurst & Blackett 1854. Bright blue morocco cloth. Steel-engraved front. in each vol.—in Vol. I Portrait, in Vol. II view of Three Mile Cross, in Vol. III view of Swallowfield. [These engravings are identical with those in 'Dramatic Works', 2 vols. 1854, q.v.]

Vol. I (x) + (320) X_8 blank
II (ii) + (304) Publishers' cat., 16 pp. undated, at end.
III (ii) + 296 Publishers' cat., 24 pp. undated, at end.

Presentation Copy: 'To dear Mrs (?) Ford from her faithful and affectionate friend the Author' in ink on fly-leaf of Vol. I. Very fine.

[1742] *BELFORD REGIS, or Sketches of a Country Town

3 vols. Bentley 1835. Boards, labels.

Half-title in Vol. I

Vol. I (xii) + ? (320) ? P_4 blank or adverts.
II (iv) + ? (320) ? P_4 blank or adverts.
III (iv) + 348

Note. Description taken from Bodleian copy, bound three-vols.-in-one. Vols. I and II end with P_3 (p. 318). B.M. and U.L.C. copies similar.

CHARLES THE FIRST: an Historical Tragedy in Five Acts [1743]

8vo. John Duncombe 1834. New boards uncut.

pp. (viii) + 80

CHRISTINA: The Maid of the South Seas. A Poem [1744]

8vo. Valpy & Rivington 1811. New boards and label; marbled edges.

Half-title. pp. (xii) + (336) Y_3 Errata, Y_4 blank.

Presentation Copy: 'To the Rev[d] R. Nares. With the respectful compliments of the Author' in ink on fly-leaf, and long notes in ink (? by Nares) on Y_4.

COUNTRY STORIES [1745]

Saunders & Otley 1837. Half-cloth boards, label.

Half-title. pp. (viii) + (328) P_8 adverts. Text ends Q_{12} (p. (312)); P_1–P_7 'Note on the Lost Dahlia'.

Ink signature: 'Adeline Newton', on fly-leaf.

DRAMATIC SCENES: Sonnets and other Poems [1746]

Geo. B. Whittaker 1827. Boards, label.

Half-title. pp. (viii) + 392

Ink signature: 'W. Wissenden', on fly-leaf.

DRAMATIC WORKS [1747]

2 vols. Hurst & Blackett 1854. Grey-purple morocco cloth. Steel-engraved portrait front. and view of Three Mile Cross in Vol. I; view of Swallowfield in Vol. II.

Vol. I (xxxvi) + (332)
II (iv) + 412

Ink signature: 'Arabella Hewit Sams, June 1855', on fly-leaf in each vol.

FOSCARI: a Tragedy [1748]

8vo. Geo. B. Whittaker 1826. Stitched as issued, uncut. Title serves as front wrapper.

pp. iv + (80) F_8 adverts.

FOSCARI AND JULIAN: Tragedies [1749]

Geo. B. Whittaker 1827. Boards, label [reading: TRAGEDIES / BY / M. R. MITFORD / 8*s*. BOARDS].

Half-title. pp. (iv) + viii [signed *a*] + (252)

Book-plate of Henry Deane. Lacks fly-leaf at end.

MITFORD

[1750] LIGHTS AND SHADOWS OF AMERICAN LIFE (Edited by Mary Russell Mitford)
3 vols. Colburn & Bentley 1832. Boards, labels.
Vol. I (viii) + 340
II (iv) + (340)
III (iv) + 344

[1751] NARRATIVE POEMS ON THE FEMALE CHARACTER IN THE VARIOUS RELATIONS OF LIFE
8vo. Valpy & Rivington 1813.
Vol. I (all published).

Copy I. Boards, label (worded: 'Miss Mitford's Poems on the Female Character').

Half-title. pp. (xii) + (332) Page (332) is printed with adverts.

'From the Author' (not in Miss Mitford's hand) in ink on fly-leaf. Spine defective.

[1751*a*] **Copy II.** Boards. Spine and label renewed. Collation as Copy I, but p. (332) blank.

Ink signature: 'George Prentiss 1838' on title.

Note. Page (332) in Copy I advertises *The Classical Journal*, No. XI for September 1812. Either because this was out of date by the time the book was published or because mistakes were made in the advert., I suggest that this was cancelled and that the regular issue showed p. (332) blank.

[1752] OUR VILLAGE: Sketches of Rural Character and Scenery
[Vol. I.] G. & W. B. Whittaker 1824. Boards, label.

Four leaves of publishers' adverts. paged (1)–8, on text paper and forming part of first sheet, and half-title precede title. pp. (xvi) [paged 8 + viii] + 292

Book-plate of H. B. Fielding. Booksellers' ticket: 'Willmer & Co. Liverpool', and ink signature: 'Julia R. Roundell', on inside front cover. Fine.

[1752*a*] Vol. II. Geo. B. Whittaker 1826. Boards, label.

Half-title. pp. viii [mispaged vii] + (312)

Ink signature: 'Madalina F. Palmer', on fly-leaf. Fine.

[1752*b*] Vol. III. Geo. B. Whittaker 1828. Boards, label.

Half-title. pp. viii + (316)

'Miss Peacock. Her Book 1828' in ink on inside front cover. Label a little torn.

[1752*c*] Vol. IV. Whittaker, Treacher & Co. 1830.

Copy I. 'Vol. IV' on label, 'Fourth Series' on title. Boards, label.

Half-title. pp. viii + (348) Z_6 adverts.

Ink signature: 'Madalina F. Palmer', on fly-leaf.

[1752*c*(i)] **Copy II.** 'Fourth Series' both on label and title. Half-cloth boards, label. Collation as Copy I.

Ink signature: 'M. M. Roberts, July 1858', on half-title.

Vol. V. Whittaker, Treacher & Co. 1832. Original half-leather, green watered cloth. [1752*d*]

pp. iv + (364) Bb_2 adverts.

Ink signature: 'H. D. Forbes', on inside front cover.

POEMS [1753]

Copy I: First Edition. A. J. Valpy & Longman 1810. Boards, no label or lettering.

Half-title. pp. (viii) [paged (vi)] + (160) Text ends K_8; (L_1)–(L_6) [unsigned and unfoliated] Notes; (L_7) 'Alterations' [i.e. Errata]; (L_8) Imprint leaf.

'Miss Mitford' written in ink on spine.

Copy II: Second Edition 'With Considerable Additions'. 8vo. Valpy & Rivington 1811. New boards, leather spine and label; marbled edges. [1753*a*]

pp. (viii) + (280) S_2 blank or adverts. (lacking in this copy). R_1–S_1 (unfoliated) 'Notes'.

SADAK AND KALASRADE, or the Waters of Oblivion. A Romantic Opera in Two Acts [1754]

Printed for the Proprietors of the Lyceum Opera House 1835. Stitched as issued, uncut. Title serves as front wrapper.

pp. (32)

MONTGOMERY, FLORENCE (1843–1923)

BLUE VEIL (The): a New Series of Moral Tales for Children [1755]

Bentley 1883. Smooth navy-blue cloth, blocked in pale blue and lettered in gold; dark chocolate end-papers.

pp. viii + (344) Z_3 recto advertises books by same author; Z_4 blank. Erratum slip faces p. viii.

Binder's ticket: 'Burn', at end. B

Note. This volume contains *Why does she Wear a Blue Veil? A Seaside Friendship* and *Introductions.*

See also *Moral Tales for Children.*

COLONEL NORTON: a Novel [1756]

3 vols. Bentley 1895. Smooth dark blue cloth; monogram end-papers. Edges marbled in gold and dark blue.

Half-title in each vol. Titles printed in red and black.

Vol. I (viii) + (280) 18_4 blank. Corrigenda slip faces p. 278.
II (vi) [paged iv] + (220) 32_6 blank, followed by cat. of Bentley's Favourite Novels, 32 pp. dated Spring 1895.
III (vi) [paged iv] + (228) Publishers' cat., 16 pp. dated April 1895, at end. B

[1757] HERBERT MANNERS and Other Tales

Bentley 1880. Scarlet diagonal-fine-ribbed cloth; black end-papers.

No. XIV of Bentley's Half-Crown Empire Library, and containing, in addition to the title-story, *The Town Crier* and *The Children with the Indian Rubber Ball*. See also *Moral Tales for Children*.

[1758] MISUNDERSTOOD

Pl. 23 **Copy I: First Edition, First Issue.** Bentley 1869. Claret dot-and-line-grain cloth; chocolate end-papers.

pp. vi + (322) pp. (v) vi and final leaf, Y_1, single insets. B

Binders' ticket: 'Edmonds and Remnants', at end.

[1758*a*] *Pl. 23* **Copy II: First Edition, Second Issue.** Differs from Copy I in following particulars: Title and Author's name on spine are in more condensed type, with a full stop after 'Montgomery'. The title is a cancel, and carries the words *All rights reserved* below imprint. There is no printer's imprint (Spottiswoode & Co.) on verso of title. B

[1758*b*] *Pl. 23* **Copy III: Illustrated Edition.** Large sq. 8vo. Bentley 1874. Grass-green diagonal-fine-ribbed cloth, pictorially blocked in black and gold. Bevelled boards. All edges gilt. Wood-engraved front. and 7 full-page illustrations after George du Maurier.

pp. (viii) + (212) B

A short preface to this edition occupies p. (vii).

[1759] MORAL TALES FOR CHILDREN

Bentley 1886: 'New Edition.' Bright blue patterned-sand-grain cloth, blocked (uniform with *Town Crier*, *Thwarted* and *Wild Mike*) in black and gold; black end-papers. Wood-engraved front. after H. Miles.

Half-title. pp. (viii) + (432) Publishers' adverts., 4 pp. on text paper undated, at end. B

Binder's ticket: 'Burn', at end. George Bentley has written 'also other Stories' in pencil on tissue covering front.

Note. This volume is a collected edition of Florence Montgomery's stories *for* children as opposed to her stories *about* children. It contains: *Herbert Manners—The Town Crier—The Children with the Indian Rubber Ball—Why does she Wear a Blue Veil?—A Seaside Friendship* and *Introductions.*

The Town Crier and *The Children with the Indian Rubber Ball* were first published in 1874 (the latter, according to the Bentley Private Catalogue, had previously been printed—one assumes privately—as 'a miniature square booklet bound in mottled cloth'); *Herbert Manners* in 1880 and the other three, under the title *The Blue Veil*, in 1883.

SEAFORTH [1760]

3 vols. Bentley 1878. Olive-green diagonal-fine-ribbed cloth; dark chocolate end-papers; bevelled boards.

Half-title in Vol. I; blank leaf and half-title precede title in Vols. II and III

Vol. I viii + (260) S_2 carries list of works by same author.

II (viii) [paged vi] + (232)

III (viii) [paged vi] + (256) R_8 carries list of works by same author. B

Binder's ticket: 'Burn', at end of Vol. I.

THROWN TOGETHER: a Story (by the author of 'Misunderstood') [1761]

2 vols. Bentley 1872; Second Edition. Smooth brown cloth, bevelled boards; milk chocolate end-papers.

Half-title in Vol. I

Vol. I (viii) + (292)

II iv + 392 B

Binders' ticket: 'Edmonds & Remnants', at end of Vol. I. Covers of Vol. II damp-stained at bottom.

Note. According to the Bentley Private Catalogue, the first edition of this novel appeared on 3 June and the second about three weeks later. The compilers could not trace a copy of the first edition, and make the odd comment that the second 'probably coincided with it'.

THWARTED, or Ducks' Eggs in a Hen's Nest. A Village Story (by the author of 'Misunderstood') [1762]

Bentley 1874. Bright blue sand-grain cloth, blocked (uniform with *The Town Crier*) in black and gold, and with author's name on front and spine; dark chocolate end-papers.

Half-title. pp. viii + (256) B

TOWN CRIER (The): to which is added 'The Children with the Indian Rubber Ball'. A Christmas Story Book for Young Children [1763]

Bentley 1874. Crimson sand-grain cloth, blocked in black and gold; dark chocolate end-papers.

Half-title. pp. (viii) + (216) B

See also *Moral Tales for Children.*

TRANSFORMED, or Three Weeks in a Life-Time [1764]

Bentley 1886. Olive-green diagonal-fine-ribbed cloth; dark chocolate end-papers.

Half-title. pp. viii + (352) Z_8 advertises works by the same author. Errata slip faces p. viii. B

[1765] VERY SIMPLE STORY (A): being a Chronicle of the Thoughts and Feelings of a Child

Copy I: First Edition. 4to. Bentley [for W. Fawcett, Sleaford] 1867. Blue bead-grain cloth. Bevelled boards. All edges gilt. Title blocked in fancy lettering in gold on front. No spine lettering. Wood-engraved front. and 3 full-page illustrations after the Marchioness of Queensberry and M.R.

Half-title. pp. 60 **B**

[1765*a*] **Copy II.** A VERY SIMPLE STORY AND WILD MIKE. Bentley 1878. Scarlet diagonal-fine-ribbed cloth; black end-papers.

No. II of Bentley's Half-Crown Empire Library.

[1766] WILD MIKE and his Victim (by the author of 'Misunderstood')

Bentley 1875. Slate-grey diagonal-fine-ribbed cloth blocked (uniform with *Town Crier* and *Thwarted*) in black and gold, and with author's name on front and spine; black end-papers.

Leaf, carrying list of works by the same author on verso, and half-title precede title.

pp. (xii) + (148) L_2 adverts., followed by publisher's cat., 24 pp. on text paper, dated July 1875. **B**

See also *A Very Simple Story*, Copy II.

MOORE, GEORGE (1857–1933)

[1767] MODERN LOVER (A)

3 vols. Tinsley 1883. Smooth grey-blue cloth, lettered and dated in black on front, gold-lettered on spine.

Vol. I (iv) + (256) R_7 R_8 blank.
II (iv) + (240)
III (iv) + (212) P_2 blank. Inset between P_1 and P_2 is a publishers' cat., 32 pp. undated.

Ink signature: 'Annie Mackay July 1883.' on fly-leaf of each vol. Fine.

Notes. (i) See Carter, *Binding Variants* (face p. 142), for illustration (B) of this, the normal binding of the novel. A third variant, probably a trial issue, was sold with the Esher Library in November 1946. This was in black diagonal-fine-ribbed cloth, lettered, etc., in gold on front as well as on spine, and with the date higher in top left corner than on the normal blue issue described above.

(ii) In 1917 Moore published a rewritten version of this story under the title *Lewis Seymour and Some Women*. A copy of this version (which incidentally involved author, publisher and printers in a libel action) is in the Collection, in new condition with dust-jacket.

MORGAN, LADY (SYDNEY OWENSON) (1776–1859) and MORGAN, SIR T. CHARLES

All Lady Morgan's fiction is in the Collection. Of her non-fiction the following are lacking: *Patriotic Sketches of Ireland* (1807), *Italy* (1821) and *Absenteeism* (1825).

BOOK OF THE BOUDOIR (The) [1768]

2 vols. 8vo. Colburn 1829. Boards, label.

Half-title in Vol. I

Vol. I xii + (340)
II iv + (324)

Book-label of 'R. J. Ll. Price, Rhiwlas Library' and bookseller's ticket: 'Seacome Chester', on inside front cover of each vol. Fine.

BOOK WITHOUT A NAME (The) (by Sir T. Charles and Lady Morgan) [1769]

2 vols. Colburn 1841. Green ribbed cloth. Lithographed portrait of Sir T. C. Morgan in Vol. I after Josephine Clarke.

Half-title in Vol. I, preceded by publisher's cat., 16 pp. dated January 1841.

Vol. I (viii) + (360) Q_{11} Q_{12} adverts.
II (iv) + (360) Q_{12} adverts.

Presentation Copy: 'To the Lady Molesworth—Sydney Morgan, Janu^y^ 5th 1846. William St., Albert Gate' in ink on title of Vol. I.

Book-plate of Sir William Molesworth in each vol. Spines faded.

FLORENCE MACARTHY: an Irish Tale (by Lady Morgan) [1770]

4 vols. Colburn 1818. Boards, labels.

Vol. I vi + (332) Text ends (322); (324)–(332) Notes.
II (ii) + (284) Text ends (276); (278)–(284) Notes.
III (ii) + (296) Text ends 288; (289)–(296) Notes.
IV (ii) + (284) Text ends 282; (283) (284) Note (recto), Errata (verso).

Very fine. From the Bellew Library.

FRANCE (by Lady Morgan) [1771]

Large 4to. Colburn 1817. Boards, label.

pp. (xvi) [*a*, 4 leaves, *b*, 4 leaves] + 252 (Part I) + 248 (Part II) + (i)–(cxvi) signed *a*–p_2 and endorsed 'VOL. II' on fly-title but 'Part II' elsewhere.

I have recorded prelims. as xvi because the requirements of normal collation (as well as the pagination) call for a half-title or blank leaf or extra leaf of some kind. But this copy, in fine original state, shows no sign of ever having contained more than seven leaves in the prelims. Of these leaves b_1, verso, carries a Publisher's Advertisement attacking Lady Morgan for delaying the book and damaging its prospects; b_2, recto and verso, carries Errata.

[1772] FRANCE IN 1829–30 (by Lady Morgan)
2 vols. 8vo. Saunders & Otley 1830. Boards, labels. Engraved portrait front. to Vol. I after J. P. Davis, dated August 29, 1830.

Leaf, inset and signed *a* 2, carrying publishers' note and adverts. precedes portrait in Vol. I

Vol. I (ii) + (x) + (528) Advert. slip of a Guide to Birmingham on thin pink paper and a 4 pp. undated cat. of Whittaker, Treacher at end.
II iv + (564) NN_9 NN_{10} adverts., followed by pink slip and Whittaker, Treacher adverts. as in Vol. I.

Vol. I rebacked, labels discoloured.

[1773] LAY OF AN IRISH HARP (The), or Metrical Fragments (by Miss Owenson)
Richard Philips 1807. Boards, label. Wood-engraved vignette on title.

pp. (xvi) + (200)

Very fine. From the Bellew Library.

[1774] LIFE AND TIMES OF SALVATOR ROSA (The) (by Lady Morgan)
Copy I. 2 vols. 8vo. Colburn 1824. Boards, labels. Engraved front. in each vol.—in Vol. I Self-portrait, in Vol. II Two Airs.

Half-title in Vol. II

Vol. I xvi + (408) $2D_4$ adverts.
II viii + (384) $2B_7$ $2B_8$ adverts.

Ink signature: 'Charlotte King 1825', inside front cover of each vol. Fine.

[1774*a*] **Copy II: Another.** Dark mushroom-brown glazed linen, black labels lettered in gold. Collation etc. as Copy I, except that the plate serving as frontispiece to Vol. II appears facing p. (313), i.e. first page of Appendix.

Pencil signature: 'Mrs ffolliott', inside front cover of each vol.

[1775] MISSIONARY (The): an Indian Tale (by Miss Owenson)
3 vols. Stockdale 1811: Second Edition (same year as First). Pale brown boards, printed in black on front, spine and back. Engraved portrait front. in Vol. I after Godby, dated 13 February 1811.

Half-title in Vols. II and III

Vol. I (iv) + 228
II (iv) + (256)
III (iv) + (224) L_4 adverts., followed by publisher's cat., 12 pp. undated.

Fine. From the Bellew Library.

Note. The unusual style of boarding on this novel is similar to that on *St Clair*, Copy II (q.v.).

MOHAWKS (The): a Satirical Poem. With Notes. [anon: by Sir Charles and Lady Morgan] [1776]
8vo. Colburn 1822. Boards, label.

pp. (vi) + (168) pp. (v) (vi) Errata, and a single inset. M_3 M_4 adverts. Text ends (128); (129)–(164) Notes.

O'BRIENS AND THE O'FLAHERTYS (The): a National Tale (by Lady Morgan) [1777]
4 vols. Colburn 1827. Pink boards, glazed black paper spines, labels.

Half-title in each vol.

Vol. I (xii) + (296)
II (iv) + 340
III (iv) + 332
IV (iv) + (364) R_2 adverts.

In this copy Vol. I, pp. (v)–(xii) [Preface dated October 1, 1827] are misbound to follow prelims. in Vol. III.

ODD VOLUME (An), extracted from an Autobiography (by Sydney, Lady Morgan) [1778]
Bentley 1859. Green bead-grain cloth. Engraved portrait front. after Berthan and coloured litho. plate of Lady Morgan's drawing-room.

Half-title. pp. (xii) + (340) Publishers' cat., 28 pp. dated January 1859 on text paper, at end.

Binders' ticket: 'Westleys', at end. Fine.

Note. The binding is gold-lettered on spine: THE DIARY OF LADY MORGAN.

O'DONNEL: a National Tale (by Lady Morgan, late Miss Owenson) [1779]
3 vols. Colburn 1814. Boards, labels.

Half-title in Vols. II and III

Vol. I (x) [paged xii] + (296) Text ends 290; (291)–(296) Notes. (ix) (x), probably conjugate with label-leaf, form a single inset.
II (iv) + (332) Text ends 314; (315)–(332) Notes.
III (iv) + (348) Text ends 332; (333)–(339) Notes; (340)–(348)—Q_3 Q_6—adverts.

Very fine. From the Bellew Library.

POEMS: Dedicated by permission to Rt. Hon. Countess of Moira (by Sidney (*sic*) Owenson) [1780]
Dublin: Alex Stewart, and London: Mr Phillips 1801. Cont. marbled boards, new morocco spine, leather label, sprinkled edges.

Half-title (missing from this copy). pp. (iv) + (160) L_4 blank or adverts. (missing from this copy).

Ink signature: 'Mrs Scott', inside front cover, and ink scribble on p. 156.

MORGAN

[1781] PRINCESS (The), or The Beguine (by Lady Morgan)

3 vols. Bentley 1835. Full cream straight grained morocco, leather lettering pieces, fully gilt; glazed green end-papers. All edges gilt.

Half-title in each vol. (missing from this copy).

Vol. I (iv) + 340
II (iv) + (334) P_{12} blank or adverts. (missing from this copy)
III (iv) + (384)

From the Library of Thomas Wildman of Newstead Abbey.

Note. From the collation given in the Bentley Private Catalogue I conjecture that half-titles should be present. That P_{12} should appear in Vol. II is deduced from the needs of normal collation.

[1782] ST CLAIR, or the Heiress of Desmond (by S. O.)

Copy I: First Edition. Printed for Harding & Highley, London, and Archer, Dublin 1803. New marbled boards, leather label, marbled edges.

pp. (252) [paged (i)–vi + (7)–248] L_5 L_6 adverts.

[1782*a*] **Copy II: Third Edition. Corrected and Greatly Enlarged** (by Miss Owenson). 2 vols. Stockdale 1812. Drabbish yellow boards, printed in black on front, back and spine. Engraved portrait front. after Dighton in Vol. I, dated September 1811.

Half-title in Vol. II

Vol. I (224) [paged (i)–viii + (13)–(228)] K_{12} blank.
II (256) M_6 adverts.

Very fine. From the Bellew Library.

Note. The binding style of this edition is very unusual, suggesting rather a wrappered chapbook than a standardised two-volume novel. Front covers carry a replica of the titles; spines carry title, author, etc. between double rules suggesting (and placed like) paper labels; the backs are printed with publishers' advertisements, virtually repeating those on M_6 of Vol. II. Cf. *Missionary* above.

[1783] WILD IRISH GIRL (The): a National Tale (by Miss Owenson)

3 vols. Richard Phillips 1806. Boards, labels.

Vol. I (264) [paged (ii) + (i)–(xxxiv) + (35)–(262)]
II (ii) + (272) N_2–N_4 adverts.
III (ii) + 264

Spines defective; label of Vol. I torn and that of Vol. III missing. Front fly-leaf of Vol. III torn.

[1784] WOMAN AND HER MASTER (by Lady Morgan)

2 vols. Colburn 1840. Dark grey-purple ribbed cloth.

Vol. I viii + 334 First leaf of final sig., P_1, a single inset. Text ends (320); (321)–334 Notes.
II (iv) [p. (iv) mispaged v] + 420 Text ends 416; (417)–420 Notes.

Book-plate of Sir Moses Montefiore, Bart. in each vol. Very fine.

WOMAN, or Ida of Athens (by Miss Owenson) [1785]

4 vols. Longman etc. 1809. Grey paper wrappers, white paper spines, labels.

Half-title in each vol.

Vol. I (xxx) [paged xxviii] + (224) Text ends p. (212); (213)–(224) Notes.
II (iv) + 272 Text ends p. 266; (267)–272 Notes.
III (iv) + 192 Text ends p. 190; (191)–192 Notes.
IV (iv) + (292) Text ends p. 290; (291) (292) Notes.

Fine. From the Bellew Library.

French Editions

FLORENCE MACARTHY (par Lady Morgan). [1786]
Traduite de l'anglais et précédée d'une notice historique sur Lady Morgan par le traducteur de *La France* [A. J. B. D.†]

4 vols. Paris: H. Nicolle 1819. Half-red roan gilt, red morocco paper sides; edges uncut. Engraved portrait front. to Vol. I.

Half-title in each vol.

Vol. I (iv) + xxiv + 252
II (iv) + (288)
III (iv) + (262) First leaf of final sig., 22_1, a single inset.
IV (iv) + (272)

From the Library of the Empress Marie Louise with her monogram on front and back covers.

GLORVINA ou La Jeune Irlandaise ['The Wild Irish Girl'] (par Miss Owenson). Traduite de l'anglais par le traducteur de Ida et du Missionaire, ouvrages du même Auteur [1787]

4 vols. Paris: Gide Fils 1813. Half-red roan gilt, red morocco paper sides; edges uncut

Half-title in each vol.

Vol. I (xxii) + 216
II (iv) + (236)
III (iv) + (224)
IV (iv) + 176

From the Library of the Empress Marie Louise but without her monogram.

† This is clearly M. Defauconpret, who later became the translator of Marryat.

[1788] NOVICE DE SAINT-DOMINIQUE (La) (de Miss Owenson [Lady Morgan]). Traduit...par Madame de R***

4 vols. Paris: H. Nicolle 1817. Half-red roan, gilt, red morocco paper sides; edges uncut.

Half-title in each vol.

Vol. I (iv) + 250 First leaf of final sig., 11_1, a single inset.
II (iv) + 240
III (iv) + 284
IV (iv) + 288

From the Library of the Empress Marie Louise with her monogram on front and back covers.

MORGAN, SIR T. C., M.D. (1783–1843)

[1789] ROYAL PROGRESS (The): A Canto with Notes written on occasion of his M——y's Visit to Ireland, August 1821 (by 'Humphrey Oldcastle' [Sir T. Charles Morgan])

J. Green 1821. Cont. half-calf, marbled boards, sprinkled edges.

pp. (96) Text ends p. 70; (71)–(96) Notes.

Book-plate of Sir T. Charles Morgan, M.D. Ink signature on title 'Sydney Morgan' and her husband's name written in under 'Oldcastle'. On leaf facing title inscription in Lady Morgan's hand:

'This *bagatelle de circonstance* was written by my dear husband in the idleness of our escape from Dublin (during the king's visit to Ireland) to a cottage in the mountains of Wicklow, when our laughter at all that was passing in Town was mingled with bitter indignation at the servile baseness of the Irish people, and the false assumptions of the falsest of all men—O'Connell—played a disgraceful part in this farce.
Sydney Morgan.'

A few pencil corrections in the text.

[1790] SKETCHES OF THE PHILOSOPHY OF MORALS

8vo. Colburn 1822. Boards, label.

Half-title. pp. (xxx) + (370) Final leaf, $(2B_1)$, a single inset.

Very fine. From the Bellew Library.

Morganiana

[1791] LETTERE A MILEDI MORGAN ('LE MORGANICHE')

Pamphlet. Tait, 'Edimburgo', 1824. Stitched, uncut, as issued.

Half-title serves as front wrapper. pp. (iv) + (84) G_2 blank.

Fine. From the Bellew Library.

[*See also* HAMILTON, WALTER, *above*]

MORIER, JAMES (1780–1849)

This is a complete collection of Morier's fiction and verse.

ABEL ALLNUTT: a Novel (by the author of 'Hajji Baba', 'Zohrab the Hostage', 'Ayesha', etc.) [1792]

3 vols. Bentley 1837. Half-cloth boards, labels.

Half-title in Vol. I

Vol. I vi + 318 Final leaf, P_3, a single inset.
II (ii) + (312)
III (ii) + (308)

Label of Vol. III defective.

ADVENTURES OF HAJJI BABA OF ISPAHAN (The) [anon] [1793]

Copy I: First Edition. 3 vols. Murray 1824. Boards, labels.

Half-title in each vol.

Vol. I (lxxvi) + 272
II (iv) + (404)
III (iv) + (388) [p. 387 mispaged 388.]

In this edition the Contents of all three vols. appear in Vol. I

Very fine.

Copy II: Second Edition. 3 vols. Murray 1824. Boards, labels. The words 'Second Edition' appear on the labels. [1793*a*]

Half-title in Vol. II

Vol. I (xl) + (312)
II viii + (352)
III viii + (384) BB_8 imprint leaf.

pp. (iii)–xxxiv of Vol. I are occupied by an 'Advertisement to the Second Edition', now first printed.

Book-label: 'Chillingham Castle' and ink signature: 'Earl of Tankerville', inside front cover of each vol. Fine.

ADVENTURES OF HAJJI BABA OF ISPAHAN IN ENGLAND (The) [anon] [1794]

2 vols. Murray 1828. Mustard-brown boards, rose-pink paper spines, labels.

Half-title in Vol. II

Vol. I xxxii + (308) O_{10} imprint leaf.
II (iv) + 352

Fine.

ADVENTURES OF TOM SPICER (The), who Advertised for a Wife (by the author of 'Hajji Baba') [1795] *Pl. 17*

Small 8vo. 'Printed, not Published' 1840. Stiff lilac (or cream) moiré-paper wrappers, printed in black on front only.

pp. 16

Two copies, both fine. (i) From the Library of Lord Esher. (ii) *Presentation Copy:* Ink inscription on title: 'From the Author—Written for a Bazar.'

[1796] AYESHA: the Maid of Kars (by the author of 'Zohrab', 'Hajji Baba', etc.)
3 vols. Bentley 1834 Boards, labels.

Vol. I (viii) + (318) Final leaf, P_3, a single inset.
II (ii) + 330 Final leaf, P_9 (and signed), a single inset.
III (ii) + (336)

Externally very fine; some signatures loose.

[1797] MARTIN TOUTROND

Copy I: First Edition. MARTIN TOUTROND: A FRENCHMAN IN LONDON IN 1831 [anon]. 'Translated from an unpublished French MS.' Bentley 1849. Three-quarter morocco, marbled edges. Etched front. signed 'G. Measom' and a few wood-engraved cuts in the text.

Half-title (missing from this copy). pp. xii + 392

Note. The original First Edition binding is of 'blue-bag'-blue fine-ribbed cloth, blocked on front with decorative frame in blind and circular centrepiece with Gallic cock in gold; gold-lettered on spine and blind blocked on back.

[1797*a*] **Copy II: New Edition.** MARTIN TOUTROND: OR ADVENTURES OF A FRENCHMAN IN LONDON. By James Morier. 'New Edition.' Bentley 1849. Blue morocco cloth. Illustrations as Copy I.

Half-title. pp. (xiv) [paged xii] + 392

The irregularity in the prelims. is caused by a reprinted title and following leaf (declaring Morier's authorship), both of which are pasted on the stub of the cancelled title. Otherwise the two editions are composed of identical sheets.

[1798] MIRZA (The)
3 vols. Bentley 1841. Half-cloth boards, labels.

Half-title in each vol.

Vol. I (iv) + (320)
II (iv) + 320
III (iv) + (310) First leaf of final sig., O_1, a single inset.

Book-plate of George Gilpin in each vol.

[1799] MISSELMAH: a Persian Tale (by the author of 'Hajji Baba', etc.)
8vo. Brighton: Printed by W. Saunders, St James's Street 1847. (PRINTED FOR SALE, IN AID OF THE FUNDS OF THE IRISH CHARITIES.)

Powder-blue paper boards, cut flush, lettered in gold on front, spine and back unprinted. All edges gilt. Double end-papers front and back.

Half-title. Pp. (viii) [paged (iv)] + (56) [paged (5)–(58) + ii. Text ends 57, (58) blank, (i) ii Appendix].

From the Library of Lord Esher. Spine defective.

ORIENTAL TALE (An) (by the author of 'Hajji Baba', etc.) [1800]
8vo. Printed (not published) by W. Leppard, Brighton (1839). PRINTED FOR SALE IN AID OF THE FUNDS OF THE SUSSEX COUNTY HOSPITAL.

Buff paper wrappers, printed in black on front only. All edges gilt. Tinted lithographic front. after a drawing by the author.

pp. (iv) + 72

Ink signature on front cover and title: 'Sophia Dungannon, 1840.' Wrappers slightly dust-soiled.

ZOHRAB THE HOSTAGE (by the author of 'Hajji Baba') [1801]
3 vols. Bentley 1832. Boards, labels.

Leaf advertising Bentley's Standard Novels precedes title in Vol. I, half-titles in Vols. II and III

Vol. I (xii) [paged (x)] + (320)
II (iv) + 326 Final leaf, Q_1, a single inset.
III (iv) + 324 B

Ink signature: 'S. & J. Bentley', on fly-leaf of Vol. I.

Note. This was the first book published by Richard Bentley as an independent publisher after his separation from Colburn. The copy came from the Bentley Collection and the inscription is probably a clerk's mistake for S. & R. Bentley.

Edited by Morier

BANISHED (The): a Swabian Historical Tale (edited by James Morier, Esq.) [1802]
3 vols. Colburn 1839. Half-cloth boards, labels.

Half-title in Vols. II and III

Vol. I (xii) + 312
II (iv) + 300
III (iv) + 298 First leaf of final sig., O_1, a single inset. Publisher's cat., 4 pp. dated April 1839, at end.

Ink signature: 'John Aldridge 1839', inside front cover of each vol. Fine.

Note. This story is from the German of Hauff. Morier's contribution consists of a 2 pp. 'Editor's Notice' in Vol. I.

ST ROCHE: a Romance, from the German. [1803]
3 vols. (edited by James Morier) Bentley 1847. Navy-blue wavy-grain cloth, paper labels.

Half-title in each vol.

Vol. I (viii) + 296
II (iv) + 252
III (iv) + (332) Text ends p. 330; (331) (332) Genealogical Table and printers' imprint. B

Note. This book was also issued in half-cloth boards, labels. The Bentley Private Catalogue says that Morier's connection with it was 'purely nominal'. The translator of *St Roche* (unidentified) also translated *The Birthright* by Emilie Carlen, 3 vols, 1851.

Partly by Morier

[1804] LITERARY CONTRIBUTIONS BY VARIOUS AUTHORS in aid of the Funds of The Hospital for Consumption, etc. at Brompton

Large 8vo. Printed by Vizetelly Brothers & Co. 1846. Stiff glazed pale-yellow paper wrappers, illuminated in colours and fancy-lettered on front; cream cloth spine, unlettered; back cover plain. All edges gilt.

pp. 60

Binders' ticket: 'Remnants and Edmonds', at end.

Note. A Poem by Morier, previously unprinted, occupies pp. (11) and 12. Other contributors include Horace Smith, Mrs Opie, John Poole and J. Heneage Jesse.

Ink inscription inside front cover: 'Inez Harriot Antoinette Augusta Cotton from her affectionate Father Henry Percy Cotton. Friday. July the [date omitted] 1851.'

MOTT, ALFRED. See BARROWCLIFFE, A. J.

MULOCK, DINAH MARIA (MRS CRAIK) (1826–1887)

[1805] ADVENTURES OF A BROWNIE (The): as told to my child (by the author of 'John Halifax, Gentleman'.)

Fcap 4to. Sampson Low, etc. 1872. Olive-green diagonal-fine-ribbed cloth, pictorially blocked and fancy lettered in gold and black on front and spine, blind-blocked on back. Bevelled boards; all edges gilt. Wood-engraved front. and 5 illustrations after H. Paterson, all on plate paper; also head and tail pieces in the text to each story.

Blank leaf (signed A) and half-title precede front.

pp. (viii) + (120) Q_2 imprint leaf, Q_3 Q_4 adverts.

Very fine.

Note. I include this juvenile (of which I am not conscious of having seen another copy) as an interesting consequence of the popularity of Mrs Ewing's famous story *The Brownies*, which was first published in 1870.

AGATHA'S HUSBAND: a Novel (by the author of 'Olive', 'The Head of the Family', etc.) [1806]

3 vols. Chapman & Hall 1853. Olive-brown wavy-grain cloth. In Vol. I front and back end-papers printed with adverts.; back end-papers unprinted in Vols. II and III.

Half-title in each vol.

Vol. I (vi) + 338 Final leaf, Z_1, a single inset.
II (iv) + 320
III (iv) + 312

Binders' ticket: 'Bone & Son', at end of each vol.

Note. I bought this book in Germany. On the title of Vol. I and fly-leaf of Vol. II are partially erased pencil attributions of the novel to 'Austen', 'Miss Bell' and 'Char Yonge', presumably experiments by a foreign bookseller in effective cataloguing. In ink on inside cover of Vol. I is written '9 Nov. 1853'.

BRAVE LADY (A) (by the author of 'John Halifax, Gentleman', etc.) [1807]

3 vols. Hurst & Blackett 1870. Magenta fine morocco cloth; red-chocolate end-papers.

Half-title in each vol.

Vol. I (vi) + (320) X_8 blank.
II (iv) + (298) Final leaf, U_5, a single inset.
III (iv) + (304) U_8 serves as fly-title, to Publishers' cat., 16 pp. undated, at end.

Book-plate of Joseph Beausire and ink signature: 'Fanny Adela Mary Beausire March 1870', in each vol. Cloth faded and back hinge of Vol. I split at base.

BREAD UPON THE WATERS: a Governess's Life (by the author of 'John Halifax, Gentleman') [1808]

Small 8vo. Governesses' Benevolent Institution, (1852). Red ribbed cloth, all edges gilt.

pp. (ii) + (110) First leaf of final sig., G_1, a single inset.

Ink inscription on title: 'Mary Ann Pittam. With Rev. C. Batchelor's best wishes. Jan. 13, 1875.' Bookseller's ticket: 'Cope Wolverhampton', inside front cover. Binder's ticket: 'W. Ellison' at end.

Notes. (i) 'Bread Upon the Waters' ends p. 96. pp. 97–109 are occupied with description of the work of the Governesses' Benevolent Institution, dated at the end March 17 1852.

(ii) The title of this copy is an inset on different paper. Probably a reprint-title and sheets of the original edition.

COLA MONTI, or the Story of a Genius (by the author of 'How to Win Love', 'Michael the Miner', etc.) [1809]

Small 8vo. Arthur Hall & Co. n.d. [1849]. Claret

ribbed cloth. Wood-engraved front. and 3 full-page illustrations after Franklin.

pp. (iv) + (260) Fine.

[1810] HALF-CASTE (The): an old Governess's Tale, etc. (by the author of 'John Halifax, Gentleman')

W. & R. Chambers 1897. Navy-blue ribbed cloth. Front. in half-tone on text paper signed H. C. P. M. and a few wood engravings in text.

pp. (240) O_8 adverts. Publishers' cat., 32 pp. undated, at end. A volume of early contributions to *Chambers' Journal*, issued as a posthumous tribute.

[1811] HEAD OF THE FAMILY (The): a Novel (by the author of 'Olive' and 'The Ogilvies')

Copy I: First Edition. 3 vols. Chapman & Hall 1852. Dark green fine-ribbed cloth, blocked in blind and lettered in gold. Primrose end-papers, of which the front ends in Vols. I and II are printed with publishers' adverts., but those in Vol. III and all back ends are blank.

Vol. I (iv) + (388)
II (ii) + 326 Final leaf, Z_1, a single inset.
III (ii) + 344

Binders' ticket: 'Bone & Son' at end of Vol. I. Pencil signature: 'W. D. Gainsford' on fly-leaf of each vol. and an approving comment on the story on last page of Vol. III. The novel is dedicated to Elizabeth Barrett Browning. Fine.

[1811*a*] **Copy II: First Illustrated Edition.** Macmillan 1875. Maroon diagonal-fine-ribbed cloth, blocked in black and gold on front and spine, in blind on back. Black end-papers. Wood-engraved front. and 5 illustrations on plate-paper after Walter Crane.

Half-title. pp. (viii) + (504) $2K_4$ blank.

Very fine.

[1812] JOHN HALIFAX, GENTLEMAN (by the author of 'The Head of the Family', 'Olive', etc. etc.)

3 vols. Hurst & Blackett 1856.

Copy I. Olive-brown wavy-grain cloth; primrose-yellow end-papers.

Vol. I (ii) + (324) Y_2 adverts. Publishers' cat., 24 pp. undated, at end.
II (ii) + (332)
III (ii) + (314) X_5 (single inset leaf) adverts.

Very fine. Small ink spot on hinge of Vol. III.

[1812*a*] **Copy II.** Earth-brown wavy-grain cloth; yellow-drab end-papers. Collation as Copy I, save that there is no catalogue at end of Vol. I.

Ink signature: 'Eliz[th] Villiers', inside front cover of each vol. Very fine. Small grease spot on front cover of Vol. II.

Note. These two copies show variations of spine lay-out and cloth-colour. For a detailed description and argument as to priority, see *More Binding Variants* by John Carter, pp. 28 seq. My notes, originally contributed to *Bibliographical Notes and Queries* (Oct. 1935), are reprinted in Carter's book.

LIFE FOR A LIFE (A) (by the author of 'John Halifax, Gentleman', 'A Woman's Thoughts about Women', etc. etc.) [1813]

3 vols. Hurst & Blackett 1859. Grey-purple diagonal-ripple-grain cloth.

Vol. I (iv) + (304)
II (ii) + (312) X_4 adverts.
III (ii) + 316 Publishers' cat., 16 pp. undated, at end.

Binders' ticket: 'Leighton, Son & Hodge' at end of Vol. I. Very fine.

NOTHING NEW: Tales (by the author of 'John Halifax, Gentleman') [1814]

2 vols. Hurst & Blackett 1857. Grey-purple morocco cloth.

Vol. I (ii) + 360
II (ii) + (316) Publishers' cat., 24 pp. undated, at end.

Presentation Copy: 'Marian. June 1857' in ink in author's hand on title of Vol. I. 'Marian James' (presumably in the hand of the recipient) on title of Vol. II. Fine.

OGILVIES (The): a Novel [anon] [1815]

3 vols. Chapman & Hall 1849. Grey-purple ribbed cloth.

Vol. I (iv) + 322 Final leaf, Y_1, a single inset.
II (ii) + (302) Final sigs., U 4 leaves, X 3 leaves; X_1 a single inset.
III (ii) + (320) X_8 adverts.

Booksellers' ticket: 'Cawthorn & Co. Cockspur St', on inside cover of Vol. I.

Traces of labels removed from inside cover of each vol., but cloth fine.

UNKIND WORD (The) and other Stories (by the author of 'John Halifax, Gentleman') [1816]

2 vols. Hurst & Blackett 1870. Bright brown fine-bead-grain cloth; dark violet end-papers.

Half-title in each vol.

Vol. I (vi) + (330) Final leaf, Y_5, a single inset.
II (iv) + (300) Publishers' cat., 16 pp. undated, at end.

Front covers damp-spotted at tail.

WOMAN'S KINGDOM (The): a Love Story (by the author of 'John Halifax, Gentleman', etc. etc.) [1817]

3 vols. Hurst & Blackett 1869. Smooth chocolate cloth, black end-papers.

Half-title in each vol.

Vol. I (vi) + (306) pp. (v) (vi), Dedication, and final leaf, X_1, single insets.
II (iv) + (296)
III (iv) + (296) U_4 serves as fly-title to Publishers' cat., 16 pp. undated, at end.

Bookseller's ticket: 'May, Bristol', inside front cover of each vol.

MURRAY, HON. CHARLES AUGUSTUS (1806-1895)

[1818] PRAIRIE BIRD (The)
3 vols. Bentley 1844. Boards, labels.
Vol. I iv + 336
II (ii) + 352
III (ii) + 372

Ink signature: 'Lord Carbery. 1844', on title of each vol. Spines renewed, but original labels, in fine condition, retained.

NEALE, W. JOHNSON (1812–1893)

[1819] CAPTAIN'S WIFE (The) (by the author of 'Cavendish', etc.)
3 vols. T. & W. Boone 1842. Half-cloth boards, labels.

Half-title in each vol.

Vol. I (vi) + (304) P_2 blank.
II (iv) + (304)
III (iv) + (312) O_{12} blank.

Booksellers' ticket: 'Meyler & Son, Bath', inside front cover of Vol. I.

[1820] GENTLEMAN JACK: a Naval Story (by the author of 'Cavendish', etc.)
3 vols. Colburn 1837. Boards, labels.

Half-title in Vol. II

Vol. I (iv) + (318) First leaf of final sig., P_1, a single inset.
II (iv) + (312) O_{12} adverts.
III (ii) + 356

Fine.

[1821] LAUREAD (The): a Literary, Political and Naval Satire (by the author of 'Cavendish')
Fcap 8vo. James Cochrane 1833. Glazed chocolate boards, black label up-lettered in gold.

Half-title and leaf of adverts. precede title. pp. (xvi) [paged (xii)] + (128) I_5–I_8 adverts.

Book-plate of Oliver Pemberton and ink signature: 'Jane Leech Feby. 14th 1833', on half-title. Small piece missing from foot of spine.

LOST SHIP (The), or the Atlantic Steamer (by the author of 'Cavendish', 'The Flying Dutchman'), etc. [1822]
3 vols. Colburn 1843. Half-cloth boards, labels.

Half-title in Vols. II and III

Vol. I iv + 300
II (iv) + 348
III (iv) + (334) P_{10} P_{11} adverts. First leaf of final sig., P_1, a single inset.

Book-plate of Sir William Symonds. Bookseller's ticket: 'Hearne, Strand', inside front cover of each vol. Ink signature: 'Sir Wm. Symonds R.N.', on title of each vol. Labels slightly defective.

WILL WATCH: from the Auto-biography of a British Officer (by the author of 'Cavendish', etc.) [1823]
3 vols. Cochrane 1834. Boards, labels.

Half-title in each vol.

Vol. I (vi) [paged viii] + (332) pp. (v) (vi) 'Preface', and a single inset.
II (iv) + (324) P_6 adverts.
III (iv) + (404) Text ends p. 376; [377]–[403] 'Statement and Correspondence relative to Captain Marryat', signed 'William Johnson Neale. November, 1834.'; (404) blank.

A poor copy: spines worn and discoloured.

Note. Marryat's version of his quarrel with Neale appeared in the *Metropolitan Magazine*, December 1834.

NEWMAN, JOHN HENRY (1801–1890)

CALLISTA: a Sketch of the Third Century [anon] [1824]
Fcap 8vo. Burns & Lambert (Cologne: J. P. Bachem) 1856. Dark blue straight-grain-morocco cloth, blocked in blind on front and back and gold-lettered on spine. Yellow end-papers printed in blue with advert. of The Catholic's Popular Library. Wood-engraved front. and decorative title, preceding printed title.

pp. iv + 296 Fine.

Note. This is No. XI in the Catholic's Popular Library. The advert. of the Series should reach No. X at the foot of inside back end-paper and final back end-paper should begin: NEW VOLUMES SHORTLY TO APPEAR / Callista: / a Tale of the Third Century. / Lives of St Francis of Sales and St Vincent / of Paul. / Alice Sherwin: / A Tale of the Times of Sir Thomas More, etc. etc.

LOSS AND GAIN [anon] [1825]
Sm. 8vo. James Burns, 17 Portman Street. 1848.

Dark gun-metal-blue fine-ribbed cloth, blocked with blind framing on front and back, with blind bands and gold-lettered (title only) on spine.

pp. (iv)+(390) CC_2 adverts., CC_3 blank. First leaf of final sig., CC_1, a single inset.

Ink signature: 'Frederick Bulley, 1848' on fly-leaf. Fine.

NICHOLSON, RENTON ('THE LORD CHIEF BARON NICHOLSON') (1809–1861)

[1826] COCKNEY ADVENTURES and Tales of London Life

8vo. W. M. Clark, 19 Warwick Lane and A. Forrester, 310 Strand. 1838. Dark green ribbon-embossed cloth, paper label up-printed with title and price (2*s.* 6*d.*) only. Two wood-engraved vignettes on text-paper in every 8 pp.

pp. (viii)+168

Issued from Nov. 4, 1837 to March 24, 1838, in 21 penny weekly numbers, each of 8 pp. printed d/c. Except in No. 1, where a cut appears on p. 1 and p. 8, the first page of each number carries two cuts. At the foot of each first page appears the words 'Vol. I'. Whether this indicates that the series continued I do not know. Neither label nor overall title gives any indication that the work is not complete.

Renton Nicholson was successively proprietor of the Garricks Head in Bow Street and of the Coal Hole, Fountain Court. He was also the creator of 'Judge and Jury' and founder and editor of *The Town*, a folio weekly paper of a relatively outrageous kind which ran to five volumes, 1837–1842. A 'New Series', frankly scabrous, appeared in 1849–1850. With this revival Nicholson had no concern.

[1827] DOMBEY AND DAUGHTER: a Moral Fiction

Royal 8vo. Thomas Farris, 340 Strand. n.d. [circ. 1850]. Twelve penny weekly parts, each of 8 pp., with a wood-engraving on the first page of each part, bound, uncut as issued, in new boards.

pp. (ii)+94 (final part, 6 pp., was originally completed by title-page, now prefixed to the series).

NOEL, LADY AUGUSTA (1838–1902)

[1828] FROM GENERATION TO GENERATION

2 vols. Macmillan 1879. Red-brown sand-grain cloth, gold-lettered on spine in the special angular caps affected by Macmillan at this period (cf. F. Marion Crawford, Henry James, Mrs Oliphant); black end-papers.

Half-title in each vol.

Vol. I vi+(288)
II vi+(312)

Book-plate of Macmillan & Co. in each vol. and blind stamp: 'FILE COPY', on back covers.

HITHERSEA MERE [1829]

3 vols. Macmillan 1887. Red-brown sand-grain cloth, uniform style with *From Generation to Generation*; black end-papers.

Blank leaf and half-title precede title in each vol.

Vol. I (viii) [paged vi]+(272)
II (viii) [paged vi]+248
III (viii)+(232)

Binder's ticket: 'Burn', at end of Vol. I. Blind stamp: 'FILE COPY' on front covers.

NORMANBY, CONSTANTINE HENRY PHIPPS, EARL MULGRAVE AND 1ST MARQUIS OF (1797–1863)

CONTRAST (The) (by the author of 'Matilda', 'Yes and No', etc.) [1830]

3 vols. Colburn & Bentley 1832. Boards, labels

Half-title in each vol.

Vol. I (viii)+288
II (iv)+258 First leaf of final sig., N_1, a single inset.
III (iv)+(252) M_5 M_6 adverts.

Book-label of 'R. J. Ll. Price, Rhiwlas Library' inside front cover of each vol. Very fine.

ENGLISH IN ITALY (The) [anon] [1831]

3 vols. Saunders & Otley 1825. Boards, labels.

Half-title in each vol.

Vol. I (vi) [paged ii]+(306) First leaf of final sig., P_1, a single inset.
II (iv)+(324)
III (iv)+(320) P_4 adverts.

Apart from pencil scribble on front end-papers of Vol. II, very fine.

HISTORIETTES, or Tales of Continental Life (by the author of 'The English in Italy') [1832]

3 vols. Saunders & Otley 1827. Boards, labels.

Half-title in each vol.

Vol. I xii+(ii) [single inset leaf, serving as fly-title to the first story]+(336) P_{12} blank. Longman etc. cat., 4 pp. dated February 1827, inserted between front end-papers.
II (iv)+352
III (iv)+(320) P_{11} P_{12} adverts.

Ink inscription: 'Dissington Hall', inside front cover of Vol. I. A rather frail copy—clean and unimproved, but a little weak at spines and hinges.

[1833] MATILDA: a Tale of the Day [anon]
Colburn 1825. Boards, label.
Half-title. pp. (viii) [paged (vi)]+(384) R_{11} R_{12} adverts.
Ink signature: 'Mary Chandos', on title. Very fine.

[1834] YES AND NO: a Tale of the Day (by the author of 'Matilda')
2 vols. Colburn 1828. Boards, labels.
Half-title in each vol.
Vol. I (viii)+(336)
II (iv)+(276) N_4–N_6 adverts.

NORTH, WILLIAM (1824–1854)

[1835] SLAVE OF THE LAMP (The): a Posthumous Novel
New York. H. Long & Brother, 121 Nassau St. 1855. Plum diagonal-ripple-grain cloth, blocked in blind on front and back, blocked and lettered in gold on spine.
Blank leaf and half-title precede title. pp. (444) [paged (i)–(xvi)+(17)–(444)] pp. (439)–(444) [19_4–19_6] adverts.
Cloth faded. Some internal foxing.
Note. William North, author of *Anti-Coningsby* (709*b*, above) left England for America in 1852, full of idealist enthusiasms for the liberty he expected to find. Two years later he committed suicide in New York. The MS. of this autobiographical novel, found in his room, was published within a year of his death with a brief but sympathetic memoir anonymously prefixed. The characters of *The Slave of the Lamp* are declared mainly recognizable, the most interesting to posterity being Fitzjames O'Brien, who appears as 'Fitzgammon O'Bouncer'.

NORTON, CAROLINE (1808–1877)

[1836] LOST AND SAVED
3 vols. Hurst & Blackett 1863. Grass-green dot-and-line-grain cloth; ox-blood end-papers.
Half-title in each vol.
Vol. I x+294 Owing to recasing I cannot say whether U_1 or U_3 is the single inset.
II vi+(304) U_8 blank
III vi+308 Publishers' adverts., 8 pp. undated, at end.
Presentation Copy: 'His Grace the Duke of Newcastle. With affectionate remembrance from the Author' in ink on half-title of Vol. I. Vol. I re-cased.

OLD SIR DOUGLAS [1837]
3 vols. Hurst & Blackett 1868. Dark green moiré-ribbed cloth; slate-purple end-papers.
Half-title in each vol.
Vol. I (viii)+308
II (iv)+(308)
III (iv)+308 Publishers' cat., 16 pp. undated, at end.
Presentation Copy: 'Marcia Sheridan with affectionate love from the Author Caroline Norton 1867' in ink, surrounded by hand-drawn decorative frame, facing half-title in Vol. I. Bookplate: 'R. B. S.' (Sheridan family plate), in each vol.

STUART OF DUNLEATH: a Story of Modern Times [1838] *Pl. 24*
3 vols. Colburn 1851.
Copy I. Half-cloth boards, labels.
Half-title in each vol.
Vol. I (xii)+290 Final leaf, O_1, a single inset.
II (iv)+(300)
III (iv)+(348) Q_6 blank.
Copy II. Green fine-ripple-grain cloth; yellow end-papers printed with adverts. [1838*a*] *Pl. 24*
Half-title in Vols. I and II. None in Vol. III. Otherwise collation as Copy I.
Binders' ticket: 'W. Johnson, Leicester St', at end of each vol. Ink inscription in each vol.: 'Emily Garthorne. Accept this as a trifling offering of *sincerest* affection from Rebecca Player, January 1st, 1855.'
Note. The half-title of Vol. III of Copy II was evidently omitted by the binder. The book is in fine condition and shows no trace of dismemberment.

WIFE AND WOMAN'S REWARD (The) [anon] [1839]
3 vols. Saunders & Otley 1835. Boards, labels.
Half-title in each vol.
Vol. I (iv)+308
II (iv)+(312)
III (iv)+(300) O_6 adverts.
Publishers' 4 pp. leaflet, undated, inset between front end-papers of Vol. I. Spines defective.
Note. The authorship of this novel is openly ascribed to Mrs Norton in Saunders & Otley's advert. at the end of the first edition of *Japhet in Search of a Father* and in *The Quarterly Advertiser*, February 1835.

VOLUME OF PAMPHLETS [1840]
The five pamphlets, which appear in their alphabetical order below, are described as 'Rosebery' copies. They are bound in one volume half-calf, marbled sides, red spine label lettered MRS NORTON. Rosebery

book-plate and blind stamp: 'The Durdans, Epsom', on title and p. 49 of *Separation of Mother and Child.*

[1840*a*] ENGLISH LAWS FOR WOMEN IN THE NINETEENTH CENTURY (by C. Norton)

8vo. 'London 1854.'

Half-title. pp. (vi) [paged iv] + (182) N_3 carries extract from *The Times* on recto. Text ends p. 170; (171)–(180) Appendix, paged (171)–176, but thereafter 7, 8, 9, 10. Final leaf, (181) (182), unpaged. As p. 176 ends M, and the first page of N is paged 7, I imagine that the last five leaves were conjugate with the three leaves of the prelims.

Ink inscription: 'A.D. 1854', on half-title. Rosebery copy.

[1840*b*] LETTERS etc. Dated from June 1836 to July 1841 (*Privately printed*)

No title or imprint, wording above appearing on fly-title. pp. 66 [paged (i)–vi + (7)–66] + (ii) + (56) + (52) The leaf following p. 66 is a fly-title to the Third and Fourth Correspondence. No 'Second Correspondence' is included in the volume.

Ink inscription: 'A.D. 1841', on first fly-title. The text of a letter (seven lines) printed on p. 50 of central section has been completely erased. Rosebery copy.

[1840*c*] LETTER TO THE QUEEN (A) on Lord Chancellor Cranworth's Marriage and Divorce Bill (by the Hon. Mrs Norton)

8vo. Longman etc. 1855. Pale green wrappers (front wrapper only preserved) with white side-label printed in black. pp. (156).

Inscribed in ink by the author on front wrapper: 'The Editor of the Caledonian Mercury, begging his attention from pp. 14–35 and pp. 141–149.'

Two holograph letters from Mrs Norton (3 leaves), endorsed on first blank recto by J. W. D. Grant (Editor of the *Caledonian Mercury*) with a message to (presumably) a reviewer, are bound before title.

The pages to which the author specially refers on the cover are heavily marked and underlined in red ink (? by her). Rosebery copy.

Note. I have seen a copy in dark-green wrappers of stouter quality, with same side-label.

[1840*d*] PLAIN LETTER (A) TO THE LORD CHANCELLOR ON THE INFANT CUSTODY BILL (by Pearce Stevenson, Esq.)

8vo. James Ridgway 1839.

Half-title. pp. (iv) + (126) I_7 Errata.

Ink inscription: 'A.D. 1839', on half-title. On title in ink in author's hand, the name Pearce Stevenson is crossed through and over-written 'Hon[b]. Mrs Norton under that name'. Rosebery copy.

SEPARATION OF MOTHER AND CHILD (THE) BY THE LAW OF 'CUSTODY OF INFANTS' CONSIDERED [anon] [1840*e*]

8vo. Roake & Varty, 31 Strand 1838.

Half-title. pp. (iv) + (76) F_6 adverts. Text ends p. 30; (31) (32) fly-title to Appendix; (33) to 73 Appendix; (74) blank; (75) (76) adverts.

Ink inscription: 'A.D. 1838', on half-title. Rosebery copy.

OLIPHANT, LAURENCE (1829–1888)

ALTIORA PETO [1841]

2 vols. large 8vo. Blackwood 1883. Smooth light brown cloth, pictorially blocked in dark brown and gold; dark brown end-papers. Wood-engraved front., pictorial title (printed in buff ochre and brown) and 1 full-page plate in each vol. after 'J.W.'

Half-title in each vol.

Vol. I (vi) + 286 A–S in eights, except K, which is 7 leaves, with K_1 a single inset.

II vi + (274) S_3–S_4 adverts. followed by a single advert. leaf. The vol. collates A–S in eights, except I and S, each 5 leaves. I_1 a single inset.

Armorial book-plate: 'Bertodano Solo', in each vol.

Note. This novel was published in four parts, dated 1883. It is, in my experience, very uncommon in cloth, and in such clean state as this copy, definitely rare.

MASOLLAM: a Problem of the Period. A Novel [1842]

3 vols. Blackwood 1886. Smooth pearl-grey cloth, elaborately blocked in chocolate and green; pale coffee end-papers with all-over design of peacock's feathers.

Half-title in each vol.

Vol. I (viii) + 278 First leaf of final sig., S_1, a single inset.

II (viii) + 284

III (viii) + (264) R_4 adverts. Publishers' cat., 24 pp. undated, at end.

Fine.

Note. Also issued in drab cloth, similarly blocked.

OLIPHANT, MRS MARGARET (1828–1897)

That few collectors at present care sufficiently for Mrs Oliphant to tackle her formidable bibliography may partially account for the fact that this series of first editions only includes 62 of her 95 published fictions. Nevertheless, even so incomplete a survey would have proved impossible but for the generosity of Messrs Macmillan & Co. Some years ago this firm decided to dispose of their office-file of lesser Victorian fiction, and were kind enough to allow me to choose and take away any titles I wanted. Without this exceptional contribution I should have been hard put to it to find a quarter of her output, so utterly do most of her books in original state seem to have vanished.

As will be seen, most of the Macmillan Oliphants are blind-stamped 'FILE' or 'FILE COPY' on their covers, a feature which seems to me as welcome a disfigurement as a review-copy stamp on a title, for it would be hard to have better evidence of a book's 'firstness' than that it went into the publishers' file. All these Macmillan copies are naturally in unused condition, but of varying brightness. Some are slightly darkened; others (notably *Joyce*, *The Second Son* and those in green diaper cloth) are brilliant.

Several of the earlier novels (of the Colburn and the Hurst & Blackett period up to 1858) end one of their volumes with a seven-leaf signature. I think this indicates that a leaf of labels (one actually survives in *Merkland*) originally completed the signature.

[1843] ADAM GRAEME OF MOSSGRAY, Memoirs and Resolutions of (by the author of 'Passages in the Life of Mrs Margaret Maitland', etc.)

3 vols. Colburn & Co. 1852. Grass-green ribbed cloth.

Vol. I (ii) + (302) U_7 adverts. (U is a seven-leaf sig., U_4 being a single inset). Publishers' cat., 16 pp. undated, at end.

II (ii) + 302 (final sig. U constructed as in Vol. I). Publishers' cat., 24 pp. undated, at end, followed by single inset leaf of adverts.

III (ii) + (332) Publishers' cat., 8 pp. undated, at end.

Fine.

Presentation Copy: 'Mrs. Barbour, with the Author's Compliments' in ink on fly-leaf of Vol. I.

Also issued in half cloth boards. Collation as above, but without publishers' catalogues.

[1844] ATHELINGS (The), or the Three Gifts

3 vols. Blackwood 1857. Dark bluish-green morocco cloth; chocolate end-papers.

Half-title in each vol.

Vol. I (iv) + (270) First leaf of final sig., R_1, a single inset.

II (iv) + (262) First leaf of final sig., R_1, a single inset.

III (iv) + 254 First leaf of final sig., Q_1, a single inset.

Binders' ticket: 'Edmonds & Remnants', at end of Vol. I. Fine.

[1845] AT HIS GATES

3 vols. Tinsley 1872. Claret sand-grain cloth, blocked in black on front and back, blocked in black and gold and gold-lettered on spine.

Half-title in each vol.

Vol. I (iv) + 304

II (iv) + 276

III (iv) + (288)

Presentation Copy: 'For my dear grandmamma (?). M.O.W.O. October 1872' in ink on title of Vol. I.

BELEAGUERED CITY (A): being a Narrative of Certain Recent Events in the City of Semur, in the Department of the Haute Bourgogne. A Story of the Seen and the Unseen [1846]

Macmillan 1880.

Copy I: Smooth dark blue cloth, unblocked but gold-lettered on front and spine; green flowered end-papers.

Half-title. pp. viii + (272) S_7 S_8 adverts. Publishers' cat., 40 pp. dated December 1879, at end.

Pencil signature: 'L. Tennyson, 4 Sussex Place, Regents Park', on half-title. This copy is rather used.

Copy II: Slate sand-grain cloth, blocked with bands of black and gold and gold-lettered on spine; black end-papers. Collation as Copy I.

Note. John Carter in *More Binding Variants* (p. 31) gives reasons for regarding Style I (dark blue cloth) as the earlier.

CALEB FIELD: a Tale of the Puritans (by the author of 'Passages in the Life of Mrs Margaret Maitland') [1847]

Colburn & Co. 1851. Bright blue morocco cloth; yellow end-papers printed with adverts.

pp. (xxiv) + (248) R_4 adverts. Publishers' cat., 24 pp. undated, at end.

Binders' ticket: 'Westleys', at end.

CHRONICLES OF CARLINGFORD [1848]

(First Series) THE RECTOR AND THE DOCTOR'S FAMILY [anon] [1848*a*]

Blackwood 1863. Red-brown dot-and-line-grain cloth; light chocolate end-papers.

Half-title. pp. (vi) + (292)

Binders' ticket: 'Edmonds and Remnants', at end. Front fly-leaf torn from this copy.

(Second Series) SALEM CHAPEL [anon] [1848*b*]

2 vols. Blackwood 1863. Cloth and end-papers uniform with First Series.

Half-title in each vol.

Vol. I (iv) + 362 Final leaf, $2A_1$, a single inset.

II (iv) + 354 Final leaf, Z_1, a single inset.

Binders' ticket: 'Edmonds and Remnants', at end of Vol. I. Book-label of Rev. Wm. Major Scott, M.A. in each vol. Ink inscription: 'With the Publishers Compts', on half-title of Vol. I.

(Third Series) THE PERPETUAL CURATE [anon] [1848*c*]

3 vols. Blackwood 1864. Cloth uniform with preceding series, but end-papers darker brown.

Leaf of adverts. and half-title precede title in Vol. I; half-title in Vols. II and III

Vol. I (viii) + 312 Publishers' cat., 20 pp. undated and in smaller format, followed by 4 pp. adverts. in same format as the novel, at end.
II (iv) + (328)
III (iv) + (296)

Binders' ticket: 'Edmonds & Remnants', at end of Vol. I. Very fine.

[1848*d*] **(Fourth Series)** MISS MARJORIBANKS [anon]

3 vols. Blackwood 1866. Cloth and end-papers uniform with First and Second Series.

Half-title in each vol.

Vol. I (iv) + 284
II (iv) + 292
III (iv) + 296 Publishers' cat., 20 pp. undated, at end.

Binders' ticket: 'Edmonds & Remnants', at end of Vol. I. Fine.

[1848*e*] **(Fifth and Last Series)** PHŒBE, JUNIOR: a Last Chronicle of Carlingford

3 vols. Hurst & Blackett 1876. Smooth red-brown cloth, in colour and style of spine-lettering vaguely reminiscent of the Blackwood Series. Black end-papers.

Half-title in each vol.

Vol. I (iv) + (316) X_6 adverts.
II (iv) + 310 Second leaf of final sig., X_2, a single inset.
III (iv) + 330 Third leaf of final sig., Y_3, a single inset. Publishers' cat., 16 pp. undated, at end.

[1849] COUNTRY GENTLEMAN AND HIS FAMILY (A)

3 vols. Macmillan 1886. Slate sand-grain cloth; black end-papers.

Half-title in each vol.

Vol. I (iv) + (244)
II (iv) + (244) R_2 adverts.
III (iv) + (228) Q_2 adverts.

Fine.

[1850] DAYS OF MY LIFE (The): an Autobiography (by the author of 'Margaret Maitland', etc.)

3 vols. Hurst & Blackett 1857. Slate straight-grain morocco cloth.

Vol. I (iv) + 290 Final leaf, U_1, a single inset. Publishers' cat., 24 pp. undated, at end.
II (ii) + (296)
III (ii) + 294 Final leaf, U_3, a single inset.

Traces of booksellers' price ticket on spine of Vol. I.

DIANA TRELAWNEY: the History of a Great Mistake [1851]

2 vols. Blackwood 1892. Blue morocco cloth; very dark grey end-papers.

Blank leaf precedes title in each vol.

Vol. I (vi) + (228) Publishers' cat., 24 pp. undated, at end.
II (vi) + (238) First leaf of final sig., P_1, a single inset. Publishers' cat., 24 pp. undated, at end.

Violet ink stamp: 'With the Publishers Compliments', on title of Vol. I. Very fine.

DUKE'S DAUGHTER AND THE FUGITIVES (The) [1852]

3 vols. Blackwood 1890. Smooth violet-blue cloth; very dark brown end-papers.

Half-title in each vol.

Vol. I (x) + 256 Half-title a single inset.
II (vi) + 252 Publishers' cat., 24 pp. undated, at end.
III (iv) + (284) S_6 blank.

Blind stamp: 'With the Publishers' compliments', on title of Vol. I. This copy is a little used.

EFFIE OGILVIE: the Story of a Young Life [1853]

2 vols. Glasgow: James Maclehose & Sons 1886. Smooth blue cloth.

Half-title in each vol.

Vol. I (242) Final leaf, (Q_1), a single inset. Publishers' cat., 20 pp. dated August 1884, at end.
II (258) Final leaf, (R_1), imprint leaf and a single inset.

Ink signature: 'Jeanie N. Boschette A.H.N.B.', on titles.

HARRY JOSCELYN [1854]

3 vols. Hurst & Blackett 1881. Brown diagonal-fine-ribbed cloth, blocked and lettered in black on front, gold-lettered and black-blocked on spine. Grey-chocolate end-papers.

Half-title in each vol.

Vol. I (iv) + 316
II (iv) + 304
III (iv) + 312 Publishers' cat., 16 pp. undated, at end. 'B. Hoddinott' rubber-stamped, facing half-title in each vol.

HARRY MUIR: a Story of Scottish Life (by the author of 'Passages in the Life of Mrs Margaret Maitland') [1855]

3 vols. Hurst & Blackett 1853. Olive-green morocco cloth.

Vol. I (ii) + 290 Final leaf, U_1, a single inset. Publishers' cat., 8 pp. dated February 1853, followed by a second cat., 16 pp. undated, at end.
II (ii) + 302 Fourth leaf of final sig., U_4, a single inset. Publishers' cat., 8 pp. undated, at end.
III (ii) + (312) X_4 adverts.

'Sedbury' in ink inside front covers. The fly-leaves of Vol. I are partially stuck down to covers.

[1856] HEART AND CROSS (by the author of 'Margaret Maitland', etc.)
Hurst & Blackett 1863. Scarlet coarse-morocco cloth.
Half-title. pp. (iv) + (304) Publishers' cat., 8 pp. undated, at end.

[1857] HESTER: a Story of Contemporary Life
3 vols. Macmillan 1883. Slate sand-grain cloth; dark grey end-papers.
Half-title in each vol.
Vol. I (viii) + (264)
II (viii) + (256) Publishers' cat., 32 pp. dated October 1883, at end.
III (viii) + 264
Blind stamp: 'FILE COPY', on front covers.

[1858] HE THAT WILL NOT WHEN HE MAY
3 vols. Macmillan 1880. Slate sand-grain cloth; black end-papers.
Half-title in each vol.
Vol. I (viii) + 280
II (viii) + 280
III (viii) + (280) T_3 T_4 adverts.
Book-plate of Macmillan & Co. in each vol. and blind stamp: 'FILE COPY', on back covers.

[1859] HOUSE DIVIDED AGAINST ITSELF (A)
3 vols. Blackwood 1886. Smooth dark blue cloth; buff-on-white designed end-papers with acorns and oak leaves.
Half-title in each vol.
Vol. I (iv) + 310 Last 3 leaves, sig. U (2 leaves) + X_1, a single inset.
II (iv) + (308) (U_2) blank.
III (iv) + 310 Last 3 leaves as in Vol. I.
Book-label: 'Martha Napier', in each vol. Very fine.

[1860] HOUSE ON THE MOOR (The) (by the author of 'Margaret Maitland', etc.)
3 vols. Hurst & Blackett 1861. Violet wavy-grain cloth.

Vol. I (iv) + 338 Final leaf, Z_1, a single inset.
II (ii) + 340
III (ii) + 300 Publishers' cat., 6 pp. undated, at end.
Book-plate of Richard Urwick in each vol.

IT WAS A LOVER AND HIS LASS [1861]
3 vols. Hurst & Blackett 1883. Dark red diagonal-fine-ribbed cloth; black end-papers.
Half-title in each vol.
Vol. I (iv) + 324
II (iv) + 332
III (iv) + (336) Y_8 serves as fly-title to publishers' cat., 16 pp. undated, at end.
Monogram book-plate 'JRSS' (?) in each vol.

JANET [1862]
3 vols. Hurst & Blackett 1891. Smooth crimson cloth; light milky-green end-papers.
Half-title in each vol.
Vol. I (iv) + (300) U_6 blank.
II (iv) + (292)
III (iv) + 276 Publishers' cat., 16 pp. dated 1891, at end.

JOHN DRAYTON: being the History of the Early Life and Development of a Liverpool Engineer [anon] [1863]
2 vols. Bentley 1851. Plum ribbed cloth.
Half-title in each vol.
Vol. I (iv) + (284)
II (iv) + (272)
Presentation Copy: 'Jane Orr Moir from Mrs Oliphant 15th March, 1868' in ink in Mrs Oliphant's hand on half-title of Vol. I. Cloth shabby.
Note. This book, like *The Melvilles*, was written for the benefit of Mrs Oliphant's brother, Rev. William Wilson.

JOYCE [1864]
3 vols. Macmillan 1888. Slate sand-grain cloth, angular lettering of the style favoured by the publishers at the period; black end-papers.
Half-title in each vol.
Vol. I (iv) + (316) X_6 adverts.
II (iv) + 316
III (iv) + (308) X_2 adverts.

KIRSTEEN: a Story of a Scotch Family Seventy Years Ago [1865]
3 vols. Macmillan 1890. Grass-green diaper cloth, uniform with *Neighbours on the Green* (q.v. below).
Half-title in each vol.

Vol. I (iv)+(272) S_8 adverts. Publishers' cat., 60 pp. dated August 1890, at end.
II (iv)+(272) S_8 adverts.
III (iv)+(300) U_5 U_6 adverts.

Binder's ticket: 'Burn', at end of Vol. I. Blind stamp: 'FILE', on front covers.

Note. As a comment on *Kirsteen* I append the following utterance by Henry James concerning the work of Mrs Oliphant, reputed to have been recorded verbatim by A. C. Benson very shortly after it had been made, and quoted by Simon Nowell Smith (without guarantee) in *The Legend of the Master* (London 1947):

'I had not read a *line* that the poor woman had written for *years*, not for years. When she died, Henley—do you know the rude, boisterous, windy, headstrong Henley?—Henley, as I say, said to me: "Have you read *Kirsteen*?" I replied that, as a matter of fact—h'm—I had not read it. Henley said: "that you should have any pretensions to interest in literature and should dare to say that you have not read *Kirsteen*!" I took my bludgeoning patiently and humbly, my dear Arthur, went back and read it, and was at once confirmed, after twenty pages, in my belief—I laboured through the book—that the poor soul had a simply *feminine* conception of literature; such slipshod, imperfect, halting, faltering, peeping, down-at-heel work—buffeting along like a ragged creature in a high wind, and just struggling to the goal, and falling in a quivering mass of faintness and fatuity.'

[1866] LADIES LINDORES (The)
3 vols. Blackwood 1883. Smooth olive-green cloth; dark brown end-papers.

Half-title in each vol.

Vol. I (iv)+300
II (iv)+300
III (iv)+(336) X_8 adverts.

Very fine.

[1867] LADY WILLIAM
3 vols. Macmillan 1893. Grass-green diaper cloth, uniform in style with *Neighbours on the Green.*

Half-title in each vol.

Vol. I (iv)+288
II (iv)+(288)
III (iv)+(284)

Blind stamp: 'FILE', on front covers.

[1868] LAIRD OF NORLAW (The): a Scottish Story (by the author of 'Margaret Maitland', etc.)
3 vols. Hurst & Blackett 1858. Dark green morocco cloth.

Vol. I (ii)+318 First leaf of final sig., X_1, a single inset.
II (ii)+338 Final leaf, Z_1, a single inset.
III (ii)+(346) Final leaf, Z_5, a single inset.

Very fine.

LAST OF THE MORTIMERS (The): a Story in Two Voices (by the author of 'Margaret Maitland', etc.) [1869]
3 vols. Hurst & Blackett 1862. Green coarse-morocco cloth.

Vol. I (ii)+306 Final leaf, X_1, a single inset.
II (ii)+(322) Final leaf, Y_1, a single inset.
III (ii)+(318) First leaf of final sig., X_1, a single inset. Publishers' cat., 16 pp. undated, at end.

Library labels inside front covers. Vol. II loose in covers.

LILLIESLEAF: being a concluding Series of Passages in the Life of Mrs Margaret Maitland of Sunnyside. Written by herself [anon] [1870]
3 vols. Hurst & Blackett 1855. Dark blue morocco cloth; deep rose end-papers.

Vol. I (ii)+306 First leaf of final sig., O_1, a single inset. Publishers' cat., 16 pp. undated, at end.
II (ii)+(308) O_{10} adverts.
III (ii)+300 Publishers' cat., 24 pp. undated, at end.

Binders' ticket: 'Leighton, Son & Hodge', at end of Vol. I. Book-label of Eliza Farnaby in each vol. and ink signature: 'Miss Traill', facing title in each vol. Fine.

LITTLE PILGRIM IN THE UNSEEN (A) [anon] [1871]
Macmillan 1882. Smooth pale grey cloth.

Half-title. pp. (viii)+(148)

Ink signature: 'L. Done, Christmas 1882', on half-title. Board of front cover creased.

LUCY CROFTON (by the author of 'Margaret Maitland', etc.) [1872]
Hurst & Blackett 1860. Dark green morocco cloth.

pp. (ii)+(318) First leaf of final sig., X_1, a single inset.

Presentation Copy: 'Jane O. Moir, with love and best wishes M.O.W.O. 28 Dec[r] 1860' in ink on fly-leaf. A worn copy.

MADAM [1873]
3 vols. Longmans, etc. 1885. Scarlet diagonal-fine-ribbed cloth. Pale grey-on-white flowered end-papers.

Half-title in each vol.

Vol. I (iv) + (292)
II (iv) + (296) U_4 blank.
III (iv) + 264 Publishers' cat., 12 pp. dated July 1884, at end.

A composite set, for Vol. III has W. H. Smith Library label inside front cover, but clean and uniform in state.

[1874] MADONNA MARY
3 vols. Hurst & Blackett 1867. Smooth purple cloth, bevelled boards; dark grey end-papers.

Half-title in each vol.

Vol. I (iv) + 300
II (iv) + 304
III (iv) + 280 Publishers' cat., 16 pp. dated October 1866, at end.

Ink signature: 'John Cordy Jeaffreson', on title in each vol. Spines darkened and cloth rather chafed.

[1875] MAGDALEN HEPBURN: a Story of the Scottish Reformation (by the author of 'Passages in the Life of Mrs Margaret Maitland')
3 vols. Hurst & Blackett 1854. Grey-purple wide-wavy-grain cloth.

Vol. I (ii) + 300 Publishers' cat., 24 pp. undated, at end.
II (ii) + (296) O_4 adverts.
III (ii) + (308) P_4 adverts.

Spines faded and cloth a little marked, but sharp and sound.

[1876] MARRIAGE OF ELINOR (The)
3 vols. Macmillan 1892. Grass-green diaper cloth, uniform in style with *Neighbours on the Green.*

Half-title in each vol.

Vol. I (iv) + (276) Publishers' cat., 4 pp. dated '20. 1. 92', at end.
II (iv) + (284) T_6 blank. Publishers' cat., 4 pp. dated '20. 1. 92', inset between pp. (282) (283).
III (iv) + 260 Publishers' cat., 44 pp. dated December 1891, at end.

Binder's ticket: 'Burn', at end of Vol. I. Blind stamp: 'FILE', on front covers.

[1877] MELVILLES (The) (by the author of 'John Drayton')
3 vols. Bentley 1852. Grey-purple perpendicular-fine-ribbed cloth, blocked in blind and lettered in gold.

Advert. leaf precedes title in Vol. I

Vol. I (iv) + (290) Final leaf, O_1, a single inset.
II (ii) + 304
III (ii) + (298) Third leaf of final sig., O_3, a single inset.

Fine.

MERKLAND: a Story of Scottish Life (by the author of 'Passages in the Life of Mrs Margaret Maitland') [1878]
3 vols. Colburn 1851.

Copy I. Half-cloth boards, labels.

Vol. I (ii) + 322 Second leaf of final sig., P_2, a single inset.
II (ii) + 292
III (ii) + (304) O_8 undivided leaf of spine-labels. The binder evidently used a set in error from the sheets of another copy.

Copy II. Grass-green ribbed cloth. Collation as Copy I, except that in Vol. III O_8 is cut away and a publisher's cat., 24 pp. undated, follows p. (302). [1878*a*]

Presentation Copy: 'Mrs Barbour, with the Author's compliments' in ink on fly-leaf of Vol. I.

MINISTER'S WIFE (The) [1879]
3 vols. Hurst & Blackett 1869. Smooth green cloth, bevelled boards; grey lilac end-papers.

Half-title in each vol.

Vol. I (vi) + 304 Publishers' cat., 16 pp. undated, at end.
II (iv) + (338) Final leaf, Z_1, a single inset.
III (iv) + 352

Bookseller's ticket: 'May, Bristol', inside front cover of each vol. Very fine.

MYSTERY OF MRS BLENCARROW (The) [1880]
Richard Edward King, Tabernacle Street, E.C., n.d. Olive-green diagonal-fine-ribbed cloth.

pp. (iv) + 186 Final leaf, 12_5, a single inset. Fine.

Note. This has an inset title on different paper. The book was originally published in [1890] by Spencer Blackett and issued in smooth black cloth, blocked and lettered in white.

NEIGHBOURS ON THE GREEN [1881]
3 vols. Macmillan 1889. Grass-green diaper cloth; black end-papers. The lettering is in the angular style favoured by the publishers at this period (cf. F. Marion Crawford, Henry James, Lady Augusta Noel).

Half-title in each vol.

Vol. I (viii) + 312 Publishers' cat., 32 pp. dated April 1888, at end.
II (viii) + (344)
III (viii) + (276) BB_2–BB_4 adverts.

Binder's ticket: 'Burn', at end of each vol. Blind stamp: 'FILE', on front covers.

ORPHANS: a Chapter in a Life (by the author of 'Margaret Maitland', etc.) [1882]
Hurst & Blackett 1858. Black ripple-grain cloth.

pp. (ii)+(318) X_7 adverts. Title-page and first leaf of final sig., X_1, single insets. Publishers' cat., 24 pp. undated, at end.

Binders' ticket: 'Leighton, Son & Hodge', at end.

Fine.

[1883] PASSAGES IN THE LIFE OF MRS MARGARET MAITLAND OF SUNNYSIDE. Written by Herself [anon]

3 vols. Colburn 1849. Grass-green ribbed cloth.

Vol. I (ii)+300 Publisher's cat., 16 pp. undated on text paper, at end.
II (ii)+(316) (P_2) adverts.
III (ii)+324

Presentation Copy: 'Robert Barton Esq. with the Author's respectful compliments' in ink on fly-leaf of Vol. I.

Also issued in half-cloth boards.

[1884] POOR GENTLEMAN (A)

3 vols. Hurst & Blackett 1889. Smooth dark-sage-green cloth; dark grey end-papers.

Half-title in each vol.

Vol. I (vi)+(298) First leaf of final sig., U_1, a single inset.
II (vi)+298 First leaf of final sig., U_1, a single inset.
III (vi)+298 First leaf of final sig., U_1, a single inset. Publishers' cat., 8 pp. undated, at end.

[1885] PRIMROSE PATH (The): a Chapter in the Annals of the Kingdom of Fife

3 vols. Hurst & Blackett 1878. Blue-green diagonal-fine-ribbed cloth; plum end-papers.

Half-title in each vol.

Vol. I (vi)+332
II (iv)+(332)
III (iv)+(346) First leaf of final sig., Z_1, a single inset. Publishers' cat., 16 pp. undated, at end.

[1886] PRODIGALS AND THEIR INHERITANCE (The)

2 vols. Methuen 1894. Brown ribbed cloth.

Half-title in each vol.

Vol. I 188 Publishers' cat., 24 pp. dated April 1894, at end.
II (iv)+(189)–380 Publishers' cat., 24 pp. dated April 1894, at end.

Fine.

Note. The pagination runs through from start to finish. Presumably two-vol. issue was an afterthought, unless continuous pagination was in prudent preparation for a one-vol. novel if the outcry from the Libraries proved louder than the publishers could endure.

QUIET HEART (The) (by the author of 'Katie Stewart') [1887]

Blackwood 1854. Royal-blue morocco cloth, blocked in blind on front and back, blocked and lettered in gold on spine.

Half-title. pp. (iv)+320

Binders' ticket: 'Edmonds and Remnants' at end. Fine.

RAILWAY MAN AND HIS CHILDREN (The) [1888]

3 vols. Macmillan 1891. Grass-green diaper cloth, uniform in style with *Neighbours on the Green.*

Half-title in each vol.

Vol. I (iv)+(284) T_6 adverts.
II (iv)+(280)
III (iv)+264

Blind stamp: 'FILE', on front covers.

SECOND SON (The) [1889]

3 vols. Macmillan 1888. Slate sand-grain cloth; black end-papers.

Blank leaf and half-title precede title in each vol.

Vol. I (viii)+(288)
II (viii)+(256)
III (viii)+(264) S_3 S_4 adverts. Publishers' cat., 32 pp. dated September 1887, at end.

Violet ink stamp: 'With the Publishers' compliments', on each title.

Note. This novel was written in collaboration with Thomas Bailey Aldrich, but his name only appears on half-titles, not on titles or covers.

SIR ROBERT'S FORTUNE: the Story of a Scotch Moor [1890]

Methuen 1895. Red ribbed cloth.

Half-title. pp. (iv)+(412) Publishers' cat., 32 pp. dated April 1895, at end.

Black stain along fore-edge of front cover.

SIR TOM [1891]

3 vols. Macmillan 1884. Slate sand-grain cloth; dark grey end-papers.

Half-title in each vol.

Vol. I (viii)+(264) S_4 adverts. Publishers' cat., 32 pp. dated May 1884, at end.
II (viii)+(276)
III (viii)+(268) S_6 adverts.

Binder's ticket: 'Burn', at end of each vol. Blind stamp: 'FILE COPY', on front covers.

SON OF HIS FATHER (The) [1892]

3 vols. Hurst & Blackett 1887. Smooth olive-green cloth.

Half-title in each vol.

Vol. I (vi)+322 Final leaf, Y_1, a single inset.
II (vi)+(318) Final leaf, X_7, a single inset.
III (vi)+(312) X_4 serves as fly-title to Publishers' cat., 16 pp. undated, at end.

[1893] SONS AND DAUGHTERS: a Novel
Blackwood 1890. Olive-drab sand-grain cloth, blocked with all-over design in red-brown, and gold-lettered; chocolate end-papers.
Half-title. pp. (iv)+(220) O_5 O_6 adverts. Publishers' cat., 24 pp. dated '9/90', at end. Fine.

[1894] SQUIRE ARDEN
3 vols. Hurst & Blackett 1871. Violet sand-grain cloth, blocked in black on front and back with ornate framing and on front lettered in black also; on spine elaborately blocked in black and lettered in gold. Reddish chocolate end-papers.
Half-title in each vol.
Vol. I (iv)+320
II (iv)+(336)
III (iv)+(332) Final leaf, Z_2, serves as fly-title to publishers' cat., 16 pp. undated, at end.
Ink signature: 'Mrs Andrew Becker, Whitchurch Rectory' on title of Vol. I; name only in II and III. Booksellers' ticket: 'E. J. and F. Blackwell, Reading' inside front cover of each vol.
Spines faded and cloth a little used, but a sound decent copy.

[1895] STORY OF VALENTINE AND HIS BROTHER (The)
3 vols. Blackwood 1875. Violet bubble-grain cloth, blocked in black and gold on front, in blind on back; gold-lettered on spine. Chocolate end-papers.
Half-title in each vol. (that in Vol. III torn from this copy).
Vol. I (vi)+314 Half-title and first leaf of final sig., V_1, single insets.
II (iv)+(308) U_2 blank.
III (iv)+(300)
'From the Author' in a clerk's hand in ink on half-title of Vol. I. A poor copy.

[1896] THAT LITTLE CUTTY: DOCTOR BARÈRE: ISABEL DYSART
Macmillan 1898. Pale apple-green ribbed cloth.
Blank leaf and half-title precede title. pp. (viii)+(244) R_2 adverts. Publishers' cat., 16 pp. dated '50' (*sic*). 1. 98' at end.

[1897] TWO STRANGERS
Slim 8vo. T. Fisher Unwin 1894. Terra-cotta paper wrappers printed in black; also in brownish-buff linen, blocked and lettered in dark blue.
Leaf of adverts. and half-title precede title. pp. (208) N_3–N_8 publisher's cat., undated.
No. 5 in Unwin's Autonym Library.

UNJUST STEWARD (The), or the Minister's Debt [1898]
W. & R. Chambers 1896. Light blue ribbed cloth.
Half-title. pp. (viii)+(312)

WHO WAS LOST AND IS FOUND: a Novel [1899]
Blackwood 1894. Dark red linen-grain cloth.
Half-title. pp. (iv)+372 Publishers' cat., 32 pp. dated '10/94', at end.

WIDOW'S TALE (A) and Other Stories. With an Introductory Note by J. M. Barrie [1900]
Blackwood 1898. Green linen flecked with white; olive-green end-papers.
Half-title. pp. (x)+418 Half-title a single inset. Publishers' cat., 32 pp. dated '5/98', at end.
Blind stamp: 'With the Publishers Compliments', on title.

WIZARD'S SON (The): a Novel [1901]
3 vols. Macmillan 1884. Slate sand-grain cloth; black end-papers.
Half-title in each vol.
Vol. I (iv)+(296) U_4 adverts.
II (iv)+(296) U_4 adverts.
III (iv)+292
Binders' ticket: 'Burn', at end of Vol. I. Book-plate of Macmillan & Co. in each vol. and blind stamp: 'FILE COPY', on front covers.

YOUNG MUSGRAVE [1902]
3 vols. Macmillan 1877. Slate sand-grain cloth; black end-papers.
Half-title in each vol.
Vol. I (viii)+276
II (viii)+(268) S_6 adverts.
III (viii)+(224) P_7 P_8 adverts. Publishers' cat., 40 pp. dated October 1877, at end.
Book-plate of Macmillan & Co. in each vol. (too lavishly pasted-in and stuck to the fly-leaf) and blind stamp: 'FILE COPY', on back covers.

ZAIDEE: a Romance [1903]
3 vols. Blackwood 1856. Pinkish-maroon wavy-grain cloth; terra-cotta end-papers.
Half-title in each vol.
Vol. I (iv)+268
II (iv)+286 First leaf of final sig., S_1, a single inset.
III (iv)+(312)
The spine of Vol. I is slightly torn at head.

OLLIER, CHARLES (1788–1859)

[1904] FERRERS: a Romance of the Reign of George the Second

3 vols. Bentley 1842. Dark green fine-morocco cloth, unblocked; paper labels.

Half-title in each vol.

Vol. I (iv)+(304)
II (iv)+312
III (iv)+314 Final leaf, P_1, a single inset.

Fine. A few sections loose.

Ink-inscription on inside front cover of Vol. I. 'This wretched work is said to be now rare, having been suppressed. L. M. Shirley. 1867.' The Bentley Private Catalogue makes no reference to suppression, merely describing the story as in the manner of Ainsworth but greatly inferior.

OUIDA (LOUISA RAMÉ; LOUISE DE LA RAMÉE) (1839–1908)

This is a complete collection of the first editions of Ouida, except for one novel (*In a Winter City*, 1876), an anti-vivisection tract (*The New Priesthood*, 1893) and a volume of essays (*Views and Opinions*, 1895). Descriptions of these are provided from copies in the Statutory Libraries.

It will add to the interest of the important series of presentation and association copies to make clear the principal personalities concerned. Ouida's godmother (to whom in her teens she became passionately attached) was a Mrs Le Neve. This lady, after the death of her husband, became Mrs Harding and had a son named Claud. When Mr Harding died, she married a third time and became Mrs Drane. She and Mr Drane remained on terms of intimate affection with Ouida all their lives, and Mrs Drane's son, Commander Harding, R.N., was naturally of their circle. Ouida had played with Claud as a small boy, and the friendship lasted. Evidently he inherited his mother's copies of the novelist's works.

It should be observed that from *Two Little Wooden Shoes* (1874) onwards, the inscriptions in Mrs Drane's copies are not in Ouida's hand but (presumably) in her own. Ouida settled permanently in Florence in 1874, and would naturally cause copies of her books to be sent direct to her old friend from the publishers.

The survival of this ample series of presentation copies provides welcome evidence of Ouida's propensity for special bindings on books destined for intimate friends. Sometimes she chose a cloth of a different colour and texture and elaborated the blocking; sometimes she added extra gold and her name or monogram to the regulation cloth; sometimes she used white or cream cloth additionally gilt. Frequently these special copies had all edges gilt and end-papers of peculiar elegance. To the best of my knowledge *Puck* (1870) was the first book to receive this treatment; and although there are among the later titles several I have never seen in presentation bindings, such may well have been produced.

In *Private Angelo* by Eric Linklater (London 1946) we read: 'The Countess was devoted to the novels of Ouida, and in every one of the several houses belonging to the Count there was a complete set of her works. Here, in Pontefiore, was the finest of them all. Bound in a soft white leather, adorned with golden blossoms, it had been Ouida's own property—and poor Ouida had sold it in the sad years before her death.' Is this Mr Linklater's invention? I can hardly believe it, for such a set would be so absolutely 'right'. I hope one existed, and still survives, despite the vandalism of the Germans as described in *Private Angelo*.

ALTRUIST (An) [1905]

Slim 8vo. Fisher Unwin 1897. Smooth apple-green cloth, blocked and lettered on front in brick-red, dark green and gold, gold-lettered on spine.

Leaf bearing publisher's device, leaf advertising Autonym Library, etc., and half-title precede title. pp. (240) K_5–K_{12} adverts. dated 1897.

Not a fresh copy.

ARIADNÊ: the Story of a Dream [1906]

3 vols. Chapman & Hall and Chatto & Windus 1877. Royal-blue diagonal-fine-ribbed cloth, blocked in black and lettered in gold.

Blank leaf and half-title precede title in Vol. I; half-title only in Vols. II and III

Vol. I (viii)+308
II (iv)+(268) Chatto & Windus cat., 32 pp. dated May 1877, at end.
III (iv)+(262) First leaf of final sig., S_1, a single inset. Chatto & Windus cat., 32 pp. dated May 1877, at end.

Book-plate of Claud Harding, R.N., in each vol. Fine.

Note. Apart from stating that with *Ariadnê* Ouida definitely changed her publishers, Miss Yvonne ffrench (in *Ouida: a Study in Ostentation*, London 1938) does not explain the curious double imprint. Presumably it was a compromise between the old love and the new, made to satisfy some conflict of claim.

BEATRICE BOVILLE and Other Stories [1907

New York: Carleton 1867. Dark maroon sand-grain cloth; pale blue end-papers.

Blank leaf and half-title precede title. pp. 384 [paged (i)–(viii), mispaged vi, +(9)–384]

Note. The second of the five stories in this volume (*Lady Marabout's Troubles*) was included in *Cecil Castlemaine's Gage*, London, 1867 (q.v.): the rest appeared here for the first time in book form.

[1908] **BIMBI**: Stories for Children
Chatto & Windus 1882. Smooth light blue-green cloth, blocked and lettered in brown and gold; grey flowered end-papers.

Half-title. pp. (viii) + (340) Z_2 publishers' device. Publishers' cat., 32 pp. dated November 1881, at end.

Binder's ticket: 'Burn', at end.

[1909] **CECIL CASTLEMAINE'S GAGE** and Other Novelettes
Chapman & Hall 1867. Crimson sand-grain cloth. Wood-engraved front. illegibly signed.

pp. (iv) + (492)

Binders' ticket: 'Bone & Son', at end.

Presentation Copy: 'To L. N. Drane from Ouida' in fanciful and violent lettering on verso of fly-leaf.

Rather loose in covers and spine slightly bubbled.

[1910] **CHANDOS**: a Novel
3 vols. Chapman & Hall 1866. Bright brown fine-morocco cloth.

Vol. I (vi) + 346 Final leaf, $2A_1$, a single inset.
II (vi) + 348
III (vi) + 400

Presentation Copy: 'To L. N. Drane with the most affectionate regards of true friendship' in fanciful ink lettering on fly-leaf of Vol. I. Very fine.

[1911] **CRITICAL STUDIES**: a Set of Essays
8vo. T. Fisher Unwin 1900. Smooth pale green cloth, blocked and lettered in gold; bevelled boards.

Half-title. pp. (viii) + (316) X_2 adverts. Final sigs., U 4 leaves, X 2 leaves.

Back cover damp-stained.

[1912] **DOG OF FLANDERS** (A) and Other Stories
8vo. Chapman & Hall 1872. Dark green sand-grain cloth, blocked in black and lettered in gold. Wood-engraved front. and 3 full-page illustrations after Enrico Mazzanti.

Half-title. pp. (viii) + (296) U_4 adverts. Fine.

[1913] **DOGS**
Simpkin Marshall 1897. Buff paper wrappers pictorially printed in red and black on front, unlettered on spine and printed in black with adverts. on inside front and both back covers. Six full-page half-tone illustrations of different types of dog.

Leaf of adverts., half-title and photograph of the Bull Dog precede title. pp. (124) I_5 I_6 adverts.

Lower corner of pages faintly damp-stained.

DON GESUALDO [1914]
Small 8vo. Routledge 1886.

Copy I: as published. Buff paper wrappers, printed with title, author and decoration in green, red and black on front, title and author in black on spine, and in black with adverts. on inside front and both back covers.

Half-title. pp. (176) Inset advert. leaf at end.

Note. This is a volume in Tillotson's Shilling Fiction and uniform with *Betty's Visions* by Rhoda Broughton.

Copy II: specially bound for presentation to the [1914*a*]
Earl of Lytton. Full vellum, with panels of dark blue, a coronet on front and elaborate gold tooling; bevelled boards; pale blue satin end-papers.

Neither half-title nor title has been bound up and advert. leaf has been cut away.

On blank leaf facing first page of text is written in Ouida's hand in purple ink: 'Written in June 1885, Ouida.'

FOLLE FARINE [1915]
3 vols. Chapman & Hall 1871. Smooth bright blue cloth, blocked in gold on front with single frame, title and author's name; on back with single frame; on spine with title, etc. in reverse on gold panels. Bevelled boards, all edges gilt.

Half-title in each vol.

Vol. I (viii) + (280)
II (iv) + (336)
III (iv) + 332

Binders' ticket: 'Leighton, Son & Hodge', at end of Vol. I.

Presentation Copy: 'To the Lord Lytton, with the sincere regard and reverence of the Author. L. de la R.' in fanciful ink-writing facing half-title of Vol. I.

Covers rather soiled and stained.

Note. This copy is in the author's presentation binding. The regular binding is a smooth apple-green cloth with a triple frame in blind on front and back and the title in blind in centre of front cover. Ordinary boards, and edges uncut.

FRESCOES, etc.: Dramatic Sketches [1916]
Chatto & Windus 1883.

Copy I: Author's Presentation Binding. White buckram, blocked and lettered in gold. Bevelled boards, all edges gilt. Thick white end-papers, patterned in gold.

Half-title. pp. (vi) + (312) X_4 publishers' device.

Covers rather soiled.

Copy II: Regular Binding. Smooth light slate [1916*a*]
cloth, blocked in light blue and maroon (design entirely different from Copy I); pale green-on-white flowered end-papers.

Blank leaf and half-title precede title. pp. (viii) + (312) X_4 publishers' device. Publishers' cat., 32 pp. dated October 1883, at end.

Presentation Copy. 'L. N. Drane from Ouida, Xmas 1883' in ink on title in same hand as inscription in *Two Little Wooden Shoes.* Fine.

[1917] FRIENDSHIP: a Story
3 vols. Chatto & Windus. 1878. Smooth blue cloth, blocked in black and lettered in gold.

Half-title in each vol.

Vol. I viii + 328 Publishers' cat., 36 pp. dated March 1878, at end.
II (iv) + (360) AA_4 publishers' device.
III (iv) + (372) BB_2 publishers' device.

Book-plate of Claud Harding, R.N., in each vol. Bookseller's ticket: 'John Bumpus, Oxford St', inside front cover of Vol. I. Binders' ticket: 'Leighton, Son & Hodge', at end of Vol. I.

Presentation Copy: Ink inscription: 'L. N. Drane from "Ouida" Nov. 1878', on half-title of Vol. I, in same hand as inscription in *Two Little Wooden Shoes.* The spine of Vol. I is torn near the head.

[1918] GUILDEROY
3 vols. Chatto & Windus 1889. Smooth dark red cloth, blocked in black and lettered in gold; olive-brown-on-white floral end-papers.

Half-title in each vol.

Vol. I (iv) + (280) T_4 publishers' device. Publishers' cat., 32 pp. dated June 1889, at end.
II (iv) + (288) T_8 publishers' device
III (iv) + (304) U_8 publishers' device.

[1919] 'HELD IN BONDAGE', or Granville de Vigne. A Tale of the Day
3 vols. Tinsley 1863. Grass-green diagonal-wide-bead-grain cloth.

Half-title in each vol.

Vol. I (vi) + (320)
II (vi) + 314 Final leaf, Y_1, a single inset.
III (vi) + 316

Presentation Copy: 'To L. N. Drane from Ouida' in fanciful ink lettering on fly-leaf of Vol. I and book-plate of Claud Harding, R.N. Very fine.

[1920] HELIANTHUS: a Novel
Macmillan 1908. Navy-blue patterned-sand-grain cloth.

Blank leaf and half-title precede title. pp. (viii) + (448) $2F_8$ adverts. Publishers' cat., 8 pp. dated Autumn 1908, at end. Fine.

HOUSE PARTY (A): a Novel [1921]
Hurst & Blackett 1887. Scarlet diagonal-fine-ribbed cloth, blocked in black and gold and lettered in gold; black end-papers.

Half-title. pp. (iv) + (332) W_2–W_6 adverts. Publishers' cat., 16 pp. undated, at end.

Presentation Copy: 'With affectionate remembrance, Ouida' in author's hand in purple ink facing title.

IDALIA: a Romance [1922]
3 vols. Chapman & Hall 1867. Violet-blue fine-morocco cloth.

Half-title in each vol.

Vol. I vi + (336)
II vi + (336) Y_8 blank.
III vi + 374 First leaf of final sig., BB_1, a single inset.

Presentation Copy: 'With the affectionate remembrances of the Author. L. de la R' in flowing but normal writing in ink facing title. Also a few pencil notes at end of Vol. III, not in author's hand.

Long review of the novel, from the *Saturday Review*, April 13, 1867, inserted. Fine.

Note. I have seen a secondary binding in grass-green bead- (or sand-) grain cloth, spine gold-lettered from type and without publishers' imprint.

*IN A WINTER CITY: a Sketch [1923]
Chapman & Hall 1876. Dark green diagonal-fine-ribbed cloth, blocked and lettered in black on front, in gold on spine; blind blocked on back.

pp. (ii) + (390) Final leaf, CC_3, a single inset.

IN MAREMMA: a Story [1924]
3 vols. Chatto & Windus 1882. Dark blue diagonal-fine-ribbed cloth, blocked in black and lettered in black and gold; flowered end-papers.

Half-title in each vol.

Vol. I (viii) + 324 Publishers' cat., 32 pp. dated October 1881, at end.
II (iv) + (332)
III (iv) + 328

Presentation Copy: 'L. N. Drane from Ouida, March 30/82' in ink on title of Vol. I in same hand as inscription in *Two Little Wooden Shoes.* Fine.

LA STREGA and Other Stories [1925]
Sampson Low, etc. 1899. Black linen flecked with white, blocked and lettered in yellow and black and lettered in gold.

Blank leaf and half-title precede title. pp. (viii) + (268) T_1 T_2 adverts. Very fine.

[1926] LE SELVE

T. Fisher Unwin 1896. Smooth apple-green cloth, blocked in dark green and brick red and lettered in gold.

Blank leaf, leaf carrying publisher's device, and half-title precede title. pp. (216) (I_2)–(I_{12}) adverts.

Book-plate of Viscountess Wolseley. Blind stamp: 'W. H. Smith & Son', on fly-leaf. Fine.

See also *The Silver Christ*, etc. 1898.

[1927] MASSARENES (The): a Novel

Ex. Cr. 8vo. Sampson Low etc. 1897. Smooth olive-green cloth.

Half-title. pp. (iv) + (576) 20_8 blank. Pp. (1) (2) Dedication, verso blank; (3) (4) 'Notice', verso blank; text begins (5).

[1928] MOTHS: a Novel

Pl. 24

3 vols. Chatto & Windus 1880. Bright blue diagonal-fine-ribbed cloth, blocked in gold in generally uniform style with *Two Little Wooden Shoes*, etc. Bevelled boards, all edges gilt. Thick glazed white end-papers patterned in gold, the fly-leaves backed with two leaves of white paper to form a double fly-leaf front and back.

Half-title in each vol.

Vol. I (viii) + (360)
II (iv) + (388)
III (iv) + (300) CC_8 publishers' device.

Very fine.

From the Drane collection, but uninscribed, this copy is in the author's presentation binding. The regular binding is dark blue fine-ribbed cloth, blocked in black with floral design and title, gold-lettered on spine; edges uncut; chocolate end-papers.

[1929] *NEW PRIESTHOOD (The)

Square 12mo (almost literally square: 6″ × 6¼″). E. W. Allen, 4 Ave Maria Lane 1893. Bluish-white morocco paper wrappers, cut flush, printed in crimson on front and back.

pp. (80) (E_4) adverts.

Note. The only copy discoverable being bound in a volume of pamphlets I cannot say whether the spine was lettered or plain.

[1930] OTHMAR

3 vols. Chatto & Windus 1885. White buckram, blocked in gold, generally uniform in style with *Frescoes* (author's binding). Bevelled boards, all edges gilt. Thick glazed white end-papers patterned in gold.

Half-title in each vol.

Vol. I (iv) + (328) Y_4 publishers' device.
II (iv) + (328)
III (iv) + (344) Z_4 publishers' device.

Covers a little soiled.

Note. This copy is in the author's presentation binding, but not from the Drane collection and uninscribed. The regular binding is dark blue fine-ribbed cloth, blocked in black and lettered in gold, ordinary boards, edges uncut.

PASCAREL: only a Story [1931]

3 vols. Chapman & Hall 1873. Grass-green sand-grain cloth, blocked in black and gold.

Half-title in Vols. I and II; blank leaf and half-title precede title in Vol. III

Vol. I xii + (302) First leaf of final sig., U_1, a single inset.
II (viii) + (320) X_8 blank.
III (viii) [paged vi] + 356

PIPISTRELLO and Other Stories [1932]

Chatto & Windus 1880. Dark blue diagonal-fine-ribbed cloth, blocked in black and lettered in gold; dark chocolate end-papers.

Leaf carrying advert. on verso and half-title precede title. pp. (viii) + (312) X_2 publishers' device, X_3 X_4 adverts. Publishers' cat., 32 pp. dated April 1880, at end.

Presentation Copy: 'L. N. Drane from Ouida June 22nd 80' in pencil on half-title in same hand as inscription in *Two Little Wooden Shoes*.

PRINCESS NAPRAXINE [1933]

3 vols. Chatto & Windus 1884. Royal-blue diagonal-fine-ribbed cloth, blocked and lettered in black and gold; olive-green-on-white decorated end-papers.

Blank leaf and half-title precede title in Vol. I; half-title only in Vols. II and III

Vol. I (viii) + (380) BB_6 publishers' device.
II (iv) + (344) Z_4 publishers' device. Publishers' cat., 32 pp. dated March 1884, at end.
III (iv) + (380) CC_2 publishers' device.

Fine.

PUCK: his Vicissitudes, Adventures, Observations, Conclusions, Friendships and Philosophies (related by Himself and edited by Ouida) [1934]

Copy I: Author's Presentation Binding. 3 vols. Chapman & Hall 1870. Smooth apple-green cloth, blocked in blind and lettered in gold, with OUIDA in gold in centre panel on front.

Half-title in each vol.

Vol. I (viii)+(340)
II (vi)+(338) Final leaf, (22_1), a single inset.
III (vi)+(426) Final leaf, 28_1, a single inset carrying L'Envoi on recto. Text of novel ends p. 424.

Presentation Copy: 'To L. N. Drane from the Author' in Ouida's fanciful writing facing title of Vol. I. The front fly-leaf of Vol. II has been carefully cut away.

[1934*a*] **Copy II: Regular Binding.** 3 vols. Chapman & Hall 1870. Royal-blue bead-grain cloth, similar blind blocking and spine lettering to Copy I, but without OUIDA on front. Collation as Copy I.

Bookseller's ticket: 'Walter T. Spencer, Oxford St', inside front cover of Vol. I.

Note. This—as stated above—I believe to have been the earliest novel for which Ouida had a special binding on her author's copies.

[1935] RAINY JUNE (A): a Novelette
Small 8vo. J. & R. Maxwell, n.d. [1885]. Brown diagonal-fine-ribbed cloth, blocked and lettered in black and lettered in gold.

pp. (ii)+(152) G_1–G_4 adverts.

[1936] RUFFINO, etc.
Copy I: First Edition. Chatto & Windus 1890. Crimson coarse-morocco cloth; black glazed end-papers.

Half-title. pp. (vi)+(312) X_4 publishers' device. Publishers' cat., 32 pp. dated November 1890, at end. Fine.

Note. This collection of four stories was issued as a volume in the standard 3*s.* 6*d.* uniform edition of Ouida's works.

[1936*a*] **Copy II: American Edition.** New York: J. W. Lovell & Co., October 7, 1890. Pale green paper wrappers printed in dark green.

No. 131 in Lovell's International Series.

[1937] SANTA BARBARA, etc.
Chatto & Windus 1891 White diagonal fine-ribbed cloth, blocked in gold. Bevelled boards, all edges gilt; thick glazed white end-papers patterned in gold.

Half-title. Pp. (viii)+(320) X_8 adverts.

From the Drane collection but uninscribed. Fine.

Note. This is an 'author's binding', the regulation binding is of smooth black cloth lettered in silver and blocked with circles and willow-sprays in terra-cotta and silver. Dark greenish-blue end-papers; ordinary boards.

SIGNA: a Story [1938]
3 vols. Chapman & Hall 1875.

Copy I: Presentation Binding. Smooth bright blue cloth, uniform in style, boards, edges and end-papers with *Two Little Wooden Shoes.* Extra plain end-paper at front and back of each vol.

Half-title in each vol.

Vol. I (iv)+(368)
II (iv)+(364) AA_6 blank.
III (iv)+(376) BB_4 blank.

Presentation Copy: 'L. N. Drane from Ouida 1875' in ink on half-title of Vol. I, in same hand as inscription in *Two Little Wooden Shoes.*

Copy II: Regulation Binding. Blue diagonal-fine-ribbed cloth, blocked and lettered in black on front, blocked and lettered in black and gold on spine, blocked in black on back. Top edges uncut; cream end-papers (single only). Collation as Copy I, but an Errata Slip not present in Copy I is tipped on to p. (1) of Vol. I. [1938*a*]

Ink signature: 'F. H. Playne', inside front cover of each vol. Binders' ticket: 'Leighton, Son & Hodge', at end of Vol. I.

SILVER CHRIST (The) and A LEMON TREE [1939]
Slim 8vo. T. Fisher Unwin 1894. Yellow paper wrappers printed in black.

Half-title. pp. 208 Publisher's cat., 16 pp. on text paper undated, at end.

No. 41 in Unwin's Pseudonym Library. On front cover is violet stamp: 'PRICE 1 F. 80 c.' Also issued in buff linen, blocked and lettered in dark blue.

See next item.

SILVER CHRIST (The): A Lemon Tree, Le Selve, An Altruist, Toxin [1940]
T. Fisher Unwin 1898. Dark green ribbed cloth.

Blank leaf and half-title precede title, which is printed in red and black. pp. (viii)+(364)

Book-plate of Albert Laker. Inside back-hinge broken.

A new edition in one tall 8vo volume of short novels previously published separately.

STRATHMORE: a Romance [1941]
3 vols. Chapman & Hall 1865. Dark green honeycomb-grain cloth.

Vol. I viii+324
II iv+(332)
III iv+328

Presentation Copy: 'To L. N. Drane from the Author' in Ouida's fanciful lettering on fly-leaf of Vol. I. Fine.

[1942] STREET DUST and Other Stories

F. V. White & Co. and George Bell & Sons 1901. Sage-green sand-grain cloth, blocked and lettered on front in olive green and white, gold-lettered on spine.

Blank leaf (signed *a*) and half-title precede title. pp. (viii)+248

[1943] SYRLIN

3 vols. Chatto & Windus 1890. Royal-blue diagonal-fine-ribbed cloth, blocked in black and pale blue and lettered in gold; light apple-green-on-white flowered end-papers.

Leaf carrying adverts. on recto and half-title precede title in Vol. I; half-title only in Vols. II and III

Vol. I (viii)+(332) Y_6 publishers' device.
II (iv)+(340) Publishers' cat., 32 pp. dated January 1890, at end.
III (iv)+(360)

Presentation Copy: 'L. N. Drane from Ouida. April 5. 90' in ink on first leaf of Vol. I and on half-titles of Vols. II and III in same hand as inscription in *Two Little Wooden Shoes*. Very fine.

[1944] TOWER OF TADDEO (The)

3 vols. Heinemann 1892. Pink linen flecked with white, blocked in dark red and gold-lettered.

Half-title in each vol.

Vol. I (iv)+(224) 14_8 blank.
II (iv)+(224)
III (iv)+(212) (42_2) blank.

Ink signature: 'Mary C. Ingram, 1893', in each vol. Spines a little faded and front cover of Vol. III stained.

[1945] TOXIN: a Sketch

Slim 8vo. T. Fisher Unwin 1895. Yellow paper wrappers printed in black. Gravure front. and 8 line-engraved and half-tone full-page illustrations on plate paper.

Leaf of adverts. and half-title precede title. pp. (192) 12_5–12_8 adverts.

A volume in Unwin's Pseudonym Library. On front cover is violet stamp: 'PRICE 1 F. 80 c.'

The 'series' status of this book is obscure. Facing title it appears as No. 48; but my cloth set of Pseudonyms (from which *Toxin* is absent) includes a different 48, and the English Catalogue does not mention it at all in their list of the series.

See also *The Silver Christ*, etc. 1898.

[1946] TRICOTRIN: the Story of a Waif and Stray

3 vols. Chapman & Hall 1869. Apple-green patterned (pansy-face)-grain cloth (a series of inter-fitting conventional flower-faces).

Half-title in each vol.

Vol. I (vi)+(332)
II (iv)+(320)
III (iv)+(414) First leaf of final sig., 26_1, a single inset, carrying 'Note' on recto, verso blank. Text of novel ends p. 412.

Double Presentation Copy: 'To Major Whyte Melville, with the kind regards of the Author. L. de la R.' ink-written on Ouida's flowing but regulation hand, facing half-title in Vol. I; and 'To L. N. Drane with the affectionate souvenirs of the Author. L. de la R.' in fanciful lettering on verso of the same half-title. Fine.

TWO LITTLE WOODEN SHOES: a Sketch [1947]

Chapman & Hall 1874. Smooth bright blue cloth, blocked in gold on front with title, 'OUIDA' in monogram on shield, the whole enclosed in single frame, on spine with title and author in reverse on gold panels. Bevelled boards, all edges gilt; thick white moiré end-papers.

Inset blank leaf and half-title precede title. pp. (vi)+(324) Y_2 blank.

Presentation Copy: 'L. N. Drane, Oakhurst from "Ouida"' in ink on first blank in a pointed, somewhat cramped feminine hand, presumably that of Mrs Drane.

Book-plate of Claud Harding, R.N. Spine rather bubbled and worn; inside hinges broken.

Note. This copy is in the author's presentation binding. The regular binding is smooth ultramarine cloth, blocked in black and lettered in gold. Ordinary boards.

TWO OFFENDERS [1948]

Chatto & Windus 1894. Smooth dark green cloth, blocked and lettered in yellow and black and lettered in gold; dark green end-papers.

Half-title. pp. (viii)+(256) R_8 publishers' device. Publishers' cat., 32 pp. dated November 1893, at end.

Presentation Copy: 'L. N. Drane from Ouida, 1894' in pencil on half-title in same hand as inscription in *Two Little Wooden Shoes*.

This copy is damp-stained on fore-edge of front and back cover.

UNDER TWO FLAGS: a Story of the Household and the Desert [1949] *Pl. 24*

3 vols. Chapman & Hall 1867. Crimson sand-grain cloth.

Vol. I viii+(324) Y_2 blank.
II iv+320
III iv+(348)

Author's signature: 'Louise de la Ramé, Langham. Nov. 20', in ink on fly-leaf of Vol. I, with review of the novel cut from a paper unnamed pasted on inside cover. Book-plate of Claud Harding,

R.N., in Vols. II and III. Some inside joints are broken and there are ink spots on front covers of Vols. I and III, but this is a remarkable copy of an outstandingly rare book.

Note. I think this was the author's own copy, and passed into Commander Harding's possession, either after his mother's death or as a direct gift from Ouida.

The former is the more probable; and there are certain indications suggesting that, because for some reason Ouida was short of author's copies of this title, she was constrained to give Mrs Drane her own.

She spells Ramé with one 'e'; she gives an abbreviated address 'Langham', and a month-date but no year; a favourable review is pasted inside the cover. Miss Yvonne ffrench, in her book, dated the move to the Langham Hotel as 1867 (the year in which *Under Two Flags* was published) and implies that the second 'e' in Ramée did not make its appearance until after 1868 and before 1876. Ouida would hardly write her name, an abbreviated address and a precise date (? of publication) in a copy meant for Mrs Drane, to whom she had already written several ornate, undated inscriptions in earlier books. Finally, favourable reviews of her work were uncommon phenomena in those days, and she might well have treasured this one for her own comfort.

[1950] *VIEWS AND OPINIONS

Methuen 1895. Unglazed crimson buckram.

Half-title. pp. (viii) + (400) Publishers' cat., 32 pp. dated January 1895, at end.

[1951] VILLAGE COMMUNE (A)

2 vols. Chatto & Windus 1881. Smooth bright blue cloth, blocked in black and lettered in black and gold; yellowish buff-on-white flowered end-papers.

Blank leaf and half-title precede title in Vol. I; half-title only in Vol. II

Vol. I (viii) + (360) AA_4 publishers' device. Publishers' cat., 32 pp. dated October 1880, at end.
II (iv) + (396) CC_5 CC_6 adverts. Text ends p. 356; (357)–392 Appendix.

Book-plate of Ilam Hall and booksellers' ticket: 'Sharp and Hall, Berkeley Square', inside front cover of each vol. Covers rubbed and spines darkened.

[1952] WANDA

3 vols. Chatto & Windus 1883. Smooth bright blue cloth, blocked in gold in generally uniform style with *Moths.* Bevelled boards, all edges gilt; thick glazed white end-papers patterned in gold.

Blank leaf and half-title precede title in Vol. I; half-title only in Vols. II and III

Vol. I (viii) + (344) Z_4 publishers' device.
II (iv) + (352)
III (iv) + (356) AA_2 publishers' device.

Presentation Copy: 'L. N. Drane from "Ouida"' in ink on half-title of Vol. I in same hand as inscription in *Two Little Wooden Shoes.*

Note. This copy is in the author's presentation binding. The regular binding is of royal blue fine-ribbed cloth, blocked and lettered in black and gold, ordinary boards, edges uncut, pale green flowered end-papers.

WATERS OF EDERA (The) [1953]

T. Fisher Unwin 1900. Dark green ribbed cloth. Title printed in red and black.

Half-title. pp. (iv) + (352) 23_7 'Note', 23_8 adverts.

WISDOM, WIT, AND PATHOS (selected from the works of Ouida, by F. Sydney Morris) [1954]

Chatto & Windus 1884. Smooth navy-blue cloth, blocked in pale blue and brown and lettered in gold; blue-on-white decorated end-papers; orange edges.

Leaf carrying advert. on verso and half-title precede title. pp. (viii) + 472 Publishers' cat., 32 pp. dated October 1883, at end.

Presentation Copy: 'L. N. Drane from Ouida, Xmas 1883' in ink on half-title in same hand as inscription in *Two Little Wooden Shoes.*

ana

FERNDYKE, by CLAUD HARDING, R.N. [1955]

London Literary Society, 376 Strand, n.d. [1855] Smooth dark blue cloth, fancy lettered in red; blue-grey flowered end-papers.

Half-title. pp. (iv) + (344)

This is the author's own copy, corrected in ink for a new edition. Chapter headings are supplied throughout and the text is revised.

[*See also* HAMILTON, WALTER, *above*]

O'SULLIVAN, MORTIMER (?1791–1859)

NEVILLES OF GARRETSTOWN (The): a Tale of 1760 [anon] [1956]

3 vols. Saunders, Otley & Co. 1860. Grey-purple ripple-grain cloth; pale coffee end-papers.

Vol. I viii + 280
II (ii) + (304) U_8 imprint leaf.
III (ii) + (276) Publishers' cat., 8 pp. undated, at end.

Covers stained.

Note. Vol. I, pp. (iii)–viii are occupied by a Preface signed: 'The Author of "Emilia Wyndham" (Mrs Marsh).'

PEACOCK, THOMAS LOVE (1785–1866)

THE HALLIFORD EDITION OF THE WORKS OF THOMAS LOVE PEACOCK, edited by H. F. B. Brett-Smith and C. E. Jones (10 vols. London 1924–1934) contained at the end of each vol. bibliographical analyses of the Peacock titles therein reprinted. These analyses (edited by Dudley-Massey) are, one hopes, to be issued in one volume by Rupert Hart-Davis, Ltd., so that a reliable Peacock Bibliography in convenient shape shall be available to collectors.

On this account I here include the Gaisford set of Peacock First Editions without bibliographical comment, referring students to what may fairly claim to be the Standard Bibliography.

Three of Peacock's novels constitute No. 57 of Bentley's Standard Novels (*Headlong Hall*, *Nightmare Abbey* and *Crotchet Castle*). This issue (1837) is not here recorded, as it appears under Bentley's Series in Section III.

[1957] SET OF FIRST EDITIONS (from the Gaisford Library)

15 Vols. Uniform full polished calf, extra gilt (twelve vols. by Bedford, two by Lloyd and one by Riviere). Top edges gilt; other edges uncut or trimmed.

[1957*a*] PALMYRA AND OTHER POEMS 1806

Book-plate of Thos. Gaisford and (?) A.F.L.

[1957*b*] PHILOSOPHY OF MELANCHOLY (The) 1812

Book-plates as in *Palmyra*.

Note. Inserted in this copy before title is Peacock's holograph MS. of his poem 'A Bill for the Better Promotion of Oppression on the Sabbath Day'. 3 pp. 4to.

This poem was first issued in printed form by H. V. Marrot, in a private edition of 50 copies, October 1926. The little book, printed on pale green paper and bound in stiff boards of the same colour, contains twelve unfoliated pages and occasional decorations after Lovat Fraser.

[1957*c*] SIR PROTEUS: a Satirical Ballad 1814

Front wrapper bound in at end of this copy. Book-plates as in *Palmyra*.

[1957*d*] HEADLONG HALL 1816

Book-plates as in *Palmyra*.

[1957*e*] MELINCOURT 3 vols. 1817.

Book-plates as in *Palmyra*.

Note. Bound in with this copy are full-page drawings in Indian ink—the work of a fairly skilful amateur with a talent for the grotesque. On fly-leaf of Vol. I is a query: '? Drawings by Miss Parker.' There is one drawing in Vol. I; three in Vol. II and three in Vol. III.

1957*f*] NIGHTMARE ABBEY 1818

Book-plates as in *Palmyra*.

RHODODAPHNE, or The Thessalian Spell: a Poem 1818 [1957*g*]

Book-plates as in *Palmyra*.

MAID MARIAN 1822 [1957*h*]

Book-plates: two Gaisford (variants) and one ? A.F.L.

Note. This copy contains the advert. leaf, M_{12}, which is sometimes missing.

MISFORTUNES OF ELPHIN (The) 1829 [1957*i*]

Book-plates as in *Palmyra*.

CROTCHET CASTLE 1831 [1957*j*]

Book-plates as in *Palmyra*.

Note. In this copy, the leaf of adverts. is absent, but a fourth preliminary leaf appears in the form of a duplicate fly-title inserted before the title and taken from another copy.

GRYLL GRANGE 1861 [1957*k*]

Book-plates as in *Palmyra*.

CALIDORE AND MISCELLANEA. Edited by Richard Garnett 1891 [1957*l*]

Book-plates as in *Palmyra*. First book-edition of *Calidore* and *Last Day of Windsor Forest*.

Wrong Attributions

The late Lord Justice Coleridge seems to have had a fancy for attributing to Peacock works written by others. By a curious coincidence I have two such faulty attributions deriving from him, one bound uniform with the Gaisford set, the other in mottled russia. Both have ink signature: 'J. D. Coleridge, 1 Sussex Square, 1870', on half-title or fly-leaf. Why one found its way into the Gaisford set and the other did not, I do not know; but it looks as though *Miserrimus* (a copy of which book was sold in May 1896 with Lord Coleridge's set of Peacock 'firsts') was detached from that set and bound uniform with the Gaisford set by the then owner of that set (presumably 'A.F.L.'). It is strange that *Arthur Courtenay* was not also taken over.

The only explanation I can offer of the faulty attributions is that at the end of the B.M. copy of *Arthur Courtenay* is a publishers' cat. advertising the recent publication of *Headlong Hall*, *Miserrimus* and the *Ionian Anthology*, no author's names being given.

(i) MISERRIMUS [anon. By Frederic Mansel Reynolds] [1958]

'Not published.' Printed by Davison Simmons & Co. 1832. Full polished calf, extra gilt, by Lloyd.

Half-title. pp. (iv)+(116)

Book-plates as in *Palmyra* in the Gaisford set.

(ii) ARTHUR COURTENAY [anon. ? author] [1959]

Hookham 1834. Full mottled russia.

Half-title. pp. (iv)+216

PEACOCK, W. F.

[1960] ADVENTURES OF ST GEORGE AFTER HIS FAMOUS ENCOUNTER WITH THE DRAGON

Large square 8vo. James Blackwood, n.d. [1858]. Red morocco cloth, blocked on front with vignette and fancy titling in gold, in blind with conventional framing. Spine unlettered. Red edges.

Wood-engraved front. and 9 plates after Gustave Doré, all on plate paper.

pp. (48)

Ink signature: 'J. R. A. V. Godley (?), Bath, April 1/60', on fly-leaf.

Notes. (i) It is curious, seeing that the Doré plates are all provided with good quality tissues, that no mention of illustration appears on binding or title.

(ii) *Catalogue de l'Œuvre Complet de Gustave Doré*, by Henri Leblanc, Paris, 1931 (p. 275), dates this book as above. The book was not in the compiler's possession and he quotes from the Preface to G. F. Pardon's *Boldheart the Warrior* (same date), which states Peacock's book to be 'pure invention' and a 'companion volume' to *Boldheart.*

PHILIPS, F. C.

[1961] AS IN A LOOKING GLASS

Demy 4to. Ward & Downey 1889. Pinkish-ochre diagonal-fine-ribbed cloth, pictorially blocked and lettered in gold on front and spine, back plain. Cream end-papers. Line-engraved front., vignette title, and 12 full-page illustrations after George du Maurier, all on plate paper. Title printed in red and black.

Half-title. pp. (viii) [front. and title not reckoned in collation] + (296) U_4 blank.

Fine.

Note. Published in an edition limited to 1000 copies, this is the best example known to me of du Maurier's work as illustrator. The story first appeared in 2 vols. in 1885, and scandalised the critics to a degree which nowadays seems unreasonable.

PHILLIPS, SAMUEL (1814–1854)

[1962] CALEB STUKELY [anon]

Copy I: First Edition. 3 vols. Blackwood 1844. Earth-brown horizontal-fine-ribbed cloth, gold-lettered on spine with title and volume number only (no imprint).

Half-title in each vol.

Vol. I (vi) + (318) First leaf of final sig., $2D_1$, a single inset.
II (iv) + (290) Final leaf, $2A_5$, a single inset.
III (iv) + (336)

Binders' ticket: 'Remnant & Edmonds', at end of Vol. I. Portion of back end-paper of Vol. I missing. Cloth slightly spotted.

Copy II: First Illustrated Edition (revised and abbreviated by the author). Nathaniel Cooke 1854. Maroon morocco cloth. Wood-engraved front., vignette title and 6 full-page illustrations after W. McConnell. [1962*a*]

pp. (iv) + (318) Final leaf, X_7, a single inset.

A volume in the Illustrated Family Novelist (3747 in Section III).

PHILLPOTTS, EDEN (b. 1862)

SOME EVERY-DAY FOLKS [1963]

3 vols. Osgood, McIlvaine & Co. 1894. Smooth grey-blue cloth, lettered in gold and blocked in scarlet and dark blue on front, gold-lettered on spine.

Vol. I iv + (292) U_2 blank.
II iv + (296) U_4 blank.
III iv + (280) T_4 blank.

Book-plate of Leonard James Shrubsall; book-label of Hugh Walpole. Not a nice copy; cloth dingy, spine of Vol. I repaired.

Note. Each vol. has a second front fly-leaf, which one would assume had been inserted by a previous owner. Yet the vols. are not re-cased and the end-papers look original.

PICKEN, ANDREW (1788–1833)

BLACK WATCH (The) (by the author of 'The Dominie's Legacy') [1964

3 vols. Bentley 1834. Boards, labels.

Half-title in Vol. III

Vol. I (iv) + (320) P_4 adverts.
II (ii) + 322 Final leaf, Q_1, a single inset.
III (iv) + 332

The dedication is signed by Picken's son in his father's name.

Book-label of R. J. Ll. Price, Rhiwlas Library, and bookseller's ticket: 'Harding, Chester', inside front cover of each vol. One label defective.

DOMINIE'S LEGACY (The) (by the author of 'The Sectarian') [196

3 vols. William Kidd, 6 Old Bond Street 1830. Boards, labels.

Half-title in Vols. I and III; leaf of adverts. and half-title precede title in Vol. II

Vol. I xx + (244)
II (viii) + 264
III (vi) + (280) T_4 advert. The stub of pp. (vii) (viii), of the original 8 pp. prelim., probably label-leaf, survives in this copy.

Ink signature: 'Frances Price, Rhiwlas. 1830' and bookseller's ticket: 'Harding, Chester', inside front cover of each vol.

[1966] SECTARIAN (The), or the Church and the Meeting House [anon]

3 vols. Colburn 1829. Boards, labels.

Vol. I (ii) + (284) N_{10} advert. The stub of pp. (i) (ii), of an original 4 pp. prelim., probably label-leaf, survives in this copy.
II (ii) + (308) O_{10} adverts.
III (ii) + 324

Ink signature: 'Frances Price, Rhiwlas, 1829' and bookseller's ticket: 'Seacome, Chester', inside front cover of each vol. Fine.

[1967] TRADITIONARY STORIES of old Families and Legendary Illustrations of Family History. With Notes, historical and biographical

2 vols. Longman etc. 1833. Boards, labels.

Half-title in Vol. II

Vol. I xii + 360
II (iv) + 342 First leaf of final sig., Q_1, a single inset.

Book-label of R. J. Ll. Price, Rhiwlas Library, inside front cover of each vol. Fine.

Edited by Picken

[1968] CLUB BOOK (The): being original Tales etc. by various Authors (edited by the author of 'The Dominie's Legacy')

3 vols. Cochrane & Pickersgill 1831. Boards, labels.

Half-title in Vols. II and III

Vol. I (xvi) + (312) O_{11} O_{12} adverts. paged (1)–4.
II (vi) + 314 Final leaf, P_1, a single inset.
III (vi) + 330 Final leaf, R_1, a single inset.

Book-label of R. J. Ll. Price, Rhiwlas Library, inside front cover of each vol. and bookseller's ticket: 'Harding, Chester', in Vol. I. Fine.

Note. This collection comprises hitherto unpublished stories by Alan Cunningham, John Galt (5), James Hogg (2), G. P. R. James, William Jerdan, Lord Francis Leveson Gower, D. M. Moir, Tyrone Power, Leitch Ritchie and the Editor (3).

POLWHELE, REV. RICHARD (1760–1838)

[1969] RURAL RECTOR (The), or a Sketch of Manners, Learning and Religion in a Country Parish [anon]

3 vols. Small 8vo. Printed by W. Polyblank [Truro] for J. B. Nichols, Longman, Simpkin & Marshall and G. B. Whittaker 1831. Boards, labels.

Vol. I xviii + (114) pp. (xvii) (xviii) and final leaf, M_1, single insets. Penultimate sig., L, two leaves.
II (196) [paged (i) (ii) + (3)–(194)]
III (iv) + (48) [end of text] + (1)–(78) [Appendix] Final leaf, H_3, imprint leaf and a single inset.

Note. An undisciplined and, in an elementary way, a scurrilous production satirising the personalities and educational arrangements in the rural parish of 'Manathon'. Its hostility is mainly directed against the so-called 'Madras' System of Education, devised by Dr Andrew Bell; but it finds occasion also to deplore the influence of Mary Wollstonecraft, of Methodism and of the Romish Clergy. Polwhele was Rector of Manaccan, near Helston, in Cornwall, from 1794 to 1821.

POOLE, JOHN (? 1786–1832)

LITTLE PEDLINGTON AND THE PEDLINGTONIANS [1970]

2 vols. Colburn 1839. Half-cloth boards, labels.

Half-title in each vol.

Vol. I (xvi) + (312) O_{11} O_{12} adverts.
II viii + 346 Q_6 cut away, probably label leaf.

Note. This fictional harlequinade satirises, under the name 'Hobbleday', Thomas Hill, bibliomaniac and bon-vivant, who was also the original of 'Hull' in Hook's, *Gilbert Gurney*.

PORTER, JANE (1776–1850)

SCOTTISH CHIEFS (The): a Romance [1971]

5 vols. Longman etc. 1810. Blue-grey paper boards, white paper spines, labels. *Pl. 19*

Half-title in each vol.

Vol. I (xii) + (364) Text ends p. 357; (358) blank; (359)–(362) Notes, paged (i)–iv; (363) (364), R_2, Leaf of Errata.
II (iv) + (368) Text ends p. 360; (361)–367 Notes; (368) blank.
III (iv) + (412) Text ends p. 405; (406) blank; (407)–411 Notes; (412) blank.
IV (iv) + (388) Text ends p. 381; (382) blank; (383)–386 Notes; (387) (388), S_2, blank.
V (iv) + 396 Text ends p. 390; (391)–396 Notes.

From the Bellew Library. Very fine.

[1972] THADDEUS OF WARSAW
4 vols. 12mo. T. N. Longman and O. Rees 1803. Cont. half calf, marbled boards, red lettering pieces, sprinkled edges.

Half-title in each vol.

Vol. I (xii)+(248)
II (iv)+224
III (iv)+236
IV (iv)+(240) [L_{12} adverts]+(2) [inset leaf of Errata in all four vols. paged (1) 2].

Ink signature: 'C. J. Fountayne' on title of Vol. I and initials 'C.J.F.' on half-titles of II to IV. One lettering piece renewed.

Note. Thaddeus of Warsaw ranks with Mrs Radcliffe's *Castles of Athlin and Dunbayne* as a super-rarity among Gothic Romantic novels.

POWER, MARGUERITE A. (niece of LADY BLESSINGTON) (?1815–1867)

[1973] NELLY CAREW
2 vols. Saunders, Otley & Co. 1859. Blue bead-grain cloth.

Vol. I viii+(268) Advert. slip, on blue paper, inserted between pp. (iv) and (v).
II vi+(230) L_6 imprint leaf, L_7 advert. and a single inset. Publishers' advert., 2 pp., followed by cat., 8 pp. dated November 1859, at end.

Ink signature: 'Emily Louisa Fitzroy', on title of each vol.

[1974] SWEETHEARTS AND WIVES
3 vols. Saunders, Otley & Co. 1861. Magenta coarse-morocco cloth; chocolate end-papers.

Half-title in each vol.

Vol. I (viii)+(292)
II (viii)+(268)
III (viii)+(256) M_5–M_8 adverts.

Binder's ticket: 'Burn', at end of Vol. I. Covers damp-stained.

POWER, TYRONE (1797–1841)

[1975] LOST HEIR (The) and THE PREDICTION [anon]
3 vols. Edward Bull 1830. Boards, labels.

Half-title in each vol.

Vol. I (iv)+(314) Final leaf, (P_1), a single inset.
II (iv)+316
III (iv)+(310) O_{10} O_{11}, the latter a single inset, adverts.

Book-label of R. J. Ll. Price, Rhiwlas Library, and bookseller's ticket: 'Harding, Chester', inside front cover of each vol.

PRYCE, RICHARD (circ. 1870–1942)

The books marked † were the author's own copies. In this country, despite laudatory reviews, Pryce never had the success he deserved. In America one or two of his novels (particularly *David Penstephen*) were widely read; but his neglect at the hands of the British public shook what little assurance he possessed and drove him inwards on his unpretentious and diffident self. Yet he was a writer of sensibility and integrity, and deserved some such concerted support from his fellow-novelists as was given to Leonard Merrick.

Six of Pryce's fictions are not in the Collection, and descriptions (asterisked) of all save one are provided from copies in Statutory Libraries. I have been unable to locate a copy of *The Ugly Story of Miss Wetherby* (1889), although I possess the original MS.

*BURDEN OF A WOMAN (The) [1976
A. D. Innes & Co. 1895. Smooth light sand-coloured cloth, blocked and lettered in chocolate on front, blocked in chocolate and gold-lettered on spine; publishers' monogram in chocolate on back.

Half-title. pp. (iv)+(316) Publishers' cat., 8 pp. undated, at end.

CHRISTOPHER [1977
Hutchinson 1911. Dark red linen-grain cloth, lettered in gold on front and spine. Title printed in light brown and black.

Half-title. pp. (viii)+(344) Publishers' cat., 32 pp. on text paper dated August 1911, at end.

DAVID PENSTEPHEN [1978
Methuen 1916. Dark greenish-blue linen-grain cloth, blocked and lettered in blind on front, in gold on spine.

Half-title. pp. (iv)+(344) 22_3 22_4 adverts. Publishers' cat., 32 pp. dated '5/1/16', at end. Very fine, with dust-jacket.

DECK CHAIR STORIES [1979
Ward & Downey 1891. Smooth sand-brown cloth, pictorially blocked on front in pink and black and black-lettered; gold-lettered on spine; publishers' monogram in black on back.

Half-title follows title. pp. (256) 16_4–16_7 adverts.; 16_8 blank. Very fine.

†DIEUDONNÉE: a Study (by Richard Ap Rhys) [1980
Remington & Co. 1884. Sage-green diagonal fine-ribbed cloth, blocked in black and lettered in gold; very dark green end-papers.

Half title. pp. (xii) [paged (vi)]+(236) Q_2 blank. Very fine.

[1981] *ELEMENTARY JANE
Hutchinson 1897. Crimson buckram, lettered in gold.
Half-title. pp. (iv) + (332)

[1982] †EVIL SPIRIT (An)
2 vols. Fisher Unwin 1887. Smooth black cloth, blocked in yellow with author's handwriting and signature on front, gold-lettered on spine; publisher's monogram in yellow on back; ochre-on-white floral end-papers.
Blank leaf and half-title precede title in each vol.
Vol. I xii + 184 Publisher's cat., 32 pp. on text paper dated Autumn–Christmas 1886, at end.
II viii + (184) Publisher's cat., as in Vol. I, at end.
Cloth dull and rubbed. Base of spine of Vol. I defective.

[1983] *JEZEBEL
Hutchinson 1900. Smooth crimson cloth flecked with scarlet, lettered in gold. Title printed in red and black.
Half-title. pp. (iv) + (354) Z_6 blank.

[1984] †JUST IMPEDIMENT
2 vols. Ward & Downey 1890. Dark red diagonal-fine-ribbed cloth, blocked and lettered in black on front, gold-lettered on spine; publishers' monogram in blind on back; fawn-on-white floral end-papers.
Blank leaf and half-title precede title in each vol.
Vol. I (viii) + (236)
II (viii) + (236)
Very fine.

[1985] †MISS MAXWELL'S AFFECTIONS: a Novel
2 vols. Chatto & Windus 1891. Sand-brown morocco cloth, blocked in dark green with design of leaves on front, spine and back; lettered in dark green on front; gold-lettered on spine; pale grey-on-white leaf-design end-papers.
Vol. I (ii) + (248) 8 pp. on text paper adverts. of novels by same author.
II (ii) + 248 Publishers' cat., 32 pp. dated June 1891, at end.

[1986] *MORGAN'S YARD
Square extra crown 8vo. Collins 1932. Black cloth, lettered in gold.
Half-title. pp. 288

[1987] †QUIET MRS FLEMING (The)
Methuen 1891. Smooth scarlet cloth, fancy-lettered on front in black, gold-lettered on spine; dark green end-papers.
Half-title. pp. (vi) + 258 Final leaf, R_1, a single inset. Publishers' cat., 12 pp. dated September 1890, at end.
Cloth damp-stained.

ROMANCE AND JANE WESTON [1988]
Collins 1924. Navy-blue diagonal-fine-ribbed cloth, blocked and lettered in red.
Half-title. pp. (304) [paged (i)–(vi) + (1)–(298)] T_6–T_8 adverts.
Fine, with dust jacket.

*STATUE IN THE WOOD (The) [1989]
Collins 1918. Scarlet linen-grain cloth, lettered in blind and black.
Half-title. pp. (vi) + (306)

SUCCESSOR (The): a Novel [1990]
Hutchinson 1904. Smooth dark blue cloth, title gold-blocked on white panel on front and author's autograph facsimiled in gold; gold-lettered on spine.
Half-title. pp. (iv) + 332 Publishers' cat., 16 pp. on text paper dated February 1904, at end.
Not a fresh copy. Damp ring on front cover.

†TIME AND THE WOMAN: a Novel [1991]
2 vols. Methuen 1892. Light blue ribbed cloth, blocked and lettered in gold; dark olive-green end-papers.
Half-title in each vol.
Vol. I (iv) + 212 Publishers' cat., 6 pp. printed in blue and dated October 1892, at end.
II (iv) + (220) Publishers' cat., as in Vol. I, at end.
Cloth damp-stained.

TOWING-PATH BESS and Other Stories [1992]
Chapman & Hall 1907. Smooth salmon cloth, gold-lettered on front and spine.
Half-title. pp. (viii) + (252) R_6 blank. Fine.

†WINIFRED MOUNT: a Novel [1993]
2 vols. Methuen 1894. Light blue ribbed cloth, lettered in gold on front and spine.
Half-title in each vol.
Vol. I (iv) + (1)–188 Publishers' cat., 24 pp. dated April 1894, at end.
II (iv) + (189)–372 Publishers' cat., as in Vol. I, at end.
Very fine.
Note. Another example (cf. Mrs Oliphant and Stanley Weyman) of a Methuen two-decker paged continuously.

RAIKES, HARRIET

[1994] MARRIAGE CONTRACT (The)
2 vols. Bentley 1849. Half-cloth boards, labels.
Half-title in Vol. II
Vol. I (iv)+(300)
II (iv)+(290) Final leaf, O_1, a single inset.
'Guys Cliffe' in ink on front covers.

Note. This novel is dedicated to Lady Georgiana Fullerton. In 1861 the author edited her father's (Thomas Raikes') correspondence with the Duke of Wellington.

REACH, ANGUS B. (1821–1856)

[1995] CLEMENT LORIMER, or the Book with the Iron Clasps
David Bogue, Fleet Street. 1849. Plum fine-ribbed cloth, pictorially blocked in gold on front and spine (spine-design, which incorporates fancy titling, is signed J. L. [John Leighton]), front design repeated in blind on back. Etched front. and 11 plates by George Cruikshank.
pp. (viii) [paged vi]+280
The copy in the collection is in full polished calf by Riviere, top edges gilt, others trimmed, cloth covers preserved.

[1996] LEONARD LINDSAY, or the Story of a Buccaneer
2 vols. David Bogue, 86 Fleet Street 1850. Navy-blue fine-ribbed cloth, blocked in blind on front, spine and back; gold-lettered on spine.
Vol. I (xvi)+328
II iv+352 Publisher's cat., 4 pp. undated, at end.
Bookseller's ticket: 'Davies, Hereford', inside front cover of Vol. I. Oval stamp: 'Hereford Permanent Library', on verso of title in each vol. Cloth fine. Some pages foxed.

READE, CHARLES (1814–1884)

For further bibliographical detail see Parrish, *Wilkie Collins and Charles Reade*, London, 1940.

[1997] BIBLE CHARACTERS [*Parrish* p. 276
Fcap 8vo. Chatto & Windus 1888. Dark red morocco-grained paper wrappers, cut flush, printed in gold and black; black end-papers.
Half-title. pp. (vi)+106 Final leaf, 7_5, a single inset. Publishers' cat., 32 pp. dated September 1888, at end. Very fine.

Note. Parrish, doubtless by a slip, describes the binding of his copy as 'original dark red limp morocco'. He does not record any cat. at end.

CHRISTIE JOHNSTONE: a Novel [1998]
[*Parrish* p. 173
Bentley 1853. Half-cloth boards, label.
pp. (iv)+(336) Text ends p. 334; (335) Note; (336) printers' imprint.

Note. A 'New Edition' with a frontispiece was published in 1857. The book was reset and issued in grey-purple morocco cloth.

CLOISTER AND THE HEARTH (The): a Tale of the Middle Ages [1999]

Copy I: First Edition. 4 vols. Trübner 1861. Grey-green morocco cloth. [*Parrish* p. 206
Vol. I (iv)+360
II pp. 384
III pp. 328
IV pp. (436)
Ink signature: 'John Burns' on fly-leaf of each vol. Binders' ticket: 'Westleys' at end of Vol. I. A magnificent copy.

Note. Parrish records that in his copy the fullstop is missing after 'Hearth' from the title-page of Vol. III only. This was the case with my previous copy. But in the copy here described it is also missing from Vol. IV.

Copy II: Second Edition. 4 vols. Trübner 1861. Binding as Copy I. [*Parrish* p. 207 [1999*a*]
Vol. I (iv)+360
II pp. 376
III pp. 328
IV pp. (436)
Ink signature: 'Mrs Marriott, Avonbank', on title, and blind stamp: 'The Bredon Book Club', on fly-leaf of each vol. Fine.
Parrish gives a valuable schedule of the important textual differences between this edition and the first.

Copy III: Third Edition. 4 vols. Trübner 1861. Binding as Copies I and II. Collation and text as Copy II. [1999*b*]
Ink signature: 'Lady Selina Henry', on title of each vol. Very fine.
See also Carter, *Binding Variants*, p. 148, and *More Binding Variants*, p. 34.

COMING MAN (The): Letters contributed to Harper's Weekly [*Parrish* p. 256 [2000]
Pott 8vo. New York: Harper 1878.

Copy I. Green diagonal-fine-ribbed cloth; pale grey end-papers.
Two leaves of adverts. precede title. pp. (96) F_4–F_8 adverts.
Ink signature: 'D. MacM. Niven', on title.
Fine. Top edge of front cover very slightly damp-spotted.

Copy II. Drab wrappers printed in red and black. Collation as Copy I. [2000*a*]
No. 69 in Harper's Half Hour Series.

[2001] COURSE OF TRUE LOVE NEVER DID RUN SMOOTH (The) [*Parrish* p. 193
Pl. 25

Bentley 1857.

Copy I: Pictorial boards printed in pink and black on front and back with lithographed picture after Alfred Crowquill.

pp. (272) S_8 blank.

Bookseller's ticket: 'Cann, Harleston', inside front cover.

[2001*a*] **Copy II.** Royal-blue morocco cloth. Collation as Copy I. B
Pl. 25

Both copies very fine.

[2002] CREMONA VIOLINS AND VARNISH: a Lost Art Revived [*Parrish*, p. 247

8vo. Gloucester: John Bellows, Steam Press 1873. Deep cream wrappers, cut flush, printed in black, red and green. Spine unlettered. Back wrapper blank. All edges gilt.

pp. (40) unsigned. Pp. (39) (40) blank.

Elaborate title, printed in black, brown, red, violet and green. Text throughout framed in red and with red initial letters.

Note. Consists of four letters from Reade to the *Pall Mall Gazette* reprinted by permission by George H. M. Muntz. This copy was presented by Muntz to his nephew Mendel Albrecht.

[2003] GOOD FIGHT (A) and other Tales [*Parrish* p. 204

New York: Harper 1859. Black ripple-grain cloth; red chocolate end-papers.

Blank leaf precedes title. pp. (iv)+(344) P_4 adverts.

Book-plate of Philip Greely Brown and ink signature: 'Philip Henry Brown', on fly-leaf. Very fine. Issued in various colours.

A Good Fight is the first version of *The Cloister and the Hearth.* The volume also contains *Autobiography of a Thief* and *Jack of All Trades.*

[2004] GRIFFITH GAUNT, or Jealousy [*Parrish* p. 214

Pl. 25 3 vols. Chapman & Hall 1866. Violet pebble-grain cloth.

Half-title in each vol.

Vol. I (iv)+302 Final leaf, U_7, a single inset.
II (iv)+318 First leaf of final sig., X_1, a single inset.
III (iv)+328 Publishers' cat., 16 pp. dated October 1866, at end.

The only fine copy of this book I have ever seen. Copies in green cloth are 'secondaries'.

ana

[2005] LIFFITH LANK OF LUNACY, by C. H. WEBB

New York: Carleton 1867. Very dark chocolate sand-grain cloth, blocked and lettered in gold on front, spine unlettered. Bevelled boards, chocolate end-papers. Vignettes in the text after Sol Eytinge Jr. Fly-title precedes title, recto reading: AUTHOR'S EDITION, verso printed with 'Overture of Select Texts'. pp. 48.

Note. In his prefatory note, 'By way of Explanation' on p. (5), the author confesses indebtedness to Charles Reade's *Griffith Gaunt* for the 'leading idea' of his story, its style and 'topographical effects'. On the first page of text a sub-title is added: 'A Tale that he who runs may reade'. The heroine is called Kate Phaeton, and there are frequent references to other works by Reade.

HARD CASH: a Matter of Fact Romance [2006]
[*Parrish* p. 211

3 vols. Sampson Low etc. 1863. Grey-green morocco cloth (as used on *The Cloister and the Hearth).*

Vol. I iv+356
II (ii)+(366) First leaf of final sig., $2A_1$, a single inset.
III (ii)+(370) Final leaf, $2B_1$, a single inset. Publishers' cat., 4 pp. dated December 10, 1863, at end. Text ends p. 358; (359)–369 Appendix; (370) printers' imprint.

Very fine.

To the details given by Parrish it may be added that, on its second appearance (Vol. III, p. 316), the facsimile of the 'receipt' is *tinted,* in such a way as to show discoloration round the white mark left by the dead man's thumb.

HERO AND A MARTYR (A): a True and Accurate Account of the Heroic Feats and Sad Calamity of James Lambert, a Living Man [2007]

8vo. Samuel French 1874. Dark yellow wrappers, cut flush, printed in black. Spine unlettered, inside wrappers and back-cover printed with adverts. Wood-engraved portrait front. on text paper. [*Parrish* p. 250

Half-title. pp. (viii)+40

Ink signature: 'M. Boyle', on front cover.

IT IS NEVER TOO LATE TO MEND: a Matter of Fact Romance [*Parrish* p. 183 [2008]
Pl. 25

Copy I: First Edition. 3 vols. Bentley 1856. Pinkish-maroon ripple-grain cloth, uniform with that used on *Peg Woffington*

Vol. I (iv)+(396)
II (ii)+(350) Final leaf, R_1, a single inset.
III (ii)+344 B

Parrish states that at foot of title of Vol. I there is no full stop after *Translation.* In this copy there is a full stop in each vol.

This, the publisher's personal copy, has signature M of Vol. I inserted in untrimmed form. Cloth very fine.

[2008*a*] **Copy II: Second Edition.** 3 vols. Bentley 1856. Half-cloth boards, labels (reading: 'IT IS NEVER / TOO LATE / TO MEND.' / *rule* / VOL. I [II. III]). Collation as Copy I. Fine.

[2009] JILT (The): a Novel [*Parrish* p. 254

Pott 8vo. New York: Harper 1877. Green diagonal-fine-ribbed cloth; pale grey end-papers. Wood-engraved front. and 3 plates.

Two leaves of adverts. precede front. pp. (126) H_4–H_8 adverts.

Ink signature: 'D. MacM. Niven', on title. Fine.

No. 20 in Harper's Half Hour Series.

[2010] LOVE ME LITTLE, LOVE ME LONG [*Parrish* p. 201

2 vols. Trübner 1859. Grass-green bead-grain cloth (also issued in blue).

Blank leaf and half-title precede title in Vol. I; half-title only in Vol. II

Vol. I (viii) + (392) $2C_4$ imprint leaf.
II (360) $2A_8$ blank. B

Presentation Copy: 'George Bentley Esq. with the Author's Kind regards' in ink on fly-leaf of Vol. II.

Book-label of George Bentley in each vol. Binders' ticket: 'Westleys', at end of Vol. I. Very fine.

[2011] *Pl. 25* PEG WOFFINGTON: a Novel [*Parrish* p. 171

Bentley 1853. Pinkish maroon ripple-grain cloth.

pp. (iv) + (332)

Copy I. A (i) in Carter's *More Binding Variants*, p. 32. B

[2011*a*] *Pl. 25* **Copy II.** A (ii) in Carter's *More Binding Variants*, p. 33. (See also Carter, *Binding Variants*, p. 148.)

The grain of cloth appears identical in each case. End-papers of Copy I deep cream, of Copy II primrose. Both copies very fine.

[2012] *Pl. 25* PERILOUS SECRET (A) [*Parrish* p. 271

2 vols. Bentley 1884. Crimson sateen-damask cloth with floral design; green-on-white foliage end-papers.

Vol. I (iv) + 296
II (iv) + 312 B

To the details given by Parrish it may be added that preceding Vol. I, p. (1) is an inset slip, announcing that this is the last work written by Charles Reade.

[2013] PROPRIA QUAE MARIBUS: a Jeu d'Esprit, and THE BOX TUNNEL: a Fact [*Parrish* p. 195

Boston. Ticknor and Fields 1857. Pinkish brown wrappers, cut flush, printed in black on front and back; spine unlettered. Inside wrappers printed with adverts.

Half-title, reading: TWO NEW STORIES / BY / CHARLES READE. pp. 108. Publishers' cat., 12 pp. on text paper dated October 1857, at end.

Book-plate of Lord Esher.

READIANA: Comments on Current Events [2014]
[*Parrish* p. 262 seq.

Chatto & Windus 1883. Scarlet diagonal-fine-ribbed cloth, blocked and lettered in black and gold in the style of the publishers' Piccadilly Novels; purple-brown flowered end-papers. Steel-engraved portrait front. and wood-engraved vignette on title, both on plate paper.

Half-title. pp. vi + (330) Final leaf, Z_1, a single inset. Publishers' cat., 32 pp. dated July 1882, at end. Fine.

WHITE ELEPHANT (The): a Story [2015]
[*Parrish* p. 275

New York: Gibson & King (1884). Smooth cream cloth, blocked in black; spine unlettered.

Blank leaf and half-title precede title. pp. (86) [paged 88] See Parrish for description of make-up. No signature-numbers.

Ink signature: 'Max Beck, 139 N 120 St. City', on fly-leaf.

READE, W. WINWOOD (1838–1875)

LIBERTY HALL, OXON [2016]

3 vols. Skeet 1860. Red bead-grain cloth, gold-lettered on spine with title, author's name and imprint, and on fronts: A STORY / of / COLLEGES.

Vol. I (viii) [paged (vi)] + (354) Final sig., [R], a single unsigned leaf, adverts.
II iv + (312) O_{12} blank.
III iv + (370)

Ink signature: 'W. T. Hews', on fly-leaf of each vol.

This novel is dedicated to the author's uncle Charles Reade. It was written at the age of 21, after the author had gone down from Magdalen Hall, Oxford.

The covers of Vols. II and III are somewhat stained by damp.

REDE, LEMAN (1802–1847)

ROYAL RAKE (The), and the Adventures of Alfred Chesterton [2017]

Large 4to. 'Printed for Private Circulation only.' Chapman & Elcoate, Peterborough Court 1842. Grey-purple ribbon-embossed cloth, up-lettered on spine. Fifteen 'fierce' woodcuts (none after p. 75).

pp. (iv) + (274) Second leaf of final sig., $2Z_2$, a single inset.

Pencil inscription: 'Very scarce, only 250 printed', inside front cover. No authority given.

Note. Printed in double column (presumably from the type of the *Sunday Times* in which it appeared serially) this curious work describes fast life at the end of the eighteenth century, introducing Lord Barrymore, Col. Hanger, the Prince of Wales, Grattan, Curran and many other historical characters. Ainsworth's *Lancashire Witches* and Knowles' *Fortescue* were first issued in this form.

REID, CAPTAIN THOMAS MAYNE (1818–1883)

Such juveniles as I possess are omitted. Of non-fiction titles I include only *Croquet* for the sake of its unexpectedness in such a bibliography. It is one of Carter's examples of 'off-subject books', which he suggested as a 'new path in book-collecting' in *The Colophon*, New Series, Vol. I, No. 2, 1935.

The curious may be recommended to an article: 'Novels in Newspapers', based on some Mayne Reid letters, contributed by Graham Pollard to the *Review of English Studies*, January 1942. This article is of much interest to students of the development of serial-fiction.

[2018] BANDOLERO (The), or A Marriage among the Mountains

Bentley 1866. Dark grass-green sand-grain cloth, blocked with gold vignette on front and gold-lettered on spine. Front. and 9 full-page illustrations, wood-engraved and unsigned.

Half-title. pp. (iv) + 308 B

[2019] CHILD WIFE (The): a Tale of the Two Worlds

3 vols. Ward, Lock & Tyler 1868. Green fine-morocco cloth.

Vol. I iv + (312)
II iv + (312)
III iv + (292) U_2 blank.

[2020] CROQUET

8vo. Skeet 1863. Salmon-pink bead-grain limp cloth, cut flush, lettered in gold with title and author's name on front, unlettered on spine. Diagram of croquet field as front.

pp. (48) C_8 blank.

Ink inscription: 'C. & L. Elam from Hedingley (?) 1864', on fly-leaf.

[2021] FLAG OF DISTRESS (The): a Story of the South Sea

3 vols. Tinsley 1876. Royal-blue diagonal-fine-ribbed cloth, blocked in black and lettered in gold.

Half-title in Vols. II and III

Vol. I (viii) + 272
II (viii) + 268
III (viii) + 276

A tired copy.

FREE LANCES (The): a Romance of the Mexican Valley [2022]

3 vols. Remington 1881. Pinkish-ochre diagonal-fine-ribbed cloth, blocked in black and lettered in gold.

Blank leaf and half-title precede title in each vol.

Vol. I viii + 232
II viii + 232
III viii + 216

Fine.

HEADLESS HORSEMAN (The): a Strange Tale of Texas [2023]

Copies I and II: Part Issue. Twenty 8vo sixpenny wrappered parts (8vo in format but collating in twelves). Parts I to XVII published by Chapman & Hall, monthly from March 1, 1865 to July 2, 1866; Parts XVIII–XX published by Bentley, monthly from August 1 to October 1 (1866). Pale salmon-pink wrappers printed in black on front (Parts I–XVII): IN TWENTY PARTS, PRICE SIXPENCE EACH / large wood-engraved illustration (unsigned but after R. J. Hamerton) incorporating title and author's name / [*All Rights Reserved.*] / PART I etc.] LONDON: CHAPMAN & HALL, PICCADILLY. [March 1 etc. (Parts XVIII–XX ditto, except that imprint at foot is: RICHARD BENTLEY, NEW BURLINGTON STREET). Back and inside covers printed with adverts. *Pl. 2*

Points of difference between Set I and Set II of Parts and other irregularities are recorded under the Parts concerned.

Part I: Inside front cover: J. Willing & Co. Publishers' cat., 4 pp. dated February 28, 1865.

Frontispiece. pp. (1)–24 of text.

Inset slip on blue paper advertising 'The People's Pickwick'.

Single advert. leaf: recto Peter Robinson; verso Adam & Charles Black.

Inside back cover: 'Shops and Companies of London.'

Outside back cover: Peter Robinson.

Part II: Inside front cover: Chatwood's Safes. Two advert. leaves (4 pp.): (i) Adam & Charles Black; (ii) J. Willing & Co.; (iii) Gillott's Pens, etc.; (iv) Peter Robinson.

Frontispiece. pp. 25–48 of text.

Inset slip on yellow paper advertising *Half a Million of Money*.

Single advert. leaf: recto 'People's Pickwick'; verso blank.

Inside back cover: Colman's Mustard.

Outside back cover: Peter Robinson.

Part III: Inside front cover: Colman's Mustard.
Frontispiece. pp. 49–72 of text.
Single advert. leaf: recto Gillott's Pens, etc.; verso blank.
Inside and outside back covers: Peter Robinson.

Part IV: Inside front cover: Chatwood's Safes.
Frontispiece. pp. 73–96 of text.
Single advert. leaf: recto Gillott's Pens, etc.; verso Colman's Mustard.
Inside and outside back covers: Peter Robinson.

Part V: Inside front cover: J. Willing & Co.
Single advert. leaf: recto Colman's Mustard; verso Gillott's Pens, etc.
Frontispiece. pp. 97–120 of text.
Two leaves on pale pink paper advertising Liverpool & London Globe Insurance Co.
Inside and outside back covers: Peter Robinson.

Part VI: Inside front cover: Chatwood's Safes.
Frontispiece. pp. 121–144 of text.
Single advert. leaf: recto Gillott's Pens, etc.; verso Colman's Mustard.
Inside and outside back covers: Peter Robinson.

Part VII: **Wrapper variant.** Set II front wrapper lacks single bracket preceding date of issue: September 1.
Inside front cover: Colman's Mustard.
Frontispiece. pp. 145–168 of text.
Single advert. leaf: recto Gillott's Pens, etc.; verso J. Willing & Co.
Inside and outside back covers: Peter Robinson.

Part VIII: Inside front cover: Chatwood's Safes.
Frontispiece. pp. 169–192 of text.
Single advert. leaf; recto Gillott's Pens, etc.; verso Colman's Mustard.
Two leaves on pink paper advertising Liverpool & London Globe Insurance Co.
Inside and outside back covers: Peter Robinson.

Part IX: **Wrapper variant.** Set II front wrapper lacks single bracket following words: PART 9.
Inside front cover: J. Willing & Co.
Single advert. leaf: recto Colman's Mustard; verso Gillott's Pens, etc.
Frontispiece. pp. 193–216 of text.
Inside and outside back covers: Peter Robinson.

Part X: **Wrapper variant.** Set I front wrapper lacks single bracket following words: PART 10. and CHAPMAN is badly spaced.
Inside front cover: Chatwood's Safes.
Frontispiece. pp. 217–240 of text.
Single advert. leaf: recto Colman's Mustard; verso Gillott's Pens, etc.
Inside and outside back covers: Peter Robinson.

Part XI: Inside front cover: J. Willing & Co.
Single advert. leaf: recto Colman's Starch; verso Gillott's Pens, etc.
Frontispiece. pp. 241–264 of text.
Two leaves advertising Rimmel's Perfumery.
Inside and outside back covers: Peter Robinson.

Part XII: Inside front cover: J. Willing & Co.
Single advert. leaf as in XI.
Frontispiece. pp. 265–288 of text.
Single leaf on yellow paper advertising Mappin & Webb.
Inside and outside back covers: Peter Robinson.

Part XIII: **Wrapper variants.** Both Set I and Set II give date of issue simply as 'March', i.e. without day-number. Set II shows final '*d*' of *reserved* dropped, and lead not removed between PART 13 and LONDON: CHAPMAN & HALL.
Inside front cover: Chatwood's Safes.
Single advert. leaf as in XI.
Frontispiece. pp. 289–312 of text.
Inside and outside front covers: Peter Robinson.

Part XIV: Inside front cover: J. Willing & Co.
Single advert. leaf as in XI.
Frontispiece. pp. 313–336 of text.
Inside and outside back covers: Peter Robinson.

Part XV: Inside front cover: Chatwood's Safes.
Single advert. leaf as in XI.
Frontispiece. pp. 337–360 of text.
Single leaf printed in blue, brown and black, advertising Keating.
Inside and outside back covers: Peter Robinson.

Part XVI: Inside front cover: 'Reconnoiterer Glass' and J. Willing & Co.
Frontispiece. pp. 361–384 of text.
Two leaves advertising Rimmel's Perfumes.
Inside back cover: Gillott's Pens, etc.
Outside back cover: Colman's Starch.

Part XVII: Inside front cover: as XVI.
Frontispiece. pp. 385–408 of text.
Set I: crown 8vo pamphlet, 16 pp. printed in red advertising Thorley's Cattle Food.
Set II: nil.
Inside and outside back covers: as XVI.

Part XVIII: Inside front cover: as XVI.
Frontispiece. pp. 409–432 of text.
Inside and outside back covers: as XVI.

Part XIX: Inside front cover: as XVI.
Frontispiece. pp. 433–456 of text.
Inside and outside back covers: as XVI.

Part XX: Inside front cover: as XVI.
Set I: Chapman & Hall cat., 4 pp. n.d.
Set II: nil.
Frontispiece. pp. 457–470 of text + X_{12} blank. X_5–X_8 are titles and Contents Lists for book issue. X_5 is an overall title for one-vol. book-issue, carries no vol. number, is dated 1866 and conjugate with X_6, a Contents List for the entire work from Prologue to Chap. C. X_7 is title for Vol. II only, carries the words 'VOL. II', is undated and conjugate with X_8, a Contents List for Chaps. XLIX–C only, i.e. the chapters ultimately contained in Vol. II. Both titles bear the Bentley imprint.

Copy III: Volume Issue. 2 vols. Chapman & Hall (Vol. I) and Bentley (Vol. II) [1866]. Red [2023*a*] morocco cloth blocked in gold, on front with large vignette of the Headless Horseman, on spine pictorially and with lettering. Wood-engraved front. and 9 illustrations in each vol., as in Parts.

Vol. I iv+240
II iv+241–(472) X_8 blank. B

Notes. (i) This was George Bentley's own copy. The spine imprint on both volumes is Chapman & Hall. The title to Vol. I, imprinted Chapman & Hall, carries the words 'VOL. I', is undated, and conjugate with a Contents List from Prologue to Chap. XLVIII only. The title and Contents of Vol. II are as in Parts.

(ii) The publishing history of *The Headless Horseman* is obscure. Mayne Reid's widow gives no information nor does the Bentley Private Catalogue state why the book was taken over from Messrs Chapman & Hall. It says, however, that a Supplementary Part (XXI) was recorded as issued on October 23, 1866; but, no copy having been found, it is presumed this 'Part' merely consisted of a 'cancel title for the First Volume to render it uniform with the second one owing to the change of publishers'.

This, however, as is seen above, could not have been the case, for the titles in the two volumes are different; nor (seeing that according to the Bentley Catalogue the 2-vol. edition was *published* on August 1, 1866) is it easy to understand why a Supplementary Part should have been issued nearly three months later.

This date of publication is curious, as it synchronises with the appearance of the first Bentley-imprinted Part. Did serious inter-publisher trouble develop, and compel a premature book-issue?

I am inclined to believe that the following was the sequence of events. When Bentley took over (the reason for his doing so remains unexplained) he assumed the novel was to be published in one thick volume (it is continuously paged) and accordingly prepared a title without volume number and dated 1866. At the last moment Chapman & Hall insisted on a continuing share in the venture, and were so far able to enforce their claim, that a 2-volume book was hastily devised, divided as to title-page imprints between the rivals.

But why are both *cases* imprinted Chapman & Hall? I have no idea. It could not have been that their cases were ready, for clearly they intended single-volume book issue when they paged continuously, and would not have had two-volume cases prepared ahead.

Probably no explanation will ever be forthcoming; but it would be interesting to know of any 2-vol. copies in original cloth with Bentley on the spines, or of 1-vol. copies using the overall title-page from the Parts. Copies bound from the Parts must surely exist, though possibly only half-bound or in binders' cloth.

On January 5, 1867 Bentley published an edition in one volume, dated 1866 and with the same gold vignette on the red-cloth cover.

LONE RANCHE (The): a Tale of the 'Staked Plain' [2024]

2 vols. Chapman & Hall 1871. Apple-green fine-morocco cloth.

Vol. I iv+(284)
II iv+(292)

Ink signature: 'Eva Blanche Freeman. 1872', on first page of text in each vol. Bookseller's blind stamp: 'Bishop. Rye', on fly-leaves. Fine.

MAROON (The) [2025]

3 vols. Hurst & Blackett 1862. Brown wavy-grain cloth.

Half-title in each vol.

Vol. I (iv)+336
II (iv)+336
III (iv)+356 Publishers' cat., 8 pp. dated January 1864, at end.

Though it has no specific disfigurement, this is a jaded and unattractive copy. Also copies with earlier advertisements must certainly exist.

NO QUARTER! [2026]

3 vols. Swan Sonnenschein, Lowrey & Co., Paternoster Square 1888. Navy-blue diagonal-fine-ribbed cloth, lettered in gold on front and spine. Fawn-on-white patterned end-papers.

Blank leaf and half-title precede title in each vol.

Vol. I viii+(272)
II viii+272
III viii+(264) S_4 blank.

Note. There is a binding variant probably of later date. The cloth is almost black; the lettering on front is in blind, not in gold; the end-papers are plain yellow; and 'Vol. I' etc. on spines are set in sans serif caps with tall initials, instead of in even serif caps.

OCEOLA [2027]

3 vols. Hurst & Blackett 1859. Dark green morocco cloth. Wood-engraved front. and a title-page vignette (the latter identical in each vol.), all after H. Weir and printed on plate paper.

Vol. I (iv) [on plate paper]+320. Publishers' cat., 16 pp. undated, at end.
II (iv) [on plate paper]+(324) Y_2 adverts.
III (iv) [on plate paper]+(324)

Binders' ticket: 'Westleys' at end of Vol. I. Fine.

QUEEN OF THE LAKES (The): a Romance of the Mexican Valley [2028]

London and Belfast: William Mullan 1880. Scarlet diagonal-fine-ribbed cloth, with all-over pictorial blocking in black and gold on front and gold-lettering up spine.

Half-title. pp. viii + (216) 14_2–14_4 adverts. Publisher's cat., 16 pp. undated, at end.

Gold blocking tarnished.

Note. Mullan was the publisher of Henry Kingsley's last story, *The Mystery of the Island* (1355 above), and his catalogue shows a strong temperance list, featuring the works of Edward Jenkins, author of *Ginx's Baby*.

[2029] RIFLE RANGERS (The), or Adventures of an Officer in Southern Mexico

2 vols. Shoberl 1850. Red perpendicular-fine-ribbed cloth, blind-blocked on front and back, gold-lettered on spine; pale blue end-papers, starred in gold. Lithographed front. to Vol. I and front. and 2 plates in Vol. II—all drawn on stone by R. J. Hamerton.

Vol. I xii + 296
II vi + 334 First leaf of final sig., P_1, a single inset.

Very fine. See note to Creasy, *Fifteen Decisive Battles*, p. 100 above.

[2030] SCALP HUNTERS (The), or Romantic Adventures in Northern Mexico

3 vols. Skeet 1851. Half-cloth boards, labels.

Half-title in Vols. I and II

Vol. I x + (308)
II (iv) + (310) First leaf of final sig., O_1, a single inset.
III (ii) + (300) Text ends p. 228; 229–299 Explanatory Notes.

Fine.

Note. This edition was also issued in full cloth—blue, green and red copies have been noted—blind-blocked on front and back, gold-lettered on spine, and (usually) with pale blue end-papers starred in gold. There is a cloth copy in the Collection, in olive-green ripple-grain cloth, with pale yellow end-papers.

Subsequent editions include an undated quarto issue ($6\frac{3}{4}'' \times 7''$) with illustrations by W. Harvey. This issue was published in 31 parts, subsequently bound to make a cloth volume of 248 pp. Two imprints have been noted on this edition—J. C. Brown & Co. (in light brown cloth pictorially blocked in gold) and Henry Lea (in green cloth, pictorially blocked in gold). The original preface, dated June 1851, is retained, with the first words altered from 'About a year ago' to 'Some years ago'.

[2031] WHITE CHIEF (The): a Legend of Northern Mexico

3 vols. David Bogue 1855. Claret ripple-grain cloth, blocked in blind and lettered in gold.

Vol. I (ii) + 308
II (ii) + (306) Final leaf, X_1, a single inset.
III (ii) + (308) Text of novel ends p. 250, (251) + 307 Explanatory Notes, (308) Printers' imprint.

A soiled copy.

WHITE GAUNTLET (The): a Romance [2032]

3 vols. Skeet 1865. Red sand-grain cloth, blocked in black on front, in blind on back, in gold and black on spine (also seen in blue).

Vol. I (ii) + (308)
II (ii) + (302) First leaf of final sig., U_1, a single inset.
III (ii) + (304)

Stain on lower corner of front cover of II and III

Note. This is a secondary binding, on sheets cut down from post to crown octavo. The original binding was of blue dot-and-line-grain cloth, with blind framing on front and back, and gold lettering on spine.

WILD HUNTRESS (The) [2033]

3 vols. Bentley 1861. Orange coarse-morocco cloth; dark orange end-papers.

Vol. I iv + (316)
II iv + (320)
III iv + (344) Z_4 blank.

Fine, although front cover of Vol. III shows a faint stain where ink-damage was remedied.

Note. I think that the earliest binding was of magenta bead-grain cloth, with gold blocking and lettering on spine somewhat eccentrically placed. The orange-style here described is more conventional in design, and was probably a 'substituted', rather than a 'secondary' binding. Copies were also issued in orange moiré fine-ribbed cloth, similarly blocked and, I imagine, of simultaneous date.

WOOD-RANGERS (The) (from the French of Luis de Bellemare) [2034]

3 vols. Hurst & Blackett 1860. Grey-purple morocco cloth. Wood-engraved front. in each vol. after J. B. Zwecker.

Vol. I (ii) + (320) X_8 adverts.
II (ii) + 290 Final leaf, U_1, a single inset.
III (ii) + (296)

Fine.

Mayne Reidiana

SKULL HUNTERS (The): a Terrific Tale of the Prairie (by Captain Rayne Meade) [2035]

Judy Publishing Office, 73 Fleet Street 1868. Grey-blue wrappers, pictorially printed in black on front; inside and outside back covers printed with adverts.; spine unlettered. Wood-engraved front. and numerous illustrations, all on text paper and reckoned in collation.

Half-title. pp. 128

No. 1 of 'Judy's Library'. The series name appears on front cover and half-title.

[*See also* HAMILTON, WALTER, *above*]

REYNOLDS, G. W. M. (1814–1879)

This is deliberately a 'marginal' collection of Reynolds. I had once a very extensive series of his familiar 8vo romances, as well as a long (virtually a complete) run of the *Miscellany*. But the novels were mostly issued undated, were liable to continual re-issue and were ugly in themselves; while the *Miscellany* occupied yards of shelf. I decided, therefore, to collect only his more obscure and individualised works, with the meagre (though uncommon) results which follow.

[2036] DRUNKARD'S PROGRESS (The): a Tale

8vo. George Henderson, 2 Old Bailey 1841. Drab paper wrappers, printed in black on front and back; up-lettered on spine. Inside covers blank. Steel-engraved front. and one plate facing it, both after J. Marshall, and a few illustrations in the text.

Half-title. pp. (iv) + (156)

[2037] GRACE DARLING, or the Heroine of the Fern Islands: a Tale founded on recent facts

8vo. G. Henderson, 2 Old Bailey 1839. Grey-green ribbed cloth. Etched front., vignette title and 18 plates by J. Phillips.

pp. x + 158 Cloth dull.

[2038] PICKWICK ABROAD, or the Tour in France

8vo. Thomas Tegg 1839. Blue-black ribbed cloth. Etched front., vignette title and 39 plates by Alfred Crowquill and John Phillips, and 33 wood-engravings in the text by Bonner.

pp. xvi + 628 Re-cased.

[2039] PIXY (The), or the Unbaptised Child: a Christmas Tale

Small 8vo. John Dicks 'at the office of Reynolds Miscellany' 1848. Dark olive-green horizontally-ribbed cloth, blocked and lettered in gold and blocked in blind.

Wood-engraved front. and 1 plate on text paper precede title. pp. (viii) + 136

Presentation Copy: 'With the kind regards of the Author, G. W. M. Reynolds' in ink on fly-leaf.

Published at one shilling and priced on spine.

ROBERT MACAIRE IN ENGLAND [2040]

3 vols. Thomas Tegg 1840. Grey-purple ribbed cloth, gold pictorial and scroll blocking on spine, blind blocking on front and back. Etched front. and 5 plates in each vol. by Phiz.

Vol. I (iv) + 300
II (ii) + (336)
III (ii) + 358 First leaf of final sig., Q_1, a single inset.

Booksellers' ticket: 'Stassin et Xavier, Paris', inside front cover of Vol. I.

YOUTHFUL IMPOSTOR (The): a Novel [2041]

3 vols. Paris: Bennis, Baudry, Amyot & Truchy; London: Longman & Washburne 1835. Publishers' half dark maroon leather, marbled boards, sprinkled edges; spine gilt and with green lettering-piece.

Half-title in Vols. II and III

Vol. I (viii) + 348
II (iv) + (308) (26_2) blank.
III (iv) + 336

Fine. This novel was re-issued in 1847 as *The Parricide.*

REYNOLDS, REV. H. R. (1825–1896), and SIR JOHN RUSSELL (1828–1896)

YES AND NO, or Glimpses of the Great Conflict [anon] [2042]

3 vols. Macmillan 1860. Brown coarse morocco cloth, 'Kingsley style' (with slight modification).

Half-title in each vol.

Vol. I (vi) + (298) First leaf of final sig., U_1, a single inset. Publishers' cat., 24 pp. dated '7. 11. 59', at end.
II (vi) + (324) Publishers' cat., 24 pp. dated '31. 10. 59', at end.
III (vi) + (288) Publishers' cat., as in Vol. I, at end.

Binder's ticket: 'Burn', at end of Vol. I. Bookplate of Alexander Macmillan.

Note. This scarce novel (it was never reprinted) by a Congregational Minister and his younger brother, a celebrated physician, deals with the religious controversies of the fifties. It was the third three-decker published by Macmillan (the two first were *Westward Ho* and *Two Years Ago*) and should be read in conjunction with the non-fictional works of Frederick Denison Maurice and Charles Kingsley which Macmillan were publishing at the time. Alexander Macmillan, to whom this copy belonged, wrote to Maurice about the book in October 1858, stating that he had urged the author to modify certain 'ultra-Protestant parts'.

RIDDELL, MRS J. H. (1832–1906)

This may not at first sight seem a discreditable series of Mrs Riddell's books, especially as several of them are in admirable condition. But when it is confessed that the twenty-eight titles here listed (and including both first and later editions) are only a little over half of her output; that eight of the three-deckers came at one swallow with the Bentley collection, and that I have collected her assiduously for more than ten years, the achievement, however meritorious, is revealed as far from exhaustive. Mrs Riddell is an outstanding example of a prolific and popular Victorian novelist whose books in fine state (and many of them irrespective of condition) seem to have disappeared. A useful list of her works and an interesting essay about her are included in *Wilkie Collins, Le Fanu and Others* by S. M. Ellis. A description of her key-title is provided from a copy in a Statutory Library.

[2043] BERNA BOYLE: a Love Story of the County Down
3 vols. Bentley 1884. Smooth greenish-blue cloth, blocked in dark blue and white, and lettered in gold; olive-brown flowered end-papers.

Half-title in each vol.

Vol. I (iv)+(280)
II (iv)+280
III (iv)+(276) B

Note. All the titles from the Bentley collection are in new and unused condition; but as they are mostly in light-coloured cloths, they show traces of dust-darkening, either on spines or along fore-edges.

[2044] CITY AND SUBURB: a Novel
Tinsley 1866: 'A New Edition.' Crimson sand-grain cloth.

This is the first one-vol. edition of a novel published in 3 vols. in 1861.

[2045] DAISIES AND BUTTERCUPS: a Novel
3 vols. Bentley 1882. Pinkish-ochre diagonal-fine-ribbed cloth, blocked on front in dark brown, on spine blocked and lettered in gold; pale grey flowered end-papers.

Half-title in Vol. I

Vol. I (viii)+(316)
II (iv)+(308)
III (iv)+(336) B

[2046] DISAPPEARANCE OF MR JEREMIAH REDWORTH (The)
Routledge's Christmas Annual (1878). White pictorial wrappers, printed in red, blue and black. Wood-engraved front. and 5 illustrations after D. H. Friston.

pp. 96 Fine.

Note. This story, like *Fairy Water, The Haunted River, Long Ago, My First Love* described below, constituted an entire Annual.

EARL'S PROMISE (The): a Novel [2047]
3 vols. Tinsley 1873. Grass-green sand-grain cloth.

Blank leaf and half-title precede title in Vols. I and II; half-title only in Vol. III

Vol. I (viii)+(304) U_8 blank.
II (viii)+312
III (vi)+322 Final leaf, Y_1, a single inset.

Very fine.

FAIRY WATER: a Christmas Story [2048]
Routledge's Christmas Annual (1873). White pictorial wrappers printed in red, grey and black. Wood-engraved front. and 5 illustrations after R. Caldecott.

pp. 96 Spine worn.

FAR ABOVE RUBIES: a Novel [2049]
3 vols. Tinsley 1867. Claret moiré fine-ribbed cloth.

Vol. I iv+(312) X_4 adverts.
II iv+(304)
III iv+(304)

Red chalk signature: 'Georgiana W. Codrington, Dodington. Chipping Sodbury', on title of Vol. II; ink signature: 'Georgiana W. Codrington', on titles of Vols. II and III. Fine. Small stain on front cover of Vol. III.

*GEORGE GEITH OF FEN COURT: a Novel [2050]
(by F. G. Trafford, author of 'Too Much Alone', etc.)
3 vols. Tinsley 1864. Red-brown sand-grain cloth, blocked in blind on front and back, with triple frame and central oval medallion, gold-lettered on spine: GEORGE / GEITH / OF / FEN COURT / BY / THE AUTHOR OF / 'TOO MUCH ALONE'. / *Leaf ornament* (followed by vol. no. and imprint). Cream end-papers.

Half-title in each vol.

Vol. I viii+318 First leaf of final sig., X_1, a single inset.
II vi+314 First leaf of final sig., X_1, a single inset.
III vi+288 Publishers' cat., 4 pp. undated on text paper, at end.

In a copy examined, binders' ticket 'Bone & Son', at end of Vol. I.

Note. A Second (of which I have a copy) and a Third Edition of this novel were published in 3 vols. in 1865, and the title-pages show a curious variation. Whereas the titles of the Third Edition are uniform in typography and wording (date and statement of edition apart) with the First, those of the Second are in larger and clearer type, the words SECOND EDITION are in sans serif rom. caps. and not gothic caps. and l.c. as are 'Third Edition', and the authorship is thus expressed:

BY F. G. TRAFFORD, AUTHOR OF 'TOO MUCH ALONE', 'THE WORLD IN THE CHURCH', 'CITY AND SUBURB', etc. There is no printer's imprint on verso of title, as there is in First and Third Editions.

[2051] GOVERNMENT OFFICIAL (The): a Novel [anon. Written by Mrs Riddell in collaboration with A. H. Norway]

3 vols. Bentley 1887. Salmon-pink silky cloth, with damask pattern of leaves, blocked in dark brown; pale grey flowered end-papers.

Half-title in each vol.

Vol. I (viii) + 300
II (vi) + (302) First leaf of final sig., 38_1, a single inset.
III (vi) + 306 **B**

The board of front cover of Vol. I has been bent.

[2052] HANDSOME PHIL and other Stories

F. V. White 1899. Dark royal-blue diagonal-fine-ribbed cloth.

Half-title. pp. 320

[2053] HAUNTED RIVER (The): a Christmas Story

Routledge's Christmas Annual (1877). White pictorial wrapper, printed in red, blue and black. Wood-engraved front. and 5 illustrations after D. H. Friston.

pp. (96) Fine.

[2054] LIFE'S ASSIZE (A): a Novel

3 vols. Tinsley 1871. Chocolate sand-grain cloth.

Half-title in each vol.

Vol. I (viii) + 298 Final leaf, X_1, a single inset.
II (vi) + (300)
III (vi) + 282 Final leaf, U_1, a single inset. Publishers' cat., 16 pp. dated November 1870, at end.

Presentation Copy: 'Mrs Greene. With the Author's Love Xmas 1870' in ink on title of Vol. I. Slight smear on back cover of Vol. II.

[2055] LONG AGO: Part I (by the author of 'George Geith', 'Austin Friars', etc.)

8vo. F. Enos Arnold, 49 Essex Street (1870). White wrappers cut flush, pictorially printed and lettered in red and black; spine unlettered; back and inside covers printed with adverts. Wood-engraved front. and 5 full-page illustrations.

32 pp. of adverts. dated December 1870 precede front. pp. (88) 6_2–6_4 adverts.

Note. Although the advert. pages are headed 'St James' Magazine Christmas Box Advertiser' the cover gives no indication that the book has any connection with that periodical. A footnote to p. (1) states that the second half of the tale will appear in January (1871). This second half is not in the Collection.

MAXWELL DREWITT: a Novel (by F. G. Trafford) [2056]

Copy I: First Edition. 3 vols. Tinsley 1865. Brown sand-grain cloth, blocked in blind on front and back, gold-lettered on spine in a style generally uniform with *George Geith.*

Half-title in Vol. I

Vol. I vi + 306
II iv + 300
III iv + (268) S_6 adverts. Publishers' cat., 16 pp. undated, at end.

Note. This is a collaborative and partially conjectural entry. Vols. II and III only of the first edition are in the Collection; the collation of Vol. I comes from the Bodleian whose copy (the only one in original state locatable) is of the third edition. But as this third edition collates, as to II and III, identically with the first, I think we can assume the collation of I to be equally correct.

Copy II: First one-vol. and first illustrated edition (by the author of 'George Geith of Fen Court', etc.) [2056*a*]

F. Enos Arnold, 49 Essex Street 1869: 'New Edition.' Rose-pink morocco cloth; pale chocolate end-papers. Wood-engraved front., vignette on title and plates in text.

MITRE COURT: a Tale of the Great City [2057]

3 vols. Bentley 1885. Smooth bright-chalky-blue cloth, blocked in chocolate and lettered in gold; lilac decorated end-papers.

Vol. I (iv) + (306) Final leaf, (20_1), a single inset.
II (iv) + 324
III (iv) + (318) First leaf of final sig., 60_1, a single inset. **B**

MOORS AND THE FENS (The) (by F. G. Trafford) [2058]

3 vols. Smith, Elder 1857. Dark sage-green ripple-grain cloth.

Vol. I (iv) + 324
II (iv) + (324)
III (iv) + 308 Publishers' cat., 16 pp. dated December 1858, at end.

Binders' ticket: 'Westleys', at end of Vol. I. Very fine.

MORTOMLEY'S ESTATE: a Novel [2059]

3 vols. Tinsley 1874. Very dark grey-black fine-morocco cloth.

Half-title in each vol.

Vol. I (viii) + (304) U_8 blank.
II (viii) + 310 First leaf of final sig., X_1, a single inset.
III (viii) + (328)

The hinge of Vol. I has been affected by damp, without result to the cloth but sufficiently to loosen pp. 6–10 of the first signature. Blind stamp: 'W. H. Smith Library', on fly-leaf of Vol. I.

Note. This novel was also issued in brown and in red cloth, with tall gilt spine-lettering.

[2060] MY FIRST LOVE (by the author of 'George Geith', 'Austin Friars', etc.)

8vo. F. Enos Arnold, 49 Essex Street 1869. White wrappers, cut flush, armorially printed and lettered in gold, red, blue and black, up-lettered on spine: NEW SERIES, ST JAMES' MAGAZINE, CHRISTMAS. 1869. Back and inside covers printed with adverts. Front. and 9 full-page illustrations, some lithographed, some wood-engraved.

40 pp. of adverts. dated December 1869 precede front. pp. 80 5_7 Publishers' Notice; 5_8 advert. 2 pp. of adverts. (inset and of different sizes) at end. Single leaves of adverts. on coloured papers inserted between pp. 8–9, 32–33, 40–41, 72–73.

Fine. This is the *St James' Magazine Christmas Box* for 1869.

[2061] MYSTERY IN PALACE GARDENS (The): a Novel

3 vols. Bentley 1880. Light drab diagonal-fine-ribbed cloth, blocked in black on front, spine and back with a design of tree branches and a seated owl, and with spine-lettering over-blocked in gold.

Half-title in Vol. I

Vol. I (vi)+(314) Final leaf, X_5, a single inset.
II (iv)+(308)
III (iv)+(292) **B**

[2062] NUN'S CURSE (The): a Novel

3 vols. Ward & Downey 1888. Smooth dark green cloth; pale grey foliage end-papers.

Half-title in Vol. I

Vol. I (viii)+(298) Final leaf, U_5, a single inset.
II (iv)+(292)
III (iv)+(326) Final leaf, Y_3, a single inset.

Presentation Copy: 'To Dear Mrs Harley with Charlotte E. Riddell's love. Dec. 2, 1887' in ink on half sheet of notepaper pasted to half-title in Vol. I. (Mrs Harley was one of the dedicatees of the novel.)

Book-plate of Francis Woodcock Goodbody in Vols. I and II. Covers of Vols. II and III slightly spotted.

[2063] PHEMIE KELLER: a Novel (by the author of 'George Geith of Fen Court', etc.)

F. Enos Arnold, 49 Essex Street 1870. Salmon-pink morocco cloth; pale chocolate end-papers. Wood-engraved front.

This is the first one-vol. and first illustrated edition of a novel published in 3 vols. in 1866.

RACE FOR WEALTH (The): a Novel [2064]

3 vols. Tinsley 1866. Bright brown fine-morocco cloth.

Half-title in each vol.

Vol. I vi+(342) Final leaf, Z_3, a single inset of commercial adverts.
II (vi)+(346) Final leaf, Z_5, a single inset.
III (vi)+374 First leaf of final sig., BB_1, a single inset.

Ink signature: 'Georgiana W. Codrington', on title, and 'Lady Georgiana Codrington' on front cover of each vol. Fine. Unobtrusive damp-stain on covers of Vol. I.

RULING PASSION (The) (by Rainey Hawthorne) [2065]

3 vols. Bentley 1857. Half-cloth boards, labels.

Half-title in each vol.

Vol. I (iv)+(320)
II (iv)+(284) T_6 blank.
III (iv)+(292) U_2 blank.

Back fly-leaf of Vol. I lacking.

Note. This novel was also issued in dark olive-grey diagonal-fine-ribbed cloth, blind-blocked and gold-lettered.

SENIOR PARTNER (The): a Novel [2066]

3 vols. Bentley 1881. Apple-green diagonal-fine-ribbed cloth, blocked in dark green with design of ivy leaves and lettered in gold; pale grey flowered end-papers.

Half-title in each vol.

Vol. I (vi)+298 Final leaf, X_1, a single inset.
II (vi)+310 First leaf of final sig., X_1, a single inset.
III (vi)+290 Final leaf, U_1, a single inset. **B**

STRUGGLE FOR FAME (A): a Novel [2067]

3 vols. Bentley 1883. Smooth light blue cloth, blocked in chocolate and lettered in gold.

Vol. I (vi)+336
II (iv)+332
III (iv)+358 Final leaf, 65_3, a single inset. **B**

SUSAN DRUMMOND: a Novel [2068]

3 vols. Bentley 1884. Smooth lilac-blue cloth, blocked with floral spray in green and red-brown, and lettered in gold; olive-brown flowered end-papers.

Half-title in Vol. I; blank leaf and half-title precede title in Vols. II and III

Vol. I (viii)+(ii) [a single inset leaf of different paper carrying 'Prefatory Note']+(336)
II (viii)+(330) Final leaf, 43_5, a single inset.
III (viii)+(388) **B**

[2069] UNINHABITED HOUSE (The)
Routledge's Christmas Annual (1875). White pictorial wrappers in red, blue and black. Wood-engraved front. and 5 illustrations after A. C. Corbould.
pp. 96 Fine.

[2070] WEIRD STORIES
James Hogg, n.d. (1882). Dark green diagonal-fine-ribbed cloth.
Blank leaf and half-title precede title. pp. (viii) + (320) X_6–X_8 adverts.

'RITA' (MRS DESMOND HUMPHREYS) (?*circ.* 1860–1938)

[2071] ENDING OF MY DAY (The): the Story of a Stormy Life
3 vols. F. V. White 1894. Dark red fine-diaper cloth; cream end-papers patterned in pale brown.
Half-title in each vol.
Vol. I (viii) + 244 Pp. (vii) (viii) are a repetition of the half-title.
II (viii) + (256) Pp. (vii) (viii) are a repetition of the half-title.
III (viii) + 236 Pp. (vii) (viii) are a repetition of the half-title. Publishers' cat., 16 pp. undated on text paper, at end.
'Author's Corrected Copy', as stated in Rita's hand on slip of paper pasted on front of each vol. Numerous pencil corrections throughout the text. 'Anderson' in ink on title of each vol., in Vol. I scored through by Rita. Back cover of Vol. I and spine of Vol. II heavily ink-stained.

[2072] PEG, THE RAKE
3 vols. Hutchinson 1894. Claret unglazed buckram, blocked in blind and lettered in gold.
Blank leaf and half-title precede title in each vol.
Vol. I (viii) + (236) 15_6 adverts.
II (viii) + (244) 16_2 adverts.
III (viii) + (256)
The dedication is repeated in each volume. Fine. Spines very slightly faded.

ROBINSON, EMMA (*fl.* 1844–1868)

[2073] CAESAR BORGIA: an Historical Romance (by the author of 'Whitefriars')
3 vols. Colburn 1846. Half-cloth boards, labels.
Vol. I (viii) + (364) R_2 adverts.
II (ii) + (326) Final leaf, P_7, a single inset.
III (ii) + (388) S_2 adverts.
Book-plate and label of the Llanover Library in each vol.; circulation list of the Abergavenny Book Club on fly-leaf of Vol. I; bookseller's ticket: 'Rees, Abergavenny', in each vol.

DOROTHY FIREBRACE, or the Armourer's Daughter of Birmingham (by the author of 'Whitefriars') [2074]
3 vols. Bentley 1865. Crimson-lake 'hexagon-grain' cloth.
Half-title in each vol.
Vol. I (iv) + 330 First leaf of final sig., Y_1, a single inset.
II (iv) + (332)
III (iv) + (324) B
Notes. (i) The titles are cancels. Judging from half-titles and running headlines the novel was originally entitled: THE ARMOURER'S DAUGHTER. A last-minute change was effected, perhaps because the first chosen title had already been used.
(ii) I am not aware of this cloth-grain on any other book. It consists of small hexagons, each with a raised dot in the centre and set very close together. Copies in green cloth are secondaries.

GOLD WORSHIPPERS (The), or the Days We Live In: a *Future* Historical Novel (by the author of 'Whitefriars') [2075]
3 vols. Parry & Co. 1851. Half-black leather, dark slate board sides and dark grey cloth corners; dark grey-purple end-papers.
Vol. I (iv) + 292
II (iv) + 316
III (ii) + 342 First leaf of final sig., Z_1, a single inset.
Book-plate of A. H. Christie.
Note. This book has a very peculiar binding—certainly original and to all appearance emanating from the publishers. Probably a special library binding, but suspiciously aesthetic.

OWEN TUDOR: an Historical Romance (by the author of 'Whitefriars', 'Caesar Borgia', etc.) [2076]
3 vols. Colburn 1849. Half-cloth boards, labels.
Half-title in Vols. I and II
Vol. I (iv) + 344
II (iv) + 336
III (ii) + 316
Book-plate and labels of the Llanover Library.

RICHELIEU IN LOVE, or the Youth of Charles I: an Historical Comedy in Five Acts, as accepted at the Theatre Royal, Haymarket and prohibited by Authority of the Lord Chamberlain. With a Preface Explanatory. [2077]
Copy I: First Edition [anon]. 8vo. Colburn 1844. Brown paper wrappers, printed in black.
Half-title. pp. (xxxii) + 80
'From the Author' in ink on front cover. Names of caste, when the play was ultimately licensed in 1852, inserted in pencil on p. (xxxii). Spine missing.

[2077*a*] **Copy II: Second Edition** ('by the author of Whitefriars'). Charles Westerton, 20 St George's Place 1852. New boards. Original brown paper wrappers printed in black preserved.

pp. (60) [paged (i)–vi + (7)–(60)] A new Dedication, dated October 9, 1852 and a new 'Preamble' occupy pp. (iii)–vi.

[2078] WESTMINSTER ABBEY, or the Days of the Reformation (by the author of 'Whitefriars', 'Caesar Borgia', etc.)

3 vols. John Mortimer 1854. Bright blue morocco cloth.

Half-title in each vol.

Vol. I (iv) + (344)
II (iv) + (352)
III (iv) + (488) $2T_4$ blank.

Book-plate of A. H. Christie.

[2079] WHITEFRIARS, or the Days of Charles II: an Historical Romance [anon]

3 vols. Colburn 1844: 'Third Edition.' Half-cloth boards, labels.

Vol. I (viii) [paged vi] + (324)
II (ii) + (340)
III (ii) + 334 First leaf of final sig., Y_1, a single inset. Single advert. leaf on thin paper inset at end.

Ink signature: 'E. Hunt, July 30, 1844', on fly-leaf of Vol. II.

[2080] WHITEHALL, or the Days of Charles I: an Historical Romance (by the author of 'Whitefriars')

3 vols. John Mortimer 1845. Cont. half-leather marbled boards (library binding).

Half-title in each vol.

Vol. I (xvi) + 278 Final leaf, O_1, a single inset.
II (iv) + (300) O_6 blank.
III (iv) + (278) Final leaf, O_1, a single inset.

Label of 'Millards Circulating Library, Lee' in each vol.

ROMER, MRS ISABELLA F.

[2081] STURMER: a Tale of Mesmerism. To which are added Other Sketches from Life

3 vols. Bentley 1841. Boards, labels.

Half-title in each vol.

Vol. I (iv) + 294 First leaf of final sig., O_1, a single inset.
II (iv) + (300)
III (iv) + (324)

Fine. Spine of Vol. I slightly split at head.

ROWCROFT, CHARLES (*fl.* 1840–1855)

CHRONICLES OF 'THE FLEET PRISON', from the Papers of the late Alfred Seedy, Esq. [2082

3 vols. H. Hurst 1847. Half-cloth boards, labels.

Half-title in Vols. I and II

Vol. I (iv) + 300
II (iv) + (312) O_{12} blank.
III (ii) + (312)

Ink signature: 'Lord Cloncurry', on title of each vol. Fine.

Note. A rare imprint. Hurst, who published Marryat's *Children of the New Forest* and *The Little Savage*, only lasted three or four years.

CONFESSIONS OF AN ETONIAN [2083

3 vols. Colburn & Co. 1852. Grey-purple morocco cloth.

Vol. I (ii) + (326) Final leaf, Y_3, a single inset.
II (ii) + (324)
III (ii) + (298) Final leaf, X_1, a single inset.

Book-plate of Alfred Charles Twentyman. Fine.

Note. This was published during the last year or two of the Colburn imprint—after Henry Colburn was dead and the short-lived style Colburn & Co. (which ran from middle or late 1851 to early or middle 1853) was in existence. The book's style is directly a forecast of that adopted by Hurst & Blackett during the fifties.

RUFFINI, JOHN (1807–1881)

DOCTOR ANTONIO: a Tale (by the author of 'Lorenzo Benoni') [208

Edinburgh: Thomas Constable & Co. 1855. Crimson morocco cloth, with fancy gold titling on front and spine, uniform with *Lorenzo Benoni.*

Leaf of adverts. and half-title precede title. pp. viii + (480) $2G_5$–$2G_8$ adverts.

Ink signature: 'L. W. Bangs', on fly-leaf. Bookseller's ticket: 'Dorman, Northampton', inside front cover.

LAVINIA (by the author of 'Lorenzo Benoni' and 'Doctor Antonio') [208

3 vols. Smith, Elder 1860. Dark grey-blue morocco cloth.

Vol. I (iv) + (308)
II (iv) + (316) $4O_6$ adverts.
III (iv) + 308 Publishers' cat., 16 pp. dated December 1860, at end.

Library labels have been removed from front covers and the colour of Vol. II is not quite uniform with Vols. I and III.

[2086] LORENZO BENONI, or Passages in the Life of an Italian. Edited by a friend [anon]

Copy I: First Edition. Large square 8vo. Edinburgh: Thomas Constable & Co. 1853. Crimson ripple-grain cloth, with fancy gold titling on front and spine.

pp. (viii) + (508) $2U_2$ blank.

Binder's ticket: 'John Gray, Edinburgh', at end. Bruise on front cover, cloth blistered, corners slightly worn.

[2086*a*] **Copy II: Half Crown Edition.** Thomas Constable 1853. Glazed white boards, printed in black, up-lettered on spine; yellow end-papers.

Half-title. pp. viii + (328) X_4 adverts.

Booksellers' ticket: 'Gilbert Bros.', inside front cover. Very fine.

Note. This edition, published in the same year as the first, carries on back cover an advert. of the first, with quotes, described as 'Library Edition'.

[2087] PARAGREENS (The), on a Visit to the Paris Universal Exhibition (by the author of 'Lorenzo Benoni', 'Doctor Antonio')

Fcap 8vo. Edinburgh: Thomas Constable & Co. 1856. Blue ripple-grain cloth, pictorially blocked in gold on front and spine. Wood-engraved front. and 4 plates after John Leech.

pp. (iv) + (236) P_4–P_6 adverts.

Blind stamp: 'W. H. Smith & Son', on fly-leaf.

[2088] QUIET NOOK IN THE JURA (A) (by the author of 'Doctor Antonio', etc.)

Edinburgh: Edmonston & Douglas 1867. Smooth brown cloth; chocolate end-papers.

Half-title. pp. (x) + 342 Final leaf, Y_3, a single inset.

Lower right-hand corners damp-stained.

[2089] VINCENZO, or Sunken Rocks

3 vols. Macmillan 1863. Blue morocco cloth, blocked and lettered in 'Kingsley' style.

Half-title in each vol.

Vol. I (viii) + 288
II (viii) + (288) T_8 blank.
III (viii) + (296) U_4 adverts.

This was the publishers' file copy. FILE is stamped in blind on front covers and a label 'Sample' has been partially removed from each cover. The end-papers in Vol. II are chocolate, in other vols. yellow. Vols. II and III are damp-stained at foot of front covers.

RUSSELL, W. CLARK (1884–1911)

AS INNOCENT AS A BABY: a Novel [anon] [2090]

3 vols. Bentley 1874. Grass-green fine-ribbed cloth.

Half-title in Vol. I

Vol. I (viii) + 286 1st leaf of final sig., 18_1, a single inset.
II (iv) + (286) Final leaf, 18_7, a single inset.
III (iv) + (272) 17_7 17_8 adverts. B

The title in each vol. is a cancel. According to the Bentley Private Catalogue the novel appeared as by 'James Remington Potts' and the cancels were printed in order to append this name; but the titles are actually anonymous, so probably in fact the process was reversed.

BOOK FOR THE HAMMOCK (A) [2091]

Chatto & Windus 1887. Smooth pinkish-ochre cloth, pictorially blocked in black, dark blue and white, and lettered in gold; black end-papers. *Pl. 25*

Half-title. pp. (viii) + (304) U_8 publishers' device. Publishers' cat., 32 pp. dated July 1887, at end.

Book-plate of John Browne. Very fine.

CAPTAIN FANNY ('by the author of "John Holdsworth, Chief Mate", etc.') [2092]

3 vols. Bentley 1876. Chocolate diagonal-fine-ribbed cloth.

Vol. I (iv) + (288)
II (iv) + (272) 17_8 adverts.
III (iv) + 272 Publishers' cat., 4 pp. undated on text paper, at end. B

Binders' ticket: 'Leighton, Son & Hodge', at end of Vol. I.

DARK SECRET (A) ('by Eliza Rhyl Davies') [2093]

3 vols. Bentley 1875. Dark sage-green sand-grain cloth, irregularly flecked with raised spots, giving the effect of a scattered bubble-grain.

Half-title in Vol. I

Vol. I (viii) + (272)
II (iv) + (252) 16_6 adverts.
III (iv) + (236) 15_4–15_6 adverts. B

The true authorship of this novel is revealed by the Bentley Private Catalogue. The cloth is of a grain I have not noted elsewhere.

DECEASED WIFE'S SISTER (The) and MY BEAUTIFUL NEIGHBOUR [anon] [2094]

3 vols. Bentley 1874. Chocolate diagonal-fine-ribbed cloth.

Vol. I (ii) + 292
II (ii) + 280
III (ii) + 282 3rd (central) leaf of final sig., T_3, a single inset. B

[2095] EMIGRANT SHIP (The)
3 vols. Sampson Low etc. 1893. Smooth grey-blue cloth; pale salmon decorated end-papers.

Half-title in Vol. I

Vol. I (viii) + (288) T_8 blank.
II (iv) + (296)
III (iv) + 288

Fine.

[2096] GOOD SHIP 'MOHOCK' (The)
2 vols. Chatto & Windus 1894. Navy-blue morocco cloth; pale grey flowered end-papers.

Blank leaf and half-title precede title in each vol.

Vol. I (viii) + (200) N_4 publishers' device. Publishers' cat., 32 pp. dated September 1894, at end.
II (viii) + 216

Fine.

[2097] IN THE MIDDLE WATCH
Pl. 25 Chatto & Windus 1885. Smooth greenish-grey cloth, pictorially blocked in dark blue and bronze, and lettered in gold; grey chocolate end-papers.

Half-title. pp. (viii) + (292) Publishers' cat., 32 pp. dated October 1885, at end.

Book-plate of John Browne. Very fine.

[2098] MRS DINES' JEWELS: a Mid-Atlantic Romance
Sampson Low etc. 1892. Smooth scarlet cloth; pale blue end-papers printed with adverts.

Half-title. pp. vi + 258

Book-plate of John Browne.

[2099] MY SHIPMATE LOUISE: the Romance of a Wreck
3 vols. Chatto & Windus 1890. Dark blue wavy-grain cloth; pale grey flowered end-papers.

Half-title in Vol. I; blank leaf and half-title precede title in Vols. II and III

Vol. I (viii) + (308) Publishers' cat., 32 pp. dated June 1890, at end.
II (viii) + (312)
III (viii) + (328)

Fine.

[3000] MYSTERY OF ASHLEIGH MANOR (The): a Romance ('by Eliza Rhyl Davies')
3 vols. Bentley 1874. Chocolate sand-grain cloth.

Vol. I iv + (300)
II (iv) + 298 Final leaf, 19_5, a single inset.
III (iv) + (274) Final leaf, (18_1), a single inset. **B**

The true authorship of this novel is revealed by the Bentley Private Catalogue.

MYSTERY OF THE 'OCEAN STAR' (The): a Collection of Maritime Sketches [3001] *Pl. 25*

Chatto & Windus 1888. Smooth turquoise-blue cloth, pictorially blocked in black, dark green and white, and lettered in gold; pale grey flowered end-papers.

Advert. leaf precedes title. pp. (viii) + (312) Publishers' cat., 32 pp. dated December 1887, at end.

Book-plate of John Browne. Very fine.

Note. A Publishers' Note describes this as the 'sixth annual volume of Mr Clark Russell's contributions to the public journals and the monthly magazines' and declares that the series 'form a marine encyclopaedia of almost every subject of interest connected with the British Mercantile Marine'. All six volumes are here represented in mint condition (the others are: *Book for the Hammock*, *In the Middle Watch*, *On the Fo'k'sle Head*, *Round the Galley Fire*, *Voyage to the Cape*) and constitute the most striking examples known to me of pictorial colour-blocking on cloth, as used at this period.

MY WATCH BELOW, or Yarns Spun when off Duty ('by a Seafarer') [3002]

Sampson Low etc. 1882. Smooth dark royal-blue cloth, blocked in red and yellow; pale grey end-papers. Wood-engraved front.

pp. viii + (252) S_1 S_2, paged (1)–4, adverts. Publishers' cat., 32 pp. dated December 1881, at end.

Published at 2*s*. 6*d*. and price blocked on spine.

OCEAN FREE LANCE (An): from a Privateersman's Log, 1812 [3003]

3 vols. Bentley 1881. Smooth sand-coloured cloth.

Vol. I (vi) + (298) Final leaf, 19_5, a single inset.
II (iv) + (272) 36_8 adverts.
III (iv) + (312) 56_3 56_4 adverts. **B**

ON THE FO'K'SLE HEAD [3004]

Chatto & Windus 1884. Smooth blue-grey cloth, pictorially blocked in black and white, and lettered in gold; grey-chocolate end-papers. *Pl. 25*

Half-title. pp. viii + 308 Publishers' cat., 32 pp. dated October 1884, at end.

Binder's ticket: 'Burn', at end. Book-plate of John Browne. Very fine.

ROMANCE OF JENNY HARLOW (The), and Sketches of Maritime Life [3005]

Chatto & Windus 1889. Smooth scarlet cloth, pictorially blocked in light blue and black, and lettered in gold; pale grey flowered end-papers. Wood-engraved front. after Fred Barnard.

pp. (iv) + 396 Publishers' cat., 32 pp. dated September 1889, at end.

Book-plate of John Browne. Fine.

[3006] **ROUND THE GALLEY FIRE**
Pl. 25 Chatto & Windus 1883. Smooth navy-blue cloth, pictorially blocked in red and black, and lettered in gold; grey-chocolate end-papers.

Half-title. pp. (viii) + 308 Publishers' cat., 32 pp. dated August 1883, at end.

Book-plate of John Browne. Very fine.

[3007] **STRANGE ELOPEMENT (A)**
Macmillan 1892. Scarlet diaper cloth. 15 half-tone illustrations after W. H. Overend.

Half-title. pp. viii + 248 Publishers' adverts., 4 pp. on thin paper of rather smaller size, dated '20. 1. 92', followed by publishers' cat., 44 pp. dated September 1891.

Book-plate of John Browne. Fine.

[3008] **STRANGE VOYAGE (A)**
3 vols. Sampson Low, etc. 1885. Light blue-grey diagonal-fine-ribbed cloth, blocked in blind on front and back, gold-lettered on spine.

Vol. I (iv) + (300) U_6 blank.
II (iv) + (292) U_2 blank.
III (iv) + 266 First leaf of final sig., S_1, a single inset. Publishers' cat., 32 pp. dated October 1885, at end.

Fine.

[3009] **VOYAGE TO THE CAPE (A)**
Pl. 25 Chatto & Windus 1887. Grey-blue diagonal-fine-ribbed cloth, pictorially blocked in dark blue and orange-brown, and lettered in gold; grey-chocolate end-papers.

pp. (viii) + 360 Publishers' cat., 32 pp. dated October 1887, at end.

Book-plate of John Browne. Very fine.

[3010] **WHICH SISTER?** a Story ('by Sydney Mostyn, author of "The Surgeon's Secret", etc.')
2 vols. Bentley 1873. Royal-blue fine-morocco cloth.

Half-title in each vol.

Vol. I (iv) + (296) U_4 blank.
II (iv) + (304) U_8 blank. B

[3011] **WRECK OF THE GROSVENOR (The)**: an Account of the Mutiny of the Crew and the Loss of the Ship, when trying to make the Bermudas [anon]
3 vols. Sampson Low, etc. 1877. Grass-green diagonal-fine-ribbed cloth, blocked in blind on front and back with triple frame and circular publishers' monogram; gold-lettered on spine.

Half-title in each vol.

Vol. I (iv) + (296) U_4 blank.
II (iv) + (296) U_4 blank.
III (iv) + (292) U_2 blank.

Fine.

RUTHERFORD, MARK (WILLIAM HALE WHITE) (1831–1913)

For further bibliographical detail, see *Bibliographies of Modern Authors (Third Series)*, London, *Bookman's Journal*, 1931 which contains a Bibliography of Mark Rutherford by Simon Nowell-Smith, issued as a Supplement to the *Bookman's Journal* in 1930. References which follow are to this monograph, or to a supplementary note published by S.N.S. in *Bibliographical Notes and Queries*, Vol. II, No. 1 (January 1936). In addition to the fiction and part-fiction described below, the collection also includes EXAMINATION OF THE CHARGE OF APOSTASY AGAINST WORDSWORTH, 1898 (by William Hale White) (S.N.S. p. 16); No. 13 of fifty large paper copies of COLERIDGE'S POEMS, 1899 (S.N.S. p. 20); JOHN BUNYAN, 1905 (S.N.S. p. 17) and the recent volumes: LETTERS TO THREE FRIENDS (S.N.S. p. 23) and Mrs Hale White's *Groombridge Diary*, both published in 1924.

AUTOBIOGRAPHY OF MARK RUTHERFORD, DISSENTING MINISTER (The) [3012]
(Edited by his Friend, Reuben Shapcott) [*S.N.S.* p. 13
Trübner & Co. 1881. Blue-green paper boards, label; dark chocolate end-papers.

Blank leaf and half-title precede title. pp. (xii) + 180 Fine. Spine slightly darkened.

CATHARINE FURZE (by Mark Rutherford. Edited by his friend, Reuben Shapcott) [3013]
2 vols. T. Fisher Unwin 1893. [*S.N.S.* p. 16

Copy I. Half apple-green cloth; dark olive-green sides, blocked and lettered in gold on front and spine.

Half-title in each vol.

Vol. I pp. (184) 12_4 imprint leaf.
II pp. (192) 12_8 imprint leaf.

Copy II. Brown diagonal-fine-ribbed cloth, blocked uniform with Copy I except that title on spine is in a single panel. Collation as Copy I. [3013*a*]

Cloth worn; labels removed from front covers.

Note. This is the copy referred to by Simon Nowell-Smith in *Bibliographical Notes and Queries*, Vol. II, No. 1 (January 1936) as one of four known to him, and as evidence (thanks to the traces of labels) that at least one copy in this style actually came upon the market. He is satisfied that the brown cloth was discarded in favour of the two greens; but I record the book here as Copy II because, although of earlier issue than Copy I, its status as a 'published' style is still uncertain. The copy was given to me by S.N.S.

[3014] CLARA HOPGOOD (by Mark Rutherford. Edited by his friend, Reuben Shapcott) [*S.N.S.* p. 16
T. Fisher Unwin 1896. Dark green ribbed cloth. Title printed in red and black.

Half-title. pp. (iv) + (300) U_2 blank. Very fine.

[3015] LAST PAGES FROM A JOURNAL, with Other Papers (Edited by his Wife) [*S.N.S.* p. 18
Fcap 8vo. Humphrey Milford 1915. Blue cloth. Half-tone front.

pp. viii + (322) Final leaf, Y_1, a single inset. As new, in dust wrapper.

[3016] MARK RUTHERFORD'S DELIVERANCE: being the Second Part of his Autobiography (Edited by his Friend, Reuben Shapcott) [*S.N.S.* p. 14
Trübner & Co. 1885. Boards, label and end-papers uniform with *Autobiography.*

Half-title. pp. viii + (212) O_2 blank. Erratum slip tipped on to p. (1).

[3017] MIRIAM'S SCHOOLING and Other Papers (by Mark Rutherford. Edited by his friend, Reuben Shapcott) [*S.N.S.* p. 15
Kegan Paul, Trench, Trübner & Co. 1890. Smooth blue-black cloth; black end-papers. Line-engraved front. after Walter Crane on plate paper.

Half-title. pp. viii + (196) N_2 imprint leaf. Very fine.

[3018] MORE PAGES FROM A JOURNAL, with Other Papers [*S.N.S.* p. 18
Fcap 8vo. Henry Frowde 1910. Blue cloth.

Half-title. pp. viii + (304) As new in dust wrapper.

[3019] PAGES FROM A JOURNAL, with Other Papers [*S.N.S.* p. 17
T. Fisher Unwin 1900. Smooth blue-green cloth.

Blank leaf and half-title precede title. pp. (viii) [paged vi] + (288) T_7 T_8 adverts. Fine.

[3020] REVOLUTION IN TANNER'S LANE (The) (by Mark Rutherford. Edited by his friend, Reuben Shapcott) [*S.N.S.* p. 14
Trübner & Co. 1887.

Copy I. Boards, label and end-papers uniform with *Autobiography.*

Blank leaf and half-title precede title. pp. viii + 388

Ink signature: 'S. C. Gordon', on title. Fine. Corners a little bruised.

[3020*a*] Copy II. Smooth blue-black cloth; dark green end-papers. Otherwise identical.

Spine imprint: 'Paul, Trench, Trübner & Co.' Very fine.

ST LEGER, FRANCIS BARRY (1799–1829)

A writer of great promise, whose mature work might well have been of importance. He collaborated with Charles Knight in the editing of *The Brazen Head* (a periodical founded by Knight after the cessation of *Knight's Quarterly Magazine*) and edited *The Album* from 1822 to his death.

MR BLOUNT'S MSS. Being Selections from the Papers of a Man of the World (by the author of 'Gilbert Earle') [3021]
2 vols. Small 8vo. Charles Knight, Pall Mall East 1826. Boards, labels.

Half-title in each vol.

Vol. I (iv) + (256)
II (iv) + (280)

Presentation Copy: 'Edward Oakeley, Esqr—from his very sincere friend, the Author' in ink on half-title of Vol. I.

Spines worn and Vol. II damp-stained in places, both externally and internally.

SOME ACCOUNT OF THE LIFE OF THE LATE GILBERT EARLE, ESQ. WRITTEN BY HIMSELF [anon] [3022]
Chas. Knight 1824. Boards, label.

pp. (viii) + (256) R_6 R_7 adverts., R_8 imprint leaf. Longman etc. cat., 12 pp. dated July 1824, inserted between front end-papers. Fine.

STORIES FROM FROISSART (by the late Barry St Leger, Esq.) [3023]
3 vols. Colburn 1832. Boards, labels.

Vol. I (lxiv) [paged lx] + (224) P_8 imprint leaf.
II (iv) + (396)
III (iv) + (362) $2A_5$ adverts. First leaf of final sig., $2A_1$, a single inset.

Ink signature: 'John Forbes', on fly-leaf of each vol.

Note. Also in the Collection is a copy in grey-purple morocco cloth, with black labels lettered in gold.

TALES OF PASSION (by the author of 'Gilbert Earle') [3024]
3 vols. Colburn 1829. Boards, labels.

Half-title in each vol.

Vol. I (vi) + (316)
II (iv) + (320)
III (iv) + (360) Q_{11} Q_{12} adverts.

Ink signature: 'Lord Clive', on front cover of each vol. Fine.

SALA, GEORGE AUGUSTUS (1828–1896)

An exhaustive check-list of the publications of Sala is provided by Ralph Straus at the end of his book, *Sala, the Portrait of an Eminent Victorian*, London, 1941.

[3025] AFTER BREAKFAST, or Pictures done with a Quill
2 vols. Tinsley 1864. Grass-green morocco cloth.
Half-title in Vol. I; blank leaf and half-title precede title in Vol. II
Vol. I (328) X_8 adverts.
II (328) [paged (326)].
Book-plate of John Browne. Very fine.

[3026] DEAD MEN TELL NO TALES, but Live Men Do. Nine complete stories
Bow Bells Annual, 1884–85, John Dicks. Glazed white pictorial wrappers in full colour. 9 illustrations on plate paper.
pp. (128) [paged 118] The first 2 and last 3 leaves carry adverts.
Fine.

[3027] MARGARET FORSTER: a Dream within a Dream. With a Preface by Mrs Sala
Fisher Unwin 1897. Smooth navy-blue cloth, blocked with a design of pansies in mauve, scarlet and white, and gold-lettered. Title printed in red and black.
Half-title. pp. xxiv + (368) Very fine.

[3028] SHIP CHANDLER (The) and Other Tales 1862. See 3711 (17) in Section II.

[3029] STRANGE ADVENTURES OF CAPTAIN DANGEROUS (The)
3 vols. Tinsley 1863. Chocolate dot-and-line-grain cloth; chocolate end-papers.
Vol. I xx + (320) X_8 adverts.
II iv + (316)
III iv + (312) X_3 X_4 adverts.
Ink signature: 'Lord Fitzhardinge, Berkeley Castle', inside front cover of each vol.

[3030] TERRIBLE TALES
Bow Bells Annual, 1873, John Dicks. White ornamental wrappers printed in green, red and violet. Front. (on verso of half-title) and 9 plates.
(128) [paged (iv) + (106)] The 9 illustrations in the text form part of the signatures and are correctly signed, but are omitted from pagination. The 4 final leaves carry adverts.
Fine.

TWO PRIMA DONNAS AND THE DUMB DOOR PORTER (The) [3031]
Tinsley 1862. Grass-green morocco cloth.
pp. viii + (248) R_4 adverts.
This copy belonged to Miss Braddon (I had it from a bookseller who cleared the books from her London home) but has no signature or book-plate.

SAVAGE, MARMION W. (1803–1872)

BACHELOR OF THE ALBANY (The) (by the author of 'The Falcon Family') [3032]
Chapman & Hall 1848. Rose-madder ribbed cloth.
Series half-title (an inset leaf) and individual half-title precede title. pp. (xiv) [paged xii] + (300) Publishers' cat., fcap 8vo, 32 pp. and dated June 1847, at end. Fine.
No. XII of CHAPMAN & HALL'S MONTHLY SERIES (3742 (15) in Section III). Here the series is no longer described as 'monthly' in incidental advert. nor does its imprint appear on spine.

FALCON FAMILY (The), or Young Ireland [anon] [3033]
Chapman & Hall 1845. Rose-madder diagonal-fine-ribbed cloth.
Half-title. pp. 348 Publishers' cat., fcap 8vo, 16 pp. and dated October 1845, at end. Fine.
No. IV of CHAPMAN & HALL'S MONTHLY SERIES (3742 (6) in Section III). The story was announced for two volumes, but actually issued in one. The series imprint appears at foot of spine.

MY UNCLE THE CURATE (by the author of 'The Bachelor of the Albany' and 'The Falcon Family') [3034]
3 vols. Chapman & Hall 1849. Dark brown fine-diaper cloth.
Fly-title conjugate with title in each vol.
Vol. I (iv) + (384) $2B_8$ adverts.
II (iv) + 304
III (iv) + (328) Y_4 adverts.
Ink signature: 'Charles Edwards 1849', on fly-leaf of each vol. Top corners of each vol. damp-stained.

REUBEN MEDLICOTT, or the Coming Man [3035]
3 vols. Chapman & Hall 1852. Dark green ripple-grain cloth; yellow end-papers, printed with adverts. in front in Vols. I and II, but blank at back; in Vol. III all blank.
Half-title in each vol.
Vol. I viii + (300)
II viii + 284
III viii + (352)
Fine.

SCOTT, LADY LYDIA

[3036] **MARRIAGE IN HIGH LIFE** (A) [anon] Edited by the authoress of 'Flirtation' (Lady Charlotte Bury)
2 vols. Colburn 1828. Boards, labels.

Half-title in Vol. II

Vol. I iv+(304) O_7 O_8 errata and adverts.
II (iv)+308

Book-label of 'Gräfl. Blome'sches Fideicommis Arnold Blome' in each vol. Front fly-leaf of Vol. II imperfect. Fine.

[3037] **OLD GREY CHURCH** (The) (by the author of 'Trevelyan' and 'A Marriage in High Life')
3 vols. Bentley 1856.

Copy I. Olive-brown wavy-grain cloth, blocked in blind and lettered in gold; yellow end-papers.

Half-title in each vol.

Vol. I (iv)+308
II (iv)+(312)
III (iv)+312

Ink signature: 'Countess of Jersey', on fly-leaf of each vol. and pencil note: 'Bed Room No. 1, Shelf 3', inside front covers. Fine.

[3037*a*] **Copy II: Another.** Claret morocco cloth, unblocked, labels; white end-papers. Collation as Copy I.

[3038] **TREVELYAN** (by the author of 'A Marriage in High Life')
3 vols. Bentley 1833. Boards, labels.

Half-title in each vol.

Vol. I (iv)+296
II (iv)+292
III (iv)+(288) N_{12} adverts.

Ink signature: 'Frances Price, Rhiwlas, 1833', and bookseller's ticket: 'Seacome, Chester', inside front cover of each vol. Very fine.

SCOTT, MICHAEL (1789–1835)

For a discussion of the variant bindings of Scott's two novels see Carter, *More Binding Variants* (London, 1938), pp. 34–37. To the argument there developed may be added the consideration that the cloth of *Tom Cringle* 'A' binding was also used on Smith, Elder's 'Library of Romance' (1833), Colburn's 'Modern Novelists' (1831–34), Macfarlane's 'Lives of Banditti & Robbers', new edition, Bull 1833. This seems to suggest that 'A' is more normally a period cloth than 'B' and, for this reason also, may well be judged earlier.

CRUISE OF THE MIDGE (The) (by the author of 'Tom Cringle's Log') [3039]
2 vols. Small Cr. 8vo. Edinburgh: Blackwood, and Cadell: London 1836.

Copy I: First Edition. 'A' Binding. Dark green fine-morocco cloth, blocked on front and back in blind with decorative panel in strap design and vignette of ship in full sail, on spine with simple gold lettering; white end-papers, over-printed with a mesh design in brown.

Half-title in each vol.

Vol. I (vi)+(388)
II (vi)+452

Book-plate of Fredk Heisch Junr. Fine.

Note. Vol. I, sig. A, consists of eleven leaves, of which the last is a single inset. The pagination is irregular, viz. 1, 2, 3*–8*, 3–16.

Copy II: First Edition. 'B' Binding. Dark green fine-diaper cloth, blind-blocked on front and back, and in gold on spine with design incorporating anchor, rope and lettering (uniform with *Tom Cringle's Log* 'B'); yellow end-papers. Collation as Copy I. [3039*a*]

Book-plate of Ralph Sanders.

TOM CRINGLE'S LOG [anon] [3040]
2 vols. Small Cr. 8vo. Edinburgh: Blackwood, and Cadell: London 1833. *Pl. 25*

Copy I: First Edition. 'A' Binding. Dark green morocco cloth, unblocked save for gold lettering on spine; white end-papers.

Half-title in each vol.

Vol. I (vi)+(372)
II (vi)+384

Fine.

Copy II: First Edition. 'B' Binding. Dark green fine-diaper cloth, blind-blocked on front and back and in gold on spine with design incorporating anchor, rope and lettering; yellow end-papers. Collation as I. Fine. [3040*a*] *Pl. 25*

Copy III: Second Edition. 2 vols. Edinburgh: Blackwood and Cadell, London 1834. Dark green fine-morocco cloth, unblocked save for gold lettering between rules surmounted by a small anchor on spines; white end-papers, over-printed with a mesh design in brown. Collation as Copies I and II. [3040*b*]

Ink signature: 'M. Daly', on slip pasted to inside cover of Vol. I. Bottom corner of front cover of Vol. II damaged by damp.

Note. P. S. O'Hegarty reports a Second Edition in First Edition 'B' Binding. This further strengthens the assumption that the sequence of 'A' and 'B' is correct.

SEWELL, ELIZABETH MISSING (1815–1906) AND REV. WILLIAM (1804–1874)

The Sewells, brother and sister, were intimate friends of the Tractarian leaders; but, alarmed by the movement's Romanizing tendency, withdrew from association with them. Their works (many of which have now become very scarce in clean original editions) were influential in the cause of Anglicanism, whether as an essential part of plans for University Reform or as an element in the education of young girls. *Laneton Parsonage* deserves authoritative description, but I have failed to locate first editions of Parts I and III.

[3041] AMY HERBERT (by a Lady. Edited by the Rev. W. Sewell, B.D., Fellow of Exeter College, Oxford)

2 vols. 12mo (collating in sixes). Longman, etc. 1844. Pinkish-straw-colour fine-ribbed cloth, blocked in blind on front and back, blocked and lettered in gold on spine.

Half-title in Vol. II

Vol. I (iv) + 284

II (iv) + (248) X_5 X_6 Y_1–Y_4 adverts. Publishers' cat., 32 pp. dated March 1844, at end.

Ink inscription: 'Guys Cliffe', on fly-leaf of each vol.

[3042] GERTRUDE (by the author of 'Amy Herbert' and 'Stories Illustrative of the Lord's Prayer'. Edited by the Rev. W. Sewell, B.D., etc.)

2 vols. 12mo (collating in sixes). Longman, etc. 1845. Dark brown fine-ribbed cloth, blocked in blind on front and back, gold-lettered and blind-blocked on spine.

Half-title in each vol.

Vol. I (iv) + (276) AA_6 adverts

II (iv) + 244 Publishers' cat., 32 pp. dated July 1845, at end.

Ink inscription: 'Guys Cliffe', on fly-leaf of each vol. Bookseller's stamp: 'Reeve, Leamington', inside front covers.

[3043] GLIMPSE OF THE WORLD (A) (by the author of 'Amy Herbert', etc.)

Small 8vo. Longman, etc. 1863. Violet wavy-grain cloth, blocked in blind on front and back, blind-blocked and gold-lettered on spine. Café-au-lait end-papers.

Half-title. pp. (iv) + (540) MM_6 adverts. Publishers' cat., 32 pp. dated January 1863, at end.

Booksellers' ticket: 'Cooke & Son, Warwick', inside front cover. Binders' ticket: 'Westleys', at end. *Ex* Guys Cliffe library. Fine. Spine very slightly faded.

[3044] HAWKSTONE: a Tale of and for England in 184– [Anon; by Rev. William Sewell]

2 vols. Small 8vo. John Murray 1845. Brown-orange fine-ribbed cloth, blocked in gold and blind on front, in blind on back, blocked and lettered in gold on spine.

Half-title in each vol.

Vol. I viii + 396

II (iv) + (424) EE_4 adverts. Publisher's cat., 16 pp. dated February 1845, at end.

Ink inscription: 'Guys Cliffe', on fly-leaf of each vol.

Binders' ticket: 'Remnant & Edmonds', at end of Vol. I. Fine.

KATHARINE ASHTON (by the author of 'Amy Herbert', etc.) [3045]

2 vols. Small 8vo. Longman, etc. 1854. Royal-blue morocco cloth, blocked in blind on front and back, gold-lettered and blind-blocked on spine. Terracotta end-papers printed with adverts. on inside front and back covers.

Half-title in Vol. II

Vol. I (iv) + (380) BB_6 adverts.

II (iv) + (364) AA_6 adverts. Publishers' cat., 24 pp. dated March 1854, at end.

Ink signature: 'A. C. Bertie Percy' [of Guys Cliffe] on fly-leaf of each vol. Bookseller's stamp: 'Reeve, Leamington', inside front covers. Binders' ticket: 'Westleys', at end of each vol. Fine.

LANETON PARSONAGE: A Tale for Children, on the Practical Use of a portion of the Church Catechism (by the Author of 'Amy Herbert', etc. Edited by the Rev. W. Sewell, B.D., etc.) [3046]

†[First Part.] 12 mo. (collating in sixes). Longman, etc., 1846. Claret horizontal-fine-ribbed cloth, blocked in blind on front and back, banded in blind and gold-lettered on spine.

No half-title. pp. (iv) + 248 Publishers' catalogue, 32 pp., dated May 1846, bound in at end.

Binders' ticket: 'Westleys & Clark', at end.

[Second Part.] Title as I, but with words 'SECOND PART' preceding author. [3046*a*]

12mo. (collating in sixes). Longman, etc. 1848. Binding as First Part.

pp. (iv) + (230) Final leaf, U_7, a single inset.

Publishers' catalogue, 32 pp. dated October 1847, at end.

†[Third Part.] Title as I, but with words 'THIRD PART' preceding author. [3046*b*]

12mo. (collating in sixes). Longman, etc. 1848. Claret perpendicular-fine-ribbed cloth, blocked and lettered in the style of I and II but not quite uniform.

Half-title. pp. (iv) + (338) Final leaf, GG_1, a single inset.

† Description adapted from Bodleian copy of 'Third Edition'. No 'first' locatable.

[3047] MARGARET PERCIVAL (by the author of 'Amy Herbert', etc. Edited by the Rev. William Sewell, B.D., etc.)

2 vols. 12mo. (collating in sixes). Longman, etc. 1847. Grey-purple perpendicular-fine-ribbed cloth, blocked in blind on front and back, banded in blind and gold-lettered on spine.

Half-title in each vol.

Vol. I (iv) + 460 Publishers' cat., 4 pp. undated, inset before half-title, and another, 32 pp. dated October 1846, bound in at end.

II (iv) + (486) 2nd leaf of final sig., TT_2, a single inset.

Binders' ticket: 'Westleys & Clark', at end of vol. I. Bookseller's stamp: 'Reeve, Leamington', inside front covers. *Ex* Guys Cliffe library.

[3048] URSULA: a Tale of Country Life (by the author of 'Amy Herbert', 'Ivors', etc.)

2 vols. Small 8vo. Longman, etc. 1858. Royal-blue morocco cloth, blocked in blind on front and back, gold-lettered and blind-blocked on spine, uniform with *Katharine Ashton*. Terracotta end-papers printed with adverts. on inside front and back covers.

Half-title in each vol.

Vol. I (iv) + 460 Publishers' cat., 32 pp. dated November 1857, at end.

II (iv) + (460)

Ink-signature: 'A. C. Bertie Percy' [of Guys Cliffe], and booksellers' stamp, 'Cooke & Son, Warwick', on fly-leaf of each vol. Binders' ticket: 'Westleys', at end of Vol. I. Fine.

SHEPPARD, ELIZABETH SARA (1830–1862)

[3049] ALMOST A HEROINE (by the author of 'Charles Auchester', 'Rumour', etc.)

3 vols. Hurst & Blackett 1859. Olive-brown morocco cloth.

Vol. I (ii) + 310 First leaf of final sig., X_1, a single inset.

II (ii) + 304

III (ii) + (284) U_2 adverts.

Binders' ticket: 'Leighton, Son & Hodge', at end of Vol. I. A poor copy. Library labels on covers and some sections loose.

[3050] CHARLES AUCHESTER: a Memorial [anon]

3 vols. Hurst & Blackett 1853. Grey-purple morocco cloth.

Vol. I (iv) + 334 First leaf of final sig., P_1, a single inset. Publishers' cat., 24 pp. undated, at end. First leaf of adverts. torn from this copy.

II (ii) + (310) First leaf of final sig., O_1, a single inset.

III (ii) + 294 First leaf of final sig., O_1, a single inset. Cat. of 'Interesting Books published for Henry Colburn by his successors Hurst and Blackett', paged 1–8 and undated, at end.

Ink inscription on title of Vol. I: 'Lady Morgan—the Publishers. August 1853', in Lady Morgan's hand. Armorial unnamed book-plate in Vol. I.

Note. To the kindness of Mr Andrew Boyle I owe the sight of a manuscript 'Key' to this novel, which was inserted in a copy belonging to him. One identification was illegibly written.

Seraphael = Mendelssohn
Charles Auchester = Joachim
Clara Benette = Jenny Lind
Anastase = Berlioz
Aronach = Zelter
Starwood Burney = Sterndale Bennett
St Michel = Costa
Maria Cerinthia = Fanny (?) Heval

Miss Sheppard wrote *Charles Auchester* at the age of 16. The novel is dedicated to Disraeli, who highly praised it.

COUNTERPARTS, or the Cross of Love (by the author of 'Charles Auchester') [3051]

Copy I: First Binding. 3 vols. Smith, Elder 1854. Grey-purple moiré horizontal fine-ribbed cloth, blind-blocked with simple framing.

Vol. I (iv) + 328 Publishers' cat., 16 pp. dated April 1854, at end.

II (ii) + 352

III (ii) + 328

Booksellers' ticket: 'Smith, Elder & Co. East India & Colonial Agents', inside front cover of each vol. Binders' ticket: 'Westleys', at end of Vol. I. Cloth a little rubbed.

Note. This novel is dedicated to Mrs Disraeli.

Copy II: Later Binding. Dark grey-purple morocco cloth, with considerable blind blocking on front and back, blind decorative bands at head and tail of spine. As Copy I, but no cat. at end of Vol. I.

Note. This was the publishers' file-copy and came to light in John Murray's warehouse in 1942 (cf. G. P. R. James). It is in new condition.

RUMOUR (by the author of 'Charles Auchester', 'Counterparts', etc.) [3052]

3 vols. Hurst & Blackett 1858. Light claret morocco cloth.

Vol. I (iv) + (312)

II (ii) + 336 Inset advert. leaf at end.

III (ii) + (348)

Binders' ticket: 'Leighton Son & Hodge', at end of Vol. I.

SHERIDAN, CAROLINE [mother of CAROLINE NORTON] (1779–1851)

[3053] AIMS AND ENDS and OONAGH LYNCH (by the author of 'Carwell')
3 vols. Bull 1833. Boards, labels.

Half-title in each vol.

Vol. I (vi) + 312
II (iv) + (316)
III (iv) + (330) Final leaf, P_9, a single inset.

Book-label of R. J. Ll. Price, Rhiwlas Library. Bookseller's ticket: 'Harding, Chester', inside front cover of each vol. Very fine.

SHORTHOUSE, JOSEPH HENRY (1834–1903)

[3054] JOHN INGLESANT: a Romance [anon]
8vo. Birmingham: Cornish Brothers. 1880.

Copy I: White parchment, lettered in red on front and spine. Half-title. pp. (578) Final leaf, MM_5, a single inset.

Bookplate of W. T. Wiggins Davies. Fine. The cleanest copy I have ever seen.

[3054*a*] **Copy II**: Full dark red morocco, blind-tooled and gold-lettered on spine by Rivingtons, Waterloo Place. Dark grey end-papers; t.e.g. others uncut. Collation as Copy I, except that a blank leaf of text paper is inset before half-title.

Presentation Copy. 'The Revd. G. D. Boyle, Dean of Salisbury, with respectful regards from the Author' in ink on verso of first blank leaf. Very fine.

The binding of this copy is clearly a presentation binding specially ordered by the author.

Note. Sig. X (pp. 345–60) of Copy II has the pagination disordered owing, undoubtedly, to the sheet having been *turned* after the first forme had been printed.

SINCLAIR, CATHERINE (1800–1864)

[3055] BEATRICE, or the Unknown Relatives
3 vols. Bentley 1852. Dark sage-green ripple-grain cloth, blocked in blind and lettered in gold.

Half-title in Vol. II; advert. leaf precedes title in Vol. III

Vol. I (i)–xxxvi + (37)–312
II (iv) + (320)
III (iv) + 344

Fine.

Notes: (i) An 'Advertisement by the Publisher', prefixed to *London Homes* (q.v. below), states that one hundred thousand copies of *Beatrice* were sold in America in a few weeks. The motto of the novel is 'Beware of Romanism!'

(ii) I suspect the above to be a 'substituted' (not 'secondary') binding style. The Bodleian copy of *Beatrice* is in bright-blue ripple-grain cloth and is uniform with the first bindings of *Peg Woffington* and *Basil*. The style of *Peg Woffington* was quickly changed, and I think the same thing happened to *Beatrice*. Probably the lettering was considered cramped and unclear.

CROSS PURPOSES: a Novel [3056]
3 vols. Bentley 1855. Three-quarter polished calf, gilt; marbled end-papers. T.e.g.: other edges uncut.

Vol. I (viii) + (320)
II (ii) + (332)
III (ii) + 356

The original binding was of grey-purple morocco cloth, blocked in blind and lettered in gold.

LONDON HOMES: including The Murder Hole, The Drowning Dragoon, The Priest and the Curate, Lady Mary Pierrepoint, and Frank Vansittart [3057]

Fcap 8vo. Bentley 1853. Blue ripple-grain cloth; terracotta end-papers.

pp. vi + (1)–86 + (1)–(14) + (1)–(10) + iv + (1)–(64) + iv + (1)–64 + (viii) + (1)–(64) E_8 blank.

Scribbles on end-papers. Binders' ticket: 'Remnant & Edmonds', at end.

Note. This curious volume is a combination of four stories separately issued between January and April 1853 in drab paper wrappers under the heading COMMON SENSE TRACTS I–IV, plus additional fragments.

LORD AND LADY HARCOURT, or Country Hospitalities [3058]
Bentley 1850. Pink morocco cloth; yellow end-papers printed with adverts.

Leaf of adverts. and half-title precede title. pp. (viii) + (328)

MODERN FLIRTATIONS, or a Month at Harrowgate [3059]
3 vols. Edinburgh: William Whyte & Co. 1841. Half-cloth boards, labels.

Vol. I xiv + 386 Title and final leaf, R_1, single insets.
II (ii) + 362 Title and final leaf, R_1, single insets. There is no gathering signed E in this volume.
III (ii) + 348

Very fine.

SIR EDWARD GRAHAM, or Railway Speculators [3060]
3 vols. Longman etc. 1849. Half-cloth boards, labels.

Half-title in Vols. II and III

Vol. I xii + (344)
II (iv) + 348
III (iv) + (376)

Labels discoloured, hinges a little frayed.

Note. This is a continuation of *Holiday House*, presenting many of the same characters in maturity. The story was re-issued in 1854 as *The Mysterious Marriage, or Sir Edward Graham*. See 3673 (5) in Section II.

[3061] PRESENTATION SET OF HER WORKS
10 vols. Full white vellum, elaborately gilt on front, spine and back. Initials 'C.S. to D.P.' centred on front; title on inlaid dark green panel on spine; gilt doublures and pale blue patterned-silk panel inside covers, faced by a leaf of vellum singly framed in gold. Bevelled boards. All edges gilt and goffered. (Titles in caps are first editions.)

There is no indication as to the identity of 'D.P.' for whom this lavishly bound set was prepared.

[3061*a*] BUSINESS OF LIFE (The)
2 vols. Fcap 8vo. Longman etc. 1848.
Vol. I viii + 364
II (iv) [paged vi] + 380 Half-title probably lacking

Inside back cover of Vol. II affected by damp.

[3061*b*] *Hill and Valley*, or Wales and the Welsh
Edinburgh: William Whyte 1848: 'Fourth Thousand.' Inside front cover and early pages affected by damp.

[3061*c*] *Holiday House*: a Series of Tales dedicated to Lady Diana Boyle
Fcap 8vo. Edinburgh: William Whyte 1849: 'Fifth Thousand.'

[3061*d*] *Jane Bouverie*, or Prosperity and Adversity
Fcap 8vo. Edinburgh: William Whyte 1848: 'Third Thousand.'

[3061*e*] *Journey of Life (The)*
Fcap 8vo. Longman etc. 1848: 'Third Edition, with Additions and Corrections.'

[3061*f*] *Modern Accomplishments*, or the March of Intellect
Edinburgh: William Whyte 1841: 'Eighth Thousand.'

[3061*g*] *Modern Society*, or the March of Intellect. The conclusion of 'Modern Accomplishments.'
Edinburgh: William Whyte 1847: 'Ninth Thousand.'

[3061*h*] *Scotland and the Scotch*, or the Western Circuit
Edinburgh: William Whyte 1840: 'Second Thousand.'

[3061*i*] SHETLAND AND THE SHETLANDERS, or The Northern Circuit
Edinburgh: William Whyte 1840.
pp. iv + 428 Folding map between pp. (420) (421).

SMART, HAWLEY (1833–1893)

AT FAULT: a Novel [3062]
3 vols. Chapman & Hall 1883. Pale olive-green diagonal-fine-ribbed cloth.

Half-title in each vol.

Vol. I vi + (280)
II vi + (272) S_8 blank.
III vi + 278 1st leaf of final sig., T_1, a single inset.

Presentation Copy: 'With kindest regards from H. Smart' in ink on title of Vol. I.

Fine. Small rust spots on cover of Vol. I.

BEATRICE AND BENEDICK: a Romance of the Crimea [3063]
2 vols. F. V. White 1891. Scarlet sand-grain cloth; very dark brown end-papers.

Half-title in each vol.

Vol. I (viii) + (248)
II (viii) + (232) 31_4 imprint leaf. Publishers' cat., 16 pp. undated on text paper, at end.

Presentation Copy: 'With best love, ever sincerely yours, Hawley Smart' in ink on p. (1) of text in Vol. I. Fine.

BELLES AND RINGERS: a Novelette [3064]
Chapman & Hall 1880. Scarlet diagonal-fine-ribbed cloth; black end-papers.

Half-title. pp. (viii) + (228) Q_2 blank.

Book-plate of John Browne. Fine.

BITTER IS THE RIND [3065]
3 vols. Bentley 1870. Brown sand-grain cloth.

Vol. I (ii) + 292
II (ii) + 308
III (ii) + (318) First leaf of final sig., X_1, a single inset. B

Note. Author's name on titles but not on spines, where are the words: 'by the author of "Breezie Langton".'

BLACK BUSINESS (A): a Novelette [3066]
F. V. White, n.d. [1890]. Black diagonal-ribbed cloth; orange decorated end-papers.

Leaf of adverts. (commercial) precedes title. pp. (viii) + (104) 7_4 adverts. (partly commercial). Publishers' cat., 16 pp. undated on text paper, at end.

Covers a little rubbed so that the black cloth has gone rusty.

BOUND TO WIN: a Tale of the Turf [3067]
3 vols. Chapman & Hall 1877. Olive-green diagonal-fine-ribbed cloth.

Vol. I (iv) + 280
II (iv) + 296
III (iv) + 292 U_2 blank.

Ink signature: 'C. G. Lawrance' (Smart's sister), on verso of front fly-leaf in each vol. Fine.

A second copy in the Collection, also fine, has ink inscription on title of Vol. I: 'J. Ashby Sterry with kind regards Hawley Smart'.

[3068] BREEZIE LANGTON: a Story of Fifty-Two to Fifty-Five

3 vols. Bentley 1869. Violet moiré fine-ribbed cloth.

Vol. I (ii) + 296
II (ii) + (288) [paged (292); 280–287 mispaged 284–291]
III (ii) + (298) Final leaf, U_5, a single inset. B

Note. The title on the spines reads: BREEZIE LANGTON OF MODERN SOCIETY.

[3069] BROKEN BONDS

3 vols. Hurst & Blackett 1874. Mauve diagonal-fine-ribbed cloth; dark green end-papers.

Half-title in each vol.

Vol. I (iv) + (302) First leaf of final sig., U_1, a single inset.
II (iv) + (302) First leaf of final sig., U_1, a single inset.
III (iv) + 304 Publishers' cat., 16 pp. undated, at end.

Ink signature: 'C. G. Lawrance', on half-title of Vol. I and with date added: 'Jan. 8, 1874', in same position in Vols. II and III. Binders' ticket: 'Leighton Son & Hodge', at end of Vol. I.

This is a poor copy, the cloth badly faded and somewhat stained.

[3070] CECILE, or Modern Idolaters

3 vols. Bentley 1871. Smooth bright blue cloth.

Vol. I (iv) + (304) U_8 adverts.
II (iv) + (284) T_6 adverts.
III (iv) + 320 B

[3071] COURTSHIP in Seventeen Hundred and Twenty, in Eighteen Hundred and Sixty

2 vols. Chapman & Hall 1876. Magenta sand-grain cloth; grey end-papers.

Blank leaf and half-title precede title in each vol.

Vol. I (viii) + (284)
II (viii) + (260)

Presentation Copy: 'Gina Lawrance with the author's love' in ink on title-page of Vol. I.

Ink signature: 'C. G. Lawrance', on verso of first blank leaf in Vol. II. Cloth rather faded.

[3072] FALSE CARDS

3 vols. Hurst & Blackett 1873. Brown sand-grain cloth; very dark green end-papers.

Half-title in each vol.

Vol. I (iv) + 320
II (iv) + (302) Final leaf, U_7, a single inset.
III (iv) + (318) Final leaf, X_7, a single inset. Publishers' cat., 16 pp. undated, at end.

Ink inscription: 'C. G. Lawrance 1872', on titles of Vols. I and II and half-title of Vol. III.

FALSE START (A): a Novel [3073]

3 vols. Chapman & Hall 1887. Pearl-grey fine-morocco cloth.

Half-title in each vol.

Vol. I vi + 256 Slip of 'Errata: Vol. I' precedes p. (1).
II vi + (256) Slip of 'Errata: Vol. II' precedes p. (1).
III vi + 308

Ink signature: 'C. G. Lawrance', on half-title of each vol.

FROM POST TO FINISH: a Novel [3074]

3 vols. Chapman & Hall 1884. Scarlet diagonal-fine-ribbed cloth.

Half-title in each vol.

Vol. I (viii) + (276) Pp. (v) (vi)—dedication to George Meredith—a cancel.
II (vi) + (280) T_4 blank.
III (vi) + 282 Final leaf, T_5, a single inset.

Ink signature: 'C. G. Lawrance', on half-title of each vol. Covers of Vol. I water-splashed.

GREAT TONTINE (The): a Novel [3075]

3 vols. Chapman & Hall 1881. Olive-brown sand-grain cloth; black end-papers.

Half-title in Vol. I; blank leaf and half-title precede title in Vols. II and III

Vol. I vi + (282) 1st leaf of final sig., T_1, a single inset.
II (viii) [paged vi] + (280)
III (viii) [paged vi] + 292

Fine. Small rust mark on one cover.

A second copy in the Collection, not quite so fine, has ink inscription on title of Vol. I: 'Ashby Sterry from his sincere friend Hawley Smart'.

Note. The cover-blocking represents a page in a ledger, with ruled columns for £ *s. d.* and the date '1881' at head of date-column.

HARD LINES: a Novel [3076]

3 vols. Chapman & Hall 1883. Dark grass-green diagonal-fine-ribbed cloth.

Half-title in Vols. I and III; blank leaf and half-title precede title in Vol. II

Vol. I vi + (282) Final leaf, T_5, a single inset.
II (viii) [paged vi] + (288)
III vi + 266 Final leaf, S_5 [signed S*], a single inset.

Presentation Copy: 'With the author's best love, your affec^ate Brother, Hawley Smart' in ink on title of Vol. I.

Ink signature: 'C. G. Lawrance', on verso of front fly-leaf of Vols. II and III. Very fine.

A second copy in the Collection, fine, has ink inscription on title of Vol. I: 'In the week of his marriage from Yours ever Hawley Smart'.

[3077] LONG ODDS: a Novel

3 vols. F. V. White 1889. Apple-green diagonal-fine-ribbed cloth; pale grey flowered end-papers.

Half-title in each vol.

Vol. I (viii) + 244 Slip of 'Errata: Vol. I' precedes p. (1).
II (viii) + (240) P_8 blank. Slip of 'Errata: Vol. II' precedes p. (1).
III (viii) + (240) P_8 blank. Slip of 'Errata: Vol. III' precedes p. (1).

Covers slightly darkened.

[3078] MASTER OF RATHKELLY (The): a Novel

2 vols. F. V. White 1888. Scarlet sand-grain cloth; pale grey flowered end-papers.

Half-title in each vol.

Vol. I (viii) + (252) 17_2 imprint leaf.
II (viii) + (264) 34_4 blank.

Ink signature: 'C. G. Lawrance', on verso of half-title in each vol.

[3079] MEMBER OF TATTERSALLS (A): a Novel

F. V. White 1892. Smooth scarlet cloth; very dark brown end-papers.

Leaf of adverts. (commercial) precedes title. pp. (viii) + (104) 7_4 adverts. (commercial). Publishers' cat., 16 pp. undated on text paper, at end.

Pencil signature: 'C. G. Lawrance 1890' (sic), on title. Cloth rather soiled.

[3080] OUTSIDER (The): a Novel

2 vols. F. V. White 1886. Scarlet morocco cloth; light olive-green patterned end-papers.

Half-title in each vol.

Vol. I (viii) + (256) 16_8 blank.
II (viii) + 256

[3081] PLAY OR PAY: a Novelette

Chapman & Hall 1878. Dark blue-green diagonal-fine-ribbed cloth.

Half-title. pp. (viii) + (244) R_2 adverts.

Presentation Copy: 'Capt. Cookworthy from the Author' in ink inside front cover.

Binders' ticket: 'Leighton, Son & Hodge', at end.

[3082] 'PLUNGER' (The): a Turf Tragedy of Five and Twenty Years ago

2 vols. F. V. White 1891. Smooth scarlet cloth, blocked with a broad band of white and lettered in black and gold; pale grey decorated end-papers.

Half-title in each vol.

Vol. I (viii) + (240) 15_8 imprint leaf.
II (viii) + (232) Publishers' cat., 16 pp. undated on text paper, at end.

Presentation Copy: 'Lily Cookworthy, ever affectionately yours Hawley Smart' in ink on p. (1) of text of Vol. I, and pencil signature: 'Lily Cookworthy, Recd Jan. 10th, 91', on title of each vol.

RACE FOR A WIFE (A): a Novel [3083]

Bentley 1870. Magenta sand-grain cloth, blocked in black on front and back, black-blocked and gold-lettered on spine. Bevelled boards. Dark sea-green end-papers. pp. (iv) + 308

Fine. Spine slightly darkened.

RACING RUBBER (A): a Novel [3084]

2 vols. F. V. White & Co. 1895. Apple-green sand-grain cloth, blocked and lettered in black on front, blocked in black and gold-lettered on spine. Ochre-on-white patterned end-papers.

Half-title in each vol.

Vol. I (xii) [paged viii] + 256
II (viii) + (372) 33_8 blank. Publishers' cat., 16 pp. on text paper undated, at end.

Fine.

Note. Smart's last novel, virtually finished at the moment of his sudden death. Pp. (ix)–(xii) of Vol. I are occupied by a preface by his widow, signed A. H. S. and dated 'Jersey. Sept. 19th, '94' in which, with much spirit, she defends horse-racing as a subject for fiction, and asserts how thorough and long-standing was her husband's knowledge of the technicalities of the turf.

SADDLE AND SABRE: a Novel [3085]

3 vols. Chapman & Hall 1888. Scarlet diagonal-fine-ribbed cloth.

Half-title in each vol.

Vol. I vi + (280)
II (vi) + (272) S_8 imprint leaf.
III vi + (278) T, 2 leaves; final leaf, U_1, a single inset.

Ink signature: 'C. G. Lawrance', on verso of front fly-leaf in each vol. Fine. Small stain on front cover of Vol. I.

SALVAGE: a Collection of Stories [3086]

Chapman & Hall 1884. Lightish sage-green diagonal-fine-ribbed cloth.

Half-title. pp. (vi) + (318) Y_3 adverts. and a single inset.

Ink signature: 'C. G. Lawrance', on half-title.

[3087] SOCIAL SINNERS: a Novel

3 vols. Chapman & Hall 1880. Dark blue diaper cloth; dark chocolate end-papers.

Half-title in each vol.

Vol. I vi+292
II vi+(290) Final leaf, U_1, a single inset.
III vi+(288)

Binder's ticket: 'Burn', at end of Vol. I. Very fine.

A second copy in the Collection, fine, has ink inscription on title of Vol. I: 'To their Godfather with the author's kind regards Hawley Smart'.

[3088] STRUCK DOWN: a Tale of Devon

Warne, n.d. [1885]. Pale grey paper wrappers printed in red, on front and spine with title, etc., on back with advert.

Half-title. pp. (xii) [pp. (i) (ii) are pasted to front cover and (ii) printed with adverts.; p. (iii) is printed with adverts., p. v half-title, etc.]+(180) N_7, recto blank, verso adverts.; N_8, recto adverts., verso pasted to back cover.

[3089] SUNSHINE AND SNOW: a Novel

3 vols. Chapman & Hall 1878. Grass-green diagonal-fine-ribbed cloth.

Half-title in each vol.

Vol. I (viii)+(264) S_4 blank.
II (viii)+282 Final leaf, U_1, a single inset.
III (viii)+292

Presentation Copy: 'Capt. Cookworthy from the Author' in ink on inside front cover of Vols. I and III. Fine.

A second copy in the Collection, also fine, has ink inscription on title of Vol. I: 'J. Ashby Sterry from yours ever Hawley Smart'.

[3090] THRICE PAST THE POST: a Novel

F. V. White 1891. Smooth scarlet cloth; very dark brown end-papers.

Leaf of adverts. (commercial) preceded title but has been cut away when cancel title was printed.

Original prelims. (viii), actual prelims. (vi)+(104) 7_4 adverts. (commercial). Publishers' cat., 16 pp. undated on text paper, at end. Slip headed 'Explanatory Note' precedes p. (1) and states that the book's title was changed at the last moment from 'A Family Failing'. This title still appears throughout the text. The new title is a cancel.

Ink signature: 'C. G. Lawrance, Aug. 1891', on title.

[3091] TIE AND TRICK: a Melodramatic Story

3 vols. Chapman & Hall 1885. Blue-grey diagonal-fine-ribbed cloth.

Half-title in each vol.

Vol. I (vi)+300
II (vi)+(312)
III (vi)+(270) The text of this vol. collates in eights to R_8; thereafter S_1–S_4, T_1 (a single inset), U_1–U_2.

Covers of Vol. II slightly stained.

TWO KISSES [3092]

3 vols. Bentley 1875. Bright blue sand-grain cloth.

Vol. I (iv)+(304)
II (iv)+280
III (iv)+284 B

Front cover of Vol. III shows scattered rust marks.

WITHOUT LOVE OR LICENCE: a Tale of South Devon [3093]

3 vols. Chatto & Windus 1890. Powder-blue sand-grain cloth, blocked in white; pale grey decorated end-papers.

Blank leaf and half-title precede title in each vol.

Vol. I (viii)+(292)
II (viii)+(284) T_6 publishers' device.
III (viii)+(276) T_2 publishers' device. Publishers' cat., 32 pp. dated January 1890, at end.

Presentation Copy: 'From yours ever Hawley Smart. March 1st 1890' in ink on title of Vol. I, and ink signature: 'Mrs Spicer Cookworthy', on half-title of each vol. Fine.

SMEDLEY, FRANK E. (1818–1864)

FRANK FAIRLEGH; or Scenes from the Life of a Private Pupil [anon] [3094]

8vo. A. Hall, Virtue & Co. 1850.

Part Issue. Fifteen monthly 8vo parts, published at one shilling (except Part 15, 1*s.* 6*d.*) from January 1849 to March 1850. Pale green paper wrappers printed in black—on front: PART I (etc.) PRICE 1*s.* [1*s.* 6*d.* on Part 15] / all-over pictorial design by Cruikshank, incorporating vignette scenes from the story, and fancy titling as follows: FRANK / FAIRLEGH / OR / SCENES / FROM THE / LIFE / OF / A PRIVATE PUPIL / ILLUSTRATED / BY / GEORGE CRUIKSHANK; imprint at foot: London: ARTHUR HALL & CO. 25 PATERNOSTER ROW [Parts 1–4; thereafter: ARTHUR HALL, VIRTUE & CO., etc.]; on back with adverts. Inside front and back wrappers printed with adverts. *Pl. 1*

The Parts are throughout undated. Until the prelims. at the end of Part 15, the only indications of date occur in Moses' back-wrapper adverts.

Part I. Inside front wrapper: Southee's Advertising Agency, *The Family Friend*, *The Weekly Despatch*, Brande's Enamel.

Two etchings by Cruikshank. pp. (1)–32 of text, followed by publishers' cat., 20 pp. undated. Inside back wrapper: Rowland's Preparations, Keatings' Cough Lozenges, Holloway's Ointment, Loader's Cabinet Warehouse.
Outside back wrapper: E. Moses & Sons, tailors, advert. headed by a poem 'The New Year, 1849'.

Part 2. Inside front wrapper: Southee's Agency (as in 1), Keating's Cough Lozenges, Brande's Enamel (as in 1).
Two etchings by Cruikshank. pp. 33 [mis-signed F]–64 of text.
Inside back wrapper: Rowland's Preparations (as in 1), Bentley's Extract of Honey, Holloway's Ointment and Loader's Cabinet Warehouse (both as in 1).
Outside back wrapper as 1.

Part 3. Inside front wrapper: Holloway's Ointment, Bentley's Extract of Honey, Loader's Cabinet Warehouse, Keating's Cough Lozenges. Leaf of publishers' adverts. on cheap paper.
Two etchings by Cruikshank. pp. 65–96 of text.
Inside back wrapper: Barry's Saline Lozenges, Measam's Medicated Cream.
Outside back wrapper: E. Moses & Son, headed by a new poem 'A Sketch for the Spring'.

Part 4. Inside front wrapper: Hoby, Publisher, 123 Mount Street, advertising *Seven Tales by Seven Authors*, edited by the author of *Frank Fairlegh*; Keating's Cough Lozenges, Slack's Cutlery. Leaf of publishers' adverts. on cheap paper.
Two etchings by Cruikshank. pp. 97–128, of text, followed by 2 leaves of cheap paper advertising Norton's Camomile Pills and other products of Ben[n]. Godfrey Windus.
Inside back wrapper: Rowland's Kalydor, Holloway's Pills, Bentley's Extract of Honey, Loader's Cabinet Warehouse.
Outside back wrapper: E. Moses & Son, headed by a new poem 'To My Eyeglass'.

Part 5. Inside front wrapper: Holloway's Pills, Keating's Cough Lozenges and Slack's Cutlery (these last as in 4). Leaf of publishers' adverts. on cheap paper, imprinted on recto 'George Virtue', on verso 'Arthur Hall & Co.'.
Two etchings by Cruikshank. pp. 129–160 of text.
Inside back wrapper: *Scripture Sites* published by Hall, Virtue. Loader's Cabinet Warehouse, Brande's Enamel.
Outside back wrapper as 4.

Part 6. Inside front wrapper: Keating's Cough Lozenges, Holloway's Pills, Slack's Shower Bath. Leaf of publishers' adverts., imprinted both sides 'George Virtue'.
Two etchings by Cruikshank. pp. 161–192 of text.
Inside back wrapper: Loader's Cabinet Warehouse, Brande's Enamel (both as in 5), Brande's Tooth Powder.
Outside back wrapper as 4.

Part 7. Inside front wrapper: Brande's Enamel Tooth Powder and Bronchial Sedative. Leaf of publishers' adverts. ('George Virtue').
Two etchings by Cruikshank. pp. 193–224 of text. followed by 2 leaves of publishers' adverts. (Tegg, London, and Griffin, Glasgow) on cheap paper.
Inside back wrapper: Holloway's Pills, Slack's Shower Bath, Loader's Cabinet Warehouse.
Outside back wrapper: E. Moses & Son, headed by a new poem 'The Stylish Young Gentleman'.

Part 8. Inside front wrapper as 7. Leaf of publishers' adverts. ('A. Hall, Virtue').
Two etchings by Cruikshank. pp. 225–256 of text.
Inside back wrapper as 7.
Outside back wrapper: E. Moses & Son, headed by a new poem 'Au Fait'.

Part 9. Inside front wrapper as 7. Leaf of publishers' adverts. ('Arthur Hall, Virtue').
Two etchings by Cruikshank. pp. 257–288 of text.
Inside back wrapper: Southee's Agency, Holloway's Pills, Slack's Fender, Nickel Silver, Cutlery and Tea Trays.
Outside back wrapper: E. Moses & Son, headed by a new poem 'September'.

Part 10. Inside front wrapper: Southee's Agency, Brande's Bronchial Sedative and Enamel. Leaf of publishers' adverts. ('George Virtue').
Two etchings by Cruikshank. pp. 289–320 of text.
Inside back wrapper: Bentley's Toilet Articles, Keating's Cough Lozenges, Slack's Fender, etc. (as in 9).
Outside back wrapper: E. Moses & Son, headed by a new poem 'Monopoly's Moan'.

Part 11. Inside front wrapper: Taylor's Dietetic Cocoa, Brande's Bronchial Sedative, *Modern Domestic Medicine*. Leaf of publishers' adverts. ('George Virtue').
Two etchings by Cruikshank. pp. 321–352 of text.
Inside back wrapper as 10.
Outside back wrapper: E. Moses & Son, headed by a new poem 'Frankly and Fairly'.

Part 12. Inside front wrapper: Taylor's Dietetic Cocoa, Slack's Nickel Silver, etc. 2 leaves of publishers' adverts., the first 'Arthur Hall, Virtue', the second (*Art Journal*) 'George Virtue'.
Two etchings by Cruikshank. pp. 353–384 of text.
Inside back wrapper: Bentley and Keating (as in 9); *Modern Domestic Medicine*, Brande's Bronchial Sedative.
Outside back wrapper: E. Moses & Son, headed by two paragraphs 'The Four Cardinal Points'.

Part 13. Inside front wrapper as 12. Publishers' cat., 20 pp. undated, on post 8vo paper.
Two etchings by Cruikshank. pp. 385–416 of text.
Inside back wrapper: Publishers' advert. of *Juvenile Calendar*, etc., Bentley's Toilet Articles, Keating's Cough Lozenges, Brande's Bronchial Sedative.
Outside back wrapper: E. Moses & Son headed by 'A Fancy' entitled 'The Twelve Months'.

Part 14. Inside front wrapper: Brande's Bronchial Sedative, Slack's Nickel Silver, etc. Leaf of publishers' adverts. ('Longman' and 'Virtue').

Two etchings by Cruikshank. pp. 417–448 of text.

Inside back wrapper: Brande's Enamel, Bentley's Toilet Articles, Keating's Cough Lozenges.

Outside back wrapper: E. Moses & Son, headed by six paragraphs 'The Month of February'.

Part 15. Inside front wrapper as 14. Leaf of publishers' adverts. ('Arthur Hall, Virtue').

Etched composite front. and vignette title (undated) by Cruikshank. pp. 449–496 of text. There follows a 16-page signature (A): p. (i) title, dated 1850; (ii) printers' imprint; (iii) (iv) Dedication, verso blank; (v)–vii Preface, dated Feb. 1850; (viii) blank; (ix)–xii Contents; (xiii) (xiv) List of Illustrations, verso blank; (xv) (xvi) publishers' adverts. ('A. Hall, Virtue') intended to be bound at end of book-issue.

Inside back wrapper as 14.

Outside back wrapper: E. Moses & Son, headed by four paragraphs 'Wool'.

Note. Never having been fortunate enough to find a copy of the book-issue of *Frank Fairlegh* in decent state, I here record a set of the Parts which, though extremely uncommon, are to my mind a 'second best'.

Nevertheless, a precise description of these Parts may prove of service, as the set described is absolutely untouched (no spine repairs whatsoever) and the details of wrapper adverts. may therefore be taken as reliable. There is an ink signature 'Pedder' and a partially erased 'Miss Pedder' in pencil on the front cover of every Part.

[3095] LEWIS ARUNDEL, or the Railroad of Life

8vo. Virtue, Hall & Virtue 1852. Lilac-grey morocco cloth pictorially blocked in gold on front and spine, blind-blocked front and back and gold-lettered on spine. Etched front., vignette title and 40 plates by Phiz.

pp. viii+(664) Publishers' cat., 16 pp. undated, at end.

SMITH, ALBERT (1816–1860)

[3096] FORTUNES OF THE SCATTERGOOD FAMILY (The)

3 vols. Bentley 1845. Plum ribbed cloth, blocked in blind front and back, blind-blocked and gold-lettered on spine. Etched front. and 6 plates in Vol. I; front. and 5 plates in Vol. II; front. only in Vol. III, all by John Leech.

Vol. I (ii)+(292)
II (ii)+320
III (ii)+332

Presentation Copy: 'Mrs Evans, with best regards from the author. January 1845' in ink on title of Vol. I. Apart from a small splash-mark on back cover of Vol. II, a fine copy.

Notes. (i) No mention of Leech's name appears anywhere, and there is neither a List of Plates nor an indication that the book is illustrated.

(ii) *The Scattergood Family* ran in 'Bentley's Miscellany' during 1844 and until February 1845, and the plates were prepared for this serial issue. The format of the 'Miscellany' being demy 8vo, the illustrations are disproportionately large for the post 8vo. page of the book edition. The dated imprint: 'London. Richard Bentley. 1844' only survives in the book issue at the base of such plates as originally carried the imprint sufficiently high on the sheet to escape off-cutting.

(iii) *The Scattergood Family* ends on p. 58 of Vol. III. pp. (59)–(176) are occupied by *Marguerite de Bourgogne: a Tradition of Ancient Paris*, and pp. (177)–332 by *The Armourer of Paris: a Romance of the Fifteenth Century.* Neither of these tales (which assort oddly with *The Scattergood Family*) is illustrated.

SMITH, HORACE (1779–1849)

ARTHUR ARUNDEL: a Tale of the English Revolution (by the author of 'Brambletye House', etc.) [3097]

3 vols. Colburn 1844. Half-cloth boards, labels.

Half-title in each vol.

Vol. I (iv)+(324) Longman etc. cat., 8 pp. undated, inserted between front end-papers.
II (iv)+312
III (iv)+(298) O_5 adverts. 1st leaf of final sig., O_1, a single inset.

Book-plate of William Holmes, Brookfield. Labels rubbed. Front fly-leaf of Vol. II missing and covers loose.

BRAMBLETYE HOUSE, or Cavaliers and Roundheads: a Novel (by one of the authors of 'Rejected Addresses') [3098]

3 vols. Colburn 1826. Boards, labels.

Vol. I (ii)+378 First leaf of final sig., S_1, a single inset.
II (ii)+(400)
III (ii)+(416) T_4 adverts.

Re-boarded at an early date: labels original.

GAIETIES AND GRAVITIES: a Series of Essays, Comic Tales and Fugitive Vagaries now first collected (by one of the authors of 'Rejected Addresses') [3099]

3 vols. Colburn 1825. Boards, labels.

Half-title in Vol. I

Vol. I viii+(354) First leaf of final sig., R_1, a single inset.
II iv+336
III iv+(348) Q_6 adverts.

[3100] GALE MIDDLETON: a Story of the Present Day (by the author of 'Brambletye House')
3 vols. Bentley 1833. Boards, labels.
Half-title in each vol.
Vol. I (iv)+(304) Final leaf, O_8, cut from this almost new copy. ? Label leaf.
II (iv)+320
III (iv)+(288)
Book-label: 'R. J. Ll. Price, Rhiwlas Library', and bookseller's ticket: 'Harding, Chester', inside front cover of each vol. Very fine.

[3101] HORACE IN LONDON: consisting of Imitations of the First Two Books of Horace (by the authors of 'Rejected Addresses', etc.) [Horace and James Smith]
12mo. John Miller, 25 Bow Street and John Ballantyne & Co. Edinburgh 1813. Boards, label.
Half-title. pp. (xii)+(180) (I_4) cancelled; (I_5) (I_6) adverts.
Ink signatures: 'Peacock' inside front cover, 'Hugh Parkin' on title. A few pages stained, others roughly opened.
Note. Text ends on p. 173, at the foot of which is printed: END OP (*sic*) VOL. I. No second volume was published.

[3102] JANE LOMAX, or a Mother's Crime (by the author of 'Brambletye House', 'Reuben Apsley', etc.)
3 vols. Colburn 1838. Boards, labels.
Vol. I (viii)+(312) O_{11} O_{12} adverts.
II (ii)+(298) Final leaf, O_5, a single inset.
III (ii)+(288) N_{11} N_{12} adverts.
Bookseller's ticket: 'Josiah Fletcher, Norwich', inside front cover of each vol. Spines and hinges defective.

[3103] MIDSUMMER MEDLEY FOR 1830 (The): a Series of Comic Tales, Sketches and Fugitive Vagaries in Prose and Verse (by the author of 'Brambletye House', etc.)
2 vols. Fcap 8vo. Colburn & Bentley 1830.
Vol. 1 (viii)+(264) S_4 adverts. Longman etc. cat., 12 pp. dated August 1830, inserted between front end-papers.
II iv+260

[3104] MONEYED MAN (The), or the Lesson of a Life
3 vols. Colburn 1841. Half-cloth boards, labels.
Vol. I iv+316 Longman etc. cat., 16 pp. dated January 1841, inserted between front end-papers.
II (ii)+338 Final leaf, Q_1, a single inset.
III (ii)+(332)
Ink signature: 'Helen Gawen 1841', inside front cover of each vol.

NEW FOREST (The): a Novel (by the author of 'Brambletye House') [3105]
3 vols. Colburn 1829. Boards, labels.
Half-title in Vol. III
Vol. I (ii)+(308) P_4 adverts.
II (ii)+(312)
III (iv)+(332) Q_3 Q_4 adverts.
Book-label: 'R. J. Ll. Price, Rhiwlas Library', and bookseller's ticket: 'Seacome, Chester', inside front cover of each vol. Fine. Spine of Vol. II repaired at head.

REJECTED ADDRESSES, or the New Theatrum Poetarum [anon] [3106]
12mo. John Miller, 25 Bow Street 1812. Boards, label.
Half-title. pp. (xvi)+(128) (G_4) adverts.
Ink signature: 'Joseph Warner Henley. Feb^{ry} 13th, 1813', on title.

REUBEN APSLEY (by the author of 'Brambletye House', 'The Tor Hill', etc.) [3107]
3 vols. Colburn 1827. Boards, labels.
Vol. I viii+340 Longman etc. cat., 4 pp. dated Feb. 1827, inserted between front end-papers.
II (ii)+(372) R_6 adverts.
III (ii)+392
Book-label: 'R. J. Ll. Price, Rhiwlas Library', inside front cover of each vol. Very fine.

TALES OF THE EARLY AGES (by the author of 'Brambletye House', 'Zillah', etc.) [3108]
3 vols. Colburn & Bentley 1832. Boards, labels.
Vol. I (ii)+(340) Pp. (1) (2) fly-title.
II (iv)+332 Pp. (iii) (iv) fly-title.
III (iv)+300 Pp. (iii) (iv) fly-title.
Book-label: 'R. J. Ll. Price, Rhiwlas Library', and bookseller's ticket: 'Harding, Chester', inside front cover of each vol. Very fine.

TIN TRUMPET (The), or Heads and Tales for the Wise and Waggish. To which are added Poetical Selections by the late Paul Chatfield, M.D. ('Edited by Jefferson Saunders Esq.') [3109]
2 vols. Whittaker 1836. Grey-purple diaper cloth. Engraved portrait front. in Vol. I.
Half-title in each vol.
Vol. I (xvi)+(296) Publishers' cat., 16 pp. dated July 1836, inserted between front end-papers.
II (iv)+(280) Publishers' adverts., 4 pp. on text paper, at end.
Spines worn at head.

TOR HILL (The) (by the author of 'Brambletye House', 'Gaieties and Gravities', etc.) [3110]
3 vols. Colburn 1826. Boards, labels.

Vol. I (ii) + 310 Seventh leaf of final sig., O_7, a single inset. Errata slip for Vols. I and II tipped in before p. (1) of text.
II (ii) + 350 Final leaf, R_1, a single inset.
III (ii) + 330 Q_2 Q_3 adverts, paged 327–330; Q_3 a single inset.

Ink signature: 'Frances Price 1832', inside front cover of each vol. and 'Rhiwaedog, 1826' on each title. Very fine.

[3111] WALTER COLYTON: a Tale of 1688 (by the author of 'Brambletye House', etc. etc.)
3 vols. Colburn & Bentley 1830. Boards, labels.
Vol. I (iv) + (332) Q_4 adverts.
II (ii) + 372
III (ii) + (336)
Ink signature: 'Frances Price, Rhiwlas, 1830', and bookseller's ticket: 'Harding, Chester' inside front cover of each vol. Very fine.

[3112] ZILLAH: a Tale of the Holy City (by the author of 'Brambletye House', 'The Tor Hill', 'Reuben Apsley', etc.)
4 vols. Colburn 1828. Boards, labels.
Half-title in each vol.
Vol. I (xxiv) + 300
II (iv) + (312) P_6 adverts.
III (iv) + (308)
IV (iv) + 316
Ink signature: 'Frances Price, Rhiwlas, 1828', inside front cover of each vol. Very fine.

Edited by Horace Smith

[3113] OLIVER CROMWELL: an Historical Romance [anon]. Edited by Horace Smith, Esq.
3 vols. Colburn 1840. Half-cloth boards, labels.
Vol. I xii + 336 'Editor's Preface' dated 'Brighton, August 1840' occupies pp. (iii)–xii. Pp. (1) (2) fly-title.
II (ii) + 294 First leaf of final sig., O_1, a single inset. Pp. (1) (2) fly-title.
III (ii) + 360 Pp. (1) (2) fly-title.
Labels rubbed.

SOMERVILLE, E. Œ. (1861–1949) and ROSS, MARTIN (1865–1915)

From this collection of the works of Somerville and Ross are missing two early 4to picture-books (*A St Patrick Day's Hunt* (1902) and *Slipper's ABC of Fox Hunting* (1903)), two or three recent non-fiction titles and the latest novel *French Leave* (1928). Of this last a description is provided from another source.

[3114] ALL ON THE IRISH SHORE: Irish Sketches
Longman etc. 1903. Smooth grey linen-grain cloth, pictorially blocked and lettered in black and gold; black end-papers. Front. and 9 full-page line-block illustrations on text paper after drawings by E. Œ. Somerville.
Half-title. pp. (viii) + (276) 18_2 adverts. Inset between 18_1 (last page of text) and 18_2 are 4 pp. of publishers' adverts. on thinner paper.
Very fine.

BEGGARS ON HORSEBACK: a Riding Tour in North Wales [3115]
Blackwood 1895.
Copy I: Primary Binding. Light blue unglazed canvas, blocked in black and lettered in gold; glazed grey-blue end-papers. Thirty-one half-tone illustrations on text paper (no front.) after drawings by E. Œ. Somerville.
Half-title. pp. vi + (188) M_6 serves as fly-title and first leaf of publishers' cat., 32 pp. dated '6/95' and on text paper.
Copy II: Secondary Binding. Smooth, slightly glazed linen-grain cloth, a shade darker blue than Copy I, identically blocked, but with glazed greenish-grey end-papers. Collation as Copy I, but no publishers' cat. at end, the volume ending on p. 186, i.e. with M_5. (Cf. Carter, *Binding Variants*, p. 153.) [3115*a*]

BIG HOUSE OF INVER (The) [3116]
Heinemann 1925. Navy-blue diagonal-fine-ribbed cloth.
Half-title. pp. (320) U_6–U_8 adverts. paged 1–6.
With dust jacket.

DAN RUSSEL THE FOX: an Episode in the Life of Miss Rowan [3117]
Methuen 1911. Smooth orange-brown cloth, blocked and lettered in black and white and spine-lettered in gold.
Blank leaf and half-title precede title. pp. (viii) + 340 Publishers' cat., 32 pp. dated March 1911, at end. Fine.

ENTHUSIAST (An) (by E. Œ. Somerville in collaboration with Martin Ross) [3118]
Longman etc. 1921. Smooth light green linen-grain cloth.
Half-title. pp. (viii) + (272) Sig. (A), 8 leaves, is paged (viii) + (1)–8. S_2 imprint leaf, S_3 blank (inside back end-paper), S_4 pasted to back cover.
With dust jacket. Inside front end-paper torn out.

*FRENCH LEAVE [3119]
Heinemann 1928. Dark red diagonal-fine-ribbed cloth.
Blank leaf and half-title precede title. pp. (viii) + (288)

[3120] FURTHER EXPERIENCES OF AN IRISH R.M.

Longman etc. 1908. Smooth pale green linen-grain cloth, with broad band of white cloth, overlaid all round at head, front-lettered in black and spine-lettered in gold. Front. and 19 full-page half-tone illustrations on art paper and 15 line-block illustrations in text after drawings by E. Œ. Somerville.

Half-title. pp. viii + (320) U_7 U_8 adverts., paged 1–(4).

As new, in dust jacket.

[3121] IN MR KNOX'S COUNTRY

Longman etc. 1915. Light green linen-grain cloth flecked with white, front-lettered in black and white, spine-lettered in gold. Front. and 7 full-page tinted plates in half-tone on art paper after drawings by E. Œ. Somerville.

Half-title. pp. (viii) + (312) Very fine.

[3122] IN THE VINE COUNTRY

W. H. Allen & Co. 1893. Smooth olive-green cloth, pictorially blocked in black and lettered in gold; very dark grey end-papers. Numerous half-tone illustrations on text paper (no front.) after F. H. Townsend from sketches by E. Œ. Somerville.

Half-title. pp. (240) 15_8 adverts. Publishers' cat., 32 pp. dated January 1893, at end.

This copy is in the primary binding (cf. Carter, *Binding Variants*, p. 152).

[3123] IRISH COUSIN (An) [by Geilles Herring and Martin Ross]

2 vols. Bentley 1889. Smooth black cloth, blocked in lime green and lettered in gold.

Vol. I (viii) + (304) 19_8 blank.
II viii + (304) B

Note. The first edition consisted of only 500 copies. Miss Somerville has told the amusing story of this book's vicissitudes, both before and after publication, in her notes to Miss Hudson's Bibliography. Both names used on the title-page were pseudonyms; 'Martin Ross' retained hers; but Miss Somerville, having found her first choice degraded to 'Grilled Herring', and having experimented with a change to 'Viva Graham' in the second edition of *An Irish Cousin*, thereafter used her real name on all the later books.

[3124] IRISH MEMORIES

Medium 8vo. Longman etc. 1917. Half dark green diagonal-fine-ribbed cloth, dark green board sides, label. Half-tone portrait front. and 15 full-page half-tone plates from photographs or after drawings by E. Œ. Somerville.

Blank leaf and half-title precede title. pp. (xii) [paged x] + (340)

Book-plate of John Robert O'Connell.

MOUNT MUSIC [3125]

Longman etc. 1919. Light green linen-grain cloth, side-lettered in black, spine-lettered in gold.

Half-title. pp. (312) U_4 blank.

Ink signature: 'C. E. Barnett, Xmas 1919', on fly-leaf. Very fine.

NABOTH'S VINEYARD: a Novel (by E. Œ. Somerville and Martin Ross, authors of 'An Irish Cousin') [3126]

Spencer Blackett 1891. Dark red diagonal-fine-ribbed cloth, blocked in black and lettered in gold; dark brown end-papers. Half-tone front.

Blank leaf and half-title precede title. pp. (viii) [paged vi] + 280 Publisher's cat., 8 pp. undated, at end. Very fine.

A volume in Spencer Blackett's Standard Library, the series title serving as imprint on spine. The book, like several other Spencer Blackett titles, was taken over by Griffith, Farran & Co. Undated copies with their imprint are secondaries.

REAL CHARLOTTE (The) [3127]

3 vols. Ward & Downey 1894. *Pl. 26*

Copy I: Primary Binding. Scarlet bubble-grain cloth, lettered in gold; fawn flowered end-papers.

Half-title in each vol.

Vol. I (iv) + (236)
II (iv) + 272
III (iv) + 268

Very fine.

Copy II: Secondary Binding. Smooth violet (or brown) cloth, blocked in black and lettered in gold; white end-papers. Collation as Copy I. [3127*a*] *Pl. 26*

Spines faded, cloth a little tired.

Note. Apart from the intrinsic qualities of size and style (cf. Carter, *Binding Variants*, p. 152) which suggest the priority of Style I above, it may be noted that Copy I came, with other three-deckers, from the Library of a reviewer named Ingram, and was in all probability the copy sent him on publication.

SILVER FOX (The) [3128]

Lawrence & Bullen Ltd. 1898. Smooth scarlet cloth, blocked and lettered in silver.

Half-title. pp. (iv) + (196)

Edges etc. sharp and fresh, but cloth a little soiled.

SOME EXPERIENCES OF AN IRISH R.M. [3129]

Longman etc. 1899. Smooth light sage-green cloth, pictorially blocked and lettered in red and black and spine-lettered in gold; black end-papers. Front. and numerous line-block illustrations, all on text paper, after drawings by E. Œ. Somerville.

Half-title. pp. viii + (312) U_4 blank. Very fine.

[3130] SOME IRISH YESTERDAYS

Longman etc. 1906. Smooth buff linen-grain cloth blocked in black. Numerous half-tone illustrations after drawings by E. Œ. Somerville.

Half-title. pp. viii + (252) [text paper] + (20) [art paper]. Very fine.

Note. The make-up is unusual. Pp. (1)–(252) represent A–P in eights + Q (4 leaves) + R (2 leaves). Then follow ten leaves of art paper, unfoliated but signed S (8 leaves) + T (2 leaves). These ten leaves are occupied by reduced reproductions of *Slipper's ABC of Fox Hunting*, the final leaf of text paper (R_2) serving as fly-title to *Slipper's ABC.* The full-page plates throughout the text are on art paper and not reckoned in collation.

[3131] STRAY-AWAYS

8vo. Longman etc. 1920. Smooth blue linen-grain cloth. Half-tone front. and 33 illustrations in half-tone and line (some full-page, some in text. but all on text paper and reckoned in collation) after drawings by E. Œ. Somerville.

Blank leaf and half-title precede title. pp. (xvi) [paged (xiv)] + 280

[3132] THROUGH CONNEMARA IN A GOVERNESS CART (by the authors of 'An Irish Cousin')

W. H. Allen & Co. 1893.

Copy I. Smooth green cloth, pictorially blocked in ochre, mauve, white and black and lettered in gold; black end-papers. Twenty-five half-tone illustrations on text paper (no front.) after W. W. Russell from sketches by E. Œ. Somerville.

Half-title. pp. viii + 200 Publishers' cat., 32 pp. undated, at end. Very fine.

[3132*a*] **Copy II.** Scarlet cloth, similarly blocked. Otherwise identical with Copy I. Book-plate of R. D. Jackson.

[3133] WHEEL-TRACKS

8vo. Longman etc. 1923. Half smooth brown cloth, pale brown board sides, label. Half-tone portrait front., 15 full-page half-tones from photographs or drawings by E. Œ. Somerville, and line illustrations in text.

Half-title. pp. x + (286) Sig. (A), 8 leaves, is paged x + 1–6. T_4 blank.

SOUTHESK, JAMES CARNEGIE, 9TH EARL OF (1827–1905)

[3134] HERMINIUS: a Romance [anon]

Sm. 8vo. Edinburgh: Edmonston & Douglas 1862. Smooth glazed dark crimson cloth, blocked in gold on front, blocked and lettered (title only) in gold on spine, blind blocked on back, with a design almost identical with that devised by D. G. Rossetti for Christina Rossetti's *Goblin Market.* Dark chocolate end-papers.

Half-title. pp. viii + (234) [paged (232)]. Q_4 blank. Between Q_2 and Q_3 [pp. 228 and (229)] is inset a leaf, not reckoned in pagination, with ADDENDUM on recto and verso blank. Very fine.

Note. This book was given me by Sir Sydney Cockerell, to whom it had been given by Lady Helena Carnegie, the author's daughter. The verso of front end-paper is inscribed to this effect. The text is prettily printed by R. & R. Clark in 'period' style, with decorative title and head-and-tail ornaments to chapters.

STANHOPE, M. SPENCER [MRS ROBERT HUDSON]

ALMACKS: a Novel [anon] [3135]

3 vols. Saunders & Otley 1826: 'Second Edition.' Boards, labels.

Half-title in each vol.

Vol. I (xii) + (392) S_4 pasted to back cover as end-paper.

II (iv) + 346 First leaf of final sig., Q_1, a single inset.

III (iv) + (416) T_4 adverts.

Boards fine. Front fly-leaf missing from Vol. I, back fly-leaf from Vol. II.

ana

KEY TO ALMACKS: reprinted from the *Literary Gazette* of December 9, 1826 [3136]

8vo. W. A. Scripps, Literary Gazette Office 1827.

No wrappers, p. (1) serving as front cover and title. pp. 16

This reprints the whole *Literary Gazette* review, at the end of which are certain identifications, e.g.

Beaulieu Family . . .	The Anglesea Pagets
Lady Hauton . . .	Lady Jersey
Lady Stavordale . . .	Duchess of Bedford
Lady Bellamont . . .	Countess of Sefton
Baroness Wallestein . .	Princess Pxxxxc
Lady Birmingham . .	Mrs Beaumont
Lord Derwent . . .	Duke of Portland
Lord Tresilian (son of Derwent)	Marquis of Titchfield
Lord Castlemaine. . .	Duke of Devonshire
The N's	Northumberlands
Dean and Lady Margaret Carlton	Dr and Lady Charlotte Bury†
Lord Clanalpin . . .	Duke of Argyll
Lady Lochaber . . .	Lady Keith
Miss Bevil	Miss Hxxxon

† This attribution was anonymously denied in the press, it being suggested that 'another title north of the Tweed of the same initial might be a more successful conjecture'.

In a third edition of this book I found a MS. key, clearly based on the above, but giving 'Wallestein' as Princess Lieven and omitting 'Miss Bevil'.

[3137] OBADIAH'S ADDRESS FROM IRELAND TO THE WORSHIPFUL AND ALL-POTENT PEOPLE OF ALMACKS [anon]

Fcap 8vo. Hatchard 1827. Boards, label.

Half-title. pp. (iv) + 76 (E_2) adverts.

Note. This curious little work addresses by name (and severely censures) all the chief characters in *Almacks.* Their identity is assumed (or known) by the writer to be as stated in the *Literary Gazette,* for the accusations of arrogance, snobbery, godlessness, dissipation and what-not, brought personally against 'Lady Hauton', 'Lady Stavordale', 'Lady Bellamont' and the rest, are recognisably directed against their *originals.*

STEEL, FLORA ANNIE (1847–1929)

Even though I aspire only to those of Mrs Steel's works which were published up to, and including, the year 1900, I have failed to find several titles in adequate condition.

[3138] HOSTS OF THE LORD (The)

Heinemann 1900. Apple-green sand-grain cloth, blocked on front with all-over design of streams, storks and trees and with title of novel, in black and metallic blue. Black-lettered on spine. Publishers' monogram in black on back.

Half-title. pp. (viii) + 344 Publisher's cat., 32 pp. signed A and undated, at end. Very fine.

[3139] IN THE PERMANENT WAY and Other Stories

Heinemann 1898. Uniform with *The Hosts of the Lord.* Blank leaf and half-title precede title. pp. (viii) + (308) U_2 blank.

Publisher's cat., 16 pp. dated Autumn 1897, at end. Very fine.

[3140] IN THE TIDEWAY

Archibald Constable 1897. Sand-coloured canvas, decoratively blocked and lettered in dark blue.

Half-title. pp. (iv) + (252) Final sigs., R 2 leaves, S 4 leaves, S_1–S_4 adverts.

[3141] *MISS STUART'S LEGACY

3 vols. Macmillan 1893. Dark blue fine-diaper cloth, gold-lettered in a modified 'Marion Crawford' style.

Half-title in each vol.

Vol. I (iv) + 260
II (iv) + 248
III (iv) + 248

[3142] ON THE FACE OF THE WATERS

Heinemann 1897. Uniform with *The Hosts of the Lord.*

Half-title. pp. viii + 432 Publisher's cat., 32 pp. signed A and undated, at end.

Very fine.

POTTER'S THUMB (The): a Novel [3143]

3 vols. Heinemann 1894. Dark red ribbed cloth, lettered in bronze on front and in gold on spine. Publishers' monogram in bronze on back.

Half-title in each vol.

Vol. I (iv) + 228
II (iv) + (208)
III (iv) + (224)

Ink signature: 'P. H. Pye Smith, 1894', on half-title of Vol. I. A poor copy, covers soiled and spotted.

VOICES IN THE NIGHT [3144]

Heinemann 1900. Uniform with *The Hosts of the Lord.*

Half-title. pp. (vi) [paged viii] + (368) Z_8 blank. Publisher's cat., 32 pp. undated, at end. Very fine.

Note. The irregular paging the of prelims. is due to the cancellation of pp. (v) (vi), probably a dedication leaf. This cancellation has occurred in each of several copies seen.

WIDE AWAKE STORIES: a Collection of Tales told by little children, between Sunset and Sunrise, in the Panjab and Kashmir (by F. A. Steel and R. C. Temple) [3145]

Copy I: First Edition. Bombay: Education Society's Press; London: Trübner & Co. 1884. Dark green diagonal-fine-ribbed cloth, on front lettered and blocked in black and lettered in gold, on spine and back lettered and blocked in black.

pp. xii + (446) Publishers' cat., 12 pp. on text paper and undated, at end. Text of 'Tales' ends p. 312; 313–347 Notes to Tales; 348–385 Analysis of the Tales; 386–436 Survey of the Incidents in Modern Indian Folk Tales; (437)–445 Index; (446) blank.

The book collates in sixes from 1–37. The final leaf, (38_1), is a single inset.

Binders' ticket: 'Bound at Education Society's Press, Byculllah', at end. Rubber stamp: 'D'Arcy Power', on fly-leaf. Cover a little spotted and spine darkened.

Copy II: New and First Illustrated Edition.
TALES OF THE PUNJAB. Told by the People [3145*a*]

Macmillan. 1894. Smooth very dark green cloth, pictorially and decoratively blocked and lettered in gold on front and spine, black plain. Very dark green end-papers. All edges gilt. Numerous line-illustrations, full-page and in the text, all on text paper after drawings by J. Lockwood Kipling, C.I.E.

Blank leaf and half-title precede front. and title.

pp. (xx) [paged xvi] + (396) Text of the Tales ends p. 296; (297) vignette; (298) blank; (299)–326 'Notes to Tales' by R. C. Temple; (327)–355

Analysis of the Tales; (356)–395 A Survey of the Incidents in Modern Indian Folk Tales.

Publishers' blind stamp 'Presentation Copy' on title.

Note. This was No. 15 of the Cranford Series, as described and listed by T. Balston in the *Book Collectors' Quarterly*, October 1933. The book carries no indication of having been previously published.

STEPNEY, LADY (MRS C. RUSSELL MANNERS) (?–1845)

[3146] COURTIER'S DAUGHTER (The)
3 vols. Colburn 1838. Boards, labels.

Vol. I (ii)+(320) 8 pp. prospectus of Colburn's Standard Novelists inserted between front end-papers.
II (ii)+(318) First leaf of final sig., P_1, a single inset.
III (ii)+(316)

Very fine.

[3147] HEIR-PRESUMPTIVE (The)
3 vols. Bentley 1835. Boards, labels.

Vol. I (ii)+(300)
II (ii)+(316)
III (ii)+314 Final leaf, P_1, a single inset.

Ink signature: 'Louisa Manners', on fly-leaf of each vol. Fine.

Note. Mrs Hofland wrote to Miss Mitford on July 6, 1835: 'I find Miss Landon wrote Lady Stepney's book—I never read it. She had a hundred pounds and grumbles much, as she says it took her more time than writing a new one would have done.' The Bentley Private Catalogue says 'Edited by Laetitia E. Landon'.

[3148] NEW ROAD TO RUIN (The)
3 vols. Bentley 1833. Boards, labels.

Half-title in each vol.

Vol. I (iv)+(312)
II (iv)+(300)
III (iv)+(288) N_{10}–N_{12} adverts.

Author's signature: 'Catharine Stepney, 8 Henrietta Street', in ink on fly-leaf of Vol. I. 'From the Stepney-Manners Library April 1924' in pencil inside front cover of Vol. I. Some notes, partially erased, on half-title of Vol. I.

STERLING, JOHN (1806–1844)

[3149] ARTHUR CONINGSBY [anon]
3 vols. Effingham Wilson 1833. Half-cloth boards, labels.

Vol. I (iv)+324
II (ii)+340
III (ii)+396

Ink signature: 'S. W. Fox', on title of Vol. I. Label of Vol. I imperfect.

Note. This is a very loquacious novel of the French Revolution. The author was a friend of Coleridge, Wordsworth, F. D. Maurice, R. C. Trench and Thomas Carlyle (who wrote his life in 1851). An intimate Account of him appears in the Journal of Caroline Fox recently re-edited by H. Wilson Harris.

STRETTON, HESBA (SARAH SMITH) (1832–1911)

'Hesba Stretton' was principally known as a writer for children and particularly as the author of *Jessica's First Prayer*. The two adult three-volume novels here described were her first works.

ALONE IN LONDON (by the author of 'Jessica's First Prayer', 'Little Meg's Children', etc.) [3150]
Small square 8vo. Religious Tract Society, n.d. Grass-green very small bead-grain cloth, blocked and lettered in gold and with single blind frame on front, spine unlettered, back blocked with single blind frame. The binding is signed on front and back: LEWIS BINDER. Cream end-papers. Wood-engraved front., 6 full-page illustrations and 6 vignettes in the text signed 'AWB', all on text paper and reckoned in collation.

pp. 144

Ink inscription: 'Louis and Cecil Ponsonby from E. S. St Michaels, Shoreditch. Epiphany '71', on fly-leaf.

See *Note* below on *Jessica's First Prayer*.

CLIVES OF BURCOT (The): a Novel [3151]
3 vols. Tinsley 1867. Royal-blue fine-morocco cloth.

Half-title in each vol.

Vol. I (iv)+(320)
II (iv)+(316) X_6 adverts.
III (iv)+300

Blind stamp of W. H. Smith & Son on fly-leaf.

Fine. Front board of Vol. I creased.

JESSICA'S FIRST PRAYER (by the author of 'Fern's Hollow', 'Fishers of Derby Haven', 'Pilgrim Street', etc.) [3152]
Small square 8vo. Religious Tract Society, n.d. Red-brown sand-grain cloth, blocked and lettered in gold and with single blind frame on front; spine unlettered; back blocked with single blind frame, uniform (except in detail of gold

blocking) with *Alone in London.* This binding also is signed on front and back: LEWIS BINDER. Deep cream end-papers. Wood-engraved front., 6 full-page illustrations and 3 vignettes in text signed 'AWB', all on text paper and reckoned in collation.

Half-title. pp. (96) [paged (i)–viii + (9)–92 + (93)–(96)] G_3 G_4 adverts.

Bookseller's ticket: 'Rice. 16 Mount St.'

Note. I believe the facts as to the first edition of this famous little book have never been established. The *D.N.B.* and the *C.B.E.L.* give the date as 1867, that of *Little Meg's Children* as 1868 and that of *Alone in London* as 1869.

Now although it is, of course, possible that the uniform style of binding, as shown on the copies of *Jessica* and *Alone in London* here described, was evolved in 1867, I confess that it looks to me of a rather later date—more suitably that of the inscription in *Alone in London*, i.e. 1871. Further, it is unlikely that a copy of *Alone in London* bought for two children in 1871 would have been anything but a *new* copy, belonging to the edition then on sale; and with a book so enormously successful the edition in the shops in 1871 would hardly have been that first published in 1869.

I incline, therefore, to regard my copies of these little books as of the format and interior-appearance (maybe printed from the plates) of the original editions, but in a binding adopted as a 'Stretton juvenile' style about 1870. It seems, however, justifiable to provide descriptions of them as, internally at any rate, they probably retain the original structure.

In conclusion it may be noted that the advert. of books by the same author on *Jessica* G_3 gives the titles of the first two books mentioned on the title-page, plus two more: *The Children of Cloverley* and *Enoch Roden's Training.*

[3153] PAUL'S COURTSHIP: a Novel

3 vols. Charles W. Wood 1867. Grass-green fine-morocco cloth.

Half-title in each vol.

Vol. I (vi) + (320) Half-title a single inset.
II (iv) + (306) Final leaf, X_1, a single inset.
III (iv) + 288 Single leaf of adverts. on thin paper inset after p. 288.

Book-plate: 'Ingram.' Fine. Slight stain on front cover of Vol. II. Carries the rare imprint of the son of Mrs Henry Wood.

STRUTT, JOSEPH (1749–1802)

QUEENHOO HALL: a Romance, and ANCIENT TIMES: a Drama (by the late Joseph Strutt) [3154] *Pl. 19*

4 vols. Fcap 8vo. John Murray & Archibald Constable 1808. Marbled board sides, white paper spines, labels.

Vol. I (xviii) [paged (ii) + (viii) + (viii)] + (254)
II (iv) [paged (ii) + ii] + (248)
III (iv) [paged (ii) + ii] + 242 Final leaf, Q_1, a single inset.
IV (iv) + (212) *Queenhoo Hall* ends p. (80); pp. (81)–(180) [paged (97)–(196)] *Ancient Times*; (181)–(196) [paged (197)–(212)] Glossary, i.e. 16 pp. (81–96) have been dropped from foliation. Sig. N (pp. 193–208) is garbled, but nothing is lacking. Final sig., O, 2 leaves.

Bookseller's ticket: 'Figgis, Dublin', inside front cover of Vol. I. Very fine. From the Bellew Library.

Note. The last chapter of this novel, left incomplete by Strutt, was written by Sir Walter Scott.

SUE, EUGÈNE (1804–1857)

MYSTERIES OF PARIS (The): from the French of M. Eugène Sue by J. D. Smith Esq. [3155]

3 vols. D. N. Carvalho, 147 Fleet Street 1844. Grey-purple fine-ribbed cloth, blocked in blind and lettered in gold. In Vol. I seven, in Vol. II five, in Vol. III seven etched plates by Onwhyn. No fronts. and no list of plates.

Half-title in each vol.

Vol. I (iv) + (336) P_{12} blank.
II (iv) + 336
III (iv) + 296

Cloth rather stained and spines faded.

PROTESTANT LEADER (The): a Novel [3156]

3 vols. Newby 1849. Dark grey-purple fine-diaper cloth.

Advert. leaf precedes title in Vol. III

Vol. I (iv) + 420 [paged (i)–xvii, Preface by the Translator + (xviii), blank + (19)–420]
II (ii) + 336
III (iv) + (372) Text ends 349, (350) blank, 351–371 Appendix, (372) blank. Publishers' cat., 12 pp. dated April 1849, at end.

Bookseller's blind stamp: 'Hayward, Bath', on fly-leaf of each vol.

[3157] RIVAL RACES (The), or the Sons of Joel: a Legendary Romance

3 vols. Trübner & Co., 60 Paternoster Row; David Nutt, 270 Strand 1863. Green morocco cloth.

Half-title in Vols. I and III

Vol. I xii+(328) Y_4 adverts.
II iv+336
III (viii) [paged vi]+(388) CC_2 adverts.

[3158] TEMPTATION, or the Watch Tower of Koat-Vën

8vo. G. Vickers 1845. Brown paper wrappers printed in black, on front with vignette and lettering, on back with advert. Fourteen wood-engraved illustrations in the text, one every eight pages.

pp. (iv)+116

Issued jointly by Vickers and Galignani, Paris, in Penny and Sixpenny parts from October 1844. Volume issue, described as 'Translated from the Original French', published at 1*s*. 6*d*. This copy in new boards, wrappers preserved, uncut.

[3159] WANDERING JEW (The)

8vo. 3 vols. Chapman & Hall. 1844 (Vol. I), 1845 Vols. II and III). Scarlet fine-morocco cloth, pictorially blocked in gold on front and spine, gold-lettered on spine, blind-blocked on back. 104 full-page illustrations on plate-paper, wood-engraved by Heath after various artists. The price: £2. 2. 0, is blocked on each spine.

Vol. I iv+(492)
II iv+(376)
III iv+372

Note. This work was published bi-weekly in numbers at threepence and bi-monthly in parts at one shilling, concurrently with its appearance in the original French in Paris.

With the completion of Vol. I and its issue in scarlet cloth, Chapman & Hall began the publication of a series of twenty-six sixpenny parts, containing the illustrations alone and entitled: HEATH'S ILLUSTRATIONS TO THE WANDERING JEW. Each part contained four plates, imprinted 'London: Chapman and Hall' and dated from January 1, 1845 (Part I) to February 15, 1846 (Part XXVI) and was wrappered in buff paper printed in black. All wrappers are dated 1845 on front and the inside back wrappers carry interesting adverts. of the Monthly Series (q.v. in Section III). The publication of the three volumes of the book edition are recorded on the inside front wrappers, thus: Part I announces Vol. I as 'now completed, price 9*s*. in cloth boards'; Part X (plates dated May 1845) announces Vol. II, price 7*s*.; Part XVIII (plates dated October 1845) announces Vol. III, price 7*s*.

Late in 1845 (but with title-pages unaltered) the three-volume book edition was re-issued, without the plates, and bound in dark green fine-ribbed cloth.

SULLIVAN, MRS ARABELLA JANE

RECOLLECTIONS OF A CHAPERON [anon]. [3160]
'Edited by Lady Dacre'

3 vols. Bentley 1833. Boards, labels.

Half-title in each vol.

Vol. I (iv)+(306) First leaf of final sig., P_1, a single inset.
II (iv)+332
III (iv)+320

Ink signature: 'Frances Price, Rhiwlas, 1833', inside front cover of each vol. Fine.

Mrs Sullivan was the only daughter of Barbarina, Lady Dacre. See also BENTLEY'S STANDARD NOVELS in Section III.

SURTEES, ROBERT SMITH (1803–1864)

[For further bibliographical detail see C. F. G. R. Schwerdt, *Hunting, Hawking, Shooting, etc.*, Privately Printed, 1928. The collations are unreliable.]

'ASK MAMMA', or the Richest Commoner in England [3161]
(by the author of 'Handley Cross', etc.)

8vo. Bradbury & Evans 1858. Rose-madder perpendicular-fine-ribbed cloth, pictorially blocked and lettered in gold, and blocked in blind; plain cream end-papers. Coloured engraved front., wood-engraved vignette on title and 12 plates by John Leech; also numerous wood-engraved illustrations in the text.

pp. (xii)+412

Ink inscription: 'George Gilford from J. F. G. Jany 1/59' on fly-leaf. Very fine.

HANDLEY CROSS, or the Spa Hunt: a Sporting [3162]
Tale (by the author of 'Jorrocks's Jaunts and Jollities')

Copy I: First Edition. 3 vols. Colburn 1843. Half-cloth boards, labels.

Half-title in Vols. II and III

Vol. I viii+328
II (iv)+316
III (iv)+(308) O_{10} adverts. paged (i)–iv.

Copy II: First Illustrated Edition. HANDLEY [3162*a*]
CROSS: or Mr Jorrocks's Hunt (by the author of 'Mr Sponge's Sporting Tour', etc.)

8vo. Bradbury & Evans 1854. Darkish-salmon perpendicular-fine-ribbed cloth, pictorially blocked and lettered in gold, and blocked in blind; plain primrose end-papers. Coloured engraved front. (listed as facing p. 1), wood-engraved vignette on title, and 16 plates by John Leech; also numerous wood-engraved illustrations in text.

pp. (x)+550 pp. (ix) (x) and final leaf, NN_3, single insets.

Ink inscription: 'George Gilford from J. F. G. Jany 1/59' on fly-leaf. Very fine.

[3163] HILLINGDON HALL, or the Cockney Squire: a Tale of Country Life (by the author of 'Handley Cross', etc.)

3 vols. Colburn 1845. Boards, labels.

Vol. I (vi)+312 Title-page a single inset. Publisher's cat., paged (i)–iv undated, precedes title.

II (ii)+324

III (ii)+296 [mispaged '96']

Book-label: 'Hamsterley Hall Library' in each vol. Very fine.

Note. Presumably Surtees' own copy. My previous copy (in boards, half-cloth) had 4 pp. adverts. (O_5 O_6) at end of Vol. III and no cat. preceding title of Vol. I.

[3164] JORROCKS'S JAUNTS AND JOLLITIES, or the HUNTING, SHOOTING, RACING, DRIVING, SAILING, EATING, ECCENTRIC AND EXTRAVAGANT EXPLOITS OF THAT RENOWNED SPORTING CITIZEN, MR JOHN JORROCKS, OF ST BOTOLPH LANE AND GREAT CORAM STREET [anon]

8vo. Walter Spiers, New Sporting Magazine Office, 399 Oxford Street 1838. Bronze-olive-green morocco cloth, pictorially and decoratively blocked in gold on front and spine, decoratively blocked in blind on front and back. Etched front. and 11 plates by Phiz.

Half-title. pp. (viii)+(360) $2A_4$ imprint leaf. Publisher's adverts., 8 pp. undated, at end. Bookplate of G. D. A. Clark. Loose in covers.

[3165] MR FACEY ROMFORD'S HOUNDS (by the author of 'Handley Cross', etc.)

8vo. Bradbury & Evans 1865. Old-rose perpendicular-fine-ribbed cloth, pictorially blocked and lettered in gold, and blocked in blind; plain cream end-papers. Coloured engraved front. and 13 plates by John Leech; also wood-engraved vignette on title and 10 coloured plates by Phiz.

Half-title. pp. (viii)+(392)

Ink inscription: 'George Gilford from A. G. Jany 3/71' on fly-leaf. Very fine.

[3166] MR SPONGE'S SPORTING TOUR (by the author of 'Handley Cross', etc.)

8vo. Bradbury & Evans 1853. Dark-salmon ribbed cloth, pictorially blocked and lettered in gold, and blocked in blind. Yellow end-papers printed in red with Publishers' adverts., including announcement of *Handley Cross* in Numbers and Christmas Books for 1853. Coloured engraved front. (listed as facing p. 385), wood-engraved vignette on title, and 12 plates by John Leech; also numerous wood-engraved illustrations in text.

Half-title. pp. (xii)+408 Very fine.

Note. Another copy, also very fine, inscribed: 'George Gilford from J. F. G. Jany 1/59', has biscuit-coloured end-papers overprinted with fine mesh and carrying publishers' adverts. in black. These are of later issue than those described above.

PLAIN OR RINGLETS? (by the author of 'Handley Cross', etc.) [3167]

8vo. Bradbury, Agnew & Co. 1860. Dark-salmon horizontally-ribbed cloth, pictorially blocked and lettered in gold, and blocked in blind; plain cream end-papers. Coloured front. (listed as facing p. 385), pictorial title (dated 1860, preceding printed title, also dated 1860, both imprinted 'Bradbury & Evans') and 11 plates by John Leech; also numerous wood-engraved illustrations in text.

pp. (x)+406 pp. (ix) (x) and final leaf, EE_1, single insets. Publishers' cat., 12 pp. dated August 1860, at end.

Very fine, apart from narrow band of fading at head of front cover.

SWEPSTONE, W. H.

CHRISTMAS SHADOWS: a Tale of the Times [3168]

Newby, n.d. [? late forties]. Red morocco cloth, all edges gilt. Etched front. and pictorial title and 4 full-page etched plates by Alfred Ashley.

pp. (ii)+222 Final sig. P seven leaves: P_1 single inset leaf.

Note. For other Ashley illustrations, see HORT.

TWO WIDOWS (The), or Matrimonial Jumbles [3169]

Newby, n.d. Grey-green diagonal-ripple-grain limp cloth, blocked in blind and lettered in gold on front; spine unlettered. Etched front., pictorial title (preceding printed title) and 4 etched plates by Alfred Ashley.

Pp. (ii)+(150) First leaf of final sig., L_1, a single inset. Worn.

Notes. (i) The etched title is imprinted 'J. C. NEWBY'; the printed title reads correctly 'THOMAS CAUTLEY NEWBY'.

(ii) *Christmas Shadows* is credited to Swepstone on the printed title, so that the authorship of that work is for the first time established.

TABLEY, JOHN LEICESTER WARREN, LORD DE (1835–1895)

[3170] HENCE THESE TEARS: a Novel [anon]
3 vols. Bentley 1872. Red-brown dotted-line-ribbed cloth.

Vol. I (vi)+(306) pp. (v) (vi) carrying 'Errata' for the three vols. form an inset leaf.
II (iv)+300
III iv+(292) B

Covers of Vols. I and II slightly damp-stained at head.

[3171] ROPES OF SAND: a Novel (by W. P. Lancaster)
3 vols. Bentley 1869. Green fine-morocco cloth.

Half-title in each vol. In each vol. pp. (v) (vi), Contents, form a single inset.

Vol. I (vi)+(276)
II (vi)+(262) First leaf of final sig., 17_1, a single inset.
III (vi)+(286) First leaf of final sig., 18_1, a single inset. B

[3172] SALVIA RICHMOND: a Novel [anon]
3 vols. Bentley 1878. Earth-brown diagonal-fine-ribbed cloth.

Vol. I (iv)+(304) 19_8 blank.
II (iv)+(272)
III (iv)+(280) 54_4 blank. B

[3173] SCREW LOOSE (A): a Novel (by William P. Lancaster, M.A.)
3 vols. Bentley 1868. Claret patterned sand-grain cloth.

Half-title in each vol.

Vol. I (viii)+(282) Collates in eights to S_8; thereafter T_1–T_4 and U_1 a single inset.
II (viii)+(272) S_8 imprint leaf.
III (viii)+278 Collates in eights to S_8; thereafter T_1, T_2 and U_1 a single inset. B

TAUTPHOEUS, BARONESS (JEMIMA MONTGOMERY) (1807–1893)

This is a complete collection of the works of the Baroness Tautphoeus.

[3174] AT ODDS: a Novel
2 vols. Bentley 1863. Magenta wavy-grain cloth.

Vol. I iv+(336) Y_8 imprint leaf.
II iv+(348) Z_6 blank.

Binders' ticket: 'Westleys', at end of Vol. I. Ink signature: 'H. Maunsell, Landsend 1863', on fly-leaf of each vol. Cloth stained and faded.

CYRILLA: a Tale [3175]
3 vols. Bentley 1853. Half-cloth boards, labels.

Half-title in each vol.

Vol. I (iv)+(312) O_{12} blank.
II (iv)+(336)
III (iv)+330 Final leaf, Q_1, a single inset.

Very fine.

INITIALS (The): a Novel [anon] [3176]
3 vols. Bentley 1850. Dark-maize morocco cloth; yellow end-papers printed in black with publisher's adverts.

Half-title in each vol.

Vol. I (iv)+324
II (iv)+(308) P_2 adverts.
III (iv)+304

Booksellers' ticket: 'Ebers & Co. Old Bond St', inside front cover of Vol. I. Very fine.

QUITS: a Novel [3177]
3 vols. Bentley 1857.

Copy I. Half-cloth boards, labels.

Vol. I iv+300
II iv+(288) T_8 blank.
III iv+304

Label of Vol. II blotched with ink.

Copy II. Dark grey-green ripple-grain cloth. [3177*a*]
Collation as Copy I.

Book-plate of Syston Park in Vol. I and booksellers' ticket: 'Cawthorn & Co. Cockspur Street', inside front cover of each vol. Fine.

TAYLOR, CAPTAIN PHILIP MEADOWS (1808–1876)

This is a complete collection of the fiction of Captain Meadows Taylor.

CONFESSIONS OF A THUG [3178]
3 vols. Bentley 1839. Half-cloth boards, labels.

Vol. I xxiv+324 Publishers' cat. (Whittaker & Co.), 16 pp. dated 1838, inset between front fly-leaf and title.
II (ii)+338 Final leaf, Q_1, a single inset.
III (ii)+424

Very fine.

NOBLE QUEEN (A): a Romance of Indian History [3179]
3 vols. Kegan Paul etc. 1878. Olive-green diagonal-fine-ribbed cloth; dark chocolate end-papers.

Blank leaf and half-title (reading: 'A Romance of Indian History') precede title in each vol.

Vol. I (xii) [paged x] + 292
II (viii) [paged vi] + 280 Publishers' cat., 32 pp. dated '77', at end.
III (viii) [paged vi] + 288 Text ends p. 285; (286) Note; (287) 288 Glossary.

Very fine.

Note. A later binding-up, with cat. in Vol. II dated '10. 79', shows a variant blocking on spine. At head and foot are three plain bands, instead of one patterned and one plain band as on first issue.

[3180] RALPH DARNELL
3 vols. Blackwood 1865. Smooth glazed dark green cloth; red-chocolate end-papers.

Half-title in each vol.

Vol. I (xii) + (322) Final leaf, (X_1), a single inset. Publishers' cat., 20 pp. undated, at end.
II vi + (308) Half-title a single inset.
III vi + 348 Half-title a single inset.

Binder's ticket: 'Burn', at end of Vol. I. Ink signature: 'Jno Brook Greaves (?) Junr', on title of each vol. Fine.

[3181] SEETA
3 vols. Henry S. King & Co. 1872. Green bubble-grain cloth; chocolate end-papers.

The fly-leaves carry a panel of adverts. on their white verso, facing title.

Vol. I xii + (280) Publishers' cat., 32 pp. dated December 1872, at end.
II (iv) [mispaged vi] + (328)
III iv + (320) X_8 adverts.

Ink inscription on each title: 'From his admirer Balvantras Vinasell Shastree (?) 11th March, 1875.' Cloth spotted.

[3182] TARA: a Mahratta Tale
3 vols. Blackwood 1863. Brownish-slate diagonal-fine-ribbed cloth.

Half-title in each vol.

Vol. I xii + 364
II (iv) + 364
III (iv) + (336) X_8 blank.

[3183] TIPPOO SULTAUN: a Tale of the Mysore War
3 vols. Bentley 1840. Half-cloth boards, labels.

Half-title in each vol.

Vol. I viii + 320
II (iv) + 360
III (iv) + 428

Very fine.

THACKERAY, ANN (LADY RITCHIE) (1837–1923)

OLD KENSINGTON [3184]
8vo. Smith, Elder 1873. Dark green patterned-sand-grain cloth, blocked on front in gold and black with open gateway enclosing a panel of lighter green smooth cloth pictorially blocked in black; on spine decoratively blocked in black and gold lettered; pinkish buff end-papers. Wood-engraved front. and 12 plates after 'G.D.L.'

Blank leaf and half-title precede front. pp. (xii) [paged (x)] + (532)

Presentation Copy: 'Dear Neighbour Dolly from her affectionate A.E.T.' in ink on title. Fine.

This is the Yates Thompson copy (Sotheby, Aug. '41) and 'Dolly' was Dorothy Smith, later Mrs Yates Thompson.

STORY OF ELIZABETH (The) [anon] [3185]

Copy I: First Edition. Smith, Elder 1863. Dark grey dot-and-line-grain cloth. Wood-engraved front. and 1 other plate after Frederick Walker.

pp. (iv) + (288)

Cloth fine. Front. and title faintly water-stained.

Copy II: 'Illustrated Edition.' Smith, Elder 1868. Smooth brown cloth, blocked in black and gold in standard style of the publishers' 'Illustrated Editions'. Wood-engraved front. (as in Copy I), pictorial title, and 2 plates (1 as in Copy I) after Frederick Walker. [3185*a*]

pp. (iv) + (252)

THACKERAY, WILLIAM MAKEPEACE (1811–1863)

ADVENTURES OF PHILIP (The) on his way through the World, etc. [3186]
3 vols. 'Smith & Elder' 1862.

Copy I. Brown coarse-morocco cloth [issue (i), below].

Half-title in Vol. I

Vol. I (viii) + (332) 21_6 blank.
II (iv) + 304
III (iv) + (304) 59_8 blank.

Copy II. Cloth and collation as Copy I, but differently blocked [issue (ii) below]. Very fine.

Copy III. Violet-blue bubble-grain cloth [issue (iii) below]. Collation as Copy I. Fine; spines slightly faded.

Note. I am not satisfied that the publishing history of this book has been correctly interpreted. We are aware of three distinct issues:

(i) Brown morocco cloth, blocked in blind on front and back with an eight-pointed, more or less geometrical design enclosed in wide-set double framing with squares at the four corners; and on spine under titling with a gold ornament involving trefoils to right and left of a circle enclosing a quatrefoil. The period which should follow the volume-number on the spine of Vol. II is missing. There is a catalogue dated July 1862 at the end of Vol. III. This issue is imprinted on spine: SMITH, ELDER & CO. and the Statutory copies in B.M. and Bodley (that in U.L.C. is re-bound) belong to it.

(ii) Brown morocco cloth, blocked in blind on front and back with a panel conventionally ornamented with scroll design in the corners and enclosed in wide-set double framing which does *not* cross over to form corner squares; and on spine, under titling, with gold ornament of four bell-shaped flowers and a spikey circle hanging from a straight line with curled-in ends. This issue is imprinted on spine: SMITH & ELDER. No catalogue is included.

(iii) Darkish violet-blue bubble-grain cloth, blocked in blind on front and back with plain triple frame; on spine, gold-lettered as (i) and (ii) with bands at head and tail but no ornament. Spine imprint: SMITH & ELDER. No catalogue is included in any copy seen.

Now the imprint 'Smith & Elder' was abandoned in favour of 'Smith, Elder & Co.' some time between the spring of 1824 and the winter of 1826. That is to say, it was discontinued at least 36 years before the publication of *Philip*, *and was never, to my knowledge, used during the cloth-period—which means that no brass for use on a cloth spine could reasonably have been in existence during the currency of the imprint.*

It follows, therefore, that the brass used on the 'Smith & Elder' copies of *Philip* was cut specially for that book, and the sudden recrudescence of a long obsolete imprint must have been due to error. *All* blue copies reported are 'Smith & Elder', as also are all brown copies with scroll as opposed to geometrical blocking. The correct imprint only appears on brown geometrical copies, and (as stated above) the two principal Statutory copies are of this type.

Hitherto it has been assumed (*cf.* Carter p. 158) that the blue copies, being less ornamented and generally meaner in appearance, were secondaries, but I cannot on this basis reasonably account for their 'Smith & Elder' imprint. As for the two brown variants, no argument as to priority has, to my knowledge, been published.

The only reasonable sequence of publishing events —given the character of George Smith and his veneration for Thackeray—seems to me to be the following:

The blue copies were the first to be bound, and on them was made the strange blunder over the publishers' imprint. Smith, who was a very particular man, saw the mistake and condemned it. At the same time, he decided that the binding design was not worthy of the author he so much admired. He, therefore, ordered an entirely new case, with richer ornamentation and a correct imprint. The first official edition was in consequence brown cloth, furnished with a publishers' catalogue, and Statutory copies were sent out in that style. As is known, the novel was unsuccessful. In 1863 Thackeray died, and at some subsequent date the publishers ordered a second binding of the residual sheets. Brown cloth was again used (probably the balance of the original order), but the binders carelessly applied the condemned imprint in place of the correct one. They used side-blocking of a stock pattern, with less character than that on brown cloth (i). By the time brown cloth (ii) came into stock, George Smith either never saw a copy or did not think it was worth while to condemn a delivery of an unpopular book by an author no longer alive. Finally came a selling-off of the blue copies, which, though in fact the earliest, reached the market last and are usually in very fine state.

Any other reconstruction than this seems to me to outrage possibility. If brown (i)—'Smith, Elder & Co.'—were truly the first binding, there would have been no conceivable reason for the subsequent making of a faulty imprint-brass. Brown (ii) not only looks less important than brown (i), but is almost proved a subsequent style by the evidence of the Statutory copies. Whence then the faulty imprints on brown (ii)? They could only have arisen from the mistaken use of an already made brass; and that brass could only have been made for the remaining binding style, viz. no. (iii) in violet-blue.

HISTORY OF HENRY ESMOND, ESQ. (The): a Colonel in the Service of Her Majesty Q. Anne (written by Himself) [3187]

3 vols. Smith, Elder 1852. White vellum spine and corners, leather lettering pieces, puce morocco cloth sides; marbled end-papers; all edges gilt. (Issued in olive-brown fine-ribbed cloth, paper labels.)

Half-title in each vol.

Vol. I pp. 344
II vi+(320)
III vi+324

Book-plate: 'Delane', on inside front cover. Book-plate: 'John Roche Dasent', on front fly-leaf of each vol. Ink signature: 'Manuel Dasent, Ascot April 1872', on half-title of Vol. I.

Note. This charmingly bound copy has a curious family resemblance to the copy of *Uncle Silas* specially bound by Le Fanu (1386*a*, above) for presentation to J. T. Delane. It seems possible that the style—three-quarter vellum, rather gay colouring and marbled end-papers—was a personal preference of the famous *Times* editor.

[3188] PUNCH'S PRIZE NOVELISTS: THE FAT CONTRIBUTOR and TRAVELS IN LONDON

New York: Appleton 1853. Dark brown morocco cloth, blocked in blind and lettered in gold.

Blank leaf and half-title precede title. pp. (312) 13_{10}–13_{12} adverts. Fine.

First book edition of all the material concerned. *Punch's Prize Novelists* consists of parodies of Bulwer Lytton, Lever, G. P. R. James, Mrs Gore and Disraeli.

TOLSTOY, COUNT LEO (1828–1910)

[3189] CHILDHOOD AND YOUTH: a Tale (by Count Nicola Tolstoi)

Translated from the Russian by Malwida von Meysenbug (*sic*). Bell and Daldy, 186 Fleet St. 1862.

Copy I: ? Regulation Issue. Brown coarse-morocco cloth, blocked in blind with plain triple framing on front and back, gold-lettered and blind-banded on spine. Red-chocolate end-papers.

Half-title. pp. (xii) + (272) S_8 imprint leaf.

Ink signature: 'A. B. Isabel Percy' on half-title.

Very fine.

Copy II: ? Presentation Issue. Grass-green coarse-morocco cloth, pictorially and ornamentally blocked in gold and blind on front, pictorially blocked and gold-lettered on spine, blind-blocked on back. Primrose end-papers. All edges gilt. Steel-engraved front. Collation as Copy I.

Very fine.

Note. This very scarce book is the first English translation of Tolstoy to be published. It appeared in Russian in 1856, when the author was 28 years of age.

Both copies are in virtually new condition, and there is no sign, either that the front. is lacking from Copy I, or has been inserted in Copy II. The gold vignette on the front cover of Copy II is signed J. L[eighton].

[3190] PRINCE SEREBRENNI (by Count A. Tolstoy) Translated by Princess Galitzine.

2 vols. Chapman & Hall 1874. Grass-green sand-grain cloth, blocked in black on front, back and spine; also blocked and lettered in gold on spine.

Half-title in each vol.

Vol. I (viii) + 288
II (viii) + 308

Ink signature 'Redfern Hampstead' inside front cover, and 'Redfern' on title of each vol.

[3191] RESURRECTION: a Novel (by Leo Tolstoy)

First Edition in English. Translated by Louise (Mrs Aylmer) Maude.

Copy I: Part Issue. Thirteen parts, published at irregular intervals at one penny each from 14 April 1899 to 10 March 1900, in tall slim 8vo format ($3\frac{5}{8} \times 8\frac{7}{16}$) each page carrying a narrow column of 49 lines printed from the type of the newspaper 'New Order'.

The wrappers vary in colour and illustration, but are all printed in black, and are constant in layout and wording, thus: *New Order* Extra / ONE PENNY / BY / LEO TOLSTOY / *double rule* / Resurrection [set sloping upward in fancy cap. and l.c.] / A / NOVEL / *short double rule* / PART I. [*II*, *III*, etc.] / *illustration* / LONDON / BROTHERHOOD PUBLISHING C°: / 26 PATERNOSTER SQ. E.C. / 1899. [Parts XII and XIII: 1900.] Spines unlettered. Inside front and back wrappers printed with adverts. of Tolstoy's works. Outside back wrapper of Parts I to XII advertises this part-issue of *Resurrection*, states that all proceeds of sale will be devoted to the assistance of the Russian Doukhobors now fleeing to Canada from the persecution of the Russian Government, announces the date of appearance of the next Part, and at foot repeats publishers' imprint and gives the date of issue of the present Part. Back wrapper of Part XIII is described below.

Part I. Salmon-pink wrappers, with half-tone portrait of Tolstoy. pp. (1)–48 of text. Date on back: April 14, 1899.

Part II. Pale green wrappers, with line illustration of an incident in the story. pp. 49–96 of text. Date on back: April 28, 1899.

Part III. Yellow wrappers, illustration as II. First leaf of text paper is a title-page, omitted from page-reckoning, dated 1899 and carrying on verso chapter titles of Parts I and II. Then follow pp. 97–128 of text. Final leaf adverts.—on recto, of a book by Tolstoy published by Walter Scott; on verso, of 'Brotherhood' publications. Date on back: May 15, 1899.

Part IV. Colour and illustration as II. First leaf of text paper, title-page as in III but headed: PART IV; on verso chapter titles of I–III. pp. 129–160 of text. Final leaf adverts., similar to that in III. Date on back: June 5, 1899.

Part V. Colour and illustration as III. First leaf of text paper 'Brotherhood' adverts.; Second leaf, title, verso Contents, as in IV but brought up to date. pp. 161–188 of text. Penultimate and final leaves, 'Brotherhood' adverts. Date on back: June 16, 1899.

Part VI. Colour as II. New line illustration of an incident in the story. First leaf of text paper 'Brotherhood' adverts. pp. 189–220 of text. At foot of p. 220: END OF VOL. I. Date on back: July 12, 1899.

Part VII. Colour as III, illustration as VI. First leaf of text paper, Press Notices of *Resurrection* to date, some highly unfavourable. pp. (221)–252 of text, the first headed: VOL. 2. Final leaf 'Brotherhood' adverts. Date on back: August 4, 1899.

Part VIII. Colour and illustration as VI. First two leaves of text paper, Press Notices, 'Brotherhood' adverts. and chapter titles of *Resurrection* to date. pp. 253–292 of text. Two final leaves 'Brotherhood' adverts. Date on back: Sept. 1, 1899.

Part IX. Colour and illustration as VII. First two and last two leaves as VIII. pp. 293–332 of text. Date on back: Sept. 22, 1899.

Part X. Colour and illustration as VI. First two and last two leaves as VIII. pp. 333–372 of text. Date on back: October 27, 1899.

Part XI. Colour and illustration as VII. First two and last two leaves as VIII. pp. 373–408 of text. At foot of p. 408: END OF VOLUME II. Date on back: November 27, 1899.

Part XII. Colour and illustration as VI. First two and last two leaves as VIII. pp. (409)–448 of text, the former headed: VOL. 3. Date on back: February 10, 1900.

Part XIII. Colour and illustration as VI. pp. 449–(496) of text. Story ends p. 495, with words THE END at foot. Outside back wrapper announces 'Illustrated Edition' as 'Now Ready. Complete in one volume. Cr. 8vo. 565 pp. in Art Canvas. Price 6s net. Published March 10, 1900 by Francis Riddell Henderson, 26 Paternoster Square, E.C.'; also that the complete set of *New Order* Extras can be had post free for 1*s.* 4*d.*

The top two inches of the front wrapper of Part I has been torn away, and skilfully repaired and facsimiled. The back wrapper of XIII is slightly defective.

Bookseller's ticket (in one case rubber stamp): 'Harrison, Lower Clapton Road' in the majority of Parts. As the tickets are in several cases loosely inserted, it is a reasonable presumption that originally each part was ticketed.

[3191*a*] **Copy II: Book Issue** Brotherhood Publishing Co. 1900. Green paper wrapper, mounted on board-stiffening and strongly grained to suggest woodwork in section. Gold-lettered on front: Resurrection [o.e., cap and l.c.] / *rule* / LEO TOLSTOY. Spine unlettered. Back plain.

Half-title. pp. (iv) + (500) pp. (497)–(500) adverts.

This is a binding-up of the Parts, with all incidental intermediate titles and advert. leaves omitted, and a new 4 pp. prelim. on whiter paper which was certainly printed with the 4 pp. of adverts. at the end.

On the title-page appears the vignette used on the covers of Parts II–V, and facing title is a slightly revised version of the statement about the Doukhobors printed on the back wrappers of the Parts. On the verso of title the 'Illustrated Edition' (cf. Part XIII) is announced as 'Now Ready'.

Ink signature: 'A. M. Broadbank' on fly-leaf. Covers rather faded.

WAR AND PEACE: I. Before Tilsit; II. The Invasion; III. The French at Moscow (by Count Lyov Tolstoi) [3192]

3 vols. Vizetelly & Co. 1886. Smooth greenish-grey cloth, blocked and lettered on front and spine in dark blue and red, blocked in blind on back with publishers' device and plain bands; dark maroon end-papers.

Half-title in each vol.

Vol. I pp. (432) [paged (430)] Half-title and final leaf, EE_3, single insets, former probably printed as EE_4.

II pp. 360 Advert. leaf on thin paper precedes half-title. Publishers' cat., 32 pp. dated September 1886, at end.

III pp. (392) CC_1 CC_2 adverts. Advert. leaf on thin paper precedes half-title as in Vol. II

Vol. I re-cased and end-papers renewed; Vols. II and III fine.

TOURGENEF, J. [TURGENIEFF, I.] (1818–1883)

FATHERS AND SONS: a Novel. Translated from the Russian with the approval of the Author by Eugene Schuyler, Ph.D. [3193]

Ward, Lock & Co. n.d. (1883). Smooth light-chocolate cloth, blocked in black, lime-green and gold; pale green floral end-papers.

pp. viii + 248 Publishers' cat., 12 pp. undated, at end.

Ink signature: 'Caroline Davidson, November 1883', on title. Fine.

This is a volume in the Select Library of Fiction and, I think, the first *English* edition of the first English translation. The book almost certainly had previously appeared in U.S.A. The author's name is spelt in the second of the two ways given above.

FIRST LOVE and PUNIN AND BABÚRIN (from the Russian of Iván Turgénev by Sidney Jerrold) [3194]

W. H. Allen & Co., 13 Waterloo Place 1884. Dark green diagonal-fine-ribbed-cloth, blocked with blind framing on front and back, blocked and lettered in gold on spine.

Portrait front.

Half-title. pp. (xii) + (240) 15_8 adverts.

pp. (1)–57 Introduction; 58–155 *First Love*; 156–237 *Punin and Babúrin.*

Fine.

LIZA. Translated from the Russian by W. R. S. Ralston [3195]

2 vols. Fcap. 8vo. Chapman & Hall 1869. Red-brown sand-grain cloth, blocked in blind and lettered in gold.

Half-title in each vol.

Vol. I xviii + (246) b_1 (pp. xvii, xviii) and final leaf, R_3, single insets.

II (iv) + (232)

Ink signature: 'G. E. Alma Tadema', on title of Vol. I. One signature loose in Vol. I.

[3196] ON THE EVE: a Tale (by Ivan S. Tourguéneff, translated from the Russian by C. E. Turner)

Sq. fcap 8vo. Hodder & Stoughton 1871. Royal-blue sand-grain cloth, blocked in black and gold and gold-lettered on front and spine, blind-blocked on back. Chocolate end-papers.

pp. vi + 306 Title and final leaf, 20_1, single insets. Publishers' cat., 16 pp. on text-paper undated, at end.

Fine.

[3197] SMOKE, or Life at Baden: a Novel

Pl. 27 2 vols. Bentley 1868. Dark reddish-brown patterned-sand-grain cloth.

Half-title in each vol.

Vol. I (iv) + 244

II (iv) + 236 **B**

First edition in English? The author's name is spelt in the first of the two ways given above.

TRELAWNY, EDWARD JOHN (1792–1881)

[3198] ADVENTURES OF A YOUNGER SON [anon]

Pl. 27 3 vols. Colburn & Bentley 1831. Boards, labels (worded: THE/YOUNGER/SON/*rule*/Vol. I [*II*, *III*]).

Half-title in each vol.

Vol. I (iv) + (336) P_{12} adverts.

II (iv) + (344) Q_4 adverts.

III (iv) + (340) Q_2 adverts.

Fine. Spines of Vols. I and III slightly imperfect at base, of Vol. II at head.

Note. The story of this really remarkable copy of *Adventures of a Younger Son* (for despite the slight damage to the spines, the volumes are really fine—sides clean and sharp and labels white and perfect) is a curious one and, like all collecting stories, will interest my fellow maniacs.

In my capacity of publisher I went, one day many years ago, to visit one of our bookseller-clients in the City. We talked over our business in his small room above the shop, and, as I was about to leave, I saw, lying on their sides on a shelf in the corner, three volumes in grey paper boards. Even in a second-hand bookshop such a sight would have meant investigation; how much keener was my curiosity at seeing an unmistakable relic of the early nineteenth century in an up-to-date City shop, which had never consciously sold a second-hand book in its life! The volumes were those of this set of the first edition of Trelawny's *The Younger Son.*

My bookseller friend then told me this almost incredible story.

A customer wanted a copy of the book. Any copy. He wanted to read it. It happened that at that moment no contemporary reprint was available, so the booksellers advertised. The only reply offered them three volumes in boards dated 1831. The price seemed rather high; but as no other copy was reported, they had the books sent to London on approval and advised their customer that this was the best they could do. He indignantly refused to pay any such sum for a book he expected to buy for about five shillings, and the volumes were, that very afternoon, to be sent back to their original offerer.

This incident is one of the most remarkable in my book-collecting experience. A routine advertisement for a copy of *The Younger Son* (any text at all, mark you) produced a first edition in a state of unsophisticated beauty, and a publishing call at a City bookshop I hardly ever visited put the volumes in my way two or three hours before they were due to disappear.

TROLLOPE, ANTHONY (1815–1882)

Having already published a Bibliography of Anthony Trollope, I have decided to omit from this Catalogue descriptions of those of his first editions which I now possess. They constitute my second Anthony-collection and, although for the most part in very fine condition, are not by any means complete.

There are, however, a few additions and one or two corrections to the text of the published Bibliography which can here be suitably recorded; and readers are asked to regard the Notes which follow as a sort of Appendix to the full-length book issued in 1929.

AUSTRALIA and NEW ZEALAND [3199

Australian Edition in Parts and Cloth.

[*Sadleir* p. 136

The record of this edition in my Bibliography is condensed and imperfect, because, when it was written, I had only seen an odd Part and a copy of the cloth edition, and was compelled to argue from insufficient data. Now that I possess a complete set in Parts an adequate description can be offered.

(i) **Part-Issue.** This consisted of Seven Parts, dated 1873 and published by George Robertson, Melbourne, wrappered in blue paper, cut flush, pictorially printed and lettered in black, and up-lettered on spine. Inside front and back wrappers of Parts 1, 2, 4, 5, 6, 7 blank; inside back wrapper of Part 3 printed with a publisher's advert. Outside back wrapper of each Part advertises either a forthcoming Part of Trollope's work or its issue in book-form.

The Parts are not numbered on front wrappers, but on spine and title-page of Parts 1–6 are described as Division I–Division VI; Part 7 has no individual title, and is described on spine as Appendix. Parts 1 and 6 are priced Three Shillings; Parts 2–5 Half a Crown; Part 7 One Shilling.

(*Part* 1): DIVISION I: QUEENSLAND. pp. (iv) [general half-title and individual title] + 1–119 of text, (120) blank.

(*Part* 2): DIVISION II: NEW SOUTH WALES. pp. (iv) [as in 1] + 121–226 of text, (227) (228) [Q_6] blank.

(*Part* 3): DIVISION III: VICTORIA. pp. (iv) [as in 1, 2] + 227–334 of text.

(*Part* 4): DIVISION IV: TASMANIA AND WESTERN AUSTRALIA. pp. (iv) [as in 1, 2, 3] + 335–433 of text, (434) blank.

(*Part* 5): DIVISION V: SOUTH AUSTRALIA. pp. (iv) [as in 1, 2, 3, 4] + 435–528 of text, (529) (530) [NN_8] blank.

(*Part* 6): DIVISION VI: NEW ZEALAND. pp. (iv) [as in 1, 2, 3, 4, 5] + 529–658 of text.

(*Part* 7): APPENDIX. pp. (viii) [general half-title, general title, Contents of the whole work] + 659–684 of text, 685–(691) Index, (692) blank.

[3199*a*] (ii) **Book-Issue.** Crimson sand-grain cloth, pictorially blocked in black (differently from Parts), blocked and lettered in gold. Bevelled boards, café-au-lait end-papers. Published at eighteen shillings.

The general half-titles and individual titles which appeared in Parts 1–6 were suppressed in book-issue, only the general prelims. included in Part 7 being retained. Neither Part nor Volume Issue contains any maps.

Note. Part 1 of the Melbourne Issue was advertised as 'ready' on March 10, 1873. Chapman & Hall advertised their 2 vol. cloth edition at the end of March. Ostensibly, therefore, the first (and maybe even the second) Melbourne Part pre-dated London issue. This is fewer than might be expected, seeing that Robertson supplied no maps and—Trollope having finished the book early in December 1872 before sailing (he arrived home with the MS. on December 20)—could have started manufacture well ahead of Chapman & Hall.

[3200] BARCHESTER TOWERS

[*Sadleir* p. 21 (*Second Binding*)

3 vols. Longman etc. 1857. Pale brown horizontally grained morocco cloth; liver-brown end-papers printed with adverts. on inside front and back covers, fly-leaves blank.

Notes. (i) A few words of comment are desirable on the term 'Second Binding' as used in my Bibliography in connection with this title. In *The Times Literary Supplement* report of the Yates Thompson Sale in August 1941 occurred the following: 'A very nice copy of *Barchester Towers* sold [to the trade] for the reasonable sum of £20. The price was probably due to the fact that the bibliography compels the description "second" binding. A copy of the "first" binding was recently offered for £115. The absurdity of such discrimination will be clear when it is said that the difference consists in the colour of the end-papers and the books they advertise. Mr Sadleir, the bibliographer's, own copy is, if memory serves, in the "second" binding.'

I agree with the writer of the above that to a collector the difference between a fine 'first' binding and an equally fine 'second' binding of *Barchester Towers* is not equivalent to the difference between £20 and £115. But I must point out that the former price having been *paid*, and the latter *asked*, we cannot know from the auction record at what price the 'second' binding would be offered for sale by the bookseller-buyer, nor whether the 'first' binding found a buyer at the price asked.

Further, there can be no doubt whatsoever that the Yates Thompson copy (like my own) actually belonged to a binding-up made after publication. The books advertised on the end-papers and the catalogue in Vol. I prove this to be the case. Both are, therefore, literally specimens of the 'second' binding. But this is not the same thing as a *secondary binding*; and it may be that to persons unfamiliar with the practices of publishing, my use of the word 'second' implied something inferior in status—indeed almost a remainder binding. Of course it does nothing of the kind. Chronologically these copies belong to the *second binding*: and I do not see how the fact could otherwise be stated.

(ii) The absence of two advert. leaves from Vol. I of my copy (a_1 and X_2) is curious. The book is in virtually new condition and the omission can only have been deliberately made by the binders. Possibly the advert.-copy prepared for the first binding-up of 1857 was out of date by 1860 and therefore removed.

CAN YOU FORGIVE HER? [*Sadleir* p. 56 [3201]

2 vols. 8vo. Chapman & Hall 1864/5.

When the sheets of the Second Edition were issued two-volumes-in-one, a new title was printed, describing the book as 'Third Edition. With 40 Illustrations by Phiz and Marcus Stone'. The mention of Stone must have been an undetected slip, for, as a letter from Trollope quoted in my biography shows, the illustrator of Vol. II was a Miss Taylor.

[3202] CASTLE RICHMOND: a Novel [*Sadleir* p. 28
3 vols. Chapman & Hall 1860.

My Bibliography failed to distinguish between the survival conditions governing the first and second issues of this novel. The discovery and analysis by the late Carroll Wilson of an undeniable first issue were recorded in my book at the last moment and, having previously been ignorant that a first issue existed, I had no evidence to guide me in estimating its rarity. Consequently I stressed (and rightly) the greater frequency with which copies *quâ copies* of *Castle Richmond* survive in comparison with copies of *The Bertrams*. Now, however, all these years later, we know that a first issue of *Castle Richmond* ranks near the top of Trollope scarcities; and is so recorded in the Comparative Table at the end of this Section of the present Catalogue.

[3203] MACDERMOTS OF BALLYCLORAN: a Novel (First American Edition) [not previously recorded]

Philadelphia: T. B. Peterson, n.d. (probably about 1871). Black sand-grain cloth, blocked in blind on front and back, blocked and lettered in gold on spine; dark chocolate end-papers.

pp. (448) [paged, for some mysterious reason, (17)–(464)] Text ends 27_5; 27_6–27_8, (28_1)–(28_8) Publisher's cat., undated and paged 11, 12+1–16+4 pp. unfoliated. Fine.

This cat. contains some fantastic attributions, e.g. to Sir E. L. Bulwer 'The Roué', 'The Oxonians' (both by Samuel Beazley) and 'The Courtier' (by Mrs Gore); to Captain Marryat 'The Sea King' (? 'The Sea Kings' by Atherstone); to Ainsworth eight biographies of criminals.

[3204] PRIME MINISTER (The) [*Sadleir* p. 148

First Edition (American) [pre-dating English by one month. *Brussel* p. 157]. 8vo. New York: Harper 1876. Buff paper wrappers, printed in black with the design of the English part issue.

Two advert. leaves precede title. pp. (256) 16_7 16_8 adverts. Publishers' cat., 8 pp. undated, at end.

[3204*a*] **First English Edition.** 4 vols. Chapman & Hall 1876. The collation can be more clearly expressed as follows:

Vol. I (iv) [paged vi]+(338) Sig. M one leaf and a single inset.
II iv+342 Sig. M five leaves, M_1 a single inset.
III (iv) [paged vi]+346 Sig. M seven leaves, M_1 a single inset.
IV (iv) [paged vi]+(348) Sig. M four leaves.

[3205] 'ST PAUL'S MAGAZINE' prospectus
8vo. Virtue & Co. October 1867. [not previously recorded]

A 4 pp. leaflet announcing the first number of *St Paul's* and consisting (apart from title, contents, etc. in upper half of p. (1) and publishers' imprint at foot of p. 4) of an editorial address, unsigned but written by Trollope. This address formed the basis of the 'Editor's Introduction' to No. 1 of the magazine, but was rewritten and expanded for that purpose. As the 'Introduction' appeared in the magazine with matter by other hands, it cannot rank, as can this prospectus, as a separate Trollope issue.

WAY WE LIVE NOW (The) [*Sadleir* p. 143 [3206]
2 vols. 8vo. Chapman & Hall 1875.

Note. The illustrations to this novel are signed 'L. F.', but are nowhere attributed to any named artist. In my Trollope Bibliography (p. 143) I stated that they were the work of Luke Fildes. This was mere assumption, and is now proved to have been incorrect.

Three or four years after the bibliography was published, a copy of *The Way We Live Now* came to light, which had belonged to one Edith Mary Fawkes; and she had written on the title of each volume under the legend 'With Fifty Illustrations', the words 'by Lionel Fawkes. Royal Artillery'.

I noted this discovery for eventual incorporation in the present Catalogue (its compilation had started as long ago as 1938), hoping that my original error would pass unnoticed until it could be formally confessed. But unluckily a near relative of Sir Luke Fildes spotted the attribution and challenged it—not surprisingly, seeing that the illustrations are very inferior and are so described. It became necessary, therefore, to admit my mistake in public and ahead of this Catalogue's completion; and a brief correspondence in *The Times Literary Supplement* not only exonerated Fildes from the blame of having produced such unworthy drawings, but also elicited some personal details about the true culprit. These I now summarize, so that the matter may be finally ventilated.

Lionel Grimston Fawkes was born in 1849 and died in 1931. He became a Colonel in the Royal Artillery; and, both as Major and Colonel Fawkes, was well known to his intimates as a skilful portraitist in water-colours, and as a man whose extempore drawings delighted the children of his acquaintance. In 1879 (four years after the publication of *The Way We Live Now*), he illustrated *The Washburn and Other Poems* by his aunt, Miss Fawkes; and she, presumably, was the lady who annotated the copy of Trollope's novel to which I refer above.

Partly by Trollope

THACKERAY, The Humourist and the Man of Letters [by Theodore Taylor, to which is added [3207

'In Memoriam' by Charles Dickens and a Sketch by Anthony Trollope]

[*Sadleir* p. 216; no description given

New York: Appleton 1864. Dark grey-green morocco cloth; yellow end-papers. Etched front. signed Jackman, a few line vignettes on text paper and a facsimile on plate paper.

pp. viii+(244) 11_2 blank. The book collates in twelves to 9_{12}; thereafter 10_1–10_4; $11*_1$–$11*_8$; 11_1, 11_2.

Trollope's 'Sketch' occupies pp. 232–242.

[3208] THIRD REPORT OF THE POSTMASTER GENERAL ON THE POST OFFICE

[not previously recorded

8vo. H.M. Stationery Office 1857.

pp. (68) [paged (i)–(vi)+(3)–64] Text of Report ends p. 34; pp. (35)–64 Appendices. pp. 56–62 are occupied by Appendix J: HISTORY OF THE POST OFFICE IN IRELAND signed ANTHONY TROLLOPE.

Note. This report was probably issued stitched, title serving as front cover. I have noted two copies: Copy I in a volume from a run of the P.M.G.'s Reports (1855–1873) bound in official scarlet roan; Copy II in marbled paper wrappers with a spine of black linen.

[3209] VICTORIA REGIA (The) [*Sadleir* p. 213

8vo. Emily Faithfull & Co. 1861.

Two bindings have been noted, in addition to those recorded in my Bibliography. The first is a Regulation binding of royal-blue morocco cloth, bevelled boards, all edges gilt; dark red-chocolate end-papers.

The second is a Gift binding of full olive-brown morocco, tooled and lettered in gold and blind. Gold doublures; double white end-papers; all edges gilt.

[3210] WELCOME (A): Original Contributions in Poetry and Prose [*Sadleir* p. 215

Square 8vo. Emily Faithfull 1863. Full cream calf, blocked and lettered in gold, uniform with the ordinary green cloth edition; double pale-pink end-papers; gold doublures; all edges gilt.

pp. (viii)+(292) pp. (239)–283 are occupied by *Miss Ophelia Gledd* by Anthony Trollope.

Presentation Copy: 'Presented to His Royal Highness Prince Arthur, pp. Emily Faithfull' in ink on second front end-paper. From the Royal Library, Windsor Castle.

Note. In my *Trollope Bibliography* I noted this gift-binding from a report and unseen. I can now confirm that the blocking is as on the ordinary edition, and the inscription and provenance suggest that the 'gift' style was indeed specially prepared for presentation to members of the Royal Family.

TROLLOPE, CECILIA (sister to ANTHONY; became MRS JOHN TILLEY) (1816–1849)

CHOLLERTON: a Tale of Our Own Times (by a Lady) [3211]

Small 8vo. John Ollivier 1846. Dark green ribbed cloth.

Blank leaf precedes title. pp. (iv)+(384) $2B_8$ adverts.

Note. I have never seen another copy outside a Library of this little High Church story—the only book Anthony Trollope's sister wrote.

TROLLOPE, FRANCES (mother of ANTHONY) (1780–1863)

A complete schedule of Mrs Trollope's work. All titles in boards or half-cloth should have white end-papers.

ABBESS (The): a Romance (by the author of 'Domestic Manners of the Americans', etc.) [3212]

3 vols. Whittaker, Treacher 1833. Boards, labels.

Half-title in each vol.

Vol. I (iv)+320
II (iv)+(332)
III (iv)+344

Book-label of R. J. Ll. Price, Rhiwlas Library, Bala, Merionethshire, and bookseller's ticket: 'Seacome, Chester', inside front cover of each vol. Back fly-leaf of Vol. I lacking.

ATTRACTIVE MAN (The): a Novel [3213]

3 vols. Colburn 1846. Full fine-bead-grain cloth labels.

Vol. I (vi)+314 pp. v (vi), signed *b*, and final leaf, Y_1, single insets.
II (ii)+322 Final leaf, Y_1, a single inset.
III (ii)+296

Very fine. Also issued in half-cloth boards.

Note. The discrepancy in collation between Vols. I and II is due to the fact that in Vol. I sig. X is 4 leaves and in Vol. II 8 leaves.

BARNABYS IN AMERICA (The), or Adventures of the Widow Wedded [3214] *Pl. 28*

3 vols. Colburn 1843. Dark ink-blue fine-ribbed cloth, blocked in blind and lettered in gold; pale yellow end-papers. Etched front. in each vol. and, in Vol. I, 2, in Vol. II, 1 and in Vol. III, 3 etched plates—all by Leech. Those in Vols. I and II are dated '1842' at foot, those in Vol. III '1843'

Vol. I (iv)+(322) First leaf of final sig., P_1, a single inset.
II (ii)+312
III (ii)+306 First leaf of final sig., O_1, a single inset.

Very fine.

[3215] BELGIUM AND WESTERN GERMANY IN 1833; including Visits to Baden-Baden, Wiesbaden, Cassel, Hanover, the Harz Mountains, etc. etc.

2 vols. John Murray 1834. Grey-green morocco cloth, paper labels. White end-papers.

Half-title in each vol.

Vol. I viii + (332) P_{10} advert., dated July 1834.
II viii + (300) O_6 imprint leaf.

Fine.

Note. It is stated on Vol. I, p. viii that the sketches by Hervieu frequently alluded to in the text were intended to have been reproduced, but the expense of engraving was found to be too great.

[3216] BLUE BELLES OF ENGLAND (The)

3 vols. Saunders & Otley 1842. Half-cloth boards, labels.

Vol. I (ii) + (304)
II (ii) + (304) O_8 adverts.
III (ii) + 296

A poor copy.

[3217] CHARLES CHESTERFIELD, or the Adventures of a Youth of Genius

3 vols. Colburn 1841.

Copy I: First Binding. Light blue fine-diaper cloth uniform with *The Widow Married*; pale yellow end-papers. Etched front. and 3 plates by Phiz in each vol.

Vol. I (iv) + 324
II (ii) + 328
III (ii) + 340 Publisher's cat., 8 pp. dated May 1841, at end.

Crest over 'G.C.' ink-stamped inside front cover of each vol. Spines soiled and rather greasy. A somewhat squalid copy, with no outstanding defect but unpleasing.

[3217*a*] **Copy II: Secondary Binding.** Dark brown fine-diaper cloth, spine lettered from type without publishers' imprint. Collation as Copy I, but no publishers' cat. at end of Vol. III. Fine.

[3218] *Pl. 27* DOMESTIC MANNERS OF THE AMERICANS

Copy I: First Edition. Regulation Issue. 2 vols. Whittaker, Treacher 1832. Smooth navy-blue linen, paper labels, lettered: *double rule*/THE/DOMESTIC/MANNERS/OF THE/AMERICANS/*short rule*/TWO VOLS./VOL. I [*II*]/*short rule*/21*s.*/*double rule.* Front. and 13 lithographed plates in Vol. I, front. and 9 lithographed plates in Vol. II, after A. Hervieu. White end-papers.

Half-title in each vol.

Vol. I (xii) + 336
II (viii) [paged (vi)] + (280) N_5–N_8 adverts., paged (1)–8.

Very fine.

Copy II: First Edition. Presentation Issue. Publishers' full dark red morocco, tooled in gold and blind, fully gilt; all edges gilt; glazed pale yellow end-papers. Plates as in Copy I, printed on India paper mounted on plate paper. Collation as Copy I, except that half-titles and N_5–N_8 advert. leaves in Vol. II, are suppressed. Very fine. [3218*a*] *Pl. 27*

Copy III: American Edition. 8vo. (though collating in twelves). New York: 'Reprinted for the booksellers' 1832. Dark green linen, paper label. Lithographed facsimiles of the Hervieu plates in the English edition. [3218*b*]

The collation is highly irregular. pp. (xvi) [paged (i)–viii + (i) [mispaged ix]–viii [misprinted iiiv]] + (304) [paged (25)–(328)] O_8 blank.

Ink signature: 'George Pardow Esq.', on title. Cloth rubbed and label discoloured and slightly defective.

A fighting preface by the 'American Editor' (7 pp.) 'inquires into the real name and character of the author of this book' with surprising results.

Copy IV. Fifth (and first one-vol.) English Edition. Small 8vo. Bentley 1839. Grey-purple ribbed cloth; steel-engraved portrait front. after Greatbatch. The illustrations to the first edition are reproduced, two in original etched form, the rest re-drawn for wood-engraving and printed in the text. [3218*c*]

Series half-title. pp. (viii) + 384

A new preface of two pages dated April 27, 1839 occupies pp. (v) (vi) and is followed on pp. (vii) (viii) by the original preface.

Notes. (i) A volume in Bentley's Standard Library of Popular Modern Literature and imprinted on spine 'BENTLEY'S LIBRARY'.
(ii) There are two variants of blind blocking for front and back covers, but I do not know what priority (if any) they imply.
(iii) The fourth edition in 2 vols. had appeared with Whittaker in January 1834.

Copy V: Modern Revival Reprint. 8vo. Routledge 1927. With an Introduction, 16 pp., by Michael Sadleir. [3218*d*]

A volume in Routledge's English Library, the text is that of Copy IV above and 8 of Hervieu's etchings are reproduced in half-tone.

ana

AMERICAN CRITICISMS ON MRS TROLLOPE'S 'DOMESTIC MANNERS OF THE AMERICANS' [3218*e*]

8vo. O. Rich, 12 Red Lion Square 1833.

Half-title. pp. (iv) + 64 Publisher's cat., 8 pp. undated, at end. Probably issued stitched, the half-title (which reads: AMERICAN CRITICISMS ON MRS TROLLOPE./*Price One Shilling*) serving as front cover. This copy is wholly uncut and was bound for me in full green buckram.

[3219] FASHIONABLE LIFE, or Paris and London

3 vols. Hurst & Blackett 1856. Light claret ripple-grain cloth, blocked in blind and gold (style uniform with that of *John Halifax, Gentleman*); dark yellow end-papers.

Vol. I (ii)+(310) First leaf of final sig., X_1, a single inset.

II (ii)+(286) First leaf of final sig., T_1, a single inset. Publishers' cat., 24 pp. undated, at end.

III (ii)+316 Inset advert. leaf on text paper at end.

Small ticket of Hodgson's Library inside front cover of each vol. Very fine.

[3220] FATHER EUSTACE: a Tale of the Jesuits

3 vols. Colburn 1847. Boards, labels,

Vol. I (ii)+344

II (ii)+(332)

III (ii)+326 First leaf of final sig., Y_1, a single inset. Publishers' cat., 24 pp. undated, at end.

Fine.

[3221] GERTRUDE, or Family Pride

3 vols. Hurst & Blackett 1855. Flesh-pink morocco cloth, blocked on front and back with publishers' monogram and decoration, on spine in blind and gold and lettered in gold; royal-blue chalk-surfaced end-papers.

Vol. I (ii)+(304)

II (ii)+306 Final leaf, X_1, a single inset. Publishers' cat., 24 pp. undated, at end.

III (ii)+(312) X_4 adverts.

Binders' ticket: 'Leighton, Son & Hodge', at end of Vol. I. Very fine.

[3222] *HARGRAVE, or the Adventures of a Man of Fashion

3 vols. Colburn 1843. Boards (and/or half-cloth boards), labels.

Vol. I (ii)+312

II (ii)+(312)

III (ii)+(326) P_8 probably label-leaf (lacking from B.M., Bodleian and U.L.C. copies, which end with P_7).

[3223] *Pl. 2* JESSIE PHILLIPS: a Tale of the New Poor Law

Copy I: Part Issue. Eleven 8vo Shilling Parts, published monthly by Colburn from December 31, 1842 to (presumably) November 30, 1843. No monthly date of issue appears on any part, but a leaf announcing the work and inset in Part 1 gives date of appearance for that Part. Pale grey-green paper wrappers printed in black; on front with ornamental frame and wording as follows: *Part* 1. [etc.] *Price* 1s./*top of frame*/JESSIE PHILLIPS:/A Tale/OF THE/NEW POOR-LAW./WITH ILLUSTRATIONS BY LEECH./TO BE COMPLETED IN TWELVE PARTS./By Frances Trollope,/AUTHORESS OF 'MICHAEL ARMSTRONG, THE FACTORY BOY',/etc. etc./LONDON:/HENRY COLBURN, GREAT MARLBOROUGH ST;/BELL AND BRADFUTE, EDINBURGH;/JOHN CUMMING, DUBLIN./1843./*bottom of frame*/MOYES AND BARCLAY. CASTLE ST. LEICESTER SQ.; on back with adverts.

Inside front and back covers blank.

Part 1: Single inset leaf headed THE POOR LAW SYSTEM and announcing the appearance of Part 1 of *Jessie Phillips* for December 31, 1842. Steel-engraved portrait signed 'J. Brown', and etched plate by Leech. (Publisher's imprint and date: 1843, at foot of these and all subsequent plates.)

pp. (1)–32 of text.

Outside back cover: 'Thomas Harris. Opticians.'

Part 2: Etched plate by Leech.

pp. 33–64 of text.

Outside back cover: Rowland's Macassar Oil, etc. headed 'Caution to Families'.

Part 3: Single inset leaf reproducing 'correspondence passing' between G. R. Wythen Baxter, Colburn, and Frances Trollope. Baxter, who lived near Llanidloes, wrote to Colburn that he was grossly caricatured in *Jessie Phillips* and would use his influence among opponents of the New Poor Law 'to *curtail*, if not altogether *confound*, the circulation of the novel'. He would further, on the least extra provocation, begin proceedings for libel. He also sent an open letter to Mrs Trollope for publication in the *Sheffield Iris* which is here reprinted. Frances Trollope assures Colburn she has never heard of Mr Baxter. Etched plate by Leech.

pp. 65–96 of text.

Outside back cover as Part 1.

Part 4: Etched plate by Leech.

pp. 97–128 of text.

Outside back cover: Rowland's Preparations, headed 'Spring'.

Part 5: Etched plate by Leech.

pp. 129–160 of text.

Outside back cover: Colburn's Publications.

Part 6: Etched plate by Leech.

pp. 161–192 of text.

Outside back cover: Rowland's Preparations headed by Royal Arms.

Part 7: Single inset leaf advertising Fraser's *Scientific Wanderings*. Etched plate by Leech.

pp. 193–224 of text.

Outside back cover: Colburn's advert. of illustrated edition of Ainsworth's *Windsor Castle*.

Note. The front cover of this part is numbered '8' and the figure is corrected in ink on this copy.

Part 8: Etched plate by Leech.

pp. 225–256 of text.

Outside back cover as Part 6.

Part 9: Etched plate by Leech.

pp. 257–288 of text.

Outside back cover advert. of Ainsworth's *Windsor Castle*, with press quotations instead of List of Illustrations as on Part 7.

Part 10: Etched plate by Leech.

pp. 289–320 of text.

Outside back cover as Part 9 but with the addition, under Colburn's imprint, of the words: '*To be had of all Booksellers*, etc.'

Part 11: Etched plate by Leech.

pp. 321–352 of text. Prelims. for volume issue, paged (i)–viii, at end. Title dated 1844.

Outside back cover: advert. of *Jessie Phillips* in one-vol. form as 'now ready...price 12*s*.'

Note. On the front cover of this part it is still stated that the novel 'is to be completed in twelve monthly Parts'. The word twelve is deleted and the figure '11' written above it in ink in the same hand as made the alteration on Part 7.

[3223*a*] **Copy II: First Book Edition, in three vols. post 8vo.** Colburn 1843. Sage-green ribbed cloth, blocked in blind and lettered in gold; pale yellow end-papers. Engraved portrait front. signed J. Brown and 3 etchings by Leech in Vol. I; in Vols. II and III etched front. and 3 plates—all by Leech.

Vol. I (iv) + 326 Final leaf, P_7, a single inset.
II (ii) + (312)
III (ii) + (326) Final leaf, P_7, a single inset.

Fine.

[3223*b*] **Copy III: First Book Edition, in one vol. 8vo.** Colburn 1844. Sage-green fine diaper cloth; pale yellow end-papers. Illustrations as in Parts.

pp. viii + 352. Loose in cover and stained.

[3224] JONATHAN JEFFERSON WHITLAW (The Life and Adventures of), or Scenes on the Mississippi

3 vols. Bentley 1836. Boards, labels. Etched front. and 4 plates in each vol. by A. Hervieu.

Half-title in Vols. II and III

Vol. I (iv) + (328)
II (iv) + (332)
III (iv) + 348

The spine of Vol. I has been partially renewed, and original label replaced.

LAURRINGTONS (The), or Superior People [3225]

3 vols. Longman etc. 1844. Half-cloth boards, labels.

Half-title in each vol.

Vol. I (iv) + 344
II (iv) + (340)
III (iv) + (340)

Ink signature: 'William Dacres Adams. Sydenham. 21 Dec. 1844', on half-title of each vol. Spines soiled and faded and labels worn. These defects apart, an honest decent copy if a little tired.

LIFE AND ADVENTURES OF A CLEVER WOMAN (The): illustrated with Occasional Exttracs from her Diary [3226]

3 vols. Hurst & Blackett 1854. Sage-green morocco cloth, blocked in blind and lettered in gold; pale yellow end-papers.

Vol. I (ii) + (302) First leaf of final sig., U_1, a single inset. Publishers' cat., 24 pp. undated, at end.
II (ii) + 304
III (ii) + 322 Final leaf, Y_1, a single inset.

Fine. Spines very slightly faded.

LOTTERY OF MARRIAGE (The): a Novel [3227]

3 vols. Colburn 1849. Half-cloth boards, labels; white end-papers.

Vol. I (ii) + 328
II (ii) + (320)
III (ii) + 336

Labels chipped and boards bruised.

Note. About 1862 this novel appeared as No. 270 in the Parlour Library.

MICHAEL ARMSTRONG, THE FACTORY BOY (The Life and Adventures of) [3228]

Copy I: Part Issue. Twelve 8vo Shilling Numbers, published monthly by Colburn from March 1, 1839 to (presumably) February 1, 1840. Monthly dates of issue appear only on Nos. 1 and 2, the advertisement sheets for which are headed 'March 1, 1839' and 'April 1, 1839'. *Pl. 2*

Pale buff paper wrappers, printed in black: on front No. 1. PRICE 1*s*./large wood-engraved symbolic design incorporating title, author's name, publisher's imprint and address, and year of issue (Nos. 1–11 1839, No. 12 1840)/*Agents for Scotland*—Messrs BELL and BRADFUTE, Edinburgh. *Agent for Ireland*—MR JOHN CUMMING, Dublin. WHITING. LONDON; on back with publisher's adverts. Inside front and back covers blank.

Small points of difference between duplicate copies of two of the Numbers are recorded under each Number concerned.

No. 1: 'Advertising Sheet', 8 pp. unfoliated and dated March 1, 1839. Etched front. and 1 plate by Hervieu dated February 20, 1839.

pp. (1)–32 of text. Publisher's cat., 16 pp. dated March 1839.

Outside back cover: 'Popular New Novels' and 'Modern Standard Novelists'.

No. 2: 'Advertising Sheet', 4 pp. dated April 1, 1839. Two etched plates by Hervieu, dated March 20, 1839.

pp. 33–64 of text.

Outside back cover: 'Life of Wellington'.

[It may be observed that p. (3) of the Advertising Sheet announces *Michael Armstrong* as to be published in '20 shilling monthly parts'.]

No. 3: Two etched plates (?) by Buss, dated April 20, 1839.

pp. 65–96 of text.

Outside back cover as No. 1.

No. 4: Two leaves on yellow paper advertising Rippon and Burton's Ironmongery Warehouse. Two etched plates, one by Onwhyn, the other by Hervieu, dated May 20, 1839.

pp. 97–128 of text.

Outside back cover: 'Burke's Landed Gentry', 'Beauties of the Court of Charles II', 'Cheap Editions of Celebrated Works of Modern Fiction'.

No. 5: Slip on buff paper, tipped in, headed MRS TROLLOPE REFUTED, and advertising the issue in ten monthly shilling numbers of MARY ASHLEY: OR FACTS UPON FACTORIES, by Frederic Montagu. Two etched plates, one by Onwhyn, the other (?) by Hervieu, dated June 20, 1839.

pp. 129–160 of text.

Outside back cover as No. 1.

No. 6: Two etched plates, one by Onwhyn, one by Hervieu, dated July 20, 1839.

pp. 161–192 of text.

Outside back cover: Colburn's 'Interesting New Works'.

No. 7: Two etched plates, one by Onwhyn, one by Hervieu, dated August 20, 1839.

pp. 193–224 of text.

Outside back cover as No. 4.

[Variant advert.: 'Life of Wellington'.]

No. 8: Prospectus of Colburn's Standard Novelists, fcap 8vo. 8 pp., tipped in. Two etched plates by Hervieu, dated September 20, 1839.

pp. 225–256 of text.

Outside back cover as No. 1, but different titles in upper section and below 'Modern Standard Novelist' (*sic*).

No. 9: Two etched plates, one by Buss, the other by Hervieu, dated October 21, 1839.

pp. 257–288 of text.

Outside back cover: 'Life of Wellington'.

No. 10: Two etched plates by Hervieu, dated December 1, 1839.

pp. 289–320 of text.

Outside back cover: 'Complete Edition of Michael Armstrong...in a few days...in 3 vols. post 8vo.'

[Variant advert.: the first five words as just quoted are on one line in condensed sans serif, instead of on two lines in serif caps.]

No. 11: Two etched plates by Hervieu, dated November 20, 1839.†

pp. 321–352 of text.

Outside back cover as No. 10.

No. 12. ['AND LAST']: Slip of pink paper tipped in announcing CHARLES CHESTERFIELD as 'preparing for publication'. Two etched plates by Hervieu dated '1840'.

pp. 353–387 of text + (388) blank + (389)–(392) [$2C_3$ $2C_4$] adverts. Prelims. for volume issue, 4 leaves paged (i)–viii, at end.

Outside back cover as No. 10 (variant) except that Onwhyn's name is here *not* given among the illustrators.

Copy II: First Book Edition in three vols. post 8vo [published December, 1839] [3228*a*] *Pl. 28*

Colburn 1840. Grey-green fine-diaper cloth; pale yellow end-papers. Etched front. in each vol. and, in Vol. I, 6, in Vol. II, 8, and in Vol. III, 7 plates by Hervieu, Buss and Onwhyn.

Vol. I (vi) + 308 pp. (v) (vi) 'Illustrations' a single inset.
II iv + (340) Q_2 adverts.
III iv + (334) First leaf of final sig., P_1, a single inset.

Very fine.

Copy III: First Book Edition in one vol. 8vo [published March, 1840] [3228*b*]

Colburn 1840. Plum fine-horizontal-ribbed cloth; pale yellow end-papers. Illustrations as in parts

pp. (x) + (392) $2C_3$ $2C_4$ adverts. Publisher's cat., 8 pp. dated May 1841, followed by another, 16 pp. dated January, 1841, at end. Fine. Front fly-leaf missing.

Note. The discrepancy between the prelims. in this edition and No. 12 is due to the insertion in the former of the single inset leaf carrying List of Illustrations.

† The discrepancy of date will be observed as against plates in Part X. It was, I imagine, due to delays on the part of Hervieu or some misfortune in the engraving and not to subsequent tampering with the actual parts. The same phenomenon occurs in two sets examined, neither of which shows any trace of 'sophistication'.

[3229] MOTHER'S MANUAL (The), or Illustrations of Matrimonial Economy. An Essay in Verse [anon] Large 8vo. Treuttel and Würtz and Richter 1833.

Copy I: Drab moiré paper boards, green side-label lettered in gold; spine of drab morocco cloth (not original); rose pink end-papers. Lithographed front. and vignette title (preceding printed title) and 18 plates, all lithographed in outline, after Hervieu.

Extra white fly-leaf follows pink fly-leaf in front and precedes pink fly-leaf at end. pp. (iv)+(84) M_2 imprint leaf.

Note. I have seen an alternative binding of pink moiré paper boards with yellow side-label, printed in black and bearing the author's name. This was probably of later date, although contemporary reviews show that the authorship was very soon an open secret.

[3229*a*] **Copy II:** Identical with Copy I, except that the lithographs are throughout hand-coloured. Full polished calf; marbled end-papers; top edges gilt, others uncut.

[3230] MRS MATHEWS, or Family Mysteries. A Novel
3 vols. Colburn & Co. 1851.

Copy I: Half-cloth boards, labels.

Vol. I (ii)+346 Final leaf, $2A_1$, a single inset. Publishers' cat., 8 pp. dated October 1851, inserted before title.
II (ii)+344
III (336) [paged (ii)+334] Title not a single inset, but A_1.

Fine. Labels slightly discoloured.

Copy II: Pale sage-green fine-ripple-grain cloth, blocked in blind and lettered in gold. Yellow end-papers printed with adverts.

Collation as Copy I, but no cat. in Vol. I. Instead, an 8 pp. cat. dated October 1, 1851, followed by an inset leaf of adverts. at end of Vol. III. Save for slight damp stain on one cover, very fine.

Blind-stamp of Hodgson's Library on fly-leaves.

[3231] OLD WORLD AND THE NEW (The): a Novel
3 vols. Colburn 1849. Half-cloth boards, labels.

Vol. I (ii)+326 First leaf of final sig., Y_1, a single inset.
II (ii)+318 First leaf of final sig., X_1, a single inset.
III (ii)+(320)

Label of Vol. I repaired, fore-edges of boards a little frayed: but a sound copy.

[3232] ONE FAULT: a Novel
3 vols. Bentley 1840. Boards, labels.

Half-title in each vol.

Vol. I (iv)+332
II (iv)+348
III (iv)+312

PARIS AND THE PARISIANS 1835 [3233]
2 vols. 8vo. Bentley 1836. Grey-purple ribbon-embossed cloth; white end-papers. Etched vignette title (preceding printed title) and 6 plates by Hervieu in each vol.

Half-title in each vol.

Vol. I (xvi)+418 Final leaf, $2E_1$, a single inset.
II (x)+412 pp. ix (x) form a single inset.

Book-label: coronet over S.E.H.B. & C.; and ink initials inside front cover and on engraved title or fly-leaf of each vol.

PETTICOAT GOVERNMENT: a Novel [3234]
3 vols. Colburn 1850. *Pl. 26*

Copy I: Sage-green fine-ribbed cloth, blocked in blind and lettered in gold; pale yellow end-papers.

Vol. I (ii)+310 Second leaf of final sig., X_2, a single inset. Publisher's cat., 16 pp. undated, at end.
II (ii)+326 First leaf of final sig., Y_1, a single inset.
III (ii)+332

Very fine.

Copy II: Half-cloth boards, labels. [3234*a*]

Collation as Copy I, but no cat. in Vol. I.

Very fine.

Note. Entries transposed to save correction. I only obtained Copy II when the catalogue was in type.

REFUGEE IN AMERICA (The): a Novel [3235]
3 vols. Whittaker, Treacher 1832. Boards, labels. *Pl. 28*

Half-title in each vol.

Vol. I (iv)+294 First leaf of final sig., O_1, a single inset.
II (iv)+(312)
III (iv)+(304) O_8 adverts.

Ink signature: 'Frances Price, Rhiwlas 1832', and bookseller's ticket: 'Harding, Chester', inside front cover of each vol. Very fine.

ROBERTSES ON THEIR TRAVELS (The) [3236]
3 vols. Colburn 1846. Half-cloth boards, labels. *Pl. 26*

Half-title in Vols. I and II

Vol. I (iv)+(336) P_{11} P_{12} adverts.
II (iv)+336
III (ii)+264

Fine.

ROMANCE OF VIENNA (A) [3237]
3 vols. Bentley 1838. Boards, labels.

Half-title in Vol. I

Vol. I (iv)+(308)
II (ii)+324
III (ii)+(348) Q_6 blank.

[3238] SECOND LOVE, or Beauty and Intellect: a Novel
3 vols. Colburn 1851.

Copy I: Half-cloth boards, labels.

Vol. I (ii)+304
II (ii)+308
III (ii)+(316) X_6 adverts.

Vol. III has new end-papers.

[3238*a*] **Copy II:** Grass-green ribbed cloth, blocked in blind and lettered in gold. Yellow end-papers printed with adverts.

Collation as Copy I. Two publisher's cats., 24 pp. and 4 pp., both undated, at end of Vol. I. Binder's ticket: 'W. Johnson', at end of each vol.

Very fine.

[3239] SUMMER IN BRITTANY (A) (by T. Adolphus Trollope, B.A. Edited by Frances Trollope)
2 vols. 8vo. Colburn 1840. Sky-blue ribbed cloth, blocked in blind and lettered in gold; glazed pale yellow end-papers. In each vol. coloured lithographic front. after Hervieu and etched vignette title by him (no printed title) and, in Vol. I, 4, Vol. II, 6 etched plates by Hervieu.

Vol. I (x) [paged (xii)]+(436) (FF_2) adverts. pp. xi (xii) form a single inset.
II (vi) [paged (viii)]+(412) DD_6 adverts. Publisher's cat., 16 pp. dated January 1841, followed by a second cat., 8 pp. dated May 1841, at end. pp. vii (viii) form a single inset.

Book-plate of John Noble. Very fine.

Note. This work (and *A Summer in Western France*) are catalogued under Frances Trollope because, although written under her guidance by her eldest son (at that time aged twenty-nine), they represented, to the publisher and public, Frances Trollope items. Her name alone appears on the spines, and on the titles she is much larger than the actual author. Whatever her share in their text, it was a paramount element in their appearance on the market.

[3240] SUMMER IN WESTERN FRANCE (A) (by T. Adolphus Trollope, B.A. Edited by Frances Trollope)
2 vols. 8vo. Colburn 1841. Sky-blue ribbed cloth, blocked in blind and lettered in gold; glazed cream end-papers. In each vol. coloured lithographic front. after Hervieu and etched vignette title by him (no printed title), and in Vol. I, 2, in Vol. II, 3 etched plates by Hervieu.

Half-title, a single inset, in each vol.

Vol. I (x)+(408) DD_4 adverts. Publisher's cat., 16 pp. dated 4 January 1841, inserted before half-title.
II (x)+428

Bookseller's ticket: 'Charles Hutt, London', inside front cover of Vol. I.

THREE COUSINS (The): a Novel [3241]
3 vols. Colburn 1847. Boards, labels.

Half-title in Vols. I and II

Vol. I (iv)+(324) P_4–P_6 adverts.
II (iv)+324
III (ii)+348

Fine.

TOWN AND COUNTRY: a Novel [3242]
3 vols. Colburn 1848. Half-cloth boards, labels.

Vol. I (ii)+300
II (ii)+(324)
III (ii)+(304)

Book-plate of B. B. Pegge-Burnell.

Note. In 1857 this novel appeared as No. 172 in the Parlour Library, under the title *Days of the Regency.*

TRAVELS AND TRAVELLERS: a Series of Sketches [3243]
2 vols. Colburn 1846. Sage-green fine-ribbed cloth, blocked in blind and lettered in gold; pale yellow end-papers.

Vol. I (ii)+(300) Publisher's cat., 24 pp. undated, at end.
II (ii)+(312)

Ink signature: 'Isabella H. Hinde, 1848', on fly-leaf of each vol. Spines faded; Vol. I partly out of cover.

TREMORDYN CLIFF [3244]
3 vols. Bentley 1835. Boards, labels. *Pl. 28*

Half-title in each vol.

Vol. I (iv)+(336)
II (iv)+(332)
III (iv)+(352) Q_8 adverts.

'1835' in ink on each paper label. Very fine.

UNCLE WALTER: a Novel [3245]
3 vols. Colburn & Co. 1852. *Pl. 26*

Copy I. Half-cloth boards, labels;

Half-title in each vol.

Vol. I (iv)+(330) Final leaf, Y_5, a single inset.
II (iv)+312
III (iv)+304

Label of Vol. I slightly chipped.

Copy II. Green morocco cloth, blocked in blind and lettered in gold; pale yellow end-papers. Collation as Copy I, plus at end of Vol. I a Publishers' cat., 16 pp. undated, and at end of Vol. III a Publishers' cat., 8 pp. undated. Very fine. [3245*a*] *Pl. 26*

VICAR OF WREXHILL (The) [3246]
3 vols. Bentley 1837. Half-cloth boards, labels. Etched front. and 2 plates in each vol. by A. Hervieu.

Half-title in Vols. II and III

Vol. I (iv) + 324 Publisher's cat. (Whittaker & Co.), 16 pp. dated January 1837, inserted between front end-papers.
II (iv) + 328
III (iv) + (344)

Bookseller's ticket: 'Smith, Inverness', inside front cover of Vol. I. Not a nice copy. Covers rubbed and stained, labels darkened and the front cover of Vol. I re-covered with brown paper.

Note. About 1860 the novel appeared as No. 216 in the Parlour Library.

ana

[3246*a*] THE VELVET CUSHION (anon)
Cadell & Davies 1814. Boards, labels (defective).

This is the first edition of a work, in its day notorious, by the Rev. W. Cunningham, Vicar of Harrow, who was known to Mrs Trollope and was said to be in part the original of 'The Vicar of Wrexhill'.

[3246*b*] THE LEGEND OF THE VELVET CUSHION (by Jeremiah Ringletub)
Williams & Son, Burton & Briggs and T. Hamilton 1815. Boards, label. Rather worn.

A satirical commentary on the tenets and popularity of *The Velvet Cushion*.

[3247] VIENNA AND THE AUSTRIANS; with Some Account of a Journey through Swabia, Bavaria, The Tyrol and the Salzbourg
2 vols. 8vo. Bentley 1838. Cobalt ribbed cloth, blocked in blind and gold and lettered in gold; glazed cream end-papers. Etched front. and vignette title (preceding printed title) in each vol. and, in Vol. I, 7, in Vol. II, 3 plates, all by Hervieu.

Half-title in each vol.

Vol. I (xviii) + 388 pp. (xvii) (xviii), 'Embellishments', form a single inset.
II xii + (420)

[3248] VISIT TO ITALY (A)
2 vols. 8vo. Bentley 1842. Brownish maroon fine-diaper cloth, blocked in blind and lettered in gold; yellow end-papers.

Half-title in each vol.

Vol. I xii + (404) $2D_2$ blank.
II xii + 396

[3249] *WARD OF THORPE-COMBE (The)
3 vols. Bentley 1842. Boards (and/or half-cloth boards), labels.

Half-title in each vol.

Vol. I (iv) + 304
II (iv) + ? (328) Q_4 blank or adverts. or label-leaf.
III (iv) + ? (316) P_2 blank or adverts. or label-leaf.

Note. II Q_4 and III P_2 are lacking from B.M., Bodleian and U.L.C. copies (all rebound) and the Bentley Private Catalogue does not record them. But it seems almost certain that they were present in some capacity.

WIDOW BARNABY (The) [3250]
3 vols. Bentley 1839. Half-cloth boards, labels.

Half-title in each vol.

Vol. I (iv) + 348
II (iv) + 380
III (iv) + 368

An unusual feature of this novel is that the price—twenty-four shillings—is printed under the imprint on each title. A frail copy, but wholesome and unsophisticated. The label of Vol. I is rubbed and chipped, Vol. III is loose in cover and the spines are faded.

Note. About 1860 the novel appeared as No. 215 in the Parlour Library.

WIDOW MARRIED (The): a Sequel to 'The Widow Barnaby' [3251]
3 vols. Colburn 1840. Light blue fine-diaper cloth; glazed yellow end-papers. Etched front. in each vol. and, in Vol. I, 7, in Vol. II, 6, in Vol. III, 5 other plates by R. W. Buss.

Vol. I (iv) + 324 Publisher's cat., 8 pp. fcap 8vo, inserted between front end-papers.
II (ii) + (344)
III (ii) + (332) P_{10} adverts.

Vol. I loose in cover, cover and spines a little faded, but a nice fresh copy.

YOUNG COUNTESS (The), or Love and Jealousy [3252]
3 vols. Colburn 1848. Half (ribbon-embossed) cloth boards, labels.

Vol. I (ii) + 306 Final leaf, X_1, a single inset.
II (ii) + 316
III (ii) + (296) Inset leaf of adverts. at end.

Vol. I out of covers, Vol. III partially detached, but general condition of copy very good.

Note. In 1860 the novel, under the title *Love and Jealousy*, appeared as No. 209 in the Parlour Library.

YOUNG HEIRESS (The): a Novel [3253]
3 vols. Hurst & Blackett 1853. Grey-purple morocco cloth, blocked in blind and lettered in gold; pale yellow end-papers.

Vol. I (ii) + 326 Final leaf, Q_1, a single inset.
II (ii) + 290 Publishers' cat., 24 pp. undated, at end.
III (ii) + 302 Final leaf, P_1, a single inset.

Ink signature: 'W. Selby Lowndes' on fly-leaf and p. (1) of Vol. II.

[3254] *YOUNG LOVE: a Novel
3 vols. Colburn 1844. Boards (and/or half-cloth boards), labels.

Vol. I (ii) + 330 Final leaf, Z_1, a single inset.
II (ii) + 322 Final leaf, Y_1, a single inset.
III (ii) + 376

Frances Trollopeana

[3255] TROLLOPIAD (The), or Travelling Gentlemen in America. A Satire by Nil Admirari, Esq.
New York: C. Shephard; Providence: Shephard Tingley & Co. 1837. Grey-purple cloth, ribbed and strongly embossed; bright yellow end-papers.

pp. (152) [paged xxviii + (29)–(152)]

Ink signature, illegible (? 'Cotton'), dated 'Philadelphia 1837', on first white leaf.

Note. A satirical poem on the various English visitors to America who afterwards wrote books about their journey. It is dedicated to Mrs Trollope, has a long ironical introduction, and the footnotes are crowded with sarcastic comments on Fanny Wright, Mrs Butler, 'Cyril Thornton' (Capt. Hamilton), the Rev. Isaac Fiddler and, of course, Mrs Trollope herself. Written with verve, point and knowledge, the work is much above the average of its kind.

TROLLOPE, FRANCES ELEANOR (second wife of THOMAS ADOLPHUS) (? 1834–1913)

[3256] AMONG ALIENS: a Novel
2 vols. Spencer Blackett 1890. Claret cloth three-quarter morocco-grain, sides smooth; black end-papers.

Half-title in each vol.

Vol. I (viii) + (232)
II (vi) + 218 pp. (v) (vi), Contents, and final leaf, 29_5, single insets. Publisher's cat., 32 pp. dated September 1889, at end.

Ink signature: 'D. von Braun', on half-title of each vol. A poor copy, with library labels inside front covers.

[3257] AUNT MARGARET'S TROUBLE ('by a New Writer')
Chapman & Hall 1866. Carmine honeycomb-grain cloth; pale chocolate end-papers.

pp. (iv) + 292

Ink signature: 'Mudie, Muswell Hill', on verso of fly-leaf.

[3258] BLACK SPIRITS AND WHITE
3 vols. Bentley 1877. Brownish-slate diagonal-fine-ribbed cloth. Cream end-papers.

Half-title in each vol.

Vol. I (iv) + (304) 19_8 blank.
II (iv) + 300
III (iv) + 304 B

Front cover of Vol. I damp-stained.

LIKE SHIPS UPON THE SEA: a Novel [3259]
2 vols. Chapman & Hall 1883. Blue-green diagonal-fine-ribbed cloth. Pinkish-cream end-papers.

Half-title in each vol.

Vol. I (iv) + 296
II (iv) + (272) S_7 S_8 adverts.

Ink signature: 'Maria Taylor', on title of each vol.

MABEL'S PROGRESS: a Novel (by the author of 'Aunt Margaret's Trouble') [3260]
3 vols. Chapman & Hall 1867. Apple-green sand-grain cloth. Cream end-papers.

Vol. I iv + (304)
II iv + (320) X_8 blank.
III iv + 288

Presentation Copy to the author's husband: 'T.A.T. from F.E.T. 1867' in ink on title of Vol. I.

Cloth rather used and spine of Vol. I crinkled.

MADAME LEROUX [3261]
3 vols. Bentley 1890. Olive-green morocco cloth. Cream end-papers.

Half-title in each vol.

Vol. I (iv) + (320)
II (iv) + (320) 40_7 40_8 adverts.
III (iv) + (328) B

SACRISTAN'S HOUSEHOLD (The): a Story of Lippe-Detmold (by the author of 'Aunt Margaret's Trouble', 'Mabel's Progress', etc.) [3262]
2 vols. Virtue & Co. 1869. Apple-green fine-dotted-line-grain cloth (identical with that used by the same publishers on Anthony Trollope's *Phineas Finn*). Cream end-papers. Wood-engraved front. to each vol. after Marcus Stone.

Half-title in each vol.

Vol. I (viii) + (284)
II (viii) + (268)

THAT UNFORTUNATE MARRIAGE [3263]
3 vols. Bentley 1888. Three-quarter smooth blue cloth, marbled paper sides; olive-brown end-papers.

Half-title in each vol.

Vol. I (iv) + (316)
II (iv) + 288
III (iv) + (304) B

'THAT WILD WHEEL' [3264]
3 vols. Bentley 1892. Smooth dark red cloth; grey monogram end-papers. Titles printed in red and black.

Vol. I (iv)+(316)
II (iv)+(316) 40_6 blank.
III (iv)+(316) 60_6 blank. B

[3265] VERONICA: a Novel (by the author of 'Aunt Margaret's Trouble', 'Mabel's Progress', etc. etc.). Reprinted from *All the Year Round*

3 vols. Tinsley 1870. Plum sand-grain cloth. Pale cream end-papers.

Vol. I iv+324
II iv+(320)
III iv+(320)

TROLLOPE, HENRY MERIVALE (son of ANTHONY) (1846–1926)

[3266] MY OWN LOVE STORY: a Novel

Copy I. 2 vols. Chapman & Hall 1887. Earth-brown smooth-morocco cloth, blocked in black and lettered in gold; pale yellow end-papers.

Half-title in each vol.

Vol. I (vi)+220 pp. (v) (vi), Contents, form a single inset.
II (vi)+(194) pp. (v)(vi), Contents, and final leaf, O_1, single insets.

Presentation Copy: 'To dear Mother from her affectionate son Harry Trollope' in ink on half-title of Vol. I and Rose Trollope's monogram book-label inside front cover of each vol.

[3266*a*] **Copy II.** Ochre diagonal-fine-ribbed cloth.

Presentation Copy: 'T. A. Trollope from his affectionate nephew Harry Trollope' in ink on half-title of Vol. I.

Both fine.

TROLLOPE, THOMAS ADOLPHUS (elder brother of ANTHONY) (1810–1892)

[3267] ARTINGALE CASTLE

3 vols. Chapman & Hall 1867. Dark maroon sand-grain cloth. Pale cream end-papers.

Vol. I iv+320
II iv+(304)
III iv+312

Presentation Copy: 'Ellen Ternan from her aff^e brother-in-law the author' in ink on title of Vol. I.

Frances Eleanor Trollope, née Ternan, came of an American family, and her actress-sister Ellen was on intimate terms with Charles Dickens.

[3268] BEPPO THE CONSCRIPT: a Novel

2 vols. Chapman & Hall 1864. Earth-brown dot-and-line-grain cloth. Cream end-papers.

Vol. I iv+(304) U_8 adverts.
II iv+(300) U_6 blank.

A poor copy, cloth used and loose in covers.

DIAMOND CUT DIAMOND: a Story of Tuscan Life [3269]

New York: Harper 1874. Green horizontal-dotted-line-grain cloth; red-chocolate end-papers.

Half-title pp. (312) N_6–N_{12} adverts.

Presentation Copy: 'Nelly Ternan with brotherly affection from the author' in ink on half-title.

Strawboard of front cover creased.

DURNTON ABBEY: a Novel [3270]

3 vols. Bentley 1871. Red brown diagonal-dot-and-line-grain cloth. Pale cream end-papers.

Vol. I (iv)+308
II iv+344
III iv+320 B

FAMILY PARTY (A) in the Piazza of St Peter, and other Stories [3271]

3 vols. Chatto & Windus 1877. Lime-green bubble-grain cloth; cream end-papers in Vol. I; grey end-papers in Vols. II and III.

Half-title in each vol.

Vol. I (viii)+304 Publishers' cat., 36 pp. dated January 1877, at end.
II (viii)+296
III (viii)+308

Ink inscription: 'Anne C. Mendey. With love from Constance S. Ward, February 5th, 1882', on half-title of Vols. II and III.

Note. One must presume from the difference in end-papers and the absence of an inscription in Vol. I, that this is a mixed set. The three volumes, however, are absolutely uniform in appearance and condition.

GARSTANGS OF GARSTANG GRANGE (The) [3272]

3 vols. Smith, Elder, 1869. Smooth grass-green cloth. Cream end-papers.

Vol. I (iv)+(304)
II (iv)+(296) 38_4 imprint leaf.
III (iv)+304

GEMMA: a Novel [3273]

3 vols. Chapman & Hall 1866. Crimson morocco cloth. Pale yellow end-papers.

Half-title, a single inset, in each vol.

Vol. I vi+(322) Final leaf, Y_1, a single inset.
II vi+312
III vi+310 First leaf of final sig., X_1, a single inset. Publishers' cat., 16 pp. dated October 1866, at end.

Binders' ticket: 'Virtue & Co.', at end of Vol. I. Cloth rather stained: inner hinges weak.

[3274] GIULIO MALATESTA: a Novel
3 vols. Chapman & Hall 1863. Dark green morocco cloth. Cream end-papers.

Vol. I iv+(328)
II iv+312
III iv+(320)

Book-plate of A. H. Christie. Yellow slip, pasted to inside back cover of Vol. III, lists Recent Fiction 'in circulation at Mudies Library'.

[3275] LA BEATA
2 vols. small 8vo. Chapman & Hall 1861. Dark green morocco cloth. Cream end-papers.

Half-title, a single inset, in each vol.

Vol. I (vi) [paged iv]+(300) U_6 imprint leaf.
II (vi) [paged iv]+(280)

[3276] LEONORA CASALONI: a Novel
2 vols. Chapman & Hall 1868. Red-brown sand-grain cloth. Pale yellow end-papers.

Half-title, a single inset, in each vol.

Vol. I viii+288
II (viii)+(282) Final leaf, T_5, a single inset.

Ink signature: 'John E. Walsh 1890', on fly-leaf of each vol. and half sheet of note paper with list of novels signed Thos. Woodall (a previous owner) pasted to inside cover of Vol. I. Cloth rather used.

[3277] SIREN (A)
3 vols. Smith, Elder 1870. Orange-scarlet sand-grain cloth. Cream end-papers.

Vol. I iv+(288)
II iv+(284) 36_6 blank.
III iv+(292) 55_2 blank.

Binders' ticket: 'Leighton, Son & Hodge', at end of Vol. I.

[3278] STILLWINCHES OF COMBE MAVIS (The): a Novel
3 vols. Bentley 1872. Grass-green sand-grain cloth; chocolate end-papers.

Vol. I iv+(310) Final leaf, 20_3, a single inset.
II iv+312
III iv+(354) B

TURGENIEFF, I. See TOURGENEF, J.

TWAIN, MARK (SAMUEL L. CLEMENS) (1835–1910)

[3279] ADVENTURES OF HUCKLEBERRY FINN (Tom Sawyer's Comrade) (The). Scene: The Mississippi Valley. Time: Forty to Fifty Years Ago
Chatto & Windus 1884. Scarlet diagonal-fine-ribbed cloth, pictorially blocked in black and lettered in gold on front and spine, publishers' monogram in black on back; olive-brown-on-white foliage end-papers. Wood-engraved front. and numerous illustrations after E. W. Kemble on text paper.

Half-title. pp. xvi+(440) FF_4 publishers' device. Publishers' cat., 32 pp. dated October 1884, at end. Very fine.

GILDED AGE (The): a Novel (by Mark Twain and Charles Dudley Warner). First English Edition [3280]
3 vols. Routledge 1874. Grass-green fine-morocco cloth, blocked in black on front and back, black-blocked and gold-lettered on spine. Numerous wood-engraved illustrations in the text.

Half-title in each vol.

Vol. I (xii)+(256) R_8 blank. pp. (v)–vii AUTHOR'S PREFACE TO THE LONDON EDITION, signed MARK TWAIN and dated 'Langham Hotel, December 11, 1873'. pp. (ix)–xi PREFACE TO THE AMERICAN EDITION, signed S.L.C. / C.D.W. and undated.
II (iv)+(260)
III (iv)+(264) Novel ends S_2 recto. S_3 APPENDIX signed 'THE AUTHORS'. S_4 blank.

Autograph and snapshot of Mark Twain pasted to front end-papers of Vol. I. Spine of Vol. III dulled, otherwise fine.

WARD, MRS HUMPHRY (1851–1920)

This is a complete record of Mrs Ward's fiction up to (and including) the year 1911. I owed my first sight of *Milly and Olly* (1881) to the courtesy of Messrs Macmillan, whose file-copy was, at that time, the only one discoverable. Titles asterisked are not in the Collection. Also included is an early non-fiction item (probably her first production) not recorded in the *C.B.E.L.*

*CANADIAN BORN [3281]
Smith, Elder 1910. Bright blue linen-grain cloth. Half-tone front. after Albert Sterner and 2 illustrations signed NR.

Blank leaf and half-title precede title. pp. (xii)+(354) Final sigs., Z (6 leaves), end of text; AA (4 leaves), adverts.

CASE OF RICHARD MEYNELL (The) [3282]
Smith, Elder 1911. Smooth grey-blue linen-grain cloth. Gravure front. and 2 illustrations after C. E. Brock.

Half-title. pp. (viii)+(532) $2L_8$, $(2M_1)$ $(2M_2)$ adverts.

Presentation Copy: 'Louise Creighton with the writer's love' in ink on front fly-leaf. Fine.

[3283] DAPHNE, or Marriage à la Mode

Cassell 1909. Smooth dark grey-blue linen-grain cloth, flecked with white. Half-tone front. and 3 illustrations after Fred Pegram, of which the first is printed in colours and the others in black on a tinted background.

Half-title. pp. (vi)+(316)

Presentation Copy: 'Louise Creighton with the writer's love. June 1909' in ink on fly-leaf. Fine.

[3284] DIANA MALLORY

Smith, Elder 1908: 'Second Edition.' Scarlet linen-grain cloth.

Half-title. pp. (viii)+(528) LL_6–LL_8 adverts.

Pencil signature: 'J. Browne 1909. 4/6d', inside front cover. Fine.

[3285] *ELEANOR

Smith, Elder 1900. Smooth light blue-green linen-grain cloth, flecked with white. Half-tone front. and 5 plates after Albert Sterner.

Blank leaf and half-title precede title. pp. (xii)+(508) KK_5 KK_6 adverts.

A slip worded: WITH ILLUSTRATIONS BY ALBERT STERNER, is tipped on to title below the author's name.

[3286] FENWICK'S CAREER

Smith, Elder 1906.

Copy I: Regular Edition. Smooth crimson linen-grain cloth, flecked with white. Half-tone front. and 3 illustrations after Albert Sterner.

Half-title. pp. (xii)+(472) Final sigs. HH (2 leaves) end of text; II (2 leaves) adverts.

From the Creighton Collection, but uninscribed. Fine.

[3286*a*] **Copy II: Limited, Signed Edition in Two Volumes on Large Paper.** Demy 8vo. 2 vols. Cream paper wrappers lettered in red on front. Spine and back plain. In Vol. I front. and 3 illustrations, in Vol. II 3 illustrations in gravure on simili-vellum, after Albert Sterner.

Leaf carrying Limitation Note (250 copies), Number of Copy and Author's Signature, and half-title precede title in Vol. I; half-title in Vol. II

Vol. I (xiv) [paged (xii)]+(240) Q_8 blank. (i) (ii) form a single inset.
II (viii)+(232) Q_4 blank.

Printed on hand-made paper. Titles printed in red and black.

Note. There is no indication as to priority of this or the ordinary edition. As the L.P. edition is paged for two vols. and the prelims. and fly-titles are differently set, the book was reimposed throughout. Vol. I Q_8 becomes in the ordinary edition fly-title to Part III, while Vol. II Q_4 is suppressed and substituted by 2 leaves of adverts. It should be noted that there are three more illustrations in the L.P. edition than in the ordinary and that the plates in the former are gravure and not half-tone.

It is curious, in view of these differences, which must have made the L.P. issue an expensive venture, that it is so flimsily wrapped. I suspect there was originally a special binding, but that the edition did not sell and the balance was sold off in remainder wrappers.

HELBECK OF BANNISDALE [3287]

Smith, Elder 1898. Smooth glazed dark green cloth; dark chocolate end-papers.

Half-title. pp. (viii)+(472) HH_1–HH_4 adverts.

Presentation Copy: 'To my old friends—from the writer. June 10 1898' in ink on half-title.

Book-plate of Mandell Creighton.

HISTORY OF DAVID GRIEVE (The) [3288]

3 vols. Smith, Elder 1892. Dark red fine-diaper cloth, style uniform with Robert Elsmere; fawn decorated end-papers.

Blank leaf and half-title precede title in Vols. I and III; half-title only in Vol. II

Vol. I (xii)+388
II (viii)+388
III (viii)+396

Presentation Copy: 'To my dear old friends, the Bishop of Peterborough and Louise Creighton, from the writer. Jan. 22, 1892' in ink on first blank leaf of Vol. I.

Book-plate of Mandell Creighton in each vol. Fine.

LADY ROSE'S DAUGHTER [3289]

Smith, Elder 1903. Smooth rose-pink linen-grain cloth, flecked with white. Half-tone front. and 5 illustrations after Howard Chandler Christy.

Blank leaf and half-title precede title. pp. (xii)+(460) GG_4 and HH_1 HH_2 adverts.

Presentation Copy: 'Louise Creighton with the writer's love Feb. 26, 1903' in ink on fly-leaf.

MARCELLA [3290]

3 vols. Smith, Elder 1894. Light green canvas-grain cloth.

Blank leaf and half-title precede title in each vol.

Vol. I (xii)+316
II (viii)+(336)
III (viii)+376

Presentation Copy: 'To my old friends. With the affection of the writer' in ink on a slip of paper pasted to first blank leaf in Vol. I.

Book-plate of Mandell Creighton in each vol. Spines a little faded.

[3290*bis*] MARRIAGE OF WILLIAM ASHE (The)

Smith, Elder 1905. Smooth blue-green linen-grain cloth, flecked with white. Half-tone front. and 8 illustrations after Albert Sterner, of which the first is printed in orange-brown ink.

Half-title. pp. (xii) + (508) KK_6 adverts.

Presentation Copy: 'To my dear old friend with the writer's love. March 1905' in ink on front fly-leaf. Fine.

[3291] *MILLY AND OLLY: a Holiday among the Mountains (by Mrs T. H. Ward)

Fcap 8vo. Macmillan 1881. Smooth light olive-green cloth, blocked and lettered in purple and scarlet. Wood-engraved front., vignette-title and 6 illustrations after Mrs Alma Tadema, all on plate paper.

Blank leaf and half-title precede front. and vignette-title.

pp. (viii) + 224

Note. As this signature was going to press, a second copy of *Milly and Olly* came to light. It is bound in greenish-blue, fine-diaper cloth, pictorially and decoratively blocked on front and spine in gold and black. The end-papers are dark chocolate. A publisher's cat., 32 pp. dated September 1881, is bound at end. I believe this to be the primary style, and that the Macmillan copy described above represents a re-clothing of sheets for the juvenile gift-book market.

[3292] MISS BRETHERTON

Macmillan 1884. Smooth salmon cloth spine, dark cherry-red cloth sides; black end-papers.

Blank leaf and half-title precede title. pp. (viii) + (300) U_6 adverts.

Book-plate of Mandell Creighton. Not a good copy. The spine is soiled and a little worn, and the book is shaken in covers.

[3293] ROBERT ELSMERE

3 vols. Smith, Elder 1888.

Copy I: First Edition. Very dark blue-green fine-diaper cloth; pale grey floral end-papers.

Blank leaf and half-title precede title in Vols. I and III; half-title only in Vol. II

Vol. I (xii) + (372)

II (vi) + (376) BB_4 adverts. pp. (v) (vi), Contents, form a single inset.

III (viii) + (412)

Presentation Copy: 'To my old friends Max and Louise Creighton. From the writer' in ink on first blank leaf of Vol. I.

Book-plate of Mandell Creighton in each vol.

SIR GEORGE TRESSADY [3294]

Copy I: Private First Edition. 2 vols. Smith, Elder 1896. Smooth apple-green linen-grain cloth; white end-papers.

Blank leaf and half-title precede title in each vol.

Vol. I (viii) + 270 First leaf of final sig., S_1, a single inset. Vol. II begins with S_8, also a single inset.

II (viii) + (271)–(576) Text ends OO_6 recto, OO_6 verso printers' imprint, OO_7 OO_8 adverts.

Presentation Copy: 'To my old friends, with the writer's love. Sept. 1896' on fly-leaf of Vol. I; '(one of six copies bound in two vols. for the Author)' in ink in the writer's hand inside front cover of Vol. I.

Book-plate of Mandell Creighton in each vol. Fine.

Note. The double prelims. include titles over-printed with single and double asterisks and, in Vol. II, a repetition of the Dedication.

Copy II: Regular First Edition. Smith, Elder 1896. Cloth uniform with Copy I; dark chocolate end-papers. [3294*a*]

Blank leaf and half-title precede title. pp. (viii) + (576) OO_7 OO_8 adverts.

STORY OF BESSIE COSTRELL (The) [3295]

Small square 8vo. Smith, Elder 1895. Grey-blue ribbed cloth, blocked and lettered in black and gold.

Half-title. pp. (iv) + 140 Insert advert. leaf of thinner paper inset at end. Pencil signature: 'Radclyffe Walters 1895' on fly-leaf. Very fine.

No. 1 of the Novel Series (3753 in Section III).

UNBELIEF AND SIN: (a Protest Addressed to those who attended the Bampton Lecture of Sunday, March 6) [anon] [3296]

8vo. 'Printed for the Author' 1881. White wrappers, cut flush, printed in black, and forming part of the sheet.

pp. (including front and back covers) (32)

Ink inscription on p. (2) [inside front cover]: 'This pamphlet was written by Mrs Humphry Ward—& sold in Oxford, but quickly withdrawn owing to a threat of prosecution for suppression of the printer's name. R.W.M.[acan].'

WARD, ROBERT PLUMER (1765–1846)

This is a complete collection of Ward's fiction and semi-fiction. Such non-fiction as I possess is omitted.

DE CLIFFORD, or the Constant Man (by the author of 'Tremaine', 'De Vere', etc.) [3297]

4 vols. Colburn 1841. Half-cloth boards, labels.

Half-title in Vols. I and II

Vol. I (xvi) + 376
II (iv) + (308)
III (ii) + (310) First leaf of final sig., O_1, a single inset.
IV (ii) + (312) O_{12} adverts.

Fine.

[3298] DE VERE, or the Man of Independence (by the author of 'Tremaine')
4 vols. Colburn 1827. Boards, labels.

Half-title in Vols. I, II and IV

Vol. I (xxviii) [paged (i)–(viii) + (i)–(xx)] + (344)
II (iv) + 388
III (ii) + 338 Final leaf, Q_1, a single inset.
IV (iv) + (332) P_8–P_{10} adverts.

Fine.

[3299] ILLUSTRATIONS OF HUMAN LIFE (by the author of 'Tremaine' and 'De Vere')
3 vols. Colburn 1837. Boards, labels.

Vol. I viii + (358) Q_{11} adverts. First leaf of final sig., Q_1, a single inset.
II (viii) + 324
III (iv) + (302) Final leaf, O_7, a single inset.

Very fine.

[3300] PICTURES OF THE WORLD at Home and Abroad (by the author of 'Tremaine', etc.)
3 vols. Colburn 1839. Dark green morocco cloth, labels.

Half-title in each vol.

Vol. I xii + (390) First leaf of final sig., S_1, a single inset.
II (iv) + (332) P_{10} adverts.
III (iv) + (336) P_{11} P_{12} adverts.

Ink signature: 'William L. Lechmere', on fly-leaf of each vol. and book-plate of same owner in Vol. I. Labels discoloured and back end-paper of Vol. III torn, owing to cuttings from a newspaper having been stuck on both sides of it with a too lavish supply of gum.

[3301] TREMAINE, or the Man of Refinement [anon]
3 vols. Colburn 1825. Boards, labels. Copper-plate front. 'Evelyn Hall' in Vol. I.

Half-title in Vols. II and III

Vol. I xii + 356
II (iv) + (404) S_{10} adverts.
III (iv) + (360) Q_{12} adverts.

Book-plate of Colville Frankland. Spines a little worn at head and tail, but a fine copy.

Edited by R. Plumer Ward

[3302] CHATSWORTH, or the Romance of a Week [anon]. Edited by the author of 'Tremaine'
3 vols. Colburn 1844. Half-cloth boards, labels.

Half-title in Vol. I

Vol. I (iv) + (286) First leaf of final sig., T_1, a single inset. Longman etc. cat., 32 pp. dated March 1844, at end.
II (ii) + (288)
III (ii) + (312) X_3 X_4 adverts.

Ink signature: 'Helen (?) Gawen 1844', on fly-leaf of each vol.

Note. Written by P. G. Patmore, this novel introduces under fictitious names d'Israeli ('The Lion'), Hon. Mrs Norton ('The Lady Penthea'), Mrs Gore ('The Lady Bab Brilliant'), Coventry Patmore ('the Boy Poet').

WARDEN, FLORENCE

HOUSE ON THE MARSH (The) [3303]
W. Stevens, 421 Strand, n.d. [circ. 1883]. Stiff silurian-grey paper wrappers cut flush, printed on front with decoration and lettering in dark blue and red. 'No. 22' in left-hand bottom corner. Up-lettered on spine and printed with advert. of Cadbury's Cocoa on back. White end-papers, printed all over with adverts.

Half-title. pp. 210 Final leaf, P_1, a single inset.

A yellow slip (probably advertising a forthcoming volume in the same series) was tipped in following title, but has been torn away from this copy.

Note. This volume is No. 22 in The Family Story Teller Series, a bye-product of *The Family Herald.* A publisher's advert. on recto of back fly-leaf gives twenty-five titles in the series and announces a Sixth Edition of *The House on the Marsh.* This copy, therefore, can hardly have belonged to the original wrappering-up of the first edition sheets. Copies in blue wrappers, without Series number on front and advertising Curzon's Furniture Depositories on outside back cover, are of later issue.

I have a copy of No. 38 in The Family Story Teller bound in dark green diagonal-fine ribbed cloth, blocked and lettered in black and gold. As the series is advertised at 1*s.* in wrappers and 1*s.* 6*d.* in cloth I presume *The House on the Marsh* also appeared in this cloth binding.

WARREN, SAMUEL (1807–1877)

TEN THOUSAND A YEAR [anon] [3304]
6 vols. Philadelphia: Carey & Hart 1840 (Vols. I–IV), 1841 (Vols. V, VI). Half (pale claret) cloth boards, labels.

Blank leaf (not part of a sheet) precedes title in Vols. II, III, V and VI. In Vol. IV a blank leaf and two leaves of adverts. (all part of the first sheet) precede title.

Vol. I **First Issue.** pp. (200) On the title of this issue, no volume number is given.
Ink signature: 'Gouverneur Morris, U.S. Army, to his afcte sister A. M. Stont', on title.
Second Issue. Collation as First Issue. 'Vol. I' on title.
II pp. (212)
III pp. (258) [paged (260), the first page of text being wrongly paged (5) instead of (3)] 22_4 blank.
IV (viii) + (220) 19_4 blank.
V pp. (204) 17_2–17_6 adverts.
VI pp. (212)

Ink signature: 'Hetty B. Hart', on titles of Vol. I (Second Issue), Vol. II and Vol. III.

Notes. (i) The labels of Vols. I–V are all worded *cross rule* / TEN / THOUSAND / A YEAR / *short rule* / Vol. I [*II* etc.] / *cross rule.* The label of Vol. VI carries the words: IN SIX VOLS. immediately above volume number.
(ii) This is the first edition of *Ten Thousand a Year*, which did not appear in book form in Great Britain until 1841.

WATSON, H. B. MARRIOTT (1863–1921)

[3305] LADY FAINT HEART: a Novel
3 vols. Chapman & Hall 1890. Brown morocco cloth, blocked in black on front, blocked and lettered in gold on spine.

Half-title in each vol.

Vol. I xii + (292)
II vi + (292) Half-title a single inset.
III vi + 308 Half-title a single inset.

The author's second book and only three-decker.

Watson was a frequent contributor to the *Scots* and *National Observer*, and became one of Henley's most intimate collaborators. The bulk of his best-known book, *Diogenes in London*, originally appeared under Henley's editorial auspices.

WESTBURY, HUGH (HUGH FARRIE)

[3306] 'ACTE': a Novel
3 vols. Bentley 1890. Smooth brown cloth spines, paper-board sides with a design of peacock's feathers elaborately and realistically coloured; grey monogram end-papers.

Half-title in each vol.

Vol. I (vi) + 264 Half-title a single inset.
II (iv) + 268
III (iv) + 270 Final leaf, 51_7, a single inset. **B**

Note. A novel of Rome under Nero. See Note to 1218 above.

WEYMAN, STANLEY J. (1855–1928)

Descriptions are given only of the 'difficult' titles of the early period, and of three scarce items elsewhere unrecorded and probably unknown to collectors.

GENTLEMAN OF FRANCE (A): being the Memoirs of Gaston de Bonne Sieur de Marsac [3307]
3 vols. Longman etc. 1893. Smooth red-brown cloth, blocked and lettered in black; pale grey end-papers with publishers' device.

Blank leaf and half-title precede title in Vol. I

Vol. I (viii) + (288) Publishers' cat., 24 pp. dated '11. 93', at end.
II (iv) + (284) 18_6 blank.
III (iv) + (296) 19_4 blank.

Fine. Spines slightly darkened.

HOUSE OF THE WOLF (The): a Romance [3308]
Longman etc. 1890. Smooth pale grey cloth; on front florally blocked in scarlet, green, violet and black, and black-lettered; gold-lettered on spine; pale grey end-papers with publisher's device.

Half-title. pp. (viii) + (280) 18_4 imprint leaf. Publishers' cat., 16 pp. dated '3.90', at end.

Presentation Copy: 'To A. P. Watt. With Stanley J. Weyman's compliments and cordial thanks. April 1890' in ink on fly-leaf.

Book-plate of A. P. Watt. Fine. Presented to me by his son, W. P. Watt.

KING'S STRATAGEM (The) and Other Stories [3309]
Fcap 8vo. New York: Platt, Bruce & Co. 1895. Pale olive-green buckram, blocked and lettered in black. Line-block front. and 6 illustrations unsigned but after different artists, on text paper but not reckoned in collation.

pp. (iv) + 224 Two blank leaves at end.

Some pages roughly opened.

LITTLE WIZARD (A) [3310]
New York: R. F. Fenno & Co. 1895. Smooth greenish-grey cloth, blocked on front in red and dark green, gold-lettered on front and spine. Half-tone portrait front. and 8 illustrations.

Half-title. pp. (192) 12_8 blank.

MY LADY ROTHA: a Romance [3311]
8vo. A. D. Innes & Co. 31/2 Bedford Street 1894. Brick red wrappers, printed in black; spine unlettered. Publishers' monogram on back.

pp. (328)

A printed note on the verso of title states: 'This edition, printed in February 1894, consists of twenty copies only, of which this is No. 11 (signed) A. D. Innes & Co.'

On the front cover is printed 'Price ten guineas'. The author, in a letter dated May 19, 1923, stated that he had no knowledge of this special edition but considered it '*possible* that a few were published earlier for some purpose of copyright and not for sale'.

Note. The ordinary edition was also published in 1894. It is a crown 8vo in smooth red-ochre cloth, blocked and lettered in dark brown and gold.

[3312] NEW RECTOR (The)

2 vols. Smith, Elder 1891. Smooth dark blue cloth, blocked and lettered in black on front, gold-lettered on spine.

Blank leaf and half-title precede title in each vol.

Vol. I (viii)+(296) U_4 adverts.
II (viii)+(280)

Very fine.

[3313] STORY OF FRANCIS CLUDDE (The)

Small demy 8vo (leaf measure $5\frac{1}{2}'' \times 8\frac{1}{4}''$). Cassell 1891. Smooth claret cloth, blocked and lettered on front and back in salmon, gold-lettered and blocked in salmon on spine. Greenish-buff-on-white flowered end-papers.

Blank leaf and half-title precede title. pp. (viii)+(444) CC_6 blank. Publishers' cat., 16 pp. dated '9. 91', at end.

Presentation Copy: 'A. P. Watt, with Stanley J. Weyman's hearty and grateful acknowledgements. Nov. 13.th 1891' in ink on fly-leaf. Book-plate of A. P. Watt. Presented to me by his son, W. P. Watt.

Note. The rare first issue, as a volume in Cassell's International Series. The Series name appears as imprint on spine and the verso of the inside front end-papers is printed with an advert. of the Series' aims and early volumes dated '10. 91'. The venture was designed to take advantage of the passing of the American Copyright Act. The book is usually seen in smaller format (leaf measure $5'' \times 7\frac{1}{2}''$), bound in plain dark blue cloth, and with the Series (Copyright Novels) advert. dated '9. 93' and the publishers' cat. '5. 93'.

[3314] UNDER THE RED ROBE

2 vols. Methuen 1894. Scarlet ribbed cloth lettered in gold. Half-tone front. and 5 illustrations in Vol. I, 6 illustrations in Vol. II after R. Caton Woodville.

Half-title in each vol.

Vol. I (viii)+172 Publishers' cat., 24 pp. dated April 1894, at end.
II (viii)+(173)–(360) $2B_2$ blank. Publishers' cat., 24 pp. dated April 1894, inset between $2B_1$ and $2B_2$.

WHITE, CHARLES

HERBERT MILTON [anon] [3315]

3 vols. Saunders & Otley 1828. Boards, labels.

Half-title in Vols. II and III

Vol. I (iv)+(384) R_{12} adverts.
II (iv)+(328)
III (iv)+(368) R_4 adverts.

Book-plate of R. J. Ll. Price, Rhiwlas Library, in each vol. Very fine.

Note. p. (iii) carries an 'Author's Note' stating that this book was originally written under the title 'Almacks', but was retitled 'Herbert Milton' before publication in order to avoid confusion with M. Spencer Stanhope's novel (q.v.). The book was re-issued in the same year under yet a third title 'Almacks Revisited' with new prelims. consisting of advert. leaf, half-title and title, but retaining the Author's Note as in the first edition.

The former owner of this copy has written 'Almacks Revisited' in ink on each title and half-title.

WILSON, JOHN ('CHRISTOPHER NORTH') (1785–1854)

LIGHTS AND SHADOWS OF SCOTTISH LIFE: a Selection from the Papers of the late Arthur Austin [anon] [3316]

Edinburgh: Blackwood 1822. Boards, label

Half-title. pp. viii+(432) Dd_8 blank.

Bookseller's ticket: 'Seacome, Chester', inside front cover.

NOCTES AMBROSIANAE (by the late John Wilson, Wm. Maginn, J. G. Lockhart, James Hogg and Others). Edited by R. Skelton Mackenzie [3317]

5 vols. New York: W. J. Middleton 1863: 'Revised Edition.' Green cloth.

Note. This, the first book edition of the *Noctes*, was first published in 1854, pre-dating Professor Ferrier's edition by two years. The 'Revised Edition' here recorded contains considerable new material.

WINGFIELD, HON. LEWIS (1842–1891)

ABIGEL ROWE: a Chronicle of the Regency [3318]

3 vols. Bentley 1883. Scarlet fine-ribbed cloth, lettered in gold.

Vol. I (viii)+(344) 22_4 blank.
II (iv)+(308) 42_2 blank.
III (iv)+(304) 61_8 blank. B

[3319] BARBARA PHILPOT: a Study of Manners and Morals (1727 to 1737)

3 vols. Bentley 1885. Dark slate diagonal-fine-ribbed cloth, blocked and lettered in gold; black end-papers.

Half-title in Vol. I

Vol. I xii + 304
II (iv) + (316)
III (iv) + 304 B

[3320] CURSE OF KOSHIU (The): a Chronicle of Old Japan

Ward & Downey 1888. Smooth olive-brown cloth, pictorially blocked in red, white and black on front, gold-lettered on spine. Pale-grey-on-white floral end-papers.

pp. iv + (320) U_8 blank. Publishers' cat., 16 pp. dated October, 1888, at end. Binder's ticket 'Novello' at end.

Presentation Copy: 'J. Ashby Sterry—from his old friend, the Author', in ink on title.

[3321] LADY GRIZEL: an Impression of a Momentous Epoch

3 vols. Bentley 1878. Slate diagonal-fine-ribbed cloth, blocked and lettered in gold.

Half-title in Vol. I

Vol. I (viii) + 316
II (iv) + 336
III (iv) + (380) B

[3322] MAID OF HONOUR (The): a Tale of the Dark Days of France

3 vols. Bentley 1891. Smooth grey-blue cloth, blocked in black and yellow with an all-over design of poppies, and gold-lettered on spine; grey monogram end-papers.

Half-title in each vol.

Vol. I viii + (300)
II viii + (300) 38_6 adverts.
III viii + (314) Final leaf, 58_5, carries Errata for all 3 vols. and is a single inset. B

The Dedication is repeated in each vol.

[3323] MY LORDS OF STROGUE: a Chronicle of Ireland, from the Convention to the Union

3 vols. Bentley 1879. Dark grass-green diagonal-fine-ribbed cloth, blocked in pink and lettered in gold.

Half-title in Vol. I

Vol. I (viii) + (294) First leaf of final sig., 19_1, a single inset.
II (iv) + 290 Final leaf, 38_1, a single inset.
III (iv) + (316) 58_6 advert. Text ends p. 308; (309)–313 'To the Reader' and List of Authorities; (314) blank; (315) advert., (316) blank. B

WOOD, MRS HENRY (1814–1887)

I have been unusually lucky with Mrs Henry Wood. In the very early twenties I found some half dozen titles in Exeter, all presented to John A. Dorsett and in good state. Then I had several late ones with the Macmillan file (cf. Mrs Oliphant), blind-stamped on covers but in unused condition. Then was sold at Hodgson's the brilliant series of copies presented to Mrs Wood's daughter Ellen. Then, with the Bentley Collection, I acquired a number of variants, as well as copies in regular binding of novels which hitherto I had only possessed in presentation style. Finally a Christie sale in February 1946 remedied practically all the titles not already in perfect condition.

This collection of her first editions published in England is complete except for one volume of collected short stories published late in her life.

I am unable to account for a statement in the Bentley Private Catalogue to the effect that *East Lynne* was her first independent publication in book form, with the three exceptions of *Danesbury House*, *Ashley* and *Bessy Wells*. Of the first we are well aware; but I can find no trace of *Bessy Wells* prior to 1875, and as for *Ashley*, it was serialised in *The Argosy* in 1891 and published by Bentley (again according to the Private Catalogue) in the same year, together with some other stories. I have failed to locate a copy of this volume.

On the subject of the several variant bindings of Mrs Henry Wood's books, reference should be made to my notes, included in Carter's *More Binding Variants*, London, 1938.

It is curious to note that, prior to the publication of *The Red Court Farm* (1868), Mrs Henry Wood's name never appeared on the *binding* of her novels (the little one-vol. *William Allair* hardly ranks as an exception), although it was in every case printed on the titles. Of the thirteen regulation novels here described as preceding *The Red Court Farm*, seven show the title only on their spines and six are described as 'by the author of East Lynne'.

ABOUT OURSELVES [3324]

Small square 8vo. Nisbet 1883. Brown diagonal-fine-ribbed cloth.

Blank leaf and half-title precede title. pp. (viii) + (152) I_8 and K_1–K_4 adverts.

A companion volume to *Our Children*. Fine.

ADAM GRAINGER: a Tale [3325]

Copy I: First Edition. Bentley 1876. Pinkish-grey diagonal-fine-ribbed cloth, bevelled boards.

Half-title. pp. (viii) + (300) U_6 adverts.

Presentation Copy: 'For John. With ever kind regards E.W. 1876' in ink on fly-leaf. Very fine.

Copy II: New Edition, with Other Stories. [3325*a*]
Bentley 1890. Scarlet diagonal-fine-ribbed cloth blocked and lettered in gold in the style of the first one-vol. uniform edition; dark café-au-lait end-papers.

Blank leaf and half-title precede title. pp. (viii) [paged vi] + (472) 30_3 advert., 30_4 blank.

Recased. Cloth a little used.

Contents: Adam Grainger—Gina Montani—A Tomb in a Foreign Land—Katarina Orsini—The Self-Convicted—A Mysterious Visitor—Rupert Hall—All Souls' Eve.

Note. See Note to 3343 below. Of the stories in this volume, other than *Adam Grainger*, *The Self-Convicted* and *All Souls' Eve* appeared in *Told in the Twilight* (3362). The remainder were now first published in book form.

[3326] ANNE HEREFORD: a Novel
3 vols. Tinsley 1868. Violet moiré cloth.

Half-title in each vol.

Vol. I (vi) + (296)
II (vi) + (320)
III 316, followed by single inset leaf advertising *The Argosy*. Sig. (1) is 9 leaves, of which (1_3) (Contents) is an inset. The final sig. (20) is 5 leaves, 20_2 being an inset.

Presentation Copy: 'Ellen Mary Wood. From Mamma' in ink on fly-leaf of Vol. I.

Spines faded, but very fine.

[3327] BESSY RANE: a Novel
3 vols. Bentley 1870. Bright blue fine-morocco cloth.

Vol. I (iv) + 330 Final leaf, 21_5 [signed 21_3], a single inset.
II (iv) + (318) First leaf of final sig., 20_1, a single inset.
III (iv) + 322 Final leaf, 21_1, a single inset.

Presentation Copy: 'For Ellen. From Mamma' in ink on fly-leaf of Vol. I. Very fine.

[3328] BESSY WELLS
Fcap 8vo. Daldy, Isbister 1875. Dark brown diagonal-fine-ribbed cloth.

Half-title and wood-engraved front. on text paper precede title. pp. (96) [paged (i)–viii + (9)–(96)] 6_8 adverts.

Binders' ticket: 'Virtue & Co.', at end.

[3329] CHANNINGS (The)
3 vols. Bentley 1862. Violet morocco cloth.

Vol. I (ii) + 312
II (ii) + (316)
III (ii) + (330) Final leaf, Z_1, a single inset. B

Front covers of Vols. I and II slightly discoloured (? by paste action), but very fine.

Note. Also issued in a (presumably secondary) binding of red cloth, with gold bands across spine and no publisher's imprint.

COURT NETHERLEIGH: a Novel [3330]
3 vols. Bentley 1881.

Copy I: First Edition in Regular Binding. Dark blue diagonal-fine-ribbed cloth, blocked in black and silver and lettered in gold; pale grey floral end-papers.

Vol. I (iv) + (320)
II (iv) + (324) Y_2 blank.
III (iv) + 330 Final leaf, Z_1, a single inset. B

Very fine.

Copy II: Second Edition in Presentation Binding. [3330*a*]
Brighter blue diagonal-fine-ribbed cloth, blocked entirely in gold (same design as Copy I); bevelled boards; same end-papers. Collation as Copy I, except that Vol. III has (332) pages of text with Z_2 blank.

Presentation Copy: 'For Ellen. With Mamma's love March 1882' in ink facing title. Very fine.

DANESBURY HOUSE [3331]
Small square 8vo. Glasgow: Scottish Temperance League; London: Houlston & Wright and W. Tweedie 1860. Royal-blue bead-grain cloth.

pp. (iv) + (348)

Copy I. Limp cloth, all edges cut flush. 'Danesbury House / by / Mrs Henry Wood. / (*rule*) / Prize Tale.' in Old English lettering in gold on front; spine unlettered. Text printed on thin paper.

'Swinton, Malvern 1860' in ink on fly-leaf. Bookseller's ticket: 'H. W. Lamb, Malvern', inside front cover.

Copy II. Stout cloth boards, unlettered on front; gold-lettered in ordinary rom. caps on spine: 'DANESBURY HOUSE / (*rule*) / PRIZE TALE.' Text printed on thicker paper. [3331*a*]

Note. I have also seen a copy in blue morocco cloth, spine all gilt with conventional decoration and the title: DANESBURY HOUSE, printed from type in a narrow interval of the decoration three-quarters high. Front: with conventional blind blocking and in centre gold ornamentation framing THE / PRIZE / TALE.—also set from type. Back: with frame and corner decorations in blind. Yellow end-papers; all edges gilt.

The style of decoration, as well as the lettering on this copy, were so cheap and perfunctory in appearance that I am inclined to suspect the binding is a secondary. The strawboards are not so thick as on Copy II above.

DENE HOLLOW: a Novel [3332]
3 vols. Bentley 1871. Red-brown morocco cloth.

Vol. I (iv) + (324) 21_2 adverts.
II (iv) + (320) 20_8 adverts.
III (iv) + (320)

Presentation Copy: 'Ellen Mary Wood From Mamma 1871' in ink on fly-title of Vol. I. Very fine.

Note. There was a secondary binding of dark green sand-grain cloth, with Bentley spine-imprint and Chapman & Hall printed end-papers.

[3333] EAST LYNNE

Copy I: First Edition. 3 vols. Bentley 1861. Maroon morocco cloth, blocked in blind front and back, gold-lettered on spine.

Vol. I (ii)+(320)
II (ii)+(324)
III (ii)+(306) Final leaf, (X_1), a single inset.

Spines rather soiled.

[3333*a*] **Copy II: Second Edition.** 3 vols. Bentley 1862. Violet morocco cloth (as used for gift-binding of *East Lynne* and *The Shadow of Ashlydyat*) blocked and lettered uniformly with Copy I (i.e. no gold save spine-lettering). Collation as Copy I. Spines darkened and that of Vol. I repaired. In general a somewhat dingy copy.

Note. In 1938 I contributed to John Carter's *More Binding Variants* (pp. 43–5) an attempted reconstruction of the chronology of the ordinary and presentation bindings of *East Lynne* and of *The Shadow of Ashlydyat.* I drew a moving picture of the Wood household, with the great authoress sitting in her chair while her husband and children flocked around, presenting with fond ceremony copies of these two novels in vivid violet cloth, heavily gilt. A letter from Mrs Wood to her publishers has now come to light which proves my reconstruction to be entirely false; and although I regret the disappearance of so charming a domestic scene, I am most grateful to Dave Randall of Scribner's for providing a perfect documentation of the problem.

Here is the letter:

2 September, 1861

May Bank Villa,
Gipsy Hill,
Upper Norwood.

'I called at Mower's to-day, and saw the binding chosen for "East Lynne". I like it very much; but I think it would have had a more pleasing appearance to the eye had a prettier colour been chosen. I saw a colour there, a sort of dark mauve, a beautiful colour. I enquired whether it would have been more expensive than the other; he said only by about one halfpenny per book. However, the binding chosen will look very well —and of course it is of no consequence what colour a book may be bound with—the only thing is, that I think the ladies, going into a circulating library, are apt to be attracted to any book when it looks very pretty to the eye. You will laugh at this theory, but I believe it to be a correct one.

'Mr George Bentley told me that half-a-dozen copies would be given to me—I have requested Mr Mower to bind these with the colour I like; I have also ordered half-a-dozen more done like them; they, all the twelve, are to be gilt-edged and some gilt on the outside—of course the one half-dozen will be at my expense, and the gilding in the half-dozen you give me—he said it would cost about 8*d.* per book. Therefore when the dozen books go in to you gilded, you will know that they are for me.'

Everything is now explained. The bindings of *East Lynne* were simultaneous; but the gift-copies, twelve in number, never came on the market. When a second edition of the novel was called for, Bentley, at an additional cost of one half-penny per copy, thoughtfully used the violet cloth his client admired. Naturally he omitted the eight-pennyworth of extra gilding.

For her next three books Mrs Wood, so far as I know, accepted regulation cloths chosen by the publishers (*The Channings* in any case was issued in violet); but with her favourite *Ashlydyat* she repeated the presentation experiment of *East Lynne*.

EDINA: a Novel [3334]

3 vols. Bentley 1876. Bright brown diagonal-fine-ribbed cloth, bevelled boards.

Half-title in Vols. I and II; blank leaf and half-title precede title in Vol. III

Vol. I (viii)+288
II (vi)+(292) U_2 adverts. pp. (v) (vi), Contents, form a single inset.
III (viii)+(300)

Presentation Copy: 'For Ellen. From Mamma' in ink on fly-leaf of Vol. I. Fine.

ELSTER'S FOLLY: a Novel [3335]

3 vols. Tinsley 1866. Royal-blue dot-and-line-grain cloth. *Pl. 28*

Blank leaf and half-title precede title in Vol. I

Vol. I (viii)+(312)
II (iv)+324
III (iv)+(312) X_4 blank.

Presentation Copy: 'For Ellen. With Mamma's love' in ink on fly-leaf of Vol. I.

Of this set (in absolutely new condition and undoubtedly as presented) Vol. I is a Second Edition, Vols. II and III are First Editions. It therefore provides further ground for presuming (cf. 302, *Lady Audley's Secret*) that publishers sometimes printed simultaneously more than one edition of their three-deckers and were liable to issue mixed sets.

FEATHERSTON'S STORY: a Tale ('by Johnny Ludlow [Mrs Henry Wood]') [3336]

Bentley 1889. Smooth pale grey cloth, pictorially blocked and lettered in blue and brown; pale grey acorn-design end-papers.

pp. (ii)+(302) First leaf of final sig., 19_1, a single inset.

Fine. Back cover slightly dust-marked.

[3337] FOGGY NIGHT AT OFFORD (The): a Christmas Gift for the Lancashire Fund
James Nisbet 1863. Violet wavy-grain cloth.
pp. (vi) + (212) O_2 blank or adverts. (missing from this copy).
Spine darkened.
Note. Although title reads as above, the spine-lettering is A / FOGGY / NIGHT / AT / OFFORD.

[3338] GEORGE CANTERBURY'S WILL: a Novel
Pl. 28 3 vols. Tinsley 1870
Copy I: Regular Binding. Claret fine-morocco cloth.
Half-title, a single inset, in each vol.
Vol. I (vi) + 288
II (vi) + 294 First leaf of final sig., U_1, a single inset.
III (vi) + (288) T_8 adverts.
'Stella. November 1870' in ink on fly-leaf of each vol.

[3338*a*] **Copy II: Presentation Binding.** Bright blue fine-morocco cloth, with variant and more ornate blocking (see *More Binding Variants*). Collation as Copy I.
Presentation Copy: 'For Ellen. From Mamma' in ink on fly-leaf of Vol. I.
Very fine. A few mildew-spots on covers of Vol. II.

[3339] HOUSE OF HALLIWELL (The): a Novel
3 vols. Bentley 1890. Sage-green diagonal-fine-ribbed cloth; fawn acorn-design end-papers.
Vol. I vi + 330 Title-page and final leaf, 21_5, single insets.
II (iv) + (308) (41_2) adverts.
III (iv) + 316 B
Very fine.

[3340] JOHNNY LUDLOW [anon]
Pl. 28 3 vols. Bentley 1874. Bright blue diagonal-fine-ribbed cloth; bevelled boards; chocolate end-papers.
Vol. I (iv) + 292
II (iv) + (308)
III (iv) + (312) X_4 blank.
Presentation Copy: 'John A. Dorsett. With ever kind regards E. W. July 1874' in ink facing title of Vol. I. Fine.
Contents: (*Vol. I*) Losing Lena—Finding Both of Them—Wolfe Barrington's Taming—Major Parrifer—Coming Home to him—Lease, the Pointsman—Aunt Dean—Going through the Tunnel—Dick Mitchell. (*Vol.* 2) A Hunt by Moonlight—The Beginning of the End—Jerry's Gazette—Sophie Chalk—At Miss Deveen's—The Game Finished—Going to the Mop—Breaking Down—Reality or Delusions. (*Vol.* 3) David Garth's Night-Watch—David Garth's Ghost—Seeing Life—Our Strike—Bursting Up—Getting Away—Over the Water—At Whitney Hall.

JOHNNY LUDLOW: Second Series [3341]
3 vols. Bentley 1880. Grass-green diagonal-fine-ribbed cloth, bevelled boards.
Advert. leaf precedes title in Vol. I
Vol. I (viii) + (312)
II (iv) + 324
III (iv) + (312) 20_4 blank.
Presentation Copy: 'For Ellen. With Mamma's love' in ink on fly-leaf of Vol. I. Very fine.
Contents: (*Vol.* 1) Lost in the Post—A Life of Trouble—Hester Reed's Pills—Abel Crew—Robert Ashton's Wedding-Day—Hardly Worth Telling—Charles van Rheyn—Mrs Todhetley's Earrings. (*Vol.* 2) A Tale of Sin—A Day of Pleasure—The Final Ending to it—Margaret Rymer—The other Earring. (*Vol.* 3) Anne—The Key of the Church—The Syllabub Feast—Seen in the Moonlight—Rose Lodge—Lee, the Letter-man.
Note. This is a more ornate binding than Series I or III and may possibly be a presentation style.

JOHNNY LUDLOW: Third Series [3342]
3 vols. Bentley 1885. Scarlet diagonal-fine-ribbed cloth, light olive-brown floral end-papers; bevelled boards.
Blank leaf and half-title precede title in each vol.
Vol. I (viii) + (300) X_2 adverts.
II (viii) + 288
III (viii) + (304) U_8 adverts.
Presentation Copy: 'For Ellen. From Mamma. February 1885' in ink on half-title of Vol. I.
Spines a little faded, but very fine.
Contents: (*Vol.* 1) The Mystery of Jessie Page—Crab Ravine—Our Visit—Janet Carey—Doctor Knox. (*Vol.* 2) Helen Whitney's Wedding—Helen's Curate—Mr Jellico—Caromel's Farm—A Day in Briar Wood. (*Vol.* 3) The Story of Dorothy Grape—Lady Jenkins—The Angels' Music.

JOHNNY LUDLOW: Fourth Series [3343]
Bentley 1890: 'New Edition.' Scarlet diagonal-fine-ribbed cloth, blocked and lettered in gold in the style of the first one-volume uniform edition; dark olive-green end-papers.
Blank leaf and half-title precede title. pp. (viii) + 470 First leaf of final sig., 30_1, a single inset.
Very fine.
Contents: A Mystery—Sandstone Torr—Chandler and Chandler—Verena Fontaine's Rebellion—A Curious Experience—Roger Bevere—Ketira the Gipsy—The Curate of St Matthews—Mrs Cramp's Tenant.
Note. I imagine that 'New Edition' appears on the title-page of this book (as also on 3325*a* and on 3344) because an overall instruction was given to the printers of the uniform edition, which

was officially known as the 'New Edition'. This 4th Series of *Johnny Ludlow* is nevertheless the first edition in book form of these stories.

[3344] JOHNNY LUDLOW: Fifth Series
Bentley 1890: 'New Edition.' Scarlet diagonal-fine-ribbed cloth; dark café-au-lait end-papers.

Blank leaf and half-title precede title. pp. (viii) + (416) 26_8 advert.

Fine.

Contents: Featherston's Story—Watching on St Mark's Eve—Sanker's Visit—Roger Monk—The Ebony Box—Our First Term at Oxford.

Note. Over half of this volume is occupied by *Featherston's Story*, already published in 1889 (3336 above). The remaining five short stories were now first published in book-form. For explanation of 'New Edition' on title, see Fourth Series above.

[3345] JOHNNY LUDLOW: Sixth Series
Macmillan 1899. Smooth olive-green cloth in the standard style of the uniform cheap edition of Mrs Henry Wood's novels.

Blank leaf and half-title precede title. pp. (viii) + (408) $2C_8$ $(2D_1)$–$(2D_4)$ publishers' cat. undated.

Contents. The Mystery at Number Seven—Caramel Cottage—A Tragedy—In Later Years—The Silent Chimes.

Note. A strange obscurity surrounds this book. No such work is catalogued by Bodley or the U.L.C. and it seems to have escaped general notice that the volume, although listed by Macmillan as No. 34 of the 'New Edition' of Mrs Wood's works, was in fact a First Edition. On the title-page are the words 'Sixth Series' only, the additional phrase 'New Edition' appearing only in the publishers' advertisement.

[3346] LADY ADELAIDE'S OATH
3 vols. Bentley 1867.

Copy I. Claret fine-dotted-line-grain cloth.

Vol. I (iv) + 328
II (iv) + 332
III (iv) + 304 B

This copy, from the collection of the publisher, seems to have been bound with the last signature of Vol. I $(Y_1$–$Y_4)$ in proof-form.

[3346*a*] **Copy II.** Apple-green sand-grain cloth, blocked as Copy I. Collation as Copy I.

'Manse (?) of Hurton' in pencil on fly-leaf of Vol. I. Small stain on back cover of Vol. II.

The Bentley Catalogue gives 'claret' as the binding colour of this novel, and the copy presented by Mrs Wood to her daughter and sold at Hodgson's in October 1935 was uniform with Copy I above.

LADY GRACE and Other Stories [3347]
3 vols. Bentley 1887. Smooth sage-green cloth; pale grey floral end-papers.

Blank leaf and half-title precede title in each vol. Titles printed in red and black.

Vol. I (viii) + (284) U_2 adverts.
II (viii) + 280
III (viii) + 284 B

Contents: (*Vols. I and II*) Lady Grace. (*Balance of Vol. II and Vol. III*) A Soldier's Career. (*Balance of Vol. III*) The Surgeon's Daughters—The Unholy Wish.

LIFE'S SECRET (A) [3348]
2 vols. Charles W. Wood 1867. Magenta sand-grain cloth.

Half-title, a single inset, in each vol.

Vol. I x + (300) U_6 blank.
II (vi) + 284, followed by single inset leaf of text paper advertising *The Argosy*, and Wood's publications.

Presentation Copy: 'For Ellen. From Mamma, October 1867' in ink on fly-leaf of Vol. I. Fine, though spines faded.

The publisher of this book was the author's son and, later, her biographer. His monogram is blocked in blind on front covers.

LORD OAKBURN'S DAUGHTERS [3349]
3 vols. Bradbury & Evans 1864. Maroon sand-grain cloth, gold-lettered on spine with title and volume number only (no imprint).

Vol. I iv + 366 First leaf of final sig., AA_1, a single inset.
II iv + (344) Z_4 blank.
III iv + 352

Presentation Copy: 'For Ellen—from Mamma' in ink on fly-title of Vol. I. Very fine.

MASTER OF GREYLANDS (The): a Novel [3350]
3 vols. Bentley 1873. Bright blue diagonal-fine ribbed cloth.

Vol. I (iv) + (336) 21_8 adverts.
II (iv) + (340)
III (iv) + 296

Presentation Copy: 'For Ellen. From Mamma' in ink on fly-leaf of Vol. I. Very fine.

MILDRED ARKELL: a Novel [3351]
3 vols. Tinsley 1865. Violet sand-grain cloth.

Half-title, a single inset, in each vol.

Vol. I (vi) + (328), followed by single inset leaf of publishers' adverts.
II (vi) + 334 First leaf of final sig., 21_1, a single inset.
III (vi) + 334 First leaf of final sig., 21_1, a single inset.

Presentation Copy: 'For Jane—with kind love. E.W.' in ink on fly-leaf of Vol. I. Very fine.

[3352] MRS HALLIBURTON'S TROUBLES
3 vols. Bentley 1862. Dark green honeycomb-grain cloth.

Vol. I iv+(344) Z_4 imprint leaf.
II iv+336
III iv+(348) $2A_2$ blank.

Presentation Copy: 'Ellen Mary Wood from Mamma' in ink on fly-leaf. Very fine.

[3353] ORVILLE COLLEGE: a Story
2 vols. Tinsley 1867. Royal-blue fine-morocco cloth.

Advert. leaf and half-title (worded: Orville College / *rule* / From Routledge's 'Magazine for Boys' / *rule* / In Two Volumes / *short rule* / VOL: I [*II*]) precede title in each vol.

Vol. I (viii)+(288) T_8 blank.
II (viii)+(304) U_8 blank.

Presentation Copy: 'For Harry. From Mamma' in ink on fly-leaf of Vol. I. Very fine.

Note. In magazine issue, as well as in *Routledge's Every Boy's Annual* for 1868, this story was entitled *The Orville College Boys.* There was a secondary binding of blue wavy-grain cloth without spine-imprint.

[3354] OSWALD CRAY
3 vols. Adam & Charles Black 1864. Dark green morocco cloth.

Half-title in each vol.

Vol. I (iv)+(368) R_4 blank.
II (iv)+(364) $Q2_6$ blank.
III (iv)+(360) $Q2_4$ [missigned Q] blank.

Presentation Copy: 'For Ellen, from Mamma' in ink on fly-leaf of Vol. I. Very fine.

Vols. I and III are printed by R. & R. Clark; Vol. II by Neill & Co. Throughout the book the signatures are alternately eight and four leaves and signed B, B2; C, C2, etc. with the exception of the final signature of Vol. II (Q2), which is 6 leaves.

[3355] OUR CHILDREN
Small square 8vo. Daldy, Isbister 1876. Dark olive-green diagonal-fine-ribbed cloth; dark green end-papers.

Half-title. pp. (iv)+(92) G_5–G_6 adverts. Fine.

This is neither a story nor a family reminiscence, but an exhortation to mothers to train their children in firm religious faith.

[3356] POMEROY ABBEY: a Romance
3 vols. Bentley 1878.

Copy I: First Edition: Regular Binding. Dark olive-green diagonal-fine-ribbed cloth, pictorially blocked and decoratively lettered in gold.

Blank leaf and half-title precede title in Vols. I and III; half-title only in Vol. II

Vol. I (viii)+322 Final leaf, Y_1, a single inset.
II vi+312 Half-title a single inset.
III (viii) [paged vi]+300 **B**

Copy II: Second Edition: Presentation Binding. [3356*a*]
Grass-green diagonal-fine-ribbed cloth, with an additional blocking in black. Design as Copy I. Bevelled boards. Collation as Copy I except that in Vol. I, final sig., Y is 2 leaves, Y_2 adverts.

Presentation Copy: 'For Ellen. From Mamma' in ink on fly-leaf of Vol. I. Very fine.

RED COURT FARM (The): a Novel [3357]
3 vols. Tinsley 1868. Royal-blue sand-grain cloth.

Half-title in each vol.

Vol. I (viii)+(312) 20_4 adverts.
II (vi)+284 pp. (v) (vi), Contents, form a single inset.
III (vi)+(264) 17_2–17_4 adverts., followed by publishers' cat. on text paper, 16 pp. undated. pp. (v) (vi), Contents, form a single inset.

Presentation Copy: 'Ellen Mary Wood from Mamma' in ink on fly-leaf of Vol. I. Very fine.

Note. There were two secondary bindings, one similar in colour, but more plainly lettered and lacking spine imprint, the other of brown-orange pebble-grain cloth, also lacking imprint.

ROLAND YORKE: a Novel [3358]
3 vols. Bentley 1869.

Copy I. Purple fine-morocco cloth.

Vol. I (iv)+312
II (iv)+312
III (iv)+316 **B**

In pencil on p. (iii) of Vol. I in George Bentley's hand 'No part the First'—calling attention to an imperfection in the Contents List.

The covers of Vols. I and II are somewhat discoloured, probably by paste-action. The copy is otherwise in new condition.

Copy II. Purple very small close-set bead-grain [3358*a*]
cloth, showing a variation in the blind framing on front and back covers. Collation as Copy I.

'A.B.' in ink on inside front cover of Vol. I. Fine. Spines a little faded.

ST MARTIN'S EVE: a Novel [3359]
3 vols. Tinsley 1866. Blue diagonal-dot-and-line-grain cloth.

Half-title in each vol.

Vol. I vi+352, followed by single inset leaf of publishers' adverts. pp. (v) vi, Contents, form a single inset.
II (vi)+320 Half-title a single inset.
III (vi)+332 Half-title a single inset.

[3360] SHADOW OF ASHLYDYAT (The)
3 vols. Bentley 1863.

Copy I: Regular Binding. Pinkish-maroon diagonal-dot-and-line-grain cloth, gold-lettered on spine with title and imprint.

Vol. I iv + 354
II iv + (342) Collates in eights to Y_8; thereafter Z_1 a single inset; $2A_1$, $2A_2$.
III iv + 324

[3360*a*] **Copy II: Presentation binding.** Violet morocco cloth, ornately blocked on front and spine in gold and gold-lettered with title on front and spine, no imprint. All edges gilt. Collation as Copy I.

'Mrs Henry Wood' in ink in her hand on fly-leaf of Vol. I.

Note. There is also a secondary binding in dark green ribbed cloth, without imprint but with 'by the Author of East Lynne' on spine.

[3361] STORY OF CHARLES STRANGE (The): a Novel
3 vols. Bentley 1888. Sage-green diagonal-fine-ribbed cloth; bevelled boards; pinkish brown floral end-papers.

Vol. I (vi) + 296 pp. (v) (vi), fly-title or misplaced half-title, form a single inset.
II (iv) + (296)
III (iv) + 282 Final leaf, 56_5, a single inset. B

[3362] TOLD IN THE TWILIGHT
3 vols. Bentley 1875. Olive-green diagonal-fine-ribbed cloth; bevelled boards.

Vol. I (iv) + 308
II (iv) + 304
III (iv) + (304) 19_8 adverts.

Presentation Copy: 'For Ellen. From Mamma' in ink on fly-leaf of Vol. I. Very fine.

Contents: (*Vols. I and II*) Parkwater. (*Balance of Vol. II*) All Souls' Eve—Martyn Ware's Temptation—The Dream of Gertrude Lisle—Cyrilla Maude. (*Vol. III*) The Self-Convicted—Mr North's Dream—My Cousin Caroline's Wedding—A Night-Walk over the Mill-Stream—An Incident in the Life of Lord Byron—Feathers and Spangles.

[3363] TREVLYN HOLD, or Squire Trevlyn's Heir
3 vols. Tinsley 1864.

Copy I: First Edition. Regular Binding. Maroon pebble-grain cloth.

Half-title, a single inset, in each vol.

Vol. I vi + (328) Y_4 adverts.
II vi + (316)
III vi + 306 Final leaf, X_1, a single inset.

Presentation Copy: 'Charles W. Wood. From Mamma' in ink on fly-leaf of Vol. I. Very fine.

Copy II: First Edition in variant Binding. Sand-brown pebble-grain cloth, blocked as Copy I. Collation as Copy I. [3363*a*]

Presentation Copy: 'For Jane—with kind love. E.W.' in ink on fly-leaf of Vol. I. Very fine.

Copy III: Second Edition in Presentation Binding. Green pebble-grain cloth, blocked as Copy I, but with all edges gilt. Collation as Copy I. [3363*b*]

Presentation Copy: 'Ellen Mary Wood. From Mamma' in ink on fly-leaf of Vol. I. Very fine.

Note. I have another copy, of which Vols. I and II are First and Vol. III Second Edition, in the same green cloth as Copy III and identically gold-blocked on spine. The blind frame on front and back is different, and the edges are uncut so that the book is slightly taller. Are we to deduce from this mixed set that, after the first binding-up, the novel was issued in green?

*UNHOLY WISH (The), and other Stories [3364]
Bentley 1890: 'New Edition.' Scarlet diagonal-fine ribbed cloth; dark café-au-lait end-papers.

Blank leaf and half-title precede title. pp. (viii) [paged vi] + (452)

Note. pp. (47)–165 are occupied by *The Foggy Night at Offord*, already published in 1863 (3337 above). The remaining nine stories were now first published in book-form.

VERNER'S PRIDE [3365]
3 vols. Bradbury & Evans 1863. Grass-green pebble-grain cloth. No imprint on spines.

Vol. I iv + 370 Final leaf, BB_1, a single inset.
II iv + (356) AA_2 blank.
III iv + (376), followed by 2 leaves adverts. undated and paged (1)–4.

Presentation Copy: 'For Jane with love and best wishes. E.W.' in ink on fly-leaf of Vol. I. Very fine.

WILLIAM ALLAIR, or Running away to Sea [3366]
Fcap 8vo. Griffith & Farran 1864. Bright-brown horizontal-dot-and-line-grain cloth, blocked pictorially and lettered in gold; red chocolate end-papers. Wood-engraved front. after F. Gilbert.

pp. iv + 192 Publishers' cat., 36 pp. dated 1864, at end.

Presentation Copy: 'Ellen Mary Wood. From Mamma' in ink on recto of front. Very fine.

Note. A copy of this book was reported to me in violet-blue morocco cloth with similar cat. and an inscription on end-paper dated 'Xmas 1863'. The report did not make clear whether the blocking on the binding was the same as on the brown copy.

[3367] WITHIN THE MAZE: a Novel
Pl. 28 3 vols. Bentley 1872. Claret fine-morocco cloth.

Vol. I (iv)+308
II (iv)+(324)
III iv+(312) **B**

WOODS, MARGARET L. (1856–1945)

[3368] ESTHER VANHOMRICH
3 vols. Murray 1891. Medium-red fine-diaper cloth; fawn decorated end-papers with publisher's monogram.

Half-title in Vols. I and III; blank leaf and half-title precede title in Vol. II

Vol. I (viii)+260
II (viii)+(260)
III (iv)+(244) R_2 blank.

[3369] VILLAGE TRAGEDY (A)
Small 8vo. Bentley 1887. Navy-blue fine-diaper cloth.

Half-title. pp. (iv)+(232) 15_4 adverts. **B**

YONGE, CHARLOTTE M. (1823–1901)

[3370] HEIR OF REDCLYFFE (The) (by the author of 'The Two Guardians', 'Henrietta's Wish', 'The Kings of England', etc., etc.)

Copy I: First Edition. 2 vols. Small 8vo. John W. Parker 1853. Rose-madder fine-ripple-grain cloth, blocked in blind on front and back with decorative frame, gold-lettered on spine with title and volume number only (no imprint) in roman caps and l.c.; pale primrose end-papers.

Half-title in each vol.

Vol. I (iv)+(360)
II (iv)+(368) AA_8 adverts.

Ink signature: 'Alice Lambton 1853', on verso of half-title in each vol. Fine.

Note. The British Museum copy contains a publishers' cat., 8 pp. undated, at the end of Vol. I.

[3370*a*] **Copy II: 'Second Edition, Revised.'** 2 vols. Parker 1853. Binding, end-papers and collation as Copy I.

Ink signature: 'Ellen France. April 1853', on fly-leaf of each vol. Base of spines a little frayed.

[3370*b*] **Copy III: Third Edition.** 2 vols. Parker 1853. Binding, end-papers and collation as Copy I. Publishers' adverts, 6 pp. on thinner paper undated, are inserted at the end of Vol. I.

Ink signature: 'M. C. Sparkes Nov. 17th 1853', on half-title of each vol., and bookseller's blind stamp: 'Roberts, Exeter', on fly-leaf of each vol.

Note on the differences between these three editions. It is of particular interest to have in one collection copies of the first three editions of this famous book, each with a dated inscription, because of the several minor differences which exist between them. These differences render impossible the apparently easy task of creating a First Edition by making-up with portions of a Second or a Third.

Cecil Hopkinson, formerly of the First Edition Bookshop, compiled a schedule of the differences, and I have his kind permission to reproduce it here (see p. 372), in order (in his words) 'to forearm collectors against what should be easily detectable fakes'. It may be observed that the same firm printed the First and Third Editions (the type of which is the same) but that another firm was employed for the Second Edition.

ZANGWILL, ISRAEL (1864–1926)

BACHELORS' CLUB (The) [3371]
Henry & Co. 1891. Smooth grey cloth, pictorially blocked and fancy-lettered in dark brown on front, gold-lettered on spine. Dark brown end-papers. Line-engraved front. printed on verso of half-title, and numerous text illustrations after George Hutchinson.

Half-title. pp. (viii)+(340) Y_2 adverts. Fine.

The author's first book.

CHILDREN OF THE GHETTO [3372]
3 vols. Heinemann 1892. Salmon diagonal-fine-ribbed cloth, blocked in gold in front with six pointed star composed of interlocking triangles, in blind on back with publisher's monogram, and gold-lettered on spine; white end-papers.

Half-title in each vol. In each vol. pp. (v) (vi), Contents, form a single inset.

Vol. I (vi)+316
II (vi)+(306) Final leaf, unsigned, a single inset.
III (vi)+(336)

Ink signature: 'Frances E. White', on fly-leaf of each vol. Very fine.

Note. This book was also issued (I think subsequently) in dark red morocco cloth.

See also BREEZY LIBRARY, 3457 in Section II.

ZOLA, EMILE (1840–1902)

LADIES' PARADISE (The) 'Translated by Frank Belmont (with the author's special permission)' [3373]

3 vols. Tinsley 1883. Scarlet diagonal-fine-ribbed cloth, blocked and lettered in black on front, blocked in black and gold lettered on spine.

Half-title in each vol.

Vol. I (iv) + 260
II (iv) + 264
III (iv) + 224

Bookplate of John Sharp. Nail-stab (repaired) in spine of Vol. III; otherwise fine.

Note. Published in the same year as the French original, this was the first Zola novel to be translated in England.

Vizetelly's Series of English Translations. 18 vols. 1884–1888 (*in order of publication*).

On 31 October, 1888, for publishing this series of translations, Vizetelly was prosecuted. He was fined £100 and undertook to withdraw the books from circulation.

In 1889 Vizetelly re-issued the works of Zola in an expurgated form, was again charged with publishing obscene libels, and again pleaded guilty. This time he was sentenced to three months' imprisonment. He was at this date 69 years of age, and died less than four years later.

Vizetelly's taste in binding-design, illustration and typographical lay-out is not that of to-day. Indeed his cover-lettering, the design of his catalogues, and the capacities of the artists he engaged are so stridently unsuitable as to compel a kind of inverted admiration. Nevertheless, as a publisher he showed intelligence and care. There is nothing botched about his various series of translations, and the Zola series is no exception. The Introductions, whether by Zola or others, are informative and to the point; the printing is clear and even; the illustrations are reproduced with an enterprise and generosity worthy of better material.

In my experience the original (condemned) run of eighteen volumes is uncommon in any state, and very scarce in the fine condition of all save one or two of the books described below.

[3374] 'ASSOMMOIR' (The) (*the Prelude to 'Nana'*): a Realistic Novel

Vizetelly 1884. Smooth plum cloth, pictorially blocked on front with a panel-illustration in gold on a scarlet ground, surrounded by an ornamental frame in black and with gold lettering above and below; blocked in blind on back with triple plain frame; on spine blocked with scarlet bands at head and tail and gold-lettered. Bright blue-on-white flowered end-papers. Wood-engraved front., pictorial title (preceding printed title) and 14 illustrations after Bellenger, Clairin, André Gill, Leloir, Rose and Vierge, printed in brown and all on plate paper.

Half-title. pp. xvi + (412) [paged (9)–(420)] Publisher's cat., 20 pp. dated Sept. 1884, at end.

Ink signature: 'W. Myers' inside front cover. Fine.

[3375] NANA: a Realistic Novel

Vizetelly 1884. Brownish-ochre diagonal-fine-ribbed cloth, pictorially blocked on front with a panel-illustration in gold on dark red ground, surrounded by an ornamental frame in black and with gold lettering above and below; blocked in blind on back with triple plain frame; on spine blocked with dark red bands at head and tail and gold-lettered. Olive-on-white flowered end-papers. Wood-engraved front., pictorial title (preceding printed title) and 14 illustrations after Bellenger, Clairin and André Gill, printed in orange and all on plate paper.

Advert. leaf and half-title precede title. pp. xvi + (396) [paged (4)–(400)] $2B_8$ adverts. Fine. The copy in the Collection is a 'Second Edition'.

Note. In 1885 Vizetelly published a Royal 8vo. edition of this novel, bound in bright chalky-blue diagonal-fine-ribbed cloth, pictorially blocked and lettered in crimson, dark blue and gold, with pale-green-on-white decorated end-papers. The words: ILLUSTRATED EDITION appear on spine. There are a wood-engraved front. vignette title and 32 full-page illustrations after various French artists, all on plate-paper but reckoned in pagination; also numerous illustrations in the text. The illustrations from the preceding Cr. 8vo. edition are repeated and many others added. [3375*a*]

Advert. leaf and half-title precede front. pp. (xvi) [paged (xiv)] + (308) Final leaf adverts. The copy in the Collection is very fine.

PIPING HOT (*Pot-Bouille*): a Realistic Novel [3376]

Vizetelly 1885. Smooth purple-brown cloth, pictorially blocked on front with a panel-illustration in gold on a terra-cotta ground, surrounded by an ornamental frame in black and with gold lettering above and below; blocked in blind on back with publisher's monogram and triple plain frame; on spine blocked with terra-cotta bands at head and tail and gold-lettered. Pinkish-brown-on-white flowered end-papers. Wood-engraved front., pictorial title (preceding printed title) and 14 illustrations after Bellenger, all on plate paper.

Advert. leaf and half-title precede title. pp. (xx) [paged xviii] + (376) [paged (9)–(348)] Publisher's cat., 20 pp. dated December 1884, at end.

Note. In 1886 appeared a Royal 8vo. edition, uniform with that of *Nana* described above. It is bound in greenish blue diagonal-fine-ribbed cloth, pictorially blocked and lettered in royal blue, scarlet and gold, and has brown-on-white decorated end-papers. Wood-engraved front. vignette title and 46 full-page illustrations, all on plate paper but reckoned in pagination. Also numerous illustrations in the text.

Half-title. pp. xvi + (314) Final leaf adverts. The copy in the Collection is soiled and rather loose.

Other titles were announced to appear in this shape, but I think only *L'Assommoir* was actually published.

ZOLA

[3377] GERMINAL, or Master and Man: a Realistic Novel

Vizetelly 1886. Brownish-ochre diagonal-fine-ribbed cloth, pictorially blocked and lettered in gold on front; back plain; spine gold-lettered. Pink-ochre-on-white flowered end-papers. Wood-engraved front., pictorial title (preceding printed title) and 14 illustrations after J. Ferat, all on plate paper.

Advert. leaf and half-title. pp. (466) Final leaf, $2B_1$, adverts. (commercial) and a single inset. Publisher's cat., 20 pp. dated May 1885, at end.

[3378] THERESE RAQUIN: a Realistic Novel

Vizetelly 1886. Brownish-ochre diagonal-fine-ribbed cloth, pictorially blocked on front with a panel-illustration in gold on a dark terra-cotta ground, surrounded by an ornamental frame in black and with gold lettering above and below; blocked in blind on back with publisher's monogram and triple plain frame; on spine blocked with terra-cotta bands at head and tail and gold-lettered. Pale-olive-brown-on-white flowered end-papers. Wood-engraved front., pictorial title (preceding printed title) and 14 illustrations after Castelli, printed in brown and all on plate paper.

Inset advert. leaf and half-title precede title. pp. (ii) + 254 [paged (i)–xii + (13)–254] Publisher's cat., 24 pp. dated Nov. 1885, at end.

Fine. Spine lettering somewhat oxidised.

[3379] HIS MASTERPIECE? (*L'Œuvre*), or Claude Lantier's Struggle for Fame: a Realistic Novel

Vizetelly 1886. Dark olive-green diagonal-fine-ribbed cloth, pictorially blocked on front with a panel-illustration in gold, dark brown and cream, surrounded by an ornamental frame in gold and with gold lettering above and below; blocked in blind on spine with publisher's monogram and triple plain frame; on spine blocked with brown bands at head and tail and gold-lettered. Pale-olive-brown-on-white flowered end-papers. Etched portrait front. by Bocourt.

Half-title. pp. (372) [paged (i)–viii + (9)–(372)] Publisher's cat., 24 pp. dated April 1886, at end.

Ink signature: 'W. Myers 1886' on p. (9). Fine. Spine lettering slightly oxidised.

[3380] LADIES' PARADISE (The) (*A Sequel to 'Piping Hot'*): a Realistic Novel

Vizetelly 1886. Dark olive-green diagonal-fine-ribbed cloth, pictorially blocked on front with a panel-illustration in gold on a chocolate ground, surrounded by an ornamental frame in bright green and with gold lettering above and below; blocked in blind on back with publisher's monogram and triple plain frame; on spine blocked with bright green bands at head and tail and gold-lettered. Olive-green-on-white flowered end-papers. Wood-engraved front., pictorial title (preceding printed title) and 6 illustrations after an artist unnamed, printed in brown and cream and all on plate paper.

Half-title. pp. (384) Publisher's cat., 24 pp. dated April 1886, at end. Fine.

ABBE MOURET'S TRANSGRESSION: a Realistic Novel [3381]

Vizetelly 1886. Dark olive-green diagonal-fine-ribbed cloth, pictorially blocked on front with a panel-illustration in gold and dark green, surrounded by an ornamental frame in scarlet and with gold lettering above and below; blocked in blind on back with publisher's monogram and triple plain frame; on spine blocked with scarlet bands at head and tail and gold-lettered. Olive-brown-on-white flowered end-papers. Wood-engraved front., pictorial title (preceding printed title) and 6 illustrations signed 'H. Leask', printed in brown and cream and all on plate paper.

Half-title. pp. (352) [paged (i)–viii + (9)–(352)] Y_8 adverts. 4 pp. of adverts. of George Moore's novels on thin paper, and publisher's cat., 32 pp. dated Sept. 1886, at end. Cloth very fine. One signature loose.

FORTUNE OF THE ROUGONS (The): a Realistic Novel [3382]

Vizetelly 1886. Olive-green diagonal-fine-ribbed cloth, pictorially blocked on front with a panel-illustration in gold and cream, surrounded by an ornamental frame in scarlet and with gold lettering above and below; blocked in blind on back with publisher's monogram and triple plain frame; on spine blocked with scarlet bands at head and tail and gold-lettered. Green-on-white flowered end-papers. Wood-engraved front., pictorial title (preceding printed title) and 6 illustrations signed 'H. Leask', all on plate paper. A folding 'Pedigree of the Rougon-Macquart Family' follows title-page.

Half-title. pp. 324 [paged (i)–viii + (9)–324] Publisher's cat., 32 pp. dated Sept. 1886, at end.

Fine.

HOW JOLLY LIFE IS! a Realistic Novel [3383]

Vizetelly 1886. Dark olive-green diagonal-fine-ribbed cloth, pictorially blocked on front with a panel-illustration in gold and chocolate, surrounded by an ornamental frame in bright green, and with gold lettering above and below; blocked in blind on back with publisher's monogram and triple plain frame; on spine blocked with chocolate bands at head and tail and gold-lettered. Pale-olive-brown-on-white flowered end-papers. Wood-engraved front., pictorial title (preceding printed title) and 6 illustrations after an artist unnamed, printed in brown and all on plate paper.

Half-title. pp. (360) [paged (i)–viii + (9)–(360)] Publisher's cat., 32 pp. dated Sept. 1886, at end.

Fine. Spine lettering somewhat oxidised.

[3384] RUSH FOR THE SPOIL (The) (*La Curée*): a Realistic Novel

Vizetelly 1886. Dark olive-green diagonal-fine-ribbed cloth, blocked on front with a panel-illustration in gold and chocolate, surrounded by an ornamental frame in bright green and with gold lettering above and below; blocked in blind on back with publisher's monogram and triple plain frame; on spine blocked with chocolate bands at head and tail and gold-lettered. Olive-brown-on-white flowered end-papers. Wood-engraved front., pictorial title (preceding printed title) and 10 illustrations, of which a few are signed 'A. M.', printed in brown-orange and all on plate paper.

Half-title. pp. (296) [paged (i)–(iv) + (i)–viii + (9)–(292)] T_2 adverts. Publisher's cat., 24 pp. dated April 1886, at end. pp. (i)–viii are occupied by a Preface by George Moore.

Cloth very fine. Spine lettering slightly oxidised.

[3385] LOVE EPISODE (A): a Realistic Novel

Vizetelly 1887. Cloth, style and colour of blocking, and end-papers uniform with *The Rush for the Spoil.* Half-tone front., pictorial title (preceding printed title) and 6 illustrations after an unnamed artist, all on plate paper.

Half-title. pp. 320 [paged (i)–(viii) + (9)–320] Publisher's cat., 32 pp. dated Sept. 1886, at end.

Very fine.

[3386] CONQUEST OF PLASSANS (The), or the Priest in the House: a Realistic Novel

Vizetelly 1887. Cloth, style and colour of blocking, and end-papers uniform with *The Rush for the Spoil.* Wood-engraved front., pictorial title and 6 illustrations after an unnamed artist, all on plate paper.

Half-title. pp. 356 [paged (i)–viii + (9)–356] Publisher's cat., 32 pp. dated Sept. 1886, at end.

Fine. Spine lettering oxidised.

[3387] HIS EXCELLENCY EUGENE ROUGON: a Realistic Novel

Vizetelly 1887. Cloth, style and colour of blocking uniform with *The Rush for the Spoil.* Pale grey-blue patterned end-papers. Wood-engraved front., pictorial title (preceding printed title) and 6 illustrations after an unnamed artist, all on plate paper.

Half-title. pp. 400 [paged (i)–viii + (9)–400]

Corners slightly worn and some signatures loose.

SOIL (The) (*La Terre*): a Realistic Novel [3388]

Vizetelly 1888. Dark olive-green diagonal-fine-ribbed cloth, blocked with scarlet bands at head and tail and lettered in gold on front and spine; back plain. Grey-on-white flowered end-papers. Gravure front. after H. Gray.

Half-title. pp. (474) $2G_4$ blank.

MADELEINE FERAT: a Realistic Novel [3389]

Vizetelly 1888. Cloth and blocking uniform with *The Soil,* save that the coloured bands are dark red. Grey-on-white foliage end-papers. Wood-engraved front. after H. Gray.

Half-title. pp. 336

FAT AND THIN (*Le Ventre de Paris*): a Realistic Novel [3390]

Vizetelly 1888. Cloth, blocking and end-papers uniform with *Madeleine Férat.* Wood-engraved front., pictorial title (preceding printed title) and 6 illustrations after Bellenger and others, printed in brown and all on plate paper.

Half-title. pp. 336 Publisher's cat., 32 pp. dated Sept. 1887, at end.

SOLDIER'S HONOUR (A) and Other Stories [3391]

Vizetelly 1888. Cloth, blocking and end-papers uniform with *Madeleine Férat.* Wood-engraved front. after H. Gray. Blank leaf and half-title precede title. pp. (308) [paged 306] The third leaf (Contents) is a single inset and not allowed for in pagination. Final leaf, U_1, also a single inset.

Publisher's cat., 32 pp. dated Sept. 1887, at end.

ana

An interesting pendant to the run of Zola's novels is a volume prepared by Vizetelly in his own defence and addressed personally to the Solicitor to the Treasury. According to Thomas Seccombe in the *D.N.B.* only 12 copies were printed. [3392]

The book is a square medium 8vo (not a 4to), bound in brown paper boards with a black cloth spine and without any external lettering. Inserted loosely before page one is a four-page letter from Vizetelly to the Solicitor to the Treasury, dated from 10 Henrietta Street on Sept. 18, 1888. This letter explains the purpose of the volume it introduces.

The volume itself contains 88 pages. Page (1) is title-page, dated 'London, 1888' and reading: EXTRACTS / PRINCIPALLY FROM / ENGLISH CLASSICS: / SHOWING / THAT THE LEGAL SUPPRESSION OF M. ZOLA'S NOVELS / WOULD LOGICALLY INVOLVE / THE BOWDLERIZING OF SOME OF THE GREATEST WORKS IN ENGLISH LITERATURE. The extracts run from Shakespeare to Swinburne.

[3370] THE HEIR OF REDCLYFFE

SCHEDULE OF DIFFERENCES BETWEEN THE FIRST THREE EDITIONS

Volume One	First Edition	Second Edition	Third Edition
Half-title	THE/HEIR OF REDCLYFFE./ VOL. 1.	THE/HEIR OF REDCLYFFE./ IN TWO VOLUMES./VOL. 1.	THE/HEIR OF REDCLYFFE./ (*rule*)/IN TWO VOLUMES./ VOL. 1.
Title	'THE TWO GUARDIANS,' 'HENRIETTA'S WISH,'/'THE KINGS OF ENGLAND,'/ETC. ETC./IN TWO VOLUMES./VOL. 1.	'THE TWO GUARDIANS,' 'HENRIETTA'S WISH,'/'KENNETH,' 'THE KINGS OF ENGLAND,'/ (10 line quotation from LYRA INNOCENTIUM.)/VOL. 1./THE SECOND EDITION REVISED.	'THE TWO GUARDIANS,' 'HENRIETTAS WISH,'/'KENNETH,' 'THE KINGS OF ENGLAND,'/ (10 line quotation from LYRA INNOCENTIUM)/VOL. 1./THE THIRD EDITION.
Title verso	LONDON:/SAVILL AND EDWARDS, PRINTERS, CHANDOS-STREET, COVENT GARDEN.	LONDON:/PRINTED BY WOODFALL AND KINDER,/ANGEL COURT, SKINNER STREET.	Blank
Page 359 foot	No imprint	Under a long line WOODFALL AND KINDER, PRINTERS, ANGEL COURT, SKINNER STREET, LONDON.	No imprint
Page 360	Blank	Blank	LONDON/SAVILL AND EDWARDS, PRINTERS, CHANDOS-STREET,/COVENT GARDEN.

VOLUME TWO. In this volume the differences in the three editions are exactly as in Volume I down to the printer's imprint at the end, which only occurs in the second edition (on p. (366)), and is the same as that at the foot of page 359 in the first volume.

Pp. (367) and (368) in the First Edition carry advertisements of 'New Books and New Editions'. In the Second Edition p. (367) carries a list of seven books 'by the same author', while p. (368) is blank. In the Third Edition p. (367) is the same as in the Second Edition but in the centre of p. (368) appears printers' imprint: LONDON:/ SAVILL AND EDWARDS, PRINTERS, CHANDOS-STREET,/COVENT GARDEN.

Evidence that the book was reset for each of the three editions is conveniently supplied by the final page of Vol. II. In the First Edition the last line of text begins with the word 'and'; in the Second with 'that'; and in the Third with 'was'.

COMPARATIVE SCARCITIES

For a discussion of the influences which at the time of first publication went to create in our own day a greater or lesser rarity of specific Victorian novels, I would refer readers to my *Trollope: a Bibliography.* There I set out a considerable argument, demonstrating how publishing history, the stage of a writer's development at which a book appeared, general political or social conditions and even the author's private life might affect the survival-chances of his various works. I illustrated this argument, not only in terms of Trollope 'firsts', but also with reference to specific titles by several other novelists, all of whom make an appearance in their own right in this catalogue. To the general argument I have little to add; but among the particular examples adduced in its support are a few about which I have, in the light of further experience, revised my opinion. It will be found below that, although I still rank *Rhoda Fleming* as Meredith 1, and *Henrietta Temple* as Disraeli 1, I have degraded *The Children of the New Forest* from Marryat 3 to Marryat 8, *Venetia* from Disraeli 2 to Disraeli 3, and slightly modified the previously implied rarity of Henry Kingsley's *Mademoiselle Mathilde.*

In only a few cases have I attempted to explain *why* one of an author's novels is rarer than another. This is partly because I have not (as I had in Trollope's case) a series of publishing agreements and a file of correspondence with publishers and editors to help me construct a detailed argument; mainly it is because students of this catalogue can easily apply for themselves the broader reasoning put forward by John Carter in his masterly and more recent work: *Taste and Technique in Book-Collecting* (Cambridge, 1948).

The simple schedule provided under each author's name is in every case limited to fiction, begins with the rarest title and ends with the commonest. In some cases it runs only to the end of the author's three-decker period because, where a bibliography ends with a considerable list of one-volume (and therefore comparatively recent) titles, grading according to conditions governing the survival of books of the three-decker period is neither possible nor permissible. The normal grading is of copies in original boards or cloth *irrespective of condition.* 'Secondaries' and re-bound copies have been strictly excluded from calculations. To distinguish between the rarity of a really fine and a moderate or poor copy of the same book has (save in one or two cases) proved impossible, because the survival in fine condition of almost any of the works listed is so exceptional that a sight of a copy is a piece of individual good fortune and offers no basis for a general judgment.

In compiling the schedules I have had the advantage of the advice of a few friends, collectors and booksellers, whose hobby or job it has been over a period of years to watch out for copies of significant nineteenth-century novels in original state. Therefore, although the lists are naturally not infallible, they do make publicly available a body of experience as comprehensive as one could hope to find.

The publication dates of the titles listed are given in each schedule. This helps the student to note that frequently a writer's first book is nowadays *not* his rarest, while his last, sometimes posthumous, work is often among those hardest to find. It is also interesting to see that 'key' titles are only seldom at the top of the list. This in the main is due to the fact that 'key' titles (*Lorna Doone* is a good example) have been regularly wanted and, therefore, noticed and stocked by the trade, whereas other neglected titles by the same authors have been passed over, and now have disappeared. Other suggestive conclusions also can be drawn from a careful study of the schedules and an examination of the publishing history of particular titles.

In conclusion, I must paraphrase a statement on p. 257 of the Trollope Bibliography, as it is essential that its content be impressed upon the reader's mind and never forgotten.

The word 'rarity', and its implied counterpart, must be understood in a purely relative sense. With perhaps half a dozen exceptions (those which appear in the pages following are signalised) no Victorian two- or three-decker in original condition is 'common' in the accepted meaning of the word. How should it be otherwise, when we consider the lapse of time, the destructive voracity of the Circulating Libraries, the taste for uniform calf-binding which beset our ancestors and (perhaps as damaging as any) the wholesale pulping of then unwanted old novels which, owing to paper shortage, took place in 1917 and 1918? This same threat again beset us not long ago and in a more acute form; but one must hope that first editions of significant nineteenth-century fiction were sufficiently valued by their possessors to have been withheld from the salvage-drive of the years 1939–1945.

N.B. At the risk of seeming tiresomely repetitive, I must impress on readers of these schedules that, except where a grading of fine copies is specifically offered, the order of scarcity *takes no account of condition.* Rebound copies and secondary bindings are excluded; but no distinction is made between clean and soiled specimens, *provided they survive in original boards or cloth.*

AINSWORTH, WILLIAM HARRISON

Ignoring the Dicks Sixpenny firsts.

1. **Hilary St Ives** (1870)
2. **James the Second** (1848)
3. **Guy Fawkes** (1841)
4. **Rookwood** (1834, his first independent novel) —**Myddleton Pomfret** (1868)—**Good Old Times** (1873)—**Preston Fight** (1875)
5. **Constable of the Tower** (1861)
6. **Goldsmith's Wife** (1875)—**Leaguer of Lathom** (1876)
7. **Miser's Daughter** (1842)
8. **Windsor Castle,** 3 vol. edition (1843)
9. **Lord Mayor of London** (1862)—**John Law** (1864)—**Spanish Match** (1865)—**Constable de Bourbon** (1866)
10. **Cardinal Pole** (1863)—**Boscobel** (1872)—**Merrie England** (1874)—**Chetwynd Calverley** (1876)—**Fall of Somerset** (1877)—**Stanley Brereton** (1881, his last novel)
11. **Crichton** (1837)—**Lancashire Witches** (1849)
12. **Beatrice Tildesley** (1878)—**Beau Nash** (1879)
13. **Jack Sheppard** (1839)—**Old St Paul's** (1841)—**St James's** (1834)—**Mervyn Clitheroe** (1858)—**Old Court** (1867).
14. **Tower of London** (1840)—**Windsor Castle,** 8vo edition (1844)—**Star Chamber** (1854)—**Flitch of Bacon** (1854)—**Spendthrift** (1857)—**Ovingdean Grange** (1860)

Remarks. This Schedule well illustrates two of the influences affecting subsequent survival—influences which, adapted to circumstances, will be found active in the case of other authors also.

(i) The *Illustrated* Ainsworths (with two exceptions) are among the most frequently met with of all his works. This is because, before the collecting of fiction quâ fiction came into its own, there was a period of enthusiasm for Cruikshank, Phiz and other illustrators of the kind, with the result that books illustrated by them were watched for by booksellers for the sake of their pictures alone, and preserved.

(ii) Ainsworth was an author who outlived his popularity and fell on straitened days. It is nearly always the case that among the last desperate money-earning books of a once triumphant author are several which have become very scarce because of the neglect of contemporaries and of posterity.

BLACKMORE, RICHARD DODDRIDGE

To the end of the three-decker period.

1. **Clara Vaughan** (1864, his first novel)
2. **Kit and Kitty** (1890)
3. **Springhaven** (1887)
4. **Lorna Doone** (1869)—**Maid of Sker** (1872)—**Tommy Upmore** (1884)
5. **Cradock Nowell** (1866)—**Cripps the Carrier** (1876)
6. **Alice Lorraine** (1875)—**Mary Anerley** (1880)
7. **Erema** (1877)
8. **Perlycross** (1894, his last three-decker)
9. **Christowell** (1882)

BRONTËS

In the case of this short bibliography one grading holds good for copies in any state of original condition, for fine copies in original condition and for re-bound copies. In any form, in fact, the Brontë books survive in this sequence:

1. **Tenant of Wildfell Hall** (1848)
2. **Wuthering Heights + Agnes Grey** (1847)
3. **Jane Eyre** (1847)
4. **Shirley** (1849)
5. **Villette** (1853)
6. **Professor** (1857)

BULWER LYTTON (*cf.* also p. 61 above).

1. **Godolphin** (1833)
2. **Night and Morning** (1841)
3. **Alice** (1838)
4. **Pelham** (1828)
5. **Pausanias** (1876, his last, unfinished and posthumous, romance)
6. **Devereux** (1829)—**Paul Clifford** (1830)—**Maltravers** (1837)—**Lucretia** (1846)
7. **Eugene Aram** (1832)
8. **Rienzi** (1835)
9. **Disowned** (1828)
10. **Zanoni** (1842)
11. **Last of the Barons** (1843)—**Harold** (1848)
12. **Last Days of Pompeii** (1834)
13. **Parisians** (1873)
14. **Falkland** (1827, his first novel)—**What Will he Do With it?** (1859)
15. **Leila** (1837)
16. **Pilgrims of the Rhine** (1834)
17. **Caxtons** (1849)—**My Novel** (1853)—**Strange Story** (1862)
18. **Coming Race** (1871)
19. **Kenelm Chillingley** (1873)

Remarks. I can only offer a few disjointed comments on this schedule. *Godolphin* holds first place because it appeared anonymously. As Trollope found when he experimented with *Linda Tressel* and *Nina Balatka,* the public are guided by a novel's authorship and are more or less unaware of its texture and quality.

They could not ticket *Godolphin*, so they ignored it; and in 1840 Bulwer Lytton avowed his authorship.

Pausanias as No. 5 may be noted, as an example of the rarity which often overtakes a late (in this case a posthumous) work by a prolific and out-dated author.

The comparative frequency with which Nos. 15 and 16 survive is, of course, due to their being 'plate' books and therefore bought as gifts or to adorn a drawing-room table.

No. 19, though not so overwhelmingly available as *Felix Holt* or *Endymion* or *One of Our Conquerors*, is a common book.

With a few definite rarities at one end and a few comparative frequencies at the other, Bulwer's books in original condition, shabby or otherwise, keep a high level of scarcity. I have graded Nos. 6–14 on the basis of my personal experience; but I suspect that a pooling of Bulwer-hunting adventures would bring all these titles on to an equal footing.

COLLINS, WILKIE

1. **Man and Wife** (1870)
2. **Queen of Hearts** (1859)
3. **Armadale** (1866)—**Moonstone** (1868)
4. **Dead Secret** (1857)
5. **Hide and Seek** (1854)—**Two Destinies** (1876)
6. **New Magdalen** (1873)—**Jezebel's Daughter** (1880)
7. **Fallen Leaves** (1879)—**Rogue's Life** (1879)—**Black Robe** (1881)—**Guilty River** (1886, in first issue wrappers)
8. **Woman in White** (1860)—**Haunted Hotel** (1879)
9. **Law and the Lady** (1875)—**I Say No** (1884)
10. **Miss or Mrs** (1873)—**Little Novels** (1887)—**Blind Love** (1890, his last, posthumous, novel)
11. **Basil** (1852)—**After Dark** (1856)—**Poor Miss Finch** (1872)
12. **Evil Genius** (1886)
13. **Antonina** (1850, his first novel)
14. **Legacy of Cain** (1889)
15. **Frozen Deep** (1874)
16. **No Name** (1862)
17. **Heart and Science** (1883)
18. **Mr Wray's Cash Box** (1852)

Remarks. On pp. 252 seq. of *Trollope: a Bibliography* I suggested three ways in which a publisher's imprint might create, decades after publication, a first-edition scarcity; and I am inclined to think that this schedule of Wilkie Collins' novels illustrates all three. I have no documents to support the argument (none, so far as I know, exist) which must therefore be recognised as deductive or, if you prefer it, conjectural.

No. 1 came from a firm (F. S. Ellis & Co.) whose imprint in this form was short-lived and sparingly used, and one which I have never seen on another novel. Ellis was a distinguished antiquarian bookseller; but his publishing activity was small and specialised, being chiefly concerned with certain of the books of Morris and Rossetti, both of whom were his close personal friends. Into the bargain the firm's name was changed early in the seventies to Ellis & White.

Why the novel (which ran serially in *Cassell's Magazine*) went to Ellis at all, I do not know (unless, being a violent attack on the 'cult' of athleticism, its theme recommended it to a firm whose list—and perhaps personal inclination also—tended to the aesthetic); but there can be little doubt that its rarity to-day is due to it having appeared with a small firm unknown to the fiction market, and one naturally ill-equipped to distribute a commercial product like a three-volume novel.

No. 2 is an admirable example of the subsequent scarcity so apt to distinguish an isolated imprint, plus, in this case, a more or less made-up volume. It also well illustrates one aspect of a publisher's mentality. Consider the books which preceded it. In 1856 Smith, Elder had published *After Dark*—a collection of long-short stories—and clearly over-estimated its chances, for it comes low in the list of scarcities. There followed in 1857 a *Household Words* serial—*The Dead Secret*, published in book-form (and fumbled) by inexpert novel-publishers whose real job was the printing and circulation of a popular periodical. (*The Dead Secret* is referred to in *Trollope: a Bibliography* (p. 255) and I now confirm my estimate of its scarcity by making it No. 4.) Two years later, either Collins collected some stories from various magazines with a view to book-issue, or was approached with an offer for a book of some kind by the ambitious successors to Henry Colburn, who were willing to consider taking a sprat in order to get a whale. From whichever end the impulse came, *The Queen of Hearts* as a proposition could hardly *in itself* have seemed to Hurst & Blackett a promising one. But, because they hoped for more or because the author was a good salesman, they accepted the manuscript, and then produced it with so much prudence that to-day copies are rarely seen.

No. 3(*a*) provokes consideration of an interesting phenomenon—the extremes of scarcity and non-scarcity which nowadays characterise the book-issues of *Cornhill* serials. Smith, Elder were accustomed to pay an outright sum for the serial rights, and for a period (or for a stipulated number of editions) of book-rights of a story they fancied. I conjecture that they were guided in producing their book-edition by the success a story had had in the Magazine. Thus, during the fifties and sixties, *Framley Parsonage*, *The Small House at Allington* and *The Claverings*—all highly successful serials—survive with comparative frequency in cloth; but *Romola* and three of the hardest Levers to find in cloth did not 'pull' in *Cornhill*, and as book-issues were purposely short-printed. There are of course exceptions—notably Thackeray's *Philip*, which was greatly over-produced in three-volume form, although it was not popular as a serial. But Thackeray was *Cornhill*'s 'great man', and the publisher would insist on doing him proud in book-form whatever the prospects of sale.

Whether *Armadale* was beneficial or otherwise to *Cornhill* there is no evidence to show. The historian of the firm of Smith, Elder merely comments on its excellent construction, 'which in critical estimation upheld the reputation of a skilful weaver of plots'—a remark which may be taken to imply whatsoever one chooses. But it is certain that Wilkie Collins was never 'comfortable' with Smith, Elder (who lost *The Woman in White* through a too-hasty decision and beside *Armadale* only published one other book of his—*After Dark*—and that ten years earlier); and I suspect that what they wanted was a Collins' novel as a feature in their monthly, and were not particularly interested in its adventures as a *book*, seeing that no successors were likely to come their way.

The Moonstone (No. 3 (*b*)) is another case of an isolated imprint, but with a difference. The novel, so far from being a plug, was read to pieces in the Libraries, and went rapidly into a series of one-volume editions.

Only one other observation need be made. No. 16, *No Name*, was the 'follow' to *The Woman in White*, which had had an at-that-time phenomenal sale in three volumes. Inevitably Sampson, Low printed a huge edition of *No Name*, and the novel is therefore nearly the commonest Collins of them all.

DICKENS, CHARLES

(i) *Original cloth but regardless of condition*

1. **Sketches by Boz**, 2nd Series (1836)
2. **Sketches by Boz**, 1st Series (1836, his first book of fiction)
3. **Pickwick** (1837)
4. **Great Expectations** (1861)
5. **Martin Chuzzlewit** (1844)
6. **David Copperfield** (1850)
7. **Our Mutual Friend** (1865)
8. **Tale of Two Cities** (1859)
9. **Oliver Twist** (1838, ignoring issues)
10. **Nicholas Nickleby** (1839)—**Dombey and Son** (1848)—**Bleak House** (1853)—**Hard Times** (1854)—**Little Dorrit** (1857)
11. **Master Humphrey's Clock** (1841)
12. **Edwin Drood** (1870, his last, unfinished and posthumous, novel)

Nos. 7–12, in poor state, rank more or less equal.

(ii) *Fine*

1. **David Copperfield** (1850)
2. **Sketches by Boz**, 2nd Series (1836)—**Pickwick** (1837)—**Tale of Two Cities** (1859)
3. **Martin Chuzzlewit** (1844)—**Great Expectations** (1861)
4. **Sketches by Boz**, 1st Series (1836)
5. **Dombey and Son** (1848)
6. **Oliver Twist** (1838)—**Little Dorrit** (1857)—**Our Mutual Friend** (1865)
7. **Bleak House** (1853)
8. **Hard Times** (1854)
9. **Nicholas Nickleby** (1839)
10. **Master Humphrey's Clock** (1841)
11. **Edwin Drood** (1870)

Remarks: I would emphasise that these lists are of Book-issues only; no account has been taken of Parts. The *Christmas Books* are omitted, as complications of 'State' make their grading too complex to be worth attempting.

DISRAELI, BENJAMIN

1. **Henrietta Temple** (1837)
2. **Alroy** (1833)
3. **Venetia** (1837)
4. **Contarini Fleming** (1832)
5. **Vivian Grey** (1826–7, his first novel)
6. **Coningsby** (1844)
7. **Young Duke** (1831)
8. **Popanilla** (1828)
9. **Sybil** (1845)—**Tancred** (1847)
10. **Lothair** (1870)
11. **Endymion** (1880, his last novel)

Remarks. I have no data on which to base an argument in defence of this schedule. The order given reflects my experience and that of others also, and offers one or two problems I am no more able to solve than when I published *Trollope: a Bibliography*. Why, for example, is *Henrietta Temple* so high and *The Young Duke* so low? Disraeli, like George Eliot and Meredith, ends with a three-decker which by any standards is a common book.

ELIOT, GEORGE

(i) *Original cloth but regardless of condition*

1. **Scenes from Clerical Life** (1858, her first fiction)
2. **Romola** (1863)
3. **Daniel Deronda**, cloth only (1876, her last novel)
4. **Middlemarch**, cloth only (1871–2)
5. **Adam Bede** (1859)
6. **Mill on the Floss** (1860)
7. **Silas Marner** (1861)
8. **Felix Holt** (1866)

(ii) *Fine*

1. **Romola**
2. **Adam Bede**
3. **Middlemarch**
4. **Daniel Deronda**
5. **Scenes from Clerical Life**
6. }
7. } As in (i)
8. }

Remarks. A fairly simple case. The unknown (and pseudonymous) author's first book (*Clerical Life*) is published in a two-volume edition of 1050 copies only, so that in any state it is now rare. But it had a success with a small intelligent public, and a higher proportion of copies than normally were *bought* and a smaller proportion went into Circulating Libraries. Therefore when it *does* turn up to-day, it is more frequently in good state than many of its successors.

The still unknown author's second book (*Adam Bede*) is produced in double the quantity, the first three-volume edition numbering 2100 copies. From the start it makes a hit with a different and much larger public: the Libraries re-order: and second and third editions (still in three volumes and numbering 730 and 520 copies respectively) follow quickly. I venture a guess that the cognoscenti, slightly resentful that an author they had spotted should now have become popular, bought *Adam Bede* sparingly, taking the line that as it was a Library success they might as well borrow a copy and save their money. Therefore the first edition is to-day high on list (ii), but comparatively low on list (i).

The demand for *Adam Bede* does not abate, and later in 1859 five printings of a cheaper two-volume edition (over 11,000 copies in all) are called for. The natural consequence is that *The Mill on the Floss*, published in 1860, starts off with a large first edition in three volumes (about 4000 copies), which is rapidly followed by 2018 copies of a second edition still in three volumes.

This 'George Eliot' has now broken into the consciousness of the non-literary well-to-do, and is clearly someone to be read. So they send to town and borrow or, if this means delay, buy 'his' latest book. As a result *The Mill* is frequently met with, alike in used-and-labelled state and 'fine'.

Silas Marner is in similar case, with the added complication that its handsome first edition 'stuck', and (I suspect) some sort of a remainder went to swell the supply of fine copies when, as happened in the late seventies and early eighties, a demand sprang up and was met by a new and cheaper edition.

As comment on the remarkable scarcity of *Romola* (published by a first-rate firm who had paid £7,000 for serial rights and certain book-rights and who would have done all in their power to get their money back) I can only quote George Smith: '*Romola* did not increase the sale of the *Cornhill* and as a separate publication it had not, I think, the success it deserved.'* Unpopular as a serial, the three-volume edition may have been purposely of modest size and destined to quick replacement by a one-volume cheap.

Middlemarch and *Daniel Deronda* are difficult in fine state. This is due to their method of publication. Both came out in fat five-shilling parts, which were widely circulated and were issued in wrappers and in cloth. Many wrappered sets were bound locally in half calf or binders' cloth; many fell to pieces and were never bound at all; many *Derondas* were abandoned as dull (with the result *Deronda* parts are now commoner than *Deronda* cloth). The Libraries took cloth-bound parts as a first course and four-volume book-issues as a second. They took more of *Middlemarch* than of *Deronda* because the book was more popular; and it is a fair guess that the book-edition of *Deronda* was smaller than that of its predecessor.

In conclusion it may be noted that *Felix Holt* (an unpopular title and therefore over-produced) is one of the few three-deckers which to-day is *really common* both in good and bad state.

* *The House of Smith, Elder.* Privately printed, 1923.

GASKELL, MRS

Principal fiction only.

1. **Mary Barton** (1848, her first novel)
2. **Cranford** (1853)—**Sylvia's Lovers** (1863)
3. **Dark Night's Work** (1863)—**Grey Woman** (1865)
4. **Wives and Daughters** (1866, her last, unfinished, novel)
5. **Lizzie Leigh** (1854)
6. **Cousin Phillis** (1864)
7. **Right at Last** (1860)
8. **Round the Sofa** (1859)
9. **Moorland Cottage** (1850)
10. **Ruth** (1853)—**North and South** (1855)

GISSING, GEORGE

Omitting posthumous publications.

Although this schedule ends with the last fiction published in Gissing's lifetime (*Our Friend the Charlatan*), it cannot pretend to grade more than very roughly the one-volume titles which followed on the three-decker period. One of the best known of all Gissing's works (*The Private Papers of Henry Ryecroft*) is ignored as non-fiction.

1. **The Unclassed** (1884)
2. **Isabel Clarendon** (1886)
3. **Born in Exile** (1892)
4. **The Nether World** (1889)
5. **Workers in the Dawn** (1880, his first novel)
6. **In the Year of Jubilee** (1894)
7. **The Odd Women** (1893)
8. **A Life's Morning** (1888)
9. **New Grub Street** (1891)
10. **Demos** (1886)—**Thyrza** (1887)—**The Emancipated** (1890)
11. **Denzil Quarrier** (1892)
12. **Eve's Ransom** (1895)—**Whirlpool** (1897)—**Human Odds and Ends** (1898)
13. **Paying Guest** (1895)—**Sleeping Fires** (1895)—**Our Friend the Charlatan** (1901)
14. **Town Traveller** (1898)—**Crown of Life** (1899)

HARDY, THOMAS

Down to *Jude the Obscure*.

1. **Pair of Blue Eyes**, green cloth, Carter A (1873)
2. **Desperate Remedies** (1871, his first novel)
3. **Laodicean**, normal issue (1881)
4. **Hand of Ethelberta** (1876)

5. **Under the Greenwood Tree** (1872)
6. **Far From the Madding Crowd** (1874)
7. **Two on a Tower** (1882)
8. **Mayor of Casterbridge** (1886)
9. **Return of the Native** (1878)
10. **Tess** (1891)
11. **Woodlanders** (1887)—**Wessex Tales** (1888)
12. **Trumpet Major** (1880)
13. **Group of Noble Dames** (1891)—**Life's Little Ironies** (1894)
14. **Jude** (1896)

JAMES, HENRY

An attempt to grade the comparative scarcities of Henry James has had to be abandoned. Only English 'firsts' (and 'partial firsts') could be treated on the basis of our experience; and a schedule of such titles would have been too patchy and incomplete to be either convincing or helpful.

JEFFERIES, RICHARD

1. **World's End** (1877)
2. **Restless Human Hearts** (1875)
3. **Scarlet Shawl** (1874, his first story)
4. **Green Ferne Farm** (1880)
5. **Dewy Morn** (1884)
6. **Bevis** (1882)
7. **Wood Magic** (1881)
8. **After London** (1885)—**Amaryllis at the Fair** (1887, his last novel)

KINGSLEY, CHARLES

1. **Yeast** (1851)
2. **Alton Locke** (1850, his first novel)
3. **Westward Ho!** (1855)
4. **Two Years Ago** (1857)
5. **Hereward** (1866)
6. **Hypatia** (1853)
7. **Water Babies** (1863)
8. **Heroes** (1856)

KINGSLEY, HENRY

The first editions of Henry Kingsley are, with two or three exceptions, markedly scarce in any sort of original condition, and really fine copies of the majority of the titles (particularly the later ones) seem unfindable. This can, I think, be explained by the fact that he started authorship with the prestige of his famous brother's name and with the first-rate firm of Macmillan, but gradually lost ground as a novelist and caste as a publisher's client, with the result (a generalisation, but one which will serve) that the two books furthest from us were successful and widely distributed, and most of those nearest to us were obscure and negligently handled.

The schedule which follows must be regarded as keyed up to a high standard of scarcity, and (with the possible exception of *Geoffry Hamlyn*) the titles included under No. 5 considered only as more frequently met with than their predecessors and not as, in the accepted sense, books easily obtainable.

1. **Austin Elliot** (1863)—**Leighton Court** (1866)—**Stretton** (1869)
2. **Hillyars and the Burtons** (1865)—**Silcote of Silcotes** (1867)—**Mademoiselle Mathilde** (1868)—**Oakshott Castle** (1873)
3. **Boy in Grey** (1871)—**Harveys** (1872)—**Hornby Mills** (1872)—**Mystery of the Island** (1877, his last, posthumous, fiction)
4. **Ravenshoe** (1861)—**Old Margaret** (1871)—**Valentin** (1872)—**Number Seventeen** (1875)
5. **Geoffry Hamlyn** (1859, his first novel)—**Hetty** (1871)—**Reginald Hetherege** (1874)—**Grange Garden** (1876, his last full-length novel)

LE FANU, JOSEPH SHERIDAN

1. **House by Churchyard**, *Irish* (1863)
2. **Chronicles of Golden Friars** (1871)
3. **Cock and Anchor** (1845, his first novel)
4. **Checkmate** (1871)
5. **Guy Deverell** (1865)—**Tenants of Mallory** (1867)—**Haunted Lives** (1868)—**Wyvern Mystery** (1869)—**Willing to Die** (1873)
6. **Uncle Silas** (1864)
7. **All in the Dark** (1866)—**Lost Name** (1868)—**In a Glass Darkly** (1872)
8. **Wylder's Hand** (1864)
9. **Rose and Key** (1871)
10. **Ghost Stories** (1851)
11. **House by Churchyard**, *English* (1863)
12. **Purcell Papers** (1880, his last, posthumous, three-decker)
13. **Torlogh O'Brien** (1847)

Remarks. As with Henry Kingsley, the standard of rarity (except in the case of Nos. 12 and 13) is a very high one. *The Cock and the Anchor* is only No. 3 when in original boards or boards, half cloth. In some sort of library rebinding, it ranks under No. 5.

LEVER, CHARLES

1. **Horace Templeton** (1848)—**A Rent in a Cloud** (1865)
2. **Paul Gosslett's Confessions** (1868)
3. **Sir Brooke Fossbrooke** (1866)—**Bramleighs of Bishop's Folly** (1868)—**Lord Kilgobbin** (1872, his last novel)
4. **Sir Jasper Carew** (1855)—**Davenport Dunn** (1859)
5. **Tony Butler** (1865)
6. **The O'Donoughue** (1845)—**Dodd Family Abroad** (1854)—**Maurice Tiernay** (1854)
7. **A Day's Ride** (1863)
8. **Tales of the Trains** (1845)—**Nuts & Nutcrackers** (1845)

9. **Con Cregan** (1850)—**That Boy of Norcotts** (1869)
10. **Harry Lorrequer** (1839, his first novel)—**Arthur O'Leary** (1844)—**The Daltons** (1852)
11. **Our Mess** (1843–4)—**Knight of Gwynne** (1847) —**Roland Cashel** (1850)
12. **Martins of Cro' Martin** (1856)—**One of Them** (1861)
13. **Cornelius O'Dowd** (1864–5)
14. **Barrington** (1863)
15. **Charles O'Malley** (1841)
16. **Fortunes of Glencore** (1857)— **Luttrell of Arran** (1865)
17. **St Patrick's Eve** (1845)

Remarks. There is a certain element of improvisation in this schedule, and I am prepared for the grading from 9–13 to be variously challenged. Critics, however, must please bear in mind that the sequences and the groupings are of copies in primary bindings only and, subject to their being in original cloth, irrespective of condition.

The picture as presented (and it is in the main, I believe, an accurate one) is unusually illustrative of certain phenomena of survival which show themselves in the bibliography of a prolific mid-nineteenth-century novelist.

We begin with a two-volume anonymous work of a very different kind from those hitherto published by Lever. There was nothing to suggest *Templeton* was by an already popular author, and it was probably 'printed short' (and justifiably) in consequence. The second title under 1 and that under 2 are minor (also anonymous) works which might be termed bye-products—again like *Linda Tressel* and *Nina Balatka* by Trollope. No. 3 consists of Lever's three late three-deckers, which are pathetic instances of the efforts of a dog who has had his day. Compare their high grading with the low grading of *Glencore* (No. 16), a similar three-decker, but one published nearly ten years earlier before the author's reputation had begun to wilt. *Glencore* itself was not a popular title; but it was extensively produced because in those days Lever's editions were large. It did not sell, and many copies survived. The others (including *Tony Butler*, despite its slightly greater frequency) were only wanted as *serials*; and, when the serials were done, their publishers had no illusions as to the stories' prospects in three-volume form.

Nos. 4(*a*) and 6(*c*) demonstrate the influence toward subsequent rarity of the inclusion in a popular-price series, mainly consisting of reprints, of stories not previously published. Both *Tiernay* and *Carew* were volumes in the *Parlour Library*, and therefore subject to the wastage inevitable among cheaps of flimsy manufacture and of little repute as *books* in their own right.

Our central groups are dominated by illustrated octavo titles which were published in parts. These have been sure of a respectable degree of survival for the sake of their illustrators (as have similar works by Ainsworth, Frances Trollope and others); but the order in which I have placed them has no sanction but individual experience. Other students, as said above, will almost certainly differ.

One overall fact may be noted. Lever's comparative scarcities take less account of chronology of publication than that of any other author examined. Dates of first appearance appear to have had no influence whatsoever on the chances of ultimate survival.

In conclusion I would point out that *Gerald Fitzgerald* (Dublin, 1899) has been purposely omitted. Although an American edition was published at the time the story was serialised, no book-issue was made in the British Isles for nearly thirty years after Lever's death. The novel is very uncommon; but its scarcity cannot be gauged by the standards of contemporary publication.

MARRYAT, FREDERICK

1. **Naval Officer** (1829, his first novel)
2. **Jacob Faithful**, *Illustrated Edition* (1837)
3. **Newton Forster** (1832)
4. **Peter Simple** (1834)
5. **Phantom Ship** (1839)
6. **Joseph Rushbrook** (1841)—**Peter Simple**, *Illustrated Edition* (1837)
7. **King's Own** (1830)—**Jacob Faithful** (1834) **Japhet** (1836)
8. **Children of the New Forest** (1847)
9. **Pacha of Many Tales** (1835)—**Snarleyyow** (1837)—**Valerie** (1849, his last, unfinished, novel)
10. **Olla Podrida** (1840)
11. **Privateersman** (1846)
12. **Midshipman Easy** (1836)—**Poor Jack** (1840)
13. **Little Savage** (1848–9)
14. **Percival Keene** (1842)
15. **M. Violet** (1843)
16. **Settlers in Canada** (1844)
17. **Pirate and Three Cutters** (1836)
18. **Masterman Ready** (1841–2)—**Mission** (1845)

Remarks. Marryat, like Bulwer Lytton, is mostly very difficult in *fine* original state throughout his board-and-label period. He is harder than Bulwer when it comes to cloth, *Masterman Ready* and *Mission* being the only titles which can fairly be said to survive with frequency.

MEREDITH, GEORGE

To the end of the two- and three-decker period (*Amazing Marriage*).

Meredith, like Disraeli and George Eliot, attains the extremes of rarity and commonness in first edition survival. Few Victorian fictions are more seldom seen than those numbered 1 to 4 below: few so persistently met with as those numbered 11 to 13. Although the slant from rarity does not accurately follow the chronology of publication, it runs sufficiently close to it to make the survival of Meredith first editions normal and comprehensible. In *Trollope: a Bibliography* I instanced *Rhoda Fleming* (the only Tinsley Meredith) as an example of a rarity caused by an isolated imprint.

1. **Rhoda Fleming** (1865)
2. **Farina** (1857)—**Harry Richmond** (1871)
3. **Evan Harrington** (1861)
4. **Richard Feverel** (1859)
5. **Vittoria** (1867)
6. **Shaving of Shagpat** (1856, his first novel)
7. **Emilia in England** (1864)—**Beauchamp's Career** (1876)
8. **Egoist** (1879)
9. **Diana of the Crossways** (1885)
10. **Tragic Comedians** (1880)
11. **Amazing Marriage** (1895, his last more-than-one-volume novel)
12. **Lord Ormont** (1894)
13. **One of our Conquerors** (1891)

OUIDA

To the end of the three-deckers (*Tower of Taddeo*).

1. **Under Two Flags** (1867)
2. **Held in Bondage** (1863, her first novel)—**Strathmore** (1865)—**Chandos** (1866)—**Cecil Castlemaine's Gauge** (1867)
3. **Idalia** (1867)—**In a Winter City** (1876)—**A House Party** (1887)—**Santa Barbara** (1891)
4. **Signa** (1875)—**Friendship** (1878)—**Frescoes** (1883)—**Don Gesualdo** (1886)
5. **Tricotrin** (1869)—**Bimbi** (1882)
6. **Two Little Wooden Shoes** (1874)—**Pipistrello** (1880)—**Othmar** (1885)—**Rainy June** (1885)—**Ruffino** (1890)
7. **Folle Farine** (1871)—**Pascarel** (1873)—**Ariadne** (1877)—**Village Commune** (1881)—**In Maremma** (1882)—**Syrlin** (1890)
8. **Puck** (1870)—**Moths** (1880)—**Wanda** (1883)—**Princess Napraxin** (1884)
9. **Guilderoy** (1889)—**Tower of Taddeo** (1892, her last three-decker)
10. **Dog of Flanders** (1872)

Remarks. It is beyond my capacity to account for the various survival-powers of Ouida's novels. They are too numerous to be treated otherwise than in groups, and we have little knowledge of her publishing relationships. This schedule, therefore, is based entirely on experience—and experience of Ouida firsts in original state is necessarily limited, as only a few turn up with any frequency and some hardly ever. It is worth noting that Ouida is one of the very few novelists treated in this book whose 'key-title' is also the rarest.

PEACOCK, THOMAS LOVE

Original boards and cloth, *regardless of condition, but excluding remainder boards.*

1. **Headlong Hall** (1816, his first novel)
2. **Maid Marian** (1822)
3. **Nightmare Abbey** (1818)
4. **Misfortunes of Elphin** (1829)
5. **Melincourt** (1817)
6. **Crotchet Castle** (1831)
7. **Gryll Grange**

[The remainder-board issues of *Crotchet Castle* and *Misfortunes of Elphin* would, if included, be equal with No. 7.]

READE, CHARLES

1. **It's Never Too Late to Mend** (1856)
2. **Griffith Gaunt** (1866)
3. **Foul Play** (1868)—**Perilous Secret** (1884, his last, posthumous, novel)
4. **Peg Woffington** (1853, his first novel)—**Cloister and the Hearth** (1861)—**Good Stories of Man, etc.** (1884)
5. **Put Yourself in His Place** (1870)
6. **Woman Hater** (1877)—**Single Heart** (1884)
7. **Trade Malice** (1875)—**Jilt** (1884)
8. **Cream** (1858)—**Love Me Little** (1859)—**Hard Cash** (1863)
9. **Terrible Temptation** (1871)—**Simpleton** (1873)
10. **White Lies** (1857)
11. **Christie Johnstone** (1853)
12. **Course of True Love** (1857)

Remarks. If one had the data, it would be interesting to analyse the survival-schedules of Collins and Reade. There are more frequencies in Reade than in Collins; yet he is as difficult to complete, owing to two or three obstinate rarities which equal anything Collins can offer.

The reason for such Reade availabilities as Nos. 8 and 9 is partly, I imagine, that, as a contentious propagandist, he found a number of serious readers (both for and against) who *bought* his books in order to argue about them. *Christie Johnstone* is No. 11 because the success of *Peg Woffington* provoked overproduction of that story's very inferior successor. Looking at No. 8 from another angle and in conjunction with No. 10, one suspects a touch of hysteria in the optimism with which Trübner, having taken Bentley's place with *White Lies*, launched their important (and aggressive) new author. Did their nerve fail them, when he brought them four volumes of *The Cloister*? Whatever the cause, their last (and greatest) Reade title is the only major rarity of the lot.

I cannot explain the unfindability of No. 2 (1866). Here is a normal three-decker, by a writer of high and established reputation, published by a prominent and experienced firm. Why does the first edition so rarely turn up? At first sight one might see a parallel case to Dickens' *Great Expectations*. But I suspect (without authority) that the reason for the scarcity of *Great Expectations* in first edition is that Dickens' public were accustomed to illustrated part-issues and book-issues in 8vo, and did not take kindly to an unillustrated three-decker. Consequently Chapman & Hall played the game they played (at about the same date) with *Rachel Ray*, and divided a normal first printing into a series of 'editions' hoping to stimulate a flagging demand. None of this can apply to Reade, who was not a part-issue author. *Griffith Gaunt*, therefore remains a mystery.

SOMERVILLE, E. Œ. AND ROSS, MARTIN

To 1915 (*In Mr Knox's Country*).

1. **An Irish Cousin** (1889)
2. **The Real Charlotte** (1894)
3. **Silver Fox** (1898)
4. **Naboth's Vineyard** (1891)
5. **Through Connemara in a Governess Cart** (1893)—**In the Vine Country** (1893)—**Some Experiences of an Irish R.M.** (1899)
6. **All on the Irish Shore** (1903)
7. **Beggars on Horseback** (1895)
8. **Some Irish Yesterdays** (1906)—**Dan Russell the Fox** (1911)
9. **Further Experiences of an Irish R.M.** (1908)—**In Mr Knox's Country** (1915)

THACKERAY, W. M.

Principal novels, and in book-editions only.

(i) *Original cloth, regardless of condition*

1. **Vanity Fair** (1848)
2. **Esmond** (1852)
3. **Newcomes** (1854–5)—**Virginians** (1858–9)
4. **Denis Duval** (1867)
5. **Adventures of Philip** (1862)
6. **Lovel the Widower** (1861)
7. **Pendennis** (1849–50)

(ii) *Fine*

1. **Vanity Fair—Esmond**
2. **Lovel the Widower—Denis Duval**
3. **Virginians**
4. **Newcomes**
5. **Pendennis**
6. **Adventures of Philip**

Note. Whereas *Vanity Fair* and *Esmond* hold their place whether in any condition or fine, *Philip* is commoner fine than used, and is an interesting example of the result of over-producing an unsuccessful book.

TROLLOPE, ANTHONY

It has seemed desirable to divide this long bibliography into four sections, from A, the rarest, to D, the most frequently met with. Trollope scarcities are very difficult to estimate, and the experience of some collectors will incline them to dispute the points of division. In the main, however, bearing in mind its date and standard three-volume form, I consider that JOHN CALDIGATE belongs with A rather than B, even though some readers may have seen copies more frequently than of B1. Similarly, I include three 8vo titles (C6 and C7) under C rather than early under D, because they are markedly scarcer than all the other octavos, which crowd together at the end of the fourth category.

This schedule of scarcities excludes rebound copies, and refers to copies in original boards or cloth *irrespective of condition.*

A

1. **The Macdermots** (1847)
2. **Dr Thorne** (1858)
3. **Castle Richmond**, 1st Issue (1860)
4. **The Kellys** (1848)—**Rachel Ray** (1863)
5. **Harry Heathcote** (1874)
6. **The Belton Estate** (1866)
7. **Nina Balatka** (1867)—**Linda Tressel** (1868)
8. **La Vendée** (1850)
9. **The Bertrams** (1859)
10. **John Caldigate** (1879)

B

1. **Tales of All Countries**, 2nd Series (1863)
2. **The Three Clerks** (1858)—**Miss Mackenzie** (1865)—**Is He Popenjoy** (1878)
3. **Barchester Towers** (1857)—**An Eye for an Eye** (1879)
4. **Framley Parsonage** (1861)
5. **Castle Richmond**, 2nd Issue (1860)—**Frau Frohmann** (1882)
6. **Phineas Redux** (1874)
7. **Lotta Schmidt** (1867)—**Kept in the Dark** (1882)
8. **The Duke's Children** (1880)—**Dr Wortle's School** (1881)

C

1. **An Editor's Tales** (1870)—**Ayala's Angel** (1881)
2. **The Golden Lion of Grandpère** (1872)—**Cousin Henry** (1879)
3. **Ralph the Heir** (1871)
4. **The Fixed Period** (1882)—**The Landleaguers** (1883)
5. **Tales of all Countries**, 1st Series (1861)—**Lady Anna** (1874)
6. **The Vicar of Bullhampton** (1870)—**Sir Harry Hotspur** (1871)—**An Old Man's Love** (1874)
7. **Can You Forgive Her?** (1864)—**He Knew He Was Right** (1869)

D

1. **The Eustace Diamonds** (1873)—**Mr Scarborough's Family** (1883)
2. **Marion Fay** (1882)
3. **The American Senator** (1877)
4. **The Warden** (1855)
5. **The Claverings** (1867)—**Brown, Jones and Robinson** (1870)
6. **Phineas Finn** (1869)
7. **Orley Farm** (1862)—**The Small House at Allington** (1864)—**The Prime Minister** (1876)
8. **The Way We Live Now** (1875)
9. **The Last Chronicle of Barset** (1867)

TROLLOPE, MRS FRANCES

It is phenomenal to find in bookshops fine copies of any of the *unillustrated* novels of Mrs Trollope—and indeed unusual to see copies of any kind, for I gather from friends in the trade that she sells readily even in re-bound condition. When I began collecting her, things were to this extent different—that decent copies of her then forgotten books (where such existed) had remained on the shelf and fell to my lot. But this is not to say they were anything but very uncommon.

Her *illustrated* novels (cf. Ainsworth and Lever) survived more frequently, for while the period when Phiz, Leech, Buss, Onwhyn, and even Hervieu were collected *as illustrators* was in its heyday, the trade took notice of a book with etched plates, though its author may well have been considered of no interest.

This state of affairs was even more noticeable in the case of the 8vo editions of *Michael Armstrong* and *Jessie Phillips* than of the illustrated three-deckers, because they offered the extra attraction of part-issue, and therefore appealed to yet another collecting taste which prevailed prior to the war of 1914. It is, perhaps, hardly necessary to add that the travel books—both illustrated and otherwise—were (and still are) more frequently met with than the novels.

If, therefore, one were now to attempt to gauge the general prospects of collecting Mrs Trollope in good original condition, one would arrive at the paradoxical (but to collectors not unfamiliar) conclusion that her showier books will be obtained with somewhat less difficulty than her regulation three-deckers, though maybe at higher prices; that the 8vo illustrateds in parts and in cloth (the latter frequently secondary) will be found a shade more easily still; that *The Domestic Manners of the Americans*, her most famous book, will—just because it *is* famous—be secured by booksellers wherever possible and offered for sale in heavy type; but that the long run of undistinguished three-volume novels in boards and labels or in cloth will, save by the merest chance, prove almost undiscoverable.

I cannot attempt to grade the scarcity of a string of novels, all of which in decent condition are now ultra-scarce. I will only say that, in so far as my experience is any guide, the following in good or fine state have been seen by me on two occasions or more, whereas the remainder of the unillustrated novels have been seen once (and bought) or never seen at all.

The Refugee in America (1832)
Tremordyn Cliff (1835)
Father Eustace (1847)
The Lottery of Marriage (1849)
Petticoat Government (1850)
Uncle Walter (1852)

To revert to the more frequent survival of the illustrated novels, I would ask collectors to note that the first of the Barnaby trilogy (the only unillustrated one) is the rarest. As a tentative grading of the scarcities *inter se* of the illustrated titles (including two non-fiction but excluding the travel books except *Domestic Manners*) I suggest the following (beginning with the rarest):

1. **The Widow Married** (1840)
2. **The Barnabys in America** (1843)
3. **Jessie Phillips,** 3 vol. edition (1843)
4. **Charles Chesterfield** (1841)
5. **Jessie Phillips,** 8vo edition (1843)
6. **Vicar of Wrexhill** (1837)
7. **Mothers Manual** (1833)
8. **Jonathan Jefferson Whitlaw** (1836)
9. **Domestic Manners of the Americans** (1832)
10. **Michael Armstrong,** 3 vol. edition (1840)
11. **Michael Armstrong,** 8vo edition (1840)

WOOD, MRS HENRY

To the last three-decker (*House of Halliwell*), excluding collections of stories first published in the uniform edition. Original cloth, regardless of condition.

1. **Shadow of Ashlydyat,** *ordinary binding* (1863)—**Orville College** (1867)—**Anne Hereford** (1868)—**Within the Maze** (1872)
2. **East Lynne,** *ordinary binding* (1861)
3. **Trevlyn Hold** (1864)—**George 'Canterbury's Will** (1870)—**Bessy Rane** (1870)—**Johnny Ludlow, I and II** (1874, 1880)—**Pomeroy Abbey** (1878)—**Lady Grace** (1887)—**Featherston's Story** (1889)
4. **Mildred Arkell** (1865)—**Lady Adelaide's Oath** (1867)—**A Life's Secret** (1867)—**Roland Yorke** (1869)—**Story of Charles Strange** (1888)—**House of Halliwell** (1890, her last, posthumous, three-decker)
5. **Foggy Night at Offord** (1863)—**William Allair** (1864)—**St Martin's Eve** (1866)—**Red Court Farm** (1868)—**Adam Grainger** (1876)
6. **East Lynne,** *presentation binding*—**Ashlydyat,** *presentation binding*—**Bessy Wells** (1875)
7. **Lord Oakburn's Daughters** (1864)—**Elster's Folly** (1866)
8. **Dene Hollow** (1871)—**Told in the Twilight** (1875)—**Court Netherleigh** (1881)

9. **Danesbury House** (1860, her first fiction)—**Mrs Haliburton's Troubles** (1862)—**Edina** (1876)
10. **Verner's Pride** (1863)—**Master of Greylands** (1873)—**Johnny Ludlow, III** (1885)
11. **Oswald Cray** (1864)
12. **Channings** (1862)

Remarks. The grading of these dozen groups—with the exception of No. 12, which is definitely the most frequent survivor among Wood 'firsts'—is so disputable as to be little more than a personal estimate. The gap between any two numbers is of the narrowest; but I think that the *ranking* of the numbers is correct, however close together the whole series may be.

Mrs Wood survives with noticeable frequency (in striking contrast to Ouida), and for the reason that she was a keen business woman. She stuck to one publisher for virtually her whole output; and her correspondence with Bentley shows her well aware of her sales-figures and sale-prospects, and anxious that her successive first editions should be adequately graded. Also she liked solid (if ornate) book-making, and her novels are all durably produced.

PLATE 1

21

21

1375

3094

PLATE 2

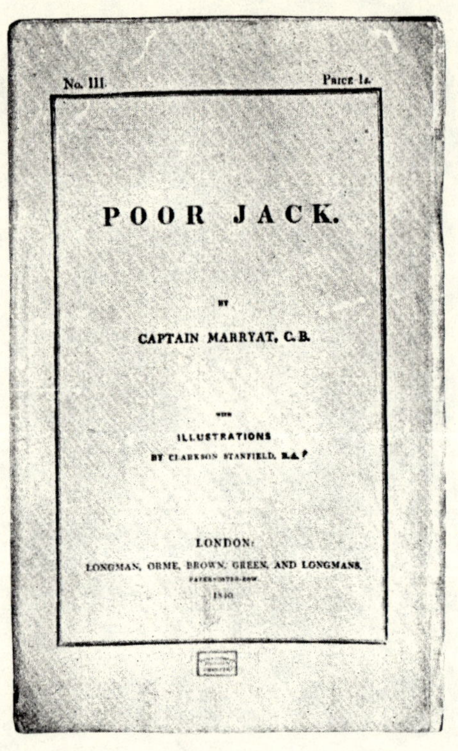

No. III. Price 1s.

POOR JACK.

BY

CAPTAIN MARRYAT, C.B.

WITH

ILLUSTRATIONS

BY CLARKSON STANFIELD, R.A.

LONDON:

LONGMAN, ORME, BROWN, GREEN, AND LONGMANS,

PATERNOSTER-ROW.

1840.

1595

IN TWENTY PARTS, PRICE SIXPENCE EACH.

THE

HEADLESS HORSEMAN

A Strange Tale of Texas

By

Capt Mayne Reid

LONDON: CHAPMAN AND HALL, PICCADILLY

2023

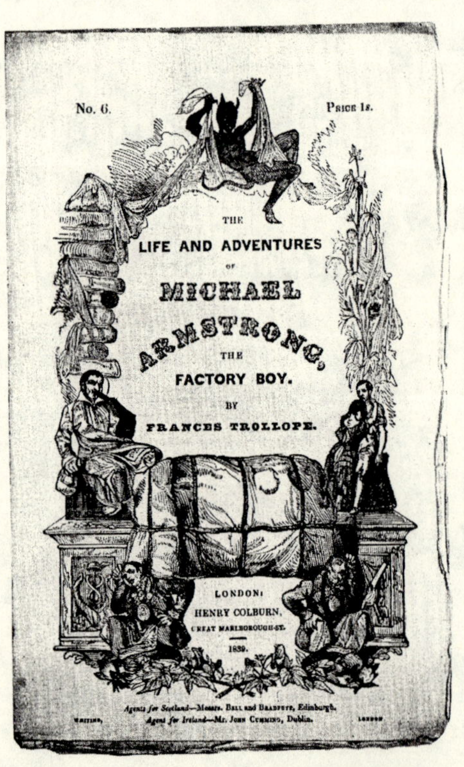

No. 6. Price 1s.

THE

LIFE AND ADVENTURES

OF

MICHAEL

ARMSTRONG,

THE

FACTORY BOY.

BY

FRANCES TROLLOPE.

LONDON:

HENRY COLBURN,

GREAT MARLBOROUGH-ST.

1839.

Agents for Scotland—Messrs. Bell and Bradfute, Edinburgh.

Agents for Ireland—Mr. John Cumming, Dublin.

3228

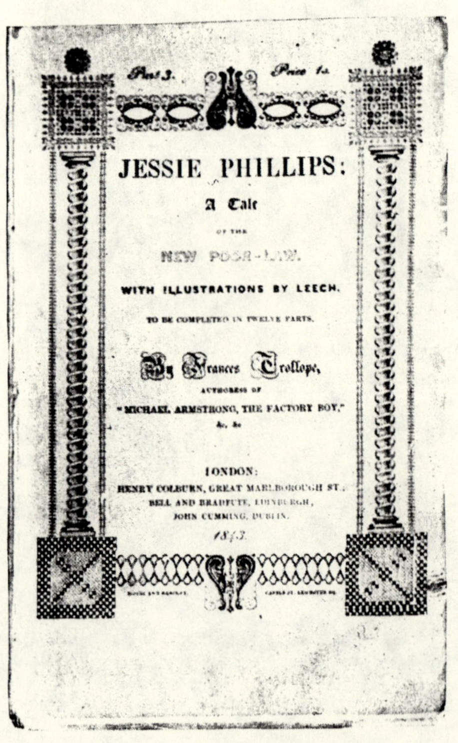

Part 3. Price 1s.

JESSIE PHILLIPS:

A Tale

OF THE

NEW POOR-LAW.

WITH ILLUSTRATIONS BY LEECH.

TO BE COMPLETED IN TWELVE PARTS.

By Frances Trollope,

AUTHORESS OF

"MICHAEL ARMSTRONG, THE FACTORY BOY,"

&c. &c.

LONDON:

HENRY COLBURN, GREAT MARLBOROUGH ST.;

BELL AND BRADFUTE, EDINBURGH,

JOHN CUMMING, DUBLIN.

1843.

3223

130 103 117

127 104 114 113 119

PLATE 4

156*a*

156*b*

221 222 227 228

350

1234

302 *a*

269

291

304

PLATE 6

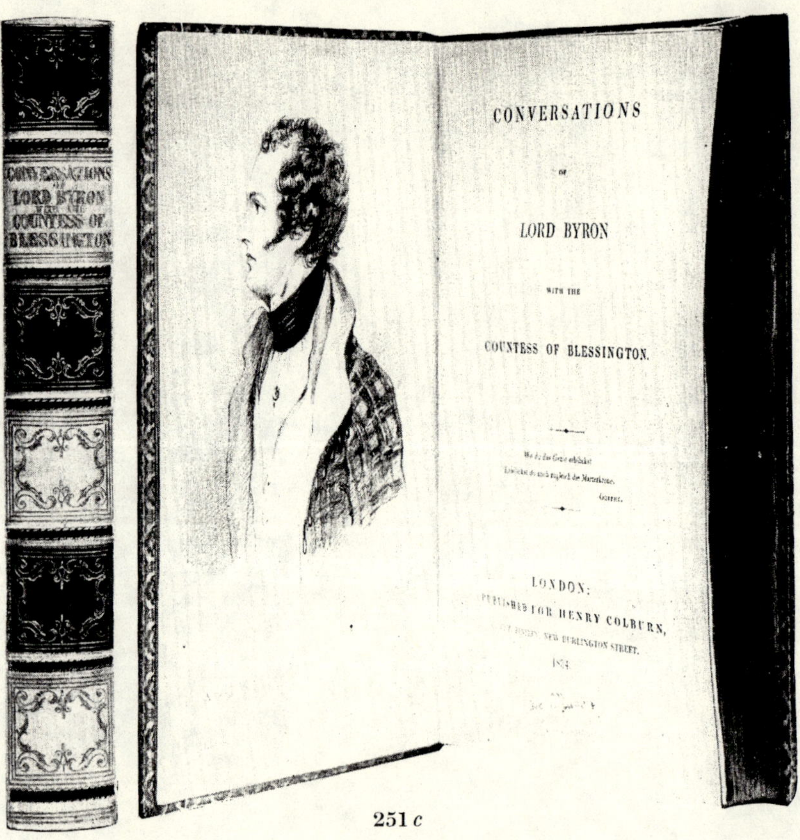

251 *c*

506

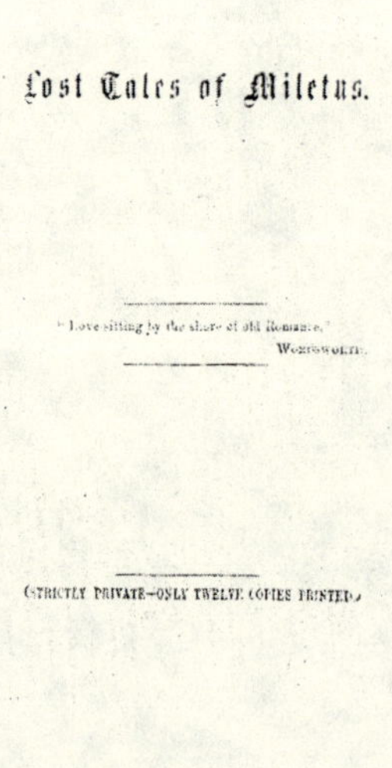
Lost Tales of Miletus.

"Love sitting by the shore of old Romance."
WORDSWORTH.

(STRICTLY PRIVATE—ONLY TWELVE COPIES PRINTED.)

418

512

PLATE 7

518 519 520

516 502 482 496 496*a* 496*b* 517 499 514 500

PLATE 8

495 495*a*

515*a* 495*b* 520*a*

PLATE 9

560

560*a*

718 725 734 735 711 714

PLATE 10

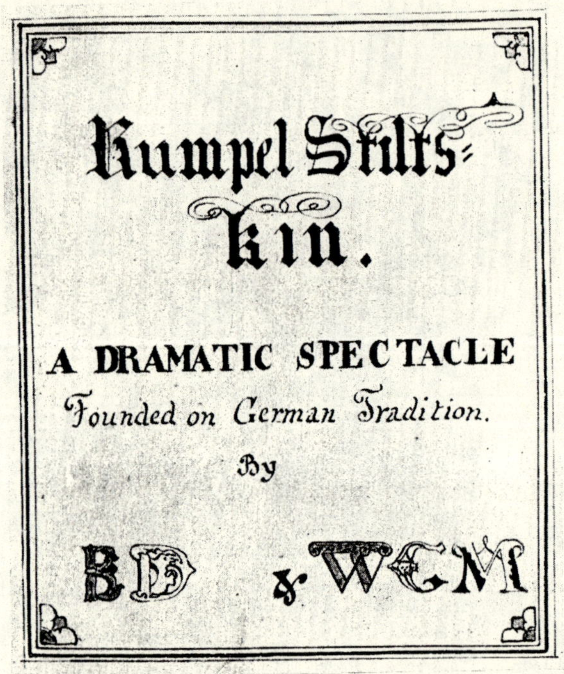

724

731

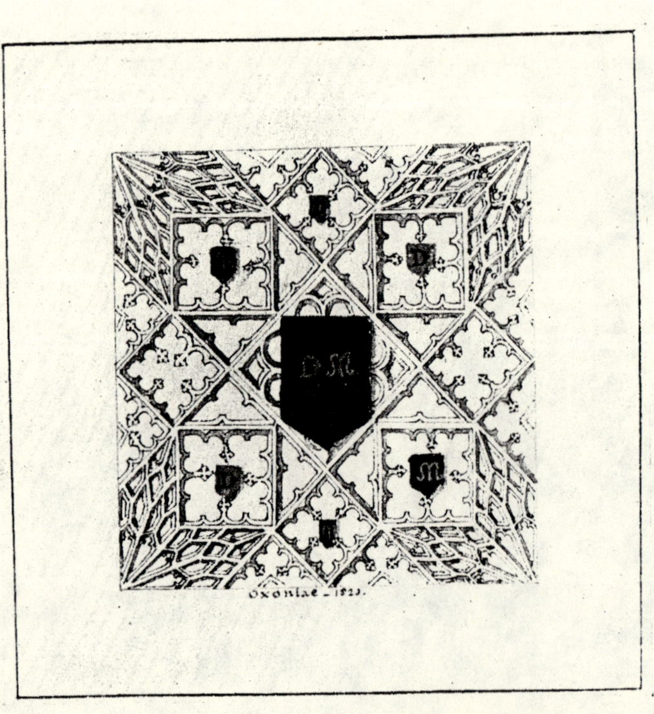

724

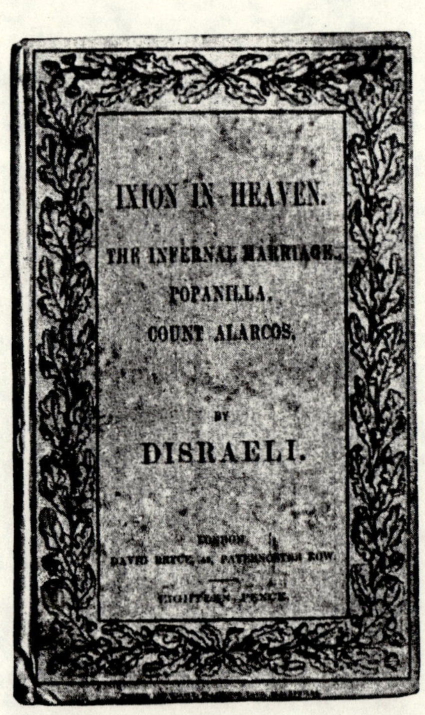

721g

PLATE 11

1018 1003 1027 993

1015 1034 1020 1020*a* 1008 996 1004

PLATE 12

550

555 873 875 1456 1656

771 763 786 780 788 777 783 766

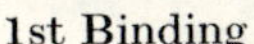

1st Binding

2nd Binding

PLATE 14

1344 1350 1362 1363 1349*b*

1379 1379*a* 1379*b* 1379*d*

1423 1418 1395 1408

1419

PLATE 16

1479

1479*a*

1523

1523*a*

THE BEAUTIFUL POEM

OF

SHAMUS O'BRIEN:

A STORY OF 'NINETY-EIGHT.

ERIN GO BRAGH

MANCHESTER:
JOHN HEYWOOD, 141 AND 143 DEANSGATE.
1867.

PRICE THREEPENCE.

1370

THE

JUVENILE

LIBRARY

BY

CAPTAIN MARRYAT, R.N.

No. I.

THE CHILDREN OF THE NEW FOREST.

LONDON:
H. HURST, 27 KING WILLIAM STREET,
STRAND.

Price One Shilling.

1573

? advance style　　1573*a–c*　　regulation style

PLATE 18

1587 1588 1578*a* 1590

1579 1598 1227 1224

1578*c*

3154 1971 1667

PLATE 20

BIRMAN

EIGHTEEN VIEWS Taken at and near RANGOON.

EMPIRE.

1610*a*

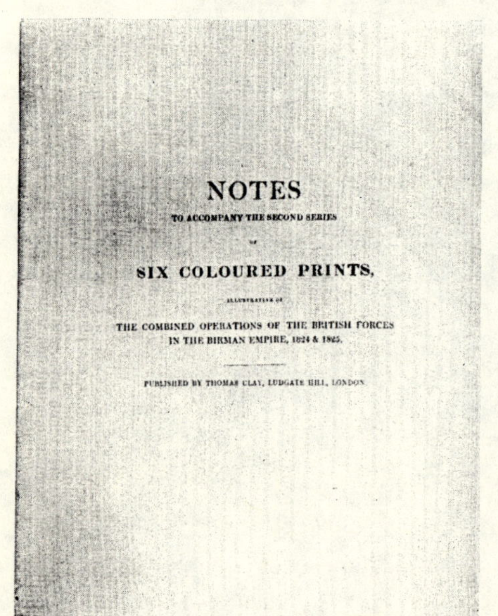
NOTES

TO ACCOMPANY THE SECOND SERIES

OF

SIX COLOURED PRINTS,

ILLUSTRATIVE OF

THE COMBINED OPERATIONS OF THE BRITISH FORCES
IN THE BIRMAN EMPIRE, 1824 & 1825.

PUBLISHED BY THOMAS CLAY, LUDGATE HILL, LONDON

1610

NOTES

TO ACCOMPANY

THE RANGOON VIEWS.

1610

SIX COLOURED PRINTS

Illustrative of the Combined Operations

OF THE

BRITISH FORCES,

IN THE

BIRMAN EMPIRE.

1824 and 1825

Second Series.

1610*a*

THE
BY
THE TWO MOUNTED SENTRIES.
with twelve colored Illustrations
LONDON.
J & D A Darling, 126, Bishopsgate Street,
1850.

1221

The Progress of a
MIDSHIPMAN
exemplified in
the Career of
Master Blockhead
in seven Plates

1611

PLATE 22

1451

1679

1682 1680 1524 1626 1617

1758 1758*a*

1758*b*

1838 1838*a*

1949 1928

2011 2011*a* 2008 2004 2001 2001*a* 2012

3040

3040*a*

3127

3127*a*

3236 3234 3245 3245*a*

3198

3218

3218*a*

PLATE 28

3235 3244 3228*a* 3214

3335 3338 3340 3367

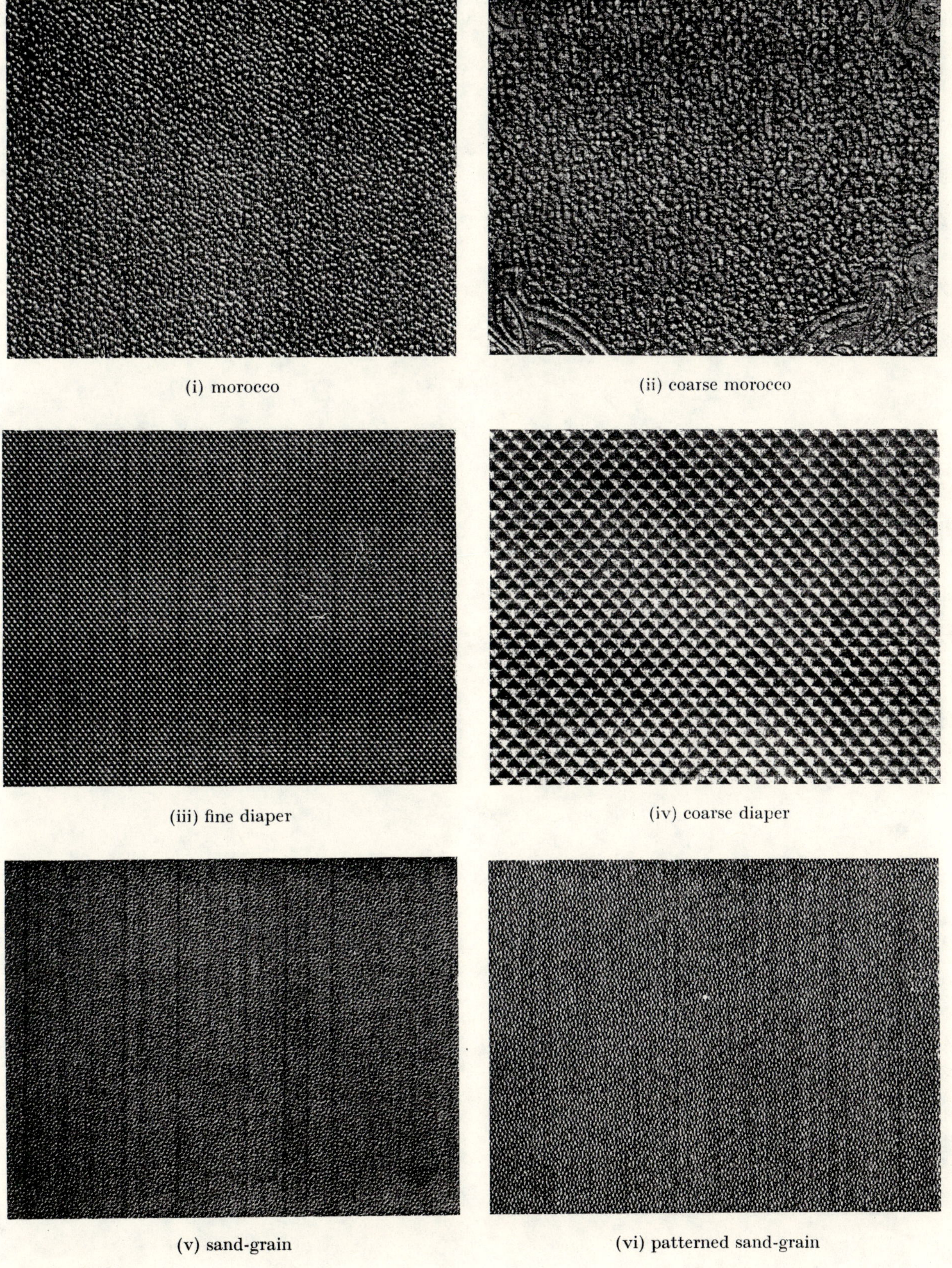

(i) morocco

(ii) coarse morocco

(iii) fine diaper

(iv) coarse diaper

(v) sand-grain

(vi) patterned sand-grain

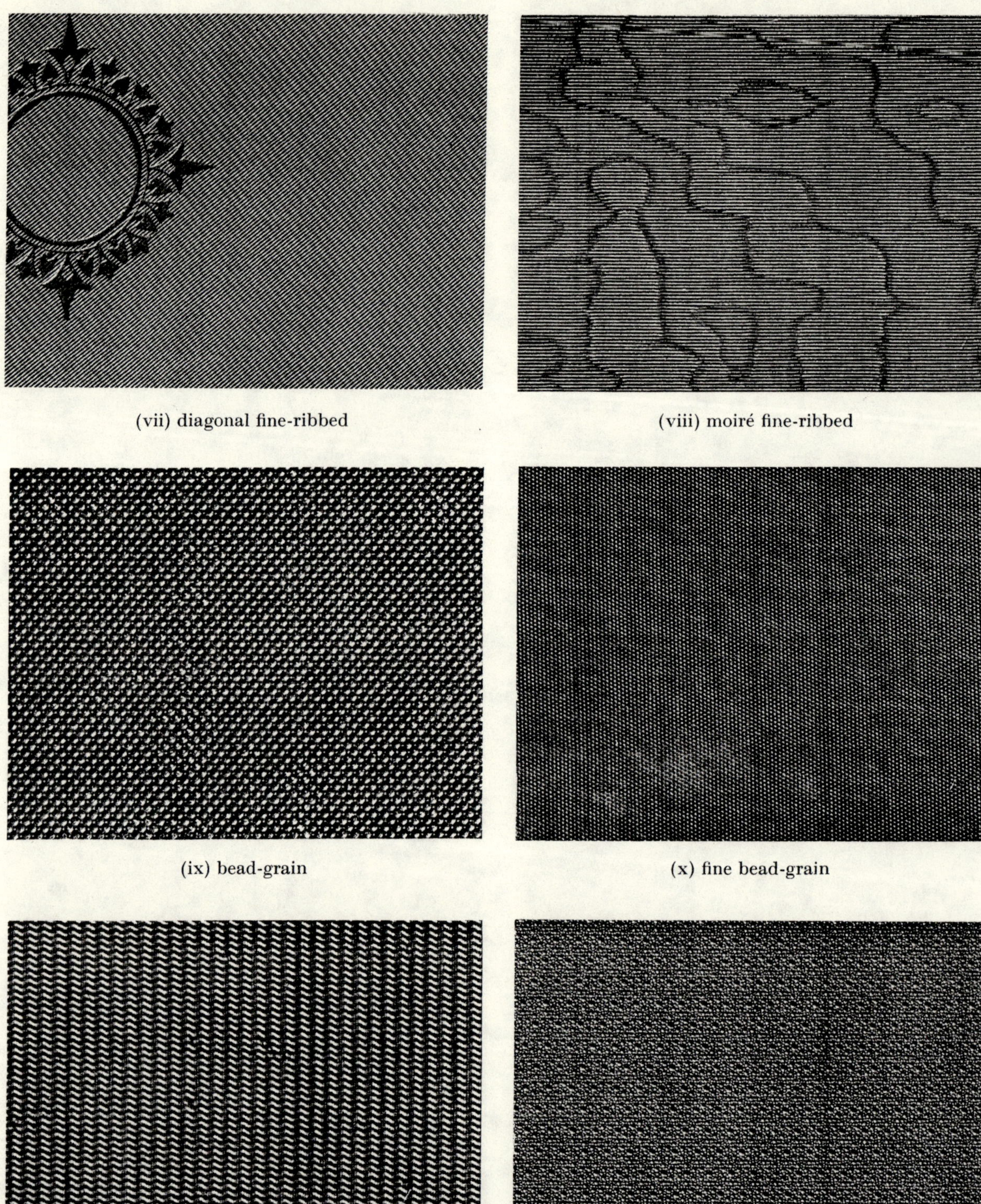

(vii) diagonal fine-ribbed

(viii) moiré fine-ribbed

(ix) bead-grain

(x) fine bead-grain

(xi) wavy-grain

(xii) bubble-grain

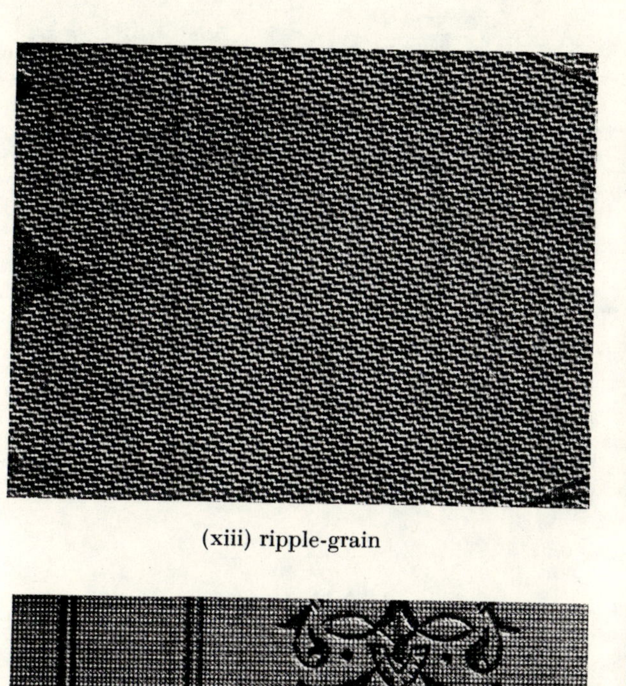

(xiii) ripple-grain

(xiv) fine ripple-grain

(xv) dotted-line-ribbed

(xvi) fine dotted-line-ribbed

(xvii) dot-and-line-grain

(xviii) fine-dotted-diaper

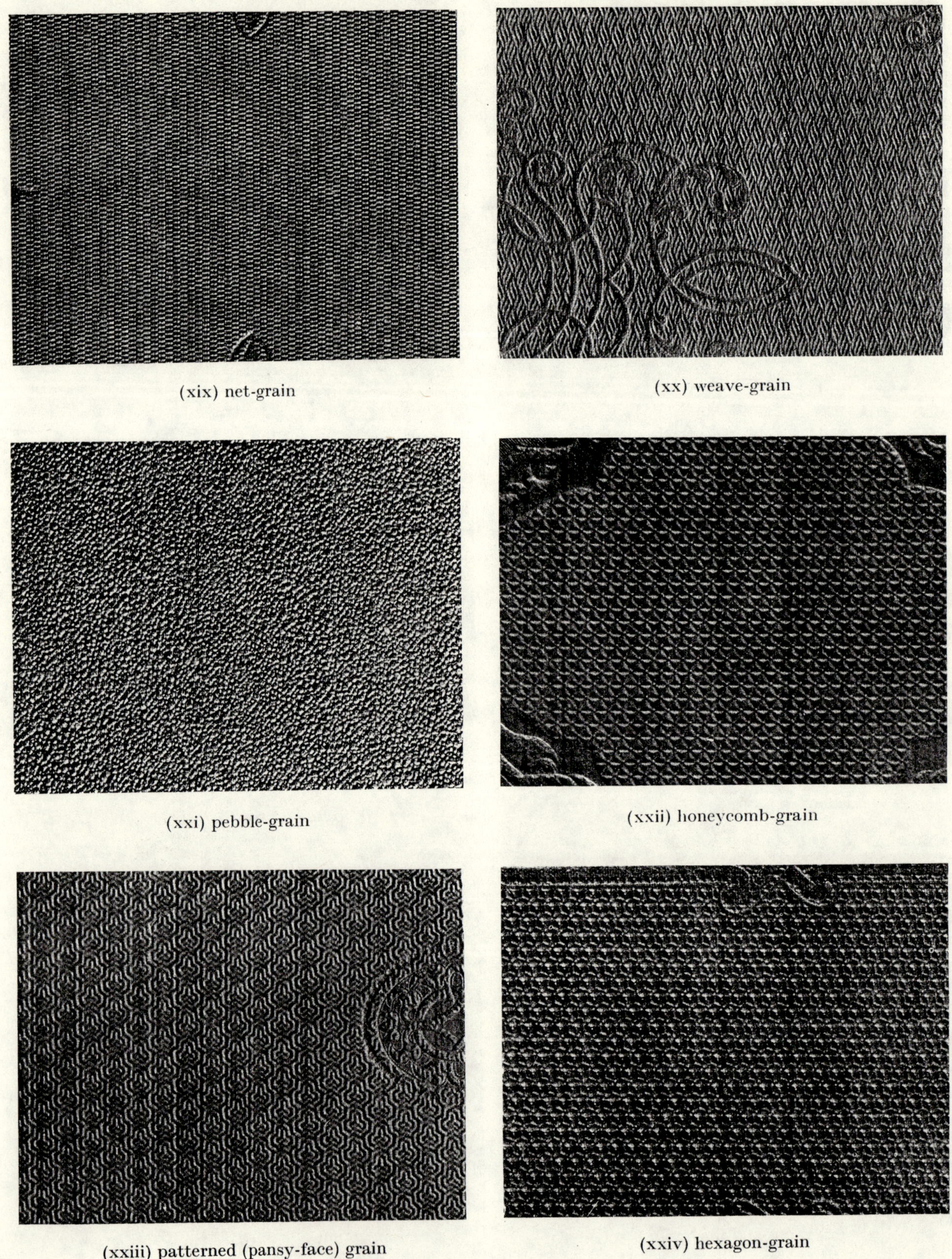

(xix) net-grain

(xx) weave-grain

(xxi) pebble-grain

(xxii) honeycomb-grain

(xxiii) patterned (pansy-face) grain

(xxiv) hexagon-grain

INDEX OF TITLES

INDEX OF TITLES

INDEX OF TITLES

INDEX OF TITLES

INDEX OF TITLES

INDEX OF TITLES

INDEX OF TITLES

INDEX OF TITLES

INDEX OF TITLES

INDEX OF TITLES

INDEX OF TITLES

INDEX OF TITLES

XIX CENTURY FICTION

A BIBLIOGRAPHICAL RECORD

BASED ON HIS OWN COLLECTION

BY

MICHAEL SADLEIR

IN TWO VOLUMES

VOLUME II

Martino Publishing

Mansfield Centre, CT

2004

Martino Publishing
P.O. Box 373,
Mansfield Centre, CT 06250 USA

web-site: www.martinopublishing.com

ISBN 1-57898-032-1

Library of Congress Cataloging-in-Publication Data

Sadleir, Michael, 1888-1957.
XIX century fiction: a bibliographical record based on his own collection / by Michael Sadleir.
p. cm.
Originally published: London: Constable, 1951, in 2 v.
Includes indexes.
ISBN 1-57898-032-1
1. English fiction--19th century--Bibliography. 2. Fiction--19th century--Bibliography. I. Title: 19th century fiction. II. Title: Nineteenth century fiction. III. Title.

Z2014.F4S16 2004
[PR861]
016.823'8--dc22 2003064873

Printed in the United States of America On 100% Acid-Free Paper

XIX CENTURY FICTION

A BIBLIOGRAPHICAL RECORD

BASED ON HIS OWN COLLECTION

BY

MICHAEL SADLEIR

IN TWO VOLUMES

VOLUME II

PRINTED AT THE UNIVERSITY PRESS, CAMBRIDGE

AND PUBLISHED

in Great Britain by

CONSTABLE & CO LTD
10–12 ORANGE STREET
LONDON W.C. 2

in the U.S.A. by the

UNIVERSITY OF CALIFORNIA
PRESS
BERKELEY AND LOS ANGELES

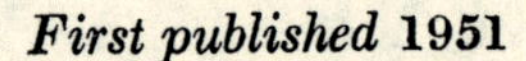

First published 1951

CONTENTS

ILLUSTRATIONS

AT END

SECTION TWO

YELLOW-BACK COLLECTION

NOTES ON THE NUMBERING OF SECTION TWO

I was strongly advised (and I think rightly) to carry the number-sequence of this Catalogue straight through from start to finish, so that anyone wishing to refer to some specific entry need not trouble to designate Section I or II or III. But, because the frame-work of Sections II and III differs from that of Section I, continuous numbering has involved me in inconsistencies and, occasionally, in what may appear to be actual mistakes.

To inconsistencies I admit; but plead that I have aimed at facilitating reference where likely to be needed, and at avoiding a clutter of non-essential numbers. The following main principles have been observed:

(1) Titles in their own right (other than those already numbered in series, e.g. Blackwood's London Library) are individually numbered, e.g. those under "Anonyma" and "Coming K——", as well as first editions of Bede, Grant, Harte, Twain and others.

(2) Alternative issues or variant copies are numbered *a*, *b* etc.

(3) Where several ordinary yellow-back reprints are grouped under an author's name, the number is attached to the author, e.g. Baring Gould, G. P. R. James, Anthony Trollope and many more. Individual reference by title to such reprints is unlikely to be required.

In a few cases we are confronted with the awkward problem of an indexed author whose yellow-back publications are partly first editions, partly mere reprints. Such cases have been dealt with in a spirit of pure opportunism. For example, Sala and Albert Smith carry author-numbers which cover their reprints, while their first editions carry numbers of their own.

Typographically, no less than in numbering, this Section is occasionally erratic. First editions are mainly set in small even caps; but where intrinsic interest or clarity seemed to me to demand a larger size, I have asked the printers to employ one.

CONTENTS

The following Series are here incorporated with Authors' names in a single alphabet

SECTION II: YELLOW-BACK COLLECTION

Containing: Books first published in pictorial or printed boards or in wrappers. Reprints of Popular Titles in pictorial or decorated boards. Translations issued in boards or wrappers (many of works not previously published in English). Significant boarded or wrappered Series (even if simultaneously published in cloth), incorporating both Original and Reprint Titles.

For this section it has seemed practical to compile a single mixed alphabet, comprising authors, classifications and names of series. All authors and titles appear in the Index at the end of the volumes. Series and classifications which constitute the Contents List on the page opposite are not included in the Index.

The term 'Yellow-Back' must be understood to cover many books not actually issued in the pictorial boards to which the expression properly applies. In every case sufficient detail is given of the style of boarding or wrappering to ensure identification.

No cloth-bound book is included in this section *in its own right.* The occasional cloth-bound items recorded were simultaneously issued in boards or wrappers.

The terms 'small format' and 'large format', used to indicate size, refer—the first to the early yellow-backs (measuring with slight variations $4'' \times 6\frac{5}{8}''$), the second to the regulation crown 8vo size ($4\frac{5}{8}'' \times 7\frac{1}{8}''$) of the conventionalised yellow-backs of the prolific middle and late periods.

As the section is a mixture of first editions and reprints, the two classes are typographically distinguished. Titles which, to the best of my knowledge, are first editions are set in caps; reprints in heavy caps and l.c.

It may well be that I have wrongfully assumed some of the volumes to be first or first English editions, or, conversely, failed to capitalise some which are. The continual transfer of cover-blocks, type-plates and copyrights from one publisher to another; the issue (in the case of translations) of unauthorised English versions; and the absence of dates (which after about 1860 becomes virtually general) often make positive identification of issues impossible.

A brief technical statement about the making of yellow-backs may here suitably be given, in the form of an extract from the Reminiscences of Edmund Evans, the pioneer of pictorial covers.

'The popular artists of the day (Birket Foster, John Gilbert, Phiz (H. K. Browne), George Cruikshank, Harrison Weir, Kenny Meadows, John Absolon, W. S. Coleman, Charles Keene, F. S. Skill, Albert H. Warren, Charles H. Bennett, Walter Crane, A. W. Cooper, D. H. Friston, E. H. Corbould, William McConnell, Matt Stretch, W. Rainey, A. Chantry Corbould, R. Caldecott, John Sturges, and many others) were asked to supply drawings which were engraved on wood. Then two 'transfers' from the engraved block were made, i.e. impressions which while wet were laid face-down on plain blocks, and then passed through the press so that the wet impression was 'set off' on the plain blocks. These transfers were used, one for a *Red* printing, the other for a *Blue* printing—the Red being engraved in gradation to get the light tints, such as faces, hands, etc.; the Blue block being engraved to get the best result of texture, patterns or sky, and the blue being crossed over the red to get good effects of light and shade. There were generally only three printings used—Black, Blue and Red, or Black, Green and Red; the very most was made of each block by engraving, so as to get the best result for the money.'

One or two incidental facts, also gathered from Edmund Evans' notes, merit record:

(i) Wood-blocks signed 'E. Evans' prior to 1847 were not the work of Edmund Evans, but of another, unconnected engraver. Evans' first pictorial yellow-back for Routledge was THE LAMPLIGHTER (*Railway Library* 1854) drawn by Anelay.

(ii) Mayhew's LETTERS LEFT AT THE PASTRY COOK'S (q.v. below), reputedly the first book produced in pictorial covers by Evans' process, had a white paper base. The trade asked for a *toned* paper to lessen risks of soiling, and yellow-glazed paper was found the most practical solution.

In conclusion I would state that this section does not cover my entire yellow-back collection, but only those titles which are in themselves of some interest or importance.

ACME LIBRARY

Practically all 'small format' items are included, however obscure their authorship, because the small format yellow-backs are the aristocrats of their kind and, almost without exception, have elegance and 'style'. Of minor authors whose yellow-backs belong to the period of mass-production I have tried to select only those represented by cloth-bound 'firsts' in Section I.

In the present Section 'condition' is rarely recorded. The vast majority of the items described are very fine, and to say so repeatedly would be tedious. Wherever a serious defect occurs I have noted it. Similarly 'provenance' is only given in the case of large-scale yellow-back collectors such as J. R. Molineux, John Browne and one or two others. I benefited so greatly from the assiduity and care shown by these individuals that it would have been ungracious not to register them as former owners.

I would like in this place—if possible once and for all—to scotch the legend that W. H. Smith invented (and published) yellow-backs, and that a *Cranford* of 1857 was the first specimen to be published. Smith did *not* invent yellow-backs, nor did he *publish* yellow-backs over his firm's name. Dozens of yellow-backs appeared prior to 1857, including a *Cranford* (Chapman & Hall). This *canard* (it is nothing less) was started by a privately printed house-history of W. H. Smith & Son, and, despite reiterated denials, was still current in 1948 when these lines were written.

For a general essay on the 'Yellow-Back' as a publishing phenomenon, I may be permitted to refer to my contribution to *New Paths in Book-Collecting* (edited by John Carter, 1934), which contribution was separately issued in 1938 in the series *Aspects of Book-Collecting*.

[3393] ACME LIBRARY (The) 1894–1896

Published by Archibald Constable & Co. in narrow fcap 8vo at 1*s.* in wrappers, 1*s.* 6*d.* in cloth, this series of original novelettes was designed to profit by the success of Fisher Unwin's 'Pseudonym' Library. Unfortunately, like Cassell's Pocket Library (3741 below), it was just too late, the public taste for such ventures having faded.

The wrappered issue was in grey-green, lettered in dark blue; the cloth issue in dark blue ribbed cloth, blocked and lettered in gold. Series title appears on front cover of both issues and on spine and back of wrappered issues, as well as on half-title of Vol. I and, from Vol. II onward, on leaf preceding half-title. The volumes, as listed on this leaf, are numbered. Titles asterisked are not in the Collection.

1 THE PARASITE by CONAN DOYLE (see 748 in Section I)
2 *THE WATTER'S MOU' by BRAM STOKER
3 *A QUESTION OF COLOUR by F. C. PHILIPS
4 A BUBBLE by L. B. WALFORD
5 *FROM SHADOW TO SUNLIGHT by THE MARQUIS OF LORNE
6 *THE RED SPELL by FRANCIS GRIBBLE
7 *AN IMPRESSIONIST DIARY by HELMUTH SCHWARTZE
8 A FEMININE CONVICTION by GEORGE ST. GEORGE
9 *AN ENGAGEMENT by SIR ROBERT PEEL, BART
10 DR KOOMAHDI OF ASHANTEE by F. FRANKFORT MOORE
11 *ANGELA'S LOVER by DOROTHEA GERARD

Note. Under 'Doyle' in Section I will be found mention of a re-issue of *The Parasite* in yellow cloth. No. 10 above was similarly re-issued, in scarlet cloth. I am not aware whether the entire series was so treated.

[3394] ADAMS, HENRY

Democracy: an American Novel [anon]

I. Walter Scott, n.d. Cream boards patterned in red and blue.

II. Ward and Lock, n.d. [1882]. Pictorial boards.

[3395] AIMARD'S (GUSTAVE) TALES OF INDIAN LIFE 1860–1864; 1877

Original Issue. This series (which ran to 26 vols.) was edited by Sir Lascelles Wraxall, who grouped such stories as had affiliations and from time to time provided a schedule of each group in a Foreword, showing the order in which the tales should be read. This order is here retained, although it was not necessarily the order of actual publication.

Unless otherwise stated, each volume is in bright-coloured paper boards, decoratively and effectively lettered in two different and contrasting colours. Series title: 'Aimard's Tales of Indian Life', appears on front cover and on spine. All are of small format and were published at 2*s*. each. Titles asterisked are not in the Collection.

Group I:

THE TRAPPERS OF ARKANSAS, or the Loyal Heart. Ward & Lock 1864.

THE BORDER RIFLES: a Tale of the Texan War. Ward & Lock 1861.

THE FREEBOOTERS: a Story of the Texan War. Ward & Lock 1861.

THE WHITE SCALPER: a Story of the Texan War. Ward & Lock 1861.

Group II:

THE ADVENTURERS: a Story of a Love Chase. Ward & Lock 1863.

The Pearl of the Andes: a Tale of Love and Adventure. J. A. Berger, n.d. Yellow-back pictorial boards with series title: 'The Aimard Library', on spine.

Undoubtedly this is a re-issue by another publisher of a book originally published by Ward & Lock. Judging from an advert. on back cover Berger took over the whole list of Aimard titles.

*THE TRAIL HUNTER 1861 [March]

THE PIRATES OF THE PRAIRIES: Adventures in the American Desert. Ward & Lock 1861 [April 1].

*THE TRAPPER'S DAUGHTER. Ward & Lock 1861.

†THE TIGER SLAYER: a Tale of the Indian Desert. Ward & Lock 1860.

THE GOLD SEEKERS : a Tale of California. Ward & Lock 1861 [January 1].

THE INDIAN CHIEF: the Story of a Revolution. Ward & Lock 1861 [February 1].

*THE RED TRACK. Ward & Lock 1862.

Group III:

PRAIRIE FLOWER: Adventures on the Indian Border. Ward & Lock 1861.

THE INDIAN SCOUT: a Story of the Aztec City. Ward & Lock 1861.

Ungrouped:

THE LAST OF THE INCAS: a Romance of the Pampas. Ward & Lock 1862.

This title was re-issued after 1884 in pictorial boards with no series title, but on spine 'With Illustrations', which were certainly never present in this edition.

THE SMUGGLER CHIEF: a Novel. Ward & Lock 1864.

† This was the first of the whole Aimard Series to be published [December 1, 1860]. Wraxall, in his Foreword, states that the French regard Aimard as their Fenimore Cooper, and that he lived for many years *as an Indian* among the Indians of North America, actually experiencing most of the adventures described in his novels.

In addition to those mentioned, the following Aimard titles are not in the Collection:

Queen of the Savannah	Stoneheart	Insurgent Chief
Buccanier (sic) Chief	The Bee Hunters	Flying Horseman
Stronghand	Guide of the Desert	

All these were of later issue than the grouped titles, and I cannot be certain that all were originally published by Ward and Lock.

Second Issue: 'Revised and Edited by Percy B. St John' Twenty-nine volumes, issued in white [3395 *a*] wrappers cut flush, pictorially printed and lettered in brown and black. All are imprinted either 'J. & R. Maxwell and George Vickers' or 'J. & R. Maxwell' only, except No. 10 (imprint: 'George Vickers' only) and No. 19 (imprint: 'Spencer Blackett, succ. to J. & R. Maxwell'). Only No. 10 is dated. Titles asterisked are not in the Collection.

1	***Trappers of Arkansas**	11	**Indian Scout**	21	**Trail Hunter**
2	**Border Rifles**	12	**Stronghand**	22	**Pirates of the Prairies**
3	**Freebooters**	13	**Bee Hunters**	23	**Trapper's Daughter**
4	**White Scalper**	14	**Stoneheart**	24	**Tiger Slayer**
5	**Guide of the Desert**	15	***Queen of the Savannah**	25	**Gold Seekers**
6	**Insurgent Chief**	16	**Buccaneer Chief**	26	**Indian Chief**
7	**Flying Horseman**	17	***Smuggler Hero**	27	**Red Track**
8	**Last of the Incas**	18	**Rebel Chief**	28	**Treasure of Pearls**
9	**Missouri Outlaws**	19	**Adventurers**	29	**Red River Half Breed**
10	**Prairie Flower** 1877	20	***Pearl of the Andes**		

See also ROUTLEDGE'S ORIGINAL NOVELS (3672 (18) below).

AINSWORTH

AINSWORTH, W. H.

[3396] (A) FIRST UNIFORM COLLECTED EDITION, **which includes the First Book Edition of 'Auriol'.** 14 vols. Small slim 8vo. Chapman & Hall 1850–1851.

This 'Cheap Uniform Edition' was issued monthly from December 1849, at first at 1*s.* and 1*s.* 6*d.* in boards, then alternatively at 2*s.* and 2*s.* 6*d.* in cloth. In my experience the series is very uncommon, and I have not succeeded in acquiring a complete set in either binding. The volumes are extremely elegant
Pl. 1 in design, both in boards and cloth. The cloth issue was not made until the series had been under way for at least four months and was then retrospective. A slip in Vol. VI announces Vol. VII in boards *and* cloth, and the advert. on back covers makes no mention of cloth until at about the same juncture. This delay in cloth issue accounts for the discrepancies on individual titles between the numbers of copies stated to have been printed of certain titles, e.g. Vol. I boards is 15th thousand, cloth 19th thousand; Vol. VII boards has no statement, cloth 9th thousand. Vols. I–XII are dated 1850, Vols. XIII and XIV 1851. In each a series title, bearing volume number, precedes individual title.

Board Issue. Yellow paper boards, printed in very dark blue and red—on front with all-over design and lettering; on spine up-lettered in blue with design, title and volume number; on back with advert. of series. White end-papers unless otherwise stated.

Cloth Issue. Olive-green fine-ribbed cloth, blocked in blind on front and back; on spine in gold with design; AINSWORTH'S / WORKS / VOL. I (etc.) at head, title of novel at tail. Yellow end-papers unless otherwise stated.

In the schedule which follows items asterisked are not in the Collection. Vol. XII, AURIOL, is set in caps and analysed because this is the first book edition of the unfinished romance which, with fine illustrations by Phiz, appeared serially, first in *Ainsworth's Magazine* during 1844 and 1845 under the title 'Revelations of London', then in the *New Monthly Magazine* during 1845 and 1846 under the title 'Auriol'. Strangely enough, this book edition of 1850 has not previously been noticed by bibliographers. Slater in *Early Editions*, Ellis in *Ainsworth and his Friends* and Locke in his *Bibliographical Catalogue of Ainsworth*, all state that no book edition was published until the ugly Routledge 8vo of 1865; and this mis-statement is repeated in the *C.B.E.L.* (doubtless on the authority of Slater, Ellis and Locke) even though the existence of a Collected Edition of 1850–51 is recorded.

Vol. I **Windsor Castle** *Boards* *Cloth*
Both editions have pale blue flowered end-papers and contain a 'Memoir of the Author' by Laman Blanchard, originally printed in *The Mirror* in 1842.

Vol. II **Rookwood** * Cloth (end-papers as I)

Vol. III **Crichton** Boards Cloth
This edition contains a new dedication to Mrs James Touchet, dated January 10, 1850.

Vol. IV **The Miser's Daughter** * *

Vols. V, VI **The Tower of London** * Cloth

Vol. VII **St James's** Boards Cloth

Vols. VIII, IX **Old St Paul's** * Cloth

Vol. X **Guy Fawkes** * *

Vol. XI **Jack Sheppard** Boards *

Vol. XII AURIOL: Fragment of a Romance. Also 'The Old London Merchant' and 'A Night's Adventure in Rome'.
pp. 128 Pp. (1) (2) Series title, verso blank; (3) Individual title; (4) Printer's imprint; (5) (6) Fly-title to 'Auriol', verso blank; (7)–110 'Auriol'; (111)–116 'The Old London Merchant'†; (117)–128 'A Night's Adventure in Rome'. * Cloth

Vols. XIII, XIV **The Lancashire Witches** * *

† Curiously enough this story had already appeared in book form in Vol. I of *The Pic Nic Papers*, 3 vols. 1841. (See 703 in Section I.)

[3396*a*] (B) INDIVIDUAL TITLES

Boscobel. Routledge, n.d. Yellow-back pictorial boards. Small format.

Flitch of Bacon (The). 'Fourth Edition.' Routledge 1855. Yellow-back boards, printed in dark blue. Small format.

Ditto: Another. n.d. Pictorial yellow-back wrappers, cut flush. Small format.

Mervyn Clitheroe. 'New Edition.' Routledge 1859. Yellow-back pictorial boards, with cover picture re-drawn from the Phiz plate facing p. 17 of first edition. Small format. *Railway Library.*

Miser's Daughter (The). 'New Edition.' Routledge, n.d. (1877). Yellow pictorial wrappers, cut flush, with cover picture an adaptation from a Cruikshank plate in first edition. Small format. Signature dated 1877 on title.

Pl. 4 **Ovingdean Grange.** Routledge 1861. Yellow-back boards with portrait of author on front cover and vignette of the Grange on spine. Small format. *Railway Library.*

Tower of London (The).

Copy I: 'New Edition.' Routledge 1858. Flame pictorial boards. Small format. *Pl. 4*

An exceptionally striking production, brilliant in colour and well drawn. The price on front is given as 'TWO SHILLINGS OR FIFTY CENTS'.

Copy II. Routledge, n.d. Pale yellow pictorial wrappers, cut flush.

A commonplace production of the eighties or even later.

ALEXANDER, MRS

Blind Fate. 'New Edition.' Chatto and Windus, 1897. White pictorial boards [3397]

AMUSING LIBRARY (The) 1885 [3398]

Lambert & Co., 63 Paternoster Row and, later, 462 New Oxford Street. Published in decorated boards at two shillings (or in cloth or half-bound at half-a-crown, or in cloth gilt at three shillings), the volumes in this series are described as 'Original Tales, also Translations and Reprints of Popular Works'. Below are given only those titles in the Collection which are first, or first English, editions. The series is not of sufficient general interest to justify listing in full, being mainly collections of regional legends and historical tales. Each volume is of small format, with end-papers printed with adverts.

CONSCIENCE, HENDRIK

The four volumes which follow are uniformly bound in primrose yellow boards, decoratively printed in red and green and lettered in black. The spine is headed 'Conscience's Tales' and at base reads 'London. 1855'. No series title on outside covers. The adverts. of the series on the end-papers make clear that these are authorised translations from the Flemish, of material not previously published in English. The title asterisked is not in the Collection. [3398 *a*]

I THE CURSE OF THE VILLAGE and THE HAPPINESS OF BEING RICH 1855

Wood-engraved front. on text paper and occasional text decorations.

pp. (viii)+(134) S_8–T_3 adverts.

II THE LION OF FLANDERS, or The Battle of the Golden Spurs 1855

Wood-engraved front. and vignette title on plate paper, but reckoned in collation. No printed title.

pp. x+360

III VEVA: or the War of the Peasants. An Historical Tale 1855

Wood-engraved front. and vignette title on plate paper and not reckoned in the collation. No printed title.

pp. xii+256

IV *TALES OF OLD FLANDERS

V THE MISER and RICKETICKETACK 1855

Wood-engraved vignette title, faced by a decoration, on plate paper, and not reckoned in the collation.

pp. 64 Publishers' cat., 16 pp. undated, at end.

GÉRARD, JULES

LIFE AND ADVENTURES OF JULES GÉRARD, THE 'LION KILLER' (1855) [3398 *b*]

Pink boards printed in black. Series title 'Amusing Library' on front cover and spine. Wood-engraved front. and vignette title on plate paper precede printed title and are not reckoned in the collation.

Half-title pp. xx+202 [First leaf of final sig., O_1, a single inset.] Publishers' cat., 16 pp. undated, at end.

Book-plate of P. Z. Cox.

HALL, MRS S. C.

POPULAR TALES AND SKETCHES 1856 [3398 *c*]

Rose pink boards, printed with floral decorations in green and crimson and lettered in black. Series title 'Amusing Library' on front cover and spine. Wood-engraved front. on text paper.

pp. viii+248 Publishers' cat., 16 pp. undated, at end.

'ANONYMA' SERIES

[3399] ANON

Terrible Tales: French and German. W. W. Gibbings, 18 Bury Street, n.d. Cream pictorial boards.

Terrible Tales: Italian and Spanish. Uniform with above.

Note. These tales were originally issued in four volumes in cloth.

[3400] 'ANONYMA' SERIES 1864; 1884

The authorship of this reputedly licentious series of stories about the smart world, the half-world and the underworld of Victorian London (and elsewhere) has never been established. The books have been attributed to Bracebridge Hemyng, to W. Stephens Hayward and to E. L. Blanchard. The attribution to Hemyng is the most categorical. In *A Brief History of Boys' Journals* by Ralph Rollington (Leicester, H. Simpson [1913]) appears the following: 'Brace Hemyng was a most prolific writer....I am indebted to J.S.G. of Sheffield for the following list, which was published in a recent letter to T.P.'s Weekly. He wrote several serials for the *London Journal*,...etc....etc....etc....The *Skittles* and *Kate Hamilton* group...etc....etc.' In support of this direct attribution may be added the reminder that Hemyng was the avowed author of the Prostitution section in Mayhew's *London Labour and the London Poor* (1861); and the two together seem to me convincing evidence that Hemyng was responsible for at least the earlier 'Anonyma' books.

But I hesitate to regard it as proof that he was the author of the whole series, which, in all probability, developed into a product of a syndicate. Certainly, as time went on and new titles of a somewhat different kind were added, the 'Author of Skittles' or the 'Author of Anonyma' became credited with stories for which previously credit had been given elsewhere. Further, the later writer or writers were worse equipped for authorship than Hemyng, the style becoming deplorable and the dialogue so stilted as to be comic. Nevertheless, although to anyone in search of impudicity the whole series proves a grave disappointment, the books provide much evidence of the lives, manners and haunts of the men upon town, their women and their hangers-on, and the descriptive background is certainly authentic.

Perhaps it is misleading to speak of the 'Anonyma' Series; and I hope no one will so far misunderstand the term as to imagine a formal series of the *Parlour Library* class. Actually the success of the first two volumes created a sort of group-popularity for books of a more or less similar kind. Several appeared within two or three years over various imprints; and then, in the middle eighties, were all reprinted by C. H. Clarke in a uniform edition. The issue of this (virtually) sham collected edition not only gave the impression that the books were all from one hand, but also that they belonged together from the first, and therefore created a 'series', even though no series title was given them. For convenience sake alone, I make use of this imaginary series title, but endeavour, in describing the individual books, to show how unreal it is.

The actual first editions of the 'Anonyma' Series in original condition are of the greatest rarity, and some I have never seen. Even the Clarke re-issue is very uncommon; but as it is a graceless production (a yellow-back of the most mechanical kind) failure to locate copies need only provoke a passing regret.

Where there is doubt whether a book is a first edition, I have said so in the entries which follow. The Clarke re-issue is frankly so described. It may be noted that all the Clarke volumes carry on their back end-papers (i) an announcement of a 'New and Uniform Two Shilling Edition of the following Popular Works', i.e. 14 volumes from *Anonyma* to *Delilah*, all anonymous;* (ii) a new edition at Two Shillings of the novels of W. Stephens Hayward. Probably the juxtaposition of these adverts. has encouraged the general attribution of the 'Anonyma' Series to Hayward.

[3401] ANONYMA, or Fair but Frail. A Romance of West End Life, Manners and 'Captivating' People [anon]

Copy I: First Edition. George Vickers, Angel Court 1864. Pictorial yellow-back boards. Small format.

Half-title. pp. (viii)+(328)

Note. Outside back cover printed with advert. of (Ward & Lock's) 'Shilling Volume Library'.

Very fine. Spine slightly chipped at head.

Copy II: C. H. Clarke re-issue, entitled: [3401 *a*]
'Anonyma, or Fair but Frail.' n.d. [1884].

* Of these 14 titles, the only one not in the Collection, either in first edition or reprint, is *Agnes Willoughby*, while of titles hereafter noticed Clarke's 'Series' does not include *London by Night*, *Bel Demonio*, *Cora Pearl*, *The Women of Paris*, *The Women of London* (which I have never seen), *Leah* and *Mabel Gray*—nor, of course, *Fast Life* and *Lola Montez*.

Large format. Pictorial cream-back boards. Same picture on cover. Description of authorship as on *Love Frolics of a Young Scamp*, Copy II (q.v.).

[3401 *b*] **Copy III: Unauthorised reprint,** entitled: 'Anonyma: a Tale of Female Life and Adventure' [anon]. 'Sold by all booksellers', n.d. Pictorial yellow-back boards. Same picture on cover. Small format.

Note. Judging by its format this edition pre-dated Clarke's re-issue. But on the back cover, headed 'Uniform with Anonyma', is a list of no fewer than 20 titles. This list includes the usual 14, with, in addition: *Diary of a Physician*, *Diary of a Judge*, *Paul Peabody*, *The Wild Irish Girl*, *Rich Relations*, *Larry Lynch*, *The Love Match*, *The Lady With Golden Hair* and *The Deserted Wife*. The implied connection between *Anonyma etc.* and novels known to be by (among others) Lady Morgan, R. B. Brough and Cockton exemplifies the bewilderment caused to later investigators by the slapdash methods of yellow-back pirates.

This is a poor copy.

[3402] ANNIE, or the Life of a Lady's Maid. Carrying a full description of all the Curious Occurrences, Intrigues, Amours, Expedients of Fashionable Gay Life among the Aristocracy

Copy I: First Edition. 'Never before Printed' [anon]. George Vickers, Angel Court 1864. Cont. half-calf (originally pictorial boards). Small format.

pp. (iv) + 316

Described on title as 'Uniform with Skittles etc.'

[3402 *a*] **Copy II: C. H. Clarke re-issue.** n.d. [1884]. Pictorial cream-back boards. Soiled. Large format. Description of authorship (virtually) as on *Love Frolics of a Young Scamp*, Copy II.

Only the first sub-title used on this edition.

[3403] BEAUTIFUL DEMON (The): a Romance (by the author of 'Leah', 'Hunted to Death', etc., i.e. W. Stephens Hayward). 'Never before printed'

George Vickers 1864. Pictorial yellow-back boards. Small format.

Half-title. pp. viii + 296

Described on front cover as 'Uniform with "Incognita"'. Many of the 'Anonyma' titles are advertised on back cover without hint of authorship, but including *The Beautiful Demon* itself, which is recorded as 'by the author of *The Black Angel*' (i.e., once again, W. Stephens Hayward). The Preface is initialled 'W.S.H.'

Ink signature: 'Charles Penruddock', on title. Fine.

Note. This is an adaptation of Féval's *Bel Demonio*, condensed and with altered names, but largely the same story. The Preface admits the tale to be founded on a French romance, while claiming virtuously that 'many episodes, scenes and dialogues at variance with English notions have been wholly avoided'.

BEL DEMONIO: a Love Story (by Paul Féval. Translated by Bertha Browne). 'Never before Published' [3404]

Ward & Lock 1863. Pictorial yellow-back boards. Small format.

pp. iv + (396)

Described on front cover as 'Uniform with "The Duke's Motto"' (also by Féval).

Ink signature: 'Charles Penruddock', on title. Very fine.

CORA PEARL (by the author of 'Anonyma', 'Skittles', 'Left Her Home', 'Kate Hamilton', 'Incognita', 'Soiled Dove', 'Skittles in Paris', etc. etc.) [3405]

E. Griffiths, Catherine Street, n.d. Pictorial yellow-back boards. Small format.

pp. iv + 316

Outside back-cover advert. identical with that on *Love Frolics of a Young Scamp* and *Lady Detective*.

Note. In contrast to *Revelations of a Lady Detective*, this volume looks like an inferior issue. The pictorial cover is coarsely designed and printed, and the end-papers, instead of being plain, are printed with commercial adverts. But the type is clean and the format of the same small size as companion volumes which are certainly first editions.

DELILAH, or the Little House in Piccadilly [3406]

C. H. Clarke re-issue, n.d. [1884]. Pictorial cream-back boards. Large format.

Description of authorship (virtually) as on *Love Frolics of a Young Scamp*, Copy II.

Spine torn and partially detached.

FAST LIFE: an Autobiography. Being the Recollections, Rencounters, Reverses and Reprisals of a Man Upon Town in London and Paris:... together with Details of the Amours of the Marquis of Waterford, etc. etc. [anon] [3407]

Vickers, n.d. [1859]. Pale yellow boards overprinted in orange, and lettered in pale yellow in reverse and also directly in dark blue. Small format.

pp. 256 [paged (i)–iv + (5)–256]

Soiled and spine lacking.

Note. I include this book (written by J. Lennox) under 'Anonyma' Series on grounds of subject. It is unconnected with the 'Anonyma' group and almost certainly of earlier date. The dating suggested above is based on a catalogue entry and MS note in my copy.

[3408] FORMOSA: the Life of a Beautiful Woman

Copy I: First Edition (by the author of 'Anonyma' 'Agnes Willoughby', 'Incognita', 'Skittles', 'Left Her Home', 'Soiled Dove', 'Mabel Gray', 'Cora Pearl', etc. etc.)

E. Griffiths, 13 Catherine Street and Evans, Oliver & Co. 81 Fleet Street, n.d. Pictorial yellow-back boards. Back cover advertises as 'Never before Published' 'Mabel Gray, by the author of 'Formosa', 'Cora Pearl' and a list of thirteen numbered titles of which XII is 'Love Frolics of a Young Scamp' and XIII 'Formosa', here (and here only) described as 'Never before published'.

Half-title. pp. viii+(312) pp. (i) (ii) and (311) (312) are pasted down to inside front and back covers to serve as end-papers.

Note. Probable date 1869/1870, being based on a Boucicault melodrama of the same name produced in 1869.

[3408 *a*] **Copy II: C. H. Clarke re-issue,** n.d. [1884]. Pictorial cream-back boards. Large format.

Description of authorship (differently arranged) as on *Love Frolics of a Young Scamp*, Copy II. Fine.

[3409] INCOGNITA: a Tale of Love and Passion

C. H. Clarke re-issue, n.d. [1884]. Pictorial cream-back boards by Phiz. Large format.

Description of authorship (differently arranged) as on *Love Frolics of a Young Scamp*, Copy II. Fine.

[3410] KATE HAMILTON: an Autobiography

C. H. Clarke re-issue, n.d. [1884]. Pictorial cream-back boards (? by Phiz). Large format.

Description of authorship as on *Love Frolics of a Young Scamp*, Copy II.

[3411] LEAH: the Jewish Maiden [anon]. 'Never before published'

Ward & Lock 1864. Cont. half-calf (originally pictorial yellow-back boards). Small format.

pp. (iv)+316

[3412] LEFT HER HOME: a Tale of Female Life and Adventure, in which the fortunes and Misfortunes of a Charming Girl are narrated (by 'Anonyma', 'Never before printed')

George Vickers, Angel Court 1864. Pictorial yellow-back boards (by Phiz). Small format.

pp. iv+(316)

This copy lacks spine.

[3413] LOLA MONTEZ (Countess of Lansfeld), Lectures of; including her Autobiography

Ward & Lock 1858. Yellow-back pictorial boards. Small format.

Half-title. pp. 192

Ink stamp: 'J. R. Molineux', on verso of half-title. Very fine.

Note. Front cover gives title as LECTURES AND LIFE OF LOLA MONTEZ (with inverted z), GILBERT'S EDITION. Like *Fast Life*, this book has no connection with the 'Anonyma' Series, but was frequently reprinted and sold with them, and was treated by the trade as in their category.

LONDON BY NIGHT (by the author of 'Anonyma', 'Skittles', 'Left Her Home', 'Kate Hamilton', 'Agnes Willoughby', 'Incognita', 'The Soiled Dove', 'Woman (sic) of London', 'Skittles in Paris', 'The Woman (sic) of Paris', 'Annie, or the Life of a Lady's Maid') [3414] *Pl. 3*

Copy I: First Edition. 8vo. William Oliver, 3 Amen Corner, n.d. [? early seventies. See note]. Pictorial white-back boards. Back outside cover advertises a work called *Social Contrasts,* consisting of 22 coloured lithographs by William Gray. Yellow end-papers. Coloured lithographic front., pictorial title and 10 plates (of which one a double folding one) by William Gray.

Half-title. pp. (viii)+176

Note. This is the most remarkable piece of yellow-back publishing I have ever seen. Full 8vo in format, elaborately illustrated (with a cover drawing not repeated inside) and priced at five shillings, it deserves commemoration as a show-piece of book-making, if for no other reason. The plates are only in two cases illustrations to the story; but the majority are really valuable in that they depict the interiors of actual taverns and night-houses and scenes in pleasure gardens. The folding plate shows the Alhambra underground canteen; others of the plates show the Argyll Rooms, Cremorne, The Holborn, Scotts, Rose Young's and Paddy's Goose.

The only hint as to date of publication is that Renton Nicholson and Kate Hamilton have been dead a few years and that *London by Night* has been 'greatly shorn of its glories of late years'. Nicholson died in 1861 and Kate Hamilton in the middle sixties. It seems almost certain therefore that *London by Night* appeared in the early seventies, after the clean-up of 1870 and during the final decadence of the Argyll Rooms.

Copy II: Re-issue. The book was re-issued at an unspecified date over the imprint of Evans & Co., 81 Fleet Street. This imprint appears on front and back covers, but the pictorial title still carries the original imprint of William Oliver. The text is printed from the plates (considerably worn) of the first edition; and the cover drawing and illustrations are printed from the same *basic* blocks, but differently and more economically coloured. For example, the pictorial title in Copy I is printed on a greenish-drab ground in black, rose, yellow and blue; in Copy II it is printed in black only. The plates in the book mostly show one colour-printing less in Copy II than in Copy I. [3414*a*]

The covers of Copy II are of dull, not glazed paper. The outside back cover, actually under the heading: 'THE ANONYMA SERIES', advertises at 2s. 4d. each in 'fancy coloured boards' *Anonyma, Skittles, Annie, Soiled Dove, Love Frolics of a Young Scamp, Kate Hamilton, Incognita, Beautiful Demon, Lady Detective, Agnes Willoughby, Skittles in Paris, Left Her Home*; and as 'uniform with the above' *The Lady with the Golden Hair*. This list does not include *Delilah* and *Formosa*, which formed volumes of Clarke's re-issue. I have never seen any of these books with Evans' imprint.

[3415] LOVE FROLICS OF A YOUNG SCAMP

Copy I: First Edition. 'Related by Himself and edited by Charles Martel. Never before printed.' E. Griffiths, 13 Catherine Street 1864. Pictorial cream-back boards [I think by Phiz]. Small format.

pp. iv + 316

Note. Outside back cover, over Griffiths' imprint, advertises: *Cora Pearl* (as 'never before printed'); *The Finest Girl in Bloomsbury* [by Augustus Mayhew] and as 'Companion volumes to *Cora Pearl*'; *Anonyma, Skittles, Annie, Left Her Home, Kate Hamilton, Agnes Willoughby, Incognita, Lady Detective, Beautiful Demon, Skittles in Paris, The Soiled Dove*,....

It will be observed that 1864 is the year of first publication (by Vickers) of *Anonyma* and *Skittles* and one wonders whether Griffiths' date on this volume is a false one or whether, maybe, his imprint and Vickers' (and perhaps others) were interchangeable conveniences in case of trouble.

[3415 *a*] **Copy II: C. H. Clarke re-issue.** n.d. [1884]. Large format. Same picture on cover.

Note. In this edition the book is described as 'By the author of *Anonyma, Skittles, Annie, Left Her Home, The Soiled Dove, The Lady Detective, The Beautiful Demon, Delilah, Skittles in Paris, Agnes Willoughby, Incognita, Kate Hamilton, Formosa*'.

As can be seen, on the first edition of one at least of these books* a quite different authorship was given, and one should, I think, view Clarke's wholesale attributions with some suspicion.

[3416] MABEL GRAY, or Cast on the Tide (by the author of 'Anonyma', 'Skittles', etc.)

F. W. Garnham, 44 Ludgate Hill, n.d. Cont. half-calf (originally pictorial boards). Small format.

pp. (iv) + 316

Note. This imprint occurs nowhere else in my experience. Perhaps the ascription to the author of *Skittles* was an unscrupulous attempt at 'passing-off'. It should be noted that *Mabel Gray* is *not* included in C. H. Clarke's standard list of the 'Anonyma' Series, nor does it appear on his title-pages among the works regularly attributed to one writer. Date 1869/1870.

* *Beautiful Demon* (3403 above).

REVELATIONS OF A LADY DETECTIVE (by the author of 'Anonyma', 'Incognita', 'Skittles', etc.) [3417] *Pl. 2*

Copy I: First Edition. E. Griffiths, Catherine Street, n.d. Pictorial yellow-back boards. Small format.

pp. (iv) + 308

Outside back-cover advert. identical with that on *Love Frolics of a Young Scamp* Copy I, i.e. without 'Formosa'. Very fine.

Note. Presumably published in the late 'sixties between 'Love Frolics' and 'Formosa'.

Copy II: C. H. Clarke re-issue. n.d. Pictorial yellow-back boards (picture totally different and very inferior to Copy I). Large format. Fine. Price-label on spine. [3417 *a*]

Description of authorship as on *Love Frolics* Copy II, but differently arranged.

SKITTLES: a Biography of a Fascinating Woman. Companion to 'Anonyma'. 'Never before published' (anon) [3418] *Pl. 2*

George Vickers 1864. Pictorial yellow-back boards. Small format.

pp. iv + 316 Very fine.

Note. Outside back cover printed with advert. of three publications by Vickers, including *Anonyma*, which is here described (though not on the book itself) as 'never before published'.

SKITTLES IN PARIS: a Biography of a Fascinating Woman [3419] *Pl. 2*

C. H. Clarke re-issue, n.d. [1884]. Pictorial cream-back boards [I think by Phiz]. Large format.

Description of authorship (virtually) as on *Love Frolics of a Young Scamp*, Copy II. Loose in covers.

SOILED DOVE (The): a Biography of 'The Kitten', a Pretty Young Lady who...etc. etc. 'Never before printed' [3420]

Copy I: First Edition. Published for the Proprietors. Sold by all booksellers, 1863. Pictorial yellow-back boards. Small format.

pp. iv + 316

This is a poor copy. The picture on cover is totally different from that on Copy II.

Note. Although the cover of this book is poorly reproduced, the dated title and the appearance of the type suggest that it is a first edition. The back cover advertises Mayhew's *Finest Girl in Bloomsbury*, Dumas' *Lady with the Golden Hair* and St John's *Paul Peabody*.

Copy II: C. H. Clarke re-issue. n.d. [1884]. Pictorial cream back boards, by Phiz. Large format. [3420 *a*]

Description of authorship (virtually) as on *Love Frolics of a Young Scamp*, Copy II.

'ANONYMA' SERIES

[3421] WOMEN OF PARIS (The): a Romance (by the author of 'Women of London', etc. etc.)

George Vickers, Angel Court, n.d. Pictorial yellow-back boards. Large format. Outside back cover advertises Miss Braddon's novels over the imprint of J. and R. Maxwell. Spine worn.

Note. This looks like an original issue, probably dating from the mid-seventies. It complicates still further the general problem of authorship, for it and its companion volume *Women of London* are surely the books listed as *The Woman of Paris* and *Woman of London* on the half-title of *London by Night* (q.v.) and there attributed to the author of *Anonyma*, *Skittles* and the rest.

[3422] ARMSTRONG, CAPT. C. F.

Cruise of the Daring (The)

I Ward & Lock, n.d. Yellow pictorial boards. Small format. *Library of Popular Authors.*

II Ward & Lock, n.d. [circa 1881]. *Select Library.*

Lily of Devon (The). Henry Lea, n.d. [1861]. Yellow pictorial boards, specially drawn spine. Small format.

Sailor Hero (The), or The Frigate and the Lugger. Ward & Lock, n.d. Yellow pictorial boards. Small format. *Library of Popular Authors.*

The following are all in pictorial boards, pink, yellow and greenish white. Large format.

Sunny South (The). Ward & Lock, n.d. [after 1884]. *Select Library.*

Two Midshipmen (The). Routledge, n.d. [after 1884].

War Hawk (The). Routledge, n.d. [after 1885].

Young Commander (The). Ward & Lock, n.d. [after 1882]. *Select Library.*

[3423] ARROWSMITH'S BRISTOL LIBRARY 1884–1906

Certain titles in this long and important series appear under their authors' names in Section I (e.g. Besant, Conway). It has not seemed worth while recording the series in full in the present section, as a complete list of titles is easily available in the *English Catalogue*, and the later volumes nearly always contain clear and consistent schedules of the books published. The Library ran to 95 volumes.

One word of warning may save the first edition hunter occasional disappointment. Make sure, before assuming that a volume in the Bristol Library is a 'first', that the work had not previously been published as an Arrowsmith Christmas Annual, and then, when its seasonal career was over, been incorporated in the publishers' flourishing permanent series.

[3424] ARROWSMITH'S TWO SHILLING SERIES 1889

8 vols. Crown 8vo. Greenish white morocco-grain paper boards, decoratively printed and lettered in dark brown and salmon. Series title and volume number at base of spine and on verso of title. Back cover printed with advert. Every story is a first edition. Those asterisked are not in the Collection.

I *DEAD MEN'S DOLLARS, by May Crommelin

II *ON THE WRONG TACK, by A. E. Wilton

III THE TRUTH ABOUT CLEMENT KER. Edited by George Fleming

IV ELIZABETH MORLEY, by Katherine S. Macquoid (q.v. in Section I)

V FRANCIS AND FRANCES, by H. Edwards

VI *LAL, by Lorin Lathrop and Annie Wakeman

VII *MONSIGNOR, by Mrs Compton Reade

VIII *MARIA AND I, by Edgar Lee

AUTHORSHIP UNKNOWN

[3425] FATAL FITZ (The). A Sensation Novel in Six Parts, by Six 'Parties', for Six Pence

$7\frac{3}{4}'' \times 10\frac{5}{8}''$. 'Echoes from the Clubs' Offices, 19 Catherine Street 1868 [probably published in December, 1867]. Buff wrappers printed in red, dark blue and black—on front with all-over design incorporating fancy lettering in blue and in reverse, and six oval vignettes illustrating the tale; on back with advert. of 'Echoes from the Clubs', a 3*d.* weekly. Spine unlettered.

pp. 24 Very fine.

Note. This is a skilful parody of six prominent novelists, who are supposed in turn to have improvised a chapter of a sensation tale.

Part I, THE WHITE MASK, is in the style of Ouida, and introduces such Ouidaesque characters as Granville Fitz-Fulke ('The Fatal Fitz'); Louise de la Ramage; Idalia, Countess Vassilis; Lord Strathmore; Ernest Chandos and Bertie Cecil, 'The Seraph'.

Part II, SHOWING HOW THE SPECIAL CORRESPONDENT TURNED SNEAK, brings in Luke Framley, a Rural Dean; Old Mr Palliasse; Lady Glenmorris; Nora Geraghty; Sir Ram Shackle of the Income-Tax Office, and is suitably written with Trollopian nonchalance and calm.

Part III, THE DUEL, is after either Lever or the author of *Guy Livingstone* or both.

Part IV, THE FENIAN LANDING—with its opening storm; 'Well it was a night—there never was such a night. I don't know what the wind did not do that night. It blew the heads off four pots of porter the Southampton potboy was carrying to the three tide-waiters from the Yellow Dragon', etc. etc.—is of course Dickens.

Part V, THERE IS SELDOM FIRE WITHOUT SMOKE, is a fine piece of sonorous Charles-Readean indignation, with a private lunatic asylum and a lurid mansion-fire.

In Part VI, IN WHICH EVERYTHING EXPLODES, the shade of Thackeray, with the help of Philip the Widower, Lady Crawley and several flunkeys, winds up the story with playful and disjointed whimsicality.

Another work by 'the authors of The Fatal Fitz', entitled *Tales of the Twelve Calenders,* is announced on the back cover as due to appear in 'Echoes from the Clubs' 'commencing with the New Year'. The serial duly started publishing in January 1868.

PUPPET SHOWMAN'S ALBUM (The). With Contributions by the Most Eminent Light and Heavy Writers of the Day [anon] [3426]

Sq. 8vo. 'Published at the Office, 334 Strand', n.d. [1848]. Buff paper wrappers, stiffened with yellow end-papers (? by W. Hamilton), over-printed in mustard yellow with lettering in reverse. On front there are four, on back one cut-out panel, in which drawings by Gavarni are printed in black. Vignette on title and numerous cuts in the text, after Gavarni. Eight full-page wood-engravings after Gavarni (one appearing as front.) are also in this copy, but have no relevance to the text and are Grangerisations.

pp. iv + (48) [paged (i)–iv + (5)–52]

This copy is bound in half leather, marbled boards, original wrappers preserved. It belonged to Walter Hamilton, editor of *Parodies*, 6 vols. 1884–1889 (see No. 1102 in Section 1), and contains his book-plate, his signature dated May 1886, and in his hand: 'Parody Collection (very scarce, no copy in B.M. Library) W.H.' He has made several notes in the text and pasted an extract from 'Parodies Part 45' on inside back end-paper. The dating given above is his.

Note. The parodies, in prose and verse, are of Macaulay, Bulwer, Leigh Hunt, G. P. R. James, Disraeli, Dickens, T. K. Hervey, Lever, Tennyson, Carlyle, Thackeray, Ainsworth, Jerrold, Landor, Gilbert à Beckett, Charles Mackay, Mrs Trollope, Croker, Albert Smith and Coventry Patmore.

AUTONYM LIBRARY 1894–1896 [3427]

Terra-cotta wrappers 1*s.* 6*d.*, buff linen 2*s.*

This series ran to eighteen volumes and is more rarely met with than the *Pseudonym Library* on which it was modelled. The titles are listed in the *English Catalogue*. They include works by the following authors represented in the present work: Robert Buchanan, Marion Crawford, George Gissing, and Mrs Oliphant, which works are noted under their writers' names. A complete cloth set in very fine state is in the Collection.

BALZAC, HONORÉ DE

(A) YELLOW-BACKS [3428]

Eugénie Grandet. Routledge 1859. Dark yellow-back pictorial boards. Small format.

BALZAC

Country Doctor (The). 1887 [announced for inclusion in *The Balzac Series*, see below]

Cousin Pons. 1886

Magic Skin (The) 1888

Père Goriot. 1886 [English edition came out in 1878]

Apart from *Eugénie Grandet,* these are uniform large format yellow-backs, with conventional spine designs and inferior pictures on front covers. All published by Routledge.

[3428 *a*] (B) THE BALZAC SERIES

Vol. I. CÉSAR BIROTTEAU (translated by John Hawkins Simpson). Saunders, Otley & Co. 1860. Orange linen, printed in black. Series title and 'Vol. I' appear on front cover and spine.

pp. (viii) + (436) Fcap 8vo slip, printed in red, advertising *The Constitutional Press Magazine*, etc., and publishers' cat., 8 pp. dated January 1860, at end.

Booksellers' ticket: 'Coombe, Worcester', inside front cover.

Note. This cloth-bound volume is included with no justification beyond the desirability of keeping Balzac translations together. It is the only specimen of 'The Balzac Series' I have ever seen. The translator, in a Preface which ranks high among the moralising pomposities of the period, announces that his second volume will be *The Country Doctor*. Whether the book ever came out and, if so, what followed it, I do not know; but neither the B.M. nor Bodley show any trace of further volumes.

[3428 *b*] (C) LOVE IN A MASK (translated by Alice M. Ivimy)

'Copyright' A. M. Gardner & Co., 111 Shoe Lane, n.d. Coloured pictorial wrappers cut flush and lettered on front: 'The recently discovered Unpublished Novel by Honoré de Balzac.' Up-lettered on spine. Back cover printed with adverts.

Half-title. pp. (128) Publishers' adverts., 6 pp. on text paper undated, at end.

The translator's introduction states that this brief novel was first published in Paris in 1911, and the English edition probably appeared in 1912 or 1913. It is a degraded production of the 'rubber-shop' type.

[3429] BARHAM, R. H. ('Ingoldsby')

My Cousin Nicholas. 'A New Edition.' Routledge 1856. Flame pictorial boards, cover drawing by Leech. Small format. *Railway Library.*

[3430] BARING-GOULD, SABINE

Arminell. 'Third Edition.' Methuen 1891. Cream boards, printed in red-brown. Extra large format.

Eve. Chatto & Windus 1890. Pale yellow pictorial boards.

†Gaverochs (The). 'New Edition.' Smith, Elder 1890.

†John Herring. 'New Edition.' Smith, Elder 1892.

†Mehalah. 'New Edition.' Smith, Elder 1892.

Red Spider. 'New Edition.' Chatto & Windus 1890. Yellow pictorial boards.

†Richard Cable. 'New Edition.' Smith, Elder 1891.

Note. Volumes marked † are in the regulation style of Smith, Elder yellow-backs, with solid black and red design on spines.

[3431] BARKER, M. H.

Nights at Sea and Other Yarns. Henry Lea, n.d. [1857]. Bright yellow pictorial boards, specially drawn spine. Small format.

Ditto ('or Naval Life during the War'). Ward, Lock & Tyler, n.d. Yellow pictorial boards. Small format. *Household and Railway Novels.*

Top Sail-Sheet Blocks. 'New Edition.' Routledge, Warne & Routledge 1859. Yellow pictorial boards. Small format. *Railway Library.*

Warlock (The). 'New Edition.' Routledge, Warne & Routledge 1860. Yellow pictorial boards, specially drawn spine. Small format.

BEDE, CUTHBERT (Edward Bradley)

[3432] ADVENTURES OF MR VERDANT GREEN (The): an Oxford Freshman

Nathaniel Cooke (late Ingram, Cooke & Co.), Milford House 1853. Cream paper wrappers, cut flush, printed in red and black with portrait of the hero, fancy lettering and decoration after drawing by the author. Down-lettered on spine. Back cover printed with publisher's advert. Ninety wood-engraved illustrations in the text after drawings by the author.

pp. iv+(124) I_4–I_6 adverts. Spine renewed.

Note. Published at one shilling. A Second Edition, issued in the same year, shows a changed imprint on front cover. In other respects the two wrappers are identical and the words 'Second Edition' appear only on the title page. The imprint on the First Edition is: LONDON: NATHANIEL COOKE. (LATE INGRAM, COOKE & CO.) On the Second Edition it is: LONDON: NATHANIEL COOKE, MILFORD HOUSE, STRAND.

Also issued in maroon morocco cloth, pictorially blocked and lettered in gold. Spine unlettered.

[3433] FURTHER ADVENTURES OF MR VERDANT GREEN (The): an Oxford Under-Graduate

H. Ingram & Co., Milford House 1854. Cream paper wrappers, cut flush, printed in red and black in similar style to *Adventures*, but redesigned. Up-lettered on spine. Back cover printed with publishers' adverts. over the imprint: 'Office of the National Illustrated Library.' Wood-engraved front. and 49 illustrations in the text after drawings by the author.

Half-title. pp. viii+(112) H_7H_8 adverts. Fine.

Published at one shilling. A second edition was issued in the same year and is identical in collation and appearance except that the wrapper is printed in green and red instead of black and red. The words 'Second Edition' appear only on the title page.

[3434] MR VERDANT GREEN MARRIED AND DONE FOR: being the Third and Concluding Part of the Adventures of Mr Verdant Green, an Oxford Freshman

James Blackwood, Paternoster Row 1857. Cream paper wrappers, cut flush, printed in red and green with vignette of Cupid after a drawing by the author, type-set lettering and adverts. even on front cover and spine. Inside covers also printed with adverts. Numerous wood-engraved illustrations in the text after drawings by the author.

Four leaves of adverts. on thin paper precede title.

pp. iv+112 Eight pages of adverts. on text paper (paged 9–24), followed by 4 unpaged leaves of adverts. on thin paper, at end.

Published at one shilling. Spine imperfect and back cover chipped. First leaf of adverts. at beginning pasted down to front cover.

LITTLE MR BOUNCER AND HIS FRIEND, VERDANT GREEN [3435]

James Blackwood, 8 Lovell's Court, n.d. [1873]. Brown-orange bubble-grain cloth, blocked and lettered in gold. Numerous illustrations by the author on text paper.

Half-title. pp. 200 Publisher's cat., 32 pp. undated, at end.

Ink initials: 'W.H.A.', on fly-leaf. Very fine.

Note. This book was also issued in wrappers.

LOVE'S PROVOCATIONS; being Extracts... from the Diary of Miss Polly C—— [3436]

Ward & Lock 1855. Cream paper wrappers, cut flush, lithographed in red and green with a design by the author. Up-lettered on spine. Back cover, inside covers and end-papers printed with adverts. Wood-engraved front. and illustrations in the text after drawings by the author, all on text paper.

pp. 104

Published at one shilling.

MEDLEY [3437]

James Blackwood, Paternoster Row 1856. Cream paper wrappers, cut flush, printed in red and dark blue with drawing and fancy lettering after design by the author, and dated. Up-lettered on spine. Back cover printed with publisher's adverts. Wood-engraved front. and decorative title (undated), no printed title, and 27 illustrations in the text after drawings by the author, all on text paper.

pp. (112) [mispaged 114] Two leaves of adverts., publishers' and commercial, at end.

Published at one shilling. Fine.

MOTLEY: Prose and Verse: Grave and Gay [3438]

James Blackwood, Paternoster Row 1855. Cream paper wrappers, cut flush, printed in blue and black with drawing and fancy lettering after design by the author. Up-lettered on spine. Outside back cover printed with adverts. Wood-engraved front. and pictorial title (preceding printed title) and numerous illustrations in the text after drawings by the author.

Half-title. pp. (viii)+(106) Final leaf, H_5, a single inset, carrying an illustration on recto and blank on verso.

Published at one shilling.

NEARER AND DEARER: a Tale out of School: a Novelette [3439]

Bentley 1857. Cream paper boards, printed in scarlet and black with a design and fancy lettering on front and spine after a drawing by the author. Front cover design repeated on back cover. Wood-engraved front. and numerous illustrations (5 full-page and many in the text) after drawings by the author.

Half-title. pp. (x) [paged as (viii)] + (184) N_4 imprint leaf.

Ink signature: 'G. F. Truscott', inside front cover.

[3440] SHILLING BOOK OF BEAUTY (The). Edited and illustrated by Cuthbert Bede

James Blackwood, n.d. [1858 or 1859]. White wrappers, cut flush, printed in pale blue and red with design and fancy lettering after a drawing by the 'editor'. Down-lettered on spine. Back cover printed with adverts. Wood-engraved front., pictorial title and numerous text illustrations after drawings by the 'editor'.

pp. (iv) + (128) Fine.

Notes. (i) I have seen back-cover advert. in two settings—one much larger than the other.

(ii) This book contains parodies of Mrs Gore, Tennyson, Thackeray, Disraeli, Lady Blessington, Lord Carlisle and other contributors to *The Book of Beauty*.

TALES OF COLLEGE LIFE [3441]

C. H. Clarke 1856. White paper wrappers cut flush, printed in red and dark blue with design and fancy lettering. End-papers printed with adverts. Up-lettered on spine. Back cover advertises publications of David Bryce. Spine defective.

pp. (120) [mispaged (i)–vi + (9)–(120)] H_5H_6 adverts. (See 3605 (6) below.)

[3442] BESANT, WALTER (and BESANT & RICE)

All in pictorial boards, yellow or white, published by Chatto & Windus and all described as 'New Edition' unless otherwise stated. Large format.

All in a Garden Fair 1885

All Sorts and Conditions of Men 1887

Bell of St Paul's (The) 1891

Beyond the Dreams of Avarice 1897

By Celia's Arbour n.d.

Chaplain of the Fleet (The) 1884

City of Refuge (The) 1899

Dorothy Forster 1886

For Faith and Freedom 1891

Golden Butterfly (The) (B. & R.) 1886

Herr Paulus 1890

Monks of Thelema (The) (B. & R.), n.d.

Ready-Money Mortiboy (B. & R.). Extra large format. 'A New Edition with a Frontispiece.' Chatto & Windus 1877 on title; Henry S. King on spine and back cover.

Revolt of Man (The) 1898

Seamy Side (The) (B. & R.) n.d.

This Son of Vulcan (B. & R.) n.d.

T'was in Trafalgar's Bay and other Stories (B. & R.) 1887

Uncle Jack, etc. 1886

Verbena, Camellia, Stephanotis, etc. 1894

With Harp and Crown (B. & R.) n.d.

World Went Very Well Then (The) 1889

[3443] BENNETT, JOHN

REVELATIONS OF A SLY PARROT

Ward & Lock n.d. [early '60s]. Yellow pictorial boards. Small format. Numerous text illustrations. pp. viii + 312.

Bennett is described on title as author of *Tom Fox* (3535 below), *Family Mysteries, Night and Day* and *Career of an Artful Dodger* (3503 below), which authorships are now first established.

[3444] BENTLEY'S RAILROAD LIBRARY (alias 'Bentley's Shilling Series') 1851–1854

Pl. 7 Published in fcap 8vo and bound in bright green boards pictorially printed in brown, up-lettered on spine, back cover printed with adverts. The series title on front cover is BENTLEY'S SHILLING SERIES, but facing title BENTLEY'S RAILROAD LIBRARY.

Like the rest of Bentley's (remarkably few) board issues, the books were fragile, and are rarely seen in fine state. *Only the titles asterisked are in the Collection.* Those in caps are first book editions or first editions in English. Original publication dates of reprints are given in brackets.

The binding was changed to one of glazed yellow wrappers printed in black, with (or approximately with) No. 18. The numbering is mine, as the volumes are not numbered in series.

1 Comic English Grammar 1851 [1840]

2 *Notes on Noses (anon; by George Jabet) 1851 (dated 1852) [1848 as 'Naseology by Eden Warwick']

3 TURF CHARACTERS (anon; by James White) 1851 (dated 1852)

4 Martin Toutrond (Morier) 1852 [1848]

5 NIGHTS AT SEA ('THE OLD SAILOR', i.e. M. H. BARKER) 1852

6 LOSS OF THE AMAZON STEAM-VESSEL (anon) 1852

7 *Border Tales (Maxwell) 1852 [1847]

8 Glimpse at the Great Western Republic (Cunynghame) 1852 [1851]

9 *Comic Tales and Sketches (Albert Smith) 1852 [1848, extracted from *The Wassail Bowl*]

10 Broad Grins from China (Sealy) 1852 [1841 as *The Porcelain Tower*]

11 *Pictures of Life at Home and Abroad (Albert Smith) 1852 [1848, extracted from *The Wassail Bowl*]

12 Sketches of English Character (Gore) 1852 [1846]

13 *Battle of Waterloo (Creasy) 1852 [Extracted, with additions, from *The Fifteen Decisive Battles of the World*, 1851]

14 BRILLIANT MARRIAGE (A) (CARLEN) 1852

15 COLUMBA (MÉRIMÉE) 1853

16 CHRONICLE OF THE REIGN OF CHARLES IX (MÉRIMÉE) 1853

17 John Drayton (Oliphant) 1853 [1851]

18 Stella and Vanessa (de Wailly) 1853 [1850]

19 Ned Myers (edited by Cooper) 1853 [1843]

20 *Two Brothers (from the German of M. Raven 1853 [1850] (yellow wrappers)

21 Stanley Thorn (Cockton) 1853 [1841]

22 Basil (Collins) 1854 [1852]

23 Lord and Lady Harcourt (Sinclair) 1854 [1850]

24 Rubber of Life (Dalton Barham) 1854 [1841, with *My Cousin Nicholas*]

BENTLEY'S SHILLING SERIES

See BENTLEY'S RAILROAD LIBRARY

[3445] BENTLEY'S TWO SHILLING SERIES (fiction and non-fiction) 1857–1858

Published in square 8vo and bound in flat-backed boards with (in some cases) pictorial covers by Crowquill and others.

This is a curiously uncommon series and, owing to the fragile boards used for casing, is, when found, generally in poor condition. *Only the three titles asterisked are in the Collection* and most of the remainder I have never seen. Titles in caps are first editions. The books were also issued in cloth at 3*s*. The numbering is mine, as the volumes are not numbered in series.

1 It's Never Too Late to Mend (Reade). 'New Edition.' 1857 [1856]

2 *THE COURSE OF TRUE LOVE (READE) 1857. See 2001 in Section I.

3 Delhi (Mrs John Mackenzie) 1857 [1853]

4 Roughing it in the Bush (Mrs Moodie) 1857 [1852]

5 *NEARER AND DEARER (CUTHBERT BEDE) 1857. See 3439 above.

6 Conquest of Canada (Warburton) 1857 [1849]

7 Our Antipodes (Mundy) 1857 [1852]

8 Confessions of a Thug (Meadows Taylor) 1857 [1839]

9 Aspen Court (Shirley Brooks) 1857 [1855]

10 The Initials (Tautphoeus) 1858 [1850]

11 The Cardinal (Boyd) 1858 [1854]

12 *GHOST STORIES AND PHANTOM FANCIES (FRISWELL) 1858. See 909 in Section I.

[3446] BLACKMORE, R. D.

Cradock Nowell. 'New and Cheaper Edition.' Sampson Low 1893. Very pale blue pictorial boards.

Lorna Doone. '33rd edition.' Sampson Low 1889. Uniform pictorial boards.

Volumes in Low's Standard Novels, the first presenting the revised text of 1873.

BLACKWOOD'S LONDON LIBRARY

[3447] BLACKWOOD'S LONDON LIBRARY (published by James Blackwood, Paternoster Row) 1855–1858 or 1859 (thereafter a hotch-potch)

This seldom-seen series started as a collection of *new* works, fiction and otherwise, but soon degenerated into a more or less ordinary series of yellow-back reprints of popular titles. In the list which follows, titles in caps are those which I know to be first (or first English) editions; those in caps and l.c. are certainly or probably reprints; those asterisked are not in the Collection. The numbering is taken from the back cover of No. (?) 22 and was later modified. Only one of the volumes described is numbered, but all but one carry the series title on front cover. All save one are of *small* format. All back covers are printed with adverts.

1 *LIVING FOR APPEARANCES, by the BROTHERS MAYHEW 1855

2 STANHOPE BURLEIGH, by HELEN DHU [Charles Edward Lester]

Pl. 4 **Copy I: First Edition.** 1855. Pink boards, printed in black with a design after McConnell. Wood-engraved front. and pictorial title after McConnell precede printed title.

Half-title reading: BLACKWOOD'S / LONDON LIBRARY. / 2. pp. xii + 260

Pl. 4 **Copy II: Fifth Thousand,** under new title and with new cover. n.d. Pictorial yellow-back boards, with title reading: THE JESUITS IN OUR HOMES on front and spine.

Internally the book is still pictorially-titled *Stanhope Burleigh* and is identical with Copy I except (*a*) there is no half-title, (*b*) the printed title reads: *Stanhope Burleigh, or The Jesuits in our Homes,* and is undated.

This is the first English edition of an American novel published in New York in the same year.

3 *KITTY LAMERE, by AUGUSTUS MAYHEW 1855

4 ***The Duchess of Mazarin*** (? first issue of this version)

5 **Basil,** by **Wilkie Collins** 1856

6 ***The Two Brothers,** by **M. Raven**

7 ***The Husband in Utah,** by **Maria Ward**

8 ***The Ghost Seer,** by **Schiller**

9 WONDERFUL ADVENTURES OF MRS SEACOLE IN MANY LANDS (Edited by W.J.S. With a Preface by W. H. Russell) 1857

Pictorial yellow-back boards, *not* carrying series title. Double spread wood-engraved front. precedes title. Publishers' cat., 8 pp. undated, precedes half-title. It is on text-paper and actually part of first sheet, but is not reckoned in the pagination.

pp. xii + 200

Rubber stamp: 'J. R. Molineux', on front cover and title.

10 ***Costal** by **Gabriel Ferry** (probably first English edition)

11 ***Hargrave,** by **Mrs Trollope**

12 ***The Robertses on Their Travels,** by **Mrs Trollope**

13 ***The Three Cousins,** by **Mrs Trollope**

14 ***Men of Capital,** by **Mrs Gore**

15 ***Preferment,** by **Mrs Gore**

16 ***The Man About Town,** by **Cornelius Webbe** (? first English edition)

17 ***The Absent Man,** by **Cornelius Webbe** (? first English edition)

18 ***De Clifford,** by **Plumer Ward**

19 ***The Mysterious Parchment,** by **J. Wakeman**

(?) 20 **The Captain's Daughter and the Queen of Spades** (no author given)

(?) 21 THE CAVALIERS AND FREE LANCES OF NEW SPAIN, by Gabriel Ferry. n.d. [1858 or 1859].

Pictorial deep-salmon-coloured boards.

pp. (iv) + (224) O_6 adverts. Publishers' cat., 8 pp. undated, at end. Yellow slips advertising books tipped on to front fly-leaf and inside back cover.

Pencil signature: 'Charles Penruddock, Compton Park', on title.

(?) 22 HOW I TAMED MRS CRUISER, by Geo. Augustus Sala. n.d. [1858 or 1859].

Pictorial yellow boards. Wood-engraved front., 5 full-page illustrations and a vignette after Phiz, all on text paper. The drawings on front cover and spine are also by Phiz and are not repeated in the book.

Half-title. pp. (192) N_3 N_4 adverts., Publisher's cat., 16 pp. undated, on text paper at end. Outside back cover lists Nos. 1–19 of Blackwood's London Library, which numbering has been here adopted.

Note. There were several re-issues of this book, with lengthening series lists on back covers and slowly vanishing illustrations.

Finally, the adverts. at the end of No. (?) 22 show that by 1859 the series also included: **The Woman Hater,** by Capt. A. F. Clarence; **The Autobiography and Letters of Lola Montez; The Arts of Beauty,** by

Lola Montez; **Adventures on the Mosquito Shore,** by S. A. Bard, and **Tales from the Operas,** edited by G. F. Pardon.

From this point I can no longer attempt to give the sequence of titles in this series. The publisher's adverts. become disordered and, as earlier volumes go out of print, he re-numbers those which are left. Different lists were issued in 1865, 1873 and 1874 and maybe still more frequently. In one case 71 titles are given, of which some certainly appeared in ordinary yellow-back form without series affiliation, and I suspect Blackwood came to use his 'London Library' as a convenient label for all his cheap issues.

There are three more items in the collection which carry the series title on front covers but cannot be numbered. These are:

Sea Drift, by Admiral Hercules Robinson. (Third Thousand.) n.d. (No. 18 in the 1873 list and 19 in the 1874 list above referred to.)

Second Love, by Mrs Trollope. 1875. (No. 33 in the lists of *Blackwood's London Library* above referred to.)

Wanderings of a Pilgrim, by G. B. Cheever. n.d. (No. 22 in the lists of *Blackwood's London Library* above referred to, but of large format and probably dating from the early '80s.)

[3448] BLENKINSOP, ADAM

Larry Lynch or Paddiana. 'New Edition.' C. H. Clarke, n.d. Yellow pictorial boards. Small format. Originally published as *Paddiana* in 2 vols. 1847.

BOHN'S CHEAP SERIES 1851–1855

[3449] THE HOUSE OF THE SEVEN GABLES: a Romance, by NATHANIEL HAWTHORNE. 1851 (Series No. 31)
Bright green glazed boards printed in dark blue and red. Series title on front and list of series (ending at No. 31) on back cover. Up-lettered on spine. End-papers printed in blue. 'Price one shilling.'

pp. (viii)+(256) pp. (iii)–vi carry an Author's Preface dated 'Lenox. January 27, 1851'.

Book-label of John Bell Sedgwick. ? First English edition. First American edition published in same year.

[3450] TWICE TOLD TALES, by NATHANIEL HAWTHORNE. 'New Edition.' 1851 (Series No. 35)
Bright green glazed boards printed in dark blue. Series title on front and list of series (ending at No. 35) on back cover. Up-lettered on spine. End-papers printed in blue. 'Price one shilling.'

pp. vi+176 Publishers' cat., 32 pp. undated, at end. pp. (iii)–vi carry an Author's Preface dated 'Lenox. January 11, 1851'.

[3451] WOLFERT'S ROOST AND OTHER TALES, by WASHINGTON IRVING. 'Now first collected.' 1855
Bright green glazed boards printed in black. 'Fine Edition. Price 1/6.' At front and back are publishers' adverts., printed in blue and treated as multiple end-papers. In front these are paged 2*b*–8*b*, (1*b*) pasted down to front cover; at back 1*e*–7*e*, (8*e*) pasted down to back cover. Engraved portrait front.

Blank leaf and half-title precede title. pp. (viii) [paged vi]+280 'Author's Edition' on title.

Book-label of John Bell Sedgwick. ? First *authorised* English edition. See below No. 3599.

BOHN'S SHILLING SERIES 1850

[3452] GENEVIEVE, or the History of a Servant Girl, by ALPHONSE DE LAMARTINE (translated by A. R. Scoble) 1850 (Series No. 25)
Bright green glazed boards printed in dark blue and red. Series title on front and list of series (ending at No. 25) on back cover. Up-lettered on spine. A 'double volume', price 1*s*. 6*d*. End-papers printed in blue. ? First English edition. French First edition published in same year.

Half-title. pp. (xlii) [paged (xl)]+(180) Publishers' cat., 32 pp. undated, at end.

[3453] BOISGOBEY, FORTUNÉ DE

I. Vizetelly Shilling Edition. Published at one shilling each, in orange-scarlet or crimson wrappers, uniform with the novels of Gaboriau (3556). Unless otherwise stated, pale blue printed end-papers. No series number on covers, but each volume numbered on title. Titles asterisked are not in the Collection.

BOISGOBEY

1 THE OLD AGE OF LECOQ, THE DETECTIVE, and An Omnibus Mystery. 2 vols. 'Twentieth Thousand.' 1886

2 IN THE SERPENT'S COILS. 'Tenth Thousand.' 1885

3 THE DAY OF RECKONING. 2 vols. 'Thirtieth Thousand.' 1887

Crimson wrappers, entitled on front: 'The Gaboriau & Boisgobey Sensational Novels.' Priced as well as lettered on spine. Plain white end-papers. Back covers plain.

Note. I have seen a re-issue of this by Richard Butterworth n.d. printed from Vizetelly plates on cheap paper and bound in green cloth.

4 THE SEVERED HAND. 'Twentieth Thousand.' 1886

[Later issued by Richard Butterworth, 16/17 Devonshire Square, E.C. at 6*d.* in similar wrappers, but unlettered on spine.]

5 BERTHA'S SECRET 1885

6 WHO DIED LAST? or The Rightful Heir 1885

7 THE CRIME OF THE OPERA HOUSE. 2 vols. 1886

8 THE MATAPAN AFFAIR 1886

9 THE FIGHT FOR A FORTUNE 1886

10 THE GOLDEN PIG, or The Idol of Modern Paris. 2 vols. 1886

11 PRETTY BABIOLE 1886 (white end-papers)

12 THE THUMB STROKE 1886

13 THE CORAL PIN. 2 vols. 1886

14 THE JAILER'S PRETTY WIFE 1886

15 THE ANGEL OF THE CHIMES 1886

16 HIS GREAT REVENGE. 2 vols. 1887

17 THE CONVICT COLONEL. 'Twentieth Thousand.' 1887 (plain white end-papers)

18 A RAILWAY TRAGEDY 1887

19 THE PHANTOM LEG 1887

20 THIEVING FINGERS 1887

21 *THE STEEL NECKLACE and CECILE'S FORTUNE (1887). For *Cecile's Fortune* see 3710 (3) below.

22 *THE DETECTIVE'S EYE and THE RED LOTTERY TICKET (1887)

23 THE GOLDEN TRESS 1887

24 THE RED BAND. 2 vols. 'The only Unabridged Translation' [on cover: 'Edition']. 1887

25 FERNANDE'S CHOICE 1887 (very pale green end-papers)

26 THE NAMELESS MAN 1887

27 THE RED CAMELLIA. 2 vols. 1887

28 THE RESULTS OF A DUEL 1888 (very pale green end-papers)

29 WHERE'S ZENOBIA? 2 vols. 1888 (very pale green end-papers)

30 SAVED FROM THE HAREM. 2 vols. 1888 Vol. I: very pale green end-papers; Vol. II: yellow end-papers)

31 THE FATAL LEGACY 1888 (very pale green end-papers)

32 THE MYSTERIES OF NEW PARIS. 2 vols. 1888 (plain white end-papers)

II. **Parisian Library.** Published by J. & R. Maxwell at one shilling, in white paper wrappers, printed in red, green and black. Series title on front. Back-wrappers printed with adverts.

DEATH OR DISHONOUR [*Jean Coupe-en-deux*]; CASH ON DELIVERY [*Rubis sur l'Ongle*] etc. See below 3649.

For Boisgobey see also 3454 and 3710.

[3454] BOULEVARD NOVELS (The) 1885–1888

Pl. 5 9 vols. Vizetelly. Published at half a crown in morocco paper boards of various colours, blocked in gold and other colours with a daring picture of a roguish young person, considerably décolletée and reading a book in the most uncomfortable position imaginable, these volumes are among the richest absurdities of their kind. Series title appears on front cover, spine, half-title and title, and the volumes are numbered on the title. All, I believe, are first English translations. The title asterisked is not in the Collection.

1 NANA'S DAUGHTER: a Story of Parisian Life, by ALFRED SIRVEN and HENRI LEVERDIER. With a letter from the authors to Emile Zola 1885
Plum boards, blocked in gold, black and blue. Cream end-papers.
Advert. leaf and half-title precede title. pp. (292) [paged (288)] I_{16} adverts. Publisher's cat., 24 pp. dated April 1886, at end.

2 THE YOUNG GUARD: a Picture of Paris Morals and Manners, by VAST-RICOUARD 1886
Dark purple boards, blocked in gold, scarlet and black; grey-green end-papers.
Half-title. pp. 248

Pl. 5 3 ODETTE'S MARRIAGE, by ALBERT DELPIT 1886
Deep-sea-blue-green boards, blocked in gold, scarlet and chocolate; grey-green end-papers.
Half-title. pp. 200 Publishers' cat., 24 pp. dated April 1886, at end.

4 THE WOMAN OF FIRE, by ADOLPHE BELOT 1886
Plum boards, blocked in gold, chocolate and blue; grey-green end-papers.
Half-title. pp. (208) Publisher's cat., 32 pp. dated September 1886, at end.

5 THE VIRGIN WIDOW, by A. MATTHEY 1887
Purple boards, blocked in gold, scarlet and black; grey-green end-papers.
Half-title. pp. (260) Publisher's cat., 32 pp. dated September 1886, at end.

6 SEALED LIPS, by F. DU BOISGOBEY 1887
Deep-sea-blue-green boards, blocked in gold, scarlet and chocolate; dark milky-green end-papers.
Half-title. pp. 288 Publisher's cat., 32 pp. dated March 1887, at end.

7 *A LADY'S MAN, by GUY DE MAUPASSANT

8 A WOMAN'S LIFE, by GUY DE MAUPASSANT 1888
Purple boards, blocked in gold, scarlet and black; dark blue-green end-papers.
Half-title. pp. (256) K_{15} K_{16} adverts. Publisher's cat., 32 pp. dated September 1887, at end.

9 A MYSTERY STILL, by F. DU BOISGOBEY 1888
Deep-sea-blue-green boards, blocked in gold, scarlet and chocolate; dark chocolate end-papers.
Half-title pp. 272

Notes. (i) Facing title in Nos. 6–9, under a list of the series, is printed a 'quote' from *The Academy*: 'Messrs Maxwell cannot vie with Messrs Vizetelly in the get-up of their translations from the French.' It is no longer considered good form (indeed it might well lead to unpleasantness) for one publisher to print in his books remarks which disparage the publications of another. (ii) Although other volumes are announced as 'in preparation' I cannot state for certain whether more were published. B.M. Cat. records Vols. 1–5, 8 and 9, and I think probably this represents the limit of the series.

BRADDON, M. E.

[3455] **Series I: Small Format.** All in pictorial boards, published by Ward, Lock & Tyler, and described as 'Stereotyped Edition' unless otherwise stated.

Birds of Prey n.d.

Captain of the Vulture n.d.

Charlotte's Inheritance n.d.

Dead Men's Shoes. (No statement of edition.) 1876

Fenton's Quest n.d.

Hostages to Fortune n.d.

John Marchmont's Legacy 'Revised Edition.' n.d.

Lucius Davoren n.d.

Open Verdict (An) John & Robert Maxwell 1878

Taken at the Flood n.d.

To the Bitter End John Maxwell & Co. 1873.

Trail of the Serpent (The) (No statement of edition.) 1867

[3455*a*] **Series II: Large Format.** All in pictorial boards, published by Maxwell or Simpkin, Marshall, and mostly described as 'Stereotyped Edition' and undated, unless otherwise stated.

Asphodel. (No statement of edition.)

Aurora Floyd

Birds of Prey

Eleanor's Victory

Gerard 1892

Golden Calf (The)

Henry Dunbar

Ishmael

Just as I am

Joshua Haggard's Daughter 1893

BRADDON

Lady Audley's Secret

Lost for Love

Lucius Davoren 1893

Mohawks

One Life One Love 1891

Only a Clod

Ralph the Bailiff and other Stories

Rupert Godwin

Sons of Fire

Thou Art the Man

Under Love's Rule

Venetians (The) 1893

Vixen

'*Edited by the author of Lady Audley's Secret*'

Put to the Test (by Ada Buisson). Ward, Lock & Tyler 1876

[3455*b*] **Series III: Cloth Edition. Small Format.**

All Along the River. 'Stereotyped Edition.' Simpkin, n.d. Red.

Golden Calf. 'Stereotyped Edition.' Simpkin, 1891. Red.

Lady Audley's Secret. 'Stereotyped Edition.' Simpkin, 1891. Red.

Mohawks (with front.). 'Stereotyped Edition.' Maxwell (1887). Green.

Mount Royal. 'Stereotyped Edition.' Maxwell, n.d. Green.

One Life One Love. 'Stereotyped Edition.' Simpkin 1891. Red.

One Thing Needful (with front.). 'Stereotyped Edition.' Maxwell (1886). Green.

Rough Justice. Simpkin 1899. Red.

Sons of Fire. 'Stereotyped Edition.' Simpkin, n.d. Red.

Thou Art the Man. 'Stereotyped Edition.' Simpkin, n.d. Red.

Venetians. 'Stereotyped Edition.' Simpkin, 1893. Red.

Vixen. 'Stereotyped Edition.' Maxwell, n.d. Green.

Wyllard's Weird (with front.). Maxwell, n.d. Green.

[3456] BRAY, MRS ANNA ELIZA

Fitz of Fitz-Ford: a Legend of Devon. 'A New Edition, Revised and Corrected. With Notes by the Author' Longman etc. 1845. Yellow decorated boards with series design for 'Bray's Novels and Romances'; up-lettered on spine; list of 10 vols. in this series at 1*s.* 6*d.* each on back cover. Engraved front. and vignette title after Stothard. Small format.

Note. This edition was originally published in cloth. The board issue probably dates from the mid-fifties.

[3457] BREEZY LIBRARY (The) 1893

Published at one shilling by Raphael Tuck & Sons, this series according to a publishers' note was 'an attempt to dissociate a shilling from a shocker and to supply a series of "Shilling Soothers", especially in the matter of paper, print and cover. The book in fact will be as much a work of art as the story.'

Certainly considerable (if mis-directed) pains were taken to produce an unusual piece of book-making. The volumes are in stiff glazed cream paper wrappers, cut flush and unlettered on spine and back. The front cover is pictorially printed and lettered in white, pale green, pink and gold—the detail being raised in bas-relief, as on many Christmas cards. At the foot of the design is printed: 'Designed at the Studios in England and completed in cameo in Saxony.'

I am only aware of two titles in the series, each with a half-tone portrait front. signed in facsimile; a coloured illustration of a sylvan Christmas-cardy kind and half-tone illustrations in the text.

1 'MERELY MARY ANN', by ISRAEL ZANGWILL. Illustrated by Mark Zangwill.

2 SUMMER CLOUDS and Other Stories, by EDEN PHILLPOTTS. Illustrations by Harold Copping.

No. 2 (not in the Collection) is announced at the end of No. 1, but itself contains no announcement of a future volume.

[3458] BROUGH, ROBERT B.

MISS BROWN: a Romance. And Other Tales in Prose and Verse

Ward & Lock 1860. Pictorial yellow-back boards. Numerous wood-engraved illustrations on text paper after McConnell, Kenny Meadows, H. G. Hine and T. Macquoid. Small format.

pp. (iv) [paged ii] + (332)

Note. What I take to be the first issue has boards of *primrose* yellow and the back cover advert. begins with *Marston Lynch* and *Ulf the Minstrel.* A later binding in darker yellow boards has back advert. beginning with *The Hooded Snake* and including *Miss Brown* itself.

[3459] BROUGHTON, RHODA

Not Wisely but Too Well (by the author of 'Cometh Up as a Flower'). 'New Edition'

Tinsley 1871. Yellow pictorial and decorated boards. 'Tinsley's Cheap Novels' on front cover and list of Tinsley's Two Shilling volumes on back cover. Chapman & Hall end-papers.

[3460] BULWER LYTTON, EDWARD

Edition I: Routledge's Railway Library. All, unless otherwise stated, in pale green boards printed in dark blue, with conventional design and lettering. Author's name 'Sir Edward Bulwer Lytton Bart' on front, 'Bulwer' on spine; series title on both front and spine. End-papers and back covers printed with adverts. Small format.

Devereux 1855

Disowned 1855

Ernest Maltravers 1854

Harold 1855

Leila and Calderon the Courtier. 1855. Preface—one page, undated and unsigned—probably written for this edition.

Lucretia 1855

My Novel. 2 vols. 1855

Night and Morning 1854

Pelham 1854

Rienzi 1854

What Will He Do With It? 'A New Edition.' 2 vols. 1864

These volumes belong to a later period of the Railway Library, and are in pictorial yellow-back boards with spine design of sword and lyre uniform with that earlier used on Edition II, below. Author's name: 'Bulwer Lytton', on front only, and series title on front.

[3460*a*] **Edition II.** Yellow-back pictorial boards, spine design of sword and lyre. Author's name on front: 'Bulwer Lytton', and ditto on spine. End-papers printed with adverts. Small format.

Last Days of Pompeii. 'A New Edition.' 1858

Pilgrims of the Rhine. 'A New Edition.' 1866

Zanoni. 'A New Edition.' 1858

Leila and The Pilgrims of the Rhine. 'New Edition.' n.d.

This is a later issue than the foregoing, though still small format. Same spine design. Author's name: 'Lord Lytton', on front and spine.

[3460*b*] **Edition III.** Yellow-back pictorial boards, spine conventional and uniform, with 'Lord Lytton's Novels' in a circle. End-papers printed with adverts. Small format. Undated (about 1876).

Falkland and Zicci

Kenelm Chillingley

Night and Morning. 'A New Edition.'

Pelham.

[3460*c*] *Pl. 6* **Edition IV.** Front cover and spine specially designed by Walter Crane, printed in black and cream on boards, coloured either brown, green or blue. Author's name: 'Lord Lytton', on front and spine. Full-page advert. pasted on to some back covers, printed on others. End-papers printed with adverts. Large format. All but one undated [1878].

BULWER LYTTON

Caxtons (The)
Coming Race (The)
Devereux
Disowned (The)
Ernest Maltravers
Eugene Aram
Godolphin
Kenelm Chillingley
Last Days of Pompeii (The)
Last of the Barons (The)
Leila, Calderon and Pilgrims of the Rhine 1878
Lucretia
My Novel. 2 vols. (Vol. II lacking from the Collection)
Night and Morning
Parisians (The). 2 vols.
Paul Clifford
Pelham
Rienzi
Strange Story, A
What Will He Do With It?
Zanoni.

Note. This edition was re-issued circa [1885] in slightly larger format and with Publishers' New York address: '9 Lafayette Place', instead of '416 Broome Street'.

[3461] BULWER LYTTON, ROSINA

Cheveley. Weldon, n.d. Cream pictorial boards.

[3462] BUNGENER, L. LOUIS FELIX

Wolf and His Prey, The: or The Priest and the Huguenot. Dean & Son, n.d. Yellow pictorial boards, specially designed down-lettered spine. Small format.

[3463] BURNS' FIRESIDE LIBRARY 1845

Published by James Burns, Portman Street, at prices from sixpence to three shillings, the volumes of the *Fireside Library* are fiction and non-fiction, new works (or translations) and reprints. The specimen in the Collection appears to be the only fictional first edition originally written in English.

FRANK'S FIRST TRIP TO THE CONTINENT, by the Rev. W. Gresley. 1845

Cream wrappers printed in dark blue and red, on front with all-over design incorporating series title, book title, imprint and 'Price Three Shillings', on back with book title surrounded by fancy frame. Unlettered spine. Wood-engraved front., vignette title and tail-piece very finely engraved by Branston after W. H. Prior.

pp. vi+290 Final leaf, CC_1, a single inset. Publisher's cat., 12 pp. undated, at end.

Note. This volume is produced with considerable care, though the un-lettered spine suggests a certain naïveté of inexperience. Burns published books of an improving kind, and a lavish use of Gothic letter gives this specimen of his work an ecclesiastical tinge.

In the prospectus of *The Fireside Series* at the end of the volume he announces a plan I have nowhere else seen candidly admitted. He proposes to include in the Series several of his former publications which were too highly priced to reach the big public. But these re-issues will not only be more cheaply produced; they will undergo 'occasional retrenchments in matter, while the editions originally published will remain on sale in their full form at the usual prices. In this way the views of all classes of readers will be met.'

[3464] CAINE, HALL

Both Chatto & Windus, in pictorial boards, one yellow, one ivory. Large format.

Deemster (The) 'Twenty-fourth Edition.' 1896
Shadow of a Crime. 'New Edition.' 1894

[3465] CARLETON, WILLIAM

Irish Life and Character

Henry Lea, n.d. [circ. 1855]. Yellow pictorial boards, after Phiz. This volume, printed from the plates of *Tales and Sketches of the Irish Peasantry* 1845 (Section I: 515), omits the final essay dealing with Second Sight.

Traits and Stories of the Irish Peasantry

Routledge 1853. Pale green glazed boards, pictorially printed in dark green. Printed end-papers. Two wood-engravings after Phiz.

This volume contains only three stories: The Station—The Party Fight and Funeral—The Hedge School.

Valentine McClutchy, the Irish Agent, and Solomon M'Slime, his Religious Attorney. 'Eighth Edition' Dublin: James Duffy & Co. n.d. [middle '60s]. Yellow pictorial boards. Wood-engraved front. and vignette title after George Measom. The front. is reproduced in colours on front cover. Spine title reads: THE IRISH AGENT AND HIS RELIGIOUS ATTORNEY BY CARLETON, and binders' imprint: 'Morison & Co., Dublin', appears at base of spine. Small format.

Willy Reilly and His Dear Colleen Bawn: a Tale Founded Upon Fact. 'Author's Copyright Edition.' Routledge, n.d. Yellow pictorial boards.

[3466] CHAMBERS' JOURNAL, TALES FROM 1884–1885

Published at 6*d*., small sq. 8vo, in lilac wrappers cut flush, printed in purple and with series name on front and spine, this venture was presumably inspired by the example of Blackwood's Magazine and Bentley's Miscellany. There was no cloth issue.

Of the first 8 titles (? the complete series) only Nos. 1 (*The Silver Lever*, by David Christie Murray) and 6 (*Chewton Abbot*, by Hugh Conway) carried authors' names, the rest being collections of anonymous tales. The only specimen in the Collection is No. 8, *The Arab Wife*, 1885.

Note. Thirty years earlier than the above was issued another series of 'Tales from Chambers'. Sufficient evidence of this undertaking is not available to justify my treating it as an item on its own, but the following particulars are appended as a note to the 1885 series, so that the previous venture is at least on record.

It would appear that during the early fifties stories from *Chambers' Miscellany* and a few other periodicals were issued by Messrs Chambers of Edinburgh in 32 pp. numbers, each with a wood-engraved vignette at the head of p. 1 and paginated separately. Whether the individual numbers were wrappered, and if so what general title was given to them, I do not know. The price was probably 1*d*. or 2*d*. per number. In 1855 (according to the *English Catalogue*) five selections of these stories were bound up in cloth volumes for regular bookshop sale, and one such volume is in the Collection.

This volume, bound in grey-purple morocco cloth, blocked in blind and gold-lettered on spine: TALES / FOR / ROAD / AND / RAIL, opens with a 4 pp. prelim.—title (reading: TALES FOR ROAD AND RAIL FROM CHAMBERS MISCELLANY and imprinted W. & R. Chambers, London and Edinburgh 1855,) verso: Contents and verso. It then offers, from what was manifestly a long series of 1*d*. or 2*d*. numbers, Nos. 116, 118, 126, 129, 134, 138, 145, 147, 148, 149, 156, 158, 163, 165, 171, 176. Each number contains 32 pp. except the last which contains only 16. The stories are for the most part unsigned; but include several by Mrs S. C. Hall, which are the only ones whose provenance is stated. There is no indication anywhere of similar collections having preceded or having been planned to follow this volume, so that I cannot say which of the five issued volumes it represents.

[3467] CHAMIER, CAPT. FREDERICK

Jack Adams, or The Mutiny of the Bounty. C. H. Clarke, n.d. Yellow pictorial boards. Small format. 'Naval and Military Library, Vol. 3' (on half-title); 'Naval and Military Library' on spine.

Pl. 8 **Life of a Sailor, The.** 'New Edition'
Ward & Lock 1856. Yellow-pictorial boards, specially drawn spine. Small format.

Pl. 8 **Tom Bowling:** a Tale of the Sea. Henry Lea, n.d. Yellow pictorial boards; cover picture repeated on back cover. Small format.

[3468] CLARKE'S CABINET SERIES 1844–1845

Imp. 32mo, published by H. G. Clarke & Co., 66 Old Bailey, in 'illuminated wrappers' or cloth or full morocco gilt.

This was a mixed series of fiction and non-fiction, of standard titles and translations of works not earlier published in English. A list at the end of Vol. II (below) gives 67 titles, but I have never seen other specimens than the following, which, in the list, are numbered 1 and 57.

[1] **Psyche,** by **Mrs Tighe.** 1844
Full dark red original morocco, gilt, enclosing illuminated front wrapper, imprinted at foot: 'PRINTED IN COLOURS BY SMART AND HOLMES, 10 LEATHER LANE.'

pp. (i)–xx + (21)–(168) L_7 L_8 adverts. Half-title or blank leaf originally preceded title.

CLARKE'S CABINET SERIES

[57] **Ulrich**: a Tale, by **Ida, Countess Hahn-Hahn** (translated from the German by J.B.S.)
2 vols. 1845. Red morocco cloth, enclosing illuminated front wrapper, reckoned in pagination.
Vol. I (i)–(xii) + (13)–(256) Q_8 adverts.
II (272) R_6–R_8 adverts.

Notes. (i) In his preface, dated February 1845, J.B.S. defends himself against reviewers who have attacked him for having translated *The Countess Faustina* by the author of *Ulrich*, which was No. 45 in CLARKE'S CABINET SERIES. It is refreshing to find a translator standing up to the outraged disapproval with which almost every English version of a Continental story was received. J.B.S. goes so far as to say (he words it gently) that if *Faustina* shocked them, let them beware of *Ulrich*.

(ii) Several of the titles in this series, and others from Clarke's Home Library and Clarke's Cabinet Series, were re-issued in 1849 and 1850 by George Slater, 252 Strand, in Slater's Shilling Series, Slater's Shilling Library, Slater's Home Library and Slater's edition of the novels of Frederika Bremer. The books were 32mo and bound in green or red morocco cloth with gold decoration and titling on spine.

[3469] CLARKE'S HOME LIBRARY 1845

Published by H. G. Clarke & Co., 66 Old Bailey, in 1845 in cream wrappers, patterned and lettered in red and black, this series included a considerable proportion of fiction. But all the fiction titles in the first twenty numbers are eighteenth-century novels or reprints of American books or unimportant translations, and I do not think space need be used to record them.

[3470] CLIFFORD, MRS W. K.

Marie May. Warne, n.d. Cream pictorial boards. *Warne's Library of Fiction.*

[3471] CLIVE, MRS ARCHER

Paul Ferroll. 'A New Edition' (by the author of 'Why Paul Ferroll Killed his Wife'). Chatto & Windus, n.d. (1882).

Why Paul Ferroll Killed his Wife. 'A New Edition' (by the author of 'Paul Ferroll'). Chatto & Windus, n.d. (1882).

COBBOLD, REV. RICHARD (See above in Section I 569*a*, 573*a*, 573*b*, 576*a*, 577*a*)

[3472] COCKTON, HENRY

Master-Passion (The). Henry Lea, n.d. Yellow pictorial boards, cover drawing by Phiz, specially designed spine. Wood-engraved front. Small format.
Note. Originally published in 1852 as *Lady Felicia.*

Pl. 4 **Valentine Vox.** '42nd Thousand.' Routledge 1856. Flame pictorial boards, printed and shaded in bronze green and black, specially designed spine. Wood-engraved front. and vignette title signed 'J.G.' Small format.
Note. This is one of the most original and imaginative yellow-backs I have seen. The shaded bronze, the proportion of the lettering, and the grotesque heads on the spine are admirably conceived.

[3473] COLE, ALFRED W.

HONEYMOON (THE)
James Blackwood 1855. White glazed boards, pictorially printed after McConnell and fancy-lettered in terra-cotta and dark brown. Spine up-lettered, back cover printed with adverts. Wood-engraved front. and vignette title after McConnell, on plate paper.
pp. (iv) + 156 Small format.

[3474] COLLINS, C. A.

A Cruise Upon Wheels. 'New Edition.' Routledge 1893. Cream pictorial boards.

[3475] COLLINS, WILKIE

All in yellow-back pictorial boards (unless otherwise stated). Large format.

Antonina. 'New Edition.' Smith, Elder 1872.

Basil. 'New Edition.' Chatto & Windus 1887.

Dead Secret (The) 'New Edition.' Chatto & Windus, n.d.

Fallen Leaves (The). 'New Edition.' Chatto & Windus, n.d.

Jezebel's Daughter. 'New Edition.' Chatto & Windus, n.d.

Miss or Mrs? and Other Stories in Outline. 'New Edition.' Chatto & Windus, n.d.

Moonstone (The). 'New Edition.' Chatto & Windus, n.d.

My Miscellanies. 'New Edition.' Chatto & Windus, n.d.

Queen of Hearts (The). 'New Edition.' Smith, Elder on title; Sampson, Low on covers, 1865. Orange-back.

Rogue's Life (A). 'New Edition.' Chatto & Windus 1890.

[3476] 'COMING K——' SERIES (The) 1872–1877

Whether this is a complete run of these notorious, enormously successful and often insulting satires on Queen Victoria, the Prince of Wales, the Court, the Ministers and the hangers-on-to-Royalty in general, I cannot say for certain. The series seems to date compactly enough; and the record is, I hope, sufficiently coherent to give the entry reference-value, if not guaranteed completeness.

The majority are written in doggerel verse; but there are numerous passages of prose narrative which qualify the books for inclusion in a Fiction Catalogue. I believe that the authorship has never been established. Halkett & Laing suggest E. C. Grenville Murray; and on grounds of theme, scurrility and agile impertinence the suggestion is a likely one. But after having been horse-whipped in St James's Street by Lord Carrington in 1869, Murray became a virtual exile in Paris, and it would have been hard for him to deal in topical minutiae unless he had active collaborators on the spot in London. Perhaps (as is implied on some of the books) the series was a group-effort, and Grenville Murray's job was to put the spice in the pudding. The numbering of the titles in sequence is mine.

[3477] 1 THE COMING K—— (anon). **Beeton's Christmas Annual, Thirteenth Season.**

Royal 8vo. Ward, Lock & Tyler, n.d. [1872]. White paper wrappers printed in red, blue and black—on front with all-over design incorporating titling, imprint, price, etc. and with THE COMING K—— printed on a diagonal white panel cut out across the design; up-lettered on spine: BEETON'S CHRISTMAS ANNUAL—ONE SHILLING; on back printed with adverts. Inside front and back covers also printed with adverts.

Make-up of a complete copy. 4 pp. demy 8vo, advertising the publications of Cassell, Petter & Galpin, tipped on to first page of the 'Advertiser'. 'Beeton's Christmas Annual Advertiser', 8 pp., of which (7) is title-page to *The Coming K——*; 8 pp. small demy 8vo, advertising Pulvermacher's Cures; 4 pp. demy 8vo, advertising Camomile Pills.

Text of the Annual. pp. (1)–(96) *The Coming K——* ends p. 47. Pp. (48)–(94) carry miscellaneous contributions and illustrations, often with adverts. printed on versos. Pp. (95) (96) adverts. 2 pp., demy 8vo, advertising Cadbury's products and printed in colours, tipped on to p. 17; 4 pp., advertising Beeton's publications, tipped on to p. 33 and 2 pp. advertising Booth & Fox's quilts, followed by 4 pp. advertising Willcox & Gibbs' Sewing Machines, tipped on to p. 73. Numerous wood-engraved illustrations throughout the text.

Note. This is the only item in the series which is combined with other matter to form an annual issue. Henceforward the popularity of the satires justified each one standing alone. The Beeton leaflet at p. 33 announces *The Coming K——* as 'A Series of Prophetic Views in Verse and Wood, by a Modern Seer and Poet, with Engravings of What Is Going To Happen. Soaring up to Heights Unthought of: Descending into Depths Undreamt of.'

The poem is in the form of a parody of *Idylls of the King*, with such dispiriting sub-titles as 'Heraint and Shenid' and 'Loosealot and Delaine'. The Prince of Wales appears as 'Guelpho'. It is, however, amusing to know that a few copies for private circulation were produced at six shillings, with illustrations, uniform with the current edition of *Idylls*. I have never seen one.

2 THE SILIAD, or The Siege of the Seats (by the authors of 'The Coming K——'). **Beeton's Christmas Annual, Fourteenth Season** [3478]

Royal 8vo. Ward, Lock & Tyler (1873). Wrappered uniform with 1.

Make-up of a complete copy. 4 pp. on orange paper, advertising John Edgington's Marquees, Flags, etc.; Beeton's Christmas Annual Advertiser', pp. i–viii; 4 pp. unfoliated of text paper, of which the first is title-page to *The Siliad*, the second adverts., the third and fourth 'The Coming K——: a Prologue to The Siliad'; 4 pp. cr. 8vo, advertising the publications of Cassell, Petter & Galpin; 4 pp. cr. 8vo (of which the first in colours), advertising Pavy's Felted Fabric; 4 pp. of Ward, Lock Announcements, paged (1)–4.

Text of *The Siliad.* pp. (92) [paged (9)–(100) *Siliad* ends p. 97, 98–(100) adverts. Continuation of Beeton's Christmas Advertiser, pp. ix–xxxii; 4 pp. demy 8vo, advertising Camomile Pills, tipped on to p. 25 and another, advertising *Beeton's Young Englishwoman*, tipped on to p. 57. Folding coloured front. facing first page of text, and numerous wood-engraved illustrations throughout the text.

Ward, Lock's Announcement of the Annual (which is described as 'for 1874', i.e. issued in December 1873) says: 'Without decyphering the Riddle, it may be, without breaking confidence, here imparted that the more remarkable Men, Women and Events of Modern Days are the subjects of the New Epic. Herein figure the commanding forms of GLADIMEMNON and DUDIZZY.'

Eight 'Books' of rhyming narrative verse, each with a mock-heroic title, celebrate the preparations for the General Election of February, 1874, which upset the Gladstone administration and made Disraeli for the second time Prime Minister.

[3479] 3 THE FIJIAD. English Nights Entertainments (by an author of 'The Siliad' and others). **Beeton's Christmas Annual, Fifteenth Season**

Sq. royal 8vo. Ward, Lock & Tyler (1874). Wrappered uniform with 1 and 2, except that three diagonal white panels are cut out across front cover to carry titling, etc. and that an abbreviated Contents List is printed perpendicularly on the margins of the coloured design.

Make-up of a complete copy. 'Beeton's Christmas Annual Advertiser', pp. i–viii, of which vii serves as title-page to *The Fijiad*; 4 pp. demy 8vo, advertising Kays, Chemists, Stockport; 6 pp. 16mo, of which first and last in colours, advertising Pavy's Felted Fabric, etc.; 4 pp. demy 8vo, advertising Moxon's publications (now handled by Ward, Lock); 4 pp. demy 8vo, advertising the publications of Cassell, Petter & Galpin.

Text of *The Fijiad.* pp. (1)–96+97–120 adverts. 4 pp. demy 8vo, on yellow paper, of Ward, Lock's Announcements, tipped on to p. 17, describes this new annual as for 1874, i.e. the year of issue. Wood-engraved front. on plate paper and numerous illustrations in the text.

Predominantly in prose, *The Fijiad* is a sort of up-to-date *Hajji Baba*—the account of a Prince of Fiji who comes to England and observes with growing astonishment the manners, morals and formalities which he encounters.

4 JON DUAN (by the authors of 'The Coming K——' and 'The Siliad') Sq. royal 8vo. Weldon & Co., 15 Wine Office Court 1874. Pictorial wrappers, showing Queen Victoria on her throne with the Prince of Wales standing before her. Up-lettered on spine. Inside and outside back covers printed with adverts. [3480]

Make-up of a complete copy. 'Jon Duan Advertisements', 4 pp. unfoliated, of which p. (iii) is title-page to *Jon Duan*; 12 pp., carrying Dedicatory Poem; extracts from Press comment (see Note); and adverts.

Text of *Jon Duan.* pp. (1)–94+95, 96 adverts. Four full-page illustrations printed in two colours and numerous wood-engravings in the text, all on text paper.

Note. It is evident from the Press extracts, dated December 1874 (misprinted 1875) and January 1875, that there was a row in Beeton's (Ward, Lock's) office over the scurrility of the 'Authors of the Coming K———'. Beeton personally split from the outraged Ward, Lock & Tyler, perforce leaving them the title 'Beeton's Annual', but stating that he would start an annual of his own. *Jon Duan* was the first of these individual speculations. On the eve of its publication 'a gigantic financier' threatened libel proceedings if the satirical poem appeared, and W. H. Smith in alarm asked to be relieved of their order of 10,400 copies. Weldon went ahead with publication (whether after expurgation or not is not stated) and declared in a letter to the *South Durham Herald*, herein quoted, that they were on January 15, 1875 'marching on to 250,000 copies without a symptom of slackness in the sale'.

5 FAUST AND 'PHISTO (anon). **Beeton's Christmas Annual, Sixteenth Season** [3481]

Royal 8vo. Ward, Lock & Tyler (1875). Wrappered uniform with 1 and 2.

Make-up of a complete copy. Beeton's Christmas Annual Advertiser, pp. i–viii, of which (vii) serves as title-page to *Faust and 'Phisto*; 2 pp. of yellow paper, advertising Fox, Chemist, Stratford; 8 pp. demy 8vo of Ward, Lock Announcements; 4 pp. large demy, advertising the publications of Cassell, Petter & Galpin; slip of grey paper advertising Queen Insurance Co.

Text of *Faust and 'Phisto.* pp. 1–96+97–120 adverts. 8 pp. demy 8vo, advertising publications of Ward, Lock & Moxon, tipped on to p. (49). Wood-engraved illustrations throughout text.

Mainly in the form of doggerel poetic drama, this is Ward, Lock's attempt to keep the continuity of 'Coming K——' popularity, and at the same time to keep it clean. A rather subdued announcement in the advertisements preceding p. 1 refers warmly to public favour in the past and claims for the new issue 'a pleasant tone of burlesque, untainted by personality' and 'legitimate amusement at a time of year when such amusement is most welcome'.

The contemporary London scene is humorously surveyed and the last half of the text under the title 'Childe Albert's Pilgrimage' makes respectful fun of the Prince's visit to India.

[3482] 6 EDWARD VII (by the authors of 'The Coming K——', 'The Siliad' and 'Jon Duan')

Sq. royal 8vo. 'Published for the Proprietors at 40 Bedford Street, Covent Garden' 1876. Pictorial wrappers (generally uniform with *Jon Duan*) showing the Coronation of Edward VII in Westminster Abbey.

Make-up of a complete copy. 'Edward VII Advertisements', 8 pp. unfoliated, of which p. (vii) is title-page to *Edward VII.* 4 pp., paged (i)–iv, Prologue.

Text of *Edward VII.* pp. (1)–90+(91) (92) adverts. Three folding wood-engraved plates and 4 single plates on plate paper. Leaflet in colour tipped on to p. 5, advertising Nye's Mincing Machines; another (plain), advertising Weldon's Publications at p. 7; and 4 pp. cr. 8vo, advertising Camomile Pills, inset at p. 37.

This is a parody of a Shakespearean historical play. The folding front is entitled 'Multiform Portraits of the Authors of the Coming K—— (1837–1876)' and presents caricatures of the Royal Family and Court functionaries between those dates.

The slightly sinister imprint did not apparently signify that Weldon also had taken fright, for not only is a Weldon leaflet inserted, but in the next item (7 below) they advertise *Edward VII* and its predecessor as obtainable from their office.

It is in this work that an advert. on p. (v) announces that 'a few copies of *The Coming K——* have been printed for private circulation uniform with Tennyson's Idylls of the King'.

ana

[3482*a*] KEY TO EDWARD THE SEVENTH (The), being an Elucidation of the Dark Allusions in that Libellous Lampoon, with Brief and Authentic Biographies of the various distinguished personages therein mentioned ('by One Behind the Scenes').

Will Williams, Falcon Court, Fleet Street, n.d. [1876]. White paper wrappers, printed on front in scarlet and black with the word 'Key' pictorially presented, spine unlettered, inside and outside back wrapper printed with adverts. Four full-page line engravings on text paper.

pp. 32 [paged (i)–v+6–32]

Note. This purports to be an indignant protest against the *lèse majesté* and scurrility of *Edward VII*, but it carefully identifies each character (appending sub-ironical notes of them). The engravings, described on the front cover as 'Portraits of the Authors' are caricatures of S. O. Beeton, Doughty, Evelyn and Weldon. The presence of the first and fourth shows that, despite the disguised imprint, they were responsible for the issue of *Edward VII.* Among the characters identified, apart from Royalty and its entourage, are Sala, Swinburne, Locker, W. H. Russell, W. S. Gilbert and various theatrical persons of both sexes.

MRS BROWN AT BALMORAL or A CROWN FOR EDWARD VII [3482*b*]

Demy 8vo. Morris & Newman, 34 Booksellers Row, Strand, n.d. White wrappers pictorially printed on front in red and black; spine unlettered; back wrapper printed with advert. of 'The Castigator'. Double spread wood-engraving on plate paper between pp. 16 and 17.

No title. pp. 32

Note. A scurrilous pamphlet attacking the Queen, satirising her relations with Brown the ghillie, and treating the Prince of Wales (spoken of as 'Ned') with pert contempt.

7 BENJAMIN D—. HIS LITTLE DINNER [3483]
(anon. Illustrated by 'Whew')

Sq. royal 8vo. Weldon & Co. 1876. Pictorial wrappers (generally uniform with 4 and 6) showing Disraeli and his Cabinet at the dinner table.

Make-up of a complete copy. 4 pp. cr. 8vo on yellow paper, advertising Weldon's New Books (including the Parlour Library); 'Benjamin D—— Advertisements', 10 pp. unfoliated, of which (v) is half-title, (vii) title and (ix) Contents for *Benjamin D——*; 12 pp., foliated (i)–x+2 pp. unfoliated, of which (i)–x Dedicatory Poem and the 2 unfoliated pp. a continuation of the 'Advertisements'.

Text of *Benjamin D——.* pp. (1)–72+2 pp. unfoliated (continuation of 'Advertisements') +73–76 ('Our Agony Column')+4 pp. unfoliated (completion of 'Advertisements'). 4 pp. demy 8vo, advertising Camomile Pills, tipped in at end. This complete paging (including all adverts.) is signed straight through in eights from B–H except that D and G are inadvertently unsigned. Four full-page wood-engravings on plate paper and numerous illustrations in the text. Loose inset on green paper advertises *Belgravia* of January 1877.

Mainly in prose, this work satirises the policy and personal foibles of the Disraeli Government. Facing the Contents List is a Weldon advert. stating that copies of *Jon Duan*, *Edward VII*, 'also the Original Edition of *The Coming K——* and *The Siliad*', may be obtained from their offices.

[3484] 8 PAN THE PILGRIM: a Vision of Judgement (by the authors of 'Benjamin D——')
Sq. royal 8vo. Weldon & Co. 1877. Pictorial wrappers (generally uniform with 4, 6 and 7) showing the Queen, the politicians, the law, the police and other symbols of established order, fleeing before the doom of the modern Sodom and Gomorrah.

Make-up of a complete copy. 'Pan the Pilgrim Advertisements', 12 pp., the first 4 unfoliated, the next 6 paged (i)–vi, of which (i) is half-title, (iii) title, (v) vi Dedication to *Pan the Pilgrim*; the next 2 unfoliated pp. a continuation of 'Advertisements'. Text of *Pan the Pilgrim.* pp. (1)–68+(69)–74, a Poem and adverts.+(75)–(84) unfoliated, completion of 'Advertisements'. Slip of blue paper, advertising Dome Black Lead, tipped on to p. 33. The book is signed A (6 leaves)+B–F in eights+balance of A (2 leaves). Two full-page wood-engravings on plate paper and numerous illustrations in the text.

A lurid poem, castigating the vices of Society. Finance, Priestcraft, Gambling, Women (both Fallen and Aggressive) and a dozen other grave threats to national survival are treated with mock horror, and the Prince of Wales is, as usual, one of the cast.

[3485] THE OSWALD ALLAN DERIVATIVES 1876–1878

Anti-monarchism, though strongly evident in the Coming K—— Series, was not the only element in their general campaign of ridicule and impertinence against the prominent persons and established conventions of the day. In 1876, however, appeared over obscure imprints (one from the same address as Weldon & Co.) the first of three (maybe of more, but I am unaware of them) satires almost wholly directed against the Royal Family. They were manifestly imitated from *The Coming K——* and its successors, alike in appearance and manner. Their author, Oswald Allan, was a music-hall performer who wrote and acted his own 'pantomimes'.

[3486] OA 1 WORTHY A CROWN? (by Oswald Allan)
Sq. royal 8vo. Head & Meek, 15 Wine Office Court 1876. Pictorial wrappers, with a composite page of little pictures centred by an empty Crown, from which hang ribbons lettered CANT, BALMORAL BOOTS, TWADDLE, HUMBUG and THE MORNING POST. The vignettes around the Crown show (among other things) the Prince of Wales and his lights o' love, the Queen dancing a reel with John Brown, piles of unpaid bills and the British Lion on his death-bed making his will. Spine unlettered. Inside and outside back covers printed with adverts.

pp. (iv) (prelim. pages and adverts.)+60 4 pp. on thinner paper at end advertise Rimmel's Perfumes. Demy 8vo leaflet, advertising Poupard's Fruit Spirit, tipped on to p. 9; publishers' advert. leaf inserted between pp. 32, 33; pp. 53, 54 (in the middle of the text of poems which follow the satire) advertise Poupard's products. A few illustrations in the text.

A mixture of verse and prose, depicting the Queen in contented domesticity with her ghillie while the Prince ranges the world for dissipation.

[3487] OA 2 THE VACANT THRONE (by Oswald Allan)
Sq. royal 8vo. E. Head, 10 Red Lion Court 1877. Pictorial wrappers, showing Albert Edward standing by the empty throne smoking a cigar while his family are grouped smilingly behind him. A portrait of John Brown hangs over the throne and in the smoke of the cigar is a vision of Queen Victoria on a pony with John Brown walking at her side.

pp. (64), of which (1) title, advert. on verso, (3) Index, ditto, (5)–51 text of *The Vacant Throne*, (52)–(64) adverts. and full-page wood-engravings irrelevant to the satire. At end, 8 pp. on yellow paper, advertising Ewart's Baths. Four full-page wood-engravings on plate paper and a few illustrations in the text after R. Prowse Junior.

OA 3 YE RED HOTTE REPUBLICK (by Oswald Allan) [3488]
Sq. royal 8vo. H. Pearce, 'The Publishing and Literary Agency, 12 Pilgrim Street, E.C., n.d. [1878]. Pictorial wrappers with an allegorical picture of the regime of crowns and great cities going up in flames, while a white robed angel hovers over a new world. 'Second Edition.'

pp. (72) 4 pp. unfoliated, of which (i) (ii) title, verso blank, (iii) (iv) adverts., +(1)–(3) adverts., (4) Index, (5)–64 text, (65)–(68) adverts. Wood-engravings (full-page and in the text) throughout and all on text paper.

Note. The date 1878 is suggested because the words THIRD YEAR appear on the front cover. I doubt there having been any fourth issue. This is a more degraded production than either OA 1 or OA 2 and the advertisements have clearly fallen off. The text is entirely in prose.

COMPANION LIBRARY. See note under 3668 below

[3489] COOPER, JAMES FENIMORE

Published by Routledge in pictorial or decorated boards of various colours; specially designed spines. Front cover design repeated on back cover unless otherwise stated. Small format.

Afloat and Ashore: Sequel to Miles Wallingford. 'A New Edition.' 1856. Green-back, printed in blue and brown. Back cover printed with adverts.

Bravo (The). 1854. Cream-back, printed in black and red.

Pl. 4 **Deerslayer (The), or the First War-Path.** 1855. Green-back, printed in red and blue.

Eve Effingham: Sequel to Homeward Bound. 'A New Edition.' 1855. Green-back, printed in navy blue and brown.

Headsman (The). 1855. Cream-back, printed in red and black.

Heathcotes (The), or the Wept of Wish-Ton-Wish. 1854. Yellow-back, printed in green and black.

Homeward Bound, or the Chase. 'A New Edition.' 1855. Cream-back, printed in blue and brown.

Last of the Mohicans (The). 'Twenty-Seventh Thousand.' 1854. White-back, printed in blue and brown.

Miles Wallingford, or Afloat and Ashore. 1854. White-back, printed in blue and brown.

Oak Openings (The), or the Bee Hunter. 1855. Cream-back, printed in blue and brown.

Pathfinder (The), or the Inland Sea. 1855. Magenta-back, printed in olive-brown and black.

Pilot (The). 'Thirty-fourth thousand.' 1855. Cream-back, printed in blue and brown.

Pioneers (The), or the Sources of the Susquehanna. 1854. Cream-back, printed in blue and brown.

Satanstoe, or the Littlepage Manuscripts. 'Fourth Thousand.' 1856. Green-back, printed in blue and brown.

Sea-Lions (The), or the Lost Sealers. 1854. Yellow-back, printed in green and black.

Spy (The): a Tale of the Neutral Ground. 'Thirty-Fourth Thousand.' 1855. White-back, printed in blue and red. *Pl. 4*

Two Admirals (The). 'New Edition.' 1854. Green-back, printed in black and red.

Note. The earlier volumes of this charming edition had spine and front-cover specially designed for each title. For the later volumes (and for re-clothing the earlier ones) two front-cover and spine designs were standardised. The Indian stories carried the standing figure of an Indian Brave with wigwams in the background; the Sea-stories carried a bearded sailor, seated, with decorative frame of flag, anchor and cordage. There was an intermediate issue of a few titles with standard front-covers but individual up-lettered spines.

The specimens in the Collection of the earliest individualised styles are: *Bravo*, *Deerslayer*, *Headsman*, *Heathcotes*, *Pathfinder*, *Sea Lions*, *Spy* and *Two Admirals*.

COSTELLO, DUDLEY

[3490] JOINT STOCK BANKER (THE): a Tale of the Day

J. & C. Brown, Ave Maria Lane 1856. Yellow pictorial boards. Wood-engraved front. on text paper after H. Anelay. Small format. pp. (288) S_8 blank. *Pl. 4*

[3491] MILLIONAIRE OF MINCING LANE (THE): a Tale of the Day

Routledge 1858. Yellow pictorial boards. End-papers printed with adverts. Small format. pp. (viii) + (336)

Note. I cannot be certain that this book is a first edition, though it has every appearance of one. It is a volume in Routledge's Railway Library, a series in which new works were rarely included. But examples do exist (e.g. 3563–64 below) and maybe this is another of them. The *English Catalogue* gives the date of first publication as 1858.

[3492] COSTELLO, LOUISA STUART

Queen Mother (The): Catherine de Medici. C. H. Clarke, n.d. Yellow pictorial boards, specially designed spine, front cover drawing repeated on back. Small format. Originally published in 1848 as *Catherine de Medici, the Queen Mother*.

COUNTRY HOUSE LIBRARY

[3493] COUNTRY HOUSE LIBRARY (The) 1875–1876

Published at 1*s*. each by Ward, Lock & Tyler, in glazed cream wrappers, ornately printed in black, lilac and red, with series title on front and spine, the volumes in this 'Library' are first editions and a mixture of fiction and non-fiction. Originally published from November 1875 to February or March 1876 they were re-issued in the eighties in bright blue covers, printed in black and red. I cannot trace more than six titles, of which only No. 2 is in the Collection.

1 THE MAD WILLOUGHBYS and Other Tales, by Mrs Lynn Linton [November 1875]

2 FALSE BEASTS AND TRUE, by Frances Power Cobbe [November 1875]

3 THE BLOSSOMING OF AN ALOE, by Mrs Cashel Hoey [January 1876]

4 COUNTRY HOUSE ESSAYS by John Latouche [January 1876]

5 NO SIGN, by Mrs Cashel Hoey [? February 1876]

6 GRACE TALMAS, by John Dangerfield [? February/March 1876]

[3494] CROLY, REV. GEORGE

Marston, or the Soldier and Statesman. 'Third Edition.' Henry Lea 1860. Yellow pictorial boards, specially drawn spine. Cover drawings by Phiz. Small format.

[3495] CROWE, MRS CATHERINE

Light and Darkness. 'New Edition.' Routledge 1856. Yellow pictorial boards. Small format.

Susan Hopley

Copy I. 'New Edition.' Routledge 1856. Salmon decorated boards, printed in black and dark green, up-lettered in large fancy caps on spine. Cover design repeated on back. Small format.

Copy II. Routledge, n.d. Yellow pictorial boards. *Railway Library.*

[3496] CROWQUILL, ALFRED

BUNDLE OF CROWQUILLS (A); dropped by A.C. on his Eccentric Flights over the Fields of Literature. Routledge 1854.

Copy I. Cream paper boards, printed in black, purple and red, with a design and fancy lettering by the author. End-papers printed with adverts. Cover design repeated on back cover. Small format. Wood-engraved front. and numerous illustrations in the text after drawings by the author and all on text paper.

pp. (248) Q_8 adverts., forming the first leaf of a ten-page publishers' cat. on text paper.

[3496*a*] **Copy II.** Orange paper boards, printed in black on front only with a different design and lettering by the author. Spine-design and end-papers identical with Copy I. Back cover printed with adverts. Illustrations and collation as Copy I, but an additional cat., 32 pp. undated, is inserted at end.

[3497] ELECTRIC TELEGRAPH OF FUN (THE). Edited and Illustrated by Alfred Crowquill.
Routledge 1854. Yellow decorated and lettered boards designed by the author and printed in red and black. Spine up-lettered: FUN. Cover design repeated on back cover. End-papers printed with adverts. Wood-engraved front. and 7 illustrations after Crowquill, all on plate paper, also a few text vignettes.

pp. 224. Folded advert. leaf at end. Small format.

CUMMINS, MARIA S.

[3498] LAMPLIGHTER (The) [anon]
Small 8vo. Nelson 1854. White boards, printed in red, green and black—on front and back with all-over decoration, lettering and circular vignette; on spine with lettering and decoration. pp. 288

On covers appears series title: NELSON'S LIBRARY. ? First English edition. First American edition published in same year.

[3499] MABEL VAUGHAN (by the author of 'The Lamplighter'). Edited by arrangement with the author by Mrs Gaskell, author of 'Mary Barton'
Sampson Low 1857. Yellow boards, pictorially printed on front in red and black, on spine with decoration in red, on back in red with adverts. Pale yellow end-papers printed with adverts. dated on inside front cover 'September 19, 1857'.

Half-title. pp. viii+(312) X_4 adverts. Pp. (v)–viii are occupied by Mrs Gaskell's Preface, signed E.C.G.

[3500] DETECTION, CRIMINOLOGY, VARIOUS PROFESSIONAL AND SPECIALIST 'EXPERIENCES' 1856–1884

This, from more than one point of view, is perhaps the most interesting class of yellow-backs published. Virtually all made their first appearance in yellow-back form—mainly during the early period, when the volumes were of small format, set in good readable type, and provided with carefully designed and individual covers. The majority are nowadays so uncommon that their very existence is almost unknown. The early titles came to publication (and to popularity) so suddenly and so plentifully that they must hold the record among novelties in publishing history for speed in attracting and holding public notice. Their success depended entirely upon their *subject* (hardly ever do they rise above mediocrity in a literary sense); and to their *subject* they owe their interest to-day, for, as evidence of primitive methods of detection and as records of actual incidents in various walks of life, they are in some respects the only sources available. Finally, their florescence (so far as they deal with adventures in detection) can be directly traced to a development in police procedure popularised by the powerful pen of Charles Dickens.

In *The Bookman* of February 1932 Mr E. A. Osborne published a valuable article on the literature of detection from a bibliographical angle, and this article was used by Mr John Carter in his essay 'Detective Fiction' in *New Paths in Book-Collecting* (London, 1934). To these two authorities I am glad to acknowledge the following facts. In 1845, when Sir James Graham detailed twelve police officers for exclusive plain-clothes detective work, the idea of the C.I.D. (actually established in 1876) was first conceived. In 1850 (July–September) Dickens printed four articles in *Household Words* describing these officers' work; and to the interest created by his articles may largely be attributed the flood of 'curiosities', 'experiences', 'secrets', 'diaries' and other narratives of detective activity, which burst on the world within the next few years.

After consideration I decided to catalogue the books alphabetically under titles, although, as the fashion was rather sociological than literary, there were arguments for a chronological arrangement. But a chronological list makes search for any particular book tedious and difficult, and I felt a natural inclination to keep the system of this catalogue as uniform as possible. To emphasise the dates of issue, these are outset to the extreme right of the column. As all the books are original editions (in one case a second issue of an original edition), I give the normal amount of bibliographical detail.

[3501] ACTOR (RECOLLECTIONS OF AN) 1865
By WALTER DONALDSON, Comedian. 'Never before printed.' John Maxwell & Co. Yellow boards, designed and lettered in scarlet and black. Small format.

pp. viii + 360

[3502] ALL AT SEA, or Recollections of a Half-Pay Officer 1864
By LT.-COL. H. R. ADDISON. Author of 'Recollections of an Irish Police Magistrate', 'Diary of a Judge', 'Traits and Stories of Indian Life', 'Belgium as She Is', 'Who's Who?' etc. Ward & Lock. Yellow pictorial boards (by Phiz). Small format.

Half-title. pp. viii + 312

The spine design on this volume is repeated on several other similar issues by Ward & Lock at the same period.

[3503] ARTFUL DODGER (THE CAREER OF AN) [by John Bennett, see 3443 above] n.d. [1860 or 1861]
George Vickers, Angel Court. Yellow pictorial boards. Wood-engraved front. on text paper and very numerous text illustrations.

pp. viii + 216

Estimated dating by another copy, with ink signature: 'Thomas Hughes Davies. May 28th, 1861', on fly-leaf.

BARRISTER (THE EXPERIENCES OF A) 1856 [3504]
By Sxxx xxxxxx xxxxxx, D.C.L. J. & C. Brown, Ave Maria Lane. Yellow pictorial boards. Wood-engraved front. after Anelay on text paper. Small format.

pp. 320

These papers appeared in *Chambers' Journal* and are now first issued in book-form.

CRIME IN EDINBURGH (CURIOSITIES OF) [3505]
n.d. [1867]
By JAMES M'LEVY. William P. Nimmo. White paper wrappers cut flush, designed and lettered in scarlet, green, dark blue, yellow and black. Small format.

Half-title. pp. xvi + 304

No. 10 of Nimmo's Popular Tales. This series ran from 1866 to 1867 and the Bodleian Cat. records Nos. 1–12.

CRIMINAL CELEBRITIES: a Collection of Memorable Trials
By LASCELLES WRAXALL.
See 3553 (3) below: FIRST CLASS LIBRARY

[3506] DARK DEEDS n.d.
By the author of 'The Gaol Chaplain' [ERSKINE NEALE]. George Vickers, Angel Court. Yellow pictorial boards (by Jewitt). End-papers and outside back cover printed with Ward & Lock adverts. Small format.
Pl. 4
pp. viii + 216

[3507] DETECTION (CURIOSITIES OF), OR THE SEA-COAST STATION and other Tales 1862
By ROBERT CURTIS, author of 'The Irish Police Officer.' Ward & Lock. Yellow pictorial boards. Small format.
pp. 320 [paged (i)–viii + (9)–320]
Ink signature: 'J. Browne' on title.

[3508] DETECTIVE'S NOTE-BOOK (THE) 1860
Edited by CHARLES MARTEL. Ward & Lock. Yellow pictorial boards (by Jewitt). Small format.
Half-title. pp. (viii) + 312

[3509] DETECTIVE POLICE OFFICER (RECOLLECTIONS OF A) 1856
By 'WATERS' [William Russell, alias 'Lieut. Warneford'].
Pl. 5 **Copy I: First Issue.** J. & C. Brown, Ave Maria Lane. Yellow pictorial boards. Wood-engraved front. on text paper. Small format.
pp. (312) [paged (i)–(viii) + (9)–(312)] U_8 adverts. Printers' imprint on p. (310): LONDON: / PRINTED BY W. CLOWES AND SONS, / STAMFORD-STREET, AND CHARING-CROSS. Back cover advertises: *Marriage Settlement, Experiences of a Barrister. Tales of the Coast Guard.*

[3509 *a*] **Second Issue** (not in the Collection) differs from Copy I in the following particulars: (i) no date on title; (ii) prelims. re-set to 4 pp.; (iii) printers' imprint on p. (310): LONDON: / PRINTED BY WILLIAM CLOWES AND SONS, / STAMFORD STREET.; (iv) back cover advertises four novels by Mayne Reid, *Experiences of a Barrister* (as published) and *Detective Police Officer* itself. Cover identical with Copy I.

[3509 *b*] **Copy II: Third Issue.** Red morocco cloth, blocked in blind front and back, spine blocked and lettered in gold. Yellow end-papers. No date on title. Prelims. 4 pp. (as Second Issue). Advert. leaf, U_8, lists books on back cover of Second Issue *plus* others, including 'A New Novel by James Grant. Shortly will be published.'
Binders' ticket: 'Leighton, Son & Hodge', at end.
Note. First edition (including the above three issues) 5000 copies, June 1856; reprint 5000, September 1856; reprint 5000, Spring, 1857.

[3510] DETECTIVE POLICE OFFICER (RECOLLECTIONS OF A) Second Series 1859
Pl. 5 By 'WATERS'. W. Kent & Co., 51–52 Paternoster Row. Yellow pictorial boards. Small format.
Half-title. pp. (viii) + (264) S_4 adverts. Leaf of orange paper, tipped on to front fly-leaf, advertises books by Mayne Reid over imprint of C. H. Clarke, 23 Paternoster Row.
Note. It should be noted that adverts. on S_4 have imprint: 'W. Kent & Co. (late D. Bogue), 86 Fleet Street', and lead off with the First Series of the *Detective Police Officer* of which over 75,000 copies are stated to have been sold, boards, 1*s.* 6*d.*
The adverts. etc. in this volume illustrate the complexity and interworking of the various obscure and ephemeral imprints active in yellow-back publishing.

DOCTOR'S NOTE BOOK (THE), or Tales of My Patients 1864 [3511]
By SAMUEL GUY, M.D. Ward & Lock. Yellow boards, designed and lettered in scarlet and black. Spine uniform with *All at Sea* (q.v.). Small format.
pp. (viii) + (312) 20_3 20_4 adverts., paged 1–4.
Ink signature: 'J. Browne', on title.
Sub-title on p. 1 of text is 'Revelations of a Fashionable Medical Practice'.

EX-DETECTIVE (DIARY OF AN) 1860 [3512]
Edited by CHARLES MARTEL. Ward & Lock. Yellow pictorial boards (I think by Phiz). Small format.
pp. (iv) + (316)
Ink signature: 'J. Browne', on title.

FEMALE DETECTIVE (THE) 1864 [3513]
By ANDREW FORRESTER, JUN., author of 'The Private Detective', 'Secret Service', etc. 'Never before published.' Ward & Lock. Yellow pictorial boards. Small format.
pp. (iv) + 316
Described on front cover as 'Uniform with Secret Service'.

FRENCH DETECTIVE (AUTOBIOGRAPHY OF A) from 1818–1858 1862 [3514]
By M. CANLER. Ward & Lock. Yellow boards, designed and lettered in scarlet and black. Spine uniform with *All at Sea* (q.v.). Small format.
pp. iv + (316)
Ink signature: 'J. Browne', on title.
Note. The book has an intelligent preface by Lascelles Wraxall, showing that he sponsored (maybe translated) this edition of a work suppressed in France.

FRENCH DETECTIVE-OFFICER (EXPERIENCES OF A) n.d. [3515]
Adapted from the manuscript of Theodore Duhamel by 'WATERS'. C. H. Clarke. Yellow pictorial boards, printed end-papers.
Half-title. pp. (310) [paged (318)]
Parlour Library, No. 134.

HEIR-AT-LAW (THE) and other Tales n.d. [3516]
By 'WATERS', author of 'Recollections of a Detective Police Officer', 'A Skeleton in Every House',

etc. Henry Lea. Yellow pictorial boards. End-papers printed with publisher's adverts. Small format.

pp. (352) Publisher's cat., 8 pp. undated, at end.

[3517] HORSE-COPER (CONFESSIONS OF A) n.d.
By 'BALLINASLOE', author of 'Recollections of a Horse Dealer', etc. George Vickers, Angel Court. Plum boards, designed and lettered in dark blue. Small format.
pp. (ii)+(174)

[3518] IRISH POLICE MAGISTRATE (RECOLLECTIONS OF AN), and other Reminiscences of the South of Ireland 1862
By HENRY ROBERT ADDISON, author of 'Who's Who?', 'Stories of Indian Life', 'The Diary of a Judge', etc. Ward & Lock. Bright green boards, designed and lettered in scarlet and black. Spine uniform with *All at Sea* (3502). Small format.
Half-title. pp. xii+(308) [20_2] adverts.
Ink signature: 'J. Browne', on title.

[3519] IRISH POLICE MAGISTRATE (Twenty Years' Recollections of a) 1880
By Frank Thorpe Porter, A.M., J.P. Dublin: Hodges Figgis; London: Simpkin. 'Eighth Edition.' Pale yellow pictorial (by lithography) boards. Small format.
Half-title. pp. xii+(412) $2D_6$ adverts.
Ink signature: 'J. Browne', on title.
Note. Judging from date to Preface, this book was first published in 1875.

[3520] IRISH POLICE OFFICER (THE). Comprising 'The Identification' and Other Tales founded upon remarkable Trials in Ireland 1861
By ROBERT CURTIS. Ward & Lock. Yellow pictorial boards. End-papers printed in blue with publishers' adverts. Small format.
pp. (viii)+216
Ink signature: 'J. Browne', on title.

[3521] ITALIAN DETECTIVE (AUTOBIOGRAPHY OF AN) [anon] n.d. [1880]
J. & R. Maxwell. 'Never before published.' Yellow pictorial boards.
pp. (iv)+316
Ink signature: 'J. Browne', on title, by whom the date of issue was supplied below imprint.
Note. Title as given above on front cover and spine. On title: 'Autobiography of an Italian Police Officer.'

[3522] JOHN HORSLEYDOWN, OF THE CONFESSIONS OF A THIEF 1860
Written by himself, and revised by THOMAS LITTLETON HOLT. Ward & Lock. Yellow pictorial boards (I think by Phiz). Small format.
Half-title. pp. (viii)+312

KIRKE WEBBE: THE PRIVATEER CAPTAIN n.d. [3523]
By 'WATERS', author of 'The Detective Police Officer', 'Game of Life', etc. Knight & Son, Clerkenwell Close. Yellow pictorial boards. End-papers printed in blue with publishers' adverts. (Knight & Son).
Half-title. pp. 260 Cat. of publications of J. & C. Brown, 8 pp. undated, at end.
Note. Did Knight succeed to the business of J. & C. Brown?

LADY DETECTIVE (REVELATIONS OF A)
By the author of 'Anonyma', 'Incognita', 'Skittles', etc. See 3417 above.

LAW AND LAWYERS: a Sketch Book of Legal Biography, Gossip and Anecdote 1858 [3524]
By ARCHER POLSON. Routledge. Yellow pictorial boards. End-papers printed with publishers' adverts. Small format.
pp. (200) Publishers' cat., 16 pp. undated, at end. Slip of salmon-coloured paper, tipped on to front fly-leaf, advertises *Walker's Pronouncing Dictionary.*
Rubber stamp: 'J. R. Molineux', on verso of title.

LAW-CLERK (LEAVES FROM THE DIARY OF A) (1857) [3525]
By the author of 'Recollections of a Detective Police Officer' ['WATERS']. J. & C. Brown, Ave Maria Lane.
Copy I. Pictorial yellow *cloth.* Small format.
pp. (296) Slip of violet paper, tipped on to front fly-leaf, advertises four juvenile books.
Ink signature: 'J. P. Stocker', on fly-leaf.
Copy II. Pictorial yellow *boards.* Cover picture and collation identical with Copy I. Violet paper advert. slip not present in this copy. [3525*a*]
Note. This pair of volumes is interesting as providing a specimen (i) of a cloth-bound book designed in imitation of a yellow-back, (ii) of the same book in actual yellow-back form. (Cf. Dumas, 3543 (20))

LONDON LIFE AT THE POLICE COURTS 1864 [3526]
By W. H. WATTS. Ward & Lock. Yellow pictorial boards (by Phiz). Small format.
pp. iv+316

NEW YORK DETECTIVE POLICE OFFICER (THE) 1865 [3527]
Edited by JOHN B. WILLIAMS, M.D. 'Never before Printed.' John Maxwell & Co. Yellow boards, designed and lettered in scarlet and black. Small format.
pp. iv+(316)

PHYSICIAN (RECOLLECTIONS OF A), or Episodes of Life. Collected from Thirty Years' Practice 1861 [3528]
By WILLIAM HEARD HILLYARD. Ward & Lock. Yellow boards, designed and lettered in

scarlet and black. Spine uniform with *All at Sea* Small format.

Half-title. pp. (viii)+(376) BB_3 BB_4 adverts. Advert. of W. H. Smith's Library, 4 pp. undated, inserted between front end-papers.

[3529] PRIVATE DETECTIVE (REVELATIONS OF A) 1863
By ANDREW FORRESTER, JUN. 'Never before Printed.' Ward & Lock. Yellow pictorial
Pl. 5 boards (? by Leech). Small format.

pp. 320 Leaf of pink paper tipped on to front fly-leaf advertises W. H. Smith's Subscription Library.

[3530] PRIVATE ENQUIRY OFFICE (SECRETS OF A) n.d. [circa 1884]
By JAMES PEDDIE. C. H. Clarke. Pictorial yellow back boards. Large format.

pp. 320

Ink signature: 'J. Browne', on title.

[3531] SECRET SERVICE, OR RECOLLECTIONS OF A CITY DETECTIVE 1864
By ANDREW FORRESTER, JUN., author of 'The Private Detective'. 'Never before published.' Ward & Lock. Pictorial yellow-back boards. Small format.

pp. (iv)+(316) X_6 blank. Slip of blue paper, tipped on to front fly-leaf, advertises 2*s.* edition of *My Uncle the Curate* over imprint of Chapman & Hall.

Rubber stamp: 'Quendon Court, Bishops Stortford', on title.

Described on front cover as 'Uniform with Private Detective'.

[3532] STORIES FROM SCOTLAND YARD 1890
By INSPECTOR MOSER and CHARLES F. RIDEAL. Routledge. Large format.

Half-title. pp. (256) R_8 adverts.

[3533] TALES IN THE CABIN, or Nights on the Ocean 1861
By a Ship's Surgeon (DR W. M. HILLYARD, author of 'Recollections of a Physician').

Copy I: First Edition. Ward & Lock. Pale blue boards, designed and lettered in dark blue. Spine uniform with *All at Sea.* pp. iv+380

Ink signature: 'J. Browne', on title.

[3533*a*] **Copy II: Re-issue.** 'Published for the Proprietors.' 1863. Yellow pictorial (and amorous) boards, spine still uniform with *All at Sea.* Collation as Copy I. Back cover advert. (over Ward & Lock imprint) of Aimard's Works.

Note. This re-issue is curious. Manifestly printed from the plates of Copy I and carrying a Ward & Lock advert. on back, it has the elusive imprint: 'Printed for the Proprietors.' It seems possible that Ward & Lock diverted some of their potentially more sensational titles into Holywell Street channels, and dressed them pictorially to fit their new role.

THEATRICAL LIFE (SHIFTING SCENES IN) 1859 [3534]
By ELIZA WINSTANLEY, Comedian. Routledge. Yellow pictorial boards (? by Phiz). End-papers printed with publishers' adverts. Small format.

pp. iv+(296) 8 pp. adverts. at end.

TOM FOX, OR THE REVELATIONS OF A DETECTIVE [3535]
[by John Bennett, 3443 above] 1860
George Vickers, Angel Court. White boards, designed and lettered in pale blue and black. Wood-engraved front. on text paper and very numerous text illustrations, largely of a humorous and skilful kind. Small format.

pp. viii+(216) [mis-paged (3)–218]

TOM ROCKET, &C. &C. &C. 1860 [3536]
By ALBANY FONBLANQUE, JUN., author of 'Rights and Wrongs', 'The Man of Fortune', 'How we are Governed', etc. etc. Ward & Lock. Yellow pictorial boards. Small format.

pp. (iv)+(348) Z_6 blank.

Ink signature: 'Charles Penruddock, Compton Park', on title.

These stories are collected from *The Welcome Guest* and other periodicals.

TRADITIONS OF LONDON: Historical and Legendary 1859 [3537]
By 'WATERS', author of 'Recollections of a Police Officer', 'The Serf Girl of Moscow', 'Kirke Webbe', etc. etc. W. Kent & Co., Paternoster Row and (late D. Bogue) 86 Fleet Street. Yellow pictorial boards. End-papers printed in blue with Ward & Lock adverts. Small format.

pp. (iv)+258 Final leaf, S_1, a single inset (see *Note*).

Rubber stamp: 'J. R. Molineux', on verso of title.

Note. Although this consists of first edition sheets, it is in fact a secondary issue. The volume was originally a full post-8vo, bound in maroon ripple-grain cloth, blocked in blind and lettered in gold. The two issues collate identically, save that in the cloth edition S_2 (adverts.) completes the final signature.

UNDISCOVERED CRIMES 1862 [3538]
By 'WATERS', author of 'Recollections of a Police Officer', 'Experiences of a Real Detective', etc. Ward & Lock. Yellow boards designed and lettered in scarlet and dark green. Spine uniform with *All at Sea.* Small format.

pp. (iv)+316

[3539] DICKENS, CHARLES

Dombey & Son. 2 vols. Chapman & Hall 1865. Bright green boards, printed in black. Large format. Front. to each volume from first edition. Set in double column and called 'The People's Dombey'.

Oliver Twist

Copy I. Chapman & Hall 1877. Greenish-white pictorial boards. Large format.

Copy II. Warne, n.d. (after 1881). Yellow pictorial wrappers, cut flush. No. 63 of *Warne's Notable Novels.*

Pickwick Papers (The). Chapman & Hall, n.d. Uniform with *Oliver Twist.*

Sketches by Boz. Chapman & Hall 1877. Uniform with *Oliver Twist.*

Picnic Papers (The).

Copy I. Five Parts. Ward & Lock, n.d. [circa 1856]. Yellow wrappers printed in black and cut flush. Parts III and IV have fronts. by Cruikshank, probably printed from the original plates. Part IV has printed end-papers, others plain. Square format.

Copy II. Ward & Lock, n.d. Grey pictorial boards. Small format.

[3540] DISRAELI, BENJAMIN

Uniform large format, published by Longman etc. Pale yellow pictorial boards, with conventional spine designs and printed end-papers. Undated [1881]. All except *Endymion* described as 'New Edition' and all listed as volumes in *Longman's Modern Novelists Library.*

Endymion
Tancred (inscription dated 1881)
Henrietta Temple
Venetia
Sybil
Young Duke (The) and Count Alarcos

[3540*a*] *Note.* Longman's yellow-back edition of Disraeli's novels was also published in olive brown pebble-grain cloth blocked in black and gold, with all edges gilt and dark green end-papers. This is the handsomest 'cloth version' of a yellow-back edition known to me. The complete series of 10 vols., in new condition, is in the Collection.

[3541] DRURY, A. H.

Misrepresentation. 'New Edition.' Ward & Lock, n.d. (after 1881). Pale green pictorial boards. *Select Library.*

[3542] DUFFY'S LIBRARY OF IRELAND 1845–1847

Although this series is predominantly non-fictional, I include it here because it contains certain titles (both fictional and otherwise) of real importance; because the volumes are with two exceptions first editions; and because, owing to its considerable scarcity, a schedule of the contents so far as I can establish them may prove of value to students of Irish history and letters.

The volumes (published monthly at one shilling from 1 July 1845 to early in 1847) are 12mo, and bound in glazed white wrappers cut flush and printed in two colours, on front with decorative frame enclosing titling, etc., on spine down-lettered on decorative panel, on back printed with list of the series, as it develops.† The imprint throughout is: 'Dublin: James Duffy.' The volumes are not numbered, but for convenience sake I have numbered them in the order of their appearance. Titles asterisked are not in the Collection.

1 THE IRISH VOLUNTEERS OF 1782. By T. MACNEVIN. July 1845
Wrappers printed in green and black. This copy is 'Fourth Edition', so the back wrapper is of late state, listing six titles as published. 'Fourth Edition' is printed on wrapper only, not on title, but a 'Preface to the Fourth Edition' dated August 16, 1845 occupies pp. (vii) (viii). Pp. (viii) [paged vi] + (9) [paged (7)]–(252) [paged 250]

2 *BALLAD POETRY OF IRELAND. Edited by C. GAVAN DUFFY. August, 1845

3 RODY THE ROVER. By W. CARLETON. September 1845 (see 512 in Section I)

4 LIFE AND TIMES OF AODH O'NEILL, Prince of Ulster. Called by the English Hugh, Earl of Tyrone. By JOHN MITCHEL. October 1845
Wrappers printed in green and bronze-brown. pp. 252 [paged (i)–xii + (13)–252]

† The series was also issued in a 'presentation binding' of black morocco, with a harp in gold on front and back, spine fully gilt and all edges gilt.

5 PARRA SASTHA. By W. CARLETON. November 1845 (see 506 in Section I)

6 THE SONGS OF IRELAND. Edited by M. J. BARRY. December 1845
Wrappers printed in green and red. Inset leaf of adverts. precedes title. pp. (ii) + xvi + (25)–(240) (N_4) adverts. Pagination and signing irregular in this volume, but the copy is in excellent condition and nothing is missing. Contents and Index both form part of the prelims.

7 LITERARY AND HISTORICAL ESSAYS. By THOMAS DAVIS. Christmas Eve 1845. Dated 1846
Wrappers printed in green and black. Leaf of adverts. precedes title. pp. 252 [paged (i)–(xii) + (13)–252]

8 THE IRISH WRITERS OF THE SEVENTEENTH CENTURY. ('Gallery of Irish Writers') By THOMAS D'ARCY M'GEE. January 1846
Wrappers printed in red and grey. pp. 252 [paged (i)–(xii) + (13)–252]

9 THE CASKET OF IRISH PEARLS. Edited by THORNTON MACMAHON. (?) February 1846
Wrappers printed in red and grey. Half-title. pp. xxiv + (13)–240 Once again an apparently causeless irregularity in pagination.

10 *THE POETS AND DRAMATISTS OF IRELAND. Vol. I. By DENIS FLORENCE M'CARTHY. (?) March 1846

11 THE POEMS OF THOMAS DAVIS, now first collected. April 1846
Wrappers printed in blue and black. 'Duffy's Literary Advertiser', 24 pp. undated, precedes title. pp. xxx + 232

12 THE CONFISCATION OF ULSTER. By THOMAS MACNEVIN. (?) May or June 1846
Wrappers printed in blue and black. Folding map follows last page of text. 'Library of Ireland Advertiser', 32 pp. on thin paper dated May 1846, followed by the first (blank) of two leaves of same paper wrapped round prelims., precede title. These two thin leaves are reckoned in pagination, thus: pp. (xii) [of which (i) (ii) and (xi) (xii) are on thin paper and included 'as the work went to Press'] + (13)–260

13 THE HISTORY OF THE AMERICAN REVOLUTION. By MICHAEL DOHENY. July 1846
Wrappers printed in blue and black. pp. (xvi) + (13)–248 Similar irregularity in pagination to No. 9. It looks as though text were paged from (13) onward before the extent of the prelims. had been decided.

14 THE CONFEDERATION OF KILKENNY. By REV. C. P. MEEHAN. (?) August 1846
Wrappers printed in blue and black. pp. 234 [paged (i)–xii + (13)–234] Final leaf, O_3, a single inset. Pp. (229)–254 Appendix.

15 THE LIFE OF THE RT. HON. J. P. CURRAN, by THOMAS DAVIS and A MEMOIR OF THE LIFE OF RT. HON. HENRY GRATTAN, by D. O. MADDEN. With Addenda and Letter in reply to Lord Clare. September 1846
Wrappers printed in blue and black. Inset leaf of adverts. precedes title. pp. (ii) + iv + (5)–232

16 THE BOOK OF IRISH BALLADS. Edited by D. F. M'CARTHY. October 1846
Wrappers printed in blue and black. pp. 252 [paged (i)–(x) + (11)–252]

17 HISTORICAL WORKS OF THE RT. REV. NICHOLAS FRENCH, D.D., Bishop of Ferns. Vol. I (containing *The Bleeding Iphigenia*, *The Settlement and Sale of Ireland*, Letters, etc.) (?) November 1846
Wrappers printed in blue and black. pp. lxxx + (81)–84 + (1)–144

18 DITTO. Vol. II (containing *The Unkind Deserter*). (?) December 1846
Wrappers printed in blue and black. pp. (vi) + 10 pp. unfoliated + (5)–(204) M_{10} blank.

19 ***Art Maguire** by **W. Carleton** (? month) 1847
This is not a first edition, the work having originally appeared in 1845 (see 492 in Section I).

20 ***History of the Rebellion of '98. By Edward Hay.** (? month)
This is not a first edition, the work having originally appeared in 1803.

21 THE GERALDINES, EARLS OF DESMOND, and the Persecution of the Irish Catholics. Translated by REV. C. P. MEEHAN. (? month) 1847
Wrappers printed in blue and black. pp. xii + (240) O_{12} adverts. Preface dated January 30, 1847.

22 *MEMOIRS OF ART MACMURROUGH. By MCGEE. (?) 1847

Here the series officially ended; but in February 1849 was published in the same format *Songs of Ireland: Second Series*, edited by Hercules Elliss, and this volume is generally accepted as belonging to the Library of Ireland.

In 1848 the series proper was re-issued in 11 vols., each containing two of the original volumes, bound in green cloth at two shillings and also in green morocco. New titles were printed for this re-issue.

A moving spirit in this whole venture was Thomas Davis, and a *Life of Wolfe Tone* by him was advance-announced as No. 4 in the series, together with a long list of works by other authors. Davis died suddenly in September 1845; and the plans (maybe also the possibilities) for publication on an extensive scale were severely curtailed. It will have been noted that posthumous tributes to Davis in the form of volumes of his writings were a feature of the series, but that these did not include a biography of Tone.

[3543] DUMAS, ALEXANDRE, THE ELDER

Such precision as this section (and the Dumas entries elsewhere in the Catalogue) may possess is due entirely to the researches of Mr Douglas Munro. He has for years been at work on the huge and obscure subject of English translations of Dumas, and, pending the completion of his own full-length bibliography, has most generously supplied me with the facts regarding the various Dumas items in my Collection. I am able, therefore, with fair certainty to record which among them are 'first editions in English', which 'first English editions' (i.e. published in England later than in U.S.A.), and which mere reprints.

The titles listed below exclude those Dumas translations which belong to *named* Series represented in the Collection and elsewhere recorded under their Series heading. The books which follow are, so to speak, the 'unattached' Dumas translations, and are arranged alphabetically under title irrespective of publisher and date. All, except where otherwise stated, are in pictorial boards with backgrounds of various colours. Only 'first editions in English' are set in caps. The numbering, of course, is mine.

1 **Ascanio: an Historical Romance**

C. H. Clarke, n.d. [1858 or 1859]. Small format. 1*s.* 6*d.*

A reprint. The first edition in English was Baltimore, Philadelphia and New York, Taylor & Co. 1845 or 1846. First English edition, C. H. Clarke 1847.

2 **Beau Tancrede**

Routledge, n.d. Yellow paper wrappers cut flush and printed with a portrait of Dumas, patterning and lettering in red and black. Small format. Price 1*s.* This (like 5, 15, 17 and 20) belongs to a rather degraded cheap uniform edition of Dumas, published in the late seventies.

3 **Catherine Blum**

Routledge 1861. Small format. A volume in Routledge's Railway Library. 1*s.* 6*d.*

First English edition. The first edition in English was New York, Appleton 1854, under the title *The Foresters.*

4 **Château Rouge, or the Reign of Terror**

Routledge 1859.

Small format. A volume in Routledge's Railway Library. 1*s.* 6*d.*

A reprint. The first English edition appeared in 1846 and between 1846 and 1859 versions of the novel (*Le Chevalier de Maison Rouge*) were published by eight different firms. This Railway Library edition is mainly remarkable for its mistranslations.

5 **Chevalier de Maison Rouge.** Uniform with 2 above.

6 **Corsican Brothers (The)**

Routledge, n.d. [1885]. Pictorial wrappers, cut flush. Small format. 1*s.*

A reprint. This version (by Henry Frith) had first been published in 1880. Several other editions in English, variously relevant to Dumas' original, had earlier appeared between 1852 and the late seventies.

7 GARIBALDI: AN AUTOBIOGRAPHY (edited by Alexandre Dumas). Translated by William Robson

Routledge 1860. Yellow boards with portrait of Garibaldi; lettering, etc. in the green, yellow, red of Italian freedom. End-papers printed with publishers' adverts. dated 1860. Lithographed portrait front. Small format.

Half title. pp. (352) Y_2–Y_8 publishers' cat. paged (1)–14, undated.

First edition in English.

8 **Half Brothers (The), or the Head and the Hand**

Routledge, n.d. Small format. A volume in Routledge's Railway Library. 2*s.*

A reprint of a translation of *Le Bâtard de Mauléon.* The first edition in English was by Appleyard, London 1848. The first Routledge edition was 1858.

9 **Isabel of Bavaria: an Historical Romance**

David Bryce, n.d. [1860]. Small format. 2*s.*

In part a first English edition of this version. The first edition in English was from Bruce and Wyld, London 1846. The present Bryce edition offers a new translation of Chaps. I–VI, but thereafter is a garbled version of the Bruce and Wyld text. The author's preface is omitted.

10 **Marguerite de Valois: an Historical Romance**

Routledge, n.d. [1856]. Small format. 2*s.* *Pl. 4*

A reprint of the first edition in English of *La Reine Margot,* published in Bogue's European Library in 1846.

11 **Mary Stuart**

Henry Lea, n.d. [1860]. Small format. 2*s.*

A reprint, omitting the wood-blocks, of the version published by Clarke in 1853 in 'Illustrated Literature of all Nations' under the title *Mary, Queen of Scots.* The first edition in English was that published by G. Pierce, London 1846 or 1847.

12 **Memoirs of a Physician**

Routledge, n.d. [circa 1866–7]. Large format.

A reprint. The first English edition of *Les Mémoires d'un Médecin: Joseph Balsamo* was practically contemporaneous with the first French edition 1846–8, forming Nos. 2 and 10 of the Parlour

Library. This imperfect version, without revision, was several times reprinted by Routledge.

13 OTTO THE ARCHER
Henry Lea, n.d. [1860]. Small format. 1*s*.
First edition in English.

14 **Page of the Duke of Savoy (The).** Uniform with 2 and 5 above.

15 **Queen's Necklace (The): a Sequel to Memoirs of a Physician**
Routledge, n.d. [circa 1885]. Large format.
A reprint. The first edition in English of *Le Collier de la Reine* was New York, W. F. Burgess 1850. The first English edition was Parlour Library No. 132, and this is the translation reprinted in the present edition.

16 **Regent's Daughter (The).** Uniform with 2, 5 and 14 above.

17 **Russian Gipsy (The), or The Palace of Ice**
Henry Lea, n.d. [1860]. Small format. 2*s*.
First English edition. The first edition in English of *La Maison de Glace* was New York, E. D. Long 1860, and this first English edition was the same translation issued later in the same year.

18 SPECTRE MOTHER (The), or LOVE AFTER DEATH
C. H. Clarke 1864. Small format. Pp. (288) [paged 292] 2*s*.
First edition in English of *Albine.*

19 **Twenty Years After.** Uniform with 2, 5, 14 and 16 above

20 **Vicomte de Bragelonne (The), or Ten Years Later**
2 vols. Routledge 1857. Yellow pictorial cloth. Small format. Per vol. 2*s*. 6*d*.
First English edition. The first edition in English was New York, Dean 1848.
Examples are very uncommon of books bound in yellow *cloth* and pictorially blocked exactly as though they were regulation yellow-backs. Such specimens perhaps represented a specially strengthened issue for library use. This work was also published in yellow-back *boards* with identical pictorial and decorative blocking. The price of the two issues, oddly enough, was the same.
The public undoubtedly got its money's worth, although in painfully small type. Vol. I contains 679 pages and Vol. II, 600. The same picture appears on both front covers.

21 **Watchmaker (The)**
Henry Lea, n.d. [1860]. Small format. 1*s*. 6*d*. Imprint on title, front cover and end-papers, as above. But outside back cover advertises the 'Popular Publications' of David Bryce, among them *The Watchmaker* at 2*s*.
A reprint. The first edition in English was a translation by Eugene Plunkett entitled *The Devil's Wedding-Ring or the Adventures of a Watchmaker*, New York, Williams Bros (?) 1844. This was re-issued in 1847. The first English edition (same translation) came from Bryce in 1860 and was immediately reprinted by Henry Lea (i.e. the present edition). Subsequently both C. H. Clarke and Routledge reprinted Plunkett's translation. None of these English pirates acknowledge the translator's name.
L'Horloger has the peculiar distinction of having completely disappeared in its original edition. No serial issue in French, or book-issue published in France or Belgium, has been located.

For other Dumas titles under Series-headings, see HODGSON'S NEW SERIES OF NOVELS (below); PARLOUR NOVELIST and PARLOUR LIBRARY (in Section III).

[3544] DUMAS, ALEXANDRE, THE YOUNGER

Denise (The Story of) [Founded on the Drama *Denise*]
Spencer Blackett 1891. Large format. 2*s*. Imprint on title as above; imprint on front cover 'J. & R. Maxwell'.

Harriet, or The Adventures of a Lady of Title
E. Harrison, Salisbury Court, n.d. Small format. 2*s*.

Lady with the Camelias (The)
E. Harrison, Exeter Change, n.d. Small format. No price on covers, but advertised on outside back cover of *Harriet* at 1*s*. 6*d*.
This volume has a preface by Jules Janin and is described as 'Translated without Abridgement from the Eighth Paris Edition'. The picture on the front cover is repeated on the back cover. The spine is unlettered.
Mr Munro informs me that he believes the first edition in English was New York, Dewitt & Davenport 1855, under the title *Camille, or the Fate of a Coquette.*

[3545] EDEN, HON. ELEANOR

Dumbleton Common. 'New Edition.' Chapman & Hall 1868. Yellow pictorial boards. *Select Library.*

[3546] EDWARDS, AMELIA B.

Half-a-Million of Money. Routledge, n.d. (after 1891). Pale buff pictorial wrappers, up-lettered on spine.

In the Days of My Youth. Ward & Lock, n.d. (after 1891).

Monsieur Maurice and Other Tales. 'New Edition.' Ward & Lock, n.d. (after 1881). Yellow pictorial boards. *Select Library.*

[3547] EDWARDES, ANNIE

Archie Lovell. 'New Edition.' Chatto & Windus, n.d. (1899). Yellow pictorial boards.

[3548] EDWARDS, M. BETHAM

Bridget. Routledge 1893. Yellow pictorial boards.

Flower of Doom (The). 'Third Edition.' Ward & Downey, n.d. [1885]. Buff pictorial wrappers, up-lettered on spine. *Ward & Downey's Shilling Library of Fiction.*

[3549] ELLIS, SARAH S.

MY BROTHER, OR THE MAN OF MANY FRIENDS (by 'An Old Author')
Slim 8vo. Sampson, Low 1855. Thick white boards, bevelled edges, printed in chocolate, dark blue and black with design of Christmas Tree and fancy lettering. Design repeated on back cover. Bright apple-green end-papers. Wood-engraved front. after George Cruikshank, on special paper used also for printed title, though the latter alone is reckoned in collation. pp. (vi) + (228) (Q_2) adverts.
Binders' ticket: 'Bone & Son', at end.
Note. A very unusual piece of production for a paper-board book. The front cover is signed: 'Bradbury & Evans Printers, Whitefriars', on the bottom bevel.

[3550] ERCKMANN-CHATRIAN (Emile Erckmann and Alexandre Chatrian)

I. **Smith, Elder Edition.** Published in cloth at 3*s*. 6*d*. and in ornamental stiff wrappers, cut flush, at 1*s*. The numbering is mine.

1 THE CONSCRIPT: a Tale of the French War of 1813. 1870
Green bubble-grain cloth, blocked in black and gold; chocolate end-papers. Wood-engraved front. and 24 illustrations. pp. (viii) + 288 Publishers' adverts., 4 pp. undated, at end.
Binder's ticket: 'Burn', at end.

2 WATERLOO: a Story of the Hundred Days. Being a Sequel to 'The Conscript'. 1870
Dark cream wrappers printed in grey blue and black; cream end-papers. Wood-engraved front. and 3 illustrations. pp. (iv) + (316) 20_5 20_6 adverts. (as in 1).
Book-label of John Bell Sedgwick.

3 BLOCKADE OF PHALSBURG (The): an Episode of the Fall of the First French Empire. 1870
Dark cream wrappers, uniform with 2 but printed in green and black. End-papers, illustrations and book-label as 2. pp. (iv) + 272 Publishers' adverts. as in 1 at end.

4 INVASION OF FRANCE IN 1814 (The)
Dark cream wrappers, uniform with 2 and 3 but printed in chocolate and black. Portrait front. End-papers and book-label as 2 and 3. pp. xii + 276 Pp. (v)–xii carry a Memoir of the Authors.

According to the *English Catalogue* only these 4 vols. were published.

[3550*a*] **II. Ward & Lock (S. O. Beeton's) Edition.** Only one title of this poor quality series is in the Collection. In contrast to the good manufacture, elegant appearance and evident authority of the Smith, Elder volumes, this book looks very inferior; and it and its fellows were probably pirated from early French editions. The series started in February or March 1871 and the first volume was *Madame Thérèse.* The specimen in the Collection (POPULAR TALES AND ROMANCES) is undated and in white pictorial stiff wrappers cut flush, with printed end-papers. The front cover is headed: BEETON'S ERCKMANN-CHATRIAN LIBRARY (this series title also appears on spine) and the back cover advertises eight titles in cloth at 3*s*. 6*d*. and in paper at 1*s*., as well as two others then running serially.

ERCKMANN-CHATRIAN

Among the titles listed at 1*s*. is THE STORY OF A PEASANT in two parts. I have seen these two parts bound in one volume in natural-coloured canvas, patterned and fancy lettered in blue and red, and described on front cover as: 'S. O. Beeton's Edition of Erckmann-Chatrian. Price Two Shillings.' It appears from the series-advert. on the back of this volume that only this title was re-issued in this form.

[3551] FARJEON, B. L.

House of White Shadows (The). 'Fifth Edition.' Ward & Downey, n.d. Yellow pictorial boards.

[3552] FERRIER, SUSAN

All Routledge, n.d., in yellow pictorial boards, small format.

Destiny. 'New Edition, Revised and Corrected by Miss Ferrier.'

Inheritance. 'New Edition, Revised and Corrected by the Authoress.'

Marriage.

Note. These are almost certainly reprints (? in the seventies) from the plates of the edition of [1856].

[3553] FIRST CLASS LIBRARY (The) 1861

'Published for the Proprietor by Kent & Co., Paternoster Row', this (I fancy) short-lived series was heralded by a spirited Prospectus, from which a few sentences merit perpetuation.

The Library is to contain First Class Copyright Works, 'each volume to have no coercive connection with preceding or succeeding volumes'....'It is idle to assume that first-class literature must be confined to the old three-volume novel and guinea and a half fashion. The Proprietors of the FIRST CLASS LIBRARY honestly believe they can afford to produce approved copyright works of some of our best living Authors at a price which will put them within reach of the great reading public....Hitherto the perusal of works of celebrated authors at a low price was accompanied in too many cases by a terrible risk to the eyes. Take up any of the mis-named railway books, and try to read it as the train dashes along through cuttings or over viaducts, and the result is a dazing of the eyesight and a feeling of misery. The Proprietors of the F.C.L. wish to obviate these and other evils. In the first place they will give clear type and good paper; in the next they will insure that the cover does not remain in the reader's hand, so soon as the leaves are opened.'

The volumes in the series are given hereafter in the order of appearance. They are not themselves numbered. All are of small format, and cased in bright green boards, designed and lettered in red and either dark green or dark blue. The series title and price appear on front cover and spine. Titles given in caps are first editions; those asterisked are not in the Collection.

1 AFTER OFFICE HOURS, by EDMUND YATES
No date on title; Preface dated 1861. Dedicated to Charles Dickens (misprinted 'Dicken'). Price Two Shillings. pp. (viii) + 312

2 *THE FINEST GIRL IN BLOOMSBURY, by AUGUSTUS MAYHEW

Pl. 6 3 CRIMINAL CELEBRITIES: a Collection of Memorable Trials, by LASCELLES WRAXALL
Title dated 1861. Price Two Shillings. pp. viii + (360) AA_4 adverts., of which recto over imprint of Ward & Lock.
Ink signature: 'J. Browne', on title.

4 **Twice Round the Clock,** by G. A. Sala
Title dated 1861. Price Half a Crown. pp. 424 Two leaves dated September 1, 1861, inserted between front end-papers advertise surplus library books from W. H. Smith's Library.
Rubber stamp: 'J. R. Molineux', on verso of title.
Note. Mr Ralph Straus informs me that he has a copy of this book in full purple morocco cloth, blocked in blind and gold-lettered on spine with title and name of series. Presumably the other volumes, also, were published in cloth as well as in boards.

At this point, order of publication (and indeed facts of publication) become obscure. The back cover of No. 4 announces as 'In the Press' *The Honour of the Family* by Watts Phillips. But the back cover of the only other volume in the Collection (see below) announces as 'Now Ready' the four titles above given and *Maids of Honour* by Robert Folkestone Williams; also as 'In the Press' Sala's *Baddington Peerage*, Aylmer's *Memoirs of a Lady in Waiting* and Braddon's *Lady Lisle.* It makes no mention of *The Honour of the Family* nor of the book on whose back cover the advertisement appears.

For convenience sake alone, we proceed to describe as No.

5 JEST AND EARNEST, by GODFREY TURNER

Title dated 1861. Price Two Shillings. Half-title. pp. 336

Note. It is worth remarking that of the titles announced as 'In the Press' on the back cover of No. 5, Aylmer's *Lady in Waiting* and Braddon's *Lady Lisle* actually appeared a year later (1862) in Ward & Lock's Shilling Volume Library (3711). I suspect they never came out in the First Class Library, and that that venture failed, its commitments being taken over by Ward & Lock (unless indeed Kent were a 'cover' for Ward & Lock or for some one connected with them—possibly John Maxwell). Finally, Mr Ralph Straus informs me that he has never seen *The Baddington Peerage* in this series and doubts its having ever appeared, especially as an abbreviated version of the novel ran serially from August 1861 in *The Welcome Guest.*

[3554] FISHER, ADMIRAL

Petrel (The). Piper, Stephenson & Spence, n.d. Yellow pictorial boards. Small format.

[3555] FLAUBERT, GUSTAVE

Salammbo. Translated by J. S. Chartres. Vizetelly 1886. Pale yellow pictorial boards. Specially drawn spine.

GABORIAU, ÉMILE

[3556] **I. Original Vizetelly Issue.** Published at one shilling each, in orange-scarlet (or crimson) stiff wrappers, cut flush and printed in black—on front, with decorative frame, portrait, title, imprint and, at head, series title: GABORIAU'S SENSATIONAL NOVELS, and price; up-lettered on spine; on back printed with adverts. (unless otherwise stated). Pale blue printed end-papers. No series number on covers, but each volume numbered on title.

1 IN PERIL OF HIS LIFE 1881

pp. (256) The paging calls for a half-title, and there may originally have been one in this copy for A_8 is a single leaf. Four-page leaflet advertising 'Select Library of Fiction' as on sale at Smith's bookstalls, inset after p. (256).

2 THE LEROUGE CASE 1881

Half-title. pp. (224) O_6–O_8 adverts.

3 OTHER PEOPLE'S MONEY 1881

Half-title. pp. (248) Q_3 Q_4 adverts.

4 LECOQ THE DETECTIVE. 2 vols. 1881

Half-title in each vol.

Vol. I pp. (232) P_4 adverts.

II pp. (208) N_8 adverts. Four-page inset advertising 'Vizetelly's Popular French Novels' at end.

5 THE MYSTERY OF ORCIVAL and PROMISE OF MARRIAGE 1883

Half-title. pp. (216) O_3 O_4 adverts. This volume has pale yellow printed end-papers.

6 THE GILDED CLIQUE. 'Twentieth Thousand.' 1885

Half-title. pp. (256) This volume has plain white end-papers.

7 DOSSIER NO. 113. 'Twenty-fifth Thousand.' 1885

Half-title. pp. (240) I_2 adverts.

8 THE LITTLE OLD MAN OF BATIGNOLLES and Other Stories. 'Twenty-fifth Thousand.' 1885

Half-title. pp. (200) G_4 adverts.

9 THE SLAVES OF PARIS. 2 vols. Vol. I, 'Second Edition', 1884. Vol. II, 'Thirtieth Thousand', 1886

Half-title in each vol.

Vol. I pp. (228)

II pp. (212)

10 THE COUNT'S MILLIONS. 2 vols. 'Twentieth Thousand.' 1886

Half-title in each vol.

Vol. I pp. (192)

II pp. (200)

These volumes have very pale green printed end-papers.

11 THE CATASTROPHE. 2 vols. 1885

Half-title in each vol.

Vol. I pp. (196)

II pp. 196

12 THE INTRIGUES OF A POISONER and CAPTAIN COUTANCEAU. 'Twentieth Thousand.' 1886
Half-title. pp. (200) G_4 adverts. This volume has very pale green printed end-papers.

[3556*a*] **II. Re-issue in cloth: Double volumes at Half a Crown.** 8 vols. Vizetelly 1885. Scarlet diagonal-fine-ribbed cloth, blocked on front in dark brown with decorative design enclosing title and incorporating general heading SENSATIONAL FRENCH NOVELS and imprint. Gold-lettered on spine. Blind blocked on back. Cambridge blue chalk surface end-papers.

These volumes consist of sheets of the original issue with new 4 pp. prelims., incidental adverts. removed, and 8 pp. of undated adverts. at end.

The volumes are not numbered and each includes two volumes of the original issue. The titles are arranged as follows: 1 and 12; 2 and 3 (this vol. not in the Collection); 4; 5 and 6; 7 and 8; 9; 10; 11.

[3557] GERSTAECKER, FREDERICK

THE HAUNTED HOUSE: a Tale
Routledge 1857. Yellow pictorial boards (? by Phiz). End-papers printed with adverts. Small format.
pp. (176) Publishers' cat., 8 pp. dated November 1856, at end. Slip of lilac paper tipped on to front end-papers advertises cheap edition of Bulwer Lytton.

[3558] GLEIG, G. R.

Both Routledge, small format.

Light Dragoon (The). 'Twenty-eighth Thousand.' 1854. Cream boards, design printed in red and black (probably by Crowquill). Specially drawn spine, front cover design repeated on back.

Veterans of Chelsea Hospital (The). 'New Edition.' 1857. Yellow pictorial boards, specially designed spine. *Railway Library.*

[3559] GRANT, JAMES

I. First Editions. The two titles imprinted 'J. & C. Brown' are listed as first editions despite the fact that they also appeared in the series ROUTLEDGE'S ORIGINAL NOVELS (3672 below). Quite apart from that series' claim to offer only new fiction, Routledge would be a more probable imprint for Grant than Brown; but I cannot reconcile the apparent dates of the Brown editions with what would seem to be the Routledge dates for Nos. 20 and 21 of the 'Original Novels'.

[3560] ARTHUR BLANE, or the Hundred Cuirassiers
J. & C. Brown, n.d. (1858). Yellow pictorial cloth in imitation of yellow-back boards. Small format.
pp. viii + (368)
Booksellers' ticket: 'Mann Nephews', inside front cover.

[3561] CONSTABLE OF FRANCE (THE), and other Military Historiettes
Routledge, n.d. (1866). Pale yellow pictorial boards, spine with conventional design common to the uniform yellow-back editions. End-papers printed with adverts. Small format.
Half-title. pp. viii + (368) $2A_8$ adverts.

[3562] HIGHLANDERS OF GLEN ORA (THE)
J. & C. Brown, n.d. [1857]. Yellow pictorial cloth, in imitation of yellow-back boards. Small format.
pp. iv + 404
Note. Bodley received their copy from the Copyright Agent on July 25, 1857. Later re-titled *Laura Everingham* (see 3568 below).

LEGENDS OF THE BLACK WATCH, or Forty-Second Highlanders [3563]
Routledge 1859. Yellow pictorial boards (by Phiz). End-papers printed with adverts. Small format.
pp. (viii) + (388) [mispaged (5)–(392)] Publishers' cat., 12 pp. undated, at end.
Pencil signature: 'J. Browne', on title.
Note. This is a volume in *Routledge's Railway Library.*

OLIVER ELLIS, or the Fusiliers [3564]
Routledge 1861. Yellow pictorial boards. End-papers printed with adverts. Small format.
pp. (viii) + 432
Note. This is a volume in *Routledge's Railway Library.*

ROYAL HIGHLANDERS (THE), or the Black Watch in Egypt [3565]
Routledge (1885). Pale yellow pictorial boards, spine with conventional design common to the uniform yellow-back editions. End-papers printed with adverts. Large format.

pp. (384) 24_7 24_8 adverts., paged 3–6.

Blind stamp: 'W. H. Smith & Son', on fly-leaf and title.

Note. I date this book from adverts. inside back cover which have printers' date at foot, from one dated advert., and from the fact that the Bodleian copy was sent in December 1885.

[3566] ROYAL REGIMENT (THE), and Other Novelettes
Routledge [1879]. Pale yellow pictorial boards, spine with conventional design common to the uniform yellow-back editions. End-papers printed with adverts. Small format.

Half-title. pp. viii+(312) X_2–X_4 adverts. paged (3)–8.

'SCOTS BRIGADE (THE)', and Other Tales [3567]
Routledge 1882. Pale yellow pictorial boards, spine with conventional design common to the uniform yellow-back editions. End-papers printed with adverts. Large format.

Half-title. pp. (320) 20_3–20_8 adverts., the final leaf being pasted to inside back cover.

Ink signature: 'J. Browne', on half-title.

YELLOW FRIGATE (THE). 1855. See 3672 (8) below.

[3568] *II. Reprints.*

Series I: Small Format. Unless otherwise stated these are in pale yellow pictorial boards, with uniform spine design, undated and published by Routledge.

Arthur Blane.
- **Copy I.** 'A New Edition.' 1862. Uniform with first edition of 1858.
- **Copy II.** Uniform with the other volumes in this small format series.

Black Watch (The)

Cavaliers of Fortune (The)

Dick Rodney
- **Copy I.** 'New Edition.' *Railway Library.* Dark yellow-back, not in series style.
- **Copy II.** Uniform small format, series style.

Did She Love Him?

Duke of Albany's Own Highlanders (The) 1881

Fairer than a Fairy

First Love and Last Love n.d.

Girl He Married (The) n.d.

Harry Ogilvie

Jack Manly

Jane Seton

King's Own Borderers (The)

Lady Wedderburn's Wish. 'A New Edition.' 1878

Laura Everingham or The Highlanders of Glen Ora

Letty Hyde's Lovers

Lucy Arden (originally published—1859—as *Hollywood Hall*)

Morley Ashton

Oliver Ellis. 'New Edition.' 1865. Dark yellow-back, not in series style. *Railway Library.*

Only an Ensign

Phantom Regiment

Queen's Cadet and Other Tales 1877

Romance of War (The)

Scottish Cavalier (The)

Second to None

Shall I Win Her?

Six Years Ago

Vere of Ours

White Cockade

[3568*a*] **Series II: Large Format.** Unless otherwise stated these also are in pale yellow pictorial boards, with spine design identical with the small format uniform edition but slightly extended; undated and published by Routledge.

Cameronians (The) 1882

Captain of the Guard

Colville of the Guards

Dead Tryst (The)

Dulcie Carlyon 1886

Derval Hampton 1887

Morley Ashton. This copy is in red cloth, blocked in black and gold, a style in which this uniform series of Grant was simultaneously issued.

Playing with Fire 1887

Ross-shire Buffs (The)

Secret Despatch (The). 'New Edition.' Chapman & Hall. 1874. *Select Library of Fiction.* Not in series style.

Sketches in London. 'New Edition.' Ward & Lock, n.d. Not in series style. Specially designed spine. Contains: 'Preface to the Present Edition.'

Vere of Ours. Red cloth, blocked in black and gold, uniform with Morley Ashton.

Violet Jermyn

[3569] GRATTAN, T. C.

Heiress of Bruges (The). Walter Scott, n.d. Cream boards patterned in red and blue (uniform with Adams' *Democracy*). Coloured front. and 3 plates.

Jacqueline of Holland. Weldon, n.d. Pale yellow pictorial boards.

[3570] GREY, MRS

Bosom Friend (The). J. & C. Brown 1858. Yellow pictorial boards. Small format.

Old Country House (The). 'New Edition.' Routledge 1859. Yellow pictorial boards. Small format. *Railway Library.*

Rectory Guest (The). J. & C. Brown, n.d. [circa 1858]. Yellow pictorial boards, specially drawn spine. Small format.

Sybil Lennard. Walter Scott, n.d. Cream boards patterned in red and blue (uniform with Adams' *Democracy*). Coloured front. and 3 plates.

[3571] GRIFFIN, GERALD

Collegians (The). 'New Edition.' Routledge 1861. Yellow pictorial boards. Small format. *Railway Library.*

[3572] HALL, MRS S. C.

LUCKY PENNY (THE), and Other Tales
Routledge 1857. Yellow pictorial boards, end-papers printed with adverts. Small format.
Half-title. pp. (viii) + 312
Ink signature: 'J. Browne', on title. See also above: AMUSING LIBRARY.

[3573] RIFT IN THE ROCK (THE)
Groombridge & Sons, n.d. [1871]. Cream paper wrappers printed in brown, green and red with design adopted for *The Rainbow Stories.* Wood-engraved front. and 1 illustration.
pp. 49–96 (no title) 4 pp. adverts. precede front.; inside covers printed with adverts.
Blind stamp: 'Presentation copy', on front cover.
Note. No. 2 of THE RAINBOW STORIES, published at 4*d.* and paginated straight through from No. 1.

[3574] **Whiteboy (The). Copy I:** 'Cheap Edition.' Chapman & Hall 1855. Yellow printed boards. *Select Library of Fiction.*

Copy II. Chapman & Hall (1880). Cream pictorial boards.

[3575] HANNAY, JAMES

King Dobbs. 'New Edition.' Routledge 1856. Yellow pictorial boards. Cover designed by McConnell. Small format.

[3576] HARDY, THOMAS

Pictorial boards. Large format.

Desperate Remedies. 'Fourth Edition.' Ward & Downey 1891.

Far From the Madding Crowd. 'New and Cheaper Edition.' 1889.

Hand of Ethelberta (The). 'New and Cheaper Edition.' 1892.

Pair of Blue Eyes (A). 'New and Cheaper Edition.' 1892.

Two on a Tower. 'New and Cheaper Edition.' 1890. [The above four titles are in pale blue boards and volumes in [Sampson] *Low's Standard Novels Series.*]

Under the Greenwood Tree. 'A New Edition.' Chatto & Windus 1892.

[3577] HARLAND, HENRY

Yoke of the Thorah (The) ('by Sidney Luska'). Cassell, n.d. (1888). Pictorial boards—front. and spine printed all-over in dark blue, with cut-out lettering and picture.

HARTE, BRET

These titles are wholly or in part First Editions (see Brussel, *Anglo-American First Editions*) except possibly *Jeff Briggs* which Brussel does not record.

[3578] FLIP and Other Stories
Chatto & Windus 1882. Yellow pictorial boards. Printed end-papers. Large format.
Advert. leaf precedes title. pp. 256 Publishers' cat., 32 pp. dated July 1882, at end.
Ink-signature: 'Elizabeth Izou', on title.
[Brussel, p. 33, describes copy in cloth.]

[3579] FOOL OF FIVE FORKS (The)
Routledge [1875]. Yellow boards printed in black and red. Up-lettered on spine. Printed end-papers. Small format.
pp. 128 [Brussel, p. 25.]

[3580] HEIRESS OF RED DOG (An)
Chatto & Windus 1879. Yellow pictorial boards. Printed end-papers. Large format.
Half-title. pp. viii + 300 Publishers' cat., 40 pp. dated August 1879, at end.
[Brussel, p. 31, describes copy in cloth.]

[3581] IN THE CARQUINEZ WOODS
Longman etc. 1883. Yellow pictorial boards. Printed end-papers. Large format.
Half-title. pp. (iv) + (252) Q_5 Q_6 adverts.
Ink signature: 'Elizabeth Izou', on title.
[Brussel, p. 33.]

JEFF BRIGG'S LOVE-STORY and Other Sketches [3581*a*]
Chatto & Windus 1880. Yellow pictorial wrappers, cut flush. Up-lettered on spine. Printed end-papers. Small format.
Half-title. pp. 128 Publishers' cat., 32 pp. dated December 1879, at end.
Ink signature: 'E. Izou', on half-title.

STORIES OF THE SIERRAS, etc. [3581*b*]
Hotten (1872). Cream pictorial wrappers, cut flush. Up-lettered on spine. Printed end-papers. Small format. Wood-engraved front. and vignette on title.
Two advert. leaves (the first pasted to front cover) precede half-title. pp. (156) [paged 152] Inset advert. leaf also precedes half-title. Publishers' cat., 28 pp. dated 1872, at end.
Ink-signature: 'E. Izou', on title. [Brussel, p. 22.]

STORY OF A MINE (The) [3581*c*]
Routledge, n.d. [1877]. Yellow pictorial boards, up-lettered on spine, back cover printed with advert. of 'Routledge's American Library'. Printed end-papers. Small format.
pp. (192) N_7 N_8 adverts.
Ink signature: 'A. H. Izou', on title.
Note. Cf. Brussel, p. 28, where there is a reproduction of the front cover.

[3582] HAYWARD, W. STEPHENS

Unless otherwise stated, all published by C. H. Clarke, undated, in uniform pictorial boards, lettered on spine: 'W. S. Hayward's Novels.' The title in caps is a First Edition.

ANDREW LORIMER, or the Young Surgeon of Featherstonehaugh. Wood-engraved front.
pp. (viii) + 312 A Publisher's Note explains that Hayward left this story unfinished. It has been completed by Dr Charles M. Clarke.

Black Angel (The). Wood-engraved front.

Black Flag (The). J. & R. Maxwell, n.d. Bright blue cloth, blocked in black and gold. (Cloth issue of the yellow-back edition.)

Demons of the Sea

Fiery Cross (The)

Love's Treason

Mutiny of the Thunder (The)

Copy II. Uniform cover, but on spine: 'Clarke's Standard Novel Library.' Back end-papers Chapman & Hall adverts.

One in a Thousand

Ran Away from Home [circa 1879]

Rebel Privateer (The)

Rodney Ray [circa 1879]

Star of the South. Wood-engraved front. 'Clarke's Standard Novel Library' on spine. End-papers: Chapman & Hall adverts.

Stolen Wall (The). J. & R. Maxwell, n.d.
I Bright blue cloth, uniform with *Black Flag*.
II Yellow pictorial boards (1890).

Three Red Men. Spencer Blackett, n.d. [circa 1892]. Yellow pictorial boards.

[3583] HAWTHORNE, JULIAN

Section 558 or The Fatal Letter. Cassel, n.d. (1888). Pale yellow boards, pictorially printed in red and blue. *American Library of Fiction.*

[3584] HELPS, SIR A.

Ivan de Biron. 'New Edition.' Chatto & Windus 1883. Yellow pictorial boards.

[3585] HOLMES, O. W.

Elsie Venner. 'Fifth Edition.' Chapman & Hall, n.d. Drab pictorial boards. *Select Library of Fiction.*

HEMYNG, BRACEBRIDGE

[3586] HELD IN THRALL (by B.H., 'author of 'The Gambler's Last Throw', 'Secrets of the Turf', etc.')
C. H. Clarke, n.d. [? sixties]. Pictorial wrappers, cut flush. Spine up-lettered. Back printed with Clarke adverts. Green and yellow end-papers printed with Chapman & Hall adverts.

pp. (ii) + (150) 1st leaf of final sig., L_1, a single inset.

Ink signature of George Cruikshank on title.

[3587] MAN OF THE PERIOD (THE), or the Girl he Loved and the Girl he Married
C. H. Clarke, n.d. [circa 1870]. Pictorial wrappers, cut flush. Spine up-lettered. Back wrapper printed with commercial advert. End-papers printed with Chapman & Hall adverts.

pp. (iv) + (156)

[3588] STOCKBROKER'S WIFE (THE) (by B.H.,' author of "Called to the Bar", "On the Line", etc.'). Edited by John Shaw
J. & R. Maxwell, n.d. [circa 1885]. Yellow pictorial boards. Large format.

pp. (224) O_2–O_8 adverts. (commercial).

Note. John Shaw, Stock and Share Broker, occupies two of the end-pages and the back cover with adverts. of his firm. His name is more prominent than Hemyng's on the front cover. One suspects the whole publication to have been at his cost and charged to 'Publicity'.

STRANGE JOURNEYS ('By a Commissionaire'). [3588*bis*]
Edited by Bracebridge Hemyng, author of 'On the Rank', 'On the Line', 'Rat-Tat Papers', 'Telegraph Secrets', 'Secrets of the Dead Letter Office', 'In the Brigade', 'Secrets of the River', 'Toilers of the Thames'
J. A. Berger, n.d. [? early seventies]. Pictorial wrappers, cut flush (title spelt 'Strange Journies'). Spine up-lettered (correctly). Back printed with Berger advert. End-papers printed with adverts. of Select Library of Fiction, but without imprint of Chapman & Hall.

pp. (ii) + 126 1st leaf of final sig., I_1, a single inset.

Note. Although described as 'edited by' Hemyng, I have little doubt that he was the author of these sensational stories. The back wrapper advert. lists five of the titles frankly credited to him on the title-page, but gives as their authors 'a Postman', 'a Railway Guard', 'a Fireman', etc.

[3589] HODGSON'S NEW SERIES OF NOVELS (published by Thomas Hodgson, Paternoster Row) 1859–1860

Published at two shillings each with covers by Alfred Crowquill, these Novels are partly reprints of established favourites, partly translations from Dumas (first English editions) and occasionally an English story which may have been first issued in this form. The series started publishing in 1859, continuing during 1860. I cannot record beyond twelve titles. All the volumes are undated, numbered in the series, of small format, and carry cover picture both on front and back covers. First editions and first editions in English (*not* first English editions) are in caps. Titles asterisked are not in the Collection.

I ***The Rose of Ashhurst,** by the author of *Emilia Wyndham*

II ***The King's Secret,** by Tyrone Power

III ***Smugglers and Forresters,** by Rosa Mackenzie Kettle

IV ***Evelyn Marston,** by the author of *Emilia Wyndham*

V ***Stephen Dugard,** by J. S. Mudford

VI **Ingenue, or The Death of Marat,** by the author of *Monte Cristo* (Alexandre Dumas) [1860]
Pictorial yellow back boards. End-papers printed with adverts. Small format.

Half-title. pp. (viii) + (304) U_8 adverts.

Ink signature: 'J. Browne', on title.

First English edition. The first edition in English was Philadelphia, Lippincott, Grambo and Co. 1855, under the title *Ingenue: or the First Days of Blood.* Hodgson's text (which omitted Chaps. XVI, XVII and XVIII of the French) was reprinted by Clarke in 1861 and Routledge in 1873.

VII *Fabian's Tower, by the author of *Smugglers and Forresters*

Pl. 6 VIII **Pauline or Buried Alive,** by the author of *Monte Cristo* (Alexandre Dumas) [1860]

Pictorial pink-back boards. End-papers printed with adverts. Small format.

Half-title. pp. (iv) + (308) X_2 pasted down to inside back cover. Publishers' adverts., 20 pp. undated, inserted between X_1 and X_2.

Ink signature: 'J. Browne', on title.

First English edition of this translation. The first edition in English was New York, Winchester 1842, under the title *Pauline: a Tale of Normandy.* The Winchester version was reprinted by H. G. Clarke in 1844 (?).

IX **Julian Mountjoy, or the Non Pareil Family.** An Historical Romance by Captain Curling [1860]

Pictorial white-back boards. End-papers printed with adverts. Small format.

Half-title. pp. (viii) + (316)

Pencil signature: 'Charles Penruddock. Compton Park', on title.

This story was first published in 3 vols. in 1855 under the title *Non Pareil House or the Fortunes of Julian Mountjoy.*

X ***The Bushranger,** by Charles Rowcroft

XI ***The Wreck Ashore,** by the author of *Tales of a Voyager*

XII CHARLES THE BOLD: AN HISTORICAL ROMANCE, by the author of *Monte Cristo* (Alexandre Dumas) [1860]

Pictorial yellow back boards. End-papers printed with adverts. Small format.

Half-title preceded by advert. leaf. pp. (viii) + (344) $Z_3 Z_4$ blank. First and last leaves pasted to inside-covers.

Ink signature: 'J. Browne', on title and date on half-title '3.7.1.' (? 1861).

First and only edition in English of *Charles le Téméraire.*

[3590] HOOK, THEODORE

Cousin Geoffrey. Routledge, Warne 1859. Yellow pictorial boards. Cover drawing by Phiz. Small format. *Railway Library.*

Jack Brag. Ward & Lock, n.d. (after 1891). Yellow pictorial boards. *Select Authors.*

Ned Musgrave, or the Most Unfortunate Man in the World. 'A New Edition.' Bryce 1853. Bright green glazed boards, printed in black.

Ink signature: 'J. R. Molineux 1854', facing title and highly unfavourable comment on the novel in pencil on fly-leaf signed 'J.R.M. '54'.

This is a new edition of Hook's first novel, *The Man of Sorrow.* (1206 in Section I.)

Peregrine Bunce. Routledge 1857. Yellow pictorial boards, specially designed spine. Cover drawing by Phiz. Small format. *Railway Library.*

Precepts and Practice. Bryce, n.d. Yellow pictorial boards, small format.

Widow and the Marquess (The). Routledge, n.d. (after 1885). Yellow pictorial boards, small format. Spine carries lettered panel 'Hook's Novels'. A late boarding-up of sheets dating from the fifties.

[3591] HOWARD, HON. E. G.

All in pictorial boards and small format unless otherwise stated.

Pl. 8 **Jack Ashore.** Bryce, n.d. Cover-drawing repeated on back-cover.

Old Commodore (The). 'Eighth Thousand.' Routledge 1855.

Pl. 8 **Outward Bound.** 'Copyright Edition.' J. & C. Brown, n.d.

Pl. 8 **Rattlin the Reefer.** 'Edited by Captain Marryat.'

Copy I. Routledge 1856. Cover by Phiz.

Copy II. Routledge, n.d. Large format, with different drawing on cover.

[3592] HUGO, VICTOR

HANS OF ICELAND, or the Demon Dwarf (followed by CLAUDE GUEUX)

George Pierce, 310 Strand, n.d. [? forties]. Pink wrappers printed in black and cut flush. Spine up-lettered: back wrapper blank. Steel engraved front. and vignette title on plate paper (no printed title).

pp. (176) [paged (1)–(174)] L_8 adverts. ? First Edition in English.

HUGO

Note. This book belongs to a 'Library of French Romance' advertised on L_8, and was issued in weekly numbers. The other titles in the 'Library' were: (by Hugo) *La Esmeralda or The Hunchback of Notre Dame, The Noble Rival*; (by Dumas) *Marie Antoinette, Margaret of Navarre, The Prisoner of If, Pascal Bruno*; (by J. la Cecilia) *Masaniello.*

Hunchback of Notre Dame (The). 'New Edition.' Chapman & Hall (1869). Yellow pictorial boards. Large format. *Select Library.*

Les Misérables

Copy I. 3 vols. Ward, Lock & Co. I **Fantine,** n.d.; II **Cosette & Marius** (1882); III **Jean Valjean** (1882). Pictorial boards, I and III uniform in standard *Favourite Authors* style; II in *Select Authors* style. Large format.

Copy II. 'Authorised Copyright English Translation.' Routledge, n.d. Yellow pictorial boards. Large format.

Toilers of the Sea

Copy I. 'Tenth Edition.' 'Authorised Translation by W. Moy Thomas.' Sampson, Low 1875. Cream pictorial boards. Large format.

Copy II. ['Workers of the Sea']. 'Translated by Sir Gilbert Campbell, Bart.' Ward & Lock, n.d. Greenish-white pictorial boards. Large format.

HUME, FERGUS

[3593] CREATURE OF THE NIGHT (A): an Italian Enigma
Sampson, Low 1891. Glazed carmine wrappers cut flush pictorially printed in dark blue. Inside covers printed with adverts.

pp. (iv) + 156

Blind stamp: 'W. H. Smith & Son', on last page of text and back cover.

[3594] GIRL FROM MALTA (THE)
Hansom Cab Publishing Co., n.d. [1889]. 'Fiftieth Thousand.' Buff wrappers, cut flush, printed in black. Inside covers printed with adverts.

pp. (196) Pp. (1) (2) adverts.; (3) half-title; (4) adverts.; (5) title; (6) adverts.; (7) Contents; (8) adverts.; (9) Portrait of the Author; (10) adverts.; (11) Dedication; (12) adverts.; (193)–(196) adverts.

[3595] MADAM MIDAS: Realistic and Sensational Story of Australian Mining Life
Hansom Cab Publishing Co. 1888. 'One Hundredth Thousand.' White wrappers, cut flush, pictorially printed in black. Inside covers printed with adverts.

pp. (224) Pp. (1) (2) adverts.; (3) half-title; (4) adverts.; (5) title; (6) adverts.; (7) Contents, Part I; (8) adverts.; (9) Contents, Part II; (10) adverts.; (11) Dedication; (12) adverts.; (223) (224) adverts.

MISS MEPHISTOPHELES: a Sequel to Madam Midas [3596]
F. V. White 1890. White pictorial boards, endpapers printed with adverts.

pp. vi + (316) X_1–X_8 publishers' cat., 16 pp. undated.

MYSTERY OF A HANSOM CAB (THE) [3597]
Hansom Cab Publishing Co., n.d. [1887]. 'One Hundredth Thousand.' Greenish-grey wrappers, cut flush, pictorially printed in black. Inside-front, spine, and both back covers printed with adverts.: Plesse & Lubin and 'The Secret'; Warner's 'Safe' Cure; Sapolio; Beecham's Pills. Inset leaf, with advert. on verso, precedes title.

pp. (ii) + (232) Pp. (231) (232) adverts.

Note. John Carter, in his essay 'Detective Fiction' (*New Paths in Book Collecting*, London, 1934), quotes from a publisher's pamphlet a statement that the first London edition numbered 25,000 copies. He states that the earliest copy so far discovered is labelled 'One Hundredth Thousand'. Such post-one-hundred-thousand specimens as I have seen are wrappered in *white*, and the adverts. are mostly different.

The story was originally published in Melbourne over the imprint: Kemp and Boyce. The book was undated. The London edition exactly reproduced the Melbourne front wrapper (imprint apart) and virtually repeated the wording of the title-page. I am inclined to suspect that the first London edition was labelled 'One Hundredth Thousand', Australian sales having been taken roughly in account.

[3598] ILLUSTRATED PENNY TALES FROM THE 'STRAND' LIBRARY [1894]

4to. 'Published at the Offices of "Tit-Bits"' (by George Newnes Ltd.). Nos. 1–10, undated and with no indication of periodicity, were issued in wrappers of different colours printed in black—on front with series-title, number of Part, Contents, and violent illustration after various artists, on inside-wrappers and outside-back-covers with adverts. Each Part contains 16 pp., with numerous text-illustrations and paged separately.

The series has issue-importance within the narrow limits of its author-significance, because its Parts represent first book-issues of stories hitherto only printed in a magazine. It has also some interest as a precursor of NEWNES PENNY LIBRARY OF FAMOUS BOOKS (3643 below).

Space need not be given to a full schedule of Contents. The following are the authors worth noting: Grant Allen (Nos. 1, 9, 10); A. Conan Doyle (No. 2); de Maupassant (No. 3); Frank R. Stockton (No. 4); Pushkin (No. 4); Dumas (No. 6); G. Manville Fenn (Nos. 7, 8).

[3599] IRVING, WASHINGTON

Salmagundi. Routledge 1855. Yellow pictorial boards, cover drawing by Crowquill, up-lettered on spine. Small format.

Wolfert's Roost. Routledge 1855. Cream pictorial boards, printed in blue, brown and black, up-lettered on spine, front cover design repeated on back. Small format. See 3451 above.

[3600] JAMES, G. P. R.

Uniform small format edition published by Routledge. Pictorial boards on pale blue or pale yellow grounds. Conventional spines with JAMES'S NOVELS on panel. Advert. pasted to some back covers. End-papers printed with adverts. 'G. P. R. JAMES NOVELS AND TALES' on some front covers. Undated.

Agincourt
Arabella Stuart
Arrah Neil
Attila
Beauchamp
Black Eagle (The) (or Ticonderoga). 'New Edition.'
Brigand (The) (or Corse de Leon). 'New Edition.'
Castelnau
Castle of Ehrenstein (The)
Charles Tyrrell
Convict (The). 'New Edition.'
Dark Scenes of History
Darnley
Delaware
De L'Orme
False Heir (The)
Forest Days
Forgery (The)
Gentleman of the Old School
Gipsy (The). 'New Edition.'
Gowrie. 'New Edition.'
Heidelberg
Henry of Guise
Huguenot (The)
Jacquerie (The)
John Marston Hall
King's Highway (The)
Leonora d'Orco
Man at Arms (The)
Margaret Graham
Mary of Burgundy
Morley Ernstein
My Aunt Pontypool
One in a Thousand
Philip Augustus
Robber (The). 'New Edition.'
Rose d'Albret
Russell. 'New Edition.'
Sir Theodore Broughton
Smuggler (The)
Stepmother (The)
Whim and Its Consequences (A)
Woodman (The)

Note. Judging from the format and style of cover picture, this series originally appeared about 1860—probably just after James's death. The present set is of much later binding (some of the end-papers are dated 1891), but in outward appearance they are as they first appeared. The following cover drawings are certainly, or in all probability, by Phiz: *Arrah Neil*; *Beauchamp*; *Darnley*; *Delaware*; *De L'Orme*; *False Heir*; *Forgery*; *Gowrie*; *Huguenot.*

[3601] JAMES, HENRY

Daisy Miller (etc.). Macmillan 1888. Ivory ornamental boards, printed in black and red with standard Macmillan design (signed L. F. Day) for two-shilling issues.

Princess Casamassima (The). Macmillan 1889. Buff ornamental boards, printed in black and bright red with same design as foregoing.

[3602] JERROLD, BLANCHARD

CHRONICLES OF THE CRUTCH. 'Reprinted from *Household Words*.' Ward & Lock 1861. Yellow pictorial boards, cover drawing by Phiz. Small format. pp. viii + 264

[3603] JEWSBURY, GERALDINE

Constance Herbert. 'New Edition.' Ward & Lock, n.d. (1882). Bright green pictorial boards. *Select Library.*

[3604] KAVANAGH, JULIA

John Dorrien. Routledge 1893. Pale yellow pictorial boards. Cover drawing by A. Corbould.

Madeleine. Ward & Lock, n.d. (1884). Very pale green pictorial boards. *Select Library.*

Queen Mab. Spencer Blackett, n.d. (after 1892). Dark yellow pictorial boards.

[3605] KENT'S SHILLING STANDARD LIBRARY 1861

'Published for the Proprietor by W. Kent & Co., Paternoster Row' (cf. 'First Class Library') only six titles can be recorded as having appeared in this series, of which only the first is a first edition.

The books are of small format, in boards of varying colour, uniformly printed in dark blue or black with a commonplace design and lettering, and up-lettered on spine. No. 1 has cover design repeated on back cover; on other volumes back cover advertises the titles in the series. The series title is part of the front-cover design and the volumes are numbered. Titles asterisked are not in the Collection.

1 TWO LOVE STORIES, by 'WATERS' (on title: TWO LOVE STORIES: an Anglo-Spanish Romance, by the author of 'A Skeleton in Every House'). Yellow boards, printed in black. Title dated 1861. pp. 192
Ink signature: 'Mary Harradene October 1866', on fly-leaf.

2 ***Comic Tales,** by Albert Smith

3 **Wonderful Adventures of A. Gordon Pym,** by Edgar Allan Poe. Royal blue boards, printed in black. Title undated.

4 ***Fascination,** by Mrs Gore

5 ***Leaves from the Diary of a Law Clerk,** by 'Waters' [cf. 3525 above].

6 **College Life,** by Cuthbert Bede. Cream boards, printed in dark blue. Title undated. (See 3441 above.)

[3606] KINGSLEY, CHARLES

Alton Locke. 'Cheap Edition.' Chapman & Hall 1856. Yellow pictorial boards, specially drawn spine. Small format. *Select Library.*

[3607] KINGSLEY, HENRY

All in pictorial boards on bases of various colours. Large format.

Austin Elliot. 'Third Edition.' Macmillan 1865.

Hornby Mills and Other Stories. Ward Lock, n.d. *Select Authors.*

Old Margaret. 'New Edition.' Ward & Lock, n.d. *Select Library.*

Ravenshoe. 'Fifth Edition.' Chapman & Hall 1872. *Select Library of Fiction.*

Valentin. 'Revised and Corrected. Copyright Edition.' Routledge, n.d. (after 1884).

[3608] KNIGHTON, WILLIAM

Private Life of an Eastern King (The). 'New Edition Revised.' Routledge 1857. Yellow pictorial boards. Wood-engraved front. and other illustrations after Harrison Weir. Small format.

[3609] LAWRENCE, G. A.

Anteros. Routledge, n.d. [circ. 1891]. Cream pictorial wrappers.

Guy Livingstone. 'Sixth Edition.' Routledge, n.d. Yellow pictorial boards. *Railway Library.*

Hagarene. 'Sixth Edition.' Ward & Lock, n.d. (1883). Yellow pictorial boards. *Select Library.*

Sword and Gown. Routledge, n.d. [circa 1891]. Cream pictorial wrappers.

[3610] LE FANU, J. SHERIDAN

All in pictorial boards and large format.

All in the Dark. 'New Edition.' Warne, n.d. *Companion Library.*

Checkmate. 'Third Edition.' Chapman & Hall, n.d. *Select Library of Fiction.*

Guy Deverell. 'New Edition.' Warne, n.d. *Companion Library.*

House by the Church-Yard (The). 'New Edition.' Warne, n.d. *Companion Library.*

An earlier yellow-back was published by Chapman & Hall in (1870).

Morley Court (see No. 1373*d* in Section I).

Tenants of Malory (The). 'New Edition.' Warne, n.d. *Companion Library.*

Uncle Silas. 'New Edition.' Chapman & Hall, 1879. *Select Library of Fiction.*

Willing to Die. 'New Edition.' Warne, n.d. *Companion Library.*

Wyvern Mystery (The). 'New Edition.' Ward & Downey, n.d.

[3611] LEVER, CHARLES

All in pictorial boards on bases of various colours. Unless otherwise stated, large format.

Pl. 4 **Arthur O'Leary.** Routledge 1856. Yellow-back. Cover and spine drawings by Phiz. Small format.

†**Charles O'Malley.** 2 vols. Chapman & Hall 1862.

Con Cregan. Copy I. Routledge 1856. Yellow pictorial cloth in imitation of a yellow-back; yellow end-papers. Cover design and 12 plates by Phiz. Large format.

Copy II. 'New Edition.' Routledge 1862. Grey boards. Uniform spine design with *Select Library* volumes (see Note), but with 'Select Library' blacked out on spine. No illustrations.

Davenport Dunn. 2 vols. Chapman & Hall 1863. Cover drawing by Phiz.

†**Fortunes of Glencore (The).** 'Fourth Edition.' Chapman & Hall, n.d. Cover design by Phiz.

†**Harry Lorrequer.** Chapman & Hall 1862. Front. by Phiz; cover drawing by or adapted from him.

†**Jack Hinton.** Chapman & Hall 1857. Front. and cover drawing by Phiz.

Luttrell of Arran. 'New Edition.' Chapman & Hall 1867. Cover drawing by Phiz.

†**One of Them.** Chapman & Hall 1863. Cover drawing by Phiz.

†**Tom Burke of Ours.** 'New Edition.' Chapman & Hall, n.d. (1869). Cover drawing by Phiz.

Tony Butler. 'New Edition.' Ward & Lock, n.d. (after 1891). *Select Authors.*

Note. Titles marked † are volumes in Chapman & Hall's *Select Library of Fiction* and, with slight variations, are uniform in front lay-out and spine design. Most have printed end-papers, and covers on a grey base.

[3612] LINTON, E. LYNN

With a Silken Thread and Other Stories. Chatto & Windus (1897). Yellow pictorial boards.

[3613] LONDON CITY TALES [1853]

Published by Ingram, Cooke & Co., 227 Strand, at one shilling each, in yellow boards printed with all-over design and lettered in red and black, the books in this series were all written by Miss E. M. Stewart. They are undated, but were issued in 1853. Each volume is of small format and has yellow end-papers printed with adverts. The series title appears on front cover and spine. Titles asterisked are not in the Collection.

1 OSBERT OF ALDGATE: a Tale of the Goldsmith's Company

Wood-engraved front., decorative title and 4 full-page illustrations all on text paper and included in the collation. pp. (160)

Pencil signature: 'John Hayden', on printed title.

2 QUEEN PHILIPPA AND THE HURRER'S DAUGHTER: a Tale of the Haberdashers' Company

Illustrated as 1. pp. 160

3 *CLARIBEL, THE SEA MAID: a Tale of the Fishmongers' Company

4 THE BRIDE OF BUCKLERSBURY: a Tale of the Grocers' Company

Illustrated as 1. pp. 160

5 WHITTINGTON AND THE KNIGHT SANS-TERRE: a Tale of the Vintners' Company

Illustrated as 1. pp. 152 Publishers' cat., 8 pp. undated, at end.

6 *FITZ-ALWYN, THE FIRST LORD MAYOR

Notes. (i) It may be noted that Nos. 2 and 5 of the above have double pagination, i.e. at the *top* of the page each is foliated (1)–160 [or (1)–152] but at the *bottom* from (161) to 320 [or (161)–312]. Presumably the six boarded numbers were later bound into two cloth volumes, each containing 480 pages, but that can only be established by examining a copy of No. 3 or No. 6, both of which are unfortunately missing from the Collection. This double pagination is, in my experience, an unusual device.

(ii) A Second Series of LONDON CITY TALES was announced as 'in the Press' in (I think) 1869 by the proprietors of The Illustrated Monthly Novelist, from their offices at 8 Palsgrave Place, Temple Bar. I have seen no specimen of this Second Series nor is there one in the Guildhall Library, but from the back wrapper of Miss Stewart's *Snowed Up* (3688 below) take the following particulars. The books were cr. 8vo and sold in pictorial wrappers cut flush at 1*s*., or in cloth gilt at 1*s*. 6*d*. Each volume had a frontispiece on toned paper and other illustrations. The six titles of the series, promised monthly from January onward, were: 1. *Walter Lenham, or the Tradesman's Truth*: a Tale of the Clothworkers' Company. 2. *The Novice of St Helens*: a Tale of the Merchant Tailors' Company. 3. *Evil May-Day, or the 'Prentice of Fenchurch Street*: a Tale of the Ironmongers' Company. 4. *Sir Thomas Gresham and The Maiden's Dower*: a Tale of the Mercers' Company. 5. *The Merchant of Dowgate*: a Tale of the Skinners' Company. 6. *The Betrothed of St Mildreds, or the Merry Monarch and the Warden's Son*: a Tale of the Salters' Company.

The first of these titles was announced in 1853 as No. 6 of the First Series, but was substituted at the last moment by *Fitz-Alwyn*.

The date 1869 is deduced from the first sentence of Miss Stewart's tale *Snowed Up*: 'Forty years ago, in the Year of Our Lord 1828, railways were a marvel.' *Snowed Up* was manifestly a Christmas volume, and I conclude was published late in 1868. The back wrapper announces *Walter Lenham* for 'Early in January'.

[3614] LOVER, SAMUEL

Handy Andy. Routledge, n.d. Pale blue pictorial boards. Cover-design by Phiz. Printed end-papers. Large format.

He Would be a Gentleman: or Treasure Trove. A Romance. 'A New Edition.'

Copy I. Bryce, n.d. [circa 1855]. Bright green glazed boards, printed in black. Small format.

Copy II. Chapman & Hall, n.d. (1879). Pale pink pictorial boards. Large format.

Rory O'More. 'New Edition.' Routledge 1864. Yellow pictorial boards. Cover design by Phiz. Printed end-papers. Small format. *Railway Library.*

[3615] MABERLY, HON. MRS

Love Match (The). 'New Edition.' Bryce, n.d. Yellow pictorial boards, specially drawn spine. Small format.

[3616] MALET, LADY

Violet or the Danseuse. Routledge 1857. Yellow pictorial boards. Small format. *Railway Library.*

[3617] MALLOCK, W. H.

Romance of the Nineteenth Century (A). 'New Edition.' Chatto & Windus, 1894. Yellow pictorial boards.

[3618] MARRYAT, CAPT. FREDERICK

First Yellow-Back Edition. Small format, pictorial spines specially designed for each title. Pictorial boards, except where otherwise stated. Titles asterisked have 'Routledge's Railway Library' on front covers.

Pl. 8 ***Dog Fiend (The), or Snarleyyow.** Routledge 1856.

Pl. 8 ***Jacob Faithful.** Routledge 1856.

***Japhet in Search of a Father.** 'A New Edition.' Routledge 1857.

King's Own (The). Routledge 1856.

Monsieur Violet, Travels and Adventures of. Thomas Hodgson on cover: Simms & McIntyre 1849 on title. Yellow boards, printed in cherry red and black with design and fancy lettering.
This is a specimen of a *Parlour Library* volume re-clothed 'in brilliant cover by Alfred Crowquill'. Design repeated on back cover.

***Newton Forster or The Merchant Service.** Routledge 1856.

Pl. 8 ***Pacha of Many Tales (The).** 'A New Edition.' Routledge 1856.

***Percival Keene.** 'A New Edition with a Memoir of the Author.' Routledge 1857. *Pl. 8*

Peter Simple. 'Thirtieth Thousand.' Routledge 1856. *Pl. 8*

Phantom Ship (The). Routledge, n.d. [circa 1877]. Yellow pictorial wrappers, cut flush. Represents a late re-issue of an original board edition.

Poacher (The). 'A New Edition.' Routledge 1857. *Pl. 8*

***Valerie: an Autobiography.** 'A New Edition.' Routledge 1857. *Pl. 8*

[3618*a*] *Second Yellow-Back Edition.* Medium format, conventional uniform spine design. Pictorial boards. All published by Routledge and undated.

Dog Fiend (The), or Snarleyyow. 'New Edition.'

Frank Mildmay. 'New Edition.'

Jacob Faithful

Japhet in Search of a Father. 'New Edition.'

King's Own (The)

Mr Midshipman Easy

Newton Forster

Pacha of Many Tales (The)

Percival Keene

Peter Simple

Poacher (The)

Note. The cover pictures are all different from those on the first yellow-back edition and carried out by inferior artists in (I imagine) the early eighties.

[3619] MARSH, ANNE

Emilia Wyndham. 'New Edition.' Ward & Lock (1882). Pale green pictorial boards. *Select Library.*

Mount Sorel. 'New Edition.' Ward & Lock (1882). Yellow pictorial boards. *Select Library.*

[3620] MARTINEAU, HARRIET

Hour and the Man (The). Routledge 1873. Yellow pictorial boards. Small format.

[3621] MATHERS, HELEN

'Cherry Ripe.' Routledge (1893). Pale yellow pictorial boards.

Jock o' Hazelgreen. Routledge 1884. Pale green pictorial boards.

Story of a Sin. Routledge 1882. Pale blue pictorial boards.

[3622] MAXWELL, W. H.

Adventures of Captain O'Sullivan 'by H. B. Maxwell, Esq.' (sic, on cover)
Bryce, n.d. [1855]. Bright green glazed boards, printed in black. Small format.
Ink signature: 'J. R. Molineux 1855', facing title.

Border Tales and Legends of the Cheviots and the Lammermuir
David Bryce, n.d. Yellow pictorial boards. Cover drawing by Phiz. Small format.

Captain Blake, The Adventures of, or My Life
Routledge 1857. Bright green pictorial boards. Cover-drawing by Phiz. Small format. *Railway Library.*

Erin-go-Bragh. 'New Edition.' *Pl. 4*
Bentley 1860. Yellow pictorial boards. Cover-drawing by Phiz. Small format.
Note. Bentley yellow-backs are almost unknown. This appeared a year after the first edition.

Flood and Field, or the Recollections of a Soldier of Fortune
Routledge 1857. Yellow pictorial boards. Engraved plates after H.K.B. (Phiz). Small format.
Note. Originally published as *The Bivouac.*

Hector O'Halloran, The Fortunes of
Routledge 1858. Yellow pictorial boards. Cover drawing by Phiz. Small format. *Railway Library.*

MAXWELL

Stories of Waterloo
Routledge 1856. Yellow pictorial boards. Small format. *Railway Library.*

Wild Sports and Adventures
Routledge 1853.

Copy I. White boards, printed in dark green and red with titling and vignette, specially designed spine, front cover design repeated on back.

Copy II. Uniform with Copy I as to front, but plain type-set spine and adverts. on back.
Both small format.

Wild Sports of the West. 'New Edition.'
Routledge, n.d. (1873). Yellow pictorial boards. Cover drawing by Phiz. Small format.
A late re-issue, with pencil dating 1873 on title.

MAYHEW, HORACE

[3623] LETTERS LEFT AT THE PASTRY COOK'S: being the Clandestine Correspondence between Kitty Clover at School and her 'Dear, Dear Friend' in Town

Ingram, Cooke & Co. 1853. White wrappers, cut flush, pictorially printed and fancy-lettered on front in blue-black and dull brick-red. Up-lettered on spine: PRICE ONE SHILLING (no title). Back printed with advert. Wood-engraved front. and 6 full-page illustrations after Phiz, all on text paper.

Half-title. pp. (viii) [paged vi]+(120) Publishers' adverts., 4 pp. on text paper, at end.

Booksellers' ticket: 'Mann Nephews, Cornhill', on back cover.

Notes. (i) This is reputed to be the first pictorial cover printed by Edmund Evans by his colour-block process, and, if this be so, can claim to be the first yellow-back.

(ii) Later printings of the wrapper (there were at least five editions in the year of publication) are in bright red instead of dull brick.

(iii) The blue-black background was produced by printing blue on red.

(iv) The book was also issued in limp dark blue morocco cloth, with a reduced adaptation of the central portion of the pictorial wrapper blocked in gold on front cover with lettering above and below. Also blind-blocked on front and back; spine unlettered. A copy of this cloth issue is in the Collection.

[3624] MAYHEW, HORACE and AUGUSTUS

Image of His Father (The). H. G. Bohn 1859. Yellow boards printed in black. Etched front., vignette titles and plates by Phiz. Small format.

Whom to Marry. Routledge, n.d. (1872). Yellow pictorial boards, cover drawing by Phiz, specially designed spine. Etched front. and plates by Cruikshank.

[3625] MAYO, W. STARBUCK

Mountaineer of the Atlas (The). Routledge 1856. Yellow pictorial boards. Small format.

[3626] MEREDITH, GEORGE

Farina: a Legend of Cologne. 'Third Edition.' Chapman & Hall 1868. Yellow pictorial wrappers cut flush, up-lettered on spine. *Standard Authors.*

Shaving of Shagpat (The). 'New Edition.' Chapman & Hall, n.d. (dated inscription 1877). Yellow pictorial boards, soiled.

Tragic Comedians (The). Ward & Lock, n.d. (about 1881). Yellow pictorial boards. *Select Authors.*

[3627] MILLS, JOHN

Briefless Barrister (The). Ward, Lock & Tyler, n.d. (after 1871). Yellow pictorial boards, cover drawing by Phiz, specially drawn spine. Small format. *Library of Popular Authors.*

Too Fast to Last. Routledge, n.d. (inscription dated 1884). Pale yellow pictorial boards.

[3628] M'INTOSH, M. J.

Lofty and the Lowly (The). 'Eighth Thousand.' Routledge 1855. Cream boards, printed with all-over decoration in orange, scarlet and black, specially drawn up-lettered spine, front cover design repeated on back cover. Small format.

[3629] MODERN ARABIAN NIGHTS (The) 1877. By Arthur à Beckett and Linley Sambourne. Nos. I–IV (all published)

Format fcap 4to, but collating in eights. Bradbury Agnew & Co. n.d. (1877).

No. I. ALLEY BABER AND SON. A Mock Exchange Story

Lilac wrappers, printed on front in orange and black with an all-over humorous pseudo-oriental design after Sambourne, incorporating series title, individual title, names of author and artist. 'Price One Shilling' and imprint. Uplettered on spine with series title, 'No. I', and individual title. Inside covers and back outside cover printed with adverts. Coloured engraved front. (signed 'Linley Sambourne inv.sd.del. June 1877') 1 full-page uncoloured engraving (both on plate paper) and several illustrations in the text, all after Sambourne.

Two leaves of adverts. on light blue paper precede front. No title-page. pp. viii [Introduction] + 40 4 pp. leaflet, fcap 8vo, printed in lilac and advertising *Select Library of Fiction*; and one leaf of adverts. on light blue paper at end. Single advert. slips (Feltoe & Sons and Jay's Mourning Warehouse) tipped on to pp. (i) and 17.

No. II. NED REDDING AND THE BEAUTIFUL PERSIAN. A Tale of Turkish Home Rule

Glazed white wrappers, printed uniformly with No. I in orange and black. Coloured engraved front. and one coloured plate (the latter signed 'Linley Sambourne, July 1877') and occasional illustrations in the text, all after Sambourne.

Three leaves of adverts. on lilac paper (of which the first pasted to inside front cover to stiffen it) precede front. No title-page. pp. (40) [paged (41)–(80)] Single advert. leaf of lilac paper at end, pasted to inside back cover.

No. III. RIDE OF CAPTAIN ALF RASHIT TO KEVERE-STREET (THE)

Wrappers as No. II. Coloured engraved front., 1 coloured plate, both signed 'Linley Sambourne', and occasional illustrations in the text.

Single advert. leaf of lilac paper at beginning and end, pasted to inside covers. No title-page. pp. (40) [paged (81)–120] Advert. of Jay's Mourning Warehouse tipped on to p. 97.

No. IV. MR O'LADDIN AND THE WONDERFUL LAMP. A Story of Obstruction and the Emerald Isle

Wrappers as Nos. II and III. Coloured engraved front., 1 uncoloured plate, both signed 'Linley Sambourne', and occasional illustrations in the text.

Single advert. leaf at front and back as in No. III. No title page. pp. (40) [paged (121)–160]

Note. This is a very scarce specimen of mid-Victorian facetiae. As political and social satire it was probably inspired by The Coming K—— series (3476 above); but it is entirely in prose, more light-heartedly written and less scurrilous. Accompanying the set described are a letter from Linley Sambourne and one from Bradbury, Agnew & Co., both dated February 1902, and written to a Mr N. C. Forman. Each letter states that only four numbers were issued, Sambourne adding that the books were published in 1877 but 'did not catch on with the Public'.

It was evidently the intention (note the continuous pagination) to carry the series further; and in a final number to provide title, contents, etc., which would presumably have been dated. As it is, no date, save those attached to two of Sambourne's signatures on the plates, appears anywhere.

Presumably, had the work been completed, it would have been published in volume-form. As it remained unfinished, the four numbers were issued in a cardboard case, with elaborate and highly coloured arabic decoration on front and back, and on one edge a long label printed in red with title and authors' names. The red of the lettering had clearly almost faded out, for an owner (presumably Mr Forman) has lightly inked it over in black. The numbers slip (not without risk to their lower corners) into this case from the top and are extractable with the help of a ribbon of pale pink watered silk.

In all my experience (and this is not the sort of publication I should fail to notice) I have only seen this one complete set and two odd numbers. Mr T. Balston informs me that at one time he owned the four numbers in binders' cloth.

[3630] MORIER, JAMES

Hajji Baba in England. 'New Edition.' Ward & Lock 1856. Yellow pictorial boards, specially drawn spine. Small format.

Maid of Kars, 'Ayesha'. Ward & Lock 1856. Yellow pictorial boards printed in black. Small format.

Note. This edition contains the engraved front. originally published in No. 100 of Bentley's Standard Novels. It is described on cover and title as by 'Miss Morier'.

Pl. 4 **Zohrab.** 'New Edition.' Ward & Lock 1856. Yellow pictorial boards, specially drawn spine. Small format. Generally uniform with *Hajji Baba in England.*

'MRS BROWN' SERIES

[3631] 'MRS BROWN' SERIES by ARTHUR SKETCHLEY [George Rose] 1866–1882

Although this is not an absolutely complete collection of the 'Mrs Brown' books, it is sufficiently nearly so to make possible a fuller and more accurate list than is elsewhere available. Dating is sometimes difficult; but the dates given by the *D.N.B.* and Allibone to such titles as they record, checked and reinforced by topical references and internal evidence, have served as basis for what I hope is a correct and comprehensive survey.

The first appearance of 'Mrs Brown' was in *Routledge's Annual* for 1866. She then became a regular and popular feature of *Fun*. Later Sketchley devised a series of recitations and readings based on her adventures which he gave with huge success in England, America, Australia and India.

The humour of Mrs Brown is not altogether that of to-day; but the enormous contemporary popularity of Sketchley's heroine more than justifies the inclusion of her opinions and adventures in a library of significant nineteenth-century fiction.

'Mrs Brown' (who doubtless derived from Mrs Gamp) was the forerunner of 'Mr Dooley', 'Mrs Green', 'Mrs Wiggs of the Cabbage Patch', W. W. Jacobs' 'Night Watchman' and even A. P. Herbert's 'Topsy'. Her particular idiom took the public fancy and, while she lasted, 'Mrs Brown' on the latest sensation or social event or popular scene was a compulsory part of up-to-date proficiency. Nor did her reputation die with her. As recently as 1914 she provided weekly material for a headmaster to read aloud to the senior boys of a large preparatory school.

The bracketed number after each title shows the order of its appearance in the whole series, the volumes themselves not being numbered. Each volume unless otherwise stated is printed with adverts. on back cover, has white end-papers and is up-lettered on spine. The asterisked titles are not in the Collection.

[3631] (1)–(4) *Pl.* 1

BROWN PAPERS (The) (1)

'Fun' Office, 80 Fleet Street 1866. Brown chalk-surfaced paper wrappers, printed in black with portrait of the author, title, etc. Spine unlettered. Back wrapper printed with adverts. Wrappers cut flush. White end-papers printed with adverts. The book is printed throughout in brown ink. Inset leaf of yellow paper advertising Dunn's Discount Bookshop; 4 leaves of adverts. on text paper (the first pasted down to form inside front cover) unfoliated.

pp. (192) [paged (1)–4 + (v)–viii + (9)–190 + (2)] Text ends p. 190; (191) (192) adverts.; 4 leaves of adverts., the fourth pasted down to form inside back cover. Signed in thirty-twos, last signature, G_1–G_{14}.

MRS BROWN'S VISIT TO THE PARIS EXHIBITION (2)

Routledge (1867). Yellow pictorial boards.

Half-title. pp. vi + (140) 9_6 adverts. Publishers' cat., 16 pp. undated, at end.

MRS BROWN IN AMERICA (3)

'Fun' Office 1868. Brown chalk-surfaced paper wrappers, uniform with *The Brown Papers*, pictorially printed and lettered in black. Wrappers cut flush. 6 leaves of adverts. (the first pasted down to form inside front cover).

pp. (136) [paged (i)–viii + (9)–134 + (2)] Final leaf, F_2, is pasted down to form inside back cover. 6 leaves of adverts. inserted between F_1 and F_2.

MRS BROWN AT THE SEASIDE (4)

Routledge, n.d. [*D.N.B.* says 1868]. Yellow pictorial boards. pp. (ii) + 126

MRS BROWN'S VISITS TO PARIS (5) [3631] (5)–(11)

Routledge, n.d. [not listed by *D.N.B.*, but announced in 6 as already published]. Yellow pictorial boards. pp. (150)

MRS BROWN IN LONDON (6)

Routledge, n.d. [*D.N.B.* says 1869]. Yellow pictorial boards.

Half-title. pp. viii + (152)

MRS BROWN UP THE NILE (7)

Routledge, n.d. [announced as 'in preparation' in 6. *D.N.B.* says 1869]. Yellow pictorial boards.

pp. (156) [paged (iii)–(x) + (5)–152 + (4)] Signatures: 2 leaves unsigned; 1–9 in eights + 10 –10_6. Text ends 10_4, 10_5, 10_6 adverts.

MRS BROWN IN THE HIGHLANDS (8)

Routledge, n.d. [*D.N.B.* says 1869]. Yellow pictorial boards.

Half-title. pp. (160) [paged (i)–(x) + (11)–158 + (2)] 10_8 adverts.

BROWN PAPERS (The), Second Series (9)

Routledge 1870. Paper wrappers cut flush, pictorially printed and lettered in black, red and green.

pp. (156) [paged 152]

MRS BROWN AT THE PLAY (10)

Routledge, n.d. (Dec. 1870—see Introduction and *Mrs Brown's Budget*, No. 21, Dec. 14, 1870). Yellow back pictorial boards.

pp. 120 [paged (i) + x + (11)–120]

*MRS BROWN ON THE GRAND TOUR (11). *D.N.B.* says 1870.

[3631] (12)–(24) MRS BROWN'S CHRISTMAS BOX (12)
Routledge, n.d. [Christmas, 1870. Not listed by *D.N.B.* or Allibone; announced in 14 as already published]. Yellow pictorial boards.
Half-title. pp. 152 [paged (i)–(xx) + (21)–152] 4 leaves of adverts. at end.

MRS BROWN'S "'OLLIDAY OUTINS" [thus on title; 'OLIDAY HOUTINGS on cover] (13)
Routledge, n.d. [May, 1871. Not listed by *D.N.B.*]. Yellow pictorial boards. pp. 152

MRS BROWN ON THE BATTLE OF DORKING (14)
Routledge, n.d. [1871]. Yellow pictorial wrappers, cut flush. Spine unlettered. pp. (64) [paged (60)] (1) (2) and (63) (64) pasted down as inside covers.

MRS BROWN AT THE INTERNATIONAL EXHIBITION AND SOUTH KENSINGTON (15)
Routledge, n.d. [*D.N.B.* says 1872]. Yellow pictorial boards. pp. (152)

MRS BROWN ON THE TICHBORNE CASE (16)
Routledge 1872. Yellow pictorial boards. pp. 152

MRS BROWN ON THE ALABAMA CASE (17)
Routledge, n.d. [1872]. Yellow pictorial boards. pp. 152

MRS BROWN ON THE NEW LIQUOR LAW (18)
Routledge, n.d. [1872]. Yellow pictorial boards. pp. 152

MRS BROWN ON WOMEN'S RIGHTS (19)
Routledge, n.d. [*D.N.B.* says 1872]. Yellow pictorial boards.
pp. (156) 10_8 (adverts.) is pasted down to inside back cover.

MRS BROWN ON THE SHAH'S VISIT (20)
Routledge, n.d. [1873]. Yellow pictorial boards.
pp. (156) 10_8 (adverts.) is pasted down to inside back cover.

Pl. 1 MRS BROWN ON THE TICHBORNE DEFENCE (21)
Routledge, n.d. [*D.N.B.* says 1873]. Yellow pictorial boards. pp. 152

MRS BROWN ON THE ROYAL RUSSIAN MARRIAGE (22)
Routledge, n.d. [1874]. White pictorial boards.
pp. (156) 10_8 (adverts.) is pasted down to inside back cover.

MRS BROWN AND DISRAELI [on cover: Mrs Brown on 'Dizzy'] (23)
Routledge [1874]. Yellow pictorial boards.
pp. (156) 10_8 (adverts.) is pasted down to inside back cover.

MRS BROWN AT MARGATE (? 24)
Routledge, n.d. [*D.N.B.* says 1874, but latest volume listed facing title is *Women's Rights* (1872)]. Yellow pictorial boards.
pp. (156) 10_8 (adverts.) is pasted down to inside back cover.

MRS BROWN AT BRIGHTON (25) [3631] (25)–(36)
Routledge, n.d. [*D.N.B.* says 1875]. Yellow pictorial boards.
pp. (156) 10_3–10_8 adverts., 10_8 pasted down to inside back cover.

MRS BROWN AT THE CRYSTAL PALACE (26)
Routledge, n.d. [*D.N.B.* says 1875 and outside back cover advertises the title in the order given here]. Yellow pictorial boards. pp. 156

MRS BROWN AT THE SKATING RINK (27)
Routledge, n.d. [*D.N.B.* says 1875]. Yellow pictorial boards. pp. 156

MRS BROWN ON THE PRINCE'S VISIT TO INDIA (28)
Routledge, n.d. [1875]. Not listed by *D.N.B.*]. Yellow pictorial boards.
pp. (156) 10_8 (adverts.) is pasted down to inside back cover.

MRS BROWN ON CLEOPATRA'S NEEDLE (29)
Routledge, n.d. [? 1876. Not listed by *D.N.B.*]. Yellow pictorial boards.
pp. (156) 10_8 (adverts.) is pasted down to inside back cover.

MRS BROWN ON SPELLING BEES (30)
Routledge, n.d. [*D.N.B.* says 1876, and List of other vols. in series is the same as in *Cleopatra's Needle*]. Yellow pictorial boards. pp. 152

MRS BROWN ON THE TURF (31)
Routledge, 1877 (not listed by *D.N.B.*). Yellow pictorial boards. pp. (152)

MRS BROWN AT THE PARIS EXHIBITION (32)
Routledge, 1878 (not listed by *D.N.B.*). Yellow pictorial boards. pp. 152

MRS BROWN ON CO-OPERATIVE STORES (33)
Routledge, 1879. White pictorial boards. pp. 152
*MRS BROWN ON CETEWAYO (34) (1879)

MRS BROWN ON JUMBO (35)
Routledge, n.d. [*D.N.B.* and Allibone say 1882]. White pictorial boards. pp. 152

MRS BROWN ON HOME RULE (36)
Routledge, n.d. [1882 *D.B.N.* and Allibone say 1881]. Buff pictorial wrappers, cut flush. pp. 124
Contains a *Memoir of the Author* by 'C.S.' Sketchley died in 1882. Wrappers not original issue.

Associated Items [3632]

MRS BROWN'S BUDGET. 'Conducted by Arthur Sketchley'
Published weekly at one penny, each number 8 pp. 4to, with wood-engraved full-length seated portrait of Mrs Brown on p. 1.
Nos. 1–25: August 1, 1870–January 11, 1871; and Christmas Number for 1870, cover printed in

red and black, with different portrait of Mrs Brown (head and shoulders only), 24 pp., price twopence.

Uncut as issued. Also a Poster and two Handbills announcing the periodical as forthcoming.

[3633] MINCEMEAT FOR CHRISTMAS PARTIES. 'Prepared from Mrs Brown's Receipts by Arthur Sketchley and Other Professed Cooks'.

4to. 44 Catherine Street, Strand, n.d. [probably 1872]. Blue wrappers, cut flush, printed in red and black. On front cover same picture of Mrs Brown as appeared on the Christmas Number of *Mrs Brown's Budget* (q.v.). Unlettered spine. Back and inside covers printed with adverts.

pp. 48 [paged (i)–viii + (9)–48] 12 pp. of adverts. on cheaper paper at end (one of which quotes an extract from the *Morning Post* of November 20, 1872).

This book contains an Introduction in 'Brownese' by Sketchley and two stories by him in ordinary English. Other contributions by 'B.A.W.' and Henry Frith.

[3634] MRS BROWN AT HOME AND ABROAD. Mr Arthur Sketchley's New Entertainment at the Egyptian Hall, Piccadilly. (Also 'Mrs Brown at the Seaside'.)

Small 8vo. n.d. Brownish yellow wrappers, cut flush, printed in brown. pp. 16, printed throughout in brown ink.

This is an elaborate programme of an Entertainment given every evening except Saturday at 8 o'clock, and on Saturday afternoons at 3 o'clock. Part One consisted of Introductory Remarks and six adventures of Mrs Brown, recited in 'Brownese'. Part Two was a travelogue describing a voyage up the Rhine and delivered in ordinary English.

pp. (10)–16 are occupied by 'Mrs Brown at the Sea Side', reprinted from *London Society*. The book issue of 'Mrs Brown at the Seaside' is a wholly different text.

'Mrs Browniana'

MR BROWN ON THE GOINGS-ON OF MRS BROWN at the Tichborne Trial and in her own Family [3635]

Hotten, n.d. (April, 1872). Cream glazed pictorial wrappers, cut flush. pp. (192) A_1 (adverts.) pasted down to inside front cover. A_2 adverts. L_6–L_8 Publisher's cat., dated 1872; (M_1)–(M_8) continuation of cat.; (N_1)–(N_4) continuation of cat., (N_4) pasted down to inside back cover.

[*See also* HAMILTON, WALTER, *in Section I.*]

[3636] MULOCK, D. M.

Domestic Stories. 'A New Edition.' Smith, Elder 1872. Yellow pictorial boards.
This volume contains some of the stories originally published in 3 vols. as *Avillion and Other Tales*.

Olive. 'New edition.' Chapman & Hall 1875. Pink pictorial boards. *Select Library*.

[3637] NAVAL AND SEAFARING YELLOW-BACKS 1854–1865

This small group of 'yellow-back firsts' parallels that which combines under one heading books dealing with Detection and Crime. They are spirited, vivacious, skilfully designed; and date from the same period as the more numerous and equally elegant reprints of Armstrong, Barker, Chamier, Howard, Marryat and Neale, which appear in this section under their authors' names.

[3638] COAST GUARD (TALES OF THE), by LIEUTENANT WARNEFORD, R.N. [William Russell, alias 'Waters']

Copy I: First Edition. J. & C. Brown, Ave Maria Lane 1856. Grey-blue boards, pictorially printed in black. Wood-engraved front. and pictorial title precede printed title. Small format.

pp. (232) P_8 adverts.

Note. The adverts. on P_8 are of 'Works published by David Bryce and sold by J. & C. Brown'. They include the 'Popular Edition' (in pink boards) of Disraeli's works (721 in Section I).

[3638*a*] **Copy II: Second Edition.** J. & C. Brown 1857. Pictorial yellow *cloth*, designed in imitation of a yellow-back (cf. 3525 and 3543 (20), above) Small format.

pp. (i)–(iv) + (9)–(270)

Note. The irregular pagination is due to the dropping of the front. and pictorial title. A new story, *Captain Larpent*, occupies pp. (231)–(269).

MARINES (TALES FOR THE), by HARRY GRINGO Lieutenant Wise), author of 'Los Gringos' [3639]

Ward & Lock 1855. Yellow boards, pictorially printed and lettered in black. End-papers printed with adverts. Small format.

pp. 256

Ink signature: 'J. Browne', on title.

MIDSHIPMAN (THE), or Twelve Years at Sea, by the Rev. F. W. MANT, late R.N. [3640]

Pl. 8 Routledge 1854. White-back boards, printed in blue, brown and red with design of red-ensign and fancy lettering. End-papers printed with adverts. Small format.

pp. viii + 246

[3641] PHANTOM CRUISER (THE). Edited by LIEUT. WARNEFORD, R.N., author of 'Tales of the Coast Guard', etc. [William Russell, alias 'Waters']. 'Never before printed.'

John Maxwell & Co. 1865. Yellow paper wrappers, cut flush, printed in dark green with fancy lettering. Up-lettered on spine. Small format.

pp. (iv) + (236) Q_6 adverts., over the imprint of Ward & Lock.

[3642] NEALE, W. JOHNSON

All small format, and in pictorial yellow-back boards. The three Bryce titles have the cover pictures repeated on back covers.

Pl. 8 **Cavendish,** or The Patrician at Sea. 'New Edition.' David Bryce, n.d.

Pl. 8 **Flying Dutchman (The):** a Legend of the High Seas.

Copy I. David Bryce, n.d. **Copy II.** 'New Edition.' Routledge, n.d.

Pl. 8 **Port-Admiral (The):** a Tale of the War. 'New Edition.' David Bryce, n.d.

Will Watch. J. and C. Brown, n.d. The Appendix to the first edition, describing the quarrel with Marryat, is omitted.

[3643] NEWNES' PENNY LIBRARY OF FAMOUS BOOKS [1896–1899]

Published weekly from January 1896, Nos. 1–46 were crown 8vo in size and issued in cream wrappers, lettered in red, blue, green or violet; Nos. 47–177 were demy 8vo, issued—as to Nos. 47–170 in pale blue wrappers pictorially printed (after Menzies) in dark blue, as to Nos. 171–177 in pink wrappers pictorially printed after an unnamed artist.

This series, wholly without issue-importance and of an undistinguished appearance suitable to a popular library of the last decade of the century, is here recorded for the sake of the titles included in it. Each number has an Editorial Note signed 'C.S.C.', and every student of nineteenth-century fiction will admit that the selection of texts (for a penny-market in the 'nineties) shows both intelligence and enterprise. The list which follows omits certain titles—either obvious or eighteenth century or too recent to be relevant (e.g. a few Scott novels; such Dumas perennials as *Monte Cristo* and the rest; translations of Eugene Sue, Merimée, Féval, etc.; and an occasional copyright English text—by Conan Doyle, Grant Allen and others—introduced to give topical flavouring to a dish mainly revivalist). This has been done in order to emphasise the overwhelming majority of reprints of significant nineteenth-century fiction. I know of no better evidence than this series of the survival power of novels well known in their day but (one would have thought) forgotten by the mid-nineties. C.S.C. knew his subject; Messrs Newnes had the courage to trust his judgement. The longevity of the series is their justification; though it is clear that as time went on they were fighting a losing battle. It is interesting to observe that only one Jane Austen was included (evidently her revival was not yet), no Morier or Trollope or Le Fanu or Collins, and very little Marryat. Also that C.S.C. successfully resisted G. P. R. James until the eleventh hour.

1 **Vicar of Wakefield** (had this not been the first title to be issued, I should have omitted it as too obvious to merit record)

2 **Tales of Adventure, Mystery and Imagination** (Poe)

3 **Suil Dhuv, the Coiner** (Griffin)

4 **Feats on the Fiord** (Martineau)

5 **Scarlet Letter** (Hawthorne)

6 **Great Hoggarty Diamond** and **Major Gahagan** (Thackeray)

8 **Peep o' Day or John Doe** (Banim)

10 **Admiral's Daughter** (Mrs Marsh)

11/12 **Ben Brace** (Chamier)

13 **Peg Woffington** (Reade)

14 **Deformed** and **Professional Visits of the Black Doctor** (Mrs Marsh)

15/16 **Stories of Waterloo** (Maxwell)

18 **Pirate** (Marryat)

19/20 **Nick o' The Woods** (Bird)

21 **Christie Johnstone** (Reade)

NEWNES' PENNY LIBRARY

22 **Barney O'Reirdon and Other Irish Legends and Stories** (Lover)

23/24 **Rifle Rangers** (Mayne Reid)

25 **Mrs Caudle's Curtain Lectures** (Jerrold)

26 **Some Tough Yarns by the Old Sailor** (Barker)

27/28 **Sense and Sensibility** (Austen)

29 **Wild Adventures in Texas and Other Tales from Blackwood** (anon)

30 **Popanilla** (Disraeli)

31/32 **Crohoore of the Bill Hook** (Banim)

34 **Sketches of Young Gentlemen, etc.** (Dickens)

35/36 **Plant Hunters** (Mayne Reid)

38 **Phelim O'Toole's Courtship; Ned McKeown, etc.** (Carleton)

41 **Love and Duty** (Mrs Marsh)

42/43 **Robber of the Rhine** (Leitch Ritchie)

44 **Half-Sir** (Griffin)

45/46 **Cliff Climbers** (Mayne Reid)

49/50 **Christmas Books** (Dickens) [Carol, Chimes—Cricket on Hearth, Battle of Life.]

51/52 **Old St Paul's** (Ainsworth)

53 **Old St Paul's (conclusion)** and **Haunted Man** (Dickens)

55 **Money-Seekers and Other Tales** (Mrs Crowe)

56/57 **Rienzi** (Bulwer Lytton)

60/61 **Harry Lorrequer** (Lever)

65/66 **Marchioness of Brinvilliers** (Albert Smith)

67 **Father's Curse** (Grattan). From *Highways and Byways*

72 **Three Cutters** (Marryat) and **Mosaic Masters** (Sand)

73/74 **Windsor Castle** (Ainsworth)

76 **Game of Life** (Leitch Ritchie)

79 **John Manesty** (Maginn)

81/82 **Last Days of Pompeii** (Bulwer Lytton)

83 **Fetches** (Banim)

87 **Dark Lady of Doona** (Maxwell)

91 **Gold Finders of California** (Mayne Reid) and **Shawn Dhuv** (? Griffin)

92/93 **Rory O'More** (Lover)

95/96 **Guy Fawkes** (Ainsworth)

97 **Demon Pilot and Other Tales** (Kingston)

99/100 **Fardarougha the Miser** (Carleton)

101 **Fireside Stories** (Ingoldsby) and **Inundation** (Gore)

105 **Soldier's Fortune** (Mrs Marsh)

107/108 **Hard Times** (Dickens)

109 **Calderon the Courtier** (Bulwer Lytton) and **Count Ludwig** (from *The Picnic Papers*)

112 **Bit o' Writin** (Banim) and **Esther** (Horace Smith; from *The Picnic Papers*)

115 **Chronicles of Clovernook** (Jerrold)

116/117 **Phantom Ship** (Marryat)

119/120 **Night and Morning** (Bulwer Lytton)

122/123 **Hunter's Feast** (Mayne Reid)

129 **Dozen Pair of Wedding Gloves** (anon. C.S.C. states he cannot identify the author)

130/131 **Rookwood** (Ainsworth)

132/133/134 **Westward Ho!** (Kingsley)

136/137 **Mary Barton** (Gaskell)

139/140 **Saucy Arethusa** (Chamier)

145/146 **Miser's Daughter** (Ainsworth)

148/149 **Richard Savage** (Whitehead)

151/152 **Richelieu** (James)

160/161/162 **Tower of London** (Ainsworth)

[Nos. 171–177—wrappered in pink—present the religious stories of one Charles M. Sheldon, a popular American pastor. A note in No. 177 states that the series is now at an end. It cannot be denied that this finale amounts to a capitulation. C.S.C., after a gallant fight, had surrendered.]

[3644] NOTLEY, MRS F. E. M.

All Ward & Lock, in yellow pictorial boards.

Forgotten Lives. n.d. [circa 1889]. *Favourite Authors.*

In the House of a Friend. n.d. [circa 1889]. *Select Library.*

Love's Bitterness. 1877. *Favourite Authors.*

[3645] NORRIS, W. E.

Mademoiselle de Mersac. 'New Edition.' Smith, Elder 1883. Pale yellow pictorial boards.

[3646] **OLIPHANT,** MRS MARGARET

All large format.

At His Gates. 'New Edition.' Ward & Lock, n.d. Greenish white pictorial boards.

†**Days of My Life (The).** 'New Edition.' Ward & Lock, n.d. (after 1889). Greenish white pictorial boards.

‡**Greatest Heiress in England (The).** 'New Edition.' Chatto & Windus 1891. Cream pictorial boards.

Lilliesleaf. 'New Edition.' Chapman & Hall 1876. Yellow pictorial boards. *Select Library of Fiction.*

†**Lucy Crofton.** 'New Edition.' Ward & Lock, n.d. (after 1889). Pale lilac pictorial boards

†**Madonna Mary.** 'New Edition.' Ward & Lock, n.d. (after 1882). Pale green pictorial boards.

Margaret Maitland. Weldon, n.d. Cream pictorial boards.

‡**Primrose Path (The).** 'New Edition.' Chatto & Windus 1892. Deep cream pictorial boards.

Second Son (The). Macmillan 1888. Pale cream decorated boards, with design in black and red common to Macmillan's board issues.

‡**White Ladies.** 'New Edition.' Chatto & Windus, n.d. (1898). Cream pictorial boards.

Note. Titles marked † are volumes in Ward & Lock's *Select Library* or *Select Authors* and have spines roughly uniform. Titles marked ‡ have spines wholly uniform.

[3647] **OUIDA**

All in yellow pictorial boards and published by Chatto & Windus unless otherwise stated. Large format.

Cecil Castlemaine's Gage, etc. 'New Edition.' n.d. (cat. dated April 1887).

Chandos 'New Edition.' n.d. (cat. dated June 1879).

Dog of Flanders (A). 'New Edition.' 1892.

Frescoes. 'New Edition.' 1890.

Friendship. 'New Edition.' n.d. (cat. dated 1880).

Held in Bondage. 'New Edition. n.d. (cat. dated May 1879).

House-Party (A). 'New Edition.' Spencer Blackett, n.d.

Idalia. 'New Edition.' n.d. (cat. dated June 1879).

In a Winter City. 'New Edition.' 1901

In Maremma. 'New Edition.' 1893.

Moths. 'New Edition.' 1893.

Othmar. 'New Edition.' 1890.

Pipistrello. 'New Edition.' 1882.

Puck. 'New Edition.' 1893.

Ruffino. 'New Edition.' 1891.

Signa. 'New Edition.' n.d. (cat. dated February 1880).

Strathmore. 'New Edition.' 1894.

Tricotrin. 'New Edition.' n.d. (cat. dated October 1879).

Two Little Wooden Shoes. 'New Edition.' 1890.

Under Two Flags. 'New Edition.' 1895.

Village Commune. 'New Edition.' 1890.

Wanda. 'New Edition.' 1901.

Wisdom, Wit and Pathos. 'New Edition.' 1890.

[3648] **'OUR NOVEL SHILLING SERIES'** 1878–1881

Sm. 8vo. Bradbury, Agnew & Co. Glazed paper boards, cut flush, printed in red and black on front and back with drawings after Linley Sambourne and lettering. Up-lettered in black on spine.

Written by F. C. BURNAND (described by *The Examiner* as 'the one living English writer whose fun is always hearty, fresh and spontaneous'), the level of these parodies of prominent contemporary novelists can be gauged by the burlesque titles of their books. They hit off the obvious foibles of the authors concerned with the cheerful ingenuity which gives humour to *Happy Thoughts* and its kind; but they neither intend subtlety nor achieve it. I am not aware of more than five titles having been published, although out of the Series, but uniform, Burnand issued THE RIDE TO KHIVA, 1877. The numbering is mine.

1 STRAPMORE: a Romance by WEEDER. Author of *Folly and Farini, Under Two Rags, Arryad'nty, Chuck, Two Little Wooden Jews, Nicotine, A Horse with Glanders, In Somers Town, Shamdross*, etc. 1878. Half-title. pp. viii+(120) I_2–I_4 publishers' adverts. paged i–vi.

2 ONE AND THREE! By (that distinguished French Novelist) FICTOR NOGO. 1878 Half-title. pp. viii+112 Publishers' adverts., paged i–viii on text paper, at end.

'OUR NOVEL SHILLING SERIES'

3 WHAT'S THE ODDS? or The Dumb Jockey of Jeddington. A Genuine Sporting Novel by Major Jawley Sharp, author of *Squeezing Langford, Two Kicks*, etc. 1879

Half-title. pp. xvi + (96) G_8 adverts.

4 CHIKKIN HAZARD. A Novel by CHARLES READIT and DION BOUNCEYCORE. 1881

Half-title. pp. viii + 120

5 GONE WRONG. A New Novel by Miss RHODY DENDRON, authoress of *Cometh Down Like a Shower, Red in the Nose is She! Buy Sweet Tart, Not Silly, but don't Tell.* 1881

Half-title. pp. (viii) + (120) H_3–end, publishers' cat. paged (i)–(xx) on text paper and dated 1881.

[3649] PARISIAN LIBRARY 1887–(?)

J. & R. Maxwell n.d. Published at one shilling each in what are described as 'Appropriate Illuminated Covers'. Inside and outside back wrappers printed with adverts. Titles asterisked are not in the Collection. The numbering is mine (and conjectural).

1 *THE RED BAND by Boisgobey. 2 vols.

2 *THE CONDEMNED DOOR by Boisgobey. 2 vols.

3 DEATH OR DISHONOUR by Boisgobey. 'The Sole and Authorised Copyright Translation by Sir Gilbert Campbell Bart.' Front. of extreme ineptitude in Vol. I after Shirley Hodson. 2 vols.

4 *THE BLUE VEIL by Boisgobey.

5 CASH ON DELIVERY by Boisgobey. 'Sole and Authorised Copyright Translation.' 2 vols. Front. in Vol. I on a level with that in 3, and after the same artist.

6 *THE CRY OF BLOOD by Boisgobey. 2 vols.

7 *THE FELON'S BEQUEST by Boisgobey. 2 vols.

8 *FICKLE HEART by Boisgobey. 2 vols.

Note. Other authors were included in this series, but only Boisgobey is here listed, because he was evidently the main bone of contention between Maxwell and Vizetelly (cf. Note to 3454 above).

'These translations', say Maxwell, 'are not only fully protected, but NO other Versions are sanctioned, authorised or allowed by the Author. *These are the only approved translations.*'

Whether this claim were justified or not, Maxwell certainly beat Vizetelly in blurb-eloquence. They describe the Parisian Library as:

'A new choice Series of Striking, Alluring and Entertaining Masterpieces of Fiction. Special arrangements ensure thoroughly fluent translations, which read like English-wrought originals, whilst preserving all the pristine vivacity, fervid colour, full spirited wit, and torrid yet refined passion.'

PARODIES

See AUTHORSHIP UNKNOWN, above, and HAMILTON, WALTER, in Section I.

[3650] PAYN, JAMES

All large format, with printed end-papers. Unless otherwise stated, all in cream pictorial boards, and published by Chatto & Windus.

Burnt Million (The). 'New Edition.' 1891.

Cecil's Tryst. 'New Edition.' 1890.

†Foster Brothers (The). 'New Edition.' n.d. (1884.)

Gwendoline's Harvest. 'New Edition.' 1881.

Halves, etc. 'New Edition.' 1888.

***Humorous Stories.** 'New Edition.' 1881. Pink boards. Cover drawing by Phiz. This has a *Select Library of Fiction* case (i.e. Chapman & Hall) but Chatto & Windus end-papers and text.

***Like Father Like Son.** 'New Edition.' Chapman & Hall 1872. Yellow back. Cover drawing by Phiz.

Lost Sir Massingberd. 'Third Edition.' Sampson Low 1865. Orange back. Cover drawing by Walter Crane. Re-issued by Chatto & Windus 1891.

Mystery of Mirbridge (The). 'New Edition.' 1890.

Talk of the Town (The). 'New Edition.' 1887. Cover drawing by Harry Furniss.

†Two Hundred Pounds Reward, etc. 'New Edition.' n.d. (1881). Cover drawing by Phiz.

Word and the Will (The). 'New Edition.' 1892.

Note. All the Chatto & Windus titles, save those marked †, have uniform conventional spines. The two asterisked are uniform with one another.

[3651] PEACOCK, THOMAS LOVE

Headlong Hall and Nightmare Abbey. Ward & Lock 1856. Yellow pictorial boards, specially drawn spine. Small format. Spine defective.

Note. The same publishers in the same year published *Maid Marian* and *Crotchet Castle* in one (presumably uniform) yellow-back volume, price one shilling. These issues were made over Peacock's name.

[3652] PHILLIPS, SAMUEL

WE ARE ALL LOW PEOPLE THERE, and other Tales (by the author of 'Caleb Stukely') Routledge 1854. Yellow boards, printed in green and black with design and fancy lettering signed 'Alfred Crowquill'. End-papers printed with adverts. Small format.

Half-title. pp. (viii) + (256) Slip of lilac paper tipped on to front end-paper advertises *The Lamplighter.*

Ink signature: 'J. R. Molineux 1854', on title.

Note. These stories are reprinted from *Blackwood's Magazine.*

[3653] POE, EDGAR ALLAN

Mystery of Marie Roget and other Tales. Chatto & Windus, n.d. (adverts. dated June, 1879). Yellow pictorial boards.

654] PORTER, JANE

Pastor's Fireside (The). Routledge, n.d. [circa 1892]. Cream pictorial boards.

Scottish Chiefs (The). Routledge, n.d. Cream pictorial boards.

[3655] PSEUDONYM LIBRARY 1890–1896

Mustard yellow wrappers 1*s.* 6*d.*, buff linen 2*s.*

Two titles in this series are recorded in Section I under Ouida. Complete lists are easily available in the *English Catalogue*, and the representation of three-decker novelists is virtually nil. Fifty of the fifty-two titles are in the Collection, in cloth and in fine state; but of these ten are not first editions.

[3656] PUSHKIN, A. S.

QUEEN OF SPADES (The), and Other Stories. With a Biography. Translated from the Russian by Mrs Sutherland Edwards. Chapman & Hall 1894. Pale yellow pictorial boards. Illustrations in the text.

[3657] RAINBOW SERIES OF ORIGINAL NOVELS 1885

Published by Cassell & Co. at one shilling in stiff paper wrappers, cut flush, shading from orange, through yellow, to pale green, and printed in black. Up-lettered on spine. Back cover printed with adverts. (commercial). Plain white end-papers. The title asterisked is not in the Collection.

1 AS IT WAS WRITTEN: a Jewish Musician's Story, by SIDNEY LUSKA [Henry Harland]. (1885)
pp. (iv) + (254) 1st leaf of final sig., 16_1, a single inset. (i) (ii) and the original 16_8 pasted to front and back covers. Publishers' cat., 16 pp. dated '5.8.85', at end.

2 *A CRIMSON STAIN, by A. BRADSHAW

3 MORGAN'S HORROR: a Romance of the 'West Countree', by GEORGE MANVILLE FENN. 1885
Half-title. pp. 192. Publishers' cat., 16 pp. undated, at end.

Whether this series ran beyond three titles I do not know. No. 3 contains no indication of future volumes in preparation.

[3658] REACH, ANGUS B.

Clement Lorimer. Routledge 1856. Yellow pictorial boards, specially drawn up-lettering on spine. Small format.

Leonard Lindsay. J. & C. Brown 1857. Yellow pictorial *cloth.* Specially drawn spine. Small format.

[3659] READABLE BOOKS 1852–1853

Published in Penny Weekly Numbers, in sixpenny parts, and in decorated board volumes at one shilling, by Henry Vizetelly, 15–16 Gough Square as to No. I); by Vizetelly and Clarke & Co., 148 Fleet Street (as to Nos. II–? V); and thereafter by Clarke, Beeton & Co., 148 Fleet Street, this series can be listed so far as No. XIV. The volumes are numbered on title; series title appears on front and back cover and on title. At some stage (probably when Clarke, Beeton became sole publishers) a cloth edition was issued at one and sixpence, but I have never seen a specimen, neither have I seen the weekly numbers or sixpenny parts.

The board editions carry an all-over design in the cameo manner, printed in various colours on various backgrounds. Front cover design repeated on back cover. The books are attractive, carefully produced and remarkable value for one shilling. The series is predominantly non-fiction. Fiction is, however, well represented by two important collections of Poe's Tales. Titles asterisked are not in the Collection.

I TALES OF MYSTERY, IMAGINATION AND HUMOUR; AND POEMS, by EDGAR ALLAN POE

Henry Vizetelly 1852 (? February or March). Covers printed in terracotta and dark brown on biscuit. Dark strawberry end-papers. Wood-engraved front., vignette title and 24 illustrations on text paper. The two first are on plate paper but reckoned in the collation.

pp. xxiv+256 [Pp. (v) vi 'Prospectus' of the series; (vii) (viii) 'Preface' by the Publisher; (xi)–xxiv Memoir of Poe, unsigned.

Note. An advert. of this volume in No. II of the series states: 'The present is the first occasion of the re-publication in this country of the above remarkable tales.'

II PHILOSOPHERS AND ACTRESSES: Scenes, Vivid and Picturesque, from the Hundred and One Dramas of Art & Passion. By ARSÈNE HOUSSAYE

Vizetelly and Clarke & Co., n.d. [April 20, 1852] Covers printed in blue and black on light brown. Dark strawberry end-papers. Wood-engraved front., vignette title and 33 illustrations. The two first, although on plate paper, are reckoned in the collation.

pp. (viii) [paged vi]+(228) I_2 adverts.

III LETTERS OF PETER PLYMLEY, ESSAYS AND SPEECHES by the REV. SYDNEY SMITH

Vizetelly and Clarke & Co., n.d. [June 1, 1852]. Covers printed in scarlet and black on biscuit. Dark strawberry end-papers. Wood-engraved front., vignette title and full-page portraits in the text. None is on text paper, but the two first are reckoned in the collation; the remainder are not.

pp. (228) H_{12} adverts. Publishers' adverts. (of the series), 4 pp. undated, at end. Pp. (v)–x occupied by Memoir of Sydney Smith, unsigned.

IV NILE NOTES OF A 'HOWADJI', OR THE AMERICAN IN EGYPT, by G. W. CURTIS

Vizetelly and Clarke & Co., n.d. [? July, 1852]. Covers and end-papers uniform with III. Wood-engraved front., vignette title and 27 illustrations. Although the two first are on plate paper they are reckoned in the collation.

pp. viii+(228) Publishers' advert. (of the series), 4 pp. undated, at end.

V *THE OLD GUARD OF NAPOLEON, by J. T. HEADLEY

VI *WELLINGTON, by ALFRED COOKE

VII *PICTURES OF EUROPEAN CAPITALS

VIII REVERIES OF A BACHELOR, by IK. MARVEL [Donald Grant Mitchell]

Clarke, Beeton & Co., n.d. [? 1853]. Covers printed in dark red and black on grey-lilac. Yellow end-papers. Wood-engraved front., pictorial title, vignette title and 10 illustrations. The two first are on plate paper and not reckoned in the collation.

pp. (xii)+(9)–220 Publishers' adverts. 4 pp. undated, both at front and at end.

First edition (American) 1850.

IX TALES OF MYSTERY, IMAGINATION AND HUMOUR, by EDGAR ALLAN POE. Second Series *Pl. 7*

Clarke, Beeton, n.d. [? 1853]. Covers printed in orange-scarlet and black on pale yellow. Yellow end-papers. Wood-engraved front., vignette title and 14 illustrations. The two first are on plate paper and not reckoned in the collation.

pp. (ii)+(252) Publishers' adverts., 2 pp. undated, at end.

X *THE CAVALIERS OF ENGLAND

XI THE ADIRONDACK OR LIFE IN THE WOODS, by J. T. HEADLEY

Clarke, Beeton, n.d. [1853]. Covers and end-papers uniform with No. IX. Wood-engraved front. and vignette title and 10 illustrations. The two first are on plate paper and not reckoned in the collation.

pp. xvi+(ii)+(17)–222 [A single leaf 'List of Illustrations' was added to prelims. after continuous pagination had been adopted.]

Ink signature dated 1853 on title.

XII *THE GUARDS

XIII *THREE TALES, by COUNTESS D'ARBOUVILLE

XIV *SOUTHEY'S LIFE OF NELSON

I suspect the series went to pieces about this point. Even as early as No. IX records of its progress (which Vizetelly had provided with care and intelligence) were dropped from the volumes—a sure sign of a publisher losing interest in a serial venture. No. XIII (Arbouville's *Tales*) reappeared shortly afterwards (? about 1855) in Clarke, Beeton's *Illustrated Railway Library*, and manifestly consists of *Readable Books* sheets with series decoration removed from title. By 1856 certain titles in the series appeared over the imprint of C. H. Clarke, but without distinctive covers or coherent sequence.

This series must not be confused with the wrappered and very commonplace reprint-fiction series of the same name published by Warne from 1877 onward.

[3660] READE, CHARLES

All large format (one extra-large); all (with one exception) cream pictorial boards.

Cloister and the Hearth (The). Chatto & Windus 1888.

†Griffith Gaunt. Ward, Lock & Tyler, n.d. (pencil inscription on title dated 1881).

Hard Cash. Chatto & Windus 1892.

It is Never Too Late to Mend. 'New Edition.' Bentley 1857. Buff boards, printed in black. Dated on spine 1857. Vignette on back cover. Extra large format.

Love Me Little, Love Me Long. Chatto & Windus 1890

†Peg Woffington. Ward, Lock & Tyler, n.d.

Perilous Secret (A). Chatto & Windus 1891.

Put Yourself in his Place. Chatto & Windus 1894.

Readiana. Chatto & Windus, n.d. (1883).

Note. The Chatto & Windus titles are all 'New Edition' and have uniform spines. Titles marked † are themselves uniform.

[3661] REID, THOMAS MAYNE

Series I. Small format. Covers specially designed. The title in caps is a First Edition.

[3662] HUNTERS' FEAST (THE), or Conversations around the Camp Fire

Copy I: First Edition. Thomas Hodgson, n.d. [1855]. White pictorial boards.

Half-title. pp. 336

This is No. 120 in *The Parlour Library* and was also issued in the regulation glazed green paper-board style of this series, with 2 additional leaves inserted in prelims.: Dedication and Preface. A few titles were specially issued in 'brilliant coloured covers by Alfred Crowquill', and of these this copy is a specimen (cf. Lever, *Sir Jasper Carew* [1419*a* above]).

[3662*a*] **Copy II: New (unavowed) Edition with Illustrations.** C. H. Clarke, n.d. Royal-blue bead-grain cloth, pictorially blocked in gold on spine. Wood-engraved front. and 8 illustrations after Harrison Weir.

This edition is from the type of the Parlour Library edition (the publisher of which Clarke became in succession to Hodgson) and collates as Copy I. An additional eight-leaf signature, unsigned, on text paper, is added—a Catalogue of Clarke's Publications. The illustrations appear for the first time in this edition.

Maroon (The)

C. H. Clarke, n.d. Yellow pictorial boards, the [3663]
spine incorporating series title: 'The Mayne Reid Library.' Half-title with the same series title.

pp. (iv) + (492)

The end-papers advertise nine titles in *The Mayne Reid Library*, but over the imprint of Ward & Lock, and cloth-bound at 3*s.* 6*d.* with illustrations.

Quadroon (The): or Adventures in the Far West [3664]
J. & C. Brown, n.d. Yellow pictorial boards.

pp. (448)

Rubber stamp: 'J. R. Molineux', facing title.

White Chief (The): a Legend of Northern Mexico [3665]
J. & C. Brown, n.d. Yellow pictorial boards

pp. (ii) + 444

Rubber stamp: 'J. R. Molineux', on fly-leaf.

[3666] **Series II. Large format.** Varying pictorial fronts. but standard spine design, incorporating series legend 'Capt. Mayne Reid's Novels'. All published by Routledge and undated.

Afloat in the Forest—Boy Hunters—Boy Slaves—Bush Boys—Cliff Climbers—Desert Home—Giraffe Hunters—Guerilla Chief—Half-Blood—Headless Horseman (demy 8vo)**—Lost Lenore—Maroon—Ocean Waifs—Quadroon—Rifle Rangers—Scalp Hunters—Tiger Hunter—White Squaw—Wild Huntress—Wood Rangers—Young Voyageurs.**

REID

[3667] **Mayne Reidiana**

SKULL HUNTERS (The): a Terrific Tale of the Prairie!! By Captain Rayne Meade

Judy Office, 73 Fleet Street 1868. Pale blue wrappers, cut flush, pictorially printed in black. Spine unlettered. Inside and back covers printed with adverts. Wood-engraved front. and numerous illustrations on text paper.

Half-title. pp. (i)–(x)+(11)–128 *Judy Library*, No. 1.

[3668] RIDDELL, MRS J. R.

All large format, and (unless otherwise stated) in pale yellow pictorial boards. All, save *A Life's Assize*, described as 'New Edition'.

Austin Friars. Warne, n.d. (probably late seventies).

Fairy Water. Chatto & Windus 1885.

George Geith. 8vo. Warne 1868. Yellow-back, with front.

Note. Re-issued in cr. 8vo in The Companion Library (n.d.) in brilliant blue and in pink boards, with same cover-design (cut down) and no front.

Life's Assize (A). Warne, n.d.

Nun's Curse (The). Ward & Downey 1889.

†Phemie Keller. Gall & Inglis, n.d.

Prince of Wales's Garden Party (The). Chatto & Windus 1884.

Weird Stories. Chatto & Windus 1891.

World in the Church (The). Warne, n.d.

Note on the 'Companion Library'. This series (one of popular reprints without issue-significance) was started by Gall & Inglis of Edinburgh and London, but was taken over by Warne. During the Gall & Inglis regime a cloth style was issued as well as pictorial boards. I have only one specimen—*City and Suburb*, by Mrs Riddell—bound in pale sage-green diagonal-fine-ribbed cloth blocked and lettered in brown and gold. The series title appears on front., the end-papers are printed with adverts. and the book is undated.

Of the yellow-backs above listed, the Warne titles are all *Companion Library*, with spines of two styles. The title marked † (imprint Gall & Inglis) is also *Companion Library*, with spine uniform with *The World in the Church* (imprint Warne). The Chatto & Windus titles have uniform spines.

[3669] RITCHIE, LEITCH

Robber of the Rhine (The). Routledge, n.d. Yellow pictorial boards. Small format.

[3670] ROBINS, REV. ARTHUR

Miriam May (anon). 'A New Edition.' Routledge, Warne & Routledge 1861. Yellow pictorial boards, specially drawn spine. Small format. *Railway Library.*

[3671] ROBINSON, EMMA (author of 'Whitefriars')

All small format, published by Routledge.

Caesar Borgia. n.d.

Madeleine Graham. n.d.

Maid of Orleans. n.d. Cover drawing by Phiz.

Westminster Abbey. n.d. (after 1884). Cover drawing probably by Phiz.

Whitehall. 'New Edition.' n.d. This has specially designed spine. Cover and spine drawings probably by Phiz.

[3672] ROUTLEDGE'S ORIGINAL NOVELS 1855–1859

This series represents another of the several attempts (cf. *First Class Library* in this section and in Section III *Chapman & Hall's Monthly Series* and *Smith Elder's Library of Romance*) made by fiction publishers during the nineteenth century to break the guinea-and-a-half convention in novel-publishing. Similar attempts to lure the public to *buy* new novels by publishing them at less than standard price have been made in our own time. These ventures always fail because (1) the public dislikes buying new books at any price, until it has sampled them from a library; (2) the Lending Libraries throw their great influence against the pioneering publisher; (3) the best authors will not write for the small rewards which are all that cheap original publication can afford. As a result, each of the price-breaking series has begun with loud trumpetings and a serious attempt to maintain a good standard of home-produced fiction, but has gradually been forced to introduce translations of foreign authors, unauthorised reprints of American books, and works by British authors of minor quality or phenomenal fertility.

It will be seen that I have been very unsuccessful in locating fine examples of Routledge's Original Novels. They are scarce even beyond the usual scarcity of yellow-backs of the early period. But I give the complete list, so far as I can establish it, because the series, for the sake of what it tried to do, should have a place in publishing history. Titles asterisked are not in the Collection.

The titles in the series were published in decorated boards at the prices stated, and the first ten were also issued in cloth at 6*d.* extra. Series title appears on covers, but the numbering is mine.

1 *THE CURSE OF GOLD, by R. W. JAMESON (1*s.*)

2 *THE FAMILY FEUD, by THOMAS COOPER, author of *Alderman Ralph* ('Adam Hornbook') (2*s.*)

3 *THE SERF SISTERS, by JOHN HARWOOD (1*s.*)

4 *THE PRIDE OF THE MESS, by the author of *Cavendish* (W. JOHNSON NEALE) (1*s.* 6*d.*)

5 *FRANK HILTON, or the Queen's Own, by the author of *The Romance of War* (JAMES GRANT) (2*s.*)

6 MY BROTHER'S WIFE, by AMELIA B. EDWARDS (1*s.* 6*d.*). 1855

Yellow boards, pictorially blocked and fancy-lettered in green and brown. Cover-design repeated on back cover. Small format. End-papers printed with adverts.

pp. 304 Publishers' cat., 8 pp. undated, at end.

7 *ADRIEN, by A. M. MAILLARD (1*s.* 6*d.*). 1855

8 THE YELLOW FRIGATE, or the Three Sisters, by JAMES GRANT (2*s.*). 1855

Pl. 4 Pale yellow boards, pictorially printed and fancy-lettered in black and pale blue. End-papers printed with adverts. Small format.

pp. (444) EE_6–EE_8 adverts. Slip of yellow paper tipped on to front fly-leaf advertises Hannay's *King Dobbs.*

Ink signature: 'J. R. Molineux. 1855', facing title.

9 *EVELYN FORESTER, by MARGUERITE A. POWER (niece of the Countess of Blessington) (1*s.* 6*d.*)

10 *HARRY OGILVIE, by JAMES GRANT (2*s.*)

11 *THE LADDER OF LIFE, by AMELIA B. EDWARDS (1*s.* 6*d.*)

12 *THE TWO CONVICTS, by FREDERICK GERSTAECKER (2*s.*)

13 *DEEDS NOT WORDS, by M. BELL (2*s.*)

14 *THE FEATHERED ARROW, by FREDERICK GERSTAECKER (2*s.*)

15 *TIES OF KINDRED, by OWEN WYNN (1*s.* 6*d.*)

16 *WILL HE MARRY HER? by JOHN LANG (2*s.*)

17 *SECRET OF A LIFE, by M. BELL (2*s.*)

18 THE LOYAL HEART, or the Trappers, by GUSTAVE AIMARD (1*s.* 6*d.*). 1858

Pictorial yellow boards. End-papers printed with adverts. Small format.

Half-title. pp. xvi + (296) U_4 adverts. Slip of green paper tipped on to front fly-leaf advertises *Horse Taming* by Rarey.

19 THE EX-WIFE, by JOHN LANG (2*s.*). 1859

Pictorial yellow boards. End-papers printed with adverts. Small format.

pp. viii + (400) Publishers' cat., 8 pp. dated December 1858, at end.

20 *ARTHUR BLANE, by JAMES GRANT (2*s.*)

21 *THE HIGHLANDERS OF GLEN ORA, by JAMES GRANT (2*s.*)

[3673] RUN AND READ LIBRARY (The), for Railway, Road and River 1853–1856

Published at 1*s.* 6*d.* and 2*s.* by Clarke, Beeton & Co. in various coloured boards printed in black, this series deserves brief record, partly for the sake of its cover design and the none-too-grammatical unction of its preliminary blurb, partly also because a few of its volumes were first or revised editions. At (or about) No. 20 the series was taken over by Simpkin, Marshall. Later still, in the late sixties, the Library (consisting of 40 titles, with numbering rearranged) passed to Ward, Lock & Tyler who re-issued the books in conventional small-format pictorial yellow-back form at 2*s.* per vol. The spine-design incorporated the series-title. One specimen of this re-issue (*Beatrice*) is in the Collection.

RUN AND READ LIBRARY

The cover design was originally used on the front cover but was soon relegated to the back, its place being taken by a vignette and more emphatic titling. The 'Announcement' defends the reading of *wholesome* fiction (with quotations from Dr Johnson and Mrs Beecher Stowe), and proclaims the publishers' 'conviction that persons who have the taste, invention, sprightliness, humour and command of diction that qualifies for a successful novelist may become the greatest of public benefactors by skilfully providing the *healthful aliment* that may be employed in supplanting the pernicious leaven'.

'It is', continues the Announcement, 'to supply this acknowledged desideratum that the RUN AND READ LIBRARY has been projected. *Taste, sprightliness, humour and command of diction, combined with sound principles,* will be the leading qualification of the works admitted into this Series.'

It will be observed that Protestantism and anti-popery rank high among Messrs Clarke, Beeton's 'sound principles'.

The volumes are not themselves numbered, but some advertisements give a numbered sequence. I could list the titles up to No. 68 (published in 1861), but it is sufficient to go to No. 22, by which time Simpkin, Marshall were certainly in charge. Titles asterisked are not in the Collection. Where a volume has 'edition significance' the fact is stated.

1 *I'VE BEEN THINKING, by A. S. ROE. 1853. A first English edition (revised and edited) of an American story, originally published in 1850, as *James Mountjoy or I've been Thinking*

2 *THE AUTOBIOGRAPHY OF A £5 NOTE, by MRS WEBB. 1853. A First Edition.

3 *THE CONFESSOR: a Jesuit Tale of the Times, by the author of *Michael Cassidy*. 1853. A First Edition, described by *The British Banner* as 'pervaded by an earnest anti-papal spirit'.

Pl. 7 4 JANE RUTHERFORD OR THE MINER'S STRIKE, by A FRIEND OF THE PEOPLE. With a Preface by Peter Richards, a Coal Miner. 1854

Dark crimson boards. Wood-engraved front., pictorial title and 12 double-spread illustrations.

pp. (i)–viii + (9)–(288) 12_{12} adverts. A First Edition.

5 *THE MYSTERIOUS MARRIAGE, by CATHERINE SINCLAIR. 1854. Originally published in 3 vols. 1849, as *Sir Edward Graham or Railway Speculators* (3060 in Section I).

6 MARY ANNE WELLINGTON, by RICHARD COBBOLD. 1854

Note. This issue is not in the Collection, but 573*a* described in Section I is so similar in appearance (though without series title) that I suspect it to be a 'Run and Read' issue re-clothed.

7 *THE LAMPLIGHTER, by MISS CUMMINS. 1854

8 *MODERN FLIRTATION, by CATHERINE SINCLAIR. 1854

9 *JULAMERK, by MRS WEBB. 1854

10 ZENON THE MARTYR, by RICHARD COBBOLD. 1855. See 576*a* in Section I

11 *TO LOVE AND TO BE LOVED, by A. S. ROE. 1855. A first English edition.

12 *BEATRICE, by CATHERINE SINCLAIR. 1855. Described as 'the great Protestant Tale'.

13 *THE PILGRIMS OF NEW ENGLAND, by MRS WEBB. 1855

14 *A LONG LOOK AHEAD, by A. S. ROE. 1855. A first English edition.

15 JANE BOUVERIE, by CATHERINE SINCLAIR. 1855

16 *THE WIDE WIDE WORLD, by MISS WETHERELL. 1855

17 THE MONK, by MRS SHERWOOD. 'A new and Improved Edition.' n.d. [1855] *Pl. 7*

Bright green boards, wood-engraved front. and pictorial title.

pp. 360 Publishers' adverts., 16 pp. on text paper, at end.

Originally published as *The Monk of Cimies*. Described on front cover as 'A vivid picturing of the life and system of Monkery. A companion to the Anti-Nunnery "Beatrice" and the Anti-Jesuit "Confessor".'

18 FRESTON TOWER, by RICHARD COBBOLD. (1856). See 569*a* in Section I.

19 *HOLIDAY HOUSE, by CATHERINE SINCLAIR. (1856)

20 *MODERN ACCOMPLISHMENTS, by CATHERINE SINCLAIR. (1856)

21 *ADONIJAH, by JANE MARGARET STRICKLAND. (1856)

22 *MODERN SOCIETY, by CATHERINE SINCLAIR. (1856)

[3674] RUSSELL, W. CLARK

Heart of Oak. 'Special Edition for Sale in India and the British Colonies.' Chatto & Windus 1896. Cream pictorial boards.

[3675] SALA, GEORGE AUGUSTUS

I. *First Editions*

[3676] MAKE YOUR GAME: or the Adventures of the Stout Gentleman, the Slim Gentleman and the Man with the Iron Chest

Ward & Lock 1860. Yellow pictorial boards. Folding wood-engraved front. and numerous illustrations in the text, all on text paper. Small format.

Half-title. pp. xii + (272) S_6–S_8 adverts. 32 pp. of publishers' (various) adverts. at end on text paper, but unsigned. Two leaves advertising W. H. Smith's Library inserted between front end-papers.

Rubber stamp: 'J. R. Molineux', on verso of title.

Note. The adverts. at the end of this volume merit examination. They include the following imprints: 'Office, 122 Fleet Street' (i.e. the address from which *Robin Goodfellow* and the *St James's Magazine*, both started by John Maxwell, were published); 'Houlston, Wright, 65 Paternoster Row' (several pages stressing *The Welcome Guest*); Ward & Lock themselves (158 Fleet Street); C. J. Skeet (advertising a Sala novel); W. Kent (The Comic Library); and G. Vickers.

The connection between these various imprints was no doubt partly a shared interest in Sala; but I must repeat my suspicion that Ward & Lock had concealed tie-ups with more than one small publishing firm, perhaps using imprints suited to certain types of books when this seemed prudent.

PAPERS HUMOROUS AND PATHETIC. Being selections from the Works of George Augustus Sala. Revised and abridged by the author for public reading. [3677]

Tinsley 1872. Dark yellow boards, printed in black and red with a portrait of Sala, titling, etc. End-papers printed with Chapman & Hall adverts. Large format.

Leaf of Tinsley adverts. precedes half-title. pp. (xii) [paged (x)] + (340) 21_8 and 22_1 22_2 Tinsley adverts.

Ink signature: 'J. Browne', on title.

II. *Reprints*

Captain Dangerous. C. H. Clarke, n.d. Yellow pictorial boards. Cover drawing by Phiz. Chapman & Hall end-papers. *Select Library of Fiction*

Gaslight and Daylight. 'A New Edition.' Chatto & Windus, n.d. (adverts. dated 1893). Pale yellow pictorial boards.

London Up to Date. 'Cheap Edition.' Adam & Charles Black 1896. Yellow ornamental boards.

See also: FIRST CLASS LIBRARY (above) and WARD & LOCK'S SHILLING VOLUME LIBRARY (below).

[3678] SAND, GEORGE

Consuelo. Weldon & Co., n.d. (inscription dated 1887). Pale yellow pictorial boards.

Countess of Rudolstadt. Weldon, n.d. (about mid-eighties). Pale yellow pictorial boards.

Old Convents of Paris (Madame Charles Reybaud) and **The Haunted Marsh** (Sand). Weldon, n.d. (about mid-eighties). Pale yellow pictorial boards. *Weldon's Two Shilling Library.*

Note. These two stories formed No. 8 of the Parlour Library (1847) and the present re-issue is printed from the plates (or type) of that edition, with prelims. re-set.

[3679] SCOTT, MICHAEL

Tom Cringle's Log. 'A New Edition.' Routledge 1876. Yellow pictorial boards.

[3680] SHELLEY, MARY W.

Fortunes of Perkin Warbeck. Routledge 1857. Yellow pictorial boards, specially designed spine. Small format. *Railway Library.*

[3681] SKETCHLEY, ARTHUR

Match in the Dark (A). 'New Edition.' Chatto & Windus 1881. Yellow pictorial boards.

See also MRS BROWN SERIES above.

[3682] SMART, HAWLEY

Pl. 6 **Cecile.** Chapman & Hall 1881. Illuminated decorative boards, uniform with Trollope's *Miss Mackenzie*, etc. Imprint of Ward & Lock on spine and series title; *Select Library of Fiction*, on front and spine. Also on spine 'The Works of Hawley Smart'.

Note. This attractive 'illuminated' binding is, in my experience, very uncommon, and I have only acquired three specimens for the Collection. But, owing to the kindness of Dr John Johnson of the Clarendon Press and another correspondent, I can record that the following titles (over and above those here noted) were published in this style: **Trollope:** *Belton Estate*; *He Knew He was Right*; *Lotta Schmidt*; *Phineas Finn* (probably *Phineas Redux* also); *Rachel Ray*; *Tales of All Countries.* **Whyte Melville:** *Market Harborough*; *Rosine*; *Tilbury Nogo.*

Outsider (The). F. V. White & Co., n.d. (inscription dated 1888). Yellow pictorial boards.
Note. Not identical with Copy II in Section I, though very similar.

Play or Pay. Chapman & Hall 1878. Pale blue pictorial boards, cover drawing by Corbould. *Select Library of Fiction.*
Note. Type similar to that of first edition, but a different printer's imprint and clearly a later impression.

Salvage, etc. Ward & Lock, n.d. (after 1884). Pink pictorial boards. *Select Authors.*

[3683] SMITH, ALBERT

I. *First Edition*

[3684] THE LONDON MEDICAL STUDENT (Edited by Albert Smith)
Small 8vo. Routledge 1861. Yellow pictorial boards, up-lettered on spine. Back cover and end-papers printed with adverts. pp. (iv) + (124) I_6 adverts.
Bookseller's stamp: 'Hickson, Bridlington', on title.

II. *Reprints.* All small format and, with one exception, published by Routledge. Conventionalised spines, except where stated.

Christopher Tadpole

Pl. 4 **Copy I:** '22nd Thousand.' 1854. White boards, printed in red and black with front and spine design by Alfred Crowquill. Front cover design repeated on back. Front. and vignette title, wood-engraved after Phiz illustrations in first edition.

Copy II: n.d. Yellow back, with same front design as Copy I in red and green, new specially drawn spine design. Advert. pasted on back cover.

Comic Tales and Pictures of Life

1st re-issue. David Bryce, n.d. Yellow pictorial boards after Leech. No front. but text illustrations. Printed from Bentley's plates, with new prelims. Small format.

2nd re-issue. C. H. Clarke, n.d. Yellow pictorial boards after Leech (different picture) and same text illustrations. Printed from Bentley's plates (now worn) with new prelims. and adjusted fly-titles. A coarse production.

Marchioness of Brinvilliers (The)

Copy I: 1856. Bright green pictorial boards. Cover drawing by Phiz. Up-lettered in fancy type on spine.

Copy II: n.d. Cream boards. Same cover-drawing as I but lettering re-arranged. Conventional spine advert. pasted to back cover.

Mont Blanc. Ward & Lock, n.d. Yellow pictorial boards. Wood-engravings in text.

Mr Ledbury (The Adventures of) *Pl. 4*

Copy I: 'New Edition.' 1856. Yellow boards, printed with all-over portrait of the author and fancy titling; spine-design by Phiz. *Railway Library.*

Copy II: n.d. Pale blue pictorial boards.

Scattergood Family, Fortunes of the. n.d. Yellow pictorial boards. Cover-drawing by Phiz.

[3685] SMITH, HORACE

All small format.

Adam Brown. C. H. Clarke, n.d. Yellow pictorial boards. Front cover drawing repeated on back. Conventional spine.

Arthur Arundel. C. H. Clarke, n.d. Yellow pictorial boards. Front cover drawing repeated on back. Spine uniform with *Adam Brown.*

Jane Lomax

Copy I. Henry Lea, n.d. Yellow pictorial boards. Cover drawing by Phiz repeated on back. Specially designed spine also by Phiz.

Copy II. J. A. Berger, n.d. (inscription dated 1877). Dark yellow pictorial boards. Cover drawing as Copy I, conventional spine, advert. on back cover. Printed from the type of Copy I on poor quality paper. Title a cancel.

New Forest (The). 'Copyright Edition.' Blaney & Fryer, n.d. Yellow pictorial cloth, in imitation of a yellow-back. Specially designed spine.

Walter Colyton. 'Second Edition.' Knight & Son, n.d. Yellow pictorial boards, specially designed spine.

[3686] SOUTHWORTH, MRS D. E. NEVITT

Lost Bride (The). Henry Lea, n.d. Pale yellow pictorial boards, specially drawn spine, front cover design repeated on back. Small format.

Retribution. Henry Lea, n.d. Yellow pictorial boards. Small format.

[3687] STEVENSON, R. L.

New Arabian Nights. 'New Edition.' Chatto & Windus 1885. Yellow pictorial boards.

Wrecker (The) (with Lloyd Osbourne). 'Colonial Edition.' Cassell 1893. Yellow pictorial boards.

[3688] STEWART, MISS E. M.

SNOWED UP, or Lost on the Wold. Edited by Miss E. M. Stewart, authoress of 'London City Tales', 'Lord Dacre' of Gilsland', 'Royalists and Roundheads', 'Hermione', 'Lillias Davenant', 'Rival Roses', etc. Offices of the Illustrated Monthly Novelist, 8 Palsgrave Place, Temple Bar, n.d. (1868). Pictorial wrappers, cut flush. Spine unlettered. Back printed with advert. of Second Series of 'London City Tales' (q.v.). Wood-engraved front. on plate paper.

pp. (iv) + 156

Note. This is yet another derivative from the Canterbury Tales. The occupants of a mail coach, snow-bound near York—a Young Author, a Sailor, a Farmer, a Lawyer, etc.—tell stories to pass the time. It was clearly a Christmas issue, for the wrapper, to sensational effect, combines sprigs of holly with a knight in armour and a ghost. For suggested dating see LONDON CITY TALES (3613 above), Note (ii).

[3689] ST JOHN, BAYLE

Maretimo. 'Cheap Edition.' Chapman & Hall, n.d. (1856). Yellow pictorial boards. Small format. *Select Library.*

[3690] STOWE, HARRIET BEECHER

Agnes of Sorrento. 'New Edition.' Smith, Elder 1869. Deep cream pictorial boards in standard Smith, Elder style.

Dred. Sampson, Low 1856.

Binding I. Cream boards, pictorially printed in black on front, spine and back; dark green end-papers.

Binding II. White boards, printed all over in red maroon, lettering in reverse; dark green end-papers.

Mayflower (The). E. Farrington, 2 Bath Street, Newgate Street 1853. Blue boards, pictorially printed and lettered in black. Imprint on cover: 'C. H. Clarke', and 2 wood-engraved plates.

Sunny Memories of Foreign Lands

Copy I: 'Author's Edition.' Sampson, Low 1854. Greenish white boards, pictorially printed in black on front cover and spine. Wood-engraved front. and illustrations in text.

Copy II: 'Thirtieth Thousand.' Routledge 1854. Yellow decorated boards. Front cover design repeated on back. Wood-engraved front. and title, but no other illustration.

[3691] SUE, EUGENE

Refugees of Martinique (The). Walter Scott, n.d. Cream boards, patterned in red and blue (uniform with Adams' *Democracy*).

Wandering Jew (The). Routledge, n.d. Yellow pictorial boards.

[3692] SURTEES, ROBERT SMITH

Jorrocks' Jaunts. Routledge, n.d. (after 1889). Cream pictorial boards; cover drawing by John Sturgess.

Soapy Sponge's Sporting Tour. Routledge 1893. Cream pictorial boards (by Sturgess) uniform with foregoing.

[3693] THACKERAY, W. M.

History of Samuel Titmarsh (The) and The Great Hoggarty Diamond. Sq. Cr. 8vo. Smith, Elder (on title), Bradbury & Evans (on front cover). n.d. 'New Edition.' Cream glazed boards printed in dark blue and light green.

[3694] THOMAS, ANNIE

Allerton Towers. F. V. White 1883. Yellow pictorial boards.

Best for Her. Ward & Lock, n.d. (1882). Yellow pictorial boards. *Select Library.*

Eyre of Blendon. F. V. White 1884. Cream pictorial boards.

[3695] TINSLEY'S COMIC LIBRARY 1854–(?)

Mainly for the sake of the imprint, which is distinct from, and pre-dates, that of Tinsley Bros., I include a brief note on this series, of which I have never seen more than the one specimen here described.

OUR HOLIDAY IN PARIS, by Percy B. St John.

Edward Tinsley & Co., 58 Fleet Street 1854. Glazed yellow wrappers cut flush, printed in black on front with an elaborate, skilful and humorously conceived design, incorporating series title, names of contributors to the series, and individual book-title. Spine up-lettered. Back wrappers printed with advert. of series. Wood-engraved front. on text paper.

Half-title. pp. (120) 2 leaves of adverts. at end stressing the works of Percy B. and Bayle St John.

The advert. on back wrapper promises for the same series a Christmas Book by Mayhew and *Lobster Salad* by Percy B. St John. It announces as published *Our Own Correspondent at the Seat of War* by William Brough.

[3696] TROLLOPE, ANTHONY

Though this collection of Trollope in yellow-back form is not complete (I have seen a few of the missing titles, but only in bad shape) nor wholly of earliest issue, it is complete enough to suggest certain publishing happenings—a rare event in the uncharted and largely undated wilderness of yellow-backs of the middle and late period.

No one of the Smith, Elder titles is present, indicating that Smith, Elder (who published few yellow-backs and those mainly in the eighties and nineties) were also unwilling to lease their books for yellow-back issue. The two Longman titles are published by Longman themselves and with a complete absence of commercial advertisement. Chapman & Hall freely included Trollope in their *Select Library of Fiction*, and in several cases leased their plates to Ward & Lock for later issue of the titles in that firm's *Library of Select Authors*. But in 1881 Ward, Lock & Co. must have acquired the right to use the series title also of the *Select Library of Fiction*, even re-clothing in the attractive 'illuminated' style novels which had already been published in their *Library of Select Authors*. For how long Ward, Lock & Co. published the *Select Library* I do not know. The *Library of Select Authors* continued long after 1881; and several Trollopes in the Series have Ward & Lock on spine, Ward, Lock & Co. on title. The latter imprint dates from about 1880.

Chatto & Windus, who were Trollope's last publishers, seem to have acquired a few late Chapman & Hall titles for their yellow-back series, in which of course they also included the three novels of their own.

American Senator (The). 'A New Edition.' Chatto & Windus 1886.

Barchester Towers. 'New Edition.' Longman etc. n.d. [circa 1870]. The imprint on front cover is 'Longmans, Green, Reader & Dyer'.

Belton Estate (The).

Copy I. 'Third Edition.' Chapman & Hall 1868. *Select Library of Fiction.*

Copy II. Ward, Lock & Bowden, n.d. [later than 1894]. *Select Authors.*

Bertrams (The).

Copy I. 'Eighth Edition.' Chapman & Hall, n.d. [1869]. *Select Library of Fiction.*

Copy II. 'New Edition.' Ward & Lock, n.d. [later than 1878]. *Select Authors.*

Castle Richmond. 'New Edition.' Ward & Lock, n.d. [later than 1878]. *Select Authors.*

Cousin Henry. 'New Edition.' Chapman & Hall 1881.

Copy I. Pictorial boards. *Select Authors.*

Copy II. Illuminated decorative boards. *Select Library of Fiction* (cf. 3682 above).

In both cases title imprint is Chapman & Hall, but imprint on cover Ward & Lock.

Doctor Thorne. 'Ninth Edition.' Chapman & Hall 1866. *Select Library of Fiction.*

Doctor Wortle's School. Ward & Lock, n.d. [1881]. *Select Authors.*

Duke's Children (The). 'Third Edition.' Chapman & Hall 1881. *Select Library of Fiction.*

Eustace Diamonds (The). 'New Edition.' Ward & Lock, n.d. [later than 1881]. *Select Library of Fiction.*

Frau Frohmann and other Stories. 'A New Edition.' Chatto & Windus 1884.

Golden Lion of Granpere (The). 'New Edition.' Tinsley 1873. The imprint on front cover and end-paper adverts. are those of Routledge.

He Knew He Was Right. 'New Edition.' Chapman & Hall, n.d. [1871]. *Select Library of Fiction.*

Is He Popenjoy? 'New Edition.' Ward & Lock, n.d. [later than 1883]. *Select Authors.*

Kellys and the O'Kellys (The). 'Eighth Edition.' Chapman and Hall, n.d. [1868]. *Select Library of Fiction.*

Kept in the Dark. 'A New Edition.' Chatto & Windus 1891.

Landleaguers (The). 'A New Edition.' Chatto & Windus 1885.

La Vendée. 'Fourth Edition.' Chapman & Hall 1875. *Select Library of Fiction.*

Macdermots of Ballycloran (The). 'New Edition.' Chapman & Hall 1866. *Select Library of Fiction.*

Marion Fay. 'A New Edition.' Chatto & Windus 1885.

Mary Gresley and An Editor's Tales. 'New Edition.' Chapman & Hall, n.d. [1871]. *Select Library of Fiction.*

For note on this title see Sadleir, pp. 113–14.

Miss Mackenzie.

'New Edition.' Ward, Lock & Co. on both title and spine. n.d. [1882]. *Select Library of Fiction.* Illuminated decorative boards, uniform with *Cousin Henry.*

Copies exist with Chapman & Hall imprint.

Phineas Finn. 'New Edition.' Ward & Lock, n.d. *Select Authors.*

Phineas Redux. 'New Edition.' Ward & Lock, n.d. [1882]. *Select Authors.*

This edition is printed from the plates of the Chapman & Hall yellow-back edition of [1878].

Rachel Ray. 'Eleventh Edition.' Chapman & Hall, n.d. (1869). *Select Library of Fiction.*

Ralph the Heir. 'New Edition.' Chapman & Hall, n.d. [1872]. *Select Library of Fiction.*

At the end of the volume an anonymous essay on Charles Lever, reprinted from *Blackwood's Magazine* and occupying 30 pages, acts as advert. for the Lever titles in the *Select Library.*

Sir Harry Hotspur. Chapman & Hall 1881. *Select Library of Fiction.*

Tales of All Countries.

Copy I. Chapman & Hall 1867. *Select Library of Fiction.*

Copy II. 'New Edition.' Ward & Lock, n.d. [later than 1878]. *Select Authors.*

Printed from same plates as Copy I. Pictorial cover identical.

Warden (The). 'New Edition.' Longman etc. n.d. [circa 1870].

New South Wales and Queensland—South and West Australia—Victoria and Tasmania

3 vols. 'New Edition.' Chapman & Hall 1875. Stiffened pictorial paper covers, with uniform design on strong yellow ground.

New Zealand. Ward, Lock & Co., n.d. [circa 1884]. Pale yellow unstiffened wrappers printed in colours with a different picture.

Note. These four volumes constitute the work *Australia and New Zealand,* and are yellow-back re-issues of the four small volumes first published in cloth in 1874 (cf. Sadleir, pp. 134–6). Presumably there was also a 'New Zealand' in the Chapman & Hall series, dated 1875. Whether Ward, Lock's later issue comprised all four parts, I do not know. The one noted above is the only specimen I have ever seen.

[3697] TROLLOPE, MRS FRANCES

Barnabys in America (Adventures of the). Ward & Lock, n.d. [circa 1857]. Pictorial boards. Small format.

Love and Jealousy. J. & C. Brown, n.d. [1859]. Pictorial boards. Small format. Date established from advert. on back cover of *Traditions of London* by 'Waters', 1859. Originally published as *The Young Countess.*

Widow Barnaby (The). 'New Edition.' Ward & Lock 1856. Pictorial boards. Dark yellow printed end-papers (very unusual in a yellow-back). Small format. Re-issued by Routledge in (1885) in inferior pictorial boards.

Widow Married (The). Ward & Lock, n.d. [circa 1856]. Pictorial boards. Small format.

[3698] TROLLOPE, T. A.

La Beata. 'New Edition.' Ward & Lock, n.d. [circa 1884]. Greenish white pictorial boards. *Select Library.*

[3699] TUPPER, MARTIN FARQUHAR

Stephen Langton

Copy I. 'New Edition Revised.' Ward & Lock 1863. Pictorial boards and decorated spine.

Copy II. 'New Edition.' Guildford: Frank Lasham 1880. Pictorial boards but plain spine.

This issue contains steel-engraved front. and title from Vol. I of the first edition, badly cut down: also a new Preface, written for this edition, dated June 1880. The coloured picture on front cover is the same as that on Copy I.

[3700] TWAIN, MARK

I. *First Editions*

[3701] CURIOUS DREAM (A) and other Sketches. Selected and revised by the Author. Copyright.

Routledge, n.d. [1872]. Yellow pictorial boards with a picture of a seated skeleton; up-lettered on spine; advert. (*Routledge's American Library*) on back.

pp. (152) L_4 advert.

Ink signature: 'E. Izou', on title.

Notes. (i) All the items in this book except the fourth: 'The Facts in the case of George Fisher deceased', are here first printed in book-form. (ii) A later issue has designed cover with moonlight view in half circle above panel with author and title, and on back cover advert. of Storel & Grant, Tailors. 'Copyright' does not appear on title, but in its place is the sentence set out in Note (ii) to *Information Wanted.* I am indebted to Mr I. R. Brussel for these and other details of Twain 'first appearances in book-form'.

[3702] INFORMATION WANTED and Other Sketches

Routledge, n.d. [circa 1875]. Yellow boards, printed in vermilion and black, up-lettered on spine, advert. (Clark & Co.'s Shutters) on back cover. Printed end-papers.

Half-title. pp. (144) Publishers' cat., 16 pp. undated, at end.

Notes. (i) The following items in the Contents List are here first printed in book-form: *Two Poems* (by Moore and Twain); *The Experiments of the MacWilliamses etc.*; *After Dinner Speech*; *A True Story Just as I Heard it*; *Speech at the Scottish Banquet in London*; *A Ghost Story*; *A Curious Pleasure Excursion.* (ii) On the title appear the words: 'Messrs George Routledge and Sons are my only authorised London publishers. Mark Twain.'

INNOCENTS AT HOME (The). 'Copyright Edition' [3703]

Routledge, n.d. [1872]. Yellow pictorial boards, up-lettered on spine, advert. (*Routledge's American Library*) on back cover. Printed end-papers. pp. 224

Note. This is a sequel to *Roughing It*, and preceded American issue by one week.

ROUGHING IT. 'Copyright Edition' [3704]

Routledge, n.d. [1872]. Dark yellow pictorial boards, up-lettered on spine, advert. (*Routledge's American Library*) on back cover. Printed end-papers.

Half-title. pp. xii + 244

Note. Described on front cover as 'Companion volume to The Innocents Abroad'. Preceded American issue by one week.

[3704*a*] II. *Reprints.* Large format, all in cream or yellow pictorial boards and published by Chatto & Windus (unless otherwise stated).

Idle Excursion (An) and Other Papers. 1878

Innocents Abroad (The). Hotten, n.d. (1872). Cream pictorial wrappers, cut flush.

†**Innocents Abroad (The) and The New Pilgrim's Progress.** 1877. Entitled 'The Pleasure Trip' on cover.

Jumping Frog (The) and other Humorous Sketches. Hotten, n.d. (1874). Cream pictorial wrappers, cut flush.

Mark Twain's Sketches. 'New Edition.' 1892

Mississippi Pilot (The). Ward, Lock & Tyler, n.d. White pictorial wrappers, cut flush.

Screamers. Ward, Lock & Tyler, n.d. White pictorial wrappers, cut flush. Cover drawing by Phiz.

Tom Sawyer (Adventures of). 'New Edition.' n.d. (1877)

Tramp Abroad (A). 'A New Edition.' 1890

Note. The Chatto titles, except that marked †, have uniform conventional spines.

[3705] VARIOUS AUTHORS

LOVER'S LEAP (The) and Other Tales, by Leitch Ritchie, Mrs Norton, Mrs S. C. Hall, Charles Knight, Thomas Pringle, Mrs Howitt, John Banim, Miss Mitford, Mrs Hofland, Miss Jewsbury.

Routledge, Soho Square 1849. Deep-cherry decorated boards, patterned in pink and gold and fancy-lettered in gold on spine: THE / LOVER'S / LEAP. All edges gilt. Steel-engraved front. and 11 plates after J. Wood (3); J. M. W. Turner, G. Arnald, David Wilkie, W. Purser, C. R. Leslie, William Finden, J. Stephanoff, W. Kidd and J. Stothard.

pp. viii + 316 Small format.

Ink inscription on fly-leaf: 'Miriam Wright Anderson. From her affectionate Brother E. A. W. Anderson. Jany 1st/49.'

Note. Conceived in the style of the Annuals, this elegant and carefully produced little volume was presumably on the market for Christmas 1848. No Editor's name is given, nor is there any suggestion that earlier volumes have been or that later ones are to be published. The title-story is by Leitch Ritchie; and in addition to contributions by the authors listed on the title the volume contains a 25 page story 'By the O'Hara Family' (i.e. John *and* Michael Banim); a story by J. Baillie Fraser; and poems or prose by The Ettrick Shepherd, Allan Cunningham, George Darley and John Clare.

[3706] VERNE, JULES

The English editions of Jules Verne present a complicated problem, and the notes here provided of issues in pictorial wrappers do not pretend to elucidate more than a corner of it. It may, however, be put on record that in 1875 Sampson Low etc. made a formal arrangement with Hetzel of Paris, Jules Verne's publishers, by which they became the sole authorised English publishers of such of Verne's works as were still in 'translation copyright'. On the strength of this arrangement they were able, in March 1876, to proceed against Weldon & Co., who published a Shilling Series of Verne, and compel them to withdraw their editions of *Around the World in* 80 *Days* and *The Adventures of Three Russians* (these titles being covered by the Hetzel agreement) and announce that in future they would only publish works by Verne of which the copyright had not been secured by Sampson Low.

Nevertheless there were on the market yet other editions of Verne, published by Routledge and by Ward, Lock & Tyler. The specimens I have seen are undated and may have pre-dated Sampson Low's exclusivity, and thereafter been withdrawn. In any event, of the Routledge titles listed quite a number, and of the Ward & Lock titles one at least, are on the list published by Sampson Low as in their sole control.

Sampson Low published their Verne editions in various forms. There was a 'very handsome cloth' edition with gilt edges, containing 350–600 pp. and 50 to 100 full-page illustrations at prices from 6*s.* to 10*s.* 6*d.* per vol.; there was a plainer cloth edition from 3*s.* 6*d.* to 5*s.*; there was an edition in smaller type with a few of the illustrations at 1*s.* per vol. in 'coloured boards', at 3*s.* or 2*s.* per vol. in cloth. It is with the last two only that I am now concerned, and with such boarded or wrappered competitors as I can record.

VERNE

[3706*a*] SAMPSON LOW'S 'AUTHORISED AND ILLUSTRATED EDITION'

Square 8vo, glazed white stiff wrappers, cut flush, printed with vignette, lettering and decoration in black and either grey or pale blue, up-lettered on spine. Inside and back covers printed. 'JULES VERNE'S WORKS. LOW'S AUTHORISED EDITION' appears on front cover and spine. The cloth editions are in smooth scarlet linen pictorially blocked and lettered in grey-blue and black, up-lettered on spine, back cover blocked with advert. Each volume contains a wood-engraved front., often a title vignette and 2 or 3 illustrations in the text. The volumes are not numbered, and I give them in the order of an advert. in an early volume which presumably represented sequence of publication. It may be noted that the first eight titles were announced in the Publishers' Circular of December 31, 1875, with a statement that as these titles were just coming out of copyright, the publishers were deliberately launching a shilling series in order to forestall similar cheap editions from other houses. Titles asterisked are not in the Collection.

1876 ***Adventures of Three Englishmen and Three Russians in South Africa**

„ **Five Weeks in a Balloon**

„ **A Floating City**

„ **The Blockade Runners**

„ ***From the Earth to the Moon**

„ **Around the Moon: a Sequel** (copy dated 1886, clearly a late issue)

„ **Around the World in 80 Days**

„ **Twenty Thousand Leagues under the Sea.** 2 vols.

„ **A Winter Amid the Ice**

„ **Dr Ox's Experiment** and **Master Zacharias**

„ **Martin Paz**

1877 **The Fur Country.** 2 vols.

1877 **Hector Servadac.** 2 vols. Third Edition (copy dated 1882)

1881 **Michael Strogoff: the Courier of the Czar.** 2 vols. (translated by W. H. G. Kingston)

1882 **The Child of the Cavern.** Translated by W. H. G. Kingston

1884 **The Green Ray**

1885 **The Giant Raft: I. Eight Hundred Leagues on the Amazon; II. The Cryptogram**

1887 **Keraban the Inflexible: I. The Captain of the Guidara** (cloth); **II. Scarpante the Spy** (cloth)

1893 **North Against South: I. Burbank the Northerner** (cloth); **II. Texar the Southerner** (cloth)

„ **The Flight to France** (cloth)

Note. The following titles were also issued in wrappers and cloth, but are not in the Collection: **Dick Sands** (2 vols.)—**Survivors of the 'Chancellor'** (2 vols.)—**Mysterious Island** (3 vols.)—**Begum's Fortune**—**Tribulations of a Chinaman**—**Steam House** (2 vols.)

[3706*b*] ROUTLEDGE EDITIONS

Yellow pictorial boards, uniform specially designed spine, n.d. Each volume contains two stories individually paged, so presumably an earlier separate issue was made.

Adventures of Captain Hatteras: I. The English at the North Pole; II. The Field of Ice.

Journey to the Centre of the Earth and **Five Weeks in a Balloon.** (Front. to each story in this volume.)

20,000 Leagues under the Sea. 2 vols. in one (front. to each volume).

A panel-advert. announces as also published (presumably uniform with these Routledge issues): **Floating City** and **Blockade Runners**—**Voyage Round the World**—**From the Earth to the Moon** and **Around the Moon**—**Three Englishmen and Three Russians**—**Around the World in 80 days**—**The Fur Country.**

[3706*c*] WARD, LOCK & TYLER EDITIONS

Yellow pictorial and decorated wrappers printed in black, red and green, cut flush. Inside covers and back cover printed with adverts. THE JULES VERNE LIBRARY on front cover and spine. n.d. [1886, according to a label pasted into the only specimen in the Collection].

The English at the North Pole (Voyages and Adventures of Captain Hatteras) [1886].

A panel-advert. announces 'in fancy wrappers 1*s*., cloth 1*s*. 6*d*., cloth gilt 2*s*.' the following other titles: **Journey Into the Interior of the Earth** (*sic*)—**Ice Desert**—**Five Weeks in a Balloon.**

Note. In no case where the same title appears in two or more publishers' lists have the books been printed from the same type or plates. Each publisher's edition is specially set and the texts of the translations vary.

[3707] VIZETELLY'S CAPITAL STORIES 1888–1890

Published at one shilling each in various coloured wrappers, cut flush, pictorially printed in black. Bracketed numbers are mine, and the order of publication is not necessarily correct. Titles asterisked are not in the Collection.

1 THE CHAPLAIN'S SECRET, by LÉON DE TINSEAU. 1888. Lilac wrappers; grey-green printed end-papers.

2 *AVATAR, by GAUTIER

3 *COLONEL QUAGG'S CONVERSION, by SALA

4 *THE MONKEY'S REVENGE, by GOZLAN

5 *THE PENSIONER WITH THE WOODEN HEAD, by MOUTON

6 *THE MARCHIONESS' TEAM, by DE TINSEAU

7 THE EMOTIONS OF POLYDORE MARASQUIN, by GOZLAN. 'Second Edition.' 1890

8 *FOR JACQUES' SAKE, by DE TINSEAU

[3708] VIZETELLY'S POPULAR FRENCH NOVELS 1880–(?) 1882

Published at one shilling each in pink paper wrappers, cut flush, printed in maroon with titling, etc. in decorative frame. Blue printed end-papers. Titles asterisked are not in the Collection. Some volumes are numbered, others unnumbered. I have numbered the latter in their correct sequence. I cannot establish the order of subsequent volumes in the series, three of which are listed in Grenville Murray's *Sidelights* (1881).

1 FROMONT THE YOUNGER AND RISLER THE ELDER, by ALPHONSE DAUDET. 1880

2 *SAMUEL BROHL AND PARTNER, by CHERBULIEZ

3 *THE DRAMA OF THE RUE DE LA PAIX, by BELOT

4 *MAUGARS JUNIOR, by THEURIET

5 WAYWARD DOSIA, by H. GREVILLE. 'Twentieth Thousand.' 1886†

6 A NEW LEASE OF LIFE and SAVING A DAUGHTER'S DOWRY, by EDMOND ABOUT. 'Fifteenth Thousand.' 1886‡

7 *COLOMBA and CARMEN, by MÉRIMÉE

8 *A WOMAN'S DIARY, by FEUILLET

9 *BLUE-EYED META HOLDENIS and A STROKE OF DIPLOMACY, by CHERBULIEZ

10 *THE GODSON OF A MARQUIS, by THEURIET

11 THE TOWER OF PERCEMONT and MARIANNE, by GEORGE SAND. 1881

12 *THE LOW-BORN LOVER'S REVENGE, by CHERBULIEZ

13 *THE NOTARY'S NOSE, etc., by ABOUT

14 *DOCTOR CLAUDE, by MALOT

15 *THE THREE RED KNIGHTS, by FÉVAL

[3709] VIZETELLY'S SENSATIONAL NOVELS 1888

Published at one shilling each in orange-scarlet wrappers, uniform with the novels of Boisgobey and Gaboriau. Titles asterisked are not in the Collection.

1 *BEWITCHING IZA, by BOUVIER

2 LECOQ THE DETECTIVE'S DAUGHTER, by BUSNACH and CHABRILLAT§

3 *DESPATCH AND SECRECY, by GRISON

4 A WILY WIDOW, by BOUVIER. 1888

5 THE CONVICT'S MARRIAGE, by BOUVIER. 1888

6 *THE MEUDON MYSTERY, by JULES MARY

[3710] VIZETELLY'S SIXPENNY SERIES of Amusing and Entertaining Books 1886–(?)

1 ? *BLACK CROSS MYSTERY, by HENRIETTA CORKRAN and MATRIMONY BY ADVERTISEMENT, by CHARLES G. PAYNE

2 ? *VOTE FOR POTTLEBECK, by CHARLES G. PAYNE

3 CECILE'S FORTUNE, by BOISGOBEY. 1886
In 1887 this story was combined with *The Steel Necklace* to form No. 21 of Vizetelly's Shilling Edition (see 3453 above)

4 THE THREE CORNERED HAT, and other Spanish Stories by P. A. DE ALARCON. 1886

† This volume is wrappered in pale yellow, printed in black and without decorative blocking.
‡ This volume is wrappered in dark red, blocked in black, uniform with standard pink wrappers.
§ Apparently re-numbered 5, although regularly listed as 2.

VIZETELLY

Note. This series continued with the following titles, but I cannot record for certain in what order they appeared:

The Steel Necklace, by Boisgobey

The Great Hoggarty Diamond, by Thackeray

Captain Spitfire and the Unlucky Treasure, by Alarcon

Young Widows, by Grenville Murray

The Detective's Eye, by Boisgobey
Combined with *The Red Lottery Ticket* in 1887 to form No. 22 of Vizetelly's Shilling Edition (3453 above).

The Strange Phantasy of Doctor Trintzius, by Auguste Vitu

A Shabby Genteel Story, by Thackeray

The Fiddler among the Bandits, by Dumas

The Red Lottery Ticket, by Boisgobey

Tartarin of Tarascon, by Daudet

King Solomon's Wives, by Hyder Ragged

The Manchester Merchant. From the German

Matrimony by Advertisement, by C. G. Payne

The Abbé Constantin, by Ludovic Halévy

[3711] WARD AND LOCK'S SHILLING VOLUME LIBRARY 1862

I have found this at once the most elusive and most obscure of all the Fiction Series of the period. Over years I have only succeeded in finding five titles of the original issue and two others in wrappers of a later design, while the lists of titles and future arrangements on back covers become so contradictory and confusing that it is impossible to reconstruct the series' publishing history beyond a comparatively early point.

The 'Shilling Volume Library' was announced as to be published on the 1st and 15th of every month, 'fcap 8vo, paper covers, in the French style of Binding'. The publishers led off with a brief exordium:

The Chancellor of the Exchequer, when proposing the Repeal of the Paper Duty, used as an argument for its removal the superiority both in paper and print of French popular literature over the same class of works produced in England. This distinction exists no longer. Therefore the *Shilling Volume Library* is projected with the view of giving to the reading public the full benefit of the abolition of the Paper Duty. Each book will present to the buyer the utmost possible value both in quantity and quality, and the greatest care will be taken so as to render the series in all respects unexceptional reading both for the young as well as for the old.

The original issue was in pale greenish-blue wrappers, printed in black, on front with series and other titling, on spine with book title, author and price, on spine with advert. of the series itself. Inside front and back covers blank. Edges uncut. The books had, in fact, exactly the appearance of French books of the period. The list of titles on back covers is numbered, but not the volumes themselves.

The following is the best I can do in the way of a chronological list of titles. Those asterisked are not in the Collection.

1 *THE FAMILY CREDIT, by WESTLAND MARSTON

2 *WHICH WINS—LOVE OR MONEY? by the author of *Whitefriars* (EMMA ROBINSON)

3 *RECOLLECTIONS OF A RELIEVING OFFICER, by E. P. ROWSELL (sic)
Note. As early as No. 3 the listing becomes slapdash. This book (later issued by J. & R. Maxwell as a large format yellow-back, poorly printed from the type of plates of the *Shilling Volume Library* edition) was by Francis W. Rowsell, C.B., C.M.G.

4 LADY LISLE, by M. E. BRADDON 1862
See 303 in Section I. The book is there described because it is in cloth, not wrappers. No mention is made of a cloth style in the back-cover adverts., and I do not know whether all or only a few of the titles were so issued.

5 THE ROUND OF WRONG, by ABOUT. (Translated by Lascelles Wraxall.) 1862
pp. (iv)+(256) Publishers' adverts., 4 pp. on text paper undated, at end.
Booksellers' ticket: 'Upward, Newport', inside front cover.

6 MEMOIRS OF A LADY IN WAITING, by MRS FENTON AYLMER. 1862
pp. (248)

7 *THE CRUISE OF THE BLUE JACKET, by LIEUT. WARNEFORD (WILLIAM RUSSELL, alias 'WATERS')

8 *SCENES WHERE THE TEMPTER HAS TRIUMPHED, by the author of *The Gaol Chaplain* (ERSKINE NEAL)

9 *THE KING OF THE MOUNTAINS, by ABOUT. (Translated by Wraxall.)

At this point a rearrangement takes place, and the back-cover lists promise but do not perform. In time they are corrected, but meanwhile the series has proceeded as follows:

10 THE YOUNG COUPLE and MISCELLANIES, by HAIN FRISWELL. 1862

pp. (viii) + 248

Note. The title-novelette occupies pp. (1)–55 only, and Friswell's Preface, dated July 1861, implies that it had been previously printed. But as 'Miscellanies' (pp. 56–248) are now first collected in book-form, and as the original printing of *The Young Couple* was probably in a periodical, I capitalise the whole volume as a first book-edition.

11 *LEONARD HARLOWE, by 'WATERS'

12 *THE NIGHT MAIL: ITS PASSENGERS AND HOW THEY FARED, by PERCY FITZGERALD

13 STORM-BEATEN, or Christmas at the Old Anchor Inn, by ROBERT BUCHANAN and CHARLES GIBBON. 1862

pp. (viii) + 248

This volume is in a totally different wrapper from its fellows—buff paper, printed in dark blue with an all-over design of branches, leaves and snow flakes. No series title on front, but series advert. on back cover—and (into the bargain) the early uncorrected advert. giving No. 11 as No. 13 and two titles for 12 and 14 which did not actually appear until Nos. 17 and 19. I can only surmise the special wrapper was devised for the Christmas market and as in keeping with the tale. The story was later re-issued in the Parlour Library: Shilling Series 3755 *b* (i).

14 THE CAPTAIN OF THE VULTURE, by M. E. BRADDON. 1863

See 272 in Section I.

We now run into fresh trouble. No. 14 above is undeniably dated 1863. Yet there are in the Collection copies of two books with this title steadily listed in the revised schedule as No. 17, and of another title not included at all up to No. 20, and both these books are dated 1862. I cannot with any certainty give beyond No. 20, nor explain the apparent discrepancy of dating.

15 *THE SILVER ACRE, by WILLIAM CARLETON. 1862

See 513 in Section I.

16 *HUNTED TO DEATH, by W. STEPHENS HAYWARD

17 THE SHIP CHANDLER AND OTHER TALES, by GEORGE AUGUSTUS SALA. 1862

pp. (iv) + (220)

18 *RALPH THE BAILIFF AND OTHER TALES, by M. E. BRADDON. 1862

See 322 in Section I.

19 *BUSH LIFE, by MRS AYLMER

20 *CYNTHIA THOROLD, by EMMA ROBINSON

Two further volumes are in the Collection, the first of which I have seen numbered 22 in one list and 19 in another, the second of which, in two later obviously renumbered lists, was recorded as 23 and 26.

Between 1863 and 1865 the series was—if not actually taken over, at any rate handled by John Maxwell, who not only renumbered but mixed reprints with original titles, so that to attempt a reliable record is hopeless. Here therefore, numbered for convenience sake only, are:

(21) THE KING'S PAGE, by PONSON DU TERRAIL. Translated by Wraxall. 1862

pp. (iv)–252

Ink signature: 'J. Browne', on title

(22) THE PERFIDY OF CAPTAIN SLYBOOTS, by GEORGE AUGUSTUS SALA. 1863

pp. (iv) + (220)

Violet wrappers, printed in dark purple and green. series title on front cover, but variant advert. on back. Soiled and spine defective.

[3712] WARD, LOCK AND TYLER'S SIXPENNY VOLUME LIBRARY

Coloured pictorial wrappers, cut flush. Series title on front, back cover printed with list of series.

THE NICHE IN THE WALL: A TALE OF TERROR (anon). n.d. [1866] Pp. 128.

The other titles listed are all of a sensational kind. The series ran to 22 vols., and my dating is taken from an advert. in the Publishers' Circular for July 16, 1866 announcing the purchase of the series by Ward, Lock & Tyler.

[3713] WARDEN, FLORENCE

All large format, cream or pale yellow pictorial boards.

Perfect Fool (A). F. V. White 1895.

Scheherazade. 'New Edition.' Ward & Downey 1889.

St Cuthbert's Tower. Cassell 1891.

Wild Wooing (A). F. V. White 1894.

Woman's Face (A). F. V. White 1890.

Young Wife's Trial (A). F. V. White 1893.

The four F. V. White titles have uniform conventional spines.

[3714] WARREN, SAMUEL

Diary of a Late Physician. Routledge, n.d. (after 1884). Cream pictorial boards.

Ten Thousand a Year. Routledge, n.d. (after 1884). Cream pictorial boards, uniform with preceding.

[3715] WHYTE MELVILLE, GEORGE JOHN

All large format in pictorial boards. The Ward & Lock titles are volumes in the *Library of Select Authors* and have uniform spines with series title at tail and 'The Works of Whyte Melville' at head. The Chapman & Hall titles all have uniform spines except one. Ditto the two Longman etc. titles.

Bones and I. 'New Edition.' Ward, Lock & Bowden, n.d. (after 1891). Yellow boards. Cover drawing by Phiz.

Cerise. 'New Edition.' Ward & Lock, n.d. (inscription dated 1881). Pink boards.

Digby Grand. 'New Edition.' Longman etc. n.d. (1874). Yellow boards.

Kate Coventry. 'New Edition.' Longman etc. n.d. (1871). Yellow boards.

Katerfelto. 'Fifteenth Thousand.' Chapman & Hall 1876. Yellow boards.

M. or N. 'New Edition.' Ward & Lock, n.d. (1881). Pink boards.

Riding Recollections. 'Eighth Edition.' Chapman & Hall 1880. Pale blue boards.

Roy's Wife. 'Seventh Edition.' Ward & Lock, n.d. (1883). Yellow boards.

Sarchedon. 'New Edition.' Chapman & Hall 1872. Yellow boards.

Satanella. 'Eleventh Thousand.' Chapman & Hall 1873. Yellow boards.

Songs and Verses. 'New Edition.' Ward & Lock, n.d. (after 1889). Yellow boards.

True Cross (The). 'New Edition.' Chapman & Hall, n.d. Yellow boards.

Uncle John. 'New Edition.' Chapman & Hall. n.d. Pale pink boards. *Select Library of Fiction*, The spine of this volume differs from others from the same publishers.

[3716] WILLIS, N. P.

Paul Fane. C. H. Clarke, n.d. Yellow pictorial boards, specially drawn spine, front cover design repeated on back. Small format.

[3717] WINTER, ANDREW

ODDS AND ENDS FROM AN OLD DRAWER (by Werdna Retnyw, M.D.)

Routledge 1855. White pictorial wrappers, cut flush, wood-engraved front., pictorial title and 6 illustrations after McConnell, all on plate paper.

Half-title. pp. viii + 120.

[3718] WINTER, JOHN STRANGE (Mrs Stannard)

All first editions or in first edition format. Some (probably all) of the titles were also issued in cloth.

[3719] BOOTLE'S BABY: a Story of the Scarlet Lancers. 'Seventh Edition.'

Warne, n.d. (1886). Buff pictorial wrappers, cut flush, up-lettered on spine. Printed end-papers. Front. and numerous illustrations after W. Ralston on text paper.

Two leaves of adverts. precede front. pp. (128) Pp. (1) (2) and (127) (128) are pasted to front and back covers. H_4–H_8 [(119)–(128)] adverts.

'Warne's London Library, 55th Thousand.' Dated by original invoice still inside book.

Ink signature: 'S. A. Creuze', on title.

[3720] BOOTLE'S CHILDREN
F. V. White & Co. 1888. Buff pictorial wrappers, printed in dark blue and red, cut flush. Inside covers, outside back cover and spine printed with adverts. Illustrations in the text after Bernard Partridge, whose name as illustrator appears on a pennant at top of front cover drawing.
Leaf of adverts. precedes title. pp. (viii) + (120) 7_8–(8_4) adverts.
Ink signature: S. A. Creuze', on title.

[3721] FERRERS COURT: a Novel
F. V. White 1890. Uniform with *Bootle's Children* but no illustrations and pennant blank. Spine down-lettered with title of book.
Leaf of adverts. precedes title. pp. (viii) + (120) 7_8–(8_4) adverts.

[3722] HE WENT FOR A SOLDIER: a Novel
F. V. White 1890. Uniform with *Bootle's Children* but no illustrations and WINTER'S ANNUAL on pennant. Spine down-lettered with title of book.
Leaf of adverts. precedes title. pp. (viii) + (120) 7_7 7_8 and (8_1)–(8_4) adverts.

[3723] HOUP-LA. 'Fourth Edition.'
Warne, n.d. (1886). Uniform with *Bootle's Baby* and same illustrator.
Two leaves of adverts. and half-title preceded front. pp. (128) First and last leaves pasted to covers as in *Bootle's Baby*. 8_3–8_8 [(117)–(128)] adverts.
'Warne's London Library, 45th Thousand.' Dated by original invoice still inside *Bootle's Baby* and covering both books.
Ink signature: 'S. A. Creuze', on title.

LITTLE FOOL (A): a Novel [3724]
F. V. White 1889. Uniform with *Bootle's Children* but no illustrations and pennant blank. Spine down-lettered with title of book.
Leaf of adverts. precedes title. pp. (viii) + (120) 7_8–(8_4) adverts.

MIGNON'S HUSBAND: a Novel [3725]
F. V. White, n.d. [1887]. Uniform with *Bootle's Children* but no illustrations and WINTER'S ANNUAL on pennant. Spine up-lettered with title of book.
Leaf of adverts. precedes title. pp. (viii) + (128) 8_4–(9_4) adverts. paged (1)–8.
Signature on title as in *Bootle's Children.*

MIGNON'S SECRET: the Story of a Barrack Bairn [3726]
F. V. White 1886. Uniform with *Bootle's Children* but no illustrations and WINTER'S ANNUAL on pennant. Spine up-lettered with title of book.
Half-title. pp. xii + (116) G_6–H_4 adverts.
Signature-letter H printed in error on H_2. Signature on title as in *Bootle's Children.*

MY POOR DICK [3727]
F. V. White 1888. Uniform with *Bootle's Children* but with illustrations by Maurice Greiffenhagen and WINTER'S ANNUAL on pennant. Spine printed with advert.
Leaf of adverts. precede title. pp. (viii) + (120) pp. (111)–(120) adverts. No signature numbers or letters.

[3728] WRAXALL, LASCELLES

WILD OATS
J. and C. Brown, Ave Maria Lane, n.d. Yellow cloth, pictorially printed in imitation of a yellow back. Small format.
Half-title. pp. (x) + 370
Note. Recorded as a first edition without certainty. It has all the appearance of one, but the imprint and absence of date are suspicious.

[3729] YATES, EDMUND and BROUGH, ROBERT

OUR MISCELLANY (Edited by E. H. Yates and R. B. Brough)
Routledge 1856. Pictorial yellow boards. End-papers printed with adverts. Small format.
Pp. (192) M_8 adverts.
Note. This is a volume of parodies of Ainsworth, Macaulay, G. P. R. James, E. A. Poe, Tennyson, Samuel Warren, Martin Tupper, J. G. Lockhart, Dickens, Longfellow, Mrs Browning and others.

[3730] ZOLA, ÉMILE

Assommoir (The). 'New Edition.' Vizetelly 1887. Cream pictorial boards, specially drawn spine.

His Masterpiece. 'New Edition.' Vizetelly 1886. Cream pictorial boards, specially drawn spine.

SECTION THREE

'NOVELIST'S LIBRARIES' 'STANDARD NOVELS' 'THE PARLOUR LIBRARY'

and other cloth (or cloth and board) bound fiction (or part-fiction) series

CONTENTS

BALLANTYNE'S NOVELIST'S LIBRARY [edited by Sir Walter Scott] 1821–1824 [3731]

10 vols. Royal 8vo. Hurst, Robinson & Co. Printed by James Ballantyne & Co. at the Border Press. Issued in boards, paper labels. This set is in three-quarter dark green morocco, fully gilt, marbled sides and end-papers. Top edges gilt, others trimmed. Book-plate of Stephen G. Holland.

Vol. I. THE NOVELS OF HENRY FIELDING, ESQ. 1821

Half-title: BALLANTYNE'S / NOVELIST'S LIBRARY (between rules) precedes individual title on which series name is not repeated.

pp. (xvi) + (i)–xxiv [PREFATORY MEMOIR, unsigned but dated 'Abbotsford, October 25, 1820'] + xxv–xxvi [LIST OF WORKS OF FIELDING] + (xxvii) xxviii [APPENDIX] + (1)–794. Final leaf, $3D_5$, a single inset.

Contents: JOSEPH ANDREWS; TOM JONES; AMELIA; JONATHAN WILD.

Vol. II. THE NOVELS OF TOBIAS SMOLLETT, M.D. 1821

Half-title: BALLANTYNE'S / NOVELIST'S LIBRARY / VOL. II (three lines between rules) precedes individual title.

pp. xii + (i)–xlii [PREFATORY MEMOIR, unsigned but dated 'Abbotsford, June 1, 1821'] + (1)–684.

Contents: RODERICK RANDOM; PEREGRINE PICKLE; HUMPHRY CLINKER.

Vol. III. THE NOVELS OF TOBIAS SMOLLETT, M.D. AND THE TRANSLATION OF CERVANTES' DON QUIXOTE 1821

Half-title as II (with, of course, volume number as called for).

pp. x + (1)–(722)

Contents: FERDINAND COUNT FATHOM; SIR LANCELOT GREAVES; Smollett's translation of DON QUIXOTE, preceded by his LIFE OF CERVANTES.

Vol. IV. THE NOVELS OF LE SAGE AND CHARLES JOHNSTONE 1822

Half-title as I (i.e. no volume number).

pp. xviii + (i)–xxvii [PREFATORY MEMOIR TO LE SAGE, unsigned and undated] + xxviii–(xxxviii) [PREFATORY MEMOIR TO CHRYSAL, unsigned but dated 'Abbotsford, September 20, 1822'] + (1)–(842).

Contents: GIL BLAS; THE DEVIL UPON TWO STICKS; VANILLO GONZALES; CHRYSAL OR THE ADVENTURES OF A GUINEA.

Vol. V. THE NOVELS OF STERNE, GOLDSMITH, DR JOHNSON, MACKENZIE, HORACE WALPOLE AND CLARA REEVE 1823

Half-title as II.

pp. viii + (i)–xxii [PREFATORY MEMOIR TO STERNE] + (xxiii)–xxxix [ditto to GOLDSMITH] + (xl)–xlvi [ditto to JOHNSON] + (xlvii)–lix [ditto to MACKENZIE] + (lx)–lxxviii [ditto to WALPOLE] + (lxxix)–(lxxxviii) [ditto to REEVE, all unsigned, but final Memoir dated 'Abbotsford, March 1, 1823'] + (1)–(660).

Contents: TRISTRAM SHANDY; SENTIMENTAL JOURNEY; VICAR OF WAKEFIELD; RASSELAS; THE MAN OF FEELING; THE MAN OF THE WORLD; JULIA DE ROUBIGNE; THE CASTLE OF OTRANTO; THE OLD ENGLISH BARON].

Vol. VI. THE NOVELS OF SAMUEL RICHARDSON, ESQ. In Three Volumes. 1824.

Half-title as II.

pp. (xxiv) [p. xxiii mispaged xxv] + (i)–xlviii [PREFATORY MEMOIR TO RICHARDSON, unsigned but dated 'Abbotsford, January 1st, 1824'] + (1)–728.

Contents: PAMELA; CLARISSA HARLOWE.

[3731] Vol. VII. [RICHARDSON, Vol. II]

Half-title as II. pp. (xx)+(1)–786

Contents: CLARISSA HARLOWE concluded.

Vol. VIII. [RICHARDSON, Vol. III]

Half-title as II. pp. xxii+(i)–iv+(1)–(792)

Contents: SIR CHARLES GRANDISON.

Vol. IX. THE NOVELS OF SWIFT, BAGE AND CUMBERLAND 1824

Half-title: BALLANTYNE'S / NOVELIST'S LIBRARY (between rules) VOL. IX (below lower rule).
pp. (iv)+(vi)+(i)–xv [PREFATORY MEMOIR TO SWIFT]+xvi–xxxiv [ditto to BAGE]+xxxv–lx (mispaged lxx) [ditto to CUMBERLAND, all unsigned, but final Memoir dated 'Abbotsford, December 1824']+(1)–776.

Contents:
GULLIVER'S TRAVELS; MOUNT HENNETH; BARHAM DOWNS; JAMES WALLACE; HENRY.

Vol. X. THE NOVELS OF MRS ANN RADCLIFFE 1824

Half-title as XI.
pp. (vi)+(i)–(xl) [PREFATORY MEMOIR TO MRS ANN RADCLIFFE, unsigned but dated 'Abbotsford, September 1, 1824']+(1)–764.

Contents: A SICILIAN ROMANCE; THE ROMANCE OF THE FOREST; THE MYSTERIES OF UDOLPHO; THE ITALIAN; THE CASTLES OF ATHLIN AND DUNBAYNE.

Note: For later news of Ballantyne's Novelist's Library, see below under Bentley's Standard Novels, p. 94.

[3732] BARBAULD'S BRITISH NOVELISTS 1810 ('The British Novelists; with an Essay; and Prefaces Biographical and Critical by Mrs Barbauld')

50 vols. 12mo ($4\frac{1}{8}'' \times 6\frac{1}{2}''$). Printed for F. C. & J. Rivington etc. 1810. Issued in drab paper boards, labels $1\frac{3}{4}''$ deep. In each volume series title precedes individual title, and is dated '1810' throughout the series. Published at twelve guineas the set.

Vols. I–VIII. CLARISSA.. 'A New Edition, with the Last Corrections by the Author'

I xii [(i) (ii) series title; (iii) (iv) novel title; (v) (vi) 'Sonnet to the Author of Clarissa', verso blank; (vii)–xi Preface (unsigned); xii 'Names of the Principal Persons']+(1)–62 'On the Origin and Progress of Novel Writing' (unsigned)+(i)–xlvi 'Richardson' (biographical and critical study, unsigned)+(1)–357 [CLARISSA]+(358)–(360) blank.

II (iv)+378+(379) (380) blank.
III (iv)+394+(395) (396) blank.
IV (iv)+408
V (iv)+388
VI (iv)+424
VII (iv)+414+(415) (416) blank.
VIII (iv)+427+(428) blank.

Labels worded: BRITISH / NOVELISTS / WITH / PREFACES / BY / MRS BARBAULD / *rule* / I. [VIII] / CLARISSA. Change of title apart, the labels are uniform throughout.

Vols. IX–XV. THE HISTORY OF SIR CHARLES GRANDISON

IX (xii)+336
X (iv)+376
XI (iv)+393+(394) blank.
XII (iv)+320+(321) blank+(322) printers' imprint+(323) (324) blank.

XIII (iv) + 312 [3732]
XIV (iv) + 390 + (391) blank + (392) printers' imprint + (393)–(396) blank.
XV (iv) + 324 + FF–OO_2 (in sixes) Index + OO_3 OO_4 'Similes and Allusions' + OO_5 imprint leaf + OO_6 blank (all these leaves unfoliated).

Vols. XVI–XVII. ROBINSON CRUSOE

XVI (xii) ['Defoe', unsigned, paged (i)–viii occupies (v)–(xii)] + 342
XVII (iv) + 318 + (319) (320) blank.

Vol. XVIII. JOSEPH ANDREWS

(xxxvi) ['Fielding', unsigned, paged (i)–xxxii, occupies (v –(xxxvi)] + (1)–10 [Preface, unsigned] + (11)–395 + (396) blank.

Vols. XIX–XXI. TOM JONES

XIX (iv) + 349 + (350) printers' imprint + (351) (352) blank.
XX (iv) + 428
XXI (iv) + 372

Vol. XXII. THE OLD ENGLISH BARON. THE CASTLE OF OTRANTO

(xii) ['Clara Reeve', unsigned, paged (i)–iii occupies (v)–(vii) and 'Walpole', unsigned, paged (i)–iii occupies (ix)–(xi)] + (304).

Vol. XXIII. POMPEY THE LITTLE. THE VICAR OF WAKEFIELD

(xvi) ['Goldsmith', unsigned, paged (i)–xii occupies (v)–(xvi)] + (1)–378 (mispaged 380)

Vols XXIV–XXV. THE FEMALE QUIXOTE

XXIV (viii) ['Mrs Lennox', unsigned, paged (i)–iv occupies (v)–(viii)] + (234)
XXV (iv) + 270

Vol. XXVI. RASSELAS. ALMORAN AND HAMET

(xiv) ['Johnson' paged (i)–viii and 'Hawkesworth' paged (i) ii, both unsigned, occupy (v)–(xiv)] + (1)–(252)

Vol. XXVII. HISTORY OF LADY JULIA MANDEVILLE. NATURE AND ART

(vi) ['Mrs Brooke', unsigned, paged (i)–ii, occupies (v) (vi)] + (1)–375 + (376)–(380), blank save for printers' imprint on (378).

Vol. XXVIII. A SIMPLE STORY

(viii) ['Mrs Inchbald', unsigned, paged (i)–iv, occupies (v)–(viii)] + (1)–(354) + (355) (356) imprint leaf.

Vol. XXIX. THE MAN OF FEELING. JULIA DE ROUBIGNE

(viii) ['Mackenzie', unsigned, paged (i)–iii, occupies (v)–(vii), (viii) blank] + (1)–274 + (275) (276) blank.

Vols. XXX–XXXI. HUMPHREY (sic) CLINKER

XXX (xxii) ['Smollet' (sic), unsigned, paged (i)–xviii, occupies (v)–(xxii)] + 246 + (247) (248) blank.
XXXI (iv) + 238 + (239) (240) blank.

Vols. XXXII–XXXIII. THE SPIRITUAL QUIXOTE

XXXII (iv) + 314 + (315) (316) blank ['Life of the Author' (Graves), unsigned, occupies pp. (1)–5]
XXXIII (iv) + 330 + (331) (332) blank.

Vols. XXXIV–XXXV. ZELUCO

XXXIV (xii) ['Dr Moore', unsigned, paged (i)–vii, occupies (v)–(xi), (xii) blank] + 244
XXXV (iv) + (258)

[3732] Vols. XXXVI–XXXVII. THE OLD MANOR HOUSE

XXXVI (xii) ['Mrs Charlotte Smith', unsigned, paged (i)–viii, occupies (v)–(xii)]+354+(355)–(360) blank.

XXXVII (iv)+(348)

Vols. XXXVIII–XXXIX. EVELINA

XXXVIII (xvi) ['Miss Burney', unsigned, paged (i)–xi, occupies (v)–(xv), (xvi) blank]+(1)–250+(251) (252) blank.

XXXIX (iv)+280

Vols. XL–XLII. CECILIA

XL (iv)+378 XLI (iv)+(396) XLII (iv)+364

Vols. XLIII–XLIV. THE ROMANCE OF THE FOREST

XLIII (xii) ['Mrs Radcliffe', unsigned, paged (i)–viii, occupies (v)–(xii)]+214

XLIV (iv)+(242)+(243) (244) blank.

Vols. XLV–XLVII. THE MYSTERIES OF UDOLPHO

XLV (iv)+(322)+(323) (324) blank.

XLVI (iv)+(322)+(323) (324) blank.

XLVII (iv)+(334)+(335) (336) blank.

Vol. XLVIII. MAN AS HE IS NOT or HERMSPRONG

(viii) ['Mr Bage', unsigned, paged (i)–iii, occupies (v)–(vii), (viii) blank]+352

Vols XLIX–L. BELINDA. THE MODERN GRISELDA

XLIX (x) [blank leaf precedes series title; 'Miss Edgeworth', unsigned and unpaged, occupies (ix); (x) blank]+352

L (viii) [blank leaf precedes series title, (vii) Contents, (viii) blank]+(1)–(328)

GENERAL NOTES ON BARBAULD'S BRITISH NOVELISTS

(i) The pagination of these volumes is given in detail, because it is so unusual to find them in original boards that I felt the opportunity of registering blank and imprint leaves should not be missed.

(ii) The series was re-issued in 1820, without any indication of earlier publication.

(iii) It seems almost certain that Scott deliberately supplemented Mrs Barbauld's collection when choosing the titles for *Ballantyne's Novelist's Library* (3731). Of the thirty-four novels he reprinted, only twelve had also been printed by Mrs Barbauld; of his remaining twenty-two, many seem to have been chosen in order to amplify her selection from certain authors, while others (notably the novels of Sterne and some by Smollett) could appear without offence under masculine editorship, whereas Mrs Barbauld, a stickler for feminine decorum and an editor with an eye to family reading, might well have hesitated to include them.

(iv) A point of considerable interest should be noted with regard to Vol. XLIII (Radcliffe's *Romance of the Forest*). On the verso of the individual title-page [pp. (iii) (iv)] appears an 'Advertisement' stating that 'some of the little Poems inserted in these pages have appeared by permission of the Author in *The Gazetteer*'. This seems to indicate that Mrs Barbauld, by agreement with Mrs Radcliffe (or her husband), included certain poems in this volume which had previously only appeared in a periodical. As the *Poems of Ann Radcliffe* were not published in book-form until 1816, Vol. XLIII of *Barbauld's British Novelists* has a place in the bibliography of Radcliffe First Editions.

BENTLEY'S EMPIRE LIBRARY 1879–1881 [3733]

Published at half-a-crown each, in small 8vo; bound in scarlet diagonal-fine-ribbed cloth with black end-papers; and blocked and lettered in black on front and back, gold-lettered and black-blocked on spine, this series was a mixture of fiction and non-fiction, of first editions and reprints. The former are set in caps. below, with references to Section I where they are there described. The title asterisked is not in the collection.

1 THE LAND O' THE LEAL (1878), by HELEN MATHERS (1658 in Section I)
2 **A Very Simple Story** and **Wild Mike** (1878), by **Florence Montgomery**
3 **Ralph Wilton's Weird** (1878), by **Mrs Alexander**
4 **A Blue Stocking** (1878), by **Annie Edwardes**
5 AS HE COMES UP THE STAIR (1878), by HELEN MATHERS (1654 in Section I)
6 **Five Years Penal Servitude** (1878) (anon; the Bentley Catalogue says by 'Edward Cxxx')
7 A ROGUE'S LIFE (1879), by WILKIE COLLINS (604 in Section I)
8 *A VICTIM OF THE FALK LAWS (1879) (by 'a German Priest' [Peter Maringer])
9 **A Vagabond Heroine** (1879), by **Annie Edwardes**
10 'MY QUEEN' (1879), by MRS G. W. GODFREY
11 ARCHIBALD MALMAISON (1879), by JULIAN HAWTHORNE (1179 in Section I)
12 **Twilight Stories** (1879), by **Rhoda Broughton** (377 *a* in Section I)
13 THE MUDFOG PAPERS (1880), by CHARLES DICKENS (693 in Section I)
14 **Herbert Manners, The Town Crier etc.** (1880), by **Florence Montgomery**
15 MADE OR MARRED? (1881), by JESSIE FOTHERGILL (894 in Section I)
16 'ONE OF THREE' (1881), by JESSIE FOTHERGILL (896 in Section I)

BENTLEY'S STANDARD NOVEL SERIES* AND ITS BYE-PRODUCTS; followed by THE BENTLEY TRADITION

I. *BENTLEY'S STANDARD NOVELS* (*Three Series*) [3734]

The immediate impulse in England to fictional re-issues in handy form and on a large scale—and, therefore, the impulse to Bentley's Standard Novel Series—was the launching by Robert Cadell on June 1, 1829, of the AUTHOR'S EDITION OF THE WAVERLEY NOVELS. Royal 18mo in size; embellished with steel-engraved frontispieces and titles; 'done up in cloth' (with white paper labels); and announced for regular monthly issue, these little volumes cost five shillings each and represented a wholly new departure in the manner of presenting contemporary fiction. Serial issues at a moderate price of 'classical' British novels were, of course, not unknown.† But for a living novelist to have his comparatively recent works put out in uniform and (by the standards of that day) remarkably cheap shape was an innovation which impressed deeply both the public and the trade.

Cadell's WAVERLEY NOVELS were so popular that the edition was rapidly over-subscribed. In consequence, eighteen months after the first volume of the original 'Author's Edition' had been published, and when only nineteen of the forty volumes of the series had appeared, he began publication of a 'Reissue of the Author's Edition', uniform in size and price, but with coloured instead of white labels to distinguish the new series from the still continuing old one. The two issues ran concurrently until the earlier was complete, and thereafter the 're-issue' ran alone to its appointed end.

Without detracting from the enterprise and inventiveness of Scott and Cadell in thus exploiting a new market for their fictional property, one may reasonably suspect that the format of these handy little volumes, with their glazed canvas bindings and paper labels, was generally suggested by Archibald Constable's

* The courtesy must be thankfully acknowledged of Mr Elmer Adler and the Pynson Printers of New York City in permitting me to reprint in a revised form material first printed in *The Colophon*.

† e.g. HARRISON'S NOVELIST'S MAGAZINE (23 vols. 1781–1789); BARBAULD'S BRITISH NOVELISTS (50 vols. 1810); MUDFORD'S BRITISH NOVELISTS (5 vols. 1810–1816); BALLANTYNE'S NOVELIST'S LIBRARY (edited by Scott, 10 vols. 1821–1824); and WHITTINGHAM'S POCKET NOVELISTS (40 vols. 1823–183?).

[3734] 'Miscellany', which began publishing in January 1827.* In size the 'Miscellany' was smaller than Cadell's 'Waverley', but in appearance and basic conception was very similar.

The influence of *Constable's Miscellany* on publishing enterprise in the matter of *content* was even greater and more immediately evident than its influence on format. The series was not concerned with fiction; it provided miscellaneous works, mainly of travel and history, and consisted largely of *original monographs specially written for the series.* This idea of providing cheap and various instruction and entertainment in series-form first prompted the Society for the Diffusion of Useful Knowledge to launch their *Library of Useful Knowledge* (54 vols. 1827–1848 at various prices, originally issued in sixpenny parts) and then caused John Murray, on April 16, 1829, to publish the first volume of his *Family Library*,† a pocket-sized five-shilling book, very neatly bound in canvas.

Six months later a series was launched which combined the royal 18mo format of Cadell's 'Waverley Novels' with the idea at the back of *Constable's Miscellany* of providing serious literature, specially written for the occasion, at a cheap price and in handy shape. In December 1829 was published the first volume of *Lardner's Cabinet Cyclopaedia* (by Longmans, at six shillings), which volume was, significantly enough, written by Sir Walter Scott himself. This 'Cyclopaedia' established itself quickly and firmly, and volumes were steadily added, the 132nd volume appearing in 1849. (In December 1851 the series was re-issued at 3*s*. 6*d*., having become the sole property of Longmans.) So well known, in fact, did Dr Lardner's series become, that within the first years of its existence it turned the tables on its original inspirer, and in 1832 caused the publishers of *Constable's Miscellany* to announce that 'a large paper edition is printed of some of the volumes in the series to range with Lardner's Cyclopaedia'. This large (or 'fine') paper edition cost five shillings, as against the three and sixpence of the original and ordinary issue.

Meantime the number of popular series in pocket form multiplied rapidly. Late in 1829 was launched Charles Knight's *Library of Entertaining Knowledge*, a second venture of the Society for the Diffusion of Useful Knowledge. The volumes were peculiarly prophetic of what was to come, in that they were bound in glazed linen of a pinkish-buff colour with two dark green labels lettered in gold placed at the extreme head and foot of the spine. This series ended with Vol. 43 in 1836, and was issued in wrappered parts at 2*s*. each, or in complete cloth-bound volumes at 4*s*. 6*d*. It was taken over by Nattali about 1840 and re-issued by them in 1849 at 2*s*. 3*d*. per volume. In January 1830 *Valpy's Family Classical Library* (4*s*. 6*d*. per vol. and running ultimately to over 50 volumes) applied the Constable-Cadell-Lardner principles to another department of learning. During the year there started publishing three other 'libraries' on not dissimilar lines—*Lardner's Cabinet Library* (published by Longmans at 5*s*., and concluded in nine 8vo volumes, 1830–1832); Oliver & Boyd's *Edinburgh Cabinet Library* (completed in 38 volumes at 5*s*.; later re-issued by Nelson at a reduced price), and *The National Library* (announced at 5*s*., but almost immediately raised to 6*s*. per volume avowedly in order to range with 'a contemporary series of a similar nature', i.e. the Standard Novels themselves) published by Colburn & Bentley.

This last is rather especially the concern of the present investigation, for not only was it issued by the firm who were to be responsible for the Standard Novels and other fictional series, but its outward appearance was almost exactly that shortly afterward adopted for the Standard Novels themselves. The first volume, issued late in August 1830, was Galt's *Life of Byron*, and the fourteenth and last—Medwin's *Conversations of Lord Byron*—appeared in 1832.‡ The books were bound in grey-purple, highly glazed canvas, with *two spine labels*, set three-quarter high and three-quarter low, printed in gold on dark green paper. The upper label carried the title of the book; the lower one the legend NATIONAL / LIBRARY. / *rule* / NO. I [*II*], etc. An engraved title-page was provided.

Thus, two months before the appearance of the first 'Standard Novel', there had been evolved the pocket format and highly individual clothing which were soon to be universally regarded as characteristic of the most famous series of cheap novels ever published.

* The first volume—Hall's *Voyages*—was actually dated 1826. The series was taken over by Whittaker, Treacher in 1832, and continued until 1835, by which date over 80 volumes had appeared.

† Completed in 80 volumes, including the so-called 'Dramatic Series'. Later taken over by Tegg and re-issued at 3*s*. 6*d*.

‡ The schedule of volumes of THE NATIONAL LIBRARY is as follows: I. Galt's *Life of Byron*, 1830. II. Gleig's *History of the Bible*, vol. i, 1830. III. Thomson's *History of Chemistry*, vol. i, 1830. IV. G. P. R. James' *History of Chivalry*, 1830. V. Horace Smith's *Festivals, Games, and Amusements*, 1831. VI. Gleig's *History of the Bible*, vol. ii, 1831. VII, VIII, IX. Bourrienne's *Life of Napoleon*, 1831. X. Thomson's *History of Chemistry*, vol. ii, 1831. XI, XII, XIII. St John's *Lives of Celebrated Travellers*, 1831–1832. XIV. Medwin's *Conversations of Lord Byron*, 1832.

Before passing to a detailed examination of the Standard Novels, it is convenient to summarise the features of similar preceding ventures, in order to see how far the Standard Novels conformed to type, how far they broke new ground. [3734]

BARBAULD'S BRITISH NOVELISTS was published at approximately 5*s.* per vol. Regular monthly issue was not observed. No engravings were included. Binding: all-over paper boards, white labels.

CONSTABLE'S MISCELLANY. Engraved titles. Approximately one volume every three weeks. 3*s.* 6*d.* per vol.; later also at 5*s.* on fine paper. Binding: glazed linen, white paper labels.

MURRAY'S FAMILY LIBRARY: no engravings. Monthly, 5*s.* per vol.

CADELL'S 'WAVERLEY': engraved frontispieces and titles. Monthly, 5*s.* per vol. (but full-length novels issued in two or more volumes). Binding: glazed linen, white (and then coloured) paper labels.

LARDNER'S CABINET CYCLOPAEDIA. Monthly, 6*s.* per vol. Binding: linen, white paper labels.

VALPY'S CLASSICAL LIBRARY. Monthly, 4*s.* 6*d.* per vol.

EDINBURGH CABINET LIBRARY. Irregular, 5*s.* per vol. Wood-engraved title and plates. Binding: brown linen, brown paper labels, lettered and ornamented in white.

NATIONAL LIBRARY: engraved titles. Monthly, 5*s.* or 6*s.* per vol. Binding: glazed linen, two green paper labels, lettered in gold.

LIBRARY OF ENTERTAINING KNOWLEDGE. Irregular issue. In parts at 2*s.* and at 4*s.* 6*d.* per vol. Binding: glazed linen, two green paper labels, lettered in gold.

Thus it will be observed that the serial element was stressed in the majority of cases; that steel engravings were usual in works of a literary nature and, because they were present in the 'Waverley' novels, almost compulsory on a new fiction series; and that six shillings was not only in itself a reasonable price for volumes of the type but, if it could be applied to *complete* novels, would mark a very considerable reduction on competing books.

On serial lines, therefore (one volume a month), in avowed imitation of Cadell's 'Waverley' (advance lists were headed: 'A Companion to the Waverley Novels'), with engraved frontispieces and titles, at a price of six shillings per volume and, with very few exceptions, on the principle of one novel one volume, COLBURN AND BENTLEY'S STANDARD NOVELS led off on February 25, 1831 with *The Pilot* by Fenimore Cooper.

'*The Pilot* for six shillings!' exclaimed *The Spectator*. 'This is, indeed, a phenomenon in the history of literature.' The paper's enthusiasm was rather prophetic than topical. Certainly, in view of the future scope and achievement of the Standard Novel Series, the appearance of its first volume was a phenomenon indeed. But the publication in one handy volume of a novel of Fenimore Cooper was in itself no novelty, for there had been issued in 1828, at 5*s.* 6*d.*, as one of *Whittingham's Pocket Novelists*, Cooper's *Spy*—a piece of pioneer (if unauthorised*) publishing which seems to have passed almost entirely unnoticed by critics and public. Whittingham's series contained no other item of contemporary fiction. The remainder of its 33 volumes offered, with one or two interesting variations, the same standard texts as were included in the Barbauld and Ballantyne series. All the more remarkable, therefore, seems the isolated excursion into cheap publishing of recent fiction by a living author.

We must imagine that the public were no less impressed than *The Spectator* with Messrs Colburn & Bentley's new venture, as indeed they were justified in being. Scott's novels in two volumes at five shillings a volume had been remarkable enough; but Scott, although still alive, was in a position far above that of the ordinary popular novelist of the day, and his earlier novels (with which Cadell's series naturally began) had been published ten years or more before their re-issue in cheap and handy form. *The Pilot*, however, was only seven years old; was offered complete for six shillings; and was announced as the forerunner of a varied list of similar cheap editions of the same† and of other authors. No wonder the public rallied to Messrs Colburn & Bentley, or that the success of the new venture was immediately evident.

* Whittingham's edition may have been a mere piracy from the original American edition, but was more probably issued by arrangement with Miller, who published the first (non-copyright) English edition in 1822. In either event the text could not show the 'revisions' carried out by Cooper for the Bentley edition.

† Early advertisements of the series made a special boast of the offer of Cooper's novels at a cheap price, and stressed the fact that the copyrights had been exclusively acquired by Colburn & Bentley. This was true; and sufficient corrections and revisions were made by Cooper in the texts of the novels to ensure that Bentley's Standard editions were the only ones 'approved by the author'. But Cooper was in an unfortunate position *vis-à-vis* English piracy so far as his earlier fictions were concerned, for he could not prevent continual reprinting by all and sundry from the original American editions. Consequently, although he could arrange with Bentley for exclusive copyright editions of all works issued after his arrival

[3734] The critics gave rapturous welcome.

'This publication', said *The Literary Gazette* in the spring of 1831, 'must ensure a prodigious success, for it is wonderfully convenient, and wonderfully cheap. We have seen no periodical design more attractive in every way.' 'We cannot sufficiently applaud a design that promises to give us the best standard works of fiction at the cheapest rate and in the most elegant form', said *The Atlas*. The *New Monthly* described the series as: 'published at a price scarcely exceeding that paid for binding in its original form. The type is beautifully clear and the getting up generally in excellent taste.' And *The Spectator*, characteristically august, declared: 'When classical and highly priced standard works are thus placed within the reach of humble means, assuredly before the lapse of many years there will not be a house which gives the occupier a right to vote that has not also its little library.'

As will be seen by anyone studying the complete schedule of the Standard Novel Series printed below, the publishers did not for some while after its beginning include novels issued *less* than seven years before their own cheap edition. In other words, when they launched the series they did not deliberately foresee it as a cheap-edition series of current popular fiction, but rather as an attempt to register the permanent fame of certain novels written since the great period of eighteenth-century novel-writing, but not hitherto fittingly reprinted in handy and cheap form. Thus, one of their announcements issued in March 1831 declared: 'Messrs Colburn and Bentley intend to produce cheap editions of such Novels and Romances written subsequently to the time of Fielding and Smollett, as have, like the production of these great delineators of nature and manners, taken their rank among English classics.'

Indeed (and this is interesting), they seem to have been in advance of public taste, even with an ambition of this very moderate modernity. At the end of Vol. I of *Pin Money* by Mrs Gore (3 vols. 1831) appeared an advert. dated June 1, 1831, and avowedly issued after the publication of the *fourth* Standard Novel. From this advert. (which I have seen nowhere else) the following paragraph may be quoted:

'As many of the Subscribers to the STANDARD NOVELS have expressed a wish that the undertaking should not be restricted to the publication of Fictions written in any one stated limit of time, and have referred the Proprietors to their own Prospectus, issued more than a twelve-month ago, wherein novels of nearly every age were promised,* Messrs COLBURN and BENTLEY have purchased the copyright of that body of English Fictions originally printed by Mr Ballantyne under the immediate superintendence of SIR WALTER SCOTT and rendered specially interesting and valuable by the copious Biographical and Critical Memoirs which that illustrious writer has prefixed to the works of each Novelist. To render, therefore, the "Standard Novels" complete as a circle of the best Stories (without restriction of any period) extant on the English language, and still more worthy of companionship with the WAVERLEY NOVELS, the Proprietors are fortunately enabled to avail themselves of the above-mentioned publication edited by SIR WALTER SCOTT.'

Yet, after all this, nothing happened. Neither the Ballantyne titles nor Scott's prefaces ever appeared in the Standard Novels nor in any other form over the imprint of Colburn or of Bentley. Why? I do not know. Nor did the compilers of the Bentley Private Catalogue know either. Their only reference to the episode occurs in a 'Note to the Year 1831' written in 1893. 'On the 29th of April, 1831, the Copyright of "Ballantyne's Novelists Library" was bought for £105 from Tegg.' That is all.

The mention of Tegg may be noted. He must have bought the Novelists Library after the Ballantyne bankruptcy of 1826—and bought it cheap. By the forties the Tegg imprint was that of a professional scavenger; but I had not personally realised that he was yapping at the heels of embarrassed publishers so early as the twenties.

Then gradually, as time went on, the idea of using the series for re-issues of contemporary best-sellers took hold of the publishers and proved its value; so that a definite part of the importance of Bentley's

in Europe (he was on the Continent and in England from 1826 to 1833) he could only authorise 'corrected' editions of his earlier work, which had to run in competition with several (often cheaper) uncorrected editions, over which he had no control. Here are a few examples in the Collection. *The Spy*, published by Orlando Hodgson, 111 Fleet Street, 1831, in ribbed cloth gilt-lettered, no vignette; *The Pilot*, published by T. Allman, 42 Holborn Hill, 1835, with a vignette title dated 1831 and imprinted A. C. Baynes, Liverpool, glazed maroon linen, black paper labels lettered in gold; *The Last of the Mohicans*, published by Charles Daly, 14 Leicester Street, 1836, with vignette title after Kenny Meadows, dark green morocco cloth, black paper label lettered in gold; and *Lionel Lincoln*, Allman, 1837, with vignette title after Kenny Meadows, dark green ribbed cloth, lettered in gold.

* I cannot trace this prospectus, nor is it quoted in the Bentley Catalogue.

Standard Novel Series to students of publishing history is that it represented (in subsequent fact, if not [*3734*]
in original intention) the first sustained attempt by a publisher to exploit a cheaper market for his successful novels.

But although Messrs Colburn & Bentley did not at first plan to make this particular piece of publishing history, conscious policy caused them to make another piece, and one equally significant. Their preparations for the series had included the securing, not only of a number of Fenimore Cooper's English copyrights, but also the revision and annotation of other well-known novels whose authors happened to be still alive. This was intelligent publishing, and it so worked out as to justify the Standard Novel Series in the important claim that many of the texts therein included were *the texts finally approved by their authors*,* or at least provided with prefaces in which the author's mature judgment was passed on early work of his or her own. Where no comment from the original novelist could be obtained, introductions or apparatus of one kind or another were added. Thus it was that the great majority of volumes issued during the first ten years of the series' life were something more than plain reprints; and it will perhaps surprise those who examine the detailed list, to find how many of the novel-texts provided have a uniqueness of one kind or another, and are, therefore, of value to literary students and collectors. By the time the publishers' determination to provide special features had faded, the series had become frankly a cheap-edition series of their own best-sellers. But even in this state (as has already been said) the books deserve the respectful notice of all interested in publishing practice, for their very quality as pioneers of the cheap novel.

I hope that enough has now been said to demonstrate that the Standard Novels form a series of great interest and importance to students of nineteenth-century fiction. This being so, it is desirable to establish correct details of the books' 'original condition', and to set out as clearly as possible the 'points' which must be looked for in the search for first editions. This may at first sight seem an absurdity. What 'points' can a cheap novel series have? Is not a 'first edition' of an avowed reprint a contradiction in terms? Let us consider the second question first. The Standard Novels are, as has been said, no mere series of straight reprints. A number of them represent texts individual to the series and often the latest texts approved by their authors; a number more contain some relevant feature not included in any other edition. Surely of such books as these first editions (or at any rate 'first issues') can suitably exist? And if one sets out to find first editions of half a series, one wishes naturally to do the same for the other half also, even although that half does consist of books which, if one may say so, had lost their technical virginity in a previous existence.

As to whether it is possible for a cheap novel series to have 'points' at all, the facts about the Standard Novels speak for themselves. And they speak with a confusion of tongues delightful, if distracting, to the true amateur of bibliography.

The Standard Novels went on for so long and were so successful that they were continually reprinted and, by living on into periods of new binding fashions, continually re-clothed. In consequence, dates were altered, and bindings were altered; but not always simultaneously—so that combinations of right date with wrong binding and vice versa were continually occurring. Further, the reorganisation of the firm which started the series led to a change of imprint during its continuance, and reprints of early volumes carried through under the later imprint naturally reflected the change.

It will be useful, therefore, to set out the implications of date, imprint, and binding which are liable to be found on volumes of the series.

DATES AND IMPRINTS. Each Standard Novel of the first 92 volumes issued contained an engraved frontispiece *and* an engraved title-page with a vignette. From No. 93 onward frontispieces only were issued, the titles being type-set in the ordinary way. To this plan there were two exceptions: No. 121 B, *Uncle Tom's Cabin*, and No. 126, *The Wyandotte*, were issued without a frontispiece, and, therefore, contained no engraved work at all.

In addition to engraved frontispiece and title, the first 92 volumes also contained *two* printed title-pages, one of which preceded the engraved pages and carried the number of the volume in the series, the other of which followed the engraved pages and served as title-page proper to the novel itself. To this rule

* Advertisements of the series claim that it offered 'the only genuine edition extant of the works in question'.

[3734] also there were two exceptions, the first and second volumes of the series having been originally issued with one printed title only, that bearing the novel's number in the Standard Novel Series. Re-issues of these first two volumes were furnished with the second title-page and became uniform with their colleagues. The double printed titles outlasted the engraved title by several volumes, continuing, in fact, up to No. 114. From No. 115 to the end, the series title-page fell out and the volumes carried no evidence of their actual number in the series, save that provided by the advertisements of the series printed on their end-papers.

At the foot of the frontispieces and on the engraved titles appeared an imprint and a date. These were *engraved on the plate*, and indicated the publishing position at the moment of first issue and the year of that issue. The *printed* titles originally tallied in these details with the engraved legends; but as soon (and as often) as the book was reprinted, the printed titles were altered, so that very frequently differences of date and imprint are found between the printed and the engraved pages.

In some cases, when a re-issue was made, the dates originally engraved on the plated frontispieces and titles were erased. In other cases they were actually altered. These changes were not very frequently made, but such erasures and alterations tend, where they occur, to increase the perplexity of posterity.

The chronology of the relevant imprints is simple. The series was started by the firm of Colburn & Bentley, and the first 19 volumes appeared imprinted 'Henry Colburn and Richard Bentley'.* There were also in the great majority of cases subsidiary imprints of the series' agents in Edinburgh, Dublin and Paris, but of these no account need be taken. In August 1832 Colburn and Bentley parted company, the latter buying out the former's interest in certain of their joint publications. Among the items bought by Bentley was the Standard Novel Series, and, in consequence, as from No. XX, Bentley's name alone (although with variations and one exception)† appears as principal imprint, wheresoever such an imprint is needed.

Pl. 9 BINDINGS. There were (apart from one secondary noted below) four distinct bindings used on the Standard Novels during their history, and Plate 9 shows them more clearly than any description could do. The varieties may be referred to as A, B, C and D, and I am of opinion that each style represented the original style used for such volumes in the series as were published during the period of use. It is easy to see how continual must have been the overlapping between one style and another; also that the earlier volumes—those originally published in style A—probably survive in all four styles, those originally in style B in three styles, those originally in style C in two styles, and those originally in style D in that style only.

Overlay this complexity of binding styles on the other complexity of dates and imprints and it becomes obvious—seeing that reprintings and rebindings did not necessarily occur simultaneously—that the chances of discovering and possessing the 'loved one' rightly imprinted, in the right costume and at the right time are as faint in Standard Novel collecting as in traditional romance.

General variations in the four bindings can, as has been said, be best noted from the illustration, but of the actual fabrics a word may be said.

Style A was in highly glazed plum-coloured linen; style B in maroon T-grain (ribbed) cloth; style C in cloth almost identical, but more deeply grained and slightly less pink in tone; style D in dark brown cloth of morocco grain.

The periods during which these binding styles ruled were, so far as I can establish them, as follow:

Binding A was employed from No. 1 (Cooper's *Pilot*, 1831) to 70 (Maxwell's *Captain Blake*, 1838).
Binding B was employed from No. 71 (Edgeworth's *Helen*, 1838) to 80 (Hood's *Tylney Hall*, 1840).
Binding C was employed from No. 81 (Frances Trollope's *Widow Barnaby*, 1840) to 114 (Lady Dacre's *Recollections of a Chaperon*, 1848).
Binding D was employed from No. 115 (Neale's *Experiences of a Gaol Chaplain*, 1849) to 126 (Cooper's *Wyandotte*, 1855).

* Or 'H. Colburn & R. Bentley', or simply 'Colburn & Bentley'.

† Nos. XX–XXIII inclusive show 'R. [or Richard] Bentley (late Colburn & Bentley)'; Nos. XXIV–L inclusive show 'R. [or Richard] Bentley (successor to H. Colburn)'.

One variant occurs during this period. No. XXVI shows '(late Colburn & Bentley)' on one title, and '(Successor to H. Colburn)' on the other.

Nos. LI and LII carry the joint imprints of John Murray and Richard Bentley, the copyright of Hope's *Anastasius* being Murray's and not for sale. From No. LIII onward Bentley appears alone without mention of Colburn.

I wish I could say with absolute certainty that these were indeed the precise moments of change from [3734]
one style to another. It is surprising how extremely rare in original state and in first issue are many of Bentley's Standard Novels, and I have had to rely as much on my own luck and patience in scouring the shops as on the shelves of the great libraries. Wherefore, evidence from other collections will be most welcome of a prolongation of style A beyond No. 70, of style B beyond No. 80, or of style C beyond No. 114. I confess, however, that I shall be disappointed if I am proved to be badly at fault.

It is desirable to record, in connection with style B, an opinion expressed by the late Mr Richard Bentley, to whom in this—as in my other investigations into nineteenth-century publishing history—I owe an abiding debt of gratitude. Mr Bentley was of opinion that style B did not constitute a formal phase in the binding history of the Standard Novel Series, but was an occasional interlude, indicating shortage of the regulation cloth. With all the respect due to the knowledge and experience of Mr Bentley, I cling to my own belief that the style was deliberate and definite; but that it was quickly discarded, probably on account of the poor effect of the blind scroll-work on the spine. It had a short life in any event—according to my computation from October 1838 to July 1840 and involving ten volumes only—and *all the specimens which I have seen* fall within these narrow limits. This is surely significant. Further, although the variation in the quality of the actual cloth might well have been due to the binders failing on occasions to match the standardised quality, the variation in blocking is too marked to be other than intentional.

One minor point may be noted in conclusion. For the very earliest volumes (issued in style A) *dark green paper* labels, similar to those used on volumes of *The National Library*, were employed, and not the more familiar *black* labels. Whether this variety was fortuitous or intentional I cannot say. I have myself only seen Nos. I and II with labels of unmistakable green, and it must be left to the combined experience of all collectors interested, gradually to establish whether the first so many volumes of the series were originally green-labelled and an overall change then made to black, or whether (owing perhaps to temporary shortage of materials) a volume here and there had to be issued in green, the publisher reverting to black as soon as the necessary paper was available.

PRICE CHANGES AND MINOR BINDING VARIANTS. Up to and including No. 114 (*Recollections of a Chaperon*, published at the very end of 1848 though dated 1849) the Standard Novels were issued at the original price of 6*s*. With No. 115—at the beginning of 1849—was introduced the brown cloth binding (D), and an entirely new scale of reduced prices was imposed from the beginning of the series. Nos. 1–28, 30, 32, 33, 36, 38, 40–43, 49, 50, 55, 60, 74, 76, 77, 89–91, 94, 95 and 99 were re-issued (naturally in the new brown cloth style) at 2*s*. 6*d*. per volume; Nos. 29, 31, 35, 37, 39, 44–46, 48, 51–54, 56–59, 61–71, 73, 75, 78–88, 92, 96–98 and 100–114 (likewise in brown cloth) were re-issued at 3*s*. 6*d*. per volume; Nos. 34, 47 and 72 (all three novels by Bulwer) were re-issued at 5*s*. per volume.

These reduced prices were considerably advertised as marking a 'new edition' of the Standard Novel Series, and were blocked in gold low down on the scroll-patterned spines of the brown cloth volumes.

It was clearly the publishers' intention to carry on the series with new volumes published in the first instance at 3*s*. 6*d*.; and Nos. 115, 116, 117 and 118 duly appeared during 1849 at this price. However, No. 119 (*The Hamiltons*) was published early in 1850 at 5*s*., probably because Mrs Gore, like Bulwer, had big ideas of the value of her copyright and was sufficiently popular to enforce them. For Nos. 120–122 (which appeared at long intervals from 1850 to 1853) the 3*s*. 6*d*. price was re-established.

The slowing-up in the production of new volumes was a sign that the series had outlived its own prosperity, that the fashion in cheap fiction had changed. Nevertheless Bentley determined on one more effort to prolong its life. He realised that his first price reduction, which had more or less served in 1849 to freshen a wilting market, was no longer effective. He had been overtaken by the rapid increase in even cheaper novels, notably those in the Parlour, and in Routledge's Railway Libraries. So sometime in 1853 he reduced many of his prices a stage further, pulling down *The Hamiltons* to 3*s*. 6*d*., transferring a number of hitherto 3*s*. 6*d*. titles to the 2*s*. 6*d*. list, and fixing on 2*s*. 6*d*. as the original price of any further volumes he might publish. There were only destined to be four such further volumes (Nos. 123–126), and each of these appeared at half-a-crown.

It should be observed that the final price reductions in the series as a whole were not uniformly reflected on the spines of the bindings. In a few cases the new prices were stamped on the spines; in the majority

[*3734*] the price was simply omitted and the lowest space in the scroll-work left blank. Also several changes in the yellow end-papers were made, some listing the titles in the series according to the prices ruling at different times: others giving the titles in numerical order: others being blank. There are, accordingly, numerous variations of issue in Standard Novels in the brown cloth (D) style. Those occurring in titles originally bound in an earlier style are of course of no importance. But among the titles *originally published in binding D* (i.e. Nos. 115–126 inclusive) the varieties cannot be ignored, although their chronology is very difficult to determine. I think, however, that the first issues of Nos. 115–122 inclusive had 3*s*. 6*d*. (in the case of *The Hamiltons* 5*s*.) on the spine, and end-papers printed with the list of the series in numerical order up to (approximately) the number preceding the actual title in question. As for Nos. 123–126 inclusive, generalisation in their regard is impossible. I have never seen more than one copy of two of the titles, two of a third and four of a fourth. Only two of these eight books had any price on the spine at all, and only one had end-papers other than plain. The two priced volumes were among the four copies discovered of *Lucy Hardinge* (No. 125) and each was priced 2*s*. 6*d*. One of these had ends printed up to No. 124. I am unable to argue the problem of priorities, but would recommend those who find clean copies of any of these four titles in any form to secure them first and argue afterwards. I am equally unable to establish the date or reason of a variation in the fount of capitals used on the spines of certain issues in binding D for the words BENTLEY'S / STANDARD / NOVELS. The majority show a sort of condensed bodoni, with emphatic thicks and thins; but on a few examples the words are set in a slighter, meaner, fount, not uniform with the titling. I suspect (but cannot prove) these examples to be of late date.

In conclusion must be recorded a binding I have only seen in one example and which may or may not have been employed on other volumes. I have a copy of No. 38 (Cooper's *Bravo*) with printed title dated 1836, bound in red morocco cloth, blocked in blind and gold-lettered on spine: THE / BRAVO / *rule* / COOPER / STANDARD / NOVELS. / BENTLEY. The spine lettering is from type, but the style is well-finished and is certainly a publisher's issue.

COMPARATIVE RARITIES. Reference has already been made to the striking rarity of most of the Standard Novels in their original shape and in good condition. This rarity is in many—perhaps a majority of—cases due to the difficulty of finding actual first issues with date, imprint and binding all correct. Copies of the actual books may be plentiful, but they are nearly always 'wrong'. There is, however, a rarity of a different kind—an 'inherent rarity', one might say—about certain of the titles, which merits record, if only in order to give joy to those seekers after minor undiscoverables who may have stumbled on one or more of them.

Among the first hundred Standard Novels the following, in my now considerable experience, are 'snags': the five Jane Austens (Nos. 23, 25, 27, 28 and 30), because not only were some of the original sheets used for the uniform green cloth set described under 'Bye-Products', but also of recent years these titles in their regular Standard Novel form have been assiduously collected to form agreeable sets of Austen novels; *Frankenstein* (No. 9); and the Peacock volume (No. 57)—for the obvious reason that both offer important commentaries and texts by 'collected' authors.

From No. 101 to the end the collector's problem becomes gradually so acute as to be finally almost insoluble. There are snags sufficient between Nos. 101 and 118 to keep an active book-hunter busy, but with No. 120 the problem becomes really serious. (Note in passing that the comparative frequency of Mrs Gore's *Hamiltons*—No. 119—is an obvious result of the authoress' arrangement to treat her Standard Novel edition as also a cheap 'new edition' of a very popular novel. (See Bye-Products, p. 107.) It is evident that by about 1850 the demand for the series had greatly fallen away. Even at their reduced price the Standard Novels were no longer the bargains they used to be; competition was very keen and public favour fickle. So it is a fair assumption that the size of the editions was heavily reduced, and maybe even of the short numbers printed only a portion were bound. In consequence the last eight Standard Novels are genuine rarities. *Uncle Tom's Cabin* has for a long while been known as such; and the trade, accustomed between the wars to sell an average Standard Novel at anything between sixpence and five shillings, have paid as much as five pounds for *Uncle Tom.* Should, however, a demand for Standard Novels *quâ* Standard Novels gradually develop, not only *Uncle Tom's Cabin* but its two predecessors, its immediate successor and even more emphatically Nos. 123–126 will rapidly take their place among the undiscoverables. The bookseller of my acquaintance most knowledgeable in this and similar series once told me that during nearly forty years' experience he had *never seen a copy* of Nos. 124 and 126 and could count the copies seen of Nos. 123 and 125 on the fingers of one hand. So the job of completing a set of Standard Novels is a job indeed. *[3734]*

At the time of compiling this catalogue, my collection of the Original Series is complete but for five titles (60, 65, 69, 80, 120), and ten others could be improved as to condition. Of the Second Series I have no single volume—which rouses a suspicion (expounded below) that no such series existed. Of the Third Series the collection includes five of the ten titles. It seems more sensible to record the gaps here than to confuse the actual lists by continual asterisks.

EPILOGUE

Thus ended the long and distinguished history of the first series of Bentley's Standard Novels, whose importance in English publishing history is hard to exaggerate. During its career it produced several other series of 'Standard Novels', which are recorded in this volume in their proper places and of which one, at least, largely consisted of Bentley titles printed from Bentley plates. It established a format for the cheap cloth-bound novel during nearly a generation, not only avowedly similar mixed series borrowing the size and style of get-up, but such outstanding ventures as Smith, Elder's Library of Romance and Saunders & Otley's admirable edition of the novels of Bulwer Lytton being unmistakably designed on Bentley's Standard Novel lines. Even Bentley himself attempted in the late thirties (though without much success) to extend the principle, style and popularity of his Standard Novels to reprints of books in General Literature. BENTLEY'S STANDARD LIBRARY (6*s.* per volume, illustrated, and virtually uniform with the Standard Novels in binding C) started with Maxwell's *Wild Sports of the West* in 1838. This was followed by

2 *Astoria*, by Washington Irving 1839
3 *Chelsea Hospital*, by Gleig 1839
4 *Life of a Sailor*, by Chamier 1839
5 *Domestic Manners of the Americans*, by Frances Trollope 1839
6 *Italy, Spain & Portugal*, by Beckford Dec. 1839 (dated 1840)

Here the series ended. Some of the books were later re-issued at 3*s.* 6*d.*, first of all forming volumes in BENTLEY'S POPULAR LITERATURE (about 1850) and then reappearing a year or two later in BENTLEY'S PARLOUR BOOKCASE, a miscellaneous non-fiction series, described as 'a Repository of New and Entertaining Literature and a Companion to Bentley's Standard Novels'.

SECOND AND THIRD SERIES OF BENTLEY'S STANDARD NOVELS

The subsequent history of the series-title 'Bentley's Standard Novels', after the completion of the first great schedule, is interesting but can be briefly recorded.

(i) **Second Series.** Already, before the actual termination of the Original Series early in 1855 with *The Wyandotte*, a 'Second Series' had (in theory at any rate) been started.* It is recorded as having run from the autumn of 1854 to the winter of 1856 and comprised twenty-two titles. The books were priced at 3*s.* 6*d.* each, with the exception of the three novels by Bulwer which, as before, were priced at 5*s.* All the titles, save one (No. 22), had previously appeared in the First Series. For a list of them, see below, p. 103. The only specimen seen was bound in blue grained cloth, gold-blocked on the spine, and blind-blocked on front and back, the words 'Bentley's Standard Novels' appearing in gold on the spine and in blind on front and back. No series title or series number was printed inside the book. Whatsoever engraved material had been included in the original issues of the novels now re-issued was (we are told) reproduced, and that the volume added for the first time was supplied with an engraved frontispiece.

(ii) **Third Series.** A 'Third Series' of Bentley's Standard Novels was started in 1860, but the name 'Standard Novels' was quickly dropped, being substituted by the words, 'Bentley's Popular Novels'.

* See comment attached to complete list below.

This Third Series numbered ten volumes, all novelties to 'Standard' issue, and was complete in a little over two years. The books were offered at 2*s.* 6*d.* and 3*s.* 6*d.* in buff linen printed in black (described as 'white' or 'printed' cloth), at 3*s.* and 4*s.* in claret cloth, gilt, and contained no engravings. Their main interest from the publishing point of view is the rapidity with which (for the most part) they followed an original publication. To-day's method of prompt cheapening of popular fiction was already established.

BENTLEY'S STANDARD NOVELS: COMPLETE LISTS

[3734*a*] I. FIRST SERIES 1831–1855

TYPOGRAPHICAL EXPLANATION. In the following complete list of the volumes in the first and principal series of Bentley's Standard Novels the titles are set in capitals of those novels, either revised, annotated, or in other ways specially prepared by their authors for issue in the series, or therein published for the first time. This has been done so as to indicate clearly which volumes are definitely of textual importance to students. Novels provided with biographical or critical introductions by persons other than their actual authors are not specially identified.

The date of the *first* English edition of each novel is given in brackets after the date of Standard Novel issue.

ECCENTRICITIES OF NUMBERING. Attention is drawn to the substitution of *Hector O'Halloran* for *Agnes de Mansfeldt* as No. 109, and the consequent substitution of *Uncle Tom's Cabin* for *Hector O'Halloran* as No. 121, when the latter novel was promoted. What probably occurred was that Bentley's eagerness to share in the hysterical demand for *Uncle Tom's Cabin*, which produced no fewer than thirty editions in England during six months and sold over a million copies before the end of 1852, coincided with the exhaustion of the first edition of his re-issue of *Agnes de Mansfeldt.* So instead of reprinting Grattan's novel he let it go out of print, transferred its series number to the recently issued *Hector O'Halloran,* and without even waiting for a frontispiece, rushed out an edition of *Uncle Tom's Cabin* as the latest volume in his series.

No.	Title	Author	Date	Notes
1	PILOT	Cooper	Feb. 1831 (1824)	
2	CALEB WILLIAMS	Godwin	March 1831 (1794)	
3	SPY	Cooper	May 1831 (1822)	
4	THADDEUS OF WARSAW	Porter	May 1831 (1803)	
5	ST LEON	Godwin	June 1831 (1799)	
6	MOHICANS	Cooper	July 1831 (1826)	
7 } 8 }	SCOTTISH CHIEFS	Porter	Aug. } Sept. } 1831 (1810)	Misprinted '1331' Half-title precedes series title
9 {	FRANKENSTEIN	Mary Shelley	Oct. 1831 (1818)	
	The Ghost Seer (part)	Schiller	(1826—in vol. III of Roscoe's *The German Novelists*)	
10 {	Edgar Huntly	Brown	Nov. 1831 (1803)	
	Ghost Seer (conclusion)			
11	HUNGARIAN BROTHERS	A. M. Porter	Dec. 1831 (1807)	Actually published (and dated) 1832
12 } 13 }	CANTERBURY TALES	Lee	Jan. } Feb. } 1832 (1797–1805)	Half-title precedes series title
14	PIONEERS	Cooper	March 1832 (1823)	Half-title precedes series title
15	Self-Control	Brunton	April 1832 (1811)	
16	Discipline	,,	May 1832 (1841)	
17	PRAIRIE	Cooper	June 1832 (1827)	
18 } 19 }	PASTOR'S FIRE-SIDE	Porter	July 1832 (1817)	
20	LIONEL LINCOLN	Cooper	Sept. 1832 (1825)	
21	LAWRIE TODD	Galt	Oct. 1832 (1830)	
22	FLEETWOOD	Godwin	Nov. 1832 (1805)	
23	Sense and Sensibility	Austen	Dec. 1832 (1811)	Dated 1833
24	CORINNE	de Stael	Jan. 1833	(specially translated for this edition by Isabel Hill, with metrical versions of the Odes by L. E. L.)

[3734a]

No.	Title	Author	Date	Notes
25	Emma	Austen	Feb. 1833 (1816)	
26	A Simple Story Nature and Art	Inchbald ,,	March 1833 (1791) (1797)	
27	Mansfield Park	Austen	April 1833 (1814)	
28	Northanger Abbey Persuasion	,,	May 1833 (1818)	
29	SMUGGLER	Banim	June 1833 (1831)	
30	Pride and Prejudice	Austen	July 1833 (1813)	
31	Stories of Waterloo	Maxwell	Aug. 1833 (1829)	
32	NOTRE DAME	Hugo	Sept. 1833	(specially translated for this edition by F. Shoberl)
33	BORDERERS	Cooper	Oct. 1833 (1829)	
34	EUGENE ARAM	Bulwer	Nov. 1833 (1832)	
35	MAXWELL	Hook	Dec. 1833 (1830)	Dated 1834
36	WATER-WITCH	Cooper	Jan. 1834 (1830)	
37	Mothers and Daughters	Gore	Feb. 1834 (1831)	
38	BRAVO	Cooper	March 1834 (1831)	
39	Heiress of Bruges	Grattan	April 1834 (1830)	
40	RED ROVER	Cooper	May 1834 (1828)	
41	Vathek Otranto Bravo of Venice	Beckford Walpole Lewis	(1786) June 1834 (1765) (1805)	
42	COUNTRY CURATE	Gleig	Aug. 1834 (1830)	
43	BETROTHED	Manzoni	Oct. 1834	(specially translated for this edition by an unrecorded hand)
44	HAJJI BABA	Morier	Jan. 1835 (1824)	
45	HAJJI BABA IN ENGLAND	,,	June 1835 (1828)	
46	PARSON'S DAUGHTER	Hook	June 1835 (1833)	
47	Paul Clifford	Bulwer	July 1835 (1830)	
48	Younger Son	Trelawny	Sept. 1835 (1831)	
49	Alhambra ABENCERAGES INVOLUNTARY PROPHET	Irving Chateaubriand H. Smith	(1832) Nov. 1835	 (specially translated for this edition by Isabel Hill) (1st book edition of this story)
50	Headsman	Cooper	Jan. 1836 (1833)	
51 52	Anastasius	Hope	March April 1836 (1819)	In 51 Advert. leaf precedes front Folding map instead of engraving as front.
53	DARNLEY	James	Oct. 1836 (1830)	
54	Zohrab	Morier	Aug. 1836 (1832)	No date on engraved title
55	Heidenmauer	Cooper	Oct. 1836 (1832)	No date on engraved title
56	DE L'ORME	James	Dec. 1836 (1830)	Dated 1837
57	NIGHTMARE ABBEY MAID MARIAN CROTCHET CASTLE	Peacock ,, ,,	(1818) March 1837 (1822) (1831)	No date on engraved title
58	Trevelyan	Lady Scott	June 1837 (1833)	No date on engraved title
59	PHILIP AUGUSTUS	James	Aug. 1837 (1831)	
60	ROOKWOOD	Ainsworth	Oct. 1837 (1834)	
61	HENRY MASTERTON	James	Nov. 1837 (1832)	
62	Peter Simple	Marryat	Jan. 1838 (1834)	
63	Jacob Faithful	,,	Feb. 1838 (1834)	
64	Japhet	,,	Feb. 1838 (1836)	
65	King's Own	,,	March 1838 (1830)	
66	Midshipman Easy	,,	April 1838 (1836)	
67	Newton Forster	,,	May 1838 (1832)	
68	Pacha	,,	June 1838 (1835)	
69	Rattlin the Reefer	Howard/Marryat	July 1838 (1836)	
70	Captain Blake (originally entitled 'My Life')	Maxwell	Aug. 1838 (1835)	
71	Helen	Edgeworth	Oct. 1838 (1834)	

	No.	Title	Author	Date	Notes
[*3734a*]	72	Pompeii	Bulwer	Dec. 1839 (1834)	
	73	Bivouac	Maxwell	March 1839 (1837)	
	74	PRECAUTION	Cooper	July 1839 (1821)	
	75	JACK BRAG	Hook	Aug. 1839 (1837)	
	76	RORY O'MORE	Lover	Oct. 1839 (1837)	
	77	BEN BRACE	Chamier	Dec. 1839 (1836)	Dated 1840
	78	VICAR OF WREXHILL	F. Trollope	Feb. 1840 (1837)	
	79	BUCCANEER	A. M. Hall	April 1840 (1832)	
	80	TYLNEY HALL	Hood	July 1840 (1834)	
	81	Widow Barnaby	F. Trollope	Oct. 1840 (1839)	
	82	SOLDIER OF LYONS (originally entitled 'The Tuileries')	Gore	Dec. 1840 (1831)	Dated 1841
	83	MARRIAGE	Ferrier	March 1841 (1818)	
	84	INHERITANCE	,,	May 1841 (1824)	
	85	DESTINY	,,	July 1841 (1831)	No date on Frontispiece
	86	Gilbert Gurney	Hook	Sept. 1841 (1836)	
	87	Widow and the Marquess (originally entitled 'Love and Pride')	,,	Dec. 1841 (1833)	Actually published (and dated) 1842
	88	All in the Wrong (originally entitled 'Births, Deaths and Marriages')	Hook	May 1842 (1839)	
	89	Homeward Bound	Cooper	Aug. 1842 (1838)	
	90	Pathfinder	,,	Dec. 1842 (1840)	Dated 1843
	91	Deerslayer	,,	Feb. 1843 (1841)	
	92	JACQUELINE OF HOLLAND	Grattan	Feb. 1843 (1831)	
	93	Man at Arms	James	Jan. 1844 (1840)	
	94	Two Old Men's Tales	Mrs Marsh	May 1844 (1834)	
	95	Two Admirals	Cooper	Sept. 1844 (1842)	
	96	RICHARD SAVAGE	Whitehead	Feb. 1845 (1842)	
	97	Cecil	Gore	April 1845 (1841)	
	98	Prairie Bird	Murray	July 1845 (1844)	
	99	Jack o' Lantern	Cooper	Nov. 1845 (1842)	
	100	AYESHA	Morier	March 1846 (1834)	
	101	MARCHIONESS OF BRINVILLIERS	Albert Smith	April 1846 (1st book edition. Reprinted from Bentley's Miscellany)	
	102	Belford Regis	Mitford	July 1846 (1835)	
	103	My Cousin Nicholas	Barham	Oct. 1846 (1841)	
	104	Poacher (originally entitled 'Joseph Rushbrook')	Marryat	Nov. 1846 (1841)	
	105	Outlaw	A. M. Hall	Jan. 1847 (1835)	
	106	Phantom Ship	Marryat	March 1847 (1839)	
	107	Dog Fiend (originally entitled 'Snarleyyow')	,,	May 1847 (1837)	
	108	Mr Ledbury	Albert Smith	July 1847 (1844)	
	109	(*a*) AGNES DE MANSFELDT	Grattan	Sept. 1847 (1836)	
		(*b*) Hector O'Halloran	Maxwell	(See 121 (*a*))	
	110	Improvisatore	Hans Andersen	Nov. 1847 (1845)	
	111	Romance and Reality	Landon	Feb. 1848 (1831)	
	112	CATHERINE DE MEDICIS (originally entitled 'The Queen's Poisoner')	Costello	June 1848 (1841)	
	113	Percival Keene	Marryat	Sept. 1848 (1842)	
	114	Recollections of a Chaperon	Lady Dacre*	Dec. 1848 (1833)	Dated 1849
	115	GAOL CHAPLAIN	Neale	March 1849 (1847)	
	116	Legends of the Rhine	Grattan	May 1849 (1832)	
	117	Peerage and Peasantry	Lady Dacre*	Sept. 1849 (1835)	
	118	SIR RALPH ESHER	Leigh Hunt	Dec. 1849 (1832)	Dated 1850
	119	Hamiltons	Gore	March 1850 (1834)	
	120	Life of a Sailor	Chamier	Sept. 1850 (1832)	

* Actually by Mrs Sullivan, ed. by her mother, Lady Dacre.

121	(*a*) Hector O'Halloran . .	Maxwell	May 1851 (1843)	Later renumbered 109	[*3734a*]
	(*b*) Uncle Tom's Cabin . .	Stowe	Sept. 1852 (1852)		
122	Scattergood Family . .	Albert Smith	July 1853 (1845)		
123	LEYCESTERS (originally entitled 'The Sisters')	Mrs Moore	March 1854 (1821)		
124	Afloat and Ashore . .	Cooper	July 1854 (1844)		
125	Lucy Hardinge . .	„	Aug. 1854 (1844)		
126	Wyandotte . . .	„	Dec. 1854 (1843)	Dated 1855	

II. SECOND SERIES [3734*b*]

1	Prairie Bird . . .	C. A. Murray	(1844)	
2	Ellen Wareham . .	Lady Dacre	(1833)	This story originally constituted the 3rd vol. of *Recollections of a Chaperon* (see footnote, p. 102)
3	Emma . . .	Austen	(1816)	
4	Marriage . . .	Ferrier	(1818)	
5	Sense and Sensibility . .	Austen	(1811)	
6	Rookwood . . .	Ainsworth	(1834)	
7	Self-Control . . .	Brunton	(1811)	
8	Northanger Abbey and Persuasion	Austen	(1818)	
9	Countess of Nithisdale . .	Lady Dacre	(1835)	This story originally constituted the 1st vol. of *Tales of the Peerage and the Peasantry* (see footnote, p. 102)
10	Inheritance . . .	Ferrier	(1824)	
11	Eugene Aram . . .	Bulwer	(1832)	
12	Paul Clifford . . .	„	(1830)	
13	Pompeii . . .	„	(1834)	
14	Mansfield Park . .	Austen	(1814)	
15	Destiny . . .	Ferrier	(1831)	
16	Discipline . . .	Brunton	(1814)	
17	Pride and Prejudice . .	Austen	(1813)	
18	Leycesters . . .	Mrs Moore	(1821)	
19	Thaddeus of Warsaw . .	Porter	(1803)	
20, 21	Scottish Chiefs . . .	„	(1810)	
22	Woman's Life . . .	Carlen	1856 (1852)	

Note. I am inclined to suspect that this series is really a ghost. A Prospectus of the Standard and Favourite Novels issued in January 1882 lists the 22 volumes with all formality, but the only one recorded as appearing in the Bentley Catalogue proper is No. 22. When to this inconsistency is added the fact that I have only in my life seen one volume (No. 1) bound as described (and that in Mr Richard Bentley's own house) there seems good ground for concluding that 'Second Series' was only, either a publisher's label (for internal office convenience, perhaps) applied to the balance of sheets of certain Standard Novel titles, or maybe an unfulfilled ideal. The publication of one new title (if indeed it actually appeared) is admittedly curious; but, as the records were manifestly obscure, confusion could easily have arisen. I find it hard to believe, if these volumes had really all been issued in the blue-cloth style, I should not have come across at least a few of them somewhere; and it even seems possible that the copy of No. 1 seen at Slough was itself a trial copy and the only one ever completed.

III. THIRD SERIES (later called BENTLEY'S POPULAR NOVELS) [3734*c*]

1	Rita: an Autobiography .	[Hamilton Aïdé]	May 1859 (1858)
2	Three Clerks . . .	Trollope	March 1860 (1858)
3	Semi-Detached House .	[Emily Eden]	March 1860 (1859)
4	Ladies of Bever Hollow .	[Ann Manning]	May 1860 (1858)
5	Village Belles . . .	[„ „]	May 1860 (1838)

[3734c]	6	Easton . . .	Eleanor Eden	July 1860 (1858)
	7	Quits . . .	Tautphoeus	Sept. 1860 (1857)
	8	Season Ticket . .	[Haliburton]	March 1861 (1860)
	9	Semi-Attached Couple . .	[Emily Eden]	July 1861 (1860)
	10	Nelly Armstrong . .	[Sarah Whitehead]	Aug. 1862 (1853)

Nos. 1, 3, 4, 5, 6, 8, 9, 10 published at 2*s.* 6*d.* in smooth white cloth, printed in black with buff end-papers, and at 3*s.* in claret cloth, gilt. Nos. 2 and 7 published at 3*s.* 6*d.* in white cloth printed, at 4*s.* in claret cloth, gilt. Series title on front and spine of every white cloth issue.

Notes. (i) The above is the original numbering and order of issue. The sequence was afterwards changed. The volumes are not individually numbered, but a numbered list appears on each back cover. Nos. 1, 2, 5, 6, 9 are in the collection. Nos. 8 and 9 were again published in 1865 and 1866 at 2*s.* each, together with two of the novels of J. B. Harwood, as BENTLEY'S GLOBE NOVELS, but the series did not extend beyond four titles.

(ii) In the Bentley Private Catalogue the issue is recorded in the autumn of 1859 of *Truth Answers Best* (by Beatrice Stebbing) as a volume in white cloth in this series. But it does not appear in the complete list of the series given elsewhere.

[3735] II. *BYE-PRODUCTS OF BENTLEY'S STANDARD NOVELS*

A. The First Collected Edition of Jane Austen.
B. The First Collected Edition of Bulwer Lytton.
C. *The Hamiltons*, by Mrs Gore.

(See also: Routledge's Standard Novels 3759, below.)

[3735*a*] A. THE FIRST COLLECTED EDITION OF JANE AUSTEN

5 vols. Bentley 1833. [See Geoffrey Keynes, *Jane Austen: a Bibliography*, London 1929, pp. 157 seq.]. Dark green morocco cloth, labels.

These five volumes originally appeared as volumes in Bentley's Standard Novel Series. In each case the engraved frontispiece and title bore the date of issue; and their order of date and appearance in this series were as follows:

23	Sense and Sensibility	Dec. 28, 1832	Dated 1833
25	Emma	Feb. 27, 1833	,, ,,
27	Mansfield Park	April 29, 1833	,, ,,
28	Northanger Abbey and Persuasion . .	May 29, 1833	,, ,,
30	Pride and Prejudice	July 31, 1833	,, ,,

When the Collected Edition was issued (on October 28, 1833) the order of the volumes was changed, *Pride and Prejudice* becoming Vol. II, *Emma* Vol. III, *Mansfield Park* Vol. IV and *Northanger Abbey* Vol. V. Special printed title-pages were supplied for the Collected issue, but the engraved fronts. and titles were as in the Standard Novel editions. So far five sets have been located of the Collected Edition. In one of these, the engraved front. and title of *Sense and Sensibility* carry the date 1833. In the other four, the dates have been erased. In all four sets, Vols. II–V carry the original dates.

It must be noted that in subsequent issues of the regulation Standard Novel editions of Jane Austen's books (the volumes were reprinted again and again, with the same engraved fronts. and titles but with changing dates on the printed titles), the engraved dates are *missing* from *Sense and Sensibility* but present in the other four volumes. It seems logical, therefore, to regard a Collected set with *Sense and Sensibility dated* as an earlier state than one with the date missing. Why, however, should there be any variation, and is it possible to argue the other way on? I can think of two conceivable explanations of the existence of dated and undated engravings in *Sense and Sensibility*, each of ambiguous significance.

A. It may have been that the first Standard Novel Edition of *Sense and Sensibility* was a shorter number than the market was later shown to require. Consequently the original printing numbers of the other four volumes in the Standard Novel Edition were considerably increased. When the idea was adopted of issuing the five-volume, ex-series, Collected Edition, so few copies remained of the *dated* *Sense and Sensibility* sheets that the novel had to be reprinted, and for the reprint it was decided to erase the dates from front and title, in order that the Collected Edition might have a chance of a longer run before looking old-fashioned. What then became of the balance of *dated* engravings, and at what stage of the Collected Edition were they used up? It may be argued that they were used first, and that the idea of an undated reprint was not thought of until they were nearly exhausted. That is very possible; but there is another possibility, as will transpire toward the end of Explanation B. [3735a]

B. It is conceivable that the muddle was involved with the appearance of *Sense* at the end of 1832. Suppose that the first printing of *Sense* was actually dated 1832, and then, for some reason or other, the book could not be published until very late in the year. Might it not have been decided to advance the date (as was frequently done at the time) and so keep all five volumes in the Standard Novels uniformly dated? If this were so, Bentley would have had on hand engraved plates dated 1832, on which imprint and date lines would have to be first erased and then re-engraved. It is conceivable that, by chance or on purpose, one or more pairs of plates were not re-engraved, so that, after the first Standard Novel issue had been made with newly dated fronts. and titles, the publisher either held some sets of undated engravings from these undated plates or could, if he wished, produce such sets from the undated plates in his possession. It seems an open and insoluble question whether, in the event of either of these things occurring, he would have issued his Collected Edition with a fortuitous mixture of dated and undated engravings in *Sense and Sensibility*; or whether, reasoning as suggested in A, he would have led off with the *undated* material to give his edition an appearance of timelessness, and worked in the balance of *dated* engravings late enough to make it unlikely the trade would notice the difference.

Why, if he was anxious not to emphasise the date on the first volume of his Collected Edition, he did not also issue Vols. II–V with dates erased, is inexplicable—as also is why, throughout the subsequent selling-life of Bentley's Standard Novels, *Sense* remained undated, but all the others carried the dates of their first appearance.

It may be of interest to note that Bentley advance-advertised his Collected Edition in the *Athenaeum* for October 26, 1833, describing it as 'neatly bound for the library, so as to range with Scott's novels, Miss Edgeworth's novels, Byron's works, etc. price 30*s*.'

B. THE FIRST COLLECTED EDITION OF BULWER LYTTON [3735*b*]

13 vols. Saunders & Otley (and Colburn) 1840–1841, 1845.

It would perhaps be more accurate to describe this edition as a joint bye-product of Bentley's and Colburn's novel series, for actually three of the volumes carry Colburn's imprint and consist of his sheets, while Bentley's name does not appear on any title-page. But the inspiration came so obviously from Bentley's Standard Novels, and Bentley's collaboration was so much more prompt, generous and self-effacing than that of his rival, that accuracy can suitably yield to equity and credit be given where credit is really due.

No more attractive production of its kind and period is known to me than this elegant and carefully produced series of brown-cloth volumes. In format, appearance and illustration they are modelled on Bentley Standard Novels of the first cloth period, but are more imaginatively blocked, printed in slightly larger type, and on the whole less conventionally illustrated. In the list which follows, titles with textual significance are in capitals. Where a title is not in the Collection, it is asterisked; it is among my keener regrets that I have not been able absolutely to complete the series, but the books seem to be very uncommon. *Pl. 9*

Description and Complete List

Earth-brown ribbed cloth, blocked in blind on front, back and spine with conventional designs, gold-lettered on spine WORKS / OF / SIR E. L. BULWER / BART. / (*title of novel*) / LONDON / SAUNDERS & OTLEY [on Nos. 10–12: LONDON / COLBURN]. Pale yellow end-papers. Steel-engraved front. and vignette title (both dated) precede printed title.

The volumes were not numbered at the time of their appearance, but incidental advert. material refer to them as the 'First', 'Second', 'Third', etc. volume and this chronological sequence is maintained as

[*3735b*] bibliographically correct. The formal re-numbering, which took place when No. 12 was published, is recorded under that volume.

1 RIENZI 1840 (Feb. 1)

Contains a new Dedication to the Author's mother, 3 pp. dated Jan. 6, 1840. Engravings after Maclise and Creswick. Adverts (4 pp.) preceding half-title make a general announcement of this 'First Uniform Edition' of Bulwer's works, stating that the volumes will be published monthly at six shillings and will 'include not only all the acknowledged works of Sir Edward Lytton-Bulwer that have yet appeared (excepting only those already printed by Mr Colburn and Mr Bentley in their several Libraries of Fiction and therefore already before the public in the same popular size and form of Six Shilling Volumes) but some not hitherto published'. The prospectus concludes: 'The whole will be carefully revised by the Author and no pains spared to give to this Edition a new and distinctive value.'

Note. As will be seen, the terms of the announcement were not wholly maintained. One title from Bentley's Standard Novels was included and three from Colburn's Modern Novels appended. No new work was first published in this form. One is reminded, a little sadly, of the Illustrated Edition of Marryat's novels which started so admirably and came to grief so soon. Certainly the Bulwer Series survived for considerably longer; but it would seem that Saunders & Otley inclined to promise more than they found themselves able to perform.

2 ERNEST MALTRAVERS 1840 (March 1)

Contains a new Preface, 6 pp., written for this edition and reporting with remarkable candour the attempts made to persuade Bentley and Colburn to lease, for inclusion in this new edition, those earlier novels published in their Novel Series. Bulwer states that £1500 were offered for the mere permission to print in the new edition *Paul Clifford*, *Eugene Aram*, *Pompeii*, *Pelham*, *Disowned* and *Devereux*, but Bentley and Colburn 'paid me the inconvenient and unwelcome compliment of stating that the novels in dispute were so popular, and so valuable in aid of other fictions in their collections, that they could not allow me to use them in mine, except upon terms which would have rendered the price of each volume a third higher than it is at present'. The Preface ends with a terrific Bulwerian appeal to the public who have already purchased the Bentley and Colburn titles to buy 'these children of my later and riper years in their present comely and commodious apparel, and so unite under your kindly roof a now scattered family'. Engravings after Cattermole.

3 **Alice**, or **The Mysteries** 1840 (April 1)

Engravings after von Holst and Stephanoff.

4 GODOLPHIN and THE PILGRIMS OF THE RHINE (Chaps. I–V) 1840 (May 1)

The first edition of *Godolphin* over the author's name, with a Dedication to Count d'Orsay (2 pp. undated) and a Note to the Present Edition (1 p. dated April 17, 1840), not previously printed. A Dedication to Henry Lytton-Bulwer (2 pp. dated April 23, 1840) is prefixed to *The Pilgrims of the Rhine*. Engravings after Maclise and Creswick.

5 **The Pilgrims of the Rhine** (Chaps. VI–end) and **The Student** (to the end of *Chairolas*)

Engravings after Cattermole.

Note. Although this volume has no textual significance, advert. leaves preceding the half-title carry further the story of the new edition and the negotiations with Bentley and Colburn. Under the heading 'Advertisement' we read that correspondence between Bulwer and Bentley and Bulwer and Colburn has led to an agreement by which on fair and reasonable terms the novels controlled by them shall be included in the Uniform Edition. A note adds that the final volume of the edition will contain title-pages for each earlier volume 'so as to number the works according to the several dates of their first publication'.

6 THE STUDENT (from *Infidelity in Love* to the end) and ENGLAND AND THE ENGLISH 1840 (July 1)

On the title-page *The Student* is described as 'revised and with Additions' and *England and the English* as 'Revised and Corrected'. There is also a new Preface to the latter work, 3 pp. dated June 1840. Engravings after Cattermole.

7 ***Paul Clifford** 1840 (Aug. 1) [*3735b*]

8 EUGENE ARAM 1840 (Sept. 1)

Contains a new Preface, 7 pp. dated August 1840. Engravings after Cattermole and Creswick.

9 **Last Days of Pompeii** 1840 (Oct. 1)

Engravings after Cattermole. A Publisher's 'Notice', preceding frontispiece, announces that the remaining three volumes of the edition—*Pelham, Disowned* and *Devereux*—'will be published monthly, with the Author's last corrections, by Mr Colburn. *Pelham* will appear on 1st of November.' Evidently Colburn had left a loophole in his previous negotiations and now refused to let his three copyrights appear over any imprint but his own.

10 **Pelham** 1840 (Nov. 1)

Although uniform in binding with the Saunders & Otley volumes, this is merely a reprint of Colburn's edition of 1835 (or possibly actual sheets), with the dates on front, and vignette title altered to 1840.

11 ***Disowned** 1840 (? Dec. 1)

12 **Devereux** 1841 (? Jan. 1)

As No. 20, this is Colburn's earlier edition with altered dates. At the end of the volume, as promised, are twelve title-pages renumbering the volumes under two classifications and in order of publication. These title-pages are not dated and read THE / COMPLETE PROSE WORKS / OF / SIR E. L. BULWER, BART. / NOW FIRST COLLECTED. / (*rule*) VOL. I. / Historical Romances, etc. / RIENZI (etc.).

As rearranged, the edition runs as follows:

Historical Romances:	I	Rienzi	II	Pompeii
Novels, Tales and Essays:	III	Pelham	IV	Disowned
	V	Devereux	VI	Paul Clifford
	VII	Eugene Aram	VIII	Maltravers
	IX	Alice	X	Godolphin etc.
	XI	Pilgrims of the Rhine etc.	XII	Student etc.

13 **Supplementary volume:** NIGHT AND MORNING Saunders & Otley 1845

Contains a Dedication (1 p.) and Preface to the Present Edition (7 pp.) both dated 1845. Engravings after Cattermole.

C. *THE HAMILTONS*, by MRS GORE 1850 [3735*c*]

Simultaneously with Standard Novel No. 119 was issued a square 8vo volume ($5\frac{1}{2}'' \times 8''$) bound in red morocco cloth, gilt, printed from Standard Novel type, including the Standard Novel frontispiece (on smaller paper) and with a specially printed title-page. It can hardly be doubted that this ingenious 'large paper' issue was Mrs Gore's idea—was perhaps prepared mainly for her personal use. She was always inclined to enterprise in her publishing styles, and of the several copies I have seen of this 'bye-product' *Hamiltons*, at least five had presentation inscriptions.

The copy in the Collection is inscribed in ink on fly-leaf: 'Lady Molesworth from C. F. Gore' and has binders' ticket: 'Josiah Westley', at end.

'THE BENTLEY TRADITION' [3736]

A. SIMULTANEOUS INSPIRATION: ROSCOE'S NOVELIST'S LIBRARY, with a note on HARPER'S LIBRARY OF SELECT NOVELS

B. HENRY COLBURN, HIS CHARACTER AND PARTNERSHIP WITH RICHARD BENTLEY

C. SHARP PRACTICE: COLBURN'S MODERN NOVELISTS (post 8vo Series)—COLBURN'S IRISH NATIONAL TALES—COLBURN'S NAVAL AND MILITARY LIBRARY—THE NEW BRITISH NOVELIST

D. STEALING BENTLEY'S THUNDER: COLBURN'S MODERN NOVELISTS (small 8vo Series and Part Issue) and COLBURN'S MODERN STANDARD NOVELISTS

ROSCOE'S NOVELIST'S LIBRARY

[*3736*] The influence on English publishing of 'Bentleyism', as expressed in the Standard Novel Series, was not only immense and durable; it was also remarkably diverse. The Standard Novels, by their immediate success, implanted three distinct ideas in the public mind, all of which were soon reflected on trade practice. First, they gave nation-wide popularity to the particular small 8vo format, the clear neat type and the steel-engraved embellishments which Cadell had devised for his *Waverley* and Bentley appropriated for his far more varied list. Second, they impressed six shillings on the consciousness of the reading public as a price at which first-rate novels of full length, not many years old and cloth bound, could conceivably and conveniently be bought, and, by so doing, threw for the first time into uneasy relief the three or more boarded volumes at half a guinea apiece which by the early thirties had become the regular guise for a new fiction. Third, they made people realise that contemporary novels, as well as those of the late eighteenth century, could aspire to the epithet 'standard'; and that consequently modern fiction was not necessarily the vicious frivolity it was so often declared to be, but might conceivably be part of English literature.

Each in turn of these new comprehensions became a challenge to publishers' conservatism or a stimulus to publishers' enterprise; to each, more or less rapidly, enterprise responded or conservatism was forced to yield. Thus it was that Bentley's Standard Novel Series became a tradition almost as soon as it came into existence; thus it was, also, that the tradition expressed itself in several quite distinct ways.

[3736*a*] A. SIMULTANEOUS INSPIRATION: ROSCOE'S NOVELIST'S LIBRARY, 1831–1833, with a note on HARPER'S LIBRARY OF SELECT NOVELS

The first Bentley Standard Novel was published on February 25, 1831. On May 1 of the same year appeared the first two volumes of *Roscoe's Novelist's Library*. The interval between these two dates is too short for the later series to be accused of having imitated the earlier one. Messrs Cochrane & Pickersgill must be given the credit of having for themselves examined the Cadell *Waverley* and wondered how best to profit by the demand for small format fiction which the success of the *Waverley* Novels had unmistakably revealed. It is interesting, seeing that both must have been in the making simultaneously, to observe the difference between their scheme and Bentley's. Cochrane & Pickersgill evidently saw the Cadell *Waverley* rather as an innovation in format than as an incitement to textual enterprise. Partly no doubt because they did not want to spend money on paying authors, partly maybe because they were themselves more interested in book-design than in judging fiction and were quite content to limit their experiments to style and embellishment, they rather tamely determined to stick to the old favourites which everyone knew, and to put on the market yet another edition of *Robinson Crusoe*, of *The Vicar of Wakefield*, of Fielding and of Smollett.

'Yet another edition'—but all the same an edition like no other. They kept to Cadell's price of five shillings, but instead of a double opening in steel engraving at the beginning they decided to offer specially drawn illustrations by an artist of repute.

But although *Roscoe's Novelist's Library* was certainly not a copy of *Bentley's Standard Novels*, there is evidence that its publishers were well aware of Bentley's series. Their prospectus, which appeared on April 5, 1831 and was manifestly drafted after February 25, is headed: 'Uniform with the Waverley Novels', and continues:

'In announcing a SELECT SERIES OF CLASSICAL NOVELS Messrs Cochrane & Pickersgill disclaim any intention of trespassing on the ground occupied by other publishers. Whilst the productions of writers of fiction subsequent to the time of Fielding and Smollett are presented in a periodical form as candidates for publication, the Proprietors are encouraged to extend the field of rational entertainment by offering to English readers CHEAP EDITIONS of...such Novels and Romances as have been unequivocally stamped with popular regard....'

The prospectus continues with disputable accuracy:

'The best uniform editions of these celebrated works [i.e. Novels by Smollett, Fielding, Goldsmith, etc.] have hitherto been published in forms and at prices which have placed them beyond the reach of any but the wealthier classes of readers.*

* This was a little hard on Mrs Barbauld and Whittingham, not to mention the series of still earlier date. But perhaps Cochrane & Pickersgill based their statement on what was at the time of writing still in print. Such facility in passing from the particular to the general has ever been a feature of publishers' advertising.

'To remove this inconvenience, and supply wants which the Public has long felt, the Proprietors intend to publish the present Edition in Monthly volumes beautifully printed and embellished with Plates, at the cheap price of five shillings per volume, neatly bound.' [3736a]

The first two volumes of Roscoe (*Robinson Crusoe*) were illustrated by Jacob George Strutt, whose etchings of trees, published as *Sylva Britannica* and *Deliciae Sylvarum*, had recently brought him a great reputation. What actually occurred to displace Strutt as illustrator of the series and instal George Cruikshank in his place is not known; nor whether the new illustrator produced a marked difference in the books' contemporary sale.* But from the point of view of their venture's ultimate renown, Cochrane & Pickersgill made a sensational exchange. Thanks to Cruikshank's work in the remaining volumes of the series, *Roscoe's Novelist's Library* has until now been the best known and most sought after of the many nineteenth-century novel-series. As an achievement in book-making it deserves its reputation; but to students of publishing and to all who, in a publisher, rate textual intelligence and courage to create a public taste more highly than mere skill in production, it cannot compare with the run of Bentley's Standard Novels.

ROSCOE'S NOVELIST'S LIBRARY: A COMPLETE LIST

19 vols. [First Series, 2 vols.; New Series, 17 vols.] 1831–1833. Vols. I and II and New Series' Vol. I, published by Cochrane & Pickersgill; New Series, Vols. II–XII, published by James Cochrane; New Series, Vols. XIII–XVII, published by Effingham Wilson.

Glazed fawn watered cloth, very dark blue paper labels lettered and decorated in gold; white end-papers. The labels are at extreme head and tail of spine, the former carrying series title and number of volume, the latter, author, book title and volume number (where required). The 17 volumes of the New Series have a third label, affixed under that carrying series title and reading: ILLUSTRATED/by/GEO. CRUIKSHANK.

I & II. ROBINSON CRUSOE 1831

I. (viii) [(i) (ii) Prospectus of Series; (iii) (iv) half-title, verso; (v) (vi) title, verso; (vii) (viii) illustrations, extracts in praise of *Robinson Crusoe*] + lxiv [Biographical Sketch of Defoe by Thomas Roscoe] + (328)

Illustrations. Engraved front. portrait and 8 etchings on India paper, mounted on plate paper.

Note. The Prospectus announces the series as 'to be published in Monthly Volumes (uniform with the *Waverley* Novels)' at five shillings each, and 'with illustrations from designs original and selected by Jacob George Strutt Esq., author of "Sylva Britannica"'. Of the volumes here announced as forthcoming about half actually appeared.

II. (viii) [as in I] + (328) X_3 X_4 adverts.

Illustrations. Etched front. and 7 plates on India paper, mounted on plate paper.

New Series

I. HUMPHRY CLINKER ('Humphrey' on spine label) 1831

(xii) [(i)–(vi) adverts., including Prospectus of Series as in I but with Cruikshank's name substituted for Strutt; (vii) (viii) half-title, verso; (ix) (x) title, verso; (xi) (xii) illustrations, verso] + (xxxii) [paged (v)–xxxvi Memoir of Smollett by Thomas Roscoe] + (404). Erratum slip tipped on to (v)

Illustrations. Engraved front. portrait and 4 etchings.

II. RODERICK RANDOM 1831

(viii) [Prospectus, half-title etc. as before] + (vi) [paged (v)–x—Preface and Apologue] + (498) $2I_4$ adverts.

Illustrations. Etched front. and 4 plates.

Note. There is in the Collection an edition of *Roderick Random* published by Orlando Hodgson in 1839 with the Cruikshank plates from the Roscoe edition, still imprinted Cochrane & Pickersgill and dated 1831. I do not know whether other titles were similarly re-issued.

* The indications are that he did so. With the first Cruikshank volume (*Humphry Clinker*) the publishers began a fresh numbering of the whole series, thereafter advertising the two volumes of *Robinson Crusoe* as 'uniform with *Roscoe's Novelist's Library*'. Also they 'billed' Cruikshank on a special spine-label—a compliment they had not paid to Strutt.

[*3736a*] III, IV. PEREGRINE PICKLE 1831

III. (viii) [as in II]+(424) $2D_4$ adverts.

Illustrations. Etched front. and 3 plates.

IV. (viii) [as in III]+448

Illustrations. Etched front. and 3 plates.

V, VI. TOM JONES 1831

V. (xxiv)+(456) $2F_4$ Prospectus of Series, as previously printed preceding half-title.

Illustrations. Engraved portrait after Hogarth and 4 etchings.

VI. (viii) [Prospectus restored to original position]+448

Illustrations. Etched front. and 3 plates.

VII. JOSEPH ANDREWS 1832

(xvi) [paged (i)–(iv)+(i)–xii]+336 The Prospectus precedes half-title, but is extended to fill three instead of two pages.

Illustrations. Etched front. and 3 plates.

Note. I have seen this book in dark green ribbon-embossed cloth, gold-lettered at head and tail of spine: ROSCOE'S / NOVELS / JOSEPH / ANDREWS / *rule* / COMPLETE. I do not know whether the whole series appeared in this secondary binding.

VIII, IX. AMELIA 1832

VIII. (xii) [paged (i)–(x)+(i)–ii]+(308)

Illustrations. Etched front. and 3 plates.

IX. (viii)+344 Y_4 (foliated) carries a continuation of the Prospectus which begins on pp. (i) (ii).

Illustrations. Etched front. and 3 plates.

X. THE VICAR OF WAKEFIELD and SIR LAUNCELOT GREAVES 1832

(xvi) [paged (x)] Pp. (vii)–(xiv) Memoir of Goldsmith by Thomas Roscoe+168 [VICAR OF WAKEFIELD]+(iv)+(244) [LAUNCELOT GREAVES]

Illustrations. Engraved front. portrait of Goldsmith and 4 etchings, two to each novel.

Note. The Prospectus of the Series does not appear in this volume.

XI, XII. TRISTRAM SHANDY and A SENTIMENTAL JOURNEY 1832

XI. (xx) [paged (xii)] Pp. (ix)–(xix) Memoir of Sterne+372

Illustrations. Engraved portrait front. and 4 etchings.

Note. The Prospectus reappears in its original short form preceding half-title.

XII. (viii)+(1)–232 [conclusion of SHANDY]+(233) (234) [fly-title to SENTIMENTAL JOURNEY]+(235)–(360) [text of SENTIMENTAL JOURNEY] Z_4 (foliated) continuation of Prospectus, as in IX. Catalogue of Valpy's publications, 12 pp. fcap 8vo undated, inserted after front end-paper.

Illustrations. Etched front. and 3 plates.

Note. This volume shows symptoms of confusion. In the first place, although the title-page is imprinted 'James Cochrane', the plates are imprinted 'A. J. Valpy'. In the second place, the List of Illustrations is faulty. The first 2 plates listed relate to the earlier portion of *Shandy*, printed in Vol. XI, and the face-pages here given (327 and 345) refer to their incidence in that volume. Nevertheless the first plate appears as front. to the present volume, and the second as sub-front. facing the fly-title to *A Sentimental Journey*, to which it is wholly irrelevant. The third and fourth plates are correctly listed and face pp. 5 and 48 of the present volume.

XIII, XIV, XV. DON QUIXOTE 1833

XIII. (xxxvi) [paged (iv)+iv+(xxviii) Prelims., 'Preface to the Reader' and Memoir of Cervantes by Thomas Roscoe]+(372)

Illustrations. Wood-engraved imaginary portrait front. of Quixote after Kenney Meadows and 5 etchings by Cruikshank.

Note. No Prospectus henceforth appears in any volume.

XIV. (viii) [paged iv]+(356) [3736a]

Illustrations. Wood-engraved imaginary portrait front. of Sancho Panza after Kenney Meadows and 5 etchings by Cruikshank.

XV. viii+384 Publishers' cat., 36 pp. undated, at end.

Illustrations. Wood-engraved imaginary portrait front. of Dulcinea after Kenney Meadows and 5 etchings by Cruikshank.

Note. On p. 13 of the publishers' cat. is advertised 'An uniform continuation of Roscoe's Novelist's Library consisting of *Don Quixote* in 3 vols. at 18*s*. and *Gil Blas* in 2 vols. at 12*s*.'

XVI, XVII. GIL BLAS 1833

XVI. xxiv [(ix)–xxiv Memoir of Le Sage by Thomas Roscoe]+(1)–2 [inset leaf signed 'C' and carrying 'Author's Declaration']+(1)–418

Illustrations. Wood-engraved imaginary portrait front. of Doctor Sangrado after Kenney Meadows and 5 etchings by Cruikshank.

XVII. xii+420

Illustrations. Wood-engraved imaginary portrait front. of Gil Blas after Kenney Meadows and 5 etchings by Cruikshank.

Secondary Bindings and a Re-issue

I have noted odd volumes of this series in two, undoubtedly secondary bindings: (i) coarse light brown watered cloth, with no volume number on top label and no Cruikshank label (*Tom Jones* and *Gil Blas*); (ii) dark green large-honeycomb-grain cloth, labelled at base of spine only with title and author. No series title inside or outside and no mention of illustration on cover (*Don Quixote*).

From an odd monthly number in my possession, I gather that during the thirties the plates of at any rate some of Cruickshank's illustrations were acquired by Orlando Hodgson, an Isleworth printer with an office at 111 Fleet Street. He had already, under the series title 'Hodgson's Standard Library', issued one or more of Cooper's novels (cf. above p. 94 *note*). These he followed with *Humphry Clinker* and *Roderick Random*, in fcap 8vo. weekly parts and monthly numbers, including the illustrations originally etched by Cruikshank for Cochrane. Whether he republished the whole Roscoe Series, I do not know.

A NOTE ON HARPER'S LIBRARY OF SELECT NOVELS

This American series has as much right as *Roscoe's Novelist's Library* to claim simultaneous inspiration with *Bentley's Standard Novels*. It began in May 1831; and it is a matter of regret that I can supply so few particulars, for the books were produced with taste and care and the venture was clearly one of pioneer importance. [3736aa]

Only one specimen is in the Collection; but presumably a description of it will apply to at any rate the earlier volumes of the series.

Nos. III, IV. THE DUTCHMAN'S FIRESIDE, by the author of 'Letters from the South', 'The Backwoodsman', 'John Bull in America', etc. etc. [J. K. Paulding]. 2 vols. sm. 8vo. New York: J. & J. Harper 1831. Dark green linen, printed in black—on front and spine with series title and number, book title and volume number. Publishers' imprint on front only. Back covers printed—Vol. I with 'Advertisement' of the Select Novels, Vol. II with a list of the *Family Library*. *Pl. 9*

Although eight pages of adverts. precede the title in the first volume, no indication is given of titles already published (or to be published) in the series nor of the price at which the volumes were issued. The following list, however (taken from a Harper publication of the early thirties), gives, I hope in correct order, the first 18 titles and 36 volumes of this attractive Library. The bracketed dates are those of the first editions.

I, II	**Youth and Manhood of Cyril Thornton**	Hamilton	(1827)
III, IV	**Dutchman's Fireside**	Paulding	1st edition
V, VI	**Young Duke**	Disraeli	(1831)

[*3736 aa*] vii, viii	**Caleb Williams**	Godwin	(1794)
ix, x	**Philip Augustus**	James	(1831)
xi, xii	**Club Book**	Picken and others	(1831)
xiii, xiv	**De Vere**	Ward	(1827)
xv, xvi	**Smuggler**	Banim	(1831)
xvii, xviii	**Eugene Aram**	Bulwer	(1832)
xix, xx	**Evelina**	Burney	(1778)
xxi, xxii	**Spy**	Cooper	(1821)
xxiii, xxiv	**Westward Ho**	Paulding	1st edition
xxv, xxvi	**Tales of Glauber-Spa**	Sedgwick	1st edition. A collection of tales edited by Bryant
xxvii, xxviii	**Henry Masterton**	James	(1832)
xxix, xxx	**Mary of Burgundy**	,,	(1833)
xxxi, xxxii	**Richelieu**	,,	(1829)
xxxiii, xxxiv	**Darnley**	,,	(1830)
xxxv, xxxvi	**John Marston Hall**	,,	(1834)

[3736*b*]

B. HENRY COLBURN, HIS CHARACTER AND PARTNERSHIP WITH RICHARD BENTLEY

There is irony in the fact that the next product of Bentleyism was not only a clever disingenuity but one devised by the very firm which were publishing the Standard Novels. In order to make clear how, from the same office, could have emanated an honest piece of publishing enterprise like the Standard Novels and two new series which were little short of a fraud on the public, it is necessary to summarise the facts of the uneasy partnership then existing between Richard Bentley and Henry Colburn, and briefly to characterise the two men.

Richard Bentley was a younger brother of the well-known printer and antiquary, Samuel Bentley. This man was first apprentice and then partner of his uncle John Nichols of the *Gentleman's Magazine.* He indexed Nichols' *Literary Anecdotes* and produced on his own account more than one work of scholarship. In 1819 Samuel Bentley, desirous of greater independence, set up a printing business with his brother Richard, in Dorset Street, Salisbury Square, and it was in the early days of this business that the younger Bentley first made the acquaintance of Henry Colburn.

Colburn was at this time a pushing young publisher with an office in Conduit Street. His origin—even to the date of his birth—is obscure, but he must have been in his early thirties when Richard Bentley first knew him. According to the *D.N.B.* it was not until 1816 that he succeeded to the proprietorship of Morgan's Circulating Library in Conduit Street, where he had already for some years served as an assistant. But the date of his independent proprietorship must have been considerably earlier. Eaton Stannard Barrett's satirical poem *The Second Titan War against Heaven* was published by Colburn from 50 Conduit Street in 1807 and advertised on its final page his 'English and Foreign Subscription Library', as well as two translations from Kotzebue, a two-volume Gothic romance called *Jeannette or The Convent of Notre Dame,* and an essay on statistics—all 'recently published by H. Colburn'. In 1808 (according to advertisements in another Colburn book issued in that year) the list had been increased by four further novels and a two-volume *Memoirs of Female Philosophers.* Year by year the business developed. By 1811, when he 'reprinted' two novels by the celebrated American writer Charles Brockden Brown (*Wieland* and *Ormond*), eight other fictions were announced as on the market. In 1812 he published C. R. Maturin's *Milesian Chief,* and the advertisement pages show his list markedly increasing. In 1814 came Barrett's well-known skit on gothistic extravagance *The Heroine,* a translation of Vulpius' *Ferrandino** and a number of general books—travel and reminiscence—as well as fiction. In 1814 he secured Lady Morgan's novel *O'Donnel*—his first venture in the work of an author whose long connection with him was to produce much profit (for which he cared a great deal) and even more ridicule (for which he cared nothing at all).

* Using in this case, oddly enough, the name of Oxberry the printer as imprint, although including among the prelims. a page advertisement of his own publications.

Colburn's list was now rapidly developing. It fills nine pages at the end of *O'Donnel*, Vol. III, and has several features of interest. In the first place it contains a large number of French books (by Mesdames de Staël, de Genlis, Cottin, and de Montolieu, by Pigault le Brun and others), printed and published in French in London. Clearly Colburn had known how to exploit the foreign connections of Morgan's Library the very moment that news of Napoleon's defeat at Leipzig promised a speedy reopening of communications with the Continent. The second interesting feature of Colburn's 1814 list is the announcement that on February 1st of the year had appeared the first number of *The New Monthly Magazine*. This periodical, issued as a direct challenge to Sir Richard Phillips' *Monthly Magazine*, was destined, under a succession of distinguished editors, to run for over sixty years. In 1816 Colburn published Lady Caroline Lamb's *Glenarvon*, and commissioned Lady Morgan to write a book on France, paying her a large fee and all her expenses during a special sojourn abroad. He was well repaid for his daring and intelligence. The book appeared early in 1817 and was immediately successful. [*3736b*]

Colburn had brilliantly gauged the reading taste of a public for many years cut off from France and now devoured with curiosity about the minds and manners of their ex-enemies. In the meantime his tireless inventiveness had devised another literary periodical, and on January 1st, 1817, he published the first weekly number of *The Literary Gazette*. In six months he sold a third interest to Jerdan of *The Sun*, who became the *Literary Gazette's* editor, and a little later a second third to Messrs Longman. The paper prospered until 1862. In 1818 Colburn paid a big price for Evelyn's *Diary*, and it was over the printing of this work that he came into contact with the man who was to become his publishing partner.

There could hardly have been two beings more different or—one would have thought—more unsympathetic than Henry Colburn and Richard Bentley. The former was a small, bustling bundle of energy, with needle-sharp business acumen and no scruples whatsoever. The first of the gambling publishers, he regarded every author as having his price and the public as gullible fools. He cared nothing about book-design, nothing about craftsmanship. Cheapest was best, so long as the leaves held together; and it is hard to find a single book of Colburn's independent creation which is other than commonplace in style or (when he fancied elegance) tawdry or over-emphatic. He had no literary taste of his own, merely an instinctive sense of the taste of the moment. In consequence (being incapable of building up a list of permanent saleability) he published on the basis of quick turn-over, and made a fortune for himself by sheer topical ingenuity. His imprint died with him. Not, however, his influence on the trade. Impervious to snubs; cheerful under vilification, so long as insults meant more business; thinking in hundreds where others thought in tens, Colburn revolutionised publishing in its every aspect. He would invent a book which he judged likely to be popular, choose his author and offer a sudden dazzling fee for the copyright. His servility was as calculated as his generosity. To the socially great he would crawl, to authors he wished to tempt or to placate he was an open-handed paymaster. But those he considered his inferiors or useless to his business found him hard and insolent, and there was little enough of kindness and consideration for Colburn authors whose books had failed to sell. He developed advertising, both direct and indirect, to a degree hitherto undreamt of. He had his diners-out who talked up his books at dinner-tables and soirées; he debauched the critics and put them on his pay-sheet. Altogether a brilliant, disturbing, meanly admirable little man, who died in 1855 leaving £35,000 and, perhaps, four copyrights of lasting value. He was a book-manufacturer, not a publisher; and his kind are with us to this day.

Richard Bentley, on the other hand, was the serious-minded craftsman-booklover. To practical ability and knowledge of manufacture, he added an innate, though rather bourgeois, sense of the dignity of a publisher's calling. From his brother Samuel (nurtured on the Nichols tradition) he had learnt a respect for books as books. When he offered something to the public, he wanted it—for his own conscience sake if for no other reason—as good as he could make it; and he would no more have thought of misleading that public by tendacious or flashy advertisement than of robbing the till. Compared to Colburn he was slow-minded and unadaptable, and for these shortcomings he paid a heavy price. But having learnt his lesson and stuck out his bad times, he founded a business beside which Colburn's dazzling improvisations were but the bright stars of a falling rocket.

Such were the two men who in 1829—ten years after their first meeting—went into publishing partnership. Why did they do it? The reason was characteristic. The only way that S. & R. Bentley could hope for the payment of Colburn's printing bill was to take an interest in the gentleman's exciting but

[3736b] hazardous business. Throughout the twenties Colburn had gone his dizzy way. In 1824 he moved from Conduit Street to 8 New Burlington Street, his 'British and Foreign Public Library' passing into the control of Saunders & Otley—a new firm destined a few years later to rival Colburn himself in spectacular modernism. This same year—1824—he had astonished Theodore Hook with the offer of £600 for a novel. The result was *Sayings and Doings*, which sold 6000 copies at 31*s.* 6*d.* In 1825 he speculated in Pepys' Diaries and, though in fact he made little profit, if any, from the venture, was reputed to have triumphed and gained much prestige thereby. In 1827 he wire-pulled *Vivian Grey* into being the talk of the town, and repeated the experiment a year later with Bulwer's *Pelham.* But spectacular seasonal successes are no real protection against prolonged bad trade, and Colburn, whose genius lay in the creation of nine days' wonders, now found that solvency depended on books which sold steadily if slowly for nine years. Wherefore the evil days of 1826–7, which swept away two-thirds of the publishing houses of the time, shook him badly. Probably the Bentley brothers had no alternative but to accept the suggestion that their mounting bill be regarded as part of the resources of Colburn's re-conditioned firm. In any event they did so; and in September 1829 a joint imprint: 'H. Colburn and R. Bentley' made its first appearance in New Burlington Street.

The deed of partnership between Colburn and Bentley was valid for three years. Colburn was guaranteed, as payment for goodwill, a sum equivalent to two years' profits of his former independent business. He estimated these profits as £5000 a year, so that the first charge in the proceeds of the new business was £10,000. He also put a generous valuation on his former copyrights and in other ways over-reached his less agile-minded and less experienced colleague. Almost at once, therefore, relations became strained. Early ventures of a series-type went badly. *The National Library, The Family Classical Library, The Juvenile Library,* were all unsuccessful. An elaborate plan for a *Library of Modern Travels and Discoveries* never came to birth at all. The launching of the Standard Novels, therefore, was a very brave or a very reckless act, on the success of which everything depended. That it did succeed was largely due to the intelligence and integrity of its planning, and as these qualities were never conspicuous in Colburn's independent ventures, it is permissible to guess that Bentley had the lion's share in devising the scheme. The Standard Novels, then, came and conquered. But within six months of their first appearance an attempt was made by their publishers to exploit the market just created—an attempt whose catchpenny but skilful exaggeration was unmistakably Colburnesque.

[3736c (i)] C. **SHARP PRACTICE:** COLBURN'S MODERN NOVELISTS (post 8vo Series); COLBURN'S IRISH NATIONAL TALES; COLBURN'S NAVAL AND MILITARY LIBRARY OF ENTERTAINMENT; THE NEW BRITISH NOVELIST

In October 1831 appeared a grandiloquent announcement by Messrs Colburn & Bentley of a series of 'The best recent Works of Fiction from the pens of the most Eminent Authors, in fifty volumes, post 8vo, at six shillings per volume, bound and lettered. The impression of this cheap and unique collection is limited to 250 copies.' Prudent book-buyers were urged instantly to place an order with their bookseller, lest they be too late to secure one of these unparalleled bargains.

Colburnesque indeed. The public were in a mood for cheap novels. Very well then, it should have them; and if credulity could be so exploited as to work off a stock of unwanted sheets, so much the better for the exploiter.

For the crude fact was that this fifty-volume series of 'Modern Novelists' consisted of unsold sheets of pre-partnership Colburn fiction. The limitation number was either window-dressing or else represented the minimum number of sheets available on the list of titles which it was desired to include. In other words, just as the Standard Novels were the first cheap editions of recent fiction in the modern bookstall sense, the Modern Novels were the first series of 'jobbed' or 'remaindered' editions of novels of yesterday. With this difference—that the jobbed novel to-day is unmistakably a job, but *Colburn's Modern Novelists* pretended to be genuine cheap editions.

Whether the original venture was a success or whether the general scheme provided the most convenient outlet available for surplus sheets of three-volume fiction, its originator kept it in being for some years, and the series of disguised remainders stayed on the market for a long while. But it underwent more than one transformation; all pretence of limitation of edition was soon dropped; and it may be taken for certain that *Colburn's Modern Novelists* (8vo series) worked for their creator and not he for them. The numbers fluctuated suspiciously and finally attained enormous proportions. [3736 c (i)]

In 1833, for example, a new start was made—or at any rate a pretence of a new start. Several titles were dropped (they had probably sold out) and the price of the remainder reduced to four shillings per volume. Colburn liked to calendar fresh ventures with impressive accuracy, so it is not surprising to find an elaborate schedule of the series—'now in regular course of monthly publication'—in an advertisement of July 1833. By that date 23 volumes were formally planned. Thus the following sets were stated to have appeared:

Feb. 1. *Tremaine* [Plumer Ward], 3 vols.
March 1. *Pelham* [Bulwer], 3 vols.
April 1. *Chelsea Pensioners* [C. R. Gleig], 3 vols.
May 1. *The Disowned* [Bulwer], 3 vols.
June 1. *De Vere* [Plumer Ward], 4 vols.
July 1. *Granby* [T. H. Lister], 3 vols.
Aug. 1. 'Will appear' *Devereux* [Bulwer], 3 vols.

The novel which followed *Devereux* was something of a curiosity, in that it carried the month as well as the year of issue on its titles—surely a unique phenomenon in post 8vo three- or four-volume fiction. The book was Disraeli's *Vivian Grey* and it was issued in four volumes (the original Vols. I and II forming Vol. I of the new edition) at sixteen shillings the set. The title-pages were headed 'Colburn's Modern Novelists' and the imprints read:

LONDON
PUBLISHED FOR HENRY COLBURN
BY R. BENTLEY, NEW BURLINGTON STREET
SEPT$^{R.}$ 1833

But careful punctuality, alike on title-pages and advertisements, was discreetly abandoned as candidates for jobbing became more numerous, and the idea of a 'series' was allowed to fade into the background. By the autumn of 1834 the number of volumes had increased to forty-seven.

An advertisement of August 1834, under the heading 'Monthly Libraries', has features of interest in addition to the list of titles offered. This list repeats that of July 1833, including of course *Vivian Grey*, but omits *Pelham* and *The Chelsea Pensioners*. The former was probably temporarily out of print (it appeared in a new form in 1835), but the latter, as will be seen in a minute, had been transferred to a new, ingenious, but no more ingenuous 'series'. Thus in August 1834 the following fictions were available:

**Tremaine*, 3 vols.
**De Vere*, 3 vols.
**The Disowned*, 3 vols.
**Devereux*, 3 vols.
**Granby*, 3 vols.
Herbert Lacy [T. H. Lister], 3 vols.
**Vivian Grey*, 4 vols.
Sayings & Doings. 1st series [Hook], 3 vols.
Sayings & Doings. 2nd series [Hook], 3 vols.
Highways & Byways, 1st series [Grattan], 3 vols.
Highways & Byways. 2nd series [Grattan], 3 vols.
The Tor Hill [H. Smith], 3 vols.
The New Forest [H. Smith], 3 vols.
Yes and No [Lord Normanby], 2 vols.
†*Gaston de Blondeville* [Ann Radcliffe], 2 vols.

Some time between August and December was added:

The Romance of Real Life [Mrs Gore], 3 vols.

Very shortly after the end of 1834 any pretence of controlling the series was dropped. By December 1836 it consisted of no fewer than one hundred and ninety volumes, still at four shillings each. They were now admittedly remainders, and described as offering 'Cheap Editions of Celebrated Works of fiction adapted for Country Libraries'.

* Published by September 1833.

† This title is a good example of Colburn's skill in exploiting his publications. In 1826 he had published in 4 vols. Mrs Radcliffe's posthumous romance *Gaston de Blondeville*, a number of her poems and a memoir with extracts from her journals. He now cut the original work in half, included the prose romance among his 'Modern Novelists' and simultaneously advertised the 2 vols. of poems as *The Poetical Works of Ann Radcliffe*.

[3736*c* (ii)] COLBURN'S IRISH NATIONAL TALES

Whether or no the questionable ingenuity behind 'Colburn's Modern Novelists' justified itself in its inventor's eyes, there is no definite means of knowing. But one indication that the public were successfully rushed into considerable purchase of the ostensible bargains, at least during the first year or two of their currency, is that Colburn twice repeated his experiment in a slightly different form, the first time late the next year (1832) or early in 1833, the second late in 1833 or early in 1834.

COLBURN'S IRISH NATIONAL TALES AND ROMANCES were a series identical in format and almost identical in appearance with his 'Modern Novelists'—that is to say, they were works in original three- or four-volume shape, post 8vo, uncut, priced at 4*s*. per vol., and bound in green morocco cloth. Their labels, however, were gold-lettered on *green* instead of on red.

The series ran to 19 volumes; and was complete by July 1833. The titles were:

To-day in Ireland (by Eyre Evans Crowe), 3 vols.
Yesterday in Ireland (by Eyre Evans Crowe), 3 vols.
The Nowlans (by the Banims), 3 vols.
The Croppy (by the Banims), 3 vols.
The Anglo-Irish (by the Banims), 3 vols.
O'Briens and O'Flahertys (by Lady Morgan), 4 vols.

In June 1834 Colburn made, on their behalf, the following preposterous claim:

'That which has already been done for Scottish National History by the uniform collection of Scott's admirable tales is here done in behalf of Irish Story by the cheap reproduction of the most celebrated works of modern times illustrative of the peculiarities of the Sister Kingdom.'

It would be difficult to find a more typical piece of Colburn impudence. This precious series, which set up to represent Irish national fiction, contained no Edgeworth, no Gerald Griffin, only one late and minor novel by Lady Morgan and three minor Banims. The reason was, of course, that it was not a series at all, but a scratching together of such Irish fictions as Colburn individually happened to have published. Nevertheless, he got his press applause and, probably, fooled a certain number of ignorant book-buyers. Here, for instance, is a sample of critical enthusiasm, from *The Globe*:

'When the publication of the deservedly popular edition of the Waverley Novels commenced at the then unprecedentedly low price of 5*s*. per volume, the reading world was at once astonished and delighted. But to no one is the public more indebted for the requisite combination of quality and quantity than to the publisher of a series of works of fiction under the title *The Modern Novelists* and of the series under the denomination *Irish National Tales*.... Here the cheapness of the Waverley Novels is eclipsed. They are 5*s*. per volume; these are only 4*s*.—of a handsome size. Good paper and print and neatly lettered in green and gold.'

[3736*c* (iii)] COLBURN'S NAVAL AND MILITARY LIBRARY OF ENTERTAINMENT

On p. 115 above reference was made to the disappearance from 'Colburn's Modern Novelists' of Gleig's book *The Chelsea Pensioners*. This disappearance is explained by its having been transferred to a series formed on identical lines to those adopted for 'Irish National Tales'; entitled THE NAVAL AND MILITARY LIBRARY OF ENTERTAINMENT; advertised as a 'Monthly Library' in August 1834; and thus described:

'A Series of the Choicest Modern Works from the pens of Distinguished Officers; forming a desirable acquisition to every mess and gun-room at home or abroad. Now completed in twenty volumes:

The Naval Officer [Marryat], 3 vols.
Sailors and Saints [Glascock], 3 vols.
Tales of Military Life by the author of *The Military Sketch Book*, 3 vols.
The Chelsea Pensioners [Gleig], 3 vols.
Tales of a Voyager, 1st series [R. P. Gillies], 3 vols.
Tales of a Voyager, 2nd series [R. P. Gillies], 3 vols.
The Night Watch.'

I believe the volumes in this 'Library' were uniform with its predecessors, but with *blue* labels lettered in gold. One may be forgiven a smile at the mobilisation of poor R. P. Gillies—antiquary and poet—among 'distinguished officers'. [*3736 c* (iii)]

THE NEW BRITISH NOVELIST [3736 *c* (iv)]

One further Colburnesque ingenuity remains to be recorded. Chronologically it should precede the three ventures just described, because, although undated, its series title is imprinted 'Colburn and Bentley' and not 'Colburn' alone. But as I have only seen one specimen anywhere and cannot give any further titles of novels included, it may serve as postscript to this brief summary of the refurbishing experiments of the prototype of all book-trade refurbishers.

Mary Shelley's *Fortunes of Perkin Warbeck* first appeared in 3 vols. in 1830. I have seen a copy with a new undated series title inserted before the original first edition title in each volume, headed: THE NEW BRITISH NOVELIST. IN 50 VOLUMES, 25 GUINEAS, and going on to give the title of Mary Shelley's book, which represents Vols. VII, VIII and IX of the series. The books were in half-cloth boards and the treatment of the spines was very curious. The original *Perkin Warbeck* labels were pasted at the *base* of each spine, while at the head was the new series label, worded as above. No indication was given of other novels forming part of the series.

D. STEALING BENTLEY'S THUNDER: COLBURN'S 'MODERN' AND 'MODERN STANDARD' NOVELISTS (small 8vo Series and Part Issue) [3736 *d*]

In the late summer of 1832 Colburn dissolved partnership with Bentley. By the terms of the agreement he went personally out of publishing, and undertook never again to publish within twenty miles of London.* But he retained a number of his more valuable copyrights and even, though himself in the background, continued active to the extent of launching several new ventures through Bentley's agency. It must remain one of the puzzles of publishing history why he was able to use the machinery of a man with whom he had quarrelled in order to market books which were directly in competition with some of Bentley's own publications.

Not the least striking of these frankly competitive Colburnisms was the series started in January 1835, and described in one advertisement as a 'New and Improved Edition of Colburn's Modern Novelists. Uniform in size and format with the Waverley Novels.' This announcement went on to state that 'each novel will be completed, whenever possible, in a single volume, with corrections and occasional Notes by the several Authors expressly made for this edition'.

Another advance advertisement read as follows:

'On 1st Jan. 1835 will be published, to be continued Monthly, beautifully printed and embellished, price 5*s*. per volume, neatly bound, Vol. I of PELHAM...being the commencement of a new, revised, handsomely illustrated and more select Collection of COLBURN'S MODERN NOVELISTS....A volume of this work (the copyrights of which are the exclusive property of Mr Colburn) will be regularly published with the Magazines on the first of every month.'

The books were pocket size, bound in grey-purple ribbon embossed cloth, gilt-lettered; had engraved frontispieces and titles and were published at 5*s*. per volume. The imprint on the first issue of Vols. I–X of the series read: *Pl. 10*

Published for Henry Colburn (no address) by R. Bentley, London;
Bell & Bradfute, Edinburgh; John Cumming, Dublin; etc.

Vols. XI–XII show 'Great Marlborough Street' very small after 'Colburn' but continue to mention Bentley. Vols. XIII–XVI show similar 'Great Marlborough Street' but omit Bentley altogether. From Vols. XVII–XX Colburn's new address is larger and Bentley continuously absent.

It will be observed that the novels chosen were, with one or two exceptions, precisely those with which Colburn had launched his earlier 8vo series. His energy as an exploiter of copyrights would even to-day command the trade's rueful respect.

* Actually his exile (to Windsor) only lasted about four years. In the autumn of 1836 he paid Bentley a fine of £1000 to be released from banishment and reappeared in London with offices in Great Marlborough Street.

COLBURN'S MODERN NOVELISTS

[3736d] COLBURN'S MODERN NOVELISTS (small 8vo) imitated their Bentley prototypes to a degree which makes the presence of Bentley's name on a number of their titles more of an enigma than ever. The engravings, the style of printing, the promise of 'corrections and occasional notes'—all these are blandly appropriated, yet announced as pioneering achievements special to the new series. Once again strict punctuality marks the early volumes; once again dates drag out and progress becomes vague and spasmodic, as the venture falls short of Colburn's hopes or as his volatile attention turns to something else.

Bentley, billed though he was as publisher of the opening volumes of the series, was quick to retaliate on this obvious attempt to steal his thunder. In February 1835 he came out with advertisements of his own Standard Novels, pointing out that it was all very well for Colburn to boast of volumes at five shillings each and promise a novel a volume 'whenever possible'. The fact remained that his first title—*Pelham*—filled two volumes, and could therefore only be bought for ten shillings. Bentley's Standard Novels, on the other hand, though priced at six shillings each, only very occasionally over-ran the single-volume limit,* and in several cases contained more than one fiction per volume.

Colburn's reply was a little over-prompt and he was forced to recede from a position too rashly occupied. In April 1835 he published a full-page advertisement in the *Quarterly*, still under-cutting Bentley's price by one shilling (i.e. promising his series at five shillings each), but undertaking to publish novels complete in one volume. He went on to stress the importance of cheap editions from a publisher who 'having had the good fortune to publish during the last twenty years a very large proportion of the most masterly and popular works in the department of fiction, is obviously placed in the most favourable position for an undertaking etc. etc.' To give effect to his promise he proceeded to bind up in one volume such novels as had hitherto appeared in two, i.e. *Pelham* and *Tremaine*. This he did without any attempt at disguise, neither refoliating nor omitting the embellishments to the previous second volumes.†

For a short while he stuck to his new policy, treated *Brambletye House* and *The Disowned* as he had treated *Pelham* and *Tremaine* (they appeared both in two volumes and two-volumes-in-one), and thereafter genuinely issued texts in one volume only. But during 1836 he found that at five shillings the game was not worth the candle, and he raised the price of the whole series to six shillings per volume. Simultaneously (in order to give Bentley something fresh to think about) he changed the series name to 'Colburn's Modern *Standard* Novelists'—with an emphasis on the 'Standard'. There is reason to suspect that, in order to maintain the policy of one-novel-one-volume, he sometimes enforced abridgements on his authors but omitted to record the fact on the books themselves. At any rate, in June 1839 he wrote to Horace Smith, asking that the text of *Zillah* be *still further abridged*, for issue in a single six-shilling volume. No suggestion of abridgement is made anywhere in the book, which appeared in October 1839 as No. 18 in the series.

Details of the volumes published in the series—both as to date of issue and significance of textual content—are given in the schedule which terminates this section. It remains for the physical features of the series, and its variant bindings, to be briefly described.

Binding A (1835). The original series title was, as has been seen: COLBURN'S MODERN NOVELISTS, and the first issue of, at any rate, the majority of the 20 volumes issued, carried those words, gold-lettered and framed, at the top of the spines, as well as the number of the volume in the series and the
Pl. 10 title of the book. The volumes were bound in grey-purple ribbon-embossed cloth, with pale yellow end-papers. Inasmuch, however, as Colburn changed his series title (probably late in 1836) to MODERN STANDARD NOVELISTS and, when further binding-up was required, altered his spine-wording accordingly, it is possible that the later volumes in the series never appeared at all as 'Modern' Novelists. The latest one I have seen with 'Modern' on the spine is No. 16 (published January 1839) and that is late enough to be curious.

Binding B (1835–1836). Dark green morocco cloth, black paper label lettered in gold. This issue was bound from the weekly numbers (see below) and combined the original two-volume editions in one cover with double volume numbers on the spine-labels. The series is still called 'Colburn's Modern Novelists'. The only title in this binding which I have seen is Bulwer's *Disowned* (Weekly Numbers VII–XII, but Vols. 8 and 9).

* To this date Bentley had published 46 titles, contained in 44 volumes.

† Later, probably in the early forties, he refoliated throughout so that one-volume issues ran uninterruptedly from page one to the end. Engravings belonging to second volumes disappeared.

Binding C (? late 1836). This third issue is uniform in style with the first, but the spine reads: COLBURN'S STANDARD NOVELISTS. *[3736d]* *Pl. 10*

Binding CC. Fourth came what would appear a transitional style—similar as to cloth and colour with C, with wording 'Standard Novels' (not 'Novelists'), but lacking any volume number in the series. This I have only seen on a copy of No. 17, and there is no method of establishing the date at which it was used, for how long or on how many titles.

Binding D. The purpose of this variant I cannot explain (unless it were prepared for continental sale), and the date can only be inferred from the fact that the two volumes seen were both dated 1836. The books were closely cut all round to a small squarish format, bound in grey-purple ribbon-embossed cloth (very similar to that used for A and B), and labelled with black paper labels, gold-lettered: COLBURN'S / MODERN / NOVELISTS / VOL. I etc. The examples noted in this style were Vols. III and XII (*O'Donnel* and *Devereux*), both with engraved frontispieces and titles and printed titles dated 1836. No series title or numbering survived inside the volumes, although the labels were numbered. Presumably 12 volumes at least appeared in this style.

Binding E. Two further styles exist, both belonging to the liquidation period, when all series numbering had been dropped and prices reduced. The earlier is of scarlet cloth, with gold-blocked scroll-work on the spine. The volumes contain no printed titles, so that the only dates available are those on the engraved frontispieces. As these were printed from the original plates and (in characteristic contrast to Bentley's more scrupulous practice) only occasionally altered, they are worthless as evidence. I would, however, ascribe style D to 1847/1848. Almost certainly it marked a reduction in the price of the volumes to 3*s.* 6*d.* each—a result of competition from *The Parlour Library.* *Pl. 10*

Binding F. The final style of Colburn's series is, oddly enough, the most attractive of the lot. Finely ribbed cloth of a pleasant shade of green is agreeably lettered and restrainedly ornamented.* It should be noted that the series title now reads: COLBURN'S STANDARD NOVELS (not 'Novelists'). This style, which may have been introduced in the early forties, was certainly still in use in 1848, for although the titles previously included in the series are as devoid of reliable dates as when clothed in E, there were added a few new ones, two of which had titles dated 1848. *Pl. 10*

In 1850 Colburn sold the whole series to Tegg and in my experience the majority of books in F show Tegg ownership in one way or another. But not all; for such new titles as preceded the sale of the series had a Colburn imprint on their printed titles.

Tegg continued to publish what were outwardly COLBURN'S STANDARD NOVELS, but he put his own printed end-papers into existing volumes, when he had to bind up again, and added a few titles of his own, which he provided with printed titles bearing his own imprint. Of what may be called posthumous titles in the series (i.e. titles added after the final price-reduction by Colburn or Tegg) I know only of five, which can hardly be a complete list.

They are (the dates in brackets are those of the first editions):

Imprint—Colburn:	**The Wild Irish Girl**	(Lady Morgan)	? 1846 (1806)
,,	**Emilia Wyndham**	(Mrs Marsh)	Feb. 1848 (1846)
,,	**Mrs Armytage**	(Mrs Gore)	April 1848 (1836)
Imprint—Tegg:	**Angela**	(Mrs Marsh)	1850 (1848)
,,	**The Lake of Killarney**	(A. M. Porter)	1853 (1804)

COLBURN'S MODERN NOVELISTS: A COMPLETE LIST **[3736*e*]**
(later—COLBURN'S MODERN STANDARD NOVELISTS)

As in the schedule of BENTLEY'S STANDARD NOVELS (see above, p. 100), titles set in capitals have textual importance. Colburn being what he was, I have not taken at face value the phrase 'Revised Edition' which appears (as though automatically) on each preliminary fly-title. I have only credited a volume with qualities special to itself when such qualities are unmistakably present.

* The scroll-blocking on the spine is virtually identical with that used by Longmans in 1840 for their ten-volume collected edition of Moore's Poetical Works.

COLBURN'S MODERN NOVELISTS

[3736e] It will be seen that interest of the series is much inferior to that of Bentley's Standard Novels. Even among the volumes containing actual new material, only those by Bulwer provide matter of real importance. Bulwer was always ready with new Prefaces and other marginalia, so that Colburn would have been able to arrange without much trouble to himself that Bulwer titles at any rate should offer 'material peculiar to this edition'.

Once again I have not risked typographical confusion by indicating which titles are in the Collection and which not. The series is well represented so far as are concerned volumes with new material, but several of the others are not present in first issue.

No.	Title	Author	Date	Year	Orig.	Notes
1 2	PELHAM . . .	Bulwer	Jan. Feb.	1835 1835	(1827)	Contains a new Preface (8 pp.), Various Notes, and the preliminary sketch for the novel: *Mortimer, or Memoirs of a Gentleman*, written in 1824 but now first printed
3	O'DONNEL . . .	Lady Morgan	March	1835	(1814)	Contains a new Preface (4 pp.)
4 5	Tremaine . . .	Plumer Ward	April May	1835 1835	(1825)	
6 7	BRAMBLETYE HOUSE .	Smith	June July	1835 1835	(1826)	Contains a new Preface (4 pp.) which is interesting as it speaks in the warmest terms of the author's generous treatment at the hands of Colburn
8 9	DISOWNED . . .	Bulwer	Aug. Sept.	1835 1835	(1829)	Contains an Essay (16 pp.) 'On the Different Kinds of Prose Fiction. With some Apology for the Fictions of the Author. (Prefixed first to this edition, 1835)'
10	Frank Mildmay . .	Marryat	Dec.	1835	(1829)	
11	GRANBY . . .	Lister	(?) Jan.	1836*	(1826)	Contains a new Preface (4 pp.) explaining why the novel could not have been imitated from *Matilda* by Lord Normanby as, apparently, was widely suggested at the time of its first appearance
12	DEVEREUX . . .	Bulwer	Feb.	1836	(1829)	Contains Dedicatory Epistle to John Auldjo, dated Dec. 12, 1835 and not previously printed
13	Sayings and Doings. 1st Series	Hook	June	1836	(1824)	
14	,, ,, 2nd ,,	Hook		1838	(1825)	No month given on dated front. and vignette title
15	,, ,, 3rd Series	Hook	(Spring)	1839	(1828)	Not actually published till after No. 16. A note facing p. 1 of text of the latter apologises for the delay, due to engravings not being ready
16	Florence Macarthy . .	Lady Morgan	Jan.	1839	(1818)	
17	Richelieu . . .	James	March	1839	(1829)	
18	Zillah . . .	Smith	Oct.	1839	(1828)	
19	CHELSEA PENSIONERS .	Gleig	(late)	1840	(1829)	Contains a new Preface (4 pp.) dated Oct. 1840, stating the proportions of fact and fiction in the stories which make up the book
20	Gurney Married† . .	Hook		1842	(1838)	

* Although the engraved frontispiece is dated 'Nov. 1835', the printed title is dated 1836.

† This novel—a sequel without its leader—was obviously hurried into the series because Bentley, having secured the copyright of *Gilbert Gurney* from Whittaker, had published it in his Standard Novel Series in Sept. 1841. Colburn watched his former partner's activities with flattering assiduity.

PART ISSUE OF COLBURN'S MODERN NOVELISTS [3736*e* (i)]

Pl. 11

That COLBURN'S MODERN NOVELISTS were re-issued from October 10, 1835 (or at any rate partially re-issued) in Shilling Weekly Numbers may be stale news to persons better informed than I. But I confess that the discovery of Nos. I–XXIV and XLI–XLV astounded me. No trace of a Part Issue had appeared in such advertisements as I had seen, nor does the Bentley Catalogue make any mention of one. It seemed contrary to all likelihood that a cheap-novel series, designed to compete with Bentley's Standard Novels, should have been published in parts. Yet there the parts were—and are—and I should welcome any information as to later numbers than those here described.

Binding. Buff paper wrappers, printed in black. On front cover: [No. I] *To be continued in Weekly Numbers* [Oct. 10 (1835)] / *top of double frame* / NEW LIBRARY OF ENTERTAINMENT. / *short rule* / COLBURN'S / MODERN NOVELISTS; / A SELECT COLLECTION OF / THE BEST WORKS OF FICTION / OF THE MOST DISTINGUISHED / LIVING ENGLISH WRITERS, / WITH PORTRAITS OF THE AUTHORS, AND OTHER ILLUSTRATIONS. / *long rule* / 'A truly popular undertaking. The series so got up and embellished, and so cheap, / must extend the fame even of the author of "Pelham".' *Literary Gazette.* / *short rule* / No. I. / *Price One Shilling.* / *short rule* / PELHAM; / OR, / THE ADVENTURES OF A GENTLEMAN. / BY E. L. BULWER, ESQ. / TO BE COMPLETED IN SIX NUMBERS, / EMBELLISHED WITH A PORTRAIT AND THREE OTHER PLATES, / BY FINDEN. / *long rule* / LONDON: / PUBLISHED FOR HENRY COLBURN, / BY R. BENTLEY; BELL AND BRADFUTE, EDINBURGH; JOHN CUMMING,/ DUBLIN; AND SOLD BY ALL BOOKSELLERS.

Spine up-lettered: COLBURN'S MODERN NOVELISTS.—NO. I, etc. Back wrapper printed with praise of the series, or announcements of forthcoming titles, or disputatious references to Bentley. Inside front and back covers plain.

An attractive feature is the inclusion, with the final part of each novel, of a black paper label lettered in gold. Buyers are informed that they can obtain the green cloth morocco case for sixpence (style B above) and have their material for cloth-binding complete.

The actual numbers in the Collection (the only ones I have seen), and a few which can be assumed to have appeared, are as follows:

I–VI	**Pelham**
VII–XII	**Disowned**
XIII–XVII	**Frank Mildmay**
XVIII–XXIII	**Brambletye House**
XXIV–[XXIX]	**Tremaine** (Nos. XXV-XXIX missing)
[XXX–XL]	**O'Donnel** and **Granby** (missing)
XLI–XLV	**Devereux** (stated on wrappers to be completed in six numbers but actually complete in five)

Notes. Incidental wrapper variants and advertisement material in the twenty-nine numbers available for examination have considerable interest and are therefore briefly set out.

Wrapper variants:

(i) The date of issue ('Oct. 10' on No. I) falls out altogether from No. II to No. XII inclusive but reappears 'Jan. 2, 1836' on No. XIII. For three numbers hereafter the correct date persists, but from No. XVI (in the middle of *Frank Mildmay*) it again disappears and is no more seen.

(ii) From No. IV onward the address: '13 Great Marlborough Street', appears over Colburn's name on front covers.

(iii) From No. V onward 'Distinguished Living English Writers' becomes 'Distinguished English Writers'.

(iv) From No. IX onward an agent for Manchester, Liverpool, Leeds and Birmingham is added to the imprint.

Advertisement material on back wrappers:

Nos. I and II. Blurb of the Part Issue, dated October 1835 and headed 'Diffusion of Entertaining Knowledge'.

No. III. Press commendations. Same heading.

[*3736e*(i)] No. IV. Advert. of Las Cases' *Emperor Napoleon.*

Nos. V, VI. Note *re* binding-case and label. Announcement of *Disowned.*

Nos. VII–X. As III.

No. XI. As IV.

No. XII. (*a*) 'Notice to Binder' to cancel the printed title supplied with the first number of *Disowned* on which the novel is stated to form Vols. 3 and 4, and to substitute the new title-page supplied with the present number which describes the novel as Vols. 8 and 9. It is explained that the publisher wishes to retain the original order of issue.

(*b*) Note *re* binding-case as on V, VI.

(*c*) 'Notice to Subscribers.' This begins: 'Mr Bentley having thought proper to issue an advertisement addressed to the Subscribers of these Works and calculated to mislead the Public on the subject of Mr Bulwer's productions, Mr Colburn...begs to notify his intention speedily to issue those remaining works of Mr Bulwer of which he possesses the copyright' etc. etc.

No. XIII. A further 'Notice to Subscribers': 'In consequence of the continued efforts made to divert the attention of Subscribers to Colburn's Novelists from the next work to appear in that Collection, the public are requested to take notice that before issuing any other works of Mr Bulwer's, Mr Colburn has determined to introduce Captain Marryat's *Frank Mildmay.*'

The actual dispute between Bentley and Colburn is obscure, but it is surely extraordinary that the former should act as publisher to a series so openly in competition with himself. Not only were the two novel-series at one another's throats, but Bentley was booming Bourienne's *Napoleon* at precisely the time when Colburn produced the rival work by Las Cases.

The remaining back wrappers, though various, carry no matter of publishing significance.

[3737] BENTLEY, TALES FROM 1859–1860

In comparison with *Tales from Blackwood* (themselves by no means easy to find complete) the short series of *Tales from Bentley* is extremely uncommon. I have never succeeded in acquiring even a specimen of the part issue, and have hardly seen another set of the two book issues in tolerable condition except those described below, of which the second (by sheer bad luck) is imperfect.

It is disappointing to have to leave many anonymities unresolved, but from the usually well-preserved Bentley records the register of Contributors to *Bentley's Miscellany* (from which these tales are reprinted) is missing. Nevertheless, sufficient are evident to give the series status as a 'First Book Edition' of important material.

[3737*a*] (i) **Part Issue.** Published from June 29, 1859 to May 28, 1860 in twelve square fcap 8vo monthly parts at sixpence each, in buff paper wrappers, printed in black—on front, with reduced facsimile of Cruikshank's original cover for *Bentley's Miscellany*; on back, with list of Contents. Wrappers undated—merely Part I and 'Published Monthly' appearing above cover-block. Inside wrappers blank in Parts I–III; printed with adverts. in Parts IV–XII.

Parts I–IV contain alternatively 96 and 84 pp.; Parts V–XI, 96 pp.; Part XII, 92 pp. Each part paginated afresh: pagination not altered for book issue.

[3737*b*] (ii) **First Book Issue.** 4 vols. 1859–1860, each containing 3 parts.

Vol. I (Aug. 26) 1859	Vol. III (Feb. 29) 1860
II (Nov. 30) 1859	IV (May 28) 1860

Pl. 11

Buff canvas, printed in black—on front with ornamental design incorporating title, on back with Contents of volume. Spine up-lettered: TALES FROM 'BENTLEY'—Vol. I [etc.] and across foot of spine: PRICE / EIGHTEEN PENCE. White end-papers.

First State. Vol. measure: case $4\frac{1}{4}'' \times 6\frac{5}{8}''$; sheets $4\frac{1}{8}'' \times 6\frac{3}{8}''$. Top edges uncut, others trimmed.

Second State. Vol. measure: case $4'' \times 6\frac{3}{8}''$; sheets $3\frac{7}{8}'' \times 6\frac{1}{4}''$. All edges cut.

[3737*c*] (iii) **Second Book Issue.** 6 vols. 1865, each containing 2 parts. Blue glazed boards, printed in black—on front as first issue with the addition of the words 'PRICE ONE SHILLING' in tablet at base of design; on back with advertisements. [Vols. I–II: *Uncle Silas*; Vol. III: *Guy Deverell* and *Uncle Silas*; Vol. IV: *Semi-Attached Couple* etc.; Vols. V and VI publishers' list]. Spine up-lettered as first issue.

CONTENTS (based on First Book Issue) *[3737 c]*

Vol. I (*Part I*)

Maxwell, W. H. Terence O'Shaughessy's First Attempt to Get Married

Author of 'Tales of an Antiquary' [**Richard Thomson**]. Plunder Creek 1783. A Legend of New York

Author of 'Rattlin the Reefer' [**Hon. Ed. Howard**]. The Marine Ghost

Author of 'Headlong Hall' [**T. L. Peacock**]. Recollections of Childhood

Vol. I (*Part II*)

'T. C. D.' [**William Maginn**]. The Two Butlers of Kilkenny

'Dalton' [**Rev. R. H. Dalton Barham**]. A Tale of Grammarye (Ballad)

'L.' Richie Barter: The Man Who Should but Did Not

Maxwell, W. H. The Devil and Johnny Dixon

Mayhew, Edward. The Good for Nothing

Inman, G. E. Old Morgan at Panama (Ballad)

Vol. I. (*Part III*)

Trollope, Frances. The Patron King

McTeague, P. The Spalpeen

Wade, J. A. Paddy Blake's Echo (Ballad)

Vol. II (*Part IV*)

Author of 'The Spalpeen' [**P. McTeague**]. The Herdsman

Jones, William. The Monks of Old (Ballad)

Napier, Sir W. Griffone: a Tale of the Peninsular War

Longfellow, H. W. The Reaper and the Flowers (Ballad)

Vol. II (*Part V*)

Anon [**Michael Burke Honan**]. A Marine's Courtship

Inman, G. E. Haroun Alraschid (Ballad)

'S. Y.' What Tom Binks did when he didn't know what to do with himself

Medwin, Capt. Mascalbruni

Vol. II (*Part VI*)

Reynolds, John Hamilton. Greenwich and Greenwich Men

Anon. The Abbot's Oak (verse)

Vol. II (*Part VI*) *cont.*

McTeague, P. Worthy Flaherty

Anon. England's Queen (Ode)

Anon [**? Baroness Tautphoeus**]. The Innkeeper of Andermatt

Gore, Mrs. National Song

Vol. III (*Part VII*)

McTeague, P. Father Mathew

'Bon Gaultier' [**Theodore Martin and W. E. Aytoun**]. The Double-Bedded Room

Anon. The Handsome Clear Starcher (Ballad)

Medwin, Capt. The Contrabandista

Anon. Marie de Villemare

Vol. III (*Part VIII*)

Anon. Bonomye the Usurer

Medwin, Capt. Pasquale: a Tale of Italy

Anon. The Man in the Spanish Cloak

Vol. III (*Part IX*)

'Father Prout' [**Rev. Francis Mahony**]. Les Poissons d'Avril

McTeague, P. Irish Invention

Anon. Scenes in the Life of a Gambler

'H. J. M.' The Deathbed Confession

'H. H.' Mrs Jennings

Vol. IV (*Part X*)

Wade, J. A. Darby the Swift

Blake, Marmaduke. An Excellent Offer

Medwin, Capt. The Quarantine

Vol. IV (*Part XI*)

Author of 'The Mountain Decameron' [**Joseph Downes**]. The Father

Anon. Richelieu or the Conspiracy (parody of Bulwer Lytton)

Sheehan, John. Paddy Flynn: or the Miseries of Dining Out

Author of 'The Subaltern' [**Rev. C. R. Gleig**]. The Phantom Funeral

Anon. The Duel

Vol. IV (*Part XII*)

Whitehead, Chas. Narrative of John Ward Gibson

Note. The set of the First Book Issue in the Collection is in the First State and has book-plate of John Browne in each volume and booksellers' ticket: 'Mann Nephews, Cornhill', inside front cover of Vol. I.

The set of the Second Book Issue, by an unfortunate coincidence, was misboarded. Vol. I contains the title-page and contents of Vol. II. These are repeated in Vol. II. The spines of Vols. II, III and VI are chipped, but otherwise the set is in unread condition.

[3738] BLACKWOOD'S STANDARD NOVELS 1841–1843, 1867–1868

This series has little textual importance, for the titles are all straight reprints, apart possibly from *Valerius* which is described as 'Revised'. But the original issue is scrupulously carried out and, among the various Standard Novel Series, ranks second after Bentley's for integrity and care.

[3738 *a*] *Pl. 12* I. **Original Issue.** 1841–1843. Fcap 8vo. Very dark green fine-ripple-grain cloth, blocked in blind on front and back, blind-banded on spine and gold-lettered BLACKWOOD'S / STANDARD NOVELS / *rule* / and title of book. Yellow end-papers.

Published monthly at six shillings. Series title, with number in series, precedes printed title. Steel-engraved front. to each volume.

1 **Annals of the Parish** and **The Ayrshire Legatees**, by John Galt 1841. Portrait front. and Memoir of Galt by D. M. Moir, pp. (i)–cxiii. Also 'Illustrations, Anecdotes and Critical Remarks' (probably edited by Moir), pp. 299–321.

2 **Sir Andrew Wylie of that Ilk,** by John Galt 1841. Front. after Alex. Fraser. 'Illustrations' etc., pp. (461)–467

3 **Tom Cringle's Log,** by Michael Scott 1842. Front. after Clarkson Stanfield. Prefatory Notice, unsigned, pp. (vii) viii

4 **The Provost and Other Tales,** by John Galt 1842. Front. after Alex. Fraser. 'Illustrations' etc., pp. (363)–390 The 'Other Tales' are *The Steamboat* and *The Omen.*

5 **Youth and Manhood of Cyril Thornton** (by Thomas Hamilton) 1842. Front. after James E. Lauder.

6 **The Entail,** by John Galt 1842. Front. after Alex. Fraser. 'Illustrations' etc. signed △ (i.e. D. M. Moir), pp. (399)–409

7 **Valerius: a Roman Story** (by J. G. Lockhart) 1842. Front. after W. L. Leitch. Described as 'A New Edition, Revised'.

8 **The Cruise of the Midge,** by Michael Scott 1842. Front. anon, engraved by Lightfoot.

9 **Pen Owen** (by Dean Hook) 1842. Front. after J. E. Lauder.

10 **Reginald Dalton,** by the author of 'Valerius' 1842. Front. after W. L. Leitch.

11 **Adam Blair** and **Matthew Wald,** by the author of 'Valerius' and 'Reginald Dalton' 1843. Front. after W. L. Leitch.

[? 12 **Percy Mallory,** by Dean Hook.] Announced, but never seen by me, nor included in later lists for re-issue.

[3738 *b*] *Pl. 12* II. **Second Issue, 1845.** Very dark brown fine-ribbed cloth, blocked in blind and gold-lettered on spine with title of book only. From this issue the series titles and fronts. are omitted. I have only seen Nos. 3 and 8 in this binding.

[3738 *c*] III. **Third Issue (with additional titles). 1867–1868.** This issue appeared concurrently in cloth at 2*s*. 6*d*. or 1*s*. 6*d*. and boards at 2*s*. or 1*s*. The cloth style is red-brown sand grain, gold-lettered on spine with title, author and 'Blackwood's Standard Novels' at foot. End-papers printed with adverts.

Pl. 12 The board style is pale green or white pictorial boards, with series name on front cover and spine, and in most cases the words FLORIN SERIES on front cover. Back cover and end-papers printed with adverts.

Several new titles were added to the series for this issue. The following is a list of the Third Issue titles in the Collection, to which are added the titles not represented.

Old Titles

Tom Cringle's Log. 'The Only Complete Edition. Copyright.' Cloth, n.d.
Cruise of the Midge. Cloth, 1868; Boards 1867.
Annals of the Parish. Boards, n.d.
The Provost. Cloth, 1868.
The Entail. Boards, n.d.
Valerius. Cloth, n.d.

New Titles

Salem Chapel (by Mrs Oliphant). Boards, n.d.
The Perpetual Curate (by Mrs Oliphant). Boards, n.d.
Miss Marjoribanks (by Mrs Oliphant). Boards, n.d.

Missing from the Collection are the following old titles: *Cyril Thornton*: *Sir Andrew Wylie*: *Reginald Dalton*: *Pen Owen*: *Adam Blair*. Also the following new ones: **Lady Lee's Widowhood** (Hamley): **The Rector** and **John** (Oliphant): **Miss Molly** (Butt): **Two Years Abaft the Mast** (Symondson): **Mansie Wauch** (Moir): **Peninsular Scenes** (Hardman): **Sir Frizzle Pumpkin** (anon): **The Subaltern** (Gleig): **Life in the Far West** (Ruxton). [3738 *d*]

IV. **Fourth Issue.** Smooth scarlet cloth, printed in black, n.d. I have only seen one title: *Reginald Dalton*, in this style, which has all the appearance of a remainder cloth.

BLACKWOOD, TALES FROM 1858–1861, 1879–1881, 1889–1890 [3739]

In relation to this series and to TALES FROM BENTLEY (see above) an interesting parallel could be drawn between the history and activities of the Edinburgh firm of Blackwood and the London firm of Bentley. Both were founded by shrewd and upright, yet rather pugnacious and sometimes tactless men, who came into book-publishing—Blackwood from bookselling, Bentley from printing. Both took a place in the front rank of their profession under the auspices of the second generation—Blackwood under the founder's sixth son John, Bentley under the founder's only son George. John Blackwood and George Bentley had individually much in common. Each combined business sense with acute literary taste; each made lasting personal friendships with authors, while keeping the necessary balance between the interests of both parties—interests so often identical, yet so liable to be suddenly opposed.

And the lists of the two firms, as well as the men in charge, had many similarities. They showed the same sort of mixture of non-fiction and fiction titles, the same ambition to excel in 'quality-popularity'—that is to say, to find good specimens of the sort of books the general public like, and to eschew, on the one hand discreditable rubbish, on the other highbrow experiments. Further, each firm made skilful use of a magazine ('*Maga*' in Blackwood's case; *Bentley's Miscellany* and *Temple Bar* in Bentley's) to recruit the sort of authors they wanted to publish. Finally, each published two precisely analogous series, dividing the honours of invention.

London led off in 1831 with BENTLEY'S STANDARD NOVELS—a landmark in the history of cheap-edition publishing. Not until ten years later did Edinburgh follow suit with what proved to be a much shorter series, but one planned and produced with equal care. Then in 1858 Blackwood turned the tables. He had the idea of collecting in successive volumes at a low price selected stories from '*Maga*', and TALES FROM BLACKWOOD were duly launched. Bentley was on his heels within twelve months. TALES FROM BENTLEY appeared in 1859, and once again the second in the field was the first to leave it. Just as BLACKWOOD'S STANDARD NOVELS only ran to fourteen titles over a period of twenty-five years as against Bentley's 136 titles in thirty-one years, so TALES FROM BENTLEY only ran to twelve parts in four volumes in two years as against TALES FROM BLACKWOOD's seventy-two parts and thirty volumes over a period of thirty-two years.

FIRST SERIES [1858–1861] [3739 *a* (i)]

I. **Part Issue.** Published from (I think) June 1858 to March 1861 in 36 fcap 8vo monthly numbers at sixpence each. Terra-cotta paper wrappers, printed in black—on front: TALES FROM 'BLACKWOOD'. / [*top of single frame*] / [*List of Contents*] / [*short rule*] / ORIGINALLY PUBLISHED IN BLACKWOOD'S MAGAZINE / [*short rule*] / [*imprint*] / [*bottom of frame*] / Price Sixpence. No. 1 (2, 3 etc.). On spine up-lettered; on back printed with adverts. Inside covers printed. Tops and fore edges uncut, tails trimmed. No date appears anywhere. Each part contains about 100 pages and is paginated afresh. The pagination was not altered for book issue. *Pl. 11*

[3739*a* (ii)] II. **Book Issue.** Published in 12 quarterly volumes at one shilling and sixpence each.

First Binding. Terra-cotta ripple-grain cloth, printed in black on front with series title, volume number and price, divided by bands and in decorative frame; printed in black on back with Contents of vol. and same decorative frame. White end-papers. Top edges uncut, others cut. The prelims. consist of a blank or an advertisement leaf and an undated title, bearing List of Contents.

Note. The volumes were advertised as 'also issued half bound and in red morocco', but I have never seen either style.

Second Binding. Very dark purple-brown fine morocco cloth, plain sides, gold-lettered on spine with series title, volume number and imprint. Black end-papers.

Third Binding. Uniform with the book issue of Third Series (3739*c* (ii) below).

Note. The Collection contains only one part (No. 1) of the Part Issue. The set of volumes in first binding has book-plate of John Browne in each volume and booksellers' ticket: 'Mann Nephews, Cornhill', in Vol. I. The set in second binding has no evidence of earlier ownership. No set in third binding is included.

SECOND SERIES [1879–1881]

[3739*b* (i)] *Pl. 11* I. **Part Issue.** Published from December 1879 to February 1881 in 24 fcap 8vo monthly numbers at one shilling each. Terra-cotta paper wrappers printed in black—on front with: PUBLISHED MONTHLY / [*top of decorative frame*] / NEW SERIES / [*short rule*] / TALES / FROM / 'BLACKWOOD'. No. I [II, III etc.] / [*List of Contents*] / [*imprint*] / [*bottom of frame*] / PRICE ONE SHILLING incorporated in the design; on spine up-lettered; on back printed with adverts. Inside covers printed. All edges uncut. No date appears anywhere. Each part contains about 180 pp. and is paginated afresh. The pagination was not altered for book issue.

[3739*b* (ii)] II. **Book Issue.** Published in 1881 in 12 volumes, each containing two parts, at half a crown.

First binding. Crimson diagonal-fine-ribbed cloth, blocked on front in black and gold with series title, medallion and decoration, on back in blind, on spine in black and gold with series title, volume number and publishers' monogram. Dark chocolate end-papers. Top edges uncut, other edges cut. The prelims. consist of undated title-page and leaf bearing List of Contents.

Note. The volumes were advertised as 'also to be had in half calf, half morocco, and roxburghe', but I have never seen a specimen of these styles.

Second binding. Uniform with the book issue of Third Series (3739*c* (ii) below).

Note. Neither the set of parts nor the set of volumes in the Collection has evidence of former ownership.

THIRD SERIES [1889–1890]

[3739*c* (i)] I. **Part Issue.** Published in 12 fcap 8vo monthly numbers at one shilling each. Scarlet morocco paper wrappers, cut flush, printed in dark green—on front with all-over design incorporating: THIRD SERIES, series title, number of part, contents and imprint; on spine up-lettered; on back printed with adverts. Inside covers printed. All edges cut. No date appears anywhere. Each part contains about 200 pages and the parts are paginated in couples, each alternate part beginning p. 1. Consequently the volumes of the book issue, with two parts to a volume, are continuously paginated.

[3739*c* (ii)] II. **Book Issue.** Published in 1890 in 6 volumes, each containing two parts, at half a crown. Greenish-ochre diagonal-fine-ribbed cloth, blocked in dark brown and gold uniform with Second Series. Dark chocolate end-papers. The prelims. (which were included in alternate parts) consist of undated title and leaf bearing List of Contents.

After the appearance of the Third Series, this binding was used retrospectively on Series One and Two.

Note. The set of parts in the Collection bears no evidence of former ownership. The set of volumes have the book-plate of James J. Joicey.

CONTENTS

I owe to the courtesy of the late Mr George W. Blackwood the names of nearly all the anonymous contributors to the three series of *Tales from Blackwood*, and wish here to make grateful acknowledgement of his kindness and trouble. The schedule of authors is an impressive one; and a series, one volume of which is the first book edition of Bulwer Lytton's *Haunted and the Haunters*, while others claim similar rank in the bibliographies of Charles Lever, Anthony Trollope, William Maginn, J. G. Lockhart and Mrs Oliphant, deserves its place in any collection of front-rank Victorian 'firsts'.

FIRST SERIES [3739*a* (ii)]

(The material here collected appeared in 'Maga' between 1821 and 1859)

Vol. I.
W. E. AYTOUN. The Glenmutchkin Railway
Anon. Vanderdecken's Message Home
Anon. The Floating Beacon
[Frederick Hardman.] Colonna, the Painter
J. G. LOCKHART. Napoleon (a poem)
GEN. SIR E. B. HAMLEY. Legend of Gibraltar
WILLIAM MUDFORD. The Iron Shroud

Vol. II.
GEN. SIR E. B. HAMLEY. Lazaro's Legacy
WILLIAM MAGINN. A Story without a Tail
Anon. Enchanter Faustus and Queen Elizabeth
W. E. AYTOUN. How I became a Yeoman
MRS SOUTHEY. Devereux Hall
ROBERT MACNISH. The Metempsychosis
[Rev. W. Lucas Collins.] College Theatricals

Vol. III.
[Rev. W. Lucas Collins.] A Reading Party in the Long Vacation
[SIR SAMUEL FERGUSON]. Father Tom and the Pope or A Night at the Vatican
MRS SOUTHEY. La Petite Madelaine
WILLIAM MAGINN. Bob Burke's Duel with Ensign Brady
[Frederick Hardman.] The Headsman
JOHN GALT. The Wearyful Woman

Vol. IV.
W. E. AYTOUN. How I Stood for the Dreepdaily Burghs
WITHAM MUDFORD. First and Last
[Frederick Hardman.] The Duke's Dilemma
[J. F. Dalton.] The Old Gentleman's Teetotum
Anon. 'Woe to us' etc. (poem)
[Rev. W. Lucas Collins.] My College Friends: (i) Charles Russell, the Gentleman Commoner
JOHN HUGHES. The Magic Lay

Vol. V.
FREDERICK HARDMAN. Adventures in Texas
W. E. AYTOUN. How we got possession of the Tuileries
J. G. LOCKHART. Captain Paton's Lament (poem)
COUNTESS D'ARBOUVILLE. The Village Doctor
JAMES HOGG. A Singular letter from South Africa

Vol. VI.
FREDERICK HARDMAN. My Friend the Dutchman
[Rev. W. Lucas Collins.] My College Friends: (ii) Horace Leicester
W. E. AYTOUN. The Emerald Studs
[Rev. W. Lucas Collins.] My College Friends: (iii) Mr W. Wellington Hurst
FREDERICK HARDMAN. Christine. Trans. from Mad. d'Arbouville
Anon. The Man in the Bell

[*3739a* (ii)] Vol. VII. FREDERICK HARDMAN. My English Acquaintance
THOS. DOUBLEDAY. The Murderer's Last Night
[Rev. James White.] Narration of Herbert Willis, B.D.
[J. Forbes Dalton.] The Wags
[Sir Sam. Ferguson.] The Wet Wooing
[Rev. James White.] Ben-Na-Groich

Vol. VIII. W. E. AYTOUN. The Surveyor's Tale
[Sir Sam. Ferguson.] The Forrest-Race Romance
CHAS. EDWARDS. Dr Vasari
[Frederick Hardman.] Sigismund Fatello
[J. Forbes Dalton.] The Boxes

Vol. IX. [Frederick Hardman.] Rosaura
Anon. Adventure in the North West Territory
[Rev. W. Lucas Collins.] Harry Bolton's Curacy
Anon. The Florida Pirate
[Rev. G. Croly.] The Pandour and his Princess
[J. Forbes Dalton.] The Beauty Draught

Vol. X. [Rev. G. Croly.] Antonio di Carara
Anon. The Fatal Repast
W. CHAS. KENT. The Vision of Cagliostro
[William Mudford.] The First and Last Kiss
FREDERICK HARDMAN. The Smuggler's Leap
[BULWER LYTTON.] The Haunted and the Haunters
[Frederick Hardman.] The Duellists

Vol. XI. [Rev. G. Croly.] The Natolian Story Teller
[William Mudford.] The First and Last Crime: James Morley
[Mrs Oliphant.] John Rintoul
FREDERICK HARDMAN. Major Moss
[Rev. G. Croly.] The Premier and his wife

Vol. XII. [Samuel Warren.] Tickler among the Thieves
[B. Simmons.] The Bridegroom of Barna
[Sir Sam. Ferguson.] The Involuntary Experimentalist
[Rev. J. White.] Lebrun's Lawsuit
[Rev. J. White.] The Snowing-up of Strath Lugas
[Rev. W. Lucas Collins.] A Few words on Social Philosophy

[3739*b* (ii)]

SECOND SERIES

(The material here collected appeared in 'Maga' between 1850 and 1878)

Vol. I. [Laurence Oliphant.] Tender Recollections of Irene MacGillicuddy
L. V. WALFORD. Nan
[Capt. Chas. Hamley.] The Bells of Botreaux
GEN. SIR E. B. HAMLEY. A Recent Confession of an Opium Eater
GEN. SIR E. B. HAMLEY. Shakespeare's Funeral
LAURENCE LOCKHART. A Night with the Volunteers of Strathkinahan
[Julian Sturgis.] The Philosopher's Baby
MRS OLIPHANT. The Secret Chamber

Vol. II. [Gen. Sir George Chesney.] The Battle of Dorking
[Rev. W. Lucas Collins.] Late for the Train
W. E. AYTOUN. The Congress and the Agapedome

LORD NEAVES. Maga's Birthday (poem) [*3739b* (ii)]
R. E. FRANCILLON. Grace Owen's Engagement
W. E. AYTOUN. The Raide of Arnaboll
LORD NEAVES. How to Make a Pedigree (poem)

Vol. III. [H. Carl Schiller.] Who Painted the Great Murillo de la Merced? (signed H. Carl S——)
[Rev. James White.] A Parochial Epic (poem)
[Rev. Thomas Boys.] A Military Adventure in the Pyrenees
ALEX. ALLARDYCE. The Pundraporo Residency
[G. H. Lewes.] Falsely Accused
[Emily Joly.] Witch-Hampton Hall

Vol. IV. [Mrs Oliphant.] A Railway Junction or the Romance of Ladybank
[G. H. Lewes.] Metamorphoses
DOUGLAS CHEAPE. Betsy Brown (poem)
[Gen. Sir E. B. Hamley.] The Last French Hero by 'Alex Sue Sand'
LAURENCE LOCKHART. Unlucky Tim Griffin
[Andrew Wilson.] The Spectre of Milaggio

Vol. V. [Laurence Oliphant.] Autobiography of a Joint Stock Co. Ltd.
L. B. WALFORD. Bee or Beatrix?
[Capt. Claude Clerk.] Night Wanderer of an Afghaun Fort
NORMAN MACLEOD. Ayrshire Curling Song
COL. CHAS. HAMLEY. The Light on the Hearth
[Rev. W. Lucas Collins.] How to Boil Peas
[H. G. Keene.] Clive's Dream before Plassey (poem)

Vol. VI. [Charles Lever.] What I did at Belgrade, by 'Bob Considine'
A. I. SHAND. Wrecked off the Riff Coast
[Laurence Oliphant.] Dollie and the two Smiths
LADY MARGARET MAJENDIE. A Railway Journey
R. E. FRANCILLON. A Dog without a Tail
COL. CHAS. HAMLEY. Wassail

Vol. VII. [Rev. W. Lucas Collins.] Cousin John's Property
W. W. STORY. A Modern Magician
A. ALLARDYCE. Edgar Wayne's Escape
[J. Gladwin Jebb.] The Lost Secret of the Cocos Group
[Mrs Oliphant.] The Two Miss Scudamores
[James White.] Bates's Tom

Vol. VIII. [Rev. James White.] The Devil's Frills
R. E. FRANCILLON. A Story of Eulenburg
[J. H. Hobart.] The Shadow of the Door
[Mrs Wordsworth.] The Wreck of the Strathmore
CHAS. LEVER. Hero Worship and its Dangers
[Emily Joly.] Annie and her Master
[Sir H. Drummond Wolff.] A Feuilleton, by H. D. W.

Vol. IX. PERCY GREG. Guy Neville's Ghost
FREDERICK HARDMAN. The Great Unknown
[C. Milnes Gaskell.] The Easter Trip of Two Ochlophobists
W. E. AYTOUN. Rapping the Question
[J. Roscoe.] My After-Dinner Adventures with Peter Schlemihl
[Laurence Oliphant.] Aunt Ann's Ghost Story
GEORGE MOIR. The Blue Dragoon
EARL OF WINCHELSEA. Lord Hatton (poem)

[*3739b* (ii)] Vol. X.
[Gen. William Hamley.] The Missing Bills
W. B. CHEADLE. My Hunt of the Silver Fox
GEORGE SKENE. Narrative of Prince Charlie's Escape, transcribed
[Rev. W. Lucas Collins.] A Fenian Alarm
RUDOLPH LINDAU. The Philosopher's Pendulum
L. B. WALFORD. Lady Adelaide
[Mrs Oliphant.] Witchley Ways
[Charles Lever.] How Frank Thornton was Cured, by 'Bob Considine'
ANNE L. WALKER. In Life and in Death
[Rev. James White.] A Cause Worth Trying

Vol. XI.
[J. Gladwyn Jebb.] The Haunted Enghenio
MARGARET VELEY. Milly's First Love
[G. H. Lewes.] Mrs Beauchamp's Vengeance
FREDERICK HARDMAN. A Family Feud
JULIAN STURGIS. The Disappointing Boy
[Gen. Sir George Chesney.] The Cottage by the River
[Capt. Chenevix Trench.] A Ride for Life
[Sir H. Drummond Wolff.] A Sketch from Babylon
[W. J. M. Rankine.] Engine Driver to his Engine (poem; signed W. J. M. R.)

Vol. XII.
R. E. FRANCILLON. Left Handed Elsa
[William Chance.] The Great Earthquake at Lisbon
CHAS. LEVER. Some One Pays
[Gen. Sir E. B. Hamley.] Sir Tray (poem)
[James White.] Whittlebridge
[Miss Butt.] Nenuphar
ANTHONY TROLLOPE. Whist at our Club
[John Harwood.] My Investment in the Far West
H. KING. Brown's Peccadillo

THIRD SERIES

[3739 *c* (ii)] (The material here collected appeared in 'Maga' between 1878 and 1890)

Vol. I.
[G. H. Lewes.] Bourgonef
MRS W. K. CLIFFORD. Thomas
LAURENCE OLIPHANT. The Brigand's Bride
HENRY PROTHERO. The Misogynist
FREDK. BOYLE. A Fetish City
[Sir Sam. Ferguson.] The Gascon O'Driscol (poem), by the author of *The Forging of the Anchor*
MRS SCOTT MONCRIEFF. An Elie Ruby
[S. BARING GOULD.] Alexander Nesbitt, ex-Schoolmaster, by the author of *John Herring*
J. LANDERS. King Bomba's Point
KATHARINE M. LUMSDEN. A Vendetta
GILFRID W. HARTLEY. Master Tommy's Experiment
R. K. DOUGLAS. A Matrimonial Feud

Vol. II.
LADY MARGARET MAJENDIE. A French Speculation
LORD WELLWOOD. Rufus Hickman of St Botolphs
C. L. LEWES. Hans Preller
MAURICE KINGSLEY. The Puerto de Medino
COL. ALFRED HARCOURT. Jack and Minory
ANNETTE LYSTER. My Treasure

MARQUESS OF LORNE. Who were they? [3739c (ii)]
R. K. DOUGLAS. Within His Danger
GILFRID W. HARTLEY. The Factor's Shooting
GEN. W. G. HAMLEY. A Magnetic Mystery

Vol. III. F. S. DELLENBAUGH. A Singular Case
MARIAN BRADLEY. Pentock
C. L. LEWES. The Dragon Tree of Telde
BARING GOULD. Last Words of Joseph Barrable
K. M. LUMSDEN. How I fell among Thieves
MRS M. E. BURTON. Fiddlers Three
M. C. STIRLING. Ghost of Morcars Tower
JOHN STUART BLACKIE. Anerum Moor (poem)

Vol. IV. GEN. W. G. HAMLEY. A Medium of Last Century
ANDREE HOPE. Alive, yet Dead
MAXWELL GRAY. An Unexpected Fare
[Col. T. P. White.] Reminiscence of a March, by T. P. W.
MRS BURTON. Don Angelo's Stray Sheep
R. K. DOUGLAS. The Twins
A. G. BRADLEY. The Doctor: an old Virginian Fox Hunter
H. JOHNSTONE. The Enchanted Bridle (ballad)

Vol. V. MRS SCOTT MONCRIEFF. Such pity as a Father Hath
COL. RUSSELL. Coincidences
CAPT. BIRD. A Dead Man's Vengeance
J. LANDERS. The Story of James Barker
A. INNES SHAND. Mr Cox's Protégé
HON. EVA KNATCHBULL HUGESSEN. A Dramatic Effect
PAUL CUSHING. A Bird that Lived
STEPHEN COLERIDGE. Daniel Fosqué
LORD WELLWOOD. The Great Unloaded

Vol. VI. FRANK COWPER. Christmas Eve on a Haunted Hulk
[J. E. T. Loveday.] Dicky Dawkins, by 'Jack the Shepherd'
M. H. DZIEWICKI. Airy Nothing
MORRIS BENT. Chapter of an Unknown Life
A. G. BRADLEY. Morise Dab after the War
C. F. GORDON CUMMING. Unfathomed Mysteries
G. JENNER. A Philanthropist
F. R. OLIPHANT. The Grateful Ghosts
C. T. BUCKLAND. A Pickle of Sakt
[J. E. T. Loveday.] On the Wallaby Track
D. S. MELDRUM. Rathillet

BOHN'S ILLUSTRATED LIBRARY 1849 to middle sixties [3740]

For examples of this predominantly non-fiction series, see in Section I, Mahony (1523*b*) and Marryat (1584*a*).

CASSELL'S POCKET LIBRARY. Edited by MAX PEMBERTON 1895–1896 [3741]

Published by Cassell & Co. Ltd. at 1*s*. 4*d*. each in narrow fcap 8vo, bound in dark yellow unglazed buckram blocked and lettered in red, this series of original novelettes was, following the example of the Acme Library (3393 in Section II), an imitation of Fisher Unwin's successful 'Pseudonym' and 'Autonym' ventures. Series-title appears on front cover. After Vol. III no numbering occurs in panel advert. facing title. Titles asterisked are not in the Collection.

1. *A KING'S DIARY, by PERCY WHITE
2. *A WHITE BABY, by JAMES WELSH
3. THE LITTLE HUGUENOT, by MAX PEMBERTON
4. A WHIRL ASUNDER, by GERTRUDE ATHERTON
5. *LADY BONNIE'S EXPERIMENT, by TIGHE HOPKINS
6. THE PAYING GUEST, by GEORGE GISSING (974 in Section I)

[3742] CHAPMAN & HALL'S MONTHLY SERIES 1845–1848

This was another conscious attempt to break the conventional fiction-price and fiction-format of one guinea and a half and three volumes; and although its defeat was less manifest than that of Smith, Elder's *Library of Romance* (the quality of the books was higher and the publishers more skilful in extricating themselves from a forlorn position), it was equally melancholy and equally inevitable.

In November 1844 the series was thus introduced to the public under the sub-title: A COLLECTION OF ORIGINAL WORKS OF FICTION AND BIOGRAPHY:

'This SERIES OF BOOKS is undertaken with the belief, that while the taste for WORKS OF FICTION has in late years greatly increased, high prices and inconvenient forms of issue have so restricted their sale, that, as well with reference to authors as to readers, a change in the manner of submitting them to the public is generally called for.

'Messrs CHAPMAN & HALL acted on this belief nine years ago, when they commenced the publication of the works of a distinguished writer in monthly parts. In the present undertaking it is intended to apply similar resources of issue, on an enlarged scale, to a more extended series.'

The next announcement was more practical and omitted the ingenious reference to PICKWICK. Thus:

'This Series of Books will consist exclusively of new and original works, chiefly of the class of Novels and Romances; and the price of each work will be less than one half the sum charged for an equal amount of matter in the ordinary system of publication.

'The Novels will be published in *four monthly parts price three shillings each*, and although containing the ordinary amount at present included in three volumes, will be completed in *two* and sold for *fourteen shillings* in cloth. The Biographies will never exceed two parts or one volume.'

On, I fancy, January 1, 1845 was published Part I of THE WHITEBOY by Mrs S. C. Hall, the novel concluding with Part IV and appearing in 2 vols. at 14*s.* on April 1. May to August were occupied by four parts of MOUNT SOREL by Mrs Anne Marsh; September and October by Holmes' LIFE OF MOZART (in 1 vol. 7*s.*); November and December by Marmion W. Savage's THE FALCON FAMILY (also 1 vol. 7*s.*). 1846 opened with two parts of Kaye's LONG ENGAGEMENTS (7*s.*), followed by two of Robert Bell's LIFE OF GEORGE CANNING (7*s.*), followed by four (May to August) of FATHER DARCY by Mrs Marsh (2 vols. 14*s.*).

Then in September 1846 came the first strategic withdrawal. The part issue was abandoned and the price per cloth-volume increased by two shillings. An announcement, headed 'Enlarged Plan', stated that 'Books of Travel and General Literature' as well as fiction and biography would in future be included, and went on:

'An increase of Price, in the ratio of an additional shilling on each Part, is found absolutely essential to render the Work, with due regard to Author as well as the Public, fairly remunerative. But the separate publication of Parts having been found inconvenient to purchasers, each Work will, in future, whether in one or two volumes, be published complete in the first instance. The number of Publications in the year will continue, as at present, to average not less than a volume on the first of every alternate month.'

Then comes the final paragraph—interesting as an example of an unlucky choice of illustration to support a high-toned argument, and also as implying a criticism of another firm's policy. The paragraph reads:

'The simultaneous appearance of two Novels by a most deservedly popular writer (the author of 'Two Old Men's Tales') one of which, in compliance with the existing system, is charged £1. 11*s.* 6*d.*, while the

other, in its place in the MONTHLY SERIES is sold in two volumes for 14*s.* may be referred to as a [3742]
practical illustration of the scheme it is now proposed to enlarge.'

The author of TWO OLD MEN'S TALES was Mrs Anne Marsh; and the novels referred to were FATHER DARCY (*Monthly Series*, 2 vols. 14*s.*) and, if you please, EMILIA WYNDHAM (Colburn, 3 vols. 31*s.* 6*d.*), which became the novelist's key-title and most successful book. It was, of course, bad luck for Chapman & Hall that the conventional three-decker, which they hoped to see under-sold and thwarted by their own cheaper ventures, should have swept into immense popularity; but that it did so ought to have convinced them that they were on a wrong tack, and that the public did not *want* to buy new fiction, even at a reduced price, and would not support them in their hopeless fight against the Lending Libraries.

The next relinquishment decided upon by the publishers was the abandonment of regular publication of new volumes; and early in 1847 the word 'Monthly' was dropped, the series becoming simply 'Chapman & Hall's Series'. At (I think) the same time the series imprint, which had hitherto appeared at the base of the spine of each cloth volume, was substituted by the ordinary publishers' imprint: 'LONDON. CHAPMAN AND HALL.' Already the skilful slide-over had begun from crusading enthusiasm to orthodox publishing. G. H. Lewes' RANTHORPE (1 vol. 9*s.*) and two non-fiction titles appeared between June and November; and in December (dated forward 1848) Savage's BACHELOR OF THE ALBANY (1 vol. 9*s.*). In April 1848 appeared Geraldine Jewsbury's THE HALF SISTERS (2 vols. 18*s.*), which was the last title to be advertised as part of the series. Thenceforward the series was forgotten; and though format and style of binding persisted, with slight adaptation, for such famous novels as ALTON LOCKE and MARY BARTON, they were presented as straight two-deckers, unconnected with any idealism or trade campaign. The *English Catalogue* is at fault when it lists 33 volumes as having formed part of the series. Actually only the first 17 were so labelled by the publishers. The final incarnation of several of the titles was in cheap brown linen, lettered in black, offered for sale by Ward & Lock, two-vols-in-one, at half a crown a time.

SCHEDULE OF THE SERIES

Binding. Rose-madder fine-ribbed cloth (sometimes diagonal, sometimes perpendicular), conventionally blocked in blind on front and back, blocked in blind and blocked and lettered in gold on spine.

I have never seen a single specimen of the part issue, which was certainly made of the earlier volumes, so cannot describe it.

All the titles are first editions, and it may be noted that in February 1846 *The Life of Talleyrand* by W. M. Thackeray was announced as in preparation for series issue. The titles asterisked are not in the Collection.

1, 2 *THE WHITEBOY 1845. By Mrs S. C. Hall
3, 4 MOUNT SOREL 1845. By Mrs Marsh (1622 in Section I)
5 *LIFE OF MOZART 1845. By Edward Holmes
6 THE FALCON FAMILY 1845. By Marmion W. Savage (3033 in Section I)
7 *LONG ENGAGEMENTS 1846. A Tale of the Affghan Rebellion (by Sir W. Kaye)
8 LIFE OF GEORGE CANNING 1846. By Robert Bell
9, 10 FATHER DARCY 1846. By Mrs Marsh (1619 in Section I)
11 *CAMP AND BARRACK ROOM 1846. (By a late Staff-Sergeant)
12 *MEMOIRS OF SIMON LORD LOVAT AND DUNCAN FORBES 1847. By J. H. Burton
13 RANTHORPE 1847. By G. H. Lewes (1424 in Section I)
14 *WAYFARING SKETCHES AMONG THE GREEKS AND TURKS 1847. (Anon)
15 THE BACHELOR OF THE ALBANY 1848. By Marmion W. Savage (3032 in Section I)
16, 17 *THE HALF SISTERS 1848. By Geraldine Jewsbury

[3743] CONSTABLE'S MISCELLANY OF FOREIGN LITERATURE 1854–1855

Square crown 8vo, published by Thomas Constable & Co., Edinburgh, in cloth volumes at 2*s.* 6*d.* and 3*s.* 6*d.* per volume.

This, in my experience, is a very uncommon series. It was produced with care and scholarship and I give the complete list of books, so far as I can establish them. Titles asterisked are not in the Collection. I imagine most of the translations are first English issues.

The two specimens in the Collection are, one in olive-brown, the other in loam-brown ribbed cloth, uniformly blocked in gold and blind and gold-lettered on spine with titling and, at foot, series title and volume number. Yellow end-papers.

Vol. I. **Hungarian Sketches in Peace and War.** From the Hungarian of **Moritz Jokai.** With a Prefatory notice by Emeric Szabad. 1854

Announcement of series and series title-page (2 leaves) precede individual title. pp. (xx) [paged (xvi)] + (308) U_2 adverts. Ink signature: 'W. Wissenden', on p. (i).

Vol. II. ***Athens and the Peloponnese,** by **Hermann Hettner**

Vol. III. ***Tales of Flemish Life,** by **Hendrik Conscience** (cf. *The Amusing Library* in Section: Yellow-Back Collection)

Vol. IV. **Chronicles of Wolfert's Roost,** by **Washington Irving**

Vols. V, VI. ***Wanderings in Corsica,** by **Ferdinand Gregorovius**

Vol. VII. ***Brittany and La Vendée,** by **Emile Souvestre**

Vol. VIII. ***Recollections of Russia,** by **a German Nobleman**

Vol. IX. ***Greece and the Greeks of the Present Day,** by **Edmund About**

Vol. X. **Tolla: a Tale of Modern Rome,** by **Edmond About.** Translated by L. C. C. 1855

Leaf of adverts. and series title precede individual title. pp. (viii) + (296) S_7 S_8 and T_1–T_4 adverts., paged (1)–12 Book-label of John Bell Sedgwick. Binder's ticket: 'Alex[r]. Banks, Edinburgh, at end.

Vol. XI (announced). ***Rhine Stories,** by **W. O. von Horn**

[3744] ENGLISHMAN'S LIBRARY, THE 1840–1841

'A Series of cheap publications on the Principles of the English Church and Constitution.' Published in 20 volumes fcap 8vo, by James Burns, 17 Portman Street.

Bound in dark blue fine-diaper cloth, and with wood-engraved front. or pictorial title and cuts in the text, this series contained eight works of fiction (in sm. caps. below), seven of which are in the Collection. Various presentation bindings were also on sale at the publishers. The books are attractively produced and uniformly religious in tendency.

1. CLEMENT WALTON, or the English Citizen. By Rev. W. Gresley. Spine-titling 'The English Citizen'. Published at 3*s.* 6*d.* 1840.

2–8. *Non-fiction.*

9. TALES OF THE VILLAGE. By Rev. Francis E. Paget. Published at 3*s.* 1840.

10–12. *Non-fiction.*

13. THE SIEGE OF LICHFIELD: a Tale illustrative of the Great Rebellion. By Rev. W. Gresley. Published at 4*s.* 1840.

14. *Non-fiction.*

15. CHARLES LEVER, or the Man of the Nineteenth Century. By Rev. W. Gresley. Published at 3*s.* 6*d.* 1841. The title is a curious coincidence, the book appearing after Lever had begun to publish, but before his name as an author was avowed.

16. TALES OF THE VILLAGE: Second Series. By Rev. F. E. Paget. Published at 3*s.* 6*d.* 1841. This volume and no. 18, below, have 'Second Series' and 'Third Series' on spines.

17. *Non-fiction.*

18. TALES OF THE VILLAGE: Third Series. By Rev. F. E. Paget. Published at 3*s.* 6*d.* 1841.
19. THE FOREST OF ARDEN: a Tale illustrative of the English Reformation. By Rev. W. Gresley. Published at 4*s.* 1841.
20. RUTILIUS, or Stories of the Third Age. By Archdeacon Wilberforce. Published at 4*s.* 1841.

HARRISON'S NOVELIST'S MAGAZINE and NEW NOVELIST'S MAGAZINE 1780–1788 [3745]

23 vols. and 2 vols. 8vo. Harrison & Co., 18 Paternoster Row. Full cont. salmon-coloured morocco gilt; marbled end-papers; sprinkled edges. (*New Novelist's Magazine* in dark green, uniform style, but yellow edges and white end-papers.)

Each volume contains an over-all copper-plate title-page giving series title, volume number, contents, vignette and imprint. A sub-title precedes each separate fiction. Plates engraved on copper after Stothard and others, each imprinted and dated, appear as set out in the schedule which follows.

The work was published in weekly numbers (presumably in wrappers, but of what colour or how printed I do not know) and the various novels (each paginated separately) appeared in the order of their sub-title dates. When the series was complete, it was issued as a Magazine of Fiction in 23 volumes, with over-all titles which, like many of the illustrations, had been previously engraved.

I am inclined to think that this set (which came from the Mount Bellew Library in Ireland) was sent out by the publishers in the existing full morocco. Christopher Bellew was the kind of collector to place such an order; and, more suggestive still, the leaf of marbled paper which faces p. 100 of *Tristram Shandy* in Vol. V is absolutely identical with that used throughout for end-papers.

Vol. I. Over-all title-page dated 1780
ALMORAN AND HAMET (Hawkesworth). pp. (54) Sub-title dated 1786. 2 plates: Nov. 1779, May 1780
JOSEPH ANDREWS. pp. (180) Sub-title dated 1785. 4 plates: Dec 1779, Jan. 1780, Feb., March
AMELIA. pp. (300) Sub-title dated 1780. 7 plates: March 1780 (2), April (5)

Vol. II. Over-all title-page dated 1780
SOLYMAN AND ALMENA (Langhorne). pp. (36) Sub-title dated 1787. 1 plate: May 1780
VICAR OF WAKEFIELD. pp. 90 Sub-title dated 1785. 2 plates: May 1780
RODERICK RANDOM. pp. 262 Sub-title dated 1785. 6 plates: June 1780 (4), July (2)
ZADIG (translated by Ashmore from Voltaire). pp. (42) Sub-title dated 1784. 4 plates: July 1780 (2), Aug. (2)
THE DEVIL UPON TWO STICKS. pp. (146) Sub-title dated 1784. 4 plates: July 1780 (2), Aug. (2)

Vol. III. Over-all title-page dated 1781
TALES OF THE GENII ('Sir Charles Morrell'). pp. (236) Sub-title dated 1785. 6 plates: Aug. 1780 (2), Sept. (4)
TOM JONES. pp. (492) Sub-title dated 1787. 12 plates: Sept. 1780 (1), Oct. (4), Nov. (4), Dec. (3)

Vol. IV. Over-all title-page dated 1783
GIL-BLAS. pp. 402 Sub-title dated 1784. 10 plates: Dec. 1780 (2), Jan. 1781 (4), Feb. (4)
ROBINSON CRUSOE. pp. (292) Sub-title dated 1781. 7 plates: March 1781 (5), April (2)

Vol. V. Over-all title-page dated 1786
TRISTRAM SHANDY. pp. 290 Sub-title dated 1787. 8 plates: April 1781 (2), May (4), June (2)
CHINESE TALES (translated by Stackhouse from the French of Gueulette). pp. (116) Sub-title dated 1781. 3 plates. June 1781
THE SISTERS (Dodd). pp. (170) Sub-title dated 1781. 4 plates: July 1781

Vol. VI. Over-all title-page dated 1782
PEREGRINE PICKLE. pp. 438 Sub-title dated 1781. 11 plates: Aug. 1781 (4), Sept. (5), Oct. (2)
MORAL TALES (translated by Dennis and Lloyd from Marmontel). pp. 234 Sub-title dated 1786. 5 plates: Oct. 1781 (2), Nov. (3)

[*3745*] Vol. VII. Over-all title-page dated 1782

FORTUNATE COUNTRY MAID (from the French of de Mouhy). pp. 290 Sub-title dated 1788. 6 plates: Dec. 1781 (5), Jan. 1782 (1)

MEMOIRS OF A MAGDALEN or LOUISA MILDMAY (Kelly). pp. (86) Sub-title dated 1784. 2 plates: Jan. 1782

LETTERS BETWEEN THEODOSIUS AND CONSTANTIA (Langhorne). pp. (70) Sub-title dated 1783. 2 plates: Jan. 1782, Feb.

FERDINAND, COUNT FATHOM. pp. 220 Sub-title dated 1784. 4 plates: Feb. 1782 (3), March (1)

Vol. VIII. Over-all title-page dated 1782

DON QUIXOTE. pp. (590) Sub-title dated 1784. 16 plates: March 1782 (4), April (4), May (4), June (4)

Vol. IX. Over-all title-page dated 1782

SENTIMENTAL JOURNEY. pp. 58 Sub-title dated 1785. 2 plates: June 1782, July

GULLIVER'S TRAVELS. pp. 140 Sub-title dated 1782. 4 plates: July 1782 (3), Aug. (1)

DAVID SIMPLE (Sarah Fielding). pp. (158) Sub-title dated 1788. 4 plates: Aug. 1782

SIR LAUNCELOT GREAVES. pp. (126) Sub-title dated 1787. 4 plates: Sept. 1782

LETTERS OF A PERUVIAN PRINCESS (translated by Ashmore from the French of Madame de Grafigny). pp. 88 Sub-title dated 1787. 2 plates: Oct. 1782

JONATHAN WILD THE GREAT. pp. (102) Sub-title dated 1788. 2 plates: Oct. 1782

Vol. X. A leaf of text paper printed on verso with 'Advertisement' precedes the over-all title-page dated 1783

SIR CHARLES GRANDISON, Vols. I–IV. pp. (612) Sub-title dated 1785.

Vol. XI. Over-all title-page dated 1783

SIR CHARLES GRANDISON, Vols. V–VII. pp. (613)–(1116) No sub-title to this vol. 28 plates for the two vols.: Nov. 1782 (5), Dec. (4), Jan. 1783 (4), Feb. (4), March (4), April (5), May (2)

Vol. XII. Over-all title-page dated 1783

FEMALE QUIXOTE (Lennox). pp. (220) Sub-title dated 1787. 4 plates: May 1783 (3), June (1)

JOURNEY FROM THIS WORLD TO THE NEXT. pp. (68) Sub-title dated 1783. 3 plates: June 1783

JOE THOMPSON (Kimber). pp. (222) Sub-title dated 1783. 4 plates: July 1783 (3), Aug. (1)

PETER WILKINS (Paltock). pp. (190) Sub-title dated 1783. 6 plates: Aug. 1783 (5), Sept. (1)

Vol. XIII. Over-all title-page dated 1784

BETSY THOUGHTLESS (Heywood). pp. 312 Sub-title dated 1783. 8 plates: Sept. 1783 (3), Oct. (5)

THOUSAND AND ONE DAYS: Persian Tales (translated from the French by Ambrose Philips). pp. 306 Sub-title dated 1783. 6 plates: Nov. 1783 (4), Dec. (2)

Vol. XIV. Over-all title-page 1784

CLARISSA, Vols. I–IV. pp. 612 Sub-title dated 1784

Vol. XV. Over-all title-page dated 1784

CLARISSA, Vols. V–VIII. pp. (613)–1308 No sub-title in this vol. 34 plates for the two vols.: Dec. 1783 (1–2), Jan. 1784 (3–7), Feb. (8–11), March (12–15), April (16–19), May (20–24), June (25–28), July (29–33), Aug. (34)

Vol. XVI. Over-all title-page dated 1780 (sic)

DON QUIXOTE (Avellaneda's 'Continuation'). pp. 252 Sub-title dated 1784. 6 plates: Aug. 1784 (2), Sept. (4)

VIRTUOUS ORPHAN (from the French of Marivaux). pp. (314) Sub-title dated 1784. 10 plates: Oct. 1784 (5), Nov. (4), Dec. (1)

Vol. XVII. Over-all title-page dated 1785

ADVENTURES OF TELEMACHUS (Hawkesworth). pp. 230 Sub-title dated 1784. 6 plates: Dec. 1784 (3), Jan. 1785 (3)

HENRIETTA, COUNTESS OSENVOR (Treyssac de Vergy). pp. 70 Sub-title dated 1785. 2 plates: Jan. 1785 [*3745*]

A leaf precedes sub-title, printed on verso with 'Advertisement' explaining that this tale was written in English by a foreign author and is printed exactly as written.

JEMMY AND JENNY JESSAMY (Heywood). pp. 226 Sub-title dated 1785. 6 plates Feb. 1785 (4), March (2)

Vol. XVIII. Over-all title-page dated 1785

ARABIAN NIGHTS ENTERTAINMENTS (from the French of Galland). pp. (648) Sub-title dated 1785. 16 plates: March 1785 (2), April (6), May (3), June (4), July (1)

Vol. XIX. Over-all title-page dated 1785

HUMPHRY CLINKER. pp. (198) Sub-title dated 1785. 4 plates: July 1785

POMPEY THE LITTLE (Coventry). pp. (78) Sub-title dated 1785. 2 plates: Aug. 1785

OPHELIA (Sarah Fielding). pp. (134) Sub-title dated 1785. 3 plates: Aug. 1785 (2), Sept. (1)

TARTARIAN TALES (translated by Thomas Flloyd from the French of Gueulette). pp. (142) Sub-title dated 1785. 4 plates: Sept. 1785 (3), Oct. (1)

Vol. XX. Over-all title-page dated 1786

PAMELA. pp. 634 (last page misnumbered 364) Sub-title dated 1785. 16 plates: Oct. 1785 (1–4) Nov. (5–8), Dec. (9–13), Jan. 1786 (14–16)

Vol. XXI. Over-all title-page dated 1786

PERUVIAN TALES (translated from the French by Samuel Humphreys). pp. 268 Sub-title dated 1786. 7 plates: Feb. 1786 (4), March (3)

GAUDENTIO DI LUCCA (translated from the Italian). pp. (104) Sub-title dated 1786. 3 plates: March 1786 (1), April (2)

ADVENTURES OF AN ATOM. pp. (84) Sub-title dated 1786. 2 plates: April 1786

SINCERE HURON (translated by Ashmore from the French of Voltaire). pp. (36) Sub-title dated 1786. 1 plate: April 1786

ENGLISH HERMIT (Longueville). pp. (110) Sub-title dated 1786. 2 plates: May 1786

Vol. XXII. Over-all title-page dated 1787

LYDIA (Shebbeare). pp. 274 Sub-title dated 1786. 6 plates: May 1786 (2), June (3), July

SIDNEY BIDULPH (Mrs Sheridan). pp. 402 Sub-title dated 1786. 10 plates—*one a month*: Aug. 1785 to May 1786

Vol. XXIII. Over-all title-page dated 1788

RASSELAS pp. 56 Sub-title dated 1787. 2 plates: June 1787, July

HENRIETTA (Lennox). pp. 160 Sub-title dated 1787. 4 plates: Aug. 1787, Sept., Oct., Nov.

NOURJAHAD (Mrs Sheridan). pp. 38 Sub-title dated 1788. 1 plate: Dec. 1787

LETTERS FROM FELICIA TO CHARLOTTE (Collyer). pp. 172 Sub-title dated 1788. 4 plates: Jan. 1788, Feb., March, April

ADVENTURES OF MR GEORGE EDWARDS, A CREOLE (Sir John Hill). pp. (68) Sub-title dated 1788. 3 plates: May 1788 (1), June (2)

INVISIBLE SPY ('Explorabilis'). pp. (236) Sub-title dated 1788. 5 plates: July 1788, Aug., Sept., Oct., Sept. (sic)

NEW NOVELIST'S MAGAZINE, or Entertaining Library of Pleasing and Instructive Histories, Adventures, Tales, Romances and other Agreeable and Exemplary Little Novels [3745 *a*]

Vol. I. Over-all title-page dated 1787. pp. 418+(6) 13 plates (some unnumbered): May 1786, June, July, Aug., Sept., Oct., Nov., Dec., Jan. 1787, Feb., March, April, May

This volume contains no sub-title, but the first leaf carries on recto an 'Advertisement' describing the new venture as a companion issue to the still running *Novelists' Magazine*. 'Contents' and 'List of Authors' (6 pp. unfoliated) conclude the volume.

Vol. II. Over-all title-page dated 1787. pp. 374+(4) 11 plates (unnumbered): June 1787, July, Aug., Sept., Oct., Nov., Dec., Jan. 1788, March, Feb. (sic), May

This volume contains no sub-title. 'Contents' and 'List of Authors' (4 pp. unfoliated) conclude the volume.

[3746] HURST AND BLACKETT'S STANDARD LIBRARY. Late sixties, early seventies

This is an agreeable series of straight reprints of popular titles, fiction and non-fiction. It has no textual significance, but is attractively produced. The first binding-style was in red-brown cloth lettered in gold. This was superseded by a grey-violet morocco cloth with a leaf design in gold on spine, incorporating title, etc. The series-name appears at foot of spine in each style. Steel-engraved fronts. after Millais and other well-known artists are features of this series. A list of titles can be found in the *English Catalogue*.

[3747] ILLUSTRATED FAMILY NOVELIST, THE 1852–1854

Published at half a crown a volume in cloth, and in full morocco at seven and six, first from the 'Office of the Illustrated London Library'; then by Ingram, Cooke & Co. and finally by Nathaniel Cooke (who succeeded Ingram, Cooke in 1853), this elegant and rather miscellaneous series contained reprints of well-known titles, original fictions and translations, and even (despite its name) books not fiction at all.

The earlier titles were first published as independent works, and then incorporated in the list of the series without assuming series dress. As the volumes are not numbered and contain no standardised list of the series, I append (without guaranteeing the actual order of issue) a list of what seem to have been the first fourteen titles, printing first editions in caps., reprints in clarendon caps. and l.c. Those not in the Collection are asterisked.

The 'series binding' below referred to is of morocco cloth of various colours, with (on spine) all-over gold decoration incorporating series title, book title and imprint: on front and back a symbolic vignette and fancy frame in blind, and the series title—in gold on front, in blind on back. The end-papers are yellow.

SQUANDERS OF CASTLE SQUANDER (THE), by WILLIAM CARLETON 2 vols. 1852 (514 in Section I).

LADY FELICIA: A NOVEL, by HENRY COCKTON 2 vols.

2 vols. Office of the National Illustrated Library, 227 Strand, 1852. Bright blue horizontal-fine-wavy-grain cloth, blocked and lettered in silver on front and spine, blocked in blind on back. Wood-engraved front, and vignette title precede printed title and Contents. All four leaves are on plate paper.

pp. (viii) [plate paper]+336

Binders' ticket: 'Leighton, Son & Hodge' at end.

Except for a tarnishing of the silver along front fore-edge, very fine. The binding design is signed J. L. (John Leighton) on front and spine.

IVAR, OR THE SKJUTS-BOY, by EMILIE CARLEN. Translated from the Swedish by Professor A. L. Krause.

Office of the Illustrated London Library 1852. Pink-ribbed cloth, with all-over blocking in silver on front and spine, incorporating title and author (the design signed 'L. L.' ('Luke Limner') on front and 'J. L.' (John Leighton) on spine) and blind-blocked on back. Wood-engraved front. and vignette title, on plate paper but reckoned in collation. No printed title. No series title anywhere.

pp. (320) X_8 advert.

Binders' ticket: 'Leighton, Son & Hodge', at end. Bookseller's ticket: 'Croydon, Teignmouth', inside front cover.

AUBREY CONYERS, OR THE LORDSHIP OF ALLERDALE, by MISS E. M. STEWART (author of 'City of London Tales (sic)', 3613 in Section II) [3747]

Ingram, Cooke & Co. 1853. Series binding in green. Wood-engraved front., vignette title and 6 plates after J. Godwin.

pp. (iv)+(316) X_2–X_6 adverts., paged 1–10

Book-plate of John Browne and booksellers' ticket: 'Mann Nephews'.

***Pathway of the Faun (The)**, by **Mrs T. K. Hervey**

***Sealsfield's Cabin-Book (non-fiction)**

*ADOLPHE RENOUARD, by JAMES WARD

*MARIE LOUISE OR THE OPPOSITE NEIGHBOURS, by EMILIE CARLEN

***Life of Toussaint l'Ouverture**, by **Rev. John Beard (non-fiction)**

***Uncle Tom's Cabin**

***White Slave (The): a Tale of Slave Life in Virginia**, by **R. Hildreth**

BLANCHE THE HUGUENOT: a Tale, by WILLIAM ANDERSON

Nathaniel Cooke 1853. Series binding in light claret. Wood-engraved front., vignette title and 6 plates after G. and W. L. Thomas.

pp. (iv)+(304)

Book-plate of John Browne and booksellers' ticket: 'Mann Nephews'.

SKETCHES OF RUSSIAN LIFE IN THE CAUCASUS, by A. RUSSE [Lermontov]

Ingram, Cooke & Co. 1853. Series binding in plum wavy-grain cloth. Wood-engraved front., vignette title and 6 plates after 'F. C. C.'

pp. (320) U_7 U_8 adverts.

Book-plate of John Browne and booksellers' ticket: 'Mann Nephews'.

Caleb Stukely [anon] Nathaniel Cooke 1854. (See 1962*a*, in Section I)

KEYNOTES SERIES 33 vols. John Lane 1893–1897 [3748]

This is the most elegant fiction series of the nineteenth century. The slim format, the excellent paper and typography, the blended colours chosen for cloth and blocking, and the binding designs by Beardsley and others, combine to produce volumes which are stylish but not affected, *soignés* yet strongly made and essentially readable. Each book has, on the spine, a specially drawn Key, incorporating the author's initial, which Keys were all Beardsley's work.

The series touches the three-decker novel at six points—Grant Allen, J. S. Fletcher, Thomas Hardy, Henry Harland, George Moore and Marriott Watson—and all but one (Allen) of these writers appear as three-decker authors in Section I above. The publisher's original intention had been to issue the volumes in paper wrappers; and the first of all—*Keynotes* by George Egerton—was actually so published, but almost immediately withdrawn and re-issued in cloth. Another change of plan occurred at the end of the series. A thirty-fourth volume—*Deliverance* by Allan Monkhouse—had been scheduled, but was in fact not included but published in 1898 in full crown 8vo format (though set for a slim page) bound in pinkish brown linen-grain cloth.

An offshoot of the series was George Egerton's translation of Hansson's *Young Ofeg's Ditties* (1895), which exactly resembled a Keynotes volume in format and front-cover lay-out, but was blocked in blind instead of in colour on scarlet ribbed cloth, and had no Key on the spine. George Egerton's two earlier volumes, *Keynotes* and *Discords*, which first appeared in official Series form, were degraded to the modified non-Series style of *Young Ofeg*, when they reached their sixth and third edition respectively.

The Collection possesses a complete set of first editions of the Keynotes Series, in mint condition (eight volumes with dust-jackets) from the library of Radclyffe Walters with his dated pencil signature in each volume. *Keynotes* in wrappers, *Young Ofeg's Ditties* in semi-Series style and *Deliverance* are also present. It is unnecessary to list the Keynotes titles, as they are easily available in the *English Catalogue* and in the publisher's contemporary lists.

[3749] LIBRARY OF FOREIGN ROMANCE AND NOVEL NEWSPAPER 1846–1847, comprising Standard English Works of Fiction and Original Translations from the most Celebrated Continental Authors

Published in fortnightly penny numbers of 16 pp. and in volume form in wrappers and in cloth, of varying bulk and at various prices, by Bruce & Wyld, 84 Farringdon Street—up to and including Vol. VII, then Bruce & Co.—this series is a combination of THE LIBRARY OF FOREIGN ROMANCE and of THE NOVEL NEWSPAPER (3752 below).

The complete list is given so far as I can establish it, though only three volumes are in the Collection. Those lacking are asterisked. Presumed dates in square brackets.

Vol. I. ***The Three Musketeers**, by **Dumas.** (Translated by William Barrow.) [1846.] Cloth only, 4*s.* 6*d.* This was the first edition in English.

Vol. II. ***Lichtenstein**, by **Wilhelm Hauff.** (Translated by Frank Woodley and William Lander.) [1846.] Cloth only, 3*s.*

Vols. III, IV. ***Twenty Years After**, by **Dumas.** (Translated by William Barrow.) [1846.] Cloth only, 3*s.* 6*d.* per vol. This was the first edition in English.

Vol. V. ***Godway Castle**, by **Madame Paalzow.** (Translated by Frances K. Barnard.) [1846.] Cloth only, 3*s.* 6*d.*

Vol. VI. ***Isabel of Bavaria**, by **Dumas.** (Translated by William Barrow.) [1846–1847.] Cloth only, 3*s.* 6*d.* This was the first edition in English.

Vol. VII. **Childhood of King Erik Menved**, by **B. S. Ingemann.** (Translated by J. Kesson.) 1846. Wrappers, 2*s.* 6*d.*; cloth (uniform with Vol. IX below), 3*s.* pp. (392 [paged (i)–vi + 7–(392)] 25_4 adverts.

Vol. VIII. **Rose of Dekama (The)**, by **J. Van Lennep.** (Translated by Frank Woodley.) 1847. Wrappers, 2*s.* 6*d.*; cloth, 3*s.* Cloth bound uniform with Vol. IX below. pp. (376) 24_2–24_4 adverts.

Vol. IX. **Secret of the Confessional (The), The Last Lord of the Manor and the Count of Mansfeldt**, by **Alexander de Lavergne.** (Translated by Millicent Hack.) 1847. Greenish black fine-diaper cloth, blocked in blind and gold-lettered on spine with series title, volume number, title, and price (wrappers, 1*s.* 6*d.*; cloth, 2*s.*). Series title-page precedes individual title. pp. (208) 13_6–13_8 adverts.

Note. This binding description can be taken as applying to the whole series, which is described in the adverts. as 'Uniformly bound in embossed cloth'.

One page of the adverts., both in Vols. VIII and IX, is devoted to 'Novel Newspaper Editions of Popular Works', which include the large majority of the novels published in the eight volumes of THE NOVEL NEWSPAPER, with some additions. Among them is No. 21: *Ormond*, referred to in my 'General Note on The Novel Newspaper' as having been seen under the imprint 'Bruce and Wyld'.

It also appears from the adverts. that THE LIBRARY OF FOREIGN ROMANCE, before its amalgamation with THE NOVEL NEWSPAPER, had run to six volumes, containing 30 sixpenny parts, each of 96 pages.

[3750] MACMILLAN'S ILLUSTRATED STANDARD NOVELS 1895–1901

This series consisted of 40 volumes, each containing, in addition to the text of the Standard Novel, specially drawn illustrations by Hugh Thomson, F. H. Townsend, H. R. Millar, C. E. Brock, Chris Hammond, E. J. Sullivan and other popular artists of the period. Most of the volumes also had a critical introduction.

First Binding. Crimson ribbed cloth, blocked in blind and lettered in gold. Price 3*s.* 6*d.*

Second Binding (introduced with No. 21 and made retrospective). Smooth cloth of various colours heavily gilt on front and spine, all edges gilt. Price 5*s.*

About 1899 the prices of both styles were reduced, to 2*s.* 6*d.* and 3*s.* 6*d.* respectively. The volumes were continually reprinted.

The history and detail of this handsome and remarkably cheap series were recorded fully and authoritatively by Thomas Balston in a long article entitled 'Illustrated Series of the Nineties', published in 1933 in *The Book Collector's Quarterly*. A few copies were bound up separately for private distribution.

On pp. 42–43 of that article appears a list of MACMILLAN'S STANDARD NOVELS with dates of original issue. Of the 40 volumes four are missing from the Collection: Peacock's *Maid Marian* (1895), Borrow's *Lavengro* (1896) and Cooper's *Deerslayer* and *Pathfinder* (both 1900). The remainder are present in first issue (and with one exception in brilliant state), and include five volumes of Jane Austen, six of Maria Edgeworth and twelve of Marryat.

The complete Marryat series is also present in the Second Binding of smooth blue cloth with all-over decoration in gold on front and spine and all edges gilt.

MUDFORD'S BRITISH NOVELISTS 1810–1817 [3751]

('British Novelists', with Notes and Critical Remarks by W. Mudford, Esq.')

Issued in shilling parts, and then in five volumes royal 8vo. Published for the Proprietors by W. Clarke, New Bond Street; Goddard, Pall Mall; Taylor & Hessey, Fleet Street; J. M. Richardson, Cornhill; and Sherwood, Neely and Jones, Paternoster Row. Boards, paper labels. 'Embellished with elegant engravings.'

Vol. I PEREGRINE PICKLE AND HUMPHRY CLINKER 1810

Twelve engraved plates, 11 after Clennell, 1 after Sargent, and all imprinted: 'Sherwood Neely and Jones' with various dates in 1810.

General title precedes individual title of *Peregrine Pickle*.

pp. (ii)+(1)–4 [title, verso and LIFE OF SMOLLETT, unsigned and undated]+(5)–6 [CRITICAL OBSERVATIONS, also unsigned and undated]+(7)–(494) [mispaged (5)–492] [PEREGRINE PICKLE] +(1)–218 [HUMPHRY CLINKER]+(i)–iv [CRITICAL OBSERVATIONS, unsigned and undated].

This volume retailed separately at 17*s*.

Vol. II. RODERICK RANDOM. FERDINAND COUNT FATHOM. SIR LAUNCELOT GREAVES 1810

Seventeen engraved plates after Clennell, imprinted as in I.

pp. (ii)+(1)–(280) [RODERICK RANDOM] MM_4 advert.+(1)–(240) [FATHOM] GG_4 advert., over sole imprint of Sherwood, Neely & Jones+(1)–(134) [GREAVES]+(i)–iv [CRITICAL OBSERVATIONS on Greaves, signed 'W. M.'].

This volume retailed separately at 17*s*.

Vol. III. TRISTRAM SHANDY. SENTIMENTAL JOURNEY. GULLIVER'S TRAVELS and THE VICAR OF WAKEFIELD 1811

Three engraved portrait fronts. and 13 plates, of which 12 after Clennell and 1 after Westall, all imprinted as in I, but with dates in 1811.

pp. (ii)+(i)–vi [title, verso and LIFE OF STERNE, unsigned and undated]+(7)–(320) [TRISTRAM SHANDY]+(1)–62 [SENTIMENTAL JOURNEY]+(i)–viii [CRITICAL OBSERVATIONS, signed 'W. M.']+(1)–(8) [title, verso and LIFE OF SWIFT, unsigned and undated]+(9)–(160) [GULLIVER'S TRAVELS]+(i)–(viii) [CRITICAL OBSERVATIONS, signed 'W. M.']+(1)–(8) [title, verso and LIFE OF GOLDSMITH, signed 'W. M.']+(9)–100 [VICAR OF WAKEFIELD]+(i)–(vi) [CRITICAL OBSERVATIONS, signed 'W. M.'].

This volume retailed separately at 16*s*.

Vol. IV. TOM JONES AND JONATHAN WILD THE GREAT 1811

Engraved portrait front. and 15 plates after Clennell, imprinted as in III.

pp. (1)–10 [*general* title (no individual title), verso, and LIFE OF FIELDING, unsigned and undated]+(11)–(514) [TOM JONES]+(i)–x [CRITICAL OBSERVATIONS, signed 'W. M.']+(1)–106 [JONATHAN WILD]+(i)–iv [CRITICAL OBSERVATIONS, signed 'W. M.'].

[3751] Vol. V. AMELIA (1811). JOSEPH ANDREWS (1815). A JOURNEY FROM THIS WORLD TO THE NEXT etc. (1816). (General title dated 1817)

Five engraved plates in *Amelia* after Corbould, imprinted as before and variously dated in 1811 and 1812. No plates in the other novels.

pp. (ii)+(1)–(306) [AMELIA]+(i)–iv [CRITICAL OBSERVATIONS, signed 'W. M.']+(1)–184 [JOSEPH ANDREWS)+(i)–iv [CRITICAL OBSERVATIONS, signed 'W. M.']+(1)–(68) mispaged (9)–(76)* [JOURNEY FROM THIS WORLD]+(i) ii [CRITICAL OBSERVATIONS, signed 'W. M.'].

Note. The condition of the set in the collection is far from fresh. The spines are rather chipped and one is torn at head. But it is wholly unsophisticated, and I am as sure as is possible with a work of the date and kind that nothing is lacking which was not lacking when boarding took place. Two or three of the 'Critical Observations' are bound out of place, and the plates do not all fulfil 'Directions to Binder'; but these are commonplaces of works of this sort at the period.

GENERAL NOTE ON MUDFORD'S BRITISH NOVELISTS

It is evident that Sherwood, Neely and Jones (whose imprint is on all the plates and who have at one point an advert. leaf of their own) were the predominant partners in this group-undertaking. They were catch-penny publishers (issuing many semi-scurrilous oddments by Westmacott, editor of *The Age*, and other disreputable pamphleteers), and there is little doubt that their venture into 'British Novelists' was in parsimonious imitation of *Harrison's Novelist's Magazine* and provoked by the success in 1810 of Mrs Barbauld's *British Novelists* (q.v.).

The whole affair is jerry-built. A grandiloquent general title-page announces 'Biographical Sketches of the Authors and a Critical Preface to each Work'—a promise by no means carried out. Mudford's comments are negligible; and whereas the labels on each volume promise 71 plates, actually only 60 are included.

It will be remarked that the last two novels in the final volume have no plates at all. That fact, and the queer spread of dates (1811–1816, with an over-all title of 1817) proves, I think, that the venture was not a success and petered out in a general loss of interest. This would have meant a small printing of the final sections and would account for the remarkable scarcity of the series as a whole.

The separate pagination of each novel suggests an intention to issue the titles (or some of them) individually at a later date. Whether this took place I do not know.

[3752] NOVEL NEWSPAPER, THE 1839–1842

12 vols. [? any more]. Vols. I, II. Royal 8vo. T. L. Holt, 266 Strand, 1839. Vol. III. Royal 8vo. J. Cunningham, Crown Court, 1839. Vol. IV. Demy 8vo. J. Cunningham, Crown Court, 1839. Vols. V, VI. Demy 8vo. J. Cunningham, Crown Court, 1840. Vols. VII, VIII. Demy 8vo. J. Cunningham, Crown Court, 1841. [Vols. IX, X] untraceable. Vol. XI 'Published at the Office of the late John Cunningham, Crown Court. 1841. Vol. XII, N. Bruce, Peterborough Court, Fleet Street. 1842. Grey-purple ribbed cloth, blocked in blind. Grey-purple paper labels printed in gold with decoration, title of series, and principal contents of each volume. White end-papers. Vols. XI, XII, contemporary half-calf.

This publication appeared in numbers, printed in double column, of which 1–125 are contained in the eight volumes. The length of the numbers varies, and the system of paging shows irregularities, which make it impossible to summarise the volumes in uniform style.

Each of the principal novels has an individual title-page, sometimes an inset and not reckoned in the pagination, but sometimes part of the sheet and reckoned.

* Something curious occurred at this point. The individual title is a single inset and cannot have been conjugate with pp. 67/68 [K_1, also a single leaf] as it is on smaller paper. Clearly the issue had become disordered by this time, and possibly 8 pages of prelims. had been planned and cancelled.

Vol. I. (iv)+(ii) [title-page to Cooper's PILOT]+(1)–96+97*–102* [asterisked inset]+(ii) [title-page to Cooper's SPY]+97–(196)+(ii) [title-page to Cooper's PIONEERS]+197–304+(ii) [title-page to Cooper's LAST OF THE MOHICANS]+305–500 [pp. (401) (402) are title-page and verso to Cooper's LIONEL LINCOLN.] *[3752]*

In this volume the *individual* titles are imprinted 'J. Cunningham' and all dated 1839 except LIONEL LINCOLN, which is dated 1838.

Vol. II. (iv)+(510)

pp. (1) (2) title-page to A. M. Porter's HUNGARIAN BROTHERS. Imprint: Cunningham. 1839.
pp. (83) (84) title-page to A. M. Porter's DON SEBASTIAN. Imprint: Holt. 1839.
pp. (209) (210) title-page to Dr Bird's PETER PILGRIM. Imprint: Cunningham. 1838.
pp. (277) (278) title-page to Dr Bird's NICK OF THE WOODS. Imprint: Cunningham. 1839.
pp. (365) (366) title-page to J. P. Kennedy's HORSE SHOE ROBINSON. Imprint: Cunningham. 1839.

Note. It would appear that Holt and Cunningham were either one firm or very closely allied. In this volume the spine-imprints (which would have been clearly visible in number issue) do not necessarily tally with those on title-pages but seem to be used indiscriminately.

Vol. III. (ii)+90 [CAPTAIN KYD, by the author of 'The Southwest']+(1)–204 [PEREGRINE PICKLE]+(1)–(108) [Cooper's PRAIRIE]+(1)–80 [THE PIRATE or LAFITTE OF THE GULPH OF MEXICO, by the author of 'Captain Kyd']+(1)–(102) [ROB OF THE BOWL, by J. P. Kennedy]

All individual titles imprinted Cunningham. CAPTAIN KYD and ROB OF THE BOWL dated 1839; PEREGRINE PICKLE, PRAIRIE and PIRATE dated 1840.

It will be observed from now on the volumes are paged in sections to facilitate separate issue of indi vidual titles. (See GENERAL NOTE below.)

Vol. IV. (ii)+(1)–146 [Cooper's RED ROVER]+(1)–134 [Bird's HAWKS OF HAWK HOLLOW]+(1)–136 [Cooper's WATER WITCH]+(1)–102 [MANFRONE or THE ONE HANDED MONK, by Mary Ann Radcliffe]

All individual titles imprinted Cunningham, 1839. Label missing from this volume and front inside hinge broken away.

Vol. V. (iv)+(1)–90 [Paulding's KONINGSMARKE, THE LONG FINNE]+(1)–86 [Brockden Brown's ORMOND]+(1)–158 [Bird's ABDALLA THE MOOR AND THE SPANISH KNIGHT]+(1)–(120) [Bird's INFIDEL'S DOOM or CORTES AND THE CONQUEST OF MEXICO]+(1)–4 [an anonymous short story THE FIELD OF TERROR]

All individual titles imprinted Cunningham. The first three dated 1839, the fourth 1840.

Vol. VI. (ii)+(1)–32 [UNDINE, translated by Tracy]+(1)–(184) [Charlotte Smith's THE OLD MANOR HOUSE]+(1)–6 [THE RANSOM (by Fouqué)]+(1)–(148) [SEVENTY SIX, by the author of 'Logan']+(149)–160 [THE OLD FARM HOUSE, by Mrs Fairlie, edited by her aunt Lady Blessington, and THE ALCHYMIST, by T. K. Hervey]+(1)–200 [Miss Cuthbertson's ROMANCE OF THE PYRENEES]

All individual titles imprinted Cunningham, 1840. The stories by Fairlie and Hervey have no such titles.

Vol. VII. (ii)+(1)–(134) [Sophia Lee's RECESS]+(1)–43 [Elizabeth Helme's LOUISA]+44 [THE BROKEN LEG, a fragment from the German of Langbein]+(45)–64 [SELIM, THE BENEFACTOR OF MANKIND (anon)]+(1)–175 [LOGAN, THE MINGO CHIEF, by the author of 'Seventy Six']+176 [THE BRIDEGROOM'S PROBATION, a fragment from Langbein]+(1)–133 [Judge Thompson's GREEN MOUNTAIN BOYS]+134–136 [FRANCESCA ZAMORA, by John Malcolm]

All individual titles imprinted Cunningham, 1840. The Langbein fragments, *Selim* and *Zamora*, have no such titles, although *Selim* has a fly-title, verso blank, undated.

[3752] Vol. VIII. (iv)+(1)–120 [Bird's ROBIN DAY OF THE ROVER'S LIFE]+(121)–128 [THE DISHONOURED IRRECLAIMABLE, from the German of Schiller]+(1)–73 [A NEW HOME: WHO'LL FOLLOW? by Mrs Clavers, published in London as 'Montacute']+(74)–80 [TRY AND TRUST, by Mrs Hale]+(1)–75 [Brockden Brown's WIELAND]+(76)–80 [an anonymous short story EMILY GRAHAM]+(1)–69 [Longfellow's HYPERION]+70–72 [THE LITTLE ITALIAN BOY, by W. Anderson]+(1)–116 [Strutt's QUEENHOO HALL, described on main title-page as 'by Sir Walter Scott', on individual title as 'Edited and Partly Written by Sir W. S.']+(117)–124 [an anonymous short story THE IRISH LORD LIEUTENANT AND HIS DOUBLE]

All individual titles imprinted Cunningham, 1840. The anonymous stories and those by Schiller, Hale and Anderson have no such titles.

I can give no particulars of Vols. IX and X as I have never seen them.

Vol. XI: (ii)+(1)–142 [Godwin's CALEB WILLIAMS]+142–144 [THE BIVOUAC by J. Malcolm]+(1)–138 [Elizabeth Helme's ST CLAIR OF THE ISLES, OF THE OUTLAWS OF BARRA]+138–144 [MONKWYND, A LEGENDARY FRAGMENT. (Anon.)]+(1)–168 [FRANCIS BERRIAN, OF THE MEXICAN PATRIOT 'By Timothy Flint Esq.']+(1)–142 [G. Simms' CONFESSION, OF THE BLIND HEART]

Individual titles up to and including *Francis Berrian* are imprinted John Cunningham and dated 1841. *Confession* imprinted 'At the Office of the late John Cunningham' and dated 1841. Presumably a blank or advert. leaf at end brought the pagination of *Confession* up to 144.

A footnote on page 142 of *Confession* promises the entire series of Waverley Novels in Novel Newspaper form, beginning with *Waverley*, as and when copyright expires.

Vol. XII: (ii)+(1)–140 [Elizabeth Helme's THE FARMER OF INGLEWOOD FOREST]+(141) [fly-title to short anonyma which follow]+(142)–157 [OTTER-BAG. THE ONEIDA CHIEF (anon.)] +157–160 [THE CAPTAIN'S LADY (anon.)]+(1)–153 [CARLETON, OF PATRIOTISM, LOVE AND DUTY (anon.)]+154–160 [THE GHOST (anon.)]+(1)–(384) [paged (iv)+380] [Lee's CANTERBURY TALES]

Notes: (i) The make-up of this section is unusual. An overall title and Contents (2 leaves) precede the individual title which is paged as (1) (2) of the text. The former merely announces *The Canterbury Tales*, the latter the *First Series*. Whether the *Second Series* constituted or formed part of Vol. XIII of *The Novel Newspaper* I do not know.

(ii) Page (232), facing the beginning of *Kruitzner, The German's Tale*, carries a Publisher's Note recording Byron's acknowledged debt to *Kruitzner* when writing *Werner*, and a rather ill-tempered attack on Byron by Christopher North for using Miss Lee's story—a use which the poet admitted freely and gratefully.

(iii) Of the individual title-pages in Vol. XII, those of *The Farmer of Inglewood Forest* and *Carleton*, and the second *Canterbury Tales* title are dated 1842 and imprinted 'The Office of the late J. Cunningham'. The overall title of *The Canterbury Tales* is dated 1842 and imprinted N. Bruce.

GENERAL NOTE ON THE NOVEL NEWSPAPER

It will be observed that this publication exactly resembles the Second Series of *The Romancist and Novelist's Library* which it pre-dates by about a year. Probably the proprietors of the latter, after the close of their First Series, borrowed Cunningham's idea of so designing their publication as to permit it to appear, first in numbers, and then in separate wrappered volumes.

In connection with such separate wrappered issues, it may be noted (i) that Cunningham apparently sold individual titles in sheets to sub-publishers or to retailers who put their own imprint on the wrapper. I have in the Collection a copy of *The Hawks of Hawk Hollow* (item 2 in Vol. IV) in a buff wrapper lettered in black and imprinted E. Elliot, 14 Holywell Street, Strand, and undated. The title-page bears Cunningham's imprint and the date 1840. On the front cover are prominently displayed the words: THE NOVEL NEWSPAPER. PART XVII, and *The Hawks* was in fact the seventeenth title in Cunningham's series. Presumably, therefore, titles were marketed separately even from Vols. I–III, despite the fact that the pagination of these volumes was continuous. Whether Elliot was one of several retailers handling Cunningham's material I do not know.

The only other specimen seen of separate issue with a different imprint on wrapper and title-page belongs to another category. This was *Ormond* (item 2 in Vol. v) issued in a buff wrapper, described as THE NOVEL NEWSPAPER NO. XXI, imprinted Bruce and Wyld and dated 1844. Cunningham's original title is preserved within. Now Bruce & Wyld were successors to N. Bruce, Peterborough Court, who took over *The Novel Newspaper* from Cunningham. Bruce would have handled all Cunningham issues during the brief period of his single imprint, and they would then have passed to Bruce and Wyld. Hence the copy of *Ormond* above referred to. [*3752*]

To what lengths Bruce carried on the original issue of this periodical I cannot say. I have only one further specimen of his imprint, on *Transatlantic Tales, Sketches and Legends by various American Authors. Collected by Gilmore Simms* (1842) and Mr T. E. Elwell of Gloucester reports that in his possession are *Beauchamp, or the Kentucky Tragedy* and *Voyages, etc.* by J. P. Cleveland, both dated 1842 and neither bearing the Series title. As these items are uniform with *The Novel Newspaper*, it is a fair presumption that they formed part of Vol. XIII, but in separate state without overall title-page they provide no proof. (See also *Library of Foreign Romance and Novel Newspaper*, 3749 above.)

The main interest of *The Novel Newspaper* lies in its obvious purpose of conducting against American writers a counter-campaign of piracy. This purpose is admitted in the Preface to Vol. I:

'It has been said that...it is unfair to issue Mr Cooper's novels at such a price. To this we reply that Mr Cooper suffers in common with Sir Edward Bulwer, Captain Marryatt (sic) and other English writers, whose new works are successively reprinted in America without one farthing being paid for copyright. Nor will Mr Cooper regret the wide circulation throughout England of the five novels contained in the present volume; since, being mainly on subjects of American history, they will tend to diffuse a better knowledge of his country amongst a class of persons whose national prejudices are even yet stronger than their reason.'

This, it will be agreed, is pretty good; and shows the opinion of the publishers of the mental quality of the readers to whom they appeal.

By the time Vol. V is reached, the promoters have changed their tune. They now adopt a literary line, and take much credit to themselves for introducing to the English public distinguished but hitherto little known American writers, particularly Dr Bird.

Finally, in the Preface to Vol. VIII, they reach a climax of virtuous disingenuity. They state that many enquiries have been made as to the cause of their preference for American to English authors. This preference is due to the fact that

'we find in their delineation of character a bolder and more vigorous outline...in their tone a more manly and moral sentiment, an absence of mawkish and *missy* sentimentality, a muse less slipshod...than is usual with English novel-makers. To crown all, we find a right vein of thinking. The plots of their dramas do not turn upon adulteries or robberies; they do not seek their heroes in the prison or on the road, nor is every woman a Lucrece Borgia, modernised with sentiment and fashionable virtue.'

And so to the grand finale:

'If the reasons given serve to excuse our preference for American novel-writers over English romancists, they will avail us with double force as regards the French novelists of the days of Victor Hugo, Madame Sand and Paul de Kock, for the total exclusion of whose works from *The Novel Newspaper* we are proud to acknowledge having received the thanks of the heads of many families.'

NOVEL SERIES (The) 1895–1896

Published by Smith, Elder in small square 8vo at 2*s*., 3*s*. or 4*s*. each, according to length, these original novels were bound in blue-grey ribbed cloth, blocked and lettered in black and gold. Series title appeared on front cover. The volumes were not numbered in series. [3753]

The titles asterisked are not in the Collection.

1. THE STORY OF BESSIE COSTRELL, by MRS HUMPHRY WARD (3295 in Section I)
2. LYRE AND LANCET, by F. ANSTEY (48 in Section I)
3. *THE COMING OF THEODORA, by ELIZA ORNE WHITE.
4. THE GREY LADY, by H. SETON MERRIMAN (1719 in Section I)
5. *FREDERICK, by L. B. WALFORD
6. *PERSIS YORKE, by SIDNEY CHRISTIAN

[3754–3756]

PARLOUR LIBRARY, THE

(preceded by THE PARLOUR NOVELIST, and followed by BY-PRODUCTS)

It is, presumably, because the study of nineteenth-century publishing history is of comparatively recent date, that the sensational importance of the Parlour Library as an innovation in cheap book-making has not previously been realised. 'Sensational', nevertheless, the venture was, alike in its courage, efficiency of handling and success; and perhaps the most remarkable feature of the whole affair is that it originated in Ireland, was undertaken by a firm of *printers* who had not previously been general publishers at all, and was neither underwritten in London nor relied—except in the ordinary way of business—on the support or money of the English trade. Certainly its immediate and overwhelming popularity transformed it in a few weeks from a local Irish speculation into an international property of great value. A London office was acquired, and a London address added to the Irish address which at the outset stood alone in the imprint of the first volume. But the fact remains that the original issue of the first item in this long and triumphant series bore a purely Irish imprint and was, into the bargain, a *new* work by a man who is now regarded as perhaps the most important Irish story-writer of the time.

* * * * * *

Before getting to grips with the details of the Parlour Library itself, it is necessary to appreciate the degree to which cheap-edition publishing had developed by the middle eighteen-forties.

The relevant facts must be summarily condensed, and naturally belong to the history of the English rather than of the Irish trade. But they were facts which Simms & M'Intyre must have taken into account in estimating their chances, even though no one (maybe) was more surprised than they by their venture's instantaneous conquest of the English market.

Taking the year 1845 as our basis for generalisation, and considering first the realm of fiction, we find the three-volume novel, published at 31*s.* 6*d.*, firmly established as the standard form of a novel's first appearance. There were of course new novels in two volumes and even novels in one; but such issues were governed by *length* and were regarded as abbreviations of the three-decker and not an alternative form. Conditions were different in Ireland, for the few Dublin publishers who originated fiction favoured small 12mo single volumes, until the fashion of part issue infected Curry and McGlashan. The Irish three-decker was an unusual phenomenon, though Tinsley is wrong when he states that Le Fanu's *House by the Churchyard* was the first three-volume novel of Irish origin.* Nevertheless Dublin (and, I imagine, Belfast) technique in fiction-publishing was on a cheaper and handier scale than that of England or Scotland; and the point is worth noting, as the designers of the Parlour Library would have been vaguely accustomed to new as well as reprint fiction in one-volume 12mo form, and therefore could more naturally have visualised a series (partly of original works, partly of reprints) in that shape than if they had grown up among the lavish splendours of three post 8vo volumes. But such a possibility is only conjectural, and would not in any case have had a more than secondary influence on Simms & M'Intyre. The new novel market which they prepared to challenge was a three-decker market, and the cheap editions confronting them were those dominant in the English trade.

In 1845 the English cheap edition of contemporary fiction was strangely undeveloped. When the successful three-decker had run its course, its chances of cheaper re-issue were very slender unless it had been published by Bentley, Colburn or Blackwood—the three front-rank firms with proprietary series of cheap copyright fiction. Two of these (Colburn and Blackwood) only included titles from their own list, and Bentley's inclination to purchase copyrights elsewhere for addition to his Standard Novels was still very restrained. It must further be remarked that the price per volume of books published in any of these series was never less than five shillings and usually six.†

* Even the bibliography of Le Fanu himself provides an earlier example, and others could be named.

† Let me emphasise that the conditions above summarised were the conditions ruling in the *fiction* market. Non-fiction—mainly owing to the enterprise of Charles Knight—was in existence at one shilling in wrappers early in the thirties. Also various Cabinet Libraries, Cabinet Cyclopaedias and so forth were well-established by 1845 at prices from six shillings down to three and six. But these did not affect the problem of Simms & M'Intyre, whose Parlour Library was to be a *fiction* series and a fiction series only.

This, let us repeat, was in 1845, when Chapman & Hall had only lately started publishing; when Newby was still only a jobber; when Tinsley, Chatto & Windus, Routledge, Ward & Lock, Maxwell and other prolific fiction-publishers of the latter half of the century were still unborn. [*3754–3756*]

And yet, if we jump three or four years—to 1848 or 1849—we find Bentley's and Colburn's *Standards* reduced first to 3*s.* 6*d.* and then to 2*s.* 6*d.*; Chapman & Hall's *Select Library* starting at 2*s.*; Routledge's *Railway Library* already a dozen volumes old at 1*s.* and 1*s.* 6*d.* And just over the horizon the dawn of the yellow-back is breaking.

It is, I think, not only legitimate but almost compulsory to give the credit (if credit it be) for this revolution in cheap-novel publishing to the firm of Simms & M'Intyre, who earned it in two stages. The first stage was marked by the publication in February 1846 of the first volume of THE PARLOUR NOVELIST, a cloth-bound fiction series at half a crown (simultaneously in wrappers at two shillings). The second stage, almost exactly a year later, by the appearance of Vol. I of THE PARLOUR LIBRARY at one shilling in boards (and, very shortly afterward, also at one and sixpence in cloth). As ventures directly responsible for so complete a transformation of publishing practice, it is surely no exaggeration to acclaim these two series (and especially the latter) as landmarks in the history of the book-trade.

In conclusion, a word should be said of the phenomenal publishing career of the firm of Simms & M'Intyre, whose history can be briefly told. In 1797 the office of the Belfast newspaper *The Northern Star* was raided and wrecked. The event was a mere episode of the preliminaries to 1798, but it threw out of employment two compositors, D. Simms and J. Doherty. These men set up a press of their own and worked jointly until 1803 when they separated. In 1807 Simms entered into partnership with one M'Intyre, and the new firm developed a successful business as printers and publishers of educational books and works of reference. The original Simms and M'Intyre were in due course succeeded by their sons John and James, and it was this second generation who conceived the idea of publishing copyright fiction at a low price and launched the half-crown cloth-bound PARLOUR NOVELIST in 1846. A year later they went one better, discontinued the Parlour Novelist, and staked what must have been an enormous sum for those days on a shilling boarded series of new and reprint fiction—THE PARLOUR LIBRARY.

In October 1853 (seven and a half years later) they sold The Parlour Library to their London agent and, so far as I know, vanished from the book-publishing scene. During their short career they invented and issued at least five series (giving to each real thought, as well as manufacturing ingenuity and speculative courage) which, between them, completely revolutionised the publishing of cheap literature throughout the English-speaking world. Whose individual genius lay behind this great achievement—an achievement unique in the history of the nineteenth-century book-trade—is apparently not known. Whoever he may have been, let us salute him.

John Simms and James M'Intyre subsequently quarrelled over the desirability of publishing the works of Swedenborg, and a long and triumphant partnership ended in bitterness. What became of M'Intyre is not on record; but John Simms lived to the age of 93 and died at Banbridge in January 1911. His two sons never married, and the one who bought the firm's copyrights neglected them; so both dynasty and imprint perished.

I. *THE PARLOUR NOVELIST* 1846–1847: *A COMPLETE LIST* [3754]

(Belfast: Simms & M'Intyre; London: J. W. S. Orr)

This series ran to 14 volumes, small 8vo, and appeared monthly from February 1846 to early in 1847. *Pl. 13*

Binding. Although advertised as '2*s.* sewed' as well as in cloth, I have never been able to add to the Collection even one volume in this style. The only two specimens I have seen (quite different one from the other) were lent me by Mr P. S. O'Hegarty of Dublin. From them I took the following description:

Wrappers [Style I]. Stiff white wrappers, cut flush, printed all over in blue with elegant floral decoration and lettering in reverse. Design repeated on back cover. Series title on front, spine and back. 'Price 2*s.*' on front and spine. Plain white end-papers.

The volume thus bound was a copy of No. 1.

PARLOUR NOVELIST

[3754] **Wrappers [Style II].** Stiff glazed green wrappers, cut flush, printed in dark green—on front with decorative frame of trees, bluebells and cherubs, enclosing lettering from *type*; on spine with lettering from type; on back with list of series in conventional frame. Series title on front, spine and back. 'Price Two Shillings' on front and spine. Plain white end-papers.

The volume thus bound was a copy of No. 11. The whole effect of this style is shoddier than the foregoing and, as will be seen, the front cover design reappears on the remainder issue. Mr O'Hegarty also reported a copy of No. 7 in Style II; and Nos. 8 and 9 were advertised 'sewed' as 2*s*. each in *The Times* for September 24, 1846.

Whether the whole series first appeared in Style I and then in Style II, or whether the design was changed part-way through, I do not know.

Cloth: Regular Style. Plum-coloured horizontal fine-ribbed cloth, blocked in blind on front and back; on spine with blind decoration and gold-lettered with series title, number of volume, title, author and imprint. Plain yellow end-papers. Edges uncut. It should be added that this binding shows two styles of spine-lettering—one with seriffed caps and normal-size seriffed numerals, the other with sans-serif caps and out-size sans-serif numerals. I cannot say whether the variation has issue-significance.

Cloth: More Ornate Style. I have one volume (a copy of No. 2) bound in the same cloth as the regular issue, but with gold decoration and lettering on spine. The design differs completely from the foregoing, is heavily ornate and extremely ugly. I have never seen another copy thus bound, and it is just possible that it was one of the few *cloth* copies offered at the remainder price (see below) and got up with a cheap gaudiness in order to tickle the groundlings.

Internal Make-Up. An engraved series title-page, undated and on plate paper, is followed by a half-title on text paper, giving the title of the book and its number in the series. Then comes an individual title-page, dated.

The design of the engraved series title changed with No. 11, a different frame and style of lettering being adopted.

Remainder Issue. In June 1848 the publishers advertised on the front end-paper of *Parlour Library* No. 16 that, as they were no longer able to supply complete sets of *The Parlour Novelist,* they were offering the remaining stock of volumes still available at one shilling in paper boards and 'a few copies in cloth-boards at one shilling and sixpence'.

The volumes listed as on sale at one shilling were Nos. 2, 4, 5, 6, 7, 10, 11, 12, 13 and 14.

I have one specimen of this issue. It is a copy of No. 12 and is bound in bright green glazed boards printed in dark green—on front with the design used in Wrapper Style II but with different wording set from type; on spine with title, author and price; on back with list of Parlour Library to No. 16. Plain pale green end-papers. No series title anywhere and series title-pages suppressed. 'Price One Shilling' on front and spine.

In the list which follows, first editions and what I take to be first issues of English translations (if not necessarily first editions in English) are in caps. The only title not in the Collection is No. 14.

1 **Tales by the O'Hara Family: Part I,** by Banim. Feb. 1846 [1825] [containing *Crohoore of the Bill-Hook* and *The Fetches*]

2 COMMANDER OF MALTA, by Eugene Sue. March 1846 [First French 1841]. Translated (for this series) by Adalbert Doisy

3 CHATEAU D'IF, by Dumas. April 1846 [First French 1845]

Translated by Emma Hardy, this volume is introduced by a Note in which the publishers take credit for being 'the first to make known to the English public this charming romance' and prophesy for it 'a higher and more lasting character than either *The Mysteries of Paris* or *The Wandering Jew*'. Mr Munro informs me that in his opinion the two-vol. 8vo illustrated edition issued by Chapman & Hall in 1846 appeared earlier in the year than this Emma Hardy version. I hesitate to differ from so authoritative a view, but would like to suggest that, although Parlour Novelist Nos. 8 and 9 in all likelihood post-dated the Chapman & Hall edition, No. 3 *pre*-dated it by two or three months. [3754]

We know that Parlour Novelist No. 3 appeared at the end of March (for April 1). The *English Catalogue* dates the Chapman & Hall edition in May. This is not in itself conclusive; but other evidence can be brought in support. The work is not included in a Chapman & Hall catalogue for October 1845, but does appear in one dated September 1846. An illustrated 8vo of the kind, had it really been published prior to March 1846, would in all likelihood have been published before Christmas 1845 (for the Christmas market) and would then surely have been pre-announced in a list for October, 1845?

4 **Mansfield Park,** by Jane Austen. May 1846 [1814]

5 **Magician,** by Leitch Ritchie. June 1846 [1836]

6 **Clarence,** by Miss Sedgwick. July 1846 [1830]

7 **Tales by the O'Hara Family: Part II.** Aug. 1846 [1826] [containing *The Nowlans*]

8, 9 COUNT OF MONTE CRISTO, by Dumas. Sept., Oct. 1846 [First French 1845]. These two vols. more than probably post-dated the Chapman and Hall edition.

10 **Dark Lady of Doona,** by W. H. Maxwell; JONATHAN FROCK and FLORETTA, by H. Zschokke. Nov. 1846

The Maxwell story was first published in Smith, Elder's Library of Romance, 1833 (q.v.). Probably the first English edition of the Zschokke stories.

11 **Tales by the O'Hara Family: Part III.** Dec. 1846 [1825] [containing *John Doe* and *Peter of the Castle*]

12 **Tales of the Woods and Fields:** a Second Series of *Two Old Men's Tales* (by Mrs Marsh). ? Jan. 1847, dated 1846 [1836]

13 GEORGE, or THE PLANTER OF THE ISLE OF FRANCE, by Dumas. Feb. 1847 [First French 1843] Translated (for this series) by G. J. Knox. First edition in English.

14 VERONICA, by H. Zschokke. March 1847. Presumably first issue of this translation.

Notes. (i) Vols. 1, 3, 8, 9 were re-issued in 1848 as 'Extra Volumes' in the Parlour Library. These 'Extra Volumes' were in green boards uniform with the Parlour Library, but printed in *black*, with 'Extra Volume' on front cover, and with special decorated title-page.

(ii) Of the remaining titles in the Parlour Novelist the following were later re-issued in the Parlour Library: Vol. 4 (as P.L. 60); Vol. 5 (as P.L. 95); Vol. 7 (as P.L. 93); Vol. 10 (as P.L. 113); Vol. 11—half of it—(as P.L. 88); Vol. 12 (as P.L. 36); Vol. 13 (as P.L. 89).

(iii) In Vol. 5 are announced as 'In preparation' for issue in the Parlour Novelist: *Highways and Byways*, by Grattan, *Dark Lady of Doona* by Maxwell and *The Khan's Tale* by J. Baillie Fraser. The second title actually appeared as Vol. 10; the other two were subsequently published as 7 and 48 of The Parlour Library.

II. *THE PARLOUR LIBRARY* 1847–1863 [3755]

Begun on April 1, 1847 this series had reached its 279th volume in 1863. Whether it continued *in numbered form* beyond this point, I cannot establish; but there must have been very few, if any, numbered titles thereafter.

The books were originally fcap octavo, and bound, either in bright green glazed boards, pictorially and decoratively printed in brown; or, alternatively, in dark green ribbed cloth, blocked in blind on front and back, scroll-blocked and lettered in gold on spine. Later, they became 'yellow-backs' of various kinds, and later still full crown 8vo in size. *Pls. 13 & 15*

Thanks to the acquisition, while this Catalogue was in the press, of a very extensive run of the Library in bound form (there are 97 vols. each containing two or three titles), I am able to establish the schedule of imprints with virtual certainty. Nos. 1–101 [1847–1853] were published by Simms & M'Intyre, London

[*3755*] and Belfast, and Nos. 102–185 [1853–1858] by Thomas Hodgson, London. Nos. 186–205 [1859–1860] were published by Darton & Co.; Nos. 206–268 or 269—No. 269 is absent from the bound set—[1860–1862] by C. H. Clarke; Nos. 269 or 270–279 [1862–1863] by Darton & Hodge.

But a knowledge of the original imprints does not save us from the complications of the Clarke regime. This always date-shy and uninformative publisher took over *some* of Darton's already reclothed titles, himself reclothed others, reprinted others again, eliminating all signs of earlier control. Consequently between No. 184 and No. 279 are books with various combinations of imprints on case, end-papers and title-page. There are Hodgson titles with Darton boards and Clarke end-papers; there are volumes all-over Clarke; there are Darton titles with Clarke cases and end-papers, and so on. As the volumes are undated and the list of the series on the end-papers is grouped under authors and without reference to order of publication, the tangle cannot be unravelled.

The series achieved final degradation during the seventies, when certain titles appeared in large yellow-back format over the imprint of Weldon & Co. No series half-title or number is in the only specimen seen, which has the standardised 'book-shelf spine' (introduced by Clarke) with the series-title in one panel. The text is printed on abominable paper and the front cover picture is blurred and weak.

It is strange that Weldon should have been permitted to use the series at all, seeing that in 1869 its copyright had been acquired by Ward Lock & Tyler (see their 'Shilling' and 'Sixpenny' series described below); and stranger still, when one recalls that the later and more extreme titles in the 'Coming K——' Series (3480 etc. in Section II) were published by Weldon, after Ward Lock's subsidiary, Beeton, had drawn back in alarm. Once again one asks one's self, what were the ramifications of the firm of Ward Lock and what cover-imprints had they at their disposal?

It must be admitted that only during the Simms & M'Intyre period is the ordering of the PARLOUR LIBRARY really scrupulous and easy to establish. The following developments during this epoch may be noted:

Dates on Title-page. Nos. 1–109 are dated, i.e. the first eight Hodgson titles carrying dates, which thereafter disappear.

End-papers. Nos. 1–31—*green*, either plain or printed with series in proper order. Nos. 32–42—white, printed in blue or green with series in proper order. Nos. 43 onward—white, printed in black with series under authors and not in order, although, so long as Simms & M'Intyre are in charge, the outside back cover continues to announce recent and forthcoming titles in correct order.

Decorative Series Title (carrying number of volume). This precedes printed title in Nos. 1–33. Thereafter it disappears, being substituted by a plain half-title carrying the number of the volume in the series.

Front Covers and Spines. The number of the volume appears both on front cover and spine of Nos. 1–33. Thereafter it disappears from both places and is printed only on the half-title. The publishers thus explain this change: 'The consecutive numbering on the bindings will be dropped so that a selection may be made from the Series without having the appearance of being imperfect.'

Back Covers. The first issues of Nos. 1–25 show the front-cover design repeated on the back cover with the number and title of the forthcoming volume enclosed in the pictorial frame. From No. 26 onward back covers are printed with straightforward type-set adverts., and later binding-up of volumes, prior to No. 25, show similar treatment.

Cloth Editions. Nos. 1–33 (despite an original announcement to the contrary, see p. 151) were issued only in boards. With No. 34 a cloth style at one and sixpence was announced, introduced, and made retrospective, and henceforward the two styles were simultaneous. Cloth copies of Nos. 1–33 are not of first issue.

Extra Volumes. See above, under PARLOUR NOVELIST.

Pl. 13 Post-Simms & M'Intyre developments demand more tentative description, and concern the introduction of pictorial covers. Sometime in the autumn of 1854 Hodgson made a considerable innovation by boarding certain selected titles from those already published in 'brilliant fancy covers by Alfred Crowquill'. The first announcement I can find of this attraction is on the back cover and inside back end-papers of No. 118.

About a dozen titles are listed as available in this new dress, and the list rapidly increases as time goes on, [3755] These 'fancy covers' are in my experience very uncommon. Where specimens are in the Collection, they are recorded in the Schedule of Titles. A few of the titles so embellished are also in the Collection (or have been seen by me) in the regulation green boards, and I presume both styles were issued in every case where a book was chosen for fancy-board treatment.

When Darton took over, they began clothing both new and existing titles in conventional yellow-back pictorial boards, a process carried much further by Clarke. I doubt whether any other style was now issued, and suspect the traditional green boards died with Hodgson's control. Clarke standardised still more by introducing a uniform spine design showing book-laden shelves with a panel one-third high carrying the series title. *Pl. 14*

* * * * * *

Two associated features of the early (and most significant) career of the Parlour Library merit record.

(i) **Initial Publicity.** *The Dublin University Magazine* for February 1847 carried the following displayed advertisement:

THE BOOK FOR ALL

'ONE OF THE BOLDEST SPECULATIONS THAT HAS EVER BEEN MADE IN THE HISTORY OF BOOKSELLING'

MESSRS SIMMS and M'INTYRE, Belfast, Publishers of the 'PARLOUR NOVELIST', encouraged by the success which has attended their endeavours to diffuse really good literature in a form at the same time cheap and elegant, and convinced, by their experiment, that there exists among the mass of their fellow countrymen, an ardent desire for reading, which as yet cannot be gratified, owing to the high prices at which unexceptionable works of fiction are sold, have determined on engaging *in one of the boldest speculations that has ever been made in the history of bookselling*, viz.:

TO PRODUCE A SERIES OF NOVELS AND TALES BY THE MOST DISTINGUISHED AUTHORS, AT A PRICE WHICH WILL PLACE THEM WITHIN THE REACH OF THE WHOLE READING PUBLIC

Taking into consideration the value of the literary matter, this series will be THE CHEAPEST THAT HAS EVER BEEN ISSUED IN ANY COUNTRY OR ANY AGE, and the Publishers need scarcely say, that, to ensure their success, they must meet with wide co-operation from that class which they intend to benefit, and that nothing but a very extended circulation can prevent them from sustaining loss and abandoning the attempt.

They therefore propose, that on the 1*st of March*, their present series shall assume a new form, and appear under the title of

'THE PARLOUR LIBRARY'

Each volume (containing about 320 pages) will, with few exceptions, embrace an entire work, and will be bound in a richly gilt cover, produced in a perfectly new style, and will be sold for

ONE SHILLING

The first work will be an original novel by William Carleton called etc. etc.

In the March number of the same magazine another full-page advertisement qualified the description of the binding to 'neatly bound in a handsome cover'. It added that 'on April 1st would appear Dumas' *Memoirs of a Physician* which has just appeared in the feuilleton of *Le Constitutionnel*'; and that 'preparing for publication' was an illustrated edition of Carleton's *The Black Prophet* 'in an entirely new and gorgeous style of binding', with six designs by Harvey, post 8vo, 10*s.* 6*d.* (495*b* in Section I).

(ii) **Purchase of G. P. R. James' Copyrights.** No more striking proof exists of the enormous contemporary popularity of this now almost unread novelist than the fanfare with which Simms & M'Intyre announced that they had 'purchased the copyright of all Mr James' Works of Fiction' and intended 'to publish them in the Parlour Library varied at intervals by works of other celebrated authors'.

PARLOUR LIBRARY

This announcement was made on the front end-papers of No. 31 and was followed by a signed 'Address' specially written by James, in which he declares how gladly he has seized the opportunity of 'sending forth my own literary productions at a price which will place them within the reach of all, in the hope that I might contribute something, however small, to the improvement and to the happiness of my fellow men'.

Three volumes later (No. 34) is *The Gipsy*—the first James title in the series—and the 'Address' appears in it in greatly extended form and dated: 'Willey House, near Farnham. October, 1849.' Between No. 34 and No. 168, forty-two James novels were published in the series.

[3755*a*]

A. PARLOUR LIBRARY (Original Series)

SCHEDULE OF TITLES

(Titles marked with an asterisk are in the Collection in *bound* form only; those marked with a dagger are not present in any form.)

One or two preliminary observations on the schedule of the PARLOUR LIBRARY may usefully be made. It will be evident that up to about No. 180 a fairly constant standard of quality and kind was maintained, probably because during the Simms & M'Intyre regime plans were laid far ahead and only a moderate amount of improvisation was called for from later, less intelligent, publishers. With the early two hundreds, the series becomes rather ragged, and offers a larger proportion of new books by obscure authors, mingled with a few imprints which can only be described as scrapings.

To trace the influence on the series of the Sale by Auction in May 1857 of the copyrights which had belonged to Henry Colburn is not without interest. The following numbers were evidently purchased at the sale and successively incorporated in the series: 168, 170, 176, 202, 203, 204, 207, 214, 259, 262 and 270. It may also be noted that the arrangement come to for the inclusion of certain novels by Miss Muloch (232, 235, 249, 250) stopped short of *John Halifax*, which Hurst & Blackett clearly had no wish to part with.

The circulation of the later volumes (from the early two hundreds onwards) must have been sparse and irregular. Only a few odd titles are lodged with the British Museum and the Bodleian; and until the discovery of the bound set already referred to, I had never even seen a copy of most of the late numbers contained in it. Unfortunately, many half-titles (on which alone the number of the volume in the series was recorded) are not present in the bound set; and I have, therefore, been forced to base my list and sequence of titles on deductions from the bound volumes in my possession, checked by the schedule given in the *English Catalogue*. Even the *English Catalogue* stops at 276; and, as my own collection demonstrates that at least three further numbers were published, there may have been still more. I think the result as given below is in all probability correct, but I cannot guarantee it absolutely.

As was the case in the Bentley Standard Novel schedule, first editions and books with textual significance are set in caps, and the date of the first edition (where ascertainable) is given in brackets after the date of the PARLOUR LIBRARY issue. I have been unable to establish whether many of the later titles (particularly translations) first appeared in the PARLOUR LIBRARY or, if not, their dates of original publication.

1	BLACK PROPHET . .	Carleton	April 1,	1847	First edition of this story. 495 in Section I
2	MEMOIRS OF A PHYSICIAN I	Dumas	May 1,	1847	The French original began publishing in 1846. The first edition in English (incomplete) appeared with Pearce in that year. P.L. Nos. 2, 10 and 16 are first editions of a different (and even more incomplete) translation
3	WOOD LEIGHTON . .	Mary Howitt	June 1,	1847 (1836)	'New, re-arranged & Corrected Edition'
4	Consuelo I . . .	Sand	?June 15,	1847 (First French 1842)	
5	Consuelo II . . .	,,	July 1,	1847 (First French 1842)	

[3755a]

No.	Title	Author	Month	Year	Notes
6	Collegians	Griffin	Aug. 1,	1847 (1829)	
7	Highways and Byways	Grattan	Sept. 1,	1847 (1823)	
8	Old Convents of Paris and The Haunted Marsh	Reybaud and Sand	Oct. 1,	1847 (First French of Sand story 1846)	Re-issued by Weldon (mid-eighties) as full size yellow-back printed from old P.L. type or plates
9	MARIAN	Mrs Hall	Nov. 1,	1847 (1840)	'Second Edition' with Dedication dated April 3, 1847
10	MEMOIRS OF A PHYSICIAN II	Dumas	Dec. 1,	1847	See No. 2 above
11	EMIGRANTS OF AHADARRA	Carleton	Jan. 1,	1848	First edition of this story. 499 in Section I
12	Rosa and Gertrude. My Uncle's Library	Töpffer	Feb. 1,	1848	? First English edition
13	Schinderhannes	Ritchie	March 1,	1848 (1833)	
14	Emilia Wyndham	Marsh	April 1,	1848 (1846)	
15	Tales of Munster Festivals	Griffin	May 1,	1848 (1827)	
16	MEMOIRS OF A PHYSICIAN III	Dumas	June 1,	1848	See No. 2 above
17	Highways and Byways: Series II	Grattan	July 1,	1848 (1825)	
18	OLIVIA	Anon [Lady Lyons]	Aug.	1848	First edition of this story. Copy in the Collection dated 1849
19	Parsonage I	Töpffer	Sept.	1848 }	? First edition of this translation. An English edition appeared in 1836
20	Parsonage II	,,	Oct.	1848 }	
21	FARDOROUGHA THE MISER	Carleton	Nov.	1848 (1839)	Long Introduction dated Sept. 16, 1848, special to this edition. 502*a* in Section I
22	Confessions of an Elderly Lady and of an Elderly Gentleman	Blessington	Dec.	1848 (1836, 1838)	
23	Family Pictures	Aug. la Fontaine	Jan.	1849	? First English edition
24	TITHE PROCTOR	Carleton	Feb.	1849	First edition of this story. 517 in Section I
25	Emma	Austen	March	1849 (1816)	
26	Previsions of Lady Evelyn	Marsh	April	1849 (1844)	Extracted from *Triumphs of Time*
27	Tales and Sketches	Töpffer	May	1849	? First English edition
28	Father Connell.	Banim	June	1849 (1842)	
29	Sidonia the Sorceress I	From the German of W. Meinhold	July	1849 }	? First English edition
30	Sidonia the Sorceress II	,, ,,	Aug.	1849 }	
31	TALES OF THE FIRST FRENCH REVOLUTION	Edited Marsh	Sept.	1849	First edition of this collection
32	ANDREW THE SAVOYARD	de Kock	Oct.	1849	? First English edition
33	Adventures of M. Violet	Marryat	Nov. 1,	1849 (1843)	Also in fancy boards, unnumbered, Hodson, n.d.
34	GIPSY	James	Dec. 1,	1849 (1835)	Special Preface proclaims James' faith in the process of cheapening literature
35	One in a Thousand	,,	Jan. 1,	1850 (1835)	
36	Tales of the Woods and Fields	Marsh	Feb. 1,	1850 (1836)	
37	Robber (*Pl. 15*)	James	March 1,	1850 (1838)	
38	Mary of Burgundy	,,	Mar. (?15)	1850 (1833)	
39	Country Stories	Mitford	April	1850 (1837)	
40	Morley Ernstein	James	May	1850 (1842)	
41	Sketch-book of Geoffrey Crayon	Irving	May 1,	1850 (1820)	
42	Tales of a Traveller	,,	May 15,	1850 (1824)	
43	Two Old Men's Tales	Marsh	May	1850 (1834)	Also issued in pictorial yellow-back boards, Clarke, n.d. throughout

PARLOUR LIBRARY

	No.	Title	Author	Date	Year	Notes
[3755a]	44	Castelnau . . .	James	June 1,	1850 (1841)	Originally published as 'The Ancien Régime'
	45	Pictures of the French Revolution	Lamartine	July 15,	1850	? First English edition
	46	Darnley . . .	James	Aug.	1850 (1830)	
	47	Northanger Abbey and Persuasion	Austen	Sept. 1,	1850 (1818)	
	48	Khan's Tale . . .	Fraser	Oct. 1,	1850 (1833)	
	49	Smuggler . . .	James	Nov. 1,	1850 (1845)	
	50	Zenobia, or the Fall of Palmyra	Author of *Julia* (Rev. W. Ware)	Dec. 1,	1850 (1844)	
	51	BELLAH: A TALE OF LA VENDÉE	From the French. Ed. Marsh	Dec. 15,	1850	First English edition of this story
	52	Brigand . . .	James	Jan. 1,	1851 (1841)	Originally published as 'Corse de Leon'
	53	GENEVIEVE . . .	Lamartine, translated by Mary Howitt	Jan. 15,	1851 (First French 1850)	? First English edition
	54	SIR PHILIP HETHERINGTON	Author of *Olivia* (Lady Lyons)	Feb. 1,	1851	First edition of the story
	55	Wanderer and his Home .	Lamartine	March 1,	1851	? First English edition
	56	Philip Augustus . .	James	April 1,	1851 (1831)	
	57	HEIR OF WAST-WAYLAND .	Mary Howitt	May 1,	1851	First edition of this story
	58	Game of Life . .	Ritchie	June 1,	1851 (1830)	
	59	Gowrie or the King's Plot .	James	July 1,	1851 (1848)	
	60	Mansfield Park . .	Austen	June 15,	1851 (1814)	
	61	Henry Masterton . .	James	July 1,	1851 (1832)	
	62	Rivals . . .	Griffin	July 15,	1851 (1830)	
	63	John Marston Hall . .	James	Aug. 1,	1851 (1834)	
	64	Countess of Rudolstadt .	Sand	Aug. 15,	1851 (First French 1844)	? First English edition
	65	ADVENTURES OF AN EMIGRANT IN SEARCH OF A COLONY	Rowcroft	Sept. 1,	1851	First edition of this story
	66	Convict . . .	James	Oct. 1,	1851 (1847)	
	67	TWO FRIENDS . .	Marriott Oldfield	Nov. 1,	1851	First edition of this story
	68	King's Highway . .	James	Dec. 1,	1851 (1840)	
	69	†Agnes de Mansfeldt . .	Grattan	Jan. 1,	1852 (1835)	
	70	Ghost-Hunter . . .	Banim	Dec. 15,	1851 (1833)	
	71	*Slave-King . . .	Adapted from Hugo	Jan. 15,	1852 (1833)	
	72	Charles Tyrrell. . .	James	Feb. 1,	1852 (1839)	
	73	Discipline . . .	Brunton	Feb. 15,	1852 (1814)	
	74	Margaret Catchpole . .	Cobbold	March 1,	1852 (1845)	
	75	Pictures of Life . .	From Stifter by Mary Howitt	April 1,	1852	? First English edition
	76	Agincourt . . .	James	May 1,	1852 (1844)	
	77	Scalp-Hunters . . .	Mayne Reid	May	1852 (1851)	
	78	Forest Days . . .	James	June 1,	1852 (1843)	
	79	Wilmingtons . . .	Marsh	July 1,	1852 (1850)	
	80	Heidelberg . . .	James	Aug. 1,	1852 (1846)	
	81	Gentleman of the Old School .	,,	Sept.	1852 (1839)	
	82	CAGOT'S HUT and CONSCRIPT'S BRIDE	Grattan	Oct. 1,	1852	First edition of these stories. 1059 in Section I
	83	Jacquerie . . .	James	Nov. 1,	1852 (1841)	
	84	†Uncle Tom's Cabin . .	Stowe	Nov.	1852 (1852)	
	85	Simple Story . . .	Inchbald	Dec.	1852 (1791)	

No.	Title	Author	Date	Year	Notes
86	REMEMBRANCES OF A MONTHLY NURSE	Downing	Dec. 1,	1852	First book edition of these 'Remembrances', originally printed in *Fraser's* and the *Monthly.* Also in pictorial yellow-back boards; Darton on title, n.d.; Clarke on covers [*3755a*]
87	Whim and its Consequences	James	Jan. 1,	1853 (1847)	
88	*John Doe	Banim		1853 (1825)	Extracted from *Tales by the O'Hara Family*, 1st Series
89	George	Dumas		1853 (1846)	Inherited from the *Parlour Novelist*
90	Stuart of Dunleath	Norton	Feb. 1,	1853 (1851)	Also in pictorial yellow-back boards; Darton, n.d. (cont. signature dated October 1861)
91	Hugenot	James	March 1,	1853 (1839)	
92	Miller of Angibault	Sand	March 15,	1853 (First French 1845)	
93	Nowlans	Banim	March 15,	1853 (1826)	Extracted from *Tales of the O'Hara Family*, 2nd Series
94	Arrah Neil	James	April 1,	1853 (1845)	
95	*Magician	Ritchie		1853 (1836)	
96	Time the Avenger	Marsh	May 1,	1853 (1851)	
97	Sir Theodore Broughton	James	June 1,	1853 (1848)	
98	Rifle-Rangers	Mayne Reid	July 1,	1853 (1850)	
99	Forgery	James	Aug. 1,	1853 (1849)	
100	LOVER UPON TRIAL	Author of *Olivia* (Lady Lyons)	Sept. 1,	1853	First edition of this story
101	False Heir	James	Oct. 1,	1853 (1843)	Simms & M'Intyre, final imprint
102	Mordaunt Hall.	Marsh	Nov. 1,	1853 (1849)	Thomas Hodgson, first imprint
103	†Arabella Stuart	James	Dec. 1,	1853 (1844)	
104	Scottish Heiress	R. M. Daniels (sic)	Jan. 1,	1854 (1843)	
105	*Henry of Guise	James	Feb. 1,	1854 (1839)	
106	Tenant of Wildfell Hall	Brontë	March 1,	1854 (1848)	
107	Beauchamp	James	April 1,	1854 (1848)	
108	Rosa or the Black Tulip	Dumas	May	1854 (First French 1850)	Also in fancy boards, imprint Hodgson. No copy seen in standard green
109	Cardinal's Daughter	R. M. Daniels (sic)	June	1854 (1847)	
110	ENGLISH ENVOY AT THE COURT OF NICHOLAS I	Corner	June	1854	First edition of this story
111	*Attila	James	July 1	[1854] (1837)	Only occasional date on title-page from now on
112	*Hero of Our Days	Lermontov, trans. by Pulszky	? July	[1854] ?	? First edition of this version of Lermontov's Caucasian Tales, of which a translation, entitled *Sketches of Russian Life in the Caucasus* appeared in 1853 in the Illustrated Family Novelist 3747 above)
113	Dark Lady of Doona	Maxwell	? Aug.	[1854] (1846)	
114	*Sybil Lennard	Mrs Grey	Aug. 1,	[1854] (1846)	
115	COUNTESS OF ST ALBAN	Haeckländer	Oct.	[1854]	First English edition (by Franz Demmler) from *Stories without a Name* by Haeckländer
116	Sea Lions	Cooper	Oct.	[1854] (1849)	
117	Marks Reef	,,		[1854] (1847)	
118	Russell	James		[? 1854] (1847)	

PARLOUR LIBRARY

[3755a]	119	MAURICE TIERNAY . .	Lever	Dec. 1,	[1854]	First edition of this story. 1411 in Section I
Pl. 13	120	HUNTER'S FEAST . .	Mayne Reid		[1855]	First edition of this story
	121	Stepmother . . .	James		[1855] (1846)	
	122	Castle Avon . . .	Marsh		[1855] (1852)	
	123	SIR JASPER CAREW . .	Lever		[1855]	First edition of this story. 1419 in Section I
	124	Castle of Ehrenstein . .	James		[1855] (1847)	
	125	*Margaret Maitland . .	Oliphant		[1855] (1849)	
	126	Angela. . . .	Marsh		[1855] (1848)	
	127	Eva St Clair . . .	James	July 14,	[1855] (1843)	
	128	*BROTHERS BASSETT .	Corner		[1855]	Cannot trace an earlier edition, and imagine this to be the first
	129	*Merkland . . .	Oliphant		[1855] (1851)	
	130	Normans Bridge . .	Marsh		[1855] (1847)	
	131	Delaware . . .	James		[? 1855] (1833)	
	132	Queen's Necklace . .	Dumas		[1855] (First French 1850)	
	133	Brambletye House . .	Smith		n.d. (1826)	
	134	Mount Sorel . . .	Marsh		n.d. (1845)	Also in pictorial yellow-back boards, Clarke, n.d. on title and covers; Darton & Hodge end-papers
	135	Inheritance . . .	Ferrier		n.d. (1824)	
	136	*De l'Orme . . .	James		[? 1856] (1830)	
	137	Marriage . . .	Ferrier		[1856] (1818)	
	138	Rose d'Albret . . .	James		[1856] (1844)	
	139	Outlaw . . .	Mrs Hall		[1856] (1835)	
	140	Jack Tier . . .	Cooper		[1856] (1848—as *Captain Spike*)	
	141	Younger Son . . .	Trelawny		[1856] (1831)	
	142	PHANTOM REGIMENT .	Grant	May 10,	[1856]	First edition of this story. 1055 in Section I
	143	Heiress of Bruges . .	Grattan	June 1,	[1856] (1830)	
	144	Frankenstein . . .	Shelley		[1856] (1818)	Also in yellow fancy boards; Hodgson, n.d., on title; Darton end-papers
	145	Lettice Arnold . .	Marsh		[1856] (1850)	
	146	*Richelieu . . .	James	Aug. 1,	[1856] (1829)	
	147	*Hungarian Brothers . .	Porter		n.d. (1807)	
	148	*Cardinal Mazarin or 20 Years After	Dumas		[1856] (First French 1845)	
	149	*Margaret Graham . .	James		n.d. (1848)	
	150	Father Darcy . .	Marsh		n.d. (1846)	
	151	*Hunchback of Notre Dame .	Hugo		n.d. (First French 1831)	
	152	*Nanon or Women's War .	Dumas		[1857] (First French 1845/46)	
	153	*Widows and Widowers. .	Mrs Thomson		n.d. (1842)	
	154	*Chevalier D'Harmental or The Conspirators	Dumas		n.d. (First French 1843)	Copy seen in pictorial boards; Clarke, n.d.
	155	*Aubrey . . .	Marsh		n.d. (1854)	
	156	*My Aunt Pontypool . .	James		n.d. (1835)	
	157	*Edgar Huntly . . .	Brockden Brown		n.d. (First English 1803)	
	158	Chain-bearer . . .	Cooper		n.d. (1845)	
	159	*Ann Boleyn . . .	Mrs Thomson		[1857] (1842)	
	160	Jacqueline of Holland . .	Grattan		[1857] (1831)	Also in fancy boards; Hodgson, n.d.; ? also in standard green
	161	Two Dianas . . .	Dumas		[1857] (First French 1846)	Also in fancy boards; Hodgson, n.d.; ? also in standard green
	162	*Woodman . . .	James		[1857] (1849)	

No.	Title	Author	Date	Notes
163	FORFEIT HAND . .	Grattan	[1857]	First edition of these stories. 1061 in Section I [3755a]
164	*Buccaneer . . .	Mrs Hall	n.d. (1832)	
165	CURSE OF THE BLACK LADY	Grattan	[1857]	First edition of these stories. 1060 in Section I
166	*Hussar . . .	Gleig	n.d. (1837)	
167	*White Mask . . .	Mrs Thomson	n.d. (1844)	
168	*History of a Flirt . .	Lady C. Bury	n.d. (1840)	
169	Man at Arms . . .	James	n.d. (1840)	
170	Ethel Churchill . .	L. E. L.	n.d. (1837)	
171	*Adventures Afloat and Ashore or Harry Hamilton	Stewart	[1857] ?	I cannot trace this title as having previously appeared elsewhere
172	*Days of the Regency . .	Mrs Trollope	n.d. (1848 as *Town and Country*)	
173	*Chicot the Jester . .	Dumas	[1857] (First French 1846)	
174	CAREW RALEGH . .	Mrs Thomson	[1857]	First edition of this story. Copy in Collection in cloth
175	*Young Widow . .	Mackenzie Daniels	n.d. (1844)	
176	LADY ANNE GRANARD .	L. E. L.	n.d. (1842)	'A New Edition thoroughly Revised for the Parlour Library.' Also in fancy boards; Hodgson, n.d.; ? issued in standard green
177	*Greville . . .	Gore	n.d. (1841)	
178	*Forty-Five Guardsmen .	Dumas	[1858] (First French 1848)	
179	Katherine Randolph . .	By the author of 'The Only Daughter'. Edited by Gleig	n.d. (1842)	Copy in Collection in green boards; Hodgson, n.d.
180	Heiress of Haughton . .	Marsh	n.d. (1855)	
181	*Tracey or The Apparition	Mrs Thomson	n.d. (1847)	
182	Regent's Daughter . .	Dumas	[1858] (First French 1845)	Copy in Collection in fancy boards; Hodgson, n.d.; ? also in standard green
183	Cauth Malowney (*sic*) . .	Power	[1858] (1830 as *The Lost Heir*)	Two copies in Collection: (1) in white 'fancy' boards, printed in green and black; Hodgson, n.d.: (2) in pictorial yellow-back boards; Hodgson title, Clarke end-papers, Darton on covers
184	*Arlington . . .	Lister	[1858] (1832)	
185	Confessions of an Etonian .	Rowcroft	n.d. (1852)	Original imprint Hodgson. Copy in Collection in pictorial yellow-back boards; Darton, n.d.
186	*Breach of Promise . .	Mrs Yorick Smythies	n.d. (1845)	Darton & Co., first imprint
187	*Disgrace to the Family .	Blanchard Jerrold	[1859] (1848)	
188	*Captain Paul & the Sicilian Bandit	Dumas	[1858] (First French 1838)	
189	*Refugees of Martinique .	Sue		
190	*Tales of the Peerage and the Peasantry	Mrs Sullivan. Edited Lady Dacre	n.d. (1831)	
191	*HAND AND GLOVE . .	Amelia B. Edwards	[1859]	First edition of this story
192	*Ben Bradshaw . .	Author of 'The Mysterious Man'	[1859] (1843)	
193	*de Cliffords . . .	Mrs Sherwood	[1859] (1847)	
194	Taking the Bastile I . .	Dumas	[1859] (First French 1853)	Copies in Collection in pictorial yellow-back boards; Darton, n.d. throughout
195	Taking the Bastile II . .	,,	[1859] (First French 1853)	Copies in Collection in pictorial yellow-back boards; Darton, n.d. throughout

PARLOUR LIBRARY

	No.	Title	Author	Date	Notes
[3755a]	196	*Trial and Triumph . .	M'Gauran	[1859] (1854)	
	197?	†Handy Andy . . .	Lover	[1859] (1842)	Also listed by *Eng. Cat.* as 276
	198	†White Chief . . .	Mayne Reid	[1859] (1855)	
Pl. 14	199	Moneyed Man . . .	Horace Smith	[1859] (1841)	Copy in Collection in pictorial yellow-back boards; Darton, n.d. throughout
	200	†Marrying Man . . .	Smythies	[?1859] (1841)	
	201	*ELSTEY OF SETTLED FOR LIFE	Anne Evans	[1859]	First edition of this story
	202	*Marmaduke Wyvil . .	H. W. Herbert	[1860]	(originally published by Colburn in 3 vols.) Imprint: Darton & Co.
	203	†Lottery of Life . .	Blessington	[1860] (1842)	
	204	†Outward Bound . .	Howard	[1860] (1838)	
	205	*RED HAND OF THE FORD OF THE DEE	Sophia Kelly (Mrs Sherwood's daughter)	[1860]	First edition of this story Imprint: Darton & Co.
	206	Stories of Peninsular War .	Maxwell	[1860] (1837, as *The Bivouac*)	Copy in the Collection pictorial yellow-back boards, Clarke, n.d. throughout
	207	*Fathers and Sons . .	Hook	[1860] (1842)	
	208	†REVELATIONS OF A CATHOLIC PRIEST	Maurice	[1860]	First edition of these stories
	209	†Love and Jealousy . .	Mrs Trollope	[1860] (1848, as *The Young Countess*)	
	210	†Ben Brace . . .	Chamier	[1860] (1836)	
	211	*Say and Seal . . .	Wetherell (Susan Warner)	[1860]	Described as 'Copyright Edition', this is the first English edition. Imprint: C. H. Clarke
	212	†Twelve Months of Matrimony .	Anon	[1860] ?	
	213	Courtier . . .	Gore	[1860] (1847)	Imprint: C. H. Clarke
	214	†Daughter of Night . .	Fullom	[1860] (1851)	
	215	*Widow Barnaby . .	Mrs Trollope	[1860] (1839)	
	216	*TALES OF THE SLAVE SQUADRON	Warneford	[1860]	First edition of these stories. Imprint of Chas. H. Clarke
	217	*Vicar of Wrexhill . .	Mrs Trollope	[1860] (1837)	
	218	*MARY ROCK . . .	St John	[1860]	First edition of this story
	219	†Cavendish . . .	Neale	[1860] (1831)	
	220	†Confessions of a Pretty Woman	Pardoe	[1860] (1846)	
	221	†Warning to Wives . .	Anon [Smythies]	[1860] (1847)	
	222	*SKELETON IN EVERY HOUSE	'Waters'	[1860]	First edition of these stories (see below 'Unnumbered')
	223	OPERA-SINGER'S WIFE .	Mrs Grey	[1860]	First edition of this story. Copy in the Collection in pictorial yellow-back boards; Clarke, n.d. throughout
	224	Frank Beresford . .	Curling	[1860] (1858)	Copy in the Collection in pictorial yellow-back boards; Clarke, n.d. throughout
	225	Ascanio . . .	Dumas	n.d.	(First French 1844) Copy in Collection in pictorial yellow-back boards; Clarke, n.d. throughout. Half-title: 'Parlour Library ccxxv'; front cover and spine: 'Dumas' Historical Library'
	226	*Young Husband . .	Mrs Grey	n.d. (?1857)	
	227	*MY PRETTY COUSIN .	Author of *The Jilt* [Smythies]	[1860]	First edition of this story
	228	†Ruth . . .	Mrs Gaskell	n.d. (1853)	
	229	ROMANCE OF COMMON LIFE.	'Waters'	n.d.	? First edition of these stories. Copy in the Collection in pictorial yellow-back boards; Clarke, n.d. throughout

	No.	Title	Author	Date		Notes
	230	†Half Sisters	Jewsbury	n.d.	(1848)	
	231	*COUNTESS MIRANDA	P. B. St John	n.d.	? 1861	First edition, according to Alibone, 1861, so probably this is original issue of this story *[3755a]*
	232	†Head of the Family	Muloch	n.d.	(1851)	
	233	*Daughters	Mrs Grey	n.d.	(1847)	
	234	EXPERIENCES OF A FRENCH DETECTIVE	'Waters' (adapted from Duhamel)	n.d.		? First edition of these stories. 3515 in Section II
	235	†Agatha's Husband	Muloch	n.d.	(1853)	
	236	*Chevalier	Mrs Thomson	n.d.	(1844)	
	237	†Mary Barton	Mrs Gaskell	n.d.	(1848)	
	238	†Lady Jane Grey	T. Miller	n.d.	(1840)	
	239	†Half-Blood	M. Reid (sic in *English Cat.*)	n.d.		? First edition. Cannot trace
	240	†AMY MOSS	P. B. St John	n.d.	(? 1861)	First edition (according to Alibone) dated 1860. This may be an error for 1861, and this an original issue
	241	*Wood-rangers	Mayne Reid (trans. from Bellamare)	n.d.	(1860)	
	242	†ALICE LESLIE	P. B. St John	[1861]		First edition of this story
	243	†Legends and Stories of Ireland	Lover	[1861]	(1831–4)	
	244	*Jealous Wife	Pardoe	[1861]	(1847)	
	245	†Madman of St James's	Trans. from German of Philip Galen by T. H.	[1861]		? First English edition
	246	†White Wolf of Brittany	Favel (? Féval)	[1861]		? First English edition
	247	†Elsie Venner	Holmes	[1861]		First English edition. First American 1861
	248	*QUEEN'S DWARF	Berwick	[1861]		First edition of this story
	249	†Olive	Muloch	n.d.	(1850)	
	250	†Ogilvies	,,	n.d.	(1849)	
	251	*Rachel the Jewess	Sicard (trans. from Spanish of Gonzales)	n.d.		? First English edition.
	252	†Gambler's Wife	Mrs Grey	n.d.	(? 1835)	
	253	†Cousin William	Hook	n.d.	(1828, in Third Series of *Sayings and Doings*)	
	254	*Rival Beauties	Pardoe	n.d.	(1848)	
	255	†Peep o' Day	Banim	n.d.	(1825, as *John Doe* in First Series of *Tales of the O'Hara Family*)	
	256	*Roman Maiden	Rowcroft	n.d.	?	
	257	†Parson's Daughter	Hook	n.d.	(1833)	
	258	†Gideon Giles, the Roper	Miller	n.d.	(1840)	
	259	†Precepts and Practice	Hook	n.d.	(1840)	
	260	†Bushranger	Rowcroft	n.d.	(1846)	
	261	?				
	262	†Woman of the World	Gore	n.d.	(1838)	
	263	†Gervase Skinner	Hook	n.d.	(1828, in Third Series of *Sayings and Doings*)	
	264	†Passion and Principle	,,	n.d.	(1825, in Second Series of *Sayings and Doings*)	
	265	*Captain Fancourt	Millingen (author of *Torres Vedras*)	n.d.		? First edition
Pl. 14	266	ROMANCE OF THE SEAS	'Waters'	n.d.	?	First edition of these stories. Copy in the Collection in pictorial yellow-back boards; Clarke, n.d. throughout
	267	†Courtship and Wedlock	Author of *The Jilt*	n.d.	(1850)	
	268	*Miser Lord (sequel to 224 above)	Curling	n.d.	(1859)	Imprint: C. H. Clarke
	269	†Jilt	Author of *The Flirt* [Smythies]	n.d.	(1844)	

PARLOUR LIBRARY

	No.	Title	Author	Date	Notes
[3755a]	270	*Lottery of Marriage	Mrs Trollope	n.d. (1849)	Imprint: Darton & Hodge
	271	*TIGER-HUNTER	Mayne Reid (trans. from Bellamare)	[1862]	First edition of this story. Imprint: Darton & Hodge
	272	*Soldier Monk	Berkeley	n.d. ?	Imprint: Darton & Hodge
	273	*Fair Rosamund	T. Miller	n.d. (1839)	Imprint: Darton & Hodge
	274	*He would be a Gentleman	Lover	[1862] (1844, as *Treasure Trove*)	
	275	*Jack Brag	Hook	[1862] (1837)	
	276?†	Handy Andy	Lover	[1862] (1842)	See 197 above
	277	Hinchbridge Haunted	Author of *The Green Hand* (Cupples)	1863 (1859)	Copy in Collection in pictorial yellow-back boards; Darton and Hodge throughout, and dated
	278	*?Recollections of a Detective Police Officer	'Waters'	[1863] (1856)	Number lacking from bound copy in Collection, but imprint Darton & Hodge, n.d.
	279	ROMANCE OF MILITARY LIFE	'Waters'		? First edition of these stories. Copy in Collection in pictorial yellow-back boards; Darton & Hodge, n.d. throughout

Unnumbered

Title	Author	Notes
A Skeleton in Every House (formerly 222)	'Waters'	Copy in Collection in pictorial yellow-back boards; Darton & Co. (42 Paternoster Row, late of Holborn Hill), throughout, n.d. Series title on half-title and spine but no number

Weldon Series (1876–1877)

No.	Title	Author
1	Cheveley	Lady Bulwer Lytton
2	Lottery of Marriage	Mrs Trollope
3	Outlaw	Mrs Hall
4	Margaret Maitland	Mrs Oliphant
5	Rectory Guest	Mrs Grey
6	Courtier	Mrs Gore
7	Heir of Wast Wayland	Mrs Howitt
8	Consuelo	George Sand
9	Godfrey Malvern	Thomas Miller
10	Chevalier	Mrs Thomson

Large format. Weldon & Co., n.d. Spine block as used from 229, but no series half-title. On verso of title: 'Parlour Library: new and Improved Edition'. The list opposite, including numbers, is taken from an advert. of late 1876. The only specimen in the Collection (or seen by me) is No. 6, which actual volume is not numbered. Of the ten titles here given Nos. 1, 5 and 9 had not previously appeared in the Parlour Library.

The Series title seems to have been soon dropped, for my copy of *Cheveley* in yellow-back form (Weldon, n.d.) is labelled 'Weldons 2/- Series' and carries a list of 26 titles facing title-page, of which Nos. 1–10 are as here given.

[3755b] B. PARLOUR LIBRARY: NEW ISSUE 1869–1870

In the late sixties the right to use the series title PARLOUR LIBRARY was acquired by Ward, Lock & Tyler, and in 1869 three different editions were announced—one at two shillings per volume, one at one shilling and one at sixpence. The publishers' pronouncement (which combines a well-merited tribute to Simms & M'Intyre with considerable sanctimony) reads:

'Probably no Series of Novels ever published attained more universal acceptance than those published in the PARLOUR LIBRARY. First in quality, as a series largest in quantity, and comprising the most Popular Works of the most successful Novelists, the PARLOUR LIBRARY took and held a leading position which excited the envy and aroused the imitativeness of the Publishing Trade. An over-stocked market was the natural result. Time, however, which tries all things, has demonstrated the necessity for Cheap and Good Books, such as the PARLOUR LIBRARY only admitted, and such as it is intended henceforth to produce.

'These Books will be chosen with the most scrupulous care and Parents may order them for their children with unqualified confidence in their perfect suitability for family perusal.'

Whether the Two Shilling Series ever appeared, I cannot say. I have never seen a specimen nor found an advertisement of it. That I can give the first 20 titles of the Shilling Series and the first 23 of the Sixpenny Series is due to advertisements on the back of the single specimen of each, which is all I have ever been able to find. The scarcity of these books (as great as that of Ward & Lock's SHILLING VOLUME SERIES) is very remarkable, and one wonders whether the stock was destroyed in a warehouse fire or was overtaken by some other disaster.

PARLOUR LIBRARY: SHILLING SERIES (1869–1870) [3755*b* (i)]

White paper wrappers, cut flush, printed in black and two colours (the only specimen seen is in black, scarlet and yellow, and presumably other volumes showed other combinations) with—on front, a wood-engraved drawing, title, author and series title; on spine up-lettered with title and series title; on back printed in black with a list of the series. The books are undated, but to the best of my knowledge all appeared in 1869 and 1870. Certainly the titles which follow were on the market by July 1870 as they were advertised in *Belgravia* for that month, and as the same list was advertised in February 1874 I presume that no further titles were published. Only No. 20 is in the Collection.

1 **Lady Goodchild's Fairy Ring** (A Collection of Fairy Tales)
2 ***Cynthia Thorold** (by the author of 'Whitefriars'—**Emma Robinson)**
3 ***Leonard Harlow ('Waters')**
4 ***Blow Hot, Blow Cold (Augustus Mayhew)**
5 ***The Round of Wrong (About)**
6 **Recollections of an Irish Police Magistrate (Addison).** First published 1862. 3518 in Section II
7 **Autobiography of a French Detective** (edited **Wraxall**). First published 1862. 3514 in Section II
8 ***Something to Laugh At (Anon)**
9 ***The Funny Fellow (Anon)**
10 **Dick Diminy, The Jockey (C. J. Collins)**
11 ***Make Your Game (Sala).** First published 1860. 3676 in Section II
12 **The Greek Brigand** (illustrated by Doré)
13 ***Hunted to Death (W. S. Hayward)**
14 ***The Chain of Destiny (Vane St John)**
15 ***Memoirs of a Lady in Waiting (Aylmer)**
16 **Which Wins, Love or Money? (Emma Robinson)**
17 **Rev. Alfred Hoblush and his Curacies (Percy Fitzgerald)**
18 **Clever Jack (Anon)**
19 ***The Night Mail (Percy Fitzgerald)**
20 ***Storm-Beaten,** by **Robert Buchanan** and **Charles Gibbon**

Titles asterisked previously appeared in Ward & Lock's SHILLING VOLUME LIBRARY. 3711 in Section II

PARLOUR LIBRARY: SIXPENNY SERIES (1869–1870) [3755*b* (ii)]

White paper wrappers, cut flush, printed in black and two colours (the only specimen seen is in black, green and yellow) with wood-engraved drawing etc. uniform with the Shilling Series. The books are undated, but Mr Ralph Straus tells me that all up to No. 16 at any rate were published in 1869, and the entire list which follows was advertised in *Belgravia* for July 1870. The same list was advertised in February 1874, which suggests that no further titles were published.

1 **The Young Lady's Book of Tales**
2 **The Boy's Own Book of Tales**
3 ***The Ship-Chandler (Sala)**
4 **The Family Credit (Westland Marston)**
5 ***The Filibuster (Albany Fonblanque)**
6 **Cruise of the Blue Jacket (Lieutenant Warneford, R.N.)**
7 **Undiscovered Crimes ('Waters').** First published 1862. 3538 in Section II
8 ***Lady Lorme (Annie Thomas)**
9 **Mutiny of the Saturn (Lieutenant Warneford, R.N.)**

[*3755b* (ii)] 10 The Fair of Emy Vale (Carleton). See 501 in Section I
11 *Perfidy of Captain Slyboots (Sala)
12 Give a Dog a Bad Name, And ——' (Albany Fonblanque)
13 The Wife's Portrait (Westland Marston)
14 Mrs Waldegrave's Will (Albany Fonblanque)
15 *Experiences of a Real Detective ('Waters')
16 The Late Mr D——, and Other Tales. By G. A. Sala
17 The Book of Moral Tales
18 The Girl's Own Book of Tales
19 The Little Red Man, and Other Fairy Tales.
20 *The Silver Acre (Carleton). See 513 in Section I
21 The Dream and the Waking (Annie Thomas)
22 The Valazy Family ('Waters')
23 Turf Characters

Titles asterisked previously appeared in Ward & Lock's SHILLING VOLUME LIBRARY. 3711 in Section II

[3756]

III. *PARLOUR LIBRARY BYE-PRODUCTS*

As soon as the PARLOUR LIBRARY was well-established, Simms & M'Intyre invented and launched other series, of which some particulars can suitably be given in order to round off this account of the firm's meteoric years of publishing.

[3756*a*]

A. PARLOUR LIBRARY OF INSTRUCTION (non-fiction)

Pl. 14 Published at one shilling in small 8vo, bound in pink glazed boards printed in black with the same pictorial design as on the PARLOUR LIBRARY. Spines plainly up-lettered. Back covers printed with adverts. Volumes not numbered in series. Decorative series title (as in PARLOUR LIBRARY) precedes printed title.

1. **Autobiography of Chateaubriand,** Vol. I 1849
2. **Memoirs of my Youth,** by **Lamartine** 1849
3. **Autobiography of Chateaubriand,** Vol. II 1849
4. **Autobiography of Chateaubriand,** Vol. III 1849
5. **Autobiography of Chateaubriand,** Vol. IV 1849
6. **Autobiography of Chateaubriand,** Vol. V (not in the Collection)

I doubt if the series went beyond this point, unless there appeared a sixth volume of Chateaubriand. Both the works in the series were first English translations. *Mémoires d'Outre Tombe* were published in Paris in 12 vols. during 1849–50 while an announcement of the Lamartine in *Chateaubriand*, Vol. I, states that the work 'is now being issued in Paris under the title of "Memoirs of My Youth" and will be published in the PARLOUR LIBRARY OF INSTRUCTION immediately upon its completion in the original'.

[3756*b*]

B. PARLOUR BOOK CASE (non-fiction)

Pl. 14 Published at eighteenpence, crown 8vo, bound in pale yellow glazed boards printed in red, brown and blue with arabesque design framing lettering (including series title) on front, spine and back. Yellow end-papers printed with adverts. The volumes are numbered in the series both on front cover and half-title.

Titles asterisked are not in the collection.

1 **Across the Rocky Mountains,** by **William Kelly** March 1, 1852
2 ***A Panorama of St Petersburg,** by **J. G. Kohl** April 1, 1852
3 **The Italian Sketch Book,** by **Fanny Lewald** May 1, 1852

4 **A Stroll Through the Diggings of California,** by **William Kelly** June 1, 1852
5 **Life in Mexico,** by **Madame Calderon** July 1, 1852
6 ***Remarkable Events in the Career of Napoleon** Aug. 1, 1852
7 ***The Glacier Land,** by **A. Dumas** Sept. 1, 1852
8 **Voices from Captivity,** by **Rev. J. R. Beard** Oct. 1, 1852

C. BOOKS FOR THE PEOPLE (fiction) [3756*c*]

Published at sixpence in small 8vo, bound in pale yellow glazed boards printed in black—on front with decorative frame (same block as used on series title of Parlour Library of Instruction) and lettering; on spine with scroll-pattern (no lettering); on back cover with advert. Volumes not numbered in series. *Pl. 14*

Three specimens are in the Collection (marked with a dagger), each dated 1852 and each carrying the same advert. on back of titles 'already published'. The books are actually *portions* of PARLOUR LIBRARY (or PARLOUR NOVELIST) volumes and are not re-foliated. So far as possible I have indicated the parent volume in the list which follows:

Angela (from the German by Mary Howitt)
†Castle of Fools (from the German by Mary Howitt) } From P.L. 75
Rivals (Griffin)
Tracy's Ambition (Griffin) } From P.L. 62
Shil Dhuv (Griffin)
Card-Drawing (Griffin) } From P.L. 15
Northanger Abbey (Austen)
Persuasion (Austen) } From P.L. 47
†Crohoore of the Bill Hook (Banim)
†Fetches (Banim) } From P.N. 1
Spectre Guest (Zschokke) ? From P.N. 13
Country Stories (Mitford) From P.L. 39
Priest and the Garde du Corps (Grattan)
Vouée au Blanc (Grattan) } From P.L. 17
Inheritance (Töpffer)
Great Saint Bernard etc. (Töpffer) } From P.L. 27
Love and Duty (Marsh)
Country Vicarage (Marsh) } From P.L. 36
Soldier's Fortune (Marsh)
Professional Visits of Le Docteur Noir etc. (Marsh) } From P.L. 31

ROMANCIST, AND NOVELIST'S LIBRARY, THE 1839–1840. The Best Works of the Best Authors. ('Edited by William Hazlitt' on title-pages of Vols. III, IV) [3757]

[FIRST SERIES.] 4 vols. large 4to. J. Clements, 21–22 Little Pulteney Street 1839 (I and II), 1840 (III and IV). Navy blue fine-ribbed cloth, embossed front, back and spine, gold-lettered on front and spine. Light green glazed end-papers.

Vol. I	(iv)+412	Vol. III	(iv)+(412)
II	(iv)+412	IV	(iv)+(412)

Book-plate of Thomas Inglis, M.D. in Vols. I, III, IV.

Notes. (i) This work appeared in twopenny weekly parts, numbered 1 to 104, each of 16 pp., except the last half-yearly part (i.e. the last part in each volume) which was of 12 pp. and probably printed with the prelims.

(ii) Vol. II is dedicated to the 'Author of Eugene Aram' and Vol. IV contains an 'Address' forecasting the Second (8vo) Series.

[*3757*] (iii) The Contents of these four volumes merit careful study. From the point of view of the Gothic Romance (which, as a dominant taste in fiction, had died twenty-five years earlier) the selection is of great value as evidence of the survival and otherwise of individual reputations.

CONTENTS

Vol. I

Lewis: Bravo of Venice
Mary Shelley: A Tale of the Passions
Walpole: Castle of Otranto
Marmontel: Misanthrope Corrected
Lewis: Mistrust or Blanche and Osbright
Leigh Hunt: The Florentine Lovers
Ann Radcliffe: The Castles of Athlin and Dunbayne
Henry Mackenzie: The Story of La Roche
de Mendoza: Lazarillo de Tormes
Goethe: A Love Tale
Ann Radcliffe: The Sicilian Romance
Anon: The Palisadoes: a Tale of the Hudson
Anon: The Spy and the Traitor: a Tale of the American War
Clara Reeve: The Old English Baron
Bernardin St Pierre (sic): Paul and Virginia
Shelley: Zastrozzi
Marmontel: The Shepherdess of the Alps
Napoleon (The Emperor): Julio or the Force of Destiny
Defoe: Captain Singleton
Lewis: The Anaconda
Goldsmith: The Vicar of Wakefield
Anon: The Convict
Mme Cottin: Elizabeth or the Exiles of Siberia
[J. F. Kind]: Der Freischütz. From the German
Anon: The Midnight Embrace in the Halls of Werdendorff
Anon: Eccentricities of Colonel David Crockett of West Tennessee
Dumas: Pascal Bruno (*specially translated for R. and N.L.*)
Anon: Jamie Loon: a Tale of America
Anon: The Diamond Watch
Lamb: Rosamund Gray
Frances Sheridan: History of Nourjahad
Anon: The Husband's Revenge or the Confession of Richard Price
Anon: The Lovers of Vire
d'Arlincourt: The Renegade or The Moors in France (*specially translated for R. and N.L.*)
Henry Mackenzie: Louisa Venoni
Elizabeth Inchbald: Nature and Art
Mrs S. C. Hall: The Redderbrae
Prince Puckler Muskau: A Cross Bones, a Tale of Galway
W. B. MacCabe: The Ghost of Kilsheelan
Anon: The Bottle Imp: a Tale from the German
Anon: Nicolas Pedrosa
Anon: The Pirate Captain
J. A. St John: Hell's Hollow
Prof. Ingraham: The Snow Pile
Mrs Parsons: The Castle of Wolfenbach
Anon: The Dean of Badajoz: a Spanish Tale
Henry Mackenzie: The Man of Feeling
Anon: The Romance of a Day
Dr Johnson: Anningait and Ajut
[W. G. Simms]: Martin Faber: the Story of a Criminal (by the author of 'Yemassee', 'Pelayo the Goth', etc.)
Anon: The Pirate's Treasure

Vol. II

Hugo: Notre Dame de Paris (*specially translated for R. and N. L. 'with the addition of several chapters that have not been given in any former translation'*)
Anon: The Spectre Barber: a Tale of the Sixteenth Century
Anon: The Czar and the Czarowitz: a Russian Story
Anon: Gondibert: a Tale of the Middle Ages
Anon: The Spectre Unmasked
Karl von Miltig: The Twelve Nights
Ann Radcliffe: The Romance of the Forest
Cervantes: La Gitana: or the Little Gipsy
Washington Irving: The Young Robber
Anon: The Two Rings: a French Tale
Paul de Kock: The Barber of Paris (*specially translated for R. and N.L.*)
William Jerdan: The Sleepless Woman
Stephen Cullen: The Haunted Priory or the Fortunes of the House of Rayo
Alan Cunningham: Gowden Gibbie
Anon: The Bohemian
Mrs Sedgwick: Three Experiments of Living
Charles Brockden Brown: Edgar Huntly or the Sleep-Walker
Leigh Hunt: Ronald of the Perfect Hand
James Hogg: The Bogle o' the Brae
Anon: The Cypress Crown or the Murderer's Doom
Anon: Doukanji and the Dervish, a Turkish Tale
Goethe: Antonelli
Anon: The Devil's Ladder of the Gnomes of Redrich
Miss Sedgwick: Home
Fennimore (sic) Cooper: The Last of the Mohicans
Washington Irving: The Enchanted Island
Leigh Hunt: The Daughter of Hippocrates
Anon: The Cobbler of Bagdad
Maturin: The Wild Irish Boy
Leigh Hunt: Galgano and Madonna Minoccia

Vol. III

Schiller: The Ghost Seer
Zschokke: The Dead Ghost (*translated by Julia Sinnett*)
J. N. Reynolds: Mocha Dick: or the White Whale of the Pacific
Anon: Robin Hood
Anon: The Magic Dollar

Mrs S. C. Hall: The Drowned Fisherman
Anon: The Field of Terror
Anon: Rip van Winkle
Lewis: Amorassan
Leigh Hunt: Adventures of Cephalus and Procris
W. Herbert: Ella Rosenberg
Anon: The Sexton of Cologne
R. H. Horne: Wolmar, a German Legend
Leigh Hunt: The Nurture of Triptolemus
Shelley: St Irvyne
Anon: Lorenzo or the Robber
Leigh Hunt: The Fair Revenge
Anna Maria Porter: Walsh Colville
Lamb: The Tempest, a Tale from Shakespeare
R. H. Horne: The Last Scene of a Miser's Tragedy
James Hogg: The Laidlaws and the Scotts
Florian: Gonzalvo of Cordova (*translated by George Frederick Smith*)
Anon: Kester Hobson, a Tale of the Yorkshire Wolds
Anon: Count Roderico's Castle of Gothic Times (author unknown. Also wrote *The Carpenter's Daughter of Derham Down*)
Egerton Brydges: Mary de Clifford
Patrick Byrne: James FitzJames
Schiller: The Sport of Destiny (*specially translated for R. and N.L. and signed* 'F. W.' *at end*)
Bernardin de St Pierre: The Indian Cottage
Anon: Nannie or a Tale of the Coral Ring
Washington Irving: The Abencerages
Paul de Kock: Andrew the Savoyard (*translated by William Hazlitt*)
Duchess de Duras: Ourika or the Negress (*from the French*)
Polidori: The Vampyre
Ann Radcliffe: The Italian
Hugo: Hans of Iceland
A. Morton: The Two Hunchbacks of Bagdad
Anon: The Pedestrian
'Dr Moore': The Post Captain or The Wooden Walls Well Manned (here attributed to the author of *Zeluco*: actually by John Davis, 678 in Section I)
Anon: The Orphan of Bollenbach or Polycarp the Adventurer
Anon: Julia or the Victim of Indiscretion

Vol. IV [*3757*]

Francis Glasse: Joe Oxford or the Runaway (The Preface to Vol. II announces this feature of the R. and N.L. in such a way as to suggest that it will there appear for the first time. Glasse is described as the author of 'New Clinton' and 'Andrew Winpenny')
Christian Simplicius: The Village Pastor (*specially translated for R. and N.L.*)
Anon: Head Quarters or The Elective Franchise; a Sketch of Long Island
Anon: Calum Dhu, a Highland Tale
Anon: The Betrothed
Elizabeth Helme: St Clair of the Isles
(Miss Sedgwick): Elinor Fulton
Leigh Hunt: The Beau Miser
Anon: The Last of the Grays: a Tale
William Maginn: A Vision of Purgatory
Anon: The Midnight Murder
(Teuthold): The Necromancer
Anon: Sir Edmund, a Fragment
Anon: The Mysterious Tailor, a Romance of High Holborn
Cazotte: Pleasure, an Allegory
Anon: Oliver and Isabella
Elizabeth Inchbald: A Simple Story
Marmontel: Lauretta
Lamb: A Midsummer Night's Dream, a Tale from Shakespeare
Regina Maria Roche: The Children of the Abbey
John Leland: Longsword, Earl of Salisbury
Marmontel: Friendship put to the Test
Anon: The Deserters
Anon: Hans Carvel
(Longueville): The English Hermit
Lamb: The Winter's Tale, a Tale from Shakespeare
Anon: Azmoloch or The Castle of Linden-Woolfe
Balzac: Ginevra del Piombo
John Palmer: The Haunted Cavern
Lamb: Much Ado About Nothing, a Tale from Shakespeare
Anon: The Treacherous Friend

NEW SERIES 1841–1842 [3757 *a*]

This took the form of a series of 32 pp. 8vo parts, first collected into four volumes over the imprint of John Clements, Little Pulteney Street and dated 1841 (I–III), 1842 (IV) and then ultimately appearing as independent wrappered fictions, each with its own title-page and sold separately.

Vol. I

Maturin: Fatal Revenge. 'Published by J. Clements...for the Proprietors of the Romancist and Novelist's Library' 1840. pp. (256)
Vulpius: Rinaldo Rinaldini: Captain of Banditti. 1841. pp. 136
Hon. Judge Thompson: May Martin or The Money Diggers 1841 *and* Tyrone Power: The Gipsy of the Abruzzo. pp. 48 + 16
Andrew Picken: The Deerstalkers of Glenskiach 1840 *and* Lewis: My Uncle's Garret Window 1841. pp. 54 + 20 The second story has its own title-page.

[3757a] **Vol. II**

W. G. Simms: Guy Rivers, The Outlaw, a Tale of Georgia 1841 *and* John Galt: The Fatal Whisper 1841. pp. (214) + (10) The second story has its own title-page.

Francis W. Thomas: Howard Pinckney 1841. pp. (160)

J. Fennimore (sic) Cooper: Imagination, a Tale for Young Women. pp. (32) The over-all Contents List states (probably truly) that this tale has never before been published in England. It was first published in New York in 1823 as by 'Jane Morgan'.

De la Motte Fouqué: Undine (*translated by Rev. Thomas Tracy*) 1841 *and* Quevedo: Paul the Spanish Sharper (*translated by John Stevens*) 1841 *and* Henry L. Tuckerman: The Sad Bird of the Adriatic 1841 *and* John Galt: Haddah Ben Ahab (1841). pp. (50) + (60) + 10 + 4 These four stories spread over four parts. The first three have their own title-page. The Galt story is described in the over-all Contents List as Copyright.

Vol. III

Francis Glasse: Andrew Whinpenny, Count de Deux Sous 1841. pp. (224) Described as 'A New Work, never before published'.

Veit Weber: Woman's Revenge or the Tribunal of Blood 1841 *and* A. Morton: The Charmed Scarf 1841 *and* Schiller: The Criminal 1841. pp. 42 + 8 + (14) (*translated expressly for the R. & N.L.*) These three stories spread over two parts. Each has its own title-page.

G. P. R. James: Bertrand de la Croix 1841 *and* The Caliph's Adventure (anon) 1841. pp. (26) + 6

Anne Ker: Edric the Forester 1841. pp. 64

Matteo Bandello: Romeo and Juliet 1841 *and* Edward Morgan (anon) 1841 *and* The Wrecker (anon). pp. 18 + 12 + 2 The first and second story have their own title-page.

D. F. Haynes: The Romance of the Castle 1841 *and* Andrea Vivano 1841. pp. 100 + (12) + (6) Both stories have their own title-page. The last six pages are adverts.

Vol. IV

John R. Willis: Carleton or Duty and Patriotism. A Tale of the American Revolution 1841. pp. 188 Described in over-all Contents List and on individual title-page as Copyright.

M. G. Lewis: Raymond and Agnes or The Bleeding Nun, 1841 *and* Voltaire: Zadig 1841 *and* Andrew Picken: The Three Kearneys 1841 *and* John Galt: The Unguarded Hour 1841. These four stories spread over four parts. Each has its individual title-page. The Picken and Galt stories are described as Copyright.

Elizabeth Helme: The Farmer of Inglewood Forest, 1841 *and* Leitch Ritchie: The Cheaterie Packman. pp. 162 + 6

Andrew Picken: Eisenbach, 1841 *and* Cyrus Cranky (anon). pp. 30 + 2 The Picken story is described as Copyright.

D. M. Moir: The Bridal of Borthwick 1841. pp. 12 Described as Copyright.

John Galt: The Book of Life *and* The Painter 1841. pp. 8 + 6 Each story has its own title-page and is described as Copyright.

Note. The Collection possesses two sets. The first is of the original 1841–42 issue, bound in half-calf. The second, a re-issue made four years later, is bound in red fine-diaper cloth, spines blocked in gold with all-over decoration and lettering. Yellow end-papers. No volume numbers on title-pages but stars (one to four) on spines. Each volume is preceded by an over-all title and Contents leaf. The general imprint is: 'John Clements. Little Pulteney Street. 1846', and 'Edited by William Hazlitt' still appears on the title-pages. I do not know how the edition of 1841 was bound.

Postscript. At least two further so-called 'volumes' and one or two independent numbers of this work were published. They are not in the Collection, but such details as I can supply are here given:

Vol. V. Clements, n.d. Over-all title-page, not giving Hazlitt's name. Each of the seven items has an individual and (with one exception) undated title-page. All are described as 'translated from the French'.

Jules Janin: Prosper Chavigni *and* Letitia Laferti or Le Chemin de Traverse

Anon: The Three Rivals or Theodora the Spanish Widow

Anon: The Enchanted Horse or Claramunda and Cleomades

Balzac: Mother and Daughter or La Marana

Hugo: The King's Fool or Le Roi s'Amuse

Hugo: Lucretia Borgia (*translated by W. T. Haley*) 1842

Sue: The Negro's Revenge or Brulart, the Black Pirate

Vol. VI. Clements, n.d. Over-all title-page as in Vol. V. In the copy seen, only the first item had an individual title-page, but it seems almost certain that the second should have had one also.

Paul Eaton: Stuart Sharpe or the Demon of the Forest. London: G. Berger, Holywell Street; Strange and Steill, Paternoster Row; and Hetherington, Strand 1839.

Anon: Life and Adventures of Charley Chalk

The contents of this 'volume' and the different imprints on over-all and individual title show to what a low level of coherence the R. & N.L. had descended. Obviously Clements took over stock of fictions of suitable length (in this case from Berger etc.), slammed them into a cover and called them Vol. VI of a once reputable series. It will be recalled (see 79 in Section I) that *Charley Chalk* in first edition was a Berger title. Probably Clements bought a balance of sheets, discarding, or not being provided with, the 'Jacob Parallel' etchings.

I have never seen the original binding of Vols. V and VI of the R. & N.L., so cannot describe it.

Finally, I have a note of two isolated issues, with wrappers imprinted: 'J. Clements; dated 1842'; and carrying the words: 'ROMANCIST, AND NOVELIST'S LIBRARY. PART XXII (and PART XXIII).' The internal title-pages differ from the wrappers and from one another.

Part XXII H. J. Copson: The Gipsey's Warning or Love and Ruin. An Entirely Original Romance of Real Life. Clements, n.d.

Part XXIII Anon: Eliza Grimwood: a Domestic Legend of the Waterloo Road. B. D. Cumins, Duke Street, Lincoln's Inn Fields, n.d.

ROUTLEDGE'S RAILWAY LIBRARY 1849 onward [3758]

This long-lived, prolific and enormously successful series has been generally regarded as a pioneer venture in cheap-book publishing and as the originator of the shilling edition of popular fiction. Actually it was a deliberate and not altogether scrupulous imitation of the PARLOUR LIBRARY, which it sedulously copied in outward appearance as well as in appeal for public favour.

To provide a complete list of its several hundred volumes, even approximately in order of appearance, would be impossible; for although in its very early stages the Library was orderly and the volumes dated, it soon lost coherence—dates disappearing from title-pages, new titles taking the place of those gone out of print, and series lists being compiled without reference to chronology. That this should have been the case was perfectly natural. The volumes multiplied rapidly, and the Library became a commercial property of lively, if rather breathless, value. The publishers, therefore, had neither time to waste on accurate records of their progress nor incentive to do so. Retailers and public were only interested to know the latest additions and whether the steady selling titles still survived. To spend labour and space on recording items no longer available would have been thriftless and unprofitable.

Fortunately the detailed achievements of the RAILWAY LIBRARY are of little more interest to posterity than those of such later miscellaneous bookstall-fodder as the SELECT LIBRARY OF FICTION, the LIBRARY OF SELECT AUTHORS, the FIRESIDE LIBRARY or the COMPANION LIBRARY. Very occasionally, after the series had run for some years, a title was included which had not previously been published in book-form; but the vast majority of RAILWAY LIBRARY titles were straight 'cheaps', with no pretension to textual significance or desire to provide anything but popular fiction at a popular price.

THE RAILWAY LIBRARY AND FIRESIDE COMPANION, as it was originally called, started off in 1849 with Cooper's *Pilot*. The preliminary 'blurb' deserves to be recorded as an unusually vivid experiment in 'publisherese':

'THE RAILWAY LIBRARY AND FIRESIDE COMPANION

In Fancy Boards. One Shilling each; or 1*s.* 6*d.* in cloth, full gilt back. Published by Geo. Routledge & Co., Soho Square, London.

Under this title it is proposed to publish monthly, in a convenient size, printed on good paper, bound in fancy boards, at *the lowest possible price*, many of the most popular

STANDARD WORKS OF CELEBRATED AUTHORS

It is not only the best intellect of other nations, and the fresh genius of the New World, that is now being brought into play, but, be it remembered, some of the imperishable charms of our own dear native literature.

The splendid and spirited painting of COOPER tells its eloquent tales of oceans and prairies; and in a fine and fiery novel, like the *Romance of War*, by Grant, we recognize the work of genius glowing with

[3758] boldness and power. But turn aside, and on the same shelf of entertainment you read of the genuine country life of England, which fixed a nationality upon Jane Austen's plume; you catch the vigorous soldier-histories of Gleig; the scintillations of strong Scotch sense and shrewdness illuminating the pages of Mackay; and in the sweet, faithful, and humorous—though melancholy—narratives of the heart-warm Carleton you gain earnest and quick sympathies for the denizens of Erin's isle.'

It will be observed that no mention is made of the PARLOUR LIBRARY as having in any way instigated the new venture—a discourtesy which contrasts with the salute given twenty years earlier by Bentley's Standard Novels to Cadell's Waverley Novels.

Pl. 15 **Bindings.** The first binding of the RAILWAY LIBRARY, alike of boards and of cloth, was manifestly contrived so as to look as much as possible like that of the PARLOUR LIBRARY. Green glazed boards printed in brown, and dark green fine-ribbed cloth with gold decoration on the spine, could be counted on to catch the eye of Parlour-Library addicts and tempt them to purchase. In actual design of board-covers the RAILWAY LIBRARY was more enterprising than its prototype (see illustration), but no superiority in decorative detail can absolve it from the charge of deliberate 'passing off'. The semi-pictorial cover was soon abandoned in favour of plain lettering, which in its turn gave place to conventional decoration. The final (and longest) phase was one of yellow-back pictorial boards—the early specimens imaginative and elegant, the later ones undistinguished.

The first twenty titles in the series were as follows, but even at this early stage I am not absolutely certain of the order of appearance of two or three volumes:

1 Pilot (Cooper)
2 Jane Sinclair (Carleton)
3 Last of the Mohicans (Cooper)
4 Pioneers (Cooper)
5 (?) Red Rover (Cooper)
Pl. 15 6 Dutchman's Fireside (Paulding)
7 Spy (Cooper)
8 Sense and Sensibility (Austen)
9 (?) Water Witch (Cooper)
10 Pride and Prejudice (Austen)
11 Charms and Counter Charms (McIntosh)
12 Lionel Lincoln (Cooper)
13 (?) Puritan and His Daughter (Paulding)
14 Clarionet (Carleton)
15 Blanche Montaigne (Myers)
16 Light Dragoon (Gleig)
17 Longbeard (Mackay)
18 Hope Leslie (Sedgwick)
19 Libby Dawson (Crowe)
20 Dark Scenes of History (James) *Pl. 15*

[3758*a*] *ROUTLEDGE'S RAILWAY LIBRARY: BYE-PRODUCT*

The RAILWAY LIBRARY, as has been stated, was an imitation of the PARLOUR LIBRARY, and Routledge's admiration for the ideas of Simms & M'Intyre was not yet exhausted. In 1849 the latter firm started the PARLOUR LIBRARY OF INSTRUCTION, a non-fiction series more or less uniform with the PARLOUR LIBRARY. Forthwith, early in 1850, Routledge came out with the POPULAR LIBRARY, a shilling non-fiction series advertised as 'Uniform with the Railway Library', and consisting largely of American works.

ROUTLEDGE'S POPULAR LIBRARY

Issued in small 8vo; bound in boards of more than one colour, printed in green, black or blue with decoration, lettering and series title on front, up-lettered and decorated on spine, and printed with an advert. on back cover. White printed end-papers. The volumes were not numbered in series, and the first five titles were as follows (those asterisked are not in the Collection):

*Oliver Goldsmith (Washington Irving)
Representative Men (Emerson). Yellow boards printed in dark green
*Life of Mahomet (Washington Irving)
Typee (Melville). Yellow boards printed in light green
Omoo (Melville). Orange boards printed in black

Beyond this point I cannot give order of publication; but by the time the twenty-third volume had been reached, Irving's works were complete in sixteen volumes, there were two books by W. S. Mayo, a Life of Sir Robert Peel, and various other titles. The binding became stabilised as pale green boards printed in dark green, and two specimens in this style are in the Collection. So far as I can discover, the series has no textual significance.

ROUTLEDGE'S STANDARD NOVELS [3759]

Although it was tastefully launched as a series 'published from time to time and comprising Bijoux of Romance and Standard Works of Celebrated Authors', this was not so much a series as a miscellaneous collection of cheap editions of popular fiction, to which a series title was, for market reasons, rather fitfully applied. I content myself therefore with providing a list of the first fourteen volumes to be published (after this point the sequence becomes confused and re-numbering constant) and in addition specifying the three styles of binding noted, in what I take to be chronological order. The series has no textual significance.

The period during which the title 'Routledge's Standard Novels' was in use lasted from about 1851 to 1860 and such volumes as I have seen are dated. Many, if not most, of the novels so labelled later became yellow-backs and were either labelled 'Railway Library' or not labelled at all. These were usually undated.

I. **First Binding.** Grey-purple coarse morocco cloth, blocked in blind on front and back with series title and fancy frame, on spine in blind with publishers' monogram and decoration and gold-lettered with titling in single fancy frame. Plain yellow end-papers.

II. **Second Binding.** Crimson morocco cloth, blocked on front and back uniform with I, but on spine blocked in gold only with all-over decoration—title, author and price (2*s.* 6*d.*) being inserted in spaces provided. Yellow end-papers.

III. **Third Binding.** Dark green moiré ribbed cloth, blocked in blind with conventional decoration on front and back, on spine in gold with foliage, book title, series title and price (2*s.* 6*d.*). End-papers usually printed with advertisements.

The first fourteen volumes, published between 1851 and 1853, were works which had already appeared in two series or in two volumes in the 'Railway Library' and were now re-issued in a single cloth volume at 2*s.* 6*d.* They were as follow:

1 **Romance of War** (Grant). Two series in one vol.
2 **Pride and Prejudice** and **Sense and Sensibility.** Two novels in one vol.
3 **Aide-de-Camp** (Grant). Two series in one vol.
4 **Whitefriars** (Robinson). Complete in one vol.
5 **Scarlet Letter** and **House of Seven Gables.** Two novels in one vol.
6 **Jasper Lyle** (Ward). Complete in one vol.
7 **Grace and Isabel** and **Charms and Counter Charms** (McIntosh). Two novels in one vol.
8 **Scottish Cavalier** (Grant). Complete in one vol.
9 **Recluse of Norway** and **Knight of St John** (Porter). Two novels in one vol.
10 **Jane Sinclair, The Clarionet and Other Tales** (Carleton). Two novels and stories in one vol.
11 **Self-Control** and **Discipline** (Brunton). Two novels in one vol.
12 **Night Side of Nature** (Crowe). Complete in one vol.
13 **Uncle Tom's Cabin** (Stowe) and **The White Slave** (Hildreth). Two novels in one vol.
14 **Whitehall** (Robinson). Complete in one vol.

These early volumes had wood-engraved frontispieces, specially prepared.

One aspect of the series has an extraneous interest. Thirty-six of Routledge's Standard Novels were 'take-overs' from Bentley's series, printed from Bentley plates (if not actually composed of Bentley sheets), and therefore almost ranking as 'bye-products' of Bentley's Standard Novels as well as incidents in the Bentley Tradition.

The authors taken over (and the number and titles of novels by each) are worth recording, as showing the results of equating Routledge's sense of contemporary market possibilities (always a shrewd one) with Bentley's willingness to transfer—a willingness no less shrewd and altogether devoid of quixotry.

Marryat, 12 titles (B.S.N. Nos. 62–69, 104, 106, 107, 113)—**Maxwell**, 4 titles (B.S.N. Nos 31, 70, 73, 109 (*b*) [121])—**James**, 3 titles (B.S.N. Nos. 53, 59, 61)—**Gore**, 3 titles (B.S.N. Nos. 37, 82, 97)—2 titles each of **Porter** (B.S.N. Nos. 7/8, 18/19), **Hook** (B.S.N. Nos. 35, 86), **Horace Smith** (B.S.N. Nos. 108, 122)—and one each of **Banim** (29), **Gleig** (42), **Lady Lydia Scott** (58), **Lover** (76), **Hood** (80), **Murray** (98), **Barham** (103) and **Chamier** (120).

[3760] SMITH, ELDER'S LIBRARY OF ROMANCE, 15 vols. 1833–1835

This little-known series of original novels is historically as important as Bentley's Standard Novels, and deserves the serious attention of all students of publishing practice, trade prejudice and reader's psychology. In the first place it consists entirely of *original fiction* never before issued, and is therefore the distant forerunner of the one-volume novel of modern times. In the second place, it represents the first of a series of attempts to break the current price of new fiction—to tempt the public to *buy* instead of to *borrow*, by offering novels very much more cheaply than they could elsewhere be obtained. In the third place, its failure was as complete and as instructive as all the subsequent failures of similar experiments. It broke down (1) because the trade in its own immediate interest wished to maintain the *status quo*, (2) because the public in England were not book-buyers but book-borrowers, intended to remain so, and have remained so ever since.

The first volume of the LIBRARY OF ROMANCE appeared on January 1, 1833. The series was announced for monthly publication at six shillings per volume and as 'uniform with the Waverley Novels'. The prospectus stated:

'The experiments that have been made and are still going on in cheap literature, have not hitherto been extended to the department of ORIGINAL ROMANCE....The 'Standard Novels' have proved a most popular and widely circulated book though they consist merely of new editions.

'It is the design of the proprietors of the present undertaking to apply the same principle to ORIGINAL ROMANCES and to enquire experimentally, whether the sale of a work written by the most eminent living authors of Europe and America will not be sufficiently extended to cover the additional expense of copyright which, in the books alluded to above, cost nothing. In theory at least they know that they are correct. Novels and Romances are a most important article in the *trade* of literature....In an article like this—for which the demand is all but unlimited—a speculation which proposes at once to lower the price and increase the value, cannot be unpopular.

'One great good will be effected by the form of the LIBRARY OF ROMANCE. It will neutralize the mischievous prejudice which prevails in the trade against works in less than three volumes, and this it will do while *increasing* rather than diminishing *the profits of the Circulating Libraries*.'

The name of Leitch Ritchie appeared as editor of the Library of Romance on the series title of the first volume, and an Editor's Preface of several solemn and rhetorical pages declared the purpose of the venture. This Preface should be read by anyone interested in the history of human error, as well as by researchers into the history of novel-publishing. Leitch Ritchie was convinced that novel-publishing had stultified itself; that Colburn's experiments in the unscrupulous exploitation of ephemeral fiction had killed the three-volume novel for good and all (this already in 1833!); that the public only wanted value for their money and would support any attempt to provide it. He promised in each volume of his series to give as much matter as was contained in two volumes of the ordinary three-volume novel; he did not rule out the possibility of including works in more than one volume, but declared that these would be exceptional; he undertook to pay authors 'in bank notes immediately on the assignment of the copyright' and was careful to explain that prices paid would vary according to the merit of the work and the popularity of its writer.† Finally, he claimed that his series would diminish the number of novels in circulation, using the following strangely unconvincing argument:

'It is manifest that no work which is not presumed to be calculated for extensive circulation will be published at such a price. This will be a benefit even to the booksellers, whatever they may think of it

† A paragraph of 'Literary Chit Chat' in the *Observer*, July 27, 1834, stated that 'Messrs Smith, Elder & Co. gave £150 for the copyright of each of the works forming their admirable "Library of Romance"'.

now; for the great majority of existing novels is formed of unsuccessful ones. Henceforth the publishers will be more careful in their selection; and for that reason successful authors will be less likely to throw away their reputations by writing hastily.'

Ritchie's preface was received with severe mockery by Colburn's *Literary Gazette*; but with praise by the *Athenaeum*, which termed it 'modest and able' and prophesied that the LIBRARY OF ROMANCE, if kept to the standard of its first volume, would entitle its editor to 'canonization in the literary calendar'. Other leading critical journals—for example *The New Monthly* and the *Metropolitan*—hardly noticed the crusading element in the new series, but confined themselves to reviews of the various volumes as they appeared.

A. ORIGINAL EDITION [3760*a*]

The bibliographical record of the LIBRARY OF ROMANCE is as follows:

Small 8vo. Dark green morocco cloth, with decorative gold blocking on spine incorporating the name of the series, the number of the volume in the series and the title. No publishers' imprint. No blind blocking on front, back or spine. All edges uncut. White end-papers, over-printed with watered silk design in varying shades of blue and greenish grey. No illustrations. *Pl. 16*

Each volume contains both a series title and individual title.

I. THE GHOST HUNTER AND HIS FAMILY, by THE O'HARA FAMILY (the brothers Banim) [*Jan.* 1833
pp. (xvi) [editor's preface, fly-title and 'Advertisement'] + (332) [text ends 330; (331) announces second volume; (332) blank]

II. SCHINDERHANNES, THE ROBBER OF THE RHINE, by LEITCH RITCHIE [*Feb.* 1833
pp. (xii) [the first two paged (1) 2 and incorporating the prospectus of the series; (iii)–viii (vi mispaged iv) prelims; (xi) (xii) fly-title to the tale and verso] + (316) [text ends 314; (315) (316) printed with adverts. of Vol. I and announcement of Vol. III]

III. WALTHAM [by ANDREW PICKEN] [*March* 1833
pp. (viii) + (360) [text ends 357; (358) blank; (359) announcement of Vol. IV; (360) blank]

IV. THE STOLEN CHILD: A TALE OF THE TOWN. Founded on a Certain Interesting Fact, by JOHN GALT [*April* 1833
pp. (viii) + (340) [text ends 337; (338) blank save for printer's imprint; (339) (340) announcements of next four volumes and new prospectus of series]

*** The new prospectus on p. (340) contains matter of interest. After congratulating themselves on the support of the public and critics which determines them 'to carry on the series with redoubled spirit and energy', the publishers make the following sensational admission:

'It has been suggested to the proprietors by the Circulating Libraries, that the volumes of The Library of Romance are inconveniently long, and should be rendered capable of being divided into two, so as to enable them to supply their subscribers with the usual quantum of reading at a time. This appears to be nothing more than reasonable; and it has therefore been determined that in future each volume shall be divided into parts or books, so as to admit of its being bound up, at the option of the possessors, into separate volumes. To effect this more easily, the work will be sold to the Libraries in sheets as well as bound.'

This bland adjustment of plan was nothing less than a surrender to the dictatorship of the Circulating Libraries. It completely stultified the original challenge to 'the mischievous prejudice against works in three volumes' (see prospectus above) and proved that the Libraries were masters of the situation. Circulating Library subscriptions were for so many *volumes* at a time; to get a novel in two or three volumes required a higher subscription than to get one in a single volume. If the public could get novels of decent length (and hitherto Ritchie had handsomely fulfilled his promise as to bulk) in one volume, subscriptions

[3760a] would fall. So the Libraries brought pressure to bear on Smith, Elder, and the latter agreed it to be 'nothing more than reasonable' that their powerful customers should be enabled 'to supply their subscribers with the usual quantum of reading at a time'. Thus the public were cheated of most of the benefit which the LIBRARY OF ROMANCE might have given them, the publishers humbled themselves, and the great principle of a minimum rather than a maximum value for money was satisfactorily vindicated.

V. THE BONDMAN: A STORY OF THE TIMES OF WAT TYLER [by MRS O'NEILL] [*May* 1833

pp. (viii)+(376) [text ends 369; (370) blank save for printer's imprint; (371)–(376) announcements of future volumes and other publishers' advertisements]

*** *The Bondman* divides conveniently at p. 149 into a Second Book. One presumes that it appeared in the Circulating Library lists as a work in two volumes.

VI. THE SLAVE-KING. FROM THE BUG-JARGAL of VICTOR HUGO [translated by Elizabeth Margaret Ritchie] [*June* 1833

pp. viii [(v) (vi)—the latter mispaged iv—consist of editorial announcement, cf. below]+(320) [text ends (319); (320) announces next volume in series]

*** The Editor's Preface states that henceforward publication will be bi-monthly instead of monthly as heretofore. 'The publishers should have time to "do justice to the publication", as the booksellers say; the libraries should not be cut short of their fair proportions by a new volume pushing the old one from its stool before its *run* is half over.' Evidently things were not going well. The trade-buyers were limiting their orders, on the ground that new titles came out too quickly. So further concession must be made.

It will be observed that the metaphors of Ritchie's last sentence are as carefully mixed as the professed and true causes of the change of plan.

VII. TALES OF THE CARAVANSERAI: THE KHAN'S TALE, by JAMES BAILLIE FRASER, author of the 'Kuzzilbash' [*Aug.* 1833

pp. (iv)+(372) [text ends 371; (372) announces vol. VIII]

There is no obvious division in this volume. The spine is lettered THE KHAN'S TALE.

VIII. WALDEMAR: A TALE OF THE THIRTY YEARS' WAR, by W. H. HARRISON, author of 'Tales of a Physician' [*Oct.* 1833

pp. (viii)+(328) [text ends 327; (328) announces vol. IX]

The volume divides at p. 153 where Book II begins.

IX. THE DARK LADY OF DOONA, by the author of 'Stories of Waterloo'; 'Wild Sports of the West', etc. etc. [W. H. MAXWELL] [*Dec.* 1833

pp. (iv)+(308) [text ends 306; (307) announces vol. X; (308) blank]

There is no obvious division of this volume, or of any of its successors. Probably the publishers had found that their attempt to conciliate the Libraries had not materially increased business—was, in consequence, not worth prolonging.

X. THE BARONET, by JULIA CORNER [*Feb.* 1834

pp. (viii) [(i) blank—signed A; (ii) (iii) advert. of series; (iv) blank; (v)–(viii) prelims.]+(312) [text ends 311; (312) announces vol. XI]

*** Preceding the preliminary signature are bound in a 16 pp. signature of publishers' adverts. and an 8 pp. signature advertising THE LIBRARY OF ROMANCE and other works.

XI. THE SEA-WOLF: A ROMANCE OF 'THE FREE TRADERS' [by JOHN BRENT] [*April* 1834

pp. (iv)+(324) [text ends 323; (324) announces vol. XII] An errata slip is inserted at p. (324).

XII. THE JESUIT: CHARACTERISTIC OF THE EARLY PORTIONS OF THE EIGHTEENTH CENTURY. From the German of C. Spindler [*June* 1834

pp. (iv)+(396) [text ends 393; (394) blank; (395) announces vol. XIII; (396) blank]

XIII. THE SIEGE OF VIENNA, from the German of MADAME PICHLER [*Aug.* 1834

pp. (iv)+(340) [text ends 337; (338) blank save for printers' imprint; (339) announces vol. XIV, *but without giving date*; (340) blank]

XIV. THE ENTHUSIAST, altered from the German of C. SPINDLER [*May/June* 1835
pp. (iv)+288

*** The "*fifteenth and concluding*" volume of the series is announced on the page facing title as coming on August 1 (1835): 32 pp. of publishers' adverts., on cheaper paper than the text, are bound in at the end of this book. Three of them are occupied with an advert. of the LIBRARY OF ROMANCE, which is there announced as due to complete with this fourteenth volume. I cannot find an explanation of the gap of ten months between the appearance of Vols. XIII and XIV. One guesses that the venture was already written down a failure, and that its promoters were losing interest even in punctuality. But that is only a guess.

XV. ERNESTO: A PHILOSOPHICAL ROMANCE, by WILLIAM SMITH, author of 'Guidone'
[*Aug.* 1835
pp. viii+(320) [text ends 313; (314) blank; (315)–319 Notes; (320) blank save for printers' imprint]
A 4 pp. prospectus of the completed series on cheaper paper is bound in before the prelims. of this volume. It urges the public to complete their sets, 'as several of the volumes are nearly out of print'*, and stresses the fact that for £4. 10*s*. a buyer can acquire a Library of Original Romance which in the usual novel form would have cost twenty guineas.

B. ILLUSTRATED EDITION, 1st Issue [3760*b*]

In 1837 Smith, Elder decided to try to work off their unsold sheets of THE LIBRARY OF ROMANCE *Pl. 16*
by giving them a new and more elaborate form. With some courage, they spent more money on a hitherto unprofitable venture and produced a very charming result.

Small 8vo (as original edition). Olive brown morocco cloth, more finely grained than that of the original edition, blocked in blind on front and back with a decorative centre-piece, ingeniously pressed out on the morocco grain so as to show a finely ribbed centre space surrounded by a ribbon and leaves of smooth cloth. The spine was entirely pressed out (presumably by a single brass) and showed a finely ribbed background with raised filigree decoration in smooth. In three panels, gold lettering was added: (on Vol. I) THE / LIBRARY / OF / ROMANCE / ILLUSTRATED / EDITION. / GHOST HUNTER / *rule* / VOL. I. The first two phrases were lettered from the brass; the third phrase—the title of the book—was lettered from type. Pale yellow end-papers. Top edges uncut; fore edges and tails trimmed. Engraved frontispiece and decorative title, carefully designed and executed.

Both series titles and individual titles were reprinted, bearing the new dates, describing the series as 'Illustrated Edition' and in some cases adding the names of authors to stories which were originally published anonymously. Where possible, advertisement material on the last sheet was cut away.

The first volume (*The Ghost Hunter*) was provided with a brief new Preface in the place of Ritchie's original harangue, dated May 1, 1837, and putting so brave a face on the enterprise as a whole that anyone inclined to suspect publishers of lack of spirit should read it and repent.

'THE LIBRARY OF ROMANCE is now so well-known in all the great book marts throughout the world that it is only necessary for form's sake to remind the reader of its plan and purpose. These were nothing less than to reduce the price of works of fiction more nearly to a level with that of other books by producing a SERIES OF NOVELS AND ROMANCES, GREATLY CHEAPER THAN THE CHEAPEST AND FULLY AS GOOD AS THE BEST THAT HAD PRECEDED THEM.

'The speculation was said by good authority to be "one of the boldest to which the enterprize of the age had given birth"; but the co-operation of some of the most popular writers of the day, and the encouragement of the literary press, enabled the proprietors to surmount difficulties under which they must otherwise have sunk.'

After which, the 'Illustrated Edition' might seem to lack justification. But the publishers rise nobly to the occasion:

'Judgment has thus been unequivocably pronounced by the public; and as the present BEAUTIFULLY ILLUSTRATED EDITION, WITHOUT ANY INCREASE OF PRICE, is sent forth *after* sentence, it will not, it is presumed, be looked upon as the exercise of an undue influence attempted by the Fine Arts in favour of their sister, Romance.'

* This, in view of later developments, was clearly a *façon de parler*.

[3760*c*] C. ILLUSTRATED EDITION, 2nd Issue

Pl. 16 It is sad to record that the fine fervour of the above Preface could not transform a failure into a success. THE LIBRARY OF ROMANCE still hung fire; and in the early forties even the 'Illustrated Edition' sank to secondary issue. Thus:

Small 8vo (as before). Brown ribbed cloth, blocked in blind on front and back with decorative panel in quadruple blind frame, on spine with bands and decorative panels and, in gold lettering, the title of the story and at foot the words ILLUSTRATED EDITION. This binding is almost exactly uniform as to cloth and spine blocking with Saunders & Otley's cheap edition of the novels of Bulwer-Lytton. Top edges uncut; fore edges and tails trimmed. Yellow end-papers a shade deeper than those of the 1st issue. Engraved frontispieces and title retained unaltered. Printed titles reduced to one, bearing name of story, no reference to series and no date.

[3760*d*] EPILOGUE

Thus ended Smith, Elder's gallant attempt to turn the flank of vested book-trade interests and to break down what they regarded as an artificially high price for novels. Their undertaking was astonishingly in advance of its time; but its enlightenment had in it more than a little of naïveté and inexperience. They trusted to the retail booksellers wholeheartedly to support their enterprise and by *selling* more cheap books to wean novel readers from borrowing expensive ones. They imagined that the public would as readily buy *new* novels for six shillings as they bought Bentley's Standard reprints. Finally they forgot that both their general books and fiction, not included in THE LIBRARY OF ROMANCE, depended for their initial circulation on the goodwill of the Lending Libraries and would be made to suffer if these Libraries had reason to be displeased with any aspect of Smith, Elder's policy.

The retail booksellers (constitutionally cautious in spending money on novelties) knew their public too well to gamble heavily in THE LIBRARY OF ROMANCE. They realised that the novel-reading public liked to sample fiction from a library before they bought it; and that there was no similarity, save one of price, between the appeal of Bentley's editions of tried favourites and Smith, Elder's neat little volumes of unknown romance. Finally, as has been seen, the (in theory) admirable gesture of giving fiction readers as much reading matter for their money as was humanly possible involved in practice a direct attack on the profits of the Circulating Libraries, and steps were taken accordingly. Smith, Elder, under pressure of a kind at which one can easily guess, had no option but to submit. They tried to disguise the fact; but when they yielded on the single-volume principle, they gave away their main position. Henceforward THE LIBRARY OF ROMANCE was a prolonged exercise in face-saving.

One other point. Although the collapse of this venture was principally due to a victory of trade-practice over idealism, there can be no doubt that the actual quality of the books had an influence (if only a secondary one) on the fate of the series. Ritchie did not succeed in keeping up a uniformly high standard of work; but that he failed was more likely due to limitations in the matter of author-payments than to editorial incompetence. THE LIBRARY OF ROMANCE simply could not afford to give such high prices for copyrights as publishers of fiction in the regulation costly form. Wherefore the editor could not tempt the really popular authors and was soon reduced to taking what he could get. It is very noticeable that he found his material preponderantly in Ireland or Scotland or among possible translations, and that the stories were of foreign countries or former times rather than of the England of the day. Galt's book (which was badly received by the press) and Miss Corner's story were the only items which competed directly with the modish fiction of the time. It will, I think, be found that on later occasions also, the difficulty of getting first-rate authors on terms possible to price-breaking series contributed to those series' failure.

Altogether, therefore, the odds were too heavy against THE LIBRARY OF ROMANCE to give it a chance of success, and it remains a forlorn monument of publishing idealism—the first of a melancholy series. At intervals during the next hundred years enterprising publishers were to cherish the illusion that the public would buy novels if only they were cheap enough. At corresponding intervals they were to find themselves mistaken.

Chapman & Hall's 'Monthly Series'; two simultaneous, little-known and short-lived experiments by Bentley* and Routledge*; another, twenty years later, by Samuel Tinsley,* and, in terms of board issues, 'Routledge's Original Novels' are examples in the history of nineteenth-century publishing, while the twentieth century (no wiser or no less optimistic than its predecessor) has witnessed the blossoming and fading of Heinemann's Dollar Library, of Nash's series modelled on Tauchnitz, and of Gollancz' three and sixpenny 'Mundanus' venture.

Successful novelists will not work under market-value in the cause of cheap fiction. The English public borrow novels from the Libraries; they will not in the first instance buy them. As for the Libraries, they buy just as few copies of any novel as they dare; and the number of copies, not the price, is what interests them.

WHITTINGHAM'S NOVELISTS LIBRARY (Whittingham's Pocket Novelists) 1823–183? [3761]

40 vols. 16mo. Printed by C. Whittingham, Chiswick, for C. S. Arnold, Tavistock Street.

This series was, I feel sure, originally issued in drab boards printed in black, although no title in this style is in the Collection. One specimen representing the series (Miss Burney's *Cecilia* in 3 vols.) is bound in smooth, dark grey-purple watered linen, blocked in blind and with black paper labels lettered in gold—a binding I should imagine to date from the early thirties; the other (Bage's *Man as He is Not*) in very dark blue morocco cloth, with black label lettered in gold.

Each volume has a wood-engraved vignette on the title-page (some have a half-title giving book-title and volume-number) and contains no editorial matter.

* On October 1, 1853 Bentley inserted, facing the title-pages of Annie Tinsley's anonymous two-volume novel *Margaret, or Prejudice at Home and its Victims*, a folded sheet making the announcement that 'from the 1st October the price of all New and Original Novels and Romances by the most distinguished writers to be published by him will be TWO THIRDS LESS than the amount charged at present for these books.

'New Novels in Three Volumes will be published at 10*s.* 6*d.* instead of £1. 11*s.* 6*d.* as at present.

'New Novels in Two Volumes at 7*s.* instead of £1. 1*s.*

'New Novels in One Volume at 3*s.* 6*d.* instead of 10*s.* 6*d.*'

The announcement goes on to assure the retail booksellers that their profit 'will remain as at present' and concludes with the usual confident hope that an increased sale would compensate the publisher for thus 'bringing the works of the ablest writers within the reach of the great body of readers'.

There follows a list of forthcoming 'new works' by (among others) Wilkie Collins, Charles Reade, Julia Kavanagh, Shirley Brooks and Robert Bell.

The first work actually to appear at the new price was Miss Tinsley's *Margaret* (2 vols. 7*s.*) ; then *Walter Evelyn* by Grenville Murray (3 vols. 12*s.*—not 10*s.* 6*d.* as pre-advertised); then *John* by Emilie Carlen (2 vols. 8*s.*—not 7*s.* as pre-advertised); then *Maud* (by Miss Lupton, 3 vols. 12*s.*). But in December 1853 appeared *The Cardinal* by Archibald Boyd (3 vols. at 31*s.* 6*d.*); and from then onward no more is heard of the reduced rate of novel prices.

Virtually at the moment when Bentley was raising his prices above those which he had pre-advertised, and only a couple of weeks or so before he abandoned the experiment altogether, Routledge broke out into challenging competition. On November 26, 1853, they suddenly advertised, as published under their 'New System of One Fourth the Usual Price' for new fiction, *Linny Lockwood* by Mrs Crowe (2 vols. 7*s.*). The next week they promised the following works under the same System: *Alderman Ralph, Saville House* by A. Hill, *Percy Effingham* by H. Cockton, *Jane Seton* by James Grant and *Miles Tremenheere* by Mrs Maillard. How many of these promised Routledge novels actually appeared at 7*s.* for the 2 vols. is obscure. Certainly Ainsworth's *Star Chamber* was advertised at this price on January 21, 1854; *Walter Hurst* by H. G. Pelham on March 4, and Grant's *Philip Rollo* in April. But thereafter titles in similar format were published at 15*s.*; and Routledge, like Bentley, reverted discreetly to conventional practice.

As for Samuel Tinsley, that rather forlorn survival of the glittering (if shoddy) imprint of Tinsley Brothers, his career as publisher has at least this claim on the memory of posterity—that he earned a place among the would-be price-breakers of current fiction. On February 4, 1872, he thus announced yet another 'New System of Publishing Original Novels':

'The first of a new series of new and original Novels (usually published in three volumes at a guinea and a half) will be ready next week at every Bookstall and Library, in one volume. Cr. 8vo., handsomely printed and bound in cloth, with Frontispiece and Vignette by Perceval Skelton. Price Four Shillings. Post Free.'

After quoting from *The Times* of November 23 and *The Saturday Review* of November 11, 1871, harsh criticisms of the 3-vol.-novel system, Tinsley revealed that his first 4*s.* venture would be *The Mistress of Langdale Hall* by Rose Mackenzie Kettle. (This was the first novel of a subsequently prolific writer who, it may be observed, was back among the hated three-deckers in 1874.)

Tinsley's next novel-advert. (May 11, 1872) announced a 2-vol. fiction at 21*s.* and said nothing of the 'New System'; but this was not quite dead, for on June 29, 1872, he advertised a second 4*s.* title called *Puttyputt's Protégé* by H. G. Churchill. This, to the best of my knowledge, closed the series.

WHITTINGHAM'S NOVELISTS LIBRARY

[*3761*] The volumes were published at various prices between 2*s.* and 5*s.* 6*d.* The first thirty-four titles were as follow. The numbering is taken from a series-list but does not appear on the individual volumes and was certainly subject to re-shuffles, for oddly enough the copy of *Man as He is Not* has a label reading: 'Whittingham's Novelists Library. Thirty volumes. Vol. 14', while Vol. 14 in the series list is none other than *Cecilia*, vol. I, which is *itself* so numbered! I conclude, therefore, that the series was at some point extended and the titles re-arranged.

1, 2	Evelina	2*s.*	per vol.
3, 4	Old Manor House	3*s.*	,,
5, 6	Zeluco	2*s.*	,,
7	Simple Story	3*s.*	,,
8	Man of Feeling and Julia de Roubigné	3*s.*	,,
9, 10, 11	Tom Jones	3*s.*	,,
12	Romance of Forest	2*s.*	,,
13	Joseph Andrews	3*s.* 6*d.*	,,
14, 15, 16	Cecilia	3*s.*	,,
17, 18	Udolpho	3*s.* 6*d.*	,,
19, 20	Roderick Random	2*s.* 6*d.*	,,
21	Lady Julia Mandeville and Nature and Art	3*s.*	,,
22, 23	Edward	3*s.*	per vol.
24	O' Halloran or The Insurgent Chief	4*s.* 6*d.*	,,
25	The Recess	5*s.* 6*d.*	,,
26	The Spy	5*s.* 6*d.*	,,
27, 28	The Italian	3*s.*	,,
29	Athlin and Dunbayne	4*s.*	,,
30	Humphry Clinker	5*s.*	,,
31, 32	Tales of the Castle	4*s.*	,,
33	Placid Man	3*s.*	,,
34	Man as He is Not (1828)	3*s.* 6*d.*	,,

3396 (xi)

3396 (xii)

3631 (1)

3631 (21)

PLATE 2

3418

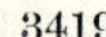

3419

3417

"LOST."

3414

LONDON WILLIAM OLIVER, 3 AMEN CORNER, E.C.
AND ALL BOOKSELLERS

3414

PLATE 4

"SPECIALLY DESIGNED SPINES"

3454 (3)

3509

3510

3529

PLATE 6

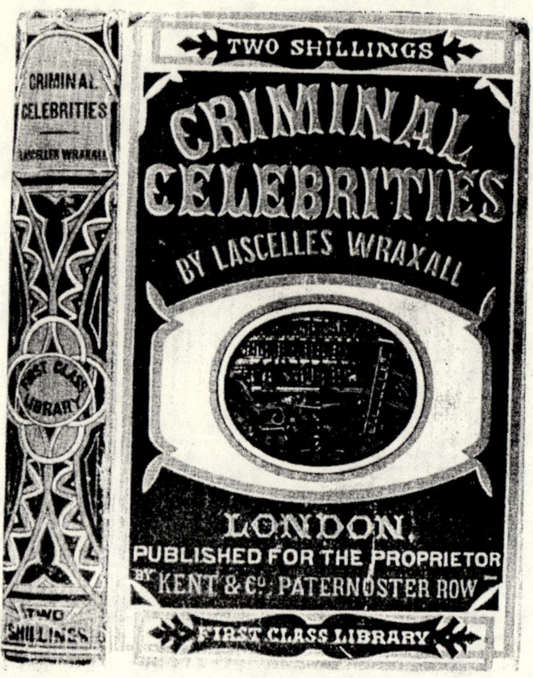

3553 (3)

3589 (viii)

3460 *c*

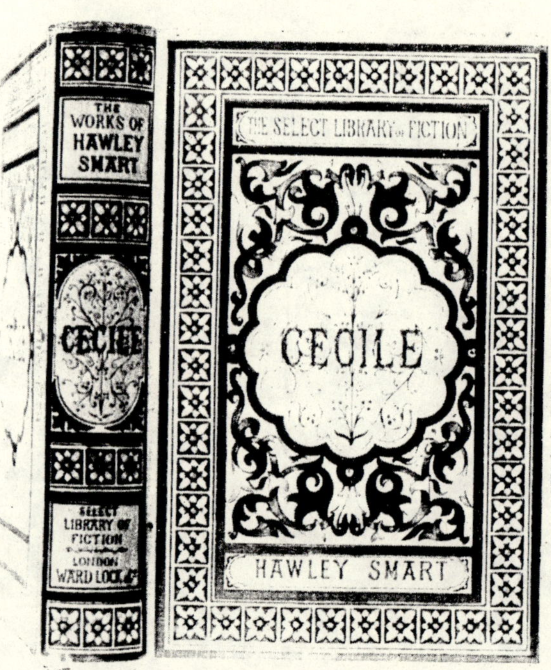

3682

3444 (7)

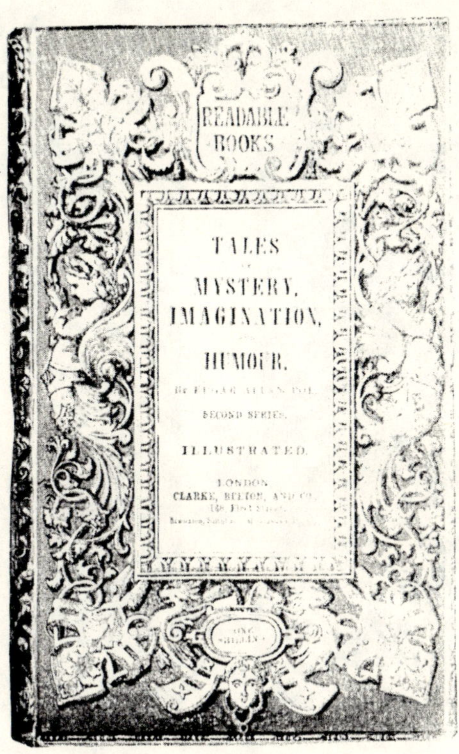

3659 (ix)

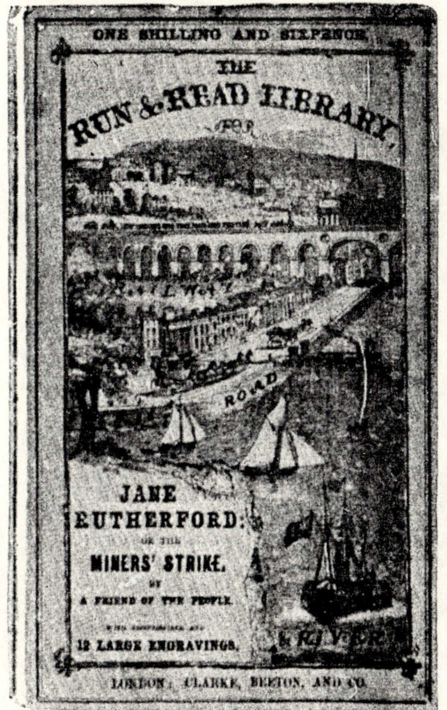

3673 (4)

3673 (17)

PLATE 8

3618

3618

3467

NAVAL YELLOWBACKS OF THE CLASSIC PERIOD

PLATE 9

BENTLEY'S
STANDARD NOVELS:
THE FOUR BINDINGS
3734 (p. 96)

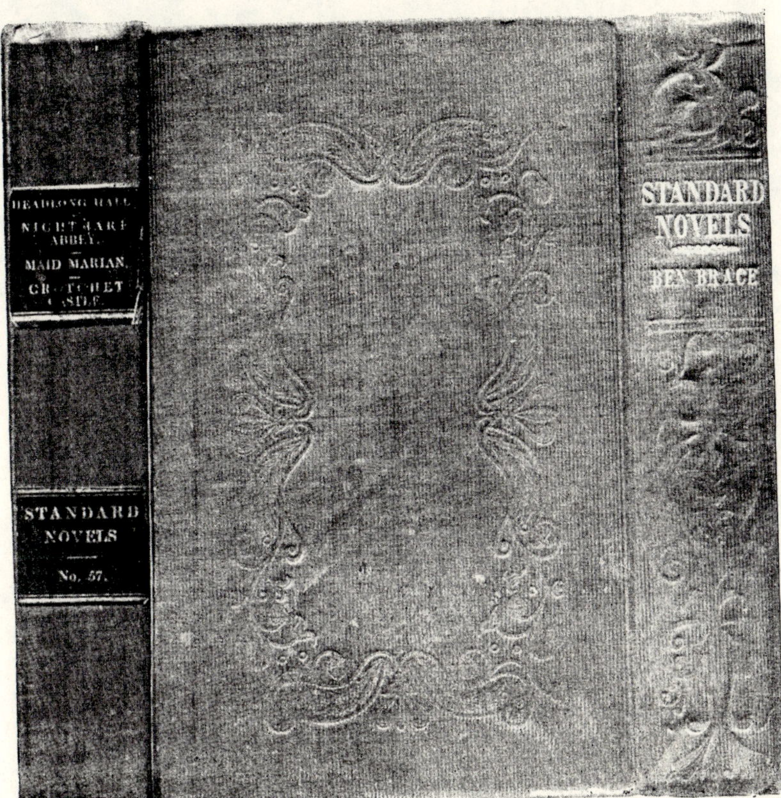

A B

C D

PLATE 10

3735 *b* (p. 105)

3736 *aa* (p. 111)

3736 *d* (pp. 117–119)

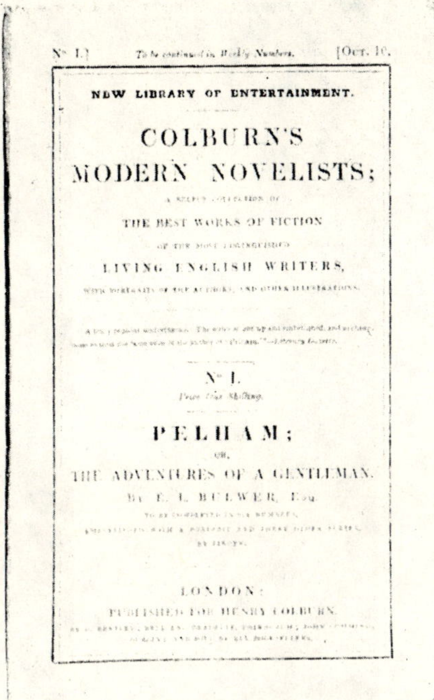

Nº 1.] *To be continued in Weekly Numbers.* [Oct. 16.

NEW LIBRARY OF ENTERTAINMENT.

COLBURN'S
MODERN NOVELISTS;

THE BEST WORKS OF FICTION

LIVING ENGLISH WRITERS,

Nº I.

PELHAM;
OR,
THE ADVENTURES OF A GENTLEMAN.
BY E. L. BULWER, Esq.

LONDON:
PUBLISHED FOR HENRY COLBURN.

3736 *d* (i)

TALES
FROM
BENTLEY

TO HER MAJESTY

3737 *b*

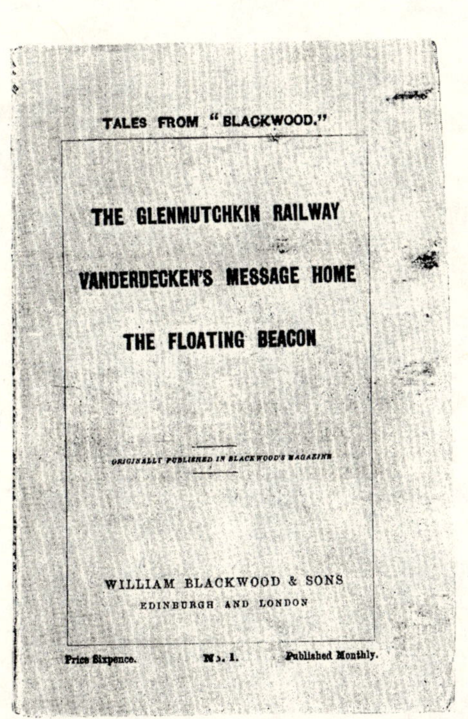

TALES FROM "BLACKWOOD."

THE GLENMUTCHKIN RAILWAY

VANDERDECKEN'S MESSAGE HOME

THE FLOATING BEACON

ORIGINALLY PUBLISHED IN BLACKWOOD'S MAGAZINE

WILLIAM BLACKWOOD & SONS
EDINBURGH AND LONDON

Price Sixpence. Nº. 1. Published Monthly.

3739 *a* (i)

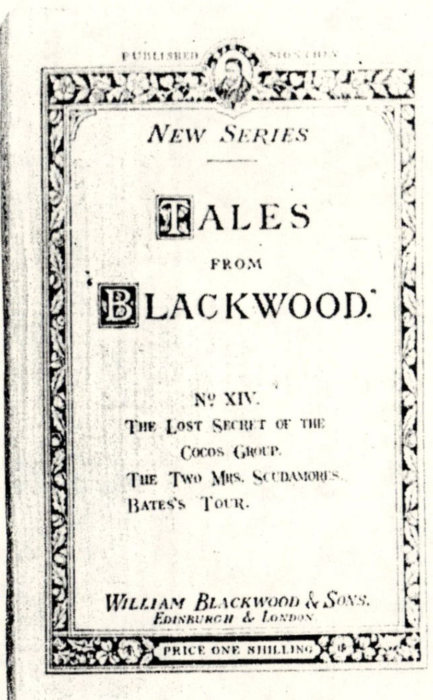

PUBLISHED MONTHLY

NEW SERIES

TALES
FROM
BLACKWOOD.

Nº XIV.
THE LOST SECRET OF THE
COCOS GROUP.
THE TWO MRS. SCUDAMORES.
BATES'S TOUR.

WILLIAM BLACKWOOD & SONS.
EDINBURGH & LONDON

PRICE ONE SHILLING

3739 *b* (i)

PLATE 12

A

B

C

D

BLACKWOOD'S STANDARD NOVELS: FOUR BINDINGS

3738 (p. 124)

3754 (pp. 147, 148)

3755 (pp. 149, 150)

3755 (p. 151)

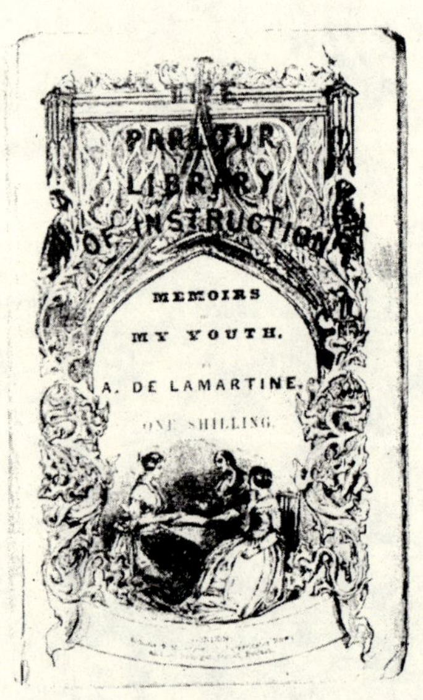

3756 *a*

3756 *b*

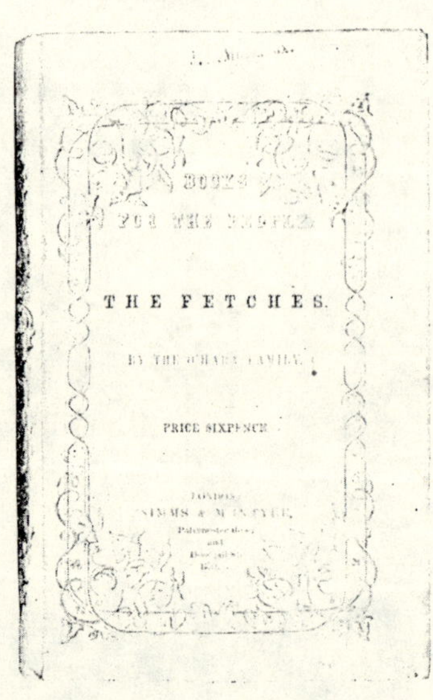

3756 *c*

3758

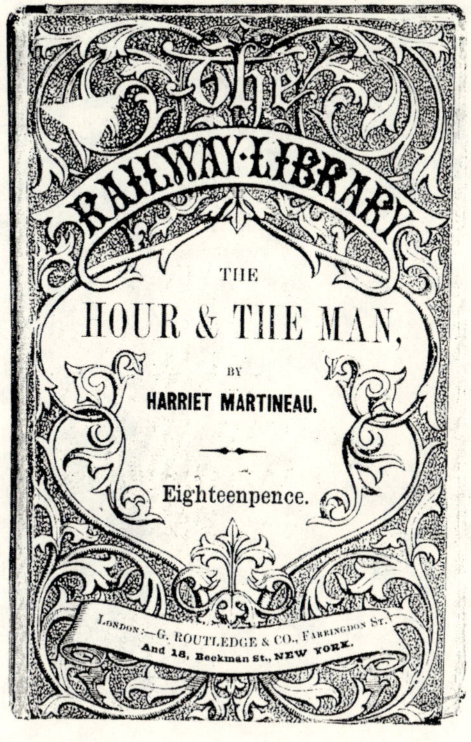

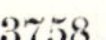

3758

3758 ("Railway")

3755 "Parlour"

PLATE 16

3760 *a*

3760 *b*

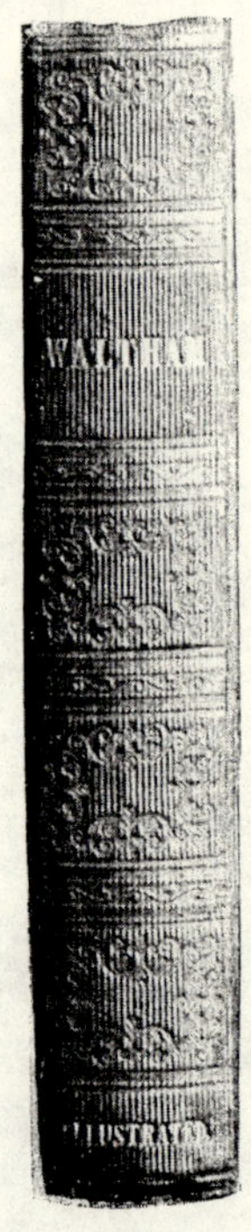

3760 *c*

INDEX OF TITLES

INDEX OF TITLES

INDEX OF TITLES

INDEX OF TITLES

INDEX OF AUTHORS

INDEX OF AUTHORS

INDEX OF AUTHORS

INDEX OF AUTHORS

mC